Professional ASP.NET

Richard Anderson
Brian Francis
Alex Homer
Rob Howard
David Sussman
Karli Watson

Wrox Press Ltd. ®

Professional ASP.NET

© 2001 Wrox Press

Published by Wrox Press Ltd,
Arden House, 1102 Warwick Road, Acocks Green,
Birmingham, B27 6BH, UK
Printed in the United States
ISBN 1-861004-88-5

Trademark Acknowledgements

Credits

Authors
Richard Anderson
Brian Francis
Alex Homer
Rob Howard
David Sussman
Karli Watson

Technical Reviewers
Maxine Bombardier
Paul Churchill
Vandana Datye
David Ebbo
Michael Erickson
Scott Guthrie
Jon Jenkins
John Kauffman
Don Lee
Shankhu Nyogi
Erik Olsen
Ranga Raghunathan
Larry Schoeneman
David Schultz

Production Manager
Simon Hardware

Proof Readers
Chris Smith
Agnes Wiggers

Project Administrator
Laura Jones

Category Manager
Kirsty Reade

Technical Architect
Chris Goode

Technical Editors
Ewan Buckingham
Matthew Cumberlidge
Gerard Maguire
Lisa Stephenson

Author Agents
Tony Berry
Sarah Bowers
Avril Corbin

Production Coordinator
Tom Bartlett

Production Assistant
Natalie O'Donnell

Index
Adrian Axinte
Michael Brinkman
Andrew Criddle

Figures
Paul Grove

Cover
Dawn Chellingworth

About the Authors

Richard Anderson

Richard Anderson is an experienced software engineer and writer who spends his time working with Microsoft technologies, day in day out. Having spent the better part of a decade doing this, he is still remarkably sane. Richard currently works for BMS software – an ADP company – where he is a technical architecture manager. Richard is currently working on the development of a large scale Internet-based payroll and HR system.

Richard would like to say thank you to his wife Sam for giving him all the love, support, and understanding a man could ever wish for. Richard would also like to say hello and thank you to all his friends, especially the other co-authors of this book, and his great work mates (Andy, Graham, Jon, Paul, Drew, Steve, Chris, etc.).

Brian Francis

Brian Francis is the Technical Sales Director for NCR's Web Kiosk Solutions. From his office in Duluth, Georgia, Brian is responsible for enlightening NCR and its customers on the technologies and tools used for Web Kiosk Applications. He spends a lot of time on planes and in airport – wondering if this is what he went to college for. He is the author/co-author of numerous Wrox books including the Professional and Beginning ASP Series of books, and is now totally immersed in the .NET world. When not working on writing, you can usually find Brian relaxing at the 19th hole after a round of golf.

Alex Homer

Alex Homer is a software developer and technical author living and working in the idyllic rural surroundings of the Derbyshire Dales, in the heart of England. Rather than doing a real job, he's discovered the raw excitement and frustration that comes with installing and playing with the latest and flakiest beta code he can find – and then he writes about it. A long-time evangelist of ASP, he has been delving deep into the world of .NET, and has emerged a confirmed convert to ASP.NET. You can contact him at alex@stonebroom.com.

Rob Howard

Rob Howard is a Program Manager on Microsoft's .NET Framework team. Within the .NET Framework team he specifically works on ASP.NET. He currently writes a column for MSDN online entitled "Nothin' but ASP.NET", as well as writing the .NET Framework column for Windows 2000 magazine. You can reach Rob at: rhoward@microsoft.com.

David Sussman

David Sussman spent most of his professional life as a developer before realizing that writing was far more fun. He specializes in Internet and data access technologies, and spends much of his time delving into beta technologies. He's just moved house, so now has no money left to add more components to his ludicrously expensive hi-fi. You can reach him at davids@ipona.co.uk.

Karli Watson

Karli Watson is an in-house author for Wrox Press with a penchant for multicolored clothing. He started out with the intention of becoming a world famous nanotechnologist, so perhaps one day you might recognize his name as he receives a Nobel Prize. For now, though, Karli's computing interests include all things mobile, and upcoming technologies such as C#. He can often be found preaching about these technologies at conferences, as well as after hours in drinking establishments. Karli is also a snowboarding enthusiast, and wishes he had a cat.

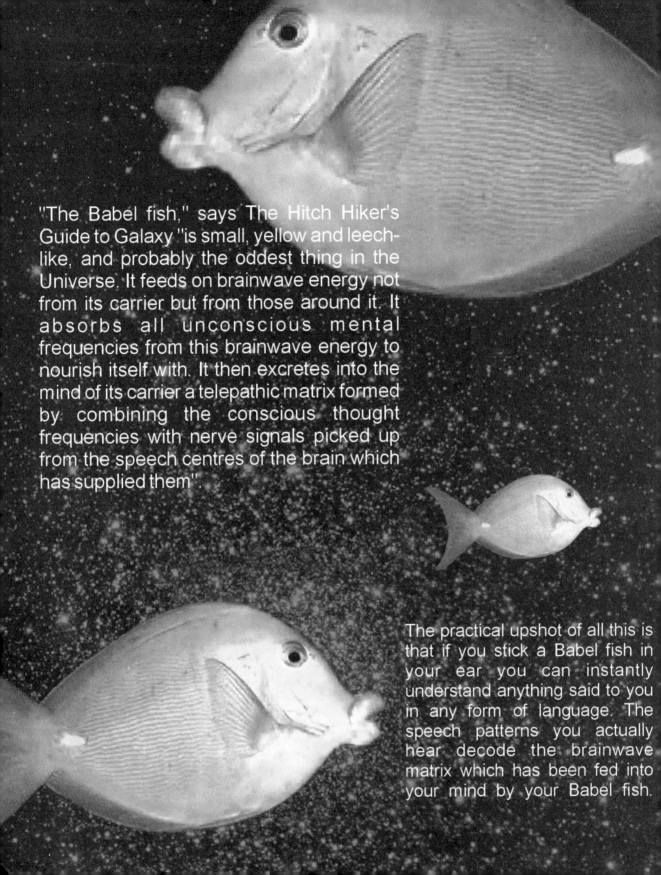

"The Babel fish," says The Hitch Hiker's Guide to Galaxy "is small, yellow and leech-like, and probably the oddest thing in the Universe. It feeds on brainwave energy not from its carrier but from those around it. It absorbs all unconscious mental frequencies from this brainwave energy to nourish itself with. It then excretes into the mind of its carrier a telepathic matrix formed by combining the conscious thought frequencies with nerve signals picked up from the speech centres of the brain which has supplied them".

The practical upshot of all this is that if you stick a Babel fish in your ear you can instantly understand anything said to you in any form of language. The speech patterns you actually hear decode the brainwave matrix which has been fed into your mind by your Babel fish.

Table of Contents

Table of Contents

Table of Contents

Table of Contents

Table of Contents

Table of Contents

Table of Contents

Table of Contents

Table of Contents

"The Babel fish," says The Hitch Hiker's Guide to Galaxy "is small, yellow and leech-like, and probably the oddest thing in the Universe. It feeds on brainwave energy not from its carrier but from those around it. It absorbs all unconscious mental frequencies from this brainwave energy to nourish itself with. It then excretes into the mind of its carrier a telepathic matrix formed by combining the conscious thought frequencies with nerve signals picked up from the speech centres of the brain which has supplied them".

The practical upshot of all this is that if you stick a Babel fish in your ear you can instantly understand anything said to you in any form of language. The speech patterns you actually hear decode the brainwave matrix which has been fed into your mind by your Babel fish

Introduction

Those of us who are Microsoft developers can't help but notice that .NET has received a fair amount of visibility over the last year. This is quite surprising considering that for most of this period, .NET has been in its early infancy and first beta version. I can't remember any unreleased product that has caused this much interest among developers. And that's really an important point, because ignoring all the hype and press, .NET really is a product for developers, providing a great foundation for building all types of applications.

Active Server Pages (ASP) has been the leading Web development tool from Microsoft, even though it's still a relatively young product. Its success is due to its ease of use and flexibility, providing a simple way to create dynamic Web sites. This success though hasn't come without problems, many of them simply because ASP has outgrown its feature set. It was designed to work with the underlying architecture of COM, which in itself has limiting features.

ASP.NET is part of the whole .NET framework, built on top of the Common Language Runtime – a rich and flexible architecture, designed not just to cater for the needs of developers today, but to allow for the long future we have ahead of us. What you might not realize is that, unlike previous updates of ASP, ASP.NET is very much more than just an upgrade of existing technology – it's the gateway to a whole new era of web development. This book will open the door to that gateway.

A New Kind of ASP

What does "A New Kind of ASP" mean for the developer? After all, many products are released as a "major breakthrough", or "revolutionary", but are in fact just point upgrades. ASP.NET isn't like that, and has been written from the ground up to provide a rich and flexible environment for developing Internet applications. Not only does it provide a host of new features, but also changes the whole way in which you need to think about designing Web-based applications.

Most of these changes come about because the architecture of ASP.NET is now much more modularized and based on the principles of components. Every page becomes a programmatically accessible fully-compiled object, and takes advantage of techniques like object-oriented design, just-in-time compilation, and dynamic caching. At the same time, the backward-compatible nature of ASP.NET means that existing pages and applications are still processed in the old way, so there's no sudden migration needed.

One of the major goals of ASP.NET is a huge improvement in the way that applications can be installed, configured and updated. Components no longer have to be registered on the Web server, and a whole application can be moved from one server to another just by using file copy commands, FTP, or specialized applications like the FrontPage Server Extensions.

What Does This Book Cover?

This book was written as Microsoft released the Beta 2 version of ASP.NET. This release is almost feature complete, and stable enough for developers to begin learning about and using the new technology as well as deploying live sites. Microsoft has several live sites running on the beta release, which have proved faster than their ASP counterparts. While we can't guarantee that the final release version will be identical, you can be sure that almost all of the concepts, examples and explanations we provide are accurate within the timeframe of the first full version of .NET.

In this book, we attempt to explain just what ASP.NET is all about, how you can use it, and what you can use it for. We start in **Chapter 1** with a look at ASP.NET, quickly explaining the concepts and providing a layout to the rest of the book. The aim is to get you up and running with some sample pages as quickly as possible.

In **Chapter 2**, we move onto the .NET framework, examining the architecture that underpins the whole of .NET. Here we talk about the Common Language Runtime (CLR), explaining why it is used and what benefits it brings. We also discuss the design goals of ASP.NET and show how they provide us with a great architecture for development.

Chapter 3 examines the .NET languages in detail, looking at the object-oriented architecture, and discusses the changes to Visual Basic and JScript, as well as the new language C#. We also discuss the benefits of the CLR with respect to these languages, and how it has freed the developer from the language wars of the past.

Chapter 4 is where we start to look at ASP.NET in detail, examining how ASP.NET pages are constructed. We take a look at a simple ASP page and show how this can be converted to ASP.NET, taking a look at how much cleaner and simpler the new page is. We look at how the code is managed within the new ASP.NET page, and how the new event model is much more reminiscent of Visual Basic than ASP.

Chapters 5, 6 and **7** examine the ASP.NET Server controls in detail, starting with what these controls are and how they work. The discussion continues with the validation controls, which provide a declarative way of validating user input, before moving on to Web Form Controls and List Controls, which provide rich content management, and finally finishing up with Data Binding, showing how controls can automatically display data from data sources.

In **Chapter 8**, we start the discussion of data management in ASP.NET, looking at ADO.NET and its design goals and architecture. Moving into **Chapter 9** we look at Relational Data, and how to manipulate data from databases, a topic continued in **Chapter 10** when we look at how to update data in those databases. The data discussion continues into **Chapter 11**, where we examine the use of XML within .NET, and how the XML objects provide a rich way of manipulating XML data.

Chapter 12 takes us to Web Applications where we look at what this term actually means, and how applications are managed. We include topics such as state management, the application event architecture, and extending the application architecture.

Once applications have been written they need to be deployed, and this is explained in **Chapter 13**, along with configuration. We look at the XML configuration file, examining its options in detail, and look at how ASP.NET can be extended.

Chapter 14 covers writing secure ASP.NET applications, and looks at Windows 2000 and IIS security, and how ASP.NET can integrate into it. We look at both declarative and programmatic security issues, covering such topics as Forms-based and Passport authentication.

Chapters 15 and **16** tackle the base class libraries, starting with a detailed look at collections and lists, continuing with file system objects, streams, network classes, and regular expressions. The base classes provide a huge array of functionality that can be used out of the box, and allow developers to implement sites with far less coding than was possible in ASP.

With the DNA architecture, the use of middle-tiers as a place for business components became commonplace. With .NET the architecture has simplified and **Chapter 17** tackles business objects and the use of transactional pages. We look at the advantages of the new architecture and how applications should be designed to make the most of the new component model.

Chapter 18 deals with the topic of extensibility, examining Server Controls and how they can be easily written. It looks at the simple coding techniques used to create these controls, and how once written they can live alongside the supplied server controls.

In **Chapters 19** and **20** we look at Web Services in detail. While this topic isn't specifically dedicated to ASP.NET, it is a major shift in the way applications are designed and written. Converting existing functionality to Web Services is extremely simple, and there's a huge amount of power that can be achieved using Web Services to provide and use the business-to-business model.

Chapter 21 deals with pervasive devices, or those that seem to be everywhere – phones, PDAs, and other such devices. The use of web sites is not just limited to computers with large screens, and the use of smaller devices is only going to increase in the future. In this chapter we examine the Mobile Internet Toolkit, and how it can be used to easily produce sites accessible by small devices.

Chapter 22 deals with two important topics, debugging and error handling. Some of the new features are down to ASP.NET, while others are part of the underlying framework, and wherever they come from, these features are a great boon to developers. They provide simple and flexible ways of debugging and handling errors.

Chapter 23 discusses the topic of migration and interoperability. There's a large amount of existing ASP code in the world, and it's important that we examine how (if at all) existing applications can be migrated to the new framework. We also examine the topic of interoperating with existing COM components, to allow the gradual migration of middle-tier layers.

Finally, in **Chapter 24**, we look at a case study, that encapsulates many of the techniques shown throughout the book. It's a sample e-commerce site, showing use of data access, server controls, class libraries and so on.

Who Is This Book for?

This book is aimed at experienced developers, who have some experience of ASP or Visual Basic. It is not aimed at beginners and does not cover general programming techniques or the basics of programming languages.

Our aim is to cover conceptual overviews of the product – including some of the background theory and explanation of why the product has developed along the lines it has. This is followed by deeper investigation of the features that developers will use first. We show how to take advantage of the new features quickly and with the minimum of fuss.

Providing that you have used ASP before, and are reasonably comfortable with the concepts, you should be able to use this book without requiring any other reference material (other than the SDK and Help files provided with the product). You should also be comfortable with the general principles of using components, and the Visual Basic and VBScript languages. Some of the samples are written in other languages, such as JScript and C# (a new language) that are supported by the CLR, but you don't need to be fluent in these languages to be able to use this book.

What You Need to Use This Book

To run the samples in this book you need to have the following:

- ❑ Windows 2000 or Windows XP
- ❑ ASP.NET. This can be either the redistributable (which is included in the .NET SDK) or the premium edition. The code in this book will not work with Beta 1 of ASP.NET.

The complete source code for the samples is available for download from our web site at http://www.wrox.com/Books/Book_Details.asp?isbn=1861004885.

Conventions

We've used a number of different styles of text and layout in this book to help differentiate between the different kinds of information. Here are examples of the styles we used and an explanation of what they mean.

Code has several fonts. If it's a word that we're talking about in the text – for example, when discussing a For...Next loop, it's in this font. If it's a block of code that can be typed as a program and run, then it's also in a gray box:

```
<?xml version 1.0?>
```

Sometimes we'll see code in a mixture of styles, like this:

```
<?xml version 1.0?>
<Invoice>
   <part>
      <name>Widget</name>
      <price>$10.00</price>
   </part>
</invoice>
```

In cases like this, the code with a white background is code we are already familiar with; the line highlighted in gray is a new addition to the code since we last looked at it.

Advice, hints, and background information comes in this type of font.

> **Important pieces of information come in boxes like this.**

Bullets appear indented, with each new bullet marked as follows:

❑   **Important Words** are in a bold type font.

❑   Words that appear on the screen, or in menus like the File or Window, are in a similar font to the one you would see on a Windows desktop.

❑   Keys that you press on the keyboard like *Ctrl* and *Enter*, are in italics.

Customer Support

We've tried to make this book as accurate and enjoyable as possible, but what really matters is what the book actually does for you. Please let us know your views, either by returning the reply card in the back of the book, or by contacting us via e-mail at feedback@wrox.com.

Source Code and Updates

As we work through the examples in this book, you may decide that you prefer to type in all the code by hand. Many readers prefer this because it's a good way to get familiar with the coding techniques that are being used.

Whether you want to type the code in or not, we have made all the source code for this book available at our web site at the following address:

http://www.wrox.com/

If you like to type in the code, you can use our files to check the results you should be getting – they should be your first stop if you think you might have typed in an error. If you don't like typing, then downloading the source code from our web site is a must!

Either way, it'll help you with updates and debugging.

Errata

We've made every effort to make sure that there are no errors in the text or the code. However, to err is human, and as such, we recognize the need to keep you informed of any mistakes as they're spotted and corrected. Errata sheets are available for all our books at http://www.wrox.com. If you find an error that hasn't already been reported, please let us know. For more information on this, see Appendix D at the end of the book.

Our web site acts as a focus for other information and support, including the code from all Wrox books, sample chapters, previews of forthcoming titles, and articles and opinions on related topics.

Subscription Discount at ASPToday

This book also gives you the opportunity to subscribe to ASPToday at a specially reduced rate.

ASPToday, at http://www.asptoday.com, is a daily knowledge site for professional programmers, delivering a new, original, free article written by ASP programmers, for ASP programmers, every day.

The full subscription service gives you additional opportunity to expand your knowledge of ASP and ASP.NET, via access to extra resources available through subscription. These include in-depth, code-heavy case studies; our collection of past ASPToday articles, "the Living Book"; a fully searchable index; tips and tricks; sneak previews of future articles; and discounts on Wrox products and services.

To get your reduced rate subscription, simply find the ASPToday page in the back of this book. On there, you'll find a URL which directs you to a special readers-only ASPToday registration page, where you can enter your details and claim your discount.

Acknowledgements

While we depend on the software manufacturers to help us out with technical support and information for almost all the books we write, we must acknowledge the special situation within which this book was produced. Wrox have been at the forefront of ASP publishing since the first beginnings of this technology, and we are grateful for the regular support we receive from the developers and product managers at Microsoft.

The authors started working with the ASP.NET team during the writing of the Preview to ASP.NET book, and this relationship has continued through the writing of this book, which certainly wouldn't have been as good as it is without the generous assistance of so many of the developers. We'd like to thank everyone who answered questions, provided help with samples, reviewed chapters, and generally helped out, notably the ASP.NET team, the ADO.NET and XML teams, and the CLR team. There are really too many people to mention, but special thanks go to Mark Anders, Scott Guthrie, Mark Fussell, Mike Pizzo, Andres Sanabria, and Erik Olsen. We'd also like to thank Carl Grumbeck for making us more than welcome every time we visit the Microsoft labs – next time we'll remember the Tea.

To all of you, thanks guys – we hope you like the result.

"The Babel fish," says The Hitch Hiker's Guide to Galaxy "is small, yellow and leech-like, and probably the oddest thing in the Universe. It feeds on brainwave energy not from its carrier but from those around it. It absorbs all unconscious mental frequencies from this brainwave energy to nourish itself with. It then excretes into the mind of its carrier a telepathic matrix formed by combining the conscious thought frequencies with nerve signals picked up from the speech centres of the brain which has supplied them".

The practical upshot of all this is that if you stick a Babel fish in your ear you can instantly understand anything said to you in any form of language. The speech patterns you actually hear decode the brainwave matrix which has been fed into your mind by your Babel fish.

A Fast-Track Guide to ASP.NET

Microsoft's .NET technology has attracted a great deal of press since Beta 1 was first released to the world. Since then, mailing lists, newsgroups, and web sites have sprung up containing a mixture of code samples, applications, and articles of various forms. Even if you're not a programmer using existing ASP technology, it's a good bet that you've at least heard of .NET, even if you aren't quite sure what it involves. After all, there's so much information about .NET, that it's sometimes hard to filter out what you need from what's available. With new languages, new designers, and new ways of programming, you might wonder exactly what you need to write ASP.NET applications.

That's where this chapter comes in, because we are going to explain exactly what is required, and how we go about using it. The aim is to get you up and running, able to write simple ASP.NET pages as quickly as possible, and give you a solid grounding in the basics of the new framework. This will not only benefit existing ASP programmers, but also people who haven't used ASP, including Visual Basic programmers who need to write Web applications. ASP.NET makes the whole job much easier whatever your skill set.

So, in particular we are going to be looking at:

- ❑ Installing and testing ASP.NET
- ❑ The benefits of the new technology
- ❑ The basic differences between ASP and ASP.NET
- ❑ The new programming model
- ❑ The rich hierarchy of server controls

Think of this chapter as a précis for the rest of the book. We start with the simple discussion of why ASP.NET has come about.

Evolution or Revolution?

As developers, we are all used to the evolutionary cycle of software product releases, where each new release adds a few features and cures a bunch of bugs. Server–side Web technology has followed this pattern, with products such as dbWeb and the IDC rapidly settling into the Active Server Pages we know and love today. ASP 1.0 was released in 1996, and although it has gone through a further two releases, it hasn't really changed that much – until now. Be prepared to throw away many of those ingrained ASP programming habits, as you've an interesting ride ahead.

ASP.NET is where the revolution begins, because it is radically different from previous versions. Its first appearance into the world was at the Wrox Conference in Washington D.C, back in 1999, where impromptu applause showed how much the audience liked the product. Then in July 2000, ASP.NET received its first public release at PDC, where around 6,000 developers were bombarded with nothing but .NET. As a consequence, they spent most of the week looking like rabbits in headlights – rather dazed and confused with all they had to take in. .NET isn't particularly difficult to understand, but ASP.NET is very different from what we are used to.

That's really the whole crux of the matter. ASP.NET is just a part of the whole .NET framework, but to use ASP.NET effectively you have to understand the underlying architecture. In the next chapter we'll outline this new architecture and the benefits it brings, but for now we need to look at ASP.NET.

Getting Started with ASP.NET

The change to ASP.NET may seem daunting to some, but in the immortal words of Douglas Adams: **don't panic!** Even though there's been a radical change, the basics of ASP.NET are easy to grasp, especially if you've only ever programmed in Visual Basic before. Another important point to highlight is that ASP.NET sits alongside ASP – it doesn't touch existing ASP applications at all. Therefore we don't have to worry about anything that we've previously done suddenly stopping working.

ASP.NET is available in two flavors:

- ❏   Standard redistributable. This is the version that is supplied with the .NET Framework SDK.

- ❏   Premium Version containing additional features.

The Premium Version, contains the following:

- ❏   Output Caching

- ❏   Web Farm Session State

- ❏   Code Access Hosting (sandboxed security for ASP.NET)

- ❏   Support for 4 CPUs and above

ASP.NET is supported on Windows 2000 (Professional and Server versions) and Windows XP. It is not supported for Windows NT or the Widows 9x platforms. You can install Visual Studio.NET on these platforms and remotely use ASP.NET on the supported platforms. ASP.NET can be obtained from Microsoft, at http://www.Microsoft.com/net, http://www.asp.net/ or http://www.gotdotnet.com/, and is also part of the MSDN Subscription service.

Installing .NET

Installation is extremely simple, consisting of a single executable. This installs the framework, including ASP.NET, and includes options for the samples and documentation. During installation you may be asked to update the Microsoft Windows Installer components, and if so, you should click the Yes button to update them. This update is required for the .NET SDK installation.

You may also see the following dialog:

This indicates the ADO 2.7 is not installed on your system. You can press the Ignore button to continue with the setup process – ADO 2.7 isn't required for .NET, although it is recommended if you use any of the data features that interoperate with ADO.

Once the Installation Wizard starts you'll have the usual license screen followed by the options screen:

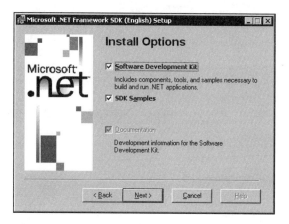

This gives you the option of installing the required components, tools and samples, as well as the SDK samples. You should leave all options ticked to ensure that everything is installed. The distributable version of the .NET framework is around 18Mb, and doesn't contain samples or documentation.

As part of the samples, a named instance of the Microsoft Data Engine (MSDE) is installed containing sample databases.

> **The Premium edition consists of an 18Mb download, and can be installed instead of the redistributable version, or after the SDK has been installed. The installation process and dialogs are similar to the SDK install.**

Configuring the Samples

The installation routine creates a folder called Microsoft .NET Framework SDK containing an HTML page titled Samples and QuickStart Tutorials. From this page you should follow the steps outlined:

Step 1: Install the .NET Framework Samples Database. Click this link and select Run this program from its current location to run the samples database installation routine. If you receive a Security Warning dialog you can select Yes to allow the program to run. At this point the program checks for MSDE, installing it if it isn't already installed, and then installs the sample databases.

Step 2: Complete the installation. Click this link and select Run this program from its current location to configure IIS and perform other installation routines. You may also receive another Security Warning dialog when you run this program, and you can select Yes to allow the program to run.

At this point the samples are installed, and you have the option to Launch them. You can also launch the samples by navigating to the Microsoft .NET Framework SDK menu (installed under the Programs) and selecting Samples and QuickStart Tutorials.

Running the Samples

From the main QuickStart page you should select Start the ASP.NET QuickStart Tutorial, where you will be presented with the following screen:

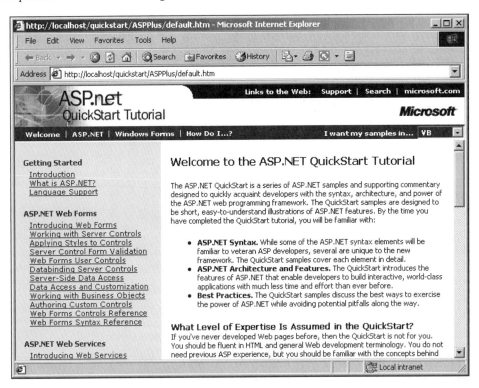

The left-hand portion of the screen shows the samples broken into their groups, which are:

Sample Group	Consists of ...
Getting Started	Introduction to ASP.NET and the .NET languages.
ASP.NET Web Forms	The basics of ASP.NET page design, including use of server controls, databases and business objects.
ASP.NET Web Services	How to create and use Web Services.
ASP.NET Web Applications	What defines an ASP.NET application, and how the global files are used.
Cache Services	The new cache features, allowing pages or data to be cached to improve performance.
Configuration	The new XML-based application configuration.
Deployment	A description of how applications are deployed.
Security	An examination of the authentication and authorization features in the .NET framework.
Localization	Examples of how internationalization can be achieved.
Tracing	How the new tracing features of ASP.NET bring increased developer productivity.
Debugging	How to use the new visual debugger.
Sample Applications	Some sample applications, described below.

We'll see examples of these topics throughout the book.

The right-hand side of the screen will show the samples, including descriptions and source code. The source code for all of the samples is available in Visual Basic, C#, and JScript. The use of these languages is discussed later in the chapter.

The Sample Applications

The sample applications should give you some good ideas of what can be achieved with ASP.NET, as well as showing how it can be achieved and some best practices for writing applications.

❑ **A Personalized Portal** is a sample portal application, allowing user login, content delivery, user preferences, configuration, and so on. It's an extremely good example of the use of User Controls, which are reusable ASP.NET pages.

❑ **An E–Commerce Storefront** is a small electronic–commerce site, based around a simple grocery store. It shows some good uses of data binding and templating, and how a shopping basket system could be implemented.

❑ **A Class Browser Application** shows how we can browse through the hierarchy of classes and objects. Not only is this useful from a learning point of view, but it also shows how the classes are queried by run-time code. This is one of the great new features of the framework, and is explained in more detail in the next chapter.

❑ **IBuySpy.com** is another electronic–commerce site, showing more features than the other sample store. It contains user logins, shopping baskets, and so on.

Additional Samples

The above list of samples describes just the ones that are installed by the SDK, but there are plenty of others available, such as a .NET version of the Duwamish site. All of the code for the samples in the book is available from the Wrox Press web site (at www.wrox.com). Microsoft has three additional sites where information and samples can be obtained:

❑ **www.asp.net** is the central site for downloads and links.

❑ **www.ibuyspy.com** is the IBuySpy application online. This code runs online as well as being available as a download (in VB.NET and C#). This site also contains links to a portal-based version of IBuySpy, allowing user customization, and a news-based version, aimed at content delivery.

❑ **www.gotdotnet.com** is a community site for all .NET developers. It's full of links and samples by both Microsoft and third parties. This site also has a list of ASP.NET hosting companies. There are also plenty of third-party sites, and since this list may change, your best bet is to go to www.gotdotnet.com and follow the links page.

Visual Studio.NET

Although this book is primarily aimed at ASP.NET, it is important that we mention Visual Studio.NET as well. The first thing to make clear is that Visual Studio.NET isn't required to write ASP.NET applications, but it does provide an extremely rich design environment. It provides features such as drag and drop for controls, automatic grid and list support, integrated debugging, Intellisense, and so on.

The installation of Visual Studio.NET comprises several steps:

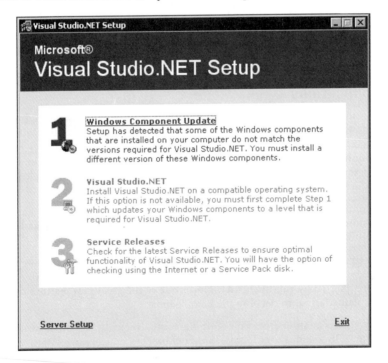

The Component Update installs the following:

- ❏ Windows 2000 Service Pack 2 (this requires a reboot)
- ❏ Microsoft Windows Installer 2.0
- ❏ Microsoft FrontPage 2000 Web Extensions Client
- ❏ Setup Run-time Files
- ❏ Microsoft Internet Explorer 6.0 and Internet Tools (this requires a reboot)
- ❏ Microsoft Data Access Components 2.7
- ❏ Microsoft .NET Framework

The Component Update install allows you to enter a login name and password to be used during the reboots, so that the entire installation can take place without user interaction.

The Visual Studio.NET install offers a similar setup to previous versions:

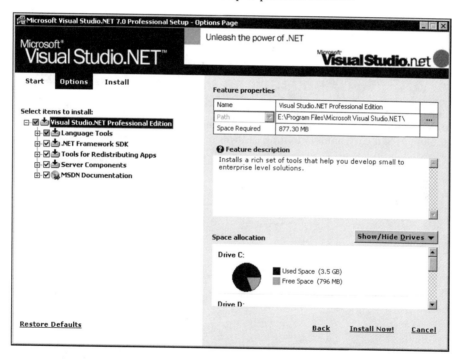

Once this step is finished, you have the option of a check for Service Releases, to allow product updates to be automatically downloaded for you.

If you've used a previous version of Visual Studio, you may think that the installed menu items are rather sparse, since you only get two or three items (depending upon your installation options). What's noticeable is that the two main items are Microsoft Visual Studio.NET 7.0 and Microsoft Visual Studio.NET Documentation. Because the underlying .NET architecture changes the way languages are used, Visual Studio.NET has been built to take this into account. So, no longer do you pick your language and then run the tool associated with that language. Now you just start Visual Studio.NET and then decide in which language you wish to write, and the type of application to create:

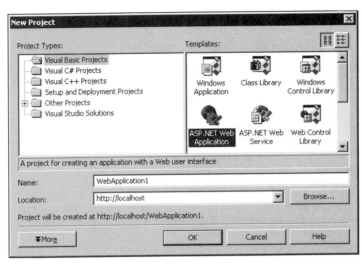

What's great about this, is that the development environment is the same, whatever the language and application. This dramatically reduces training time, as you don't have to learn a different tool to do something differently.

Creating ASP.NET Applications in Visual Studio.NET

When using Visual Studio.NET, you select ASP.NET Web Application from the New Project dialog (shown above), and this creates the named web site and some default pages. From that point onwards you just use the design environment to drag controls onto the design grid:

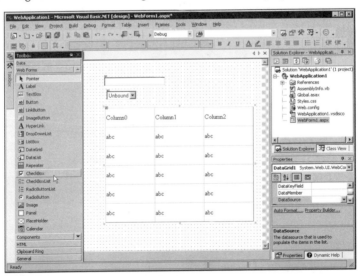

You can then use View Code (or the more familiar double-click on a control) to see the code for the web page you are creating.

We're not going to go into any more detail on using Visual Studio.NET, as it's too big a topic and really is outside the scope of this book. What we really want to concentrate on is ASP.NET itself.

How is ASP.NET Different from ASP?

This question can be answered in one word – very. ASP.NET is not just a new version, but a whole new idea and way of programming Web applications. New features weren't retrofitted into ASP to give us a new version – ASP.NET has been written from the ground up to provide the best possible application framework. This has meant that, in many areas, compatibility with ASP has been broken, but in the long term this is a good thing. It means that ASP.NET provides a much stronger platform for developing applications, and gives many more benefits.

If you're worried about the compatibility issue, then remember we mentioned earlier that ASP.NET runs alongside ASP. Even though there are many differences between the two, installing ASP.NET won't break existing applications. That's because your existing ASP pages are still processed by the same mechanism as before, and the new framework processes ASP.NET pages. This is achieved by ASP.NET pages having a new file extension (`.aspx`), meaning they are not processed in the same way as ASP pages.

Compatibility and migration issues are covered in Chapter 23.

Why Do We Need a New Version?

ASP has achieved enormous success as a way of developing web sites, so why is a new version needed? Simply put, ASP hasn't evolved to take into account the way it's now being used. Although designed with great scope and flexibility, I don't think even its authors could have seen how it would become the cornerstone of many applications. Like a tempestuous Hollywood starlet, its rapid rise to fame has led to problems:

- ❑ ASP is a scripted language, relying mainly on VBScript and JScript. Other languages are available if we install an interpreter, but it's still interpreted. The two disadvantages of interpreted languages are the lack of strong types (as supported by typed languages such as Visual Basic and C/C++), and the lack of a compiled environment. ASP does cache code, but it's still interpreted, and this inevitably leads to performance and scalability problems.

- ❑ ASP doesn't provide an inherent structure for applications. In the days of static web pages, we used to see small, focused source files. With the dynamic concept of ASP, it was possible to build code into the web page, again leading to problems. There's the eternal worry of mixing code and content, which can be a problem if you have a mixed team, with certain people designing the HTML and the interface, with different people doing the other coding. Having two sets of people working on the same files is asking for trouble. Another problem was the ability to make the code complex, leading to larger source files. Include files allow a certain amount of structure and code reuse, but it was never really a great solution.

- ❑ We have to write code in ASP to do most things, no matter how simple. For example, consider the task of validating form fields. Just to ensure that values are entered into a field requires code. Other areas such as caching content, maintaining form state, and so on, all require code. Even adding new HTML controls requires writing the raw HTML to the page.

- ❑ The world of browser compatibility has morphed into device compatibility. Whilst the majority of Web access still takes place from a PC and browser, how long will that remain the case? Mobile devices are becoming more prevalent, and more powerful, leading to more problems designing sites. If you want your web site to obtain maximum reach you need to contend with these devices, and this means writing code to detect the device and render the appropriate content.

❏ Standards compatibility also plays a big part in Web development. XHTML is becoming more widely accepted, XML and XSL/T are both now widely used, and talking to mobile devices might also mean support for WML. Support for these standards means that our ASP applications not only have to work with existing standards, but also be easily upgradeable to support future standards.

These are just some of the problems we will encounter when building ASP applications, but they aren't the only ones. The rapidly changing nature of the Internet often requires rapid changes to applications. For languages that have strong development environments, practices such as componentization, code reuse, rapid development, and so on, are a great boon to a developer, but this sort of support is lacking in ASP. The rise of Business-to-Business applications, and peer-to-peer data sharing also brings great challenges to the developer.

ASP.NET was written from the ground up to meet these needs. Not only does it answer many of the questions posed by the existing development environment, but also provides great extensibility, and brings great tool support. At its minimum, all you require is the ASP.NET redistributable, which is freely available, and you can continue to use your favorite editor of choice (come on, admit it – it's Notepad). This gives us access to everything possible with ASP.NET, including multi-language support. For a richer environment you can use Visual Studio.NET, where you get the drag and drop support, colored code (more useful than you'd think), context-sensitive help and tooltips, and all of the usual great editing features that Visual Studio has brought in the past.

Benefits of ASP.NET

From the above discussion of the problems with ASP it would be easy to say that ASP.NET solves those problems, and whilst that is so, there's a lot more to it than that. To understand what's been done, have a look at four of the main goals of ASP.NET:

❏ Make code cleaner

❏ Improve deployment, scalability, security, and reliability

❏ Provide better support for different browsers and devices

❏ Enable a new breed of Web applications

You may not see some of this support directly, as the Common Language Runtime (CLR) handles much of it. This is discussed in detail in the next chapter, but for now we are going to concentrate on how ASP.NET improves our lives.

Multiple Languages

ASP has been limited to scripting engines, notably VBScript and JScript. The .NET framework inherently supports multiple languages, so we can use whichever we feel most comfortable with. Microsoft will support VB.NET, C#, and JScript (all compiled), and there are a number of third party languages that we can use, such as managed C++. Because this language support is part of the framework, it really doesn't matter what language you, or others in your team use. Obviously, from your point of view, it's probably best to maintain some degree of compatibility (for maintenance purposes if nothing else), but as far as the framework is concerned, anything goes.

This multiple language support isn't just limited to what's available, but also to how it's used. It's quite possible to write components in one language, and use (or reuse) them from another language. The server-based controls are written in C#, but we can quite happily sub-class them from Visual Basic, and then sub-class that control in JScript (or any .NET supported language).

The framework is covered in more detail in the next chapter, while Chapter 3 delves into the languages themselves in more detail.

Server Processing

If you've done some Visual Basic programming, then you'll find the switch to the new ASP.NET Server Controls fairly painless, but they might cause some initial confusion if your programming has been limited to ASP. There's no need to worry though, as they are extremely easy to understand and use – it's just that they are very different from ASP.

One of the big problems with ASP is that pages simply define one big function, which started at the top of the page and finished at the bottom. The page content is rendered in the page order, whether it is straight HTML or ASP-generated HTML. Therefore, our logic was dependent upon its position in the page, and there's no way to target HTML controls except by rendering them as part of the stream. Anything we do requires us to write code, and that includes the output of HTML elements.

ASP.NET solves this problem by introducing a declarative, server-based model for controls. This is where the concept may seem alien to ASP programmers, because the controls are declared on the server, can be programmed against on the server, but can be event driven from the client. This sounds pretty weird, but it's simple to use. All we have to do to turn a normal HTML control into a server control is add `runat="server"` as an attribute. For example:

```
<input id="FirstName" type="text" runat="server">
```

This is a standard HTML control, but the addition of the new attribute allows the control to be programmed against with server-side code. For example, if this control is placed within a form and we submit the form back to the same page, we can do this in our server-side code:

```
Dim PersonFirstName As String

PersonFirstName = FirstName.Text
```

Making a control run on the server allows us to use the `ID` attribute to identify it directly. This allows the code to become more readable, since we don't have to refer to the form contents or copy the contents into variables. It's also more natural to refer to the control directly, which makes developing pages simpler. If you've done any Visual Basic or VBA programming then this won't seem too alien for you.

If you've only ever done scripting in ASP, then this may seem strange, but that's only because it's a different way of working with content to and from the browser. You've probably done database access, so you've used objects, called methods, and set properties, and the ASP.NET Server Controls aren't really any different from this.

The new server processing architecture is covered in Chapter 4.

Web Form Controls

Converting existing HTML controls to server-side ones is simple, but there are still several problems with this approach:

❏ **Consistency**. We are still stuck with the rather non-intuitive nature of some HTML controls. Why for example, is there an INPUT tag for single-line text entry, but a TEXTAREA tag for multi-line text entry? Surely a single control where we specify the rows and columns makes more sense?

❏ **User Experience**. How do we easily write sites that render rich content for browsers such as IE, while also preserving compatibility with down level browsers? HTML doesn't have the ability to change its content depending on the browser – we have to write the code for that.

❏ **Devices**. How do we write sites that cope with devices other than browsers? WAP-phones, PDAs, and even fridges have browsers nowadays. Like the browser issue, we'd have to manually write code for this.

To alleviate these problems Microsoft has created a set of server controls, identified by the asp: prefix. The ASP.NET server controls tackle the above problems by:

❏ Providing a consistent naming standard. For example, all text entry fields are handled by the TextBox control. For the different modes (multi-line, password, etc.) we just specify attributes.

❏ Providing consistent properties. All server controls use a consistent set of properties, making it easier to remember. For example, the Text field of a TextBox is more intuitive than a Value field.

❏ Providing a consistent event model. Traditional ASP pages often have large amounts of code handling the posting of data, especially when one page provides multiple commands. With ASP.NET we wireup controls to event procedures, giving our server-side code more structure.

❏ Emitting pure HTML, or HTML plus client-side JavaScript. With one minor exception (which is intentional) the server controls emit HTML 3.2 by default, giving great cross-browser compatibility. This can be changed so that by default we target up-level browsers such as IE, where the controls will emit HTML 4.0 and DHTML, providing a richer interface. All the user ever sees is the HTML content, not the server controls.

❏ Emitting device-specific code. Certain controls will emit HTML when requested by a browser, but WML when requested by a WAP-phone. The control handles the detection of the device and the generation of the correct markup.

The controls will be covered in detail in later chapters, but let's take a quick look at a simple example to show how these controls work:

```
<html>

<script language="VB" runat="server">

 Public Sub btn_Click(Sender As Object, E As EventArgs)

   ' some code goes here

 End Sub

</script>
```

```
<body>

<form runat="server">

 Press the button: <asp:Button runat="server"
            Text="Press Me" OnClick="btn_Click"
            runat="server"/>
</form>

</body>
</html>
```

The server control in this example is a button, added to the page using the `asp:Button` element. There are several things to note about this control:

- ❏ It has the `runat="server"` attribute set, to tell ASP.NET that it should process this control.

- ❏ It uses the `Text` attribute to set the text to be shown on the button. This is consistent with other controls.

- ❏ It uses the `OnClick` attribute to identify the event procedure to be run when the button is clicked. Since this is a server control this event procedure runs on the server.

The event procedure is automatically supplied with two parameters – the control that generated the event, and any additional arguments the procedure requires. Within the event procedure we can access any other server controls, including the contents of input fields submitted during a postback.

HTML Output

In traditional ASP pages, the ASP processor runs server-side code, stripping it out so that only HTML and client-side script is sent to the client. This process is exactly the same for ASP.NET pages (the `<% %>` tags still work), with the server controls being converted to their HTML equivalents. For example, the page code shown above renders the following HTML to the browser:

```
<html>
<body>

<form name="ctrl2" method="post" action="test.aspx" id="ctrl2">
<input type="hidden" name="__VIEWSTATE"
   value="YTB6MTU5NDYxNjE5M19fX3g=2dbab7f5" />

 Press the button: <input type="submit" name="ctrl5" value="Press Me" />
</form>

</body>
</html>
```

There are several things to note here:

- ❏ The first is that the `form` has `method`, `action`, and `id` attributes added automatically, with the default post being to the same page. We can add these in ourselves (even posting to another page) if we want to, but it's not necessary. Letting the server do this makes the page more readable, as well as allowing us to rename the page if required, without having to change the action attribute.

- ❑ A hidden input field is added, which contains (in a compressed form) the state of the server controls. This is called the ViewState, and is how ASP.NET manages the content of the controls. ViewState is covered in Chapter 4.

- ❑ The Button is converted into a standard submit button.

So, we can see that even though we have better code on the server, it doesn't affect how the code is presented on the client. It's still standard HTML, with standard forms and elements.

Server Control Hierarchy

The server controls are logically broken down into a set of families:

- ❑ **HTML Server Controls**, which are the server equivalents of the HTML elements.

- ❑ **Web Form Controls**, which map closely to individual HTML elements.

- ❑ **List Controls**, which map to groups of HTML elements that produce grids or grid-like layout.

- ❑ **Rich Controls**, which produce rich content and encapsulate complex functionality, and will output pure HTML or HTML and script. A good example of this is the Calendar control, which provides the user with a calendar from only one line of code.

- ❑ **Validation Controls**, which are non-visible controls, but allow the easy use of both server-side and client-side form validation.

- ❑ **Mobile Controls**, which output HTML or WML depending upon the device accessing the page.

Chapters 5 and 6 deal extensively with most of these controls, and Chapter 21 covers the Mobile Controls.

At this early stage in the book, you may not be able to see the implications that these controls have for you, but let's take a couple of common examples. First off, the case of displaying data from a database, perhaps in some form of grid. In ASP, we'd open the Recordset containing the data, and loop through the rows and columns building up an HTML table. We might well have this abstracted into a separate function in an include file, but we still had to write the code. With the ASP.NET DataGrid control, it's the control itself that handles this for us. The list controls (which include the DataGrid) have built-in support for extracting data from a data source and creating the HTML for us. For example, consider the following ASP code:

```
<%
Dim rs
Dim fld

Set rs = Server.CreateObject("ADODB.Recordset")

rs.Open "select * from authors", _
    "Provider=SQLOLEDB; Data Source=.; Initial Catalog=pubs; UID=sa; PWD="

If Not rs.EOF Then
  Response.Write "<table border='1'><tr>"
  For Each fld In rs.Fields
    Response.Write "<td>" & fld.Name & "</td>"
  Next
  Response.Write "</tr>"
```

```
   While Not rs.EOF
     Response.Write "<tr>"
     For Each fld In rs.Fields
       Response.Write "<td>" & fld.Value & "</td>"
     Next
     Response.Write "</tr>"
     rs.MoveNext
   Wend

     Response.Write "</table>"
   End If
%>
```

There's nothing special about this – it just creates an HTML table. Now compare this to the equivalent ASP.NET code using a DataGrid:

```
<%@ Import Namespace="System.Data.SqlClient" %>

<script language="VB" runat="server">

 Sub Page_Load(Sender As Object, E As EventArgs)

   Dim con As New SqlConnection("Data Source=.; " & _
                  "Initial Catalog=pubs; UID=sa; PWD=")
   Dim cmd As SqlCommand

   con.Open()
   cmd = New SqlCommand("select * from authors", con)

   DataGrid1.DataSource = cmd.ExecuteReader()
   DataGrid1.DataBind()

 End Sub

</script>

<asp:DataGrid id="DataGrid1" runat="server"/>
```

We can immediately see how there's much less code to write. In fact, all of the code here relates to getting the data from the database and binding it to the grid. There isn't any code to create a table as the DataGrid does this.

Data binding is covered in Chapter 7.

Another great example of the power of controls is the Calendar control, which with one line of code creates a fully functional calendar on our web page:

```
<asp:Calendar runat="server"/>
```

That's it – nothing extra is needed to get it working.

This sort of simplified approach doesn't mean that the controls are simple, just simple to use. The onus on coding has moved from the web page developer to the control developer. There are also plenty of other non-Microsoft controls, either planned or released, covering everything from more advanced grids to TreeViews. Alternatively you can write your own controls. This is covered in Chapter 18.

Language Improvements

One of the greatest new features is that scripting is dead – hooray. This is a slight exaggeration, as what's really dead is the typeless, interpreted nature of these languages. VBScript is no longer supported, and is replaced with full Visual Basic support, while JScript is still supported but has the addition of types. In addition, a new language called C# (pronounced C Sharp) is introduced, with a format similar to C/C++. As ASP.NET is entirely written in C# we can understand that this isn't a minor addition.

We look at the detailed improvements in languages in Chapter 3, but for now, all we need to understand is that all languages:

❑   Support data types.

❑   Use a common set of data types.

❑   Are fully compiled.

❑   Are object-oriented, and support inheritance.

What's also important is that the language support is built into the Common Language Runtime (CLR), which provides this common support. This means that things such as inheritance are cross-language, so we can write components in C# and inherit and extend them in Visual Basic. The CLR manages all of this for us, as well as providing cross-language debugging, giving such features as being able to use a debugger to step through Visual Basic code in an ASP.NET page into a C# component.

What's also provided is extensibility, meaning that additional languages can be supported. Microsoft supply VB.NET, JScript, and C# as standard with the .NET SDK, but many other languages are being worked on by third parties.

Code and Content Separation

I think that this is generally an unused feature of web site design, as many sites are created entirely by programmers. In itself this isn't a bad thing, but on average I think programmers don't make great designers, and I count myself firmly in this group. While I'm extremely interested in interface design and usability, I'm not particularly good at it. ASP tended to build on this problem, as the code (ASP script) is, more often than not, intermingled with the content (HTML). This makes it difficult for design and coding to be done at the same time, as well as risking potential problems if updates to the page are required.

Code Inline

ASP.NET gets around this problem in one of two ways. The first is the code inline model, where code is still held within the ASP.NET page, but is not mixed with the HTML. It's easy to separate the code and content into two sections. For example:

```
<html>

<%-- This is the code section %>
<script runat="server">

 Public Sub btn_Click(Sender As Object, E As EventArgs)

   YourName.Text = Name.Text

 End Sub
```

```
</script>

<body>

<%-- This is the content section %>
 <form runat="server">

  Enter your name: <asp:TextBox id="Name" runat="server"/>
  <br/>

  Press the button: <asp:Button OnClick="btn_Click"
            runat="server" Text="Press Me"/>
  <br/>

  Your name is: <asp:Label id="YourName" runat="server"/>

 </form>
</body>
</html>
```

This isn't that radical a design, but it is a difference from ASP where the <%...%> server blocks are often intermingled with the HTML. Don't worry about what the code does for the moment, as we'll be covering that later. What's important is that all of the script is kept separate from the content. This split is possible in ASP.NET because of the new server control architecture, which allows access to the HTML controls from server-based code. We'll be looking at this in a moment.

Code Behind

The second way of separating code from content is the code-behind model, where the code is completely removed into a separate file. Using the example we saw above, our HTML file would now look like this:

```
<%@Page Language="VB" Inherits="Ch1CodeBehind"
    Src="Components\Ch1CodeBehind.vb" %>

<html>
<body>

<%-- This is the content section %>
 <form runat="server">

  Enter your name: <asp:TextBox id="Name" runat="server"/>
  <br/>

  Press the button: <asp:Button OnClick="btn_Click"
            runat="server" Text="Press Me"/>
  <br/>

  Your name is: <asp:Label id="YourName" runat="server"/>

 </form>
</body>
</html>
```

Once again don't worry too much about the code itself – it's the structure that's important. Notice how the script block has been removed, and a special `Page` directive has been added (these are covered in Chapter 4). This tells the CLR that the current page inherits its code from the named file, which looks like:

```
Imports System
Imports System.Web.UI
Imports System.Web.UI.WebControls

Public Class Ch1CodeBehind
        Inherits System.Web.UI.Page

 Public Sub btn_Click(Sender As Object, E As EventArgs)

  YourName.Text = Name.Text

 End Sub

End Class
```

Notice that the procedure `btn_Click` is exactly the same as it was when it was inline. That's one of the great features of the code-behind model; apart from a few directives, the code remains exactly the same. And, since we're now working in a compiled environment, there's no performance loss either.

Configuration

Two things govern the configuration of ASP.NET. The first is the standard IIS settings, no different to existing ASP applications. The second is the configuration file, an XML file containing the metadata for our application. There is a machine-wide file (`machine.config`) containing the defaults for all ASP.NET applications, and each application can have its own file (`web.config`) to override the defaults. The advantage of a file containing configuration information is that we don't need to touch the registry to modify settings – each application is self-contained. This has an added advantage when we look to deploy an ASP.NET application, because the configuration is just one of the files that we deploy.

The configuration files are covered in detail in Chapter 13.

Deployment

Deployment is another area made significantly simpler in ASP.NET, and is generally called **XCopy Deployment**, for the simple reason that that's all we generally have to do. Each application is self-contained, including the configuration file and components. In the .NET framework, components no longer require registration, and copying them to their target location is all that's required.

Deployment is covered in detail in Chapter 13.

There are exceptions to this model of deployment. One is if we are interacting with COM/COM+ components, which still need to be registered. Another is if we are using Shared Assemblies, where .NET components are being used by more than one ASP.NET application. In this case the component isn't kept within the same directory as the rest of the ASP.NET files.

Interoperability with COM/COM+ is covered in Chapter 23.

Writing ASP.NET Pages

The first part of this chapter has been a brief overview of some of the differences between ASP and ASP.NET, and Chapter4 goes into this in more detail. Now it's time to show you how to get those ASP.NET pages up and running as quickly as possible. Let's consider a simple form that extracts the author details from the pubs database. We'll have a drop-down list to show the various states where the authors live, a button to fetch the information, and a grid. This will quickly show you several simple techniques you can use in your pages.

Creating the Web Site

The first thing to do is decide on where you want to create your own samples. Like ASP we can create a directory under \InetPub\wwwroot, or create a directory elsewhere and use a Virtual Site or Virtual Directory to point to it. There's no difference between the methods, it's purely a matter of preferences.

Next you can create your web pages, using whatever editor you prefer. You should give them an extension of .aspx.

The Sample Page

Now let's add the code for the sample page – call this SamplePage.aspx (we'll examine it in more detail after we've seen it running). This page assumes that the Pubs database is installed on your system.

```
<%@ Import Namespace="System.Data.SqlClient" %>

<script language="VB" runat="server">

 Sub Page_Load(Sender As Object, E As EventArgs)

  If Not Page.IsPostBack Then
    state.Items.Add("CA")
    state.Items.Add("IN")
    state.Items.Add("KS")
    state.Items.Add("MD")
    state.Items.Add("MI")
    state.Items.Add("OR")
    state.Items.Add("TN")
    state.Items.Add("UT")
  End If

 End Sub

 Sub ShowAuthors(Sender As Object, E As EventArgs)

  Dim con As New SqlConnection("Data Source=.; " & _
                "Initial Catalog=pubs; UID=sa; PWD=")
  Dim cmd As SqlCommand
  Dim qry As String

  con.Open()

  qry = "select * from authors where state='" & _
     state.SelectedItem.Text & "'"
  cmd = New SqlCommand(qry, con)
```

```
      DataGrid1.DataSource = cmd.ExecuteReader()
      DataGrid1.DataBind()

      con.Close()

    End Sub

  </script>

  <form runat="server">

    State: <asp:DropDownList id="state" runat="server" />

    <asp:Button Text="Show Authors" OnClick="ShowAuthors" runat="server"/>

    <p/>
    <asp:DataGrid id="DataGrid1" runat="server"/>

  </form>
```

When initially run we see the following:

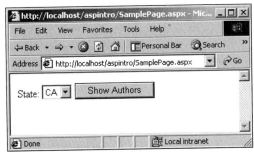

Nothing particularly challenging here, and when the button is pressed, the grid fills with authors from the selected state:

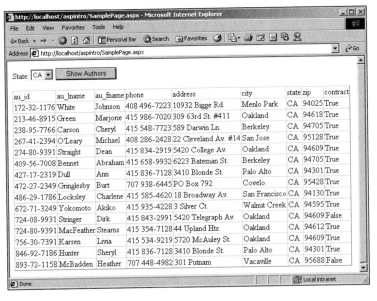

Again, nothing that couldn't be achieved with ASP, but let's look at the page code, starting with the controls:

```
<form runat="server">

State: <asp:DropDownList id="state" runat="server" />

<asp:Button Text="Show Authors" OnClick="ShowAuthors" runat="server"/>

<p/>
<asp:DataGrid id="DataGrid1" runat="server"/>

</form>
```

Here we have a form marked with the `runat="server"` attribute. This tells ASP.NET that the form will be posting back data for use in server code. Within the form there is a `DropDownList` (the equivalent of an HTML SELECT list) to contain the states, a `Button` (equivalent of an HTML `INPUT type="button"`) to postback the data, and a `DataGrid` to display the authors. The button uses the `OnClick` event to identify the name of the server-side code to run when the button is pressed. Don't get confused by thinking this is the client-side, DHTML `onClick` event, because it's not. The control is a server-side control (`runat="server"`) and therefore the event will be acted upon within server-side code.

Now let's look at the remaining code, starting with the `Import` statement. This tells ASP.NET that we are going to use some data access code, in this case code specific to SQL Server.

```
<%@ Import Namespace="System.Data.SqlClient" %>
```

Next comes the actual code, written in Visual Basic.

```
<script language="VB" runat="server">
```

Here is the first real introduction to the event architecture. When a page is loaded, the `Page_Load` event is raised, and any code within the event procedure is run. In our case, we want to fill the `DropDownList` with a list of states, so we just manually add them to the list. In reality, this data would probably come from a database.

```
Sub Page_Load(Sender As Object, E As EventArgs)

If Not Page.IsPostBack Then
  state.Items.Add("CA")
  state.Items.Add("IN")
  state.Items.Add("KS")
  state.Items.Add("MD")
  state.Items.Add("MI")
  state.Items.Add("OR")
  state.Items.Add("TN")
  state.Items.Add("UT")
End If

End Sub
```

One thing to note about this code is that it is wrapped in an `If` statement, checking for a boolean property called `IsPostBack`. One of the great things about the Web Controls is that they retain their contents across page posts, so we don't have to refill them. Since the `Page_Load` event runs every time the page is run, we'd be adding the states to the list that already exists, and the list would keep getting bigger. The `IsPostBack` property allows us to identify whether or not this is the first time the page has been loaded, or if we have done a postback to the server.

Now, when the button is clicked, the associated event procedure is run. This code just builds a SQL statement, fetches the appropriate data, and binds it to the grid.

```
Sub ShowAuthors(Sender As Object, E As EventArgs)

Dim con As New SqlConnection("Data Source=.; " & _
                "Initial Catalog=pubs; UID=sa; PWD=")
Dim cmd As SqlCommand
Dim qry As String

con.Open()

qry = "select * from authors where state='" & _
    state.SelectedItem.Text & "'"
cmd = New SqlCommand(qry, con)

DataGrid1.DataSource = cmd.ExecuteReader()
DataGrid1.DataBind()

con.Close()

End Sub

</script>
```

This code isn't complex, although it may seem confusing at first glance. The rest of the book explains many of these concepts in more detail, but we can easily see some of the benefits. The code is neatly structured, making it easy to write and maintain. Code is broken down into events, and these are only run when invoked. Chapter 4 contains a good discussion of the page events, how they can be used, and the order in which they are raised.

What's also noticeable is that there's less code to write compared to an equivalent ASP page. This means that we can create applications faster – much of the legwork is done by the controls themselves. What's also cool about the control architecture is that we can write our own to perform similar tasks. Because the whole of the .NET platform is object-based, we can take an existing control and inherit from it, creating our own, slightly modified control. A simple example of this would be a grid within a scrollable region. The supplied grid allows for paging, but not scrolling.

Summary

This chapter has been a real whistle-stop tour of why ASP.NET has come about, some of the great features it has, and how easily we can create pages. We've looked at:

❑   The problems of ASP

❑   Why ASP.NET came about

❑   The differences between ASP and ASP.NET

❑   A simple example of an ASP.NET page

ASP is still a great product, and it's really important to focus on why we had to change, and the benefits it will bring in the long term. Initially there will be some pain as you learn and move towards the .NET architecture, but ultimately your applications will be smaller, faster, and easier to write and maintain. That's pretty much what most developers want from life.

Now it's time to learn about the .NET Framework itself, and how all of these great features are provided.

"The Babel fish," says The Hitch Hiker's Guide to Galaxy "is small, yellow and leech-like, and probably the oddest thing in the Universe. It feeds on brainwave energy not from its carrier but from those around it. It absorbs all unconscious mental frequencies from this brainwave energy to nourish itself with. It then excretes into the mind of its carrier a telepathic matrix formed by combining the conscious thought frequencies with nerve signals picked up from the speech centres of the brain which has supplied them".

The practical upshot of all this is that if you stick a Babel fish in your ear you can instantl understand anything said to you in any form of language. The speech patterns you actuall hear decode the brainwav matrix which has been fed int your mind by your Babel fish

2

Understanding the .NET Framework

In the previous chapter we saw how ASP.NET is a major evolution from ASP 3.0. ASP.NET provides a powerful new server-side control architecture, which makes the development of very rich web pages easier than ever before. It has a cleaner, event-based programming model, making web development much more like traditional VB forms programming. This results in the average ASP.NET page requiring a lot less code than an equivalent ASP page, which in turn leads to great developer productivity and better maintainability. ASP.NET pages are also compiled, so web servers running ASP.NET applications can expect to far exceed the performance and scalability levels of previous ASP applications.

ASP.NET is part of the .NET Framework, a new computing platform that simplifies and modernizes application development and deployment on Windows.

The .NET Framework is many things, but here are the most important aspects of it:

❑ A platform designed from the start for writing Internet-aware and Internet-enabled applications that embrace and adopt open standards like XML, HTTP, and SOAP.

❑ A platform that provides a number of very rich and powerful application development technologies like Windows Forms, used to build classic GUI applications, and of course ASP.NET, used to build web applications.

❑ A platform with an extensive class library that provides extensive support for data access (relational and XML), directory services, message queuing and much more.

❑ A platform that has a base class library that contains hundreds of classes for performing common tasks like file manipulation, registry access, security, threading, and the searching of text using regular expressions.

❑ A language-neutral platform that makes all languages first class citizens. You can use the language you feel most comfortable and productive with, and not face any limitations (and yes, you can do multi-threaded applications in VB.NET).

❑ A platform that doesn't forget its origins, and has great interoperability support for existing components that you or third parties have written, using COM or standard DLLs.

❑ A platform with an independent code execution and management environment called the Common Language Runtime (CLR), which ensures code is safe to run, and provides an abstract layer on top of the operating system, meaning that elements of the .NET Framework can run on many operating systems and devices.

From a developer's perspective, the .NET Framework effectively supercedes the Windows development platform of old, providing an all-new, object-oriented alternative (some would say replacement) for the WIN32 API, all language run-times, technologies like ASP, and the majority of the numerous COM object models like ADO in use today.

In this chapter we'll look at:

❑ The Microsoft vision for .NET, and why we need a new platform.

❑ The role and power of the Common Language Runtime (CLR).

❑ The key elements that comprise the .NET Framework.

❑ The key design goals and architecture of ASP.NET.

What is .NET?

If you have surfed over to www.microsoft.com recently, you've no doubt read about .NET. Like a lot of people, you may be a bit confused about the scope of .NET. What precisely is .NET? What technologies and products comprise .NET? Is .NET a replacement for COM or is it built using COM?

There is no simple answer to what .NET is. Microsoft has really confused the boundaries of .NET, which is of course something we all know and love the Microsoft marketing division for. Ask anybody what Windows DNA is, and you'll get 15 different answers. The same confusion is now happening with .NET. To make the confusion worse, Microsoft has dropped the Windows DNA name, and re-branded most of their server products (like SQL Server 2000 and BizTalk Server 2000) as **.NET Enterprise Servers**. This has left many people thinking that .NET is just DNA renamed, which of course it isn't.

The Pieces of .NET

The way to break through this confusion is to divide .NET into three main pieces in your mind:

- ❑ **The .NET Vision** – the idea that all devices will some day be connected together by a global broadband network (that is, the Internet), and that software will become a service provided over this network.

- ❑ **The .NET Framework** – new technologies like ASP.NET that make .NET more than just a vision, providing concrete services and technologies so that developers can build applications to support the needs of users connected to the Internet today.

- ❑ **The .NET Enterprise Servers** – server products like SQL 2000 and BizTalk 2000 that are used by .NET Framework applications, but are not currently written using the .NET Framework. All future versions of these server products will support .NET, but will not necessarily be rewritten using .NET.

For developers, another important piece of the .NET platform is of course developer tools. Microsoft also has a major new update of Visual Studio called Visual Studio.NET that is the premier development environment for .NET. However, you can still develop .NET applications using Notepad or any other IDE you prefer, which is what a lot of the Microsoft development teams do.

The .NET Vision

For years now Microsoft has been investing heavily in the Internet, both in terms of product development, technology development, and consumer marketing. I can't think of any Microsoft product or technology that isn't web-enabled these days, and I can't think of any marketing material Microsoft has released that isn't Internet-centric. The reason for this Internet focus is that Microsoft are betting their future on the success of the Internet and other open standards such as XML succeeding and gaining widespread adoption. They are also betting that they can provide the best development platform and tools for the Internet in a world of open standards.

The .NET Framework provides the foundations and plumbing on which the Microsoft .NET vision is built. Assuming the .NET vision becomes reality, one day very soon the whole world will be predominantly Internet enabled, with broadband access available just about anywhere, at any time. Devices of all sizes will be connected together over this network, trading and exchanging information at the speed of light. The devices will speak common languages like XML over standardized or shared protocols such as HTTP, and these devices will be running a multitude of software on different operating systems and devices. This vision is not specific to Microsoft, and many other companies like IBM and Sun have their own spin on it.

The .NET Framework provides the foundation services that Microsoft sees as essential for making their .NET vision a reality. It's all well and good having a global network and open standards like XML that make it easier for two parties to exchange data and work together, but history has shown that great tools and technologies that implement support for standards are an important ingredient in any vision. Marketing dribble alone doesn't make applications, great developers with great tools and a great platform do. Enter the .NET Framework.

The .NET Framework is the bricks and mortar of the Microsoft .NET vision. It provides the tools and technologies needed to write applications that can seamlessly and easily communicate over the Internet (or any other network such as an Intranet) using open standards like XML and SOAP. The .NET Framework also solves many of the problems developers face today when building and deploying Windows DNA applications. For example, ever cursed at having to shutdown ASP applications to replace component files? Ever wished you didn't have to register components, or spend hours trying to track down binary compatibility or versioning problems? The good news is that the .NET Framework provides a solution to problems like these. No more registering components or shutting down applications to upgrade them!

> Windows DNA was the name Microsoft used to give to their n-tier development methodology before .NET was launched. The name is now somewhat defunct, but the same principles (for the most part) still hold true in .NET.

Even better news is that the .NET Framework also solves many of the problems you're likely to experience in the future. For example, ever considered how you're going to adapt your applications or web sites to run on or support small hand-held devices? Have you thought about the impact of the up and coming 64-bit chips from Intel? Microsoft has, and these are all catered for as part of .NET Framework.

So, the whole push towards the Internet stems from Microsoft's belief that all devices (no matter how small or large) will one day be connected to a broadband network: the Internet. We will all benefit in unimaginable ways from the advantages this global network will bring – your fridge could automatically send orders out to your local supermarket to restock itself, or your microwave could download the cooking times for the food you put in it, and automatically cook it. Wouldn't that be cool?

These ideas might sound a little futuristic, but manufacturers are already working on prototypes. Imagine if you were part of a team working on one of these projects. Where would you start? How many technologies and protocols would you need to use? How many languages? How many different compilers? Just thinking about some of these fairly elementary issues makes my brain hurt. However, this is just the tip of the iceberg.

If a fridge were going to restock itself automatically, wouldn't it be cool to have it connect via the Internet to the owner's local supermarket, or any other supermarket available in some global supermarket directory. The supermarket systems and fridges would need to exchange information in some standard format like XML, ordering the goods and arranging delivery. Delivery times would have to be determined, probably by the fridge, based upon the owner's electronic diary (maybe stored on a mobile device or in a central internet location – Hailstorm for example), telling the fridge when the owner will be at home to accept the delivery.

Mad as it as sounds, I do believe applications like this will be available and very common in the next five to ten years. Our lives as developers really are going to change a lot in the future, especially when web services are widely adopted. I doubt we'll all be programming fridges (although I know of people who are), but the Internet has already changed our lives and careers dramatically, and that change isn't slowing down. More and more devices are going to get connected, and if we are going to adapt quickly to these changes, we need a great toolset that enables us to meet the time-to-market requirements of the Internet, and a toolset that also provides a consistent development strategy, no matter what type of development we're doing.

Let's take a look at the current Window DNA platform, and see why the platform and the tools we have today need to be revamped for some of this next generation of web-enabled applications.

The Problems with Windows DNA

Microsoft Windows Distributed interNet applications Architecture (Windows DNA) started back in late 1996/early 1997, when Microsoft began to see the potential that the Internet offered. They released Windows DNA to help companies embrace their vision (and of course sell their platform).

> Windows DNA was a programming model or blueprint that companies could use when designing n-tier distributed component-based applications for the Windows platform. At that time, development of .NET had already begun inside of Microsoft, although back then it was called COM+ 2.0.

Windows DNA applications did not have to use the Internet, but that was the primary focus for most companies. Over the years Windows DNA has grown, and these days it also covers in some detail how the various Microsoft products and services could be used in an n-tier application to provide functionality such as messaging and data storage.

The problem with Windows DNA is not the blueprint for design, and indeed the same n-tier designs still apply for .NET applications. The problem with Windows DNA is the enabling toolset provided by Microsoft and others is primarily based upon old technologies like Microsoft Component Object Model (COM) whose origins date back to the early 90s, and the Win32 API, which utilizes proprietary languages and protocols, which we all know are a bad thing these days. You may be shocked at these statements initially, but just think of the pains you go through as a developer today when building web applications. Do you think the Windows DNA platform is easy to use? Do you think the platform is consistent? The answer is of course a resounding "no".

Let's review some of the most common problems with Windows DNA, and touch briefly on how .NET solves these problems. Once we've covered a few of these problems, we'll really start to drill down into the driving technology behind .NET, the Common Language Runtime (CLR). We'll see how these lower-level technologies really drive and enable the development of higher-level technologies like ASP.NET.

Stopping 24x7 Applications

Have you ever tried replacing a COM component in a production web server? Or even on a development machine.? Today, you have to stop the entire web site, copy a file across, and then restart the web site. Even worse, sometimes you have to reboot a machine because COM/IIS just seem to get confused, and do not release files correctly. This is a pain during the development of an application, and is unacceptable for production sites that must always be running. This problem is caused by the way COM manages files such as DLLs: once they are loaded, you can not overwrite them unless they are unloaded during an idle period, which of course may never happen on a busy web server.

.NET components do not have to be locked like this. They can be overwritten at any time thanks to a feature called **Shadow Copy** that is part of the Common Language Runtime. Any applications you write, as well as Microsoft technologies like ASP.NET, can take advantage of this feature that prevent PE (portable executable) files such as DLLs and EXEs from being locked. With ASP.NET, changes to component files that you create and place in the `bin` directory – this is where components for an application live – are automatically detected. ASP.NET will automatically load the changed components, and use them to process **all new** web requests not currently executing, while at the same time keeping the older versions of the components loaded until previously active requests are completed.

Side By Side

Another pain with Windows DNA is that it is not easy to run two **different** versions of the same application components side by side, either on the same machine, or in the same process. This will improve in the Windows XP time frame, but currently you typically have to upgrade an entire application to use the latest set of components, or go through some serious development nightmares.

.NET allows different versions of the same components to co-exist and run side-by-side on the same machine and within the same process. For example, one ASP.NET web page could be using version 1 of a component, whilst another ASP.NET web page uses version 2, which is not compatible with version 1, but for the most part uses the same class and method names. Based upon the dependencies for the web page (or another component) using a component, the correct version of a component will be resolved and loaded, even within the same process. The ability to run multiple versions of the same code simultaneously is referred to as **side-by-side execution**.

> Using side-by-side you'll be able to run all future versions of ASP.NET side by side on the same machine without conflict. The same will be true for the .NET Framework.

Scripting Limitations

If you're an ASP developer who is not that familiar with writing components (if at all), you have probably found it annoying that you can't do everything you want to from within an ASP page. You have to write, find, or buy components to expose the functionality you need to your pages, such as registry access and security, which, at the end of the day, are all a standard part of the Windows Platform.

This problem is caused by the fact that ASP pages can only be written in scripting languages, which in turn cannot directly access the Win32 API, and also have many COM-related restrictions. This can be a real pain if you haven't got the resources or time to invest in component development. I'm not advocating that component development is a bad thing, but sometimes your schedule or particular project just doesn't need or allow components. Wouldn't it be nice if you could do everything within an ASP page, and just use components when you have time, and when there is a benefit such as common code being reused? Well, with ASP.NET you can take that approach.

ASP.NET pages can use all of the functionality of the .NET Framework. You no longer have to write components to work around the problems of the scripting run-time (since there is no scripting run-time anymore). You can decide what code goes into an ASP.NET page, and/or what goes in your components. There are no scalability issues with code in ASP.NET page, although it's still good practice to create components for reasons of code reusability and maintenance.

Versioning Hell (DLL Hell)

Undoubtedly the biggest problem with Windows DNA today is versioning. When an application is built it typically consists of many intricately related pieces like standard DLLs, ASP pages, and COM DLLs hosting components. ASP page X can't run without COM component Y, which requires DLL Z, which in turn is dependent upon more DLLs or specific versions of object models like ADO 2.6. All of these dependencies are implicit (not documented, visible, or enforceable by the operating system), and have to be satisfied for an application to run smoothly.

If any of these application dependencies are broken, the application won't function correctly, or worse still, your application can break at run-time halfway through some important operation due to missing dependencies. Many components are also dependent upon system-wide DLLs shared by many applications, and the system registry. It is very easy today to break applications by simply installing another application, or accidentally changing the registry using a tool like Regedit. Tracking these problems down is a very difficult task, if not impossible.

To resolve versioning problems, .NET allows developers to specify version and dependencies between different software components. These dependencies are stored along with a component in what's called an **assembly** (think of an assembly as a DLL or EXE file for now), and .NET uses this information to ensure application integrity is maintained, reporting errors if components cannot be loaded, if missing dependencies are found, or even if tampered files have been detected.

To further reduce registration problems, .NET no longer uses the registry for component registration. Information about the types (classes, structures, enums etc.) is contained with the code, and this type information is retrieved directly from the files at run-time. When an application instantiates a new type like a business object, the common language runtime will scan the application directory for the component, then look at other predefined locations for the component. Once a component is located, information about it is cached for performance reasons, and reused on subsequent requests for the component. This decentralized registration reduces the chances of applications interfering with each other by mistake, and also removes the need to register and unregister components. This makes deploying applications much easier, since all you have do is copy files into a directory and you're done.

> The .NET Framework supports having shared components, although these are not recommended unless you're a component vendor. Shared components are installed in the global assembly cache (GAC), which you can think of as a system directory for holding component files.

Why We Need .NET

The problems we've discussed here about Windows DNA are just a few of many I'm sure you have encountered. These problems, combined with the inherent complexity of the Windows DNA platform, make it a less than optimal platform for developing next generation applications, especially those that will run on non-standard devices, like our fridge from earlier. Can you imagine the trouble you'd have to go to in order to actually implement the software required for an Internet enabled e-fridge?

The good news is that .NET avoids many of the problems associated with the Windows DNA platform, by giving us a brand-new Internet-centric platform.

.NET – A Clean Start

When programming applications for Windows platform today, there are a myriad of programming languages and technologies that we can use. Depending on what programming language you choose, the technologies available are typically very different, and can often be restricted. For example, a C/C++ programmer who has to write a GUI Application can either use the Microsoft Foundation Classes (MFC), the Windows Template Library (WTL), or the lower level WIN32 APIs. A VB programmer has to use the VB forms package.

The problems with this approach are:

- ❑ Microsoft spends more time developing two or more competing technologies, rather than focusing on improving one shared technology.

- ❑ The availability of so many technologies doing the same thing confuses people.

- ❑ Multi-faceted developers who know multiple languages have to learn multiple technologies to achieve the same results.

- ❑ Companies have to predominantly invest in one language, since cross-training can be time consuming and expensive.

- ❑ Not all languages will necessarily expose all of the same functionality, or be as productive as each other. For example, with C/C++ and MFC today we can easily write MDI applications with docking toolbars and windows. With VB, we have to buy a third-party package or write the functionality ourselves. However, I can pretty much guarantee (from experience) that VB programmers are typically more productive because they spend less time debugging low-level pointer errors.

These points and many others make the Windows DNA platform hard to understand. It often leads to confusion, and I know many companies that have fallen foul of choosing the wrong technology/language, and hitting technical implementation problems late into their schedule. Some people might argue using C/C++ for everything helps, but then of course you'll probably miss your time-to-market goal because the developers are too busy debugging their code all the time. There just aren't enough really good C/C++ programmers who actually want to develop business applications. .NET helps solve these problems.

With .NET there is now just one clean object-oriented way of accessing the functionality of the .NET Framework and building applications. All the best and most commonly used features of existing technologies have been merged together into a single framework:

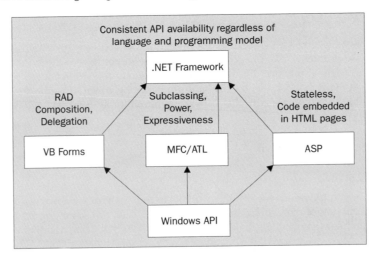

For example, when developing GUI applications you use Windows Forms (WinForms). WinForms is a consistent GUI framework that exposes the same set of classes to any language supported by the .NET Framework. All languages typically also have the same Visual Designers. This makes the development of GUI applications simple. You use one technology, and it does not matter what language you use. The same simplicity also applies to building web applications using ASP.NET. No longer do you have to choose between writing VB Web Classes, ISAPI Extensions, or ASP, you just use ASP.NET. It provides all of the features application developers need, and again all languages are equal and can access exactly the same functionality.

> **VB Web Classes are not supported in .NET. They are superceded by ASP.NET pages.**

Of course, there are some downsides to .NET. If you're writing applications that require absolute performance, such as real-time applications, or applications like SQL Server, .NET v1.0 might not be the platform for you. Although .NET has huge benefits to the average application developer, it simply doesn't have the raw performance of a well-written C/C++ application, although certain aspects of a .NET application (such as memory allocation) are faster than C/C++. For reasons of performance and investment, many Microsoft teams will not be rewriting their applications using .NET, instead they will be .NET enabling them. For example, the next major release of SQL Server will enable you to write stored procedures using .NET languages like VB and C#.

So, No More Language Functionality Debates?

If you have programmed using VB before, no doubt you have been aware that C/C++ is a much more powerful environment for low-level development, and suffers from far fewer limitations than VB. With .NET, all programming languages are first-class citizens. This means you can implement solutions in a programming language that your developers are productive with, without any penalties. With version 1.0 of .NET there will be four languages shipped by Microsoft:

- ❑ VB.NET
- ❑ C#
- ❑ JScript.NET
- ❑ MC++

There are no significant technical differentiators between these languages; so again, it's a matter of personal preference and/or company benefits. One caveat to note is that some languages may perform marginally better (about 5%) than others. My tests have shown that C# is marginally faster than VB, and MC++ (Managed C/C++) is faster than C# since it optimizes the output it creates. At the end of the day performance really comes down to the abilities of the compiler writers to generate good code, and how long the compiler has been under development for.

If performance is crucial to your applications, you may want to do some basic performance testing before choosing a language. Eventually, one would assume all languages would be as performant as each other, so I personally wouldn't recommend spending too much time worrying about this issue. Go with the language that will give you the most productivity.

In case you're wondering, my language preference as a professional developer is C#. It's a clean, modern and easy-to-use language that was designed specifically for the component-oriented world of the .NET Framework. It doesn't carry around any of the baggage or quirks other languages like VB and MC++ have.

No More ASP-imposed Limitations

When we were writing the book *Professional ASP 3.0* (*ISBN 1-861002-61-0*) we spent a lot of time explaining the limitations of ASP, and explaining that for many tasks you had to create COM components. With ASP.NET these limitations essentially go away, since it no longer uses Active Scripting engines, and instead uses proper type-safe languages like VB.NET.

Anything that we can do from within a .NET class we can do in an ASP.NET page. This means that rather than having to always use components to develop our n-tier web application, we now have the choice of when, how and if we use them. This flexibility in ASP.NET stems from the fact that all ASP.NET pages are converted into classes and compiled into a DLL behind the scenes. Of course, just because we now have this new-found flexibility, doesn't mean we should be silly and forget everything we've learnt in the past. We should still use components to encapsulate data access and other common functionality used in our applications, and we certainly shouldn't go mad and do crazy things like trying to display a WinForm in an ASP.NET page!

Multiple Platform Support

.NET has been designed with multiple platform support as key feature. For version 1.0 of .NET, this means that code written using the .NET Framework can run on all versions of Windows: Windows 95, 98, 98SE, Windows NT, Windows 2000, Windows XP, and so on. Depending upon the class libraries used, the same code will also execute on small devices under operating systems like Windows CE, which will run a special compact edition of .NET. However, unlike Java, .NET does not promise that all classes will work under all platforms.

Rather than restricting the class libraries available in .NET to cover functionality that's only available on all platforms, Microsoft has included rich support for all platforms. As developers, it's down to us to make sure we only use .NET classes supported on those platforms (although it's expected that Microsoft will provide tools to help with this process). Work in this area has already started with the definition of the Common Language Specification (CLS). Microsoft is working on the CLS with HP, Intel, IBM, and other companies, so who knows, we could also get versions of .NET not written by Microsoft, which run on other platforms.

An exciting prospect for companies is that the .NET code you write today will also work under 64-bit versions of Windows without change. If you ever ported a 16-bit application to 32-bit Windows you'll appreciate the time, effort, and pain this saves. This is possible since .NET natively supports 64-bit types such as `System.Int64`, which in VB is called the `Long` type.

Targeting multiple platforms with .NET does introduce the potential for well-known Java problems to hit companies. Since the code is being compiled dynamically on different platforms, the compilation process will result in different native code. Even with the best intentions in the world, this could lead to some bugs appearing in your code, especially if the JIT compiler for a given platform has bugs, or just compiles things differently. You should be prepared to QA your products on the .NET platforms you are going to support. Even so, the benefits and money saved by the reduced development time makes this an exciting time.

Looking forward, it is expected that .NET will run under other platforms like UNIX, although it is unlikely that the whole of the .NET Framework will be supported, probably just the languages and the base class libraries. Microsoft is keeping these plans very quiet at the moment, but they are on the table, and they are being researched. Once again though, even if Microsoft does deliver .NET on a non-Windows platform, it's unlikely they will want to invest significantly into other platforms, so the amount of functionality available to .NET applications on these platforms is likely to be reduced, since the operating system is not Windows, so you might lose COM+ services like transaction support.

Performance

Since day one, an important design goal for .NET has been great performance and scalability. For .NET to succeed, companies must be able to migrate their applications, and not suffer from poor performance due to the way code is executed by the CLR. To ensure optimal performance, the CLR compiles all application code into native machine code at some point. This conversion can either be done just in time as an application runs (on a method-by-method basis), or when an application is first installed. The compilation process will automatically make use of the microprocessor features available on different platforms, something traditional Windows applications could never do, unless you shipped different binaries for different platforms.

With the first version of ASP.NET you can expect well-written web applications to run two to four times faster than equivalent ASP applications, with similar gains in the area of scalability. In other areas of .NET like WinForms, performance is likely to be similar to VB6 for most applications, with memory usage increasingly slightly, due to overhead introduced by the CLR and a version 1.0 product release. As subsequent versions of the CLR and technologies like WinForms are released, you'll find that each release will have a smaller memory footprint and better performance.

Hopefully by now you're starting to understand how .NET can help solve many of the problems developers face today when writing software. It replaces a lot of older technologies like COM (although COM is certainly not dead), with better-designed equivalents. At the heart of this new platform is the **Common Language Runtime** (CLR).

The Common Language Runtime (CLR)

The CLR is one of the most radical features of .NET. Modern programming languages like VC++ and VB have always had runtimes. These are sometimes very small like MSCRT40.DLL (used by Visual C++ applications), and other times they can be quite big like MSVBVM60.DLL (used by Visual Basic 6).

A language runtime's role changes depending on the language: it may actually execute the code (as in the case of Java, or VB applications compiled using p-code), or in the case of native compiled languages (like C/C++), the runtime provides common functionality used by the application. Some of this runtime functionality may be used directly by an application, such as searching for a character sequence in a string, or indirectly by a compiler that injects additional code during the complication process to handle error situations or exceptions, such as the user aborting an application.

The CLR is a runtime for all .NET languages. It is responsible for executing and managing **all** code written in **any** language that targets the .NET platform.

The role of the CLR in some ways is similar to Sun's Java Virtual Machine (JVM) and the VB runtime. It is responsible for the execution of code developed using .NET languages. However, the critical point that differentiates the CLR is that it natively compiles all code. Although .NET compilers emit an **Intermediate Language** (IL) rather than machine code, the IL is **just-in-time** (JIT) **compiled** before code is executed. IL is not interpreted, and is not a byte code like p-code used by VB or the byte code used by Java. IL is a language. It is compiled, converted into machine code, and then executed. The result is applications targeting .NET, and executing on the CLR have exceptionally good application performance.

To complement IL, compilers that target the CLR also emit rich **metadata** that describes the types contained with a DLL or EXE (similar to COM type libraries but much richer) and version/dependency information. This metadata allows the CLR to intelligently resolve references between different application files at runtime, and also removes the dependency on the system registry. As we discussed earlier, these are two common problem areas for Windows DNA applications.

CLR Services

The CLR provides many core services to applications such as garbage collection, code verification, and code access security. The CLR can provide these services due to the way it manages code execution, and the fact that it can understand all types used within code thanks to the rich metadata compilers produce.

Garbage Collection is a CLR feature that automatically manages memory on the behalf of an application. You create and use objects, but you do not explicitly release them. The CLR automatically releases objects when they are no longer referenced and in use. This eliminates memory leaks in applications. This memory management feature is similar in some ways to how VB works today, but the implementation is radically different under the hood and much more efficient. A key difference is that the time at which unused memory will be released is non-deterministic. One side effect of this feature is that as a programmer, you cannot assume an object is destroyed when it goes out of the scope of a function. Therefore, you should not put code into a class destructor to release resources. You should always release them in the code using a class, as soon as possible.

Code verification is a process that ensures all code prior to execution is safe to run. Code verification enforces type safety, and therefore prevents code from performing illegal operations such as accessing invalid memory locations. With this feature it should **not** be possible for you to write code that causes your application to crash. If your code does do something wrong, the CLR will throw an exception before any damage can be done. Such exceptions can be caught and handled by an application.

Code access security allows code to be granted or denied **permissions** to do things, depending on the security configuration for a given machine, the origins of the code, and the metadata associated with types that the code is trying to use. The primary purpose of this feature is to protect users from malicious code that attempts to access other code residing on their machine. For example, with the CLR, you could write an e-mail application that denies all rights to code contained within an e-mail, and to use other classes such as the address book or file system.

Managed Code

The code produced for an application designed to run under the CLR is called **managed code**: self-describing code that makes use of the CLR and requires it to run. Code written with languages like VB6 that doesn't provide IL and doesn't need the CLR to run is called **unmanaged code**. For managed code, the CLR will:

❑   Always locate the metadata associated with a method at any point in time.

❑   Walk the stack.

❑   Handle exceptions.

❑   Store and retrieve security information.

These low-level requirements are necessary for the CLR to watch over code, provide the services we've discussed, and ensure its integrity for security/protection reasons.

Common Functionality

The CLR provides access to common base functionality (such as string searching) to all languages via the Base Class Library (BCL). The CLR is basically a replacement for the WIN32 API and COM, which solves nearly all the problems (or, should I say, features) of the Windows Platform. In doing this, it provides the foundation on which the .NET vision has been realized, since most of the Windows DNA limitations stem from features of these technologies. More importantly for VB developers, the WIN32 API provided a lot of functionality they could not easily use, like process creation and free-threaded support. Since that functionality is now part of the CLR, VB (and other languages such as COBOL) can now create high performance multi-threaded applications.

The CLR is object-oriented. All of the functionality of the CLR and the class libraries built on top of it are exposed as methods of objects. These classes are as easy to use as the ASP intrinsic objects and ADO objects you use today, but are far richer in functionality.

Using Objects

To show how to create and use objects with the CLR, let's walk through some simple examples. These will show:

❑ Creating a class in VB

❑ Creating a class in C# that inherits from the VB class

Let's start by creating our simple VB class:

```
Namespace Wrox.Books.ProASPNet

    Public Class MyVBClass

    End Class

End Namespace
```

Don't worry about what the `Namespace` statement means for the moment – we'll come onto that next.

Assuming this class is contained in a file called `base.vb`, we can compile it using the following command, which invokes the VB.NET command line compiler:

```
vbc base.vb /t:library
```

The output of the command is a DLL called `base.dll` that contains the class `MyVBClass`. The `/t:library` tells the compiler that we are creating a DLL. Any other developer can now use our class in their own code written using their preferred language.

To show the in-class **inheritance** feature of the CLR, and to show how easy inheritance is, we can create a class in any other language (in this case C#) that derives from our base VB class. This C# class inherits all of the **behavior** (the methods, properties, and events) of the base class:

```
using Wrox.Books.ProASPNet;

public class MyCSharpClass : MyVBClass
{

};
```

Assuming this is contained in a file called `derived.cs`, we could compile it using the following command, which invokes the C# command line compiler:

```
csc /t:library /r:base.dll derived.cs
```

`csc` is the name of the C# compiler executable. `/t:library` (t is short for target) tells the compiler to create a DLL (referred to as a library). `/r:base.dll` (r is short for reference) tells the compiler that the DLL being created references types (classes etc.) in the DLL `base.dll`.

You'll find a more comprehensive introduction to the syntax changes in the new .NET languages, as well as the similarities and differences between them, in the next chapter. We'll also see more on the syntax of the compiler options, and discuss JScript.NET.

This simple example doesn't have any real practical use (since there are no methods etc.), but hopefully it goes some way in demonstrating how easy and simple building components with the CLR and VB.NET and C# is. There is no nasty COM goo, just clean code.

This code example is so clean because the CLR is effectively responsible for all of the code. At run-time it can hook up the classes to implement the inheritance in a completely seamless way. The CLR really couldn't make cross-language development and integration any simpler for developers. You can create classes in any language you want, and use them in any other languages you want, either just instantiating and using them, or as in this example, actually deriving from them to inherit base functionality. You can use system classes (those written by Microsoft) or third-party classes in exactly the same way as you would any other class you'd written in your language of choice. This means the entire .NET Framework is one **consistent** object-oriented class library.

Namespaces

As we'll see in the next chapter, we'll create and use many different types when writing a CLR application. Within our code we can reference types using the `imports` key in VB.NET, and the `using` keyword in C#. In the VB class definition we had the following line:

```
Namespace Wrox.Books.ProASPNet
```

> **In .NET everything is referred to as a "type". A type can be a class, enumeration, interface, array, or structure.**

The namespace declaration tells a compiler that any types (such as classes or enumerations) defined are part of the specified namespace, which in this case is called `Wrox.Books.ProASPNET`. If we want to use these classes in another application, we need to import our namespace. In our C# code we saw this namespace import definition defined as:

```
using Wrox.Books.ProASPNet;
```

This namespace import declaration makes the types within the `Wrox.Books.ProASPNET` namespace available to any of the code in our C# file.

Namespaces have two key functions:

❑ **They logically group related types**. For example, `System.Web` contains all ASP.NET classes that manage the low-level execution of a web request. `System.Web.UI` contains all of the classes that actually render UI, and `System.Web.Hosting` contains the classes that aid in ASP.NET being hosted inside of IIS or other applications.

❑ **They make name collision less likely**. In an object-oriented world, many people are likely to use the same class names. The namespace reduces the likelihood of a conflict, since the fully qualified name of a class is equal to the namespace name plus the class name. You can choose to use fully qualified names in your code, and forgo the namespace import declaration, though you'll typically only do this if you have a name collision.

> **Namespaces do not physically group types, since a namespace can be used in different assemblies (DLLs and EXEs).**

Namespaces are used extensively in the CLR, and since ASP.NET pages are compiled down to CLR classes, you'll also use them extensively in your ASP.NET pages. For this reason ASP.NET automatically imports the most common names into an ASP.NET page. As we'll see later in the book you can extend this list to include your own classes.

It helps to think of namespaces like directories. Rather than containing files they contain classes. However, a namespace called `Wrox.MyBook` does not mean a namespace called `Wrox` exists. It is likely that it does, but it is not mandatory.

A Common Type System

For interoperability to be so smooth between languages, the CLR has a common type system. Languages like VB have built-in **primitive types** like `Integer`, `String`, and `Double`. C++ has types like `long`, `ulong`, and `char*`. However, these types aren't always compatible. If you've ever written a COM component, you'll know that making sure your components have interfaces that are usable in different languages depends a great deal on types. You'll often spend a lot of time converting types, and it's a real pain. For the CLR to make cross-language integration so smooth, all languages have to use a common type system.

The following table lists the types that form part of the **Common Language Specification** (CLS), and defines the types usable in any language targeting the CLR:

Type	Description	Range/Size
System.Boolean	Represents a `Boolean` value.	`True` or `False`. The CLS does not allow implicit conversion between `bool` and other primitive types.
System.Byte	Represents an unsigned byte value.	Positive integer between 0 and 255.
System.Char	Represents a UNICODE character value.	Any valid UNICODE character.

Table continued on following page

Type	Description	Range/Size
System.DateTime	Represents a date and time value.	IEEE 64-bit (8-byte) long integers that represent dates ranging from 1 January 1 CE (the year 1) to 31 December 9999 and times from 0:00:00 to 23:59:59.
System.Decimal	Represents positive and negative values with 28 significant digits.	79,228,162,514,264,337,593,543,950,335 to negative 79,228,162,514,264,337,593,543,950,335.
System.Double	Represents a 64-bit, double precision, floating point number.	Negative 1.79769313486231570E+308 to positive 1.79769313486231570E+308.
System.Int16	Represents a 16-bit signed integer value.	Negative 32768 to positive 32767.
System.Int32	Represents a 32-bit signed integer value negative.	Negative 2,147,483,648 to positive 2,147,483,647.
System.Int64	Represents a 64-bit signed integer.	9,223,372,036,854,775,808 to positive 9,223,372,036,854,775,807.
System.Sbyte	Represents an 8-bit signed integer.	Negative 128 to positive 127.
System.Single	Represents a 4-byte, single precision, floating point number.	Negative 3.402823E38 to positive 3.402823E38.
System.TimeSpan	Represents a period of time, either positive or negative.	The MinValue field is negative 10675199.02:48:05.4775808. The MaxValue field is positive 10675199.02:48:05.4775807.
System.String	Represents a UNICODE String.	Zero or more UNICODE characters.
System.Array	Represent a single dimension array.	Range is based upon declaration/usage. Arrays can contain other arrays.
System.Object	The base type from which all other types inherit.	N/A

Different languages use different keywords to expose these types. For example, VB will convert variables you declare as type Integer to System.Int32 during compile time, and C# will convert int into System.Int32. This makes working with different languages more natural and intuitive, whilst not compromising any goals of the CLR. You can of course declare the native CLR type names in any language, but you typically wouldn't do this unless the language did not have its own native mapping. This is another great feature of the CLR. If the language doesn't support a feature, you can usually find some .NET Framework classes that do.

All types derive from `System.Object`. This class has four methods. All of these methods are available on all types:

`Equals`	Allows two object instances to be compared for equality. Most CLR classes override this and provide a custom implementation. For example, `System.ValueType` has an implementation that compares all members' fields for equality. Value types are discussed shortly.
`GetHashCode`	Returns a hash code for the object. This function is used by classes such as `Hashtable` to get a unique identity for an object. Two objects of the same type that represent the same value will always return the same hash code.
`GetType`	Returns a `Type` object that can be programmatically used to explore the methods, properties, and events of a type. This feature of the CLR is called **Reflection**.
`ToString`	Returns a string representation of the type. The default implementation returns the fully-qualified type name suitable in aiding debugging. Most CLR types override this method and provide a more useful return value. For example, `System.Int32` will return a string representation of a number.

Common Language Specification

Some languages can require types that other languages do not support. To allow for this there are additional CLR types that support the functionality required for specific languages such as C#. However, one caveat with sharing CLR classes created with different languages means that there is the potential that a class will not be usable in certain languages if its types are not understood. For example, the C# language has types like unsigned `long`s that are not available in languages such as VB, so a C# class that uses unsigned `long`s as part of its **public member definitions** can **not** be used in VB. However, the same class can be used if such types are used in **non-public member definitions**. To help ensure types created by different languages are compatible, a common set of base types exists to ensure language interoperability. This is part of what is called the Common Language Specification (CLS). Most CLR compilers have options to flag warnings if non-CLS types are used.

Everything in the CLR is an Object

Every type in the CLR is an object. As we saw in the table above, all other types are derived from `System.Object`. When you define your own **custom types** such as classes, structures, and enumerations, they are also automatically derived from `System.Object`, even though you don't explicitly define this inheritance. When a class is compiled, the compiler will automatically do this for you.

As every type has a common base type (`System.Object`), developers can write some very powerful generic code. For example, the `System.Collection` namespace provides lots of collection classes that work with `System.Object`. For example, the `Hashtable` class is a simple dictionary class populated using a name and a `System.Object` reference. By using either a name or an index you can retrieve an object reference from the collection very efficiently. Since all types derive from `System.Object` you can hold any type in a `Hashtable`.

Value Type and Reference Types

If you're a C/C++ developer or an experienced VB programmer, you're probably thinking that having every type in the CLR as an object is expensive, since primitive types such as `integer` and `long` and `structure` in VB6 and C/C++ only require space to be allocated on the stack, where as object references require allocated space on the heap. To avoid having all types heap allocated, which would compromise code execution performance, the CLR has **value types** and **reference types**.

❑   Value types are allocated on the **stack** just like primitive types in VBScript, VB6, and C/C++.

❑   Reference types are allocated on the **managed CLR heap**, just like object types.

It is important to understand how the CLR manages and converts these types using boxing and unboxing, otherwise you can easily write inefficient code without knowing it.

Value types are **not** instantiated using `new` (unless you have a parameterized constructor) and go out of scope when the function they are defined within returns. Value types in the CLR are defined as types that derive from `System.ValueType`. All of the CLR primitive types like `System.Int32` derive from this class, and when you define structures using VB.NET and C# those types automatically derive from `System.ValueType`.

Here is an example VB.NET structure that represents a CLR value type called `Person`:

```
Public Structure Person

    Dim Name As String
    Dim Age As Integer

End Structure
```

The equivalent C# structure is:

```
Public Struct Person
{
    string name;
    int age;
}
```

Both compilers will emit IL that defines a `Person` type that inherits from `System.ValueType`. The CLR will therefore know to allocate instances of this type on the stack.

Boxing

When using CLR classes like the `Hashtable` (discussed in Chapter 15) that work with collections of `System.Object` types, you need to be aware that the CLR will automatically convert value types into reference types. This conversion happens when you assign a value type, such as a primitive type like `System.Int32`, to an `object` reference, or vice versa.

The following code will implicitly **box** an `Integer` value when it is assigned to an `object` reference:

```
//C#
int i = 32;
object o = i;
```

```
'VB
dim i as Integer = 32
dim o as object = i
```

When boxing occurs, the contents of a value type are copied from the stack into memory allocated on the managed heap. The new reference type created contains a copy of the value type, and can be used by other types that expect an `object` reference. The value contained in the value type and the created reference types are not associated in any way (except they contain the same values). If you change the original value type, the reference type is not affected.

The following code explicitly **unboxes** a reference type into a value type:

```
//C#
object o;
int i = (int) o;
```

```
'VB
dim o as object
dim i as Integer = CType(o, Integer)
```

> **In this example you need to assume the object variable o has been previously initialized.**

When unboxing occurs, memory is copied from the managed heap to the stack.

Understanding boxing and unboxing is important, since it has performance implications. Every time a value type is boxed, a new reference type is created, and the value type is copied onto the managed heap. Depending on the size of the value type, and the number of times value types are boxed and unboxed, the CLR can spend a lot of CPU cycles just doing these conversions.

To put all this type theory into practice, take a look at the following VB.NET code, which illustrates when value types and reference types are used, and when boxing and unboxing occurs:

```
Imports System.Collections
Imports System
```

We start by declaring a simple structure called `Person` that can hold a name and an age. Since structures are always value types (remember compilers automatically derive structures from `System.ValueType`), instances of this type will always be held on the stack:

```
Public Structure Person

    Dim Name As String
    Dim Age As Integer

End Structure
```

Then we begin our main module:

```
Public Module Main

  Public Sub Main()

  Dim dictionary As Hashtable
  Dim p As Person
```

First, we create a `Hashtable`. This is a reference type, so we use `New` to create an instance of the object, which will be allocated on the managed CLR heap:

```
dictionary = new Hashtable()
```

Hashtable and other collections classes are explained in more detail in Chapter 15.

Next, we initialize our `Person` structure with some values. This is a value type, so we don't have to use `New`, since the type is allocated automatically on the stack when we declare our variable:

```
p.Name = "Richard Anderson"
p.Age = 28
```

Once our `Person` structure is initialized, we add it to the dictionary using a key of `"Rich"`. This method call will implicitly cause the value type to be boxed within a reference type as we discussed, since the second parameter of the `Add` method expects an `object` reference:

```
dictionary.Add( "Rich", p )
```

Next, we change the values of the same `Person` structure variable to hold some new values:

```
p.Name = "Sam Anderson"
p.Age = 27
```

and add another person to the dictionary with a different key. Again, this will cause the value type to be boxed within a reference type and added to the dictionary:

```
dictionary.Add( "Sam", p )
```

At this point, we now have a `Hashtable` object that contains two reference types. Each of these reference types contains our `Person` structure value type, with the values we initialized.

We can retrieve an item from the `Hashtable` using a key. Since the `Hashtable` returns object references, we use the `CType` keyword to tell VB.NET that the object type returned by the `Item` function is actually a `Person` type. Since the `Person` type is a value type, the CLR knows to unbox the `Person` type from the returned reference type:

```
p = CType( dictionary.Item("Rich"), Person )
```

And now we can use the `Person` type

```
    Console.WriteLine("Name is {0} and Age is {1}", p.Name, p.Age )

    End Sub

End Module
```

Language Changes

The CLR supports a rich set of functionality. To enable languages like VB to make use of these capabilities, the language syntax has to be enhanced with new keywords. The CLR functionality may be common to all languages, but each language will expose the functionality in a way that suits that language. As our simple inheritance example showed earlier, both VB.NET and C# explicitly define the start and end of a class (VB used to do this implicitly via the file extension), but the keywords used are different.

We'll investigate the language changes fully in Chapter 3.

Assemblies – Versioning and Securing Code

We discussed earlier how one of the biggest problems with Windows DNA applications is the number of implicit dependencies and versioning requirements. One application can potentially break another application by accidentally overwriting a common system DLL, or removing an installed component. To help resolve these problems, the CLR uses **assemblies**.

An assembly is a collection of one or more files, with one of those files (either a DLL or EXE) containing some special metadata known as the **assembly manifest**. The assembly manifest defines what the versioning requirements for the assembly are, who authored the assembly, what security permissions the assembly requires to run, and what files form part of the assembly.

An assembly is created by default whenever you build a DLL. You can examine the details of the manifest programmatically using classes located in the `System.Reflection` namespace. To keep our discussion focused, we'll use a tool provided with the .NET SDK called ILDASM (Intermediate Language Disassembler). You can run this tool from either a command prompt or via the Start bar Run menu.

When the tool is running, we can use the File | Open menu to open up the `derived.dll` created in our simple inheritance sample earlier. Once loaded ILDASM shows a tree control containing an entry for the assembly manifest, and an entry for each type defined in that DLL:

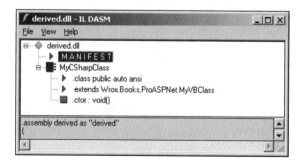

Although the type information for MyCSharpClass is part of our DLL, it is not part of the assembly manifest. It is however part of the assembly.

If we double-click on the MANIFEST entry, we'll see the manifest definition:

```
MANIFEST
.assembly extern base
{
  .ver 0:0:0:0
}
.assembly extern mscorlib
{
  .publickeytoken = (B7 7A 5C 56 19 34 E0 89 )                    // .z\V.4..
  .ver 1:0:2411:0
}
.assembly derived
{
  // --- The following custom attribute is added automatically, do not uncomment -------
  //   .custom instance void [mscorlib]System.Diagnostics.DebuggableAttribute::.ctor(bool,
  //                                                              bool) = ( 01 00 00 01 00 00 )
  .hash algorithm 0x00008004
  .ver 1:0:1:0
}
.module derived.dll
// MVID: {CFDC3A0A-B394-4DD5-84A2-AC1045D25258}
.imagebase 0x00400000
.subsystem 0x00000003
.file alignment 512
.corflags 0x00000001
// Image base: 0x031a0000
```

The manifest is stored as binary data, so what we are seeing here is a decompiled form of the manifest, presented in a readable form. The .assembly extern lines tell us that this assembly is dependent upon two other assemblies: base and mscorlib. mscorlib is the main CLR system assembly, which contains the core classes for the built-in CLR types, etc. We created the assembly base earlier when we built our file base.vb. The default name of the assembly created by a compiler reflects the output filename created, minus the extension. If we'd used the following command line to build our VB DLL from earlier:

```
vbc base.vb /out:Wrox.dll
```

the assembly created would be called Wrox, and the output from ILDASM for derived.dll should show a .assembly extern line for Wrox instead of base.

In the screenshot of the manifest you can see that the reference to the base assembly from within the derived assembly has two additional attributes:

❑   .ver – Specifies the version of the assembly compiled against. The CLR uses the format Major:Minor:Build:Revision for version numbers. An assembly is considered incompatible if the Major or Minor version numbers change.

❑   .hash – A hash value that can be used to determine if any of the files in the reference assembly are different.

The `mscorlib` assembly reference has one additional attribute worth briefly discussing:

❑ `.publickeytoken` – This specifies part of a public key that can be used by the CLR when loading the reference assembly, to 100% guarantee that only the named assembly written by a given party (in this case Microsoft) is loaded.

The `.assembly derived` section of the manifest declares the assembly information for the derived `.dll` file. This has similar attributes to the external manifests. By default the version of an assembly is 0.0.0.0. To change this you specify an assembly version attribute in one of the source files. VS.NET typically creates a separate source file to contain these attributes, but you can define them anywhere you choose, providing it's not within the scope of another type definition.

In VB.NET the format for assembly attributes is:

```
<assembly: AssemblyVersion("1.0.1.0")>
```

This would make the assembly version appear as 1.0.1.0. Within C# the format is slightly different, but has the same net effect:

```
[assembly: AssemblyVersion("1.0.1.0")]
```

> To use assembly attributes you have to import the `System.Reflection` namespace.

Attributes are a feature of CLR compilers that allow you to annotate types with additional metadata. The CLR or other tools can then use this metadata for different purposes, such as containing documentation, information about COM+ service configuration, and so on.

Are Assemblies Like DLLs?

For the most part, you can think of a DLL and an assembly as having a one-to-one relationship. Most developers will probably use them this way, but for special cases you can use the more advanced features of the command line compilers to create assemblies that span multiple DLLs, a single EXE, and either contain or link to one or more resource files.

The following diagram shows the basic structure of a typical assembly:

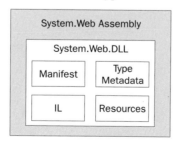

In this diagram we're looking at the `System.Web` assembly. This assembly consists of a single file, `System.Web.DLL`. The `System.Web.DLL` contains the assembly manifest, the type metadata that describes the classes etc. located within `System.Web.DLL` file, the IL for the code and resources for embedded images. The embedded resources within this `System.Web.DLL` are mainly images used in Visual Studio.NET to represent web controls.

If the designers of this assembly had chosen to do so, they could have created a multi-file assembly (**complex assembly**) like this:

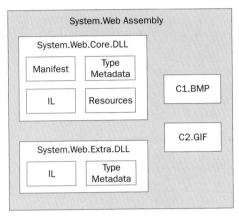

The System.Web assembly in this diagram consists of four files:

❑ System.Web.Core.DLL – contains the assembly manifest describing all the other files and dependencies of those files, the type metadata for the classes located within the file (not the whole assembly), the IL for the code within the classes, and some embedded resources.

❑ System.Web.Extra.DLL – contains the type metadata for the classes etc. located within the file (not the assembly). Also contains the IL for code within the various classes.

❑ C1.BMP – A picture in bitmap format.

❑ C2.GIF – A picture in Graphic Interchange Format (GIF).

Although the physical file structure of these assemblies is different, to the CLR they have logically the same meaning. Both expose the same types, and consumers of the types within the assembly are not affected, since they only ever reference types using namespaces.

All files within an assembly are referred to as **modules**. A namespace can span one or more modules. A namespace can also span across one or more assemblies. The physical structure of an assembly has no impact or relation to the namespace structure.

The reasons for creating a multi-file assembly vary. They may be appropriate if you're working in a large team and you want to be able to bring individual developer's modules together within a single assembly that is version controlled. Or more practically, you might want to manage memory consumption. If you know certain classes are not always needed, putting them into a separate physical file means the CLR can delay loading that file until the types within it are needed.

For a lot of applications, using complex assemblies is probably overkill. Even if you don't use the versioning features assemblies provide, you should still be aware of how type versioning within assemblies occurs.

You need to try to make sure that your business components are kept compatible with the ASP.NET pages that call them. You are creating **private assemblies** when you build component files like DLLs that are only used by your application, but for the most part this is an implementation detail you can ignore. However, if you want to share your component files across multiple web applications, you may need to create **shared assemblies** and put them in the GAC, and understand the more complex versioning implications these have.

No More DLL Hell

The CLR can load multiple versions of the assembly at the same time. This basically solves DLL hell – the problem where installing a new application might break other applications, because newer DLLs are installed that older applications are not compatible with. This is known as **side-by-side** component versioning and deployment.

Type Versioning

If you have ever written a COM component you have probably experienced **binary-compatibility** problems. This is typified by needing to change a component's public interface (adding, changing, or deleting methods) once it has already been released. The rules of COM say that once a component is released, its interface is immutable: it should not be changed. If you do need to make changes then your component should support multiple interfaces. This approach has a number of problems:

- ❑ It's difficult to manage multiple interfaces, and almost impossible not to break compatibility by mistake.

- ❑ VB6 never really supported interfaces properly, so implementing interfaces has always been a black art.

- ❑ Most application developers don't want to version individual components.

Versioning in ASP web applications to date has shielded many developers from these problems. ASP pages always used **late binding** to talk to COM components. Each time a method was called, the script engine executing the ASP page code determined if the method existed, invoking it if it did. If a method did not exist, an error would be raised.

This late-bound approach is actually pretty good in some ways. ASP developers don't have to worry too much about versioning – as long as the methods called for each object are supported, the page will still work. The only drawback of this approach, which can be a significant cost, is that small performance hit per method call to find out if this method exists.

The CLR provides late-binding versioning for types in a similar way to late binding in COM/ASP, but there is no performance hit. When the CLR loads a type such as a class, it knows what methods of other types that class is going to call. It can therefore resolve these references at run time at a method level, generating **early-bound** code to call each method. This means the programmer only has to worry about keeping method signatures the same to maintain binary compatibility. It is possible to support interfaces and use the same technique as COM, but Microsoft discourages this unless it is really necessary. If an interface changes, all classes implementing the interface have to be recompiled.

If you do break compatibility in a component it will show itself quickly. For example, if an application calls into a component that no longer supports a method it needs, the CLR will raise a `MissingMethodException`. If an application tries to use a type that has been deleted, or a type that doesn't implement all of the methods of an interface, a `TypeLoadException` will be thrown. These can be caught by the caller application, and they usually contain detailed messages to explain what went wrong.

.NET provides a platform that enables us to start implementing next generation Internet applications, with more power and speed than ever before. It also enables us to capitalize on our existing knowledge of VB, C/++, and JScript, as well as introducing enhancements to all the languages (like inheritance, polymorphism, and multi-threading) – not to mention the brand new language C#, designed to work from the ground up with the .NET Framework.

The reason for not giving .NET DLL/EXE files a different extension is for compatibility reasons.

CLR and COM

At this point you're probably beginning to ask yourself where the Component Object Model (COM) fits into the CLR. The simple answer is that it doesn't. From a technology perspective COM is **not** used as a core technology to power the CLR. The CLR is written from the ground up, and COM is only used for interoperability and hosting. Interoperability allows you to use your existing COM components within .NET languages just as if they were CLR classes, and to use your CLR classes as COM components for non-CLR applications. Hosting the CLR inside of applications (such as IIS) is done using COM, as the CLR provides a set of COM components for loading and executing CLR code.

The fact that the CLR is not COM-based does signal that COM will no longer be a mainstream technology for web applications written on the Windows platform in future. This means that most of the concepts you may use as a C/C++ programmer, or may have been aware of as a VB programmer, are not part of the .NET Framework. For example, in the world of COM, all objects were reference counted, all COM methods returned an HRESULT, etc. However, the concept of interface-based programming is still prevalent within .NET, so the COM way of thinking about things in terms of interfaces is still valid. Still, most people will probably switch interfaces to base classes for productivity reasons.

> Internally Microsoft is promoting that teams should no longer build and release new COM components. The way forward is to create .NET components that are exposed through interop as COM components.

Intermediate Language

We're not going to cover IL in any great depth in this book, but just so you can get a feel for it, examine this line of VB.NET code:

```
System.Console.WriteLine(".NET makes development fun and easy again")
```

It calls the `WriteLine` method of the `Console` class, which is part of the `System` namespace. A namespace, as we discussed, is a way of grouping related classes. When compiled and run as part of a console application, this line of code will basically output the simple message to a console window. We could write this same line of code in IL, as follows:

```
LdStr ".NET makes development fun and easy again"
Call [mscorlib]System.Console::WriteLine(class System.String)
```

This code uses the same API call, except it is prefixed with `[mscorlib]`, which tells the CLR that the API we're calling is located in the file `MSCORLIB.DLL`. The first line shown is the way in which parameters are passed to an API. The `LdStr` command loads the specified string onto the call stack, so the API being called can retrieve it.

If we took our simple VB code and used the VB.NET compiler to compile it, the output produced would be an executable file that contains IL similar to what you have just seen. The IL would not be identical since the VB compiler actually spits out some additional initialization IL, which isn't important in our example. The point to walk away with is that the DLLs and EXEs you create are **self-describing**.

Application Domains

All Windows applications run inside of a process. Processes own resources like memory and kernel objects, and threads execute code loaded into a process. Processes are protected from each other by the operating system, such that one process can in **no way** unexpectedly affect the execution of another application running in another process. This level of protection is the ultimate way of having many applications run on a machine, safe in the knowledge that no matter what one application does, if it crashes, the others should continue. Processes provide a high level of application fault tolerance, which is why IIS and COM+ use them when running in high isolation mode.

The problem with processes in Windows is that they are a very expensive resource to create and manage, and they do not scale well if used in large quantities. For example, if you're using IIS and have a large number of web sites configured to run in isolation, each one has its own dedicated process which will consume a lot of resources, such as memory. If you ran all of these applications within the same process, you'd be able to run a much larger number of web sites on one machine since fewer resources would be consumed. Less memory would be required since DLLs would also only have to be loaded into one process, and the inter-process overhead between the various processes and the core IIS worker process would be reduced. Of course, the downside to this approach is that if one site crashes, all sites would be affected.

Application Domains in .NET have the same benefits as a process, but multiple application domains can run within the same process:

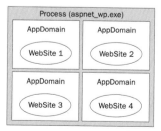

Application Domains (AppDomains) can be implemented safely within the same process, because the code verification feature of the CLR ensures the code is safe to run before allowing it to execute. This provides a huge scalability and reliability benefit. For example, now applications like IIS can achieve higher scalability by running each web site in a different application domain, rather than a different process, safe in the knowledge that inter-application isolation has not been compromised.

ASP.NET, when running as part of IIS4/5, uses AppDomains to run each instance of an ASP.NET application:

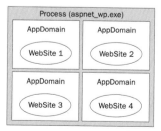

Each ASP.NET application runs in its own application domain, and is therefore protected from other ASP.NET applications on the same machine. ASP.NET ignores the process isolation you specify in IIS.

.NET Framework Drill Down

The .NET Framework consists of four major pieces:

- ❏ Application development technologies
- ❏ Class libraries
- ❏ Base class libraries
- ❏ The Common Language Runtime

These pieces sit on top of each other, with each of the higher layers making use of one or more of the lower layers, as shown in this diagram:

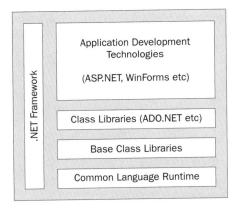

We have already discussed the CLR and base class libraries, so in the next section we'll briefly examine the top two layers: application development technologies and class libraries. These layers are the primary focus for the rest of the book.

Application Development Technologies

As we saw in Chapter 1, ASP.NET is a very exciting .NET technology for building web applications, providing us with many new features and a much cleaner programming mode. The features we're going to concentrate on here are:

- ❏ Web services
- ❏ WinForms

Web Services

In our intelligent fridge example earlier, we discussed the idea of a fridge talking to a supermarket over the Internet to automatically restock itself. To achieve this, supermarkets would have to expose APIs over the Internet that any fridge could call upon to place orders. There would also be a requirement to locate such services, giving the fridge owner the ability to pick a supermarket to order from. This concept of locating and consuming programmatic functions over the Internet is called **Web Services**.

> Web Services are programmable business logic components that serve as "black boxes" to provide access to functionality via the Internet using standard protocols such as HTTP.

Web Services are based upon an application of XML called the **Simple Object Access Protocol** (**SOAP**). SOAP defines a standardized format for enveloping XML payloads exchanged between two entities over standard protocols such as HTTP. SOAP is completely based upon open standards. The consumer of a Web Service is therefore completely shielded from any implementation details about the platform exposing the Web Service – the consumer simply sends and receives XML over HTTP. This means that any Web Service on a Windows platform can be consumed by any other platform, like Unix.

> More technical details on SOAP can be found at http://www.w3.org/TR/SOAP/ and http://www.develop.com/soap/.

Web Services are a core part of the .NET Framework. Using ASP.NET you can easily expose Web Services from your web site, and you can easily consume Web Services from other web sites. To make this whole model simple for developers, within the .NET environment you do little more than write a class to expose a Web Service, or consume a class to use a Web Service. This saves you from having to understand protocols like SOAP in detail, but you can be assured that anybody can access the functionality you provide.

The following VB code defines a simple Web Service with a single function called NameABook:

```
<%@ WebService Language="VB" class="MyWebService" %>

Imports System
Imports System.Web.Services

Public Class MyWebService

  Public Function <WebMethod> NameABook() As String
    Return "Professional ASP.NET"
  End Function

End Class
```

Here is the same Web Service, this time written in C#:

```
<%@ WebService Language="C#" class="MyWebService" %>

using System;
using System.Web.Services;

public class MyWebService
{
  [WebMethod]
  public string NameABook()
  {
  return "Professional ASP.NET";
  }
}
```

To host these Web Services within an ASP.NET page, all you have to do is copy the code into a standard text file, and save that file in your ASP.NET application directory, giving the file an extension of .asmx. When the ASP.NET run-time sees an .asmx file being requested, it knows that the file requested represents a Web Service, and will automatically decode the incoming SOAP request, invoke the appropriate function, and send out an SOAP/XML response.

There are more facets to Web Services, such as security, describing the Web Services available on a given site, and providing the ability to locate Web Services via a certain discovery service.

We'll be looking at Web Services more closely in Chapters 19 and 20.

WinForms

For developing traditional Windows GUI applications, the .NET Framework provides us with **Windows Forms (WinForms)**.

> **WinForms is an extensive class library that exposes the functionality of Windows Common Controls using the expressive object-oriented capabilities of the .NET Framework.**

If you have ever developed a form in VB6 using the forms designer, or created dialogs using VC++ and MFC, you'll be right at home, since a lot of the classes are similar. WinForms uses a similar designer to previous versions of Visual Studio, but the functionality exposed by the controls is much richer, and they are object-oriented. The net result is applications that look pretty much like they do today, but you require less code, and the code is cleaner and easier to understand.

Another important advance with WinForms is that we now have a single GUI library and forms designer for all of the supported languages. Whether you program in VB, C++, or one of the newer languages like C#, you'll be using the same classes, methods, and events, since they all use the same class library: WinForms. The benefits this brings to programmers are very important. Since the same class library is being used, all of the languages have the same capabilities. This means you can use the language you're most comfortable with, and don't have to worry about whether the language you choose has the same features as are available, say, in C/C++. This is a problem you might well have hit in the past.

Class Libraries

The .NET Framework has an extensive set of class libraries. This includes classes for:

❑ **Data Access** – High performance data access classes for connecting to SQL Server or any other OLEDB provider. See Chapter 9.

❑ **XML support** – Next generation XML support that goes far beyond the functionality of MSXML. See Chapter 11.

❑ **Directory Services** – Support for accessing Active Directory/LDAP using ADSI.

❑ **Regular Expression** – Support above and beyond that found in Perl 5. See Chapter 15.

❑ **Queuing Support** – Provides a clean object-oriented set of classes for working with MSMQ.

These class libraries use the CLR base class libraries for common functionality.

Base Class Libraries

The base class library in the .NET Framework is huge. They cover areas like:

❑ **Collections** – The `System.Collection` namespace provides numerous collection classes. See Chapter 15.

❑ **Thread Support** – The `System.Threading` namespace provides support for creating fast, efficient, multi-threaded applications.

❑ **Code Generation** – The `System.CodeDOM` namespace provides classes for generating source files in numerous languages. ASP.NET uses these classes when converting ASP.NET pages into classes, which are subsequently compiled.

❑ **IO** – The `System.IO` namespace provides extensive support for working with files and all other stream types.

❑ **Reflection** – The `System.Reflection` namespace provides support for load assemblies, examining the types within assemblies, creating instances of types, etc.

❑ **Security** – The `System.Security` namespace provides support for services like authentication, authorization, permission sets, policies, and cryptography. These base services are used by application development technologies like ASP.NET to build their security infrastructure.

The list of support base classes goes on forever in .NET, but if you ever find yourself lost looking for a specific class, you can use the `WinCV` tool to locate it. You can run this from the Start bar Run menu. The file is typically located in the `c:\program files\Microsoft.Net\FrameworkSDK\Bin` directory.

The `WinCV` tool allows you to type in a search string, and brings back a list of all the types it found that match it. The following screen shows the results of typing **HttpRequest** (the ASP.NET class that is the `Request` object, also called the `Request` intrinsic):

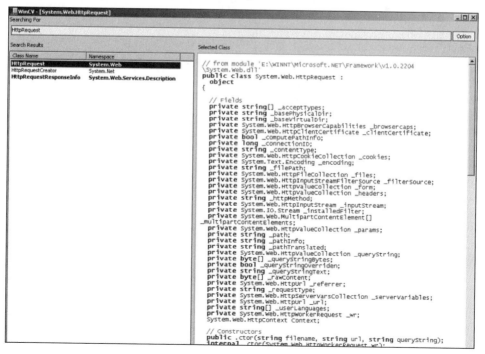

The left pane shows all of the types matched. The right side shows the type definition, retrieved using the reflection classes. Using the information shown, we can determine that the HttpRequest class is defined as part of the System.Web namespace, which is contained in the file System.Web.dll.

By now you should have a fairly good picture of how the .NET Framework fits together, so let's look at some of the ASP.NET design goals, and see how the .NET Framework was used to build ASP.NET.

ASP.NET Design Goals

To understand some of the reasons why ASP.NET works the way it does, we'll cover some of the key design goals of ASP.NET in this section. We'll be looking at these in more depth later in the book.

Some of the key goals of ASP.NET were to:

❑ Remove the dependency on script engines, enabling pages to be type safe and compiled.

❑ Reduce the amount of code required to develop web applications.

❑ Make ASP.NET well factored, allowing customers to add in their own custom functionality, and extend/replace built-in ASP.NET functionality.

❑ Make it easy to deploy web applications.

❑ Make ASP.NET a logical evolution of ASP, where existing ASP investment and therefore code can be reused with little, if any, change.

❑ Provide great tool support in terms of debugging and editing.

❑ Realize that bugs are a fact of life, so ASP.NET should be as fault tolerant as possible.

We'll examine each of these goals, and look at how they have been realized in ASP.NET.

Remove the Dependency on Script Engines

ASP is built using Active Scripting, a technology originally designed to enable developers to script and control applications in a uniform way. It isn't a technology that was really designed to write full-scale applications, which is essentially what many developers are trying to do using ASP, which is why ASP.NET was **not** written using Active Scripting.

Active Scripting has many inherent problems:

❑ Code is interpreted, not compiled

❑ It has a weak type system – just variants

❑ It only supports late-bound calling of methods

❑ Each instance of an active scripting engine consumes memory

As an ASP developer you're probably very aware of these problems, and will have experienced them when developing or profiling your applications. Interpreted code results in very average performance. A weak type system makes code harder to develop, read, and debug. Late-bound code is many times slower than early-bound code, and restricts what components you can use. You may have written lots of COM components to get around these problems, but even that solution has performance and maintenance implications. Creating COM objects from ASP is relatively expensive, and upgrading COM components today typically means stopping your web servers.

All of these problems were not something ASP.NET wanted to inherit, so the decision was made early on to target compiled code. Since the .NET platform was already in development, and had the potential to deal with the problems of COM and the Windows DNA platform in general, ASP.NET was built using C# and targeted as part of the .NET Framework. Finally, ASP.NET was built from the ground up.

Performance

To get great performance and remove the active scripting dependency, ASP.NET pages utilize assemblies (DLLs). The basic process is shown in this diagram:

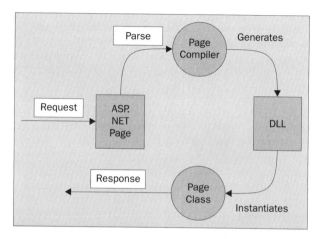

When a page is first requested, ASP.NET compiles the page into an assembly. The assembly created is assigned a unique name, and is placed in a sub-directory within the directory `%systemroot%/Microsoft.NET/Framework/v1.n.nnnn/Temporary ASP.NET Files`. The assembly created contains a single generated class that derives from the `System.Web.UI.Page` class. This class contains all the code needed to generate the page, and is instantiated by the framework to process a request each time the `.aspx` page is requested.

The page compilation process isn't cheap and can take a few seconds for complex pages. However, the compilation is only ever done **once** per `.aspx` file. All subsequent requests for the page – even after IIS has been restarted – are satisfied by instantiating the class generated, and asking it to render the page. This results in great performance. The only cost to you is a little disk space on your web servers.

> **You can change the temporary directory location used by ASP.NET by adding a `tempDirectory` attribute to the compilation element in `machine.config`.**

When a .NET class is generated for an `.aspx` page, the dependencies of that page – such as the `.aspx` page and any include files – form part of the compiled class. These dependencies are checked before a page is rendered, and if it's determined that any of the dependency files have changed since the page was compiled, the assembly is deleted and a new one is created. This ensures that the page rendered is always up to date.

The code generation and compilation classes and methods used by ASP.NET are a standard part of the .NET Framework, located within the `System.CodeDOM` namespace contained in the assembly `System.DLL`.

An Evolution of ASP

ASP.NET has been designed to try and maintain syntax and run-time compatibility with existing ASP pages wherever possible. The motivation behind this is to allow existing ASP pages to be initially migrated to ASP.NET by simply renaming the file to have an extension of `.aspx`. For the most part this goal has been achieved, although there are typically some basic code changes that have to be made, since VBScript is no longer supported, and the VB language itself has changed.

Once you've renamed your ASP pages to have an extension of `.aspx`, they become ASP.NET pages, and you'll need to go through the process of fixing any errors so that those pages will be compiled and can execute without problems. However, ASP.NET pages **cannot** share any type of state with ASP pages, so you cannot share information using any of the intrinsic objects like application or session. This means for most applications you'll typically have to convert all of your ASP pages at once, or convert groups of pages, that can work effectively together.

> You can run ASP.NET and ASP side-by-side on the same box. When future versions of ASP.NET are released, you'll also be able to run multiple different versions of ASP.NET side-by-side on the same box.

Easy to Deploy

Deploying an ASP application today onto a production web server can be a traumatic experience, especially if the application consists of COM components, and requires configuration changes to the IIS meta-data. The scope of these problems gets a lot worse in a web farm scenario. You have to copy the ASP files onto every server, copy and register the COM components, create COM+ applications and register the associated COM+ components, and update the IIS meta-data using ADSI depending on your configuration requirements. This installation isn't an easy thing to do, and typically you need a skilled administrator, and time and patience, to get a site up and running. Or, you need to write a fairly advanced setup program, which is the approach I've taken in the past.

The deployment of an ASP.NET application is radically simpler. To install an application requires two steps:

- ❏ Create a web site or virtual directory
- ❏ XCOPY your application files into the directory

Deleting an application is equally simple:

- ❏ Delete or stop the web site or virtual directory
- ❏ Delete the files

ASP.NET achieves this goal by making a few fundamental changes to the way we develop web applications:

- ❏ Configuration of applications is done using XML configuration files stored in the web application directories. This replaces the need to use the IIS meta-data. It also allows you to store your own configuration in these files, rather than a database, which simplifies deployment. IIS6 is likely to use an XML-based configuration model when it is released.

❑ ASP.NET (specifically the CLR) does not require components to be registered. As long as your component files are located within the `bin` directory (you can not change the name of this directory) on your virtual directory, your ASP.NET pages can create and use components within those files.

❑ ASP.NET is built using the services of the CLR rather than COM. This means you can copy updated DLLs into your application directory (the `bin` sub-directory), and it will automatically start using the components within those files, unloading the previous versions from memory.

To make redeployment of an existing application simple, ASP.NET uses the CLR Shadow Copy feature to ensure component files are never locked. That's right, no more IIS reset or rebooting a machine. This feature means that at any point in time you can upgrade components by simply copying newer component files over the old ones. The Shadow Copy feature of the CLR allows this, since the component file is actually copied into a cache area before they are loaded. This means the original file is never actually loaded from the original location.

The Shadow Copy feature of the CLR works on an application domain basis. Files are shadow copied for each application domain. To reload a component once it's changed, ASP.NET creates a new application domain, thus causing the changed file to be cached and used.

The Shadow Copy feature of the CLR only works for ASP.NET component files located in the `bin` directory.

Great Tool Support

ASP has always been a great technology for developing web applications, but it has never had great tool support, which has made web application development less productive than it really could be.

For most people in the world of ASP, Notepad was their editor, and `Response.Write` was the preferred and – for the most part – the only reliable debugging method. To be fair, Visual Interdev wasn't a bad editor, and when it worked, the debugging support could be pretty good (if the sun was shining and REM was playing on the radio). However, having worked on a couple of development teams where a few people were using Visual InterDev, I can quite honestly say it always seems to cause the most grief to developers (although SourceSafe is a close second). I personally never liked Visual Interdev, since debugging from ASP pages through to COM components and back again was never supported well. The good news with ASP.NET is that you no longer have to use Visual Interdev (hooray!).

Visual Studio.NET (VS.NET) has *first class* support for ASP.NET page development and debugging. When developing pages, you get the same type of designer mode as Visual Interdev, but the whole layout of the VS.NET designer is much more natural, and much more flexible. Developing an ASP.NET page is pretty much the same as developing a VB form, and very productive.

Debugging support in ASP.NET is also excellent. You can debug from ASP.NET pages, into a .NET component, back into ASP.NET pages with great ease. Since all of the compiled code is using the CLR to execute, the orchestration between your code and VS.NET is smooth and reliable, even if you debug across multiple languages. Never again will you have to use `Response.Write` or a script debugger. As if this isn't enough, ASP.NET also provides excellent tracing services, which are covered in more detail in Chapter 22.

Simpler, More Flexible Configuration

The XML based configuration model of ASP.NET makes deployment of applications much easier. The configuration is kept in text files stored with the application, so deployment is a non-issue. Furthermore, ASP.NET provides a very powerful and flexible configuration system, which is easy to utilize within your own ASP.NET pages and components.

Configuration files in ASP.NET are hierarchical – settings defined in one directory can be overridden by settings defined in a sub-directory. A base configuration for all ASP.NET applications (machine level) is defined in the web.config file located with the ASP.NET system directory. This file defines global settings and mappings that are common to most applications, which includes settings like:

❑ The time before a web request is timed out.

❑ Which .NET classes are responsible for compiling and handling files of a specific extension.

❑ How often ASP.NET should automatically recycle its worker processes.

❑ What security settings should be used by default.

A simple XML configuration file is shown here:

```
<configuration>

<!-- store the database connection info here -->

<appsettings>
<add key="DSN"
 value="server=spellbound;uid=sa;pwd=;database=aspdotnetrocks" />
</appsettings>

</configuration>
```

To access and use this configuration file we could write the following simple ASP.NET page using VB:

```
<%@Page Language="VB" %>

<h3>Simple Configuration Example</h3>

<%
 Response.Write( "The DSN is " & ConfigurationSettings.AppSettings("dsn") )
%>
```

or using C#:

```
<%@Page Language="C#" %>

<h3>Simple Configuration Example1</h3>

<%
 Response.Write( "The DSN is " + ConfigurationSettings.AppSettings["dsn"] );
%>
```

If we run either of these pages we'll see the DSN is displayed:

Configuration files once loaded by ASP.NET are cached for quick access, so performance is excellent. The files are automatically reloaded if they are changed, so configuration updates do not require you to restart the web site.

The ASP.NET configuration system is discussed in more detail in Chapter 13.

Factored "Open" Design

Like ASP, ASP.NET is in part implemented as an Internet Server Application Programming Interface (ISAPI) extension DLL. ISAPI is an arcane C API that defines a standard for having web requests processed by a DLL, rather than an EXE as with CGI. The benefit of ISAPI is that DLLs are far more efficient, as executables are very expensive to create and destroy for each web request.

IIS maps ISAPI extension DLLs to web requests by matching the extension of the URI requested to a specific DLL. These mappings are defined using the application configuration property sheet:

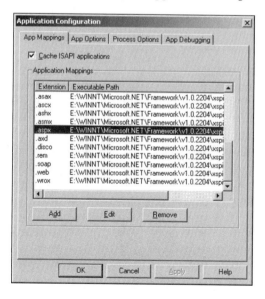

To display this property sheet, bring up the context *menu for a virtual directory, and then click the* configuration *button located on the* Virtual Directory *tab.*

In this screen shot, the `.aspx` extension is highlighted. It shows that the `aspnet_isapi.dll` located in the .NET system directory is responsible for processing this request.

ASP implemented a lot of functionality via its ISAPI extension DLL:

❑ It provided state management for web clients via the `Session` object.

❑ It enabled us to share data across web applications via the `Application` object.

❑ It integrated with MTS.

❑ It provided basic security services to protect ASP files, and helped to identify users using the security support in IIS and Windows.

Whilst this is great if you're developing an ASP application, wouldn't it have been nice if we could have used some of this functionality directly from our own ISAPI extensions, or even directly from COM components, without the need to have any interpreted ASP files? And wouldn't it have been nice to be able to easily replace or enhance the functionality ASP provides? For example, moving all ASP state into a database? With ASP.NET you can easily do this.

The designers of ASP.NET realized a couple of important points early on in the design phase:

❑ ASP.NET should provide an extensibility model that allows services like state management to be extended or replaced with custom alternative implementations.

❑ A lot of the services provided by ASP, like state management, should be usable in non-ASP.NET web applications. The services that ASP.NET requires are common requirements for all web application types.

❑ ASP.NET should not require IIS to run. It should be possible to host ASP.NET on other web servers like Apache.

To achieve these goals, the HTTP run-time was created, on which ASP.NET was built.

The HTTP Run-time

The HTTP run-time effectively provides the same base services as ISAPI extensions and ISAPI filters (filters can preprocess requests, modify them, etc.), but it's a much cleaner model. It is built using the CLR, and has a simple object-oriented approach to managing web requests:

❑ A web request is processed by an HTTP request handler class.

❑ Services like state services are exposed to the run-time using HTTP module classes.

❑ An HTTP application class manages the web execution process, effectively managing what HTTP modules are invoked when passing a request to an HTTP request handler, and sending the output of the HTTP request handler back to the client.

The basic structure of the HTTP run-time looks something like this:

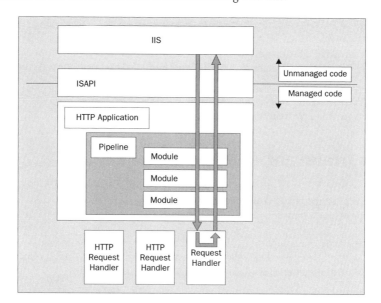

The number of HTTP modules is not limited, and they can be defined at a directory level using XML configuration files, so different services can be made available too, and consumed by different ASP.NET pages (or any type of HTTP request handler). This enables root-level configuration defined in the .NET system directory to be redefined or removed at the directory level. For example, the web.config file in the .NET system directory may define that a specific HTTP module is loaded for state management by default, but an additional web.config file in the same directory as a requested page (or a directory above the requested page) can override this, potentially replacing the state module with another one.

All in all, the HTTP run-time is very powerful, and a lot of the functionality and power of ASP.NET (except the server-side control architecture) comes from the HTTP run-time. We can easily extend this and use it within our own applications.

Web.Config for HTTP Handlers

ASP.NET is implemented as an HTTP handler. If you look at the machine.config file in the .NET system config directory you'll see a section called httphandlers:

```
<httphandlers>
 <add verb="*" path="*.aspx"
     type="System.Web.UI.PageHandlerFactory, System.Web,
        Version=1.0.2411.0, Culture=neutral,
        PublicKeyToken=b03f5f7f11d50a3a" />
 <add verb="*" path="*.asmx"
    type="System.Web.Services.Protocols.WebServiceHandlerFactory,
      System.Web.Services, Version=1.0.2411.0, Culture=neutral,
      PublicKeyToken=b03f5f7f11d50a3a" validate="false"/>

</httphandlers>
```

This cut-down version of the section shows that all web requests with an extension of `.aspx` are handled by the class `System.Web.UI.PageHandlerFactory`, and that all requests with an extension of `.asmx` are handled by `System.Web.Services.Protocols.WebServiceHandlerFactory`.

To implement our own HTTP run-time handler, we can create a class that supports the HTTP run-time interfaces, add our extension and class to this file, and hence write our own web technologies.

> *When your HTTP run-time handler is hosted in IIS, you must add your extension to the IIS configuration map. You extension should be pointed to by the `aspnet_isapi.DLL`.*

Language Is Irrelevant (Almost)

When developing ASP.NET pages the language you use is down to personal preference. Whether you use VB, C#, or even JScript.NET, you have exactly the same functionality available to you. There are no limitations or penalties imposed by ASP.NET for using a specific language.

ASP.NET uses the `compilers` section of the `machine.config` file located in `%SystemRoot%\WINNT\Microsoft.NET\Framework\V1.n.nnnn\Config` directory to define the mapping of a page's extension and available languages that can be used in ASP.NET:

```
<compilers>
 compiler language="c#;cs;csharp" extension=".cs"
    type="Microsoft.CSharp.CSharpCodeProvider, System,
    Version=1.0.2411.0, Culture=neutral,
    PublicKeyToken=b77a5c561934e089" />
  <compiler language="vb;visualbasic;vbscript" extension=".vb"
    type="Microsoft.VisualBasic.VBCodeProvider, System,
      Version=1.0.2411.0, Culture=neutral,
      PublicKeyToken=b77a5c561934e089" />
  <compiler language="js;jscript;javascript" extension=".js"
    type="Microsoft.JScript.JScriptCodeProvider,
      Microsoft.JScript" />
</compilers>
```

The compiler element has the following attributes:

❑ `language` – The abbreviations that can be specified by an ASP.NET page developer when using the `language` attribute, either as part of `<script>` block, or as part of the `page` directive.

❑ `extension` – The file extension associated with the language. When a file is included as part of an ASP.NET page using one of the page directives or attributes like assembly or code behind, the extension gives ASP.NET the hint it needs to tell it how to compile the file.

❑ `type` – The fully-qualified name of the code generator class, and the name of the assembly in which the class is located. A comma separates these two values.

For third-party languages like COBOL or Perl to be usable within an ASP.NET page, the compiler vendors must provide a Code Generator class for their language that derives from `System.CodeDOM.CodeGenerator`, and it must be registered in this configuration section, so that ASP.NET knows how to make use of it.

Less Code, Cleaner Code, More Maintainability

One of the biggest problems with ASP today is the amount of code you have to write. If you want to display data from a database, you have to write the code that connects to the database, and use `Response.Write` to output the HTML required for the table. If you want to display a calendar, you have to write the code to create the calendar. With ASP.NET you don't have to write code to do everything. ASP.NET **server controls** provide a way of declaratively building pages by using nothing but tags and attributes. These server controls encapsulate the behavior used to render the UI and respond to postback.

ASP.NET also lets you build your own server controls. You can either write these in a compiled form, where you develop a class that inherits from one of the ASP.NET server control classes (a custom server control), or you can declare other ASP.NET pages as controls, then use those pages to build up other pages (a user control). Both of these approaches are shown in Chapter 18.

The ASP.NET server controls provide a great mechanism for reusing code within ASP.NET applications. Microsoft predicts many third-party vendors will create ASP.NET server controls, and they also intend to provide more and more controls with each release of ASP.NET.

Rich Authentication Model

ASP.NET was designed to provide a rich authentication model to suit modern e-commerce application requirements. The three core modes of security supported are:

❑   Windows Authentication – targeted mainly at intranets, where domain accounts can be used to identify users.

❑   Forms Authentication – cookie-based authentication as used by sites like Amazon.

❑   Microsoft Passport Authentication – cookie-based authentication performed by Passport Manager, used by sites like Hotmail.

ASP.NET also enables different authentication models to be used within the same application. This scenario allows a single web site to be used for intranet and extranet purposes.

The authentication models of ASP.NET are discussed in detail in Chapter 14.

Realize That Bugs Are a Fact of Life

The designers of ASP.NET appreciated from day one that nobody writes bug-free code – including Microsoft. For this reason ASP.NET deals with bugs, expecting them to happen, and has a number of cool features:

❑   Detects memory leaks and automatically restarts ASP.NET applications. You define the scope of a memory leak.

❑   Detects hung or deadlocked requests, and resolves them.

❑   Automatically restarts an ASP.NET application after a specified number of requests.

❑   Allows state to be stored externally to the main ASP.NET worker process, even in a state service or a SQL Server database. This allows ASP.NET applications to be restarted without end users losing their state.

No Tools Required!

Like ASP, ASP.NET requires no additional development tools. Everything you need to develop, deploy, and debug ASP.NET applications – or any other type of .NET application – is part of the .NET Framework SDK. For hard-core developers who want to save money, or just don't like IDEs, this minimalist approach to ASP.NET application development is certainly not restrictive in any way.

When VS.NET is released, it's probably going to cost several hundred dollars. For this you'll get an all-in-one common IDE capable of developing, debugging, and deploying applications in any language. The .NET Framework SDK will still be available for free download, so you don't have to buy VS.NET, but the productivity gains from just using the cool help system, intelli-sense, and wizards that generate shell applications alone are probably worth the asking price.

Summary

In this chapter we've covered the scope of .NET, and how the .NET Framework provides the technologies that make the platform a reality.

We started the chapter by exploring the need for .NET, explaining some of the common deployment and versioning problems Windows DNA developers face, and how these problems are actually due to the underlying technologies – like COM – on which the Windows DNA platform is built.

We showed some of the design goals for .NET, and then explored the Common Language Runtime (CLR), the core technology upon which the .NET Framework is built. This included a discussion of how the CLR architecture works, and how it solves many of the problems of the Windows DNA platform.

We discussed the four key components of the .NET Framework: Application Development Technologies, Class Libraries, Base Class Libraries, and the CLR. We saw how these are built on top of each other, and together provide a very powerful and productive development platform.

Finally, we reviewed the design goals of ASP.NET, looking at how these features work.

In the next chapter, we'll take a closer look at the syntax of some of the languages you can use to build .NET applications, investigating the advantages and disadvantages of these languages, and their similarities and differences in more detail.

"The Babel fish," says The Hitch Hiker's Guide to Galaxy "is small, yellow and leech-like, and probably the oddest thing in the Universe. It feeds on brainwave energy not from its carrier but from those around it. It absorbs all unconscious mental frequencies from this brainwave energy to nourish itself with. It then excretes into the mind of its carrier a telepathic matrix formed by combining the conscious thought frequencies with nerve signals picked up from the speech centres of the brain which has supplied them".

The practical upshot of all this is that if you stick a Babel fish in your ear you can instantly understand anything said to you in any form of language. The speech patterns you actually hear decode the brainwave matrix which has been fed into your mind by your Babel fish

3

The .NET Languages

The first two chapters have clearly shown that .NET is not just a minor product release – ASP.NET is not just ASP 4.0, and Visual Studio.NET is not just another upgrade. And as to the Common Language Runtime (CLR), well that's completely new. It's a natural reaction to wonder about the changes, ask why there are new languages, why the existing ones are so different, and to question Microsoft's motive.

The Java issue has raged for a long time now and seems to continually produce holy wars of mindless banality – 'C# is just a copy of Java' they cry, without realizing that each programming language builds on the ones that have gone before. That's what developers do – they continue to improve products, and there's no reason why languages should be treated any differently to applications.

Microsoft looked at the way their languages were being used and asked several questions:

- ❑ Do our languages provide developers with what they need?
- ❑ How can we improve the languages?
- ❑ How can we leverage the existing skills of developers?
- ❑ How can we enable applications to be more robust and more scalable?
- ❑ How can we provide a better development environment?
- ❑ Is the application architecture as good as it could be?

The answers to these questions aren't necessarily compatible with each other, and with the .NET framework Microsoft has concentrated on providing the best possible platform for future development. In some areas this has come at the expense of compatibility with existing technologies, and risks alienating some die-hard developers. However, when weighing up the problems, the benefits easily compensate for the losses.

In the previous chapter we discussed the CLR and the benefits it brings, such as common functionality, namespaces, a common type system, versioning, and so on. In this chapter we'll be concentrating on the languages themselves, rather than any ASP.NET-specific details. In particular we'll look at:

- ❑ The new features in Visual Basic and JScript.
- ❑ The new language of C#.
- ❑ What other languages are available.
- ❑ How the CLR affects your use of languages.
- ❑ Examples of common tasks, in different languages, to ease conversion and migration.

The Supplied Languages

The .NET framework is supplied with three languages (Visual Basic.NET, C#, and JScript), but the whole infrastructure is designed to be language independent. We'll briefly mention some of the alternative languages you might want to use later in the chapter. The factored, open design of ASP.NET, which allows pluggable HTTP modules, also extends to the CLR, allowing pluggable languages.

In the previous chapter we saw that the compilers section of the `machine.config` file defines the languages in use:

```
<compilers>
   <compiler language="c#;cs;csharp" extension=".cs"
             type="Microsoft.CSharp.CSharpCodeProvider,System"/>
   <compiler language="vb;visualbasic;vbscript" extension=".vb"
             type="Microsoft.VisualBasic.VBCodeProvider,System"/>
   <compiler language="js;jscript;javascript" extension=".js"
             type="Microsoft.JScript.JScriptCodeProvider,System"/>
</compilers>
```

What this means is that anyone can supply a language for use in the .NET framework, as long as it's got a compiler and fits a few basic rules. That's outside the scope of this book, but later in the chapter we'll look at the other languages that will be supplied by third parties.

Whither VBScript?

During the beta program many people asked about VBScript, and some deliberately inflammatory headlines appeared on various web sites saying "Microsoft dump VBScript". While it's technically true, it's misleading and really misses the point. The .NET framework supports Visual Basic, so there's really no need for VBScript.

Visual Basic provides everything that VBScript supplied, and far more. While VBScript has indeed gone, the syntax is still supported, but you now get full compilation, data types, and the added benefits of the new language. So if you've only ever used VBScript, don't worry – you'll have a little adjusting to do, but for the most part you'll find using Visual Basic.NET simple.

Visual Studio or Notepad?

It would be very easy to assume that to use Visual Basic or C# in our ASP.NET pages we need Visual Studio.NET, but that isn't the case. Support for the languages is built into the Common Language Runtime (CLR), and the compilers are available as part of the SDK. This means that to write ASP.NET applications all you need is the (freely available) SDK and your favorite editor (great news if, like me, you're a die-hard Notepad user). For compilation there's a standalone compiler for each language (described later in the chapter), so we can compile our components from the command line.

Visual Studio.NET does of course give us far more than just an editor. It provides us with a rich environment for developing both ASP.NET applications (WebForms) and Windows applications (Windows Forms), with all the usual cool features like drag and drop, statement completion (intellisense), debugging, and so on. As a productivity tool it's great, but it's not forced on you if you don't want it.

Further, the open design of the .NET languages allows third parties to produce alternative editors with support for .NET; Notepad with color-coding and statement completion is pretty much my idea of heaven!

Visual Basic .NET

The latest version of Visual Basic is a major leap forward in terms of functionality, with several features added to take advantage of the Common Language Specification (CLS) and the CLR.

Each generation of a language brings improvements. To understand why Visual Basic.NET implements the changes it does, consider for a moment some of the problems with previous versions of Visual Basic:

❑ **The Visual Basic runtime libraries**. These are relatively large DLLs incorporating the base functionality, and are required for all Visual Basic programs to run. Common complaints were the size of these DLLs and versioning problems (different libraries for different versions of VB). You might think that these have just been replaced by the CLR, but the CLR is much more than this and addresses far more than just VB. While size may still be considered an issue, the redistributable CLR is less than 20 MB and supports multiple versions.

❑ **Poor object-oriented features**. Object-oriented gurus criticized Visual Basic for its lack of 'proper' functionality – not providing features such as inheritance, overloading, and so on. Although these are valid points, many of the problems really stemmed from the capabilities of COM rather than Visual Basic itself.

❑ **Inability to create multi-threaded applications**. With the introduction of Microsoft Transaction Server (MTS), n-tier architectures became a reality, and Visual Basic programmers started to get to grips with componentization. However, Visual Basic components were forced into an Apartment Threading model, a limitation that attracted much criticism from programmers who wanted to build multi-threaded components. Personally I think much of this condemnation is misplaced, as I wonder how many people could actually write a fully threaded component (I'm not sure I could). Think about it – managing the threads, state, and so on, isn't easy.

All of these problems disappear in Visual Basic.NET. The runtime libraries are no longer needed because they're taken care of by the CLR, and the object-oriented features have been massively improved (partly because of CLR and CLS support) and the whole threading issue has gone away. With the CLR you just don't need to think about threading (unless you explicitly want to).

> *We'll look at Visual Basic.NET in more detail than the other languages, because most ASP programmers are used to VBScript and need to understand the language changes.*

So let's take a look at some of those new features we mentioned.

Object-Oriented Features

The OO features were probably one of the enhancements most requested by programmers. I remember being at a Microsoft event when Visual Basic 6 was in beta, and the most frequently asked question was whether inheritance was going to be supported. Since this is an intrinsic feature of the CLS, it is now supported, and classes are inheritable by default. In fact, since everything in .NET is class based, you have an enormous amount of flexibility, as you can not only extend and overload your own classes, but many system ones too.

Classes

As in previous versions of Visual Basic, classes are created using the `Class` statement. However, the syntax has changed a little:

```
[ Public | Private | Protected | Friend | Protected Friend ]
[MustInherit | NotInheritable] Class className

End Class
```

Visual Basic still requires the underscore (_) for line continuation – it's not shown above just to make things clearer.

Let's take a look at the keywords in more detail:

Keyword	Description
Public	The class is publicly accessible.
Private	The class can only be accessed within the file in which it is declared.
Protected	The class is only accessible from the containing class or types derived from the containing class.
Friend	The class is only accessible from this assembly.
Protected Friend	The class only accessible from this program or types derived from the containing class.
MustInherit	This class is an abstract class, and the class members must be implemented by inheriting classes.
NotInheritable	This class is not inheritable.

Within a class the member definition follows the same rules. Members not explicitly declared with a keyword are `Public` by default.

For example:

```
Public Class Calculator

    ' implementation goes here

End Class
```

or

```
Protected MustInherit Class Calculator

    ' abstract implementation goes here

End Class
```

Methods

Methods are declared as a `Sub` or a `Function`, but there are improvements to fit in with the inheritance rules. The syntax for a `Sub` is now:

```
[Overloads | Overrides | Overridable | NotOverridable | MustOverride |
 Shadows | Shared]
[Private | Public | Protected | Friend | Protected Friend]
Sub subName [(parameters)]

End Sub
```

For a `Function` the syntax is:

```
[Overloads | Overrides | Overridable | NotOverridable | MustOverride |
 Shadows | Shared]
[Private | Public | Protected | Friend | Protected Friend]
Function functionName [(parameters)] [As type]

End Function
```

The various keywords are described below:

Keyword	Description
Overloads	The member is overloaded, with more than one declaration existing, each with different parameters.
Overrides	The member overrides an identically named member from a base class. This is useful for sub-classing situations where you want to provide your own implementation of a particular member. The overridden method must have the same signature, that is the parameters and data types must match those of the base class member.
NotOverridable	The member cannot be overridden in a derived class.
Overridable	The method can be overridden by a derived class.
MustOverride	The member must be overridden in a derived class. This implies `Overridable`.
Shadows	The method shadows a method in a parent class. This means that the method in the parent class is not available, and allows creation of methods with a different signature (parameters & data types) than that of the parent. It effectively redeclares the type.

Table continued on following page

Keyword	Description
Shared	The member is shared by all instances of the class, and exists independently of a class instance. This is equivalent to a static method in C# or C++.
Public	The member is publicly accessible.
Private	The member is only accessible within the class.
Protected	The member is only accessible from the containing class or types derived from the containing class.
Friend	The member is only accessible from this program.
Protected Friend	The member is only accessible from this program or types derived from the containing member.

For example:

```
Public Class Calculator

   Public Function Add(Op1 As Double, Op2 As Double) As Double

      Return Op1 + Op2

   End Function

End Class
```

> This shows an important change from previous function syntax – the value of the function is now returned using the **Return** keyword, rather than by setting the function name to the value.

Properties

Properties can be implemented as Public member variables, or by using the Property statement. For example:

```
Public Class Calculator

   Public Op1 As Double
   Public Op2 As Double

   Public Function Add() As Double
      Return Op1 + Op2
   End Function

End Class
```

The class could be used like so:

```
Dim calc As New Calculator
calc.Op1 = 123
calc.Op2 = 456
Response.Write(calc.Add())
```

The above example uses public variables. The alternative, and preferred approach, is to use Property, the syntax of which has changed:

```
[Default | ReadOnly | WriteOnly] Property propertyName ([parameters])
                                                        [As type]

  Get
    ' code for getting the property
  End Get

  Set
    ' code for setting the property
  End Set

End Property
```

A property defined as ReadOnly can only have the Get block. Likewise a property with only a Get block must be marked as ReadOnly. The same applies for WriteOnly and the Set block. There is also no longer a Let option, as Let and Set are both the same now.

For example:

```
Public Class Calculator

    Private _op1 As Double
    Private _op2 As Double

    Public Property Operand1() As Double

      Get
        Operand1 = _op1
      End Get
      Set
        _op1 = value
      End Set

    End Property

    Public Property Operand2() As Double

      Get
        Operand2 = _op2
      End Get
      Set
        _op2 = value
      End Set

    End Property

End Class
```

Notice the use of the keyword value in the Set block. This is the actual code you should type, as value is an implicit variable that contains the value of the property being set.

Default Properties and Property Parameters

Default properties are another area of change, as they are only supported on properties with a parameter list. So for example, we could add a property called `Result` to our `Calculator` class, to contain the last result of an operation, but we wouldn't be able to make it the `Default` property. So we can't code it like this:

```
Default Property Result() As Double
```

which stops us doing this:

```
Label1.Text = MyCalc
```

To declare a default property we have to have parameters (and these cannot be declared as `ByRef`). For more details on this consult the Visual Basic.NET documentation.

Constructors and Object Creation

The `Class_Initialize` event has been removed from classes, but has been replaced with a member function called `New`, which allows for constructors to be inherited.

One of the cool new features of Visual Basic.NET is the use of overloading, which is perfect for providing constructors. The `New` method is a special case for overloading, since the `Overloads` keyword is not required. For example, consider a `Person` class:

```
Public Class Person

  Private _firstName As String
  Private _lastName  As String

  Sub New()
    _firstName = ""
    _lastName = ""
  End Sub

  Sub New(firstName As String, lastName As String)

    _firstName = firstName
    _lastName = lastName

  End Sub

  Public Property FirstName() As String
    ' property code here
  End Property

  Public Property LastName() As String
    ' property code here
  End Property

End Class
```

In this example there are two occurrences of the `Sub New`: one without parameters and one with. This means that we can do this:

```
Dim coolDude As New Person()
coolDude.FirstName  = "Vince"
coolDude.LastName = "Patel"
```

or

```
Dim coolDude As New Person("Vince", "Patel")
```

This provides a much richer way of using classes, and simplifies code.

Destructors and Object Destruction

Like the `Class_Initialize` method, `Class_Terminate` has also been replaced by a `Destruct` method. For example:

```
Sub Destruct{}

   ' code to clean up here

End Sub
```

There has been a big change in the way destructors are called from previous versions of Visual Basic, and it revolves around the CLR. One of the good features of the CLR is **Garbage Collection** (GC), which runs in the background collecting unused object references, freeing us from having to ensure we always destroy them. However, the downside is that since it's a background task, we don't know exactly when our destructor is called.

During the beta there was a wide discussion regarding this, resulting in an extensive paper from Microsoft about garbage collection and its effects (search the MSDN Web site for Deterministic Finalization for more details). Some people were concerned that there might be cases where you needed to guarantee something happening (such as resource cleanup) when the object is no longer in use. If this is the case, then the advice is to create a method to house this functionality, and call this method when you have finished with the class instance.

In reality, the time difference between you releasing the object instance, and it being garbage collected is likely to be very small, since the garbage collector is always running.

Inheritance

As we mentioned in the previous chapter, everything in .NET is an object, so we can inherit from pretty much anything. If we take our `Person` class, again, as a base class, then we could create a new class from it:

```
Public Class Programmer
   Inherits Person

   Private _avgHoursSleepPerNight As Integer

   Public Sub New()
     MyBase.New()
   End Sub
```

```
      Public Sub New(firstName As String, lastName As String)
        MyBase.New(firstName, lastName)
      End Sub

      Public Sub New(firstName As String, lastName As String, _
                          hoursSleep As Integer)
        MyBase.New(firstName, lastName)
        _avgHoursSleepPerNight = hoursSleep
      End Sub

      Public Property AvgHoursSleepPerNight() As Integer
        Get
          AvgHoursSleepPerNight = _avgHoursSleepPerNight
        End Get
        Set
          _avgHoursSleepPerNight = value
        End Set
      End Property

  End Class
```

This class extends the existing `Person` class and adds a new property. The ways it does this are:

❑   Firstly, after the class declarations comes the `Inherits` statement, where the base class we are inheriting from is defined.

```
      Public Class Programmer
      Inherits Person
```

❑   Next come the definitions for the existing constructors. Our class is going to provide an extra one, so we need to overload the base class constructors. Notice how the definitions of these match the definitions in the base class, and how we call the constructor of the base class using `MyBase`. We are not changing the existing constructors, just adding our own, so we just want to map functionality to the base class.

```
      Public Sub New()
        MyBase.New()
      End Sub

      Public Sub New(firstName As String, lastName As String)
        MyBase.New(firstName, lastName)
      End Sub
```

❑   Now we can add our extra constructor, which calls one of the previous constructors and then sets the addition property:

```
      Public Sub New(firstName As String, lastName As String, _
                                 hoursSleep As Integer)
        MyBase.New(firstName, lastName)
        _avgHoursSleepPerNight = hoursSleep
      End Sub
```

❑ Finally we add the definition of the new property:

```
Public Property AvgHoursSleepPerNight() As Integer
  Get
    AvgHoursSleepPerNight = _avgHoursSleepPerNight
  End Get
  Set
    _avgHoursSleepPerNight = value
  End Set
End Property
```

In object-oriented terms this is fairly standard stuff, but it's new for Visual Basic and provides a great way to promote code reuse.

Classes and Interfaces

An interface is the description of the methods and properties a class will expose – it's an immutable contract with the outside world. The interface doesn't define any implementation – just the methods and properties. Derived classes then have to provide the actual implementation.

In Visual Basic.NET you automatically get a default interface that matches the class methods and properties, but there may be times when you want to explicitly define the interface. One good example of this is when creating .NET serviced components, where the interface can be used to provide versioning features. See Chapter 23 for more details on this.

To create an interface you use the `Interface` construct. For example:

```
Public Interface IPerson

   Property FirstName() As String
   Property LastName()  As String

   Function FullName()  As String

End Interface
```

As you can see, there is no implementation specified here. By convention the interface name is the class name preceded by an `I`, although this isn't enforced. To derive a class from an interface you use the `Implements` keyword on the class:

```
Public Class Person
    Implements IPerson

  Private _firstName As String
  Private _lastName As String

  Public Property FirstName() As String Implements IPerson.FirstName
    ' implementation goes here
  End Property

  Public Property LastName() As String Implements IPerson.LastName
    ' implementation goes here
  End Property
```

```
    Public Function FullName() As String Implements IPerson.FullName

      Return_firstName & " " & _lastName

    End Function

  End Class
```

Notice that both the class, and the methods and properties have to specify their implementation interface.

An interface is the only type where multiple inheritance is allowed. For example:

```
Public Interface Person
      Inherits IPerson
      Inherits ICleverPerson
End Interface
```

Language Changes

Along with the object-oriented features, there have been many changes to the language. We won't go into exhaustive detail here (it's well covered in the documentation), but here are some things to watch out for:

- ❑ **Array Bounds**. The lower bound of an array is always 0, and cannot be changed. The `Option Base` statement is not supported.

- ❑ **Array Declaration**. You can only use `ReDim` if the array has already been declared.

- ❑ **Array Sizes**. Arrays do not have a fixed size (although the number of dimensions is fixed). For example:

  ```
  Dim ConnectionTimes(10) As Date
  ```

  This defines an array with an initial size of 11 elements. Arrays can also be populated on declaration:

  ```
  Dim ConnectionTimes() As Date = {"10:30", "11:30", "12:00", "06:00"}
  ```

- ❑ **String Length**. The fixed-width string is no longer supported.

- ❑ **Variants**. The `Variant` data type is no longer supported, being replaced by a more generic `Object`. The corresponding `VarType` function is also not supported, as the `Object` has a `GetType` method.

- ❑ **Data Types**. The `Currency` data type is replaced by `Decimal`.

- ❑ **Short-Circuiting**. Multiple Boolean expressions in an `If` statement now short-circuit. So, with an `And`, if the first expression is `False`, the rest of the expression is not evaluated. Likewise, with an `Or`, if the first expression evaluates to `True`, the rest of the expression is not evaluated.

- ❑ **Short Cut Operators**. A new short form of addition and assignment has been added. For example:

  ```
  counter += 1
  name &= " Sussman"
  ```

❑ **Default properties**. As mentioned earlier, default properties are not supported, unless they take parameters.

❑ **Variable declaration**. When declaring multiple variables on the same line, a variable with no data type takes the type of the next declared type (and not `Variant` as was the case in VB6). For example, in the following declarations `Age` is an `Integer`:

```
Dim Age, Hours As Integer
Dim Name As String, Age, Hours As Integer
```

❑ **Variable Scope**. Block scope is now supported, so variables declared within blocks (such as `If` blocks) are only visible within the `If` block. In Visual Basic 6 variables could be declared anywhere, but their scope was the entire method.

❑ **Object Creation**. The `As New` keywords can be used freely on the variable declaration line. There is no implicit object creation, so objects that are `Nothing` remain set to `Nothing` unless an explicit instance is created. .

❑ **Procedure Parameters**. The rules for parameter passing and optional parameters have changed. See the section on *Parameters* later for more information on this.

❑ **Procedure Calls**. Parentheses are now required on all procedure calls, not just functions.

❑ **Function Return Values**. The return value from a function is now supplied with the `Return` statement, rather than by setting the function name to the desired value.

❑ **While loops**. The `Wend` statement has been replaced with `End While`.

❑ **String and Variant functions**. The string manipulation functions that had two types of call (`Trim` returned a `Variant` and `Trim$` returned a `string`) are replaced with overloaded method calls.

❑ **Empty and Null**. The `Empty` and `Null` keywords have their functionality replaced by `Nothing`.

There are many other changes, some of which don't really affect ASP.NET programmers, but for a full list you should consult the Visual Basic.NET documentation, or see Wrox's *VB.NET Programming With The Public Beta, ISBN 1-861004-91-5*.

References

Since we're freed from using a set design tool, some of the features we are used to now require a bit more typing. One example is referencing other components. In Visual Basic 6 for example, to access COM components you selected **References** from the **Project** menu. There's something similar in Visual Studio.NET to reference assemblies (or even COM components), but if you're using Notepad you have to provide the reference yourself. This is done using the `Imports` keyword. For example:

```
Imports System
Imports MyComponent
```

It's also possible to alias references using the following syntax:

```
Imports aliasName = Namespace
```

If an alias is used, the alias *must* be included in references to classes that the namespace contains. For example if we have a namespace called `MyComponent` containing a class called `MyClass`, and import the namespace like this:

```
Imports foo = MyComponent
```

we can't then access the class like this:

```
Dim comp As MyClass
```

we have to use this syntax:

```
Dim comp As foo.MyClass
```

Structured Error Handling

One of the best new features of .NET is a unified structured error-handling framework, which extends to Visual Basic.NET. Although `On Error` is still supported, a far better way of handling errors is to use the new `Try ... Catch ... Finally` structure. The way it works is simple, with each of the statements defining a block of code to be run.

The syntax is:

```
Try

    ' code block to run

[Catch [exception [As type]] [When expression]

    ' code to run if the exception generated matches
    ' the exception and expression defined above

    [Exit Try]

Catch [exception [As type]] [When expression]

    ' code to run if the exception generated matches
    ' the exception and expression defined above

    [Exit Try]

[Finally
    ' code that always runs, whether or not an exception
    ' was caught, unless End Try is called
    ]

End Try
```

This allows us to bracket a section of code and then handle generic or specific errors. For example:

```
Try
    ' connect to a database and
    ' retrieve some data
    ' ... code left out for clarity ...

Catch exSQL As SQLException
    ErrorLabel.Text = "SQL Error: " & exSQL.ToString()

Catch ex As Exception
    ErrorLabel.Text = "Other error: " & ex.ToString()

Finally
    FinishedLabel.Text = "Finished"

End Try
```

Notice that we can have multiple `Catch` blocks, to make our error handling specific to a particular error. You should put the most specific `Try` blocks first and the more generic ones last, as the `Catch` blocks are tried in the order they are declared.

The `Throw` statement can be used to throw your own errors, or even re-raise errors.

Errors and exceptions are covered in more detail in Chapter 22.

Data Types and Structures

There are three new data types:

- ❑   Char, for unsigned 16-bit values.

- ❑   Short, for signed 16-bit integers. This is the equivalent to the current Visual Basic `Integer` (in Visual Basic.NET the `Integer` is now 32-bits and the `Long` 64-bits).

- ❑   Decimal, for signed integers.

Custom types are now provided by the `Structure` statement, rather than the `Type` statement. The syntax is:

```
[Public | Private | Friend] Structure structureName

End Structure
```

For example:

```
Public Structure Person
    Public   FirstName As String
    Public   LastName  As String
    Private Age        As Integer
End Structure
```

The use of structures is unified with classes, allowing structures to not only contain member variables, but also methods:

```
Public Structure Narcissist
    Public  FirstName As String
    Public  LastName  As String
    Private RealAge   As Integer

    Public Function Age() As Integer
        Return RealAge - 5
    End Function

End Structure
```

Whether you use classes or structures is purely a coding and design decision, but the close linking of the two types provides added flexibility

Parameters

There are several things that have changed with regard to passing parameters to procedures. The most important is that parameters now default to ByVal. This means that to achieve reference parameters you must explicitly put ByRef in front of the parameter name.

The second, as mentioned earlier, is that all method calls with parameters must be surrounded by parentheses. In previous versions of Visual Basic we had the inconsistency of parentheses being required for functions, but not subroutines. For example, the following is no longer valid:

```
MyMethod 1, 2, "foo"
```

Instead we must use:

```
MyMethod(1, 2, "foo")
```

For optional parameters we now have to specify a default, and the IsMissing method is removed. For example, we cannot do:

```
Sub MyMethod(Name As String, Optional Age As Integer)

    If IsMissing(Age) Then
    . . .
```

We have to supply a default:

```
Sub MyMethod(Name As String, Optional Age As Integer = -1)
```

Debugging and Message Boxes

Although not relevant to ASP.NET pages, there are two things that might hit you if you are using Visual Studio.NET:

❑ The first is that the Print method of the Debug object has been replaced by four methods – Write, WriteIf, WriteLine, and WriteLineIf.

❑ The second point is that the MsgBox statement has been replaced with the Show method of the MessageBox object.

Debugging is covered in more detail in Chapter 22.

Backward Compatibility

To ease the transition from Visual Basic 6 to Visual Basic.NET, you can reference the `Microsoft.VisualBasic.Compatibility.VB6` namespace, which provides access to much of the removed or changed functionality. It's probably best not to overuse these compatibility features, though. The changes to the language have been made not only to improve it, but also to bring it in line with the CLS and the other .NET languages.

C#

Like .NET itself, C# has raised a fair amount of discussion, much of it based around phrases such as "another language? why?" and "isn't it just Java?". To understand why a new language has been introduced you have to think about what Microsoft is trying to achieve with .NET. Some of the key ideas are:

- ❑ Cross-language development, to allow programmers to use whatever language they are most familiar with.

- ❑ A unified type system, to allow true cross-language development, especially inheritance.

- ❑ Extensibility and security, providing an easy way for developers to extend and reuse code, as well as being able to secure code.

- ❑ Great support for development tools.

Now these are not the only goals, nor are they specific reasons for creating a new language, but it was clear that to build the .NET framework the existing languages wouldn't meet these requirements. C++ for example, isn't truly component oriented, and still has many hang-ups from the C language. Java is bound by its ownership by Sun (not to mention lawsuits) and is interpreted, which leads to performance problems. Object-oriented languages such as Smalltalk and Eiffel have the stigma of being thought obscure, and would also need performance increases and structural changes.

So, a new language was the simplest answer, but not so new that it wouldn't feel familiar. You can think of C# as a member of the C/C++ family – a fact that's not surprising since the majority of development at Microsoft is done in these languages. As such, C# contains the best features of C++, but leaves out all of the bits that aren't required for a language to be part of the framework (such as typedefs, templates, and so on). Leaving out functionality hasn't been a hindrance, rather it has made the language simpler to use and more efficient. Also it's not just a language being pushed on the public – ASP.NET is entirely written in C#.

> If you're a Visual Basic or VBScript programmer trying out C# for the first time then there's one really important thing to note: *C# is case sensitive*.

Classes

Even though C# is more like C and C++, Visual Basic or VBScript programmers won't have too much trouble with this new language. Classes are defined using the following syntax:

```
[public | protected | internal | protected internal | private |
 abstract | sealed ] class className
{
}
```

Let's take a look at the keywords in more detail:

Keyword	Description
public	The class is publicly accessible.
protected	The class is only accessible from the containing class or types derived from the containing class.
internal	The class is only accessible from this program. Equivalent to Friend in Visual Basic.
protected internal	The class is only accessible from this program or types derived from the containing class. Equivalent to Protected Friend in Visual Basic.
private	The class is only accessible from within the containing class.
abstract	This class is an abstract class, and the class members must be implemented by inheriting classes. Equivalent to MustInherit in Visual Basic.
sealed	No further inheritance is allowed from this class. Equivalent to NotInheritable in Visual Basic.

For example:

```
public class Calculator
{
   // implementation goes here
}
```

Methods

In C# there is no direct distinction between a Sub and a Function, and members are just implemented as functions (that may, or may not, return data). The syntax is:

```
[ public | protected | internal | protected internal | private | static |
  virtual | override | abstract | extern ]
[ type | void ] memberName([parameters])
{
}
```

The various keywords are described below:

Keyword	Description
public	The member is publicly accessible.
protected	The member is only accessible from the containing class or types derived from the containing member.
internal	The member is only accessible from this program. Equivalent to Friend in Visual Basic.
protected internal	The member is only accessible from this program, or types derived from the containing member. Equivalent to Protected Friend in Visual Basic.

Keyword	Description
private	The member is only accessible from within the containing member.
static	The member is shared by all instances of the class, and exists independently of a class instance. Equivalent to Shared in Visual Basic.
virtual	The member can be overridden by a sub-class.
override	The member overrides an identically named member from a base class, with the same signature. The base class member must be defined as virtual, abstract or override.
abstract	This member is an abstract member, and must be implemented by a sub-class.
extern	The member is implemented in an external assembly.

For example:

```
public class calculator
{
  public double Add(double op1, double op2)
  {
    return op1 + op2;
  }
}
```

For a method that does not return a result, you declare the type as void:

```
public void updateSomething()
{
}
```

Properties

Properties in C# are very similar to Visual Basic.NET, and can be implemented as public member variables or by using the property accessors. For example, the following uses public variables:

```
public class calculator
{
  public double Op1;
  public double Op2;

  public double Add()
  {
    return Op1 + Op2;
  }
}
```

The alternative (and preferred) approach is to use property accessors. For example:

```
public class calculator
{
  private double _op1;
  private double _op2;

  public double Operand1
  {
    get
    {
      return _op1;
    }
    set
    {
      _op1 = value;
    }
  }

  public double Operand2
  {
    get
    {
      return _op2;
    }
    set
    {
      _op2 = value;
    }
  }

}
```

Unlike Visual Basic there are no specific keywords to identify read-and write-only properties. If only the get accessor is provided then the property is read-only, and if only the set accessor is provided then the property is write-only. Both accessors mean a read/write property.

Constructors

Rather than using New for constructors, the C# syntax is to use a method with the same name as the class. For example:

```
public class person
{
  private string _firstName;
  private string _lastName;

  public person() {}

  public person(string firstName, string lastName)
  {
    _firstName = firstName;
    _lastName = lastName;
  }
```

```
   public string FirstName
   {
     // property accessors here
   }

   public string LastName
   {
     // property accessors here
   }
}
```

Destructors

For destructors there is no `Destruct` keyword. This functionality is provided by a method with the same name as the class, but with a tilde (~) in front of it. For example:

```
public class person
{
  private string _firstName;
  private string _lastName;

  public person() {}

  public person(string firstName, string lastName) { }

  ~person()
  {
    // destructor code here
  }
}
```

Like Visual Basic.NET, destructors in C# are called by the garbage collector, and are not guaranteed to be executed at the time you destroy the class.

Inheritance

Inheritance in C# looks more like C++, where a colon (:) is used to separate the class and the base class. For example:

```
public class programmer : person
{
  private int _avgHoursSleepPerNight;

  public programmer(): base()
  {
  }

  public programmer(string firstName, string lastName):
         base(firstName, lastName)
  {
  }
```

```
        public programmer(string firstName, string lastName, int hoursSleep):
                base(firstName, lastName)
        {
          _avgHoursSleepPerNight = hoursSleep;
        }

        public int AvgHoursSleepPerNight
        {
           get { return _avgHoursSleepPerNight; }
           set { _avgHoursSleepPerNight = value; }
        }
    }
```

The class definition defines that our class is called `programmer` and the base class is called `person`:

```
    public class programmer : person
    {
```

Next we need to provide the constructors. Here we specify the same constructors as the base class, and use the same inheritance syntax (the :) to indicate that this method inherits its implementation from the base class. Any parameters should be passed to the base class constructor.

```
    public programmer(): base()
    {
    }

    public programmer(string firstName, string lastName):
            base(firstName, lastName)
    {
    }
```

To declare an additional constructor we follow the same rules, invoking the base constructor, but also providing additional functionality:

```
    public programmer(string firstName, string lastName, int hoursSleep):
            base(firstName, lastName)
    {
      _avgHoursSleepPerNight = hoursSleep;
    }
```

And finally we have the new property:

```
    public int AvgHoursSleepPerNight
    {
      get { return _avgHoursSleepPerNight; }
      set { _avgHoursSleepPerNight = value; }
    }
  }
```

The `value` keyword is implemented automatically by the CLR, providing the property with the supplied value from the calling program.

Interfaces

Interfaces work the same as in Visual Basic.NET, providing an immutable contract to the external world.

To create an interface you use the `interface` construct. For example:

```
public interface IPerson
{
  string FirstName(get; set;)
  string LastName(get; set;)

  string FullName();
}
```

To derive a class from an interface you use the same method as inheritance:

```
public class Person : IPerson
{
  private string _firstName;
  private string _lastName;

  public string FirstName()
  {
    // implementation goes here
  }

  public string LastName()
  {
    // implementation goes here
  }

  public string FullName()
  {
    return_firstName + " " + _lastName;
  }

}
```

Notice that unlike Visual Basic.NET, only the class needs to specify the interface inheritance.

References

References use the same method as Visual Basic.NET, but with the keyword `using` instead of `Imports`. For example:

```
using System;
using MyComponent;
```

It's also possible to alias references using the following syntax:

```
using aliasName = Namespace;
```

If an alias is used, the alias **must** be included in references to classes that the namespace contains. For example if we have a namespace called `MyComponent` containing a class called `MyClass`, and import the namespace like this:

```
using foo = MyComponent;
```

We can't then access the class like this:

```
MyClass comp = MyClass
```

We have to use this syntax:

```
foo.MyClass comp = foo.MyClass
```

Exception Handling

The `try ... catch ... finally` combo is also the way exception handling is performed in C#, using the following syntax:

```
try
{
   // code block to try
}
[catch[(type exception)]
{
   // code block to run if the exception matches the type above
}]
catch[(type exception)]
{
   // code block to run if the exception matches the type above
}
finally
{
   ' code that always runs, whether or not
   ' an exception was caught
}
```

For example:

```
try
{
   // connect to a database and
   // retrieve some data
   // ... code left out for clarity ...
}
catch(SQLException exSQL)
{
    ErrorLabel.Text = "SQL Error: " + exSQL.ToString();
}
  catch(Exception ex)
{
    ErrorLabel.Text = "Other error: " + ex.ToString();
}
finally
{
    FinishedLabel.Text = "Finished";
}
```

The `throw` statement can be used to raise errors, even when in `try...catch` blocks. For example:

```
try
{
  // some code here
}
catch(SQLException exSQL)
{
  if (some expression)
    throw(exSQL);
}
```

XML Documentation

One really great feature that C# has over Visual Basic is the ability to include inline documentation. This is done by placing a set of XML tags at various places in our code, and then adding a compiler directive to pull out the comments. For example:

```
using System;

namespace peopleCS
{
    ///<remarks>
    ///The <c>programmer</c>class defines the salient
    ///attributes of every fine programmer.
    ///<seealso cref="person">Inherits from person</seealso>
    ///</remarks>
    public class programmer : person
    {
        private int _avgHoursSleepPerNight;

        ///<summary>Default constructor</summary>
        public programmer(): base()
        { }

        ///<summary>Constructor using first and last names</summary>
        ///<param name="firstName">The first name of the programmer</param>
        ///<param name="lastName">The last name of the programmer</param>
        ///<seealso cref="string"/>
        public programmer(string firstName, string lastName):
                base(firstName, lastName)
        { }

        ///<summary>Constructor using first and last names and
        ///the hours of sleep</summary>
        ///<param name="firstName">The first name of the programmer</param>
        ///<param name="lastName">The last name of the programmer</param>
        ///<param name="hoursSleep">The average number of hours of sleep</param>
        ///<seealso cref="string"/>
        ///<seealso cref="int"/>
        public programmer(string firstName, string lastName, int hoursSleep):
                base(firstName, lastName)
        {
            _avgHoursSleepPerNight = hoursSleep;
        }
```

```
///<value>Defines the average number of hours of sleep.</value>
public int AvgHoursSleepPerNight
{
  get { return _avgHoursSleepPerNight; }
  set { _avgHoursSleepPerNight = value; }
}
  }
}
```

Notice how the XML tags are placed after three /// characters – not to be confused with two, as used by comments. The tags we can use are:

Tag	Description
c	Text that indicates inline code.
code	Multiple lines of code, such as a sample.
example	Description of a code sample.
exception	Indicates an exception class. Additionally the attribute cref can be used to reference another type (such as the exception type). This reference is checked against the imported libraries.
include	Allows XML documentation to be retrieved from another file.
list	Indicates a list of items. The type attribute can be one of: ❑ bullet, for bulleted lists ❑ number, for numbered lists ❑ table, for a table You can use a listheader element to define headings, and an item element to define the items in the list. Each of these can contain two elements: item for the item being listed, and description.
para	Allows paragraph definitions within other tags.
param	Describes the parameter of a method. The name attribute should match the name of the parameter.
paramref	Used to indicate references for parameters.
permission	Describes the permissions required to access the member. The cref can be used to reference another type (such as the security permission type). This reference is checked against the imported libraries.
remarks	Overview information about the class or type.
returns	The return value of a method.
see	The attribute cref is used to reference another type (such as a related member). This reference is checked against the imported libraries.

Tag	Description
seealso	The attribute cref is used to reference another type (such as a related member), to be documented in the See Also section. This reference is checked against the imported libraries.
summary	Description of a member or type.
value	Description of a property.

In Visual Studio these tags can be processed to form HTML pages that become part of the project documentation. Outside of Visual Studio, you can produce an XML file for the comments by using the /doc compiler switch (more on these later), which produces the file like so:

```xml
<?xml version="1.0"?>
<doc>
  <assembly>
    <name>PeopleCS</name>
  </assembly>
  <members>
    <member name="T:peopleCS.programmer">
      <remarks>
      The <c>programmer</c>class defines the salient
      attributes of every fine programmer.
      <seealso cref="T:peopleCS.person">Inherits from person</seealso>
      </remarks>
    </member>
    <member name="M:peopleCS.programmer.#ctor">
      <summary>Default constructor</summary>
    </member>
    <member name="M:peopleCS.programmer.#ctor(System.String,System.String)">
      <summary>Constructor using first and last names</summary>
      <param name="firstName">The first name of the programmer</param>
      <param name="lastName">The last name of the programmer</param>
      <seealso cref="T:System.String"/>
    </member>
    <member
name="M:peopleCS.programmer.#ctor(System.String,System.String,System.Int32)">
      <summary>Constructor using first and last names and the hours of
sleep</summary>
      <param name="firstName">The first name of the programmer</param>
      <param name="lastName">The last name of the programmer</param>
      <param name="hoursSleep">The average number of hours of sleep</param>
      <seealso cref="T:System.String"/>
      <seealso cref="T:System.Int32"/>
    </member>
    <member name="P:peopleCS.programmer.AvgHoursSleepPerNight">
      <value>Defines the average number of hours of sleep.</value>
    </member>
  </members>
</doc>
```

The compiler automatically includes the namespace and builds tags for the member names. The members are given a fully qualified name starting with one of the following prefixes:

Prefix	Description
N	Namespace
T	Type: `Class`, `Interface`, `Struct`, `Enum`, or `Delegate`
F	Field
P	Property (including indexers)
M	Method (including constructors)
E	Event
!	Error string if links cannot be resolved

You could then use an XSLT stylesheet, or XML processing code to style this into your own documentation. You can also add your own XML elements to the class descriptions, and these will be extracted along with the predefined elements.

Unsafe Code

Although C# is part of the managed code environment, Microsoft has realized that sometimes developers need total control, such as when performance is an issue, when dealing with binary structures, or for some advanced COM support. Under these circumstances you are allowed to use C# code in an unsafe manner, where you can use pointers, have unsafe casts, and so on.

As an ASP.NET developer it's unlikely you'll ever need this, but knowing it's available gives you the flexibility to choose should the need arise. Consult the C# documentation or Wrox's *C# Programming With the Public Beta, ISBN 1-86004-87-7*, for more information on this.

Operator Overloading

C# is the only one of the supplied languages that supports operator overloading. This works in the same way as method overloading, but for operators. The reason for this is to allow the standard operators to be used on objects such as classes.

The classic example given is a class for handling complex numbers, which have a real and imaginary part (stored as integers). Imagine a class that has two properties for these two parts, and a constructor that takes two arguments to match the properties:

```
CNumber c1 = new CNumber(12, 4);
CNumber c2 = new CNumber(5, 6);
```

When performing addition on complex numbers we must add the real part and imaginary part independently of each other, and might consider creating this method:

```
public CNumber Add(CNumber c1, CNumber c2)
{
   return new CNumber(c1.real + c2.real, c1.imag + c2.imag);
}
```

We could then call this by:

```
CNumber c3 = CNumber.Add(c1, c2);
```

There's nothing wrong with that per se, but it would be far better to use:

```
CNumber c3 = c1 + c2;
```

To achieve this we have to overload the + operator:

```
public static CNumber operator +(CNumber c1, CNumber c2);
{
   return new CNumber(c1.real + c2.real, c1.imag + c2.imag);
}
```

This provides a much more intuitive way of developing, and is especially useful when building class libraries for other developers.

> **For more details on C#, see *C# Programming with the Public Beta*, ISBN 1-861004-87-7, from Wrox Press.**

JScript.NET

Like Visual Basic, JScript has also undergone some changes, although they aren't as radical. The first thing to realize is that JScript.NET is a full .NET language, and therefore provides the advantages that the other supported languages do. In fact, JScript.NET has been completely rewritten in C#. It now supports types and inheritance, and is fully compiled.

Although completely rewritten, JScript.NET is more evolutionary, and still supports existing JScript functionality – the new features are extra, and (apart from compilation, which is a CLR requirement) not enforced.

> **Like C#, JScript is case sensitive.**

Data Types

The first new feature is the ability to use JScript as a fully typed language. This isn't enforced, so there are two varieties of variable type usage:

❑   Type inferencing

❑   Data types

Type Inferencing

If we choose to keep the existing form of JScript, without types, then the data type of a variable is inferred from its context. For example, consider the following:

```
var idx;

for (idx = 0 ; idx < 10 ; idx++)
{
}
```

The compiler infers the type for `idx` from its usage. This doesn't really change from the way the script engine runs with previous versions of JScript, except that now it's the compiler that does the work.

Data Types

If we want to use data types, then we use a colon (`:`) to specify the type. The new syntax is:

```
var name : type[[]] [ = value ]
```

For example:

```
var firstName : String           // JScript String
var dateOfBirth : Date           // JSCript Date
var lastName : System.String     // .NET Framework string
var names : String[]             // array of JScript Strings
```

Notice that both JScript and .NET types are supported.

Namespaces

Namespaces are provided using the `package` keyword, which is equivalent to the Visual Basic and C# `namespace` keyword. For example:

```
package Person
{
  // classes go here
}
```

Classes

Because JScript.NET is implicitly supported by the CLR, the class support is just like that of the other languages. The high level syntax is:

```
[ attributes ] class className [extends baseClassName] [implements interfaceName]
{
}
```

The `attributes` can be one or more of:

Attribute	Description
expando	The class supports dynamic properties, and is given a default indexed property.
public	The class is publicly accessible.
internal	The class is only visible within the package in which it is declared. Equivalent to `Friend` in Visual Basic and `internal` in C#.
abstract	This class is an abstract class, and the class members must be implemented by inheriting classes. Equivalent to `MustInherit` in Visual Basic.
final	This class cannot be inherited. Equivalent to `NotInheritable` in Visual Basic and `abstract` in C#.

For example:

```
public class Calculator
{
  // implementation goes here
}
```

Methods

Like C#, JScript.NET uses functions for methods, using the following syntax:

```
[attributes] function memberName([parameters]) [: type]
{
}
```

The `attributes` can be one or more of:

Attribute	Description
override	The member overrides an identically named member from a base class.
hide	The member does not override an identically named member from a base class.

Modifier	Description
public	The class is publicly accessible.
internal	The member is only visible within the package in which it is declared. Equivalent to `Friend` in Visual Basic and `internal` in C#.
protected	The member is only accessible from the containing class or types derived from the containing member.
private	The member is only accessible from within the containing member.

Table continued on following page

Modifier	Description
static	The member is shared by all instances of the class, and exists independently of a class instance. Equivalent to Shared in Visual Basic.
abstract	This member is an abstract member, and must be implemented by inheriting classes. Equivalent to MustInherit in Visual Basic.
final	This method cannot be overridden, although it can be hidden or overloaded.

For example:

```
public class calculator
{
  public function Add(op1 : double, op2 : double) : double
  {
    return op1 + op2;
  }
}
```

Properties

Like both Visual Basic and C#, JScript properties can be accessed as public variables, or by accessor functions. For example, here we're using public variables:

```
public class calculator
{
  public var Op1 : double;
  public var Op2 : double;

  public function Add() : double
  {
    return Op1 + Op2;
  }
}
```

The alternative, and preferred approach, is to use property accessors. For example:

```
public class calculator
{
  private var _op1 : double;
  private var _op2 : double;

  public function get Operand1() : double
  {
      return _op1;
  }
  public function set Operand1(value: double)
  {
      _op1 = value;
  }
}
```

```
    public function get Operand2() : double
    {
        return _op2;
    }
    public function set Operand2(value: double)
    {
        _op2 = value;
    }
}
```

Like C#, the read/write ability of a property in JScript is determined by the accessor functions. Therefore, if only a get function is provided, the property will be read only.

Constructors

Like C#, the JScript syntax for class constructors is to use a method with the same name as the class. For example:

```
public class person
{
  private var _firstName : string;
  private var _lastName : string;

  public function person() {}

  public function person(firstName : string, lastName : string)
  {
    _firstName = firstName;
    _lastName = lastName;
  }
}
```

Destructors

JScript does not have explicit destructors. To implement this type of behaviour you need to create a method and ensure that this method is called before you destroy the object instance.

Inheritance

JScript uses the extends keyword to inherit from classes. For example:

```
public class programmer extends person
{
  private var _avgHoursSleepPerNight : int;

  public function programmer()
  {
    super();
  }

  public function programmer(firstName : String, lastName : String)
  {
    super(firstName, lastName);
  }
```

```
    public function programmer(firstName : String, lastName : String,
                               hoursSleep: int)
    {
      super(firstName, lastName);
      _avgHoursSleepPerNight = hoursSleep;
    }

    public function get AvgHoursSleepPerNight() : int
    {
      return _avgHoursSleepPerNight;
    }
    public function set AvgHoursSleepPerNight(a : int)
    {
      _avgHoursSleepPerNight = a;
    }

}
```

The class definition defines that our class is called `programmer` and the base class is called `person`:

```
public class programmer extends person
```

Next we need to provide the constructors. Here we specify the same constructors as the base class, and use the `super` keyword (meaning **superclass**) to call the method of the base class. Any parameters are passed to the base class constructor:

```
public function programmer()
{
  super();
}

public function programmer(firstName : String, lastName : String)
{
  super(firstName, lastName);
}
```

In JScript the overridden classes must have the same signature (number and type of parameters) as the base class. We cannot declare local methods with the same name but different parameters – that is, shadowing isn't supported.

Interfaces

Interfaces work the same way as in Visual Basic.NET, providing an immutable contract to the external world.

To create an interface you use the `interface` construct. For example:

```
public interface IPerson
{
  public function get FirstName() : String
  public function set FirstName(value:String)
  public function get LastName() : String
  public function set LastName(value:String)

  public function FullName() : String;
}
```

To derive a class from an interface you use the `implements` keyword:

```
public class Person implements IPerson
{
  private var _firstName : String;
  private var _lastName : String;

  public function get FirstName() : String
  {
    // implementation goes here
  }

  public function set FirstName(value:String)
  {
    // implementation goes here
  }

  ...

}
```

Notice that unlike Visual Basic.NET, only the class needs to specify the interface inheritance.

References

To include references we use `import`. For example:

```
import System;
import MyComponent;
```

You cannot alias references in JScript.NET.

Directives

Three directives have been introduced to bring supported CLR features to the JScript programmer. All three are set using the `@set` directive, the syntax of which is:

```
@set @directive(arguments)
```

The first directive is for debugging:

```
@set @debug(on | off)
```

Debugging is set to set to on by default, and allows hosting environments (such as ASP.NET) to emit their own code into the actual compiled code.

The second directive is to enable CLS compliance:

```
@set @option(fast)
```

When the fast option is enabled:

- ❑ All variables must be declared.

- ❑ We cannot redefine functions.

- ❑ We cannot assign values to functions.

- ❑ We cannot assign, delete, or change the predefined values of built-in objects.

- ❑ Expanded properties are not allowed on built-in objects except for the `global` object.

- ❑ The correct number of arguments must be supplied to function calls.

- ❑ We cannot use the `arguments` property within function calls.

The third directive allows us to provide positional information for debugging messages. This is useful because the code that's executed might not be the same as the code written. This occurs because some environments (such as ASP.NET) might emit their own code into the program. So, when errors occur, the line number it's reported on might not match up to the lines in our code. This directive takes the form:

```
@set @position(end | [file = name] [,line = lineNum] [, column = columnNum])
```

For example, if the environment adds extra code at the beginning of our file, we could add the following:

```
@set @position(line=1)
```

This ensures that the line numbers emitted by errors match with your files.

Other enhancements

Two other enhancements to JScript are the addition of constants and enumerations. Constants are declared using the `const` statement:

```
const variableName = value;
const variableName : type = value;
```

For example:

```
const age = 18
const age : int = 18;
```

Enumerations are declared using the `enum` statement:

```
enum enumName [: type]
{
name [= value[ [, name [= value]] [, …]
}
```

For example:

```
enum days : int
{
    Mon, Tue, Wed, Thu, Fri, Sat, Sun
}
```

If no values are explicitly given, the names are assigned incremental values starting at 0. So, this gives Mon the value of 0, Tue the value of 1, and so on. Alternatively you can specify a value anywhere in the list, and the incrementation continues from that value:

```
enum days : int
{
   Mon=1, Tue, Wed, Thu=9, Fri, Sat, Sun
}
```

This gives the following:

Name	Value
Mon	1
Tue	2
Wed	3
Thu	9
Fri	10
Sat	11
Sun	12

C++

Since C++ already has object-oriented features, the VC++ implementation supplied with Visual Studio.NET provides support for managed code. At the minimum you must include the following two lines at the top of you code:

```
#using <mscorlib.dll>
using namespace System;
```

These give you access to the .NET classes. You must also add the /CLR compiler option when building the executable.

Details of working with the managed extensions for C++ are really outside the scope of this book, so you should consult the documentation for more details.

Other Supported Languages

We've mentioned before that the open design of .NET actively encourages the use of other languages, and Microsoft is keen for this to happen. At the time of writing, the following languages were also becoming available:

- ❑ Dyalog APL/W Version 9.
- ❑ Fujitsu COBOL
- ❑ Component Pascal
- ❑ Eiffel
- ❑ Haskell
- ❑ Mercury
- ❑ Oberon
- ❑ Perl
- ❑ Python
- ❑ Scheme
- ❑ Standard ML

There are others in the pipeline, and the best resource is http://www.gotdotnet.com, which contains an up-to-date list of languages.

If you're into building your own languages, then the SDK comes with some good sample compilers that show you how you can do this. They are in the Tool Developers Guide, and there's plenty of documentation about assemblies, IL, and so on.

The .NET Language Compilers

When working within the Visual Studio.NET environment you don't need to worry about the compiler, because the editor takes care of all that for you. Likewise, when simply developing ASP.NET pages, you can rely upon the framework to compile pages as required. However, when building components or controls you'll want to compile your code into a DLL, so you need to know how the compiler works.

There is a separate compiler for each language, but luckily you use them all in the same way, and most of the switches and flags are identical. The compilers are:

- ❑ csc for C#
- ❑ vbc for Visual Basic.NET
- ❑ jsc for JScript.NET

These are automatically part of the .NET installation, and are invoked from the command line. For example:

```
vbc /t:library /out:..\bin\People.dll /r:system.dll person.vb programmer.vb
```

This compiles the `person.vb` and `programmer.vb` source files into an assembly named `People.dll`.

Compiler switches fall into two usage categories. The first is those that enable or disable an option. In this case, the switch or the switch name followed by plus enables the option, and the switch name followed by minus disables it. For example:

`/cls`	enables the option
`/cls+`	enables the option
`/cls-`	disables the option

The second category contains switches that specify a file or reference. In these cases a colon (`:`) separates the switch and the argument. For example:

```
/out:..\bin\People.dll
```

The full list of options is shown below, including a list of which languages the option is supported in:

Option	Language	Description
`@`	All	Specifies the file containing the compiler options.
`/?` `/help`	All	Display the options, without compiling any code.
`/addmodule:module`	VB / C#	Reference metadata from the specified *module*.
`/baseaddress:number`	VB / C#	Specifies, as a hexadecimal *number*, the base address of the DLL.
`/bugreport:file`	VB / C#	Create a *file* containing information that can be used when filing bug reports.
`/checked`	C#	Generate overflow checks
`/cls`	JScript	Enable or disable CLS checking. By default this is enabled.
`/codepage:id`	Jscript / C#	Specify the code page *id* use in source files.
`/debug`	All	Add debugging information to the created file. This is required if you need to debug into components.
`/define:symbols`	All	Defines conditional compiler constants. You can define multiple constants by separating them with commas. For example: `/define:DBTracing=True,CustomErrors=False`

Table continued on following page

Option	Language	Description
/doc:*file*	C#	Emit the XML documentation in the source files into the named *file*.
/delaysign	VB	Delay-sign the assembly, using only the public part of the strong name key.
/fast	JScript	Disable language features to allow better code generation.
/filealign:*n*	C#	Specify the alignment used for output file sections.
/fullpaths	C#	Generate fully qualified paths.
/imports:*list*	VB	Import a namespace from the specified assembly.
/incr /incremental	C#	Enable or disable incremental compilation.
/keycontainer	VB	Create a unique container name for a key. Used when generating shared components, as it inserts a public key into the assembly manifest, and signs the assembly with the private key. This can be used with the sn utility, which manages keys
/keyfile	VB	Specify the file containing the public and private keys to be added to a shared component. This can be used with the sn utility, which manages keys
/lcid:*id*	JScript	Use the specified locale *id* for the default code page and messages.
/lib:*directories*	C# / JScript	Specify addition *directories* to search for references.
/libpath:*directories*	VB	Specify additional *directories* to search for references.
/linkres:*resinfo* /linkresource:*resinfo*	All	Create a link to a resource file. The first argument is the file name containing the resource, and an optional second argument specifies the identifier in the resource file. For example: `/linkresource:Wrox.resource,AuthorBio`
/m:*type* /main:*type*	C#	Specifies the class or module *type* that contains the main start-up procedure.

Option	Language	Description
`/nologo`	C#	Don't show the copyright banner during compile. This makes it a lot easier to see compilation messages.
`/nowarn`	VB	Disable warnings.
`/nostdlib`	C# / JScript	Enables or disables the import of the standard library `mscorlib.dll` compilation.
`/nowarn:list`	C#	Disable warning messages specified in the *list*.
`/optimize`	C# / VB	Enable or disable compiler optimizations.
`/optioncompare:type`	VB	Specify the *type* of comparison used for strings. The values are `text` or `binary` (the default). For example: `/optioncompare:text`
`/optionexplicit`	VB	Enables (the default) or disables explicit variable declaration.
`/optionstrict`	VB	Enables (the default) or disables strict type conversions. In strict mode the only implicit conversions are those that widen types (for example an integer to a long).
`/out:file`	All	Specifies the name of the output *file*. By default a DLL will take its name from the first source code file, and an EXE will take its name from the file containing the main procedure.
`/print`	JScript	Enable or disable provision of the `print()` function.
`/quiet`	VB	Quiet output mode.
`/recurse:wildcard`	C# / VB	Recurses through subdirectories compiling files. For example: `vbc /target:library /out:Foo.dll /recurse:inc\*.vb`
`/r:list` `/reference:list`	All	Reference metadata from the specified file *list*. For multiple files use a semi-colon (`;`) to separate them.
`/removeintchecks`	VB	Enables or disables (the default) overflow error checking for integer variables.

Table continued on following page

Option	Language	Description
`/res:resinfo` `/resource:resinfo`	All	Embed a resource into the assembly. The first argument is the file name containing the resource, and an optional second argument specifies the identifier in the resource file. For example: `/resource:Wrox.resource,AuthorBio`
`/rootnamespace`	VB	Indicates the namespace in which all type declarations will appear.
`/target:type`	All	Indicate the *type* of file to be created. This can be one of: ❑ exe, for a console application ❑ library, for a DLL ❑ module, for a module ❑ winexe, for a Windows application The `module` option is not applicable in JScript.
`/time`	C#	Displays the project compile times.
`/unsafe`	C#	Enable or disable unsafe code.
`/utf8output`	C# / JScript	Output compiler messages in UTF-8 encoding.
`/verbose`	VB	Enables or disables verbose error and information messages.

`/version:string`	VB	Specifies the versioning information *string* to be inserted into the target. The syntax is:
		
		`/version:[major[.minor [.revision[.build]]]]`
		
		For example:
		
		`vbc /target:library /version:2.2 test.vb`

`/versionsafe`	JScript	Enable or disable specification of default for members that aren't marked as `override` or `new`.
`/w:n` `/warn:n`	C# / JScript	Set the warning level to *n*.
`/warnaserror`	All	Enable or disable the treatment of warnings as errors.
`/win32icon:file`	C# / VB	Specifies the icon *file* (`.ico`) to be added to the resource.
`/win32res:file` `/win32resource:file`	All	Inserts a Win32 resource *file* into the target.

Benefits of a Common Language Runtime

Let's quickly remind ourselves of the points made in the previous chapter about languages:

❑ Language functionality. The choice of language is now a lifestyle choice, rather than a functionality choice, as they are all equivalent. Use whatever language you are happiest with.

❑ Performance. The .NET languages were designed to provide high performance. The only difference between the languages is at the compilation stage, where compilers may produce slightly different MSIL.

❑ Platform Support. The languages sit on top of the Common Language Runtime, so if the CLR is available on a platform, then so are the .NET languages. For small device support and 64-bit platforms this makes portability far easier than with previous Windows languages.

Let's have a look at the practicalities of the CLR and CLS.

Common API

In the previous version of Visual Studio, common functionality was always far harder than it should have been. For C++ programmers, the Windows API is their natural home, but Visual Basic programmers had to use custom controls and libraries, or delve into the API itself. This isn't complex, and can yield great benefits, but there is no consistency.

With .NET we now have a common API and a great set of class libraries (which are covered in detail in Chapter 7). For example, consider the case of TCP/IP network applications. C++ programmers generally write directly to Winsock, whereas Visual Basic programmers prefer to use custom controls on their forms. The .NET framework provides a `System.Net.Sockets` namespace encompassing all of the networking functionality, and its usage is the same for each language.

For example, consider the case of writing to a UDP port – you can see the only differences in the code are the syntax of the language.

Visual Basic

```
Dim Client        As UDPClient
Dim HostName      As String
Dim HostIP        As IPHostEntry
Dim GroupAddress  As IPAddress
Dim Remote        As IPEndPoint

HostName = DNS.GetHostName()
HostIP = DNS.GetHostByName(HostName)

Client = New UdpClient(8080)
GroupAddress = IpAddress.Parse("224.0.0.1")
Client.JoinMultiCastGroup(GroupAddress, 500)
Remote = New IPEndPoint(GroupAddress, 8080)
Client.Send(".NET is great", 13, Remote)
```

C#

```
UDPClient   Client;
String      HostName;
IPHostEntry HostIP;
IPAddress   GroupAddress;
IPEndPoint  Remote;

HostName = DNS.GetHostName();
HostIP = DNS.GetHostByName(HostName);

Client = new UdpClient(8080)
GroupAddress = IpAddress.Parse("224.0.0.1");
Client.JoinMultiCastGroup(GroupAddress, 500);
Remote = new IPEndPoint(GroupAddress, 8080);
Client.Send(".NET is great", 13, Remote);
```

JScript

```
var Client      : UDPClient
var HostName     : String
var HostIP       : IPHostEntry
var GroupAddress : IPAddress
var Remote       : IPEndPoint

HostName = DNS.GetHostName();
HostIP = DNS.GetHostByName(HostName);

Client = new UdpClient(8080)
GroupAddress = IpAddress.Parse("224.0.0.1");
Client.JoinMultiCastGroup(GroupAddress, 500);
Remote = new IPEndPoint(GroupAddress, 8080);
Client.Send(".NET is great", 13, Remote);
```

Common Types

One of the ways in which the cross language functionality is made available is by use of common types. Those Visual Basic programmers (and I was one) who delved into the Windows API, always had the problem about converting types. Strings were the worst, because the API is C/C++ based, which uses null terminated strings, so you always had to do conversion and fixed string handling stuff. It was ugly.

With the CLS there is a common set of types, so no conversion is required. The previous chapter detailed these, showing their range and size, and explained that the various compilers will convert native types into CLS ones. The conversion works like this:

Type	Visual Basic	C#	JScript
System.Boolean	Boolean	bool	boolean
System.Byte	Byte	byte	byte
System.Char	Char	char	char

Type	Visual Basic	C#	JScript
System.DateTime	Date	No direct equivalent. Use the CLS type.	No direct equivalent. JScript has its own Date type.
System.Decimal	Decimal	decimal	decimal
System.Double	Double	double	double
			Number
System.Int16	Short	short	short
System.Int32	Integer	int	int
System.Int64	Long	long	long
System.UInt16	No direct equivalent.	ushort	ushort
System.UInt32	No direct equivalent.	uint	uint
System.UInt64	No direct equivalent.	ulong	ulong
System.SByte	No direct equivalent.	sbyte	sbyte
System.Single	Single	float	float
System.String	String	string	String

Note that not all languages have equivalents of the CLS types. For example, JScript implements dates using the standard JScript Date object. However, you can convert between various type formats, as well as declaring the CLS types directly.

Cross-Language Inheritance

Another area where the CLS has helped is the area of inheritance. Assuming that you use the common types in your class interfaces, then inheriting classes written in other languages is no different to that of inheriting from the same language. We showed a brief example in the previous chapter, when discussing the CLR and common functionality, but a fuller example makes this clear. For example, suppose that you had the following Visual Basic class:

```
Public Class Person

    Private _firstName As String
    Private _lastName  As String

    Sub New()
    End Sub


    Sub New(firstName As String, lastName As String)
```

```
      _firstName = firstName
      _lastName = lastName

   End Sub

   Public Property FirstName() As String
      ' property code here
   End Property

   Public Property LastName() As String
      ' property code here
   End Property

End Class
```

You could write another program, perhaps in C#, that inherits from it:

```
public class Programmer : Person
{
  private int _avgHoursSleepPerNight;

  public programmer(): base()
  {
  }

  public programmer(string firstName, string lastName
                 : base(firstName, lastName)
  {
  }

  public programmer(string firstName, string lastName, int hoursSleep)
                 : base(firstName, lastName)
  {
    _avgHoursSleepPerNight = hoursSleep;
  }

  public int AvgHoursSleepPerNight
  {
    get { return _avgHoursSleepPerNight; }
    set { _avgHoursSleepPerNight = value; }
  }

  ~programmer()
  {
  }
}
```

This brings great flexibility to development, especially where team development is concerned.

Another great point about this is that many of the base classes and web controls are inheritable. Therefore, in any language, you can extend them as you wish. A good example of this is the ASP.NET DataGrid control. Say you didn't want to use paging, but wanted to provide a scrollable grid, so browsers that supported inline frames would allow the entire content of the grid to be rendered within a scrollable frame. You can create your own control (say in Visual Basic), inheriting everything from the base control (perhaps written in C#), and then just output the normal content within an IFRAME. This sort of thing is extremely easy to do with the new framework.

Cross-Language Debugging and Profiling.

The cross language debugging features are really cool, and provide a huge leap forward over any debugging features we've ever had before. Both the framework and Visual Studio.NET come with visual debuggers, the only difference being that the Visual Studio.NET debugger allows remote debugging as well as edit and continue. The debuggers works through the CLR, and allow us to step through ASP.NET pages and into components, whatever the language. Along with debugging comes tracing and profiling, with the ability to use common techniques to track code.

Both of these topics are covered in more detail in Chapter 22.

Performance Issues

Performance is always a question in people's minds, and often gets raised during beta testing when there's lots of debugging code hanging around in the product. Even in the early betas it was clear that ASP.NET was faster than ASP, with figures showing a 2-3 times improvement.

One of the reasons for this performance improvement is the full compilation of code. Many people confuse Intermediate Language (IL) and the CLR with byte-code and interpreters (notably Java), and assume that performance will drop. Their belief in this deepens when they first access an aspx page, because that first hit can sometimes be slow. That's because pages are compiled on their first hit, and then served from the cache thereafter (unless explicit caching has been disabled).

Appendix B has a list of tips and tricks to help with performance.

Languages

Although all languages compile to IL and then to native code, there may be some slight performance differences, due to the nature of the compiler and the language. In some languages the IL produced may not be as efficient as others – some people have said that the C# compiler is better than the Visual Basic one, but the effects should be imperceptible. It's only under the highest possible stress situation that you may find differences, and to be honest I wouldn't even consider it a problem.

Late Bound Code

One of the greatest advantages of the CLR is fully typed languages. However, you can still use JScript without datatypes, allowing legacy code to continue working. The disadvantage of this is that types then have to be inferred, and this will have a performance impact.

In Visual Basic, if strict semantics are not being used (either by the Option Strict Off page directive or by the /optionstrict- compiler switch), then late-bound calls on object types are handled at run-time rather than compile time.

Common Examples

Experienced developers probably won't have much trouble using the new features of the languages, or even converting from one language to another. However, there are plenty of people who use ASP and VBScript daily to build great sites, but who have little experience of advanced development features, such as the object oriented features in .NET. That's actually a testament to how simple ASP is, but now that ASP.NET is moving up a gear, it's important that you make the most of these features.

To that end, this section will give a few samples in Visual Basic.NET, C# and JScript.NET, covering a few common areas. This will help, should you want to convert existing code, write new code in a language that you aren't an expert in, or perhaps just examine someone else's code. We won't cover the definition of classes and class members again in this section, as they've had a good examination earlier in the chapter.

Variable Declaration

The first point to look at is that of variable declaration.

Visual Basic.NET

Visual Basic.NET has the same variable declaration syntax as the previous version, but now has the ability to set initial values at variable declaration time. For example:

```
Dim Name     As String = "Rob Smith"
Dim Age      As Integer = 28
Dim coolDude As New Person("Vince", "Patel")
```

C#

C# follows the C/C++ style of variable declaration:

```
string Name = "Rob Smith";
int Age = 28;
coolDude = new Person("Vince", "Patel");
```

JScript.NET

JScript.NET uses the standard JScript declaration method, with the addition of optional types:

```
var Name : String = "Rob Smith";
var Age = 28;
var coolDude : Person = new Person("Vince", "Patel")
```

Functions and Procedures

Declaring procedures is similar in all languages.

Visual Basic.NET

Procedures and functions follow similar syntax to previous versions:

```
Private Function GetDiscounts(Company As String) As DataSet
Public Sub UpdateDiscounts(Company As String, Discount As Double)
```

The major difference is that by default all parameters are now passed by value, and not by reference. And remember that `Optional` parameters also now require a default value:

```
' incorrect
Function GetDiscsounts(Optional Comp As String) As DataSet

' correct
Function GetDiscountss(Optional Comp As String = "Wrox") As DataSet
```

Returning values from functions now uses the `Return` statement, rather than setting the function name to the desired value. For example:

```
Function IsActive() As Boolean

    ' some code here

    Return True

End Function
```

The way you call procedures has also changed. The rule is that arguments to all procedure calls must be enclosed in parentheses. For example:

```
UpdateDiscounts "Wrox", 5        ' no longer works
UpdateDiscounts("Wrox", 5)       ' new syntax
```

C#

C# doesn't have any notion of procedures – there are only functions that either return or don't return values (in which case the type is `void`). For example:

```
bool function IsActive()
{
    // some code here

    return true;
}
```

```
void function UpdateDiscounts(string Company, double Discount)
{
    return;
}
```

To call procedures, C# requires that parentheses are used.

JScript.NET

For JScript.NET the declaration of functions is changed by the addition of types.

```
function IsActive() : Boolean
{
    // some code here

    return true;
}
```

```
function UpdateDiscounts(Company : String, Discount : Double) : void
{
  return;
}
```

To call procedures, JScript.NET requires that parentheses are used.

Syntax Differences

There are a few syntactical differences that confuse many people when switching languages for the first time. The first is that Visual Basic isn't case sensitive, but the other languages are – it still catches me out. Other things are the use of line terminators in C# and JScript, which use a semi-colon. Many people switching to these languages complain about them, but the reason they are so great is that it makes the language free form – the end of the line doesn't end the current statement. This is unlike Visual Basic, where the end of the line is the end of the statement, and a line continuation character is required for long lines.

Listed below are some of the major syntactical differences between the languages.

Loops

Visual Basic.NET

There are four loop constructs in Visual Basic, and the syntax of one has changed in Visual Basic.NET. The first is the For...Next loop:

```
For counter = start To end [Step step]
Next [counter]
```

For example:

```
For count = 1 To 10
  ...
Next
```

The second is the While loop, for which the syntax has changed – the new syntax is

```
While condition
End While
```

For example:

```
While count < 10
  ...
End While
```

In previous versions of Visual Basic the loop was terminated with a Wend *statement.*

The third is the Do...Loop, which has two forms:

```
Do [(While | Until) condition]
Loop
```

or:

```
Do
Loop [(While | Until) condition]
```

The difference between these two is the placement of the test condition. In the first instance the test is executed before any loop content, and therefore the content may not get executed. In the second case the test is at the end of the loop, so the content is always executed at least once. For example:

```
Do While count < 10
Loop
```

```
Do
Loop While count < 10
```

The fourth loop construct is for iterating through collections:

```
For Each element In collection
Next [element]
```

For example:

```
Dim ctl As Control
For Each ctl In Page.Controls
     .
Next
```

C#

C# has the same number of loop constructs as Visual Basic. The first is the for loop:

```
for ([initializers] ; [expression] ; [iterators])
```

For example:

```
for (count = 0 ; count < 10 ; count++)
```

Each of these parts is optional. For example:

```
for ( ; count < 10; count++)
for ( ; ; count++)
for (count = 0 ; ; count++)
for ( ; ; )
```

The last of these produces an infinite loop.

The second is the while loop:

```
while (expression)
```

For example:

```
while (count < 10)
```

The third is the do...while loop:

```
do statement while (expression);
```

For example:

```
do
while (count < 10);
```

The fourth loop construct is for iterating through collections:

```
foreach (type identifier in expression)
```

For example:

```
foreach (Control ctl In Page.Controls)
```

You can also use this for looping through arrays:

```
String[] Authors = new String[]
                    {"Alex", "Brian", "Dave", "Karli", "Rich", "Rob"};

foreach (String Author In Authors)
    Console.WriteLine("{0}", Author);
```

One point to note about loops in C# is that the loop affects the code block after the loop. This can be a single line or a bracketed block. For example:

```
for (count = 0 ; count < 10 ; count++)
    Console.WriteLine("{0}", count);
```

or, if more than one line is required as part of the loop

```
for (count = 0 ; count < 10 ; count++)
{
    Console.Write("The value is now: ");
    Console.WriteLine("{0}", count);
}
```

JScript.NET

JScript has the same number of loop constructs as C# and Visual Basic, with the syntax being more C# like. The first is the `for` loop, where unlike C#, all parts of the loop are required:

```
for (initializers ; expression ; iterators)
```

For example:

```
for (count = 0 ; count < 10 ; count++)
```

The second is the `while` loop:

```
while (expression)
```

For example:

```
while (count < 10)
```

The third is the `do...while` loop:

```
do statement while (expression);
```

For example:

```
do
while (count < 10);
```

The fourth loop construct is for iterating through objects and arrays:

```
for (identifier in [object | array])
```

For example:

```
for (ctl In Page.Controls)
```

or, for looping through arrays:

```
var Authors :String= new String[]
                {"Alex", "Brian", "Dave", "Karli", "Rich", "Rob"};

foreach (String Author In Authors)
   Console.WriteLine("{0}", Author);
```

One point to note about loops in JScript is that the loop affects the code block after the loop. This can be a single line or a bracketed block. For example:

```
for (count = 0 ; count < 10 ; count++)
   Console.WriteLine("{0}", count);
```

or, if more than one line is required as part of the loop

```
for (count = 0 ; count < 10 ; count++)
{
  Console.Write("The value is now: ");
  Console.WriteLine("{0}", count);
}
```

Type Conversion

Type conversion of one data type to another is an area that causes a great deal of confusion, especially for those programmers who are used to a type-less language such as VBScript. When dealing with strongly typed languages you either have to let the compiler, or runtime, convert between types (if it can) or explicitly perform the conversion yourself. The method of conversion depends upon the language:

Visual Basic.NET

In Visual Basic.NET there are two ways to do this. The first uses CType:

```
Dim AgeString As String
Dim Age As Integer

AgeString = "25"
Age = CType(AgeString, Integer)
```

The CType function takes an object and a datatype, and returns the object converted to the data type.

The other way is to use the data type as a cast function:

```
Age = CInt(AgeString)
```

C#

In C# we just place the type in parentheses before the expression we wish to convert. For example:

```
Age = (int)AgeString;
```

JScript.NET

To cast in JScript we use a cast function. For example:

```
Age = int(AgeString)
```

Summary

In this chapter we've examined the languages supplied with .NET, and discovered that the underlying framework provides a rich development environment. The whole issue, and arguments that go along with it, of which language is better, or more suitable, has simply disappeared. The language that's best is the one you are most familiar with. Apart from in a few small areas, the major difference between the .NET languages is the syntax.

We've also looked at the enhancements to the existing languages that bring them into line with the CLR and CLS, how these features are compatible across all languages, and the benefits they brings. Features such as cross-language development, debugging, and tracing may not seem that great if you only use one language, but the flexibility it brings is immeasurable, especially when combined with the extensive class libraries.

Now that we've examined the languages, it's time to them to start to use them and look in detail at the process of writing ASP.NET pages.

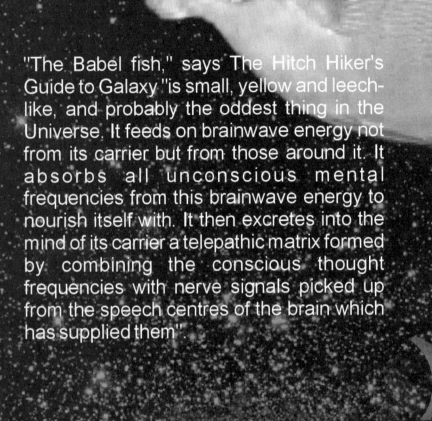

"The Babel fish," says The Hitch Hiker's Guide to Galaxy "is small, yellow and leech-like, and probably the oddest thing in the Universe. It feeds on brainwave energy not from its carrier but from those around it. It absorbs all unconscious mental frequencies from this brainwave energy to nourish itself with. It then excretes into the mind of its carrier a telepathic matrix formed by combining the conscious thought frequencies with nerve signals picked up from the speech centres of the brain which has supplied them".

The practical upshot of all this is that if you stick a Babel fish in your ear you can instantly understand anything said to you in any form of language. The speech patterns you actually hear decode the brainwave matrix which has been fed into your mind by your Babel fish.

4

Writing ASP.NET Pages

Now it's time to get serious – we've taken a high-level look at the .NET framework, and seen a few quick examples of ASP.NET pages, so now we're going to dive in and look at how we create ASP.NET pages in more detail. Whether we call them ASP.NET pages or Web Forms, these files are the core for all ASP.NET applications. In this chapter, we will look at:

- ❑   The old way of creating ASP pages versus the new way with ASP.NET.

- ❑   The steps a page goes through as it is processed.

- ❑   How to use the various features of the `Page` object.

- ❑   Breaking up a page into reusable objects called User Controls.

Once we reach the end of this chapter, we will have learned the core essentials for the rest of the ASP.NET world. Everything we do for the remainder of the book will draw on the page framework that we are about to discuss.

Coding Issues

In Chapter 1 we looked at some of the main disadvantages of existing ASP applications, showing why we needed a new version, and how ASP.NET solves some of those problems. We also saw that ASP.NET introduces a new way of coding, and for those of you who have programmed in event-driven languages, such as Visual Basic, this model will seem familiar. It might, at first, seem a little alien to programmers who have only coded in script languages such as VBScript. However, it's extremely simple, providing many advantages, and leads to much more structured code. The code is no longer intermixed with the HTML, and its event-driven nature means it is more easily structured for better readability and maintainability.

We saw in the first chapter how this worked for an `OnClick` event on a server control, and how the code to be run was broken out into a separate event procedure. That example showed a list of states in a `DropDownList` Server Control. Using lists like this is extremely common, and often the list of items is generated from a data store. To understand the difference between the existing ASP architecture, and the new event-driven ASP.NET architecture, let's take a sample page and compare the old and the new.

Coding the Old Way

To produce a list of items from a data store in ASP, you have to loop through the list of items, manually creating the HTML. When the item is selected, the form is then posted back to the server. It looks something like this (`OldAsp.asp`):

```
<html>

<form action="OldAsp.asp" method="post">

    Please select your delivery method:
    <select id="ShipMethod" Name="ShipMethod" size="1">
<%
    Dim rsShip
    Dim SQL
    Dim ConnStr
    Dim ItemField

  Set rsShip = Server.CreateObject("ADODB.Recordset")

    SQL = "SELECT * FROM Shipping_Methods"
    ConnStr = "Driver={SQL Server}; Server=localhost; " & _
          "Database=IBuyAdventure; UID=sa"

    rsShip.Open SQL, ConnStr

    While Not rsShip.EOF
    Response.Write "<option value='" & _
          rsShip("ShippingMethodID") & "'>" & _
          rsShip("ShippingMethod") & "</option>" & vbCrLf
    rsShip.MoveNext
    Wend

    rsShip.Close
    Set rsShip = Nothing
%>
    </select>
    <br>
    <input type="submit" value="Place Order">
</form>

<%
    If Len(Request.Form("ShipMethod")) > 0 Then
    Response.write "<br>Your order will be delivered via " & _
          Request.Form("ShipMethod")
    End If
%>
</html>
```

This code is fairly simple – it loops through a recordset building a SELECT list, allows the user to select a value and submit that back to the server. In many situations you'd probably build some sort of database query or update based upon the selected value, but in our example we are printing out the selected value:

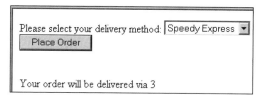

Notice that only the `value` is available in the submitted page, and not the text value selected – that's just the way SELECT lists work. This is fine if we're going to use the value in some form of data query, but not if we need to display it again. You can see how this happens by looking at the HTML generated:

```html
<html>

<form action="Shipping.asp" method="post">

  Please select your delivery method:
  <select id="ShipMethod" Name="ShipMethod" size="1">
<option value='1'>Speedy Express</option>
<option value='2'>Federal Shipping</option>
<option value='3'>Mail Company</option>
<option value='4'>Slow Shipping</option>

  </select>
  <br>
  <input type="submit" value="Place Order">
</form>

<br>Your order will be delivered via 3
</html>
```

The `option` elements have their `value` attribute as the ID of the shipping method, and it's the value that's accessible from server-side ASP code.

Coding in ASP.NET Pages

As ASP.NET is event based, you need to understand the order of events, so that you can see where the equivalent code would go. Code within these events is processed sequentially, but the events are processed only when they are raised. For example, the event order is:

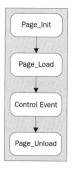

These events are:

Event	Description
Page_Init	Fired when the page is initialized.
Page_Load	Fired when the page is loaded.
Control Event	Fired if a control (such as a button) triggered the page to be reloaded.
Page_Unload	Fired when the page is unloaded from memory.

The difference between Page_Init and Page_Load, is that the controls are only guaranteed to be fully loaded in the Page_Load. You can access the controls in the Page_Init event, but the ViewState is not loaded, therefore controls will have their default values, rather than any values set during the postback.

For example, rewriting the original ASP page in ASP.NET we get (NewAspNet.aspx):

```
<%@ Import Namespace="System.Data" %>
<%@ Import Namespace="System.Data.SqlClient" %>

<html>
<head>

<script language="VB" runat="server">

    Sub Page_Load(Source As Object, E As EventArgs)

        Dim myConnection As SQLConnection
        Dim myCommand As SQLCommand
        Dim myReader  As SQLDataReader
        Dim SQL       As String
        Dim ConnStr   As String

        SQL = "SELECT * FROM Shipping_Methods"
        ConnStr = "server=localhost;uid=sa;pwd=;database=IBuyAdventure"

        myConnection = New SQLConnection(ConnStr)
        myConnection.Open()

        myCommand = New SQLCommand(SQL, myConnection)

        myReader = myCommand.ExecuteReader()

        ShipMethod.DataSource = myReader
        ShipMethod.DataBind()

    End Sub

    Sub PlaceOrder_Click(Source As Object, E As EventArgs)

    YouSelected.Text = "Your order will be delivered via " & _
        ShipMethod.SelectedItem.Text

    End Sub
```

```
    </script>

    <form runat="server">

        Please select your delivery method:

        <asp:DropDownList id="ShipMethod"
            DataTextField="ShippingMethod" DataValueField="ShippingMethodID"
            runat="server"/>

        <br/>

        <asp:button id="PlaceOrder" Text="Place Order"
            onClick="PlaceOrder_Click"
            runat="server"/>

        <br/>

        <asp:Label id="YouSelected" runat="server"/>
    </form>
    </html>
```

Let's look at this code in detail to see what the changes are, and why they've been done, starting with the HTML form:

```
    <form runat="server">

        Please select your delivery method:

        <asp:DropDownList id="ShipMethod"
            DataTextField="ShippingMethod" DataValueField="ShippingMethodID"
            runat="server"/>

        <br/>

        <asp:button id="PlaceOrder" Text="Place Order"
            onClick="PlaceOrder_Click"
            runat="server"/>

        <br/>

        <asp:Label id="YouSelected" runat="server"/>
    </form>
```

This has three ASP.NET Server Controls – a drop-down list, a button, and a label. The next chapter gives more detail on the Server Controls, but for the moment, we want to concentrate on the event side of things. So, just remember that these are server-side controls, and can therefore be accessed from within our server-side code.

At the start of the page we place the Import statements, to tell ASP.NET which code libraries we wish to use. The two below are for data access, and are covered in more detail in Chapters 8 and 9.

```
<%@ Import Namespace="System.Data" %>
<%@ Import Namespace="System.Data.SqlClient" %>

<html>
<head>
```

Next, we start the script block, and define the `Page_Load` event. Remember this will be run every time the page is loaded.

```
<script language="VB" runat="server">

    Sub Page_Load(Source As Object, E As EventArgs)
```

The parameters to this event are fixed, and defined by ASP.NET. The first defines the source object that raised the event, and the second contains any additional details being passed to the event. For the `Page_Load` event we can ignore these, but later in the book you'll see where they come in useful.

Within this event we want to query the database and build our list of shipping methods. We're not going to explain the following data access code, since it's covered in the Chapters 8 and 9, but it's roughly equivalent to the code in the previous example, simply creating a set of records from the database.

```
Dim myConnection As SQLConnection
Dim myCommand    As SQLCommand
Dim myReader     As SQLDataReader
Dim SQL          As String
Dim ConnStr      As String

SQL = "SELECT * FROM Shipping_Methods"
ConnStr = "server=localhost;uid=sa;pwd=;database=IBuyAdventure"

myConnection = New SQLConnection(ConnStr)
myConnection.Open()

myCommand = New SQLCommand(SQL, myConnection)

myReader = myCommand.ExecuteReader()
```

Once the records are created, we use data binding to fill the list (`ShipMethod`). In the ASP example we actually had to create the HTML `OPTION` elements in the loop, but in the ASP.NET page we can use the data-binding features that allow controls to automatically populate themselves from a set of data (Data binding is covered in detail in Chapter 7). We showed earlier that the list is declared to run server-side, so we can just call its methods and properties server-side. This is more like the Visual Basic programming environment, where we're dealing with controls.

```
ShipMethod.DataSource = myReader
ShipMethod.DataBind()
```

At this stage the code in the `Page_Load` event has finished. Since this is the first time the page has been executed, there are no control-specific events.

When we select an item in the list and click the button, we invoke the postback mechanism. Our button was defined as:

```
<asp:button id="PlaceOrder" Text="Place Order"
    onClick="PlaceOrder_Click"
    runat="server"/>
```

The `onClick` property identifies the name of the server-side event procedure to be run when the button is clicked. Remember that this is server-side event processing, so there is no special client-side code. When this button is clicked, the form is submitted back to itself, and the defined event handler is run (after the `Page_Load` event):

```
Sub PlaceOrder_Click(Source As Object, E As EventArgs)

    YouSelected.Text = "Your order will be delivered via " & _
        ShipMethod.SelectedItem.Text

End Sub
```

This just sets the text of a label to the value selected:

This shows an interesting point. Because the list control is a server control, we have access not only to the value, but also to the text of the selected item. Although this is possible with ASP, the code required isn't as neat as the ASP.NET solution. We haven't had to detect which control is selected and choose the value – the control, and its ViewState, handles it for us.

So, let's just reiterate these points:

- ❑ Server based controls can be accessed from server code. Even though these controls emit plain HTML, and are part of a standard HTML form, the architecture of ASP.NET ensures that they are accessible from server-side event procedures.

- ❑ The `Page_Load` event is run every time the page is executed. It's in this event that you'll want to populate controls.

- ❑ The control event is only run when fired by a server control. This is indicated by wiring up the event property on the control to an event procedure name.

Postback Identification

There is one big flaw in our code shown above. Because the Page_Load runs every time the page loads, the code in it will be run even under a postback scenario – that is, even when a button is pressed. That means we are performing the data query and filling the drop-down list every time, so whatever the user selected would be overwritten (as well as being unnecessary).

The IsPostBack property of the Page is designed to counter this problem, by allowing us to identify whether or not we are in a postback situation (as opposed to the first time the page is loaded). We can use this property in the Page_Load event so that our data access code is only run the first time the page is loaded:

```
Sub Page_Load(Source As Object, E As EventArgs)

    If Not Page.IsPostBack Then

        Dim myConnection As SQLConnection
        Dim myCommand As SQLCommand
        Dim myReader  As SQLDataReader
        Dim SQL       As String
        Dim ConnStr   As String

        SQL = "select * from Shipping_Methods"
        ConnStr = "server=localhost;uid=sa;pwd=;database=IBuyAdventure"

        myConnection = New SQLConnection(ConnStr)
        myConnection.Open()

        myCommand = New SQLCommand(SQL, myConnection)

        myReader = myCommand.ExecuteReader()

        ShipMethod.DataSource = myReader
        ShipMethod.DataBind()
    End If

End Sub
```

We've now ensured that this code runs only when the page is first loaded. We don't have to worry about the contents of the list disappearing, because the contents are held within the ViewState of the drop-down list. If we look at the HTML produced, we see that it's very similar to the old ASP example:

```
<html>
<head>

<h1>ASP.NET - The Page_Load Event</h1>
<hr/>
<form name="ctrl0" method="post" action="NewAspNet.aspx" id="ctrl0">
<input type="hidden" name="__VIEWSTATE"
value="dDwxNTY5OTcyNzI0O3Q8O2w8aTwyPjs+O2w8dDw7bDxpPDE+O2k8NT47PjtsPHQ8dDw7bDxpPDE+O2k8NT47PjtsPHQ8dDw7bDxpPDE+
+O0A8U3BlZWR5IEV4cHJlc3M7RmVkZXJhbCBCTaGlwcGluZztNYWlsIENvbXBhbnk7U2VvdyBTaGlwcGluZ
zs+O0A8MTsyOzM7NDs+Pjs+Ozs+O3Q8cDxwPGw8VGV4dDs+O2w8WW91ciBvcmRlciB3aWxsIGJlIGRlbGl2
2ZXJlZCB2aWEgU3BlZWR5IEV4cHJlc3M7Pj47Pjs7Pjs+Pjs+" />

    Please select your delivery method:
```

```
    <select name="ShipMethod" id="ShipMethod">
...<option selected="selected" value="1">Speedy Express</option>
...<option value="2">Federal Shipping</option>
...<option value="3">Mail Company</option>
<option value="4">Slow Shipping</option>

</select>

    <br/>
    <input type="submit" name="PlaceOrder" value="Place Order" id="PlaceOrder" />
    <br/>

    <span id="YouSelected">Your order will be delivered via Speedy Express</span>
</form>
</html>
```

You can see that the `asp:DropDownList` produces an HTML `select` list along with the associated `option` elements. The form posting is still handled in the same way as ASP. The major difference is the hidden VIEWSTATE field, containing control ViewState. We look at this topic a little later in the chapter.

As we saw in Chapter 1, the new model for ASP.NET is based around the separation of the visual portion of the web form (the HTML code) from the logic portion (the executable code). In this way, the operation of Web Forms is much closer to the way that Visual Basic forms have worked in the past than they are to traditional web pages.

Web Forms also help to solve a number of challenges in using a browser-based execution engine to provide a user experience that is similar to today's Windows applications. These challenges include:

❑   Delivering rich user interfaces, and delivering these user interfaces on a wide variety of platforms. Web Forms can insulate the developer from the actual client being used, which allows them to focus on providing the necessary business logic.

❑   How to merge a client-server application, where code is being executed in two different locations into a more traditional event-driven programming model. Web Forms accomplish this by providing a single methodology for dealing with application events – no matter if the event was fired on the client, or on the server.

❑   Providing state management in an execution environment that is inherently stateless. Many different methods have been used in the past to provide for a stateful execution environment for the stateless web world. These methods have ranged from cookies, to hidden form fields, to state information being held on the server. Yet each one of these methods presented a different programmatic interface to the developer, forcing them to choose at development time the type of state management to use. Web Forms insulates the developer from this by providing a standard way of maintaining state for the developer, while hiding the actual implementation details from them.

Even though the presentation, and the logic are separate for the developer as the application is being developed, it is important to know that when they are actually executed, they come together as one unit. Even if the logic exists in one file and the presentation in another, at run-time they are compiled into a single object. This object is represented by the `Page` class.

The Page Class

When a Web Form is requested from the server – a client requests a URL that has an `aspx` extension on it – the components that make up that page are compiled into one unit. The components can consist of:

❑ The `.aspx` file being requested.

❑ The .NET class file containing the code for that page.

❑ Any user controls used by the page.

This unit that the components are compiled into is a dynamically generated class that is derived from the .NET `Object.Control.TemplateControl.Page` class. All of your controls, presentation information, and logic are used to extend this class to provide you with an object that supports the functionality of the page you created.

This dynamically created `Page` class, can then be instantiated any time a request is made for the `.aspx` page. When it is instantiated, the resulting object is used to process the incoming requests and returns the data to the requesting client. Any web controls – intrinsic or custom – are in turn instantiated by this object and provide their results back to the `Page` object to be included in the response to the client. The executable page object is created from compiling all of the files (code behind, user controls and so on) associated with the page. This compilation only takes place when one of the files changes, or when the application configuration file (see Chapter 13) changes. This means that the process is extremely efficient.

In ASP, we were used to having our code and presentation integrated into one file, or split among many files if using `#include` files. When this file was executed, the server would simply start at the top of the file and spit out any HTML text that it found back to the client. When it encountered some script, the script would be executed, and any additions to the HTML response stream would be added at that point. So in effect, all we had was an HTML file with some code interspersed in it.

In ASP.NET, the page is actually an executable object that outputs HTML. But it is truly an object in that it has a series of processing stages – initialization, processing, and cleanup – just like all objects do. The differences that make the `Page` class unique is that it performs these functions EVERY time it is called – meaning it is a stateless object and no instances of it hang around in between client requests. Also, the `Page` class has a unique step, known as the rendering step, when HTML is actually generated for output to the client.

When we take a look at **code-behind** programming a little later in this chapter, you will see that the file that actually contains the code is really a class definition. The class defined in that file is derived from the `Page` class. Once you have the class derived from the `Page` class, you need to link that to the `.aspx` file in some way. This is done in the @ `PAGE` directive at the top of a `.aspx` file. So if in our code-behind file we have a class definition such as:

```
public class MyPage: Page {….. }
```

Then in the corresponding `.aspx` file, there will be the following directive:

```
<%@ PAGE Inherits="MyPage" Code="mypage.cs" %>
```

The intrinsic `Page` class serves as a container class for all of the components that make up a page. We can use the interface of the `Page` class to let us manipulate certain aspects of what happens on the page. The events, properties and methods are shown in the three tables below:

Event Table

Event	Description
Init event	Fired when the page is initialized.
Load event	Fired when the page is loaded, and all controls (including their viewstate) have been loaded.
Unload event	Fired when the page is done processing – this happens after all the information has been sent to the client.
PreRender event	Fired just prior to the information being written to the client.
AbortTransaction event	Fired when the transaction that the page is participating in is aborted.
CommitTransaction event	Fired when the transaction that the page is participating in is committed
Error event	The Error event will be fired whenever an unhandled exception occurs on the page. You can handle this event to do your custom error processing (see Chapter 22 for more details).

Property Table

Property	Description
Application property	Reference to the current Application object. For each web application, there is exactly one instance of this object. It is shared by all of the clients accessing the web application.
Cache property	The Cache property gets a reference to the Cache object that can be used to store data for subsequent server round-trips to the same page. The Cache object is in essence a dictionary object whose state is persisted through the use of hidden form fields, or some other means, so that data can live from one page request to the next.
ClientTarget property	This property allows you to override the browser detection that is built into ASP.NET and specify what specific browser you want that page to be rendered for. Any controls that then rely on the browser being detected will use the specified configuration, rather than the capabilities of the actual requesting browser.
EnableViewState property	This Boolean value indicates whether or not the server controls on this page maintain their ViewState between page requests. This value affects all of the controls on the page, and supercedes any individual settings on the controls themselves.

Table continued on following page

Property	Description
ErrorPage property	If, as the page is being compiled and run, an unhandled exception is detected, then you probably want to display some kind of error message to the user. ASP.NET generates its own default error page, but if you want to control what is being displayed, then you can use this property to set the URL of the page that will be displayed instead.
IsPostBack property	This Boolean value is set to true if the page is being run as the result of a client round-trip. When it is false, we know that it is the first time the page is being displayed, and that there is no ViewState stored for the server controls. When this is the case, we need to set the state of the controls manually – usually during the execution of the Page_Load event.
IsValid property	This Boolean value is set to true if all of the validation controls on the page report that their validation conditions have been positively met. If only one validation control fails, then this value will be set to false. We will look at the validation controls in Chapter 5 when we look at Server controls in detail. Checking this property can help to improve page performance by allowing us to avoid performing certain expensive functions when we know that a validation condition has not been met.
Request property	Reference to the Request object – allowing access to information about the HTTP Request.
Response property	Reference to the Response object – allowing access to the HTTP Response.
Server property	Reference to the current Server object.
Session property	Reference to the current Session object.
SmartNavigation property	Boolean to indicate if smart navigation is enabled (covered later in the chapter).
Trace property	This property is a reference to the Trace object for this page. If you have tracing enabled on the page, then you can use this object to write explicit information out to the trace log. We will look at this object in more detail in Chapter 22.
TraceEnabled property	This Boolean value allows us to detect whether tracing is enabled for the page.
User property	Gets information about the user making the page request.
Validators property	This property is a reference to a collection of all of the validation controls that are on the page. You can use this collection to iterate through all of the validation controls on a page to potentially check status or set validation parameters.

Method Table

Method	Property
`DataBind` method	Performs data binding for all controls on the page.
`FindControl` method	Allows you to find a control within the page.
`LoadControl` method	Dynamically loads a User Control from a `.ascx` file.
`LoadTemplate` method	Dynamically loads a template. This is examined in Chapter 7 where data binding and templating are covered.
`MapPath` method	Retrieves the physical path for a specified virtual path.
`ResolveURL` method	Converts a virtual URL to an absolute URL.
`Validate` method	Instructs any validation controls on the page to validate their content.

These members of the intrinsic `Page` class are accessible from within ASP.NET pages directly, without having to go through the `Page` object itself. For example, the following two lines of code are equivalent:

```
Page.Response.Write("Hello")
```

```
Response.Write("Hello")
```

There's no performance difference and you can use whichever form you prefer. As a general rule most samples tend to only use the `Page` object when referring to `IsPostBack` purely because it's a new feature. Using the explicit convention just makes it clearer that `IsPostBack` is an intrinsic property, rather than some form of user defined global variable, although there's no actual difference between the two forms.

HttpRequest Object

The `HttpRequest` object in ASP.NET is enhanced over its counterpart in legacy ASP. These changes will be covered in more detail in Chapter 23, but we will look at a few of the new features here.

The `HttpRequest` object is mapped to the `Request` property of the `Page` object, and is therefore available in the same way as in ASP – just by using `Request`.

One of the most evident changes is the promotion of a number of Server Variables to properties of the `HttpRequest` object itself. With ASP, you had to reference the `ServerVariables` collection if you wanted information about the User Agent, the IP Address of the client making the request, or even the physical path to the ASP.NET source file. Now, in ASP.NET, these values are now properties of the `HttpRequest` object, making it much easier and straightforward to access the information. For example, the following table lists some of these (the full list, including changes, is covered in more detail in Chapter 23).

Property and Method Table

Property/Method	Description
AcceptTypes	Indicates the MIME types supported by the client.
ApplicationPath	The virtual application path.
ContentLength	The length (in bytes) of the request.
ContentType	The MIME type of the request.
FilePath	The virtual path of the request.
Headers	A collection of HTTP headers.
HttpMethod	The HTTP method used for the request.
Path	The virtual path of the request.
PathInfo	Additional path information.
PhysicalApplicationPath	The physical path of the application root.
PhysicalPath	The physical path of the request.
RawUrl	The raw URL of the request.
RequestType	The HTTP method used for the request.
TotalBytes	The number of bytes in the input stream.
Url	A Uri object containing details of the request.
UrlReferrer	A Uri object detailing referrer information.
UserAgent	The browser user agent string.
UserHostAddress	The IP address of the user.
UserHostName	The DNS name of the user.
UserLanguages	An array of languages preferences.

Another new feature of the HttpRequest object is its Browser property. This property points to an instance of the HttpBrowserCapabilities object. This object contains information about the capabilities of the browser making the request. Previously, ASP developers had to use the Browser Capabilities component to determine the same type of information. Now, they can simply refer to the Browser property directly.

In the past, the information that the Browser Capabilities component used to determine the capabilities of a browser, was stored in the BROWSCAP.INI file. That information is now stored in the machine.config file. The information is now also stored in an XML format, and uses regular expression pattern matching to link a browser User Agent string, to the capabilities of that browser. But since the information is still contained in an updateable format, there will continue to be support for new browsers and new capabilities without requiring a completely new ASP.NET version.

The new `Params` collection is a collection of all of the `QueryString`, `Form`, `ServerVariables`, and `Cookie` items that are part of the request. In the past, this was the default collection of the `Request` object itself. To access it in ASP.NET you need to go through the `Params` collection.

```
Dim strValue As String
strValue = Request.Params("param1") ' in ASP, this could have been
                         ' written as Request("param1")
```

> *You can still use the individual `QueryString`, `Form`, `ServerVariables`, and `Cookie` collections to access information from specifically that item if you want.*

There is now a `MapPath` method of the `HttpRequest` object. This method will take a virtual path to a file as a parameter, and return the physical path to the file on the server. You can also use this method to obtain the physical path to an object in a different application on the same server.

Finally, there is now a `SaveAs` method for the `HttpRequest` object. This method will let you save the contents of the current request to disk. This can be very useful during the debugging of a web application so you can view the contents of the actual request. You can also have HTTP headers saved into the file along with the contents of the request.

```
If (bErrorCondition) Then
    Request.SaveAs("c:\currentRequest.txt", true)
                     ' true indicates to save the headers as well
End If
```

HttpResponse Object

The `HttpResponse` object allows you to send data back to the browser as the result of a request. It also provides you with information about that response. The `HttpResponse` object is mapped to the `Response` property of the `Page` object, and is therefore available directly within ASP.NET pages. There are several new features that are part of the `HttpRequest` object with ASP.NET.

The `Buffer` property from ASP has been replaced with the `BufferOutput` property. This Boolean property sets the way that the response data is sent back to the client. If it is set to `true`, which is the default, then the contents of the response are held on the server until the response is finished, or until the buffer is explicitly sent back to the client. When this value is `false`, the information is sent back to the browser as soon it is generated by the page.

In Chapter 16, we will be looking at some of the other classes that are part of the .NET framework. Two that we will look at are the `TextWriter` and `Stream` classes. These classes allow you to work with streams of text or streams of bytes. You will find that there are methods that will take a `Stream` object or a `TextWriter` object as a parameter, and send the results from that method to that object. So what does that have to do with the `HttpResponse` object?

There are two new parameters of the `HttpResponse` object – `Output` and `OutputStream` – that expose the contents of the `Response` buffer as either a `TextWriter` object or a `Stream` object. One way that this can be used, is in the dynamic creation of images using ASP.NET. The `Save` method of the `Bitmap` class can accept a `Stream` object as its destination – so if we pass in the `HttpResponse.OutputStream` property to this method, then the results of the save will be sent as the response to the client.

```
<%@ Page Language="VB" ContentType="image/jpeg" %>
<%@ Import Namespace="System.Drawing" %>
<%@ Import Namespace="System.Drawing.Imaging" %>
<%@ Import Namespace="System.Drawing.Drawing2D" %>
<%
    Response.Clear()
    Dim height As integer = 100
    Dim width As integer = 200
    Dim r As New Random
    Dim x As integer = r.Next(75)
    Dim x1 As integer = 0
    Dim a As integer = r.Next(155)
    Dim x2 As integer = r.Next(100)

    Dim bmp As new Bitmap(width, height, PixelFormat.Format24bppRgb)
    Dim g As Graphics =  Graphics.FromImage(bmp)
    g.SmoothingMode = SmoothingMode.AntiAlias
    g.Clear(Color.LightGray)
    g.DrawRectangle(Pens.White, 1, 1, width-3, height-3)
    g.DrawRectangle(Pens.Gray,  2, 2, width-3, height-3)
  g.DrawRectangle(Pens.Black, 0, 0, width, height)
    g.DrawString("Response.OutputStream Test", _
            New Font("Arial", 10, FontStyle.Bold), _
            SystemBrushes.WindowText, New PointF(10,50))
    g.FillRectangle(New SolidBrush(Color.FromArgb(a, 255, 128, 255)), _
            x, 20, 100, 50)
    g.FillRectangle(New LinearGradientBrush(New Point(x2, 0), _
                New Point(x2+75, 50+30), _
                Color.FromArgb(128, 0, 0, 128), _
                Color.FromArgb(255, 255, 255, 240)), _
        x2 ,50, 75, 30)

    bmp.Save(Response.OutputStream, ImageFormat.Jpeg)
    g.Dispose()
    bmp.Dispose()
    Response.End()
%>
```

There are four key lines that we need to look at – we will not be looking at all of the drawing functions, since they are probably worthy of an entire book to themselves! First, we need to tell the browser requesting this page that we are sending back a set of bytes that represent an image – not a set of text in HTML format.

```
<%@ Page Language="VB" ContentType="image/jpeg" %>
```

Next, just to be safe, we want to make sure that no header information has been sent back to the browser. To do this, we need to clear the buffer. Remember that when the output to the browser is buffered, as is the default, then we can clear out that buffer at any time before it is sent back.

```
    Response.Clear()
```

The next part of the page is going to dynamically create a Bitmap object in memory, and then draw to that object. Once we have completed drawing the bitmap, we will want to send it to the browser. The Save method of the Bitmap object looks like this:

```
Public Sub Save( _
    ByVal stream As Stream, _
    ByVal format As ImageFormat _
)
```

The first parameter is a `Stream` object. The `Save` method will send the bytes that make up the bitmap to this `Stream`. The second parameter defines the format that the image will be saved as. Even though the object is a `Bitmap` object, we can create more than just BMP files.

```
bmp.Save(Response.OutputStream, ImageFormat.Jpeg)
```

So to save the contents of the `Bitmap` object directly to the `Response` object, we pass the `Response.OutputStream` property as our `Stream` parameter. And since earlier in the page we defined the content type as `image/jpeg`, we set the format of the image being saved to `JPEG`. Once all of the data has been sent, we want to explicitly end the response, by calling the `End` method of the `Response` object. We have provided two files, `image_cs.aspx` and `image_vb.aspx` in our download code for you to try out. When we view the page in the browser, it looks like this:

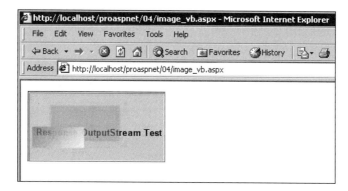

In addition to the `HttpResponse.Clear` method that we saw in the previous example, the `HttpResponse.ClearHeaders` method will just clear the headers from the response.

While the `HttpResponse.Write` method is still available in ASP.NET, the use of server controls greatly lessens the need to manually output response information using that method. However, a new method in ASP.NET, `WriteFile`, greatly simplifies the output of file-based information to the response. In previous versions of ASP, the developer was responsible for opening up a file, reading its contents into a buffer, and then outputting the contents of that buffer to the response using the `Write` method. The `WriteFile` method takes a filename as a parameter, and will do all of the necessary file handling work to open that file, read it, and then output its contents to the response buffer. For example, this allows you to stream previously created HTML directly to the browser along with the current page:

```
<html>

Some html content here

<script language="VB" runat="server">

  Sub Page_Load(Sender As Object, E As EventArgs)

    Response.WriteFile("c:\temp\Content.html")

  End Sub

</script>

</html>
```

Page Processing Steps

A Web Forms page isn't significantly different from a traditional web page. It is still created as a result of an HTTP Request. The server creates the page, sends the data back to the client, closes the HTTP connection, and then forgets about the request. But there are many enhancements that are added with Web Forms. In order to best understand these enhancements, it is important to look at the steps that the page goes through when it is processed on the server.

Server Round-trip

As with all dynamic web generation systems, like ASP, JSP, Cold Fusion, etc., there is a division of labor that goes on. There is work that the server does and there is work that the client does. The client is responsible for presenting information, capturing information from the user, and for optionally executing some client-side script. The server is responsible for dynamically creating the page and delivering the page to the client. The server may also be managing some degree of server-side state for the client – so that information about the client's task can be passed from one request by a user to the next one by that same user.

In this division of labor, it is critical to recognize that work executed on the client is usually only visible to the client and work executed on the server is only visible to the server. With the Web Forms model in ASP.NET, Microsoft has introduced a new concept of server controls. These controls act like the client-side controls that we may have used in the past with Visual Basic, but their execution happens on the server. This means that the client has no access to these controls programmatically. So how do we interact with these controls?

In order to interact with server controls, the execution must be passed from the client back to the server. The only way to do this is via an HTTP request.

There are other ways to pass information to the server to be executed without making an HTTP Request. We could use DCOM, Java RMI, or a simple socket communication. But within the pure web paradigm of ASP.NET, the HTTP Request is the only method available.

If we look at the interaction between client and server during a Web Forms application, we see that the execution gets passed back and forth between client and server – even within the context of the same .aspx page. This is what is known as a server round-trip.

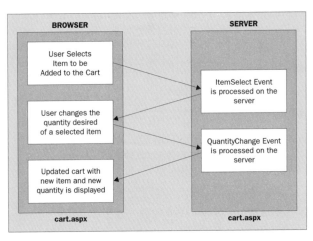

In order to trigger a round-trip, the user needs to perform some interaction with the browser. There usually isn't a case where a round-trip would be triggered without a user intervention, but there is nothing that prevents that from happening. Typically, the round-trip is triggered by the user clicking or selecting something on a page. In either case, it takes an explicit user interaction to start a round-trip. While it is possible, you wouldn't want an event like an onmouseover to cause a round-trip. That happens too frequently and would overload the server and cause the user experience to grind to a halt.

Page ViewState

In this new round-trip model of Web Forms, there are potentially more interactions with a server, than there would be in a traditional browser-server interaction. But at the core it is still stateless HTTP communication. This means that the server doesn't retain *any* information about the previous client request, such as values in form fields, or the state of objects instantiated to create the page. This would normally mean that the server is doing a lot of extra work in recreating the page each time during a round-trip. But the Web Forms architecture has a way of dealing with this.

The page will retain its **ViewState** between requests to the server. The ViewState contains the state of all user controls on the page. This information is stored as name-value pairs using the System.Web.UI.StateBag object. The ViewState is stored as a string variable that is passed back to the client in the page. Since the client probably doesn't know anything about ASP.NET and ViewState, this string is stored as a hidden form field. If we take a look at the example page from earlier in this chapter, and then view its source, we can see the ViewState being stored.

```
<html>
<head>

<form name="ctrl0" method="post" action="NewAspNet.aspx" id="ctrl0">
<input type="hidden" name="__VIEWSTATE"
value="dDwxNTY5OTcyNzI0O3Q8O2w8aTwyPjs+O2w8dDw7bDxpPDE+O2k8NT47PjtsPHQ8dDw7dDxpPDQ
+OOA8U3B1ZWR5IEV4cHJlc3M7RmVkZXJhbCBCTaGlwcGluZztNYWlsIENvbXBhbnk7U2xvdyBTaGlwcGluZz
zs+O0A8MTsyOzM7NDs+Pjs+Ozs+O3Q8cDxwPGw8VGV4dDs+O2w8WW91ciBvcmRlciBicmVhdGU3aWxsIGJlIGRlbGl
2ZXJ1ZCB2aWEgU3B1ZWR5IEV4cHJlc3M7Pj47Pjs7Pjs+Pjs+" />

   Please select your delivery method:
```

The contents of the ViewState are quite obviously not in a human-readable form. But the Web Forms processor can read this and restore the values of the server controls when this page is submitted to the server. The advantage of this method is that the state of the page is held with the page, and not within the server. Another advantage is that we can deploy the page to a web farm and not have to worry about forcing the request from a client to come back to the same server. But there are some minor disadvantages as well. For our rather simple page, there is a pretty sizeable set of text making up the ViewState. In a much more complex page, the contents of the ViewState could grow to a point where they begin to affect the speed at which the page is downloaded, although this isn't as much of a performance issue as it was in the past.

ViewState is enabled by default for all server controls. This means that you don't have to do anything explicit to take advantage of it. But as we just saw, there could be performance issues in maintaining ViewState for a page with a large number of controls on it. There are two ways that we can control whether or not the ViewState is maintained. We can disable ViewState on a page level – meaning that no state will be kept for any control on the page. To do this, you would use the @Page directive along with the EnableViewState attribute.

```
<%@ Page EnableViewState="false" %>
```

The second level at which you can control the ViewState is on a control-by-control basis. To do this, you simply add the same `EnableViewState` parameter to the declaration of the control.

ViewState is discussed in more detail in Chapters 6 and 7, where we look at how to gage the impact on performance.

```
<asp:DropDownList id="ShipMethod" EnableViewState="false" runat="server"/>
```

The `EnableViewState` attribute is also discussed in Chapters 6 and 7, where we look at its impact on performance.

Page Processing Steps

As we had mentioned earlier in the chapter, there are a set of distinct steps that the server goes through when processing a Web Forms page. At each stage, the server calls a certain set of code. This allows you to add your code at specific points during the execution of the page. Every time a page is requested, these steps are processed. The `IsPostBack` property lets us know if this is the first time a page is being viewed, or it is being viewed as a result of a server round-trip.

The four page processing stages are:

❑ Configuration

❑ Event Handling

❑ Rendering

❑ Cleanup

There are other stages that the page goes through when it is loaded, but these are not generally used in everyday page processing. These stages are primarily used for server controls to be able to initialize themselves when the page is loading, then render themselves into the page, and finally clean themselves up. We will look at these stages in Chapter 18, when we look at creating custom server controls.

Configuration Stage

This is the first stage that is encountered in processing a page. If we are on a postback (not the initial load), then the page and control ViewStates are restored. After that is done, then the `Page_Load` event is fired. This means that any code we write in this event handler can access the state of any control on the page. This is very important because it allows us to perform the processing necessary to get the page ready for display to the user.

A typical `Page_Load` event is shown below:

VB. NET

```
Sub Page_Load(Sender As Object, E As EventArgs)
    Dim cart As New IBuyAdv.CartDB
    cart = New IBuyAdv.CartDB(getDSN())

    If Len(Request.Params("ProductCode")) > 0 Then
        cart.AddShoppingCartItem(GetCustomerID(), Request.Params("ProductCode"))
    End If
```

```
      If Not Page.IsPostBack Then
          PopulateShoppingCartList()
          UpdateSelectedItemState()
      End If
   End Sub
```

C#

```
   void Page_Load(Object sender, EventArgs e) {
      IBuyAdv.CartDB cart = new IBuyAdv.CartDB(getDSN());
      if (Request.Params["ProductCode"] != null) {
         cart.AddShoppingCartItem(GetCustomerID(), Request.Params["ProductCode"]);
      }
      if (Page.IsPostBack == false) {
      PopulateShoppingCartList();
      UpdateSelectedItemStatus();
   }
```

In this `Page_Load` event from the case study we will look at in chapter 24, you can see three different steps taking place. These steps are quite common. First, we are creating an instance of a database access object:

```
   Dim cart As New IBuyAdv.CartDB
   cart = New IBuyAdv.CartDB(getDSN())
```

or in C#

```
   IBuyAdv.CartDB cart = new IBuyAdv.CartDB(getDSN());
```

This gives us access to a database object, which we will use in the methods and events of the page. The next step is to conditionally perform some processing based on a parameter passed to this page.

```
   If Len(Request.Params("ProductCode") > 0 Then
      cart.AddShoppingCartItem(GetCustomerID(), Request.Params("ProductCode"))
   End If
```

or in C#

```
   if (Request.Params["ProductCode"] != null) {
      cart.AddShoppingCartItem(GetCustomerID(), Request.Params["ProductCode"]);
   }
```

The `Request` object contains information about the request being made to the server. The `Params` collection is a collection of all the information contained in the `QueryString`, `Form`, `ServerVariables`, and `Cookies` collections. Based on the existence of a specific value, `ProductCode`, we will perform some processing.

```
   If Not Page.IsPostBack Then
      PopulateShoppingCartList()
      UpdateSelectedItemState()
   End If
```

or in C#

```
if (Page.IsPostBack == false) {
    PopulateShoppingCartList();
    UpdateSelectedItemStatus();
}
```

The last thing we do in the `Page_Load` event, is to load the data into the controls on the page. Now since these controls have their ViewState saved during a server round-trip, we only want to load the data the first time. By checking the `IsPostBack` property of the `Page` object, we can determine if this is the first time the page is being loaded. If it is, then we go ahead and retrieve the data from the database and add it to control. If the page is being viewed as a result of a round-trip, then we just let the ViewState restore the state of the control. There is no reason why we couldn't populate the control from scratch each time, but why waste the server processing time if we don't have to.

Event Handling Stage

As we saw earlier, the server controls on an ASP.NET page can generate events that get processed on the server. We already saw that an action on the client can initiate a server round-trip through an HTTP Post. Now once that round-trip gets to the server, we need to be able to detect what control caused the event to happen, and then take steps to process it.

While there can only be one event that causes a round-trip to begin, there may be other events that have occurred on the server controls at the client which haven't been processed yet. These are also processed during the event handling stage. There is no particular order in which the prior occurring events are processed, but they are always processed first. The event that actually triggered the round-trip is processed last.

Let's take a look at some event-handling routines, again from our case study:

VB. NET

```
Sub Recalculate_Click(Sender As Object, E As EventArgs)
    UpdateShoppingCartDatabase()
    PopulateShoppingCartList()
    UpdateSelectedItemStatus()
End SUb

SubCheckout_Click(Sender As Object, E As EventArgs)
    UpdateShoppingCartDatabase()
    Response.Redirect("secure/Checkout.aspx")
End Sub
```

C#

```
void Recalculate_Click(Object sender, EventArgs e) {
    UpdateShoppingCartDatabase();
    PopulateShoppingCartList();
    UpdateSelectedItemStatus();
}

void Checkout_Click(Object sender, EventArgs e) {
    UpdateShoppingCartDatabase();
    Response.Redirect("secure/Checkout.aspx");
```

The `Recalculate_Click` event is fired when the user clicks the **Recalculate** button on the page. Since this is a button control, the round-trip is started immediately. In the next section, we will look at the parameters that are passed when the event is fired. The `Checkout_Click` event is fired when the user clicks the **Checkout** button on the page. You can see that in the event handler, we are calling `Response.Redirect` to send the browser off to another page. So in an event handler, we have the ability to affect whether or not this page is even displayed.

Rendering Stage

The Rendering stage is where the rubber meets the road. Or shall we say, the HTML meets the browser. In this stage all of the static HTML in the page, the results of any `Response.Write` methods, and the output from all of the server controls on the page is sent down to the browser. Any in-line script code is run at the same time, but no event processing occurs, since that has already happened.

Cleanup Stage

This is the final stage of the page processing. All of the HTML has been rendered and sent to the browser. The primary event that happens during this stage is the `Page_Unload` event. In this event, you should do things like close any open database connections, close any files you may have opened, and properly discard any objects that you may have been using in the page. While you can simply let object references fall out of scope, it's not a good practice.

Since objects in .NET are garbage collected (as we saw in Chapter 3) the resources that an object uses will still be consumed, even after the object reference falls out of scope. It is the responsibility of the garbage collector to free up these resources of unused objects. But we can't predict when the garbage collector will run, so we can't explicitly state when the resources will be freed. So to free up the resources as soon as possible, you should explicitly close the objects you are using.

Web Form Events

As we have just seen, events in web forms are different to the events we may have been used to in the traditional event-driven programming model. While we can still have events that are raised on the client, and handled on the client, as well as events raised on the server that are handled on the server, the primary Web Form event model is for an event to be raised on the client and processed on the server. This transfer of control from the client to the server is accomplished through the use of an HTTP POST. As a developer, we need to be aware how this mechanism takes place, but the .NET Framework takes care of figuring out from the POST information what events need to be handled on the server.

There's a set of intrinsic events that server controls will support. Since we don't want to continually be passing control from the client to the server, this event set is rather limited. It's primarily user interactions, such as a button click or changing a selection, which will cause an event to be raised on the server. In this way, it takes an *explicit* user action to fire a server event – they don't usually happen without the user taking some action at the client.

The event handler function declaration is the same for all events. There are two parameters that are passed to the event handler.

```
void MyButton_OnClick(Object sender, EventArgs e)
{
    ...
}
```

or in Visual Basic

```
Sub MyButton_OnClick(Sender as Object, e as EventArgs)
    ...
End Sub
```

The first parameter, `sender`, is a reference to the server control that raised the event. When we add a server control to the page, we need to explicitly state the events we want to handle, and what function will be the event handler for that particular event.

```
<asp:Button id="PlaceOrder" Text="Place Order"
            onClick="PlaceOrder_Click" runat="server"/>
```

In this example, we're placing a `Button` server control onto the page with the ID of `PlaceOrder`. When the user clicks on this button on the client, the control will be passed to the server via an HTTP POST. On the server, the function `PlaceOrder_Click` will be called. Remember that there is a reference to the server control passed to the event handler. In this way, we could have one event handler that handles events for multiple controls – we would know the specific control based on the value of the `sender` variable.

The second parameter is an object containing a set of information about the specific event. This parameter is usually of type `EventArgs`, which in its base implementation contains little information about the event. But it also serves as a base class for derived classes, such as the `RepeaterCommandEventArgs` class. An object of this type gets passed when using a `Repeater` control, and you have wired up the `ItemCommand` event. You can see this in the example below, where we talk about event bubbling.

Event Bubbling

There are certain server controls that serve as containers for other controls. Controls such as the `Repeater`, the `DataList`, and the `DataGrid` controls, can all contain server controls as children of the parent control. These child controls will not raise their events by themselves, to be handled on the page. Rather the event is packaged by the container and passed to the page as an `ItemCommand` event. This event is raised when you click a button within the `Repeater`. In this example, we will take a look at how you can handle the events from a set of child buttons within a `Repeater` control.

```
<%@ Page Language="C#" %>
<html>
  <head>
    <script language="C#" runat="server">

    void MyRepeater_ItemCommand(Object Sender, RepeaterCommandEventArgs e) {
        ClickInfo.Text = "You selected the  " + ((Button)e.CommandSource).Text +
                                                " button <br>";

        }
    </script>
  </head>

    <form runat="server">
        <asp:Repeater id=MyRepeater OnItemCommand="MyRepeater_ItemCommand"
                                            runat="server">
```

```
        <ItemTemplate>
          <tr>
            <td> <%# DataBinder.Eval(Container.DataItem, "Name") %> </td>
            <td> <ASP:Button Text=<%# DataBinder.Eval(Container.DataItem,
                              "Initials") %> runat="server" /></td>
          </tr>
        </ItemTemplate>

        <asp:Label id=ClickInfo font-name="Verdana" font-size="12pt"
                   runat="server"/>
      </form>
    </body>
  </html>
```

When we run the page, we will see a list of authors and their initials. When we select one of the buttons, the ClickInfo label control will be populated to indicate what button was pressed.

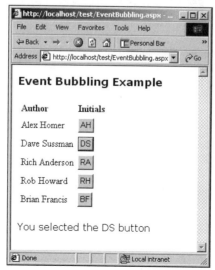

In this example, we have a repeater control that contains a table (simply for the sake of formatting). Each row of the table has a cell with the author name, and another cell with a button server control.

```
<td> <%# DataBinder.Eval(Container.DataItem, "Name") %> </td>
<td> <ASP:Button Text=<%# DataBinder.Eval(Container.DataItem,
                              "Initials") %> runat="server" /></td>
```

You can see that the button control itself does not have an event handler associated with it. It does have the all-important `runat="server"` parameter, so the events generated by this control will be handled on the server. So where is the click event from this button handled? To see that, we need to look at the container control – the `Repeater` control.

```
<asp:Repeater id=MyRepeater OnItemCommand="MyRepeater_ItemCommand"
            runat="server">
```

When we declare the `Repeater` control, we are setting up an event handler function to handle the `ItemCommand` event. This event is fired whenever a control contained by the `Repeater` raises an event. The `MyRepeater_ItemCommand` function looks like this:

```
void MyRepeater_ItemCommand(Object Sender, RepeaterCommandEventArgs e) {
    ClickInfo.Text = "You selected the  " + ((Button)e.CommandSource).Text +
                                                        " button <br>";

    }
```

The second parameter of this event handler is of type `RepeaterCommandEventArgs`. This object contains enough information about the event to allow us to determine the control that raised the event. The properties of this object that we need to look at are:

Property	Description
CommandSource	Reference to the child server control that actually raised the event.
Item	Reference to the specific item within the `Repeater` control where the event took place. This could be the header or footer template, or from an individual data row.

Since we know that the child control that caused the event is a `Button` control, we can cast the `CommandSource` object to a `Button` type, and then access the properties of that control. In this case, we are going to pull out the value of the `Text` property for the button, and display that in our `ClickInfo` label control.

Event Handling on Client AND Server

Since we are bridging the gap between client and server when it comes to handling control events, it makes sense that we need to talk about which side handles what events. Most server controls only have one or two events that actually get processed on the server. But the HTML control that they are finally rendered as, may be able to generate a great number of different events for client-side use. So the question is: what gets handled where?

Basically, those events that are supported by the server control will get handled on the server. So for a `Button` control, there is one event supported by that control – the `Click` event. All of the other events that can be generated by an HTML INPUT control (what a `Button` server control is rendered as) will need to be handled on the client. But what about the click event that can be handled at the client-side as well?

When you have an event that could be handled on either the client or the server, then the server handling of that event will take precedence. So in the case of the `Button`, if you write a server-side event handler for `Click` and also write a client-side event handler for `Click`, then the client-side code will be ignored by the Web Forms framework, and the event will be handled on the server. But you could write a client-side `onmouseup` event handler, which would continue to be run at the client – prior to the control being passed back to the server.

Page State

Since the core to the functionality in Web Forms is the server round-trip, we are constantly going back to the server and asking it to create a new page and send it to the client. It is in this merger of the stateless web world with the stateful world, that the concept of page state needs to be discussed. How do we retain information while the client has control and the server has in essence forgotten about the client and its prior request?

We have already looked at the `Page ViewState`, which is the way that the information contained in the server controls is automatically persisted during a server round-trip. So how can the developer store information from request to request, when that information may not be contained in a server control? In the past, storing information in a hidden form field, or possibly in the `Session` object would have been ways to do this. While these ways are still available, the Web Forms framework provides another more flexible option: **State Bags**.

The State Bag is a data repository that is automatically persisted from page request to page request. If we take a look at our event bubbling example from earlier in the chapter, we can easily add the use of the State Bag to the page.

```
void Page_Load(Object Sender, EventArgs e) {
   int viewCount;
   if (ViewState["viewCount"] != null)
      viewCount = (int)ViewState["viewCount"] + 1;
   else

      viewCount = 1;

   labelViews.Text = "Times page has been viewed: " + viewCount.ToString();
   ViewState["viewCount"] = viewCount;
   if (!IsPostBack) {
      ArrayList values = new ArrayList();
   ...
}
```

The `ViewState` object is a collection of the state that is maintained by the page. You can add your own keys to this collection, and that value will be persisted along with state from all of the server controls on your page. In our example, we are storing the number of times the page is viewed, and then displaying that value to see how many times the page has been viewed.

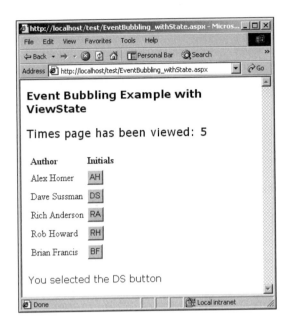

Page Directives

When you are creating a page, you can declaratively set a number of attributes about the page. Some of the ones we have seen up to this part are the @Page directive and the @Import directive. Each of these directives has a set of associated attributes that control some aspect of the page generation. We will now look at each of the directives, and the attributes associated with each.

@Page directive

This directive is used to assign page-specific attributes that are used by the Web Forms page parser and compiler to affect how the page is created. This directive, along will all the other ones we will look at, can legally be placed anywhere on the page, but by convention they are generally at the top of the file. However there can only be one @Page directive in a single file.

Attribute	Values (default in bold)	Used for
AspCompat	true or **false**	Sets the page to run in a Single-thread Apartment. Allows access to legacy COM components developed in VB, which could only create STA components.
AutoEventWireup	**true** or false	Indicates whether or not the page events are automatically wired up. If false, events such as Page_Load must be enabled by the developer.
Buffer	**true** or false	Response buffering is enabled.
ClassName	Valid class name	Class name that this page is derived from.

Attribute	Values (default in bold)	Used for
ClientTarget	Valid User Agent name	Browser (or compatible) that the page is targeting.
CodePage	Valid code page value	Sets the code page of the response, if it is different from the web server.
CompilerOptions	Valid compiler options	List of compiler options to be used when the page is compiled.
ContentType	Valid MIME type	Sets the content type of the response.
Culture	Valid culture ID	Culture ID sets the language, calendar system, and writing system.
Debug	true or **false**	Compile page with debugging enabled.
Description	n/a	Description of the page – ignored by ASP.NET.
Enable SessionState	**true**, ReadOnly, or false	Page has access to the Session object. ReadOnly – the page can read but not change session variables.
EnableViewState	**true** or false	Page ViewState is maintained for server controls.
Enable ViewStateMac	true or **false**	Page should run a machine authentication check on the View State. Validates that the ViewState has not been tampered with by the client.
ErrorPage	Valid URL	Page to be redirected to if an unhandled error occurs.
Explicit	true or **false**	Uses the Visual Basic Option Explicit mode.
Inherits	Valid class name	Code-behind class that this page inherits.
Language	Valid .NET Language name	Language used to compile all source code on the page.
LCID	Valid locale ID	Locale identifier for the page, if different from the locale of the web server.
ResponseEncoding	Valid character encoding name	Encoding format for the text sent by the response.
SmartNavigation	true or **false**	Enables or disables the Smart Navigation feature (see later for more details of this).
Src	Valid source file name	File name of the code-behind class used by this page.
Strict	true or **false**	Uses the Visual Basic Option Strict mode.

Table continued on following page

Attribute	Values (default in bold)	Used for
Trace	true or **false**	Tracing the page execution is enabled.
TraceMode	SortByTime or SortByCategory	Sort order for trace messages generated when the page is created.
Transaction	NotSupported, Supported, Required, RequiresNew	Indicates the transaction settings for this page.
Warning Level	0, 1, 2, or 4	Compiler warning level at which compilation should be aborted.

@Import directive

This directive is used to explicitly import a namespace onto the page. This will make all of the classes and interfaces contained within this namespace available to code on the page. This value can either be a .NET Framework namespace name, or a valid user-created namespace.

```
<%@ Import namespace="value" %>
```

You can only import one namespace per directive entry, so to import multiple namespaces into a page, you need to have multiple @Import statements. The .NET Framework automatically imports a set of namespaces for you, so you don't need to import these explicitly. These namespaces are:

System	System.Web
System.Collections.Specialized	System.Web.Security
System.IO	System.Web.UI
System.Text.RegularExpressions	System.Web.UI.WebControls
System.Collections	System.Web.Caching
System.Configuration	System.Web.SessionState
System.Text	System.Web.UI.HtmlControls

@Implements directive

The @ implements directive allows you to implement a .NET interface in your page. When you implement an interface, you are saying that your page will support the defined properties, methods, and events of a specific interface. This will be key when we look at implementing custom User Controls in Chapter 5. In order for our custom control to be able to respond to events like a standard server control, then our control must implement the IPostBackEventHandler interface. The directive to do this is:

```
<%@ Implements Interface="System.Web.UI.IPostBackEventHandler" %>
```

Interfaces are covered in Chapter 3.

@Register directive

Whenever you are adding a custom server control to a page, you need to tell the compiler something about that control. If the compiler doesn't know what namespace contains the control or what assembly that namespace is in, then it will not be able to recognize the control, and will generate an error. To give the compiler the information it needs, we will use the @Register directive.

There are two forms of the @Register directive, depending on how we identify the location of the custom control.

```
<%@ Register tagprefix="tagprefix" Tagname="tagname" Src="pathname" %>
<%@ Register tagprefix="tagprefix" Namespace="namespace" Assembly="assembly" %>
```

The first usage of the @Register directive is to add support for user controls to the page. The tagprefix attribute identifies the string that we will use to decorate all instances of the custom server control on the page. For example, if we have this directive at the top of the page:

```
<%@ Register TagPrefix="Ecommerce" TagName="Header"
             Src="UserControls\Header.ascx" %>
```

Then for every instance of the Header user control that we use on the page, we will have to prefix it with Ecommerce, as we can see here:

```
<Ecommerce:Header id="Header" runat="server"/>
```

The tagname attribute identifies the name that will be used to refer to the control within the page. Since a user control source file, UserControls\Header.ascx, can only have one control contained within it, the tagname attribute is simply a shortcut to allow us to reference the control.

The final parameter, src, indicates the file in which the source of the user control resides.

The second usage of the @Register directive is for adding custom server controls to the page. These custom controls are compiled and contained within assemblies. The tagprefix attribute has the same usage that we saw before – it defines the namespace of the custom server control when it is used in the page. The namespace attribute indicates the namespace in which the custom control resides. And finally, the assembly attribute indicates the assembly where the namespace resides. If we look at the directive for a custom server control, we will see:

```
<%@ Register TagPrefix="Wrox" Namespace="WroxControls" Assembly="RatingMeter" %>
```

When we use this custom server control within the page, it looks no different than if we were using a user control in the same place.

```
<Wrox:RatingMeter runat="server" Score=3.5 Votes=1
                  MaxRating=5 CellWidth=51 CellHeight=10 />
```

As you can see, when we create a custom control, or even a user control, we can pass attributes to the control by adding them to the tag in the page. We will see more about how to do this when we look at creating custom server controls later in this book.

@Assembly directive

The @Assembly directive is used to reference an assembly directly, so that the classes and interfaces that it contains become available to the code in your page. You can either pass in the name of a compiled assembly:

```
<%@ Assembly Name="assemblyname" %>
```

or you can pass in the path to a source file that will be compiled when the page is compiled:

```
<%@ Assembly Src="pathname" %>
```

This tag is usually not required, as any assembly that is in the ASP.NET application's bin directory will automatically be compiled into the page. You would use this directive if you wanted to explicitly include an assembly that is in the global assembly cache, or if you wanted to explicitly compile in an assembly source file that is residing in another directory.

@OutputCache directive

This directive is used to control how the page is cached on the server. ASP.NET Premium Edition supports a very powerful set of caching capabilities. When output caching is turned on for a page, then the first time the page is run, it is compiled and run, and its results are sent back to the browser. But instead of the server then throwing everything away, the results of the page just run are held on the server. The next time a request comes in for that page, even from a different user, the server can then just spit back the results without having to rerun the page. This can cause tremendous performance increases, especially if you have pages that may be database generated, but where the underlying data that creates the page doesn't change very often.

We will look at caching in greater detail later in this chapter, but let's take a look at how to use the @OutputCache directive. There are a series of attributes that allow you to control how the caching is performed.

```
<%@ OutputCache Duration="#ofseconds"
Location="Any | Client | Downstream | Server | None"
VaryByCustom="browser | customstring"
VaryByHeader="headers"
VaryByParam="parametername" %>
```

The duration attribute is used to control how long an item will stay in the cache before being invalidated. When a cache item is invalidated, the next time the page is requested, ASP.NET will run the page, deliver the results to the browser, and then store the results in the cache. This attribute is mandatory – there is no default value, and the page will not compile if you leave it out.

The Location attribute identifies where the actual data for the cache is stored. There are five possible values for this attribute:

Value	Use
Any	The cache can be located on the client, on a downstream server (like a proxy server), or on a server where the request was originally processed. This is the default.
Client	The cache is located on the client that made the request.
Downstream	The cache is located on a server downstream from the server that processed the request.
Server	The cache is located on the server where the request was processed.
None	This page does not have output caching enabled.

The `VaryByCustom` attribute is used to identify any custom caching requirements. If the string "browser" is passed as the value for this attribute, then the cache will be varied by browser name and version. When a cache is varied, there is a different processed page stored for each condition that the cache is varied by. For example, if the cache is varied by browser, then there will be one page version stored for IE5, another one for IE4, and yet another for Netscape 6. If someone accessed the site using Opera, then since that browser type was not cached, then a new page would be generated, passed back to the browser, and then cached for the next request from an Opera browser.

The `VaryByHeader` attribute contains a list of HTTP headers (separated by semi-colons) that are used to vary the output cache. You can vary the cache on one header, or on a group of headers.

The `VaryByParam` attribute is used to vary the cache, based on the values of parameters passed to the server, along with the request for the page. These can be `QueryString` parameters, or they can be the contents of form fields. You can pass a single parameter, multiple parameters separated by semicolons, you can pass a *, which means to vary on all parameters, or you can pass none, which means that the cache will not be varied based on any parameters. You must supply a value for this attribute. If you don't want to vary by parameter, then pass a value of none. If you don't want to be explicit in which parameters you vary the cache by, then pass a * and the cache will be varied by all parameter values.

@Reference directive

This directive is used to identify a page or control that the current page should dynamically compile and link with at runtime. This will allow you to dynamically add a user control to a page at runtime. You will use this directive in conjunction with the `LoadControl` method of the `Page` object. By adding the user control as a reference to the page, the compiler will be able to perform strong type checking against the control. We will see how to use this in Chapter 5 when we look at server controls.

Using Code Behind

In Chapter 1 we briefly looked at the idea of the Code Behind model, where we can separate the code from the actual content of the page. In the world of ever increasingly complex web applications, it's often difficult to separate the different parts of the development process. Writing web applications is hard enough without worrying about how to make them look good and stay maintainable over the years. Some companies have designers who create the look and feel of the site, allowing the programmers to concentrate on the coding. With the tradition ASP model, this is hard to achieve, as code and content are often intermixed.

The way to solve this problem in ASP.NET is by using Code Behind, where the content (HTML and Server Controls) are in one file, and the server-side code in another. Not only does this allow different people to work on the same page at once, but it also enables either part to be redesigned (as long as the controls still stay the same) without affecting the other.

The code behind model is no different in action to pages where the code is inline. Earlier we mentioned that an ASP.NET page, and its associated files are compiled into an executable object. This object is essentially (as far as performance and use goes) the same as any other page, allowing easier development with the same effect.

'Code Behind' in Development Tools

The approach you use for code may depend on how you create your ASP.NET applications. For this book, most of the samples will show code inline, simply because it's easier to show, as well as being more convenient when using text editors such as Notepad. Other tools, such as Visual Studio.NET take the opposite approach, using the code behind model as default. One reason is that it allows a standard HTML designer to be used for designing the look and feel of the page, and a code editor to be used for the actual code. This gives the user the familiar feel (comparable to the Visual Basic 6 environment) of design and code windows.

Another reason is that Microsoft has taken the view that third parties may want to use write designers or code editors that integrate with .NET. The code behind approach allows any HTML designer to be used (as long as it doesn't change ASP.NET controls) and any editor.

Using 'Code Behind'

The principle of code behind is that you create a class for your code, and inherit this class from the ASP.NET Page object. This gives your class access to the page intrinsics, and allows it to interact with the postback architecture. You then create the ASP.NET page and use a page directive to inherit from the newly created class.

There are some rules that you must follow to create the code behind class, the first of which is to reference the required namespaces. At a minimum these need to be `System` and `System.Web.UI`, although you may require others. For example, you generally need to reference controls on the page, and to define the control types you should reference `System.Web.UI.WebControls`. You can also include any other namespaces that you require, such as `System.Data.SqlClient` for accessing SQL Server.

Next you create a class that inherits from the `Page` object (this is why you need the `System.UI.Web` namespace). Within this class you should declare public instances of ASP.NET server controls that are on the web page, using the same name for the variables that the Web Control has. This provides a link between the code behind class and the actual server controls (there are other ways to do this, but this method is simplest). Within this class you can create event procedures, methods and properties, just as you would with any class. The events can be event procedures named on Server Controls in the web page.

For example, consider the simple select list with Shipping Methods we showed earlier in the chapter. The following code samples show the code behind class. With the exception of the additions required for the code behind model, the code is exactly the same as the code inline samples.

VB. NET

```
Imports System
Imports System.UI
Imports System.UI.WebControls

Public Class ShipMethodClass
   Inherits Page

   ' public variables to match the server controls
   Public ShipMethod   As DropDownList
   Public YouSelected  As Label
   Public PlaceOrder   As Button

  Sub Page_Load(Source As Object, E As EventArgs)

   If Not Page.IsPostBack Then
   Dim myConnection As SqlConnection
   Dim myCommand    As SqlCommand
   Dim myReader     As SqlDataReader
   Dim SQL          As String
   Dim ConnStr      As String

   SQL = "select * from Shipping_Methods"
   ConnStr = "server=localhost;uid=sa;pwd=;database=IBuyAdventure"

   myConnection = New SqlConnection(ConnStr)
   myConnection.Open()

   myCommand = New SqlCommand(SQL, myConnection)

   myReader = myCommand.ExecuteReader()
      ShipMethod.DataSource = myReader
      ShipMethod.DataBind()
    End If

   End Sub

   Sub PlaceOrder_click(Source As Object, E As EventArgs)

      YouSelected.Text = "Your order will be delivered via " & _
                   ShipMethod.SelectedItem.Text

End Sub
```

C#

```
using System;
using System.Data;
using System.Data.SqlClient;
using System.Web.UI;
using System.Web.UI.WebControls;
```

```
public class ShipMethodClass : Page
{
// public variables to match the server controls
public DropDownList    ShipMethod;
public Label       YouSelected;
public Button        PlaceOrder;

public void Page_Load(Object Source, EventArgs E)
{
   if (!Page.IsPostBack)
   {
      SqlConnection   myConnection;
      SqlCommand    myCommand;
      SqlDataReader   myReader;
      String       SQL;
      String       ConnStr;

      SQL = "select * from Shipping_Methods";
      ConnStr = "server=localhost;uid=sa;pwd=;database=IBuyAdventure";

      myConnection = new SqlConnection(ConnStr);
      myConnection.Open();

      myCommand = new SqlCommand(SQL, myConnection);

      myReader = myCommand.ExecuteReader();

      ShipMethod.DataSource = myReader;
      ShipMethod.DataBind();
   }
}

public void PlaceOrder_click(Object Source, EventArgs E)
{
YouSelected.Text = "Your order will be delivered via " +
                  ShipMethod.SelectedItem.Text;

}
}
```

Inheriting the Code Behind Class File in an ASP.NET Page

To connect the class file containing the code implementation to your ASP.NET page, you add an Inherits entry to the <%@Page...%> directive, and specify the location of the 'Code Behind' file:

```
<%@Page Inherits="class_name" Src="path_to_class_file" %>
```

For example, to inherit from a VB.NET class named ShipMethodClass that is implemented in a file named ShipMethodClass.vb in the same directory as the page, we would use:

```
<%@Page Inherits="ShipMethodClass" Src="ShipMethodClass.vb" %>
```

Note that it is important to use the correct file extension for your class files – .vb for Visual Basic files, .js for JScript files, .cs for C# files and .cpp for C++ files. This ensures that they are passed to the correct compiler when the page is first executed.

An alternative form of this directive allows the `Src` attribute to be omitted:

```
<%@ Page Inherits="ShipMethodClass" %>
```

In this case ASP.NET will assume that the class is pre-compiled, and in the `bin` directory of the application.

Page Caching

One of the criticisms of dynamic page creation techniques, is that they are less scalable and require more server resources than just sending static HTML files to clients. A solution that many sites have adopted is batch processing the pages, and saving the results to disk as static HTML files. However, this can only work if the content is not directly dependent on the client each time – in other words, the page is the same for all requests. This is the case for things like product catalogues and reports, and the update process only needs to be run when the data that the page is built from changes.

The Premium edition of ASP.NET includes a new feature called **dynamic output caching** that can provide the same kind of effect automatically, without the need to write the pages to disk. Instead, it can cache the dynamically created output (the content that the client receives), and use this cached copy for subsequent requests. This is even better than writing the content to a disk file, as it removes the need for a disk access each time.

Of course, this will only be of any use where the content of the page is the same for all requests for this page. However, ASP.NET is clever – the cache can be varied based on a set of parameters, either the query string, the browser type, User Controls (see Partial Page Caching, later in this chapter), or even a custom value, and ASP.NET will only use the cached copy if the parameters are the same as well. So, for example, pages that change depending on the contents of the query string will be served correctly – if the contents of the query string are different from those used when the cached copy was created, a new copy is created instead. This new copy is also cached, and is then available for use by clients that provide matching query string values.

An Output Caching Example

Output caching a page is quite straightforward. All that is necessary is to add the proper `@OutputCache` directive to the page, and ASP.NET will take care of the rest in caching the page. At its simplest, there are two pieces of information that we need to provide to the `@OutputCache` directive – how long we want the cached item to remain in the cache, and what value should be used to vary the cache. Varying the cache means defining the value supplied by the browser that if it changes, a different page will be cached.

```
<%@ Page Language="C#" %>
<%@ OutputCache Duration="10" VaryByParam="*" %>

<Script runat="server">
   public void Page_Load(){
       // Get the Date and Time, once again this should not change after the
       // first run
       DateTime NowTime = DateTime.Now;
       DateTime Expires = NowTime.AddSeconds(10);
```

```
                CreatedStamp.InnerHtml = NowTime.ToString("r");
                ExpiresStamp.InnerHtml = Expires.ToString("r");
        }
    </Script>

    <Font size="3">
    Output caching for 10 seconds...
    <HR size="1">
    Output Cache created: <Font color="red">
                            <B id="CreatedStamp" runat="server"></B></Font>
    <BR>
    Output Cache expires: <Font color="red">
                            <B id="ExpiresStamp" runat="server"></B></Font>
    </Font>
```

In this example, we are going to cache the results of the page for 10 seconds. To do this, we set the `Duration` parameter of the `@OutputCache` directive to 10. We also need to supply a value for the `VaryByParam` parameter as well. This parameter is required, and it defines what query string parameters to vary the cache by. Since our page does not rely on a query string, we want to provide the same page regardless of what parameters are passed to the page. The parameter value of `none` tells ASP.NET to always provide the same page.

If you view the page, you will see the time when the page was added to the cache, and when it will expire.

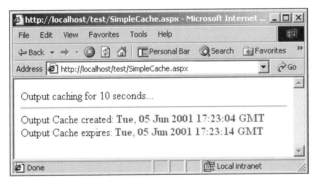

With the page displayed in the browser, you can press *F5* to cause the page to reload. You will notice that each time you press *F5* the same page will be displayed. And after 10 seconds since the first request has elapsed, a new page will be generated and the times will change.

Caching by Browser

Just as you can vary the cache based on a query string or other parameter, you can also vary the cache based on the type of browser making the request. To do this, you add the `VaryByCustom` parameter to the `@OutputCache` directive. The value for this parameter can be set to `browser`. This will tell ASP.NET to vary the cache based on the major version of the browser type. This means that IE6 will get one version of a cached page, IE5 will get another, and Netscape 6 will get a third. In this way, you don't have to worry about a Netscape browser inadvertently getting a page from the cache that has been customized to Internet Explorer.

```
<%@ OutputCache Duration="10" VaryByParam="*" VaryByCustom="browser" %>
```

Remember that `VaryByParam` is still a required parameter. If you include a parameter value other than browser, then you must override the `GetVaryByCustomString` in your `global.asax` file.

> **Remember that output caching only works in the Premium Edition of ASP.NET**

Smart Navigation

Smart Navigation is one of the coolest new features of ASP.NET, giving web applications a look and feel more like those of conventional Windows applications. One of the big drawbacks of web applications is the architecture of HTTP, requiring postback to the server and a complete redrawing of the page being viewed. Not only does this cause the screen to 'flash', but for long pages it also scrolls you to the top of the page, changes control focus and so on. With Windows applications we're used to areas of screen content being updated without the rest of the page being affected. Smart Navigation brings this to web applications.

The first thing to note is that this is an Internet Explorer feature only, requiring IE5 or higher. Whilst one of the main goals of ASP.NET is to target HTML 3.2, allowing great cross-browser compatibility, there are also plenty of cases where this isn't an issue. One such case is Intranets, where the browser can be controlled. However, you can enable or disable Smart Navigation at will, without affecting your application in any way. Even if you are targeting multiple browsers you can leave Smart Navigation enabled, as it detects the browser and only enables itself for supported browsers.

The four features of Smart Navigation are:

- ❑ No more screen flash.
- ❑ Scroll position maintained.
- ❑ Element focus maintained.
- ❑ Last page in History maintained.

This feature is really targeted at those applications that require a lot of postback, but where the content doesn't change a great deal.

Perhaps the most amazing thing about this feature is that you don't actually have to do any coding. Smart Navigation is controlled by a `Page` directive for individual pages, or in the `Web.Config` file for entire applications.

For the `Page` directive the syntax is:

```
<%@ Page SmartNavigation="true" %>
```

For `Web.Config` the syntax is:

```
<configuration>
   <system.web>
       <pages smartNavigation="true"/>
   </system.web>
</configuration>
```

There's no way we can show you a screenshot to see how great this feature is – you have to try it yourself to see it. It works by loading the page into a hidden `IFRAME`, and then only rendering those parts of the page that have changed. Try it out – it really is very cool.

Custom Controls

In addition to using HTML and server controls in your ASP.NET page, you can also create custom server controls. There are four primary ways for creating these custom controls – we will look at the first and simplest way in this chapter. A user control functions like an include file, but an include with a defined interface. You can also take an existing control and derive a new control from it – retaining the functionality that you like, and modifying or adding new functionality. A composite control can be created by combining the functionality of two or more server (or user) controls into a new control. Finally, you can create a custom server control from scratch – by starting with a base control class and extending it to support the functionality and the resulting HTML that you need.

The idea behind user controls is that you can create reusable sections of code or content as separate ASP.NET controls, and then use them in other pages without having to change the code, or even be aware of how it works! And while 'Code Behind' techniques are primarily aimed at just inheriting code classes into a page, user controls allow you to inherit parts of the user interface as well. In effect, they are a way of encapsulating other controls and code into a reusable package. The programming model for writing user controls is exactly the same as that for writing ASP.NET pages – if you know how to write ASP.NET pages, then you know how to write user controls. Because they are so easy to create, user controls enable a RAD-style development model for building reusable controls.

Approaches to Building User Control

There are two approaches that you can use to build a user control. You can take an existing ASP.NET page and convert it to a user control. Or, you can set out to build a user control from scratch. The advantage to creating one from an existing (and assumed working) page is that you can test it directly as an ASP.NET page, make sure it works, and then convert it to a user control. But to be able to do this, we need first see how to create a user control from scratch.

Creating a User Control

With what we have looked at up to this point in the book, you already have everything you need to create user controls from scratch. A user control is nearly identical to a Web Forms page, except for a few minor differences. A user control does not have a <HTML> tag, a <BODY> tag, or even a <FORM> tag. Since a user control will be inserted into another page, the other page will already have these elements. And since a page can only have one set of these elements, it is important that they are not part of the user control.

A user control can contain client script, HTML elements, ASP.NET code, and other server controls. The simplest user control would be one that simply outputs HTML when the page is rendered.

```
<hr>
<table border="0">
<tr><td colspan="2" align="center">This table is in a User Control</td></tr>
<tr><td align="right">Copyright: </td><td>2001 Wrox Press</td><tr>
<tr><td align="right">Page Created on: </td><td><%= Now() %></td></tr>
</table>
```

If we create this file on our server and save it as `standardFooter.ascx`, we have now created our first user control. User controls have to have a file suffix of `.ascx`. To test it, we need to add it to a Web Forms page. There are two steps to doing this. First, we need to use the `@Register` directive to tell the page that there is a new user control that we are going to be using in the page.

```
<%@ Register tagprefix="wrox" Tagname="footer" Src="standardFooter.ascx" %>
```

Next, we need to add it to the page where we want this information to be displayed.

```
<wrox:footer runat="server" />
```

When we view the page in the browser, we will see this on the page:

Converting a Page to a User Control

Now that we can see how easy it is to create a user control from scratch, let's look at the more common way of creating a user control. As you are developing your ASP.NET web application, you will probably come across sections of code that you are using on multiple pages. In the past, your options were to create an include file that kept the code in a single location, or maybe creating a design-time control for Visual Studio. But neither of these methods was really that simple or straightforward to use. And all developers know that if something isn't simple and straightforward, then chances are it won't get used. But now with user controls, we can take that code segment from our existing page and turn it into a control that can be easily reused in multiple pages.

At the beginning of this chapter, we saw an example that allowed you to select from a list of shipping methods. This page included the database code to retrieve the list as well as the controls to display the list. If we can package that logic into a reusable control, then we can ensure that wherever we need a list of shippers in our application (or applications) the data will be retrieved and displayed in the same way. A similar technique is used in Chapter 8 to build a control that returns data.

The first part of our control will be the display. The selection list is a drop-down list server control. We will leave what to do with the data in the control up to the page that is hosting the control. Since the server control is using data binding, the code that makes up the display will be quite simple.

```
<asp:DropDownList id="ShipMethod" runat="server"/>
```

The main work of the page is done in the code that sets up the page. Since in effect the user control is a page, we can still perform the work to read from the database in the Page_Load event that we used in the original page. We also need to check to see if the page we are converting into a user control has an @Page directive. If it does, then we will need to change this to an @Control directive.

```
<% @Control Language="Visual Basic" %>

<script language="VB" runat="server">
    Sub Page_Load(Source As Object, E As EventArgs)

    If Not Page.IsPostBack Then

        Dim myConnection As SQLConnection
        Dim myCommand    As SQLCommand
        Dim myReader     As SQLDataReader
        Dim SQL          As String
        Dim ConnStr      As String

        SQL = "SELECT * FROM Shipping_Method"
        ConnStr = "server=localhost;uid=sa;pwd=;database=IBuyAdventure"

        myConnection = New SQLConnection(ConnStr)
        myConnection.Open()

        myCommand = New SQLCommand(SQL, myConnection)

        myReader = myCommand.ExecuteReader()

        ShipMethod.DataSource = myReader
        ShipMethod.DataBind()
    End If

    End Sub

</script>
```

As you can see, this is exactly the same code that we had in our ASP.NET page. Since there are references to other .NET assemblies in our code, we need to add an @Imports tag to our user control. We can't necessarily rely on the page hosting this control to have imported these references. It doesn't matter to the compiler if these references are imported twice – but it will complain if they aren't there at all.

```
<%@ Import Namespace="System.Data" %>
<%@ Import Namespace="System.Data.SqlClient" %>
```

When we view a page that contains this control, we will see:

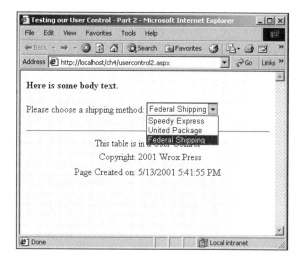

If we examine the HTML that this produces you can see that nothing special is happening on the client:

```
<html>
<head>
   <title>Testing our User Control - Part 2</title>
</head>

<body>
<form name="ctrl0" method="post" action="UserControl2.aspx" id="ctrl0">
<input type="hidden" name="__VIEWSTATE"
value="dDwzNzA5NjI5Njk7dDw7bDxpPDE+Oz47bDx0PDtsPGk8MT47PjtsPHQ8O2w8TwwPjs+O2w8dDx
0PDtwPGw8aTwwPjtpPDE+O2s8Mj47PjtsPHA8U3BlZWR5IEV4cHJlc3M7MT47cDxVbml0ZWQgUGFja2FnZ
TsyPjtwPEZlZGVyYWwgU2hpcHBpbmc7Mz47Pj47Pjs7Pjs+Pjs+Pjs+" />

<strong>Here is some body text.</strong>

<P>Please choose a shipping method: <select name="ctrl1:ShipMethod"
id="ctrl1_ShipMethod">
   <option value="1">Speedy Express</option>
   <option value="2">United Package</option>
   <option value="3">Federal Shipping</option>

</select>
</P>

   <hr>
<table border=0 align=center>
<tr><td colspan=2 align=center>This table is in a User Control</td></tr>
<tr><td align=right>Copyright: </td><td>2001 Wrox Press</td><tr>
<tr><td align=right>Page Created on: </td><td>6/6/2001 7:11:54 PM</td></tr>
</table>

</form>
</body>
</html>
```

The user control behaves just like any other control. The `Page_Load` runs and any content is transmitted to the parent page. The difference is that this user control can be dropped onto other pages.

The @Control Directive

This directive is used to assign control-specific attributes that are used by the Web Forms page parser and compiler to affect how the user control is created. There can only be one @Control directive in a single file.

Attribute	Values (default in bold)	Used for
AutoEventWireup	**true** or false	Has server controls automatically post back to server. When false, the developer must fire the server event manually from the client.
ClassName	Valid class name	Class name that this control is compiled as.
CompilerOptions	Valid compiler options	List of compiler options to be used when the page is compiled.
Debug	true or **false**	Compiles the page with debugging enabled.
Description	n/a	Description of the page – ignored by ASP.NET.
EnableViewState	**true** or false	ViewState for this user control is maintained during round-trips.
Explicit	true or **false**	Uses the Visual Basic Option Explicit mode.
Inherits	Valid class name	Code-behind class that this control inherits.
Language	Valid .NET Language name	Language used to compile all source code on the page.
Src	Valid source file name	File name of the Code-Behind class used by this page.
Strict	true or **false**	Uses the Visual Basic Option Strict mode.
WarningLevel	0, 1, 2, or 4	Compiler warning level at which compilation should be aborted.

User Control Properties

You can interact with your user control by exposing a set of properties for it. This will allow you to programmatically change the behavior of the control from the page that is hosting it. It also makes it much easier to build a control that can be used on multiple pages, even if the data being displayed is somewhat different.

There are three steps to using properties with user controls. First, you need to expose the properties from your user control. This is done using the standard property syntax that we have already seen in the book. If we take our previous example, we can add to it to expose some properties.

```
<%@ Import Namespace="System.Data" %>
<%@ Import Namespace="System.Data.SqlClient" %>

<script language="VB" runat="server">
```

```
    Private ConnStr As String

    Property ConnectionString() As String
      Get
        return ConnStr
      end Get

      Set
        ConnStr = value
      End Set
    end Property

    Sub Page_Load(Source As Object, E As EventArgs)

      If Not Page.IsPostBack Then
        Dim myConnection As SQLConnection
        Dim myCommand    As SQLCommand
        Dim myReader     As SQLDataReader
        Dim SQL          As String

        SQL = "select * from Shipping_Methods"
        If ConnStr = "" Then
          ConnStr = "server=localhost;uid=sa;pwd=;database=IBuyAdventure"
        End If

        myConnection = New SQLConnection(ConnStr)
        myConnection.Open()
```

One of the ways that we can make our user control more extensible is to not hardcode the database connection string. If we make the connection string a property of the control, then the page that is using the control can pass in the proper connection string. In the code above you can see that no matter what page the control is used in, the correct connection string for the database will be used.

The first thing to do is to create a variable to hold the connection string value. Since the property assignment statement is called before Page_Load, we need to have a place to hold the value before it is used to actually open the database.

```
    Private ConnStr As String
```

The next step is to allow the user of the control to set a value for the property, as well as read the value contained by the property. This is done using the Property statement. We provide a Get method to allow for the retrieval of the value, and a Set method to allow the property value to be set.

```
    Property ConnectionString() As String
      Get
        return ConnStr
      end Get

      Set
        ConnStr = value
      end Set
    end Property
```

177

Finally, we need to use the connection string to open the database. Since we can't guarantee that a user will have set the `Property` value, we need to have a default value that is used if there is no value present. Alternatively, if we wanted to require that a value be set, then we could throw an exception at this point if there is no value set. But in this case, we will use a default value.

```
If ConnStr = "" Then
ConnStr = "server=localhost;uid=sa;pwd=;database=IBuyAdventure"
End If
```

The last step is to use this revised user control in our ASP.NET page. To pass a property to a user control, you simply add the property name and value as a parameter when you add the user control to the page.

```
<wrox:shipment ConnectionString="server=localhost;uid=sa;
pwd=;database=IBuyAdventure"
   runat="server" />
```

User Control Events

The key thing that you need to remember when dealing with user control events, is that the event needs to be handled in the user control itself, and not in the page. In this way, all of the event handling for a user control is encapsulated within the control. You should not try to include event handlers for controls within a user control in the page that is hosting the user control (that is, the parent page) – the events will not be passed to the page, so the event will never be processed.

Since event handlers within user control, are handled in the same way as event handlers for server controls within pages, it is pretty similar to what we looked at earlier in the chapter to add an event handler to a user control. We will add to our current user control an event that will be fired when the user selects an item from the drop-down list. This event will cause the user's selection to be displayed in a label control just below the selection.

```
Sub ShipMethod_Change(Source As Object, E As EventArgs)
    SelectedMethod.text = "You have selected " &
                          ShipMethod.SelectedItem.Text &
                          " as your shipping method."
End Sub
</script>

<asp:DropDownList AutoPostBack="true"
                  OnSelectedIndexChanged = "ShipMethod_Change"
                  id="ShipMethod" runat="server"/>
<BR><asp:Label id="SelectedMethod" runat="server"/>
```

We've made two changes to the `DropDownList` control that is part of our User Control. First, we need to let ASP.NET know that we want to automatically trigger a postback when the selection in the drop down list is changed. This is done by setting the `AutoPostBack` parameter to `true`. The second change is to define what method will be called whenever the user selects an item from the drop down list. The name of the event that is fired is `OnSelectedIndexChanged` and when that event is fired, we will call the `ShipMethod_Change` event.

We will then need an event handler within the user control that will be called when the selection is made. This event handler will grab the text value of the selected item from the control, and use that to populate a label control for display back to the user.

```
Sub ShipMethod_Change(Source As Object, E As EventArgs)
    SelectedMethod.text = "You have selected " &
                        ShipMethod.SelectedItem.Text &
                    " as your shipping method."
End Sub
```

The `SelectedItem` property of the `DropDownList` control identifies the particular item object from the list that is currently selected. The `Text` property of this object contains the actual text that was in the drop down list. We can grab this value and use it to build a prompt to display for the user.

Code Behind with User Controls

Earlier in this chapter, we saw how we can use the `Page` class to create an object that will handle all of the code for our page. Then by placing that class definition into its own file, we can separate the code from the layout. This is the same as code behind technique we used earlier. Since user controls are very similar to ASP.NET pages, we can also use code-behind when creating our user controls as well.

```
Imports System
Imports System.Web.UI
Imports System.Web.UI.WebControls
Imports System.Data.SqlClient
```

The first step is to import the necessary namespaces for the user control. The `System` and `System.Web.UI` namespaces are required. Since we are using ASP.NET Server Controls, we also need to import the `System.Web.UI.WebControls` namespace. And, in order to retrieve our data from a database, we need to import the `System.Data.SqlClient` namespace as well.

The next step is to declare a class that we will use to define our user control. To provide the necessary functionality, this class needs to inherit from the `UserControl` class. This class will contain the same initialization code, object interface code, and event handling code that is in the user control we have already created. One important difference is that we must declare `Public` variables for each of the server controls that our user control needs.

```
Public Class shipMethodClass
    Inherits UserControl

    Private ConnStr As String
    Public ShipMethod As DropDownList
    Public SelectedMethod As Label
```

When we save our code-behind file, it is important to use the proper filename extension. This is the only way to inform the ASP.NET compiler what language our code-behind file is written in. If you don't use the proper extension, then the compiler will fail when trying to display this page.

```
<%@ Control inherits="shipMethodClass" src="shipMethod.vb"
        ClassName="shipMethod" %>
```

Finally, we need to remove the VB code from our user control and then add a `@Control` directive to attach the user control to the code-behind file. There are three parameters in the `@Control` directive that we need to use. The `inherits` parameter defines the name of the class that contains the code-behind code. The `src` parameter defines the source file that actually contains the code-behind source code. The `ClassName` defines a class name for the control, which we will need if we dynamically create the control on a page.

Partial Page Caching with User Controls

As we saw earlier in this chapter, you can use caching to reduce the number of processing cycles required to deliver a page when it is requested by the client. By storing the output from a page on the server, and then outputting that information to a client when the same page is requested again, we eliminate the need to execute the page again. We can use a very similar concept to allow us to cache parts of a page.

If you are wondering "how can I tag part of the page to be cached?" then think about what user controls do. They are basically separate page sections that are embedded into another page. If we could cache the output of a user control, and then insert it into a page when it is requested, then we can again achieve the benefits of caching. This technique is called partial page caching, or **fragment caching**.

The key to using fragment caching is through user controls. You must place the portions of the page that you wish to cache into a user control, and then indicate that the user control should be cached. To do this, you use the @OutputCache directive, just like we did when we cached the entire page.

```
<%@ OutputCache Duration="time" VaryByParam="none" %>
```

To see how fragment caching works, we will add caching to the user control that we have been looking at in this chapter. This specific user control, since it is performing database access, will gain great performance benefits by being cached. Since the data that is being displayed does not change very frequently, it would be of great benefit if we didn't have to go to the database each time the control is used.

```
<%@ Import Namespace="System.Data" %>
<%@ Import Namespace="System.Data.SqlClient" %>
<%@ OutputCache Duration="10" VaryByParam="none" %>

<script language="VB" runat="server">

  Sub Page_Load(Source As Object, E As EventArgs)
    Dim NowTime As DateTime
    Dim Expires as DateTime
    NowTime = DateTime.Now
    Expires = NowTime.AddSeconds(10)
    CreatedStamp.InnerHtml = NowTime.ToString("r")
    ExpiresStamp.InnerHtml = Expires.ToString("r")

    If Not Page.IsPostBack Then
      Dim myConnection As SQLConnection
      ...
```

The one line that enables fragment caching is the @OutputCache parameter. We have set the cache to hold the page for 10 seconds. By setting the VaryByParam parameter to none we have the same cached value regardless of the parameters or browser making the request.

The rest of the code that we have added to the user control is simply to help us identify that the cache is actually working. We want to display the time the user control was run as well as 10 seconds into the future – which is when the cache will expire. There are two Label server controls that will display that information for us.

```
<HR>Fragment Cache created: <Font color="red">
                            <B id="CreatedStamp" runat="server"></B></Font>
  <BR>
  Fragment Cache expires: <Font color="red">
                            <B id="ExpiresStamp" runat="server"></B></Font>
```

When we view the page in the browser, we can see the time that the page was created, the time that the user control was created, and when the cached version of the user control will expire. Here we see that the time the page was loaded was 13:31:20 – the same time shown on the fragment cache.

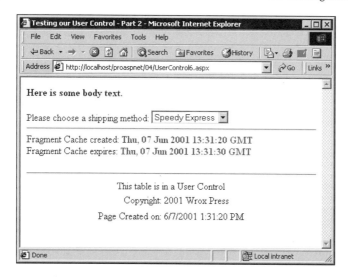

If we hit *F5* to refresh the browser, we can then see that the page creation time changes (it's now 13:31:26), but the user control creation time and cache expire time doesn't change – it is being drawn from the cache.

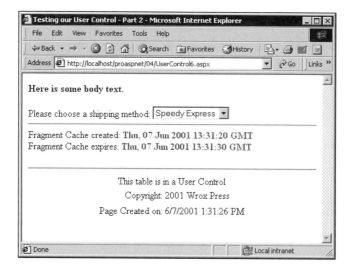

Summary

In this chapter, we have taken a look at the core for ASP.NET – the page. Whether you refer to it as a Web Form or as an ASP.NET page, the page is the central part of all that you will do with ASP.NET. The page is what embodies the interface that the user has to interact with, on your web site or web application. The page gives us plenty of power to do things, like generate non-text files such as images, or be separated into smaller segments called user controls. But with this power also comes complexity. The nice thing though about the `Page` object and all that it represents is that you can just work with the tip of the iceberg and still function. But when you need to delve deeper, the `Page` object, and all that it encompasses, has the power that you need.

In this chapter, we looked at:

- ❏ The old way of doing ASP pages, and contrasted that with the new ASP.NET style of pages.
- ❏ The `Page` class itself and the object model that it supports.
- ❏ The steps that the page goes through in its lifetime.
- ❏ How to use Code Behind to separate code from layout.
- ❏ How output caching can be used to increase performance.
- ❏ How to create and use user controls.

In the next chapter, we will begin to dive deeper into the world of server controls. As we have already seen with user controls, the ability to embed complex functionality into a control, and then drop that control onto a Web Form page with one tag is one of the revolutionary aspects of ASP.NET.

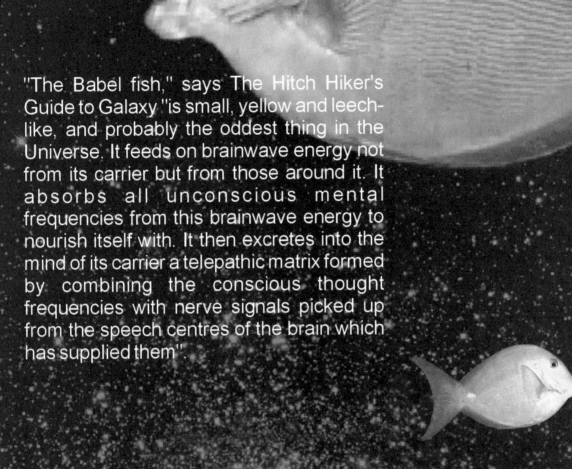

"The Babel fish," says The Hitch Hiker's Guide to Galaxy "is small, yellow and leech-like, and probably the oddest thing in the Universe. It feeds on brainwave energy not from its carrier but from those around it. It absorbs all unconscious mental frequencies from this brainwave energy to nourish itself with. It then excretes into the mind of its carrier a telepathic matrix formed by combining the conscious thought frequencies with nerve signals picked up from the speech centres of the brain which has supplied them".

The practical upshot of all this is that if you stick a Babel fish in your ear you can instantly understand anything said to you in any form of language. The speech patterns you actually hear decode the brainwave matrix which has been fed into your mind by your Babel fish

5

Server Controls and Validation

Introduction

We've already used server controls in many of the examples of building ASP.NET pages in previous chapters. However, in this and the next two chapters, we're going to be looking in more depth at exactly what server controls are and how we can use them. In fact, we'll be examining all the different types of server controls that are supplied with the standard .NET installation.

Server controls are the heart of the new ASP.NET techniques for building interactive web forms and web pages. They allow us to adopt a programming model based around server-side event handling that is much more like the structured event-driven approach we're used to when building traditional executable programs.

Of course, as the .NET framework is completely extensible, we can build our own server controls as well – or just inherit from existing ones and extend their behavior. We'll look at how we can go about building our own server controls later in this book. In the meantime, we'll stick to those that come as part of the standard .NET package.

The topics we'll cover in this chapter are:

- ❑ What are server controls?
- ❑ How we can build interactive forms and pages using them.
- ❑ The server controls that are supplied with .NET.
- ❑ A detailed look at the HTML and Input Validation controls.

We start with the obvious question: "What are server controls?"

What Are Server Controls?

As we saw in Chapter 4, ASP.NET is designed around the concept of server controls. This stems from the fundamental change in the philosophy for creating interactive pages. In particular, with the increasing power of servers and the ease of building multi-server web Farms, we can circumvent the problems of handling the increasing range of different client devices by doing much more of the work on the server.

We also end up with a client interface that looks and behaves much more like a traditional application. However, to understand how the use of server controls affects the way we build applications, it's important to grasp the way that the new ASP.NET "page" model changes the whole approach to Web page design.

The ASP.NET Page Model Revisited

In previous versions of ASP we've got quite used to the traditional way of creating pages dynamically:

❏   Capture the request in IIS and pipe it through a parsing engine like the ASP interpreter. This is achieved by setting the script mappings in IIS to direct all requests for `.asp` pages to the ASP ISAPI DLL named `asp.dll`.

❏   Within the interpreter (`asp.dll`), examine the page for server-side script sections. Non-script sections are simply piped back out to the client through the response. Script sections are extracted and passed to an instance of the appropriate scripting engine.

❏   The scripting engine executes the code and sends any output this code generates to the response at that point in the page.

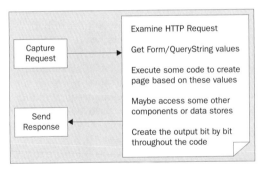

The problem is that the code usually ends up resembling spaghetti. It's really hard to get a well structured design when all we're really doing is interpreting the blocks of script that can be placed almost anywhere in the page.

ASP.NET Pages Are All About Events

Instead, if we think about how a traditional Windows executable application is created, it all depends on **events**. We create a "form" or "window" for the user to work with, and place in it the controls they'll use to accomplish the required task. Events are raised as the user interacts with the controls and the page, and we create handlers for these events. The code in each event handler is responsible for updating the page or controls, creating output, or carrying out whatever task is required:

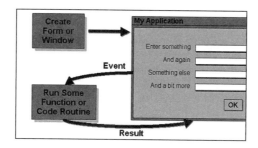

The great thing with ASP.NET is that, in conjunction with server controls and the new "page" model, we can build web pages and web applications that work in just the same way. In other words, we now have a proper **event-driven architecture**.

ASP.NET Is Compiled Code

Much of the theory of this new page structure was covered in previous chapters, so we'll confine ourselves to the actual server controls themselves in this chapter. However, the important concept to grasp is that the whole page, including all of the HTML, text, and other content, is compiled into a **class**. This class can then be executed to create the output for the client.

All the **static** or **client-based content** (text, HTML, client-side script, etc.) is sent to the client through the response when the class is executed. We have no interaction with it on the server. However, all controls or elements that are marked with the `runat="server"` attribute are themselves created as objects within the page class. This means that we can write code that uses these objects. Or, to put it more simply, if we mark an element or control as being `runat="server"`, we can access its properties, call its methods and react to the events it raises on the server. This works because ASP.NET uses `<form>` elements to create the **postback architecture** we described in earlier chapters. In the postback architecture, the page and its contents are posted back to the same ASP.NET file on the server when the user interacts with the controls on that page.

Server Controls Are Event Driven

When a user clicks a button on a page, the values of the controls on that page are posted back to the server and a click event is raised (on the server). We react to this event using an **event handler**. For example, we can define a button control like this:

```
<input type="submit" value="Go" onserverclick="MyFunction" runat="server" />
```

Then, on the server, we react to the click event (notice that the attribute name is `onserverclick`, not `onclick` – which is defined in HTML 4.0 to raise a client-side event):

```
<script language="VB" runat="server">
Sub MyFunction(objSender As Object, objArgs As EventArgs)
 ... code to handle the event here ...
End Sub
</script>
```

Server Controls Are Objects Within the Page

Another point that might seem obvious, but which is again at the heart of the new page design, is that each server control is compiled into the page class as an object that is globally available within the page. This means that, within an event handler, we can access all the controls. So, as in a traditional application, we can access the values in other textboxes, buttons, list controls, and so on, then take the appropriate actions and/or create the appropriate output. Here's an example where the `Page_Load` event is used to collect values from several server controls:

```
<div id="divResult" runat="server" />
...
<script language="VB" runat="server">
Sub Page_Load()
 Dim strResult As String
 strResult = "MyTextBox.ID = " & MyTextBox.ID & "<p />"
 strResult += "MyTextBox.Value = " & MyTextBox.Value & "<p />"
 strResult += "MyCheckBox.Checked = " & MyCheckBox.Checked
 divResult.InnerHtml = strResult
End Sub
</script>
```

And, of course, we can also set the value of the controls:

```
<script language="VB" runat="server">
Sub Page_Load()
 Dim datToday As Date = Now()
 MyTextBox.Value = datToday
End Sub
</script>
```

Experimenting with Server Controls

To show how the various server controls work, we've provided a simple example application that shows the output generated in the browser by each of the controls. You can also set the values of the common properties for each control and see the results. The example is included in the samples that you can download for this book from:

http://www.wrox.com/Books/Book_Details.asp?isbn=1861004885

The application is in the folder named `server-controls`, and has a `default.htm` page to start it:

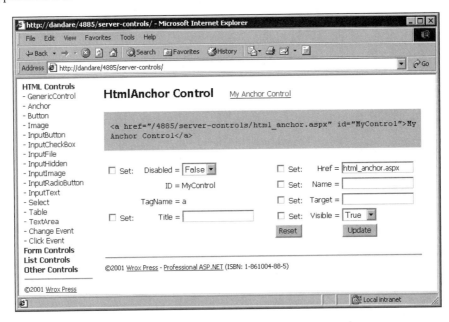

The gray background section in the main page displays the actual HTML output that the selected control generates. This is done with some client-side JScript, which creates an instance of the XMLHTTP object (an integral part of IE5) and uses it to fetch the same page again as a string, after it has finished loading into the right-hand frame of our application. The code then parses out the section containing the output of the server control and displays it (you can view the source of the page to see this code). This means that you will only be able to use IE5 or above to view this particular example; however, this was felt to be a valid course of action in order to show the actual output of the server controls.

We could simply have queried the OuterHtml property of the element itself to get the HTML content, but this is actually different from the HTML that the browser receives from the server. The IE HTML DOM parses the incoming HTML and sorts and simplifies the attributes, so you wouldn't see a true picture of the server control's output in this case.

As you can see from the previous screenshot, the left-hand frame contains a collapsible tree listing all the server controls. For each one, you can specify the values for several of the most useful properties for that control. For example, in the next screenshot we've selected the HTML Anchor control and set the Title, Href, Name, and Target properties, then clicked the Update button. You can see the effect this has on the output of the control:

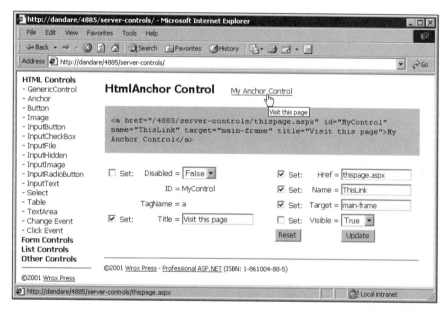

We'll be using this application throughout this and the next chapter to demonstrate the various controls. We don't have room to exhaustively examine all the methods and properties for all of the controls, but you can experiment with it yourself to see what effect each of the properties has on the output created by the different server controls.

By comparing the output that is generated to the property settings you make, you can get a feel for how these controls can be used. OK, so it's a relatively simple one-to-one connection between the properties you set and the attributes that are created with the HTML controls. However, as we'll see in the next chapter (particularly with the "rich controls" described there), the results from the other sets of server controls can be quite different.

About the Example Application

Although we won't be describing how the example application works in this chapter, the source code is available for you to look through if you want to learn more. Basically, all it does is create an instance of the selected control, then it displays a set of input elements for the properties that are specific to that control. As the page loads, it reads the values of these properties and inserts them into the input elements. When we set one or more of the properties and click the Update button, the server control is updated to reflect these property values.

We haven't provided inputs for all the properties, as there are a large number that are generic to many controls, and which are not commonly used. Where the property value is taken from an enumeration, such as the `Align` property for an `ASP:Image` control, we provide a drop-down list containing the enumeration values. To set the property when the page is submitted, we use the integer value of that enumeration member as stored in the `value` attribute of the list box item. We'll discuss this in more detail when we look at the ASP.NET Web Form controls in the next chapter. However, you can see how this works if you examine the source code for the page (`asp_image.aspx`).

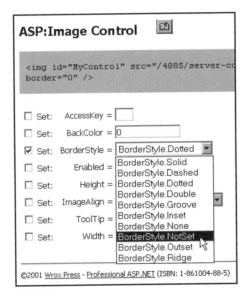

Some of the server controls demonstrated in the application (such as textboxes and lists) are interactive. However, note that any changes you make within the control itself (the control we're demonstrating) are not reflected in the property values shown in the controls where you set these values. For example, if you change the text in the `InputText` control at the top of that particular demonstration page, it is reset to the value shown in the `Value` property input control when you click Update. At any time you can return the control to its original state by clicking the Reset button.

When Should I Use Server Controls?

One very important topic to consider is when we should choose server controls over "normal" HTML elements. For example, if we want a textbox on a form, should we use a server control or a normal `<input type="text">` element? In fact, to create a text box we have three options. We can just use an ordinary HTML element that is displayed as a textbox in the browser:

```
<input type="text" name="mytext" />
```

We can also use an `HtmlInputText` server control. Again, we set the `type` attribute to `"text"`, but this time we include the `runat="server"` attribute as well:

```
<input type="text" id="mytext" runat="server" />
```

Or we can use an ASP `TextBox` control (we'll discuss the pros and cons of these controls in the next chapter):

```
<asp:TextBox id="mytext" runat="server" />
```

Adding the `runat="server"` attribute to an HTML element, or using one of the ASP Web Form controls (which must always include the `runat="server"` attribute in their definition) causes that control to be compiled into the page, and executed on the server each time the page is requested. This is obviously more resource-intensive that just including some HTML in the page output, as would be the case with an element that does not contain the `runat="server"` attribute.

However, if we want to be able to access the element's properties, methods, or events in our server-side code, we have to create it as a server control. But it's always worth considering which elements actually do need to be server controls when we build a page. For example, the following situations **do not** require a server-side control:

❑ When the element is only used to run some client-side script, for example a button that opens a new browser window, interacts with a client-side ActiveX control or Java applet, or calculates some value for display in the page using DHTML or in an `alert` dialog.

❑ When the element is a Submit button that is only used to submit a form to the server. In this case, the code in the `Page_Load` event handler can extract the values from the other controls.

❑ When the element is a hyperlink that opens a different page or URL and there is no need to process the values for the hyperlink on the server.

❑ Any other times when access to the element's properties, methods or events in server-side code is not required.

Remember that we can still use the `Request.Form` and `Request.QueryString` collections in the same way as previous versions of ASP if we wish, with both ordinary HTML control elements and with server controls. HTML control elements that are on a `<form>` but which are not marked with `runat="server"` (in other words they are not server controls), will still send their values to the server in the `Request.Form` and `Request.QueryString` collections when the form is submitted.

In general, a page that uses server controls instead of HTML elements results in something like a 30% drop in performance each time the page is generated. However, this is only an average – you don't get a compounded 30% penalty hit for every control. Besides, if you use server-side code to set the values of controls using traditional ASP techniques, you generally get worse performance compared to using the ASP.NET server controls.

The Controls Available in ASP.NET

From the previous discussion, you should now appreciate the advantages we get with server controls:

❑ HTML output that creates the elements to implement the control in the browser

❑ An object within the page that we can program against on the server

❑ Automatic maintenance of the control's value (or state)

❑ Simple access to the control values without having to dig into the `Request` object

❑ The ability to react to events, and so create better structured pages

❑ A common approach to building user interfaces as web pages

❑ The ability to more easily address different types of client device

The server controls provided with the .NET framework fall quite neatly into six groups:

❑ **HTML Server Controls** are the server-based equivalents of the standard HTML controls. They create output that is basically the same as the definition of the control within the page, and they use the same attributes as the standard HTML elements. We'll look at these controls in this chapter.

❑ **ASP.NET Validation Controls** are a set of special controls that are designed to make it easy to check and validate the values entered into other controls on a page. They perform the validation client-side, server-side or both – depending on the type of client device that requests the page. We'll also look at these controls in this chapter.

❑ **ASP.NET Web Form Controls** are a set of controls that are the equivalent of the normal HTML `<form>` controls, such as a textbox, a hyperlink, and various buttons. They have a standardized set of property names that make life easier at design time and easier for graphical page creation tools to build the page. We'll see more about these controls in the next chapter.

❑ **ASP.NET List Controls** provide a range of ways to build lists. These lists can also be data bound. In other words, the content of the list can come from a data source such as an `Array`, a `HashTable`, or a range of other data sources. The range of controls provides many different display options, and some include special features for formatting the output and even editing the data in the list. We'll see more about these controls in Chapter 7.

❑ **ASP.NET Rich Controls** are things like the Calendar and Ad Rotator, which create complex task-specific output. In many cases, the rich controls also modify the output automatically to suit the device that requests the page. We'll see more about these controls in the next chapter.

❑ **ASP.NET Mobile Controls** are a separate set of controls that provide the same kind of functionality as the Web Form, List, and Rich controls – but they have specially extended features that completely change the output of the control based on the client device so that they can also support mobile and small-screen devices. They can create output that is in Wireless Markup Language (WML) as well as HTML and other formats. We'll see more about these controls in Chapter 21.

The HTML Server Controls

The HTML server controls are defined within the namespace `System.Web.UI.HtmlControls`. There are a couple of generic base classes defined there, from which the controls inherit. There are also specific classes for each of the **interactive** controls (those controls that are usually used on an HTML `<form>`).

The HtmlControl Base Classes

The base class for all HTML controls is `System.Web.UI.HtmlControls.HtmlControl`. This exposes methods, properties, and events that are common to all HTML controls. For example, the ones we use most often include:

`Attributes` property	Returns a collection of all the attribute name/value pairs within the `.aspx` file for this control. Can be used to read and set non-standard attributes (custom attributes that are not actually part of HTML) or to access attributes where the control does not provide a specific property for that purpose.
`ClientID` property	Returns the control identifier that is generated by ASP.NET.
`Controls` property	Returns a `ControlCollection` object containing references to all the child controls for this control within the page hierarchy.
`Disabled` property	Sets or returns a Boolean value indicating if the control is disabled.
`EnableViewState` property	Sets or returns a Boolean value indicating if the control should maintain its viewstate and the viewstate of any child controls when the current page request ends. Default is `True`.
`ID` property	Sets or returns the identifier defined for the control.
`Page` property	Returns a reference to the `Page` object containing the control.
`Parent` property	Returns a reference to the parent of this control within the page hierarchy.
`Style` property	References a collection of all the CSS style properties (selectors) that apply to the control.
`TagName` property	Returns the name of the element, for example "a" or "div".
`Visible` property	Sets or returns a Boolean value indicating if the control should be rendered in the page output. Default is `True`.
`DataBind` method	Causes data binding to occur for the control and all of its child controls.
`FindControl` method	Searches within the current container for a specified server control.
`HasControls` method	Returns a Boolean value indicating if the control contains any child controls.
`DataBinding` event	Occurs when the control is being bound to a data source.

A full list of all the members for this object can be found in the Class Library Reference section `System.Web.UI.HtmlControls.HtmlControl` *within the .NET SDK*

The second base class is `System.Web.UI.HtmlControls.HtmlContainerControl`, which is used as the base for all HTML elements that **must** have a closing tag (elements such as `<i>`, `<b>`, and `<select>` that, unlike `<img>` or `<input>`, make no sense as single tags). This class inherits from `HtmlControl`, and exposes the same methods, properties, and events as shown above. And, because it's only used for "container" elements that can themselves have content, it adds two more very useful properties that allow us to read and set this content:

`InnerHtml` property	Sets or returns the HTML and text content between the opening and closing tags of the control.
`InnerText` property	Sets or returns just the text content between the opening and closing tags of the control.

The HtmlGenericControl Class

As you'll no doubt be aware, there are around 100 elements currently defined in HTML – though some are browser specific. Rather than provide a class for all of these, the .NET framework contains specific classes for only a few of the HTML elements. These mainly include those elements that we use on an HTML `<form>`, or which we use to build interactive parts of a page (such as hyperlinks or images).

This doesn't mean that we can't use other HTML controls as server controls. If there is no specific class defined for the element we use, the framework simply substitutes the `System.Web.UI.HtmlControls.HtmlGenericControl` class instead. Note that this is **not** a base class – it is a public class designed for use with all elements for which there is no specific class.

For example, you may have noticed in an example earlier in the chapter that we used a `<div>` element to display the results of some code in an event handler:

```
<div id="divResult" runat="server" />
...
Sub Page_Load()
  ...
  divResult.InnerHtml = strResult
End Sub
```

You can see that we've defined the `<div>` as being a server control (it includes the `runat="server"` attribute, and this allows us to use the XML-style shorthand syntax of specifying a forward slash instead of a closing tag). To display the result, we simply set the `InnerHtml` property on the server. So if the value of `strResult` is "This is the result", the page output will contain:

```
<div id="outResult">This is the result</div>
```

As the `HtmlGenericControl` is based on the `HtmlContainerControl` base class (which itself inherits from `HtmlControl`), it exposes the same list of members (properties, methods, and events) that we described earlier for these classes. In our previous code, we used the `InnerHtml` property to display a value within the control. We can equally well use the other members; for example, we can force the element to be displayed or hidden (included or not included in the final page output) by setting the `Visible` property.

The Specific HTML Control Classes

The `System.Web.UI.HtmlControls` namespace includes specific classes for the HTML interactive controls, such as those used on a `<form>`. Each one inherits from either `HtmlControl` or `HtmlContainerControl` (depending on whether it has a closing tag), so it has the same members as that base class.

However, for these controls to be useful, we need to be able to access the properties and events that are specific to each type of control. For example, with a hyperlink, we might want to read and set the `href`, `name`, and `target` attribute values in our server-side code. We might also want to be able to detect when a user clicks on a hyperlink.

To accomplish this, each of the controls has specific properties and events that correspond to the attributes we normally use with that element. A few also have other properties that allow access to control-specific values, such as the `PostedFile` property for an `<input type="file">` element or the specific data-binding properties of the `<select>` element. The button-type controls also have a `CausesValidation` property, which we'll see in use when we look at the `Validation` server controls later in this chapter.

HTML Element	Specific Properties	Specific Events
`<a>` ClassName: `HtmlAnchor`	`Href, Target, Title, Name`	`OnServerClick`
`<img>` Class Name: `HtmlImage`	`Align, Alt, Border, Height,` `Src, Width`	*- none -*
`<form>` Class Name: `HtmlForm`	`Name, Enctype, Method,` `Target`	*- none -*
`<button>` Class Name: `HtmlButton`	`CausesValidation`	`OnServerClick`

`<input type="button">`
`<input type="submit">`
`<input type="reset">`
Class Name: `HtmlInputButton`
	`Name, Type, Value,`
	`CausesValidation`
		`OnServerClick`

`<input type="text">`
`<input type="password">`
Class Name: `HtmlInputText`
	`MaxLength, Name, Size,`
	`Type, Value`
		`OnServerChange`

`<input type="checkbox">` Class Name: `HtmlInputCheckBox`	`Checked, Name, Type, Value`	`OnServerChange`

Table continued on following page

`<input type="radio">`
Class Name:
`HtmlInputRadioButton`
	Checked, Name, Type, Value	OnServerChange

`<input type="image">` Class Name: `HtmlInputImage`	Align, Alt, Border, Name, Src, Type, Value, CausesValidation	OnServerClick
`<input type="file">` Class Name: `HtmlInputFile`	Accept, MaxLength, Name, PostedFile, Size, Type, Value	- *none* -
`<input type="hidden">` Class Name: `HtmlInputHidden`	Name, Type, Value	OnServerChange
`<textarea>` Class Name: `HtmlTextArea`	Cols, Name, Rows, Value	OnServerChange
`<select>` Class Name: `HtmlSelect`	Multiple, SelectedIndex, Size, Value, DataSource, DataTextField, DataValueField Items *(collection)*	OnServerChange
`<table>` Class Name: `HtmlTable`	Align, BgColor, Border, BorderColor, CellPadding, CellSpacing, Height, NoWrap, Width Rows *(collection)*	- *none* -
`<tr>` Class Name: `HtmlTableRow`	Align, BgColor, Border, BorderColor, Height, VAlign Cells *(collection)*	- *none* -
`<td>` Class Name: `HtmlTableCell`	Align, BgColor, Border, BorderColor, ColSpan, Height, NoWrap, RowSpan, VAlign, Width	- *none* -

In the next sections of this chapter we'll examine these controls in more detail using the demonstration application we provide.

Using the HTML Server Controls

In most cases, the use of HTML controls is self-evident if you are familiar with the quirks of HTML and its inconsistent use of attribute names. The properties of the controls, as we've just seen, match the attribute names almost identically. There are a couple of useful techniques that apply to all the HTML controls, and in fact to most of the other server controls as well. We'll look at these next.

Setting the Control Appearance Using Style Properties

All the server controls (including the ASP Web Form controls we look at in the next two chapters) provide a `Style` property that we can use to change the appearance of the control. It defines the CSS properties that will be added to the element tag when the control is created. We simply set or add the appropriate CSS style selectors to the collection for that control, using the same values as we would in a normal CSS style sheet. For example, we can display the content of a `<div>` element in large red letters like this:

```
<div id="divResult" runat="server" />
...
<script language="VB" runat="server">
Sub Page_Load()
 divResult.InnerHtml = "Some Big Red Text"
 divResult.Style("font-family") = "Tahoma"
 divResult.Style("font-weight") = "bold"
 divResult.Style("font-size") = "30px"
 divResult.Style("color") = "Red"
End Sub
</script>
```

Here's the result:

If we examine the output that is generated by the control, we see the `style` attribute that determines the formatting we specified in our code:

```
<div id="divResult" style="font-family:Tahoma;font-weight:bold;font-
size:30px;color:Red;">Some Big Red Text</div>
```

This technique is most useful with the HTML controls, as the ASP.NET Web Form controls and most of the other server controls have specific properties that can be used to change their appearance – as we'll see in the next chapter.

Managing viewstate Across Postbacks

One important point you should be aware of is the effect that **VIEWSTATE** has on the performance of your server and the page itself. We looked at what VIEWSTATE is in the previous chapter, and we'll see more detail about the effects it has on performance in Chapter 7, when we come to look at the more complex list controls. Basically, to recap, an ASP.NET page containing a server-side `<form>` control automatically generates VIEWSTATE. This is an encoded representation of all the values in all the controls on the page, and it is persisted across page loads using a HIDDEN-type `<input>` control. If you view the source of the page in the browser, you'll see this:

```
<form name="ctrl0" method="post" action="mypage.aspx" id="ctrl0">
<input type="hidden" name="__VIEWSTATE" value="dDwxOTAwNDM2ODc1Ozs+" />
...
```

You can prevent a control from persisting its values within the VIEWSTATE by changing the `EnableViewState` property from its default value of `True` to `False`:

```
<ASP:TextBox id="MyTextBox" EnableViewState="False" runat="server" />
```

This is also useful if you use a control such as a `<div>` to display some kind of status or information value by setting the `InnerText` or `InnerHtml` property in your server-side code. When the page is posted back to the server, the value is persisted automatically. By changing the `EnableViewState` property to `False`, you start with a fresh new empty `<div>` (or whichever element you use it with) each time.

Examples of the HTML Server Controls

So that you can appreciate how each of the HTML server controls works, and how the properties we define affect the output that the control generates, the next few sections show each of the controls in detail, together with some pointers to be aware of when you use them.

The HtmlGeneric Control

There's not much to say about the HtmlGeneric control, other than this is the **only** control where the `TagName` property is read/write. It's read-only in all other controls. We can use the HtmlGeneric control to create any container-type HTML element that we need:

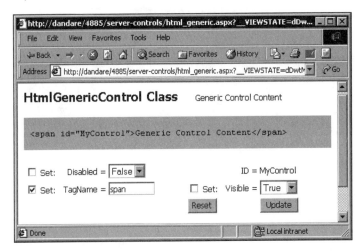

The HTML we use to create the server control in the source code for the page is:

```
<span id="MyControl" runat="server">Generic Control Content</span>
```

The HtmlAnchor Control

We saw the `HtmlAnchor` control in our demonstration application earlier in this chapter. The five attributes that we generally use with an HTML hyperlink or an HTML anchor are available as properties:

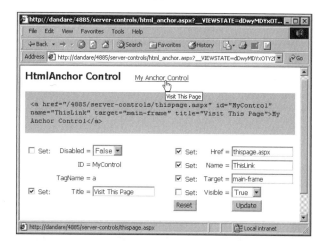

The HTML we use to create the server control in the source code for the page is:

```
<a href="html_anchor.aspx" id="MyControl" runat="server">My Anchor Control</a>
```

The HtmlImage Control

When we want to display an image, and be able interact with this `<img>` element on the server, we can use the `HtmlImage` control. The screenshot below, from the demonstration application, shows most of the properties set to custom values. You can see that we've changed the image, specified a five pixel wide border for it, set the height and width, and added a pop-up tool-tip:

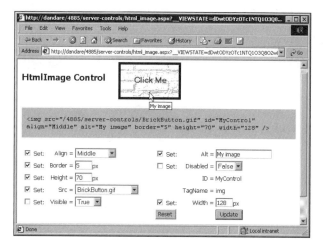

The HTML we use to create the server control in the source code for the page is:

```
<img id="MyControl" src="BookmarkButton.gif" runat="server" />
```

The HtmlForm Control

The HtmlForm control can't be demonstrated in our sample application. However, it can easily be used to create a form – in fact it's the way we usually do it when building ASP.NET interactive pages:

```
<form runat="server">
... form content defined here ...
</form>
```

ASP.NET automatically sets the remaining attributes, so that the contents of the form are posted back to the same page. What is actually generated as output is shown next – notice that the hidden VIEWSTATE element is automatically added:

```
<form name="ctrl0" method="post" action="test.aspx" id="ctrl0">
<input type="hidden" name="__VIEWSTATE" value="dDwxNTkzNjk1MzQ7Oz4=" />
... form content appears here ...
</form>
```

We can also use the HtmlForm control to create a form with some of our own specific attributes. For example, in order to make our demonstration application work properly (due to the need to fetch the page separately with the XMLHTTP component to show the content), we need to use the GET method for the form content, rather than POST:

```
<form method="get" runat="server">
```

Also remember that, if you use the HtmlInputFile control or a normal <input type="file"> element (which we look at later in the chapter), you must set the enctype attribute yourself to allow files to be uploaded to the server:

```
<form enctype="multipart/form-data" runat="server">
```

The HtmlButton Control

The HtmlButton control creates an HTML element of type <button>..</button>. This isn't a commonly used element (it isn't supported in Navigator or Opera), but is actually quite useful if you are targeting Internet Explorer. Unlike the <input type="button"> element, HtmlButton is a container control, so you can place HTML inside the element instead of just text.

This means that you can, for example, display an image and text together – and you can even use an animated GIF image if you like. All the content is rendered on top of a standard button control background, and it "depresses" just like a normal button. This is the code we used for this example:

```
<button id="cmdRemove" accesskey="R" style="font-size:9pt" runat="server">
 <img id="imgbtnRemove" src="remove.gif"<br /><u>R</u>emove
</button>
```

Note that, to change the content of an HtmlButton control, you have to set the InnerHtml property or define the content at design-time within the element. There is no specific property for the "caption", "text", or "value".

In the next screenshot, you can see one of the few properties available for the HtmlButton control in use. In this case, we've set the Disabled property to True, and you can see how the caption is dimmed to indicate that the button is disabled:

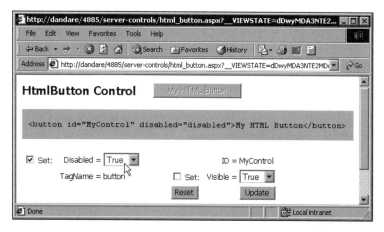

The HTML we use to create the server control in the source code for the page is:

```
<button id="MyControl" runat="server">My HTML Button</button>
```

Remember that the Disabled property, which adds the attribute disabled="disabled" to the element, only has an effect in Internet Explorer. Most other browsers don't recognize this attribute.

The HtmlInputButton Control

The type of buttons we normally use in our interactive forms are the <input type="submit">, <input type="button">, and <input type="reset"> elements. The HtmlInputButton control is used to create these three elements. The only button-specific properties we can set are the Name and Value (the caption). The Disabled and Visible properties are, of course, inherited from the base class HtmlControl. In the next screenshot, we've set a variety of values for the three variations of the HtmlButton control:

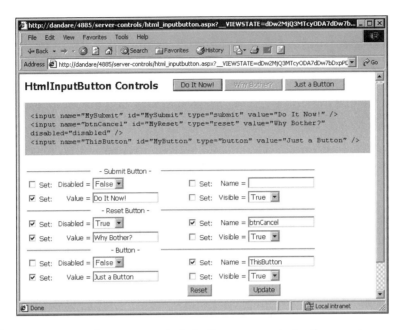

The HTML we use to create the server controls in the source code for the page is:

```
<input id="MySubmit" type="submit" runat="server" />
<input id="MyReset" type="reset" runat="server" />
<input id="MyButton" type="button" runat="server" Value="My Caption" />
```

The HtmlInputText Control

Probably the most common HTML form control is the textbox, and this is implemented as a server control by the HtmlInputText control. As usual with the HTML controls, the properties map one-to-one with the attributes of the <input type="text"> element that defines a textbox in the browser. In the following screenshot you can see that we've set the MaxLength, Size, and Name properties:

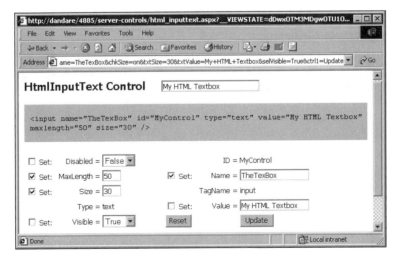

The HTML we use to create the server control in the source code for the page is:

```
<input type="text" id="MyControl" value="My HTML Textbox" runat="server" />
```

The HtmlInputCheckBox and HtmlInputRadioButton Controls

To create a checkbox or a radio button (or "option button" as they are sometimes called) we use the HTML server controls `HtmlInputCheckBox` and `HtmlInputRadioButton`. The set of properties, and the way they work, are pretty much the same for both controls – in the next screenshot we show the `HtmlRadioButton` control:

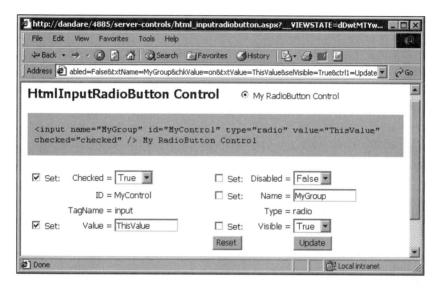

The HTML we use to create the controls in the source code for these two pages is:

```
<input type="radio" id="MyControl" name="MyGroup" runat="server" /> My RadioButton
Control
```

and

```
<input type="checkbox" id="MyControl" runat="server" /> My Checkbox Control
```

The one point to bear in mind (which applies only to radio buttons) is that to create a mutually exclusive "option" group of buttons on a form, you must assign each one the same value for the `name` attribute.

The HtmlInputImage Control

An easy way to display an image that is "clickable" is with an `<input type="image">` element. It acts like a "submit" button in that, when the button is clicked, the form containing the element is submitted to the server along with the coordinates of the mouse pointer within the image. Our demonstration page allows you set all the commonly used properties for this type of control, including the alignment, border width, alternaite text, and image source (from a selection we've provided) – as well as the name and value:

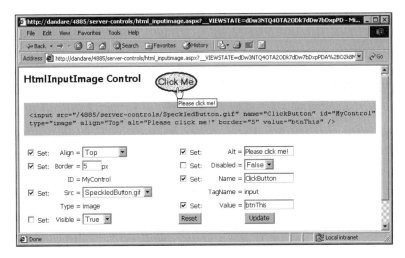

The HTML we use to create the server control in the source code for the page is:

```
<input type="image" id="MyControl" src="BookmarkButton.gif"
runat="server" />
```

The HtmlInputFile Control

If you need to allow users to upload files to your server, you can use the `<input type="file">` element. This is implemented as a server control by `HtmlInputFile`. It has a special property just for this purpose, named `Accept` (the MIME type of the file to upload). The other properties are the same as for a textbox element. In our demonstration page, you can see the settings we've made. While the Browse button that the control creates does allow you to select a file, you can't actually upload files with our demonstration application:

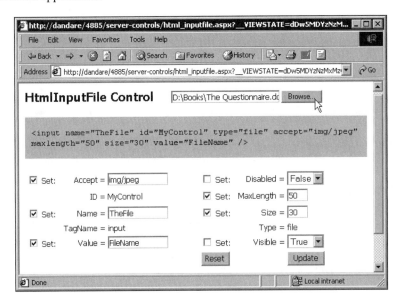

The HTML we use to create the server control in the source code for the page is:

```
<input type="file" id="MyControl" runat="server" />
```

The Code To Upload a File

To create a working file upload page, all you need is a form with the correct value for the `enctype` attribute, an `HtmlInputFile` element, and a button to start the process:

```
<form enctype="multipart/form-data" runat="server">
  Select File:
  <input type="file" id="MyFileInput" accept="image/*" runat="server" />
  <input type="button" id="SubmitButton" value="Upload Image"
      runat="server" onserverclick="UploadFile" />
</form>
<div id="outError" runat="server" />
...
<script language="VB" runat="server">
Sub UploadFile(objSource As Object, objArgs As EventArgs)
  If Not (MyFileInput.PostedFile Is Nothing) Then
   Try
     MyFileInput.PostedFile.SaveAs("c:\temp\uploaded.jpg")
   Catch objError As Exception
     outError.InnerHtml = "Error saving file " & objError.Message
   End Try
  End If
End Sub
</script>
```

The `<script>` section following the form contains the code routine that runs when the user clicks the Upload button. It checks to see that there is a file by referencing the `PostedFile` property of the control, and if so saves it to the server's disk. Any error message is displayed in a `<div>` control on the page.

Note that you will probably need to change the value of `maxRequestLength` in the `<httpRuntime>` element within the `<system.web>` section of `web.config` or `machine.config` to allow files to be posted to the server. The default value is 4096 (bytes), and you should change it to accommodate the largest file you wish to accept. See Chapter 13 for details of the `web.config` and `machine.config` configuration files.

The HtmlInputHidden Control

In the days before ASP.NET, we used `hidden`-type `input` controls to persist values between pages. In fact, this is what ASP.NET does behind the scenes to maintain the VIEWSTATE of the page, as we've seen previously in this chapter. However, there may still be uses for the control in your applications. For example, we can use them to store values within the page on the client, and have these values posted back to our server without them being visible in the page.

The demonstration page we provide shows how you can set the properties for an `HtmlInputHidden` control – basically the `Name` and `Value`:

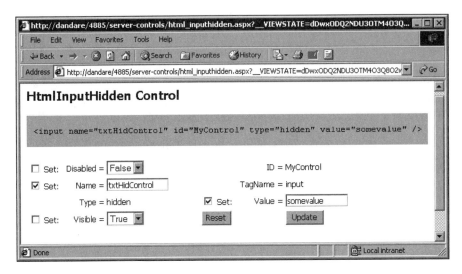

The HTML we use to create the server control in the source code for the page is:

```
<input type="hidden" id="MyControl" runat="server" />
```

Notice that we have set the value True for the Visible property. Don't be confused by this – the Visible property simply defines whether or not the HTML output generated by the control will actually be included in the output for the page, in other words in the HTML that the server returns to the client. It doesn't make the control "visible" or "hidden".

If we set the Visible property to False, the control itself will not be part of the page we create. You can try this yourself, and you'll see that the gray area that shows the output from the control is then empty. This feature allows us to dynamically hide and display controls when required.

The HtmlSelect Control

HTML defines only one way to create list box controls, the HTML <select> element. This is implemented as the server control named HtmlSelect. Our demonstration page uses data binding to create the list of options for the control, using a pre-populated HashTable object as the DataSource:

```
Dim tabValues As New HashTable(5)
tabValues.Add("Microsoft", 49.56)
tabValues.Add("Sun", 28.33)
tabValues.Add("IBM", 55)
tabValues.Add("Compaq", 20.74)
tabValues.Add("Oracle", 41.1)
MyControl.DataSource = tabValues
```

You'll see more about data binding in Chapter 7. In the meantime, you can experiment with the results here. A HashTable is similar to the Dictionary object found in ASP 3.0, with each value (in our case the numbers) being identified by a key (in our case the company names). The demonstration page allows you to set the DataTextField and DataValueField properties, which specify whether the property value should come from the Key or the Value in the HashTable. To see the effect that this has on the list, try swapping the values over in the page:

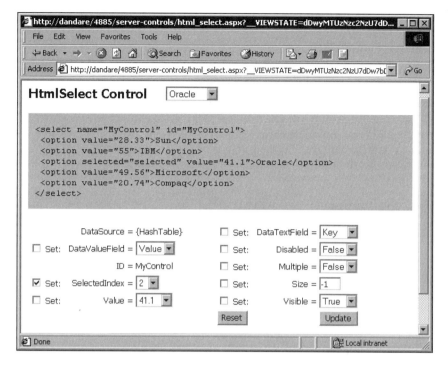

The HTML we use to create the server control in the source code for the page is:

```
<select id="MyControl" runat="server" />
```

The HashTable is very useful in this scenario, as it allows the options in the list to use some readable text, while the actual values that are submitted to the server can be different. An example would be the use of part numbers for the values, with the text of each option showing the part name or description.

Creating List Content with ListItem Objects

Instead of populating the list using data binding, we can just use <option> elements in the traditional way:

```
<select id="MyControl" runat="server">
 <option value="value1">Option 1 Text</option>
 <option value="value2">Option 2 Text</option>
 <option value="value3">Option 3 Text</option>
</select>
```

Note that we haven't marked the <option> element as runat="server". There is no need, as they will automatically be converted into ListItem objects when the page is compiled.

A ListItem object is not actually a server control, though it is part of the same namespace as the ASP.NET Web Form controls classes (which we'll look at in more detail in the next chapter). In the meantime, it's enough to know that this object exposes three useful properties:

`Selected`	Sets or returns a Boolean value indicating if this item is selected in the list. Useful for iterating through the list when the control allows multiple selections to be made by clicking while holding down the *Shift* and *Ctrl* keys.
`Text`	Sets or returns the text that is displayed in the list control for this item.
`Value`	Sets or returns the value that is returned when this item in the list is selected.

To create a multiple-selection list, just change the `Multiple` and `Size` properties in the demonstration page and click **Update**. In our example, even after doing so, you can still only select a single item using the input control for the `SelectedIndex` property, but the demonstration control at the top of the page then works as a multiple-selection list:

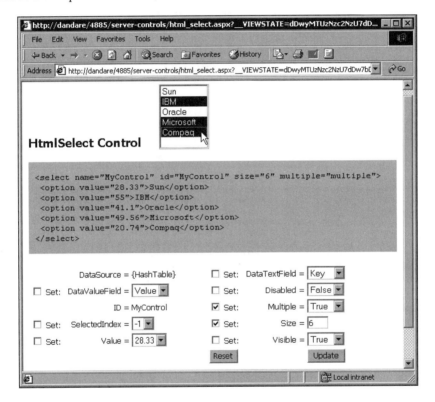

We'll look at how we use the `ListItem` *object in a list control to extract the list of selected items shortly, when we examine how we work with the events that the HTML controls raise.*

The HtmlTextArea Control

When we need to display a multi-line textbox in a Web page, we use the `<textarea>` element. This is implemented by the server control named `HtmlTextArea`. It has the specific properties required to set the number of rows and columns in the control, as well as the name and value. Notice that, in this case, the value is actually the content rather than an attribute – the text that lies between the opening and closing `<textarea>` tags:

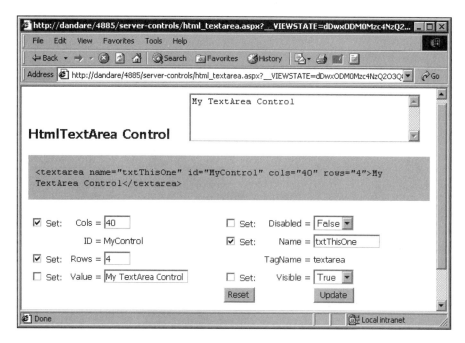

The HTML we use to create the server control in the source code for the page is:

```
<textarea id="MyControl" runat="server">My TextArea Control</textarea>
```

The HtmlTable, HtmlTableRow, HtmlTableCell Controls

The final HTML control is actually a combination of several controls. We can create tables dynamically on the server, and save ourselves a lot of hand coding, using an `HtmlTable` server control and the associated `HtmlTableRow` and `HtmlTableCell` controls. Our demonstration page shows how we can build tables with the specified number of rows and columns, and then populate the cells on demand (these controls cannot be used declaratively). The page also allows you to experiment with some of the other common properties of the `HtmlTable` control – for example changing the alignment of the table within the page, the spacing and padding of the cells, the height, width, and border styles, and so on:

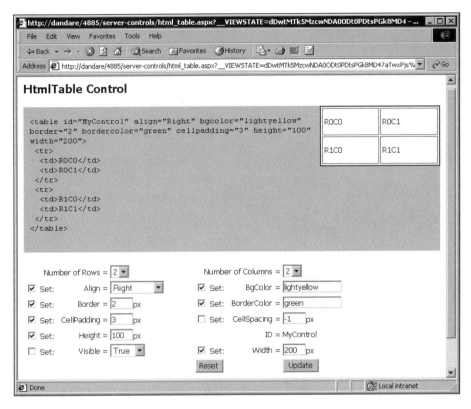

While we've only shown the properties for the HtmlTable control in our demonstration page, you can also use very similar sets of properties for the HtmlTableRow and HtmlTableCell controls. For the HtmlTableRow control, the commonly used properties are: Align, BgColor, Border, BorderColor, Height, and VAlign. For the HtmlTableCell control, they are: Align, BgColor, Border, BorderColor, ColSpan, Height, NoWrap, RowSpan, VAlign, and Width.

The Code To Create a Table

To create a table using the HtmlTable, HtmlTableRow, and HtmlTableCell server controls we first add an HtmlTable control to the page like this:

```
<table id="MyControl" runat="server" />
```

Then we have to create each cell in turn and add it to a row, then add the row to the table. In our demonstration page, we use this code:

```
'get values for number of rows and columns from drop-down lists
Dim intRows As Integer = selRows.Value
Dim intCols As Integer = selCols.Value

'declare the local variables we'll need
Dim intRowCount, intColCount As Integer

'declare variables to hold an HtmlTableRow and HtmlTableCell
Dim objRow As HtmlTableRow
Dim objCell As HtmlTableCell

'loop for the number of rows required
For intRowCount = 0 To intRows - 1

  'create a new row control
  objRow = New HtmlTableRow()

  'loop for the number of columns required
  For intColCount = 0 To intCols - 1

    'create a new table cell control and set the content
    objCell = New HtmlTableCell()
    objCell.InnerHtml = "R" & intRowCount & "C" & intColCount

    'add each cell to the new row
    objRow.Cells.Add(objCell)
  Next

  'add the new row to the table
  MyControl.Rows.Add(objRow)

Next 'go to the next row
```

Reacting to the ServerClick and ServerChange Events

Our examples so far have shown how we can change the appearance and behavior of the HTML controls by setting properties. However, we also interact with them by responding to the events that they raise. There are two events we can use, `ServerClick` and `ServerChange`. We'll look at each one in turn.

Handling the ServerClick Event

The `ServerClick` event occurs for the `HtmlAnchor`, `HtmlButton`, `HtmlInputButton`, and `HtmlInputImage` controls. Our demonstration page shows the latter three of these controls, which is where we normally use this event. As you click a button, a message indicating that the event occurred is displayed.

As you can see, for the image button we can also get extra information, the *x* and *y* coordinates of the mouse pointer within the image. This could be used to create a server-side image map – your code could easily examine the coordinates and take different actions, depending on which area of the image was clicked.

The code we use in this page defines a form and the three button controls. Notice that the onserverclick attribute is set to one of two event handlers – MyCode or MyImageCode:

```
<form runat="server">

 <input id="MyButton" type="button" value="My Button"
     onserverclick="MyCode" runat="server" />

 <input id="MySubmitButton" type="submit" value="My Submit Button"
     onserverclick="MyCode" runat="server" />

 <input id="MyImageButton" type="image" src="ClickmeButton.gif"
     onserverclick="MyImageCode" runat="server" />

</form>
```

The page also contains a `<div>` where we'll display the messages about the events. Notice that we have disabled VIEWSTATE for this control so that the message will not be persisted across postbacks:

```
<div id="divResult" runat="server" enableviewstate="false" />
```

The two event handlers are shown next. Each receives two parameters when the event occurs. The first parameter is a reference to the object that raised the event (one of our button controls) from which we can get the ID of the source of the event.

The second parameter is an "Args" object that contains more information about the event. In the case of the HtmlInputButton the second parameter is an EventArgs object, which contains no extra useful information. However, for the HtmlInputImage control, the object is an ImageClickEventArgs object, and this includes the two fields X and Y that contain the coordinates of the mouse pointer when the event was raised:

```
<script runat="server">

  Sub MyCode(objSender As Object, objArgs As EventArgs)
   divResult.InnerHtml += "ServerClick event detected in control '" _
          & objSender.ID & "'<br />"
  End Sub

  Sub MyImageCode(objSender As Object, objArgs As ImageClickEventArgs)
   divResult.InnerHtml += "ServerClick event detected in control '" _
          & objSender.ID & "' at X=" & objArgs.X _
          & " Y=" & objArgs.Y & "<br />"
  End Sub

</script>
```

Handling the ServerChange Event

The `ServerClick` event seems reasonably intuitive to use – when a button is clicked the form is posted back to the server and the event can be handled in our server-side code. But what about the `ServerChange` event? This occurs for controls that don't automatically submit the form they are on, for example `HtmlInputText`, `HtmlInputCheckBox`, `HtmlInputRadioButton`, `HtmlInputHidden`, `HtmlTextArea`, and `HtmlSelect`. So, how (and when) can our server-based code react to the event?

In fact, the event is very useful because it is raised when the page is submitted by any other control, and occurs for every control where the value has changed since the page was loaded (sent to the client). Our demonstration page shows this. It contains three different types of control that expose the `ServerChange` event, and a **Submit** button that simply submits the form to the server:

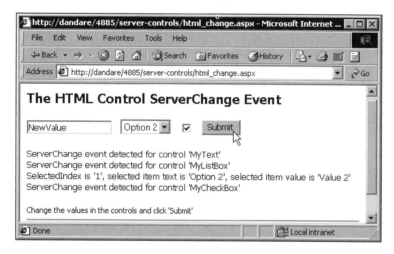

You can see that we detected three `ServerChange` events, and they occur in the order that the controls appear in the source of the page. You can also see that we're displaying the values from the option that is selected in the `HtmlSelect` control (the values for the `SelectedIndex` start at zero).

The declarative page syntax (that is the HTML source) to create the form and the server controls is shown next. You can see that the `onserverchange` attributes point to two event handlers in our page named `MyCode` and `MyListCode`. Notice also that, in this case, the **Submit** button is **not** a server control – we haven't included the `runat="server"` attribute in the `<input type="submit">` element. We don't need to access the control on our server – we just want it to submit the form:

```
<form runat="server">

  <input id="MyText" type="text" value="OriginalValue"
      onserverchange="MyCode" runat="server" />

  <select id="MyListBox" onserverchange="MyListCode" runat="server">
   <option value="Value 1">Option 1</option>
   <option value="Value 2">Option 2</option>
   <option value="Value 3">Option 3</option>
  </select>
```

```
<input id="MyCheckBox" type="checkbox"
     onserverchange="MyCode" runat="server" />

<input type="submit" value="Submit" />

</form>

<div id="divResult" runat="server" enableviewstate="false" />
```

The event handler named `MyCode` is just about identical to the previous `ServerClick` event example, simply displaying the event name and the `ID` of the control that raised the event.

```
<script runat="server">

  Sub MyCode(objSender As Object, objArgs As EventArgs)
    divResult.InnerHtml += "ServerChange event detected for control '" _
          & objSender.ID & "'<br />"
  End Sub
...
```

However, the `MyListCode` event handler needs to extract the selected value from the drop-down list created by our `HtmlSelect` control. We'll see how it does this in the next section.

Getting the Selected Values from HtmlSelect List Controls

We've seen how the server control that creates list boxes or drop-down lists is made up of an `HtmlSelect` control that contains child `ListItem` elements. The `ServerClick` event handler demonstration page we've just been looking at uses code similar to the following to create a list control:

```
<select id="MyListBox" onserverchange="MyListCode" runat="server">
<option value="Value 1">Option 1</option>
<option value="Value 2">Option 2</option>
<option value="Value 3">Option 3</option>
<option value="Value 4">Option 4</option>
<option value="Value 5">Option 5</option>
</select>
```

The simplest way to get the "value" of the currently selected item is to query the `Value` property of the list control:

```
strValue = MyListBox.Value
```

However, this may not return what you need. As with the normal HTML `<select>` list, the `Value` of the control returns the content of the `value` attribute for the currently selected item, or for the first selected item (the one with the lowest index) if there is more than one item selected. If there are no value attributes in the `<option>` elements, it returns instead the content of the first selected `<option>` element – in other words, the text that is displayed in the list.

However, it's usually better to be more specific and extract the values we actually want – and we have to do this if we want to get both the content of the `value` attribute *and* the text content. To extract the values from the `ListItem` objects for each `<option>` element, we use the `Items` collection of the parent control (the `HtmlSelect` control). The `SelectedIndex` property of the `HtmlSelect` control returns the index of the first item that is selected in the list, so we can extract the text and value of that item using:

```
    strText = MyListBox.Items(MyListBox.SelectedIndex).Text
    strValue = MyListBox.Items(MyListBox.SelectedIndex).Value
```

So, in our event handler named `MyListCode`, we first get the id of the `HtmlSelect` control that raised the event and then we can extract the text and value of the selected list item:

```
    ...
    Sub MyListCode(objSender As Object, objArgs As EventArgs)
      divResult.InnerHtml += "ServerChange event detected for control '" _
            & objSender.ID & "'<br />SelectedIndex is '" _
            & objSender.SelectedIndex _
            & "', selected item text is '" _
            & objSender.Items(objSender.SelectedIndex).Text _
            & "', selected item value is '" _
            & objSender.Items(objSender.SelectedIndex).Value   End Sub
  </script>
```

Getting Multiple Selected Values from List Controls

The technique just described is fine if the list control only allows one item to be selected: that is, in terms of the `HtmlSelect` control, the `Multiple` property is `False`. However, if it is `True`, users can select more than one item in the list by holding the *Shift* or *Ctrl* keys while clicking. In this case, the `SelectedIndex` and `SelectedItem` properties only return the **first** item that is selected (the one with the lowest index).

To detect which items are selected in a multi-selection list (none, one, or more), we query the `Selected` property of each `ListItem` object within the list. Probably the easiest way is to use a `For Each...Next` construct. In the following code, the event handler creates a `String` variable to hold the result and a variable of type `ListItem` to hold each item in the list as we iterate through it:

```
    Sub MyListCode(objSender As Object, objArgs As EventArgs)
      Dim strResult As String
      strResult = "The following items were selected:<br />"
      Dim objItem As ListItem
      For Each objItem in objSender.Items
        If objItem.Selected Then
          strResult += objItem.Text & " = " & objItem.Value & "<br />"
        End If
      Next
      outMessage.InnerHtml = strResult
    End Sub
```

In the `For Each...Next` loop we reference each member of the `Items` collection for the list control in turn. If it is selected, we add the `Text` and `Value` properties to the "results" string. After examining all the items in the list we can display the "results" string in a `<div>` control. The screenshot here shows the result.

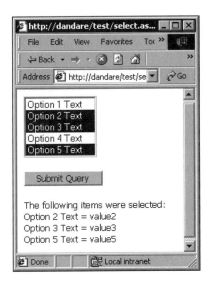

The ASP.NET Input Validation Controls

One of the most tiresome tasks when building interactive web forms is the requirement for validating values that the user enters into input controls. This is particularly the case if we need to perform client-side validation as well as validating the values on the server when the page is submitted. For maximum browser compatibility, we should be writing the client-side code in JavaScript – which is often more error-prone unless you are well practiced with this language. It's also often a long-winded and repetitive task.

Help is at hand with the range of **validation controls** that are included in ASP.NET. They cover almost all the common validation scenarios, and there is even a custom validation control that we can use to integrate our own specific non-standard validation requirements into the overall process. The controls available are:

`<ASP:RequiredFieldValidator>`	Checks that the validated control contains a value. It cannot be empty. Can be used in conjunction with other validators on a control to trap empty values.
`<ASP:RangeValidator>`	Checks that the value in the validated control is within a specified text or numeric range. If the validated control is empty, no validation takes place.
`<ASP:CompareValidator>`	Checks that the value in the validated control matches the value in another control or a specific value. The data type and comparison operation can be specified. If the validated control is empty, no validation takes place.

`<ASP:RegularExpressionValidator>`	Checks that the value in the validated control matches a specified regular expression. If the validated control is empty, no validation takes place.
`<ASP:CustomValidator>`	Performs user-defined validation on an input control using a specified function (client-side, server-side or both). If the validated control is empty, no validation takes place.
`<ASP:ValidationSummary>`	Displays a summary of all current validation errors.

What the Input Validation Controls Do

The principle is that we associate one or more validation controls with each of the input controls we want to validate. When a user submits the page, each validation control checks the value in its associated control to see if it passes the validation test. If any fail the test, the `ValidationSummary` control will display the error messages defined for these validation controls.

The validation controls also automatically detect the browser or client device type, and will generate client-side validation code in the page for Internet Explorer 5 and above (in future versions, they will probably support other browsers as well). This client-side code uses DHTML to display the content of the validation control (the text or characters between the opening and closing tags of the validation control) in the page dynamically, as the user tabs from one control to the next. It also prevents the page from being submitted if any of the validation tests fail. This gives a far more responsive interface, much like traditional handcrafted client-side validation code can do. You can see an example of this in the demonstration application we provide, under the subsection "Other Controls" in the left hand pane.

Protecting Against Spoofed Values

The validation controls also help to protect against malicious use of our pages. Client-side validation is great, but users could create their own pages (or edit the page we deliver to them) so that client-side validation does not take place. In this case, they could possibly "spoof" our server by submitting invalid values. However, even if the validation controls are performing client-side validation, they always perform the same checks server-side as well when the page is submitted, so we get the best of both worlds automatically.

We can turn off client-side validation if we don't need it, and we can also check the result for each validation control individually when the page is submitted. This allows us to create custom error messages rather than using the `ValidationSummary` control if preferred. We can also specify that particular "submit" buttons or controls will not cause validation to occur (as we'll see later in this chapter). This allows us to include a "Cancel" button in a page that allows the user to abandon the page without having to fill in valid values for the controls.

The BaseValidator Class

All of the validation controls inherit from the base class `BaseValidator`, which is part of the class library namespace `System.Web.UI.WebControls`. `BaseValidator` exposes a series of properties and methods that are common to all the validation controls. The most commonly used ones are:

`ControlToValidate` property	Sets or returns the name of the input control containing the value to be validated.
`EnableClientScript` property	Sets or returns a Boolean value indicating whether client-side validation is enabled where the client supports this.
`Enabled` property	Sets or returns a Boolean value indicating if validation will be carried out.
`ErrorMessage` property	Sets or returns the text of the error message that is displayed by the `ValidationSummary` control when validation fails.
`IsValid` property	Returns a Boolean value indicating if the value in the associated input control passed the validation test.
`Validate` method	Performs validation on the associated input control and updates the `IsValid` property.

The Specific Validation Control Members

Each of the validation controls also has properties and methods (and in one case an event) that are specific to that control type:

Control	Properties	Events
`RequiredFieldValidator`	`InitialValue`	*- none -*
`RangeValidator`	`MaximumValue`, `MinimumValue`, `Type`	*- none -*
`CompareValidator`	`ControlToCompare`, `Operator`, `Type`, `ValueToCompare`	*- none -*
`RegularExpression Validator`	`ValidationExpression`	*- none -*
`CustomValidator`	`ClientValidationFunction`	`OnServerValidate`
`ValidationSummary`	`DisplayMode`, `ShowHeaderText`, `ShowMessageBox`, `ShowSummary`	*- none -*

Most are self-explanatory, though we will look at all the validation controls in the next section and see how these properties and the single event are used.

Using the Validation Controls

The demonstration application we provide includes a page that you can use to experiment with the validation controls (open the **Other Controls** section of the left hand menu). The page contains several textboxes where you have to enter specific values in order for validation to be successful. If you enter invalid values and then click the **Submit** button, a summary of all the errors is displayed:

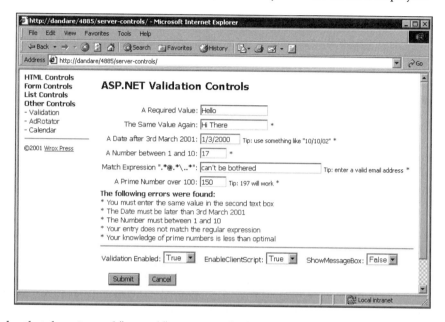

Notice also that there is a red "asterisk" next to each control where validation failed. If you are using Internet Explorer 5 or above, these asterisks appear after you tab from the control to the next one without requiring the page to be submitted. In other browsers they only appear when the page is submitted. Once you enter valid values for all the controls and click **Submit**, a message is displayed showing that validation at `Page` level succeeded:

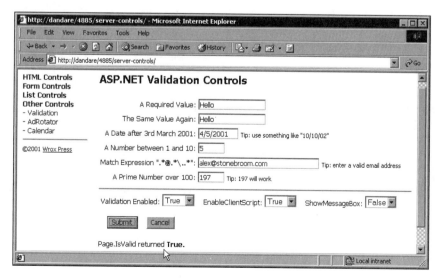

We'll examine each of the validation controls we use in this demonstration page next, then move on to look at other issues such as checking if the complete page is valid during postback, and enabling and disabling client-side and server-side validation.

The RequiredFieldValidator Control

The first textbox requires a value to be entered before validation can succeed. The source code we use for this is:

```
A Required Value:
<input type="text" id="txtRequired" size="20" runat="server" />
<asp:RequiredFieldValidator id="valRequired" runat="server"
   ControlToValidate="txtRequired"
   ErrorMessage="* You must enter a value in the first textbox"
   Display="dynamic">
   *
</asp:RequiredFieldValidator>
```

We've specified the `<input>` control named `txtRequired` as the control to be validated, and an error message that will be displayed by the `ValidationSummary` control if validation fails when the user attempts to submit the page. An asterisk character is used as the content of the control. Any text placed here will be displayed in the output (at the point where the validation control is actually located in the page) to indicate to the user that the associated control contains an invalid value. We can change the color of this text from the default of red using the `ForeColor` attribute if required.

The value of the `Display` property determines if the text content of the validation control will take up space in the page even when not displayed (that is, whether it will be set to "hidden" but still inserted into the page or just omitted from the page when not required). This means that we can control the layout of, for example, a table by setting the attribute `Display="static"` to prevent the width of the column containing the validation control from changing when the "error" characters are displayed.

The CompareValidator Control

The second text box requires the same value as the first one in order to pass the validation test. The code we use for this control and its associated validation control is:

```
The Same Value Again:
<input type="text" id="txtCompare" size="20" runat="server" />
<asp:CompareValidator id="valCompare" runat="server"
   ControlToValidate="txtCompare"
   ControlToCompare="txtRequired"
   Operator="Equal"
   ErrorMessage="* You must enter same value in the second textbox"
   Display="dynamic">
   *
</asp:CompareValidator>
```

In this case, we set the `ControlToCompare` property to the name of the first textbox, which contains the value we want to compare this textbox value with. We also get to specify the type of comparison (`Equal`, `GreaterThan`, `LessThanOrEqual`, etc.).

Remember that only the `RequiredFieldValidator` *returns an invalid result when a text control on the page is left empty. This is intentional, and you have to associate a* `RequiredFieldValidator` **and** *any other specific validation controls you require if you don't want the user to be able to submit empty values.*

The third textbox in the demonstration page also uses a `CompareValidator` control, but this time we're using it in a different way. We're comparing the value in this textbox to a fixed value, and using a comparison based on a date instead of the default `String` type (as returned by a textbox control):

```
A Date after 3rd March 2001:
<input type="text" id="txtCompareDate" size="10" runat="server" />
<asp:CompareValidator id="valCompareDate" runat="server"
   ControlToValidate="txtCompareDate"
   ValueToCompare="3/3/2001"
   Operator="GreaterThan"
   Type="Date"
   ErrorMessage="* The Date must be later than 3rd March 2001"
   Display="dynamic">
   *
</asp:CompareValidator>
```

We specify the fixed value in the `ValueToCompare` property, an `Operator` for the comparison, and the `Type` of comparison. This is simply the data type of the value we're comparing to (that is the data type of the fixed value), and can be one of `"Currency"`, `"Double"`, `"Date"`, `"Integer"`, or `"String"`.

The RangeValidator Control

The fourth textbox requires a value that is between two specified values. We use the `RangeValidator` here, and indicate the `MaximumValue` and `MinumumValue` in the respective properties. We also specify the `Type` of comparison to use when validating the content of the associated control:

```
A Number between 1 and 10:
<input type="text" id="txtRange" size="5" runat="server" />
<asp:RangeValidator id="valRange" runat="server"
   ControlToValidate="txtRange"
   MaximumValue="10"
   MinimumValue="1"
   Type="Integer"
   ErrorMessage="* The Number must between 1 and 10"
   Display="dynamic">
   *
</asp:RangeValidator>
```

The RegularExpressionValidator Control

When we want to validate complex text values, we can use a `RegularExpressionValidator` control. The fifth textbox on our demonstration page uses this control to force the entry of a valid e-mail address. An appropriate regular expression is provided for the `ValidationExpression` property:

```
Match Expression "<b>.*@.*\..*</b>":
<input type="text" id="txtRegExpr" size="40" runat="server" />
<asp:RegularExpressionValidator id="valRegExpr" runat="server"
    ControlToValidate="txtRegExpr"
    ValidationExpression=".*@.*\..*"
    ErrorMessage="* Your entry does not match the regular expression"
    Display="dynamic">
    *
</asp:RegularExpressionValidator>
```

The CustomValidator Control

For those occasions when the validation we need to perform is too complex for any of the standard validation controls, we can use a CustomValidator control. The final textbox in the page, which in fact has two validation controls associated with it, demonstrates this. We use a CompareValidator to ensure that a value greater than 100 has been entered, and a CustomValidator to validate the value itself:

```
A Prime Number over 100:
<input type="text" id="txtCustom" size="5" runat="server" />
<asp:CompareValidator id="valComparePrime" runat="server"
    ControlToValidate="txtCustom"
    ValueToCompare="100"
    Operator="GreaterThan"
    Type="Integer"
    ErrorMessage="* The Prime Number must be greater than 100"
    Display="dynamic">
    *
</asp:CompareValidator>
<asp:CustomValidator id="valCustom" runat="server"
    ControlToValidate="txtCustom"
    ClientValidationFunction="ClientValidate"
    OnServerValidate="ServerValidate"
    ErrorMessage="* Your knowledge of prime numbers is not optimal"
    Display="dynamic">
    *
</asp:CustomValidator>
```

The Custom Validation Functions

The CustomValidator control provides two properties named ClientValidationFunction and OnServerValidate, where we specify the names of custom functions we create (and include within the page) to validate the value. The ClientValidationFunction is usually written in JavaScript for maximum compatibility, as it is included in the page we send to the browser so that the validation can be carried out client-side. In our example page we used the following code:

```
<script language="JScript">
<!--
// client-side validation function for CustomValidator
function ClientValidate(objSource, objArgs) {
  var blnValid = true;
  var intNumber = objArgs.Value;
  if (intNumber % 2 == 1) {
   var intDivisor = Math.floor(intNumber / 3);
```

```
      if (intDivisor > 2) {
       for (var i = 3; i <= intDivisor; i = i + 2) {
        if (intNumber % intDivisor == 0) {
         blnValid = false;
         break;
        }
       }
      }
      else
       blnValid = false;
     }
     else
      blnValid = false;
      objArgs.IsValid = blnValid
      return;
    }
    //-->
    </script>
```

Notice how the validation control supplies a reference to itself (objSource) and an object containing the arguments for the function call (objArgs). We get the value of the associated control from the Value field of objArgs, and we set the IsValid field of objArgs to indicate whether our custom validation succeeded or not.

For server-side validation, we use the same logic. However, as our page is written in VB, we have to use VB to create the server-side validation function as well (in the current version of ASP.NET there can only be one language server-side per page). In this case, our function receives as parameters a reference to the validation control and a ServerValidateEventArgs object that contains the value of the associated control as its Value property:

```
Sub ServerValidate(objSource As Object,
          objArgs As ServerValidateEventArgs)
  Dim blnValid As Boolean = True
  Try
    Dim intNumber As Integer = objArgs.Value
    'check that it's an odd number
    If intNumber Mod 2 = 1 Then
     'get the largest possible divisor
     Dim intDivisor As Integer = intNumber \ 3
     If intDivisor > 2 Then
       Dim intLoop As Integer
       'check using each divisor in turn
       For intLoop = 3 To intDivisor Step 2
        If intNumber Mod intDivisor = 0 Then
         blnValid = False
         Exit For
        End If
       Next
     Else
      blnValid = False
     End If
    Else
     blnValid = False
```

```
     End If
   Catch objError As Exception
     blnValid =False
   Finally
     objArgs.IsValid = blnValid
   End Try
 End Sub
```

The ValidationSummary Control

The list of errors that is shown when the page is submitted with any invalid value is created automatically by a ValidationSummary control within our demonstration page. In our example, we've specified the heading we want in the HeaderText property and set the ShowSummary property to True so that the value of the ErrorMessage property of each of the other validation controls that fail to validate their associated text box is displayed:

```
<asp:ValidationSummary id="valSummary" runat="server"
    HeaderText="<b>The following errors were found:</b>"
    ShowSummary="true" DisplayMode="List" />
```

The DisplayMode allows us to choose the type of output for the error messages. The options are List, BulletList, and SingleParagraph, and we can also use the ForeColor property to set the color for the messages. Another useful property is ShowMessageBox. Setting it to True causes the validation error messages to be displayed in an Alert dialog on the client instead of in the page itself. You can try this in our demonstration page using the appropriate drop-down list:

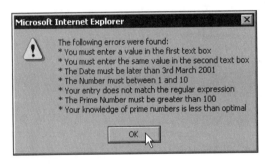

Checking If a Page is Valid

Our demonstration page contains two buttons marked "Submit" and "Cancel". Both are HTML input type="submit" buttons that submit the page to the server for processing. The "Submit" button calls the server-side routine ConfirmEntry, which would be used in a complete application to carry out the process for which you collected the values from the user:

```
<input type="submit" id="cmdConfirm" value="Submit" runat="server"
                              onserverclick="ConfirmEntry">
```

Each validation control, and the Page object itself, exposes an IsValid property. Our demonstration page displays the value of the Page.IsValid property when you click the Submit button. Just bear in mind that, unless you disable client-side validation first using the EnableClientScript drop-down list, you won't be able to submit an invalid page using this button:

```
Sub ConfirmEntry(objSender As Object, objArgs As EventArgs)
  outMessage.InnerHtml = "Page.IsValid returned <b>" _
          & Page.IsValid & ".</b>"
End Sub
```

If we only want to determine the state of an individual validation control (perhaps to check which ones contain invalid values), we can query that controls own `IsValid` property. For example, to get the value for the validation control with the `id` of `valRegExpr`, we could use:

```
blnValidated = valRegExpr.IsValid
```

Canceling Validation of a Page

The second button on our page calls the server-side routine `CancelEntry`, and the user would click this button to abandon the data entry and close the page. This button also has to submit the page to the server, but when client-side validation is in use (the default on most script-enabled browsers) the user can't submit the page while it contains invalid values. In other words, a traditional submit button that we might use as a "Cancel" button to abandon the page will still cause validation to occur and prevent the page from being submitted.

The solution is to set the `CausesValidation` property for this button to `False`. All button-type controls (`HtmlButton`, `HtmlInputButton`, `HtmlInputImage`, and the equivalents in the ASP Web Form controls that we'll look at in the next chapter) have this property. The default value is `True`, which means that they will cause validation unless we "turn it off".

So, our "Cancel" button looks like this:

```
<input type="submit" id="cmdCancel" value="Cancel" runat="server"
           CausesValidation="False" onserverclick="CancelEntry">
```

The `CancelEntry` event handler that is executed when the button is clicked, simply displays a message indicating that validation was not carried out.

The Enabled and EnableClientScript Properties

We can also disable client-side, server-side, or both types of validation in our server-side code by changing the value of the `Enabled` and `EnableClientScript` properties of the appropriate validation control(s). This allows us, for example, to force the browser to use only server-side validation even if it supports dynamic client-side validation. The following code taken from our demonstration page shows how we can iterate through the collection of validation controls and set these properties:

```
Sub Page_Load()
  Dim objValidator As BaseValidator
  For Each objValidator In Page.Validators
    objValidator.Enabled = lstEnabled.SelectedItem.Text
    objValidator.EnableClientScript = lstClientScript.SelectedItem.Text
  Next
End Sub
```

In our example, this code is executed each time the page loads, and the property settings are controlled by two drop-down lists near the bottom of the page:

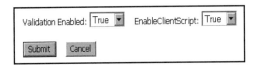

Summary

In this chapter, we've explored the concept of server controls in general, and concentrated on the set of **HTML server controls** and the **validation controls** that are provided with ASP.NET. Server controls are at the heart of ASP.NET development techniques, providing us with a programming model that is event driven, and which is much closer to the way that we build traditional executable applications using environments like Visual Basic, C++, and other languages.

In conjunction with other features in ASP.NET and the .NET framework as a whole (such as the postback architecture and the comprehensive class library), building powerful, intuitive, and attractive Web-based applications just got a lot easier.

In fact, we can summarize the advantages of using server controls. They automatically provide:

- ❑   HTML output that creates the elements to implement the control in the browser
- ❑   An object within the page that we can program against on the server
- ❑   Automatic maintenance of the control's value (or state)
- ❑   Simple access to the control values without having to dig into the Request object
- ❑   The ability to react to events, and so create better structured pages
- ❑   A common approach to building user interfaces as Web pages
- ❑   The ability to more easily address different types of client device

In the next chapter, we move on to look at another set of server controls that are provided with ASP.NET. These are the useful and powerful **Web Form controls**.

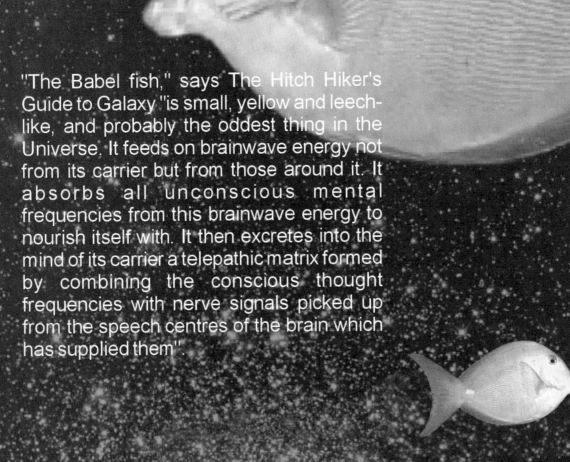

"The Babel fish," says The Hitch Hiker's Guide to Galaxy "is small, yellow and leech-like, and probably the oddest thing in the Universe. It feeds on brainwave energy not from its carrier but from those around it. It absorbs all unconscious mental frequencies from this brainwave energy to nourish itself with. It then excretes into the mind of its carrier a telepathic matrix formed by combining the conscious thought frequencies with nerve signals picked up from the speech centres of the brain which has supplied them".

The practical upshot of all this is that if you stick a Babel fish in your ear you can instantly understand anything said to you in any form of language. The speech patterns you actually hear decode the brainwave matrix which has been fed into your mind by your Babel fish.

6

ASP.NET Web Form Controls

In the previous chapter we looked at the range of HTML server controls and validation controls that are part of ASP.NET. We saw how they are one of the fundamental foundations on which ASP.NET is built. These controls cause our ASP.NET pages to output the HTML that implements the control elements in the browser (for example an `<input>` or `<select>` element). However, the server controls are also objects that are compiled within the page on our server, and so we can interact with them as we dynamically build the page.

More than this, the basic concept of using server controls allows us to change to a more structured event-driven programming model. This provides us with a programming environment that is cleaner and easier to work in, as well as being easier to debug when things go wrong.

However, the server controls we looked at in the previous chapter (with the exception of the validation controls) are really nothing more than server-side equivalents of the normal HTML elements that implement controls for use on a `<form>`. They still provide a valid model for building interactive forms, but we can do better. In this chapter you'll see how, as we look at:

❑   The ASP.NET Web Form controls in general

❑   The basic Web Form input and navigation server controls

❑   The Web Form server controls used for building lists

❑   The "rich" Web Form controls that provide complex compound interface elements

We start with the basic Web Form input and navigation controls.

The Basic ASP.NET Web Form Controls

As well as creating HTML elements using the HTML server controls, we can also use a set of controls that are part of ASP.NET, called the **Web Form controls** (or just **Web Controls**, after the namespace where they reside). These are all defined within the namespace System.Web.UI.WebControls. The controls that we can use, and the equivalent HTML output that they generate, are shown in the next table (the various types of list control will be covered in a later section of this chapter):

ASP.NET Web Form control	Creates HTML Element(s)
<ASP:HyperLink>	<a>...</a>
<ASP:LinkButton>	<a><img/></a>
<ASP:Image>	<img/>
<ASP:Panel>	<div>...</div>
<ASP:Label>	...
<ASP:Button>	<input type="submit"/> *or* <input type="button"/>
<ASP:TextBox>	<input type="text"/> *or* <input type="password"/> *or* <textarea>...</textarea>
<ASP:CheckBox>	<input type="checkbox"/>
<ASP:RadioButton>	<input type="radio"/>
<ASP:ImageButton>	<input type="image"/>
<ASP:Table>	<table>...</table>
<ASP:TableRow>	<tr>...</tr>
<ASP:TableCell>	<td>...</td>

Why Have Another Set of Controls?

It might seem odd to have a second set of server controls that appear to duplicate the existing HTML controls. In fact there are a couple of good reasons for this. The ASP.NET Web Form controls are designed primarily to achieve two things:

❑   To make it easier for manufacturers and developers to build tools or applications that automatically generate the UI.

❑   To simplify the process of creating interactive Web Forms, requiring less knowledge of the way that HTML controls work and making the task of using them less error-prone.

Both of these requirements are met by providing a consistent and structured interface for the controls. Unlike the HTML controls, the Web Form controls all use the same property name for a specific "value" for the control. Contrast this with the HTML controls, where the size property (attribute) of a control might be the number of rows visible in a list box or the number of characters width for a textbox. Meanwhile the number of characters width for a <textarea> element is actually the cols property.

In the Web Form controls, the same property name is used across the controls. The property names are also more intuitive, for example the ASP:TextBox control has properties named TextMode, Rows, and Columns. By setting these in different combinations, the control will generate the appropriately sized <input> element or <textarea> element. You don't have to know what the actual HTML output required is, you just set the properties of the control and let it get on with it. It can even create a password-type <input> element if you set the appropriate value for the TextMode.

On top of this, the controls add extra features that are not usually available in the basic HTML controls. You can specify automatic postback of a form when a value in a control is changed. Several of the controls also create more than one HTML element, for example they automatically add a text "label" to a checkbox or radio button.

The WebControl Base Class

Like the HTML controls we looked at earlier, most of the Web Form controls inherit their members (properties, method and events) from a base class. In this case it is WebControl, defined within the namespace System.Web.UI.WebControls. This class provides a wide range of members – many of which are only really useful if we are building our own controls that inherit from WebControl. However, the public members that we use most often are:

Attributes property	Returns a collection of all the attribute name/value pairs within the .aspx file for this control. Can be used to read and set non-standard attributes (custom attributes that are not actually part of HTML) or to access attributes where the control does not provide a specific property for that purpose.
AccessKey property	Sets or returns the keyboard shortcut key that moves the input focus to the control.
BackColor property	Sets or returns the background color of the control.
BorderColor property	Sets or returns the border color of the control.
BorderStyle property	Sets or returns the style of border for the control, in other words: solid, dotted, double, etc.
BorderWidth property	Sets or returns the width of the control border.
ClientID property	Returns the control identifier that is generated by ASP.NET.
Controls property	Returns a ControlCollection object containing references to all the child controls for this control within the page hierarchy.
Enabled property	Sets or returns a Boolean value indicating if the control is enabled.
EnableViewState property	Sets or returns a Boolean value indicating if the control should maintain its viewstate and the viewstate of any child controls when the current page request ends.

Table continued on following page

Font property	Returns information about the font used in the control.
ForeColor property	Sets or returns the foreground color used in the control, usually the color of the text.
Height property	Sets or returns the overall height of the control.
ID property	Sets or returns the identifier specified for the control.
Page property	Returns a reference to the Page object containing the control.
Parent property	Returns a reference to the parent of this control within the page hierarchy.
Style property	References a collection of all the CSS style properties (selectors) that apply to the control.
TabIndex property	Sets or returns the position of the control within the tab order of the page.
ToolTip property	Sets or returns the pop-up text that is displayed when the mouse pointer is over the control.
Visible property	Sets or returns a Boolean value indicating if the control should be rendered in the page output.
Width property	Sets or returns the overall width of the control.
DataBind method	Causes data binding to occur for the control and all of its child controls.
FindControl method	Searches within the current container for a specified server control.
HasControls method	Returns a Boolean value indicating if the control contains any child controls.
DataBinding event	Occurs when the control is being bound to a data source.

The Specific Web Form Control Classes

Each of the Web Form controls inherits from WebControl (or from another control that itself inherits from WebControl), and adds its own task-specific properties, methods, and events. Those that we commonly use for each control are listed in the next table:

Control	Properties	Event Properties
HyperLink	ImageUrl, NavigateUrl, Target, Text	*- none -*
LinkButton	CommandArgument, CommandName, Text, CausesValidation	OnClick, OnCommand

The Specific Web Form Control Classes

Image	AlternateText, ImageAlign, ImageUrl	- *none* -
Panel	BackImageUrl, HorizontalAlign, Wrap	- *none* -
Label	Text	- *none* -
Button	CommandArgument, CommandName, Text, CausesValidation	OnClick, OnCommand
TextBox	AutoPostBack, Columns, MaxLength, ReadOnly, Rows, Text, TextMode, Wrap	OnTextChanged
CheckBox	AutoPostBack, Checked, Text, TextAlign	OnCheckChanged
RadioButton	AutoPostBack, Checked, GroupName, Text, TextAlign	OnCheckChanged
ImageButton	CommandArgument, CommandName, CausesValidation	OnClick, OnCommand
Table	BackImageUrl, CellPadding, CellSpacing, GridLines, HorizontalAlign, Rows	- *none* -
TableRow	Cells, HorizontalAlign, VerticalAlign	- *none* -
TableCell	ColumnSpan, HorizontalAlign, RowSpan, Text, VerticalAlign, Wrap	- *none* -
Literal	Text	- *none* -
PlaceHolder	- *none* -	- *none* -

It should be obvious from the name what most of the properties are for, however we'll examine each control in the following sections and indicate some of the things to look out for when we use them. The sample application, which we have already seen in Chapter 5, contains pages for most of the ASP.NET Web Form controls, and we'll be using these pages to demonstrate the properties of each control:

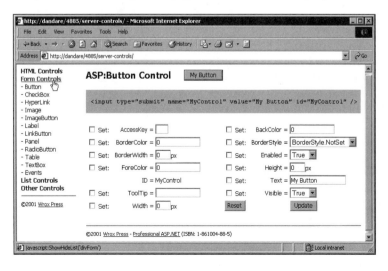

You can get the sample files for this chapter, which contain this application, from:

http://www.wrox.com/Books/Book_Details.asp?isbn=1861004885

The application is in the folder named `server-controls`.

Using the Web Form Controls

When we want to add an ASP.NET Web Form server control to our page, we define it just like an ordinary HTML element – adding the appropriate "attributes" for the properties we want to set. For example we can add an `ASP:TextBox` control to the page, in order to output an HTML textbox element, using:

```
<ASP:TextBox id="MyTextBox" BackColor="Red" Text="Enter a value..." />
```

Notice that the Web Form controls all have the `ASP` namespace prefix (upper or lowercase – it doesn't matter which) to denote that they are from the `System.Web.UI.WebControls` namespace.

One thing that makes working with the HTML server controls we used in the previous chapter easy is that all the properties are simple `String` values. For example, we specify the string value `"right"` for the `Align` property of an `HtmlImage` control to align the image to the right of any following page content. As you'll see in this section, however, it's not always as straightforward with the ASP.NET Web Form controls. Many of the properties for the ASP Web Form controls use values from an enumeration, or a reference to an object.

Setting Property Values from Enumerations

For example, to align an image to the right of any following content when using an ASP.NET `Image` server control, we set the `ImageAlign` property to the integer value that is defined for the enumeration member `ImageAlign.Right`. In this example the enumeration is named `ImageAlign`, and the member is named `Right`.

Of course, this isn't a problem when we explicitly define the properties declaratively (in other words by setting the "attributes" of a server control in the source of the page). The control knows from the property name which enumeration to use:

```
<ASP:Image Src="mypic.gif" ImageAlign="Right" runat="server" />
```

This produces the following HTML output (notice that, in the `Image` control, `border="0"` is the default if not specified otherwise):

```
<img src="mypic.gif" align="Right" border="0" />
```

However, if we need to assign a value to the property within the executable code of the page we have to use:

```
objMyImage.ImageAlign = ImageAlign.Right
```

Creating Enumeration Values Dynamically

But even this is no good if we want to assign the property values dynamically at run-time, such as when they are selected from a list (as in our demonstration pages). We have to use the **numeric value** of the appropriate enumeration member. In the case of `ImageAlign.Right` this value is 2.

If we use a `<select>` list control for the values, we can set the `Text` of each `<option>` to the name in the enumeration, and set the `Value` to the integer that this equates to. The following code shows a `<select>` list containing the complete `ImageAlign` enumeration:

```
<select id="selAlign" runat="server">
 <option value="0">ImageAlign.NotSet</option>
 <option value="1">ImageAlign.Left</option>
 <option value="2">ImageAlign.Right</option>
 <option value="3">ImageAlign.Baseline</option>
 <option value="4">ImageAlign.Top</option>
 <option value="5">ImageAlign.Middle</option>
 <option value="6">ImageAlign.Bottom</option>
 <option value="7">ImageAlign.AbsBottom</option>
 <option value="8">ImageAlign.AbsMiddle</option>
 <option value="9">ImageAlign.TextTop</option>
</select>
```

Then, to set the `ImageAlign` property, we can just assign the value from the list directly to it:

```
objMyImage.ImageAlign = selAlign.Value
```

Or we can be more specific, and use the `SelectedIndex` property of the list:

```
objMyImage.ImageAlign = selAlign.Items(selAlign.SelectedIndex).Value
```

Finding Enumeration Values

Of course, the next obvious question is how do we go about finding out the values to use for an enumeration? In fact there are a few options here. Most enumerations provide a type converter that we can use to get the value given the enumeration member as a string. In Visual Basic, we can use:

```
TypeDescriptor.GetConverter(GetType(enumeration)).ConvertFromString("member")
```

To be able to create a `TypeDescriptor` object and use its methods in our code, we must import the `ComponentModel` namespace that contains the definition of the `TypeDescriptor` class:

```
<%@Import Namespace="System.ComponentModel" %>
```

For example, to get the value of `HorizontalAlign.Left` we can use:

```
TypeDescriptor.GetConverter(GetType(HorizontalAlign)).ConvertFromString("Left")
```

Alternatively, for enumerations that don't provide a type converter, we can cast the enumeration member directly to an `Integer` variable:

```
Dim intValue = CType(HorizontalAlign.Left, Integer)
```

Another technique is to use the excellent WinCV utility that is included with the frameworks. Open it from the Run command on your .NET server's Start menu, and type in the name of the enumeration. Select the enumeration in the left-hand pane and the values are displayed in the right-hand pane. You can even click the Option button in the top right of the window to copy them to the clipboard ready to paste into your code (but note that the values are hexadecimal):

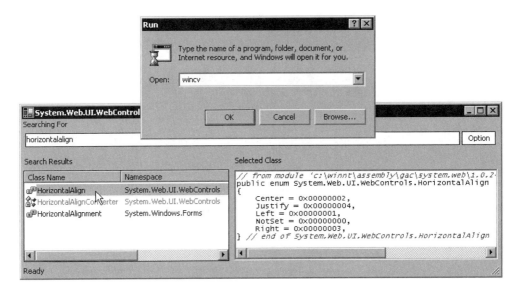

Setting Properties that are Objects

The second area where working with the ASP Web Form controls can be a little tricky, is when we want to set (or retrieve) property values that are actually references to other objects. A typical example of something that should be simple, but actually isn't when you first try it, is setting the value of a "color" property. It's not that Microsoft's developers were trying to make life awkward – it's done on purpose to provide extra features within the controls and the framework as a whole. It also allows strong type checking to be achieved by the compiler and better support in a designer tool such as Visual Studio, which would not be possible if they were string values.

As an example, the ASP Web Form controls have several properties (BackColor, ForeColor, BorderColor) that reference a Color object rather than a simple string value. When we explicitly define the colors for the controls in our source code, we can use the color names directly:

```
<asp:textbox id="MyText" Text="This is a textbox" runat="server"
            BackColor="Red" ForeColor="White" />
```

However, if we want to assign colors at run-time we have to create a Color object first and then assign this object to the appropriate property. For this, we use the shared properties and methods that the Color class exposes.

The System.Drawing.Color Class

The Color class defines shared properties for all of the standard HTML color names, such as AliceBlue, AntiqueWhite, etc. It also exposes three shared methods that create a Color object:

FromArgb	Creates a `Color` object from its 32-bit component values that define the `alpha`, `red`, `green`, and `blue` elements.
FromKnownColor	Creates a `Color` object from a specified HTML standard "known color" name, for example "AliceBlue" or "Gainsboro".
FromName	Creates a `Color` object using the specified name, which can be a "known color" name, a 32-bit value or a hexadecimal HTML-style color value such as "#ff0000" (red).

Each `Color` object also has a series of properties that returns the individual components of the current color. For example the properties A, B, G, and R return the alpha, blue, green, and red components respectively. To get the name of the color if it is one of the "known colors", we can query the Name property of the `Color` object.

To be able to create a `Color` object and use its shared properties and methods in our code, we must import the `System.Drawing` namespace that contains the definition of the `Color` class:

```
<%@Import Namespace="System.Drawing" %>
```

In our demonstration pages, we include textboxes where you can enter the colors you want for various properties of the control. For example, to set the `BackColor` property of a control we call the `FromName` method (passing it the value that was entered), and then assign the object that this method creates to the `BackColor` property of the control:

```
MyControl.BackColor = Color.FromName(txtBackColor.Value)
```

To retrieve the color from the `BackColor` property, we just have to extract the Name of the `Color` object that the property references:

```
txtForeColor.Value = MyControl.ForeColor.Name
```

The System.Web.UI.WebControls.Unit Class

Several properties of the ASP Web Form controls are references to a `Unit` object, for example the Width and Height of an `Image` control and the `BorderWidth` of a `Table` control. As with the "Color" properties, we don't have to concern ourselves with this when we explicitly define the values in our source code:

```
<asp:image id="MyImage" Src="mypic.gif" runat="server"
           Height="100px" Width="50%" />
```

However, to assign values at run-time we have to use the properties and methods exposed by the `Unit` object. The class that defines the `Unit` object is part of the same namespace as the ASP.NET Web Form controls, and so it is imported by default into our ASP pages. It exposes two properties:

Type	The type of unit that the value is measured in. One of the members of the `UnitType` enumeration (Cm, Mm, Em, Ex, Inch, Percentage, Pica, Pixel, or Point).
Value	The actual number of the units (as defined in the Type property) that make up the value.

The `Unit` class also provides three shared methods that we can use to create a `Unit` object with a specific Type property value:

Percentage	Creates a Unit object of type Percentage using the specified 32-bit signed integer.
Pixel	Creates a Unit object of type Pixel using the specified 32-bit signed integer.
Point	Creates a Unit object of type Point using the specified 32-bit signed integer.

So, if we have an Integer variable named intTheHeight that contains the value in pixels we want to set for the Height property of a control named MyControl, we can use:

```
MyControl.Height = Unit.Pixel(intTheHeight)
```

If the value comes from a textbox with the id of "txtHeight", we can use:

```
MyControl.Height = Unit.Pixel(txtHeight.Value)
```

If we want the value to be set as a percentage (say we wanted the control to be 50% of the width of the page or its container), we would use:

```
MyControl.Height = Unit.Percentage(50)
```

To retrieve the value of the Height property from the control, we query the Unit object's Value property. The following code returns "100" for the Image control we used earlier in this section:

```
txtHeight.Value = MyControl.Height.Value
```

If we want to know the type of unit, we can query the Type property of the Unit object, but this returns the integer equivalent of the UnitType enumeration. For a unit in pixels, for example, this property returns 1. However (in a similar way to the example with the HorizontalAlign enumeration), we can use a type converter to get the text name. This time we use the ConvertToString method rather than the ConvertFromString method:

```
TypeDescriptor.GetConverter(GetType(UnitType)).ConvertToString _
                                    (MyControl.Height.Type)
```

Finally, the easiest way to get the complete value in human-readable form (including the unit type) is to use the ToString method. For the same control, the following code returns "100px":

```
txtHeight.Value = MyControl.Height.Value.ToString()
```

Using the AutoPostBack Feature

When we build an interactive form using previous versions of ASP, a common technique is to use some client-side script with certain controls (such as a list box or checkbox) to automatically submit the <form> they reside on to the server for processing when the user selects a value. This allows the server to update the page in response to changes the user makes in the form.

In ASP.NET, this is now part of the feature set you get for free with the framework. Certain of the Web Form server controls (the TextBox, CheckBox, RadioButton) and all the list controls we'll look at later in the chapter, provide a property named AutoPostBack. By default this property is False. If we set it to True for a control, that control will automatically post its value, and the values of the rest of the controls on the same form, back to the server when the user selects a value.

This also raises an event on the server that we can handle and use to update the contents of the page. You can experiment with `AutoPostBack` in the samples we provide, and we'll look at how we can handle the events on the server later in this section of the chapter.

How Does AutoPostBack Work?

The mechanism to implement automatic postback is simple. It uses exactly the same techniques as we would use if we were programming it ourselves in a `<form>` page. When the `AutoPostBack` property is `True`, the server control adds a client-side event to the control – for a button-type control it's the `onclick` event, and for textboxes and list controls it's the `onchange` event:

```
<input id="MyControl" type="checkbox" name="MyControl"
       onclick="javascript:__doPostBack('MyControl','')" />
```

This causes a client-side function named `__doPostBack` to run when the control is clicked, when the selection is changed in a list, or when the user edits the content of a textbox and moves to another control. The `id` of the control is passed to this function as well.

At the same time, the `<form>` on which the control resides has two extra `HIDDEN`-type `<input>` controls added to it. These are used to pass back to the server the `id` of the control that was clicked or changed, and any value for the second parameter that the `__doPostBack` function receives:

```
<input type="hidden" name="__EVENTTARGET" value="" />
<input type="hidden" name="__EVENTARGUMENT" value="" />
```

And, of course, the client-side `__doPostBack` function is added to the page as well. It just collects the control name and any arguments, puts them into the hidden controls, and submits the form to the server:

```
<script language="javascript">
<!--
function __doPostBack(eventTarget, eventArgument) {
    var theform = document.ctrl0;
    theform.__EVENTTARGET.value = eventTarget;
    theform.__EVENTARGUMENT.value = eventArgument;
    theform.submit();
}
// -->
</script>
```

Examples of the ASP Web Form Controls

In this section, we'll briefly look at each of the basic ASP.NET Web Form controls to give you a flavor for what they do and how they can be used. We'll pick out any particularly important points about each control as we go.

The ASP:CheckBox and ASP:RadioButton Controls

We start with the controls that create individual checkboxes and radio buttons (later we'll see two controls that can create lists of checkboxes or radio buttons automatically). One extremely useful feature of the `CheckBox` and `RadioButton` controls is that they automatically create a label for the control using the value of the `Text` property – and you can place this label to the left or right of the control using the `TextAlign` property:

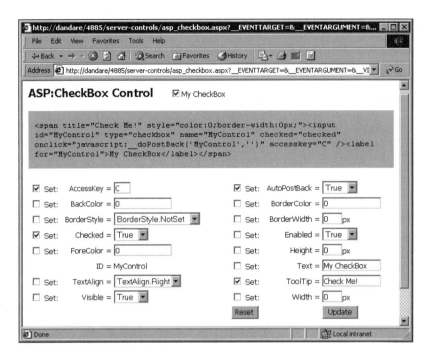

The source code we used to create the server control in this page is:

```
<ASP:CheckBox id="MyControl" Text="My CheckBox" runat="server" />
```

You can also use this page to experiment with the effects of the AutoPostBack property we discussed earlier. Also notice the AccessKey and ToolTip that make it seem like a real Visual Basic style control. These are, of course, client-side features (ToolTip sets the title attribute of the element), but they are part of the HTML 4.0 standards.

Adding Styles to Web Form Controls

The formatting features that apply to all the ASP Web Form controls are demonstrated in the next screenshot of the CheckBox control. You can see how they add a set of CSS style properties (or selectors) to the element:

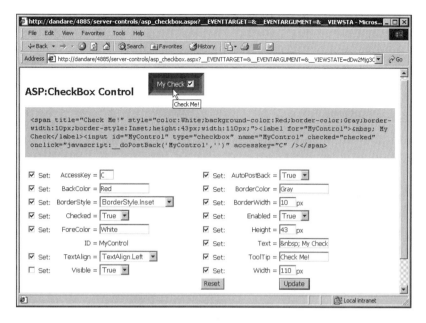

Setting the Group Name for a RadioButton Control

The `RadioButton` control is almost identical to the `CheckBox` control, except (of course) that it creates an `<input type="radio">` element instead of an `<input type="checkbox">` element. However, there is one more fundamental difference. The `RadioButton` control exposes an extra property called `GroupName`, which sets the `name` attribute of the control. You can see this in the next screenshot:

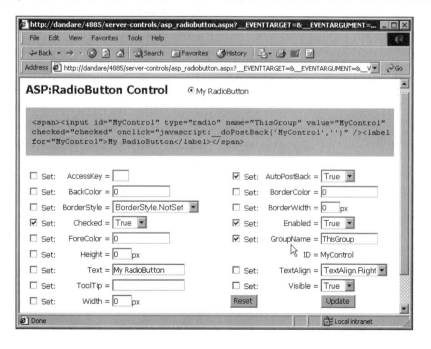

The source code we used to create the server control in this page is:

```
<ASP:RadioButton id="MyControl" Text="My RadioButton" runat="server" />
```

This feature is required for two reasons. One is the obvious reason that you must use the same name attribute for all radio buttons that you want to be part of the same mutually exclusive group. The second reason is that all the controls on a page have to have a unique id property, and this is automatically used as the name attribute as well (as you can see if you refer back to the screenshot of the CheckBox control). Unlike the HTML radio button control there is no Name property for the ASP.NET Web Form RadioButton control, so the GroupName is the only way to set the name attribute.

The ASP:HyperLink Control

This control provides an easy way to create hyperlink <a> elements. As well as the usual formatting, AccessKey, and ToolTip properties, it provides specific properties for the NavigateUrl (which sets the href attribute) and the Target property (which sets the target attribute). One other great feature is that we can set the text that appears as the hyperlink (the content of the resulting <a> element) using the Text property:

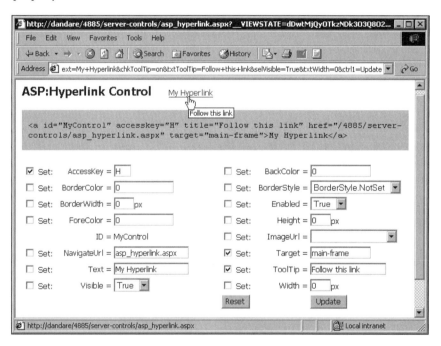

The source code we used to create the server control in this page is:

```
<ASP:Hyperlink id="MyControl" Text="My Hyperlink"
               NavigateUrl="asp_hyperlink.aspx" runat="server" />
```

Notice that there is, again, no Name property. This seems to indicate that we can't use the control to create an **anchor** in a page that another hyperlink can target. An HTML anchor element requires the name attribute to be set:

```
<a name="para1">Paragraph One</a>
```

Then we target this location in the page using an HTML element such as:

```
<a href="thepage.aspx#para1">Go To Paragraph One</a>
```

However, we can add a `name` attribute to a `Hyperlink` control either declaratively or programmatically. We do it declaratively by specifying it within the element in the source of the page:

```
<ASP:Hyperlink Name="para1" id="MyAnchor" Text="text-for-link"
               NavigateUrl="url-to-go-to" runat="server" />
```

Using the Attributes Property with Server Controls

One other solution at run-time is to use the `Attributes` property to add the attribute programmatically. This property gives us access to a collection of all the HTML attributes on a server control. So, we can access the `name` attribute using:

```
strNameAttr = MyAnchor.Attributes("name")
```

And we can set or change the `name` attribute using:

```
MyAnchor.Attributes("name") = strNewName
```

So, we can still achieve what we want without a `Name` property. This useful technique can be applied to any of the server controls – including the HTML server controls we looked at in the previous chapter. It may be useful in other cases where you want to add non-standard attributes to an element for your own purposes.

Using an Image as a Hyperlink

We often use images as hyperlinks in our pages, and the `Hyperlink` control makes this much easier than hand coding. If we specify the path to an image file as the `ImageUrl` property, that image is used in place of the `Text` property as the content of the `<a>` element. We've provided a few images to try out:

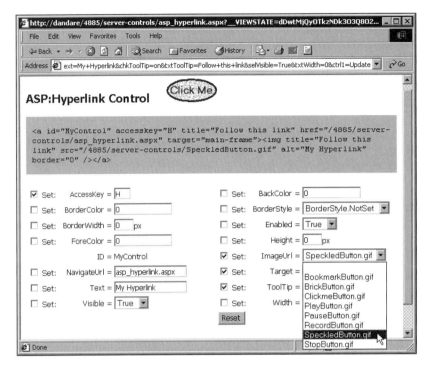

The ASP:LinkButton Control

The LinkButton control demonstrates an interesting extension to the use of an HTML `<a>` element. By default it uses the AutoPostBack feature we described earlier, specifying the client-side JavaScript function named __doPostBack as the href attribute of an `<a>` element. This means that whenever the link is clicked, the form will be posted back to the server where a Click event will be raised:

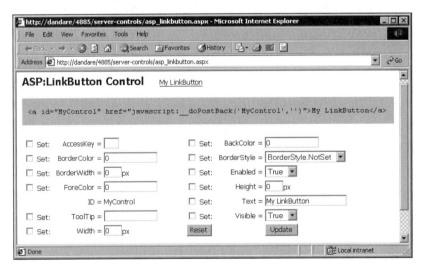

The source code we used to create the server control in this page is:

```
<ASP:LinkButton id="MyControl" Text="My LinkButton" runat="server" />
```

We specify the "clickable" text using the Text property in the same way as with a Hyperlink control, but in this control there is no option to use an image instead of text. For that we have to use an ImageButton control (described shortly) instead.

The ASP:Image Control

When we want to display an image in our page, and to be able to access the control in our server-side code, we can use the ASP.NET Image server control. There are properties available that specify all the usual attributes for an <img> element, including the size, an AccessKey, the ToolTip, the alignment in relation to surrounding content, the border style, and the border and background colors:

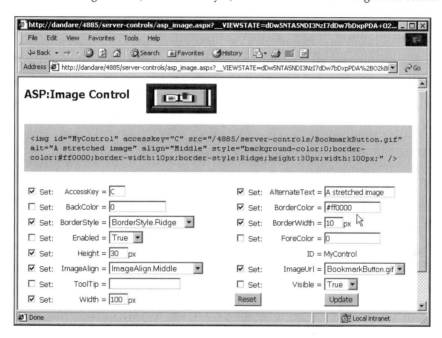

The source code we used to create the server control in this page is:

```
<ASP:Image id="MyControl" ImageUrl="BookmarkButton.gif" runat="server" />
```

Again, we've provided a few images for you to experiment with. Notice also how we can specify the values for the "Color" properties (BorderColor in the screenshot above) using a standard HTML-style hexadecimal color value.

The ASP:Panel Control

While it might sound like an exotic new feature to use in your pages, the Panel control is actually just a way of creating a formatted HTML <div> element. We can specify the size and style of the element, and add a background image (though you should realize that – as with all the server controls – some browsers may not support all the style properties we apply):

245

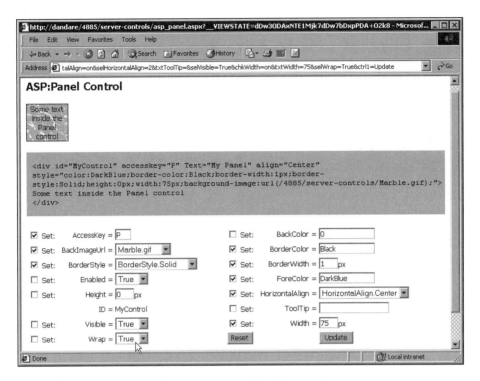

The source code we used to create the server control in this page is:

```
<ASP:Panel id="MyControl" Text="My Panel" runat="server">
Some text inside the Panel control</ASP:Panel>
```

A useful feature is the ability to set the width of the control and then turn text wrapping on and off using the `Wrap` property. Remember that we can also add our own extra style properties to any server control using the `Style` collection:

```
MyControl.Style("selector-name") = "value"
```

So we could specify that the `<div>` be absolutely positioned on the page, add scroll bars to it, change the font and so on by adding the appropriate selector values.

The ASP:Label Control

The `Panel` control we've just seen creates an HTML `<div>` element, and this is not always ideal – for example it automatically wraps to the next line and causes other content to be wrapped below it. To place content inline with other elements and text, we need an HTML `<span>` element instead. This is just what the ASP.NET `Label` control provides.

This control has the usual set of properties that define the appearance: `ToolTip`, `AccessKey` and so on. It also has the `Text` property that we use to specify the content of the `<span>` element:

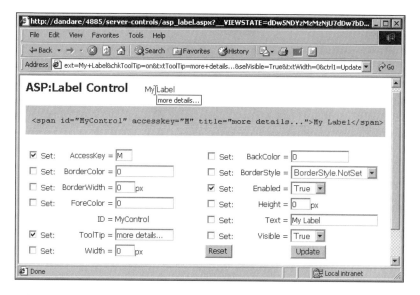

The source code we used to create the server control in this page is:

```
<ASP:Label id="MyControl" Text="My Label" runat="server" />
```

The ASP:Button Control

The ASP.NET Button control is used to create a standard HTML button that we can access in our server-side code. Again, the properties are the usual set we've seen in all the other controls. Notice that the type of <input> element it creates is a submit button, so clicking the button will automatically submit the form it resides on to our server where we can handle the Click event it raises in our server-side code:

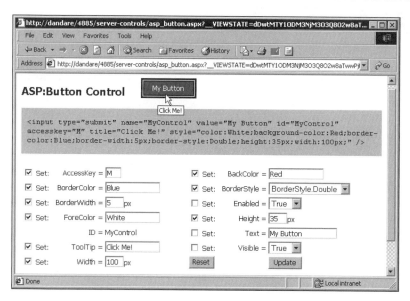

The source code we used to create the server control in this page is:

```
<ASP:Button id="MyControl" Text="My Button" runat="server" />
```

The ASP: ImageButton Control

Instead of using a normal text-captioned button to raise a Click event on the server, we can use a "clickable" image instead. The ImageButton control creates an <input type="image"> element that submits the form it resides on to the server when clicked. And, as you can see from the following screenshot, we can control the size and appearance of the image to get the effect we want:

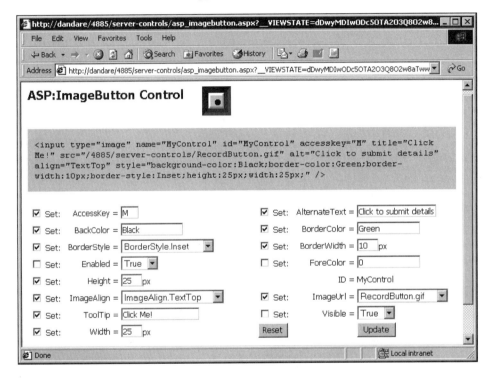

The source code we used to create the server control in this page is:

```
<ASP:ImageButton id="MyControl" ImageUrl="BookmarkButton.gif"
                 runat="server" />
```

The ASP:TextBox Control

One of the most complex of the basic Web Form input controls is the TextBox control. We can use this to create several different types of HTML element, including a normal single-line textbox, a multi-line textbox (where it actually creates an HTML <textarea> element), and a password input box that displays asterisks instead of text.

In its simplest form, to create a normal <input type="text"> element, we don't have to change any of the default property values. However, in the screenshot below you can see that we've set the MaxLength, ReadOnly, and ToolTip properties. We also set the Columns property, which equates to the size attribute for an <input type="text"> element:

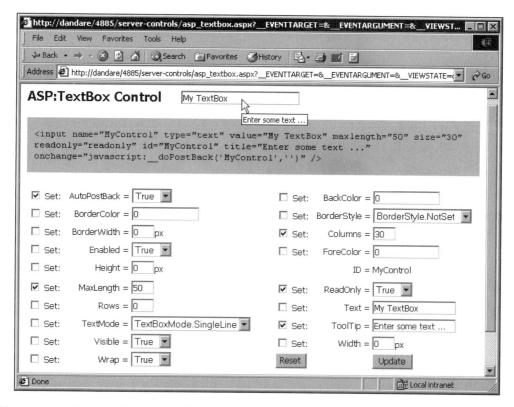

The source code we used to create the server control in this page is:

```
<ASP:TextBox id="MyControl" Text="My TextBox" runat="server" />
```

We've turned on `AutoPostBack` as well, and if you do the same and experiment you'll find that you can type in the textbox as usual, but when you move the input focus to another control (by pressing the *Tab* key or by clicking on another control with the mouse), the page is automatically submitted to the server where it will raise a `Change` event that we could create an event handler for. We'll see more about this later in this chapter.

Creating a Multi-line Text Box

The next screenshot shows how we can create an HTML `<textarea>` element that acts as a multi-line textbox using the ASP.NET `TextBox` control. We just have to change the value of the `TextMode` property to `TextBoxMode.MultiLine` and specify the appropriate number of `Rows` and `Columns`:

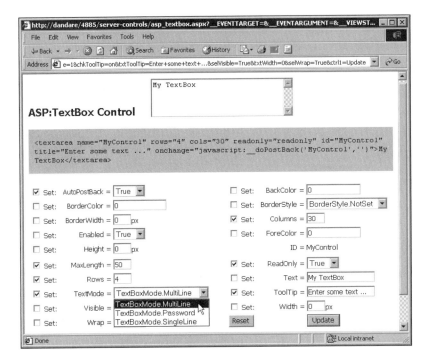

Creating a Password Input Element

The third option for the `TextMode` property is `TextBoxMode.Password`. When this is selected, as you can see in the next screenshot, the control creates an HTML `<input type="password">` element instead:

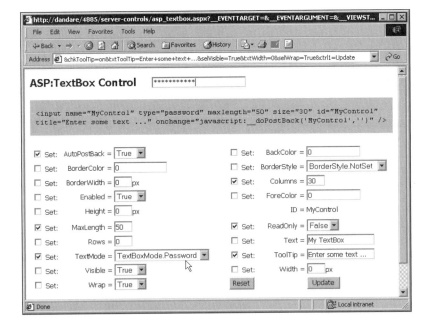

Note that textboxes always persist their state (text) when placed on an HTML form, even if you turn off VIEWSTATE by setting `EnableViewState=False`. *This is because they always post their value back to the server from a form and cause an update event.*

The ASP:Table Control

A useful ASP.NET Web Form control is the `Table` control. This is, in fact, very similar to the `HTMLTable` server control we experimented with in the previous chapter. However, it also provides the standard Web Form range of control properties for the appearance of the table. The next screenshot shows a formatted table and the first part of the output that the control creates to implement the table in the browser:

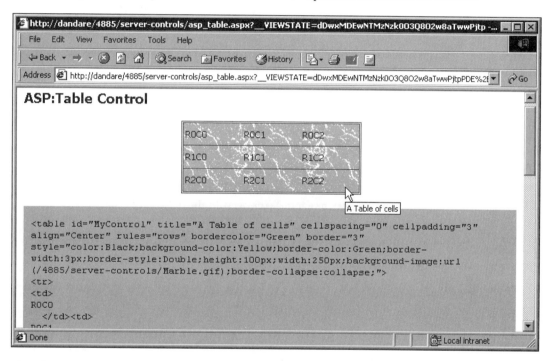

Scrolling to the bottom of the page you can see the values we set for the properties – though bear in mind that (as with the `HTMLTable` control) we have to create the table dynamically using code in the page. The drop-down lists for the number of rows and columns are there so that we can specify what size the table we generate should be:

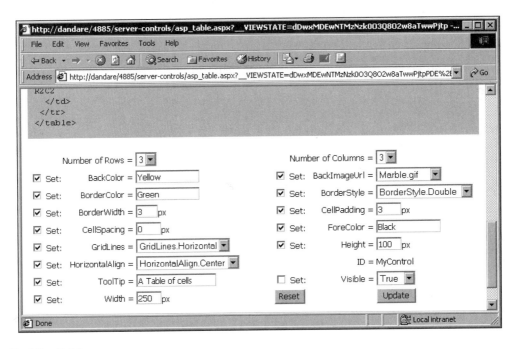

Creating the Table

The way that we create the table is very much the same as with the HTMLTable server control we used in the previous chapter. Of course, the object class names are different (TableRow and TableCell instead of HTMLTableRow and HTMLTableCell). We've highlighted the differences between the example in the previous chapter and this one:

```
Dim intRows As Integer = selRows.Value
Dim intCols As Integer = selCols.Value
Dim intRowCount, intColCount As Integer
Dim objRow As TableRow
Dim objCell As TableCell
For intRowCount = 0 To intRows - 1
  objRow = New TableRow()
    For intColCount = 0 To intCols - 1
      objCell = New TableCell()
      objCell.Controls.Add(New LiteralControl ("R" & intRowCount _
                                     & "C" & intColCount))

    objRow.Cells.Add(objCell)
  Next
  MyControl.Rows.Add(objRow)
Next
```

We also have to use a different technique to insert the values into the cells of the table. In our HTMLTable example we simply set the InnerHtml property of the cells, but we can't do that here because the TableCell object doesn't have an InnerHtml property.

252

Using a LiteralControl object to Generate Content

Instead we use a `LiteralControl` object. This object provides no inherent formatting or content of its own – in other words it doesn't create any HTML elements. It simply inserts an instruction (actually a `Write` statement) into the code when the page is compiled that outputs the value of the control.

So to output the content for each cell we just instantiate a new `LiteralControl` object and pass as the single `String`-type parameter the text, HTML or other content that we want to be generated. We can, of course, use a `LiteralControl` anywhere where we want to generate some content without placing it inside another HTML element.

The ASP:Literal and ASP:PlaceHolder Controls

Two controls that we do not include in the demonstration application, but which you may find use for in your own pages are the `ASP:Literal` and the `ASP:PlaceHolder` controls. We'll describe these two controls here for completeness.

We used the `ASP:Literal` control in the previous example where we dynamically created a table using the `ASP:Table` control. Other than the common members inherited from the base class `Control`, it has only a single property named `Text`. This defines the text that is output by the control. It generates no other output (no HTML elements, for example), and so is useful where all we want is to place some text in the page.

```
<ASP:Literal Text="Some Text Here" runat="server" />
```

The value we use for the `Text` property can, however, contain HTML – for example we can use it to create custom elements in the output for which there is no server control available:

```
<ASP:Literal Text="<gloop>A custom element</gloop>" runat="server" />
```

As you'd expect, this produces the following (probably not very useful) output:

```
<gloop>A custom element</gloop>
```

The ASP:PlaceHolder Control

The final control we'll look briefly at is the `ASP:PlaceHolder` control. This is used when we want to create controls dynamically in a page, rather than declaring them explicitly within the source of the page as we've done so far. For example, if we insert an `ASP:PlaceHolder` into the page like this:

```
<asp:placeholder id="MyControl" runat="server" />
```

we can then insert three `ASP:TextBox` controls into the page using this code:

```
<script runat="server">
Sub Page_Load()
  Dim intLoop As Integer
  Dim objTextBox As TextBox
  For intLoop = 1 To 3
    objTextBox = New TextBox()
    MyControl.Controls.Add(objTextBox)
  Next
End Sub
</script>
```

The result when viewed in the browser is just the three new textboxes – the `PlaceHolder` control doesn't create any output of its own:

```
<input name="ctrl0" type="text" /><input name="ctrl1" type="text" /><input
name="ctrl2" type="text" />
```

Reacting to Click and Change Events

As with the HTML controls, the ASP.NET Web Form controls raise events that we can react to on the server. The Events demonstration page shows the `Click` and `Change` events that are exposed by most of the Web Forms. It neatly demonstrates the way that the `Change` event is raised when you edit the content of a text box and then press the *Tab* key or move to another control by clicking with the mouse. A message indicating that a `Change` event was detected, and showing the source control's `id`, is displayed at the bottom of the page:

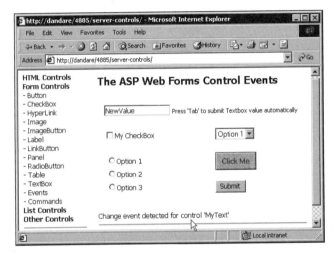

The code in the page also detects events for any of the other controls. For example, you can click the `ImageButton` control, and in this case you also get the coordinates of the mouse pointer within the control displayed:

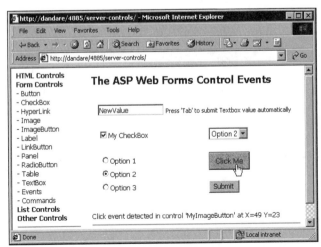

The Code in the 'Events' Demonstration Page

The code we use in this page is very similar to what we showed for the HTML controls in the previous chapter. Each of the non-button controls on the page has the AutoPostBack property set to True, so that clicking or changing the control's contents will automatically submit the page to the server (the button-type controls do this automatically). Also, each control has an event handler specified for the appropriate "Click" or "Change" property. Notice that they have specific event names depending on the control type:

```
<asp:TextBox id="MyText" Text="OriginalValue" runat="server"
    OnTextChanged="MyChangeCode" AutoPostBack="True" />

<asp:CheckBox id="MyCheckbox" Text="My CheckBox" runat="server"
    OnCheckedChanged="MyChangeCode" AutoPostBack="True" />

<asp:ImageButton id="MyImageButton" ImageUrl="ClickmeButton.gif"
    runat="server" ImageAlign="absbottom" OnClick="MyImageCode" />

<asp:Button id="MyButton" Text="Submit" runat="server"
    OnClick="MyClickCode" />
```

> *We haven't included the list controls here, as they are described in the next section of the chapter, where we'll investigate how we get the selected value(s) from these controls.*

There is also a <div> where we display the messages about the events we detect:

```
<div id="divResult" runat="server" EnableViewState="False" />
```

The event handlers for the textbox, checkbox, and button controls are shown next. You can see that the ImageButton event code accepts an ImageClickEventArgs object as the second argument (from where it extracts the coordinates of the mouse pointer), while the other controls accept an ordinary EventArgs object for the second parameter:

```
Sub MyChangeCode(objSender As Object, objArgs As EventArgs)
    divResult.InnerHtml += "Change event detected for control '" _
                    & objSender.ID & "'"
End Sub

Sub MyImageCode(objSender As Object, objArgs As ImageClickEventArgs)
    divResult.InnerHtml += "Click event detected in control '" _
                    & objSender.ID & "' at X=" & objArgs.X _
                    & " Y=" & objArgs.Y
End Sub

Sub MyClickCode(objSender As Object, objArgs As EventArgs)
    divResult.InnerHtml += "Click event detected for control '" _
                    & objSender.ID & "'"
End Sub
```

Working with Command Controls

Three of the button-type controls, namely `Button`, `ImageButton`, and `LinkButton`, provide a **command** feature as well as supporting the standard events. We can set the two properties `CommandName` and `CommandArgument` to any string values we want. When that button is clicked, it raises a `Command` event on the server to which we can respond. You can see this in the **Commands** demonstration page:

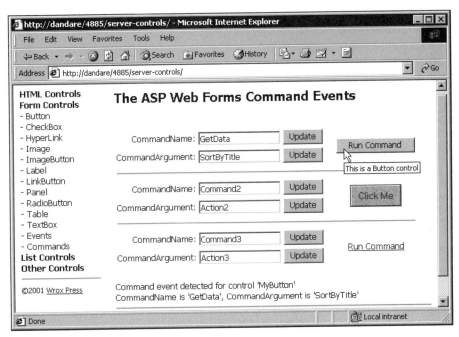

The Code in the 'Commands' Demonstration Page

Each time the page is loaded, it assigns the values from the textboxes on the page to the `CommandName` and `CommandArgument` properties of the three button controls. The page also contains the following event handler, which is executed when a `Command` event occurs. All it does is extract the `id`, `CommandName` and `CommandArgument` properties of the button control that raised the event and displays them:

```
Sub MyCommandCode(objSender As Object, objArgs As CommandEventArgs)
    divResult.InnerHtml += "Command event detected for control '" _
                        & objSender.ID & "'<br />" _
                        & "CommandName is '" _
                        & objSender.CommandName _
                        & "', CommandArgument is '" _
                        & objSender.CommandArgument & "'"
End Sub
```

This feature is useful in a couple of scenarios. If we have more than one button control on a form, we can use it to detect which button was clicked to submit that form. In previous versions of ASP, this was normally achieved by examining the `Request.Form` collection (or `Request.QueryString` if the form has its `method` set to "GET") to see which button was clicked. We just looked for the specific name or value of the button.

With a `Command` event, we can instead use a `Select Case` construct to figure out which button raised the event. All we have to do is check the `CommandName` value. This provides a far better structure to our code, and means that it is easier to add more buttons or change the caption or name of existing ones without breaking the code. We can also use different values for the `CommandArgument` property to pass our own custom control-specific or task-specific values to the event handler.

The second useful scenario is when we work with the complex list controls – in particular the `DataGrid` control. By setting pre-defined values for the `CommandName` property, we can use the buttons for control-specific tasks when we edit data in the `DataGrid` control. We'll be describing this technique in Chapter 7.

The ASP.NET List Controls

The fourth group of controls that are part of ASP.NET is the range of **list controls**. This includes the familiar list box and drop-down list, implemented using the HTML `<select>` element. However, there are several other very useful list controls as well:

`<ASP:DropDownList>`	Creates a `<select>` list element that includes the attribute `size="1"` so that only a single row is visible to create a drop-down list box. It can also populate the list using `<ASP:ListItem>` controls or through data binding.
`<ASP:ListBox>`	Creates a `<select>` list element that includes the attribute `size="x"` so that more than one row is visible to create a normal single-select or multi-select list box. It can also populate the list using `<ASP:ListItem>` controls or through data binding.
`<ASP:CheckBoxList>`	Creates an HTML `<table>` or a simple list containing HTML checkboxes.
`<ASP:RadioButtonList>`	Creates an HTML `<table>` or a simple list containing a mutually exclusive group of HTML radio buttons.
`<ASP:ListItem>`	Not actually a control, but an object that is used to create an item in a list control – depending on the type of control. For example, it creates an `<option>` element in a list box or a new checkbox control in a `CheckBoxList` control.
`<ASP:Repeater>`	Repeats content that you define once for each source item within the data source specified for the control. No integral formatting is applied except the layout and content information you define. This control is described in Chapter 7.
`<ASP:DataList>`	Creates an HTML `<table>` with a row for each source item you specify. You create templates that define the content and appearance of each row. This control is described in Chapter 7.
`<ASP:DataGrid>`	Creates an HTML `<table>` that is designed for use with server-side data binding, and includes built-in features to support selection, sorting and editing of the content rows. This control is described in Chapter 7.

These controls further reinforce the fact that the Web Form controls can save huge amounts of effort when creating interactive web pages – in particular when the values for the lists come from some dynamic data source such as a database. We'll be looking in detail at the concepts of data binding in Chapter 7, and we'll postpone the discussion of the three more complex types of list control to there. In this chapter, we'll concentrate on the first four of the controls listed above.

The ListControl Base Class

The four list controls we're describing in this chapter are derived from the base class `ListControl`, which is part of the namespace `System.Web.UI.WebControls`. This class itself inherits from `WebControl`, and so provides the same properties, methods, and events as we described in the previous section on the Web Form controls. To these, it adds some other members that are available for all the list controls:

`AutoPostBack` property	Sets or returns a Boolean value indicating whether the page will be posted back to the server automatically when the user changes the selection in the list.
`DataMember` property	Sets or returns the name of the table within the `DataSource` that will supply the values for the list when data binding is used to populate it. Used when the `DataSource` object contains more than one table, for example when using a `DataSet`.
`DataSource` property	Sets or returns a reference to the object that provides the values to populate the list.
`DataTextField` property	Sets or returns the name of the field within the current `DataSource` that provides the text to be used for the list items.
`DataTextFormatString` property	Sets or returns the formatting string that controls how the data bound to the list is displayed. For example `"{0:C}"` for currency.
`DataValueField` property	Sets or returns the name of the field within the current `DataSource` that provides the values for the list items.
`Items` property	Returns a collection of the items (rows or `<option>` elements) within the list control.
`SelectedIndex` property	Sets or returns the integer index of the first selected item in the list. To retrieve multiple selected items use the `Selected` property of each individual `ListItem` object.
`SelectedItem` property	Returns a reference to the first selected item within the list control. To retrieve multiple selected items use the `Selected` property of each individual `ListItem` object.
`OnSelectedIndexChanged` event	Occurs on the server when the selection in the list has been changed and the page is posted back to the server.

The Specific List Control Classes

Each of the list controls adds properties and a method to the base class from which they inherit. These are:

Control/Object	Properties	Methods
DropDownList	*- none -*	*- none -*
ListBox	Rows	*- none -*
ListItem	Attributes, Selected, Text, Value	FromString
CheckBoxList	CellPadding, CellSpacing, RepeatColumns, RepeatDirection, RepeatLayout, TextAlign	*- none -*
RadioButtonList	CellPadding, CellSpacing, RepeatColumns, RepeatDirection, RepeatLayout, TextAlign	*- none -*

In the next section we'll look at how we can use each of the five list controls we're featuring in this chapter.

Using the ASP List Controls

In general, we use the list controls in the same way as the basic ASP.NET Web Form controls we examined in the previous section of this chapter. Properties like AutoPostBack, AccessKey, ToolTip, and the various formatting properties work in just the same way. We've also used a HashTable as the data source for the examples in our demonstration application, in the same way as we did with the HTMLSelect control in the previous chapter.

What we'll be concentrating on here is the properties that are specific to list controls, as shown in the previous tables. We'll follow this up towards the end of this section with a look at the way we retrieve details about the selected items in a list control.

The ASP:DropDownList Control

The ASP.NET DropDownList control creates basically the same output in the browser as the default HTMLSelect list we saw in the previous chapter. It generates an HTML <select> element with no size attribute, so only one item in the list is visible and it behaves as a "drop-down" selection list.

Because we've bound the control to the same HashTable as we used with the HTMLSelect control, you can see that it creates the same five <option> elements within the <select> element. The formatting of the control is performed by setting the BackColor, BorderColor, and ForeColor properties, and we've also turned on AutoPostBack which adds the onchange attribute to the <select> element:

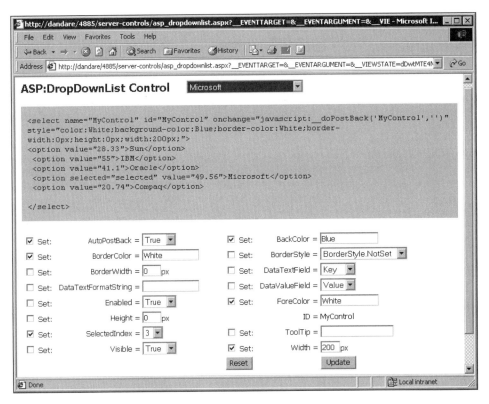

The source code we used to create the server control in this page is:

```
<ASP:DropDownList id="MyControl" runat="server" />
```

To see the effects of data binding to the HashTable data source, swap over the DataTextField and DataValueField properties. The list will show the contents of the "field" selected as the DataTextField property, and use the contents of the "field" specified as the DataValueField to fill the value attributes of each <option> element.

The ASP:ListBox Control

To create a list box rather than a drop-down list, we use the ListBox control. This has a couple of extra properties that we use to specify the size and behavior of the list. Firstly, we can specify how many items will be displayed by setting the Rows property (which sets the size attribute – notice how the property names are common across the Web Form controls, hiding the inconsistent HTML attribute names):

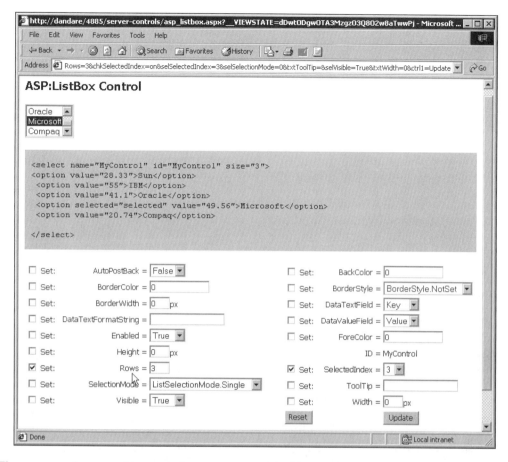

The source code we used to create the server control in this page is:

```
<ASP:ListBox id="MyControl" runat="server" />
```

We can also permit multiple selections to be made in the list by setting the SelectionMode property to a value from the ListSelectionMode enumeration. The value Multiple simply adds the multiple="multiple" attribute to the output so that the *Shift* and *Ctrl* key can be used to select more than one item in the list.

The ASP:CheckBoxList and ASP:RadioButtonList Controls

There are two exciting and useful controls that are part of the Web Form list control range – the CheckBoxList and RadioButtonList controls. These create a list containing several checkboxes or radio buttons, and they automatically set the value and the text (for the caption) of each one. When used in conjunction with data binding, as in our demonstration pages, these controls can really save development time.

The next screenshot shows the standard results for a RadioButtonList control when data-bound to the same HashTable as we used in the previous examples. The CheckBoxList control is identical except that it creates a list of checkboxes (as you'd expect). You can see that the output generated is an HTML table containing <input type="radio"> and <label> elements:

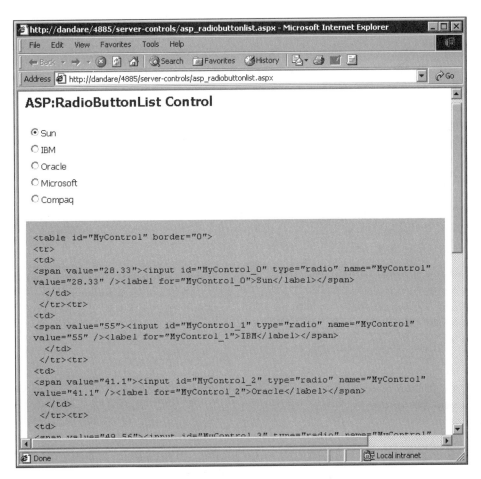

The source code we used to create the server control in this page is:

```
<ASP:CheckBoxList id="MyControl" runat="server" />
```

However, this is not the only output "format" we can create. In the next screenshot you can see that the controls are laid out inline rather than using a table. This is because we set the RepeatLayout property to Flow, and the RepeatDirection to Horizontal (using members of the appropriate enumerations). We also set the RepeatColumns property to 3 so that the controls appear three across the page:

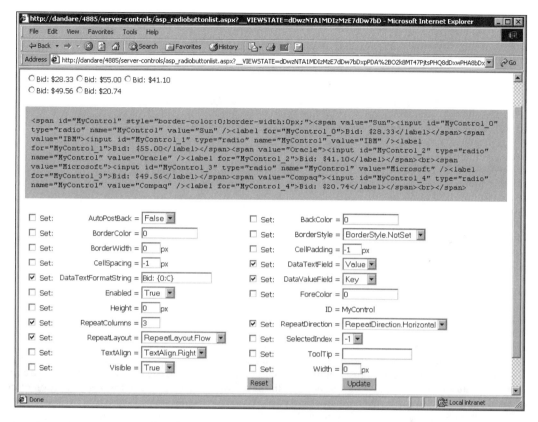

Another point to notice is that the values for each option are now formatted as currency. We do this by setting the `DataTextFormatString` to a suitable format expression. In our example we've used `Bid: {0:C}` to output the literal characters "`Bid:`" and convert the numerical value to currency format, but you can substitute others to experiment.

Reacting to Change Events

The Events demonstration page we used in the previous section to show the events for button controls also shows how we can react to the "`Change`" event that is exposed by all the Web Form list controls. When you make a selection in the `RadioButtonList` or the `DropDownList` control, the page displays information about that event:

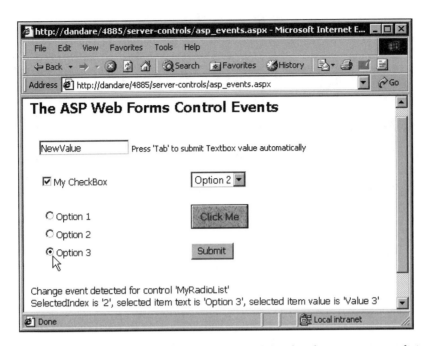

The `RadioButtonList` and `DropDownList` controls are defined in the page using explicit values for their contents, rather than using data binding as we did in the previous examples. However, as we're using the ASP Web Form list controls here, we **must** define the contents using `ListItem` elements rather than `<option>` elements. Notice that we set the `Text` property to the string we want to appear in the visible portion of the list, rather than providing it as the content of the element as we do when we're using `<option>` elements:

```
<asp:DropDownList id="MyDropDownList" runat="server"
      OnSelectedIndexChanged="MyListChangeCode" AutoPostBack="true">
 <asp:ListItem Text="Option 1" Value="Value 1" />
 <asp:ListItem Text="Option 2" Value="Value 2" />
 <asp:ListItem Text="Option 3" Value="Value 3" />
</asp:DropDownList>

<asp:RadioButtonList id="MyRadioList" runat="server"
      OnSelectedIndexChanged="MyListChangeCode" AutoPostBack="true">
 <asp:ListItem Text="Option 1" Value="Value 1" />
 <asp:ListItem Text="Option 2" Value="Value 2" />
 <asp:ListItem Text="Option 3" Value="Value 3" />
</asp:RadioButtonList>
```

You can also see how easy it is to define the individual radio buttons that make up the `RadioButtonList` control (we use exactly the same technique with a `CheckBoxList` control). We only have to specify the `ListItem` element and its properties. The list control knows what type of items to create for the list, and automatically generates the correct HTML.

Extracting Values from List Controls

The two list controls have their `AutoPostBack` property set to `True`, so the page will be submitted to our server when the current selection is changed. They also have their `OnSelectedIndexChanged` property set to point to an event handler named `MyListChangeCode`, which (as usual) is executed on the server when the page is submitted.

The code for this event handler is shown next. It displays the `id` of the control that raised the event, then extracts the selected item `Text` and `Value` and displays these as well:

```
Sub MyListChangeCode(objSender As Object, objArgs As EventArgs)
   divResult.InnerHtml += "Change event detected for control '" _
                   & objSender.ID & "'<br />SelectedIndex is '" _
                   & objSender.SelectedIndex _
                   & "', selected item text is '" _
                   & objSender.SelectedItem.Text _
                   & "', selected item value is '" _
                   & objSender.SelectedItem.Value & "'<br />"
End Sub
```

Notice how, in this case, we simply access the `SelectedItem` property of the list control, which returns a reference to the first item in the list that is selected.

Extracting Multiple Selected Values from List Controls

Both of the lists in the previous example allow only a single selection to be made. This is always the case with a `RadioButtonList`, but we can specify that a `ListBox` control will accept multiple selections by setting the `SelectionMode` property to the value `ListSelectionMode.Multiple`. And of course, in a `CheckBoxList` we will usually allow multiple selections as this is the sole reason for using this type of control.

We extract multiple selected values from a list control using exactly the same technique as we did with the `HtmlSelect` control in the previous section. We iterate through all the `ListItem` elements in the `Items` collection exposed by the list control checking the `Selected` property of each one, and extract the `Text` and `Value` properties for those that are selected:

```
Sub MyCode(objSender As Object, objArgs As EventArgs)
   Dim strResult As String
   strResult = "The following items were selected:<br />"
   Dim objItem As ListItem
   For Each objItem in objSender.Items
     If objItem.Selected Then
        strResult += objItem.Text & " = " & objItem.Value & "<br />"
     End If
   Next
   outMessage.InnerHtml = strResult
End Sub
```

Other ASP.NET Rich Controls

To finish off this chapter, we'll look briefly at three other controls that are provided with ASP.NET. These are called "rich" controls because they create the entire HTML required to implement a complex task in one simple operation. A typical example of this is the Calendar control, which can create a complete working calendar within a web page. All you do is add the control to your page and set a few properties. The three controls we'll be covering here are:

`<ASP:AdRotator>`	Displays an advertisement banner that changes on a predefined schedule.
`<ASP:Calendar>`	Displays a calendar showing single months and allows selection of a date.
`<ASP:Xml>`	Displays the content of an XML document or the result of an XSL or XSLT transformation.

Using the Rich Controls

The rich controls we're looking at in this section are very useful when you need to perform the specific tasks for which they are designed. We don't have room to provide exhaustive coverage here, but by now you should be familiar with the way that server controls work, and you should have no problem getting to grips with these. You can use the demonstration application we provide (open the Other Controls section of the left-hand menu) to see the output that they generate, and experiment with the various property settings.

The ASP:AdRotator Control

The AdRotator control has been part of ASP almost since the beginning, and is a popular way to display advertisement banners on a semi-random pre-defined schedule. A new version is included as part of the default ASP.NET installation, and it has a couple of extra features.

Probably the most useful is the ability to **filter** the list of banners that will be displayed dynamically, so that you can, for example, display banners for products or organizations that are relevant to a specific page or user. The filtering is carried out through the KeywordFilter property. You can see that we've set this property in the following screenshot from our demonstration application:

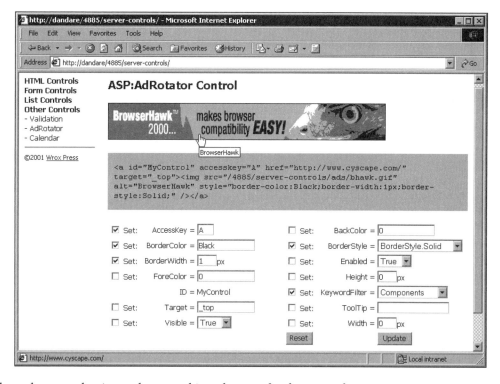

The code we used to insert the control into the page for this example is:

```
<ASP:AdRotator id="MyControl" AdvertisementFile="adverts.xml"
               runat="server" />
```

Previous versions of the AdRotator control relied on a text file to specify the advertisements and the schedule for display of each one. As the whole world is now going XML crazy, the new control follows the trend by using an XML file to define the schedules. The file path is specified in the AdvertisementFile property, as shown in the source code for the page above (you can't change this property in the demonstration page).

The AdRotator Schedule File

An example of the format of the XML schedule file is:

```
<Advertisements>
  <Ad>
    <ImageUrl>ads/asptoday.gif</ImageUrl>
    <NavigateUrl>http://www.asptoday.com/</NavigateUrl>
    <AlternateText>ASPToday</AlternateText>
    <Impressions>20</Impressions>
    <Keyword>Articles</Keyword>
  </Ad>
  <Ad>
    <ImageUrl>ads/wrox.gif</ImageUrl>
    <NavigateUrl>http://www.wrox.com/</NavigateUrl>
```

```
        <AlternateText>Wrox Press</AlternateText>
        <Impressions>20</Impressions>
        <Keyword>Books</Keyword>
      </Ad>
      ... more <Ad> elements here ...
   <Advertisements>
```

The `ImageUrl` and `NavigateUrl` are self-explanatory. The `AlternateText` is used as the HTML `alt` attribute of the `<img>` element that the `AdRotator` control creates, and the `Impressions` value is used to control how often this banner will appear. The total for this element in all the `<Ad>` elements in the schedule file is calculated, and the ratio of impressions can then be calculated by the control and used to select the advertisement to display.

The `Keyword` element is used to allocate each advertisement to a "category" with that name. When you set the `KeywordFilter` property, only advertisements with the specified value for their `Keyword` element are included in the selection and display process.

The ASP:Calendar Control

By far the most complex server control in ASP.NET is the `Calendar` control. This creates a fully interactive "one-month-at-a-time" calendar as an HTML table. The output of the control depends on the browser that has requested the page, and it includes client-side script code that allows the control to change the month without having to keep reloading the page from the server.

The next screenshot shows the default output from the `Calendar` control, and you can see that it really is a "rich" control in that it saves an incredible amount of effort on behalf of the developer:

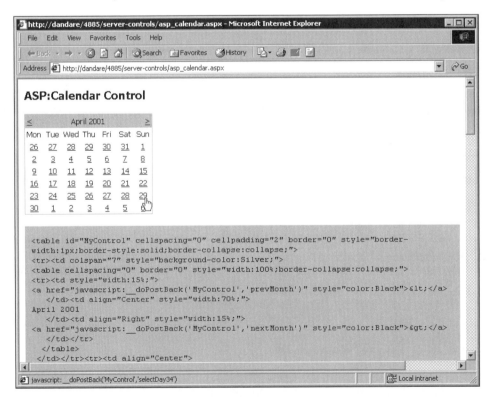

The code we used to insert the control into the source of the page is:

```
<ASP:Calendar id="MyControl" runat="server" />
```

Notice that it automatically defaults to the current date if we don't specify a date.

If you scroll to the bottom of this page, you can see some of the properties that we can set to change the appearance. These don't include the various calendar-specific style properties that are available, such as DayHeaderStyle, DayStyle, MonthStyle, and so on:

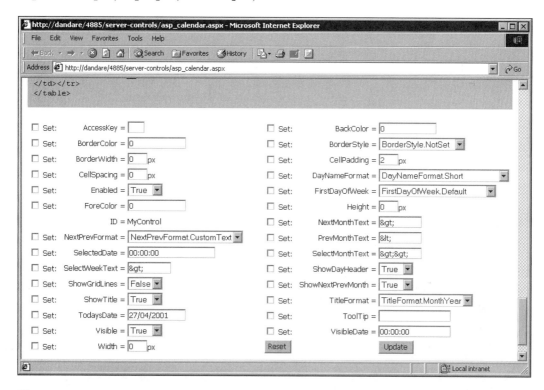

The Calendar control also exposes a couple of events that we can use to detect when the user interacts with the control. We can write an event handler for the SelectionChanged event, and obtain the date that the user selected by querying the SelectedDate property of the control within that event handler.

We can also create an event handler for the VisibleMonthChanged event. In this case, the second parameter of the event handler is a MonthChangedEventHandler object, which exposes two properties named NewDate and PreviousDate that contain the original (before the month was changed) and current dates (the date after the month was changed).

The ASP:Xml Control

The final control we're looking at is the Xml server control. This can be used to display the content of an XML document, or to perform a server-side transformation on the document using a suitable XST or XSLT style sheet. Note that this control does not inherit from WebControl. It inherits directly from Control, and so doesn't have all the display-oriented properties that the other Web Form controls do.

Don't be confused into thinking that this control creates an IE5-style <xml> element. It doesn't. It is a server-side object that outputs XML or the result of a transformation to the client.

There are six properties available for the Xml control. We specify the source document using one of the first three properties in the following table, and the style sheet (if we're using one) in one of the next two properties shown:

Document	A reference to an XmlDocument object that contains the XML document we want to display or transform. We look at how we use the XmlDocument object in Chapter 11.
DocumentContent	A string containing the text of the XML document we want to display or transform.
DocumentSource	A string that contains the physical or virtual path to the XML document we want to display or transform.
Transform	A reference to an XslTransform object that contains the XSL or XSLT stylesheet we are using to transform the XML document before displaying it. We look at how we use the XslTransform object in Chapter 11.
TransformSource	A string that contains the physical or virtual path to the XSL or XSLT stylesheet we want to use for the transformation.
TransformArgumentList	A reference to an XsltArgumentList object that contains the arguments to be passed to the stylesheet.

In the demonstration page we have set the DocumentSource property to "books.xml". The control loads this document from disk and displays it in the page. Of course the XML elements aren't visible, because the browser attempts to render the XML as though it were HTML and so only the text content of the elements is shown in the page. If you view the source in your browser, however, you'll see the XML that the control sends to the client. We've also included a hyperlink in the page so that you can open the XML document in a separate browser window and see it:

The code we used to insert the control into the source of the page is:

```
<ASP:Xml id="MyControl" DocumentSource="xml/books.xml" runat="server" />
```

If you compare the original disk file with the output of the control, you'll also see that the control has removed "insignificant whitespace" from the result. In other words, it strips out all the carriage returns, spaces, and *Tab* characters.

Using an XSL Stylesheet

We've also provided three simple XSL stylesheets that you can use to transform the XML document. They transform the XML into HTML (because we're displaying it in the browser in our application); for example, the `reportview.xsl` stylesheet generates a sales report from the data in the XML document:

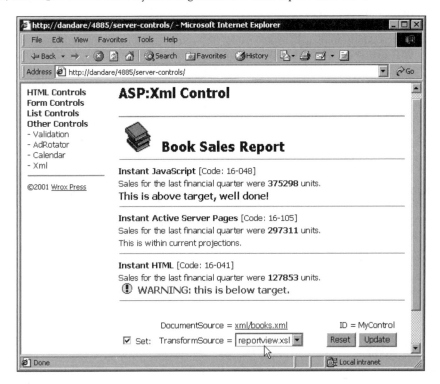

Summary

In this chapter, we've looked at the second major type of server controls that are provided as part of the default ASP.NET installation – the **Web Form** controls. These are a mixture of simple controls that emulate the HTML controls we looked at in the previous chapter, and more complex controls that provide "rich" output containing more than one HTML element.

The **Web Form** controls also have other advantages over the HTML controls. They provide a consistent object model, using the same property name in all the controls for the same "value". An example is the Text property, which sets the visible text within the control irrespective of which HTML element is output, and which HTML attribute carries the text content. This makes working with them easier, and also simplifies the task of creating tools or applications that will create a user interface automatically.

The **Web Form** controls we examined in this chapter fall into three groups:

❑   The basic controls, such as Image, Hyperlink, TextBox, and RadioButton

❑   The list controls, such as ListBox, DropDownList, and RadioButtonList

❑   The rich controls, such as AdRotator, Calendar, and Xml

We showed you the common properties for each one, and demonstrated them through a sample application that we provide. We also looked at how we react to events that these controls expose, and some of the other issues involved when we come to use them.

The topics we covered in this chapter were:

❑   The ASP.NET Web Form server controls in general

❑   The basic Web Form input and navigation server controls

❑   The Web Form server controls used for building lists

❑   The "rich" Web Form controls that provide complex compound interface elements

However, we didn't examine all the **list controls** in this chapter, as there are some very specialist ones such as Repeater, DataList, and DataGrid. We look at these in the next chapter.

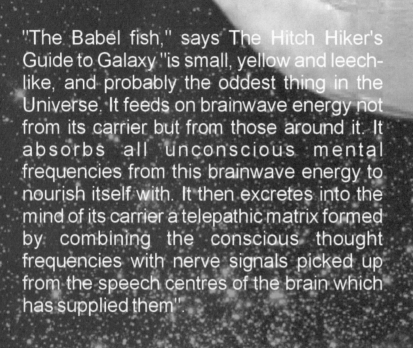

"The Babel fish," says The Hitch Hiker's Guide to Galaxy "is small, yellow and leech-like, and probably the oddest thing in the Universe. It feeds on brainwave energy not from its carrier but from those around it. It absorbs all unconscious mental frequencies from this brainwave energy to nourish itself with. It then excretes into the mind of its carrier a telepathic matrix formed by combining the conscious thought frequencies with nerve signals picked up from the speech centres of the brain which has supplied them".

The practical upshot of all this is that if you stick a Babel fish in your ear you can instantly understand anything said to you in any form of language. The speech patterns you actually hear decode the brainwave matrix which has been fed into your mind by your Babel fish

7

List Controls and Data Binding

Most dynamic web sites, and just about every web-based application, will need to access a data source at some point. ASP has long been quite capable of accessing various kinds of data store, such as relational databases, e-mail servers, XML, and text files. It's also relatively simple to manipulate, format, and display data in a range of ways. However, though it's simple to do, it always requires you to write code – and that code can become quite extensive, making it difficult to manage and debug.

ASP.NET introduces some new ways to manage and present data of all kinds. In later chapters, we'll be looking at the whole concept of data management for both relational and XML data. However, in this chapter we'll look at some of the new ways that we can display data in our pages and applications.

This might seem to be an odd ordering of topics, but in fact data presentation in ASP.NET is managed mainly through a series of new **server controls** that are specially designed to work with a whole range of types of data – not just relational or XML data. And the techniques for working with these controls are more akin to the techniques for creating ASP.NET pages that we've been examining in previous chapters.

What's more, you don't need a deep understanding of where the data comes from, or how it is extracted from a data store, to be able to use the new data presentation controls. The fundamentally disconnected design of the data management features within the .NET framework means that we can easily separate the business rules that create and expose data from the code that creates the display.

So, in this chapter, we'll deal with the way that the controls work, and how you use them. In later chapters, we'll be free to examine relational and XML data management techniques without getting bogged down in presentation issues. So, the topics we'll be covering here are:

❑   What data binding actually is, and how it works

❑   How we can bind controls to single data values

❑   How we can bind list controls to sets of data values

❑   How we can change the appearance of data-bound controls

❑   How we use data-bound controls to edit and update the source data

Obtaining the Sample Files

All the examples used in this chapter are included with the sample files available for this book from http://www.wrox.com/Books/Book_Details.asp?isbn=1861004885. You'll find a `default.htm` menu page in the subfolder named `data-binding`:

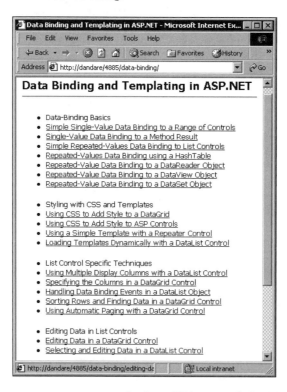

Some of the examples require a connection to a database. We've provided a Microsoft Access `.mdb` database file and two SQL scripts to create the database in SQL Server. These files, and instructions on creating the database, are included in the `data-binding/database` subfolder of the sample files. Remember that you must edit the file named `connect-strings.ascx` (found in the `data-binding/global` folder of the samples) to specify the path to the `.mdb` file and/or the name of your database server.

Data Binding – The Concepts

The term **data binding** is one of those familiar things that you've heard many times, but can actually be quite elusive to pin down exactly. In programming languages like Visual Basic, and applications like Microsoft Access, the term describes the way that values from a collection of data, such as a recordset, are connected to controls on a form. As the form is used to navigate through the records, the values of each of the columns are automatically displayed in the controls. The controls are **bound** to the columns in the recordset, and you don't have to write any code for displaying the values or updating the original data source.

However, the disconnected nature of the HTTP protocol means that the traditional client/server data binding used in Visual Basic and Access cannot be used over an HTTP-based network connection. When Internet Explorer 4 appeared, it included some clever client-side and server-side COM components that allowed a similar technique to be used over HTTP. This was referred to as **client-side data binding**, and worked well. However, the browser-specific requirements of this technology, combined with suspicions about security that it raised, meant that it didn't really catch on in a big way.

Doing It All on the Server

In fact, the continuing divergence in the types of client device that we are seeing now means that almost any browser-specific technology will have a limited appeal in the long term. Instead, the whole essence of the .NET framework vision is to provide wide support for **all** types of client. Ultimately, this means we have to build applications that either detect the client device type (and change their behavior accordingly), or we just "do it all on the server".

In many cases, to be able to exert the control over output and security we want within our applications, doing it all on the server is a good plan. Developments in server and Web farm technologies make it much easier to provide scalable and reliable servers, and ASP.NET is designed to create faster responses to client requests through pre-compilation, caching, and so on.

So how does this relate to the topics of this chapter? The answer is that we are moving in .NET towards the concept of **server-side data binding**. We can take advantage of the time saving and code saving features of data binding – just like we would with Visual Basic and Access – but have it work across HTTP in a disconnected environment like the Web.

With data binding in ASP.NET, we simply tell the controls or the page where to find the data. It extracts the values and builds the page with this data in it. We'll see how next.

Displaying Data – ASP Versus ASP.NET

In ASP 3.0 and earlier, we can use components or a technology like ADO to create a `Recordset` object that contains rows of data for display. To get them into the page, we would usually iterate through the rows extracting values, formatting them, and inserting them into the output – something like this:

```
...' assuming we've got a Recordset object containing the data ...
Response.Write "<table>"
Response.Write "<tr><th>Date</th>"
Response.Write "<th>Subject</th>"
Response.Write "<th>User Name</th>"
Response.Write "<th>Content</th></tr>"
```

```
Do While Not objRecs.EOF
strDate = FormatDateTime(objRecs("dtDate").value, vbLongDate)
  Response.Write "<tr><td>" & strDate & "</td>"
  Response.Write "<td>" & objRecs("tSubject").value & "</td>"
  Response.Write "<td>" & objRecs("tUserName").value & "</td>"
  Response.Write "<td>" & objRecs("tContent").value & "</td></tr>"
  objRecs.MoveNext
Loop
Response.Write "</table>"
objRecs.Close
```

All this just to get a simple unformatted table containing values from the rows in the recordset. In ASP.NET, using a server control, you can do the same with two lines of code:

```
<!-- the server control located in the HTML section of the page -->
<ASP:DataGrid id="MyDataGrid" runat="server" />

...' assuming we've got a DataView object containing the data ...
MyDataGrid.DataSource = objDataView
MyDataGrid.DataBind()
```

We'll be covering the data access objects such as DataView *in detail in the following chapters.*

The server control does much the same as the ASP 3.0 code shown earlier – it automatically creates an HTML table with the column names in the first row, followed by a series of rows containing the values from each of the source data rows. What's more, we can change the appearance by just setting a few properties of the ASP:DataGrid control. We can add automatic sorting with only a two-line subroutine. Or we can add automatic paging, with each page showing the number of rows we require, and with links to the other pages: all this requires is one property setting and two lines of code.

And this only scratches the surface. The ways that we can use this control will cater for almost any dataset presentation requirement. What's more, there are several other controls that are designed to display repeated data such as this, and even more that work with one single item of data at a time through server-side data binding. Throw away your MoveNext and get on the ASP.NET data-binding wagon now!

Data Binding Syntax

We actually used data binding in a couple of the examples in the previous two chapters, but we didn't discuss how it worked in any depth. We'll concentrate on the theory here, and then move on in this chapter to look at how we can really get the benefits of server-side data binding with the new ASP.NET server controls.

The principle behind server-side data binding is to get ASP to insert one or more values from a data source into the page or into a control on the page. The basic syntax uses a construct that looks like a server-side script block, with the '#' character as an indicator that this is actually a data-binding statement:

```
<%# name-of-data-source %>
```

*Note that you **cannot** place code that you want to be executed within this block – although it **looks** like a server-side script block, it isn't. Only specific data-binding syntax expressions can be used within the block.*

There are two basic scenarios when we bind a control to a value or a source of data:

- ❑ When we have a single value that we want to bind to a control, for example to set one of the properties (or attributes) of that control. The bound value is often used to set the displayed content of the control (that is, the Text or Value property), and is suited to controls that only display a single value, such as the <input>, ASP:TextBox and ASP:Hyperlink controls. This is generally referred to as "**single-value binding**".

- ❑ When the data source contains more than one value (as a list, collection, or rowset) and we want to bind it to a control that can display more than one value. Examples are the various types of list controls, such as <select>, ASP:ListBox, ASP:CheckBoxList, etc. This is generally referred to as "**repeated-value binding**".

Although the techniques for the two types of binding are fundamentally similar, we'll examine the concepts of each one separately. We'll start by looking at **single-value data binding**.

Single-Value Data Binding

When we bind controls to single values, such as properties, methods, or expressions, we use one of the following simple types of syntax:

```
<%# property-name %>
```

or:

```
<%# method-name(parameter, parameter, ...) %>
```

or:

```
<%# expression %>
```

You can see from this that there are several possible sources for the value that will be bound to the control, and we'll look at these next.

Sources of Data for Single-Value Binding

The source of the value that we can use with single-value data binding includes:

- ❑ The value of a **property** declared within a page, or the property of another control or object.

- ❑ The result returned from a **method** declared in the page, or in another control or object.

- ❑ The result of evaluating an **expression**.

All of these will return a single value for binding to a control or, in fact, for placing directly within a page. So, for example, if we declare a suitable property named ImageURL within the code of the page like this:

```
ReadOnly Property ImageURL() As String
   Get
      'read-only property for the Page
      Dim strURL As String
```

```
        'some code would be here to calculate the value
        'we just set it to a fixed value for illustration
        strURL = "myimage.gif"
     Return strURL
  End Get
End Property
```

We can insert the value directly into the page itself, or as the value of an attribute for a control, using:

```
<%# ImageURL %>
```

The only remaining task is to activate the binding when the page is loaded. This is done using the `DataBind` method – we'll look at this in detail shortly:

```
Sub Page_Load()
   DataBind()
End Sub
```

Using Controls with Bound Values

The real advantage in using bound values is that the data binding statement block can be used within other controls, and the value of one control can come from another control. For example, we can link a label to a text box by specifying the `Text` property of the `TextBox` control as the `Text` property of the `Label` control:

```
<form runat="server">
  <ASP:TextBox id="MyTextBox" runat="server" />
  <ASP:Label id="MyLabel" Text="<%# MyTextBox.Text %>" runat="server" />
  <input type="submit" />
</form>

<script language="VB" runat="server">
Sub Page_Load()
   DataBind()
End Sub
</script>
```

Now, each time the page is submitted, the value in the `Label` control named `MyLabel` will be the value that was present in the `TextBox` control named `MyTextBox` – and we don't need to write any code other than calling the `DataBind` method.

This technique isn't limited to just setting the `Text` property of a control. We can use it to insert a value into almost any control – for example to specify the `Src` property of an `ASP:Image` control:

```
<ASP:Image Src="<%# ImageURL %>" ImageAlign="middle" runat="server" />
```

to specify the text caption of an `ASP:CheckBox` control:

```
<ASP:CheckBox Text="<%# ImageURL %>" runat="server" />
```

or to specify the text and target URL for an ASP:Hyperlink control:

```
<ASP:Hyperlink Text="<%# ImageURL %>" NavigateUrl="<%# ImageURL %>"
        runat="server" />
```

It also works the same for the normal HTML controls and elements that aren't actually server controls. For example, to specify the text that appears in an HTML textbox element:

```
<input type="text" value="<%# ImageURL %>" />
```

to specify the caption of an HTML Submit button:

```
<input type="submit" value="<%# ImageURL %>" />
```

or to specify the target URL and hotlink text in an HTML <a> element:

```
<a href="<%# ImageURL %>"><%# ImageURL %></a>
```

And, of course, we can concatenate explicit values with the bound value if required. For example, we can use it to specify just the file name part of a complete URL:

```
<a href="http://mysite.com/images/<%# ImageURL %>">
  View the file named '<%# ImageURL %>'</a>
```

Activating the Binding

As we briefly noted earlier, once we've specified the data-binding statement blocks in a page we must activate the binding when the page is loaded (or some other event occurs) to get the values inserted into their respective positions. If we don't, the ASP engine ignores the data-binding blocks when the page is compiled, and they aren't replaced by the intended value.

We activate the binding process using the DataBind method. This method is available at several places within the hierarchy of the page:

❑ To activate the binding for all the controls on the page we call the DataBind method of the Page object (as in the previous examples – Page is the default object so we can use Page.DataBind or just DataBind). This is the only way to activate the binding for the controls that are not specifically designed for use with data binding, such as the examples we've looked at so far in this chapter. It also binds any values that are inserted directly into a page, rather than into a control of some kind.

❑ To bind just a single control, we call the DataBind method of that control. This only applies to the list controls designed specifically for use with data binding (we'll meet these shortly).

❑ To bind just one row or item object from the data source, within a control, we call the DataBind method of that object. Again, this only applies to the list controls designed specifically for use with data binding.

A Single-Value Data-Binding Example

As an example of some of the ways that we can use data binding with single values, we've provided a sample page, Simple Single-Value Data Binding to a Range of Controls (`simple-single-binding.aspx`):

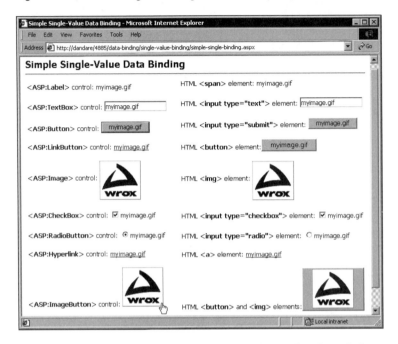

This example page shows how single-value data binding can be used with a whole range of controls. Click the [view source] link at the bottom of the page if you want to see the complete source for the page. Basically, it just uses the code we saw earlier to expose a simple property named `ImageURL`. Each of the controls in the page then uses this property value to set one or more of the properties for that control. Finally, the code in the `Page_Load` event handler calls the `DataBind` method of the `Page` object to bind all the controls on the page to the property value:

```
Sub Page_Load()
   Page.DataBind()   'bind all the controls on the page
End Sub
```

We've also provided a very similar example page that binds to the result of a method rather than a property value. This page, Single-Value Data Binding to a Method Result (`method-single-binding.aspx`) looks identical to the previous example when it's displayed in a browser. However, it does differ in the definition of a method named `ImageURL` that returns the value "`myimage.gif`":

```
Function ImageURL() As String
   Return "myimage.gif"
End Function
```

The only other difference is that now the expressions in the data-binding blocks include parentheses (because the data source is a method – though in fact in VB it works just as well without these):

```
<ASP:Label Text="<%# ImageURL() %>" runat="server" />
```

Repeated Value Data Binding

Single-value data binding is a useful technique, but data binding becomes a lot more valuable when we have repeating sets of values that we want to display – for example a rowset from a relational database, or an array of values.

ASP.NET provides eight list controls that are designed to work with repeated-value data binding. They have a set of properties and methods that allow us to connect them to a data source and they then automatically create one display row or display item for each row or item in the data source. For example, a `<select>` list control will automatically create an appropriate set of `<option>` elements to show all the rows or items in the data source.

One obvious advantage with these controls is that we don't have to provide any of the HTML ourselves. The control does it all automatically (though we can add HTML elements to the output to customize it if required).

The List Controls Designed for Repeated Binding

The eight controls specifically designed for use with server-side data binding are:

- ❏ The HTML `<select>` element, implemented by the .NET Class `System.Web.UI.HtmlControls.HtmlSelect`. It creates a standard HTML `<select>` list with repeating `<option>` elements when presented with a suitable source of repeating data values.

- ❏ The `ASP:ListBox` control, implemented by the .NET Class `System.Web.UI.WebControls.ListBox`. It also creates a standard HTML `<select>` list with repeating `<option>` elements. By default, it creates a listbox rather than a drop-down list like the `<select>` element – though the appearance of both can be changed by setting the number of items to display.

- ❏ The `ASP:DropDownList` control, implemented by the .NET Class `System.Web.UI.WebControls.DropDownList`. Again, it creates a standard HTML `<select>` list with repeating `<option>` elements. However, by default, it creates a drop-down list rather than a listbox.

- ❏ The `ASP:CheckBoxList` control, implemented by the .NET Class `System.Web.UI.WebControls.CheckBoxList`. It creates a list of standard HTML `<input type="checkbox">` elements – one for each row or item in the data source.

- ❏ The `ASP:RadioButtonList` control, implemented by the .NET Class `System.Web.UI.WebControls.RadioButtonList`. It creates a list of standard HTML `<input type="radio">` elements – one for each row or item in the data source. It also sets the HTML `Name` attribute (represented by the `GroupName` property of the control) to the same value so that each one in the list is mutually exclusive.

- ❏ The `ASP:Repeater` control, implemented by the .NET Class `System.Web.UI.WebControls.Repeater`. By default it generates no visible interface or formatting, and no HTML content – simply repeating the content you define within the control once for each row or item in the data source.

- ❏ The `ASP:DataList` control, implemented by the .NET Class `System.Web.UI.WebControls.DataList`. It repeats the content you define within the control once for each row or item in the data source, either enclosing each item in an HTML table row, or delimiting them using an HTML `<br />` element to create a list. It can also lay out the content in more than one column, and process items vertically or horizontally within the columns.

❑ The `ASP:DataGrid` control, implemented by the .NET Class `System.Web.UI.WebControls.DataGrid`. This is a full-featured grid control designed for use with data in the form of a `DataView`, `DataSet` or `DataReader` object, or a collection. It generates a visible interface in the form of an HTML table, automatically adding the column or item names to the header row. There are also many other useful features built in to make it easy to customize the display (we'll be looking at these later in this chapter).

The next screenshot (taken from the example page we'll look at shortly) shows the physical appearance of the various types of control listed above:

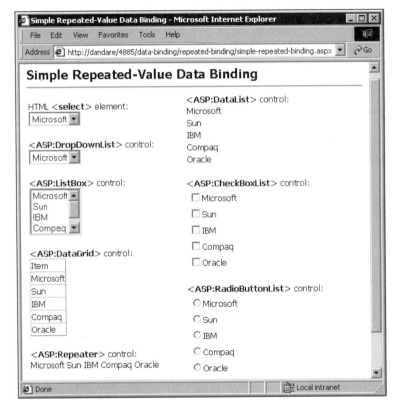

The Properties of a Repeated Binding Control

All the controls designed for use with server-side data binding expose properties and methods that we use to manage the binding. The properties are:

`DataTextField`	Specifies which field or column in the data source contains the values to be used for display, for example the values used as the text for `<option>` elements in a list box, or the captions of the checkboxes in a `CheckBoxList` control.
`DataValueField`	Specifies which field or column in the data source contains the values to be used as the `Value` property of the control elements, for example the values used as the `value` attribute for `<option>` elements in a listbox.

`DataTextFormatString`	The format string to be used for the values from the column or field specified in the `DataTextField` property when displaying these values in the control. For example, `"{0:C}"` for formatting currency values, or `"{0:dddd MMMM dd, yyyy}"` for formatting dates. We'll look at this topic in more detail later.
`DataMember`	Used to specify the set of rows to bind to when the data source contains more than one rowset, for example the name of the table when binding to a `DataSet` object.

There are many other properties that are specific to individual controls, and which govern how the content is displayed. We'll be looking at most of these as we see some example pages that use the controls later in this chapter.

The Methods of a Repeated Binding Control

All of the controls designed for use with repeated-values data binding expose at least two methods that we use when working with bound data. They are:

`DataBind`	Causes the control to populate itself with the data from the data source – in effect activating the bindings that we specify within the declaration of the control.
`FindControl`	Used to get a reference to a child control within the container (that is, within the bound control). Useful when we want to check the value in another child control (such as a table cell) within the same row as the current control. Normally used within event handlers that are executed once for each row or item – for example the `DataBinding` event.

The Events of a Repeated Binding Control

There is a wide range of events raised by the list controls, many specific to the control type. However, there are two that are common across all list controls designed for use with data binding:

`DataBinding`	Occurs for each row or item in the data source as that row or item is created within the control during the execution of the `DataBind` method. The row or item is passed to the event within the event parameters, and code can examine and modify the content of that row or item in the container control as it is populated.
`SelectedIndexChanged`	Occurs when the currently selected item changes and the page is posted back to the server. It allows code to change the display to reflect the user's selection.

Sources of Data for Repeated-Values Binding

So, having looked at the controls themselves, what kind of data sources can we bind to them? In technical terms, the list controls can be bound to any data source that implements the `IEnumerable`, `ICollection`, or `IListSource` interface. In more down-to-earth terms, this really means:

❑ A `Collection`, such as the collection of values in `Request.Form`, the collection of tables in a `DataSet` object's `Tables` collection, or a collection you create and populate yourself.

❑ An `ArrayList`, which contains a simple list of values. This is a good way to create a list of items for display in, for example, a listbox.

❑ A `HashTable`, which contains items that are identified by a key, rather like a `Dictionary` object. Each item has a `Key` and a `Value` property, making this type of data source ideal for things like listboxes, where the text to be displayed and the value to be returned when that item is selected are different.

❑ An ADO.NET `DataView` object, which contains rows from a `DataTable` that is populated from a database, or which is created and populated manually using code. This is a disconnected object that is easy to pass between the tiers of an application. We discuss the whole topic of creating and manipulating relational data in later chapters of this book.

❑ An ADO.NET `DataSet` object, which contains one or more `DataTable` objects that are populated from a database, or which are created and populated manually using code. Again, this is a disconnected object that is easy to pass between the tiers of an application. A control is bound to one of the tables through its `DataMember` property.

❑ An ADO.NET `DataReader` object, which provides connected forward-only and read-only access to a database for extracting data. It can contain one or more rows of data, and behaves basically in the same way as a `DataView` object for binding. When possible, you should aim to use a `DataReader` rather than a `DataView` or `DataSet` for performance reasons; however, some scenarios do require a `DataView` or `DataSet` to be used. We'll explore these in the examples later in the chapter.

For a full examination of the various types of collection that the .NET framework provides, see Chapter 15 "Working with Collections and Lists". For a full examination of how we can work with relational data and the `DataView`, `DataSet`, and `DataReader` objects, see Chapters 8, 9, and 10.

The Syntax for Repeated-Values Data Binding

When we bind controls to single values, such as properties, methods, or expressions (as we saw earlier), we use the simple syntax:

```
<%# name-of-data-source %>
```

However, data sources used for repeated-values binding often have more than one field (that is, more than one value in each row or "list item"). Examples are the `HashTable`, which contains a `Key` and a `Value`, and the `DataView` or `DataReader` object where each item is itself a `DataRow` object. In this case, we have to be able to specify **which** field (which value from the row or list item) we want to bind to the control.

Many of the list controls are also capable of displaying or using more than one value for each item in the list. As a simple example, a `<select>` element can use one value for the content of an `<option>` element, and one value for that `<option>` element's `value` attribute:

```
<select>
  <option value="value1">Text1</option>
  <option value="value2">Text2</option>
  ...
</select>
```

Mapping Fields in the Data Source To Control Properties

There are two ways that we can map (or connect) specific fields in each row of the data source to the properties or attributes of a control, depending on the type of control we are binding to. If the control supports **templates**, we can declaratively create a template that defines the content of each "row" or item that the control will display. If the control does not support templates, we assign the fields in the data source to the attributes of the control dynamically by setting the properties of the control at runtime.

The controls in ASP.NET that do support templates are Repeater, DataList and DataGrid. So, for one of these controls, we can declare a template within the control element and place our data binding instructions within it. We reference the row or list item as a DataItem object within the control's Container, and specify the field or column that we want. For example, when binding to a HashTable we specify either the Key property or the Value property:

```
Key: <%# Container.DataItem.Key %>
```

or:

```
Value: <%# Container.DataItem.Value %>
```

When binding to a Collection, DataView, or DataReader object, we specify the property, field, or column name itself:

```
Value from DataView/DataReader: <%# Container.DataItem("BookTitle") %>
```

or:

```
Value from Collection: <%# Container.DataItem("ForeColor") %>
```

So, for example, we could use a Repeater control to display the Key and Value in each row of a HashTable like this:

```
<ASP:Repeater id="MyRepeater" runat="server">
  <ItemTemplate>
    <%# Container.DataItem.Key %> =
    <%# Container.DataItem.Value %><br />
  </ItemTemplate>
</ASP:Repeater>
```

Then, in our Page_Load event handler, we simply assign the data source to the control and call its DataBind method (you'll see the result of this in the examples coming shortly):

```
MyRepeater.DataSource = tabValues
MyRepeater.DataBind()
```

Mapping Fields Dynamically at Runtime

For controls that don't support templates, we must set the properties listed in the earlier table at runtime. These properties specify the field from the data source that will provide the visible output for the control (the `DataTextField` property) and the field that will provide the non-displayed values for the control (the `DataValueField` property).

So, using our previous example of a `<select>` list populated from a `HashTable`, we could use one "column" (probably the Key) as the `value` attribute of each `<option>` element and the other "column" (the `Value`) as the text of the `<option>` element. We declare the control like this:

```
<select id="MySelectList" runat="server" />
```

And then set the properties of the control in the `Page_Load` event to display the appropriate fields from the data source like this (again you'll see the result of this in examples coming shortly):

```
MySelectList.DataSource = tabValues
MySelectList.DataValueField = "Key"
MySelectList.DataTextField = "Value"
MySelectList.DataBind()
```

The `DataGrid` control is also clever enough to be able to figure out fields in the data source automatically, and display all the values. This works when the data source is an `Array`, a `DataView`, a `DataSet` or a `DataReader`, but **not** when the data source is a `HashTable`. We'll look at the `DataGrid` control in detail towards the end of this chapter.

Evaluating Expressions with the Eval Method

The data-binding statement block in a control that requires templates (such as the `Repeater`, `DataList` and `DataGrid`) can contain instances of only the following expression and derivatives of it. In its simplest form, this expression is:

```
<%# Container.DataItem("field-name") %>
```

The common derivative is the use of the `Eval` method of the `DataBinder` object to specify a value within a data source (where it contains more than one value per row), and optionally format the value for display. In fact there are three ways that we can use the `Eval` method:

❑ When each row or list item in the data source contains more than one value (more than one column or field), for example a row from a `DataView` based on a database table, or a `HashTable` object.

❑ When we want to use a value from a different object than the one that the control is bound to as the source of the value.

❑ When we want to format the value for display, for example taking a numeric value and formatting it as currency.

The first of these is just an extension of the syntax we used in the previous section, and adds nothing to the process other than a performance hit. In general it should be avoided. As an example, however, in the following code the value we want is in the column named `BookTitle` within a row in a `DataView` object:

```
<%# DataBinder.Eval(Container.DataItem, "BookTitle") %>
```

It's important to realize that the `DataBinder.Eval` *method uses a technique called late-bound reflection to evaluate the expression. Therefore it carries a noticeable performance overhead compared to the standard data-binding syntax where just the value name is specified.*

Another important point is that we have to include a line-continuation character in Visual Basic when we use the `Eval` *statement, if we need to break the statement over more than one line. This shouldn't really be necessary, but bear it in mind when you are reading published code listings where the code could wrap to the next line.*

The second way we can use the `Eval` method is when we want to bind to an object that is not defined in the `DataSource` for the control. This allows us to reference specific values in that object, which are then used in every row that is displayed. For example, if we have a `DataView` named `objCityData` that contains information about cities, we can specify the value of the `CityName` column in the fourth row (rows are indexed from zero) of the `DataView` with:

```
<%# DataBinder.Eval(objCityData, "[3].CityName") %>
```

However, the most common and useful application of the `Eval` method is the third of the ways we listed earlier – to format values for display. We'll look at this topic next.

Formatting Values and Expressions with the Eval Method

The `Eval` method takes three parameters, the last of which is optional. This third parameter, which we didn't use in the previous examples, is a "format string" that defines the format of the output. For example, we can specify that the contents of the `PublicationDate` field in our data source is displayed in standard date format (depending on the regional settings of the server) using:

```
<%# DataBinder.Eval(Container.DataItem, "PublicationDate", "{0:D}") %>
```

The result from this example is something like "10 March 2001". When we use the `Eval` method we can only have one value in each expression, so the first number in the curly braces (a placeholder for the variable containing the value to be formatted) must always be zero. The character(s) after the colon (in this case "D") denote the format itself.

The common format strings we use with numeric values are:

Format character	Description	Example (US English culture)
C *or* c	Currency format	$1,234.60, ($28.15), £28.75
D *or* d	Decimal format	205, 17534, -65
E *or* e	Scientific (exponential) format	3.46E+21, -1.2e+3, 3.003E-15
F or f	Fixed-point format	34.300, -0.230
G or g	General format	Depends on actual value
N or n	Number format	3,456.23, 12.65, -1.534
P or p	Percent format	45.6%, -10%
X or x	Hexadecimal format	&H5f76, 0x4528 (depends on actual value)

The common format strings we use with dates are:

Format character	Description	Example (US English culture)
d	Short date	M/d/yyyy
D	Long date	dddd, MMMM dd, yyyy
f	Full (long date and short time)	dddd, MMMM dd, yyyy HH:mm aa
F	Full (long date and long time)	dddd, MMMM dd, yyyy HH:mm:ss aa
g	General (short date and short time)	M/d/yyyy HH:mm aa
G	General (short date and long time)	M/d/yyyy HH:mm:ss aa
M *or* m	Month and day	MMMM dd
R *or* r	RFC1123 format	ddd, dd MMM yyyy HH':'mm':'ss'GMT'
s	ISO 8601 sortable using local time	yyyy-MM-dd HH:mm:ss
t	Short time	HH:mm aa
T	Long time	HH:mm:ss aa
u	ISO 8601 sortable using universal time	yyyy-MM-dd HH:mm:ss
U	Universal sortable date/time	dddd, MMMM dd, yyyy HH:mm:ss aa
Y *or* y	Year and month	MMMM, yyyy

It's also possible to use the following characters to create a "picture" for numeric values. For example the format string "00#.##", when applied to the number 1.2345 would produce "001.23". If we want to specify positive, negative and zero formats, we separate each with semi-colons. So given the format string "00#.##;(00#.##);[0]", we would get "(001.23)" for the number -1.2345 and "[0]" for zero.

The picture format characters for numbers are:

Format character	Description
0	Displays a zero if there is no significant value – that is, it adds a zero in front of a number, or at the end of the number after the decimal point.
#	Digit placeholder, replaced only with significant digits. Other occurrences of this symbol are ignored if there is no significant digit.
.	Displays the decimal point character used by the current culture.
,	Separates number groups with the character used by the current culture, such as "1,000" in the US English culture. Can also be used to divide the value of a number, for example, the format string "0,," will display the number 100,000,000 as just 100 in the US English culture.

Format character	Description
%	Displays the percent character used by the current culture.
E+0, E-0, e+0 or e-0	Formats the output as scientific or exponent notation.
\	Displays the following character as a literal; that is, it is not interpreted as a format character.
" or '	Any characters enclosed in single or double quotes are interpreted as a literal string.
{ and }	Double curly brackets are used to display a single literal curly brace. For example "{{" displays "{" and "}}" displays "}"
;	Separates the two or three sections for positive, negative and zero values in the format string.

All other characters are copied directly to the output, so the format string "My value is: #.00" would, with the number 42, produce "My value is: 42.00".

Remember that the DataBinder.Eval method carries a noticeable performance overhead compared to the standard data-binding syntax of specifying just the value name, and you should use it only when necessary. In particular, avoid it when formatting of the value is not actually required. You can often format values as you extract them from a database, or within the definition of the property or method that provides the bound values.

Simple Repeated-Values Data Binding Examples

We've provided five example pages that are fundamentally similar, but demonstrate the different types of data source we can use with repeated-values data binding. There are examples of binding to an ArrayList, a HashTable, a DataView, a DataSet and a DataReader. We'll start with the ArrayList example, then show you the particular differences between this and each of the other examples in turn.

Repeated-Values Binding to an ArrayList Object

The simplest example of repeated-values data binding uses a one-dimensional ArrayList that is created and populated with values in the Page_Load event handler. This example page, Simple Repeated-Values Data Binding to List Controls (simple-repeated-binding.aspx) includes one of each of the eight list controls bound to our ArrayList:

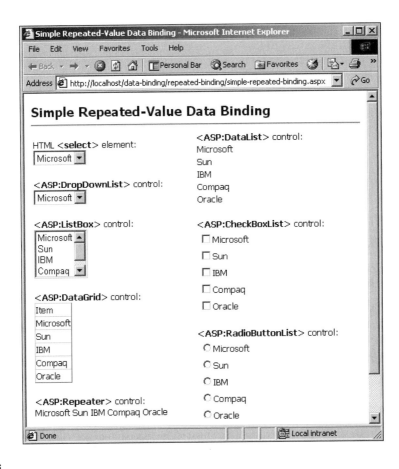

How It Works

The HTML section of the page contains the definition of the eight list controls. You can see that, with the exception of the Repeater and DataList controls, all we do is declare the control itself:

```
HTML <b>&lt;select&gt;</b> element:<br />
<select id="MySelectList" runat="server" /><p />

<b>&lt;ASP:DropDownList&gt;</b> control:<br />
<ASP:DropDownList id="MyDropDown" runat="server" /><p />

<b>&lt;ASP:ListBox&gt;</b> control:<br />
<ASP:ListBox id="MyASPList" runat="server" /><p />

<b>&lt;ASP:DataGrid&gt;</b> control:<br />
<ASP:DataGrid id="MyDataGrid" runat="server" /><p />

<b>&lt;ASP:Repeater&gt;</b> control:<br />
<ASP:Repeater id="MyRepeater" runat="server">
  <ItemTemplate>
    <%# Container.DataItem %>
  </ItemTemplate>
</ASP:Repeater><p />
```

```
<b>&lt;ASP:DataList&gt;</b> control:<br />
<ASP:DataList id="MyDataList" runat="server">
  <ItemTemplate>
    <%# Container.DataItem %>
  </ItemTemplate>
</ASP:DataList><p />

<b>&lt;ASP:CheckBoxList&gt;</b> control:<br />
<ASP:CheckBoxList id="MyCheckList" runat="server" /><p />

<b>&lt;ASP:RadioButtonList&gt;</b> control:<br />
<ASP:RadioButtonList id="MyRadioList" runat="server" /><p />
```

However, the `Repeater` and `DataList` controls require us to specify the output we want for each repeated item, and so for these we've included an `<ItemTemplate>` specification as well. Whatever we put inside the `<ItemTemplate>` is executed once for each repeated item (we look at templates in detail later in this chapter). In our code above, we're just specifying the `DataItem` itself – the value of that item within the `ArrayList`.

The Page_Load Event Handler

The remainder of the page is the event handler that runs when the page is loaded. It simply creates a new `ArrayList` and fills it with five string values. Then it sets the `DataSource` property of each of the eight list controls to this `ArrayList` and calls the `DataBind` method of the `Page` object to bind all the controls:

```
Sub Page_Load()

  'create an ArrayList of values to bind to
  Dim arrValues As New ArrayList(5)
  arrValues.Add("Microsoft")
  arrValues.Add("Sun")
  arrValues.Add("IBM")
  arrValues.Add("Compaq")
  arrValues.Add("Oracle")

  'set the DataSource propert of the controls to the array
  MySelectList.DataSource = arrValues
  MyDropDown.DataSource = arrValues
  MyASPList.DataSource = arrValues
  MyDataGrid.DataSource = arrValues
  MyRepeater.DataSource = arrValues
  MyDataList.DataSource = arrValues
  MyCheckList.DataSource = arrValues
  MyRadioList.DataSource = arrValues

  'bind all the controls on the page
  Page.DataBind()
End Sub
```

How the Controls Are Bound

To understand what the controls are doing when data binding takes place, it's worth taking a look at the actual HTML that is being created. You can do this by viewing the source of the page in your browser (right-click the page and select **View Source**). The simple list controls, the HTML `<select>`, `ASP:DropDownList`, and `ASP:ListBox`, are all persisted to the client as `<select>` elements. Each `<option>` element within the list has the value from the `ArrayList` items as both the value attribute and the text of the `<option>` element:

```
<select name="MySelectList" id="MySelectList">
  <option value="Microsoft">Microsoft</option>
  <option value="Sun">Sun</option>
  <option value="IBM">IBM</option>
  <option value="Compaq">Compaq</option>
  <option value="Oracle">Oracle</option>
</select>
```

The `DataList` control creates an HTML `<table>` and populates it with rows and cells containing the values from the `ArrayList`. The `DataGrid` control does the same, but adds a row containing the column name (in this case `Item`) as well:

```
<table cellspacing="0" rules="all" border="1">
<tr><td>Item</td></tr>
<tr><td>Microsoft</td></tr>
<tr><td>Sun</td></tr>
<tr><td>IBM</td></tr>
<tr><td>Compaq</td></tr>
<tr><td>Oracle</td></tr>
</table>
```

The `CheckBoxList` and `RadioButtonList` also both produce a table, but this time each cell contains either a checkbox control or a radio button control. The `CheckBoxList` control simply uses the values from the `ArrayList` as the captions for each checkbox – it doesn't set the value of each one:

```
<td>
  <span>
    <input id="MyCheckList_0" type="checkbox" name="MyCheckList:0" />
    <label for="MyCheckList_0">Microsoft</label>
  </span>
</td>
```

However, the `RadioButtonList` does set the value as well as the caption for each radio button. And all the radio buttons have the same name attribute (the name we gave to the control), so they operate as a radio button group – as you'd expect:

```
<td>
  <span value="Microsoft">
    <input id="MyRadioList_0" type="radio" name="MyRadioList"
         value="Microsoft" />
    <label for="MyRadioList_0">Microsoft</label>
  </span>
</td>
```

Finally, the output from the `Repeater` control is just a list of the values with no formatting:

```
Microsoft
Sun
IBM
Compaq
Oracle
```

Repeated-Value Binding to a HashTable Object

To demonstrate the differences in the way we handle other types of data source, the next example page binds the eight types of list control to a `HashTable` object rather than an `ArrayList`. You can run the example page, Repeated-Value Data Binding using a HashTable (`hashtable-binding.aspx`) to see the difference. One thing you'll notice immediately is that we've included two of each of the first three controls, and they contain different sets of values:

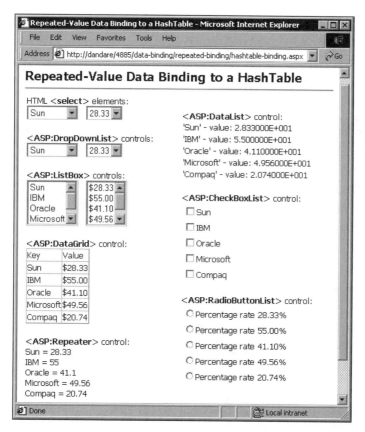

How It Works

In this case, the data source is not a simple array of values, but a `Dictionary`-style object known as a `HashTable`. Each of the repeated items in the `HashTable` contains a `Key` and a `Value`. So, in this case, we have to specify which of these we want to bind each control to. In the case of the first three list controls (the HTML `<select>`, `ASP:DropDownList`, and `ASP:ListBox`), we've bound one control to the `Key` of the `HashTable` and the other to the `Value`.

So, the HTML section of the page looks like this:

```
HTML <b>&lt;select&gt;</b> elements:<br />
<select id="MySelectList1" runat="server" />  
<select id="MySelectList2" runat="server" /><p />

<b>&lt;ASP:DropDownList&gt;</b> controls:<br />
<ASP:DropDownList id="MyDropDown1" runat="server" />  
<ASP:DropDownList id="MyDropDown2" runat="server" /><p />

<b>&lt;ASP:ListBox&gt;</b> controls:<br />
<ASP:ListBox id="MyASPList1" runat="server" />  
<ASP:ListBox id="MyASPList2" runat="server" /><p />

<b>&lt;ASP:DataGrid&gt;</b> control:<br />
<ASP:DataGrid id="MyDataGrid" runat="server" AutoGenerateColumns="false">
  <Columns>
    <ASP:BoundColumn HeaderText="Key" DataField="Key" />
    <ASP:BoundColumn HeaderText="Value" DataField="Value"
          DataFormatString="{0:C}" />
  </Columns>
</ASP:DataGrid><p />

<b>&lt;ASP:Repeater&gt;</b> control:<br />
<ASP:Repeater id="MyRepeater" runat="server">
  <ItemTemplate>
    <%# Container.DataItem.Key %> =
    <%# Container.DataItem.Value %><br />
  </ItemTemplate>
</ASP:Repeater><p />

<b>&lt;ASP:DataList&gt;</b> control:<br />
<ASP:DataList id="MyDataList" runat="server">
  <ItemTemplate>
    '<%# Container.DataItem.Key %>' - value:
    <%# DataBinder.Eval(Container.DataItem, "Value", "{0: E}") %>
  </ItemTemplate>
</ASP:DataList><p />

<b>&lt;ASP:CheckBoxList&gt;</b> control:<br />
<ASP:CheckBoxList id="MyCheckList" runat="server" /><p />

<b>&lt;ASP:RadioButtonList&gt;</b> control:<br />
<ASP:RadioButtonList id="MyRadioList" runat="server" /><p />
```

The declaration of the HTML `<select>`, `ASP:DropDownList`, and `ASP:ListBox` controls at the top of the page, and the `ASP:CheckBoxList` and `ASP:RadioButtonList` controls at the bottom of the page, is no different to the previous example – we just define the control itself. However, the definition of the other three list controls has to take into account the new structure of the data source.

Binding a DataGrid Control To a HashTable

The `DataGrid` control cannot figure out by itself how to handle a `HashTable`, and needs us to provide some help. As you'll see in more detail later in this chapter, we do this by setting the `AutoGenerateColumns` property of the control to `False`, and then using a `<Columns>` element and `<ASP:BoundColumn>` controls to specify where the values should come from.

The two columns are bound to the `Key` and `Value` fields in each item using the syntax shown below. We also specify a `DataFormatString` for the `Value` column so that it is displayed in currency format:

```
<ASP:DataGrid id="MyDataGrid" runat="server" AutoGenerateColumns="false">
  <Columns>
    <ASP:BoundColumn HeaderText="Key" DataField="Key" />
    <ASP:BoundColumn HeaderText="Value" DataField="Value"
            DataFormatString="{0: c}" />
  </Columns>
</ASP:DataGrid>
```

Binding a Repeater and a DataList Control To a HashTable

The `Repeater` and the `DataList` controls contain an `<ItemTemplate>` entry as in the previous example where we used an `ArrayList`. However, now we can include two values in each template – the `Key` property and the `Value` property. Notice how we refer to these as properties of the `DataItem` object.

You can also see that we're adding some extra layout information in these two controls. In the `Repeater` control we're adding the equals sign between the `Key` and the `Value`, and a line break after each `Key`/`Value` pair. In the `DataList` control, we're wrapping the output for each `Key` in single quotes, adding the word "value:" and formatting the `Value` property in scientific notation using the format string `"{0:E}"`:

```
<b>&lt;ASP:Repeater&gt;</b> control:<br />
<ASP:Repeater id="MyRepeater" runat="server">
  <ItemTemplate>
    <%# Container.DataItem.Key %> =
    <%# Container.DataItem.Value %><br />
  </ItemTemplate>
</ASP:Repeater><p />

<b>&lt;ASP:DataList&gt;</b> control:<br />
<ASP:DataList id="MyDataList" runat="server">
  <ItemTemplate>
    '<%# Container.DataItem.Key %>' – value:
    <%# DataBinder.Eval(Container.DataItem, "Value", "{0:E}") %>
  </ItemTemplate>
</ASP:DataList><p />
```

The Page_Load Event Handler

When the page loads, we first create the `HashTable` and fill in some values:

```
Sub Page_Load()

  'create a HashTable of values to bind to
  Dim tabValues As New HashTable(5)
  tabValues.Add("Microsoft", 49.56)
  tabValues.Add("Sun", 28.33)
  tabValues.Add("IBM", 55)
  tabValues.Add("Compaq", 20.74)
  tabValues.Add("Oracle", 41.1)
```

Then we can set the `DataSource` property of each of the controls on the page. Notice that, in this case, we have to set at least the `DataSource` and `DataTextField` properties of the `<select>`, `ASP:DropDownList` and `ASP:ListBox` controls so that they know which field in the data source contains the values to display. In fact we've exploited this by having the first control in each pair display the `Key` values from the `HashTable`, and the second display the actual values of each item in the `HashTable`: We can also provide different values for the value attribute of the control if required – we've done this for the second one of each control listed next:

```
'first <select> displays the Keys in the HashTable
MySelectList1.DataSource = tabValues
MySelectList1.DataTextField = "Key"

'second one displays the Values in the HashTable
'and uses the Keys as the <option> values
MySelectList2.DataSource = tabValues
MySelectList2.DataValueField = "Key"
MySelectList2.DataTextField = "Value"

'same applies to ASP: controls, except here
'we can also specify the format of the Key
MyDropDown1.DataSource = tabValues
MyDropDown1.DataTextField = "Key"
MyDropDown2.DataSource = tabValues
MyDropDown2.DataValueField = "Key"
MyDropDown2.DataTextField = "Value"
MyDropDown2.DataTextFormatString = "{0:F}"

MyASPList1.DataSource = tabValues
MyASPList1.DataTextField = "Key"
MyASPList2.DataSource = tabValues
MyASPList2.DataValueField = "Key"
MyASPList2.DataTextField = "Value"
MyASPList2.DataTextFormatString = "{0:C}"
```

If you look back at the screenshot, you can also see the results of setting the `DataTextFormatString` property of the `ASP:DropDownList` and `ASP:ListBox` controls. For example, in the last three lines of the code above we bound the second `ASP:ListBox` control to the `HashTable` so that the text of each `<option>` element is automatically formatted as a currency value.

Binding the `DataGrid`, `Repeater`, and `DataList` controls is easy because we specified how the columns should be mapped to the data source in the control definitions. We just need to set the `DataSource` property of each one:

```
MyDataGrid.DataSource = tabValues
MyRepeater.DataSource = tabValues
MyDataList.DataSource = tabValues
```

For the final two list controls, the `CheckBoxList` and `RadioButtonList`, we can specify both the `DataValueField` and the `DataTextField` properties. This is like the simple list controls such as the `<select>` list, and allows us to use different values from each item in the `HashTable` for the value attribute and the text for the control's caption:

```
'in the CheckboxList we'll display the Title and
'use the Value as the control value
MyCheckList.DataSource = tabValues
MyCheckList.DataValueField = "Value"
MyCheckList.DataTextField = "Key"

'in the RadioList we'll display and format the
'Value and use the Key as the control value
MyRadioList.DataSource = tabValues
MyRadioList.DataValueField = "Key"
MyRadioList.DataTextField = "Value"
MyRadioList.DataTextFormatString = "Percentage rate {0:F}%"
```

The final part of the code in the `Page_Load` event simply calls the `DataBind` method of the page to perform the data binding:

```
Page.DataBind() 'bind all the controls on the page

End Sub
```

How the Controls Are Bound

If you view the output that this page creates in the browser, you'll see that (unlike in the previous `ArrayList` example where the value and text were the same) the second of the two lists in each group has the `Key` from each item in the `HashTable` as the `value` attribute of the `<option>` elements, and the `Value` from each item in the `HashTable` as the text of each `<option>` element:

```
<select name="MySelectList2" id="MySelectList2">
  <option value="Sun">28.33</option>
  <option value="IBM">55</option>
  <option value="Oracle">41.1</option>
  <option value="Microsoft">49.56</option>
  <option value="Compaq">20.74</option>
</select>
```

In the `RadioButtonList`, this technique also gives an output that specifies the `Key` from each item in the `HashTable` as the `value` attribute, and the `Value` of each item in the `HashTable` is formatted and used as the text caption of the checkbox or radio button:

```
<span value="Microsoft">
  <input id="MyRadioList_3" type="radio" name="MyRadioList" value="Microsoft" />
  <label for="MyRadioList_3">Percentage rate 49.56%</label>
</span>
```

Repeated-Values Binding to a DataView Object

The third example of data binding is to a `DataView` object. For this example we're using a custom user control that returns a `DataView` object from a database. We've provided the scripts and instructions for creating this database with the sample files, as well as a Microsoft Access database that you can use instead.

> *We're putting off discussion of data access techniques until later in this book – it's not a vital topic here as long as you appreciate that basically each of the objects provides us with a set of data rows (a rowset) to which we can bind our controls. In the next chapter we discuss in detail how we use these objects to extract data from a relational database.*

The example page, Repeated-Value Data Binding to a DataView Object (`dataview-binding.aspx`) contains the same eight list controls as we've used in the previous two examples. However, now we are displaying information drawn from our database of Wrox books:

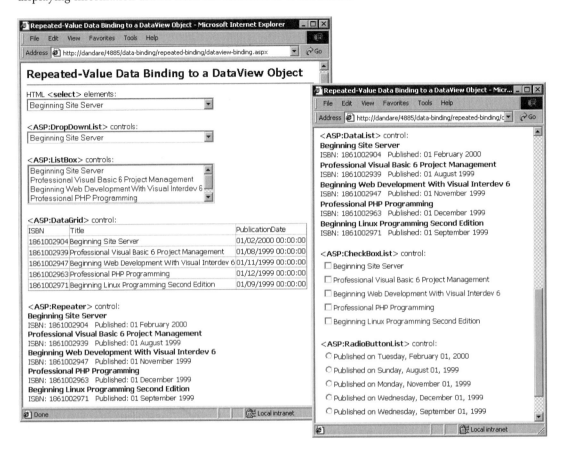

How It Works

The HTML section of this page is basically the same as the first `ArrayList` example. The exceptions are the definitions of the `Repeater` and the `DataList` controls. In each case, we need to specify the way we want to generate the content of the control from the values that are available in each "list item" (that is, each data row) within our source `DataView`.

The `Repeater` control generates no layout information by default, so we have to create a template using an `<ItemTemplate>` element (we'll look at templates in more detail later in this chapter). We specify a `<div>` element to get each item on a separate line, because the `Repeater` does not provide any intrinsic formatting. Inside the `<div>` we place the text, HTML, and definitions of the fields in the data source that we want to display. We're displaying the contents of three columns from the `DataView` – the `Title`, `ISBN`, and `PublicationDate` columns. We also format the `PublicationDate` column using the `DataBinder.Eval` method:

```
<ASP:Repeater id="MyRepeater" runat="server">
  <ItemTemplate>
    <div>
      <b><%# Container.DataItem("Title") %></b><br />
      ISBN: <%# Container.DataItem("ISBN") %>  
      Published: <%# DataBinder.Eval(Container.DataItem, _
                     "PublicationDate", "{0:D}") %>
    </div>
  </ItemTemplate>
</ASP:Repeater>
```

The `DataList` control creates an HTML table by default, so in this case we just need to specify the column and formatting information, along with any text and HTML we want to include in the table cells in each row:

```
<ASP:DataList id="MyDataList" runat="server">
  <ItemTemplate>
    <b><%# Container.DataItem("Title") %></b><br />
    ISBN: <%# Container.DataItem("ISBN") %>  
    Published: <%# DataBinder.Eval(Container.DataItem, _
                   "PublicationDate", "{0:D}") %>
  </ItemTemplate>
</ASP:DataList>
```

As we saw earlier, the `DataGrid` control is primarily designed to work with objects that are returned as the results of a database query, such as a `DataView` object, and so it will figure out what the column names and content are from the data source object automatically. Therefore we only need to place the `DataGrid` control in the page, and we don't need to provide column information:

```
<ASP:DataGrid id="MyDataGrid" runat="server" />
```

The Page_Load Event Handler

In this example, we're using two separate custom user controls that return a database connection string and a `DataView` object populated with details about some Wrox books. All the code in this page has to do is call functions in the user controls to get back the `DataView` object:

```
'get connection string from ..\global\connect-strings.ascx user control
Dim strConnect As String = ctlConnectStrings.OLEDBConnectionString

'create a SQL statement to select some rows from the database
Dim strSelect As String
strSelect = "SELECT * FROM BookList WHERE ISBN LIKE '18610029%'"

'create a variable to hold an instance of a DataView object
Dim objDataView As DataView

'get dataset from get-dataset-control.ascx user control
objDataView = ctlDataView.GetDataView(strConnect, strSelect)

If IsNothing(objDataView) Then Exit Sub
```

Details of how the control is inserted into the page, and how it gets the data from the database and creates the DataView object are contained in Chapter 8.

The next step is to set the DataSource and other properties of the controls in the page. The HTML <select> list and ASP:DropDownList and ASP:ListBox controls are mapped to the ISBN and Title columns in the DataView using the DataValueField and DataTextField properties of the controls:

```
'<select> list displays values from the Title column
'and uses the ISBN as the <option> values
MySelectList.DataSource = objDataView
MySelectList.DataValueField = "ISBN"
MySelectList.DataTextField = "Title"

'do same with ASP: list controls
MyDropDown.DataSource = objDataView
MyDropDown.DataValueField = "ISBN"
MyDropDown.DataTextField = "Title"

MyASPList.DataSource = objDataView
MyASPList.DataValueField = "ISBN"
MyASPList.DataTextField = "Title"
```

As we saw earlier, the DataGrid control can figure out what the DataView contains itself, so we just set the DataSource property:

```
MyDataGrid.DataSource = objDataView
```

And, as we specified the column information in the definition of the Repeater and DataList controls earlier on, we just set their DataSource properties:

```
MyRepeater.DataSource = objDataView
MyDataList.DataSource = objDataView
```

For the CheckBoxList control, we're using the ISBN as the value attribute, and the Title as the text to be displayed for each checkbox caption:

```
MyCheckList.DataSource = objDataView
MyCheckList.DataValueField = "ISBN"
MyCheckList.DataTextField = "Title"
```

Finally, we specify that the value property of each radio button in the RadioButtonList control should be the ISBN, but this time we're displaying the content of the PublicationDate as the caption. We also format it using a custom format string to display a "long" date:

```
MyRadioList.DataSource = objDataView
MyRadioList.DataValueField = "ISBN"
MyRadioList.DataTextField = "PublicationDate"
MyRadioList.DataTextFormatString = "Published on {0:dddd, MMMM dd, yyyy}"
```

All that's left is to activate the binding for all the controls on the page by calling the DataBind method of the Page object:

```
Page.DataBind()
```

Repeated-Value Binding to a DataSet Object

The next example of data sources is the DataSet, and this is used in the page Repeated-Value Data Binding to a DataSet Object (dataset-binding.aspx). It creates exactly the same result as the previous example, and the only differences are the creation of the datasource itself, and how we actually perform the binding. The page includes some code that creates a DataSet object, and we're leaving discussion of how this works until the next chapter. What we want to focus on here is the use of an object that has (or can have) multiple members as a data source.

As you'll see in the next chapter, a DataSet object can contain several tables of data (DataTable objects). When we bind to a DataSet, therefore, we have to specify which table we want the values for the control to come from. This is done with the DataMember property of each control. For example, to set the binding for the <select> list with the id of MySelectList we use:

```
MySelectList.DataSource = objDataSet 'specify the DataSet as the source
MySelectList.DataMember = "Books"    'use values from the table named "Books"
MySelectList.DataValueField = "ISBN" 'specify column to use for control values
MySelectList.DataTextField = "Title" 'specify column containing text to display
```

And, of course, the same technique is used for the rest of the controls on the page.

Repeated-Value Binding to a DataReader Object

The example page Repeated-Value Data Binding to a DataReader Object (datareader-binding.aspx) uses a DataReader as the data source for the bound controls. In general, using a DataReader is the preferred source of data for server-side data binding. However, there is one important difference between this and the other data sources we've used. A DataReader is really just a "pipe" to the results of executing a query in a database. Once the database has processed the query and built up the results set, the DataReader gives us a forward-only connection to that result set. We can read the rows once only.

This means that we can't create a DataReader and bind it to multiple controls as we've done in the previous examples. They worked because all of the other data sources (an ArrayList, HashTable, DataView and DataSet) are "disconnected" from the database. Unlike the DataReader, they are objects that actually hold the data, allowing us to read the contents as many times as we like. So, this example page only contains one data-bound control – a DataGrid. This is what the page looks like:

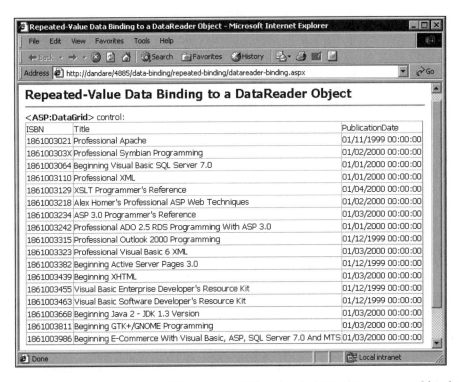

All we do is create our `DataReader` object in a variable named `objDataReader`, and bind it to the `DataGrid` control. The control can figure out what columns are in the rowset, and it displays the column names and the data automatically when we call the `DataBind` method:

```
'create a DataReader object
Dim objDataReader As OleDbDataReader
...
'code here to connect to the database and build the rowset
...

'set the DataSource property of the control
MyDataGrid.DataSource = objDataReader
MyDataGrid.DataBind() 'and bind the control
```

Notice that we are calling the `DataBind` method of the control itself, rather than the `DataBind` method of the `Page` object as we did in previous examples. As we've only got this one control, we can use its `DataBind` method whereas, in the previous example, we used the `DataBind` method of the `Page` to bind all the controls in one go.

Adding Styles and Templates

Having seen how easy data binding is to use, and how much code and effort it saves, we'll move on next to look at how we can change the appearance of the data-bound controls. This can be done in three ways:

- ❑ Add CSS styles to the control – either directly using a `<style>` element in the page, or by setting the specific style properties of the controls.

- ❑ Create templates that specify the appearance of individual sections of the control's output.

- ❑ Use a combination of the two techniques.

All of our example pages include a standard type of HTML `<style>` element in the `<head>` section of the page, which specifies the font name and font size for the page. As you'd expect, because the controls are generating ordinary HTML, their output is automatically formatted in line with these styles. The browser automatically applies the CSS styles that are active in the page:

```
<style type="text/css">
   body, td {font-family:Tahoma,Arial,sans-serif; font-size:10pt}
   input {font-family:Tahoma,Arial,sans-serif; font-size:9pt}
</style>
```

So, all of our `<input>` elements (including those that are created by the `ASP:ListBox` control, `ASP:DropDownList` control, etc.) are formatted with the style specified within our `<style>` element. We also include specific CSS style definitions for the `<td>` elements in the `<style>` section, so the HTML tables that some of the list controls create will be formatted in line with our `<style>` definition as well.

Using the Style Properties

The list controls designed for use with data binding also have a set of style properties that override the CSS styles defined in the page, and can be used to change the appearance of the control. The one exception is the `Repeater` control, which provides no visible interface elements (remember, it simply repeats the content of the templates we define within it). Some of the properties that can be set are shown in the table below (a full list is included in the .NET SDK Class Reference for each control):

`BackColor, BackImageUrl`	Sets the appearance of the control's background.
`BorderStyle, BorderColor, BorderWidth`	Sets the appearance of the control's border.
`GridLines, CellPadding, CellSpacing`	Specifies the appearance of each cell.
`Font-Name, Font-Size, Font-Bold`	Specifies the text style within the control.
`HeaderStyle, ItemStyle, FooterStyle AlternatingItemStyle`	Specifies the style for various parts of the control's output, such as the header or the content items.

Adding Style to a DataGrid Control

To see how these style properties can be used, and what effect they have on the appearance of a `DataGrid` control, run the example page Using CSS to Add Style to a DataGrid (`css-style-datagrid.aspx`). You can edit the code to experiment with the different styles:

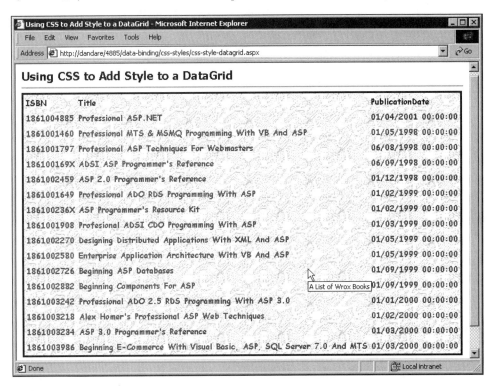

How It Works

All of the work of formatting the output of this rather garish example is done using the style properties of the `DataGrid` object. This is the definition of the `DataGrid` within the HTML section of the page:

```
<ASP:DataGrid id="MyDataGrid" runat="server"
  ShowHeader="True"
  ShowFooter="False"
  BackColor="darkgray"
  BackImageUrl="background.gif"
  ToolTip="A List of Wrox Books"
  GridLines="None"
  BorderStyle="Solid"
  BorderColor="black"
  BorderWidth="3"
  CellPadding="2"
  CellSpacing="2"
  Font-Name="Comic Sans MS"
  Font-Size="10pt"
  Font-Bold="True" >
    <HeaderStyle ForeColor="blue" />
    <ItemStyle ForeColor="red" />
    <AlternatingItemStyle ForeColor="green" />
</ASP:DataGrid>
```

You can see we're specifying that the grid should display a header but not a footer row (although, in fact, these are the defaults). We're also specifying the background color and an image to be used to fill the grid, a tool-tip that is displayed when the mouse hovers over the grid, and we're turning off display of the grid lines.

Next come the properties that define the 3-pixel wide black border for the control, and the padding within and spacing between the cells. We also specify the font name and size, and make it bold. Then, finally, come the style definitions for the header, each item (row) in the grid, and each alternating item. All we're doing here is specifying a color for the `ForeColor` property (via the `ForeColor` attribute), though in fact we can include values for the other properties such as `BackColor`, `BorderWidth`, `Font`, and so on.

In the `Page_Load` event, all we have to do now is create a `DataReader` object and set it as the `DataSource` property of the grid, then call the `DataBind` method. In this case, as we only have the one control to deal with, we've called the `DataBind` method just for our `DataGrid` control rather than calling it at `Page` level:

```
...
'create a suitable DataReader object here
...

'set the DataSource property of the DataGrid
MyDataGrid.DataSource = objDataReader

'and bind the control to the data
MyDataGrid.DataBind()
```

Using Templates with Data-bound Controls

The second way to manage the appearance of the ASP list controls designed for use with data binding is through the addition of **templates** to the control definition. In fact (as we've seen in earlier examples), templates can do a lot more than just change the appearance of a control – we can use them to specify which columns are displayed in a control, and how the values appear.

Three of the ASP list controls, the `Repeater`, `DataList` and `DataGrid`, accept a series of templates that define the appearance and content of specific parts of the output. All the templates are optional (depending on the control and the data source, as we'll see shortly), but the full list is demonstrated in the following diagram:

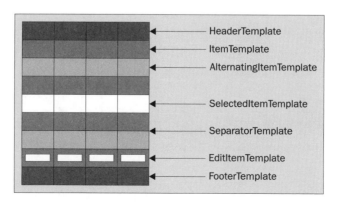

The names of each template are reasonably self-explanatory. We can optionally specify a different appearance for the header row (usually where the names of each field or column appear), the item rows themselves, the alternating item rows, the separator used between each item row, and the footer row (often used to display navigation controls if there is more than one 'page' of rows available).

The other two templates require a little more explanation:

❑ The `DataList` and `DataGrid` controls allow you to specify one item or row that is "selected" (by setting the `SelectedIndex` property). The `SelectedItemTemplate` is used to specify the appearance of this item or row.

❑ The `DataList` and `DataGrid` controls also allow you to switch them into "edit mode" by setting the `EditItemIndex` property. The `EditItemTemplate` is used to specify the appearance of this item or row (for example, by changing the controls used to display the values in the row from labels to input controls).

Specifying Style and Content in a Repeater Control

You'll recall that a `Repeater` control is the simplest of all list controls, and is designed just to repeat the content of the item or row without adding any formatting or layout information. To specify the content of each item when using a `Repeater` control (as we saw in earlier examples), we have to add at least an `<ItemTemplate>` element to the control definition. For example, to bind to an `ArrayList` we used the code:

```
<ASP:Repeater id="MyRepeater" runat="server">
  <ItemTemplate>
    <%# Container.DataItem %>
  </ItemTemplate>
</ASP:Repeater>
```

This specifies that the value in each row of the one-dimensional `ArrayList` should be displayed within the control. The `<ItemTemplate>` is used to define the content of the output.

The example page Using a Simple Template with a Repeater Control (`simple-repeater-template.aspx`) demonstrates how we can use templates to specify both the content and the appearance of a `Repeater` control. In this case, we're displaying an image, a subheading, and some text for each item. We're also displaying a header (Some of the Latest Wrox Press Books), a footer (containing the hyperlink to the Wrox web site), and separating each row with a dark red "rule" image:

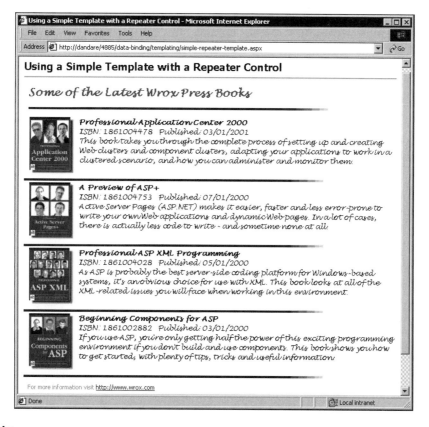

How It Works

This example applies style to a Repeater control through the use of four templates – one each for the header, item, separator, and footer of the control – and through a set of CSS styles defined within a <style> element in the <head> section of the page. Each template specifies the formatting, layout, and content of that section of the control's output – it has to do so as the Repeater control produces no layout information of its own.

So, the control definition starts with the opening <ASP:Repeater> tag, and then contains the first template definition. This is the <HeaderTemplate> (although template definitions don't have to be placed in any particular order within the control definition). It uses a <div> element to place the heading text and a ruler-style image on the page. This <div> uses the CSS style class named rHead to format the appearance of the text in the header:

```
<ASP:Repeater id="MyRepeater" runat="server">

  <HeaderTemplate>
    <div class="rHead">
      Some of the Latest Wrox Press Books<br />
      <img src="images/redrule.gif">
    </div>
  </HeaderTemplate>
```

This is followed by the `<ItemTemplate>` definition, which is again a `<div>` element. However, this time it takes its style from the CSS style class named rItem. Inside the `<div>` is an `<img>` element containing the cover image – it uses the value of the column ImageURL as the src attribute of the image. This is followed by definitions of the text and bound values – similar to those we've used in earlier examples – that display the book title, the ISBN, the publication date, and a short description obtained from a column named Precis. After all this comes a `<br>` element that prevents the next item from wrapping to the cover image in this row:

```
<ItemTemplate>
  <div class="rItem">
    <img src="images/<%# Container.DataItem("ImageURL") %>"
      align="left" hspace="10" />
    <b><%# Container.DataItem("Title") %></b><br />
    ISBN: <%# Container.DataItem("ISBN") %>  
    Published: <%# DataBinder.Eval(Container.DataItem, _
        "PublicationDate", "{0:d}") %><br />
    <%# Container.DataItem("Precis") %>
  </div><br clear="all" />
</ItemTemplate>
```

Notice that we've included a line-continuation character in the Eval statement for the "Published" value. This is code that is executed within the control at run-time to obtain the values, and so you can't have line breaks within it when using Visual Basic unless you include the line-continuation character.

Next comes the `<SeparatorTemplate>` definition. This is simply the red "rule" image:

```
<SeparatorTemplate>
  <img src="images/redrule.gif">
</SeparatorTemplate>
```

Finally, we have the `<FooterTemplate>` definition. This again contains the red "rule" image (the SeparatorItem template is only rendered between items in the control and not before the first one or after the last one). After the image comes the "more information" link, and then the closing `<ASP:Repeater>` tag:

```
<FooterTemplate>
  <img src="images/redrule.gif">
  <div class="rFoot">
    For more information visit
    <a href="http://www.wrox.com">http://www.wrox.com</a>
  </div>
</FooterTemplate>

</ASP:Repeater>
```

The Page_Load Event Handler

In this example, we provide our Repeater control with a DataView object that we create in code within the Page_Load event handler, rather than using a separate user control as we have in some of the earlier examples. So, the first part of the Page_Load event handler is responsible for creating a DataTable object from which we can obtain a DataView. The code is shown below in abridged form – we'll discuss the concepts of relational data access in depth starting in chapter 8:

```
Sub Page_Load()

    'create a new empty DataTable object
    Dim objTable As New DataTable("NewTable")

    'define four columns (fields) within the table
    objTable.Columns.Add("ISBN", System.Type.GetType("System.String"))
    objTable.Columns.Add("Title", System.Type.GetType("System.String"))
    objTable.Columns.Add("PublicationDate", System.Type.GetType("System.DateTime"))
    objTable.Columns.Add("ImageURL", System.Type.GetType("System.String"))
    objTable.Columns.Add("Precis", System.Type.GetType("System.String"))

    'declare a variable to hold a DataRow object
    Dim objDataRow As DataRow

    'create a new DataRow object instance in this table
    objDataRow = objTable.NewRow()

    'and fill in the values
    objDataRow("ISBN") = "1861004478"
    objDataRow("Title") = "Professional Application Center 2000"
    objDataRow("PublicationDate") = "2001-03-01"
    objDataRow("ImageURL") = "appcenter.gif"
    objDataRow("Precis") = "This book takes you through ... etc."
    objTable.Rows.Add(objDataRow)

    ...
    'repeat process for other rows
    ...

    'assign the DataTable's DefaultView object to the Repeater control
    MyRepeater.DataSource = objTable.DefaultView
    MyRepeater.DataBind() 'and bind (display) the data

End Sub
```

In the penultimate line of code, we simply assign the DataView object that is returned from the DefaultView property of the table to the DataSource property of the Repeater control. Then we execute the DataBind method of the control to display the contents of the DataView.

Loading Templates Dynamically at Run-time

The templates we used in the previous example are hard-coded into the source of the page. But what happens if we want to change the template we use at runtime? The next example page, Loading Templates Dynamically with a DataList Control (datalist-load-template.aspx) demonstrates how we can do this by dynamically loading templates using code. The page includes a drop-down list where you can select a color scheme for the output, and it loads the appropriate set of header, footer, item, and alternating item templates from disk each time:

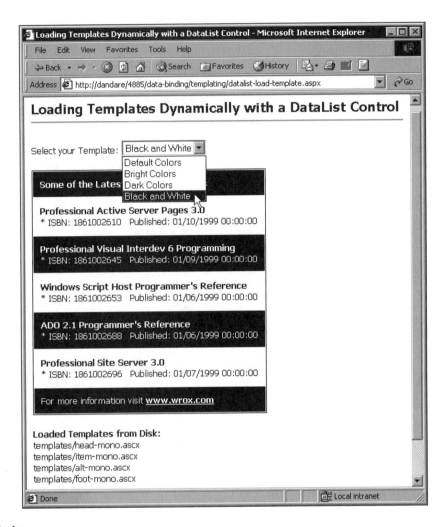

How It Works

The HTML section of the page defines a `<form>` containing the drop-down list where you select the color scheme you want. By setting the `AutoPostback` property to `True` (as we described in the previous chapter) we avoid the need for a separate button, as the form will be posted to the server automatically whenever the selection in the list is changed. The remainder of the HTML defines our `DataList` control with minimal formatting, and a `Label` control where we'll display the names of the template files currently in use:

```
<form runat="server">
  Select your Template:
  <ASP:DropDownList runat="server" id="TemplateList" AutoPostback="True">
    <ASP:ListItem Value="default" Text="Default Colors" />
    <ASP:ListItem Value="bright" Text="Bright Colors" />
    <ASP:ListItem Value="dark" Text="Dark Colors" />
    <ASP:ListItem Value="mono" Text="Black and White" />
  </ASP:DropDownList>
</form>
```

```
<ASP:DataList id="MyDataList" runat="server"
    BorderStyle="None"
    Font-Name="Tahoma"
    Font-Size="10pt" />

<p><ASP:Label id="lblFileNames" runat="server" /></p>
```

The Dynamic Template Files

Dynamically loaded templates must be disk files stored within the same application – that is within the same folder or a subfolder of the page that uses them. We've provided four templates for each color scheme (one each for the header, item, alternating item, and footer), placed in a folder named `templates` below the folder that contains our example page.

These template files contain just the contents of each of the templates, and omit the enclosing `<xxxxTemplate>` element. For example, this is the template for items when the "bright" color scheme is selected:

```
<div style="color:white; background-color:blue; padding=10px">
<b>
<%# DataBinder.Eval(CType(Container,DataListItem).DataItem, "Title") %>
</b>
<br />* ISBN:
<%# DataBinder.Eval(CType(Container,DataListItem).DataItem, "ISBN") %>  
Published:
<%# DataBinder.Eval(CType(Container,DataListItem).DataItem, "PublicationDate") %>
</div>
```

The Page_Load Event Handler

When the page loads, we create a `DataReader` object that will return some data rows from our sample database. Then we can create the filenames of the four templates we want for the selected color scheme. If this is the first time the page has been loaded (meaning it's not a postback, so no color scheme has been selected yet) we use the default templates:

```
Sub Page_Load()

  'create a suitable DataReader object here

  Dim strFileName As String
  If Page.IsPostBack Then
    strFileName = TemplateList.SelectedItem.Value & ".ascx"
  Else
    strFileName = "default.ascx"
  End If

  Dim strHeadFile As String = "templates/head-" & strFileName
  Dim strItemFile As String = "templates/item-" & strFileName
  Dim strAltIFile As String = "templates/alt-" & strFileName
  Dim strFootFile As String = "templates/foot-" & strFileName
```

Now that we have the filenames, we can load the templates by calling the `LoadTemplate` method of the `Page` object. The reference returned by this method is assigned to the appropriate property of the `DataList` control:

```
MyDataList.HeaderTemplate = Page.LoadTemplate(strHeadFile)
MyDataList.ItemTemplate = Page.LoadTemplate(strItemFile)
MyDataList.AlternatingItemTemplate = Page.LoadTemplate(strAltIFile)
MyDataList.FooterTemplate = Page.LoadTemplate(strFootFile)
```

The final tasks are to display the names of the templates in our `Label` control, and then bind the `DataReader` object containing our data rows to the `DataList` control:

```
lblFileNames.Text = "<b>Loaded Templates from Disk:</b><br />" _
    & strHeadFile & "<br />" & strItemFile & "<br />" _
    & strAltIFile & "<br />" & strFootFile & "<br />"

MyDataList.DataSource = objDataReader
MyDataList.DataBind()

End Sub
```

Multiple Column Layouts with a DataList Control

The `DataList` control we used in the previous example creates output that, by default, is an HTML table containing the items you bind it to. One very useful aspect of this control is the ability to change the layout of the table content by specifying the number of columns to use, and the order in which the columns are filled from the data source (that is from top to bottom, or from left to right).

The example page Using Multiple Display Columns with a DataList Control (`columns-datalist-template.aspx`) shows this technique in use. It displays six book cover images in two columns of three when you open the page. However, you can use the controls in the page to change the number of columns and the layout direction – as shown in the next screenshot:

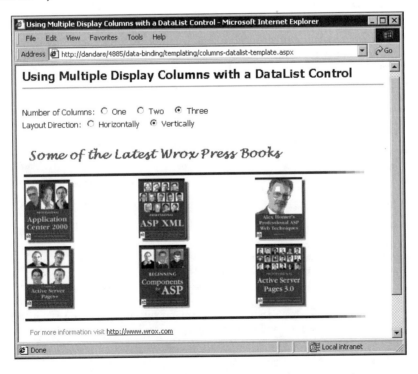

How It Works

The HTML section of this page contains a `<form>` with the five radio buttons that control how the `DataList` should lay out the content. We use the `AutoPostback` feature (as in the previous example) so that any change to the current settings automatically posts the values to our server and regenerates the page with the new layout:

```
<form runat="server">
  Number of Columns:
  <ASP:RadioButton id="Cols1" GroupName="Cols" AutoPostback="True"
        runat="server" /> One  
  <ASP:RadioButton id="Cols2" GroupName="Cols" AutoPostback="True"
        runat="server" /> Two  
  <ASP:RadioButton id="Cols3" GroupName="Cols" AutoPostback="True"
        runat="server" /> Three<br />
  Layout Direction:
  <ASP:RadioButton id="Horiz" GroupName="Dir" AutoPostback="True"
        runat="server" /> Horizontally  
  <ASP:RadioButton id="Vert" GroupName="Dir" AutoPostback="True"
        runat="server" /> Vertically<p />
</form>
```

Next comes the definition of the `DataList` control. You can see that we've specified three templates to control the appearance of the header, footer, and each item – in this case using an `<img>` element in the `<ItemTemplate>` to display the cover images:

```
<ASP:DataList id="MyDataList" runat="server" RepeatLayout="Table">

  <HeaderTemplate>
    <div class="rHead">
      Some of the Latest Wrox Press Books
    </div>
    <img src="images/redrule.gif">
  </HeaderTemplate>

  <ItemTemplate>
    <span>
      <img src="images/<%# Container.DataItem %>" />
    </span>
  </ItemTemplate>

  <FooterTemplate>
    <img src="images/redrule.gif">
    <div class="rFoot">
      For more information visit
      <a href="http://www.wrox.com">http://www.wrox.com</a>
    </div>
  </FooterTemplate>

</ASP:DataList>
```

The Page_Load Event Handler

The layout styles for the DataList are set in the Page_Load event handler code. We start by checking if this is a postback, or if it's the first time the page has been loaded. If it's a postback, we will already have the data source (an ArrayList in this example) available, so we only need to check what values were selected in the radio buttons and set the appropriate values for the RepeatColumns and RepeatDirection properties of the DataGrid. This automatically lays out the contents in the required way, without the need to rebind the data source:

```
Sub Page_Load()

  If Page.IsPostBack Then

      'set the number of columns to display
      If Cols1.Checked = True Then MyDataList.RepeatColumns = 1
      If Cols2.Checked = True Then MyDataList.RepeatColumns = 2
      If Cols3.Checked = True Then MyDataList.RepeatColumns = 3

      'set the repeat direction of the items in the columns
      If Horiz.Checked = True Then
         MyDataList.RepeatDirection = RepeatDirection.Horizontal
      End If
      If Vert.Checked = True Then
         MyDataList.RepeatDirection = RepeatDirection.Vertical
      End If
```

However, if this is the first time that the page has been loaded (so it's not a postback), we must create and populate the ArrayList, and bind it to our DataList control. We also have to set the default values for our radio buttons, and set appropriate initial values for the properties of our DataList control:

```
  Else

      'create an ArrayList of values to bind to
      Dim arrValues As New ArrayList(6)
      arrValues.Add("appcenter.gif")
      arrValues.Add("aspplus.gif")
      arrValues.Add("aspxml.gif")
      arrValues.Add("components.gif")
      arrValues.Add("webmaster.gif")
      arrValues.Add("asp3.gif")

      'bind the ArrayList to the DataList control
      MyDataList.DataSource = arrValues
      MyDataList.DataBind()

      'set default columns and direction when page first loads
      Cols2.Checked = True
      MyDataList.RepeatColumns = 2
      Horiz.Checked = True
      MyDataList.RepeatDirection = RepeatDirection.Horizontal

  End If

End Sub
```

Notice that we only have to create the data source once – when the page is first loaded, and not every time the user changes the layout. The values from the `ArrayList` are persisted through the VIEWSTATE of the page. However, you should be aware of issues that can arise from this. We'll look at the whole concept of managing the VIEWSTATE later in this chapter, when we examine how we can sort and filter the rows displayed in a list control.

Custom and Hidden Columns in a DataGrid

Templates are immensely powerful when working with the `Repeater`, `DataList`, and `DataGrid` controls. In fact when we come to use a `DataGrid` control, they become almost indispensable.

You'll recall from our earlier examples that the `DataGrid` control is very clever. It automatically figures out how many columns are needed to display the contents of a data source such as a `DataView` or `DataReader` object, and adds the column names to the header row. This means that, unlike with the `Repeater` and `DataList` controls, we aren't **required** to include templates that define the content – in other words we can just use:

```
<ASP:DataGrid id="MyDataGrid" runat="server" />
...
MyDataGrid.DataSource = objDataView
MyDataGrid.DataBind()
```

But what happens if we don't want to display all of the columns in the data source, or if we want to add custom columns to the output? It would be a shame to have to abandon the `DataGrid`, with all the extra features it provides, and go back to using a `DataList` or `Repeater` control.

Specifying a Custom Column Layout

Instead, we can use templates to specify the column layout of the `DataGrid` control. We set the `AutoGenerateColumns` property to `False`, and then use a `<Columns>` element to specify the columns to be displayed. Within the `<Columns>` element, we place a series of `ASP:BoundColumn` controls that define the column properties:

```
<ASP:DataGrid id="MyDataGrid" runat="server" AutoGenerateColumns="False">
  <Columns>
    <ASP:BoundColumn HeaderText="Book Code" DataField="ISBN" />
    <ASP:BoundColumn HeaderText="Book Title" DataField="Title" />
  </Columns>
</ASP:DataGrid>
```

So, the code above specifies that our control should display only the `ISBN` and `Title` columns from our data source, and that the columns should have the names Book Code and Book Title in the header row of the final output rather than the column name.

Adding Unbound Columns

We can also add extra columns that are not part of the original dataset using an `ASP:TemplateColumn` control and an `ItemTemplate`. For example, the following definition of a `DataGrid` control includes a column with the heading Information. In each row of this column is an (unbound) `ASP:Button` control with the caption More Info:

```
<ASP:DataGrid id="MyDataGrid" runat="server" AutoGenerateColumns="False">
  <Columns>
    ...
    <ASP:TemplateColumn HeaderText="Information">
      <ItemTemplate>
        <ASP:Button id="cmdInfo" Text="More Info" runat="server" />
      </ItemTemplate>
    </ASP:TemplateColumn>
  </Columns>
</ASP:DataGrid>
```

Formatting the Column Contents

We can also change the appearance of each of the custom columns, and format the values they contain. The following code defines a DataGrid like that we described earlier, but now it has a column with the heading **Released** that displays the value of the PublicationDate column in the source dataset. The value is formatted as a date using the format string "{0:D}", and right-aligned in the column on a yellow background:

```
<ASP:DataGrid id="MyDataGrid" runat="server" AutoGenerateColumns="False">
  <Columns>
    <ASP:BoundColumn HeaderText="Book Code" DataField="ISBN" />
    <ASP:BoundColumn HeaderText="Book Title" DataField="Title" />

    <ASP:BoundColumn HeaderText="Released" DataField="PublicationDate"
            DataFormatString="{0:D}"
            ItemStyle-BackColor="yellow"
            ItemStyle-HorizontalAlign="right" />

    <ASP:TemplateColumn HeaderText="<b>Buy Now</b>"
            ItemStyle-BackColor="silver"
            ItemStyle-HorizontalAlign="center">
      <ItemTemplate>
        <ASP:CheckBox id="chkBuy" runat="server" />
      </ItemTemplate>
    </ASP:TemplateColumn>

  </Columns>
</ASP:DataGrid>
```

There is also a column with the heading Buy Now in bold text. It has a silver background with the content aligned centrally in the column, and each row contains an unbound checkbox control. You can see all of the effects we've just been describing, plus one or two more, by running the example page Specifying the Columns in a DataGrid Control (columns-datagrid.aspx):

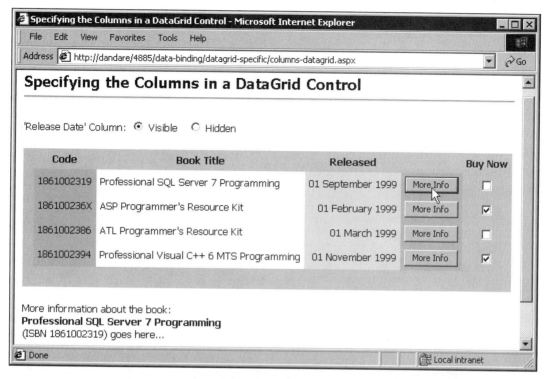

You'll also notice that clicking the **More Info** buttons produces some text at the foot of the page (it's displayed in a Label control). This text would probably be extracted from the same database table (or another table). However, we haven't implemented that in our example, as we're more interested in the way that the DataGrid control is used.

How It Works

The first part of the HTML is the definition of the two radio buttons that control the display of the "Released" column. As in previous examples, we use automatic postback to make it more intuitive in use:

```
<form runat="server">

  'Release Date' Column:
  <ASP:RadioButton id="chkVisible" GroupName="Col2Visible" runat="server"
        AutoPostback="True" /> Visible  
  <ASP:RadioButton id="chkNotVisible" GroupName="Col2Visible" runat="server"
        AutoPostback="True" /> Hidden<p />
```

Next comes the DataGrid control definition. It's on our <form> because it contains controls that we want to use to post the page back to our server (that is, the **More Info** buttons). It uses the techniques we've just been discussing to create a custom column layout – including columns that contain only a non-breaking space and are simply there to give the required appearance for the control:

```
<ASP:DataGrid id="MyDataGrid" runat="server"
   AutoGenerateColumns="False"
   CellPadding="5"
   GridLines="None"
   HeaderStyle-BackColor="silver"
   HeaderStyle-HorizontalAlign="center"
   FooterStyle-BackColor="silver"
   ShowFooter="True"
   OnItemCommand="ShowInfo">
  <Columns>
    <ASP:TemplateColumn HeaderText="" ItemStyle-BackColor="silver">
      <ItemTemplate> </ItemTemplate>
    </ASP:TemplateColumn>
    <ASP:BoundColumn HeaderText="<b>Code</b>" DataField="ISBN"
         ItemStyle-BackColor="lightblue" />
    <ASP:BoundColumn HeaderText="<b>Book Title</b>" DataField="Title"/>
    <ASP:BoundColumn HeaderText="<b>Released</b>"
         DataField="PublicationDate"
         DataFormatString="{0:D}" ItemStyle-BackColor="yellow"
         ItemStyle-HorizontalAlign="right" />
    <ASP:TemplateColumn HeaderText="" ItemStyle-BackColor="lightblue">
      <ItemTemplate>
        <ASP:Button id="cmdInfo" Text="More Info"
             CommandName="Info" runat="server" />
      </ItemTemplate>
    </ASP:TemplateColumn>
    <ASP:TemplateColumn HeaderText="Buy Now" ItemStyle-BackColor="silver"
         ItemStyle-HorizontalAlign="center">
      <ItemTemplate>
        <ASP:CheckBox id="chkBuy" runat="server" />
      </ItemTemplate>
    </ASP:TemplateColumn>
  </Columns>
</ASP:DataGrid>
```

Notice the penultimate <ASP:TemplateColumn> control. It contains an <ItemTemplate> specifying that each row will contain an ASP:Button control with the caption **More Info**. It also specifies that the CommandName property of the button is the string value "Info". You'll see how we use this when we look at the code in the page shortly.

The only other control is the Label named lblInfo that we use to display information about each book in the table:

```
<ASP:Label id="lblInfo" runat="server" />
```

```
</form>
```

Binding the DataGrid

The code in this page is divided into three subroutines:

❑   Page_Load is executed each time the page is loaded. It sets the visibility of the "Released" column and then calls the BindDataGrid routine.

❑   BindDataGrid fetches the data from the database and returns it as a DataReader object. Then it binds this to the DataGrid control to display the values.

❑   ShowInfo runs when any of the command buttons in the grid is clicked. It retrieves the ISBN and title of the book from the row and displays it in the Label control at the foot of the page.

Showing and Hiding Columns

When you click the relevant radio button at the top of the page, the Released column is hidden or shown in the grid. Compare this next screenshot with the previous one to see the difference:

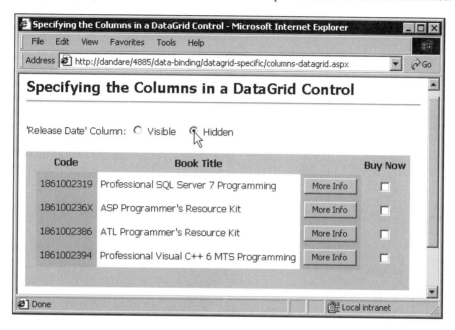

The radio buttons have their AutoPostback property set to True so that the page is reloaded each time the selection is changed. In the Page_Load event, we check to see if this is the first time the page has been loaded. If not (if it's a postback) we just set the Visible property of the appropriate column using its index within the Columns collection of the DataGrid control. If it's not a postback, we have to set the default value for the radio buttons and bind the grid to the data source. In this case, the Released column will be displayed, because the default is to show all columns:

```
Sub Page_Load()

    If Page.IsPostBack Then

        'display or hide the "Released" column
        'have to use the index of the column not the column name
        MyDataGrid.Columns(3).Visible = (chkVisible.Checked = True)

    Else

        chkVisible.Checked = True 'set default value
        BindDataGrid()           'create dataset and bind grid

    End If

End Sub
```

Reacting To the ItemCommand Event

The other feature of the page is how it displays information about each book in response to a click on the **More Info** button. In the definition of the `DataGrid` control, we specified the name of an event handler for the `ItemCommand` event by setting the `OnItemCommand` property of the `DataGrid`:

```
  . . .
  OnItemCommand="ShowInfo">
```

When any control within the grid is activated – in our case the `ASP:Button` control with the caption **More Info** – this event handler is executed. The parameters sent to the event handler contain a reference to the control that initiated the event, and a `DataGridCommandEventArgs` object that contains details of the event and references to the current row in the control (the row containing the control that was activated).

Within our event handler, we access the `CommandName` of the `CommandSource` object (our **More Info** button) to see which control it was that activated the event (there could be more than one in each row). Our button has a `CommandName` property value of `Info`, so we can choose the action to take based on this:

```
Sub ShowInfo(objSender As Object, objArgs As DataGridCommandEventArgs)

  'runs when any command button in the grid is clicked
  'see if the CommandName of the clicked button was "Info"
  If objArgs.CommandSource.CommandName = "Info" Then
    . . .
```

Now that we've identified that it was the **More Info** button that was clicked, we can access the values in that particular row of our control. The `DataGridCommandEventArgs` object (here named `objArgs`) exposes the items in the current row of a `DataGrid` control as a `Cells` collection. We access the cell we want by specifying its index within the row (starting at zero), and get the value from the `Text` property. Then we can use these values to create the output and place it in the `Label` control located below the grid on our page:

```
    . . .
    'get values of ISBN and Title from Text property of the table cells
    'for the current row returned in the objArgs parameter values
    Dim strISBN As String = objArgs.Item.Cells(1).Text
    Dim strTitle As String = objArgs.Item.Cells(2).Text

    'display the information in the page – possibly extract from database?
    lblInfo.Text = "More information about the book:<br /><b>" & strTitle _
      & "</b><br />(ISBN " &strISBN & ") goes here..."
  End If

End Sub
```

So, using this technique, we could extract the ISBN and use it to look up information about the book in another table. Or we could even use it to access another web site or a Web Service to get information and display that to the user.

Handling Data Binding Events

The content of each cell or item in a list control is created as that control is being executed, as part of the overall page creation process. This means that the content of each cell is controlled only by the value in the data source and the formatting applied by the template or style properties in the control definition. However, it's often useful to be able to access and modify the content at runtime, based on the actual value that occurs in the source dataset.

We can do this by reacting to events that the control raises. The most useful in this scenario is the DataBinding event, which occurs after the values for the column have been determined, but before they are output to the client. This event is supported in all the list controls designed for data binding, including the ASP:DataGrid, ASP:DataList, ASP:Repeater, and HTMLSelect controls.

In essence we just have to create a handler for the event and tell the control where to find this event handler. It is then called for each row in the data source as the binding takes place. Within the event handler, we can access the entire row of data, and modify the content of any of the controls within that row.

The example page Handling Data Binding Events in a DataList Object (datalist-bind-events.aspx) demonstrates this technique by adding the slogan "Great for ASP Programmers!" to any book title that contains the words "Active Server Pages" or "ADO":

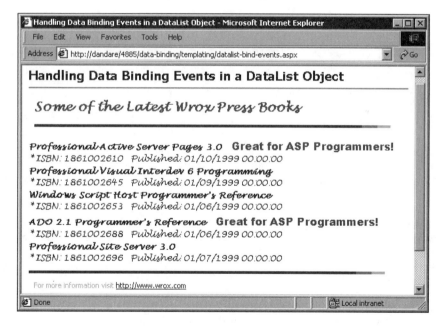

How It Works

The definition of the DataList control we use in this example is much the same as in previous examples. We use a <HeaderTemplate>, <ItemTemplate>, and <FooterTemplate> along with some CSS styles to specify and format the output from the control. What's important here is that we also set the OnItemDataBound property of the DataList object to the name of an event handler that we want to be executed as each row in the list is bound to the data source:

```
<ASP:DataList id="MyDataList" runat="server" RepeatLayout="Table"
   OnItemDataBound="CheckTitle">
   ...
</ASP:DataList>
```

We use the same Page_Load event handler as in previous examples to get a DataView object containing our source data from the separate custom user control, and bind it to the grid for display. What makes this example different is the event handler that we have specified for the ItemDataBound event.

Reacting To the ItemDataBound Event

Our event handler, named CheckTitle, is shown next. When it's called by the control, as each row is bound to the source data, it is passed two parameters. The first is the usual reference to the object that caused the event, and the second is a DataListItemEventArgs object that contains information about the event and the row that was being bound.

The first thing we do in our event handler is to check what type of row was being bound, whether it's a header row, footer row, item row, alternating item row, etc. (the type of template used to create the row determines this). We're only interested in item and alternating item rows. You can see that we obtain the row type from the ItemType property of the current row in the DataListItemEventArgs:

```
Sub CheckTitle(objSender As Object, objArgs As DataListItemEventArgs)

   'see what type of row (header, footer, item, etc.) caused the event
   Dim objItemType As ListItemType = CType(objArgs.Item.ItemType, ListItemType)

   'only format the results if it's an Item or AlternatingItem event
   If objItemType = ListItemType.Item _
   Or objItemType = ListItemType.AlternatingItem Then
      ...
```

Once we know that this is a row we want to process, we can get the values from the DataItem property of this row. This returns a DataRowView object – basically a collection of the columns within this row. So we can access the value of the column we want (the Title column) by specifying the column name:

```
   ...
   'objArgs.Item.DataItem returns the data for this row of items
   Dim objRowVals As DataRowView = CType(objArgs.Item.DataItem, DataRowView)

   'get the value of the Title column
   Dim strTitle As String = objRowVals("Title")
```

Now we can test the value to see if it's one that we want to modify. We're looking for book titles that contain the words "Active Server Pages" or "ADO". If we find one that matches, we use the FindControl method of the row to get a reference to the control with an ID value of TitleLabel. This is the control that we bound to the Title column within the definition of the DataList control earlier in our page. Once we get our reference to this control, we can append the extra text (Great for ASP Programmers!), putting it in a <span> element that specifies the large red font style:

```
        If strTitle.IndexOf("Active Server Pages") >= 0 _
        Or strTitle.IndexOf("ADO") >= 0 Then

            'get a reference to the "Title" ASP:Label control in this row
            Dim objLabel As Label = _
                CType(objArgs.Item.FindControl("TitleLabel"), Label)

            'add a message to this Label control
            objLabel.Text += "   <span class='bigRed'>" _
                & "Great for ASP Programmers!</span>"

        End If
    End If

End Sub
```

If you look back at the screenshot, you'll see that this text appears only for the two books that contain the search text within their title. So, this gives us a useful technique for dynamically modifying the contents of a list control based on the current values of the data – something we can't always do by hard-coding logic into the page.

And it isn't limited to just adding text to a Label control. We could place other controls (such as <img> elements) in the output of a DataList that are not visible, and then change their properties in the ItemDataBound event handler based on the values in the bound data. Or we could just change the formatting of existing bound content based on the current value. The possibilities are almost endless.

Sorting and Filtering Rows in a DataGrid

When we need to display more than a few rows of data, it's helpful for users to be able to sort the rows based on a specific column, and filter the rows based on specific values. Both techniques make it much easier for them to find what they are looking for. OK, so it means extra round-trips to the server using the current generation of controls, but it's a useful feature to add to your applications.

We can provide both these facilities easily when using a DataGrid control. The DataGrid can do most of the work required to provide a "sort by column" facility. And if the data source for the control is a DataView object, we can take advantage of the sorting and filtering features that it includes.

❑   To **sort** the rows within a DataView, we just have to set the Sort property to a string containing the name of the column, and optionally the keyword DESC to sort in descending order. We can sort by more than one column by separating the column names with a comma.

❑   To **filter** the rows that appear in the DataView, we set the RowFilter property to an expression that specifies the rows to be displayed. A simple example is "Title LIKE 'ASP'". More details on the Sort and RowFilter properties are provided in the data access chapters later in this book.

The big advantage in using a DataGrid control is that it has a property named AllowSorting, and it exposes an event named SortCommand. When we set the AllowSorting property to True (usually done within the definition of the control), each column heading automatically becomes a hyperlink. When clicked, a postback occurs and the event handler specified for the SortCommand property is executed.

You can see the way that we implement both sorting and filtering in the example page Sorting Rows and Finding Data in a DataGrid Control (`sort-find-datagrid.aspx`):

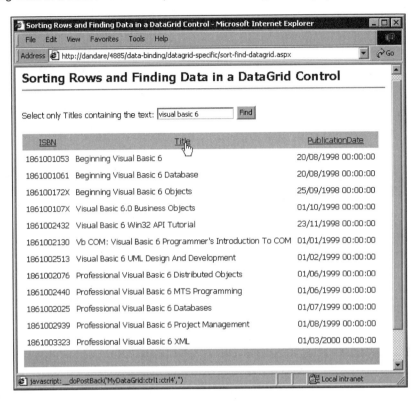

How It Works

The HTML section of this page contains the textbox and button used to filter the rows based on the title of the book. These controls are followed by the definition of the DataGrid that we use to display the matching titles:

```
<form runat="server">

  Select only Titles containing the text:
  <ASP:TextBox id="txtFindText" runat="server" />
  <ASP:Button id="cmdFind" Text="Find" runat="server" /><p />

  <ASP:DataGrid id="MyDataGrid" runat="server"
    EnableViewState="False"
    CellPadding="5"
    GridLines="None"
    HeaderStyle-BackColor="silver"
    HeaderStyle-HorizontalAlign="center"
    FooterStyle-BackColor="silver"
    ShowFooter="True"
    AllowSorting="True"
    OnSortCommand="SortRows" />

</form>
```

Other than some minimal styling information, the two properties we set for the `DataGrid` that are of interest here are the `AllowSorting` property and the `OnSortCommand` property. As we explained earlier, these properties specify the appearance of the `LinkButton` controls as the column names in the header row, and the name of the event handler that is executed when one of the column names is clicked.

The code section of the page contains three subroutines. As well as the `Page_Load` event handler, we have a `BindDataGrid` routine that is responsible for fetching the data sorted and filtered as required. The third routine, named `SortRows`, is executed when the column headings are clicked. You can see that it is attached to the `DataGrid` in the previous code listing as the `OnSortCommand` property. The page also defines two global (`Page`-level) variables that will hold the current sort order and filter expression:

```
Dim gstrSortOrder As String  'to hold the sort order
Dim gstrFindText As String   'to hold the filter expression
```

Binding the DataGrid

The first of the subroutines, named `BindDataGrid`, uses the same custom user control as some of the earlier examples to fetch a `DataView` object containing the book details from the data store. It then binds this `DataView` to our `DataGrid` control. However, it has a couple of other tasks to complete as well. It uses the two global variables to set the sort order of the rows in the `DataView` (by setting the `Sort` property) and it applies a filter to the rows controlling which ones will be displayed (by setting the `RowFilter` property):

```
Sub BindDataGrid()

    ...
    'get dataset from get-dataset-control.ascx user control
    ...

    'sort the rows in the DataView into the specified order
    objDataView.Sort = gstrSortOrder

    'select the rows in the DataView that match the filter
    objDataView.RowFilter = gstrFindText

    'set the DataSource property of the DataList and bind it
    MyDataGrid.DataSource = objDataView
    MyDataGrid.DataBind()

End Sub
```

The Page_Load Event Handler

The second subroutine is the `Page_Load` event handler. This is executed when the page first loads and when the user clicks a column heading to change the sort order, or clicks the Find button to filter the rows that are displayed. In the event handler, if this is a postback, we change the global filter expression variable to reflect the value in the textbox. If it's the first time that the page has been loaded, we set default values for the textbox and the global string that specifies the sort order of the rows.

The result is that we start out with the value "ASP" in the textbox when we first load the page, and from then on the global string variable will always hold the expression used to filter the rows. We also call our `BindDataGrid` subroutine (the one we just examined) each time the page is loaded, so that the `DataView` object and the grid are recreated with the current sort order and row filter:

```
Sub Page_Load()

  If Page.IsPostBack Then

    'set the value to be used for the RowFilter on the DataView
    gstrFindText = "Title LIKE '*" & txtFindText.Text & "*'"

  Else

    'set the default values for the sort string and filter text box
    gstrSortOrder = "ISBN"
    txtFindText.Text = "ASP"

  End If

  'recreate the data set and bind to the DataGrid control
  BindDataGrid()

End Sub
```

Sorting the Rows in the DataGrid

When our page is first loaded, the Page_Load event handler sets the Page-level variable holding the sort order to the value "ISBN", so the rows will be sorted in the order of the ISBN column values. But how do we change the sort order? Easy – the DataGrid control raises the SortCommand event whenever the user clicks on a column heading LinkButton. We specified our subroutine named SortRows as the handler for this event:

```
Sub SortRows(objSender As Object, objArgs As DataGridSortCommandEventArgs)
  'runs when the column headings in the DataGrid are clicked

  'get the sort expression (name of the column heading that was clicked)
  gstrSortOrder = objArgs.SortExpression.ToString()

  'recreate the data set and bind to the DataGrid control
  BindDataGrid()

End Sub
```

As you can see, the code required is minimal. The DataGridSortCommandEventArgs object that is automatically passed to our event handler when a column heading is clicked exposes a SortExpression property, which contains the name of the column. All we do is ensure that it's converted to a string and assign it to the Page-level "sort order" variable, then call the routine that recreates the DataView and binds it to our grid.

Controlling the Size of the VIEWSTATE

One issue that you really must be aware of when using these list controls is the effect that they have on the amount of data being transmitted across the wire with each postback and with each newly generated page. As we briefly discussed in the previous chapter, an ASP.NET page containing a server-side <form> control automatically generates **VIEWSTATE**. This is an encoded representation of all the values in all the controls on the page, and it is persisted across page loads using a HIDDEN-type <input> control. If you view the source of the page in the browser, you'll see something like this:

```
<form name="ctrl0" method="post" action="mypage.aspx" id="ctrl0">
<input type="hidden" name="__VIEWSTATE" value="dDwxOTAwNDM2ODc1Ozs+" />
...
```

If we place a list control on a page and fill it with data, all that data is encoded into the VIEWSTATE and passed across the wire with each page load and postback. In fact, it's even worse than that because when the user loads the page, we're actually sending all the values twice – once as the visible output of the list control, and once as the content of the VIEWSTATE.

Of course, we may want this to occur as a feature of the way that the page works. If we create the output for the list control and bind it only during the first page load, not during each postback, we depend on the VIEWSTATE to maintain the values in the list control. If getting the values from the data source is an expensive process in terms of resources or time, then persisting them in the VIEWSTATE is a good idea.

However, if we are limited in bandwidth, or perhaps serving devices like mobile phones that can't cope with large volumes of form content, then we might instead decide to recreate the values on each postback, and not include them in the VIEWSTATE. Bear in mind that this option requires a conscious decision – if you take no action the values will be included in the VIEWSTATE.

Persisting List Control Values Automatically Across Postbacks

If we want to persist values across postbacks, we can use the `IsPostback` property of the `Page` object so that the values are only created when the page is being executed for the first time:

```
Sub Page_Load()
  If Not Page.IsPostback Then
    objDataView = GetDataView(.....)    'get or build a DataView object
    MyDataGrid.DataSource = objDataView 'specify the data source
    MyDataGrid.DataBind()               'bind data to grid control
  End If
End Sub
```

Now, when the page is reloaded, the values that are automatically included in the VIEWSTATE will be used to populate the control.

Preventing List Control Values from Being Persisted Across Postbacks

There are occasions when we don't want to persist the values in a list control across postbacks. As well as the concern over bandwidth, we might have other reasons for recreating the dataset, or rebinding the list control each time we load the page. The simplest scenario is when the page does not actually include a `<form>`. Many of our previous examples were like this. They are not interactive pages, and so there is no requirement to post values back to the server – you just load the page and view it. In this case, there is no VIEWSTATE, but no user interaction either.

However, if the page does contain a `<form>` section, the values from the list control are automatically included in the VIEWSTATE. Of course, if the list control contains interactive elements, such as buttons or editcontrols that must be posted back to the server, the control has to be on an HTML `<form>`. This is the case with the sorting and filtering example we've just been looking at, where the column headings are automatically rendered as `LinkButton` controls.

However to sort and filter the rows, we have to rebind the data grid each time to the `DataView` object. We're actually recreating the whole `DataSet` and `DataView` with each postback, so we have no need to maintain the values in the VIEWSTATE. For this reason, we set the `EnableViewState` property of the `DataGrid` object to `False` in the control definition, so that the contents of this control are not included in the VIEWSTATE:

```
<ASP:DataGrid id="MyDataGrid" runat="server"
    EnableViewState="False"
    ...
```

You can always check how much data is included in the VIEWSTATE of a page by using **page tracing**. In the `Page` directive, add `Trace="True"`:

```
<%@Page Language="VB" Trace="True"%>
```

Then run the page locally (that is in a browser running on the web server itself). In the Control Tree section of the output in our example below, you can see that the total size of the `DataGrid` control named **MyDataGrid** – including children – is 22kB. The `<form>` itself (given the name **ctrl0** because we didn't specify a name for it) shows the size of the entire VIEWSTATE to be near to 23kB:

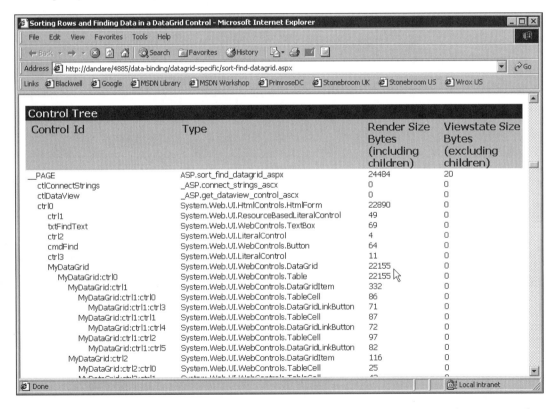

Of course, the other way to see how much VIEWSTATE is in a page is just to view the source in the browser so that you can see the `HIDDEN`-type `<input>` control. From that you can get a good idea of the amount of data being sent to the client each time.

Automatic Paging in a DataGrid

Our final example of using the DataGrid control to display data demonstrates the use of "**paging**". When there are a large number of rows to display, sending them all to the client in one go doesn't make sense. Your client will get impatient waiting for them all to arrive, and may find that they actually wanted to see something else instead. To prevent this aggravation and waste of bandwidth, we usually divide the output into pages containing 10 or 20 rows (depending on the content), and then provide navigation controls so that users can view other pages of rows.

The DataGrid control makes it easy to provide a paging feature. It contains logic that can automatically create pages containing the number of rows you require, and it can render the navigation controls in a range of ways. You can also take over paging entirely and implement all the features yourself to provide a custom interface.

To turn on the automatic paging feature, we simply set the AllowPaging property of the DataGrid control to True, and specify the name of an event handler that will run when the PageIndexChanged event occurs. We usually set these properties when we define the control in the HTML of the page. We can also specify the position of the "Pager" navigation controls. By default they are located in the footer row of the grid, aligned on the left.

Our example that uses the automatic paging feature is Using Automatic Paging with a DataGrid Control (paging-datagrid.aspx). When you run this example, you'll see that it also contains controls where you can specify other properties of the paging feature. For example you can specify the number of rows in each page, and the style of the navigation controls. After changing any of the property values, just click on one of the navigation links to reload the page with the new options set:

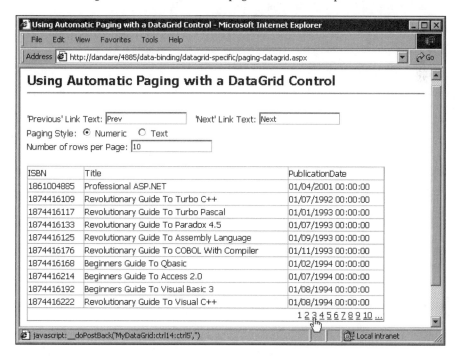

How It Works

As is usual by now, the HTML section of our page starts with the controls where you can specify how the DataGrid behaves:

```
<form runat="server">

  'Previous' Link Text:
  <ASP:TextBox id="PrevText" runat="server" />  
  'Next' Link Text:
  <ASP:TextBox id="NextText" runat="server" /><br />

  Paging Style:
  <ASP:RadioButton id="PageNumeric" GroupName="Style"
          runat="server" /> Numeric  
  <ASP:RadioButton id="PageText" GroupName="Style"
          runat="server" /> Text<br />

  Number of rows per Page:
  <ASP:TextBox id="PageRows" runat="server" /><p />
```

This is followed by the definition of the DataGrid. Notice that we set three properties that control the paging behavior – we set AllowPaging to True, specify that the paging controls should be right-aligned within the footer row, and that the event handler named ChangeGridPage – which we'll look at shortly – will be executed when the user selects a page using the paging controls:

```
<ASP:DataGrid id="MyDataGrid" runat="server"
    Width="90%"
    AllowPaging="True"
    PagerStyle-HorizontalAlign="Right"
    OnPageIndexChanged="ChangeGridPage" />

</form>
```

The Page_Load Event Handler

When the page loads each time, either when the user opens the page for the first time or in response to a click by the user on the paging controls, our Page_Load event handler is executed. We only want to execute code when the page is first opened, however, so we check the value of the IsPostback property first. If it's False, we can set the default values for the controls in the page, and then call the BindDataGrid subroutine to bind and display the source data values in the DataGrid control:

```
Sub Page_Load()
  If Not Page.IsPostback Then

    'set the default values in the controls on the page
    PrevText.Text = "Prev"
    NextText.Text = "Next"
    PageNumeric.Checked = True
    PageRows.Text = "10"

    'set the initial page in the DataGrid to zero
    '(not actually required as this is the default)
    MyDataGrid.CurrentPageIndex = 0

    'create the dataset and bind it to the DataGrid control
    BindDataGrid()

  End If
End Sub
```

The BindDataGrid Routine

When we come to bind the source data to the `DataGrid`, we first have to set the values of the properties that control the paging feature. We get the number of rows that are to be shown in each page from the textbox named `PageRows` on our page, and assign this value to the `PageSize` property of the `DataGrid` control. We see which type of paging controls the user specified (page numbers or **Previous/Next** text captions), and set the `PagerStyle.Mode` property of the `DataGrid`. We also collect the values that the user wants for the text captions if that mode is selected. In reality, we only need to set this if the pager mode is text captions (`NextPrev` rather than `Numeric`), but it makes no difference to the operation of the page:

```
Sub BindDataGrid()

  'set the value of the number of rows per page
  MyDataGrid.PageSize = CInt(PageRows.Text)

  'set the type of pager to include in the DataGrid
  If PageNumeric.Checked = True Then
    MyDataGrid.PagerStyle.Mode = PagerMode.NumericPages
  Else
    MyDataGrid.PagerStyle.Mode = PagerMode.NextPrev
  End If

  'set the text for the pager to use when in NextPrev mode
  MyDataGrid.PagerStyle.NextPageText = NextText.Text
  MyDataGrid.PagerStyle.PrevPageText = PrevText.Text
```

Now we can get the `DataView` object and bind it to the grid. We're using the same custom user control as in previous examples here:

```
  ...
  'get dataset from get-dataset-control.ascx user control
  ...

  MyDataGrid.DataSource = objDataView
  MyDataGrid.DataBind()

End Sub
```

In the next screenshot, we've selected the text-style paging option, and entered different text for the pager links. We've also changed the number of rows that should appear in each page, and you can see the result:

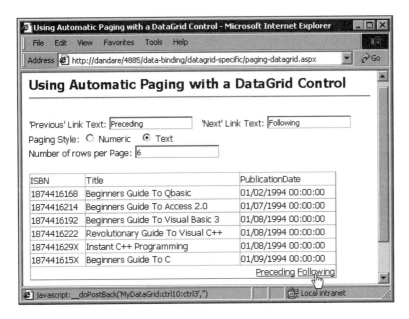

Changing the Page That's Displayed

We've set all the properties of the DataGrid control that affect the appearance, and bound and displayed the data content starting from the first "page" of rows. All that remains is to handle the PageIndexChanged event that occurs when the user clicks one of the page navigation links. We specified the event handler named ChangeGridPage in the original definition of the DataGrid control. Here is that event handler:

```
Sub ChangeGridPage(objSender As Object, _
        objArgs As DataGridPageChangedEventArgs)
  'runs when one of the pager controls is clicked

  'update the current page number from the parameter values
  MyDataGrid.CurrentPageIndex = objArgs.NewPageIndex

  'recreate the dataset and bind it to the DataGrid control
  BindDataGrid()

End Sub
```

As you can see, all we have to do is collect the index number of the page that the user selected from the NewPageIndex property of the DataGridPageChangedEventArgs object that is passed to our event handler when the event occurs. We assign this value to the CurrentPageIndex property of the DataGrid, and then call our BindDataGrid routine to fetch, bind, and display the appropriate page of data rows.

Building paging into applications that display rows of data was always a notoriously error-prone task, and you can see how easy it is with the DataGrid. You can also specify custom paging controls – building your own with buttons, hyperlinks, images, etc. This involves setting the AllowCustomPaging property, as well as the AllowPaging property, to True. Then the paging controls will not appear, but you can still react to the PageIndexChanged event to display the appropriate set of rows and display your own paging controls.

Custom paging is also useful if you want to use a `DataReader` as the data source for your control. When using the built-in paging feature of the `DataGrid`, you cannot use a `DataReader` as the data source – it must be one of the other data source types such as a `DataView`, `DataSet`, `ArrayList` or `HashTable`. However, you can use a `DataReader` if you implement custom paging. We aren't demonstrating custom paging here, but there are examples in the SDK and in the "QuickStart" samples included with ASP.NET.

Editing Data with Data-bound Controls

The final topic for this chapter shows a rather more specialized technique when using the `DataList` and `DataGrid` controls. Both these controls provide built-in editing features. They allow you to change the way that a row or item is displayed to indicate to a user that one of the rows is 'selected' (is the 'current row'), or that one of the rows is being used to edit the values in the data source. We'll look at an example of editing data with both the `DataGrid` and `DataList` controls next.

Editing Data with a DataGrid Control

The `DataGrid` provides the most automated developer support for in-line editing. We can define an `EditCommandColumn` within the grid, and it will automatically handle most of the plumbing and navigation for us. To see what it does, run the example page Editing Data in a DataGrid Control (edit-datagrid.aspx). When you first open the page it displays a list of books. However, there is an extra column on the right that contains an "Edit" hyperlink for each row. When you click on the link, that row goes into "edit mode", and the Title and Published columns show textboxes rather than just the values for that row:

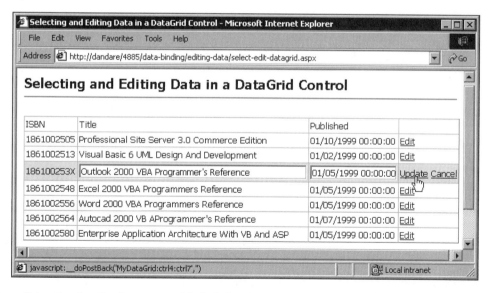

After editing the details, the user would click the Update link to save the changes, or the Cancel link to abandon them. Because we haven't looked at data management techniques so far in this book, the example page simply creates a suitable SQL statement that would perform the update and displays it. It doesn't update the original data:

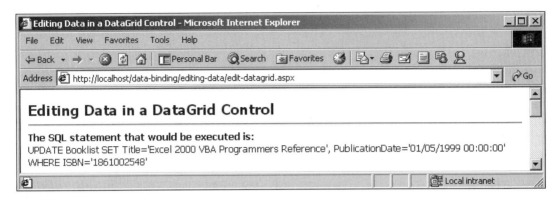

How It Works

The HTML section of this page contains a `<form>`, within which is our `DataGrid` control. The definition of the `DataGrid` specifies that the background color of the item being edited is yellow. It also specifies that the `DataKeyField` in the source dataset is the column named `"ISBN"`. This useful feature of the list controls means that we don't have to include the primary key of the source dataset in our columns – even if we need to access it to perform data updates. For any row, we can access the primary key from this collection, as you'll see later in this example.

The next three attributes in the opening `DataGrid` tag are used to specify the names of the event handlers that will be executed in response to the user clicking the Edit, Update, and Cancel links that the `EditCommandColumn` will generate for us. Finally, we set the `AutoGenerateColumns` property to `False` as we want to create our own column structure for the grid:

```
<form runat="server">

  <ASP:DataGrid id="MyDataGrid" runat="server"
     CellPadding = "2"
     EditItemStyle-BackColor="yellow"
     EditItemStyle-ForeColor="black"
     DataKeyField="ISBN"
     OnEditCommand="DoItemEdit"
     OnUpdateCommand="DoItemUpdate"
     OnCancelCommand="DoItemCancel"
     AutoGenerateColumns="False">
```

Within the `<ASP:DataGrid>` definition, because we've turned off automatic generation of the columns, we must specify the columns that we want to appear. We include a `BoundColumn` that displays values from the `ISBN` column in our data source, a custom `TemplateColumn` that displays the `Title`, followed by another `BoundColumn` that displays the `PublicationDate`. Notice that we included the attribute `ReadOnly="True"` for the `ISBN` column. We don't want the user to be able to edit values in this column because it is the primary key of the source table.

We used a custom `TemplateColumn` instead of a `BoundColumn` for the `Title` column for a couple of reasons. Firstly, the automatic editing feature displays a textbox instead of a simple text value in all the columns that are not read-only. However, this textbox isn't large enough to comfortably accommodate a long string, so we decided to specify the editing control ourselves and make it 60 characters long. Secondly, this gives you the chance to see how we can provide non-standard edit controls for a column if required. We just specify an `<ItemTemplate>` to be used to display the column values in normal mode, and an `<EditItemTemplate>` that defines the control to be used in edit mode:

```
<Columns>

  <ASP:BoundColumn DataField="ISBN" HeaderText="ISBN" ReadOnly="True" />

  <ASP:TemplateColumn HeaderText="Title">
    <ItemTemplate>
      <ASP:Label Text='<%# Container.DataItem("Title") %>' runat="server" />
    </ItemTemplate>
    <EditItemTemplate>
      <ASP:TextBox id="txtTitle" Size="60"
        Text='<%# Container.DataItem("Title") %>' runat="server" />
    </EditItemTemplate>
  </ASP:TemplateColumn>

  <ASP:BoundColumn DataField="PublicationDate" HeaderText="Published" />

  <ASP:EditCommandColumn EditText="Edit"
    CancelText="Cancel" UpdateText="Update" />

</Columns>

</ASP:DataGrid>

</form>
```

As you can see from the code, the last column is the `EditCommandColumn` we mentioned earlier. While there are plenty of attributes that we can apply to this column to control the formatting (basically the same as for the list controls themselves such as the font style, column heading, wrapping behavior, etc.) we've just specified the text we want to use for the three commands that can appear in this column. And that completes the definition of our `DataGrid` control.

The Page_Load Event Handler

When the page first loads, we must create the dataset we are using as the source of the `DataGrid` control. We do this in the `Page_Load` event handler, but only if this is not a postback – as you've seen in plenty of previous examples:

```
Sub Page_Load()
  If Not Page.IsPostback Then
    BindDataGrid() 'create dataset and bind to grid control
  End If
End Sub
```

The `BindDataGrid` routine is responsible for fetching the data from the database through a `DataReader` object, binding it to the control, then calling the `DataBind` method of the `DataGrid` to display the data. Again, this is the same routine as we've used in previous examples:

```
Sub BindDataGrid()

  ...
  'create a DataReader object to retrieve the data
  ...

  MyDataGrid.DataSource = objDataReader
  MyDataGrid.DataBind()

End Sub
```

Displaying the UPDATE SQL Statement

Another subroutine that we use in this page is responsible for displaying the SQL statement that we generate in a `Label` control in the HTML section at the top of the page:

```
<ASP:Label id="lblSQL" runat="server" />
```

This routine, named `ExecuteSQLStatement`, would normally be responsible for executing the SQL statement against the back-end database or other data source to update the values in line with the edits made in our `DataGrid`. However, in this example page, we just display the SQL statement:

```
Sub ExecuteSQLStatement(strSQL)

    lblSQL.Text = "The SQL statement is: <br />" & strSQL

End Sub
```

Handling Item Edit Events

All that remains now is to handle the three events we specified in the definition of the `DataGrid` control. We have to react to the `EditCommand`, `UpdateCommand`, and `CancelCommand` events.

The `EditCommand` event is raised when the user clicks the **Edit** link in any row within the grid. For this event, we specified our `DoItemEdit` event handler routine. Within this routine, we first clear any existing SQL statement from the `Label` at the top of the page (to avoid confusion). Then we set the `EditItemIndex` property of the `DataGrid` control to the index of the row that contained the **Edit** link the user clicked:

```
Sub DoItemEdit(objSource As Object, objArgs As DataGridCommandEventArgs)

    lblSQL.Text = ""   'clear text from label that shows SQL statement

    'set the EditItemIndex property of the grid to this item's index
    MyDataGrid.EditItemIndex = objArgs.Item.ItemIndex
    BindDataGrid() 'bind the data and display it

End Sub
```

As you can see, we get this index from the parameters of the event handler – our code is passed a `DataGridCommandEventArgs` object that exposes the `ItemIndex` property of the item that was selected. Finally we rebind the grid to display the new layout.

The default value of the `EditItemIndex` property is `-1`, which indicates that none of the rows is in "edit mode". When the `DataGrid` control comes to render the grid, it will detect that the `EditItemIndex` has been set to a different value, and will automatically render the specified row with the contents of our `<EditItemTemplate>`, or with textboxes instead of plain text for ordinary bound columns where we haven't specified a custom `<EditItemTemplate>`.

Handling the Update and Cancel Events

Now that we've got our grid into "edit mode", we just need to handle the **Update** and **Cancel** events. We specified that a click on the **Cancel** link should execute our event handler named `DoItemCancel`. In this event handler, all we need to do is switch the grid back out of "edit mode" by setting the `EditItemIndex` property back to `-1`:

```
Sub DoItemCancel(objSource As Object, objArgs As DataGridCommandEventArgs)

    'set EditItemIndex property of grid to -1 to switch out of Edit mode
    MyDataGrid.EditItemIndex = -1
    BindDataGrid() 'bind the data and display it

End Sub
```

However, if the user clicks the **Update** link, our `DoItemUpdate` event handler will be called. Here, we have to create a suitable SQL statement, or execute some stored procedure or other code to update the original source data. We're just generating a simple SQL UPDATE statement in our example, and for this we need to get the edited values from the `DataGrid` row that the user is working on.

We've used two different techniques in this example (simply to illustrate the options and show how it can be done). After declaring two variables to hold references to the textboxes that contain the edited values, we first access the **Title** textbox (named `txtTitle`) using the `FindControl` method of the item that is contained in the `DataGridCommandEventArgs` object passed to our event handler as a parameter. Notice that we have to convert (or 'cast') the return value to the correct type – in this case a `TextBox` object:

```
Sub DoItemUpdate(objSource As Object, objArgs As DataGridCommandEventArgs)

    'get a reference to the title and publication date text boxes
    Dim objTitleCtrl, objPubDateCtrl As TextBox
    objTitleCtrl = CType(objArgs.Item.FindControl("txtTitle"), TextBox)
    objPubDateCtrl = objArgs.Item.Cells(2).Controls(0)
```

For the second textbox, as shown above, we are accessing the `Cells` collection for the item contained in the `DataGridCommandEventArgs` object. From the third cell in the row (indexed 2 – our `PublicationDate` column), we can use the `Controls` collection of that cell to get a reference to the textbox it contains. This technique is best used when the column is a normal `BoundColumn` or auto-generated column – it doesn't work with a custom column created with templates (which is why we used the `FindControl` technique with our `Title` column).

Once we've got references to the two controls, we can create the SQL UPDATE statement and call our `ExecuteSQLStatement` routine to execute it against the data source (or, in our example page, just display it). Notice how we get the value of the primary key for the current row (the ISBN) from the `DataKeys` collection. You'll recall that we included the attribute `DataKeyField="ISBN"` in the definition of our `DataGrid` control, and so we can get the value of the ISBN column for this row using the row index against the `DataKeys` collection:

```
    'create a suitable SQL statement and execute it
    Dim strSQL As String
    strSQL = "UPDATE Booklist SET Title='" & objTitleCtrl.Text & "', " _
        & "PublicationDate='" & objPubDateCtrl.Text & "' " _
        & "WHERE ISBN='" & MyDataGrid.DataKeys(objArgs.Item.ItemIndex) & "'"
    ExecuteSQLStatement(strSQL)

    'set EditItemIndex property of grid to -1 to switch out of Edit mode
    MyDataGrid.EditItemIndex = -1
    BindDataGrid() 'bind the data and display it

End Sub
```

We finish off by switching the grid back out of "edit mode" by setting the `EditItemIndex` property of the `DataGrid` control back to `-1`, and rebind the control to display the result.

It's taken a while to explain this example, but you can see that there really isn't a lot of code in it. The code that is required is relatively simple and very well structured. We are just reacting to events that the `DataGrid` control raises, so debugging and modifying the page is far less error-prone than with any technique we might have used to do the same thing in previous versions of ASP.

Selecting and Editing Data with a DataList Control

The second control that provides in-line editing capabilities automatically is the `DataList`. In fact, we can actually do more with this control as far as selecting or editing data goes, but it requires more code and more effort to use. One extra feature here is the ability to easily switch the control into "selected" mode, where one row becomes the current row and we can highlight it by applying different styles or formatting to that row.

The example page Selecting and Editing Data in a DataList Control (`select-edit-datalist.aspx`) demonstrates both selecting and editing rows in a `DataList` control. When first opened, it displays a list of book titles. Each one has an Info button at the left-hand end of the row. If you click one of these buttons, that row becomes selected – and both the format and content change to reflect this:

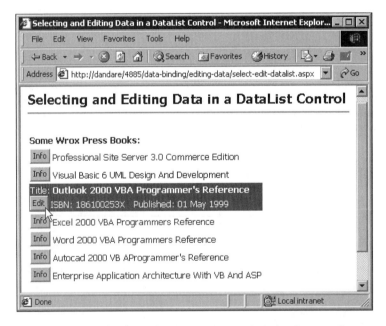

An Edit button also appears in the selected row. When you click this button, that row goes into "edit mode". The book title and publication date appear in textboxes where they can be edited. At the same time, three other buttons appear in the row – allowing you to Update the row with your changes, Delete the current row, or Cancel your updates:

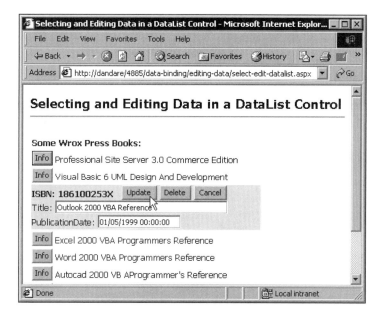

When you select the Update or Delete option, a suitable SQL UPDATE or DELETE statement is generated and displayed in the page (as in the previous example – it doesn't actually execute the statement against the data store):

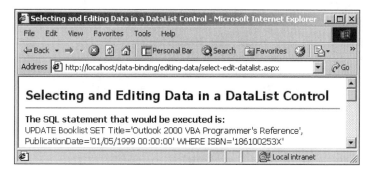

How It Works

While this example looks quite different from the previous DataGrid example, there are a lot of similarities and quite a lot of common code. The HTML section of the page contains a <form>, and within this is the definition of the DataList control. In this case, we have some extra style properties, because we now have a "selected mode" as well as an "edit mode". And, as before, we set the DataKeyField attribute to "ISBN" – the name of the primary key column in our data source.

We also have to specify the event handlers for our edit commands. In this case, we have to react to the ItemCommand event as well, so that we can detect a click on the Info button and put that row into "selected mode":

```
<ASP:DataList id="MyDataList" runat="server"
   CellSpacing = "2"
   SelectedItemStyle-BackColor="red"
   SelectedItemStyle-ForeColor="white"
   EditItemStyle-BackColor="yellow"
   EditItemStyle-ForeColor="black"
   DataKeyField="ISBN"
   OnItemCommand="DoItemSelect"
   OnEditCommand="DoItemEdit"
   OnUpdateCommand="DoItemUpdate"
   OnDeleteCommand="DoItemDelete"
   OnCancelCommand="DoItemCancel">
```

The remainder of the control definition is the four templates we need. There's a `<HeaderTemplate>` that defines what appears at the top of the control, followed by the `<ItemTemplate>` that defines the normal content for rows that are not selected or being edited. We use an ordinary `ASP:Button` control for the Info button in each row, with the `CommandName` property set to `Select`, and we just display this button and the book title:

```
<HeaderTemplate>
  <b>Some Wrox Press Books:</b><br />
</HeaderTemplate>

<ItemTemplate>
  <ASP:Button CommandName="Select" Text="Info" runat="server" />
  <%# Container.DataItem("Title") %>
</ItemTemplate>
```

Next is the `<SelectedItemTemplate>`, which is used for the row that is currently in "selected mode". This is the row specified by the `SelectedIndex` property of the `DataList` (as with the `EditItemIndex` property of the `DataGrid` control, this property is -1 if no row is selected). For the selected row, we display the book title, a button with the caption and `CommandName` value of `Edit`, the ISBN for this book, and the publication date:

```
<SelectedItemTemplate>
  Title: <b><%# Container.DataItem("Title") %></b><br />
  <ASP:Button CommandName="Edit" Text="Edit" runat="server" />
  ISBN: <%# Container.DataItem("ISBN") %>  
  Published:
  <%# DataBinder.Eval(Container.DataItem, "PublicationDate", "{0:D}") %>
</SelectedItemTemplate>
```

This provides the "selected row" appearance we saw in the previous screenshots:

List Controls and Data Binding

The Edit button will be used to put the DataList row into "edit mode". When this happens, the control will use the contents of the `<EditItemTemplate>` to render the content for this row. We display the ISBN followed by three buttons with the captions and `CommandNames` of Update, Delete, and Cancel. Then, on the next line, we display two textboxes that are bound to the `Title` and `PublicationDate` columns in the data source:

```
<EditItemTemplate>
  <b>ISBN: <%# Container.DataItem("ISBN") %></b>  
  <ASP:Button CommandName="Update" Text="Update" runat="server" />
  <ASP:Button CommandName="Delete" Text="Delete" runat="server" />
  <ASP:Button CommandName="Cancel" Text="Cancel" runat="server" /><br />
  Title:
  <ASP:TextBox id="txtTitle" Text='<%# Container.DataItem("Title") %>'
        size="46" runat="server" /><br />
  PublicationDate:
  <ASP:TextBox id="txtPubDate" size="20" runat="server"
        Text='<%# Container.DataItem("PublicationDate") %>' />
</EditItemTemplate>

</ASP:DataList>
```

Note that this is a conscious design feature of our example page, and not a requirement. In your own applications you can put a row into "edit mode" without having to put it into "selected mode" first – as we did with the previous DataGrid example. Meanwhile, in this example – when we're in "edit mode" – the row we're editing looks like this:

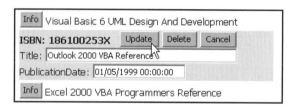

The Page_Load event handler is the same as we used for the previous DataGrid example, as is the BindDataGrid routine. The page also contains the same ExecuteSQLStatement routine that displays the SQL statement we'll build when the Update or Delete buttons are clicked. What are different – though not *that* different – are the routines that perform the switch to "select mode" and "edit mode", and which generate the SQL statements.

Selecting a Row

The ItemCommand event handler, for which we specified our routine DoItemSelect, is executed when any command button or link within the rows of the control is clicked. All we need to do to select a row in our DataList is set the SelectedIndex property of the control. Before we do this, we clear any existing text from the Label control at the top of the page that displays our SQL update or delete statements.

However, there is an important issue to be aware of here. We specified other command buttons in the templates for our DataList – those that activate the Update, Delete, and Cancel commands when the grid is in "edit mode". These three events will automatically call the event handlers that we specified for the UpdateCommand, DeleteCommand, and CancelCommand when we defined the control itself. But they also call the ItemCommand event handler – they raise the ItemCommand event as well as their "own" event. This means that we must check which control was used to raise the event in the ItemCommand event handler (our DoItemEvent routine). We only select the row if it is the Info button, which has the CommandName value of Select:

343

```
Sub DoItemSelect(objSource As Object, objArgs As DataListCommandEventArgs)

    lblSQL.Text = "" 'clear any content from SQL statement Label

    'see if it was the Select button that was clicked
    If objArgs.CommandName = "Select" Then

        'set the SelectedIndex property of the list to this item's index
        MyDataList.SelectedIndex = objArgs.Item.ItemIndex
        BindDataGrid() 'bind the data and display it

    End If

End Sub
```

Now, the grid will automatically render our `<SelectedItemtemplate>` contents for the row indicated by the `SelectedIndex` property.

Editing a Row

Once we put a row into "selected mode" in our example, it displays a button that can be used to put that row into "edit mode". The Edit button has the `CommandName` value `Edit`, which means that it will raise the `EditCommand` event (as well as the `ItemCommand` event) when clicked. We specified our `DoItemEdit` routine as the event handler for the `EditCommand` event, and in it we first "unselect" this row by setting the `SelectedIndex` property of the control to -1, then set the `EditIndex` property to this row index and rebind the grid:

```
Sub DoItemEdit(objSource As Object, objArgs As DataListCommandEventArgs)

    'set the SelectedIndex propery of the list to -1 to "unselect" it
    MyDataList.SelectedIndex = -1

    'set the EditItemIndex property of the list to this item's index
    MyDataList.EditItemIndex = objArgs.Item.ItemIndex
    BindDataGrid() 'bind the data and display it

End Sub
```

Now, the contents of the `<EditItemTemplate>` will be used when this row is rendered.

Updating a Row

Once in "edit mode", the row displays the Update, Delete, and Cancel buttons. The Update button has the `CommandName` value `Update`, and so it will raise the `UpdateCommand` event when clicked. This will execute our routine named `DoItemUpdate`, which we specified as the handler for this event in the definition of the `DataList` control.

In this routine, we do almost exactly the same as we did in the previous `DataGrid` example. We get a reference to the `txtTitle` and `txtPubDate` textboxes in this row, and use their values to build a SQL statement to update the row in the original data source. Again, we get the ISBN (the primary key for the row) from the `DataKeys` collection.

Then, after executing the SQL statement (or, in our example, just displaying it), we switch the row out of "edit mode" by setting the `EditItemIndex` of the `DataList` control to -1, and rebind the control to display the updated results:

```
Sub DoItemUpdate(objSource As Object, objArgs As DataListCommandEventArgs)

    'get a reference to the title and publication date textboxes
    Dim objTitleCtrl, objPubDateCtrl As TextBox
    objTitleCtrl = CType(objArgs.Item.FindControl("txtTitle"), TextBox)
    objPubDateCtrl = CType(objArgs.Item.FindControl("txtPubDate"), TextBox)

    'create a suitable SQL statement and execute it
    Dim strSQL As String
    strSQL = "UPDATE Booklist SET Title='" & objTitleCtrl.Text & "', " _
        & "PublicationDate='" & objPubDateCtrl.Text & "' " _
        & "WHERE ISBN='" & MyDataList.DataKeys(objArgs.Item.ItemIndex) & "'"
    ExecuteSQLStatement(strSQL)

    'set EditItemIndex property of grid to -1 to switch out of Edit mode
    MyDataList.EditItemIndex = -1
    BindDataGrid() 'bind the data and display it

End Sub
```

Deleting a Row

The `DeleteCommand` event handler we specified in our definition of the `DataList` control is the routine named `DoItemDelete`. This is a relatively simple routine when compared to the "update" event handler. We build a SQL DELETE statement, using the ISBN value obtained from the `DataKeys` collection, execute it, switch the row back out of "edit mode", and rebind the grid to display the results:

```
Sub DoItemDelete(objSource As Object, objArgs As DataListCommandEventArgs)

    'create a suitable SQL statement and execute it
    Dim strSQL As String
    strSQL = "DELETE FROM Booklist WHERE ISBN='" _
        & MyDataList.DataKeys(objArgs.Item.ItemIndex) & "'"
    ExecuteSQLStatement(strSQL)

    'set EditItemIndex property of grid to -1 to switch out of Edit mode
    MyDataList.EditItemIndex = -1
    BindDataGrid() 'bind the data and display it

End Sub
```

Canceling Edit Mode

Canceling "edit mode" is the same as we did on our `DataGrid` example previously. In the definition of the `DataList` control we specified our routine named `DoItemCancel` as the event handler for the `CancelCommand` event. In this routine we just set the `EditItemIndex` property of the `DataList` control to -1 and rebind the grid:

```
Sub DoItemCancel(objSource As Object, objArgs As DataListCommandEventArgs)

    'set EditItemIndex property of grid to -1 to switch out of Edit mode
    MyDataList.EditItemIndex = -1
    BindDataGrid() 'bind the data and display it

End Sub
```

And that's it. We've build a responsive, intuitive, and attractive data update page with only a handful of controls and relatively few lines of code. To do the same using ASP 3.0 would take a great deal longer, and require a lot more effort and a lot more code.

What we haven't done is look very deeply at how the relational data management processes are carried out. We've used fairly simple data access code to get sets of data from a database, and displayed the explicit SQL statements we could use to perform updates. However, we devote several chapters later in this book to the whole topic of data management, using both relational data and XML.

Summary

In this chapter, we've looked in some detail at a specific new feature that is available when using ASP.NET, namely **server-side data binding**. This allows us to insert values from a range of different types of data source into a page, or into controls on a page. Together with the eight special list controls that are part of the .NET framework, this allows us to build data-driven pages with the minimum of code and effort.

There are two basic types of data binding supported in ASP.NET – single-value binding to any control and repeated-values binding to the special list controls. Single-value binding can be used with a property, method result or an expression to create a value that is then used to set a property or the content of any other control – effectively just inserting this value. A simple example is setting the Text property of a Label control to the same value as is currently selected in a list box.

Repeated-value data binding takes a data source such as an ArrayList, a HashTable, a Collection, a DataView, a DataReader or a DataSet object. Using any of the eight special list controls, it will then display the contents of the data source as a series of repeated rows or items. Depending on the type of control, we can add formatting and specify the actual content in a range of ways. For example we can specify the number of columns and the layout direction for a Repeater control. We can also hide columns, add custom columns, sort and filter rows and use automatic paging in a DataGrid control.

As well as looking at how we use these list controls to display data, we also briefly introduced the features they provide for updating data. This gives us an easy way to build an intuitive interface for managing all kinds of data – in particular data extracted from and updated to a relational database.

In summary, the chapter topics were:

- ❏ What data binding actually is, and how it works
- ❏ How we can bind controls to single data values
- ❏ How we can bind list controls to sets of data values
- ❏ How we can change the appearance of data-bound controls
- ❏ How we use data-bound controls to edit and update the source data

We've talked quite a lot about working with relational data through objects like the DataReader and DataView in this chapter, without really explaining much about them. However, this is because we wanted to cover the wide range of server controls that are part of ASP.NET first so that you are comfortable with creating dynamic pages. And we make up for this omission by starting a four-chapter detailed exploration of the various ways we can work with data in ASP.NET next.

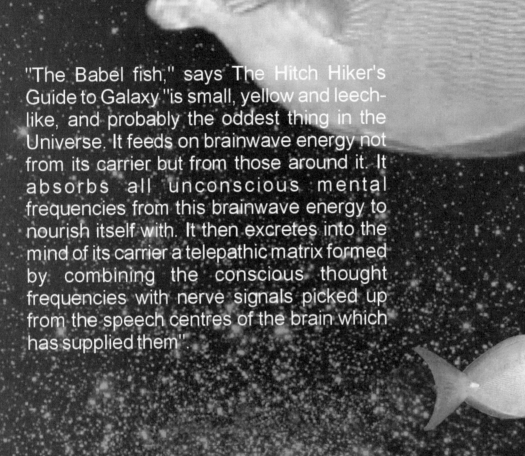

"The Babel fish," says The Hitch Hiker's Guide to Galaxy "is small, yellow and leech-like, and probably the oddest thing in the Universe. It feeds on brainwave energy not from its carrier but from those around it. It absorbs all unconscious mental frequencies from this brainwave energy to nourish itself with. It then excretes into the mind of its carrier a telepathic matrix formed by combining the conscious thought frequencies with nerve signals picked up from the speech centres of the brain which has supplied them".

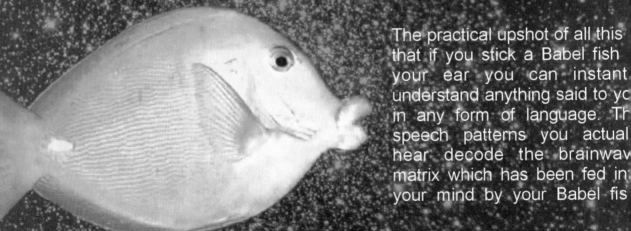

The practical upshot of all this that if you stick a Babel fish your ear you can instant understand anything said to yc in any form of language. Th speech patterns you actual hear decode the brainwav matrix which has been fed in your mind by your Babel fis

8

Introducing .NET Data Management

In previous chapters we've looked at the basics of Microsoft's new .NET Framework, and ASP.NET in particular. We've seen how it changes the way we program with ASP – adding a whole range of new techniques that make it easier to create dynamic pages, Web services, and Web-based applications. However, there is one fundamental aspect of almost all applications that we haven't looked at in detail yet. This is how we access and work with data that is stored in other applications or files. In general terms, we refer to these sources of information as **data stores**. In this chapter, we start off with a look at how the .NET Framework provides us with access to the many different kinds of data store that we might have interface with.

The .NET Framework includes a series of classes implementing a new data access technology that is specifically designed for use in the .NET world. We'll look at why this has come about, and how it relates to the techniques we've become accustomed to using in previous versions of ASP. In fact, this is the core topic that we'll be covering in this chapter, as the new framework classes provide a whole lot more than just a ".NET version of ADO". Like the move from ASP to ASP.NET, they involve fundamental changes in the approach for managing data in external data stores.

While "data management" is often assumed to relate to relational data sources such as a database, we also use this chapter to explore the other types of data that we increasingly encounter today. There is extended support within .NET for working with Extensible Markup Language (XML) and the associated technologies. As well as comprehensive support for the existing XML standards, .NET provides new ways to handle XML. This includes integration between XML and traditional relational data access methods.

So, the topics for this chapter are:

❑   The various types of data storage that we use today, and will use in the future

❑   Why do we need another data access technology?

❑   An overview of the new relational data access techniques in .NET

❑   An overview of the new techniques for working with XML in .NET

❑   How we choose an appropriate data access technology and a data format

We start with a look at the way that we store and work with data today.

Data Stores and Data Access

In the not so distant past, the term "data store" usually meant a database of some kind. Databases were usually file-based, often using fixed-width records written to disk – rather like text files. A database program or data access technology read the files into buffers as tables, and applied rules defined in other files to connect the records from different tables together. As the technologies matured, relational databases evolved to provide better storage methods such as variable-length records, and more efficient access techniques.

However, the basic storage medium was still the "database" – a specialist program that managed the data and exposed it to clients. Obvious examples are Oracle, Informix, Sybase, DB2, and Microsoft's own SQL Server. All are enterprise-oriented applications for storing and managing data in a relational way.

At the same time, "desktop" database applications matured and became more powerful. In general, this type of program provides its own interface for working with the data. For example, Microsoft Access can be used to build forms and queries that can access and display data in very powerful ways. They often allow the data to be separated from the interface over the network, so that it can reside on a central server. But, again, we're still talking about relational databases.

Moving to a Distributed Environment

In recent years, the requirements and mode of operation of most businesses have changed. Without consciously realizing it, we've moved away from relying on a central relational database to store all the data the company produces and requires access to. Now, data is stored in e-mail servers, directory services, Office documents and other places – as well as the traditional relational database.

On top of this, the move to a more distributed computing paradigm means that the central data store, running on a huge box in an air-conditioned IT department, is often only a part of the whole corporate data environment. Modern data access technologies need to be able to work with a whole range of different types of data store.

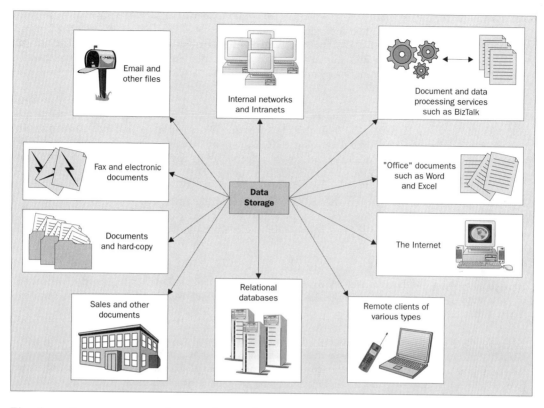

The above figure attempts to show just how wide the range of disparate storage techniques has become. It's easy to see why the term "database" is no longer appropriate for describing the many different ways that data is often stored today. Distributed computing means that we have to be able to extract data in a suitable format, move it around across a range of different types of network, and change the format of the data to suit many different types of client device. In the next section, we'll be exploring one of the areas where data storage and management is changing completely – the growth in the use of Extensible Markup Language, or XML.

XML – A Data Format for the Future?

One of the most far-reaching of the new ideas in computing is the evolution of **Extensible Markup Language**, or **XML**. The World Wide Web Consortium (W3C) issued proposals for XML some three years ago (at the time of writing), and these have matured into standards that are being adopted by almost every sector of the industry.

XML has two big advantages when it comes to storing and transferring data – it's an accepted industry standard, and it's just plain text. The former means that, at last, we have a way of transferring and exposing information in a format that is platform, operating system, and application independent. Compare this to, for example, the MIME-encoded recordsets that Internet Explorer's Remote Data Service (RDS) uses. Instead, XML means that we don't have to have a specific object to handle the data. Any manufacturer can build one that will work with XML data, and developers can use one that suits their own platform, operating system, programming language or application.

The fact that XML is just plain text also means that we no longer have to worry about how we store and transport it. It can be sent as a text file over the Internet using HTTP (which is effectively a 7-bit only transport protocol). We don't have to encode it into a MIME or UU-Encoded form. We can also write it to a disk as a text file, or store it in a database as text. OK, so it often produces a bigger file than the equivalent binary representation, but compression and the availability of large cheap disk drives generally compensate for that.

Applications are already exposing data as XML in a range of ways. For example, as we'll see in later chapters, Microsoft SQL Server 2000 includes features that allow you to extract data directly as XML documents, and update the source data using XML documents. Databases such as Oracle 8i and 9i are designed to manipulate XML directly, and the most recent office applications like Word and Excel will save their data in XML format either automatically or on demand.

And, as you'll see in other chapters, XML is already directly ingrained into many applications. ASP.NET uses XML format configuration files, and Web Services expose their interfaces and data using an implementation of XML called the Simple Object Access Protocol (SOAP).

Other XML Technologies

As well as being a standard in itself, XML has also spawned other standards that are designed to inter-operate with it. Two common example are XML Schemas, which define the structure and content a XML documents, and XSLT to perform transformations of the data into new formats.

XML Schemas also provide a way for data to be exposed in specific XML formats that can be understood globally, or within specific industries such as pharmaceuticals or accountancy applications. There are also several server applications that can transform and communicate XML data between applications that expect different specific formats (or, in fact other non-XML data formats). In the Microsoft world this is BizTalk Server, and there are others such as Oasis and Rosetta for other platforms.

Another Data Access Technology?

To quote a colleague of mine: "Another year, another Microsoft data access technology". We've just got used to ADO (ActiveX Data Objects), and it's all-change time again. Is this some fiendish plan on Microsoft's behalf to keep us on our toes, or is there some reason why the technology that seemed to work fine in previous versions of ASP is no longer suitable?

In fact there are several reasons why we really need to move on from ADO to a new technology. We'll examine these next, then later on take a high-level view of the changes that are involved in moving from ADO to the new .NET Framework data access classes.

.NET Means Disconnected Data

Earlier on in this chapter, we talked a little about how relational databases have evolved over recent years. However, it's not just the data store that has evolved – it's also the whole computing environment. Most of the relational databases still in use today were designed to provide a solid foundation for the client/server world. Here, each client connects to the database server over some kind of permanent network connection – and remains connected for the duration of their session.

So, taking Microsoft Access as an example, the client opens a Form window (often defined within their client-side interface program). This form fetches and caches some or all of the data that is required to populate the controls on the form from the server-side database program, and displays it on the client. The user can manipulate the data, and save changes back to the central database over their dedicated connection.

For this to work, the server-side database has to create explicit connections for each client, and maintain these while the client is connected. As long as the database software and the hardware its running on are powerful enough for the number of clients you anticipate, and the network has the bandwidth and stability to cope with the anticipated number of client connections, it all works very well.

But when we move this to the disconnected world of the Internet, it soon falls apart. The concept of a stable and wide-band connection is hard enough to imagine, and the need to keep this connection permanently open means that we run into problems very quickly. It's not so bad if you are operating in a limited-user scenario, but for a public web site it's obviously not going to work out.

In fact, there are several aspects to being disconnected. The nature of the HTTP protocol that we use on the Web means that connections between client and server are only made during the transfer of data or content. They aren't kept open after a page has been loaded or a recordset has been fetched. On top of this, there is often a need to use the data extracted from a data store while not even connected to the Internet at all. Maybe while the user is traveling with a laptop computer, or the client is on a dial-up connection and needs to disconnect while working with the data then reconnect again later.

This means that we need to use data access technologies where the client can access, download, and cache the data required, then disconnect from the database server or data store. Once they're ready, they then need to be able to reconnect and update the original data store with the changes.

Disconnected Data in n-tier Applications

Another aspect of working with disconnected data arises when we move from a client/server model into the world of *n*-tier applications. A distributed environment implies that the client and the server are separate, connected by a network. To build applications that work well in this environment we are moving to the use of a design strategy that introduces more granular differentiation between the layers, or **tiers**, of an application.

For example, it's usual to create components that perform the data access in an application (the **data tier**), rather than having the ASP code hit the data store directly. There is often a series of rules (usually called business rules) that have to be followed as well, and these can be implemented within components. They might be part of the components that perform the data access, or they might be separate – forming the **business tier** (or application tier). There may also be a separate set of components within the client application (the **presentation tier**) that perform specific tasks for managing, formatting, or presenting the data.

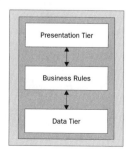

The benefits of designing applications along these lines are many, such as reusability of components, easier testing and faster development. However, here, we're more interested in how it affects the process of handling data.

Within an *n*-tier application, the data must be passed between the tiers as each client request is processed. So, the data tier connects to the data store to extract the data, perhaps performs some processing upon it, and then passes it to the next tier. At this point, the data tier will usually disconnect from the data store, allowing another instance (another client or a different application) to use the connection.

By disconnecting the retrieved data from the data store at the earliest possible moment, we improve the efficiency of the application and allow it to handle more concurrent users. However, it again demonstrates the need for data access technologies that can handle disconnected data in a useful and easily manageable way – particularly when we need to come back and update the original data in the data store.

The Evolution of ADO

Pre-ADO data access technologies, such as DAO (Data Access Objects) and RDO (Remote Data Objects) were designed to provide open data access methods for the client/server world – and are very successful in that environment. For example, if you build Visual Basic applications to access SQL Server over your local network, they work well.

However, with the advent of ASP 1.0, it was obvious that something new was needed. It used only active scripting (such as VBScript and JScript) within the pages, and for these a simplified ActiveX or COM-based technology was required. The answer was ADO 1.0, included with the original ASP installation. ADO allows us to connect to a database to extract recordsets, and perform updates using the database tables, SQL statements, or stored procedures within the database.

However, ADO 1.0 was really only an evolution of the existing technologies, and offered no solution for the disconnected problem. You opened a recordset while you had a connection to the data store, worked with the recordset (maybe updating it or just displaying the contents), then closed it and destroyed the connection. Once the connection was gone, you had no easy way to reconnect the recordset to the original data.

To some extent, the disconnected issue was addressed in ADO 2.0. A new recordset object allowed you to disconnect it from the data store, work with the contents, then reconnect and flush the changes back to the data store again. This worked well with relational databases such as SQL Server, but was not always an ideal solution. It didn't provide the capabilities to store relationships and other details about the data – basically all you stored was the rowset containing the values.

Another technique that came along with ADO 2.0 was the provision of a Data Source Object (DSO) and Remote Data Services (RDS) that could be used in a client program such as Internet Explorer to cache data on a client. A recordset can be encoded as a special MIME type and passed over HTTP to the client where it is cached. The client can disconnect and then reconnect later and flush changes back to the data store. However, despite offering several useful features such as client-side data binding, this non-standard technique never really caught on – mainly due to the reliance on specific clients and concerns over security.

So, to get around all these limitation, the .NET Framework data access classes have been designed from the ground up to provide a reliable and efficient disconnected environment for working with data from a whole range of data stores.

.NET Means XML Data

As we saw earlier in this chapter, the computing world is moving ever more towards the adoption of XML as the fundamental data storage and transfer format. ADO 1.0 and 2.0 had no support for XML at all – it wasn't around as anything other than vague proposals at that time. In fact, at Microsoft, it was left to the Internet Explorer team to come up with the first tools for working with XML – the MSXML parser that shipped with IE5 and other applications.

Later, MSXML became part of the ADO team's responsibilities and surfaced in ADO 2.1 and later as an integral part of Microsoft Data Access Components (MDAC). Along with it, the Data Source Object (DSO) used for remote data management and caching had XML support added. There were also methods added to the integral ADO objects, such as the `Recordset`, to allow it to load and save the content as XML. However, it was never really more than an add-on, and the MSXML parser remained distinct from the core ADO objects.

Now, to bring data access up to date in the growing world of XML data, .NET includes a whole series of objects that are specifically designed to manage and manipulate XML data. This includes native support for XML formatted data within objects like the `Dataset`, as well as a whole range of objects that integrate a new XML parsing engine with the framework as a whole.

.NET Means Managed Code

As we saw in previous chapters, the .NET Framework is not a new operating system. It's a series of classes and a managed runtime environment within which our code can be executed. The framework looks after all the complexities of garbage collection, caching, memory management and so on – but only as long as we use managed code. Once we step outside this cozy environment, we reduce the efficiency of our applications (the execution has to move across the process boundaries into unmanaged code and back).

The existing ADO libraries are all unmanaged code, and so we need a new technology that runs within the .NET Framework. While Microsoft could just have added managed code wrappers to the existing ADO libraries, this would not have provided either an ideal or an efficient solution.

Instead, the data access classes within .NET have been designed from the ground up as managed code. They are integral to the framework and so provide maximum efficiency. They also include a series of objects that are specifically designed to work with MS-SQL Server, using the native Tabular Data Stream (TDS) interface for maximum performance. Alternatively, managed code OLE-DB and ODBC drivers are included with the framework (or are on the way) to allow connection to all kinds of other data stores.

.NET Means a New Programming Model

As we've seen in previous chapters, one of the main benefits of moving to .NET is the ability to get away from the mish-mash of HTML, content and script code that traditional ASP always seems to involve. Instead, we have a whole new structured programming model and approach to follow. We use server controls (and user controls) to create output that is automatically tailored to each client, and react to events that these controls raise on the server.

We also write in "proper" languages, and not script. Instead of VBScript, we can use Visual Basic. As well as a compiled version of the JScript language, we can use the new C# language. And, if you prefer, you can use C++, COBOL, Active Perl, or any one of the myriad other languages that are available or under development for the .NET platform.

This move to a structured programming model with server controls and event handlers doesn't fit well with our existing data-handing techniques using traditional ADO. For example, why do we need to iterate through a recordset just to display the contents? The .NET Framework provides extremely useful server controls such as the `DataGrid`, which look after displaying the data themselves – all they need is a data source such as a set of records (a **rowset**).

So, instead of using `Recordset`-specific methods like `MoveNext` to iterate through a rowset, and accessing each field in turn, we just bind the rowset to the server control. It carries out all the tasks required to present that data, and even make it available for editing. Yet, if required, we can still access data as a read-only and forward-only rowset using the new `DataReader` object instead.

Overall, the .NET data access classes provide a series of objects that are better suited to working with data using server controls, as well as manipulating it directly with code.

Introducing Data Management in .NET

So, having seen why we need a new data access technology, let's look at what .NET actually provides. In this section, we'll give you a high-level overview of all of the .NET data management classes, and see how each of the objects fits with the disconnected and structured programming environment that .NET provides. We've divided this into two sections, relational data management (techniques such as you used traditional ADO for), and XML data management (for which, traditionally, you would use an XML parser such as MSXML).

The System Namespaces for Data Management

The new relational data management classes are in a series of namespaces based on `System.Data` within the class library. The combination of the classes from the namespaces in the following table is generally referred to as **ADO.NET**:

`System.Data`	Contains the basic objects used for accessing and storing relational data, such as `DataSet`, `DataTable`, and `DataRelation`, and which are independent of the type of data source and the way we connect to it.
`System.Data.Common`	Contains the base classes that are used by other objects, in particular the common objects for the `OleDB` and `SqlClient` namespaces. In general we do not specifically import this namespace into our applications.
`System.Data.OleDb`	Contains the objects that we use to connect to a data source via an OLE-DB provider, such as `OleDbConnection`, `OleDbCommand`, etc. These objects inherit from the common base classes, and so have the same properties, methods, and events as the `SqlClient` equivalents.

`System.Data.SqlClient`	Contains the objects that we use to connect to a data source via the Tabular Data Stream (TDS) interface of Microsoft SQL Server (only). This can generally provide better performance as it removes some of the intermediate layers required by an OLE-DB connection. Objects such as `SqlConnection`, `SqlCommand`, etc. inherit from the same common base classes as the `OleDb` objects, and so have the same properties, methods, and events.
`System.Data.SqlTypes`	Contains classes to implement the data types normally found in relational databases such as SQL Server, and which are different to the standard .NET data types. Examples are `SQLMoney`, `SQLDateTime`, and `SQLBinary`, etc. Using these can improve performance and avoid type conversion errors.

There is also a separate series of namespaces containing the classes we use to work with XML rather than relational data. These namespaces are based on `System.Xml`:

`System.Xml`	Contains the basic objects required to create, read, store, write, and manipulate XML documents in line with W3C recommendations. Includes `XmlDocument` and a series of objects that represent the various types of node in an XML document.
`System.Xml.Schema`	Contains the objects required to create, store and manipulate XML schemas, and the nodes that they contain.
`System.Xml.Serialization`	Contains objects that can be used to convert XML documents to other persistence formats such as SOAP, for streaming to disk or across the wire.
`System.Xml.Xpath`	Contains the classes required to implement reading, storing, writing, and querying XML documents using a fast custom XPath-based document object. Includes `XPathDocument`, `XPathNavigator` and objects that represent XPath expressions.
`System.Xml.Xsl`	Contains the objects required to transform XML into other formats using XSL or XSLT stylesheets. The main object is `XslTransform`.

Importing the Required Namespaces

Pages that use objects from the framework's class libraries must import the namespaces containing all the objects that they explicitly create instances of. Many of the common namespaces are imported by default, but this does not include the data management namespaces. To use any type of data access code, we must import the appropriate namespace(s) from the tables shown previously.

Importing the System.Data Namespaces

For accessing relational data, we'll need at minimum `System.Data` and either `System.Data.OleDb` or `System.Data.SqlClient` (depending on the way we're connecting to the data source). In ASP.NET, we use the `Import` page directive:

```
<%@Import Namespace="System.Data" %>
<%@Import Namespace="System.Data.OleDb" %>
```

or

```
<%@Import Namespace="System.Data" %>
<%@Import Namespace="System.Data.SqlClient" %>
```

In Visual Basic code or applications, we can use the Imports statement:

```
Imports System.Data
Imports System.Data.OleDb
```

and in C# we use the using statement:

```
using System.Data;
using System.Data.OleDb;
```

There are certain occasions when we need to specifically import the other System.Data namespaces. For example, if we want to create a new instance of a DataTableMapping object we need to import the System.Data.Common namespace, and if we want to use an SQL-specific data type we need to import the System.Data.SqlTypes namespace.

Importing the System.Xml Namespaces

To access XML data using the objects in the framework class library, we can often get away with importing just the basic namespace System.Xml. However, to create an XPathDocument object, we have to import the System.Xml.Xpath namespace as well. To use the XslTransform object to perform server-side transformations of XML documents, we also need to import the System.Xml.Xsl namespace.

The System.Xml.Schema namespace is usually only required when we are working with collections of schemas. Most of the XML validation objects are in System.Xml, so we can create an XmlValidatingReader (for example) without referencing the System.Xml.Schema namespace. But, if we want to create a new SchemaCollection object, we must import the System.Xml.Schema namespace.

"Data Type Not Found" Compilation Errors

If you forget to import the required namespaces, you'll get an error like that shown in the following screenshot. In this case, it indicates that we have forgotten to import the namespace that contains the class for SqlConnection. To solve this particular error we just need to import the namespace System.Data.SqlClient:

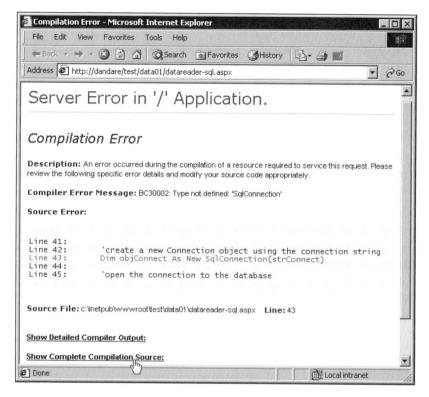

To find out which namespace contains a particular class you can simply look in the .NET SDK section named ".*NET Framework Class Library*" within the section ".*NET Framework Reference*", or search for the object/class name using the *Index* or *Search* feature of the SDK. Alternatively, use the excellent *WinCV* (Windows Class Viewer) tool that comes with the .NET installation.

> *For help on using the tools that come with .NET, check out the SDK section .NET Framework Tools and Debugger, and open the topic named .NET Framework Tools. The WinCV utility is described in detail in the subsection* Windows Forms Class Viewer (Wincv.exe).

The Fundamental ADO.NET Objects

Traditional data access with ADO revolves around the fundamental data storage object – the `Recordset`. The technique used there is to create a connection to a data store using either an OLE-DB provider or an ODBC through OLE-DB driver (depending on the data store and the availability of the provider), then execute commands against it that return a `Recordset` object containing the appropriate data. This can be done using a `Command` object, or directly against the `Connection` object. Alternatively, to insert or update the data, we simply execute a SQL statement or a stored procedure within the data store using the `Connection` object or `Command` object directly, without returning a `Recordset` object.

Data access in .NET follows a broadly similar principle, but uses a different set of objects. So, switching to .NET does not involve learning a completely different technique. However, the objects we use are quite different, providing much better performance with more flexibility and usability.

The .NET data access object model is based around one fundamental object – the DataSet. This replaces the Recordset from traditional ADO. It provides many new features that make complex data access techniques much more efficient, while remaining as easy to use as the Recordset object. The main difference is that a DataSet object can hold more than one table (in other words more than one rowset) from the same data source, as well as the relationships between them.

We can create a DataSet from existing data in a data store, or fill it directly with data one record at a time using code. It also allows us to manipulate the data held in the DataSet's tables, and build and/or modify the relationships between the tables within it. Each table within a DataSet maintains details of the original values of the data as we work with it, so that these changes can be pushed back into the data store at a later date. The DataSet also contains metadata describing the table contents, such as the columns types, rules, and keys. Remember that the whole ethos is to be able to work accurately and efficiently in a disconnected environment.

The DataSet object can also persist its contents, including more than one data table or rowset, directly as XML, and load data from an XML document that contains structured data in the correct format. In fact, XML is the standard persistence format for data sets in .NET – bringing it more into line with the needs of disconnected and remote clients.

Comparison of Techniques in ADO and ADO.NET

As we expect most of our readers to be at least partly familiar with traditional ADO programming techniques, we start with a quick overview of how the new ADO.NET objects and methods relate to these traditional techniques. We'll discuss each of the objects you see mentioned here and the basic techniques for using them in this chapter.

Traditional ADO approach	ADO.NET equivalent
Connected access to data using a Connection (and possibly a Command as well) to fill a Recordset then iterate through the Recordset.	Use a Connection and a Command to connect a DataReader object to the data store and read the results iteratively from the data store.
Updating a data store using a Connection and Command object to execute a SQL statement or stored procedure.	Use a Connection and a Command to connect a DataReader object to the data store and execute the SQL statement or stored procedure.
Disconnected access to data using a Connection (and possibly a Command as well) to fill a Recordset then remove the connection to the data source.	Use a Connection and a Command to connect a DataAdaptor to the data source and then fill a DataSet with the results.
Updating a data store from a disconnected Recordset by reconnecting and using the Update or UpdateBatch method.	Use a Connection and a Command to connect a DataAdaptor to the data source and then call the Update method of the DataSet.

The major differences you should be aware of at the start if you are already experienced in using ADO in earlier versions are:

❑ There is no direct equivalent of a `Recordset` object. Depending on the task you want to achieve, you use a `DataReader` or a `DataSet` instead.

❑ Client-side and server-side (database) cursors are not used in ADO.NET. The disconnected model means that they are not applicable.

❑ Database locking is not supported or required. Again, due to the disconnected model, they are not applicable.

❑ All data persistence is as XML. There are no MIME-encoded or binary representations of rowsets or other data structures.

So, having discussed the differences, we'll now look at the new objects in ADO.NET in more detail.

The Connection Objects

These objects are similar to the ADO `Connection` object, with similar properties. They are used to connect a data store to a `Command` object.

❑ An `OleDbConnection` object is used with an OLE-DB provider or OLE-DB/ODBC driver

❑ A `SqlConnection` object uses Tabular Data Services with MS SQL Server

In traditional ADO, it was common to use the `Connection` object to directly execute a statement against the data source or to open a recordset. This cannot be done with the .NET `Connection` objects. However, they do provide access to transactions that are in progress against a data store.

The Basic Methods of the Connection Objects

The most commonly used methods for both the `OleDbConnection` and the `SqlConnection` objects are:

Method	Description
Open	Opens a connection to the data source using the current settings for the properties such as `ConnectionString`, which specifies the connection information to use.
Close	Closes the connection to the data source.
BeginTransaction	Starts a data source transaction and returns a `Transaction` object that can be used to commit or abort the transaction.

An excellent reference to all the properties, methods, and events of the objects we discuss here is included within the .NET SDK that is provided with the framework. Simply open the ".NET Framework Class Library" within the section ".NET Framework Reference", or search for the object/class name using the Index *or* Search *feature of the SDK. We demonstrate many of the more common ones, including those shown above, later in this chapter and in the following chapters.*

Remember that there are two implementations of some of the .NET data access objects, each one being specific to the data store we are connecting to. The objects prefixed with `OleDb` are used with a managed code OLE-DB provider or ODBC via OLE-DB driver. The objects prefixed with `Sql` are used only with Microsoft SQL Server.

Other than that, the objects are identical as far as programming with them is concerned. However, you must use the appropriate one depending on which data store you connect to, so your code must be rewritten to use the correct ones if you change from one set of objects to the other. This is generally only a matter of changing the prefixes in the object declarations. For this reason you may prefer to avoid including the prefix in your variable and method names, and in comments within your code.

The Command Objects

Again these are similar to the equivalent ADO Command object, and have similar properties. They are used to connect the Connection object to a DataReader or a DataAdapter object.

- ❑   An OleDbCommand object is used with an OLE-DB provider or OLE-DB/ODBC driver
- ❑   A SqlCommand object uses Tabular Data Services with MS SQL Server

The Command object allows us to execute a SQL statement or stored procedure in a data source. This includes returning a rowset (in which case we pass the data to another object such as a DataReader or a DataAdapter), or returning a count of the number of records affected for queries that do not return a rowset.

The Basic Methods of the Command Objects

The most commonly used methods for both the OleDbCommmand and the SqlCommand objects are:

Method	Description
ExecuteNonQuery	Executes the command defined in the CommandText property against the connection defined in the Connection property for a query that does not return any rows (an UPDATE, DELETE or INSERT). Returns an Integer indicating the number of rows affected by the query.
ExecuteReader	Takes a "reader" object and executes the command defined in the CommandText property against the connection defined in the Connection property. On return the reader is connected to the resulting rowset within the database allowing the rows to be retrieved. The derivative method ExecuteXmlReader can be used with SQL server 7.0 SQLXML technology to return an XML docment fragment in a XML Reader object. We look at the various "reader" objects later in this chapter.
ExecuteScalar	Takes a "reader" object and executes the command defined in the CommandText property against the connection defined in the Connection property. Returns only the first row of the resulting rowset. Any other returned rows are discarded.

The DataAdapter Objects

These are new objects that connect one or more Command objects to a Dataset object. They provide the pipeline and logic that fetches the data from the data store and populates the tables in the DataSet, or pushes the changes in the DataSet back into the data store.

- ❑   An OleDbDataAdapter object is used with an OLE-DB provider or OLE-DB/ODBC driver
- ❑   A SqlDataAdapter object uses Tabular Data Services with MS SQL Server

These objects provide four properties defining the commands used to manipulate the data in a data store: `SelectCommand`, `InsertCommand`, `UpdateCommand`, and `DeleteCommand`. Each one of these properties is a reference to a `Command` object:

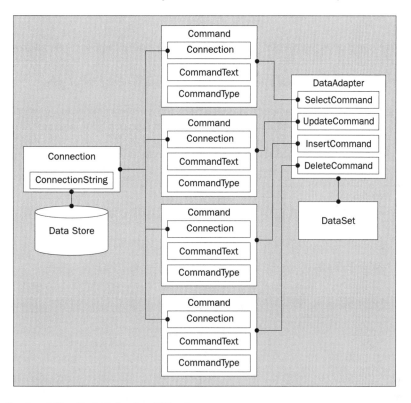

The Basic Methods of the DataAdapter Objects

Both the `OleDbDataAdapter` and the `SqlDataAdapter` objects provide a series of methods for working with the data set that they apply to. The two most commonly used ones are:

Method	Description
Fill	Executes the `SelectCommand` to fill the `DataSet` object with data from the data source.
FillSchema	Uses the `SelectCommand` to extract just the schema for a table in the data source, and creates an empty table with all the corresponding constraints in the `DataSet` object.
Update	Calls the respective `InsertCommand`, `UpdateCommand` or `DeleteCommand` for each inserted, updated or deleted row in the `DataSet` so as to update the original data source with the changes made to the content of the `DataSet`. This is a little like the `UpdateBatch` method provided by the ADO `Recordset` object, but in the `DataSet` it can update more than one table.

The DataSet Object

The `DataSet` provides the basis for disconnected storage and manipulation of relational data. We fill it from a data store, work with it while disconnected from that data store, then reconnect and flush changes back to the data store if required. The main differences between a `DataSet` and the ADO `Recordset` are:

❑ The `DataSet` object can hold more than one table (more than one rowset in other words), as well as the relationships between them.

❑ The `DataSet` object automatically provides disconnected access to data.

Each table in a `DataSet` is a `DataTable` object within the `Tables` collection. Each `DataTable` object contains a collection of `DataRow` objects and a collection of `DataColumn` objects. There are also collections for the primary keys, constraints, and default values used in this table (the `Constraints` collection), and the parent and child relationships between the tables.

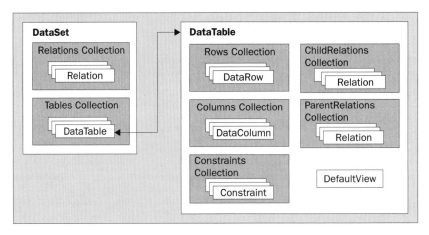

Finally, there is a `DefaultView` object for each table. This is used to create a `DataView` object based on the table, so that the data can be searched, filtered or otherwise manipulated – or bound to a control for display. We'll look at the `DataTable` and `DataView` objects shortly.

The Basic Methods of the DataSet Object

The `DataSet` object exposes a series of methods that can be used to work with the contents of the tables or the relations between them. For example, you can clear the `DataSet`, or merge data from separate `DataSet` objects:

Method	Description
Clear	Removes all data stored in the `DataSet` by emptying all of the tables it contains. However, it is often more efficient to destroy the object and create a new one unless you need to hold a reference to the existing one.
Merge	Takes the contents of a `DataSet` and merges it with another `DataSet` so that it contains all the data from both of the source `DataSet` objects.

We mentioned earlier that the default persistence format in .NET is XML, and the `DataSet` object provides methods for reading and writing this XML data:

Methods	Description
`ReadXML` and `ReadSchema`	Takes an XML document or schema and reads it into the `DataSet`.
`GetXML` and `GetSchema`	Returns a `String` containing an XML document or schema that represents the data in the `DataSet`.
`WriteXML` and `WriteSchema`	Writes the XML document or schema that represents the data in the `DataSet` to a disk file, a "reader/writer" object or stream. We look at the "reader/writer" objects later in this chapter.

The `DataSet` object, together with all the `DataTable` objects it contains, keeps a record of the values for the content when it was originally created and loaded (filled with data). This is a fundamental requirement to allow the changes to be pushed back into the original data store in a multi-user scenario. To allow you to control when and how the original values are stored, there are four methods provided:

Method	Description
`AcceptChanges`	Commits all the changes made to the tables or relations within the `DataSet` since it was loaded, or since the last time that `AcceptChanges` was executed.
`GetChanges`	Returns a `DataSet` object containing all the changes made since it was loaded, or since the last time that `AcceptChanges` was executed.
`HasChanges`	Indicates if any changes have been made to the contents of the `DataSet` since it was loaded, or since the last time that `AcceptChanges` was executed.
`RejectChanges`	Abandons all the changes made to values in the tables within the `DataSet` since it was loaded, or since the last time that `AcceptChanges` was executed. Returns it to the original state and removes all stored changes information.

The DataTable Object

Each of the tables or rowsets stored within a `DataSet` object is exposed through a `DataTable` object – as we saw in the previous schematic. Each `DataTable` has a property named `Rows` that references a `DataRowsCollection` object. This is a collection of `DataRows` objects.

The Basic Methods of the DataTable Object

The `DataTable` object exposes a series of properties and methods that allow us to interact with each table individually whilst it is stored in the `DataSet`. The most commonly used of these methods are `Clear`, `AcceptChanges`, and `RejectChanges`. These are fundamentally the same as the methods just described for the `DataSet` object, but operate only on the specific table to which the `DataTable` object refers. There are also methods that allow us to manipulate the contents of the table. For example:

Method	Description
NewRow	Creates a new row for the table. The values can then be inserted into it using code and the new row can be added to the table.
Select	Returns the set of rows that match a filter, in the order specified. Used to create subsets of rows.

The Basic Methods of the DataRowsCollection Object

This is a collection of all the rows in a DataTable, as referenced by the Rows property of the table. It provides methods to add and remove rows, and to find a row based on a value for the primary key (or more than one value for a multiple-column primary key):

Method	Description
Add	Adds a new row created with the NewRow method of the DataTable to the table.
Remove	Permanently removes the specified DataRow object from the table.
RemoveAt	Permanently removes a row specified by its index position from the table.
Find	Takes an array of primary key values and returns the matching row as a DataRow object.

The Basic Methods of the DataRow Object

This object represents the row itself within the table and within the DataRowsCollection. It has an AcceptChanges and a RejectChanges method that works the same as for the DataTable. It also has methods that we use to manipulate individual rows in a table:

Method	Description
BeginEdit, EndEdit and CancelEdit	Used to switch the row into "edit mode" and save or abandon the changes made in this mode.
Delete	Marks the row as being deleted, though it is not removed from the table until the Update or AcceptChanges method is executed.
GetChildRows	Returns a collection of rows from another table that are related as child rows to this row.
SetColumnError and GetColumnsInError	Used to set and return the error status for this row. In conjunction with the HasErrors and RowError properties, this allows bulk edit errors to be reported separately afterwards.

The DataView Object

As we saw in the earlier schematic, we can retrieve a DataView object containing the data from a table within a DataSet object. The DataView object exposes a complete table or a subset of the records from a table. It can be created using the DefaultView of the table or from a DataTable object that selects a subset of rows from a table.

The Basic Methods of the DataView Object

In general, if you want to manipulate the contents of a table within a `DataSet`, it's best to create a `DataView` object from the table and use the methods it provides. The most commonly used ones are:

Method	Description
AddNew	Adds a new row to the view. The values can then be inserted into it using code.
Delete	Removes the current or specified row from the view.
Find	Returns the row that matches the specified primary key value.

The DataReader Objects

While the `DataSet` object provides a comprehensive platform for disconnected data access, there are many occasions when we just want a fast and efficient way to access a data store without actually extracting data that will be **remoted** (disconnected). This might be to extract one or a few records or specific field values, or to execute a simple INSERT, UPDATE, or DELETE SQL statement. Or, it might be where there is too much data to fit into a `DataSet` and to remote sensibly. It's also the ideal solution for server-side data-binding in most cases, as we saw in the previous chapter. For all these tasks we can use a `DataReader` object.

❑ An `OleDbDataReader` object is used with an OLE-DB provider or OLE-DB/ODBC driver

❑ A `SqlDataReader` object uses Tabular Data Services with MS SQL Server

The `DataReader` provides the equivalent of a "firehose" cursor for direct connected access and retrieval of data from a data store. It's like the way we used an ADO `Recordset` to extract data and then iterate through it. It allows us to execute a SQL statement or stored procedure to get a set of data rows, and iterate through them – all the time being connected to the data store. It can also be used to execute SQL statements or stored procedures that update the source data without returning any rows.

❑ The `DataReader` object provides a partial equivalent of a cursor against a data store using a SQL statement or a stored procedure to extract a rowset.

❑ It also provides the ability to execute a SQL statement or a stored procedure to update the data store content.

❑ It does **not** provide disconnected access to data.

Access to the rowset referenced by a `DataReader` is read-only and forward-only.

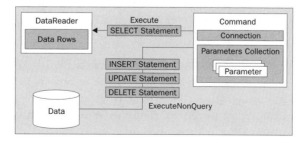

Remember that you can extract XML formatted data fragments directly from MS SQL Server 2000 using a "reader" object (in this case an XmlReader) and the built-in SQLXML technology.

The Basic Methods of the DataReader Objects

To use a `DataReader` object, we create a `Command` object and use it to execute our SQL statement or stored procedure. If the statement returns any records, the `DataReader` provides access to this data. We can then iterate through the rows and fields to extract the results. The most commonly used methods exposed by the `DataReader` objects are:

Method	Description
Read	Advances the current record pointer to the next record or row so that the values of the fields or columns can be accessed using the column name or ordinal position.
Get*XXXX*	Gets a value as a specific data type from the results. Examples are `GetBoolean`, `GetInt16`, and `GetChars`.
NextResult	Moves the current row pointer to the next set of results when the statement is a SQL stored procedure or a batch SQL statement that returns more than one result set. Note that this is not a `MoveNext` operation like that of an ADO `Recordset` object – it moves the current row pointer from one **rowset** to the first row in the **next rowset**.
Close	Closes the `DataReader` and releases the reference to the rowset.

Should I Use a DataReader or a DataSet?

When you start building applications that access a data store, you really need to think about what kind of access you actually need, and how the data will be used. It should be obvious from the preceding descriptions of the objects that the `DataSet` carries a large overhead in terms of complexity when compared to a `DataReader`, with the corresponding effect on performance and memory usage.

So, wherever it's possible you should aim to use a `DataReader` rather than a `DataSet`. The kind of occasions where a `DataSet` is a requirement are:

❑ When you need to remote the data, that is disconnect from the data store and pass the data to another tier in the application, to a client application, store it ready for use in a process, edit the data, or in some similar scenario.

❑ When you need to store, transport or access more than one table (i.e. more than one `DataTable` object), and optionally the relationships between these tables.

❑ When you need to update data in the source database using the built-in methods of the `DataSet` rather than executing individual SQL update statements or stored procedures via a `DataReader`. The `DataSet` also stores the original (as well as the current) values of each column in each row, so it better manages a situation where multiple users are concurrently updating the data.

❑ When you need to take advantage of the synchronization between an XML document and the equivalent "relational" rowset. This is a topic we look at in detail in Chapter 11.

❑ In certain data-binding scenarios, such as binding the same data to several controls, or using automatic record paging in a `DataGrid` control, you cannot use a `DataReader` as the data source. In this case, it's usual to use a `DataView` created from a table in a `DataSet`.

❑ If you are iterating through the data rows, and need the freedom to be able to move backwards and forwards in the rowset. The `DataReader` is a forward-only data source.

Relational Data Providers for .NET

As we've seen, .NET uses managed code data providers to connect to a data store. The ones that ship with the current version of the framework include:

Provider Name	Description
SQLOLEDB	OLE DB Provider SQL Server
MSDAORA	OLE DB Provider for Oracle
Microsoft.Jet.OLEDB.4.0	OLE DB Provider for Access and other Jet data sources

More managed providers are planned, such as providers for Microsoft Exchange, Active Directory, and other data stores. The existing unmanaged OLEDB providers for these data stores cannot be used in .NET.

Common Data Access Tasks with .NET

To demonstrate the basics of working with relational data in .NET, we've put together a series of sample pages that show the various objects in action. You can download the samples to run on your own server (or just to examine and use the code they contain) from our web site at http://www.wrox.com/Books/Book_Details.asp?isbn=1861004885.

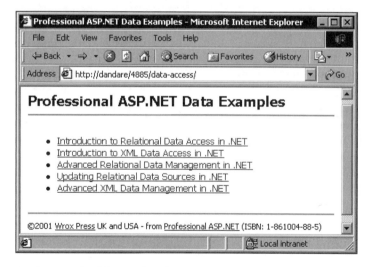

The default page for the samples (shown above) contains a link "Introduction to Relational Data Access in .NET" to the samples for this section. The default page for this section shows the list of available samples:

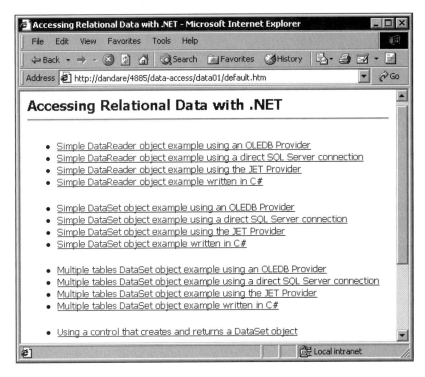

The first three groups of links show the three basic techniques for accessing relational data. Each example is shown with the three different connection types: an OLEDB provider for SQL Server, a direct SQL Server TDS connection, and via the Jet provider for Microsoft Access. There is also a sample for each group written in C# rather than VB.

Setting Up the Samples on Your System

The downloadable samples file contains both an Access database named `books.mdb` that you can use with the Jet examples, and a set of SQL scripts that you can use to create the sample `WroxBooks` database on your own local SQL Server. Instructions for using the scripts are in the `readme.txt` file located within the `database` folder of the samples.

You'll also need to edit the connection strings to suit your own setup. The file `connect-strings.ascx` is in the `global` folder of the sample files. This is an ASP.NET user control, which exposes the connection strings as properties. For example the OLEDB connection string is returned by the `OLEDBConnectionString` property like this:

```
Public ReadOnly Property OLEDBConnectionString() As String
   Get
      '*******************************************************************
      'edit the values in curly braces below as appropriate
      Return "provider=SQLOLEDB.1;data source={yourservername};" _
           & "initial catalog={databasename};uid={username};pwd={password};"
      '*******************************************************************
   End Get
End Property
```

All of the samples that access the databases use this control. They insert it into the page using a `Register` directive at the top of the page, and by defining an element within the `<body>` of the page that uses the `TagPrefix` and `TagName` (see Chapter 4 for more details on working with user controls like this):

```
<%@ Register TagPrefix="wrox" TagName="connect"
             Src="..\global\connect-strings.ascx" %>

             Src="..\global\connect-strings.ascx" %>
...
<wrox:connect id="ctlConnectStrings" runat="server"/>
```

Then the code can access the connection strings using:

```
strOLEDBConnect = ctlConnectStrings.OLEDBConnectionString
strSQLConnect = ctlConnectStrings.SqlConnection String
strJetConnect = ctlConnectStrings.JetConnectionString
```

Using a DataReader Object

The first group of links in the relational data access menu shows the `DataReader` object in use. This is the nearest equivalent to the `Connection/Recordset` data access technique used in traditional ADO. The next screenshot shows the result of running the OLEDB example, the others provide an identical output but with different connection strings:

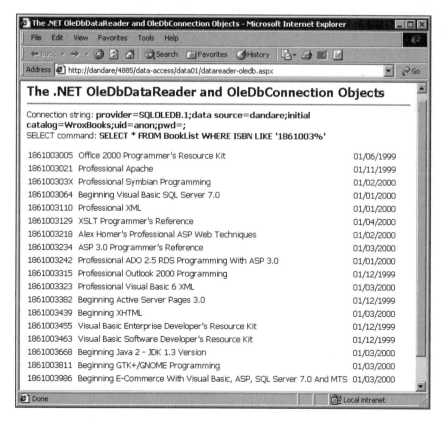

371

The code in the page (`datareader-oledb.aspx`) is placed within the `Page_Load` event handler, so it runs when the page loads. The code inserts the connection string, SQL `SELECT` statement and the results into `<div>` elements within page. All the code is fully commented, and we've included elementary error handling to display any errors. However, we're just going to show the relevant data access code here. You can examine the entire source code for any of the pages by clicking the [view source] link at the bottom.

The DataReader Example Code

The first step is to get the connection string from our custom user control, and then specify the SQL statement. These are displayed as the code runs in `<div>` elements named `outConnect` and `outSelect` (located within the HTML of the page):

```
strConnect = ctlConnectStrings.OLEDBConnectionString
outConnect.InnerText = strConnect

strSelect = "SELECT * FROM BookList WHERE ISBN LIKE '1861003%'"
outSelect.InnerText = strSelect
```

Now we can create a new instance of an `OleDbConnection` object. We specify the connection string as the single parameter of the constructor. Then we open the connection by calling the `Open` method:

```
Dim objConnect As New OleDbConnection(strConnect)
objConnect.Open()
```

Next, we need an `OleDbCommand` object. This will be used to execute the statement and return a new `ADODataAdapter` object containing the results of the query. Notice that we specify the SQL statement and the active `Connection` object as the parameters to the `OleDbCommand` object constructor:

```
Dim objCommand As New OleDbCommand(strSelect, objConnect)
```

Then we can call the `Execute` method of the `OleDbCommand` object. This returns a `DataReader` object that is connected to the result rowset:

```
'declare a variable to hold a DataReader object
Dim objDataReader As OleDbDataReader

'execute SQL statement against the command to get the DataReader
objDataReader = objCommand.ExecuteReader()
```

Displaying the Results

The `DataReader` allows us to iterate through the results of a SQL query, much like we do with a traditional ADO `Recordset` object. Note that we no longer have a `MoveNext` method. Forgetting to include this statement was found by testers to be the most common reason why developers had problems when working with the `Recordset` object in ADO. In a `DataReader`, we just have to use the `Read` method to get the next row of the results.

So, as was common practice in ASP 3.0 and earlier, we can build up an HTML `<table>` to display the data. However, as we're working with ASP.NET now, our example actually creates the definition of the table as a string and then inserts it into a `<div>` element elsewhere in the page (rather than the ASP-style technique of using `Response.Write` directly):

```
Dim strResult As String = "<table>"

'iterate through the records in the DataReader getting field values
'the Read method returns False when there are no more records
Do While objDataReader.Read()
    strResult += "<tr><td>" & objDataReader("ISBN") & "</td><td>  " _
            & objDataReader("Title") & "</td><td>  " _
            & objDataReader("PublicationDate") & "</td><td></tr>"
Loop

'close the DataReader and Connection
objDataReader.Close()
objConnect.Close()

'add closing table tag and display the results
strResult += "</table>"
outResult.InnerHtml = strResult
```

Closing the DataReader and the Connection

Notice that we have to explicitly close the DataReader object. We also explicitly close the connection by calling the Connection object's Close method. Although the garbage collection process will close it when it destroys the object in memory after the page ends, it's good practice to always close connections as soon as you are finished with them. They are a precious resource and the number available is often limited.

One useful technique is to use the optional parameter of the Command object's ExecuteReader method to force the connection to be closed automatically as soon as we call the Close method of the DataReader object:

```
objDataReader = objCommand.ExecuteReader(CommandBehavior.CloseConnection)
```

Overall, you can see that the techniques we used in this example are not that far removed from working with traditional ADO in ASP. However, there are far more opportunities available in .NET for accessing and using relational data. These revolve around the DataSet object rather than the DataReader object.

A Simple DataSet Example

A DataSet is a disconnected read/write container for holding one or more tables of data, and the relationships between these tables. In this example, we just extract a single table from our database and display the contents. This is what the "Simple DataSet object example using an OLEDB Provider" (simple-dataset-oledb.aspx) sample looks like when it runs:

The Simple DataSet Example Code

We've used the same connection string and SQL statement as in the `DataReader` example. We also create a new `OleDbConnection` object using this connection string like we did previously:

```
Dim objConnect As New OleDbConnection(strConnect)
```

To execute the SQL statement for the `OleDbDataReader` object in the previous example, we used the `ExecuteReader` method of the `OleDbCommand` object. In this example, we're aiming to fill a `DataSet` object with data, and so we use an alternative object to specify the SQL statement – an `OleDbDataAdapter` object. Again, we provide the SQL statement and the active `Connection` object as the parameters to the object constructor:

```
Dim objDataAdapter As New OleDbDataAdapter(strSelect, objConnect)
```

This technique does in fact still create and use a Command object. When we create a DataAdapter object, a suitable Command object is created automatically behind the scenes, and assigned to the SelectCommand property of our DataAdapter. We could do this ourselves, but it would mean writing the extra code and there is no advantage in doing so.

Now we can create an instance of a `DataSet` object, then fill it with data from the data source by calling the `Fill` method of the `DataAdapter` object. We specify as parameters the `DataSet` object and the name we want the table to have within the `DataSet` (it doesn't have to be the same as the table name in the database):

```
Dim objDataSet As New DataSet()
objDataAdapter.Fill(objDataSet, "Books")
```

Filling the Schema in a DataSet

The `Fill` method of the `DataAdapter` object that we used here creates the table in the `DataSet`, then creates the appropriate columns and sets the data type and certain constraints such as the column "width" (that is number of characters). What it doesn't do automatically is set the primary keys, unique constraints, read-only values, and defaults. However, we can call the `FillSchema` method first (before we call `Fill`) to copy these settings from the data source into the table:

```
objDataAdapter.FillSchema(objDataSet, SchemaType.Mapped)
```

After all this, we've now got a disconnected `DataSet` object that contains the results of the SQL query. The next step is to display that data.

Displaying the Results

In this, and many of the other examples, we're using an ASP `DataGrid` control to display the data in our `DataSet` object. We saw how the `DataGrid` control works in Chapter 7:

```
<asp:datagrid id="dgrResult" runat="server" />
```

However, we can't bind the `DataSet` object directly to a `DataGrid`, as a `DataSet` can contain multiple tables. Instead, we create a `DataView` based on the table we want to display, and bind the `DataView` object to the `DataGrid`. We get the default `DataView` object for a table by accessing the `Tables` collection of the `DataSet` and specifying the table name:

```
Dim objDataView As New DataView(objDataSet.Tables("Books"))
```

Then we can assign the `DataView` to the `DataSource` property of the `DataGrid`, and call the `DataBind` method to display the data:

```
dgrResult.DataSource = objDataView
dgrResult.DataBind()
```

However, it's actually better performance-wise, though not as clear when you read the code, to perform the complete property assignment in one statement:

```
dgrResult.DataSource = objDataSet.Tables("Books").DefaultView
```

We use both techniques in our examples.

A Multiple Tables DataSet Example

Having seen how we can use a `DataSet` to hold one "results" table, we'll now see how we can add multiple tables to a `DataSet` object. The "Multiple tables DataSet object example using an OLEDB Provider" (`multiple-dataset-oledb.aspx`) example creates a `DataSet` object and fills it with three tables. It also creates relationships between these tables. The page shows the connection string, and the three SQL statements used to extract the data from three tables in the database. Below this are two `DataGrid` controls showing the contents of the `DataSet` object's `Tables` collection and `Relations` collection:

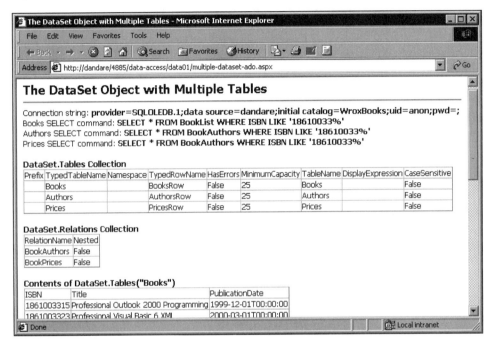

Further down the page are three more `DataGrid` controls, which show the data that is contained in the three tables within the `DataSet`:

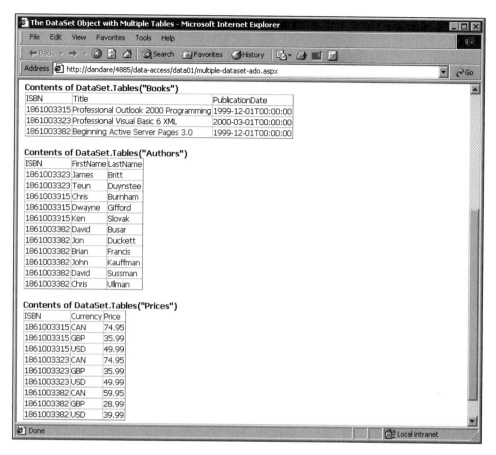

The Multiple Tables DataSet Example Code

While the principle for this example is similar to the previous "simple `DataSet`" example, the way we've coded it is subtly different. We've taken the opportunity to demonstrate another way of using the `Command` and `DataAdapter` objects.

As before, we first create a `Connection` object using our connection string. However, we create a `Command` object next using the default constructor with no parameters:

```
Dim objConnect As New OleDbConnection(strConnect)
Dim objCommand As New OleDbCommand()
```

Now we set the properties of the `Command` object in a very similar way to that you may be used to in "traditional" ADO. We specify the connection string, the command type (in our case `Text` as we're using a SQL statement), and the SQL statement itself for the `CommandText` property. By doing it this way, we can change the SQL statement later to get a different set of records from the database without having to create a new `Command` object:

```
objCommand.Connection = objConnect
objCommand.CommandType = CommandType.Text
objCommand.CommandText = strSelectBooks
```

Once we've got a `Command` object, we can use it within a `DataAdapter`. We need a `DataAdapter` to extract the data from the database and squirt it into our `DataSet` object. After creating the `DataAdapter`, we assign our `Command` object to its `SelectCommand` property. This `Command` will then be used when we call the `Fill` method to get the data:

```
Dim objDataAdapter As New OleDbDataAdapter()
objDataAdapter.SelectCommand = objCommand
```

So, we've got a valid `DataAdapter` object, and we can set about filling our `DataSet`. We call the `Fill` method three times, once for each table we want to insert into it. In between, we just have to change the `CommandText` property of the active `Command` object to the appropriate SQL statement. The code (shown below) creates three tables named `Books`, `Authors`, and `Prices` within the `DataSet`:

```
Dim objDataSet As New DataSet()
objCommand.CommandText = strSelectBooks
objDataAdapter.Fill(objDataSet, "Books")
objCommand.CommandText = strSelectAuthors
objDataAdapter.Fill(objDataSet, "Authors")
objCommand.CommandText = strSelectPrices
objDataAdapter.Fill(objDataSet, "Prices")
```

Opening and Closing Connections with the DataAdapter

In the examples where we use a `DataAdapter`, we haven't explicitly opened or closed the connection. This is because the `DataAdapter` looks after this automatically. If the connection is closed when we call the `Fill` method it is opened, the rows are extracted from the data source and pushed into the `DataSet`, and the connection is automatically closed again.

However, if the connection is open when the `Fill` method is called, the `DataAdapter` leaves it open after the method has completed. This provides us with a useful opportunity to maximize performance by preventing the connection being opened and closed each time we call `Fill` if we are loading more than one table in the `DataSet`. We just have to open the connection explicitly before the fist call, and close it again after the last one:

```
Dim objDataSet As New DataSet()
objCommand.CommandText = strSelectBooks
objConnect.Open()
objDataAdapter.Fill(objDataSet, "Books")
objCommand.CommandText = strSelectAuthors
objDataAdapter.Fill(objDataSet, "Authors")
objCommand.CommandText = strSelectPrices
objDataAdapter.Fill(objDataSet, "Prices")
objConnect.Close()
```

Adding Relationships to the DataSet

We've got three tables in our `DataSet`, and we can now create the relationships between them. We define a variable to hold a `DataRelation` object and create a new `DataRelation` by specifying the name we want for the relation (`BookAuthors`), the name of the primary key field (`ISBN`) in the parent table named `Books`, and the name of the foreign key field (`ISBN`) in the child table named `Authors`. Then we add it to the `DataSet` object's `Relations` collection:

```
Dim objRelation As DataRelation
objRelation = New DataRelation("BookAuthors", _
              objDataSet.Tables("Books").Columns("ISBN"), _
              objDataSet.Tables("Authors").Columns("ISBN"))
objDataSet.Relations.Add(objRelation)
```

Then we can do the same to create the relation between the `Books` and `Prices` tables in the `DataSet`:

```
objRelation = New DataRelation("BookPrices", _
              objDataSet.Tables("Books").Columns("ISBN"), _
              objDataSet.Tables("Prices").Columns("ISBN"))
objDataSet.Relations.Add(objRelation)
```

Usefully, as the relations are added to the `DataSet`, an integrity check is carried out automatically. If, for example, there is a child record that has no matching parent record, an error is raised and the relation is not added to the `DataSet`.

Displaying the Results

Having filled our `DataSet` with three tables and two relations, we can now display the results. We use five `DataGrid` controls to do this. The `DataSet` object's `Tables` and `Relations` collections can be bound directly to the first two `DataGrid` controls:

```
dgrTables.DataSource = objDataSet.Tables
dgrTables.DataBind()

dgrRelations.DataSource = objDataSet.Relations
dgrRelations.DataBind()
```

For the three tables within the `DataSet`, we assign the `DataView` object returned by the `DefaultView` property of the tables to the remaining three `DataGrid` controls:

```
dgrBooksData.DataSource = objDataSet.Tables("Books").DefaultView
dgrBooksData.DataBind()

dgrAuthorsData.DataSource = objDataSet.Tables("Authors").DefaultView
dgrAuthorsData.DataBind()

dgrPricesData.DataSource = objDataSet.Tables("Prices").DefaultView
dgrPricesData.DataBind()
```

A User Control That Returns a DataSet Object

The code we've just seen is used in several examples in this and subsequent chapters, and to make it easier we've encapsulated it as a user control that returns a fully populated `DataSet`. All that's needed is to change the page's file extension to ".ascx" and change the `Page` directive to a `Control` directive:

```
<%@Control Language="VB"%>
```

Then, instead of placing the code in the `Page_Load` event handler, we place it in a `Public Function` to which we provide the connection string and the `WHERE` clause for the SQL statement as parameters. The function returns a `DataSet` object:

```
Public Function BooksDataSet(strConnect As String, _
                             strWhere As String) _
                             As DataSet

    ...
    strSelectBooks = "SELECT * FROM BookList WHERE " & strWhere
    strSelectAuthors = "SELECT * FROM BookAuthors WHERE " & strWhere
    strSelectPrices = "SELECT * FROM BookPrices WHERE " & strWhere

    Dim objDataSet As New DataSet()
    ...
    ... code to fill DataSet as before ...
    ...
    Return objDataSet

End Function
```

Note that this allows us to select a different set of books by varying the `strWhere` parameter value when we use the control. The example page named "Using a control that creates and returns a DataSet object" (`use-dataset-control.aspx`) contains the `Register` directive and matching element to insert the control into the page:

```
<%@ Register TagPrefix="wrox" TagName="getdataset"
             Src="..\global\get-dataset-control.ascx" %>
...
<wrox:getdataset id="ctlDataSet" runat="server"/>
```

Then, to get a `DataSet` from the control, we just have to create a variable of the correct type and pass it, along with the connection string and `WHERE` clause, to the control:

```
Dim objDataSet As DataSet
objDataSet = ctlDataSet.BooksDataSet(strConnect, "ISBN LIKE '186100338%'")
```

We'll continue our investigation of the `DataSet` object in Chapter 10. We'll see how we can use more complex data sets, and update and edit data using the new .NET relational data access classes. We'll also explore in more detail the new ways that .NET combines the traditional relational database access techniques with the more recent developments in XML-based data storage and management. In the meantime, while we're on the subject of XML, we'll introduce the .NET classes that we use to work with XML.

An Introduction To XML in .NET

The previous section described the new features of .NET that are aimed at accessing relational data, and how they relate to the way we work with data compared to the traditional techniques used in previous versions of ADO. However, we should also look at a second technique for working with data within the .NET Framework.

Extensible Markup Language (XML) is fast becoming the lingua franca of the Web, and is being adopted within many other application areas as well. We discussed the reasons for this earlier in this chapter, and what we want to do here is to look at how XML is supported within .NET. This relates to the .NET support for relational data, as XML is the standard persistence format for data within the .NET data access classes. However, there are also several other techniques for reading, writing, and manipulating XML data and the associated technologies.

In this book, we're assuming that the reader is familiar with XML as a data storage mechanism, and how it is used through an XML parser and with the associated technologies such as XSLT. Our aim is to show the way that the .NET Framework and ASP.NET can be used with XML data.

> *For a primer and other reference materials covering XML and the associated standards and technologies, check out the Wrox Press list of XML books at http://www.wrox.com/.*

The Fundamental XML Objects

The World Wide Web Consortium (W3C at http://www.w3.org/) provides standards that define the structure and interfaces that should be provided for accessing XML documents. This is referred to as the XML Document Object Model (DOM), and is supported under .NET by the XmlDocument and XmlDataDocument objects. They provide full support for the XML DOM Level 2 Core. Within their implementation are the node types and objects that are required for the DOM interfaces, such as the XmlElement and XmlAttribute objects:

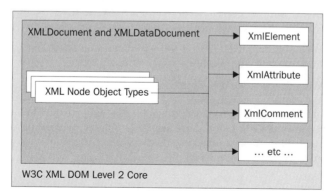

However, .NET extends the support for XML to provide much more in the way of techniques for manipulating XML documents, schemas, and stylesheets. The next schematic shows the main objects that are used when working with XML documents within your .NET applications.

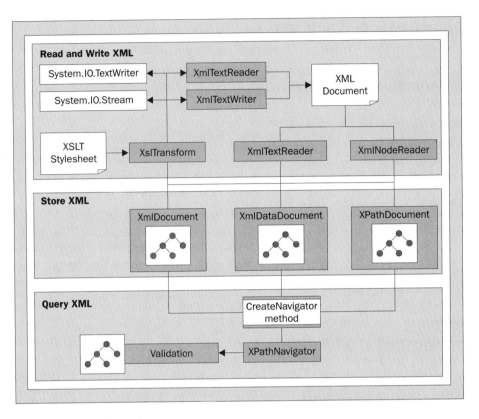

Basically, the objects fall into three groups:

- ❑ **Reading, writing, and transforming XML**, which includes the XmlTextReader, XmlNodeReader, and XmlTextWriter – plus the XslTransform object for creating files in a different format to the original XML document.

- ❑ **Storing and manipulating XML**, which is the function of the XmlDocument, XmlDataDocument, and XPathDocument objects.

- ❑ **Querying XML**, for which we use the XPathNavigator object.

There is some overlap between these functions, of course. To validate an XML document while reading it we use an XmlValidatingReader, and there are other objects for creating and editing schemas that we aren't covering in this book. You can also use the XslTransform object to perform querying of a document as well as transforming it into different formats.

In this section, we'll briefly overview the objects and their commonly used methods, and then move on to show you some simple examples. We'll then come back to XML again in Chapter 11 and see some more advanced techniques.

The Document Objects

There are three implementations of the document object for storing and working with XML:

❑   The `XmlDocument` object is the .NET implementation of the standard DOM Level 2 `XMLDocument` interface. The properties and methods it exposes include those defined by W3C for manipulating XML documents, plus some extensions to make common operations easier.

❑   The `XmlDataDocument` object is an extension of the `XmlDocument` object, providing the same set of properties and methods. However, it also acts as a "bridge" between XML and relational data access methods. Once loaded with an XML document, it can expose it as a `DataSet` object. This allows us to use relational data programming techniques to work with the data, as well the XML DOM techniques that are used with the `XmlDocument` object.

❑   The `XPathDocument` object is a fast and small implementation of an XML storage object that is designed for access via an `XPathNavigator` object, using only XPath queries or navigation element-by-element using the "pull" technique.

The Basic Document Methods

The `XPathDocument` object has no really useful public methods other than `CreateNavigator`, as it is designed solely to work with an `XPathNavigator` object. However, the other two document objects expose the full set of properties and methods specified in the W3C XML DOM Level 2 Core. The extensions to these properties and methods include several methods that we use regularly to work with XML documents. There are extensions for creating specific types of node, and accessing existing nodes:

Method	Description
Create*XXXX*	Creates a node in the XML document depending on the actual method name, for example `CreateElement`, `CreateComment`, `CreateTextNode`, etc.
CloneNode	Creates a duplicate of an XML node (for example a copy of an element).
GetElementById	Returns the single node with the specified value for its ID attribute.
GetElementsByTagname	Returns a node list containing all the elements with the specified element name.

There is also a series of methods for loading and saving XML to and from the XML document objects:

Method	Description
Load	Loads an XML document from a disk file.
LoadXml	Loads an XML document from a String.
Save	Saves the entire XML document to a disk file.
ReadNode	Loads a node from an XML document in an `XmlTextReader` or `XmlNodeReader` object.
WriteTo	Writes a node to another XML document using an `XmlTextWriter` object.
WriteContentTo	Writes a node and all its descendents to another XML document using an `XmlTextWriter` object.

If we want to use an XPathNavigator with our document, we create it using the CreateNavigator method:

Method	Description
CreateNavigator	Creates and returns an XPathNavigator object based on the currently loaded document. Applies to all the document objects. Optionally, for the XmlDocument and XmlDataDocument objects only, accepts a parameter that is a reference to a node within the document that will act as the start location for the navigator.

The XmlDataDocument object adds a single property to those exposed by the XmlDocument object:

Property	Description
DataSet	Returns the contents of the XML document as an ADO.NET DataSet object.

The XmlDataDocument object also adds methods that provide extra access to the contents of the document – treating it more like a recordset or data table.

Method	Description
GetRowFromElement	Returns a DataRow object representing the element in the document.
GetElementFromRow	Returns an XmlElement object representing a DataRow in a table within a DataSet.

The XPathNavigator Object

In order to make working with XML documents easier, the System.Xml namespace classes include this object, which can be used to navigate within an XML document, or to query the content of the document using an XPath expression. It's important to note here that an XPathNavigator can be used with **any** of the XML document objects – not just an XPathDocument. We can create an XPathNavigator based on an XmlDocument or an XmlDataDocument as well.

❑ The XPathNavigator object provides methods and properties that allow cursor-style navigation through the XML document, for example by stepping through the nodes (elements and attributes) in order, or by skipping to the next node of a specific type.

❑ The XPathNavigator object also provides methods that accept an XPath expression, the name of a node or a node type and return one or more matching nodes. We can then iterate through these nodes.

An XPathNavigator object can **only** be created from an existing document object. We do so using the CreateNavigator method:

```
Dim objNav1 As XPathNavigator = objXMLDoc.CreateNavigator()
Dim objNav2 As XPathNavigator = objXMLDataDoc.CreateNavigator()
Dim objNav3 As XPathNavigator = objXPathDoc.CreateNavigator()
```

The Basic XPathNavigator Methods

The `XPathNavigator` object is designed to act as a "pull" model interface for an XML document. It allows us to navigate across a document, and select nodes within that document. We can also create two (or more) navigator objects against the same document, and compare their positions.

To edit the XML document(s), we use the reference to the current node exposed by the navigator, or an `XPathNodeIterator` object that contains a collection of nodes, and call the methods of that node or collection. At the same time, the `XPathNavigator` exposes details about the current node directly, so we have two ways to get information about each node.

The following tables show the most commonly used methods of the `XPathNavigator` object. There are methods to move around within the document, making different nodes current in the navigator, and to create a new navigator:

Method	Description
MoveTo*XXXX*	Moves the current navigator position. Examples are `MoveToFirst`, `MoveToFirstChild`, `MoveToParent`, `MoveToAttribute`, `MoveToRoot`, etc.
Clone	Creates a new `XPathNavigator` object that is automatically located at the same position in the document as the current navigator.
IsSamePosition	Indicates if two navigators are in the same position within the document.

There are methods to access and select parts of the content of the document:

Method	Description
GetAttribute	Returns the value of a specified attribute from the current node in the navigator.
Select	Returns an `XPathNodeIterator` object (a `NodeList`) containing a collection of nodes that match the specified `XPath` expression.
SelectAncestors	Returns an `XPathNodeIterator` object (a `NodeList`) containing a collection of all the ancestor nodes in the document of a specific type or which have a specific name.
SelectDescendants	Returns an `XPathNodeIterator` object (a `NodeList`) containing a collection of all the descendant nodes in the document of a specific type or which have a specific name.
SelectChildren	Returns an `XPathNodeIterator` object (a `NodeList`) containing a collection of all the child nodes in the document of a specific type or which have a specific name.

The XmlTextWriter Object

When using an `XmlDocument` object to create a new XML document, we must create document fragments and insert them into the document in a specific way – a technique that can be error-prone and complex. The `XmlTextWriter` can be used to create an XML document node by node in serial fashion by simply writing the tags and content to the output stream using the comprehensive range of methods that it provides.

❑   The `XmlTextWriter` object takes as its source either a `TextWriter` object that refers to a disk file, the path and name of a disk file, or a `Stream` object that will contain the new XML document. It exposes a series of properties and methods that can be used to create XML nodes and other content, and output them to the disk file or stream directly.

❑   The `XmlTextWriter` object can also be specified as the output device for methods in several other objects, where it automatically streams the content of the object to a disk file, `TextWriter` or `Stream`.

The `TextReader`, `TextWriter`, and `Stream` objects are discussed in Chapter 16.

The Basic XmlWriter Methods

The most commonly used methods of the `XmlTextWriter` object are listed next:

Method	Description
WriteStartDocument	Starts a new document by writing the XML declaration to the output.
WriteEndDocument	Ends the document by closing all un-closed elements, and flushing the content to disk.
WriteStartElement	Writes an opening tag for the specified element. The equivalent method for creating attributes is `WriteStartAttribute`.
WriteEndElement	Writes a closing tag for the current element. The equivalent method for completing an attribute is `WriteEndAttribute`.
WriteElementString	Writes a complete element (including opening and closing tags) with the specific string as the value. The equivalent method for writing a complete attribute is `WriteAttributeString`.
Close	Closes the stream or disk file and releases any references held.

The XmlReader Objects

We need to be able to read documents from other sources, rather than always creating them from scratch. The `XmlReader` object is a base class from which two public classes, `XmlTextReader` and `XmlNodeReader` inherit.

❑   The `XmlTextReader` object takes as its source either a `TextReader` object that refers to an XML disk file, the path and name of an XML disk file, or a `Stream` object containing an XML document. The contents of the document can be read one node at a time, and the object provides information about each node and its value as it is read.

❑ The XmlNodeReader takes an XmlNode object as its source, allowing us to read specific portions of an XML document rather than having to read all of it if we only want to access a specific node and its children.

❑ The XmlTextReader and XmlNodeReader objects can also be used standalone to provide simple and efficient access to XML documents, or as the source for another object whereby they automatically read the document and pass it to the parent object.

Like the XPathNavigator, the XmlTextReader provides a "pull" model for accessing XML documents node-by-node, rather than parsing them into a tree in memory as is done in an XML parser. This allows larger documents to be accessed without impacting on memory usage, and can also make coding easier depending on the task you need to accomplish.

Furthermore, if you are just searching for a specific value, you won't always have to read the whole document. Taking a broad average, you will reach the specific node you want after reading only half the document. This is considerably faster and more efficient than reading and parsing the whole document every time.

The Basic XmlReader Methods

The XmlTextReader and the XmlNodeReader objects have almost identical sets of properties and methods. The most commonly used methods are:

Method	Description
Read	Reads the next node into the reader object where it can be accessed. Returns False if there are no more nodes to read.
ReadInnerXml	Reads and returns the complete content of the current node as a string, containing all the markup and text of the child nodes.
ReadOuterXml	Reads and returns the markup of the current node and the complete content as a string, containing all the markup and text of the child nodes as well.
ReadString	Returns the string value of the current node.
GetAttribute	Returns the value of a specified attribute from the current node in the reader.
GetRemainder	Reads and returns the remaining XML in the source document as a string. Useful if we are copying XML from one document to another.
MoveTo*XXXX*	Moves the current reader position. Examples are MoveToAttribute, MoveToContent, MoveToElement, etc.
Skip	Skips the current node in the reader and moves to the next one.
Close	Closes the stream or disk file.

The XmlValidatingReader Object

There is another object based on the XmlReader base class – the XmlValidatingReader. You can think of this as an XmlTextReader that does document validation against a schema or DTD. We create an XmlValidatingReader from an existing XmlReader (an XmlTextReader or XmlNodeReader), from a Stream or from a String that contains the XML to be validated.

Once we've created the `XmlValidatingReader`, we use it just like any other `XmlReader`. However, it raises an event when a schema validation error occurs, allowing us to ensure that the XML document is valid against one or more specific schemas.

The XslTransform Object

One common requirement when working with XML is the need to transform a document using Extensible Stylesheet Language. The .NET Framework classes provide the `XslTransform` object that is specially designed to perform either XSL or XSLT transformations.

The Basic XslTransform Object Methods

The `XslTransform` object has two methods we use for working with XML documents and XSL/XSLT stylesheets:

Method	Description
Load	Loads the specified XSL stylesheet and any style sheets referenced within it by `xsl:include` elements.
Transform	Transforms the specified XML data using the currently loaded XSL stylesheet, and outputs the results.

Next, we'll look at some of the common tasks that we need to carry out using XML documents.

Common XML Tasks in .NET

The default page for the samples that we saw earlier contains a link "Introduction to XML Data Access in .NET". The menu page that this opens contains links to several examples of the basic .NET framework XML data access techniques:

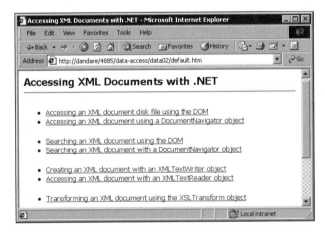

The first two pairs of links show how we can access XML data stored in a document object in two distinct ways – using the methods and properties provided by the XML Document Object Model (DOM), and through the new .NET `XPathNavigator` object.

XML Document Access via the DOM

The .NET XML classes provide an XML parser object named `XmlDocument` that is W3C DOM-compliant. This is the core object for most XML-based activities we carry out in .NET. We can use it with the same kind of code as we would (say) the MSXML parser object to access an XML document. The first example page, "Accessing XML documents using the DOM" (`xml-via-dom.aspx`), shows the results of recursively parsing a simple XML document using DOM methods:

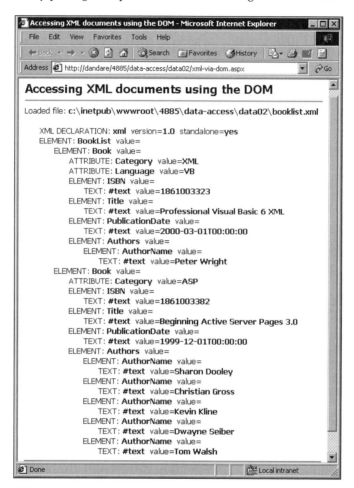

The XML DOM Example Code

This example, like the relational data access examples we saw earlier, uses code in the `Page_Load` event handler to access the data and present the results within `<div>` elements located in the page. It first creates a string containing the path to the XML document, which is located in the same folder as the ASP.NET page:

```
Dim strCurrentPath As String = Request.PhysicalPath
Dim strXMLPath As String = Left(strCurrentPath, _
                                InStrRev(strCurrentPath, "\")) & "booklist.xml"
```

Then it creates a new `XmlDocument` object and loads the XML file. The example contains some elementary error-handling code that we've removed here for clarity. You can use the [view source] link at the bottom of any of the sample pages to see the entire code:

```
Dim objXMLDoc As New XmlDocument()
objXMLDoc.Load(strXMLPath)
```

Now we can display the contents of the XML document by calling a custom function we've written that recursively extracts details of each element:

```
outResults.innerHTML = strNodes & GetChildNodes(objXMLDoc.ChildNodes, 0)
```

The function named `GetChildNodes` that we're using here accepts as parameters an `XmlNodeList` object containing the collection of child nodes of the current node – in this case the children of the document node.

> *An XML document has a single document node that has as its children the XML declaration node (such as `<?xml version="1.0"?>`), the root node of the XML (in our case `<BookList>`) and any comment nodes or processing instructions.*

The function also accepts an integer that indicates the nesting level. We use this to create the indentation of the output to show the structure more clearly. So, by calling this function initially with `objXMLDoc.ChildNodes` and 0 as the parameters, we'll start the process with the XML declaration and the root element of the document.

The Custom GetChildNodes Function

The complete listing of the `GetChildNodes` function is shown next. The techniques are standard W3C DOM coding practice. The principle is to iterate through all the nodes in the current `NodeList` object, displaying information about each one. Notice how there are different properties available for different types of nodes – we check the `NodeType` first then access the appropriate properties.

Next, if it is an `Element`-type node, we iterate through all the attributes adding information about these. Finally, we check if the node has any child nodes, and if so we iterate through these recursively calling the same `GetChildNodes` function.

```
Function GetChildNodes(objNodeList As XMLNodeList, _
                       intLevel As Integer) _
                    As String

    Dim strNodes As String = ""
    Dim objNode As XmlNode
    Dim objAttr As XmlAttribute

    'iterate through all the child nodes for the current node
    For Each objNode In objNodeList

        'display information about this node
        strNodes = strNodes & GetIndent(intLevel) _
                 & GetNodeType(objNode.NodeType) & ": <b>" & objNode.Name
```

```
      'if it is an XML Declaration node, display the 'special' properties
      If objNode.NodeType = XMLNodeType.XmlDeclaration Then
         'cast the XMLNode object to an XmlDeclaration object
         Dim objXMLDec =CType(objNode, XmlDeclaration)
         strNodes = strNodes & "</b>  version=<b>" _
                   & objXMLDec.Version & "</b>  standalone=<b>" _
                   & objXMLDec.Standalone & "</b><br />"
      Else
         'just display the generic 'value' property
         strNodes = strNodes & "</b>  value=<b>" _
                   & objNode.Value & "</b><br />"
      End If


      'if it is an Element node, iterate through the Attributes
      'collection displaying information about each attribute
      If objNode.NodeType = XMLNodeType.Element Then
         'display the attribute information for each attribute
         For Each objAttr In objNode.Attributes
            strNodes = strNodes & GetIndent(intLevel + 1) _
                      & GetNodeType(objAttr.NodeType) & ": <b>" _
                      & objAttr.Name & "</b>  value=<b>" _
                      & objAttr.Value & "</b><br />"
         Next
      End If


      'if this node has child nodes, call the same function recursively
      'to display the information for it and each of its child node
      If objNode.HasChildNodes Then
       strNodes = strNodes & GetChildNodes(objNode.childNodes, intLevel + 1)
      End If

   Next   'go to next node

   Return strNodes    'pass the result back to the caller

End Function
```

There are a couple of other minor functions that the code above uses. The GetIndent function simply takes an integer representing the current indent level and returns a string containing a suitable number of   non-breaking space characters. The GetNodeType function looks up the numeric node type value returned from the NodeType property of each node, and returns a text description of the node type. You can view the code for these functions in the sample page using the [view source] link.

XML Document Access with an XPathNavigator

The second example shows how we can achieve the same results as the previous example, but this time by using the new XPathNavigator object. The sample page "Accessing an XML document using an XPathNavigator" (xml-via-navigator.aspx) produces an output that is fundamentally similar to the previous example. Notice, however, that now we get the complete content of all the child elements for the value of an element (all the #text child nodes of all the children concatenated together):

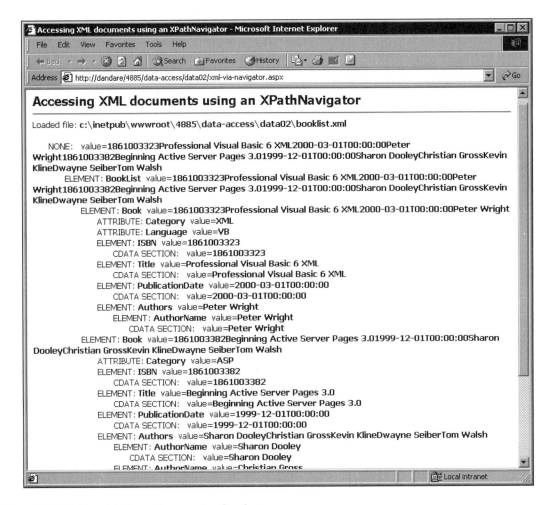

The XPathNavigator Example Code

As in the previous example, we start out by locating and loading the XML document into an XmlDocument object. If there is no error, we know that the document is well-formed and loaded successfully:

```
Dim strCurrentPath As String = Request.PhysicalPath
Dim strXMLPath As String = Left(strCurrentPath, _
                    InStrRev(strCurrentPath, "\")) & "booklist.xml"
Dim objXMLDoc As New XmlDocument()
objXMLDoc.Load(strXMLPath)
```

However, here the code differs considerably. We create an XPathNavigator object based on the XmlDocument object:

```
Dim objXPNav As XPathNavigator = objXMLDoc.CreateNavigator()
```

To display the output, we first move the current position (pointer) of the XPathNavigator to the document itself. Then we can call a custom recursive function named GetXMLDocFragment that iterates through all the nodes in the document and inserts the result into our <div> element elsewhere in the page. Note that this time we are calling our custom function with the new XPathNavigator object as the first parameter (the second is the same "indent level" parameter as we used in the previous example):

```
objXPNav.MoveToRoot()
outResults.innerHTML = GetXMLDocFragment(objXPNav, 0)
```

Our Custom GetXMLDocFragment Function

The XPathNavigator object exposes a series of properties, methods, and collections that make it easy to navigate an XML document. We use a range of these in our custom function. The first step, after declaring a couple of local variables we'll need, is to get the information about the current node. Notice that we use the same GetNodeType function as we did in the previous example to convert the numeric NodeType value into a text description of the node type:

```
Function GetXMLDocFragment(objXPNav As XPathNavigator, _
                           intLevel As Integer) _
                           As String

   Dim strNodes As String = ""
   Dim intLoop As Integer

   'display information about this node
   strNodes = strNodes & GetIndent(intLevel) _
           & GetNodeType(objXPNav.NodeType) & ": " & objXPNav.Name _
           & "  value=" & objXPNav.Value & "<br />"
```

In our previous XML DOM example, we extracted the value of the node through the XmlNode object's Value property, which returned just the value of this node. In this example, we are accessing the content of our XML document through an XPathNavigator and not using the XML DOM methods. For example, you can see that to get the value of the node we are using the Value property of our objXPNav object – an XPathNavigator that is currently pointing to the node we are querying. The Value property of a node returned by the XPathNavigator is a concatenation of all the child node values.

Reading the Attributes of a Node

Now we can see if this node has any attributes. If it does, we iterate through them collecting information about each one. You can see here how this is different from using the DOM methods, where we could iterate through the Attributes collection. Using an XPathNavigator is predominantly a forward-only "pull" technique. We extract the nodes from the document in the order that they appear. So, for a node that does have attributes we move to the first attribute, process it, move to the next attribute until there are no more to process, then move back to the previous position using the MoveToParent method:

```
   'see if this node has any Attributes
   If objXPNav.HasAttributes Then

      'move to the first attribute
      objXPNav.MoveToFirstAttribute()

      Do
```

```
                'display the information about it
                strNodes = strNodes & GetIndent(intLevel + 1) _
                        & GetNodeType(objXPNav.NodeType) & ": " & objXPNav.Name _
                        & "  value=" & objXPNav.Value & "<br />"

         Loop While objXPNav.MoveToNextAttribute()

            'then move back to the parent node (that is the element itself)
            objXPNav.MoveToParent()

      End If
```

Reading the Child Nodes for a Node

Now we can see if the current node has any child nodes by checking the HasChildren property. If it does, we need to move to the first child node and recursively call our function for that node – incrementing the "level" parameter to get the correct indenting of the results. Then we can move back to the previous position (the parent) and continue.

```
         'see if this node has any child nodes
      If objXPNav.HasChildren Then

            'move to the first child node of the current node
            objXPNav.MoveToFirstChild()

            Do
               'recursively call this function to display the child node fragment
               strNodes = strNodes & GetXMLDocFragment(objXPNav, intLevel + 1)
            Loop While objXPNav.MoveToNext()

            'move back to the parent node - the node we started from when we
            'moved to the first child node - could have used Push and Pop instead
            objXPNav.MoveToParent()

      End If
```

Reading the Sibling Nodes for a Node

So far, we've only processed the current node, its attributes and its child nodes (if any). We need to repeat the process for all the following sibling elements as well. This is achieved using the MoveToNext method, and by calling the recursive function again for each one:

```
      Do While objXPNav.MoveToNext()

            'recursively call this function to display this sibling node
            'and its attributes and child nodes
            strNodes = strNodes & GetXMLDocFragment(objXPNav, intLevel)

      Loop

      Return strNodes   'pass the result back to the caller

   End Function
```

Searching an XML Document

The second pair of links in the menu page opens two examples that search for specific element values within an XML document, rather than displaying the entire document. The two examples are "Searching an XML document using the DOM" (search-dom.aspx) and "Searching an XML document with an XPathNavigator" (search-navigator.aspx). The task is to retrieve the values of all the <AuthorName> elements within the document. You can run these samples to see the results – this is the XML DOM version:

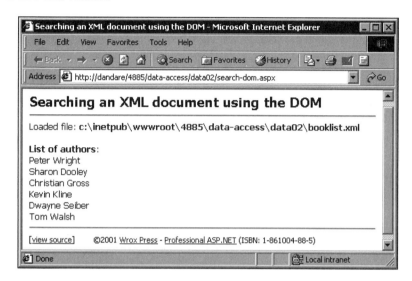

Using the DOM Methods

Using the DOM methods, we can take advantage of the very useful GetElementsByTagname method that the XmlDocument object exposes. We use this method to create a collection of matching elements as an XmlNodeList object, then iterate through the collection displaying the values of the #text child node for each one:

```
Dim strResults As String = "<b>List of authors</b>:<br />"

'create a NodeList collection of all matching child nodes
Dim colElements As XmlNodeList
colElements = objXMLDoc.GetElementsByTagname("AuthorName")

'iterate through the collection getting the values of the
'child #text nodes for each one
For Each objNode In colElements
  strResults += objNode.FirstChild().Value & "<br />"
Next

'then display the result
outResults.innerHTML = strResults    'display the results
```

Remember that an element's value is stored in a #text-type child node of the element node: it's not the value of the element node itself. You can clearly see this in the previous examples that displayed all the nodes in the document.

Using an XPathNavigator

We've already seen how we can create an XPathNavigator for an XmlDocument object, and use it to traverse the document. The XPathNavigator object also provides the Select method, which takes an XPath expression and selects all matching nodes or fragments within the document. We can then traverse the set of selected nodes and extract the values we want.

> *For full details of XPath expression syntax, check out "XSLT Programmer's Reference"*
> *(ISBN 1-861003-12-9) also from Wrox Press – see http://www.wrox.com/ for details.*

As we aren't interested in using the XML DOM methods in this example, we can also improve performance by using the lighter and faster XPathDocument object to hold our XML document rather than the W3C-compliant XmlDocument object.

Creating an XPathDocument and XPathNavigator Object

So, code in the Page_Load event handler first creates an XPathDocument object and loads the XML document into it. However, in this case, we must use the constructor for the XPathDocument to load the XML as there is no Load method for this object. While we can create an XPathDocument from a Stream, a TextReader or an XmlReader, the easiest way when we have an XML disk file is to specify the path and filename of that file:

```
'declare a variable within current scope to hold an XPathDocument
Dim objXPathDoc As XPathDocument
Try
   'create XPathDocument object and load the XML file
   objXPathDoc = New XPathDocument(strXMLPath)
Catch objError As Exception
   'display error details here
   ...
End Try
```

Then our code creates an XPathNavigator object for this document:

```
Dim objXPNav As XPathNavigator = objXPathDoc.CreateNavigator()
```

Selecting the Nodes and Displaying the Results

Now we can execute the Select method with an appropriate XPath expression. The result will be an XPathNodeIterator object that contains the matching node(s).

```
Dim strResults As String = "<b>List of authors</b>:<br />"

'select all AuthorName nodes into XPathNodeIterator object
'using an appropriate XPath expression
Dim objXPIter As XPathNodeIterator
objXPIter = objXPNav.Select("descendant::AuthorName")
```

Then it's simply a matter of iterating through the selected nodes collecting their values. Each "node" in the XPathNodeIterator is itself an XPathNavigator based on this node within the document. This new XPathNavigator has a Name and Value property that reflect the value for the current node:

```
Do While objXPIter.MoveNext()
  'get the value and add to the 'results' string
  strResults += objXPIter.Current.Value & "<br />"
Loop

outResults.innerHTML = strResults    'display the result
```

As you can see, we need to consider the task we want to achieve quite carefully when deciding whether to use an `XPathNavigator` object or the XML DOM methods. Of course, as we can create an `XPathNavigator` based on an existing `XmlDocument` object (as well as on an `XPathDocument`), we can use both where this is appropriate. Also remember to choose the lighter and faster `XPathDocument` if you don't need to access the XML DOM, in other words when you can perform all the tasks you require using an `XPathNavigator`.

An XML TextWriter Object Example

The example "Creating an XML document with an XMLTextWriter object" (`xml-via-textwriter.aspx`) demonstrates how we can use the `XmlTextWriter` object to quickly create a new XML document as a disk file. It writes to the file a series of elements and attributes that make up the document, then reads the document back from disk and displays it:

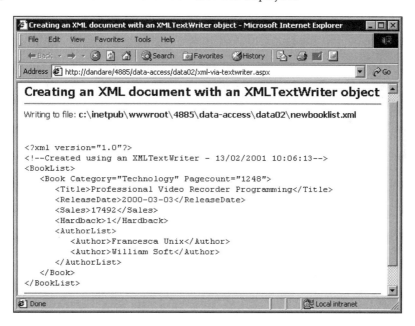

The XMLTextWriter Example Code

To create the new XML document, we first create a suitable path and filename so that the new file will be placed in the same folder as the ASP page:

```
Dim strCurrentPath As String = Request.PhysicalPath
Dim strXMLPath As String = Left(strCurrentPath, _
                InStrRev(strCurrentPath, "\")) & "newbooklist.xml"
```

Now we can create the `XmlTextWriter` object instance. We specify the path to the new file as the first parameter to the constructor, and `Nothing` for the second. The second parameter is the encoding required for the file, defined as an `Encoding` object. If we set this parameter to `Nothing`, the default encoding "UTF-8" is used:

```
Dim objXMLWriter As XmlTextWriter
objXMLWriter = New XmlTextWriter(strXMLPath, Nothing)
```

Now we can set the properties of the `XmlTextWriter`. In our example, we want the document to be indented (to show the structure more clearly), with each level of indent being three space characters:

```
objXMLWriter.Formatting = Formatting.Indented
objXMLWriter.Indentation = 3
```

We're now ready to start writing the new document. The `WriteStartDocument` method creates the opening XML declaration, and we follow this with a comment indicating the date and time that the document was created:

```
objXMLWriter.WriteStartDocument()
objXMLWriter.WriteComment("Created using an XMLTextWriter - " & Now())
```

Writing Elements and Attributes

The next step is to write the opening tag of the root element `<BookList>`. The `WriteStartElement` does this for us, and we follow it with the opening `<Book>` element tag:

```
objXMLWriter.WriteStartElement("BookList")
objXMLWriter.WriteStartElement("Book")
```

We want to add two attributes to the `<Book>` element. For these we use the `WriteAttributeString` method to create an attribute from a text string. Where the value for the attribute is a numeric (or other non-`String`) data type, we convert it to a string first:

```
'add two attributes to this element's opening tag
objXMLWriter.WriteAttributeString("Category", "Technology")
Dim intPageCount As Integer = 1248    'numeric value to convert
objXMLWriter.WriteAttributeString("Pagecount", intPageCount.ToString("G"))
```

The next step is to write the four elements that form the content of the `<Book>` element that we've already opened. We use the `WriteElementString` method, which writes a complete element (not just the opening tag like the `WriteStartElement` method we used earlier does). Note that the actual **content** of the element in the final document is always text (XML documents are just plain text). Therefore we have to convert non-`String` type values to a string first:

```
'write four elements, using different source data types
objXMLWriter.WriteElementString("Title", _
                     "Professional Video Recorder Programming")
Dim datReleaseDate As DateTime = #03/03/2000#
objXMLWriter.WriteElementString("ReleaseDate", _
                     datReleaseDate.ToString("yyyy-MM-dd"))
Dim intSales As Integer = 17492
objXMLWriter.WriteElementString("Sales", intSales.ToString("G"))
Dim blnHardback As Boolean = True
objXMLWriter.WriteElementString("Hardback", blnHardback.ToString())
```

Next we want to write the `<AuthorList>` element and its child `<Author>` elements. We need to open the `<AuthorList>` element and then write the child elements. Afterwards, we can create the closing `</AuthorList>` tag by calling the `WriteEndElement` method. This simply closes the most recently opened element:

```
'write the opening tag for the <AuthorList> child element
objXMLWriter.WriteStartElement("AuthorList")

'add two <Author> elements
objXMLWriter.WriteElementString("Author", "Francesca Unix")
objXMLWriter.WriteElementString("Author", "William Soft")

'close the <AuthorList> element
objXMLWriter.WriteEndElement()
```

To finish the document, we just need to close the `<Book>` element and the root `<BookList>` element. Then we flush the output to the disk file and close the `XMLTextWriter`. Always remember to call the `Close` method otherwise the disk file will remain locked:

```
'close the <Book> element
objXMLWriter.WriteEndElement()

'close the root <BookList> element
objXMLWriter.WriteEndElement()

objXMLWriter.Flush()
objXMLWriter.Close()
```

Displaying the New XML Document

Now that we've got our new XML document written to a disk file, we can read it back and display it. To do this we use a `StreamReader` object. We open the file, read the entire content into a string variable, and close the file.

We can then insert the string into a `<div>` element elsewhere on the page to display it. Notice that we add the `<pre>` elements (we could use `<xmp>` instead) to maintain the indentation and line breaks in the document when displayed in the browser:

```
Dim strXMLResult As String
Dim objSR As StreamReader = File.OpenText(strXMLPath)
strXMLResult = objSR.ReadToEnd()
objSR.Close
objSR = Nothing
outResults.innerHTML = "<pre>" & Server.HtmlEncode(strXMLResult) & "<pre>"
```

An XML TextReader Object Example

OK, so we can create an XML document as a disk file with an `XmlTextWriter`. The obvious next step is to read a disk file back using an `XmlTextReader` object. The example "Accessing an XML document with an XMLTextReader object" (`xml-via-textreader.aspx`) does just that (though with a different XML document).

If we run the example, we see a list of the nodes found in the sample `booklist.xml` document. For each node, the page shows the type of node, and the node name and value (if applicable – some nodes have no name and some have no value):

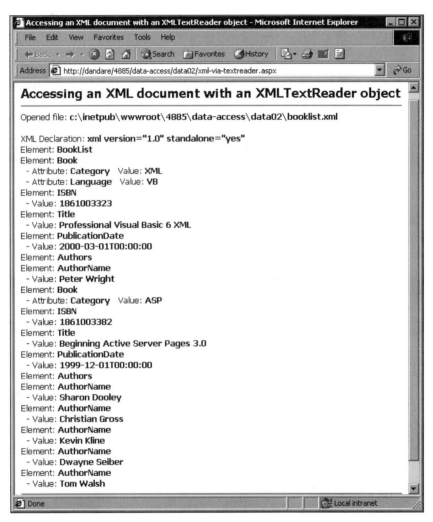

The XMLTextReader Example Code

As in the previous example, the first step is to build the path to the file we'll be opening: in this case `booklist.xml` in the same folder as the ASP page:

```
Dim strCurrentPath As String = Request.PhysicalPath
Dim strXMLPath As String = Left(strCurrentPath, _
                    InStrRev(strCurrentPath, "\")) & "booklist.xml"
```

Now we can declare an `XmlTextReader` object, passing the path to the file we want to open as a parameter to the constructor:

```
Dim objXMLReader As XmlTextReader
objXMLReader = New XmlTextReader(strXMLPath)
```

To read the XML document, it's just a matter of reading each node in turn using the `Read` method. This method returns `False` if there are no more nodes to read. For each node we find, we examine the `NodeType` property to see what kind of node it is. Depending on the node type, there are different properties available that we can access to build our `results` string:

```
'now ready to read (or "pull") the nodes out of the XML document
Dim strNodeResult As String = ""
Dim objNodeType As XmlNodeType

Do While objXMLReader.Read()

   'select the type of the node - as an illustration
   'the following are only some of the available types
   objNodeType = objXMLReader.NodeType

   Select Case objNodeType

      Case XmlNodeType.XmlDeclaration:
         'get the name and value
         strNodeResult += "XML Declaration: " & objXMLReader.Name _
                  & " " & objXMLReader.Value & "<br />"

      Case XmlNodeType.Element:
         'just get the name, any value will be in next (#text) node
         strNodeResult += "Element: " & objXMLReader.Name & "<br />"

      Case XmlNodeType.Text:
         'just display the value, node name is "#text" in this case
         strNodeResult += "- Value: " & objXMLReader.Value & "<br />"

   End Select
```

The `XmlTextReader` returns the document node by node when we call the `Read` method. However, an element-type node that has attributes is returned as a complete entity during a single `Read` method call, and so we have to examine each node as we read it to see if it is an element that has attributes. If so, we iterate through these by using the `MoveToFirstAttribute` and/or the `MoveToNextAttribute` methods:

```
           'see if this node has any attributes
        If objXMLReader.AttributeCount > 0 Then

           'iterate through the attributes by moving to the next one
           'could use MoveToFirstAttribute but MoveToNextAttribute does
           'the same when the current node is an element-type node
           Do While objXMLReader.MoveToNextAttribute()

              'get the attribute name and value
              strNodeResult +=  "- Attribute: " & objXMLReader.Name _
                          & " Value: " & objXMLReader.Value & "<br />"
           Loop

        End If
```

That's finished the current node, so we can now go back and handle the next one. After the Do loop is complete (we've processed all the nodes returned by successive Read method calls) we close the XmlTextReader object and display the results in a <div> element elsewhere in the page:

```
        Loop    'and read the next node

        'finished with the reader so close it
        objXMLReader.Close()

        'and display the results in the page
        outResults.innerHTML = strNodeResult
```

An XSL Transform Object Example

Our final example shows one other task that is regularly required when working with XML data, and which .NET makes easy. We can use XML stylesheets written in XSL or XSLT to transform an XML document into another format, or to change its structure or content.

The example page "Transforming an XML document using the XSLTransform object" (xsl-transform.aspx) demonstrates a simple transformation using the booklist.xml file from the previous example and an XSLT stylesheet named booklist.xsl. The results of the transformation are written to disk as booklist.html. You can use the links in the page to open the XML document, the stylesheet or the final HTML page:

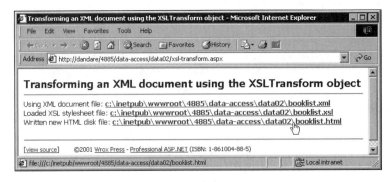

Note that you must run this page in a browser running on the same machine as the Web server to be able to open the linked files using the absolute physical paths.

The XSLTransform Example Code

There is surprisingly little code required to perform the transformation (you can view the code in the example using the [view source] link at the bottom of the page). First, we create an `XslTransform` object and load the XSL stylesheet into it from disk:

```
'create a new XslTransform object
Dim objTransform As New XslTransform()

'load the XSL stylesheet into the XslTransform object
objTransform.Load(strXSLPath)
```

Then we can perform the transformation directly using the XSL file in the `XslTransform` object and the XML file path held in a variable named `strXMLPath`. The result is sent to the disk file specified by the variable named `strHTMLPath`:

```
'perform the transformation
objTransform.Transform(strXMLPath, strHTMLPath)
```

The next screenshot shows the resulting HTML page. However, this is just one way to use the `XslTransform` object (in fact, the simplest way) but we'll see a more complex example at the end of the data management chapters when we look at XML data management techniques in more depth:

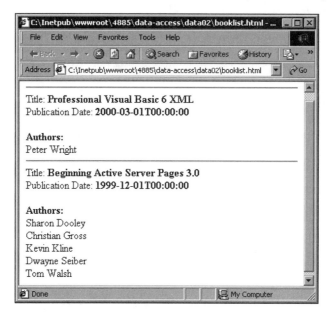

What We've Seen So Far

What we've seen in this section is a basic introduction to working with XML in the .NET environment. The next two chapters return to looking at relational data management, but we'll start to see how the relational and XML data models are quite thoroughly integrated under .NET. Then, in the chapter after that, we'll come back to XML and look in more depth at some of the more complex techniques that .NET offers. But, to finish this chapter, we'll try to make some sense of the whole "relational versus XML" issue.

Choosing a Data Storage Methodology

Having seen both relational and XML data access in action within the .NET Framework (albeit in a fairly basic way so far), how do we decide on a data storage methodology? The simple answer is that, with the advent of .NET, we really don't need to worry about this any more.

Years ago, one of the main directions in data storage and access was the construction of huge data depositaries or data warehouses, where all the data your organization requires is stored in a massive central database. While this might still suit some situations, such as a government tax office, it's become clear that it is not a realistic approach in today's distributed computing world.

In fact, there has been even less centralization of data over recent years, and the drive now is far more towards the provision of access through common methods to all kinds of remote and non-centralized data. As an example, the Internet contains vast quantities of data in myriad different formats, but more and more we need to be able to get at this data in a structured and standard way.

Likewise, in an office environment, the promised takeover of thin client computing has not really happened yet. People like to store information locally as they work, and use it when disconnected from the corporate network. In some cases, such as the traveling salesperson with a laptop computer, this is the prime requirement when working with corporate data.

Access and Manipulation is the Key

In fact, it's obvious that what's important is not **where** we store data, and not (to some extent) **how** we store data. What's really at the crux of the matter is how we can **access** and **manipulate** that data – in whatever format it's stored and wherever it resides. As we saw at the start of this chapter, this is what has been the driving force behind the adoption of XML, and the design of the .NET data access libraries.

So, what issues should we consider when we come to implement a data store, and which data access technique is most appropriate for that data? The answer lies more in the nature of our data, and the way we need to use it. For example, highly structured data, such as stock lists or customer details, is well suited to storage in a relational database such as SQL Sever or Oracle, or MS Access on the desktop. However unstructured data, such as reports, data sheets, email messages, family trees and other common everyday scenarios, is more suited to storage using the tree-like metaphor of XML.

Likewise, if we regularly need to access parts of the data in specific ways, or on a very regular basis, the relational database is probably the most efficient. It is optimized to provide indexing and other features to give the best performance. But if we usually access the entire data entity in one go, or access it only rarely, an XML-based approach is probably the best choice. And, being basically just text files, XML documents are easy to archive and retrieve.

Of course, in some cases, we don't actually get to choose the data storage format. For example, your email server and your fax server probably have dedicated storage mechanisms that can't be changed. In this case, we have to make do with what's there, or change to another product.

Transport Protocols are the Future

Once we've decided on the storage mechanism for our data, the next important decision comes when we consider how we will transport our data from one place to another. Here, there is probably only one good solution that matches the requirements of the future. There's no doubt that we'll face increasing needs to interface with other systems and other organizations as time goes by, and for this a standard data interchange format is going to be an absolute necessity.

The only obvious choice today is XML (and the associated standards such as SOAP and other industry-specific implementations of XML). XML is platform, application, and operating system independent, so it provides the best chance for interoperability. And, using the tools available today and in the near future, we can transform an XML document into any other format on demand – and often transform any non-XML document or data into XML as well.

In fact, Microsoft BizTalk Server and similar systems can handle the transmission and guaranteed delivery of data in XML format over almost any kind of network, as well as the conversion to and from other formats. Using the tools available today and in the near future, we can transform an XML document into almost any other document type on demand – and often transform any non-XML document or data into XML as well.

And .NET is a Great Solution

So, if the transport protocol and transmission format for data are going to be XML-based, and the data storage and manipulation could be through any existing or new technology, what we really need is a solid, reliable and wide-ranging technique to connect to any kind of data store, and work with any kind of data.

This is where the combination of the relational and XML data access techniques provided by the .NET Framework comes in. As we've seen in this chapter, and will see elsewhere throughout this book, we will be able to use the .NET data access classes to connect to almost any kind of data store – be it a mail server, a relational database, an office application document, an XML document, or whatever. Then, once we have extracted data, we can convert it between XML and traditional relational rowsets at will – and update the data store or save it to disk in almost any format we need.

Summary

In this chapter, we've started to explore the possibilities for working with data within the .NET Framework, based on ASP.NET, the .NET data access classes, and the extended XML technologies that they provide. We overviewed the two main topic areas, relational and XML data access, then examined in more depth the core objects that are provided within these topic areas.

One of the problems with learning to use the new techniques is the complexity that can arise from the huge number of properties, methods, and events that these new objects expose. Many are rarely used, and so we've tried to make it easier by just concentrating on the commonly used techniques rather than trying to document each one in minute detail.

> *An excellent reference to all the properties, methods, and events of all the .NET framework objects is included within the SDK that is provided with the framework. Simply open the* ".NET Framework Class Library" *within the section* ".NET Framework Reference", *or search for the object/class name using the* Index *or* Search *feature of the SDK.*

What you should have gained by now is an understanding of the core objects and the basic techniques we use when working with them. We'll continue this in the next three chapters as well.

The topics for this chapter were:

- ❑ How data storage is currently handled and will be handled in the future.
- ❑ What are the problems with the technology we have at the moment?
- ❑ Changes to relational data access techniques in .NET.
- ❑ What we can now do with XML in .NET.
- ❑ Considerations for choosing specific data access technologies and data formats.

The next chapter looks specifically at relational data access within .NET, and how we use more advanced techniques – in particular working with relational data sets and tables, editing them, and displaying the data they contain.

"The Babel fish," says The Hitch Hiker's Guide to Galaxy "is small, yellow and leech-like, and probably the oddest thing in the Universe. It feeds on brainwave energy not from its carrier but from those around it. It absorbs all unconscious mental frequencies from this brainwave energy to nourish itself with. It then excretes into the mind of its carrier a telepathic matrix formed by combining the conscious thought frequencies with nerve signals picked up from the speech centres of the brain which has supplied them".

The practical upshot of all this is that if you stick a Babel fish in your ear you can instantly understand anything said to you in any form of language. The speech patterns you actually hear decode the brainwave matrix which has been fed into your mind by your Babel fish.

Working with Relational Data

In the previous chapter, we saw how easy it is to access both relational and XML data using the .NET data access libraries. In this and the next chapter, we are concentrating on what has traditionally been the major use of data access in ASP – relational data – and we'll be seeing some of the more advanced features that .NET provides. This chapter is mainly concerned with the ways we use the `DataReader`, `DataSet`, and `DataTable` objects that we introduced in the previous chapter. In the next chapter, we'll move on to look at how we can update data sources using .NET.

While simple data access through a `DataReader` object will fulfill many of the tasks previously accomplished with an ADO `Connection` and `Recordset` object in earlier versions of ASP, we regularly want to build more complex data structures. Plus, the fundamentally disconnected nature of the .NET data access techniques means that we will often decide to use a `DataSet` to implement a selection of information as a "package" that can be easily stored and transported between application tiers – including across the network.

We saw how the `DataSet` object is at the heart of the .NET disconnected data access strategy in the previous chapter, and we'll look at all the important aspects of using one in this chapter. The overall set of topics that we'll be covering is:

- ❑ Accessing Complex Data with `DataReader` and `DataSet` Objects

- ❑ Using Stored Procedures with `DataReader` and `DataSet` Objects

- ❑ Building and Editing Data in a `DataTable` Object

- ❑ Sorting and Filtering Data with `DataTable` and `DataView` Objects

Obtaining the Sample Files

All the examples used in this chapter are available for you to run on your own server. The download file can be obtained from http://www.wrox.com/Books/Book_Details.asp?isbn=1861004885. It includes SQL scripts and instructions for creating the database that the examples use. You can also run some of the examples online at http://www.daveandal.com/profaspnet/data-access/.

The main menu page (default.htm) contains links to all the sample files. The third link, "Advanced Relational Data Management in .NET" leads to another menu page that contains links to all the examples for this chapter:

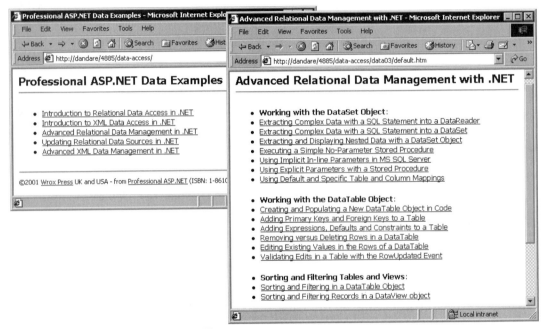

Accessing Complex Data

The relational data access examples in the previous chapter were fairly simple, concentrating on extracting data from a single table and multiple tables into the DataSet and DataReader objects. However, often the results you require are not just rows from a single table. They may require a more complex SQL query that joins several tables, or they might be the result of running a database stored procedure within the database.

In this section, we'll look at some examples that use both complex SQL statements and stored procedures to return sets of rows or just individual values from a data source. The first shows how we can use a DataReader object to efficiently extract the data for display, and the second uses the DataSet object.

Accessing Complex Data with a DataReader

We saw in the previous chapter how the `DataReader` object can be used to quickly extract a disconnected recordset from a data store. We simply create a `Connection` object, use it to create a `Command` object for this connection, and then call the `ExecuteReader` method of the `Command` object. It returns the new `DataReader` object.

The example code, like many of the relational data access examples in the previous and this chapter, uses a separate user control that exposes the specific connection strings for our database server. We described this control in the previous chapter, and we insert it into our page using:

```
<%'-- insert connection string script --%>
<wrox:connect id="ctlConnectStrings" runat="server"/>
```

> *Remember to edit this file (`connect-strings.ascx` in the `data-access\global` folder of the samples) before running the samples on your own server.*

And, as in the previous chapter, the example page uses some server-side `<div>` elements to display the connection string, the `SELECT` command we're using, and any error message. There is also an ASP `DataGrid` control to display the results:

```
<div>Connection string:
<b><span id="outConnect" runat="server"></span></b></div>
<div>SELECT command:
<b><span id="outSelect" runat="server"></span></b></div>
<div id="outError" runat="server"> </div>
<asp:datagrid id="dgrResult" runat="server" />
```

This is what the page "Extracting Complex Data with a SQL Statement into a DataReader" (`complex-datareader.aspx`) looks like when it runs:

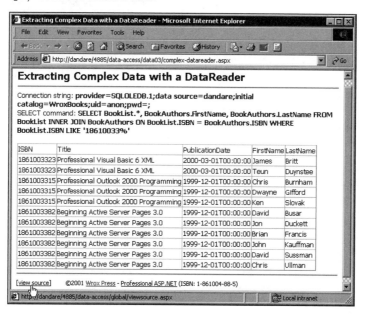

> *Note that all the examples we use contain a [view source] link at the bottom of the page that you can use to view the source code for the page.*

The Code for the DataReader Example

The code for this page is compact and quite simple. The most complex part is the SQL statement itself, which selects data from two joined tables. In the `Page_Load` event we collect the connection string from the user control we discussed earlier, and use it in the constructor for a `Connection` object. We also create the SQL statement in a string variable named `strSelect`:

```
Sub Page_Load()

    'get connection string from ..\global\connect-strings.ascx user control
    Dim strConnect = ctlConnectStrings.OLEDBConnectionString
    outConnect.innerText = strConnect 'and display it

    'specify the SELECT statement to extract the data
    Dim strSelect As String
    strSelect = "SELECT BookList.*, BookAuthors.FirstName, " _
            & "BookAuthors.LastName FROM BookList INNER JOIN " _
            & "BookAuthors ON BookList.ISBN = BookAuthors.ISBN " _
            & "WHERE BookList.ISBN LIKE '1861033%'"
    outSelect.innerText = strSelect     'and display it
```

We're using an OLEDB provider to access SQL Server in this example, so we need to use the "OleDb-prefixed" objects from the `System.Data.OleDb` namespace of the .NET class libraries. We added the appropriate `Import` declarations to the head of our page so that they are available:

```
<%@Import Namespace="System.Data" %>
<%@Import Namespace="System.Data.OleDb" %>
```

> *If you want to use the direct (TDS) driver for MS SQL Server, you will need to import the `System.Data.SqlClient` namespace instead of `System.Data.OleDb`, and use the objects prefixed with "Sql", as demonstrated in the previous chapter. Also remember to use the `SQLConnectionString` property of the "connection strings" user control instead of the `OLEDBConnectionString` property.*

Back to our example code, we first declare a variable to hold a `DataReader` object. Next, within a `Try...Catch` construct, we can create our new `Connection` object based on the connection string. Then we create a new `Command` object using the string that holds the SQL statement, and the new `Connection` object. This is much the same as we did in the previous chapter:

```
    'declare a variable to hold a DataReader object
    Dim objDataReader As OleDbDataReader

    Try

        'create a new Connection object using the connection string
        Dim objConnect As New OleDbConnection(strConnect)

        'create new Command using connection object and SQL statement
        Dim objCommand As New OleDbCommand(strSelect, objConnect)
```

Next we can open the connection and execute the SQL statement in the `Command` to return our `DataReader` object. If there is an error, we display the details in the `<div>` element we created in the HTML part of the page, and stop execution of the code:

```
        'open connection and execute command to return the DataReader
        objConnect.Open()
        objDataReader = objCommand.ExecuteReader()

    Catch objError As Exception

        'display error details
        outError.innerHTML = "* Error while accessing data.<br />" _
            & objError.Message & "<br />" & objError.Source
        Exit Sub  ' and stop execution

    End Try
```

If all goes well and we've got our rowset, we can go ahead and display it. In this example we use a `DataGrid`, but you could just iterate through the rows and create the output that way, as we demonstrated in the "Using a DataReader Object" example in the previous chapter:

```
    'assign the DataReader object to the DataGrid control
    dgrResult.DataSource = objDataReader
    dgrResult.DataBind  'and bind (display) the data

    'finished with the DataReader
    objDataReader = Nothing

End Sub
```

So, using a complex SQL statement to access multiple tables is easy enough – often the hardest part is creating the statement itself. An easy way to do this is to take advantage of the Query Designers in programs like Visual Studio or Microsoft Access, both of which can easily link to a set of database tables in SQL Server and other ODBC-enabled data sources.

Accessing Complex Data with a DataSet

Having seen how we can use a complex SQL statement with a `DataReader`, let's see how the same statement works with a `DataSet` object. The example "Extracting Complex Data with a SQL Statement into a DataSet" (`complex-dataset.aspx`) is very similar to the previous `DataReader` example. The only differences being in the declaration of the `DataSet` object (notice that we create a new `DataSet` object instance with the `New` keyword here, whereas we created a variable of type `DataReader` in the previous example), and the use of a `DataAdapter` object instead of a `Command` object:

```
Dim objDataSet As New DataSet()

Try

        'create a new Connection object using the connection string
        Dim objConnect As New OleDbConnection(strConnect)
```

413

```
          'create new DataAdapter using connection and SQL statement
          Dim objDataAdapter As New OleDbDataAdapter(strSelect, objConnect)

          'fill the dataset with data via the DataAdapter object
          objDataAdapter.Fill(objDataSet, "Books")

  Catch objError As Exception

     'display error details
     outError.innerHTML = "* Error while accessing data. " _
                        & objError.Message & " " & objError.Source
     Exit Sub  ' and stop execution

  End Try
```

Once we've filled the `DataSet`, we can display the contents of the single table within it. Again, we're using a `DataGrid` to show the results, but this time we have to use a `DataView` object (as returned by the `DefaultView` property of the table in the `DataSet`) as the `DataSource`:

```
  'assign the table DefaultView to the DataGrid control
  dgrResult.DataSource = objDataSet.Tables("Books").DefaultView
  dgrResult.DataBind()  'and bind (display) the data
```

Accessing and Displaying Nested Data

The previous two examples have demonstrated how we can use complex SQL statements that join data from several tables and return it as a single table in the `DataSet`. There is also another situation, where we extract data from the tables in the data source using simple SQL statements and store the resulting rowsets as individual tables (plus the relationships between them) in the `DataSet`.

In the previous chapter, we showed you a custom user control that creates and returns a `DataSet` object containing three tables and the relationships between these tables. In that example (use-dataset-control.aspx), we displayed the contents of the `DataSet` using several ASP `DataGrid` controls so that you could see the contents of all the tables.

In an application, however, you generally want to be able to access the data in a nested and structured fashion so that it can be displayed in a format that is meaningful to the user. In other words, you want to be able to display it in a hierarchical format, perhaps using some clever type of UI control widget. What we'll demonstrate here is how you can access the data in that way (though we're just going to display it as text in the page in our example).

The next screenshot shows the example "Extracting and Displaying Nested Data with a DataSet Object" (nested-data-access.aspx). It lists three of the books stored in our sample database, and for each one shows the authors (where available) and the prices in three currencies:

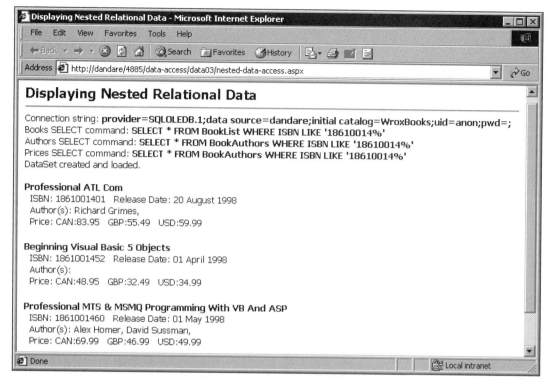

The Database Tables Structure and Relationships

From the previous chapter, you'll have seen how the database holds three tables that contain all the information shown in this page. The `BookList` table contains the ISBN (the primary key), the title and the publication date. The `BookAuthors` table contains the ISBN as a foreign key and the first and last names of each author. There is a row for each author for each book. The `BookPrices` table holds the ISBN as a foreign key, the currency name ("CAN", "GBP" or "USD"), and the price in that currency. Again, there is one row for each currency for each book.

The `DataSet` returned by the custom user control contains three tables named `Books`, `Authors`, and `Prices`, each containing matching subsets of rows from the three tables in the database. It also has the relationships between the tables defined (you can review the code in the previous chapter for creating a multiple-table `DataSet` to see how it works).

The GetChildRows Method

To be able to create the output shown above, we need a way of navigating from one table to another so that we can pull out the child rows from the `Authors` and `Prices` tables in the `DataSet` object that match each row in the `Book` table in the `DataSet`. The answer is the `GetChildRows` method that is exposed by the `DataRow` object.

All we have to do is iterate through the `Books` table one row at a time, calling the `GetChildRows` method twice on each `DataRow` object – once to get the matching `Author` rows and once to get the matching `Prices` rows. We specify the relationship that links the parent and child tables in the call to `GetChildRows` so that it can work out which rows to return. Each call to `GetChildRows` returns a collection of matching `DataRow` objects from the specified child table. We can then iterate through these collections displaying the values of each row.

> *Interestingly, there is also a converse method named* `GetParentRows` *that, in conjunction with the members of the* `ParentRelations` *collection of the* `DataTable` *object, returns a collection of the matching parent rows when called using a* `DataRow` *object that represents a child row and a relationship between the tables. This could be useful if you wanted to list the results in a different order – perhaps by author instead of by book.*

The Nested Data Example Code

We'll examine the code for the example shown in the earlier screenshot next. We aren't showing the code to build the `DataSet` here, as it's been described in the previous chapter. What we're interested in is how we use the `GetChildRows` method to create and output the nested results. The first step is to create a string variable to hold the result (we'll insert it into a `<div>` on the page in customary fashion afterwards). Then we can get references to all the objects we'll need:

```
'create a string to hold the results
Dim strResult As String = ""

'create a reference to our main Books table in the DataSet
Dim objTable As DataTable = objDataSet.Tables("Books")

'create references to each of the relationship objects in the DataSet
Dim objAuthorRelation As DataRelation = _
                    objTable.ChildRelations("BookAuthors")
Dim objPriceRelation As DataRelation = _
                    objTable.ChildRelations("BookPrices")
```

We need a reference to the `Books` table so that we can iterate through the rows. Notice also that we just need references to the relationship objects and not to any of the columns – the `GetChildRows` method uses the relationships we previously defined (and which already contain the column information) to figure out which rows we want.

Now we can iterate through the rows in the parent ("Books") table. For each row, we extract the values of the `Title`, `ISBN`, and `PublicationDate` columns and add them to the "results" string:

```
Dim objRow, objChildRow As DataRow
For Each objRow In objTable.Rows

    'get the book details and append them to the "results" string
    strResult += "<b>" & objRow("Title") & "</b><br />  ISBN: " _
            & objRow("ISBN") & "   Release Date: " _
            & FormatDateTime(objRow("PublicationDate"), 1) & "<br />"
```

Now we can get a collection of the rows that are related to the current row by specifying the reference to the relationship between the `Books` and `Authors` tables in the `DataSet` in our call to `GetChildRows`. We also add a subheading `"Author(s)"` to the `"results"` string:

```
'get a collection of all the matching Author table rows for this row
Dim colChildRows() As DataRow = objRow.GetChildRows(objAuthorRelation)
strResult += "  Author(s): "
```

Next, we iterate through the collection of `DataRow` objects returned by the `GetChildRows` method. For each one, we extract the first and last name of the author, and add it to the `"results"` string – followed by an HTML line break:

```
'iterate through all matching Author records adding to result string
For Each objChildRow In colChildRows
    strResult += objChildRow("FirstName") & " " _
               & objChildRow("LastName") & ", "
Next
strResult += "<br />"
```

Now we repeat the process, but this time using the relationship between the `Books` and `Prices` tables. For each matching child row, we extract the currency name and the price, and add them to the `"results"` string:

```
'repeat using Price table relationship for data from Price records
colChildRows = objRow.GetChildRows(objPriceRelation)
strResult += "  Price: "
For Each objChildRow In colChildRows
    strResult += objChildRow("Currency") & ":" _
               & objChildRow("Price") & "   "
Next
strResult += "<p />"
```

And, having completed one book, we can go back and repeat the process for the next book in the parent `Books` table. After we've processed all the book records, we present the results in the `<div>` element named `divResults`:

```
Next    'and repeat for next row in Books table

divResults.innerHTML = strResult    'display the results
```

So, while we can take advantage of clever client-side display controls such as the ASP `DataGrid` when we're working with tables in a `DataSet`, there is an alternative when we want to create nested output from more than one table. Of course, third-party suppliers will no doubt develop other data grid controls, perhaps ones that can bind directly to a `DataSet` and display the nested data automatically.

Using Database Stored Procedures

So far, we've used SQL statements to extract the data from our data source directly. In "real-world" applications, it is often preferable to use a stored procedure within the data store to return the required data set. This can provide better performance, allow finer control over access permissions, and help to hide the structure of the data store tables from inquisitive users.

As in traditional ADO, the .NET data access classes can work with stored procedures just as easily as they can with SQL statements. The simplest stored procedures require only that we specify the name of the procedure, and they return a set of results that can't be controlled by the ASP code we use. However, stored procedures can also be written so that they accept parameters. This allows the actual content of the returned rowset to be controlled by ASP code that sets the parameter values and calls the procedure.

We've provided three examples that demonstrate the techniques for calling a stored procedure. The first uses a simple stored procedure that does not accept parameters. The second example uses a simplified "in-line" or "implicit" syntax, by simply adding the parameters for the stored procedure to the name of the stored procedure. The third example uses an "explicit" syntax, by creating the parameter objects directly within the ASP code and then adding them to the `Command` object that executes the procedure.

This last technique often turned out to be difficult in traditional ADO. It was hard to arrive at the correct data types, and often programmers resorted to using the `Refresh` *method to create the collection of parameters with the appropriate types. This is no longer the case under .NET, as parameters of all types are easy to create.*

Using a Simple "No Parameters" Stored Procedure

The example page "Executing a Simple No-Parameter Stored Procedure" (`simple-stored-proc.aspx`) demonstrates how we can use a `Command` object to execute a stored procedure that does not accept any parameters. This is often the case with stored procedures that perform some fixed operation on the data such as removing old records, or selecting specific values like a count of products sold or the largest value in a column.

Our example uses a stored procedure named `GetBooks` that returns a fixed subset of rows from the `BookList` table – books with the word "ASP" in their title. This is what the stored procedure looks like:

```
CREATE PROCEDURE GetBooks AS
SELECT * FROM BookList WHERE Title LIKE '% ASP %'
```

The SQL scripts we provide to create the database will also create all the stored procedures we use in this chapter.

Running the example gives this result:

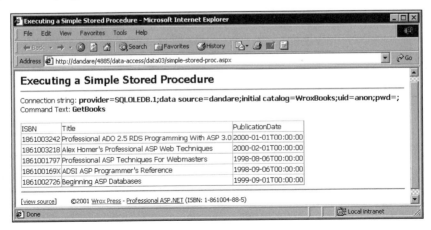

The Code for the Simple Stored Procedure Example

As usual, we're getting the connection string for the database from our custom user control, and displaying the output in an ASP `DataGrid` control. What's of interest here is the way that we call the stored procedure and get back the results in a `DataReader` object.

The first step is to create a string that will be used as the command to be executed. In this example, it's simply the name of the stored procedure, and we display it in the page as well:

```
'create the SQL statement that will call the stored procedure
Dim strCommandText As String = "GetBooks"
outCommandText.InnerText = strCommandText 'and display it
```

Now we can carry on as we did before when using a `DataReader` by creating a `Connection` object and a `Command` object. However, for maximum efficiency, we indicate to the `Command` object that the string we supplied for the first parameter of the object constructor is the name of a stored procedure. This saves SQL Server from having to look to see what objects with the name "GetBooks" the database actually contains when it executes the command:

```
Dim objCommand As New OleDbCommand(strCommandText, objConnect)

'set the CommandType to 'Stored Procedure'
objCommand.CommandType = CommandType.StoredProcedure
```

> *To specify that the type of object we're referring to is a stored procedure we set the `CommandType` property of the `Command` object to `CommandType.StoredProcedure`. The `CommandType` enumeration is defined within the `System.Data` class library, and the possible values are `StoredProcedure`, `TableDirect` (the name of a table), and `Text` (the default – a SQL statement).*

Now we can declare our `DataReader` object variable, open the connection, and execute the command:

```
'declare a variable to hold a DataReader object
Dim objDataReader As OleDbDataReader

'open the connection and execute the command
   objConnect.Open()
   objDataReader = objCommand.ExecuteReader()
```

The `DataReader` object is then bound to a `DataGrid` for display as usual (the code is not shown here).

Using Implicit In-line Parameters with a Stored Procedure

Using a non-parameter stored procedure is as easy as using a SQL statement. However, it gets more complicated when the stored procedure expects us to provide parameters as well. One option is the simple "in-line" or "implicit" technique, which works fine with Microsoft SQL Server. You can use either the `Sql`-prefixed objects (via TDS) or the `OleDb`-prefixed objects to perform the data access.

> *One important thing to note is that this syntax might not work in all database applications (that is, other than Microsoft SQL Server), because the in-line syntax for stored procedure parameters is not always supported by other database systems.*

The example "Using Implicit In-line Parameters in MS SQL Server" (`sql-stored-proc.aspx`) uses a stored procedure named `FindFromTitleAndDate`. It expects two parameters to be provided, the title (or part of it) and the publication date. It returns a rowset containing all matching books. This is the stored procedure code:

```
CREATE PROCEDURE FindFromTitleAndDate
@Title varchar(50), @Date datetime
AS
SELECT *  FROM BookList
WHERE (Title LIKE @Title) AND (PublicationDate = @Date)
```

And this is what the page looks like when you open it:

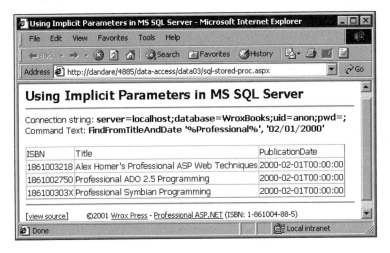

The Code for the "In-line Parameters" Stored Procedure Example

The only real differences between the ASP code for this example and the previous one are in the command text and the use of the "`Sql`"-prefixed data access objects. The command text contains the values we'll use for the parameters. In our case they're hard-coded, but of course you would usually create these dynamically from a user's input:

```
Dim strCommandText As String = _
           "FindFromTitleAndDate '%Professional%', '02/01/2000'"
```

However, there is one other important issue. SQL Server treats this command text as a SQL query (it automatically locates the stored procedure name within the string and parses out the parameter values). Therefore, we **cannot** set the `CommandText` property of the command object to `CommandType.StoredProcedure` as we did in the previous example – if we do we'll get an error saying that the stored procedure can't be found. Instead, we can either specify `CommandType.Text` (a SQL statement) or just omit setting the property as we've done in our example. The default is `CommandType.Text` anyway.

The rest of the code just does the same as previous examples – it creates a `Connection` object, a `Command` object, and declares a variable to hold a `DataReader` object. Then it opens the connection and executes the command to get the `DataReader`:

```
Dim objConnect As New SqlConnection(strConnect)
Dim objCommand As New SqlCommand(strCommandText, objConnect)
Dim objDataReader As SqlDataReader
objConnect.Open()
objDataReader = objCommand.ExecuteReader()
```

The rest of the page (not shown here) just assigns the DataReader to an ASP DataGrid as before to display the contents of the returned rows.

Using Explicit Parameters with a Stored Procedure

As we saw in the previous example of using "in-line" or "implicit" parameters when executing a stored procedure, it is quick and easy to program. It also provides more compact (and therefore faster) code. However, once you are using more than a couple of parameters, or if you need to use a return parameter to pass a result back from the database to the code, the implicit technique is not really suitable. There is also the limitation that some data stores might not support it. For a more general approach, we can create each parameter for a stored procedure explicitly, and assign values to them before executing the query.

The Command objects (both SqlCommand and OleDbCommand) expose a Parameters collection that can contain multiple Parameter objects. Each Parameter object has a range of properties that we can access and set. When we call the ExecuteReader, ExecuteNonQuery or ExecuteScalar method of the Command object, the parameters are sent to the data store as part of the command.

The example page "Using Explicit Parameters with a Stored Procedure" (parameter-stored-proc.aspx) demonstrates how we can use these Parameter objects. It uses a stored procedure named FindFromISBN that (given the ISBN code of a book) returns two values – the title and the publication date:

```
CREATE PROCEDURE FindFromISBN
@ISBN varchar(12), @Title varchar(50) OUTPUT, @Date datetime OUTPUT
AS
SELECT @Title = Title, @Date = PublicationDate
FROM BookList WHERE ISBN = @ISBN
```

Note that this differs in several key ways from the FindFromTitleAndDate stored procedure we used in the previous examples. The FindFromTitleAndDate procedure returns a set of records, or rowset, containing all books that match the criteria in the two parameters. However the FindFromISBN procedure we're using in this example returns the values as output parameters, and accepts only a single input parameter. So, to get the results we have to explicitly create the three parameters we need and feed them to the stored procedure when we execute it.

The next screenshot shows the example page in action. You can see that we're displaying not only the command text (the name of the stored procedure) but also the parameters that we explicitly create and add to the Command object's Parameters collection:

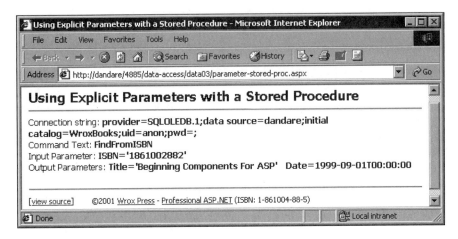

The Code for the "Explicit Parameters" Stored Procedure Example

As you'd expect by now, much of the code is the same as we've used in previous examples. The page contains <div> elements into which we insert the values you see in the screenshot. However, as there is no rowset returned from the execution of the stored procedure, we don't need a DataSet or DataReader object. Remember, all our "results" values are returned as parameters.

As we're specifying the parameters explicitly this time, we only need to use the stored procedure name as the CommandText property of our Command object:

```
'create a string to hold the name of the stored procedure
Dim strCommandText As String = "FindFromISBN"
outCommandText.InnerText = strCommandText 'and display it
```

Then we can go on and create our Connection and Command objects as before, remembering this time to set the CommandType property to CommandType.StoredProcedure:

```
Dim objConnect As New OleDbConnection(strConnect)
Dim objCommand As New OleDbCommand(strCommandText, objConnect)
objCommand.CommandType = CommandType.StoredProcedure
```

Creating the Parameter Objects

Now we can create the Parameter objects we need. We declare a variable to hold a Parameter object first:

```
'create a variable to hold a Parameter object
Dim objParam As OleDbParameter
```

The syntax for creating and adding parameters to the Command object's Parameters collection is not immediately obvious. We might be tempted to create a new Parameter object, set the properties, and then use the Add method of the Parameters collection. However, the Add method actually creates a new parameter, adds it to the Parameters collection and then returns a reference to it – so we need to do it this way:

```
'create a new Parameter object named 'ISBN' with the correct data
'type to match a SQL database 'varchar' field of 12 characters
objParam = objCommand.Parameters.Add("ISBN", OleDbType.VarChar, 12)
```

Notice the three arguments to the Add method: the name of the parameter, the data type (using the OleDbType enumeration), and optionally the size – in this case 12 characters. For numeric types, we can omit the size and the default size for that data type is automatically applied. Other common data types we use are Boolean, Char, DBDate, Single, Double, and Integer.

> *There are around 40 different data types specified for the OleDbType enumeration, and around 25 for the matching SqlDbType enumeration (as used with the SqlCommand object). Search the .NET frameworks SDK for "OleDbType enumeration" or "SqlDbType enumeration" to see the full list.*

Once we've got a reference to the parameter, we can set the other properties. In our example, we must specify the direction of the parameter (the options specified by the ParameterDirection enumeration are Input, Output, InputOutput, and ReturnValue). We also specify the Value property. This is the code for our first parameter – the one that we use to input the ISBN code we're looking for:

```
'specify that it's an Input parameter and set the value
objParam.Direction = ParameterDirection.Input
objParam.Value = "1861002882"
```

The Parameter Object Constructor

Our example doesn't demonstrate all the properties that we can set for a parameter, or all the ways of creating a Parameter object. There are several constructors available, ranging from the empty constructor:

```
objParam = objCommand.Parameters.Add()
```

to the full constructor where all the properties are specified:

```
objParam = objCommand.Parameters.Add(parameter-name, db-type, size, _
           direction, is-nullable, precision, scale, source-column-name, _
           source-column-version, value)
```

In this second case, we can specify all the properties required for the Parameter object. The various arguments are:

parameter-name	The name for the parameter.
db-type	A data type from the OleDbType or SqlDbType enumeration.
size	The size as an integer value.
direction	A value from the ParameterDirection enumeration.
is-nullable	A Boolean indicating if the parameter can accept Null values.
Precision	The total number of digits to which the value is resolved.
Scale	The number of decimal places to which the value is resolved.

Table continued on following page

source-column-name	The name of the column in a table from which the parameter value will be taken.
source-column-version	A value from the `DataRowVersion` enumeration, such as `Current`, `Original`, `Default`, or `Proposed`. A table maintains all these values for each column as the contents of the columns are changed or edited, and you can access whichever one you want. This is covered in detail in the next chapter.
Value	The specifically assigned value of the parameter.

Getting Back To the Example Code

Getting back to our example code, we now need to create the two output parameters that will hold the values returned by the stored procedure. The only real difference is that we specify the direction as `ParameterDirection.Output` rather than `ParameterDirection.Input` as we did for the `ISBN` parameter:

```
'create a new Parameter object named 'Title' with the correct data
'type to match a SQL database 'varchar' field of 50 characters
'and specify that it's an output parameter (so no value required)
objParam = objCommand.Parameters.Add("Title", OleDbType.VarChar, 50)
objParam.Direction = ParameterDirection.Output

'create another output Parameter object named 'Date' with the correct
'data type to match a SQL database 'datetime' field
objParam = objCommand.Parameters.Add("Date", OleDbType.DBDate)
objParam.Direction = ParameterDirection.Output
```

Now we can display the values of the input parameter in the page before we execute the stored procedure:

```
'display the value of the input parameter
outInParams.InnerText = "ISBN='" & objCommand.Parameters("ISBN").Value & "'"
```

Actually executing the stored procedure is easy – we just open the connection and call the `ExecuteNonQuery` method of the `Command` object (because we aren't executing a query that will return a rowset):

```
objConnect.Open()
objCommand.ExecuteNonQuery()
```

Afterwards, providing that there was no error (although not shown here, we include some basic error handling code in the example), we can extract the returned values from the two output parameters and display them:

```
'collect the values of the output parameters - note the use of
'the ToString method as they will contain DBNull if there was no
'match for the ISBN and this will cause an error if displayed
strTitle = objCommand.Parameters("Title").Value.ToString()
strDate = objCommand.Parameters("Date").Value.ToString()
outOutParams.InnerHtml = "Title='" & strTitle & "'   Date=" & strDate
```

Working with the DataTable Object

We discussed the nature of the `DataSet` object in the previous chapter, and saw how it is at the heart of the .NET disconnected data access strategy. In this section, we'll explore some of the ways that we can work with `DataSet` objects and their contents. This is by no means an exhaustive exploration of the capabilities of the `DataSet` – we'll be seeing more as we progress through this and the next chapter.

Here we're interested in looking at the ways that we can create `DataSet` objects and fill them with data – extending the techniques that we introduced in the previous chapter. Along the way, we'll see:

❑ How we can fill a `DataSet` using code

❑ The different ways that we can specify the columns in a table

❑ How we work with constraints, calculated columns and default values

❑ How we add and remove rows in the tables in a `DataSet`

❑ How we can use table and column mappings in a `DataSet`

❑ How we can sort and filter the data in a table

❑ How we can create and fill a table using code

There are often occasions where we want to create a data table directly in code, rather than filling it from a data store. Under .NET, this is a useful technique when we want to insert values into a data store – we can create a `DataTable` object containing the new data within a `DataSet`, and then push the data into a database or other type of data store. It's also handy when we just want to package data up into a format that we can pass from one tier of an application to another, or use as the `DataSource` property of a data-bound control like a `DataGrid`, a list box or some other type of ASP list control.

The example page "Creating and Populating a New DataTable Object in Code" (`create-new-datatable.aspx`) demonstrates the basic techniques for creating a `DataTable` object. In this case we aren't specifically creating a `DataSet` object – we're just creating the `DataTable` as a stand-alone object and binding it to an ASP `DataGrid` control to display the contents:

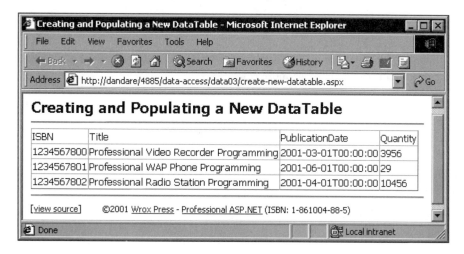

The Code to Create and Fill a New DataTable

Creating a new `DataTable` object is simply a matter of calling the constructor. We can give the table a name at the same time by providing this as the parameter to the constructor:

```
Dim objTable As New DataTable("NewTable")
```

Now we need to define the columns in the new table. We call the `Add` method of the `Columns` collection for the table, and specify the column name and the data type. The data types that we can use are listed in the `System` class library, and are basically the same as the data types that are available from all the .NET languages such as `Int16`, `Int32`, `Single`, `Double`, `Char`, `String`, `Boolean`, etc.:

```
'define four columns (fields) within the table
objTable.Columns.Add("ISBN", System.Type.GetType("System.String"))
objTable.Columns.Add("Title", System.Type.GetType("System.String"))
objTable.Columns.Add("PublicationDate", _
                     System.Type.GetType("System.DateTime"))
objTable.Columns.Add("Quantity", System.Type.GetType("System.Int32"))
```

Adding Data Rows To the Table

Having defined the four columns in our new table, we can now add some data rows. We define a variable to hold a `DataRow` object, and then call the `NewRow` method of the `DataTable` object. This creates the new row based on the schema for this table, and returns a reference to it:

```
Dim objDataRow As DataRow
objDataRow = objTable.NewRow()
```

Now we can fill in the values for that row. Once complete, we call the `Add` method of the table's `Rows` collection to add the row to the table:

```
'and fill in the values
objDataRow("ISBN") = "1234567800"
objDataRow("Title") = "Professional Video Recorder Programming"
objDataRow("PublicationDate") = "2001-03-01"
objDataRow("Quantity") = 3956
objTable.Rows.Add(objDataRow)
```

Now we repeat the process to add two more rows:

```
objDataRow = objTable.NewRow()
objDataRow("ISBN") = "1234567801"
objDataRow("Title") = "Professional WAP Phone Programming"
objDataRow("PublicationDate") = "2001-06-01"
objDataRow("Quantity") = 29
objTable.Rows.Add(objDataRow)

objDataRow = objTable.NewRow()
objDataRow("ISBN") = "1234567802"
objDataRow("Title") = "Professional Radio Station Programming"
objDataRow("PublicationDate") = "2001-04-01"
objDataRow("Quantity") = 10456
objTable.Rows.Add(objDataRow)
```

We finish by assigning the `DefaultView` property of our new table to the `DataSource` property of the ASP `DataGrid` that we placed in the HTML section of the page. A call to the `DataBind` method then causes the contents of our table to be displayed:

```
dgrResult.DataSource = objTable.DefaultView
dgrResult.DataBind()  'and bind (display) the data
```

Adding a Table to a DataSet

In the previous example we created a stand-alone `DataTable` object purely to be able to use it to populate an ASP `DataGrid` (and, of course, to demonstrate the technique). However, a physical `DataTable` object cannot exist alone, and must be part of a `DataSet`. What happened in the previous example was that a `DataSet` was created automatically behind the scenes, and our new table is part of that `DataSet`.

However, sometimes we will want the table to be part of an existing, or an explicitly created new `DataSet` object. We can create a new instance of a `DataSet` object from scratch like this:

```
Dim objDataSet As New DataSet("BooksDataSet")
```

> *The parameter is the name of the `DataSet` object, and is optional.*

Alternatively, we can use an existing `DataSet` that is empty, or that already has some tables in existence. Once we've got a reference to the `DataSet` object, we just declare a variable to hold a `DataTable` object and set it to the result of a call to the `Tables` collection's `Add` method:

```
Dim objTable As DataTable
objTable = objDataSet.Tables.Add("NewTable")

'populate the DataTable with the required values here
....
```

Managing Constraints and Default Values

If the `DataSet` object is going to be any use as a package that we can use to store and transport disconnected data, we need the ability to exert fine control over the structure and content of that `DataSet`. We saw in the previous chapter how we can add relationships between the tables in a `DataSet` to check and enforce referential integrity.

We've also seen how we can add tables to a `DataSet`, and fill them with data. In earlier examples we did this simply by filling them from an existing data source – for example with a SQL `SELECT` statement that returns a rowset from a relational database.

And in the previous example we saw how we can do the same directly, using code. The data in that example was hard-coded into the page, but could just as easily have come from user input, or from processing data collected from some other kind of data store – perhaps one that doesn't support the SQL-based data access methods we've been using so far.

When we fill a table in a `DataSet` from an existing data source using a `DataAdapter` object using the `Fill` method, information about the data type of each column is automatically collected from the data source and added to the table. And if we use the `DataAdapter` object's `FillSchema` method first, the column constraints (that is, primary keys, default values, unique values, nullability, and so on) are also added to the table. So, if a column in the original source table in the database is an integer data type that does not accept `Null` values, the table in the `DataSet` will exhibit the same properties.

Of course, when we create tables in a `DataSet` using code (or if the `FillSchema` method was not used), we have to specify all these extra properties ourselves. This and the next example demonstrate how we can do this. The example "Adding Expressions, Defaults and Constraints to a Table" (`column-constraints.aspx`) shows how we can create a table that has non-null columns, default column values, and calculated columns (that is, columns that use an expression based on other column values as their value source):

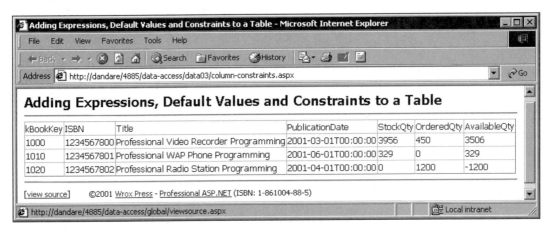

The example demonstrates several ways that we can add properties to the columns. The `kBookKey` column is an "AutoNumber" or "Auto-Increment (IDENTITY)" column that has `1000` as the seed value and `10` as the increment value – so the values in this column are created automatically as we add new rows to the table. The `ISBN` column cannot contain `Null` values, and each value must be unique.

The `StockQty` and `OrderQty` columns are `Integer` types, and have a default value specified so that they will contain zero (rather than `Null`) when a new record is created if there is no value specified for one or both of these fields. Finally, the `AvailableQty` field is based on an expression. The value in this column is automatically adjusted when rows are added or edited to reflect the actual quantity available (`StockQty` minus `OrderedQty`).

The Code for This Example

The code for this example is similar to that of the previous example in that we first create a new `DataTable` object. However, in this case we want to be able to access each of the new `DataColumn` objects as we add the columns to the table so that we can set the extra properties. So, we also declare a variable we'll use to hold `DataColumn` objects as we create them:

```
'create a new empty DataTable object
Dim objTable As New DataTable("NewBooks")

'declare a variable to hold a DataColumn object
Dim objColumn As DataColumn
```

The first column we create is the kBookKey auto-increment column with a data type o
see the property settings we make to specify that it's an auto-increment column:

```
objColumn = objTable.Columns.Add("kBookKey", _
                          System.Type.GetType("System.Int32"))
objColumn.AutoIncrement = True
objColumn.AutoIncrementSeed = 1000
objColumn.AutoIncrementStep = 10
```

Next we add the ISBN column to the table. This is a String, which cannot contain Null, can be a
maximum of ten characters, and must be unique. Again, the property settings can be seen in the
following code:

```
objColumn = objTable.Columns.Add("ISBN", _
                          System.Type.GetType("System.String"))
objColumn.AllowDBNull = False
objColumn.Unique = True
objColumn.MaxLength = 10
```

Now come two columns to hold the Title and the PublicationDate. As we don't need to set any
extra properties on these, we don't bother collecting the column reference returned from the Add
method of the Columns collection:

```
objTable.Columns.Add("Title", System.Type.GetType("System.String"))
objTable.Columns.Add("PublicationDate", _
                 System.Type.GetType("System.DateTime"))
```

Specifying Column Default Values and Expressions

The next two columns, StockQty and OrderedQty, are of data type Int32, and we want them to have
a default value of zero if no value is specified for new rows. Easy – just set the DefaultValue property
for each column:

```
'add columns for stock and order quantities with default values of zero
objColumn = objTable.Columns.Add("StockQty", _
                          System.Type.GetType("System.Int32"))
objColumn.DefaultValue = 0

objColumn = objTable.Columns.Add("OrderedQty", _
                          System.Type.GetType("System.Int32"))
objColumn.DefaultValue = 0
```

The final column is a calculated column that shows the available stock quantity. Again, it's of type
Int32. To make it a calculated column, we just set the Expression property to a string that contains
the expression to evaluate for each row:

```
'add a column containing an expression showing the quantity availability
objColumn = objTable.Columns.Add("AvailableQty", _
                          System.Type.GetType("System.Int32"))
objColumn.Expression = "[StockQty] - [OrderedQty]"
```

ntaining special characters (. ~ ( ) # \ / = > < + - * % & | ^ ' " [ ]) or spaces must be
We chose to do this anyway, and it probably makes more complex
any of your column names contains a closing square bracket you must
aracter, for example a column named `Tax[Basic]Value` would be
Value].

Table

and we can now add some rows. Although the technique is the same as
sted the code we use in this example so that you can see how the end
values we place in the columns:

```
Dim objDataRow As DataRow

objDataRow = objTable.NewRow()
objDataRow("ISBN") = "1234567800"
objDataRow("Title") = "Professional Video Recorder Programming"
objDataRow("PublicationDate") = "2001-03-01"
objDataRow("StockQty") = 3956
objDataRow("OrderedQty") = 450
objTable.Rows.Add(objDataRow)

objDataRow = objTable.NewRow()
objDataRow("ISBN") = "1234567801"
objDataRow("Title") = "Professional WAP Phone Programming"
objDataRow("PublicationDate") = "2001-06-01"
objDataRow("StockQty") = 329
'note - no "OrderedQty" provided so default value used
objTable.Rows.Add(objDataRow)

objDataRow = objTable.NewRow()
objDataRow("ISBN") = "1234567802"
objDataRow("Title") = "Professional Radio Station Programming"
objDataRow("PublicationDate") = "2001-04-01"
'note - no "StockQty" provided so default value used
objDataRow("OrderedQty") = 1200
objTable.Rows.Add(objDataRow)
```

The final step (not shown here) is to assign the `DefaultView` of the new table to a `DataGrid` object declared elsewhere in the page, so that the contents of the table are visible.

Specifying Primary and Foreign Keys

So, we've seen how we can create a `DataSet`, add tables and relationships, fill the tables with data and set several properties on each column. The one remaining aspect to consider is how we create columns that act as primary keys and foreign keys.

The example "Adding Primary Keys and Foreign Keys to a Table" (`key-constraints.aspx`) illustrates the techniques. When you open the page, you can see that we're selecting data from two tables in our data store and using them to fill a `DataSet` object. This automatically sets the appropriate data types for the columns, and copies any column constraints. What it doesn't do is specify within the `DataSet` which columns are the primary key and foreign key in the tables.

Obviously, we can create a relationship between the tables within the `DataSet`. We can then use this relationship to navigate from parent record to child record and back to parent record when accessing the data in the tables, as we demonstrated earlier in this chapter. But again, this does not change the table structure or specify which columns are the primary key and foreign key for each table.

So, we need to be able to create these keys ourselves. Unlike the previous example, where we set the values of properties for each **column** object, to define primary and foreign keys we have to create them as objects and add them to the `Constraints` collection of the **table** object.

This is because a primary or foreign key can encompass more than one column – for example the only possible primary key for the `BookPrices` table in our database is the combination of the ISBN code and the currency name. None of the individual columns has values that are unique in the table, and only a combination of columns can provide a unique key value. However, the ISBN column alone provides the link to the parent `BookList` table, and so we specify it as a foreign key in the `BookPrices` table.

The next screenshot shows what the example page looks like when it runs. You can see from the `DataSet.Tables` collection that there are two tables in the `DataSet`, named `Books` and `Authors`. These are filled with a subset of values from the `BookList` and `BookAuthors` tables in the database. Also shown is the content of the `Constraints` collection for both the tables in the `DataSet`, followed by the data in the two tables:

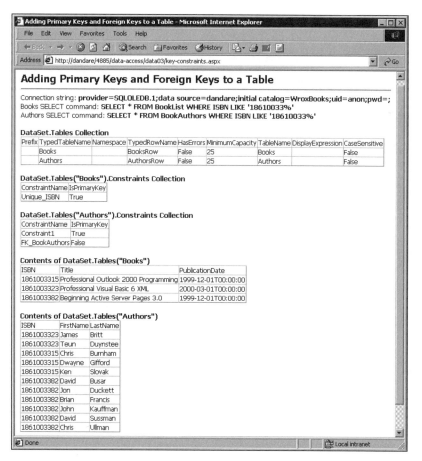

The Code for the Primary and Foreign Keys Example

The example page uses exactly the same techniques as earlier examples to fill the two tables with data from the database, so we won't be looking at that part of the code here. What we're interested in is how we specify the primary and foreign keys for the two tables within the `DataSet`, after they have been filled with data.

We start by getting a reference to each of the tables and to the columns that will become the primary and foreign keys:

```
'declare variables to refer to the DataTable and DataColumn objects
Dim objParentTable As DataTable = objDataSet.Tables("Books")
Dim objChildTable As DataTable = objDataSet.Tables("Authors")
Dim objParentColumn As DataColumn = objParentTable.Columns("ISBN")
Dim objChildColumn As DataColumn = objChildTable.Columns("ISBN")
```

For one or more columns to become the primary key, we first need to create a `UniqueConstraint` object for that table which refers to the column(s) in question, and make sure that they cannot contain `Null` values. We've named our new constraint "`Unique_ISBN`", as you can see in the screenshot:

DataSet.Tables("Books").Constraints Collection	
ConstraintName	IsPrimaryKey
Unique_ISBN	True

```
'create a new UniqueConstraint object and add to Constraints collection
Dim objUnique As New UniqueConstraint("Unique_ISBN", objParentColumn)
objParentTable.Constraints.Add(objUnique)

'prevent the column from accepting Null values
objParentColumn.AllowDBNull = False
```

Now we can specify that it is the primary key. As we discussed, the primary key could include more than one column, and so the way we specify it is through an array of columns (even though in this case there is only one). We create an array that will contain `DataColumn` objects, and set the first and only item (at index zero) to the column in our `Books` table that will be the primary key:

```
'create an array of columns containing this column only
Dim objColumnArray(0) As DataColumn
objColumnArray(0) = objParentColumn
```

Now we simply specify this array as the `PrimaryKey` property of the table itself:

```
'and set this array as the columns for the Primary Key of the table
objParentTable.PrimaryKey = objColumnArray
```

The next step is to specify the primary key for the `Authors` table. In this case, the ISBN cannot be used on its own as the values in it are not unique – there could be more than one author row for each book row. While not strictly the correct approach (the ideal would be a unique author reference number), we've chosen as an illustration to use the combination of the ISBN and the last name in each record as the primary key for the table. However, it will suffice for our example where there are no authors with the same last name for any one book.

The process is the same as for the Books table, except that – as there is more than one column in the primary key – we have to add the other (Lastname) column to the array as well before assigning it to the table's PrimaryKey property:

```
'now we can process the child table named "Authors"
'create an array of columns containing the ISBN and Lastname columns
ReDim objColumnArray(1)
objColumnArray(0) = objChildColumn      'the ISBN column
objColumnArray(1) = objChildTable.Columns("Lastname")

'prevent either of these columns containing Null
objColumnArray(0).AllowDBNull = False
objColumnArray(1).AllowDBNull = False

'set this column array as the primary key
objChildTable.PrimaryKey = objColumnArray
```

Creating the Foreign Key Constraint

Now we can add the foreign key constraint to the child table named Authors. This is just the ISBN column, which forms the link between the two tables in the DataSet. We create a ForeignKeyConstraint object (here named "FK_BookAuthors"), and we specify the parent and child columns to which it applies:

```
'create a new ForeignKeyConstraint object
Dim objFKey As New ForeignKeyConstraint("FK_BookAuthors", _
                                    objParentColumn, objChildColumn)
```

Now we can specify the other properties that apply to a foreign key. In this case, we're specifying that any deletes should cascade – in other words that deleting a row in the parent table will automatically delete all matching child rows. We also specify that any updates to the primary key value in the parent table should be cascaded to all matching child rows – the value of the foreign key in each matching row will be changed to the new value of the parent row's primary key:

```
'set the "update" properties
objFKey.DeleteRule = Cascade
objFKey.UpdateRule = Cascade
```

The DeleteRule and UpdateRule Property Values

The possible values for the DeleteRule and UpdateRule properties of a ForeignKeyConstraint object are:

Cascade	Updates to the primary key value in the parent table are copied to the foreign key in all linked child rows. Deleting a parent row deletes all linked child records.
SetDefault	Updates to the primary key value in the parent table or deletion of a parent row both cause the foreign key in all linked child rows to be set to its default value.
SetNull	Updates to the primary key value in the parent table or deletion of a parent row both cause the foreign key in all linked child rows to be set to Null.
None	Updates to the primary key value in the parent table or deletion of a parent row have no effect on child rows.

In most cases, to provide the highest level of integrity maintenance for your data, you will use `Cascade`. Other choices will leave unlinked (orphan) rows in the child table. However, depending on how you want to edit and manage your data (particularly when doing bulk updates), you may prefer to specify a different setting and perform manual integrity checks afterwards.

Finally, we add this constraint to the table's `Constraints` collection:

```
'and add it to the Constraints collection
objChildTable.Constraints.Add(objFKey)
```

You can see the new foreign key constraint, and the primary key constraint we created earlier for this table, in the `Constraints` collection (as shown in the screenshot). Notice that we haven't explicitly specified a named `UniqueConstraint` object for this table, so it has the default name "Constraint1":

DataSet.Tables("Authors").Constraints Collection	
ConstraintName	IsPrimaryKey
Constraint1	True
FK_BookAuthors	False

Displaying the DataSet Contents

Most of the code that displays the contents of the `DataSet` object is the same as we've used in previous examples, so we won't be repeating it here. You can examine the source code for this (and any other) page using the [view source] link at the bottom of the page. However, notice how we display the contents of the `Constraints` collection for the two tables. As these are collections, we can bind them directly to the `DataSource` of a couple of ASP `DataGrid` controls declared within the HTML section of the page:

```
'bind the collections of Constraints to DataGrids on the page
dgrBookCons.DataSource = objDataSet.Tables("Books").Constraints
dgrBookCons.DataBind()
dgrAuthorCons.DataSource = objDataSet.Tables("Authors").Constraints
dgrAuthorCons.DataBind()
```

Adding, Modifying, Removing, and Deleting Rows

We've now looked at all the important techniques available for building `DataTable` objects within a `DataSet`, and filling them with data. Next we'll confirm just how easy it is to add and edit the data in our `DataSet` tables, and then see how we can delete and/or permanently remove existing rows.

Adding Rows To a DataTable

Adding rows to a `DataTable` was demonstrated in several of the previous examples. The `NewRow` method of the `DataTable` object returns a new empty `DataRow` object for the table. After filling in the values, we use the `Add` method of a table's `Rows` collection to add the new row:

```
objDataRow = objTable.NewRow()
objDataRow("ISBN") = "1234567801"
objDataRow("Title") = "Professional WAP Phone Programming"
objDataRow("PublicationDate") = "2001-06-01"
objDataRow("Quantity") = 329
objTable.Rows.Add(objDataRow)
```

At a minimum, we must provide appropriate (legal) values for any primary and foreign keys in the table, and for any columns that will not accept `Null`. Any other columns that we don't set a value for will be `Null` when the row is added to the table (unless, of course, they have a default value constraint assigned to them).

Adding Rows with an Object Array

We can also add a row to a table using an array of the basic `Object` types. We simply create a one-dimension array to hold the correct number of column values, fill in the values, and call the `Add` method of the `Rows` collection with the array as the single parameter:

```
'add a new row using an array of values
Dim objValsArray(3) As Object
objValsArray(0) = "1234567900"
objValsArray(1) = "Impressionist Guide to Painting Computers"
objValsArray(2) = "05-02-2002"
objValsArray(3) = 150
objTable.Rows.Add(objValsArray)
```

Editing Values in a DataTable

To change the contents of a row in a table, we can simply access the row through the table's `Rows` collection, and access the column through the collection of items in the `DataRow` object that represents that row:

```
objTable.Rows(0)("Title") = "Amateur Theatricals for Windows 2000"
objTable.Rows(2)("PublicationDate") = "01-01-2002"
objTable.Rows(5)("ISBN") = "200000000"
```

Remember that the first row in the table is at row index zero. And if you specify a row index that is greater than the number of rows in the tables minus one (a row that is past the end of the table), you'll obviously get an error.

Using the BeginEdit, CancelEdit, and EndEdit Methods

An alternative technique is to use the `BeginEdit`, `EndEdit`, and `CancelEdit` methods of the `DataRow` object. Unlike the previous technique of just referencing the column and poking a new value into it, we can perform a controlled update to several values in a row without the values being immediately persisted to the row.

The `BeginUpdate` method effectively creates a copy of the row so that all the changes are made to this copy rather than to the original row. This means that all the updates made to any of the columns can be cancelled with a call to the `CancelEdit` method of that row – whereupon the original row is unchanged. To accept all the changes, effectively replacing the original row with the updated row, we simply call the `EndEdit` method.

The example page "Editing Existing Values in the Rows of a DataTable" (`edit-rows.aspx`) demonstrates this technique in action. After filling the `Books` table in a `DataSet` object with some rows from our database, we create a reference to this table and display the original values of the rows in the first ASP `DataGrid` control on the page:

```
Dim objTable As DataTable
objTable = objDataSet.Tables("Books")

'assign the DataTable's DefaultView object to the DataGrid control
dgrResult1.DataSource = objTable.DefaultView
dgrResult1.DataBind()   'and bind (display) the data
```

The code now calls `BeginEdit` and updates the first row in the table, after which it displays the current values in the next ASP `DataGrid` control:

```
'now edit the first row
Dim objRow As DataRow
objRow = objTable.Rows(0)

objRow.BeginEdit()

'change some of the values in the row
objRow("ISBN") = "2000000000"
objRow("Title") = "Professional Video Recorder Programming"
objRow("PublicationDate") = "2001-03-01"

'then display the contents again
dgrResult2.DataSource = objTable.DefaultView
dgrResult2.DataBind()
```

Now we perform some arbitrary test and make a decision whether to keep the changes we just made to the row. In the first case, this test fails and so the `CancelEdit` method is executed. After this, we again display the contents of the table. Notice that we reference the "copy" of the row that is being edited using the `Proposed` value of that row – we'll discuss this in more detail later on:

```
'now we can check if the values are valid
If objRow("ISBN", DataRowversion.Proposed) > "1999999999" Then
    objRow.CancelEdit()
Else
    objRow.EndEdit()
End If

'then display the contents again
dgrResult3.DataSource = objTable.DefaultView
dgrResult3.DataBind()
```

To demonstrate the effect of the `EndEdit` method, the next section of code just repeats the whole process – but this time it sets the value of the ISBN field to a number less than `"1999999999"` so that the test succeeds. This means that this time the `EndEdit` method is called. Again, the contents of the table are displayed during and after the edit process:

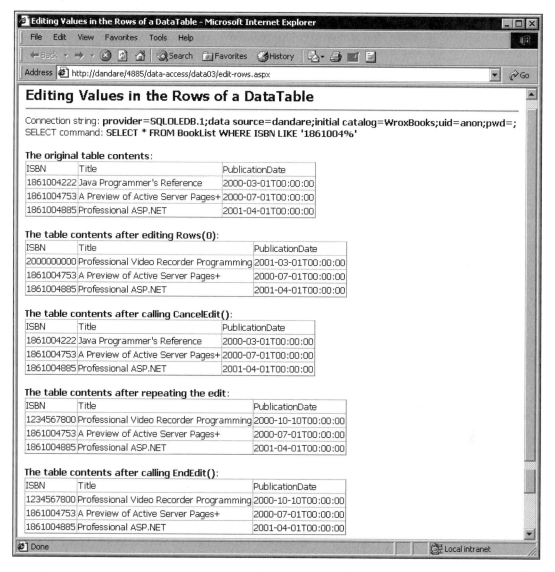

The Original, Current, and Proposed Column Values

If you were on your toes when reading the previous code listing, you'll have seen that we used a special syntax when accessing the value of a column:

```
If objRow("ISBN", DataRowversion.Proposed) > "1999999999" Then ...
```

As we'll see in more detail in the next chapter, every column in every row of a table maintains three values for that item. These values are defined in the `DataRowversion` enumeration, and they are used to help maintain concurrency when updating data:

Original	The value that was in the column when the DataTable was created and filled with data. It is compared to the value in the original database table when an update is performed, to see if another user or process has changed the value since the DataTable data was created.
Proposed	The proposed value for this column after changes have been made following BeginEdit, but before EndEdit, CancelEdit, AcceptChanges* or RejectChanges* has been executed.
Current	The actual column value after changes have been made to it, and after these changes have been accepted (after EndEdit or AcceptChanges* has been executed).

*The *AcceptChanges* and *RejectChanges* methods are described next.

Accepting and Rejecting Changes in a Row, Table, or DataSet

As we saw earlier, we can access any of the three values that are stored for every column in every row of a table at any time to get the appropriate value for a comparison test, or to check whether values in a row have been changed or are in the process of being changed.

As well as using the BeginEdit, EndEdit, and CancelEdit methods to manage updates to a table row, we can also use the AcceptChanges and RejectChanges methods. Their actions are self-explanatory, with AcceptChanges effectively calling EndEdit on any rows that are currently being edited, and RejectChanges effectively calling CancelEdit on any rows that are currently being edited.

As far as the DataRow object is concerned:

❑　After execution of the BeginEdit method, if you change the value in any column, the Current and Proposed values of all the columns become accessible. The Proposed value is the same as the Current value until you edit that particular column.

❑　After execution of the CancelEdit method, the Proposed value is discarded and the Current value is unchanged.

❑　After execution of the EndEdit method, the Current value for each column is replaced by the Proposed value.

❑　After execution of the AcceptChanges method, the Current value for each column is replaced by the Proposed value. As far as a DataRow object is concerned, this is the same as calling EndEdit.

❑　After execution of the RejectChanges, the Proposed value is discarded and the Current value is unchanged. As far as a DataRow is concerned, this is the same as calling CancelEdit.

The AcceptChanges and RejectChanges methods can also be used at DataTable and DataSet level. After execution of the DataTable (rather than the DataRow) object's AcceptChanges method, the Original value for every column in **all rows** in the table is set to the same as the Current value. After execution of the DataSet object's AcceptChanges method, the Original value for every column in every row in **all tables** in the Dataset is set to the same as the Current value.

It's important not to call these methods on a DataSet or a DataTable if you intend to update the original source data from the DataSet object, as it depends on the difference between the Original and Current values to be able to correctly detect any concurrency errors. We look at this topic in detail in the next chapter.

The RowState Property of the DataRow Object

Each row in a table exposes another useful property named `RowState`. This is related to inserting, editing, and deleting rows in a table, and provides a useful indication of the current state of each row. The `DataRowState` enumeration provides the following values:

Unchanged	No changes have been made to the row since it was created or since the last call to the `AcceptChanges` method of the row, table, or `DataSet`.
Added	The row has been added to the table and `AcceptChanges` has not yet been executed.
Modified	At least one value or property of the row has been changed since the last call to the `AcceptChanges` method of the row, table, or `DataSet`.
Deleted	The row has been deleted from the table using the `Delete` method and `AcceptChanges` has not yet been executed.
Detached	The row has been created with the `NewRow` method but has not yet been added to the table with the `Add` method. Hence, it is not actually classed as being a row within that table.

We can access the `RowState` property at any time to see the state of any row. However, it is most useful when we come to update the original source data. We'll see this in the next chapter.

Deleting and Removing Rows from a DataTable

Deleting a row from a table is easy – we just call the `Delete` method of the `DataRow` object we want to delete. We can specify the index of the row to delete:

```
'delete first and third rows in table referenced by objTable
objTable.Rows(0).Delete()
objTable.Rows(2).Delete()
```

Or we can use a reference to the `DataRow` object that we want to delete:

```
objThisRow.Delete()
objOtherRow.Delete()
```

The rows we delete remain in the table – all the `Delete` method does is set the `RowState` property to `DataRowState.Deleted` (as we saw in the previous section). However, next time we call `AcceptChanges` for the table, or for the `DataSet` object that contains the table, the row is removed from the table. This means that we can "undelete" rows simply by calling `RejectChanges` instead of `AcceptChanges`.

So, we can write code to delete some rows (or update and insert rows for that matter) in a table, and then carry out some comparison tests to decide whether to accept or reject all the changes in one go. Of course, (as we saw a little earlier) we can access the appropriate `DataRowVersion` for each column as we do so to get the `Original`, `Current`, or `Proposed` value.

Removing Versus Deleting Rows

As an alternative to deleting a row in a table, we can **remove** it instead. This is an entirely different process from deleting a row. When we execute the `Remove` method we immediately and irretrievably remove the row from the table in the `DataSet`. It isn't marked as deleted – it just disappears from the table. As a result, the row indices also change to reflect the new "row positions" as they all shuffle up to fill the gap left by the row that was removed:

```
'remove the third row from the table
objTable.Rows.Remove(2)

'using the Remove method on row 2 (rather than marking it as deleted
'with the Delete method) means that the next row then becomes row 2
'so, to remove the next row from the table as well we repeat the use of
objTable.Rows.Remove(2)
```

> *If you intend to use the `DataSet` to update the original data store, avoid using `Remove` to remove rows. Always use the `Delete` method so that the rows remain in the table but are marked as being deleted. These "deletes" will then be made in the original data source when you call the `Update` method.*

Notice the difference in syntax. The `Delete` method is a member of the `DataRow` object. The `Remove` method is a member of the `Rows` collection. To see how the `Delete` and `Remove` methods work, you can try the example "Removing versus Deleting Rows in a DataTable" (`remove-delete-rows.aspx`):

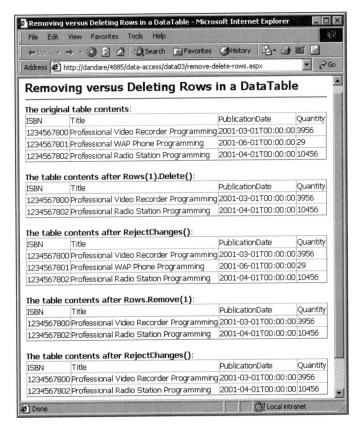

The Code for the Delete Versus Remove Example

The code in this example is relatively straightforward. We create a new `DataSet` and insert three records into it using the same kind of code as in earlier examples:

```
'create a new empty Table object
Dim objTable As New DataTable("NewTable")

'fill table with three new records using code here
'...
```

All these rows will now have a `RowState` property of `DataRowState.Added`. So, we call the `AcceptChanges` method to "fix" (accept) these changes – which updates the `RowState` property of all the rows to `DataRowState.Unchanged`. Then we display the contents of the table:

```
'call AcceptChanges to accept the changes to the table so far
objTable.AcceptChanges()

'assign the DataTable's DefaultView object to the DataGrid control
dgrResult1.DataSource = objTable.DefaultView
dgrResult1.DataBind()  'and bind (display) the data
```

Now we call the `Delete` method on the second row, and then display the contents again. The `RowState` property of the deleted row is set to `DataRowState.Deleted` and it disappears from view:

```
'now Delete the second row and display the contents again
objTable.Rows(1).Delete()
dgrResult2.DataSource = objTable.DefaultView
dgrResult2.DataBind()
```

However, the next line of code calls the `RejectChanges` method of the table, and then displays the contents again. The `RowState` property of the deleted row is set back to `DataRowState.Unchanged` and it reappears in the table:

```
'call RejectChanges to restore the deleted row
objTable.RejectChanges()
dgrResult3.DataSource = objTable.DefaultView
dgrResult3.DataBind()
```

Now we call the `Remove` method of the `Rows` collection of the table, specifying the second row as the one to be removed. Then we display the contents of the table again to show that it has been removed:

```
'now Remove the second row from the table
'note that this is a method of the Rows collection not the Row object
objTable.Rows.Remove(1)
dgrResult4.DataSource = objTable.DefaultView
dgrResult4.DataBind()
```

Finally, we call the `RejectChanges` method of the table. However, this time, the row does not reappear. It has been permanently removed from the table and cannot be restored:

```
'call RejectChanges - the deleted row is not restored
objTable.RejectChanges()
dgrResult5.DataSource = objTable.DefaultView
dgrResult5.DataBind()
```

441

Working with DataTable Events

The `DataTable` object exposes a series of events that we can use to monitor changes to the content of a table in a `DataSet`. The `ColumnChanging` event is raised for a column in a row that is being edited, before the change is applied to a column (allowing the change to be cancelled). The `ColumnChanged` event is raised after the column has been changed and the change has been persisted to the column.

There are also events that occur for the row as a whole, rather than for each column in a row. The `RowChanging` and `RowChanged` events are raised when the content of any row in the table is changed – the first event occurring before the change is applied to the row (allowing the change to be cancelled) and the second event occurring after the change has been persisted in the table.

Finally, there are two events that occur when a row is deleted from a table. The `RowDeleting` event occurs before the row is deleted, allowing the deletion to be cancelled, and the `RowDeleted` event occurs after the row has been deleted from the table. We don't have room to demonstrate all these events, however we will show you an example of how they can be used.

Using the RowUpdated Event

The example page "Validating Edits in a Table with the RowUpdated Event" (`update-check-errors.aspx`) demonstrates how we can use the `RowUpdated` event of a `DataTable` object to validate the values that were entered into each row. Code in this page fills a `DataSet` object with data from our sample database and then changes the values in two rows. It then displays the changed rows in a `DataGrid`:

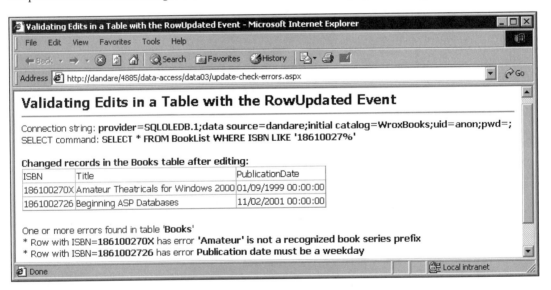

At the bottom of the page, you can see that two errors have been reported. We placed an event handler in the page that detects when a row is updated, and applies a couple of simple validation rules to the data in the row. Code in the page then checks the data for errors, and summarizes any it finds.

The Code for the Validating Edits Example

We've used the same techniques as most of the earlier examples to fill our `DataSet` with a table named "`Books`" that contains details of several books from our example database. We aren't repeating this code here. After filling the `DataSet`, we call the `AcceptChanges` method to "fix" the current contents:

```
'accept changes to "fix" current state of the DataSet contents
objDataSet.AcceptChanges()
```

Now we can set up the event handler we need to react to the RowChanged event, using the AddHandler method and specifying the event we want, and details of the event handler named "onRowChanged" that is defined elsewhere in the page:

```
'set up event handler to react to changes to rows in the table
Dim objTable As DataTable = objDataSet.Tables("Books")
AddHandler objTable.RowChanged, _
           New DataRowChangeEventHandler(AddressOf OnRowChanged)
```

This event handler will be called when any row is updated, after the changes have been applied to the table. In it, we'll apply our simple validation rules. If the update is not valid, we need to be able to flag this up – though we don't actually want to do it at this point. We want to be able to detect errors at some point in the future, perhaps before we submit the DataSet back to the database to update the original data.

If we only wanted to flag up errors at the point the user entered them, we could validate the values in the page where they were entering the data.

Row Errors and DataRow Actions

Each DataRow object has a RowError property, which is basically just a String value. We can write an error message to this string property, and then detect later if there is an error in the row (and retrieve this error message). So, all our event handler has to do if it detects an invalid value is write this error message to the RowError property of the row that has just been updated.

The event handler receives a DataRowChangeEventArgs object that contains details of the row that is being updated. This includes a reference to the DataRow object that has changed, and the Action that is being taken on the row. The Action can be one of the DataRowAction enumeration values shown in the next table:

Add	The row has been added to the table.
Change	One or more column values in the row have been changed.
Delete	The row has been deleted from the table.
Nothing	The row has not changed.
Commit	The changes to the row have been committed as part of a database transaction.
Rollback	The changes to the row have been abandoned following the rolling back of a database transaction.

The onRowChanged Event Handler

As you can see from the previous table, the RowChanged event is actually raised in several circumstances, not just when values in a row are modified. Therefore, in our example page event handler, we need to ensure that we only react to the event when the Action is DataRowAction.Change. This is the complete code for the event handler:

```
Sub OnRowChanged(objSender As Object, objArgs As DataRowChangeEventArgs)

    'only react if the action is "Change"
    If objArgs.Action = DataRowAction.Change Then

        'validate a new title
        If InStr(objArgs.Row("Title"), "Amateur") > 0 Then
            objArgs.Row.RowError = "'Amateur' is not a recognized " _
                            & "book series prefix"
        End If

        'validate a new publication date
        If objArgs.Row("PublicationDate").DayOfWeek = 0 _
        Or objArgs.Row("PublicationDate").DayOfWeek = 6 Then
            objArgs.Row.RowError += "Publication date must be a weekday"
        End If

    End If

End Sub
```

You can see that the code applies two simple validation tests and sets the appropriate value(s) in the RowError property if one or both of the tests fail.

Back To the Page_Load Event Code

Having seen what happens if an edit produces an invalid value in the row, we'll go back to where we were in the Page_Load event code that runs when the page is opened from the server. So far we've created the DataSet and filled a table within it, and set up the event handler that will validate the values in the rows as they are edited. So, the next step is to perform some edits:

```
'now change some records in the Books table
objTable.Rows(0)("Title") = "Amateur Theatricals for Windows 2000"
objTable.Rows(2)("PublicationDate") = "11-02-2001"
```

As these edits are applied to the rows, the RowUpdated event is fired and the validation tests are carried out. The values we're using will cause a validation error in both rows, and so the RowError property will be set to a description of the error for these rows.

Next we display the contents of the changed rows in the page using a DataGrid as before. To display just the changed rows, we create a DataView based on the table and then set the RowStateFilter property of the DataView to DataRowState.Modified (we'll also be looking at data row states in detail later in this chapter and in the next chapter):

```
'declare a variable to hold a DataView object
Dim objDataView As DataView

'get DataView and set to show only modified rows
objDataView = objDataSet.Tables(0).DefaultView
objDataView.RowStateFilter = DataRowState.Modified

'display the contents of the modified rows
dgrResult.DataSource = objDataView
dgrResult.DataBind()
```

Checking for Invalid DataRows

Finally we can check our data to see if any of the rows contain an error. Thankfully, we don't have to query the `RowError` property of each row in **all** the tables in a `DataSet` to find any errors. Both the `DataSet` and each of the `DataTable` objects it contains provide the `HasErrors` property, which is `True` if any row in that `DataSet` or `DataTable` has a non-empty value for its `RowError` property.

So, in our example page, we first query the `HasErrors` property of the `DataSet` to see if there are any errors at all. If so, we iterate through the `Tables` collection looking at the `HasErrors` property of each `DataTable`. We know that one (or possibly more if there are several tables) contains a row that has an error:

```
Dim strResult As String = ""   'to hold the result

'see if there are any update errors anywhere in the DataSet
If objDataSet.HasErrors Then

    'check each table for errors in that table
    Dim objThisTable As DataTable
    For Each objThisTable In objDataSet.Tables
        If objThisTable.HasErrors Then
            strResult += "One or more errors found in table '" _
                    & objThisTable.TableName & "'<br />"
```

Once we've narrowed down the search to the appropriate table, we iterate through each row checking if it contains an error. We can use the `HasErrors` property of each row here, which is much faster than comparing the string value of the `RowError` with an empty string. When we find a row with an error we add the value of the `RowError` property to our output message string:

```
            'check each row in this table for errors
            Dim objThisRow As DataRow
            For Each objThisRow In objThisTable.Rows
                If objThisRow.HasErrors Then
                    strResult += "* Row with ISBN=" & objThisRow("ISBN") _
                            & " has error " & objThisRow.RowError _
                            & "<br />"
                End If
            Next 'row
```

Having completed that row, we can go round and look for the next table that contains errors. After we've extracted all the error messages, we display them in a `<div>` at the bottom of the page:

```
        End If
    Next 'table

End If

outResult.InnerHtml = strResult    'display the result
```

The `DataTable` events we've looked at here are very useful for validating data when we have a remoted `DataSet` object. There are also similar events that are raised by the `DataAdapter` object when we come to update the original data source from our `DataSet`. We'll look at these in the next chapter.

Using Table and Column Mappings

The final topic we want to consider while we're looking at working with `DataSet` and `DataTable` objects is how we can specify custom mappings for columns and tables. When we fill a table in a `DataSet` from a data source such as a relational database, we can specify the name we want the table to have within the `DataSet` as the (optional) second parameter of the `DataAdapter` object's `Fill` method. If we don't provide this, the table will adopt the same name as the source table in that database. For example, in this code, we're naming the table "Books":

```
objDataAdapter.Fill(objDataSet, "Books")
```

However, in this case we have no direct control over the names of the **columns** in the newly filled table. They automatically adopt the names of the columns returned by the stored procedure, table name, or SQL statement that fills the table.

One way round this is to specify the column names within the SQL statement or stored procedure. For example, in a SQL statement, we can change the column names like this:

```
SELECT ISBN AS BookCode, Title AS BookTitle, PublicationDate AS Published
FROM BookList WHERE ISBN LIKE '186100022%'
```

Now the data set returned by the SQL statement will have the "new" names for the columns, and these will be used for the table's column names within our `DataSet`:

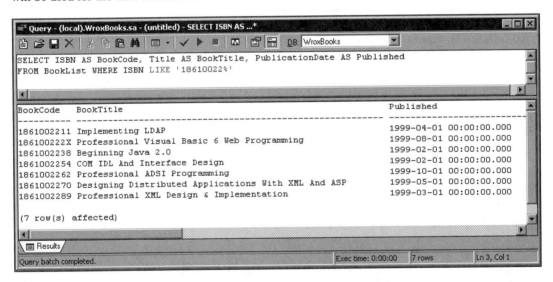

However, it's convenient to be able to specify the names of both the tables and the columns within our `DataSet`. That way, we can create reusable code that automatically maps data to the correct column and table names. It also allows us to push the changes to the data back into the database by simply calling the `Update` method – something we wouldn't be able to do if we renamed the columns in the SQL statement or stored procedure.

The example page "Using Default and Specific Table and Column Mappings" (`table-mappings.aspx`) demonstrates how we can use table and column mappings to manage the "connection" between the original table and its column names in the database with the table and column names in the `DataSet`:

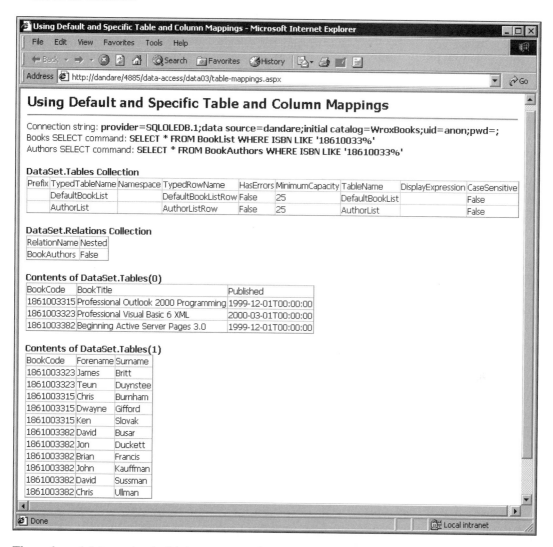

The code and data used to build the `DataSet` shown in the screenshot is the same as in many of the examples used earlier in this chapter. However, the names of the tables and the columns in each table are different from the ones we got in these earlier examples. All these are defined as custom mappings, and the conversion from the default to the custom name is automatically applied when we load the data.

All the mappings for both table names and column names are stored in the `DataSetCommand` object that we use to fill the `DataSet`. This means that we can create multiple `DataSetCommands` for a `DataSet` object with different mappings, and use the one that meets the requirements of the current task.

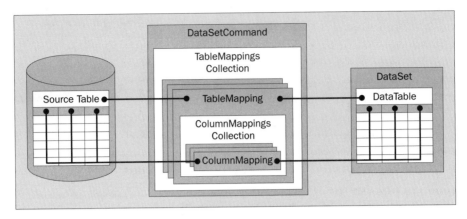

Note that the two objects we use to create custom mappings are members of a different namespace to the other objects we've used so far. To be able to create these objects, we have to add a reference to the `System.Data.Common` namespace to our page:

```
<%@Import Namespace="System.Data.Common" %>
```

The Code for the Table and Column Mappings Example

Our example page uses the now familiar code to access the database and extract subsets of rows from the `BookList` and `BookAuthors` tables. Along the way, it creates a new instance of a `DataAdapter` object to use to access the database and push the values into the `DataSet`:

```
'create a new DataAdapter object
Dim objDataAdapter As New OleDbDataAdapter()
...
```

It's at this point, before we call the `Fill` method to actually fetch the data, that we create our custom mappings for both the tables and the columns within them. We'll create a default table mapping, so that any call to `Fill` that doesn't specify the name of the table (in the second parameter) will create a table named "DefaultBookList". We first declare a variable to hold a `DataTableMapping` object:

```
'declare a variable to hold a DataTableMapping object
Dim objTableMapping As DataTableMapping
```

Now we can call the `Add` method of the `DataSetCommand` object's `TableMappings` collection. The `Add` method takes two parameters: the name of the source table that will be specified in the `Fill` method, and the name to use for the new table in the `DataSet` instead of the source table name. For a default mapping, we use the value "Table" for the first parameter:

```
'add the default table mapping "Table" - this table name will be used
'if you don't provide a table name when filling the DataSet
objTableMapping = objDataAdapter.TableMappings.Add("Table", _
                                                   "DefaultBookList")
```

Specifying the Column Mappings

Now that we've created the `TableMapping` object, we can access its `ColumnMappings` collection to create the column mappings. The simplest syntax is to use the `With` construct. We call the `Add` method of the `ColumnMappings` collection to create each column mapping, specifying the name of the column in the data source and the name we want that column to have in the table within a `DataSet`:

```
'now add the column mappings for this table
With objTableMapping.ColumnMappings
   .Add("ISBN", "BookCode")
   .Add("Title", "BookTitle")
   .Add("PublicationDate", "Published")
End With
```

Now we do the same to create the custom mappings for the `AuthorList` table. We've already got a default table mapping (using the value `"Table"`) so we can only create specific table mappings now. We first specify that a table in the data source named `BookAuthors` will create a table in the `DataSet` named `AuthorList`:

```
'add a table mapping so that data from the table named "BookAuthors" in
'the database will be placed in a table named "AuthorList"
objTableMapping = objDataAdapter.TableMappings.Add("BookAuthors", _
                                                   "AuthorList")
```

Then we finish up by specifying the column mappings from the source database table to the new table in the `DataSet`:

```
'add the column mappings for this table
With objTableMapping.ColumnMappings
   .Add("ISBN", "BookCode")
   .Add("FirstName", "Forename")
   .Add("LastName", "Surname")
End With
```

Using the Column Mappings

One point to be aware of is that the mapped table and column names are now the ones that must be used for all operations with the `DataSet` and its contents. When we create a relationship between the tables, for example, we must use the mapped table names:

```
'create a Relation object to link the two tables
'note that it uses the new mapped table and column names
objRelation = New DataRelation("BookAuthors", _
              objDataSet.Tables("DefaultBookList").Columns("BookCode"), _
              objDataSet.Tables("AuthorList").Columns("BookCode"))
```

The same applies, of course, when we come to access tables and columns in the `DataSet` in code. The only other issue is that we must be sure to specify the same table and column mappings in the `DataAdapter` that we use when we come to update the original data source. If not, the `DataAdapter` will not be able to associate the tables and columns in the `DataSet` with the ones in the source data store or database. We'll see how all this works in the next chapter.

Sorting and Filtering Data

To finish off this chapter, we'll look at one more topic that is concerned with `DataTable` and `DataView` objects. Once we've loaded a `DataTable` or a `DataView` object with data, we don't really want to go back to the data store and reload it every time we want to sort the rows into a different order, or filter the rows so that only a subset is displayed. Thankfully, both the `DataTable` and `DataView` provide sorting and filtering features, even if the way that they work is fundamentally different between the objects. We'll look at both next.

Sorting and Filtering in a DataTable Object

The example page "Sorting and Filtering in a DataTable Object" (`select-in-table.aspx`) demonstrates how we can sort and filter data that is stored in a `DataTable` object. For example, below, we've loaded the page and then clicked the "By Date" button to sort the rows into order by the values in the `PublicationDate` column and then by the values in the `Title` column. You can see from the message in the page that our code executed the `Select` method of the `DataTable` object with two parameters: an empty string and a string containing the two column names for the sort:

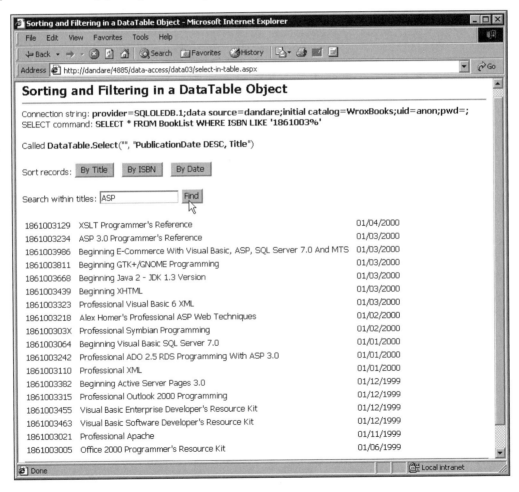

As shown in the screenshot, the page also provides a "Search" feature, where we've entered the text "ASP" in the textbox. Clicking the Find button gives the result shown in the next screenshot:

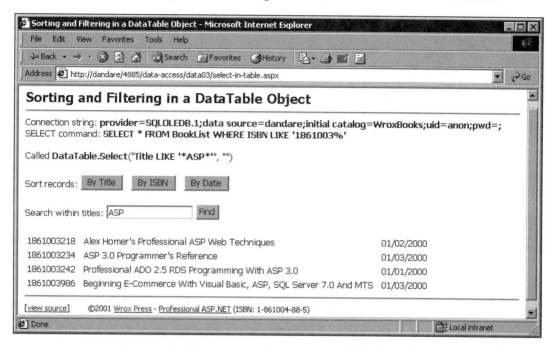

As you can see, the `DataTable.Select` method was executed again. This time the first parameter is the expression `"Title LIKE '*ASP*'"`, and the second is an empty string. Only rows containing the text `"ASP"` anywhere within the `Title` column appear in the page.

> *You'll notice that in our example page we are recreating the `DataSet` and its content each time you change the sort order or perform a search. This is only because we don't persist the data elsewhere between requests. If you remote the `DataSet` to another tier of your application, or receive it from something like a Web Service, you do not need to recreate it each time. Instead, you simply execute the `Select` method on the table within your cached `DataSet` object.*

The DataTable.Select Method

It's clear from the example that the `DataTable` object's `Select` method takes two parameters – an expression that filters the rows and a list of column names by which the rows are sorted:

```
DataTable.Select(filter-expression, sort-order)
```

Our example page only uses one of these parameters at a time, but you can of course use both together – for example:

```
objDataTable.Select("Title LIKE '*ASP*'", "PublicationDate DESC, Title")
```

Notice that we use the same syntax for the sorting parameter as most other data access techniques – add `DESC` to force reverse sort order. This second parameter is also optional, so we can use the following code if we want to filter the rows but we don't want to sort them:

```
DataTable.Select("Title LIKE '*ASP*'")
```

Specifying the DataRowState

There is also a third optional parameter supported by the `Select` method. This is used to specify the `DataViewRowState` that should be used. By using the value of each row's `RowState` property, this allows us to only include in the result rows that are unchanged, new, modified, deleted, or all rows. For example, the following code will only include records that have not been changed or deleted:

```
DataTable.Select("Title LIKE '*ASP*'", "Title", DataViewRowState.Unchanged)
```

The default for this parameter if we don't specify a different value is `DataViewRowState.None`, and the result reflects the current state of all the rows in the table. The full set of values for the `DataViewRowState` enumeration is:

CurrentRows	Includes unchanged, new, and modified rows.
ModifiedCurrent	Includes the current values of any modified rows.
OriginalRows	Includes only unchanged and deleted rows.
ModifiedOriginal	Includes the original values of any modified rows.
Unchanged	Includes only unchanged rows.
Added	Includes only new rows added to the table.
Deleted	Includes only deleted rows.
None	No filtering on the `RowState` of the rows is applied.

The Filter Expression Syntax

In general, the expression syntax used in the first parameter of the `Select` method is much as you'd expect – following the expression syntax of the .NET languages. For example, simple **comparison expressions** are:

```
"Lastname = 'Jones'"          'string literals in single quotes
"StockQty > 1000"             'numbers are not quoted
"PublicationDate > #10/10/99#" 'special syntax for date/time
```

The supported comparison operators are: `<`, `>`, `<=`, `>=`, `<>`, `=`, IN and LIKE.

For numeric column values, the operators that can be used are: +, -, *, /, % (modulus).

String concatenation is always with the ' + ' character. Case-sensitivity during string comparisons depends on the current setting of the parent `DataSet` object's `CaseSensitive` property. This property value can be changed in code as required.

The LIKE operator supports **wildcards for string comparisons**. The ' * ' or ' % ' character (these characters are equivalent) can be used to represent any series of characters, and can be used at the start, at the end, or at both the start and end of other literal text. They cannot be used within the text of a search string.

```
"Lastname LIKE 'Peter%'"    is the same as    "Lastname LIKE 'Peter*'"
"Lastname LIKE '%Peter'"    is the same as    "Lastname LIKE '*Peter'"
"Lastname LIKE '%Peter%'"   is the same as    "Lastname LIKE '*Peter*'"
```

To include the wildcards where they are part of the literal text in the search string, they must be escaped with a preceding backslash:

```
"WebWord LIKE '\*BOLD\*'"    'filters on the string "*BOLD*"
```

The AND, OR, and NOT operators are supported, with AND having precedence unless you use parentheses to force a different evaluation order:

```
"Title LIKE '*ASP*' AND StockQty > 1000"
"(LastName = 'Smith' OR LastName = 'Jones') AND FirstName = 'John'"
```

The following characters cannot be used directly in a column name within a filter expression:

~ ( ) # \ / = > < + - * % & | ^ ' " [ ]

If a **column name** contains one of these characters or a space, it must be enclosed in square brackets:

```
"[Stock#] > 1000"       'column named "Stock#"
```

If a column name contains a closing square bracket this must be escaped with a preceding backslash:

```
"[Number[\]Cols] > 1000"      'column named "Number[]Cols"
```

There is also a range of **functions** supported in filter expressions, including:

Sum, Avg, Min, Max, Count, StDev, Var, Convert, Len, IsNull, IIF, SubString

For more information, search the .NET SDK for "column and filter expressions".

The Code for the DataTable Sorting and Filtering Example

We can now look at the code for the example page we saw a little earlier. It contains a `<form>` that holds the command buttons and text box for the filter expression, and which is followed by a `<div>` where the results are displayed:

```
<form runat="server">
Sort records:
<input type="submit" id="cmdTitle" value="By Title" runat="server" />  
<input type="submit" id="cmdISBN" value="By ISBN" runat="server" />  
<input type="submit" id="cmdDate" value="By Date" runat="server" /><p />
Search within titles:
<input type="text" id="txtFind" size="20" runat="server" />
<input type="submit" id="cmdFind" value="Find" runat="server" />
</form>

<div id="outResult" runat="server"></div>
```

The code then goes off and collects a subset of rows from the original data store – our SQL Server database. It places them in a table named `Books` within a `DataSet`. This table contains all the books you saw in the first screenshot for this example. Then we can create the filter and/or sort expressions provided by the user. In the case of a filter expression, we add a preceding and trailing asterisk wildcard character so that it will match column values containing this text.

```
'create the Sorting expression
Dim strSortString As String = ""
If Len(Request.Form("cmdTitle")) > 0 Then strSortString = "Title"
If Len(Request.Form("cmdISBN")) > 0 Then strSortString = "ISBN"
If Len(Request.Form("cmdDate")) > 0 Then strSortString = _
                                "PublicationDate DESC, Title"

'or create the Filter expression
Dim strFilterExpr As String = ""
If Len(Request.Form("cmdFind")) > 0 Then
    strFilterExpr = "Title LIKE '*" & txtFind.Value & "*'"
End If
```

If this is the first time that page has been loaded, there will be no values from the `<form>` in the request, and so no filter or sort expression will be created. Otherwise, after the code above has been executed, we'll have one or the other in the strings `strSortString` and `strFilterExpr`. We display these values in another `<div>` element placed before the `<form>` section of the page:

```
'display the parameters we're using
outMessage.innerHTML = "Called DataTable.Select(""" _
                & strFilterExpr & """, """ & strSortString & """)"
```

Now we can apply the filter or sort to the table. We first get a reference to the `DataTable` object:

```
Dim objTable As DataTable = objDataSet.Tables("Books")
```

Executing the Select Method

The `Select` method returns an array of `DataRow` objects that match the filter and sort we apply, so the next step is to create a suitable array variable. Then we can execute the `Select` method and assign the result to this variable:

```
'create an array to hold the results then call the Select method
Dim objResults() As DataRow
objResults = objTable.Select(strFilterExpr, strSortString)
```

Displaying the Results

To display the results, we have to iterate through the array of `DataRow` objects that is returned by the `Select` method – we can't bind it to a `DataGrid` as we've done in earlier examples. In our example, we build an HTML table containing the column values for each `DataRow` in the array and then display this table in the `<div>` element named `outResult`:

```
'the result is an array of DataRow objects not a DataTable object
'so we have to iterate through to get the row contents
Dim objRow As DataRow
Dim strResult As String = "<table>"
For Each objRow In objResults
    strResult += "<tr><td>" & objRow(0) & "</td><td>  " & objRow(1) _
            & "</td><td>  " & objRow(2) & "</td></tr>"
Next
strResult += "</table>"

outResult.InnerHtml = strResult    'and display the results
```

Sorting and Filtering in a DataView Object

Another opportunity for sorting and filtering rows for display is within a `DataView` object. It's common to create a `DataView` based on a `DataTable` when using server-side data binding – as we've been doing throughout these chapters with the ASP `DataGrid` object. The example page "Sorting and Filtering Records in a DataView object" (`sort-find-in-dataview.aspx`) demonstrates how easy it is to sort and filter the rows in a `DataView`.

The page looks similar to the previous example of sorting and filtering a `DataTable`. However, notice the code that has been executed after we clicked the "By Date" button this time:

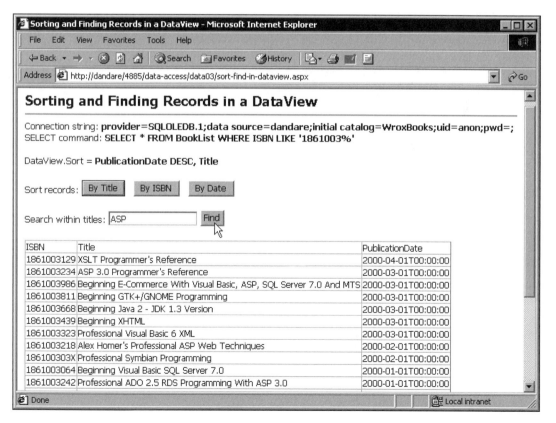

Rather than using a `Select` method, as we did with the `DataTable`, we specify the filter and sort order for a `DataView` by setting its properties. We set the `Sort` property to change the sorting order of the rows, and the `RowFilter` property to apply a filter. The next screenshot shows the result of entering the search text "ASP" and clicking the "Find" button:

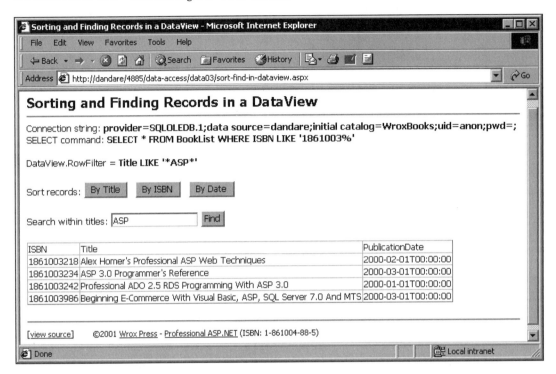

As we saw earlier in the example of using the `RowUpdated` event, the `DataView` object also has a `RowStateFilter` property. This works just the same as with the `DataTable` object, and we can also use this to filter the rows.

The Code for the DataView Sorting and Filtering Example

As you'll expect, most of the code for this example is the same as we used in the previous example. It uses the same HTML form and the same code to create and fill a `DataSet` with some book details. However, the next step is to get a reference to the `DataView` object that we'll be working with. In our example, we're creating a new `DataView` based on the `Books` table in the `DataSet`:

```
'create a DataView object for the Books table in the DataSet
Dim objDataView As New DataView(objDataSet.Tables("Books"))
```

Of course, if you already have a `DataTable` object available, perhaps as the result of some other code you've used to create it specifically, you can simply access the `DefaultView` property of the table to get back a `DataView` object.

Collecting the User's Values and Applying the Sort and Filter

Now, we can check for user's input and build the appropriate string for the `Sort` and `RowFilter` properties of the `DataView`. If the user clicked a 'sort' button, we simply build the sort expression as one or more column names (including "`DESC`" for a descending sort order) and set the `Sort` property of the `DataView` object. We also display the code we used:

```
'sort the records into the correct order
If Len(Request.Form("cmdTitle")) > 0 Then
   objDataView.Sort = "Title"
   outMessage.innerHTML = "DataView.Sort = " & objDataView.Sort
End If
If Len(Request.Form("cmdISBN")) > 0 Then
   objDataView.Sort = "ISBN"
   outMessage.innerHTML = "DataView.Sort = " & objDataView.Sort
End If
If Len(Request.Form("cmdDate")) > 0 Then
   objDataView.Sort = "PublicationDate DESC, Title"
   outMessage.innerHTML = "DataView.Sort = " & objDataView.Sort
End If
```

If the user clicked the "Find" button, we build a filter expression (using the same syntax as the previous example), and assign it to the `RowFilter` property of the `DataView` object. As in the previous example, we add a preceding and trailing asterisk wildcard character so that it will match column values containing this text. We also display the code we've just used in the page:

```
'or find matching records
If Len(Request.Form("cmdFind")) > 0 Then
   objDataView.RowFilter = "Title LIKE '*" & txtFind.value & "*'"
   outMessage.innerHTML = "DataView.RowFilter = " & objDataView.RowFilter
End If
```

Finally, we can assign our sorted or filtered `DataView` object to the `DataSource` property of an ASP `DataGrid` control declared elsewhere in the page to display the contents:

```
'assign the DataView object to the DataGrid control
dgrResult.DataSource = objDataView
dgrResult.DataBind()   'and bind (display) the data
```

Summary

In this chapter, we've looked at all the important topics regarding working with data in the three fundamental .NET data access objects – the `DataReader`, the `DataTable` and the `DataSet` objects. We've seen how we can extract data from a data store using complex SQL statements and different types of stored procedures. We've also seen how we can build `DataSet` and `DataTable` objects from scratch using code, and then set a range of properties on each data column to accurately specify their behavior.

Then we moved on to look at how we can add, delete, edit, and completely remove rows in a table. We examined the various properties that indicate the state of each row and each column in that row, and saw how we can cancel changes to a row, a table, and a complete `DataSet` object.

Finally, we looked at a couple of ways that we can filter and sort data – in a `DataTable` object and in a `DataView` object. The topics we covered as a whole were:

❑   Accessing Complex Data with `DataReader` and `DataSet` Objects

❑   Using Stored Procedures with `DataReader` and `DataSet` Objects

❑   Building and Editing Data in a `DataTable` Object

❑   Sorting and Filtering Data with `DataTable` and `DataView` Objects

Now that you are comfortable with the way that .NET data access works, and the fundamental objects, their common properties and methods, it's time to look at the final major relational data topic. How do we go about updating the original data in our database or other data store? This is the core topic of the next chapter.

"The Babel fish," says The Hitch Hiker's Guide to Galaxy "is small, yellow and leech-like, and probably the oddest thing in the Universe. It feeds on brainwave energy not from its carrier but from those around it. It absorbs all unconscious mental frequencies from this brainwave energy to nourish itself with. It then excretes into the mind of its carrier a telepathic matrix formed by combining the conscious thought frequencies with nerve signals picked up from the speech centres of the brain which has supplied them".

The practical upshot of all this is that if you stick a Babel fish in your ear you can instantly understand anything said to you in any form of language. The speech patterns you actually hear decode the brainwave matrix which has been fed into your mind by your Babel fish.

10

Updating Relational Data Sources

In the previous three chapters, we've explored how we can use the major objects that we use within the .NET framework for relational data access –the `DataReader`, `Connection`, `Command`, `DataAdapter`, `DataTable`, and `DataSet` objects. We've also explored the use of the subsidiary objects such as the `DataRelation`, `DataRow`, `Parameter`, and others. We've seen how we can use these objects in a range of combinations to extract data from a relational data store and work with that data.

The techniques we demonstrated included a examination of the ways we can update the data that we hold within the confines of the disconnected `DataSet` objects that we created. What we haven't looked at is how we perform that final step required in any application used fundamentally for updating a data store – how we get our changes back into the data store

Even in a connected environment, such as a traditional client-server application, the process of managing updates to the source data is not without its own problems, in particular the managing of concurrent updates to the source data. While .NET does not introduce any new problems, the concept of working with data in a fundamentally disconnected way (such as .NET provides) means that you need to be fully aware of the issues and know how to handle them. This is the core topic of this chapter. We'll be looking at:

- ❑ Updating data sources with a `Command` object
- ❑ Using Transactions when updating data sources
- ❑ Updating data sources from a `DataSet` object
- ❑ A detailed look inside the `DataAdapter.Update` method
- ❑ Managing concurrent updates to a data source

Obtaining the Sample Files

All the examples used in this chapter are available for you to run on your own server. The download file can be obtained from http://www.wrox.com/Books/Book_Details.asp?isbn=1861004885, and it includes SQL scripts and instructions for creating the database that the examples use. You can also run some of the examples on-line at http://www.daveandal.com/profaspnet/data–access/.

The main menu page (default.htm) contains links to all the data access sample files. The fourth link, "Updating Relational Data Sources in .NET" leads to another menu page that contains links to the examples for this chapter:

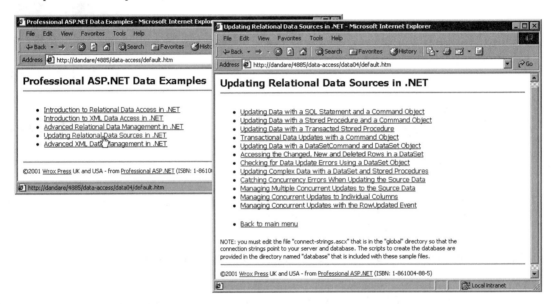

Updating Data with a Command Object

For simple single or multiple row updates to a data store, we traditionally used an ADO Connection or Command object with a SQL statement or a stored procedure. This technique is particularly useful for tasks like inserting a new record into a database, perhaps in response to a user submitting feedback to your web site or registering for your monthly e-mail bulletin. It's also useful for the equivalent 'delete' operation to remove one or more rows, or for updating row values.

Under the .NET framework, we can do the same thing using one of the new Command objects. The SqlCommand object is used only with Microsoft SQL Server (via TDS), while the OleDbCommand object can be used for any type of data store for which an OLEDB provider is available.

We provide two pages that demonstrate the technique – one that uses a SQL UPDATE statement to modify a row in the database, and one that uses a stored procedure within the database to add a new row or delete an existing row. Like all the examples, they develop on the techniques that we've covered in the previous data access chapters, and so we'll be concentrating on the new features that the examples introduce, and the code we use to implement these features.

Using a Command Object with a SQL Statement

The simplest way to perform a quick update to a data source is to create a suitable SQL statement and then execute it against that data source using a Command object. The example page Updating Data with a Command Object (update-with-command.aspx) does just that. When you open the page, code in the Page_Load event handler creates a SQL UPDATE statement that changes the title of a book with a specified ISBN code in our BookList table:

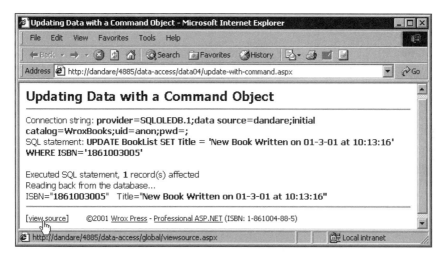

Remember that all the example pages have a [view source] link that you can use to view the source code of the page.

The SQL statement we use is visible in the screenshot, and you can see that one record was affected by the execution of that statement. The code in the page then uses a DataReader object with the same connection to read back the newly updated row from the source table and display the values.

The Code for the SQL Statement Update Example

As with most of the examples in previous chapters, the pages in this chapter work with a database named WroxBooks and the connection string specified in the user control named connect-strings.ascx (in the global folder of the data access samples). See the previous chapters for more details.

The first section of code that interests us here is how we create the SQL statement that will update the book title. We've included the current date and time in the title so that it changes every time you run the page:

```
'specify the SQL statement to update the data
Dim datNow As DateTime = Now()
Dim strNow As String = datNow.ToString("dd-M-yy \a\t hh:mm:ss")
Dim strSQL As String
strSQL = "UPDATE BookList SET Title = 'New Book Written on " _
       & strNow & "' WHERE ISBN='1861003005'"
outSQL.InnerText = strSQL    'and display it
```

After displaying the SQL statement in a `<div>` element named `outSQL` (elsewhere in the page), we create a new `Connection` object using our previously obtained connection string. Then we specify this `Connection` and our SQL statement in the constructor for a new `Command` object. We also declare an `Integer` variable to hold the number of rows that are updated:

```
Dim objConnect As New OleDbConnection(strConnect)
Dim objCommand As New OleDbCommand(strSQL, objConnect)
Dim intRowsAffected As Integer
```

Executing the SQL Statement

Now we can execute the command. We open the connection to the database, and then call the `ExecuteNonQuery` method of the `Command` object. This method is used whenever we don't expect to get a rowset back. It returns the number of rows affected by the execution of the statement, and we capture this in our `intRowsAffected` variable:

```
Try

    objConnect.Open()
    intRowsAffected = objCommand.ExecuteNonQuery()

Catch objError As Exception

    'display error details
    outError.InnerHtml = "* Error while updating original data.<br />" _
                    & objError.Message & "<br />" & objError.Source
    Exit Sub  ' and stop execution

End Try
```

Provided that we didn't get an execution error (if we do, the `Try..Catch` construct will display the error and stop execution of the code), we can display the number of records that were updated:

```
'declare a string to display the results
Dim strResult As String

'show the number of records affected
strResult = "Executed SQL statement, " & intRowsAffected.ToString() _
        & " record(s) affected<br />Reading back from the database..."
```

Displaying the Updated Row

Now we can read the updated row back from the database to prove that the process worked. We create a suitable SQL `SELECT` statement and assign it to the `CommandText` property of our existing `Command` object. Then we declare a variable to hold `DataReader` object, and execute the `SELECT` statement. The result is obtained by reading the rows returned by the `DataReader` (we demonstrated this technique several times in previous chapters):

```
objCommand.CommandText = "SELECT * FROM BookList WHERE ISBN='1861003005'"

Try

   Dim objDataReader As OleDbDataReader
   objDataReader = objCommand.ExecuteReader()

   Do While objDataReader.Read()
      strResult += "ISBN=""" & objDataReader("ISBN") _
               & """   Title=""" _
               & objDataReader("Title") & """"
   Loop

   objDataReader.Close()
   objConnect.Close()

Catch objError As Exception

   'display error details
   outError.InnerHtml = "* Error while accessing updated data.<br />" _
                     & objError.Message & "<br />" & objError.Source
   Exit Sub   ' and stop execution

End Try
```

Finally, we display the contents of the updated record that we captured in the 'result' string in another `<div>` element named `outResult`:

```
outResult.InnerHtml = strResult   'display the result
```

So, using a SQL statement and `Command` object to modify the contents of a data store is very similar to the way we would have carried out the operation in previous versions of ADO. And we can use `INSERT` and `DELETE` statements in exactly the same way as we used an `UPDATE` statement in this example.

However, it's often preferable to use a stored procedure defined within the data store to perform data updates. Stored procedures can provide a useful increase in performance, hide the structure of a database table from inquisitive users, and allow finer control over security permissions. The next example demonstrates how we can use a similar technique to that above with a stored procedure instead of a SQL statement.

Using a Stored Procedure with a Command Object

Using a stored procedure with a `Command` object is a fundamentally similar process to using a SQL statement, as we discovered in the previous chapter when we were extracting data from a data store. The example **Updating Data with a Stored Procedure** (`update-with-storedproc.aspx`) shows how we can use a `Command` object to execute a stored procedure that updates the source data.

The stored procedure named `AddNewBook` is created within the `WroxBooks` database by the SQL script we provide in the samples. It inserts a new row into the `BookList` table using values provided in parameters to the stored procedure, and returns zero (0) if it succeeds in inserting the new row:

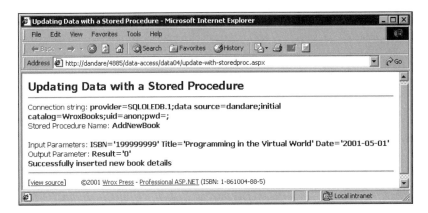

However, to make the process repeatable when you are experimenting with the samples, we've added a rather unusual twist to the procedure (one which is unlikely to be found in a real-world application). If we hadn't done this, you would only be able to run the procedure once unless you manually deleted the row in the database, or edited the procedure to insert a different row.

What the procedure does is to first check to see if a book with the specified ISBN (the primary key of the table) already exists. If it does exist, it deletes this row from the table instead – and returns minus one (-1) as the result. This way, you can run the page as many times as you wish:

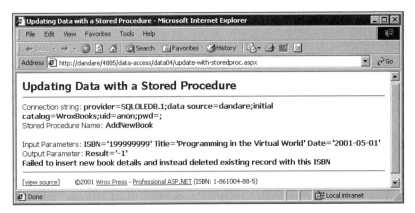

The AddNewBook Stored Procedure

The stored procedure takes as input parameters the ISBN code, title, and publication date of the book to be inserted, and it has a fourth Integer-type output parameter to hold the result. This is what it looks like:

```
CREATE PROCEDURE AddNewBook
   @ISBN varchar(12), @Title varchar(100), @Date datetime,
   @Result integer output AS
SELECT ISBN FROM BookList WHERE ISBN=@ISBN
IF @@ROWCOUNT = 0
  BEGIN
    INSERT INTO BookList(ISBN, Title, PublicationDate)
           VALUES (@ISBN, @Title, @Date)
    SELECT @Result = 0
```

```
      END
   ELSE
      BEGIN
         DELETE FROM BookList WHERE ISBN=@ISBN
         SELECT @Result = -1
      END
```

The Code for the Stored Procedure Update Example

In this example we're executing a stored procedure, so our command text is just the name of the stored procedure – that is. AddNewBook. We start by specifying this and displaying it in the page:

```
'specify the stored procedure name
Dim strSQL As String = "AddNewBook"
outSQL.InnerText = strSQL    'and display it
```

Now we create our connection and command objects as before. However, for maximum execution efficiency, we need to specify this time that the command text is the name of a stored procedure:

```
Dim objConnect As New OleDbConnection(strConnect)
Dim objCommand As New OleDbCommand(strSQL, objConnect)
objCommand.CommandType = CommandType.StoredProcedure
```

Next we create the parameters we'll need within the Parameters collection of the Command object. The first is for the ISBN code, and is of type OleDbType.VarChar and length 12 characters. We also specify that it's an input parameter, and set the value:

```
'create a variable to hold a Parameter object
Dim objParam As OleDbParameter

'create a new Parameter object named 'ISBN' with the correct data
'type to match a SQL database 'varchar' field of 12 characters
objParam = objCommand.Parameters.Add("ISBN", OleDbType.VarChar, 12)

'specify that it's an Input parameter and set the value
objParam.Direction = ParameterDirection.Input
objParam.Value = "1999999999"
```

The process is repeated for the next two input parameters, the book title and publication date. Note that the publication date parameter (named Date) is of type OleDbType.DBDate, and we have to specify the value in a format that corresponds to the column in the database. In the case of a SQL datetime column, the format "*yyyy-mm-dd*" will work:

```
'create a new Parameter object named 'Title' with the correct data
'type to match a SQL database 'varchar' field of 50 characters
'specify that it's an Input parameter and set the value
objParam = objCommand.Parameters.Add("Title", OleDbType.VarChar, 50)
objParam.Direction = ParameterDirection.Input
objParam.Value = "Programming in the Virtual World"

'create another input Parameter object named 'Date' with the correct
'data type to match a SQL database 'datetime' field
'specify that it's an Input parameter and set the value
objParam = objCommand.Parameters.Add("Date", OleDbType.DBDate)
objParam.Direction = ParameterDirection.Input
objParam.Value = "2001-05-01"
```

The final parameter is named `Result`, and is an output parameter that will return the result of executing the stored procedure. It returns an integer value, and so we specify `OleDbType.Integer` in this case:

```
'create an output Parameter object named 'Result' with the correct
'data type to match a SQL database 'integer' field
'specify that it's an Output parameter so no value required
objParam = objCommand.Parameters.Add("Result", OleDbType.Integer)
objParam.Direction = ParameterDirection.Output
```

Before executing the stored procedure, we display the input parameter values in the page – within a `<div>` element named `outInParams`. We can read their current values directly from the `Parameters` collection by specifying the name of each one:

```
'display the value of the input parameters
outInParams.InnerText = "ISBN='" & objCommand.Parameters("ISBN").Value _
                & "' Title='" & objCommand.Parameters("Title").Value _
                & "' Date='" & objCommand.Parameters("Date").Value & "'"
```

The next step is to execute the stored procedure. In this case, we don't have any returned value for the number of rows affected, so we don't need to capture the result of the `ExecuteNonQuery` method:

```
Try

    objConnect.Open()
    objCommand.ExecuteNonQuery()

Catch objError As Exception

    outError.InnerHtml = "* Error while updating original data.<br />" _
        & objError.Message & "<br />" & objError.Source
    Exit Sub

End Try
```

Once the stored procedure has been executed, the parameter named `Result` will contain the result of the process. We collect its value from the `Parameters` collection of the `Command` object. In our example, we also display the value – plus an accompanying explanation message – in a `<div>` element named `outOutParams` within the page:

```
'collect and display the value of the output parameter
Dim intResult As Integer = objCommand.Parameters("Result").Value
Dim strResult As String = "Result='" & CStr(intResult) & "'<br />"

If intResult = 0 Then
  strResult += "Successfully inserted new book details"
Else
  strResult += "Failed to insert new book details and instead " _
            & "deleted existing record with this ISBN"
End If

outOutParams.InnerHtml = strResult
```

Updating Data Sources with Transactions

One of the features of most database systems, and some other types of data store, is the ability to use **transactions**. Simply put, a transaction is a series of events that are all completed, or of which none are completed – there is never an intermediate result where some but not all of the events within the transaction occur.

The name 'transaction' comes from real-world scenarios such as purchasing an item in a store where you give the seller money in exchange for goods. Unless one of you gets cheated, the transaction will either succeed with both parties happy at the outcome (that is. you pay your money and get your goods), or fail where neither action occurs. There should never be an outcome where you pay money and don't get the goods, or where you get goods but don't pay the money.

In this section, we'll look at two types of transactions:

❑ **Database transactions**, where database-specific statements control the transaction, and it is carried out within the database itself. Usually the stored procedure within the database contains the transaction statements.

❑ **Connection-based transactions**, where the statements that control the transaction, and the execution and management of that transaction, are outside the database. Usually these are a feature of the `Connection` object that executes a SQL statement or stored procedure.

> *While it is possible to write stored procedures that perform transactions across different databases on the same server, this is outside the scope of this chapter. It is also possible to use the services of another application, such as Windows 2000 Component Services (or MTS in Windows NT4) to perform a **distributed transaction** – where a series of events spread across different databases and applications on different servers are managed as a single transaction. Again, this topic is outside the scope of the chapter.*

Database Transactions

In a database system such as SQL Server, we specify transaction operations within a stored procedure using vendor-specific statements like BEGIN TRANSACTION to start a new transaction, COMMIT TRANSACTION to accept all the updates and permanently commit the changes to the data, and ROLLBACK TRANSACTION to cancel all the changes made within the current transaction.

We've provided an example page that uses a transacted stored procedure. The stored procedure, named DoBookArchive, is created within the WroxBooks database by the SQL script that we provide with the samples.

The DoBookArchive Stored Procedure

All this stored procedure does is move a row from the BookList table into another table named ArchiveBooks, within the same database. If the process succeeds, the transaction is committed and the updates are permanently applied to the database tables. If there is an error when writing to the ArchiveBooks table, or when deleting the book from the BookList table, both actions are rolled back and the tables are left in exactly the same state as before – neither is affected by the procedure.

However, to make it repeatable while you are experimenting with the example, the stored procedure always starts by deleting any existing book with the same ISBN (the primary key) in the `ArchiveBooks` table. This action will also be rolled back if the complete transaction fails, so if a book has been archived (and hence deleted from the `BookList` table) it will not be deleted from the `ArchiveBooks` table if you run the stored procedure again with the same ISBN. In this case, the `INSERT` statement will fail because the book is not in the `BookList` table, and so the entire transaction is rolled back undoing the `DELETE` operation on the `ArchiveBooks` table.

This is the code for the stored procedure:

```
CREATE PROCEDURE DoBookArchive
    @ISBN varchar(12), @Result integer output AS
BEGIN TRANSACTION
DELETE FROM ArchiveBooks WHERE ISBN=@ISBN
INSERT INTO ArchiveBooks (ISBN, Title, PublicationDate)
    SELECT * FROM BookList WHERE ISBN LIKE @ISBN
SELECT @Result = @@ROWCOUNT
IF @@ERROR <> 0 GOTO on_error
IF @Result > 0
  BEGIN
    DELETE FROM BookList WHERE ISBN=@ISBN
    IF @@ERROR <> 0 GOTO on_error
    COMMIT TRANSACTION
  END
ELSE
  ROLLBACK TRANSACTION
RETURN
on_error:
SELECT @Result = -1
ROLLBACK TRANSACTION
RETURN
```

The Transacted Stored Procedure Example

The example page Updating Data with a Transacted Stored Procedure (`transacted-storedproc.aspx`) uses the stored procedure we've just described. We've arranged for it to use the same ISBN code as the previous example that inserts and deletes a book in the `BookList` table, so that you can see the results of this example by running it after inserting the new book and after deleting it. Providing that you have run the previous example to insert the new book row, the stored procedure in this example will succeed:

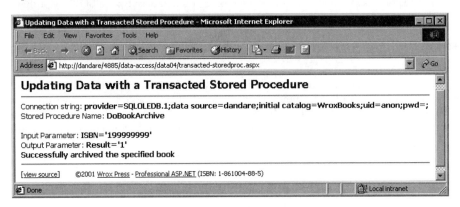

470

If you then run the page again, it will show that the stored procedure failed to find the book in the BookList table (because, of course, it's just been moved to the ArchiveBooks table):

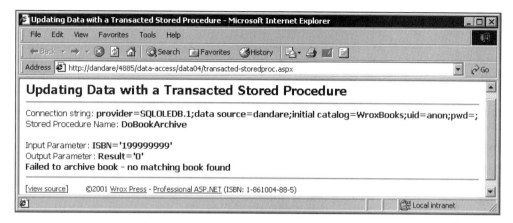

The Code for the Transacted Stored Procedure Example

As in our earlier examples, we start by specifying the name of the stored procedure and displaying it in the page, and then create the Connection and Command objects we'll need to execute it. We also set the CommandType of the Command object to indicate that we'll be executing a stored procedure:

```
'specify the stored procedure name
Dim strSQL As String = "DoBookArchive"
outSQL.InnerText = strSQL    'and display it

Dim objConnect As New OleDbConnection(strConnect)
Dim objCommand As New OleDbCommand(strSQL, objConnect)
objCommand.CommandType = CommandType.StoredProcedure
```

Now we create the parameters for the command. This time there are only two – an input parameter to hold the ISBN of the book we want to archive, and an output parameter to hold the result:

```
Dim objParam As OleDbParameter

'create an input Parameter object named 'ISBN' with the correct data
'type to match a SQL database 'varchar' field of 12 characters
objParam = objCommand.Parameters.Add("ISBN", OleDbType.VarChar, 12)
objParam.Direction = ParameterDirection.Input
objParam.Value = "199999999"

'create an output Parameter object named 'Result' with the correct
'data type to match a SQL database 'integer' field
'specify that it's an Output parameter so no value required
objParam = objCommand.Parameters.Add("Result", OleDbType.Integer)
objParam.Direction = ParameterDirection.Output

'display the value of the input parameter
outInParams.InnerText = "ISBN='" & objCommand.Parameters("ISBN").Value & "'"
```

471

The next step is to open our connection and execute the stored procedure:

```
Try

    objConnect.Open()
    objCommand.ExecuteNonQuery()
    objConnect.Close()

Catch objError As Exception

    outError.InnerHtml = "* Error while updating original data.<br />" _
        & objError.Message & "<br />" & objError.Source
    Exit Sub  'stop execution

End Try
```

Then we can collect the result from the output parameter and display it, along with some accompanying explanatory text:

```
'collect and display the value of the output parameter
Dim intResult As Integer = objCommand.Parameters("Result").Value
Dim strResult As String = "Result='" & CStr(intResult) & "'<br />"

Select Case intResult
    Case -1: strResult += "Error occurred while attempting archive"
    Case 0: strResult += "Failed to archive book -no matching book found"
    Case > 0: strResult += "Successfully archived the specified book"
End Select

outOutParams.InnerHtml = strResult
```

Notice that we didn't have to do anything extra to benefit from the transaction within the stored procedure – we just executed it and checked the result to see what actually happened. This is not the case, however, when we use the other type of transaction, a connection-based transaction. We'll see how different working with this type of transaction is next.

Connection-based Transactions

The previous example demonstrates how we can use a transaction within a stored procedure (a **database transaction**) to ensure that a series of operations on our data either all succeed or are all rolled back. A second way of using a transaction is through the capabilities of the Connection object.

Both the SqlConnection and the OleDbConnection object can be used to perform transacted data updates. While the way we actually apply a transaction is different from the stored-procedure transaction we used in the previous example, the terminology is the same:

BeginTransaction	Starts a new transaction on the connection, and all subsequent changes to the data made through the connection become part of that transaction until transaction is committed or rolled back.
Commit (Transaction)	Commits all changes to the data made since the current transaction was started. The changes are made permanent in the target data store.
Rollback (Transaction)	Abandons all changes to the data made since the current transaction was started. The changes are removed from the target data store.

The Transaction Object

In ADO.NET, we have two objects that implement transactions – SqlTransaction for use with Microsoft SQL Server via TDS, and OleDbTransaction for use with an OLE-DB provider. To start a transaction we call the BeginTransaction method of the current Connection object. This returns a Transaction object that we must then assign to any Command objects that we want to enroll into that transaction.

To end a transaction and commit all the changes to the database, we call the Commit method of the Transaction object (note that it's not a method of the Connection object as you might at first have expected). To abandon all changes to the data, we call the Transaction object's Rollback method instead.

Notice also that we have to manually enroll any Command objects into the transaction. While this might seem odd, it does allow us to have multiple transactions in progress, and use whichever is appropriate for each command we carry out on the database. We can also create a nested transaction (that is a transaction that executes within another transaction) by creating a new Transaction object and calling the Begin method.

A Connection-based Transaction Example

To see these methods in action, open the example Transactional Data Updates with a Command Object (update-with-transaction.aspx). This page creates three SQL statements that are used to update the title of three books in the BookList table to reflect the current date and time, and then it executes these statements. Afterwards, it reads the rows back from the database and displays the details to confirm that the updates were successful:

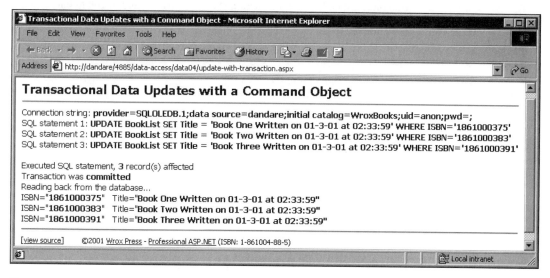

You can see in the previous screenshot that the transaction was committed, and the three rows were updated. However, this is only because the page contains logic that uses the current time in seconds to decide whether to commit or roll back the transaction. While not a real-world scenario, it is done so that you can see the result of rolling back a transaction as well as committing it. After running the page again where the time has an even number of seconds, the transaction is rolled back and so the titles are not updated:

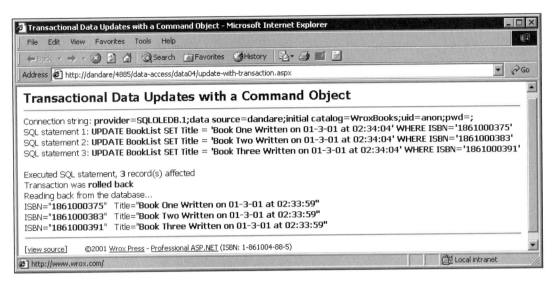

The Code for the Connection-based Transaction Example

The only real differences in the way that this page works from the other examples that use SQL statements to update the data source, is that we have to call the transaction methods at the appropriate times – effectively managing the transaction ourselves. Instead of a stored procedure within the database itself deciding whether to commit or rollback the changes (usually dependent on the outcome of one of the statements in the stored procedure), we decide within our ASP code if the transaction should be committed or rolled back.

As usual, we start by creating the SQL statements we'll be executing against the BookList table to update the book titles:

```
'specify the SQL statements to update the data
Dim strNow, strSQL1, strSQL2, strSQL3 As String
Dim datNow As DateTime = Now()
strNow = datNow.ToString("dd-M-yy \a\t hh:mm:ss")
strSQL1 = "UPDATE BookList SET Title = 'Book One Written on " _
          & strNow & "' WHERE ISBN='1861000375'"
outSQL1.InnerText = strSQL1    'and display it
strSQL2 = "UPDATE BookList SET Title = 'Book Two Written on " _
          & strNow & "' WHERE ISBN='1861000383'"
outSQL2.InnerText = strSQL2    'and display it
strSQL3 = "UPDATE BookList SET Title = 'Book Three Written on " _
          & strNow & "' WHERE ISBN='1861000391'"
outSQL3.InnerText = strSQL3    'and display it
```

Then we create our Connection and Command objects, and declare the variable to hold the number of rows affected by our updates. We've set the initial value to zero here, though this is not actually required (as zero is the default value), but it helps to illustrate how the code works and ensures that we can safely add on the result each time we execute a SQL statement:

```
Dim objConnect As New ADOConnection(strConnect)
Dim objCommand As New ADOCommand()
Dim intRowsAffected As Integer = 0
```

Starting a Transaction

We need a variable to hold the `Transaction` object that will be returned when we start a transaction, and so we declare this next:

```
'declare a variable to hold a Transaction object
Dim objTransaction As OleDbTransaction
```

Next we open our connection, and execute the `BeginTransaction` method to start a new connection-based transaction. We assign the `Transaction` object that is returned to our `objTransaction` variable:

```
Try

    objConnect.Open()

    'start a transaction for this connection
    objTransaction = objConnect.BeginTransaction()
```

Now we are ready to execute our three SQL UPDATE statements using the `Command` object we created earlier on. We created it without providing any values for the constructor parameters, so we have to assign our `Connection` object to its `Connection` property. We also set the `CommandType` to indicate that we're using a SQL statement (though this is the default if not specified). Once we've set up our `Command` object, we have to enroll it into the current transaction:

```
'specify the Connection object and command type for the Command
objCommand.Connection = objConnect
objCommand.CommandType = CommandType.Text

'attach the current transaction to the Command object
'must be done after setting Connection property
objCommand.Transaction = objTransaction
```

Notice that we can only do so after we've set the `Connection` property, and if we want to change the `Connection` property afterwards we have to un-enrol by setting the `Transaction` property of the `Command` to `Nothing`.

Then we can assign each SQL statement to the `CommandText` property in turn and execute it:

```
'specify the select statement to use for the first update
objCommand.CommandText = strSQL1

'execute the SQL statement against the command to fill the DataReader
'keep track of number of records originally updated
intRowsAffected += objCommand.ExecuteNonQuery()

'repeat using the select statement for the second update
objCommand.CommandText = strSQL2
intRowsAffected += objCommand.ExecuteNonQuery()

'repeat using the select statement for the third update
objCommand.CommandText = strSQL3
intRowsAffected += objCommand.ExecuteNonQuery()
```

The next place where we need to consider how we handle the transaction that we've started is if an error occurs while executing the SQL statements. In an error situation, we must call the Rollback method of the Transaction object to cancel any changes that have been applied to the source data:

```
Catch objError As Exception

    'error encountered so roll back all the updates
    objTransaction.Rollback()

    'display error details
    outError.InnerHtml = "* Error while updating original data.<br />" _
        & objError.Message & "<br />" & objError.Source
    Exit Sub  ' and stop execution

End Try
```

After successfully executing all three statements without an error, we would normally call the Commit method of the Transaction object to permanently apply the changes to the data store. However, in our example, we check the number of seconds in the current time and only call Commit if this is an odd number. If it's an even number, we call the Rollback method to abandon all updates:

```
'all seems OK so can now commit all the updates. However as an
'illustration of the technique only do so if the current time
'has an odd number of seconds. If not, rollback all changes
    Dim strCommit As String
    If Second(datNow) Mod 2 = 0
        objTransaction.Rollback()
        strCommit = "rolled back"
    Else
        objTransaction.Commit()
        strCommit = "committed"
    End If
```

After this, we can read the values of the rows using a DataReader object and display them in the page. This is identical to the way we did it in the first example in this chapter, so we aren't repeating the code here.

Having looked briefly at how we can use transactions to ensure multiple data updates all succeed, or all fail, we'll move on to a different topic. The DataSet object introduced in previous chapters has the facility to automatically update the source data from which it was created – or in fact any data store for which the structure and contents of the tables within the DataSet are of the appropriate format. This is the focus of the next section.

Updating Data from a DataSet Object

In previous chapters we've regularly used a DataSet object to store data extracted from a database, or to hold data that we've created dynamically using code. We also looked at the ways we can edit and modify the data that the DataSet contains. In this section of the chapter, we'll look in detail at how we get those changes back into a data source such as a relational database.

The .NET data access namespace contains an object named DataAdapter that is used to provide the connection between a data store and a disconnected DataSet. We saw this object in action in Chapter 8, but only so far as collecting rows from a database and pushing them into a DataSet. To understand how the update process works for a DataSet, we need to examine the DataAdapter object in more depth.

Inside the DataAdapter Object

In order to understand and take advantage of many of the features of the .NET disconnected data model, especially when we come to look at concurrent data update issues later in this chapter, you must be comfortable with what's going on behind the scenes when you use the `DataSet` and `DataAdapter` objects to push changes made to the data back into a data source.

The full chain of objects that are required to pull data from a data store into a `DataSet`, and push it back into the data store after updating, is shown in the next schematic. You can see the four main objects that are involved in the process –the `Connection`, `Command`, `DataAdapter`, and `DataSet`:

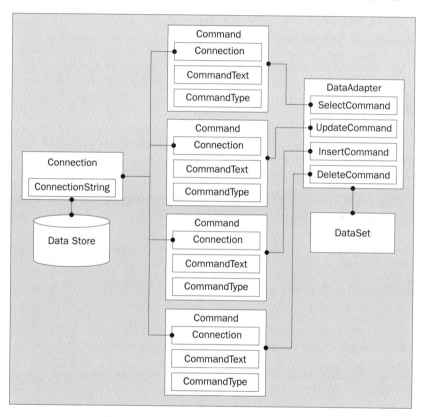

The DataSet Object Chain

The four objects in the schematic were discussed in outline in Chapter 8. However, we'll be going into more detail here as we discover how the whole process works.

- ❏ The `Connection` object defines the way that the data store will communicate with `Command` objects, using a connection string and the appropriate data store provider such as SQL TDS or OLEDB.

- ❏ The `Command` object performs the task of executing the SQL statement, query, stored procedure, etc. against the data store via the `Connection` object. It contains details about that SQL statement, query or stored procedure, and the way that it should be processed.

❑   The `DataAdapter` object is the bridge between the `DataSet` and the `Command` objects. It specifies the organization of the tables within the `DataSet` through table and column mappings, and is responsible for managing the whole process of fetching data from the data source and pushing it back to the data source.

❑   The `DataSet` is the disconnected data storage and processing unit that actually holds the data. It does so using one or more tables, and (optionally) relationships between these tables.

Notice in the schematic that there are four `Command` objects involved in the process. Why? We only need one to fill a `DataSet` from a data store – a suitable `SelectCommand` such as a SQL SELECT statement or the equivalent stored procedure (or table name). However, to be able to update the original data, we need the other three – an `UpdateCommand`, an `InsertCommand`, and a `DeleteCommand`.

All four commands share the same `Connection` object; they all have a reference to it in their `Connection` property. This technique consumes far less resources (and hence is more efficient) than using four different ones, and works because the `DataAdapter` only processes one command at a time. Connections to a data store are limited, and using the same one reduces the demands of the application considerably.

Creating the Necessary Objects

Of course, in most of our examples, we don't explicitly create all these objects every time we want to access a data store. But that doesn't mean they don't exist. In fact they are all created every time we perform data access – in particular when we are pushing data back into a data source. Allowing the system to create them on demand also reduces the code we have to write, and can provide marginally better performance.

For example, when simply extracting data, we usually create a `Connection` object, a `DataAdapter` object, and a `DataSet` object –then use the `Fill` method of the `DataAdapter` to get the data into the `DataSet`:

```
Dim objConnect As New OleDbConnection(strConnectString)
Dim objDataAdapter As New OleDbDataAdapter(strSQLStatement, objConnect)
Dim objDataSet As New DataSet()
objDataAdapter.Fill(objDataSet, "table-name")
```

However behind the scenes, when the constructor for the `DataAdapter` is executed, a `Command` object is created using the SQL statement and the connection object. This new `Command` object is then assigned to the `SelectCommand` property of the `DataAdapter` object.

We can even dispense with creating a `Connection` object ourselves. We just pass the connection string itself into the constructor for the `DataAdapter` object:

```
Dim objDataAdapter As New OleDbDataAdapter(strSQLStatement, _
                                strConnectString)
```

Again, behind the scenes, the `DataAdapter` constructor is creating a new `Command` object by calling its constructor with the SQL statement and (this time) the connection string. Then the `Command` object constructor creates a new `Connection` object using the connection string. The whole process still takes place to create the chain of four objects, even if we don't specifically code this.

Specifying the SelectCommand

At minimum, when creating a `DataAdapter` object, only the `SelectCommand` is required and this must always be provided. As you've seen, we usually specify this as a string (the SQL statement, query string, table name or stored procedure name) in the constructor for the object. Of course, there's nothing to stop us creating a `Command` object directly and assigning this to the `SelectCommand` property of the `DataAdapter`:

```
Dim objConnect As New OleDbConnection(strConnectString)
Dim objCommand As New OleDbCommand(strSQLStatement, objConnect)
Dim objDataAdapter As New OleDbDataAdapter(objCommand)
```

or, in an even more verbose way:

```
Dim objConnect As New OleDbConnection(strConnectString)
Dim objCommand As New OleDbCommand(strSQLStatement, objConnect)
Dim objDataAdapter As New OleDbDataAdapter()
objDataAdapter.SelectCommand = objCommand
```

While it's hard to see when we might use the last of these, it could be a useful technique when we already have a `DataAdapter` that we want to reuse by just changing the `SelectCommand` to reference a different `Command` object.

Specifying the Other Commands

We only need a `SelectCommand` to be able to fill a `DataSet`, but when we come to push the changes back to the data store we must provide the appropriate `Command` objects for the `UpdateCommand`, `DeleteCommand`, and `InsertCommand` properties of the `DataAdapter`.

We don't always need all three, for example if we are only changing existing rows within the data source (that is our `DataSet` object only contains modified rows and no new or deleted rows), we only need to specify a suitable `Command` object for the `UpdateCommand` property of the `DataAdapter`. The same logic applies if we are only deleting rows or inserting new rows. However, if the `DataSet` contains modified, deleted, and new rows, we have to specify suitable `Command` objects for all the matching `DataAdapter` properties.

What is a suitable `Command` object? It's pretty obvious that this is a `Command` that has a connection specified to the appropriate data store (via its associated `Connection` object), and which specifies a suitable SQL statement or stored procedure that will add, delete or update the rows. We'll see some examples later in this section that show this in more detail. However, ADO.NET can also help out by generating suitable SQL statements automatically for us.

Command Builder Objects and Auto-generated Commands

ADO.NET tries to make our life easier when we use a `DataSet` to update a data store by providing two `CommandBuilder` objects – the `SqlCommandBuilder` for use with SQL TDS and the `OleDbCommandBuilder` for use with an OLE-DB provider. These objects can create suitable "**auto-generated commands**" for use when pushing changes back to a data store via a `DataAdapter` object.

All we have to do is create a `CommandBuilder` object, specifying as the parameter to its constructor the `DataAdapter` we want to use it with. Then we call the methods of the `CommandBuilder` to create and return `Command` objects that specify the appropriate SQL statements (it can figure these out by looking at the `SelectCommand` and the table and column mappings and structure of the `DataSet`). We can then assign the returned `Command` object directly to the `DataAdapter`:

```
Dim objCommandBuilder As New OleDbCommandBuilder(objDataAdapter)

'set the update, insert and delete commands for the DataAdapter
objDataAdapter.DeleteCommand = objCommandBuilder.GetDeleteCommand()
objDataAdapter.InsertCommand = objCommandBuilder.GetInsertCommand()
objDataAdapter.UpdateCommand = objCommandBuilder.GetUpdateCommand()
```

We'll see what the SQL statements that these methods create look like in the next example in this chapter. In the meantime, however, you should be aware of a few limitations of the auto-generated command feature:

❑ The rows in a table in the DataSet must have originally come from a single table, and can be used only to update a table of the same format (generally the same source table).

❑ The source table must have a primary key defined (it can be a multiple-column primary key), or it must have at least one column that contains unique values. This column (or columns) must be included in the rows that are returned by the SELECT statement or query that is used for the SelectCommand.

❑ Table names that include special characters such as spaces, periods, quotation marks, or other non-alphanumeric characters cannot be used (even if delimited by square brackets). However, fully qualified table names that do include the period character (such as dbo.BookList) can be used.

Of course, we can create our own command strings if required, rather than using the auto-generated commands provided by the CommandBuilder, and have the DataAdapter use these instead of the auto-generated ones. In a later example, we'll see how this is useful when we are working with stored procedures that perform the updates to the data store – rather than with SQL statements.

Using the DataAdapter.Update Method

The example page Updating Data with a DataAdapter and DataSet Object (update-with-dataset.aspx) demonstrates the simplest way to use a DataAdapter object to update the source data with changes made to the rows stored in a DataSet object. The example simply reads in a rowset from the BookList table in our WroxBooks sample database, changes some of the rows, then pushes the changes back into the data store.

The code in the page deletes or removes four rows from the original table, modifies values in three other rows, and adds a new row. You can see this by comparing the contents of the table in the two DataGrid controls on the page:

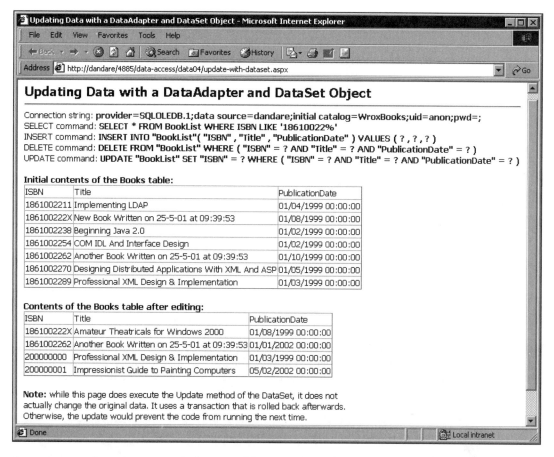

As you can see from the note at the bottom of the page, the code uses a connection-based transaction to prevent the changes being permanently applied to the source data. If they were, the example page would fail to work the next time, as some of the records would have been deleted and primary key violations would occur due to the new row already being present in the source table. However, you can change the code to commit the transaction if you wish – to see that it actually works and does update the original data.

You can also see the auto-generated commands that are used by the DataAdapter to update the source data. It's obvious that these are SQL statements – with question-mark characters as placeholders for the values used to update the table in our target data source. We'll look at them in more detail later in this section.

The Code for the 'Updating with a DataAdapter' Example

The SELECT statement that we use is simple enough – it just selects a subset of the rows in our BookList table:

```
strSelect = "SELECT * FROM BookList WHERE ISBN LIKE '18610022%'"
```

Then we can use the now familiar technique to create and fill the `DataSet` with our source data. We covered all this in detail in previous chapters, so we're simply listing the code here:

```
Dim objDataSet As New DataSet()
Dim objConnect As New OleDbConnection(strConnect)
Dim objDataAdapter As New OleDbDataAdapter(strSelect, objConnect)

Try

    objDataAdapter.Fill(objDataSet, "Books")

Catch objError As Exception

    outError.innerHTML = "* Error while accessing data.<br />" _
        & objError.Message & "<br />" & objError.Source
    Exit Sub

End Try
```

In our example, we want to be able to see which rows have been changed, and the `Update` method also depends on this information to be able to correctly update the original data in our database. Once way to "fix" the current state of all the rows in all the tables in a `DataSet` (as we saw in the previous chapter) is to call the `AcceptChanges` method to accept all the changes that have been made to the `DataSet`.

In fact, in our example, it's not strictly necessary because the `Fill` method automatically sets the status of all the rows to "Unchanged". However it illustrates the process, and would be necessary if we had made any changes since we originally filled the `DataSet` that we don't want to flush back into the database. In later examples, we'll be taking advantage of this:

```
'accept the changes to "fix" the current state of the DataSet contents
objDataSet.AcceptChanges()
```

We'll also need to reference the `Books` table in our `DataSet` in several places within our code, so we create that reference next:

```
'declare a variable to reference the Books table
Dim objTable As DataTable = objDataSet.Tables("Books")
```

And then we can display the contents of the `Books` table that is currently held in our `DataSet`. We simply bind the default view of the table to a `DataGrid` control named `dgrResult1` that is declared elsewhere in the HTML section of the page:

```
'display the contents of the Books table before changing data
dgrResult1.DataSource = objTable.DefaultView
dgrResult1.DataBind() 'and bind (display) the data
```

Changing the Rows in the DataSet

Now we're ready to make some changes to the data. This is exactly the same technique as we used in previous chapters. After making these changes to the Books table in our DataSet we display the contents again:

```
'now change some records in the Books table
objTable.Rows(0).Delete()
objTable.Rows(1)("Title") = "Amateur Theatricals for Windows 2000"
objTable.Rows(2).Delete()
objTable.Rows(3).Delete()
objTable.Rows(4)("PublicationDate") = "01-01-2002"   'see note below
objTable.Rows.Remove(5)
'notice that using the Remove method on row 5 (rather than marking
'it as deleted) means that the next row then becomes row 5
objTable.Rows(5)("ISBN") = "200000000"

'add a new row using an array of values
Dim objValsArray(2) As Object
objValsArray(0) = "200000001"
objValsArray(1) = "Impressionist Guide to Painting Computers"
objValsArray(2) = "05-02-2002"   'see note below
objTable.Rows.Add(objValsArray)

'display the contents of the Books table after changing the data
dgrResult2.DataSource = objTable.DefaultView
dgrResult2.DataBind() 'and bind (display) the data
```

Notice that we have to use a date string that is in the correct format for the column in our table. In the example where we set the value of a parameter object, we used the format "yyyy-mm-dd" as this is a suitable format for the SQL DateTime field. Here we're using the format "mm-dd-yyyy" as this is the format of the table column.

Creating the Auto-Generated Commands

OK, so now we can update our data source. The first step in this part of the process is to create the commands that the DataAdapter will use to push the changes into the database. We use the OleDbCommandBuilder object to create the three Command objects it requires, and we assign these to the appropriate properties of the DataAdapter:

```
'create an auto-generated command builder to create the commands
'for updating, inserting and deleting rows in the database
Dim objCommandBuilder As New OleDbCommandBuilder(objDataAdapter)

'set the update, insert and delete commands for the DataAdapter
objDataAdapter.DeleteCommand = objCommandBuilder.GetDeleteCommand()
objDataAdapter.InsertCommand = objCommandBuilder.GetInsertCommand()
objDataAdapter.UpdateCommand = objCommandBuilder.GetUpdateCommand()
```

Pushing the Changes Back into the Data Source

As we are using a transaction in our example (so that you have to rerun the page) we have to explicitly open the connection to the database. If we weren't using a transaction, we could remove the `Open` method call as well (the `DataAdapter` automatically opens the connection when we call the `Update` method, then closes it afterwards). We follow this with a call to the `BeginTransaction` method of the connection:

```
'start a transaction so we can roll back changes if required
objConnect.Open()
objConnect.BeginTransaction()
```

Next (only because we're using a transaction in our example) we have to explicitly enroll all the `Command` objects into the transaction. Then we can call the `Update` method of the `DataAdapter` to push all the changes we've made to the rows in the `DataSet` back into the data source automatically. Notice that we specify the name of the table that contains the changes we want to push back into the data source:

```
'attach the current transaction to all the Command objects
'must be done after setting Connection property
objDataAdapter.DeleteCommand.Transaction = objTransaction
objDataAdapter.InsertCommand.Transaction = objTransaction
objDataAdapter.UpdateCommand.Transaction = objTransaction

'perform the update on the original data
objDataAdapter.Update(objDataSet, "Books")
```

Normally that's all we would need to do. However, we are performing the update within a transaction so that we can roll it back again afterwards – allowing you to run the same page again without getting the errors that would occur from inserting and deleting the same rows again. So we finish off by rolling back this transaction:

```
objTransaction.Rollback()
```

Viewing the Auto-generated Commands

Our example page displays the auto-generated commands that were created by the `CommandBuilder` object so that you can see what they look like. At the end of the page is the following code:

```
'display the SQL statements that the DataSet used
'these are created automatically when Update is called
outInsert.InnerText = objDataAdapter.InsertCommand.CommandText
outDelete.InnerText = objDataAdapter.DeleteCommand.CommandText
outUpdate.InnerText = objDataAdapter.UpdateCommand.CommandText
```

The SQL statement (the `CommandText`) for each of the commands is displayed in a `<div>` near the top of the page. We've repeated the first part of the screenshot for this example again here:

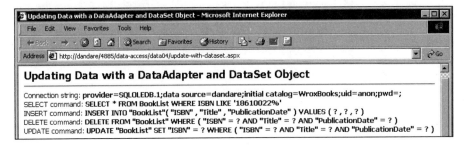

You can see that these are "outline" or "pseudo" SQL statements containing question-mark placeholders where the values from each row are placed when the statements are executed. Notice how they only perform the action on the source table if the row has not been changed by another process in the meantime (that is while the `DataSet` was holding the rows). The `DataSet` is a disconnected data repository, and so the original data could have been updated, existing rows deleted, or new rows added with the same primary key by another user or process.

Later in this chapter we'll be looking in detail at how ADO.NET manages concurrent updates to a data store, and how you can manage these yourself. In the meantime, there are a few other issues that we need to look at when using the `Update` method of the `DataAdapter` object.

Checking How Many Rows Were Updated

The `Update` method returns the number of rows that were updated in the source table. While we didn't take advantage of this in our examples, it's pretty easy to do. We simply declare an `Integer` variable and assign the result of the `Update` method to it:

```
Dim intRowsUpdated As Integer
intRowsUpdated = objDataAdapter.Update(objDataSet, "table-name")
```

Specifying the Tables When Updating Data

As we've seen, the `DataAdapter` object's `Update` method provides a really easy and efficient way to update the source data. If we have more than one table in the `DataSet`, we simply call the method once for each table to automatically update the source data with all the changes to rows in that table. The changes are applied in the order that the rows exist within the table in the `DataSet`.

There is one point to watch out for, however. If the source data tables contain foreign keys, in other words there are enforceable relationships between the tables, the order that the tables are processed can cause errors to occur. It all depends on the type of updates you're carrying out, and the rules or triggers you have inside the source database.

For example, if our `DataSet` contained rows that originally came from the `BookList`, `AuthorList`, and `BookPrices` tables, we could add a new book to the `Books` table in the `DataSet` and add matching rows (based in the ISBN that acts as the primary and foreign keys) to the `Authors` and `Prices` tables in the `DataSet`.

When we come to execute the `Update` method, however, it will only work if the `Books` table is the first one to be processed. If we try to process the `Authors` or `Prices` table first, the database will report an error because there will be no parent row with an ISBN value to match the newly inserted child rows. We are trying to insert orphan rows into the database table, and thus breaking referential integrity rules.

In other words, to insert a new book in our example, we would have to use:

```
objDataAdapter.Update(objDataSet, "Books")
objDataAdapter.Update(objDataSet, "Authors")
objDataAdapter.Update(objDataSet, "Prices")
```

However, if we have deleted a book and all its child rows from the `Authors` and `Prices` table, the opposite applies. We can't delete the parent row while there are child rows in the database table, unless the database contains rules or triggers that cascade the deletes to remove the child rows. And if it does, the delete operations carried out for the child tables would fail, because the rows would have already been deleted. This means that we probably want to process the `Books` table in our `DataSet` last rather than first:

```
objDataAdapter.Update(objDataSet, "Authors")
objDataAdapter.Update(objDataSet, "Prices")
objDataAdapter.Update(objDataSet, "Books")
```

But if we have carried out both insert and delete operations on the tables, neither method will work correctly. In this case, we need to process the updates in a more strictly controlled order. We'll look at what this involves in a short while. First, we'll briefly examine some of the other ways that we can use the Update method.

Automatically Updating the Default Table in a DataSet

If we have created a table mapping in the DataSet for the default table, we can execute the Update method without specifying the table name. We discussed how we create table mappings in the previous chapter. Basically, we create a variable to hold a TableMapping object and then call the Add method of the DataAdapter object's TableMappings collection to create the new table mapping. We specify the string "Table" to indicate that we are creating a default table mapping, and the name of the table:

```
Dim objTableMapping As DataTableMapping
objTableMapping = objDSCommand.TableMappings.Add("Table", "DefaultBookList")
```

Now we can call the Update method without specifying the name of the table:

```
objDSCommand.Update(objDataSet)
```

An error occurs if this mapping does not exist when the Update method is called without specifying the name of a table.

Updating Subsets of Rows from a Table

The DataSetCommand object's Update method can also be used to push changes from a collection or array of DataRow objects into the data source. All the rows must come from the same source table, and there must be a default table mapping set up as described in the previous section. The updates are then processed in the order that they exist in the array.

To create an array of DataRow objects we can use the All property of a table's Rows collection:

```
Dim arrRows() As DataRow
arrRows = objDataSet.Tables(0).Rows.All
```

Then we can push the changes in this array of rows into the data source using the Update method and specifying this array:

```
objDSCommand.Update(arrRows)
```

This technique is useful if we have an array of rows that contain our changed records – rather than one that contains all the rows in the original table (as shown above).

Updating from a DataSet using Stored Procedures

Near the start of the chapter, we showed you how we can use stored procedures within a database to update the source data. In that example, we used a `Command` object to execute the stored procedures. Meanwhile the previous example showed how we use the auto-generated commands with a `DataSet` to update data automatically.

Of course, we don't **have** to use auto-generated commands with a `DataSet`. Instead we can use our own custom SQL statements or stored procedures to do the same thing. We just create the appropriate `Command` objects for the `InsertCommand`, `DeleteCommand`, and `UpdateCommand` properties of the `DataAdapter`, and call the `Update` method as before. Then our custom SQL statements or stored procedures are used to push the changes back into the data store.

The previous example also updated only a single table (a prerequisite when using the auto-generated commands). However, often we have a more complex task to accomplish when updating the source data. For example, the rows in the table in our `DataSet` might have originally been created from several source tables, perhaps by using a `JOIN` statement in the SQL query or some clever stored procedure.

This was demonstrated at the beginning of the previous chapter, where we had a table containing data drawn from both the `BookList` and the `BookAuthors` tables in our sample database. When we come to push changes to data like this back into our database, we need to use some process that can disentangle the values in each row and perform a series of staged updates to the original tables, thereby maintaining integrity within the database.

The example page Updating Complex Data with a DataSet and Stored Procedures (`complex-dataset-update.aspx`) demonstrates all of these techniques and features. It extracts some data from our sample database using a SQL `JOIN` statement and displays it. It then changes some of the rows in the original table and displays the data again. Finally, it pushes the changes back into the data source using stored procedures that we've provided within the database:

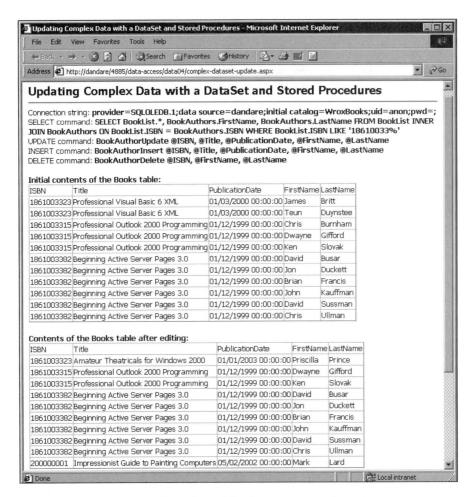

At the top of the page you can see the values of the four `Command` objects' `CommandText` properties. Notice that, while the `SelectCommand` is a SQL statement (one we specified to extract the data from the database), the other three are obviously not auto-generated SQL statements. They don't contain the question-mark placeholders. In fact they are the names of three stored procedures within our sample database (our code adds the names of the parameters to the display as well – these are not actually part of the command strings).

At the bottom of the page (not visible in the screenshot) is a note about the transaction that we use to prevent the updates being permanently committed to the data store so that you can rerun the page (without this the updates to the source data would prevent the page from working next time).

The Stored Procedures for the 'Updating Complex Data' Example

Our `DataSet` table holds rows that are created from two different tables in the database via a SQL `JOIN` statement, and so we need to update these two tables to persist any inserts, deletes or updates that are made to rows in the table in the `DataSet`. To do this, we use three stored procedures.

The `BookAuthorUpdate` stored procedure takes as parameters the ISBN of the book (which is the primary key in the `BookList` table and the foreign key in the `Authors` table), the book title and publication date, and the author's first and last names. It uses these values to update the matching row in the `BookAuthors` table and the matching row in the `BookList` table:

```
CREATE PROCEDURE BookAuthorUpdate
@ISBN varchar(12), @Title varchar(100), @PublicationDate datetime,
@FirstName varchar(50), @LastName varchar(50) AS
UPDATE BookList SET Title=@Title, PublicationDate=@PublicationDate
    WHERE ISBN=@ISBN
UPDATE BookAuthors SET FirstName=@FirstName, LastName=@LastName
    WHERE ISBN=@ISBN
```

In fact this is only a simple example, and won't work if there is more than one author for the book we are updating. While we could have created more complex procedures to handle all the scenarios, that isn't the focus of this example. As it stands, it will suffice to demonstrate the techniques of using custom commands with a DataAdapter object that we're exploring here.

The `BookAuthorInsert` stored procedure takes the same parameters as the previous one. It inserts a new row into the `BookList` table and then inserts a new row into the `BookAuthors` table using the parameter values:

```
CREATE PROCEDURE BookAuthorInsert
@ISBN varchar(12), @Title varchar(100), @PublicationDate datetime,
@FirstName varchar(50), @LastName varchar(50) AS
SELECT ISBN FROM BookList WHERE ISBN=@ISBN
IF @@ROWCOUNT = 0
  BEGIN
    INSERT INTO BookList(ISBN, Title, PublicationDate)
      VALUES (@ISBN, @Title, @PublicationDate)
  END
INSERT INTO BookAuthors(ISBN, FirstName, LastName)
  VALUES (@ISBN, @FirstName, @LastName)
```

Finally, the `BookAuthorDelete` stored procedure takes only three parameters – the ISBN of the book, and the first and last name of the author (these last two values act as the key for the `BookAuthors` table). It deletes the matching child row in the `BookAuthors` table and then deletes the matching parent row in the `BookList` table:

```
CREATE PROCEDURE BookAuthorDelete
@ISBN varchar(12), @FirstName varchar(50), @LastName varchar(50) AS
DELETE FROM BookAuthors
    WHERE ISBN=@ISBN AND FirstName=@FirstName AND LastName=@LastName
SELECT ISBN FROM BookAuthors WHERE ISBN=@ISBN
IF @@ROWCOUNT = 0
  BEGIN
    DELETE FROM BookList WHERE ISBN=@ISBN
  END
```

Again, this won't work if there is more than one author for the book we are deleting. However, it will suffice to demonstrate the techniques of using custom commands with a DataAdapter object that we're exploring here.

The Code for the 'Updating with Stored Procedures' Example

So, all we need to do now is use these three stored procedures as the command text for the Command objects in the DataAdapter object's UpdateCommand, InsertCommand, and DeleteCommand properties. The first part of the code in the page simply fills the DataSet from the database using the same techniques as we did in earlier examples and earlier chapters, so we aren't repeating that here.

Creating the Command Objects

Once we've created and filled our DataSet, changed some rows and displayed the changes, we can set to building the Command objects we need. We start with the one for the UpdateCommand. We create a new Command object and specify that the CommandType is a stored procedure:

```
Dim objUpdateCommand As New OleDbCommand("BookAuthorUpdate", objConnect)
objUpdateCommand.CommandType = CommandType.StoredProcedure
```

Creating the UpdateCommand Dynamic Parameters

Next we create the parameters that we'll use with this Command object. Notice that, in this example, we are specifying which column will provide the value for the parameter when the Command is executed rather than specifying actual values for the parameters. We are creating a **dynamic parameter** that is the equivalent to the question-mark placeholder you saw in the SQL statement for the update command in the previous example. Remember that this command will be executed once for each row in the DataSet table that has been modified (in other words has a RowState property value of DataRowState.Modified).

To specify a dynamic parameter, we set the SourceColumn property of the Parameter object to the name of the column from which the value for the parameter will come. However, you'll recall that each column can expose four different values (the DataRowVersion): Original, Current, Default, and Proposed. We specify which of these values we want the parameter to use by setting the SourceVersion property of the Parameter object as well.

This means that we can specify the original value of the column as the parameter value (useful if it is being used to look up or match a value with the original value of that column in the source table), or the Current value of the column if we are updating that column in the table. In other words, we would specify that the parameter should use the Original value of this column from each row when it's part of the SQL WHERE clause (and so should match the existing value in the database tables) or the Current value when it's part of the SET clause.

Our first parameter is used to match the ISBN code, and so it uses the Original value of that column:

```
Dim objParam As OleDbParameter
objParam = objUpdateCommand.Parameters.Add("ISBN", OleDbType.VarChar, 12)
objParam.Direction = ParameterDirection.Input
objParam.SourceColumn = "ISBN"
objParam.SourceVersion = DataRowVersion.Original
```

The code is similar for the remaining four parameters. However, this time we want to use the Current version of the data for each column in the rows, because this value is part of the SQL SET clause and will be used to update the original rows in the database tables:

```
        objParam = objUpdateCommand.Parameters.Add("Title", _
                                         OleDbType.VarChar, 100)
        objParam.Direction = ParameterDirection.Input
        objParam.SourceColumn = "Title"
        objParam.SourceVersion = DataRowVersion.Current

        objParam = objUpdateCommand.Parameters.Add("PublicationDate", _
                                         OleDbType.DBDate)
        objParam.Direction = ParameterDirection.Input
        objParam.SourceColumn = "PublicationDate"
        objParam.SourceVersion = DataRowVersion.Current

        objParam = objUpdateCommand.Parameters.Add("FirstName", _
                                         OleDbType.VarChar, 50)
        objParam.Direction = ParameterDirection.Input
        objParam.SourceColumn = "FirstName"
        objParam.SourceVersion = DataRowVersion.Current

        objParam = objUpdateCommand.Parameters.Add("LastName", _
                                         OleDbType.VarChar, 50)
        objParam.Direction = ParameterDirection.Input
        objParam.SourceColumn = "LastName"
        objParam.SourceVersion = DataRowVersion.Current
```

The parameters are now ready, and we can specify that this `Command` object be used as the update command by assigning it to the `DataAdapter` object's `UpdateCommand` property:

```
        objDataAdapter.UpdateCommand = objUpdateCommand
```

Creating the InsertCommand Parameters

The `InsertCommand` uses basically the same parameters as the `UpdateCommand`. We use the name of the "insert" stored procedure in the constructor for the `Command` object, then create the parameters as before. The only other difference is that the `InsertCommand` stored procedure uses the ISBN value in the `SET` clause of the SQL statement rather than the `WHERE` clause to set the value of the newly inserted rows. In other words it needs to use the `Current` value of the column and not the `Original` value:

```
        Dim objInsertCommand As New OleDbCommand("BookAuthorInsert", objConnect)
        objInsertCommand.CommandType = CommandType.StoredProcedure

        objParam = objInsertCommand.Parameters.Add("ISBN", _
                                         OleDbType.VarChar, 12)
        objParam.Direction = ParameterDirection.Input
        objParam.SourceColumn = "ISBN"
        objParam.SourceVersion = DataRowVersion.Current

        objParam = objInsertCommand.Parameters.Add("Title", _
                                         OleDbType.VarChar, 100)
        objParam.Direction = ParameterDirection.Input
        objParam.SourceColumn = "Title"
        objParam.SourceVersion = DataRowVersion.Current
```

```
objParam = objInsertCommand.Parameters.Add("PublicationDate", _
                                             OleDbType.DBDate)
objParam.Direction = ParameterDirection.Input
objParam.SourceColumn = "PublicationDate"
objParam.SourceVersion = DataRowVersion.Current

objParam = objInsertCommand.Parameters.Add("FirstName", _
                                             OleDbType.VarChar, 50)
objParam.Direction = ParameterDirection.Input
objParam.SourceColumn = "FirstName"
objParam.SourceVersion = DataRowVersion.Current

objParam = objInsertCommand.Parameters.Add("LastName", _
                                             OleDbType.VarChar, 50)
objParam.Direction = ParameterDirection.Input
objParam.SourceColumn = "LastName"
objParam.SourceVersion = DataRowVersion.Current
```

And finally we can specify that this Command object is the insert command by assigning it to the DataAdapter object's InsertCommand property:

```
objDataAdapter.InsertCommand = objInsertCommand
```

Creating the DeleteCommand Parameters

The third and final stored procedure is used to delete rows from the source table. It requires three parameters, and the code to create them is very similar to that we've just been using with the other Command objects:

```
Dim objDeleteCommand As New OleDbCommand("BookAuthorDelete", objConnect)
objDeleteCommand.CommandType = CommandType.StoredProcedure

objParam = objDeleteCommand.Parameters.Add("ISBN", _
                                             OleDbType.VarChar, 12)
objParam.Direction = ParameterDirection.Input
objParam.SourceColumn = "ISBN"
objParam.SourceVersion = DataRowVersion.Original

objParam = objDeleteCommand.Parameters.Add("FirstName", _
                                             OleDbType.VarChar, 50)
objParam.Direction = ParameterDirection.Input
objParam.SourceColumn = "FirstName"
objParam.SourceVersion = DataRowVersion.Original

objParam = objDeleteCommand.Parameters.Add("LastName", _
                                             OleDbType.VarChar, 50)
objParam.Direction = ParameterDirection.Input
objParam.SourceColumn = "LastName"
objParam.SourceVersion = DataRowVersion.Original

objDataAdapter.DeleteCommand = objDeleteCommand
```

Displaying the Command Properties

Now that the three new `Command` objects are ready, we display the `CommandText` and the parameters for each one in the page. Notice that we can iterate through the `Parameters` collection with a `For Each..Next` construct to get the values:

```
Dim strSQL As String   'create a new string to store vales

'get stored procedure name and source column names for each parameter
strSQL = objDataAdapter.UpdateCommand.CommandText
For Each objParam In objDataAdapter.UpdateCommand.Parameters
    strSQL += " @" & objParam.SourceColumn & ","
Next
strSQL = Left(strSQL, Len(strSQL) -1)    'remove trailing comma
outUpdate.InnerText = strSQL    'and display it

'repeat the process for the Insert command
...

'repeat the process for the Delete command
...
```

Executing the Update

Then we simply call the `Update` method of the `DataAdapter` to push our changes into the database via the stored procedures in exactly the same way as we did in previous examples. As in earlier examples, this page uses a transaction to make it repeatable, so the code is a little more complex than is actually required simply to push those changes into the database. Basically, all we need is:

```
objDataAdapter.Update(objDataSet, "Books")
```

The code to create the transaction is the same as we used in the previous example, and you can use the [view source] link at the bottom of the page to see it. To prove that the updates do actually get carried out, you can also change the code so that the transaction is committed, or remove the transaction code altogether.

Update Events in the DataAdapter

In the previous chapter we saw how we can write event handlers for several events that occur for a row in a table when that row is updated. In the examples we used, the row was held in a `DataTable` object within a `DataSet`, and the events occurred when we updated the row. There is another useful series of events that we can handle, but this time they occur when we come to push the changes back into the original data store using a `DataAdapter` object.

The `DataAdapter` exposes two events: the `RowUpdating` event occurs before an attempt is made to update the row in the data source, and the `RowUpdated` event occurs after the row has been updated (or after an error has been detected – a topic we'll look at later). This means that we can monitor the updates as they take place for each row when we use the `Update` method of the `DataAdapter`.

Handling the RowUpdating and RowUpdated Events

The example page Handling the RowUpdating and RowUpdated Events (`rowupdated-event.aspx`) demonstrates how we can use these events to monitor the update process in a `DataAdapter` object. When you open the page, you see the now familiar `DataGrid` objects containing the data before and after it has been updated by code within the page:

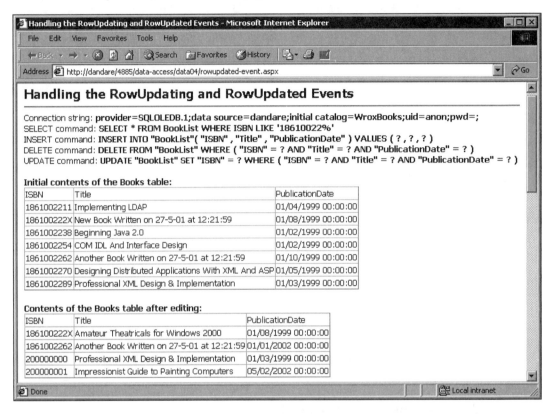

You can also see the SQL `SELECT` statement that we used to extract the data, and the three auto-generated statements that are used to perform the updates. This page uses exactly the same code as the earlier `DataAdapter.Update` example to extract and edit the data, and to push the changes back into the database.

However, you can see the extra features of this page if your scroll down beyond the `DataGrid` controls. The remainder of the page contains output that is generated by the handlers we've provided for the `RowUpdating` and `RowUpdated` events (not all are visible in the screenshot):

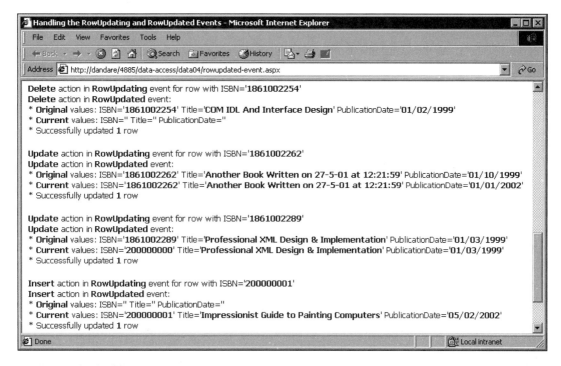

Inside the browser window:

```
Delete action in RowUpdating event for row with ISBN='1861002254'
Delete action in RowUpdated event:
* Original values: ISBN='1861002254' Title='COM IDL And Interface Design' PublicationDate='01/02/1999'
* Current values: ISBN='' Title='' PublicationDate=''
* Successfully updated 1 row

Update action in RowUpdating event for row with ISBN='1861002262'
Update action in RowUpdated event:
* Original values: ISBN='1861002262' Title='Another Book Written on 27-5-01 at 12:21:59' PublicationDate='01/10/1999'
* Current values: ISBN='1861002262' Title='Another Book Written on 27-5-01 at 12:21:59' PublicationDate='01/01/2002'
* Successfully updated 1 row

Update action in RowUpdating event for row with ISBN='1861002289'
Update action in RowUpdated event:
* Original values: ISBN='1861002289' Title='Professional XML Design & Implementation' PublicationDate='01/03/1999'
* Current values: ISBN='200000000' Title='Professional XML Design & Implementation' PublicationDate='01/03/1999'
* Successfully updated 1 row

Insert action in RowUpdating event for row with ISBN='200000001'
Insert action in RowUpdated event:
* Original values: ISBN='' Title='' PublicationDate=''
* Current values: ISBN='200000001' Title='Impressionist Guide to Painting Computers' PublicationDate='05/02/2002'
* Successfully updated 1 row
```

Attaching the Event Handlers

The only difference to the code we used in the earlier example is the addition of two event handlers. We have to attach these event handlers, which we've named OnRowUpdating and OnRowUpdated, to the DataAdapter object's RowUpdating and RowUpdated properties. In Visual Basic, we use the AddHandler statement for this:

```
'set up event handlers to react to update events
AddHandler objDataAdapter.RowUpdating, _
        New OleDbRowUpdatingEventHandler(AddressOf OnRowUpdating)
AddHandler objDataAdapter.RowUpdated, _
        New OleDbRowUpdatedEventHandler(AddressOf OnRowUpdated)
```

The OnRowUpdating Event Handler

When the DataAdapter comes to push the changes to a row into the data store, it first raises the RowUpdating event, which will now execute our event handler named OnRowUpdating. Our code receives two parameters, a reference to the object that raised the event and a reference to a RowUpdatingEventArgs object.

> *As we're using the objects from the System.Data.OleDb namespace in this example, we actually get an OleDbRowUpdatingEventArgs object. If we were using the objects from the System.Data.SqlClient namespace, we would, of course, get a reference to a SqlDbRowUpdatingEventArgs object.*

495

The `RowUpdatingEventArgs` object provides a series of "fields" or properties that contain useful information about the event:

`StatementType`	A value from the `StatementType` enumeration indicating the type of SQL statement that will be executed to update the data. Can be `Insert`, `Update` or `Delete`.
`Row`	A reference to the `DataRow` object that contains the data being used to update the data source.
`Status`	A value from the `UpdateStatus` enumeration that reports the current status of the update and allows it and subsequent updates to be cancelled. Possible values are: `Continue`, `SkipCurrentRow`, `SkipAllRemainingRows`, and `ErrorsOccurred`.
`Command`	A reference to the `Command` object that will execute the update.
`TableMapping`	A reference to the `DataTableMapping` that will be used for the update.

Our event handler collects the statement type (by querying the `StatementType` enumeration), and uses this value to decide where to get the row values for display. If it's an `Insert` statement, the `Current` value of the `ISBN` column in the row will contain the new primary key for that row, and the `Original` value will be empty. However, if it's an `Update` or `Delete` statement, the `Original` value will be the primary key of the original row in the database that corresponds to the row in our `DataSet`.

So, we can extract the primary key of the row that is about to be pushed into the database and display it, along with the statement type, in our page:

```
Sub OnRowUpdating(objSender As Object, _
                  objArgs As OleDbRowUpdatingEventArgs)

    'get the text description of the StatementType
    Dim strType = System.Enum.GetName(objArgs.StatementType.GetType(), _
                                      objArgs.StatementType)

    'get the value of the primary key column "ISBN"
    Dim strISBNValue As String
    Select Case strType
        Case "Insert"
            strISBNValue = objArgs.Row("ISBN", DataRowVersion.Current)
        Case Else
            strISBNValue = objArgs.Row("ISBN", DataRowVersion.Original)
    End Select

    'add result to display string
    gstrResult += strType & " action in RowUpdating event " _
            & "for row with ISBN='" & strISBNValue & "'<br />"
End Sub
```

The OnRowUpdated Event Handler

After the row has been updated in the database, or when an error occurs, our `OnRowUpdated` event handler will be executed. In this case, we get a reference to a `RowUpdatedEventArgs` object instead of a `RowUpdatingEventArgs` object. It provides two more useful fields:

Errors	An `Error` object containing details of any error that was generated by the data provider when executing the update.
RecordsAffected	The number of rows that were changed, inserted, or deleted by execution of the SQL statement. Expect 1 on success and zero or -1 if there is an error.

So, in our `OnRowUpdated` event handler, we can provide information about what happened after the update. Again we collect the statement type, but this time we also collect all the `Original` and `Current` values from the columns in the row. Of course, if it is an `Insert` statement, there won't be any `Original` values as the row has been added to the table in the `DataSet` since the `DataSet` was originally filled. Likewise, there won't be any `Current` values if this row has been deleted in the `DataSet`:

```
'event handler for the RowUpdated event
Sub OnRowUpdated(objSender As Object, objArgs As OleDbRowUpdatedEventArgs)

    'get the text description of the StatementType
    Dim strType = System.Enum.GetName(objArgs.StatementType.GetType(), _
                                      objArgs.StatementType)

    'get the value of the columns
    Dim strISBNCurrent, strISBNOriginal, strTitleCurrent As String
    Dim strTitleOriginal, strPubDateCurrent, strPubDateOriginal As String
    Select Case strType
        Case "Insert"
            strISBNCurrent = objArgs.Row("ISBN", DataRowVersion.Current)
            strTitleCurrent = objArgs.Row("Title", DataRowVersion.Current)
            strPubDateCurrent = objArgs.Row("PublicationDate", _
                                      DataRowVersion.Current)
        Case "Delete"
            strISBNOriginal = objArgs.Row("ISBN", DataRowVersion.Original)
            strTitleOriginal = objArgs.Row("Title", DataRowVersion.Original)
            strPubDateOriginal = objArgs.Row("PublicationDate", _
                                      DataRowVersion.Original)
        Case "Update"
            strISBNCurrent = objArgs.Row("ISBN", DataRowVersion.Current)
            strTitleCurrent = objArgs.Row("Title", DataRowVersion.Current)
            strPubDateCurrent = objArgs.Row("PublicationDate", _
                                      DataRowVersion.Current)
            strISBNOriginal = objArgs.Row("ISBN", DataRowVersion.Original)
            strTitleOriginal = objArgs.Row("Title", DataRowVersion.Original)
            strPubDateOriginal = objArgs.Row("PublicationDate", _
                                      DataRowVersion.Original)
    End Select

    'add result to display string
    gstrResult += strType & " action in RowUpdated event:<br />" _
            & "* Original values: ISBN='" & strISBNOriginal & "' " _
            & "Title='" & strTitleOriginal & "' " _
            & "PublicationDate='" & strPubDateOriginal & "'<br />" _
            & "* Current values: ISBN='" & strISBNCurrent & "' " _
            & "Title='" & strTitleCurrent & "' " _
            & "PublicationDate='" & strPubDateCurrent & "'<br />"
```

This time we can also include details about the result of the update. We query the `RecordsAffected` value to see if one row was updated (as we expect), and if not we include the error message from the `Errors` field:

```
'see if the update was successful
Dim intRows = objArgs.RecordsAffected
If intRows > 0 Then
    gstrResult += "* Successfully updated " & intRows.ToString() _
                & " row<p />"
Else
    gstrResult += "* Failed to update row <br />" _
                & objArgs.Errors.Message & "<p />"
End If

End Sub
```

AcceptChanges and the Update Process

One important point to bear in mind is how the update process affects the `Original` and `Current` values of the rows in the tables in a `DataSet`. Once the `DataAdapter.Update` process is complete (in other words all the updates for all the rows have been applied), the `AcceptChanges` method is called for those rows automatically. So, after an update, the `Current` values in all the rows are moved to the `Original` values.

However, during the update process (as you can see from our example), the `Current` and `Original` values are available in both the `RowUpdating` and the `RowUpdated` events. Therefore we can use these events to monitor changes and report errors (we'll see more in a later example).

The techniques we've used in this section of the chapter (and in earlier examples) work fine in circumstances where there are no concurrent updates taking place on the source data. In other words, there is only ever one user reading from and writing to any particular row in the tables at any one time. However, concurrency rears its ugly head in many applications, and can cause all kinds of problems if you aren't prepared for it. It's also the topic of the next section.

Managing Concurrent Data Updates

To finish off our look at relational data handling in .NET, we'll examine some of the issues that arise when we have multiple users updating our data – a problem area normally referred to as **concurrency**. It's easy enough to see how such a problem could arise:

❑   Alice in accounts receives a fax from a customer indicating that their address has changed. She opens the customer record in her browser and starts to change the address column values.

❑   Just at this moment, Dave in dispatch (who received a copy of the fax) decides to update the customer's delivery route code. He also opens the customer record in his browser and changes the routing code column value.

❑   While Dave is doing this, Alice finishes editing the address and saves the record back to the database.

❑   Shortly afterwards, Dave saves his updated record back to the database.

What's happened is that Dave's record, which was opened before Alice saved her changes, contains the old address details. So when he saves it back to the database, the changes made by Alice are lost. And while concurrency issues aren't solely confined to databases (they can be a problem in all kinds of multi-user environments) it is obviously something that we can't just ignore when we build data access applications.

Avoiding Concurrency Errors

Various database systems and applications use different approaches to control the concurrent updates problem. One solution is the use of **pessimistic record locking**. When a user wants to update a record, they open it with pessimistic locking, preventing any other user opening the same record in update mode. Other users can only open the record in 'read' mode until the first user saves their copy and releases their lock on the record.

> *For maximum run time efficiency, many database systems actually lock a 'page' containing several contiguous records rather than just a single one – but the principle is the same.*

However, in a disconnected environment (particularly one with occasionally unreliable network links such as the Internet) pessimistic locking is not really feasible. If a user opens a record and then goes away, or the network connection fails, it will not be released. It requires some other process to monitor record locks and take decisions about when and if the user will come back to update the record so that the lock can be released.

Instead, within .NET, all data access is through **optimistic record locking**, which allows multiple users to open the same record for updating – possibly leading to the scenario we described at the start of this section. It means that we have to use some kind of code that can prevent errors occurring when we need to support concurrent updates. There are a few options:

❏   We can write stored procedures that do lock records and themselves manage the updates to prevent concurrency errors. For example, we could add a column called "Locked" and set this when a user fetches a row for updating. While it's set, no other user could open the row for updating, only for reading. This is not, however, a favored approach in .NET as it takes away the advantages of the disconnected model.

❏   We can arrange for our code to only update the actual columns that it changes the value of, minimizing the risk of (but not guaranteeing to prevent) concurrency errors. For example, in the previous scenario, if Dave in dispatch had only updated the route code column that he changed the value of, Alice's changes to the address columns would not have been lost.

❏   We can compare the existing values in the records with the values that were there when we created our disconnected copy of the record. This way we can see if another user has changed any values in the database while we were working on our disconnected copy. This is the preferred solution in .NET, and there are built-in features that help us to implement it.

A Concurrency Error Example

To illustrate the way that a concurrency error can be detected, try the example page Catching Concurrency Errors When Updating the Source Data (`concurrency-error.aspx`). This page extracts a row from the source data table and displays the values in it. Then it executes a SQL statement directly against the **original** table in the database to change the Title column of the row whilst the disconnected `DataSet` is holding the original version of the row. You can see this in the screenshot after the first `DataGrid` control.

Next the code changes a couple of columns in the disconnected `DataSet` table row, then calls the `Update` method of the `DataAdapter` to push this change back into the original source table. We're using a `CommandBuilder` object to create the SQL statement that performs the update, and you can see this statement displayed in the page below the `SELECT` statement that originally fetched the row. Notice that it uses a `WHERE` clause that tests all the values of the row in the database against the values held in the `DataSet`.

499

This means, of course, that (because the concurrent process has changed the row) the update fails and an error is returned. What's happened is that the Update process expects a single row to be updated, and when this didn't happen it reports an error. The error message is displayed at the bottom of the page:

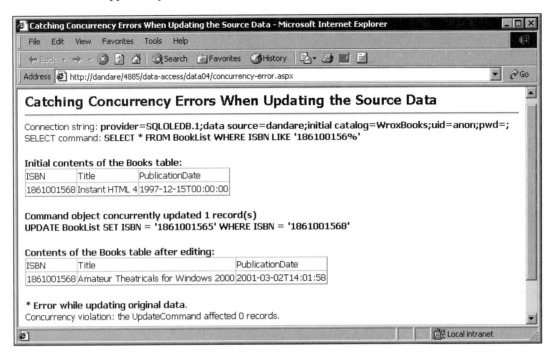

At this point, the developer would usually indicate to the user that this error had occurred, and give them the chance to reconcile the changes. Exactly how this is done, and what options the user has, depends on the application requirements. The usual process is to provide the user with the values that currently exist in the row as well as the values they entered, and allow them to specify which should be persisted into the data store.

The Code for the 'Catching Concurrency Errors' Example

The only section of the code for this example that we haven't seen before is that which performs a concurrent update to the source table in the database while the DataSet is holding a disconnected copy of the rows. It's simply a matter of creating a suitable SQL statement, a new Connection and Command object, and executing the SQL statement. We collect the number of rows affected by the update and display this in the page along with the SQL statement:

```
'change one of the rows concurrently - that is. while the
'DataSet is holding a disconnected copy of the data
Dim strUpdate As String
Dim datNow As DateTime = Now()
Dim strNow As String = datNow.ToString("dd-M-yy \a\t hh:mm:ss")
strUpdate = "UPDATE BookList SET Title = 'Book Written on " _
        & strNow & "' WHERE ISBN = '1861001622'"

Dim intRowsAffected As Integer
Dim objNewConnect As New OleDbConnection(strConnect)
Dim objNewCommand As New OleDbCommand(strUpdate, objNewConnect)
...
```

```
objNewConnect.Open()
intRowsAffected = objNewCommand.ExecuteNonQuery()
objNewConnect.Close()
...
outUpdate.InnerHtml = "Command object concurrently updated " _
        & CStr(intRowsAffected) & " record(s)<br />" & strUpdate
```

Then the code changes the disconnected copy of the row in the DataSet table:

```
'change the same row in the table in the DataSet
objTable.Rows(0)("Title") = "Amateur Theatricals for Windows 2000"
objTable.Rows(0)("PublicationDate") = Now()
```

Finally, all we have to do is execute the Update method of the DataAdapter object. The error is trapped by the Try..Catch construct (like that we've used in all the examples) and details are displayed in the page:

```
Try
    'create an auto-generated command builder and set UPDATE command
    Dim objCommandBuilder As New OleDbCommandBuilder(objDataAdapter)
    objDataAdapter.UpdateCommand = objCommandBuilder.GetUpdateCommand()

    'display the auto-generated UPDATE command statement
    outUpdate.InnerText = objDataAdapter.UpdateCommand.CommandText

    'now do the update - in this case we know it will fail
    intRowsAffected = objDataAdapter.Update(objDataSet, "Books")
    outResult.InnerHtml = "<b>* DataSet.Update</b> affected <b>" _
                    & CStr(intRowsAffected) & "</b> row."

Catch objError As Exception

    'display error details
    outError.innerHTML = "* Error updating original data.<br />" _
            & objError.Message & "<br />" & objError.Source

End Try
```

Updating Just the Changed Columns

In general, it is the process of modifying existing rows in a data store that is most likely to create a concurrency error. The process of deleting rows is usually less error-prone, and less likely to cause data inconsistencies in your database. Likewise, providing data entry programs are reasonably clever about how they create the values for unique columns, the process of inserting new rows is generally less of a problem.

One of the ways that we can reduce the likelihood of a concurrency error during row modification, as we suggested right at the start of this section of the chapter, is to push only the modified column values (the ones that have been changed by this user or process) into the original data store, rather than blindly updating all of the columns. Of course, this means that we can't use the Update method – we have to build and execute each SQL statement ourselves.

An Example of Updating Individual Columns

The example page Managing Concurrent Updates to Individual Columns (concurrency-columns.aspx) demonstrates the process we've just been discussing. Rather than updating all the columns in every row that has been modified, it only attempts to update the column values that have actually changed. The code extracts a series of rows from the BookList table and displays them, then changes some of the column values and displays the rows again:

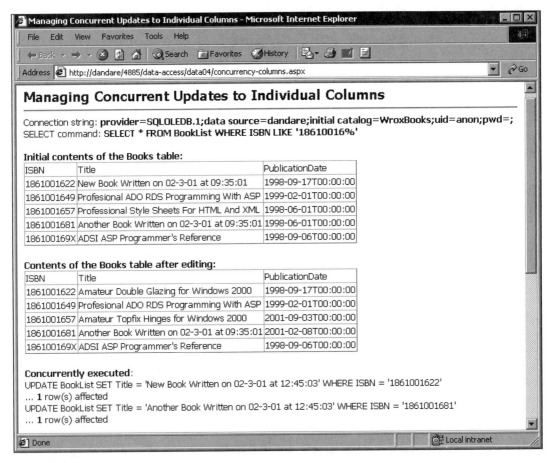

At the bottom of the page, you can see that the code concurrently updates two of the rows in the source database table while the DataSet is holding a disconnected copy of the data. Scrolling down the page, you can see that, after the concurrent updates have taken place, we attempt to push our changes in the DataSet back into the data store. However, in this case, we're processing each of the modified rows individually by executing a custom SQL statement for each one. This statement only updates the columns that have been changed within the table in the DataSet:

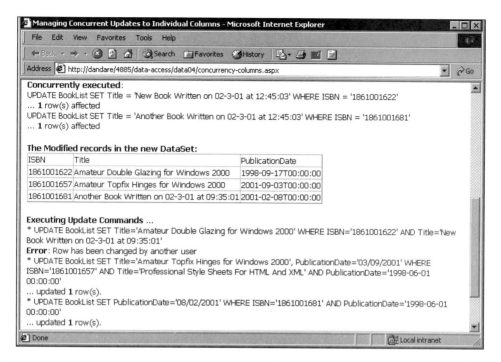

What you should be able to see here is that the first update fails because we are attempting to change the title while the concurrent process has already changed this column (look back at the previous screenshot to see the original values of the rows). Following this, the second update succeeds because the concurrent process has not changed the original row.

However, the third update **also succeeds** – even though the same row in the original table has been concurrently updated. The concurrent process changed only the title column while our disconnected copy contains an updated value for only the publication date. Hence, because our update code is clever enough to only update the changed columns, both updates can occur concurrently without risking inconsistencies arising.

The Code for the 'Updating Individual Columns' Example

There are several things going on in this example page that we need to look at in more depth. For example, we need to be able to get at just the modified rows in the table within our DataSet so that we can iterate through these rows processing the update for each one. Secondly, we need to look in more detail at how we create the values that we use in the WHERE clause of our SQL statements to compare to a DateTime column in SQL server.

Marshaling the Changed Rows in a DataSet

As we saw in the previous chapter, every row in a table within a DataSet has a RowState property that indicates whether that row has changed since the table was filled, or since the last time the AcceptChanges or RejectChanges method was called. So, to get a list of the changed rows we could iterate through the table looking at this property in each row, and extract just the ones we want into an array – or into another table.

This would allow us to take a table that contained updated, deleted and inserted rows and extract these into separate arrays of rows – one each for changed rows, deleted rows and updated rows. We could then use the `Update` *method of the* `DataAdapter` *with each table or array of rows in turn (as discussed earlier in this section of the chapter) – in the correct order to avoid any errors due to parent/child relationships within the source data tables.*

The general process of collecting together data and transferring it to another location is often referred to as **marshaling**. In our case, we want to marshal the changed rows from one table into another table, and the .NET data access classes make it easy through the `GetChanges` method of the `DataSet` object. It returns a `DataSet` object containing just the changed rows. We can use the `GetChanges` method in two ways:

❑ With no parameters, whereupon it returns a `DataSet` object with the default table (at index zero) filled with **all** the changed records – that is. all the rows that have been modified, deleted or inserted.

❑ With a `DataRowState` value as the single parameter, whereupon it returns a `DataSet` object with the default table (at index zero) filled with just the changed records having that value for their `RowState` property – that is just the rows that have been modified, or just the rows that have been deleted, or just the rows that have been inserted.

Getting the Modified Rows Into a New DataSet

The code in our page creates a variable to hold a `DataSet` object, and then executes the `GetChanges` method with the value `DataRowState.Modified` as the single parameter. The new `DataSet` object is returned and assigned to our variable `objChangeDS`, and we can display the contents in the usual way using a `DataGrid` control defined elsewhere in the page.

```
'declare a variable to hold another DataSet object
Dim objChangeDS As DataSet

'get *changed* records into the new DataSet
'copy only rows with a RowState property of "Modified"
objChangeDS = objDataSet.GetChanges(DataRowState.Modified)

'display the modified records from the table in the new DataSet
dgrResult3.DataSource = objChangeDS.Tables(0).DefaultView
dgrResult3.DataBind()   'and bind (display) the data
```

As an aside (we don't actually do it in our example here) we can use the same technique to get the inserted, deleted or unchanged rows as well. To get the inserted rows into a `DataSet` we just need to specify the value `DataRowState.Added` in the parameter to the `GetChanges` method:

```
objChangeDS = objDataSet.GetChanges(DataRowState.Added)
```

The same applies to the deleted rows, we specify `DataRowState.Deleted` in the parameter to the `GetChanges` method:

```
objChangeDS = objDataSet.GetChanges(DataRowState.Deleted)
```

However, if we then want to bind this data to a `DataGrid` object, we don't actually get anything displayed – after all the rows have been deleted so we can't really expect to see them. To get round this we have to create a `DataView` object explicitly for the table and then set the `RowStateFilter` property to `DataViewRowState.Deleted` as well (we covered this topic in the previous chapters). Then it will show the deleted records:

```
Dim objDataView As DataView = objChangeDS.Tables(0).DefaultView
objDataView.RowStateFilter = DataViewRowState.Deleted
dgrResult.DataSource = objDataView
dgrResult.DataBind()
```

Finally, to get the unchanged rows we specify `DataRowState.Unchanged` in the parameter to the `GetChanges` method:

```
objChangeDS = objDataSet.GetChanges(DataRowState.Unchanged)
```

Getting Back To Our Example

After that short aside, let's get back to the code for our example page. While there is quite a lot of code in this page, most of it is stuff that we've seen several times before. Basically, it extracts the rowset from the data store and displays it, executes a couple of SQL UPDATE statements to change the original data store contents, then changes some values in the same rows in the disconnected copy held within the `DataSet` object. All these steps can be seen in the page.

What we want to concentrate on here is how we create and execute the SQL statements that we'll use to perform the updates to the original data.

Building the SQL Statements

The plan is to create the two 'root' parts of the SQL statement (the SET clause and the WHERE clause) separately as we iterate through each column in the row, then assemble the complete statement afterwards. We've already marshaled the modified rows into a new `DataSet` named `objChangeDS`, so we can iterate through the single table in that `DataSet` processing each modified row using a For Each..Next construct. As we process each row, we create our two sections of SQL statement. For the WHERE clause we include the test for the Original value of the ISBN (the primary key):

```
'iterate through all the modified rows in the table
For Each objRow in objChangeDS.Tables(0).Rows

    'create the two root parts of the SQL statement
    strSQL = "UPDATE BookList SET "
    strWhere = " WHERE ISBN='" _
            & objRow("ISBN", DataRowVersion.Original) & "'"
```

Now we start the nested For Each..Next construct that will iterate through each column in this row, and we collect the column name in a string variable. Then we can see if the value of the column has been changed since we loaded our `DataSet` by comparing the Original and the Current values:

```
'iterate through all the columns in this row
For Each objColumn In objChangeDS.Tables(0).Columns
    strColName = objColumn.ColumnName

    'see if this column has been changed since the DataSet was
    'originally created by comparing Original and Current values
    If objRow(strColName, DataRowVersion.Current) <> _
        objRow(strColName, DataRowVersion.Original) Then
```

Note that this is nothing to do with checking the original values in the source table in the database. We're disconnected from that table, and we can't see any concurrent updates going on. What we're checking for here is if the contents of the disconnected row have been changed **within the DataSet** – since it was originally extracted from the source database.

If the column has been changed, we need to add it to both sections of the SQL statement we're constructing. However, if the value is a `DateTime`, we have to format the `Original` value (which will be used in the `WHERE` clause) to match the column in the source table in the database.

Matching a SQL Server DateTime Column

To perform a match against a SQL `DateTime` column, we have to specify the value in our disconnected row in a suitable format so that it can be compared properly. The next part of the code extracts the original value of the `PublicationDate` column from the row and formats it if it is a date/time – if not it just extracts the value:

```
'have to get format of DateTime exactly right for a comparison
If objColumn.DataType.ToString() = "System.DateTime" Then
    datRowDateValue = objRow(strColName, DataRowVersion.Original)
    strRowValue = datRowDateValue.Format("yyyy-MM-dd\ HH:mm:ss", _
                                          Nothing)
Else
    strRowValue = objRow(strColName, DataRowVersion.Original)
End If
```

Now we add the column name and values to the two sections of the SQL statement. We use the `Current` value in the `SET` clause and the `Original` value in the `WHERE` clause. Then we can go round and process the next column:

```
    strSQL += strColName & "='" _
            & objRow(strColName, DataRowVersion.Current) & "', "
    strWhere += " AND " & strColName & "='" & strRowValue & "'"

  End If

Next   'go to next column
```

Once all the changed columns have been processed, we tidy up the SQL statement by stripping off the extra comma and space we added and assemble it into one string. Then we can display it in the page:

```
'strip off extra comma and space from end of string
strSQL = Left(strSQL, Len(strSQL) -2) & strWhere

'assemble and display the SQL statement
strResults += "* " & strSQL & " ... "
objCommand.CommandText = strSQL
```

Executing the SQL Statement

Now we can execute this SQL statement and check the number of rows affected. If it is zero or -1, we know that there was a concurrency error – the original row in the source table has changed while we were holding the disconnected copy:

```
Try
   intRowsAffected = objCommand.ExecuteNonQuery()
   If intRowsAffected > 0 Then
      strResults += "... updated <b>" & intRowsAffected & "</b> row(s)"
   Else
      strResults += "<b>Error</b>: Row was changed by another user"
   End If
Catch objError As Exception
   'display error details
   strResults += "Error: " & objError.Message & " -" _
            & objError.Source & "<br />"
End Try
```

After processing this row, we go back and do the next one in our modified rows table. When all the rows have been processed, we display the result in a `<div>` element located in the HTML of the page:

```
Next                                    'repeat for next row if any
outUpdates.InnerHtml = strResults       'then display the results
```

Handling Any Concurrency Errors

Our example simply displays the errors that were encountered due to concurrent updates in the page – it doesn't provide any way to reconcile these errors. In fact, the .NET data access objects don't provide any features for this, as there is no fixed way to do it. It all depends on what your application is doing, how the updates are being carried out, and what business rules you want to apply.

Capturing Errors with the RowUpdated Event

The previous example attempted to reduce the likelihood of concurrency errors occurring by taking over the "update" process and replacing it with a custom system of SQL statements. This allows updates to be monitored individually. However, this kind of process is going to produce a performance hit when compared to the Update method exposed by the DataAdapter.

We saw in an earlier section of this chapter that the DataAdapter raises two events for each row events as the Update method is being executed. These events allow us to examine each row before it is pushed into the original table (the RowUpdating event) and after the update has been processed for that row (the RowUpdated event). By writing handlers for these events, we can deal with many concurrency issues.

Of course, we don't usually detect a concurrency error until we actually perform the update to a row against the original data source. We could use the RowUpdating event to fetch the data again from the database before we attempted to perform our update, and see if it had changed, but this is an inefficient approach unless you really need to actually prevent update attempts that might result in a concurrency error.

Generally a better solution is to trap any errors that occur during the update process and report these back so that the user (or some other process) can reconcile them. Our next example demonstrates how we can do this, and also introduces a couple more features of ADO.NET.

Concurrent Updates and the RowUpdated Event

The example page Managing Concurrent Updates with the RowUpdated Event (`concurrency-rowupdated.aspx`) demonstrates how we can capture information about concurrency errors while updating a data source. It handles the `RowUpdated` event, and creates a `DataSet` object containing a single table that details all the errors that occurred. This `DataSet` could be returned to the user, or passed to another process that will decide what to do next. In our example, we simply display the contents in the page.

So, when you open the example page, you see the rowset with its original values when we fetched it from the database, and then the contents after we've made a couple of changes to this disconnected data. Next the page shows two SQL UPDATE statements that we execute directly against the database to change the values in two of the rows that we are also holding in the `DataSet`:

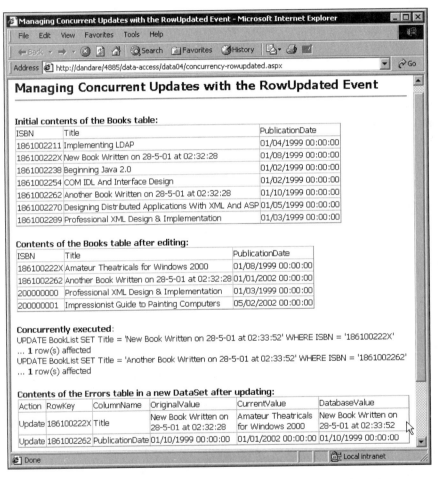

At the bottom of the page you can see a third `DataGrid` control. This displays the content of the new "errors" table that we've dynamically created in response to errors that occurred during the update process. You can see that we've got two errors, and for each one the table provides: information about the type of operation that was being executed (the "statement type"), the primary key of the row, the name of the column that was modified in the `DataSet`, and three values for this column.

These values indicate the value when the `DataSet` was first filled (that is the value that was in the database at that point), the current value after the updates we made in the `DataSet`, and the value of that column at the moment in the database (the value set by the concurrently executed SQL `UPDATE` statements).

If you look at the result, you can see that the first error row indicates that we modified the Title column in our `DataSet`, while the concurrent process changed the same column as well – the value in the database is different from the `Original` value. In the second error row, however, the update failed because the concurrent process had changed a different column than was changed in the `DataSet` within that row. The database value and the `Original` value are the same.

> *If you intend to use a page like this to extract data that will be presented to a user so that they can manually reconcile the data, you may prefer to include all the columns from rows where a concurrency error occurred in the "errors" table. We'll discuss this at the appropriate point as we work through the code.*

The Code for the 'RowUpdated Event' Example

The majority of the code in this example is the same as in our earlier "concurrency" examples. One difference you will see if you examine the whole page, however, is that we declare some of the variables we use as being global to the page, rather than within the `Page_Load` event handler as we've done before. This is because we want to be able to access these variables within our `RowUpdated` event handler:

```
<script language="vb" runat="server">

Dim gstrResult As String          'to hold the result messages
Dim gstrConnect As String         'to hold connection string
Dim gobjDataSet As DataSet        'to hold rows from database
Dim gobjErrorTable As DataTable   'to hold a list of errors
Dim gobjErrorDS As DataSet        'to hold the Errors table

Sub Page_Load()
    ...  page load event handler is here
```

In the `Page_Load` event, we fill a table in the `DataSet` with some rows from the `BookList` table in our example database and display these rows in the first `DataGrid` control. Then we change two of the rows in the `DataSet` in exactly the same way as we did in the previous examples, and display the rowset in the second `DataGrid` control.

Next we create a new connection to the source database, and through it we execute a couple of SQL `UPDATE` statements that change two of the rows. These statements are displayed in the page below the second `DataGrid` control. At this point, we are ready to push the updates back to the database. But before we do so, we add our `OnRowUpdated` event handler to the `DataAdapter` so that it will be executed each time a row is updated in the original data source:

```
AddHandler objDataAdapter.RowUpdated, _
           New OleDbRowUpdatedEventHandler(AddressOf OnRowUpdated)
```

Creating and Displaying the 'Errors' DataSet

Before we start the update process, we need to create the new `DataSet` that will contain details of errors that occur during the process. We create a `DataTable` object named `Errors`, and define the columns for this table (we saw how this works in the previous chapter):

```
'create a new empty Table object to hold error rows
gobjErrorTable = New DataTable("Errors")

'define the columns for the Errors table
gobjErrorTable.Columns.Add("Action", _
                        System.Type.GetType("System.String"))
gobjErrorTable.Columns.Add("RowKey", _
                        System.Type.GetType("System.String"))
gobjErrorTable.Columns.Add("ColumnName", _
                        System.Type.GetType("System.String"))
gobjErrorTable.Columns.Add("OriginalValue", _
                        System.Type.GetType("System.String"))
gobjErrorTable.Columns.Add("CurrentValue", _
                        System.Type.GetType("System.String"))
gobjErrorTable.Columns.Add("DatabaseValue", _
                        System.Type.GetType("System.String"))
```

Now we can create a new `DataSet` object and add the table we've just defined to it. Notice that all these objects are referenced by global variables that we declared outside the `Page_Load` event handler so that we can access them from other event handlers:

```
'create a new empty DataSet object to hold Errors table
gobjErrorDS = New DataSet()
gobjErrorDS.Tables.Add(gobjErrorTable)
```

Now we can carry on as in other examples by creating the auto-generated commands for the update and executing them by calling the `DataAdapter` object's `Update` method. Once the update is complete, we display the contents of our "errors" `DataSet` in the third `DataGrid` control at the bottom of the page:

```
'display the contents of the Errors table
dgrResult3.DataSource = gobjErrorDS
dgrResult3.DataMember = "Errors"
dgrResult3.DataBind()    'and bind (display) the data
```

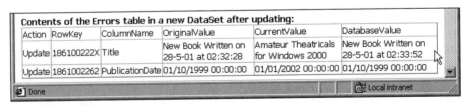

You can see that, in this case, we've bound the `DataGrid` to the `DataSet` object itself (using the `DataSource` property) and then specified that it should display the contents of the table named `Errors` within that `DataSet` by setting the `DataMember` property.

Getting the Current Value from the Database Table

Of course, the code shown so far won't actually put any rows into the "errors" `DataSet`. These rows are created within the `RowUpdated` event handler whenever a concurrency error is detected. We know that we want to include in each row the current value of the column in the original database table at the point that the update process was executed – it will be different from the `Original` value of that column in the `DataSet` if that column in the row was changed by a concurrent process.

So, we have written a short function within the page that – given a connection string, primary key (ISBN) value, and a column name – will return the value of that column for that row from the source database. The function is named `GetCurrentColumnValue` and looks like this:

```
Function GetCurrentColumnValue(strConnect As String, strISBN As String,
strColumnName As String) As String

    'select existing column value from underlying table in the database
    Dim strSQL = "SELECT " & strColumnName _
                & " FROM BookList WHERE ISBN='" & strISBN & "'"
    Dim objConnect As New OleDbConnection(strConnect)
    Dim objCommand As New OleDbCommand(strSQL, objConnect)
    Try
        objConnect.Open()
        'use ExecuteScalar for efficiency, it returns only one item
        'get the value direct from it and convert to a String
        GetCurrentColumnValue = objCommand.ExecuteScalar().ToString()
        objConnect.Close()
    Catch objError As Exception
        GetCurrentColumnValue = "*Error*"
    End Try

End Function
```

One interesting point here is that we use the `ExecuteScalar` method of the `Command` object to get the value. This method returns just a single value from a query (rather than a rowset, for which we'd have to use a `DataReader` object). This means that it is extremely efficient when compared to a `DataReader`, where we have to call the `Read` method to load the first row of results, and then access the column by name or ordinal index.

> *The `ExecuteScalar` method is especially appropriate for queries that calculate a value, such as summing values or working out the average value in a column for some or all of the rows. In our case, it's useful because our SQL statement also only returns a single value (sometimes referred to as a **singleton**).*

So, this simple function will return the value of a specified column in a specified row, or the string value `"*Error*"` if it can't access it (for example if it has been deleted).

The RowUpdated Event Handler

Finally, we have the `RowUpdated` event handler. Remember that this is called after each row has been updated in the source database, whether on not there was an error. So the first thing we do is check the `RecordsAffected` field of the `RowUpdatedEventArgs` object to see if the update for this row failed. If it did, we need to add details of the error to our "errors" `DataSet`:

```
'event handler for the RowUpdated event
Sub OnRowUpdated(objSender As Object, objArgs As OleDbRowUpdatedEventArgs)

    'see if the update was successful
    If objArgs.RecordsAffected < 1 Then
```

We want to know what type of update this is, so we extract the `StatementType` and store this in a local variable for use later. We also extract the `Original` value of the ISBN column from the row, as this is the primary key we'll need to locate the row later:

```
        'get the text description of the StatementType
        Dim strType = System.Enum.GetName(objArgs.StatementType.GetType(), _
                                         objArgs.StatementType)


        'get the primary key of the row (the ISBN)
        Dim strRowKey As String
        strRowKey = objArgs.Row("ISBN", DataRowVersion.Original)
```

Finding the Modified Columns

Now we can check which column(s) caused the concurrency error to occur. We start by getting a reference to the table in our original DataSet – the one we filled with rows from the database, and we declare a couple of other variables that we'll need as well:

```
        'get a reference to the original table in the DataSet
        Dim objTable As DataTable = gobjDataSet.Tables(0)


        Dim objColumn As DataColumn      'to hold a DataColumn object
        Dim strColumnName As String      'to hold the column name
```

The next step is to iterate through the Columns collection of this DataSet comparing the Current and Original values. If they are different we know that this column in the current row has been modified within the DataSet since it was filled from the database table:

```
        'iterate through the columns in the current row
        For Each objColumn In objTable.Columns

          'get the column name as a string
          strColumnName = objColumn.ColumnName

          'see if this column has been modified
          If objArgs.Row(strColumnName, DataRowVersion.Current) _
            <> objArgs.Row(strColumnName, DataRowVersion.Original) Then
```

Notice that this is why we only get the modified columns in our "errors" table. If the concurrent process changes a different column to the one(s) that are modified in the DataSet, that row will not appear in the "errors" table. We could simply remove this If...Then construct, which will then cause the three values from all the columns in a row that caused a concurrency error to be included in the "errors" table. However, in that case we would probably also want to change the way we extract the current values from the database, as using a separate function call for each column would certainly not be the most efficient technique.

Filling in the Column Values

Since we know that this row caused a concurrency error, and that this column has been changed since the DataSet was filled, we will add details about the values in this column to our table named Errors within the new "errors" DataSet we created earlier. We create a new DataRow based on that table, and then we can start filling in the values:

```
        'create a new DataRow object instance in this table
        Dim objDataRow As DataRow = gobjErrorTable.NewRow()

        'and fill in the values
        objDataRow("Action") = strType
        objDataRow("RowKey") = strRowKey
        objDataRow("ColumnName") = strColumnName
        objDataRow("OriginalValue") = objArgs.Row(strColumnName, _
                                        DataRowVersion.Original)
        objDataRow("CurrentValue") = objArgs.Row(strColumnName, _
                                        DataRowVersion.Current)
        objDataRow("DatabaseValue") = GetCurrentColumnValue(gstrConnect, _
                                        strRowKey, strColumnName)
```

We saved the values for the first three columns in our Errors table as strings earlier on in our event handler. The next two values come from the row referenced by the RowUpdatedEventArgs object that is passed to our event handler. The final value comes from the custom GetCurrentColumnValue function we described earlier, and contains the current value of the column for the same row in the source database.

After we've filled in the row, we add it to the Errors table, then go round and look at the next column:

```
        'add new row to the Errors table
        gobjErrorTable.Rows.Add(objDataRow)
      End If
    Next
```

Returning an UpdateStatus Value

The other important point when using the RowUpdating and RowUpdated event handlers that we haven't mentioned so far is how we manage the status value that is exposed by the Status field of the RowUpdatingEventArgs and RowUpdatedEventArgs objects. In our previous example we just ignored these values, but that was really only acceptable because we didn't get any errors during the update process.

When the DataAdapter object's Update method is executing, each call to the RowUpdating and RowUpdated event handler includes a status "flag" value. We can set this to a specific value from the UpdateStatus enumeration to tell the Update method what to do next:

Continue	The DataAdapter will continue to process rows (including this one if this is a RowUpdating event) as part of the Update method call.
ErrorsOccurred	The DataAdapter will stop processing rows and treat the RowUpdating or RowUpdated event as raising an error.
SkipAllRemainingRows	The DataAdapter will stop processing rows and end the Update method, but it will not treat the RowUpdating or RowUpdated event as an error.
SkipCurrentRow	The DataAdapter will not process this row (if this is a RowUpdating event), but will continue to process all remaining rows as part of the Update method call.

The default is `Continue`, which means that the `Update` process will stop when the first concurrency error occurs. However, as we're handling the errors ourselves, we must set the value to `UpdateStatus.SkipCurrentRow` so that it isn't reported as an error that would terminate the `Update` process. This is the last step in our event handler:

```
        'set Status property of row to skip current row update
        objArgs.Status = UpdateStatus.SkipCurrentRow
    End If
End Sub
```

In this final example, you've seen how we can capture information on concurrency errors, allowing the user or another process to take a reasoned decision on how to reconcile the values. Because we've placed the information in a disconnected `DataSet` object, it could easily be remoted to a client via HTTP or a Web Service, or passed directly to another tier of the application.

Summary

This chapter has been devoted entirely to the often-thorny problems we encounter when updating a relational data source such as a SQL database from within our applications. While the techniques have focused on using the .NET data access classes with a relational database, bear in mind that the connection between our code and the data store is via standard methods such as OLEDB and ODBC. This means that, as new managed providers become available, you can use the same techniques to work with other data stores such as mail servers, active directory, indexing services, etc.

The chapter began with a look at the techniques we often use to perform single operations against a data store – such as inserting a user's name and e-mail address into a database, or deleting rows in response to a user's input. We demonstrated how to do this with both SQL statements and with stored procedures. We also looked at how we can use transactions to provide better data integrity. We used both database transactions and .NET connection-based transactions.

However, the main focus of the chapter was on how we use the new `DataSet` object to store and then update data in a disconnected environment. We saw how we can use the `Update` method of the `DataAdapter` to push updates into a data store automatically, and how we can carry out the task ourselves in a staged and more controllable manner.

We finished up with a look at a major issue in all multi-user environments – concurrent data updates. We saw how we can work round the problem using our own custom methods, and how the .NET data access classes provide other techniques that make it much easier than with the data access technologies we used with previous versions of ASP.

Overall, the topics we examined were:

- ❏ Updating data sources with a `Command` object
- ❏ Using Transactions when updating data sources
- ❏ Updating data sources from a `DataSet` object
- ❏ A detailed look inside the `DataAdapter.Update` method
- ❏ Managing concurrent updates to a data source

This chapter completes our look at how we can work with relational data within .NET using the new data-access classes that the framework provides. However, the ceaseless advance of XML into our daily data-handling lives requires us to be competent in handling this new type of data format, as well as being proficient in handling relational data. And, to help us out, the .NET classes provide useful integration between relational and XML data. In the next chapter, we'll explore this, and see other ways that we can access and manipulate XML.

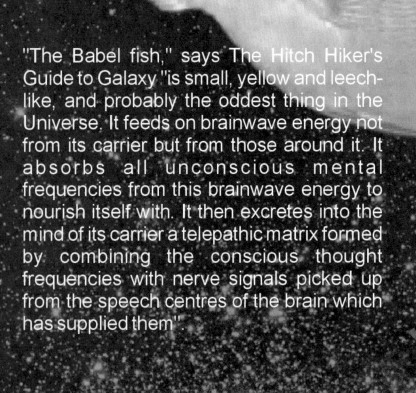

"The Babel fish," says The Hitch Hiker's Guide to Galaxy "is small, yellow and leech-like, and probably the oddest thing in the Universe. It feeds on brainwave energy not from its carrier but from those around it. It absorbs all unconscious mental frequencies from this brainwave energy to nourish itself with. It then excretes into the mind of its carrier a telepathic matrix formed by combining the conscious thought frequencies with nerve signals picked up from the speech centres of the brain which has supplied them".

The practical upshot of all this is that if you stick a Babel fish in your ear you can instantly understand anything said to you in any form of language. The speech patterns you actually hear decode the brainwave matrix which has been fed into your mind by your Babel fish.

11

XML Data Management in .NET

The previous three chapters have largely been concerned with working with relational data in ASP.NET. Even though XML is gradually spreading into most areas of computing, databases such as Microsoft SQL Server, Oracle, DB2, and Sybase still form the backbone of most commercial environments. However, to conclude our study of data management techniques within ASP.NET, we'll devote this chapter to looking in more detail at how we can work with XML documents.

Unlike the previous situation with ASP 3.0 and earlier, we don't need to use add-ons such as an XML parser or other specialist components to be able to work with XML formatted data. All the tools we need are built into the .NET Framework as a set of useful and extensible classes. We can use these to read, write, and edit XML in its native format, and convert from relational data to XML and back again.

So, in this chapter, we'll look at:

- ❑ Accessing relational data as XML and vice versa
- ❑ Synchronization between an XML document and the `DataSet` object
- ❑ Validating XML documents using a schema
- ❑ Creating and editing XML documents in a range of different ways
- ❑ Some alternatives available when transforming XML using style sheets

We spent some time in Chapter 8 exploring the whole object model for XML under .NET, and the new approach we must take when using it. We also demonstrated many of the more simple techniques. Here, we'll dive straight in with a detailed look at the major topic of the interchangeability of XML and relational data.

Obtaining the Sample Files

All the examples used in this chapter are available for you to run on your own server. The download file can be obtained from http://www.wrox.com/Books/Book_Details.asp?isbn=1861004885, and it includes SQL scripts and instructions for creating the database that the examples use. You can also run some of the examples online at http://www.daveandal.com/profaspnet/data-access/.

The main menu page (default.htm) contains links to all the sample files. The fifth link, "Advanced Relational Data Management in .NET" leads to another menu page (in the data05 folder) that contains links to all the examples for this chapter:

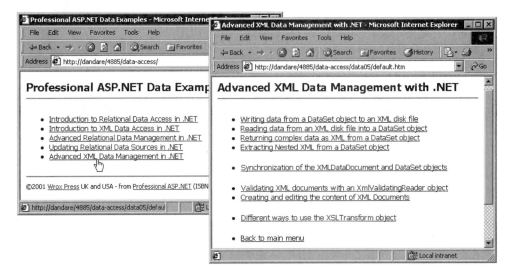

XML and the DataSet Object

Despite the ubiquitous presence of relational databases as the powerhouses of most commercial environments today, the use of XML as a data format is growing steadily. The ease of transmission and storage of XML as a text document (or within a database table as text), and its inherent cross-platform nature, make it ideal for many situations. In fact, in the .NET Framework, it is actually the foundation for all data storage and serialization. There are no more MIME-encoded recordset objects or COM objects that hold data in their own specific formats.

A good example is the DataSet object we've been using throughout the previous chapters. We've viewed it as a container for one or more data tables (rather like some wrapper around multiple recordset objects). This is a reasonable approach when we need to access the data using relational techniques. However, the DataSet can persist its contents to a disk file, or into another object such as a Stream. The format of the data at this point is XML.

The XML-based Methods of the DataSet

The `DataSet` object exposes the following methods for working with an XML representation of the data it contains or will contain:

`GetXml`	Returns a string containing the XML representation of the data stored in the `DataSet`.
`GetXmlSchema`	Returns just the schema for an XML representation of the data stored in the `DataSet`.
`InferXmlSchema`	Uses a schema provided in a `TextReader`, `XmlReader`, or `Stream` object, or in a specified disk file, to infer the structure of the data in a `DataSet`.
`ReadXml`	Reads XML data (including a schema if present) into the `DataSet` from a `TextReader`, `XmlReader`, or `Stream` object, or from a specified disk file.
`ReadXmlSchema`	Reads an XML schema only into the `DataSet` from a `TextReader`, `XmlReader`, or `Stream` object, or from a specified disk file.
`WriteXml`	Writes the contents of the `DataSet` object to an XML document via a `TextWriter`, `XmlWriter`, or `Stream` object, or directly to a specified disk file.
`WriteXmlSchema`	Writes a schema describing the contents of the `DataSet` object to a `TextWriter`, `XmlWriter`, or `Stream` object, or directly to a specified disk file.

In general, when extracting XML from a `DataSet`, unless you actually need a string representation of the data, the `GetXml` and `GetXmlSchema` methods should be avoided. It's much more efficient to create a disk file directly, using the `WriteXml` and `WriteXmlSchema` methods. We'll demonstrate these two methods, and the `ReadXml` and `ReadXmlSchema` methods, in the next two examples.

Writing Data from a DataSet to an XML File

Our first example demonstrates the way we can write data from a `DataSet`, directly to a disk file, as an XML document. As we're filling the `DataSet` from a relational database, we need to include the relevant namespaces in our page, and we also include the custom user control that returns the correct connection string for our machine:

```
<%@Import Namespace="System.Data" %>
<%@Import Namespace="System.Data.OleDb" %>

<%@ Register TagPrefix="wrox" TagName="connect"
            Src="..\global\connect-strings.ascx" %>

<%'-- insert connection string script --%>
<wrox:connect id="ctlConnectStrings" runat="server" />
```

The way we're filling the DataSet is identical to the techniques and code we used in the previous chapters, and so we won't be describing it in detail again here. For more information, refer back to Chapter 8 Introducing .NET Data Management.

The page contains three `<div>` elements where we output information and results:

```
<div>Connection string: <span id="outConnect" runat="server" / ></div>
<div>SELECT command: <span id="outSelect" runat="server" /></div>
<div id="outMessage" runat="server" />
```

Filling the DataSet

In the `Page_Load` event, we fill our `DataSet` using a SQL statement that joins two tables:

```
Sub Page_Load()

    Dim strConnect As String
    strConnect = ctlConnectStrings.OLEDBConnectionString
    outConnect.innerText = strConnect
    Dim strSelect As String
    strSelect = "SELECT BookList.*, BookAuthors.FirstName, " _
          & "BookAuthors.LastName FROM BookList INNER JOIN " _
          & "BookAuthors ON BookList.ISBN = BookAuthors.ISBN " _
          & "WHERE BookList.ISBN LIKE '186100339%'"
    outSelect.innerText = strSelect

    Dim objDataSet As New DataSet

    Try
        Dim objConnect As New OleDbConnection(strConnect)
        Dim objDataAdapter As New OleDbDataAdapter(strSelect, objConnect)
        objDataAdapter.Fill(objDataSet, "Books")
    Catch objError As Exception
        outError.innerHTML = "Error while accessing data.<br />" _
            & objError.Message & "<br />" & objError.Source
        Exit Sub
    End Try
```

Now that we have a `DataSet` containing our data, we can write it out to a disk file as XML. The next screenshot shows the results of running this page 'Writing data from a DataSet to an XML File' (`write-data-as-xml.aspx`):

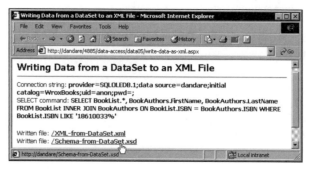

You can see that the page includes two hyperlinks to the files we've created – the XML data itself and the XSD schema that defines the structure of the XML document. The code to create these two files is shown below.

Creating the XML Data and Schema Files

All we have to do is create the appropriate virtual path and name for the two files, and then call the `WriteXml` and `WriteXmlSchema` methods. We do this within a `Try...Catch` construct to trap any errors that might arise while writing the files – for example if ASP.NET does not have the relevant permission or if the path does not exist. If all goes well, we display the confirmation messages and hyperlinks to the new files:

```
Try

    'use the path to the current virtual application
    Dim strVirtualPath As String = Request.ApplicationPath _
                                  & "XML-from-DataSet.xml"
    Dim strVSchemaPath As String = Request.ApplicationPath _
                                  & "Schema-from-DataSet.xsd"

    'write data and schema from DataSet to documents on disk
    'must use the Physical path to the file not the Virtual path
    objDataSet.WriteXml(Request.MapPath(strVirtualPath))
    outMessage.innerHTML = "Written file: <a href=" & Chr(34) _
                         & strVirtualPath & Chr(34) & ">" _
                         & strVirtualPath & "</a><br />"

    objDataSet.WriteXmlSchema(Request.MapPath(strVSchemaPath))
    outMessage.innerHTML += "Written file: <a href=" & Chr(34) _
                          & strVSchemaPath & Chr(34) & ">" _
                          & strVSchemaPath & "</a></b>"

Catch objError As Exception

    'display error details
    outMessage.innerHTML = "Error while writing disk file.<br />" _
        & objError.Message & "<br />" & objError.Source
    Exit Sub  ' and stop execution

End Try
```

Notice that we have to provide a physical path to the XML document files, not the virtual path.

The Resulting XML Document

If you click the hyperlinks in the page, you can view the XML document and schema we've created. The XML document is shown in the next screenshot. We've used IE5's ability to collapse elements so that you can see the overall structure of the document. Each `<Books>` element describes one row from the original rowset we loaded into our `DataSet` object:

The Resulting XML Schema

The second link in the original page fetches and displays the schema document we created from the disk file. You can see the structure is specified quite loosely, for example the schema allows elements to be optional (minOcccurs="0"). It means that you may want to modify the schema if you use the XML for situations where a tighter definition is required – perhaps when communicating with BizTalk Server or some other application:

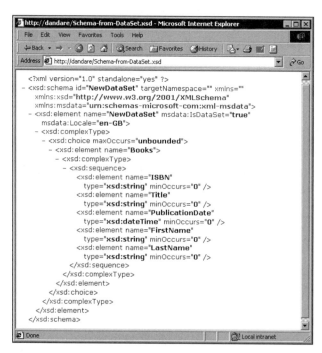

Reading Data into a DataSet from an XML File

The next example uses the XML file we've just created (you should run the previous example before you try this one). In this example we load the XML data and schema into a new `DataSet` object. We then display the content using `DataGrid` server controls, in other words the data is accessed as a data table using relational methods.

The example page, 'Reading Data Into a DataSet from an XML File' (`read-data-from-xml.aspx`) looks like this when we run it:

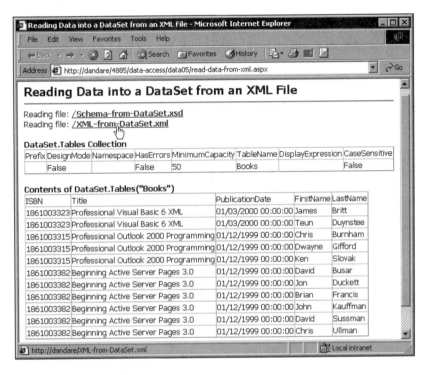

The Code for This Example

Because we're creating a `DataSet` object, we need the namespace `System.Data`:

```
<%@Import Namespace="System.Data" %>
```

Next comes a `<div>` for output messages, followed by two `ASP:DataGrid` controls:

```
<div id="outMessage" runat="server" /><br />

<b>DataSet.Tables Collection</b>
<asp:datagrid id="dgrTables" runat="server" /><br />

<b>Contents of DataSet.Tables("Books")</b>
<asp:datagrid id="dgrValues" runat="server" />
```

Loading the XML Documents

The code in our `Page_Load` event handler first creates the path and name for each of the two XML documents, the data, and the schema. Then it's simply a matter of calling the `ReadXmlSchema` and `ReadXml` methods to load the schema first followed by the data. Again, we have to provide a physical path to the XML document files, not the virtual path:

```
'create a new DataSet object
Dim objDataSet As New DataSet()

Try

    'use the path to the current virtual application
    Dim strVirtualPath As String = Request.ApplicationPath _
                                  & "XML-from-DataSet.xml"
    Dim strVSchemaPath As String = Request.ApplicationPath _
                                  & "Schema-from-DataSet.xsd"

    'read schema and data into DataSet from documents on disk
    'must use the Physical path to the file not the Virtual path
    objDataSet.ReadXMLSchema(Request.MapPath(strVSchemaPath))
    outMessage.InnerHTML = "Reading file: <a href=" & Chr(34) _
                         & strVSchemaPath & Chr(34) & ">" _
                         & strVSchemaPath & "</a><br />"

    objDataSet.ReadXML(Request.MapPath(strVirtualPath))
    outMessage.InnerHTML += "Reading file: <a href=" & Chr(34) _
                         & strVirtualPath & Chr(34) & ">" _
                         & strVirtualPath & "</a>"

Catch objError As Exception

    'display error details
    outMessage.InnerHTML = "Error while reading disk file.<br />" _
        & objError.Message & "<br />" & objError.Source
    Exit Sub  ' and stop execution

End Try
```

Displaying the Data

We now have the data loaded into our `DataSet` ready to use. In our example page, we simply bind the `Tables` collection, and the contents of the table named "Books" (the table name is automatically inferred from the repeated element name in the XML file) to a pair of `DataGrid` server controls so that you can see the results:

```
'assign the DataView.Tables collection first to the DataGrid control
dgrTables.DataSource = objDataSet.Tables
dgrTables.DataBind()  'and bind (display) the data

'create a DataView object for the Books table in the DataSet
Dim objDataView As New DataView(objDataSet.Tables("Books"))

'assign the DataView object to the second DataGrid control
dgrValues.DataSource = objDataView
dgrValues.DataBind()  'and bind (display) the data
```

With or Without a Schema – That Is the Question

Our example page explicitly tells the `DataSet` what to expect. The schema we load first contains a definition of the structure of the XML data we load later. However, you may not want to use a schema, or you may not have one available.

This is often the case if the XML structure is not constant over time. To save having to keep creating new schemas for dynamically generated XML data, you can omit the schema altogether and just use the `ReadXml` method to load the XML data. The `DataSet` will infer the structure of the data automatically from the structure of the XML document. However, if for some reason it can't (usually because the document structure is not consistent), you may not get any data in the `DataSet`.

Bear in mind, that without a schema, the `DataSet` might come to a different conclusion from you about what the structure is – so it's wise to include a schema whenever possible. As long as the XML document is well formed, it will be loaded – but the results might not be what you expect. You can create the schema like we did in the previous example by loading the appropriate data into the `DataSet` and then calling the `WriteXmlSchema` method.

> *The `DataSet` does **not** validate the document against the schema – it just uses it to infer the structure required for the tables in the `DataSet`. We'll look at the issues of validating an XML document against a schema later in this chapter.*

Remember that you can also include a schema within the XML data file or document, rather than as a separate file. In this case, the structure of the data is specified automatically when you load the document and there is (of course) no need to execute `ReadXmlSchema`.

Getting XML as a String from a DataSet

Although it is not the recommended technique for extracting XML from a `DataSet`, unless you specifically want it as a string for use in your code, you can use the `GetXml` and `GetXmlSchema` methods. We've provided a simple example page that uses these, and displays the results in the page.

The example file is 'Returning XML from a DataSet' (`get-data-as-xml.aspx`), and it looks like the following screenshot when you run it and click the 'Display XML Data' checkbox:

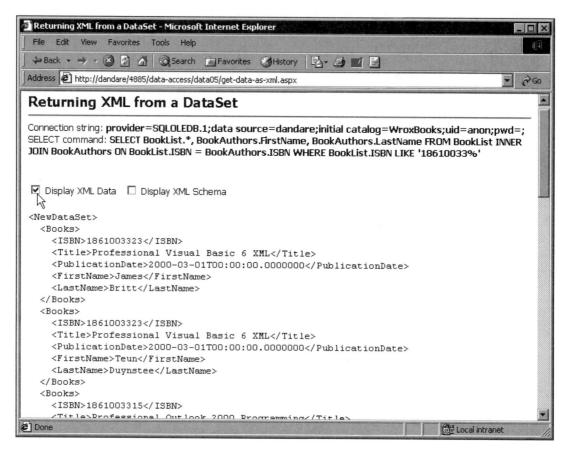

How It Works

The two checkboxes simply execute an appropriate combination of the `GetXml` and `GetXmlSchema` methods of the `DataSet` (which we fill with data using exactly the same code as the previous example). The two methods return a `String`, which we assign to the `InnerHtml` property of an HTML `<xmp>` element:

```
'display the data and/or schema in the DataSet as an XML document
xmpResults.InnerHtml = ""
If chkSchema.checked Then
    xmpResults.InnerHtml = objDataSet.GetXmlSchema() & vbCrlf & vbCrlf
End If
If chkXML.checked Then
    xmpResults.InnerHtml += objDataSet.GetXml()
End If
```

The HTML `<xmp>` element automatically displays content as text, without attempting to render it, so the XML elements are visible. An alternative approach would be to use the `Server.HtmlEncode` method on the string, and then it could be displayed directly in the page with the elements visible.

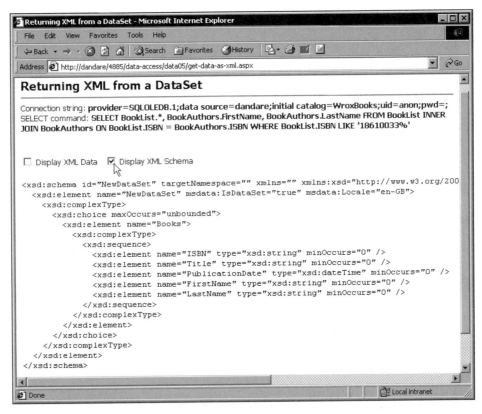

Clicking the other checkbox in the page displays just the schema (as shown in the previous screenshot), and you can check them both to display the schema and the XML data together. If you do this, and copy the result to a new document, you automatically have the appropriate combined document and schema as one file for this DataSet.

Nested XML and Related Data in a DataSet

When we export data from a DataSet as XML, we don't have much control over the actual format of the XML itself. There are several interesting arguments for and against the two basic approaches to the structure of an XML document that contains repeating data (that is, a representation of a rowset or data table):

❑   Place the data within the elements as the text content (as in the examples so far in this chapter)

❑   Use a single element for each data row and place the data itself in attributes of that element

The first option, using the data items as the text content of a hierarchical structure of elements, tends to give a more human-readable result, but produces a bigger document as there is more markup (that is, element tags). Using attributes produces smaller documents, but accessing the content using other XML techniques such as the DOM methods can be more difficult.

In a later example in this chapter, we'll see how we can use SQL Server's built-in XML data-handling function to create different formats of XML. In the meantime, we also need to consider how the format of the XML is affected when we export data from more than one data table into an XML document.

527

The DataRelation.Nested Property

We've seen in the previous few chapters that a `DataSet` can contain more than one table and also the relationships between these tables. We used these relationships in a previous chapter to extract the child rows from one table that were related to the current row in the parent table.

Each relationship (`DataRelation` object) in a `DataSet` also has a `Nested` property. This is `False` by default, and has no effect when we are accessing the data using relational techniques. For example, when we bind the data to a `DataGrid`, or iterate through the `Rows` collection of a table. However, it does affect the way that the data is exported as XML when we use the `GetXML` or `WriteXml` methods. Our next example demonstrates this.

The Nested XML Data Example Page

The example page 'Extracting Nested XML from a DataSet' (`nested-xml-from-dataset.aspx`) demonstrates how useful the `Nested` property of a `DataRelation` object is when it comes to exporting data as XML. We use the custom user control from previous chapters to create a `DataSet` object and fill it with three tables named "`Books`", "`Authors`", and "`Prices`" that contain data from our relational database. The control also creates two relationships (`DataRelations`) between these tables.

The page also includes three `ASP:DataGrid` controls. The first is used to display the `DataSet` object's `Tables` collection, and the other two show the contents of the `Relations` collection.

```
<b>DataSet.Tables Collection</b>
<asp:datagrid id="dgrTables" runat="server" /><br />

<b>DataSet.Relations Collection</b>
<asp:datagrid id="dgrRelsNormal" runat="server" />
<div id="outResultNormal" runat="server" /><p />

<b>DataSet.Relations Collection</b>
<asp:datagrid id="dgrRelsNested" runat="server" />
<div id="outResultNested" runat="server" /><p />
```

We then create the `DataSet` using our custom control:

```
Dim strConnect As String = ctlConnectStrings.OLEDBConnectionString
Dim objDataSet As DataSet
objDataSet = ctlDataSet.BooksDataSet(strConnect, "ISBN LIKE '186100338'")
If IsNothing(objDataSet) Then Exit Sub
```

Displaying the DataSet Contents

Now that we have our `DataSet` filled, related, and ready to use, we can display information about it. We bind the first `DataGrid` control on our page to the `Tables` collection, and the second to the `Relations` collection:

```
'bind the collection of Tables to the first DataGrid on the page
dgrTables.DataSource = objDataSet.Tables
dgrTables.DataBind()

'bind the collection of Relations to the second DataGrid on the page
dgrRelsNormal.DataSource = objDataSet.Relations
dgrRelsNormal.DataBind()
```

Exporting the Data to an XML Disk File

Next we write the data in our `DataSet` to an XML document on disk. We build up a virtual path and name for the file, write it with the `WriteXml` method, and display a hyperlink so that you can view it:

```
Dim strVirtualPath As String = Request.ApplicationPath _
                & "Normal-XML-from-DataSet.xml"
objDataSet.WriteXml(Request.MapPath(strVirtualPath))
outResultNormal.innerHTML = "Written file: <a href=" & Chr(34) _
                & strVirtualPath & Chr(34) & ">" _
                & strVirtualPath & "</a>"
```

The next screenshot shows the results of running the page – you can see the two `DataGrids` we've populated so far and following them is the hyperlink to the file `Normal-XML-from-DataSet.xml` we just created. And in the second `DataGrid` in the page you can see the contents of the `DataSet.Relations` collection at this point in our code. The two relations, named `BookAuthors` and `BookPrices`, both have the default value `False` for their `Nested` property:

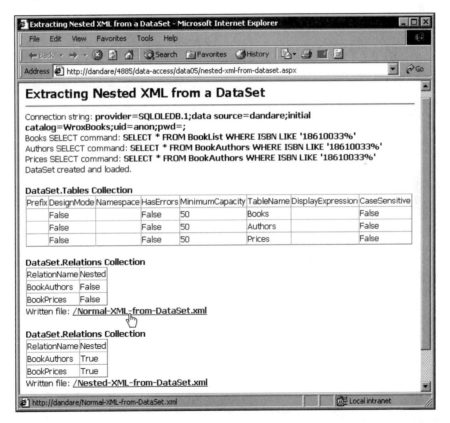

The Resulting XML Document

If you click this first hyperlink, you can see the XML file format that is created by default from a `DataSet` containing more than one table. Again, in IE5, we've collapsed some of the elements so that you can see the structure:

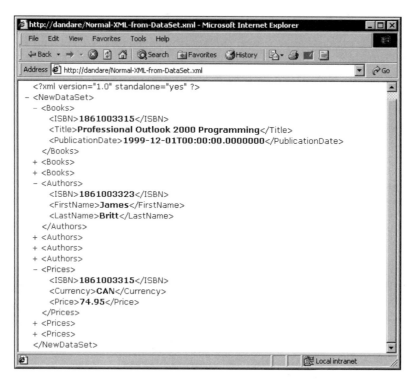

It's pretty clear that the document contains separate <Books>, <Authors>, and <Prices> elements. There is no concept of hierarchy between the parent and child elements. They are all at the same "level" (that is, are siblings in XML terminology). However, they all contain the primary key (the ISBN code) so an application could read and work with the data in a related manner if required.

Nesting the XML Result

The format we've just looked at is not really what we might expect having gone to the effort of creating the relationships between the tables. But, as you've probably already guessed, the Nested property comes to our rescue. The code in our example page continues by setting the Nested property to True for both the DataRelation objects:

```
'now set the Nested property of the two relation objects
objDataSet.Relations("BookAuthors").Nested = True
objDataSet.Relations("BookPrices").Nested = True
```

Then it redisplays the contents of the Relations collection:

```
'bind the collection of Relations to the third DataGrid on the page
dgrRelsNested.DataSource = objDataSet.Relations
dgrRelsNested.DataBind()
```

If you look back at the original screenshot for this example, you can see that the third DataGrid shows the Nested property of both Relations as being True now. So, we can create another XML document by exporting the contents of the DataSet again:

```
Dim strVirtualPath As String = Request.ApplicationPath _
                        & "Nested-XML-from-DataSet.xml"
objDataSet.WriteXML(Request.MapPath(strVirtualPath))
outResultNested.innerHTML = "Written file: <a href=" & Chr(34) _
                        & strVirtualPath & Chr(34) & ">" _
                        & strVirtualPath & "</a>"
```

The Resulting XML Document

Now, if you open and view the second XML document, you can see the difference. Each <Books> element is a child of the document root, and the <Authors> and <Prices> elements are nested within their respective book:

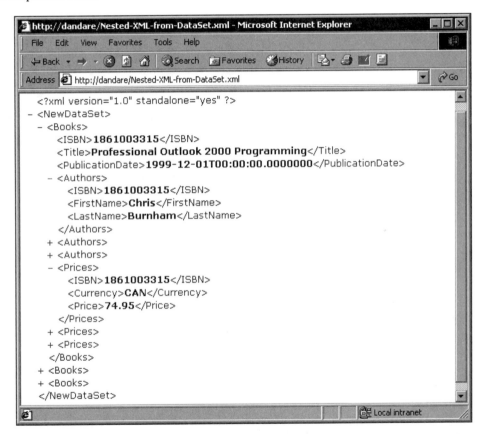

This is pretty much an ideal format both for readability and usability, and is probably something like we would have come up with if we had been crafting the XML by hand. Perhaps the only downside is the repeated occurrence of the primary key within the child elements. Later in this chapter, we'll see a way that we can extract the XML from a SQL Server database so that the values are in attributes rather than as the content of elements.

Working with the XmlDataDocument Object

The DataSet provides an excellent vehicle for transferring data from one of more relational data sets to XML documents and XML schemas, and vice versa. But we can do even better if we are predominantly concerned with accessing our data as XML, rather than starting out with relational data.

To refresh our earlier overview of the XML object model and the various members of the XML namespaces in .NET, we repeat the following diagram from the data management introduction chapter. You can see that there are three types of object we can use to access XML and hold it in memory as a document – the XmlDocument, XmlDataDocument, and XPathDocument:

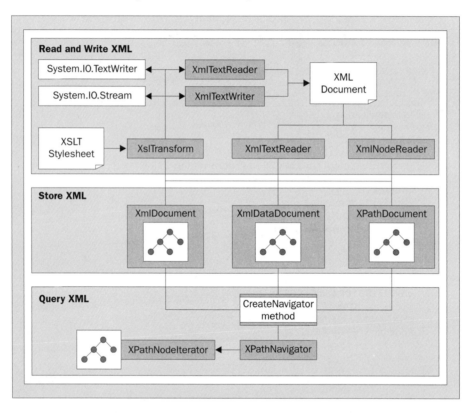

We discussed the reason for having these three different objects in Chapter 8, Introducing .NET Data Management, and you should recall that the XmlDataDocument is (like the DataSet) designed to act as a bridge between relational and XML data.

XmlDataDocument and DataSet Synchronization

The only real external difference between an XmlDocument object and an XmlDataDocument object is that the latter has a few extra properties and methods. The most useful is the property named DataSet. This returns a reference to an object that contains the data in the XML document, but which is exposed as a DataSet. The property is read-only so we can't "go the other way", but even so, it provides some useful opportunities.

The next diagram conceptualizes the way it works. The XML document can be accessed through various `Reader` objects and loaded into an `XmlDataDocument` object, as we saw in Chapter 8. It can also, as we discovered earlier in this chapter, be loaded into a `DataSet`.

However, after we load the XML into an `XmlDataDocument` object, we can reference a `DataSet` object that contains the same data, and which is equivalent to reading the data into that `DataSet`. More to the point, as we change the data in either the `DataSet` or the `XmlDataDocument`, the changes are reflected in both. They are completely and automatically synchronized – in effect, all we've got is two different views of the same data:

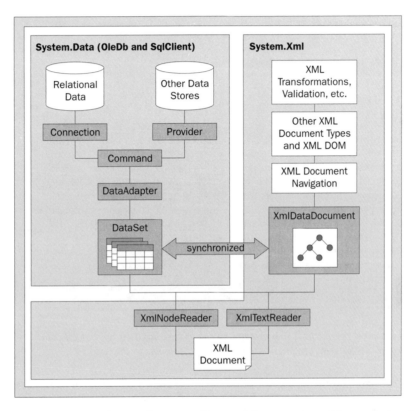

This means that we no longer have a distinction between the two types of data, relational or XML – they are just **two views of the same data**. This works in part because, underneath, the .NET Framework data management objects all use XML as their standard persistence format.

Once we've got our data in an `XmlDataDocument`, we can then access it using any of the techniques available in our relational and XML armories. The next example page demonstrates just a few.

The DataSet-XML Synchronization Example

The example page named 'Synchronization of the XMLDataDocument and DataSet objects' (`xml-to-dataset.aspx`) shows some of the features of the integration we've just been discussing. It takes an XML document and the matching XSD schema and loads them into a new `XmlDataDocument` object. There are hyperlinks in the page so that you can examine the XML and schema files – they are basically the same ones as we used in the first couple of examples in this chapter:

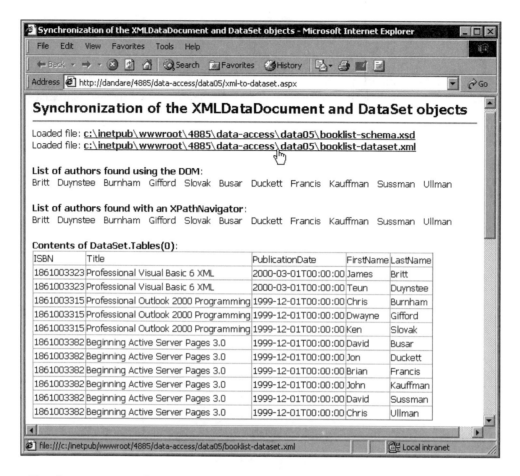

Note that you must run the page in a browser on the Web server itself to be able to open the XML document and schema using the physical paths in the hyperlinks in the page.

After loading the data into the XmlDataDocument, the code carries out four different tasks with it. The first two display a list of the last names of all the authors in our data. The first uses the standard methods exposed by the XML DOM (as per the W3C recommendations) and the second uses an XPathNavigator object with a recursive search function.

Then comes a DataGrid control that displays all the rows in the table within the DataSet. Of course, we get this DataSet from the XmlDataDocument object's DataSet property, but notice how we are already freely mixing our relational and XML terminology.

Finally, if you scroll to the bottom of this page, you'll see a heap of XML. We've extracted this from the DataSet object, using the GetElementFromRow method. Using this method, we can pull out specific rows of data and return just those rows as XML. We've got a simple and efficient automated relational-based technique for manipulating data and creating the equivalent XML:

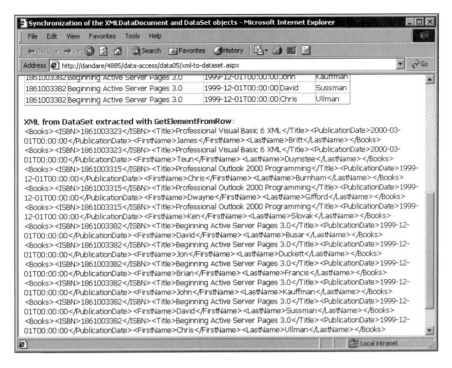

The Code for This Example Page

There is a lot of code in this page, as you can confirm if you view the source. However, it is commented and divided up into the four tasks we're performing, so is easy enough to follow. In the listings here, we'll confine ourselves to the features that are relevant to the four tasks, and omit much of the surrounding code that creates links in the page, error messages, etc.

The first step is to create the `XmlDataDocument` and load the schema and XML from disk:

```
'create a new XMLDataDocument object
Dim objXMLDataDoc As New XMLDataDocument()

'load the XML schema into the XMLDataDocument object
objXMLDataDoc.DataSet.ReadXmlSchema(strSchemaPath)

'load the XML file into the XMLDataDocument object
objXMLDataDoc.Load(strXMLPath)
```

Using the XML DOM Methods of the Document

Now we can use the `XmlDataDocument` object. First, we prove that the object behaves like a normal W3C-standard `XMLDocument` object by using the `GetElementsByTagname` method to create an `XmlNodeList` containing all the `<LastName>` elements in the document:

```
Dim objNode As XmlNode
Dim strResults As String = ""

'create a NodeList collection of all matching child nodes
Dim colElements As XmlNodeList
colElements = objXMLDataDoc.GetElementsByTagname("LastName")
```

Then we can iterate through this NodeList (collection) displaying all the element values:

```
'iterate through the collection getting the values of the
'child #text nodes for each one
For Each objNode In colElements
  strResults += objNode.FirstChild().Value & "   "
Next

'then display the result
outDOMResult.innerHTML = strResults
```

Using an XPathNavigator Object

As we saw in Chapter 8, *Introducing .NET Data Management*, the .NET Framework introduces a new object that we can use to navigate within an XML document. An XPathNavigator can be created from an XML document object of any type, by calling the CreateNavigator method of that document object. We use an XPathNavigator to fetch the values of all the <LastName> elements in our XMLDataDocument by moving to the root element of the document and then calling a recursive function, which searches each child of the current element in turn looking for matches and extracting the values:

```
'create a new XPathNavigator object using the XMLDataDocument object
Dim objXPNav As XPathNavigator
objXPNav = objXMLDataDoc.CreateNavigator()

'move to the root element of the document
objXPNav.MoveToRoot()

'and display the result of the recursive 'search' function
outXPNavResult.innerHTML = SearchForElement(objXPNav, "LastName")
```

We haven't listed our recursive SearchForElement function again here, as it's identical to the technique we used back in Chapter 8.

Displaying the Content of the DataSet

The next part of the page output is easy to create. We reference the DataSet property of the XmlDataDocument object, and from that access the first member of the Tables collection. This gives us a reference to the default DataTable within the DataSet. We can use this reference to create a DataView object, and then assign the DataView to an ASP:DataGrid control that we previously defined within the page:

```
'create a DataView object for the Books table in the DataSet
Dim objDataView As New DataView(objXMLDataDoc.DataSet.Tables(0))

'assign the DataView object to the DataGrid control
dgrResult.DataSource = objDataView
dgrResult.DataBind()   'and bind (display) the data
```

This gives us a picture of the data as a standard relational rowset – just as though we'd filled our DataSet table using a Connection, Command, and DataAdapter.

Extracting XML Elements from the DataSet

The final task in this page is to demonstrate how we can query the `DataSet` to extract individual rows as XML. The `GetElementFromRow` method takes as its parameter an object that represents a row in a `DataTable` – a `DataRow` object. It returns an XML representation of that row.

All we do is create a reference to the `DataTable` in our `DataSet`, and then iterate through the rows. For each one, we call the `GetElementFromRow` method of our `XmlDataDocument` object, which returns an `XmlElement` object. We get a string representation of the element from its `OuterXml` property, and HTML-encode this before displaying it in the page:

```
'create a DataTable object for the Books table in the DataSet
Dim objDataTable As DataTable = objXMLDataDoc.DataSet.Tables(0)

Dim objRow As DataRow
Dim objXMLElement As XmlElement

'iterate through all the rows in this table
For Each objRow In objDataTable.Rows

    'get an XML element that represents this row
    objXMLElement = objXMLDataDoc.GetElementFromRow(objRow)

    'HTMLEncode it because it contains XML element tags
    strResults += Server.HtmlEncode(objXMLElement.OuterXML) & "<br />"

Next

outFromRowResult.innerHTML = strResults     'and display the result
```

Getting a DataRow Object from an XML Element

Interestingly, there is also a mirror of this method named `GetRowFromElement`. We can iterate through the elements in an XML document using the DOM methods or an `XPathNavigator` to get an `XmlNodeList` of element objects, or individual `XmlElement` references.

For each one, the `GetRowFromElement` method of the `XmlDataDocument` object that holds the document will return a `DataRow` object. This can then be accessed to extract field information, or even used to update the original XML document:

```
objThisRow = objXmlDataDoc.GetRowFromElement(objElement)
objThisRow("MyFieldName") = "This is the new value"
```

So now we even have a way to edit an XML document using relational techniques.

Reading XML Data Direct from SQL Server

Our earlier discussion of the format of the XML returned from a `DataSet` mentioned the "alternative" format of using the attributes of a "row" element to hold the individual column or field data items. This was, in fact, the default format introduced with ADO 2.0/2.1 when XML support was added to ADO. It's also the default format for the XML created by the new features of Microsoft SQL Server 2000 (and the "SQLXML Technology Preview" that is still available for SQL Server 7.0).

We've provided an example page named 'Reading XML Direct From SQL Server With An XmlReader' (`xmldatareader-sql.aspx`) that demonstrates this feature. To use it you must have SQL Server 2000 installed – the SQLXML Technology Preview does not work with .NET.

When you run the page, you see the connection string and the SQL SELECT statement we used. Notice that it includes the "FOR XML AUTO" instruction. Below this is a series of XML elements that are created automatically by SQL Server in response to the instruction in the SQL statement:

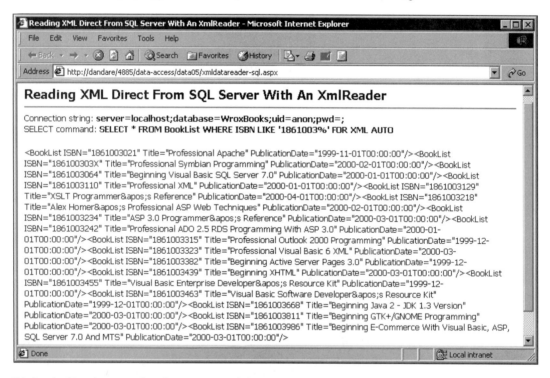

It's kind of hard to see what the structure of the XML is from the screenshot, but if we break out one of the elements you can see the structure quite clearly:

```
<BookList ISBN="1861003110" Title="Professional XML"
          PublicationDate="2000-01-01T00:00:00"/>
```

There are a couple of things to note. This is *not* an XML **document**, as there is no document type declaration or root element. All we get back is a series of elements that contain the row values as attributes. This is the default format for the "AUTO" part of the instruction we used in the SQL statement. We would probably use the elements to build up our own specific XML documents, depending on the task our application has to achieve.

> *The XML technology built into SQL Server 2000 is very powerful, allowing updates to the source data to be made as well as extracting it. The Help topic "Retrieving and Writing XML Data" within the section "XML and Internet Support" of SQL Server Books Online contains full details of the various formats and options that are available when using this technology.*

The Code for the SQLXML Example Page

The ability to extract data as XML from SQL Server using the SQLXML feature has proved very useful to developers already, and it's extremely fast and efficient. To support it in .NET simply meant including an option to return an object that could hold XML document fragments. This is an alternative to the `DataReader` object we used in the relational data examples in previous chapters.

The answer is a special version of the "execute" methods available in the `Command` object we use for relation data access, which returns an `XmlReader` object. This method is called (not surprisingly) `ExecuteXmlReader`. The code we use in our example page demonstrates it. First we collect the connection string from our custom user control (as in previous examples), and then create the SQL statement we need to extract the XML:

```
Dim strConnect As String
strConnect = ctlConnectStrings.SQLConnectionString

Dim strSelect As String
strSelect = "SELECT * FROM BookList WHERE " _
        & "ISBN LIKE '1861003%' FOR XML AUTO"
```

Now we create a `StringBuilder` object that we'll use to hold the large strings that we expect to get back from the database. We also create the customary `Connection` and `Command` objects. Notice that we're using the objects from the `SqlClient` namespace here (prefixed "Sql"). This page is only going to work with SQL Server 2000 anyway, and so we might as well take advantage of the performance boost that comes with the SQL TDS provider:

```
'create a new StringBuilder to hold the results
Dim objStrBuilder As New StringBuilder()

'create a new Connection object using the connection string
Dim objConnect As New SqlConnection(strConnect)

'create new Command using the connection object and select statement
Dim objCommand As New SqlCommand(strSelect, objConnect)
```

Executing the Command

We need an object to "receive" the results of executing the SQL statement, and for this we declare a variable to hold an `XmlTextReader` object (a public class based on `XmlReader`):

```
'declare a variable to hold an XmlTextReader object
Dim objXTReader As XmlTextReader
```

Then we can open the connection and call the `ExecuteXmlReader` method. It returns our `XmlTextReader` all ready to go:

```
'open the connection to the database
objConnect.Open()

'execute the SQL statement against the command to create the XmlReader
objXTReader = objCommand.ExecuteXmlReader()
```

Retrieving the XML Result

To retrieve the data once we've executed the SQL statement, we call the `Read` method of the `XmlTextReader` to initialize it. Then we call the `GetRemainder` method to read to the end of the results, and append it all to the `StringBuilder` we created earlier:

```
'read the first result to initialize the reader
objXTReader.Read()

'and then read remainder into the StringBuilder as well
objStrBuilder.Append(objXTReader.GetRemainder().ReadToEnd())
```

To finish off we close the reader and the connection, and display the results in the page:

```
'close the XmlReader and Connection
objXTReader.Close()
objConnect.Close()

'display the results as Text to show XML elements
outError.InnerText = objStrBuilder.ToString()
```

Validating XML Documents

An XML document must follow the specific standards laid down by W3C in order to be acceptable – in particular it must be "**well-formed**". In other words, it must:

❑ Have a single root element that encloses all other content except the document declaration, processing instructions and comments.

❑ Have matching closing tags for all the opening tags (or use the shorthand syntax of ending the element with a forward slash character).

❑ Be properly nested so that elements are fully enclosed. In other words, you can't open an element as a child of another element then close the parent element before closing the child element.

❑ Contain only valid characters. All non-valid content must be escaped or replaced by the correct entity equivalents such as & for an ampersand character.

It's possible for an XML document to be well-formed, but still not **valid**. We define the validity of a document using a schema or document type definition (DTD). This lays out the structure of the elements, attributes and other content, the ordering of the elements, and the permissible value ranges for the elements and attributes. The XML "storage" objects parse the XML to ensure it is well-formed when they load it (they can't load it if it is not), but they don't automatically validate the XML. We have to look after that part ourselves, as you'll see next.

The XmlValidatingReader Object

We validate documents against a given XML schema or DTD using the `XmlValidatingReader` object. This isn't actually a reader, but a "helper" object that we attach to a reader. The following schematic shows the way it works. The document is read using an `XmlTextReader` (or an `XmlNodeReader` if we only want to validate part of a document). This object automatically raises an error if the document is not well-formed as we read it.

When we attach an `XmlValidatingReader` to the `XmlTextReader`, it automatically checks for the presence of a schema or DTD within the document, and validates the content of the document against that schema or DTD. Any errors found during validation are raised through the `Validation` event, and this receives a `ValidationEventHandler` object that contains a description of the error. We can handle this event to determine what validation errors are present (we'll see how this is done shortly in our example page), or we can leave it to the default event handler to raise an error:

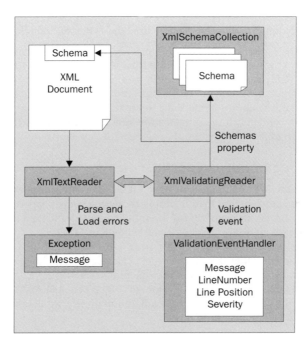

Creating an XMLValidatingReader Object

Creating an `XMLValidatingReader` for use with a document that contains an inline schema or DTD (or specifies an external schema or DTD itself) is easy. We just create the `XmlTextReader`, specifying the XML document to load, and then use this as the basis for creating the `XmlValidatingReader`. Afterwards, we can set the `ValidationType` property to specify the type of schema we're using:

```
'create the new XmlTextReader object and load the XML document
objXTReader = New XmlTextReader(strXMLPath)

'create an XmlValidatingReader for this XmlTextReader
Dim objValidator As New XmlValidatingReader(objXTReader)

'set the validation type to use an XSD schema
objValidator.ValidationType = ValidationType.Schema
```

The acceptable values for the `ValidationType` property are:

Auto	The default. Validation is automatically performed against whichever type of schema or DTD is encountered.
DTD	Validate against a Document Type Definition (DTD). This actually creates an XML 1.0 compliant parser. Default attributes are reported and general entities can be resolved by calling the `ResolveEntity` method. The `DOCTYPE` is not used for validation purposes.
Schema	Validate against a W3C-compliant XSD schema, including an inline schema. XSD schemas are specified using a `schemaLocation` attribute.
XDR	Validate against a schema that uses Microsoft's XML Data Reduced (XDR) syntax, including an inline schema. XDR schemas use the `"x-schema"` namespace prefix or the `Schemas` property.
None	No validation is performed. Can be used to "switch off" validation when not required.

The diagram also shows how we can use a separate (that is, not inline and not linked) schema or DTD to validate our document. And, as schemas can inherit from each other, there could be several schemas that we want to apply to our XML document (thought there can only be one DTD). To cope with this, the `XmlValidatingReader` exposes a reference to an `XmlSchemaCollection` through the `Schemas` property. This collection contains all the schemas we want to use. We'll see how we work with an `XmlSchemaCollection` object in the example page coming up shortly.

Validating XML in Document Objects

If you are used to using the MSXML parser in ASP 3.0 or other environments, you may expect to be able to validate a document when you load it simply by setting some property. For example, with MSXML, the `ValidateOnParse` property can be set to `True` to validate a document that contains an inline schema or DTD, or a reference to an external schema or DTD.

However, things are different under the `System.XML` classes in .NET. Loading a combined schema or DTD and the XML data content (that is, an inline schema) or an XML document that references an external schema or DTD into any of the XML "storage" objects such as `XmlDocument`, `XmlDataDocument`, and `XPathDocument`, does not automatically validate that document. And there is no property that you can set to make it do this.

Instead, you load the document via an `XmlTextReader` object. The `Load` method of all the `XmlDocument` and `XmlDataDocument` objects can accept an `XmlTextReader` as the single parameter instead of a file path and name. Meanwhile the constructor for the `XPathDocument` object also accepts an `XmlTextReader` as the single parameter.

So all we have to do is set up our `XmlValidatingReader` and `XmlTextReader` combination, and then pass this to the `Load` method or the constructor function (depending on which document object we're creating). The document will then be validated as it is loaded:

```
'create XmlTextReader, load XML document and create Validator
objXTReader = New XmlTextReader(strXMLPath)
Dim objValidator As New XmlValidatingReader(objXTReader)
objValidator.ValidationType = ValidationType.Schema
```

```
'use the validator/reader combination to create XPathDocument object
Dim objXPathDoc As New XPathDocument(objXTReader)

'use the validator/reader combination to create XmlDocument object
Dim objXmlDoc As New XmlDocument()
objXmlDoc.Load(objXTReader)
```

The `XmlValidatingReader` can also be used to validate XML held in a `String`. So we can validate XML that's already loaded into an object or application by simply extracting it as a `String` object (using the `GetXml` method with a `DataSet` object, or the `OuterXml` property to get a document fragment, for example) and applying the `XmlValidatingReader` to this.

Validating XML in a DataSet Object

Like the XML document objects, a `DataSet` does not automatically validate XML that you provide for the `ReadXml` method against any schema that is already in place within the `DataSet` or which is inline with the XML (that is, in the same document as the XML data content). In a `DataSet`, the schema is used solely to provide information about the intended structure of the data. It's not used for actual validation at all.

When we load the schema, the `DataSet` uses it as a specification for the table names, column names, data types, etc. Then, when we load the XML data content, it arranges the data in the appropriate tables and columns as new data rows. If a value or element is encountered that doesn't match the schema, it is ignored and that particular column in the current data row is left empty.

This makes sense, because the `DataSet` is designed to work with structured relational data, and so any superfluous content in the source file cannot be part of the correct data model. So, you should think of schemas in a `DataSet` as being a way to specify the data structure (rather than inferring the structure from the data, as happens if no schema is present). Don't think of this as a way of validating the data.

A Document Validation Example

We've provided an example page 'Validating XML documents with an XmlValidatingReader object' (`validating-xml.aspx`) that demonstrates how you can validate an XML document. When you first open it, it displays a list of source documents that you can use in a drop-down list and performs validation against the selected document. As you can see from the screenshot, it reports no validation errors in a valid document:

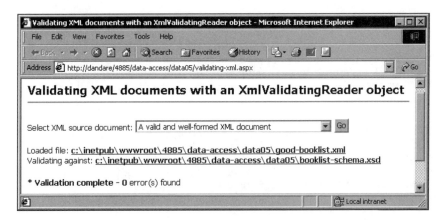

Note that you must run the page in a browser on the Web server itself to be able to open the XML document and schema using the physical paths in the hyperlinks in the page.

However, if you select the "well-formed but invalid" document, it reports a series of validation errors:

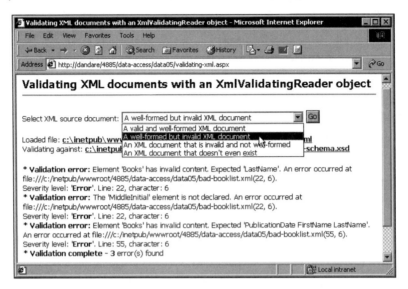

In this case the XML document contains an extra child element within one of the <Books> elements, which is not permitted in the schema that we're using to validate it (you can view the document and the schema using the hyperlinks we provide in the page):

```
<Books>
    <ISBN>1861003315</ISBN>
    <Title>Professional Outlook 2000 Programming</Title>
    <PublicationDate>1999-12-01T00:00:00</PublicationDate>
    <FirstName>Chris</FirstName>
    <MiddleInitial>J</MiddleInitial>
    <LastName>Burnham</LastName>
</Books>
```

The Code for the Validation Example

The code that performs the validation is shown in the next listings. We start by creating the paths to the schema and XML document. In this example, the document name comes from the drop-down list named `selXMLFile` that is defined earlier in the page – the filename itself is the `value` attribute of the selected item:

```
'create physical path to sample files (in same folder as ASPX page)
Dim strCurrentPath As String = Request.PhysicalPath
Dim strXMLPath As String = Left(strCurrentPath, _
    InStrRev(strCurrentPath, "\")) & selXMLFile.SelectedItem.Value
Dim strSchemaPath As String = Left(strCurrentPath, _
    InStrRev(strCurrentPath, "\")) & "booklist-schema.xsd"
```

We then declare a variable to hold the number of validation errors we find. This is followed by code to create an `XmlTextReader` object, specifying the XML document as the source. We also display a hyperlink to this document:

```
'variable to count number of validation errors found
Dim intValidErrors As Integer = 0

'create the new XmlTextReader object and load the XML document
objXTReader = New XmlTextReader(strXMLPath)
outXMLDoc.innerHTML = "Loaded file: <a href=""" & strXMLPath _
   & """>" & strXMLPath & "</a><br />"
```

Creating the XmlValidatingReader and Specifying the Schema

The next step is to create our `XmlValidatingReader` object with the `XmlTextReader` as the source, and specify the validation type to suit our schema (we could, of course, have used `Auto` to automatically validate against any type of schema or DTD):

```
'create an XMLValidatingReader for this XmlTextReader
Dim objValidator As New XmlValidatingReader(objXTReader)

'set the validation type to use an XSD schema
objValidator.ValidationType = ValidationType.Schema
```

Our schema is in a separate document and there is no link or reference to it in the XML document, so we need to specify which schema we want to use. We create a new `XmlSchemaCollection`, and add our schema to it using the `Add` method of the `XmlSchemaCollection`. Then we add this collection to the `Schemas` property, and display a link to the schema:

```
'create a new XmlSchemaCollection
Dim objSchemaCol As New XmlSchemaCollection()

'add the booklist-schema.xsd schema to it
objSchemaCol.Add("", strSchemaPath)

'assign the schema collection to the XmlValidatingReader
objValidator.Schemas.Add(objSchemaCol)

outXMLDoc.innerHTML += "Validating against: <a href=""" _
   & strSchemaPath & """>" & strSchemaPath & "</a>"
```

Specifying the Validation Event Handler

The `XmlValidatingReader` will raise an event whenever it encounters a validation error in the document, as the `XmlTextReader` reads it from our disk file. If we don't handle this event specifically, it will be raised to the default error handler. In our case, this is the `Try...Catch` construct we include in our example page.

However, it's often better to handle the validation events separately from other (usually fatal) errors such as the XML file not actually existing on disk. To specify our own event handler for the `ValidationEventHandler` event in Visual Basic we use the `AddHandler` method, and pass it the event we want to handle and a pointer to our handler routine (which is named `ValidationError` in this example):

```
'add the event handler for any validation errors found
AddHandler objValidator.ValidationEventHandler, AddressOf ValidationError
```

545

Reading the Document and Catching Parser Errors

We are now ready to read the XML document from the disk file. In our case, we're only reading through to check for validation errors. In an application, you would have code here to perform whatever tasks you need against the XML, or alternatively you would use the XmlTextReader as the source for the Load method of an XmlDocument or XmlDataDocument object, or in the constructor for an XPathDocument object:

```
Try

'iterate through the document reading and validating each element
While objValidator.Read()
'use or display the XML content here as required
End While
```

Once validation is complete, we display a count of the number of errors found, and close the reader object to release the disk file. If the document is not well-formed, or cannot be loaded for any other reason (such as it doesn't exist), a parser error occurs. So we include a statement in the Catch section that displays the error in this case:

```
'display count of errors found
    outXMLDoc.innerHTML += "Validation complete " & intValidErrors _
        & " error(s) found"

    Catch objError As Exception

    'will occur if there is a read error or the document cannot be parsed
    outXMLDoc.innerHTML += "Read/Parser error: " & objError.Message

    Finally

    'must remember to always close the XmlTextReader after use
    objXTReader.Close()

    End Try
```

That's all we need to do to validate the document. The remaining part of the code in this page is the event handler that we specified for the Validation event. We'll look at this next.

The ValidationEvent Handler

The XmlValidatingReader raises the Validation event whenever a validation error is discovered in the XML document, and we've specified that our event handler named ValidationError will be called when this event is raised. The event handler receives the usual reference to the object that raised the event, plus a ValidationEventArgs object containing information about the event.

In the event handler, we first increment our error counter, and then check what kind of error it is by using the Severity property of the ValidationEventArgs object. Then we display a message describing the error, and the line number and character position if available (although these are generally included in the error message anyway):

```
Public Sub ValidationError(objSender As Object, _
    objArgs As ValidationEventArgs)
'event handler called when a validation error is found
```

```
      intValidErrors += 1    'increment count of errors

      'check the severity of the error
      Dim strSeverity As String
      If objArgs.Severity = 0 Then strSeverity = "Error"
      If objArgs.Severity = 1 Then strSeverity = "Warning"

      'display a message
      outXMLDoc.innerHTML += "Validation error: " & objArgs.Message _
          & "<br /> Severity level: '" & strSeverity
      If objXTReader.LineNumber > 0 Then
          outXMLDoc.innerHTML += "Line: " & objXTReader.LineNumber _
                & ", character: " & objXTReader.LinePosition
      End If

  End Sub
```

We saw the validation error messages in the previous screenshot using a well-formed but invalid document. We've also provided an XML document that is not well-formed so that you can see the parser error that is raised in this case and trapped by our Try...Catch construct. This also prevents the remainder of the document from being read:

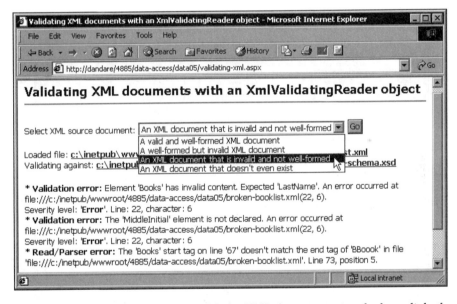

In this case, as you can verify if you try to open the XML document using the hyperlink, there is an illegal closing tag for one of the <Books> elements:

```
<Books>
   <ISBN>1861003382</ISBN>
   <Title>Beginning Active Server Pages 3.0</Title>
   <PublicationDate>1999-12-01T00:00:00</PublicationDate>
   <FirstName>David</FirstName>
   <LastName>Sussman</LastName>
</BBoook>
```

We've also provided an option that tries to load a non-existent XML document, so you can see that the page traps this error successfully as well.

Creating and Editing XML Documents

We've spent a lot of time looking at how we can read and write XML documents, access them in a range of ways, and validate the content against a schema or DTD. However, we haven't looked at how we can edit XML documents, or how we create new ones. The example page for this section, 'Creating and Editing the Content of XML Documents' (edit-xml.aspx) fills out these gaps in our coverage.

The example page loads an XML document named bookdetails.xml and demonstrates four different techniques we can use for editing and creating documents:

❏ Selecting a node, extracting the content, and deleting that node from the document

❏ Creating a new empty document and adding a declaration and comment to it

❏ Importing (that is, copying) a node from the original document into the new document

❏ Selecting, editing and inserting new nodes and content into the original document

The next screenshot shows the page when you run it. You can see the four stages of the process, though the second and third are combined into one section of the output in the page:

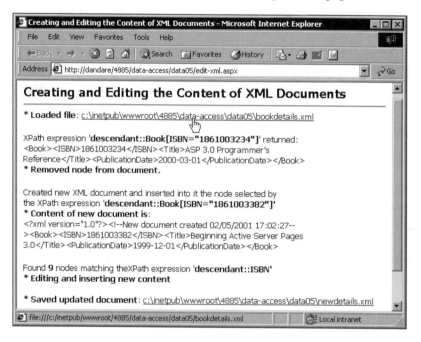

Note that you must run the page in a browser on the Web server itself to be able to open the XML documents using the physical paths in the hyperlinks in the page.

The Code for this Example Page

The page contains the customary `<div>` elements to display the results and messages, and details of any errors that we encounter. It also creates the paths to the existing and new documents and displays a hyperlink to the existing document. This is identical to the previous example, and we aren't repeating the code here. Instead, we start with the part that loads the existing document into a new `XmlDocument` object:

```
Dim objXMLDoc As New XmlDocument()

Try
    objXMLDoc.Load(strXMLPath)
Catch objError As Exception
    outError.innerHTML = "Error while accessing document.<br />" _
        & objError.Message & "<br />" & objError.Source
    Exit Sub  ' and stop execution
End Try
```

Selecting, Displaying, and Deleting a Node

To select a specific node in our document we can use an **XPath expression**. In our example the expression is `descendant::Book[ISBN="1861003234"]`, which, when the current node is the root element of the document, selects the `<Book>` node with the specified value for its `<ISBN>` child node.

We use this expression in the `SelectSingleNode` method, and it returns a reference to the node we want. To display this node and its content, we just have to reference its `OuterXml` property:

```
'specify XPath expression to select a book element
Dim strXPath As String = "descendant::Book[ISBN=" & Chr(34) _
    & "1861003234" & Chr(34) & "]"

'get a reference to the matching <Book> node
Dim objNode As XmlNode
objNode = objXMLDoc.SelectSingleNode(strXPath)

'display node and content using the OuterXml property
outResult1.InnerHtml = "XPath expression '<b>" & strXPath _
    & "</b>' returned:<br />" _
    & Server.HtmlEncode(objNode.OuterXml) & "<br />"
```

*If we only want the **content** of the node, we can use the `InnerXml` property, and if we only want the **text values** of all the nodes concatenated together we can use the `InnerText` property.*

To delete the node from the document, we call the `RemoveChild` method of the parent node (the root of the document is returned by the `DocumentElement` property of the document object), and pass it the reference to the node to be deleted:

```
'delete this node using RemoveChild method from document element
objXMLDoc.DocumentElement.RemoveChild(objNode)
outResult1.InnerHtml += "Removed node from document.<br />"
```

Creating a New Document and Adding Nodes

We create a new empty XML document, simply by instantiating an XmlDocument (or XmlDataDocument) object. Then we can create nodes and insert them into this document using code like the following. Here, we're creating a new XML declaration (the `<?xml version="1.0"?>` element) and inserting it into the new document with the InsertBefore method:

```
'create new empty XmlDocument object
Dim objNewDoc As New XmlDocument()

'create a new XmlDeclaration object
Dim objDeclare As XmlDeclaration
objDeclare = objNewDoc.CreateXmlDeclaration("1.0", Nothing, Nothing)

'and add it as the first node in the new document
objDeclare = objNewDoc.InsertBefore(objDeclare, _
    objNewDoc.DocumentElement)
```

The second and third parameters of the `CreateXmlDeclaration` *method are used to specify the encoding type used in the document, and the* `standalone` *value (in other words, if there is a schema available to validate the document). We set both to* `Nothing`*, so we'll get neither of these optional attributes in our XML declaration element. An XML parser will then assume the default values* `"UTF-8"` *and* `"true"` *when it loads the document.*

When we create the new node, we get a reference to it back from the CreateXmlDeclaration method, and we use this as the first parameter to the InsertBefore method. The second parameter is a reference to the node that we want to insert before, and in this case we specify the root of the document. Notice that DocumentElement is not the root element of the document, as it doesn't yet have one. This sounds confusing, but you can think of it as a reference to the placeholder where the root element will reside.

Next we create a new Comment element, and insert this into the new document after the XML declaration element:

```
'create a new XmlComment object
Dim objComment As XmlComment
objComment = objNewDoc.CreateComment("New document created " & Now())

'and add it as the second node in the new document
objComment = objNewDoc.InsertAfter(objComment, objDeclare)
```

Importing Nodes into the New Document

To get some content into the new document we just created, our example page imports a node from the existing document that we loaded from disk at the start of the page. We again use an XPath expression with the SelectSingleNode method to get a reference to the <Book> element we want to import:

```
strXPath = "descendant::Book[ISBN=" & Chr(34) _
    & "1861003382" & Chr(34) & "]"
objNode = objXMLDoc.SelectSingleNode(strXPath)
```

Now we create a new `XmlNode` object in the target document to hold the imported node, and call the `Import` method of this new node to copy the node from the original document. The second parameter to the `Import` method specifies if we want a "deep" copy – in other words if we want to import all the content of the node as well as the value:

```
'create a variable to hold the imported node object
Dim objImportedNode As XmlNode

'import node and all children into new doc (unattached fragment)
objImportedNode = objNewDoc.ImportNode(objNode, True)
```

Once we've got our new node into the document, we have to insert it into the tree – it is only an unattached fragment at the moment. We use the `InsertAfter` method as before, using the reference we've already got to the new node, and the reference we created earlier to our `Comment` node so that the imported node becomes the root element of the new document:

```
'insert new unattached node into document after the comment node
objNewDoc.InsertAfter(objImportedNode, objComment)

'display the contents of the new document
outResult2.InnerHtml = "Created new XML document and inserted " _
    & "into it the node selected by<br />" _
    & "the XPath expression '" & strXPath & "'" _
    & "Content of new document is:<br />" _
    & Server.HtmlEncode(objNewDoc.OuterXml)
```

We finish this section (in the code above) by displaying the contents of the new document. We've got a reference to the `XmlDocument` object that contains it, so we just query the `OuterXml` property to get the complete content. You can see the new document displayed in the example page:

```
Created new XML document and inserted into it the node selected by
the XPath expression 'descendant::Book[ISBN="1861003382"]'
* Content of new document is:
<?xml version="1.0"?><!--New document created 02/05/2001 17:02:27--
><Book><ISBN>1861003382</ISBN><Title>Beginning Active Server Pages
3.0</Title><PublicationDate>1999-12-01</PublicationDate></Book>
```

Inserting and Updating Nodes in a Document

The final part of our example page edits some values that are in the original document. This time we need an XPath expression that will match more than one node, and so we use the `SelectNodes` method of the document to return an `XmlNodeList` object containing references to all the matching nodes (in our example all the `<ISBN>` nodes). Then we can display the number of matches found:

```
strXPath = "descendant::ISBN"

'get a reference to the matching nodes as a collection
Dim colNodeList As XmlNodeList
colNodeList = objXMLDoc.SelectNodes(strXPath)

'display the number of matches found
outResult3.InnerHtml = "Found " & colNodeList.Count _
    & " nodes matching the" _
    & "XPath expression '" & strXPath & "'<br />" _
    & "Editing and inserting new content<br />"
```

Our plan is to add an attribute to all of the <ISBN> elements, and replace the text content (value) of these elements with two new elements that contain the information in a different form. After declaring some variables that we'll need, we iterate through the collection of <ISBN> nodes using a For...Each loop:

```
Dim strNodeValue, strNewValue, strShortCode As String

'create a variable to hold an XmlAttribute object
Dim objAttr As XmlAttribute

'iterate through all the nodes found
For Each objNode In colNodeList
```

Within the loop, we first create a new attribute named "formatting" and set the value to "hyphens" (all our <ISBN> nodes will have the same value for this attribute). Then we can add this attribute to the <ISBN> element node by calling the SetAttribute method. However, there is a minor hitch – the members of an XmlNodeList are XmlNode objects, which don't have a SetAttribute method. We get round this in Visual Basic by casting the object to an XmlElement object using the CType (convert type) function:

```
'create an XmlAttribute named 'formatting'
objAttr = objXMLDoc.CreateAttribute("formatting")

'set the value of the XmlAttribute to 'hyphens'
objAttr.Value = "hyphens"

'and add it to this ISBN element - have to cast the object
'to an XmlElement as XmlNode doesn't have this method
CType(objNode, XmlElement).SetAttributeNode(objAttr)
```

To change the content of the <ISBN> elements, we just have to set the InnerXml property. This is much easier than using the InsertBefore and InsertAfter methods we demonstrated previously, and provides a valid alternative when the content you want to insert is available as a String (recall that we had references to the element node and its new content node when we used InsertBefore previously).

Our code extracts the existing ISBN value, creates the new "short code" from it, formats the existing ISBN with hyphens, and then creates a string containing the new content for the element. The final step is to insert these values into the <ISBN> node by setting its InnerXml property, before going round to do the next one:

```
'get text value of this ISBN element
strNodeValue = objNode.InnerText

'create short and long strings to replace content
strShortCode = Right(strNodeValue, 4)
  strNewValue = Left(strNodeValue, 1) & "-" _
    & Mid(strNodeValue, 2, 6) & "-" _
    & Mid(strNodeValue, 8, 2) & "-" _
    & Right(strNodeValue, 1)

'insert into element by setting the InnerXml property
objNode.InnerXml = "<LongCode>" & strNewValue _
    & "</LongCode><ShortCode>" _
    & strShortCode & "</ShortCode>"

Next
```

We end the page by writing the complete edited XML document to a disk file and displaying a hyperlink to it so that you can view it:

```
'write the updated document to a disk file
objXMLDoc.Save(strNewPath)

'display a link to view the updated document
outResult3.InnerHTML += "Saved updated document: <a href=""" _
  & strNewPath & """>" & strNewPath & "</a>"
```

Viewing the Results

If you open both documents, the original and the edited version, you can see the effects of our editing process. The first contains the <Book> node with the <ISBN> value 1861003234, while it is not present in the second one (they are in order by ISBN code). You can also see the updated <ISBN> elements in the second document:

In this example we've demonstrated several techniques for working with an XML document, using the System.Xml classes provided in .NET. Some of the techniques use the XML DOM methods as defined by W3C, and some are specific "extensions" available with the XmlDocument (and other) objects. In general, these extensions make common tasks a lot easier, for example the ability to access the InnerText, InnerXml, and OuterXml of a node makes it remarkably easy to edit or insert content and markup.

We have by no means covered all the possibilities for accessing XML documents, as you'll see if you examine the list of properties, methods and events for each of the relevant objects in the SDK. However, by now, you should have a flavor for what is possible, and how easy it is to achieve.

Using XSL and XSLT Transformations

To finish this chapter, we need to come back to a topic that we first looked at in the data management introduction chapter. There, we saw how easy it is to perform an XSL or XSLT transformation against an XML document using the new `XslTransform` object. However, we only used the very basic approach of applying it to two disk files (an XML document and a style sheet) by specifying the paths to these files.

We can use the `XslTransform` object to perform transformations when the document is not actually a disk file. This could well be the case in an application that processes XML. For example it could be referenced by an `XmlTextReader`, or stored in the `XmlDocument` object returned by a Web Service or business component, or even pointed to by an existing `XPathNavigator`.

And you might not want the results to be written to disk as a file – you might need them as a `String` or a `StringBuilder` object. Our example attempts to demonstrate several of these scenarios.

An XSL Transformation Example

The example page, 'Different ways to use the XSLTransform object' (`multi-xsl-transform.aspx`) is shown next. It loads the XML document and the stylesheet from disk at the start of the page, but then references the XML document in a range of ways to demonstrate the possibilities. It also performs a transformation to a `String`, and displays this in the page before writing it to disk separately – rather than directly through the `XslTransform` object:

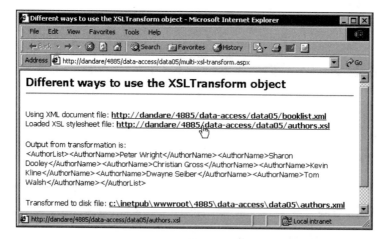

Remember that, again, you must run the page in a browser on the Web server itself to be able to open the XML document and style sheet using the physical paths in the hyperlinks in the page.

The next screenshot shows the simple stylesheet we're using. All it does is extract the `<AuthorName>` elements from the XML source document and generate a new XML document containing these – within a root element named `<AuthorList>`:

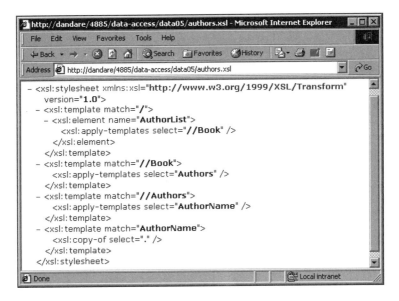

The Code for the XslTransform Example

After creating the paths to the XML document and XSL stylesheet we're using, the code displays hyperlinks to these. We haven't repeated the code for this again here. What we're interested in is the way that we load the documents and execute the transformation itself.

We start by creating a new `XslTransform` object and loading the stylesheet into it, using the `Load` method with the path and filename of the style sheet:

```
'create a new XslTransform object to do the transformation
Dim objTransform As New XslTransform()

'load the XSL stylesheet into the XSLTransform object
objTransform.Load(strXSLPath)
```

To load the XML document in this example, we use an `XmlTextReader`. What we're demonstrating here isn't the quickest or shortest way to do it, but instead it aims to give you ideas about how you can use the various objects in your own projects. For example, by loading the XML document with an `XmlTextReader`, we have the opportunity to validate it at the same time if this is a requirement. We would just need to assign an `XmlValidatingReader` to the `XmlTextReader`.

So, our code creates the `XmlTextReader` for the XML document and then creates a new `XPathDocument` from this `XmlTextReader`. The constructor for the `XPathDocument` automatically loads the XML from disk into the new `XPathDocument`:

```
'create a new XmlTextReader object to fetch XML document
Dim objXTReader As New XmlTextReader(strXMLPath)

'create a new XPathDocument object from the XmlTextReader
Dim objXPDoc As New XPathDocument(objXTReader)
```

Now we can create a new XPathNavigator based on the XPathDocument by calling the CreateNavigator method:

```
'create a new XPathNavigator object from the XPathDocument
Dim objXPNav As XPathNavigator
objXPNav = objXPDoc.CreateNavigator()
```

Displaying the Transformed Result with an XmlReader

The Transform method of the XslTransform object can only output the result of a transformation to an XmlReader object, a TextReader object or an XmlWriter object. If we want the result to be available as a string, for use elsewhere in our applications, we use an XmlReader or a TextReader object (depending on whether the result is XML that we want to parse as we use it, or some other format that we can't use with an XmlReader).

Our example transforms the XML into an XmlReader object. We declare a variable to hold the object, and call the Transform method of the XslTransform object before passing it the XPathNavigator we created for the XML document. The second argument allows us to pass in an XsltArgumentList object that can contain the parameters or arguments used by the stylesheet. As we don't have any parameters in our stylesheet, we use the value Nothing for this argument:

```
'create a variable to hold the XmlReader object that is
'returned from the Transform method
Dim objReader As XmlReader

'perform the transformation using the XSL file in the
'XSLTransform and the XML document referenced by the
'XPathNavigator. The result is in the XmlReader object
objReader = objTransform.Transform(objXPNav, Nothing)
```

Once we get back our XmlReader object we can display the contents – the result of the transformation. The easiest way is to use the ReadOuterXML method of the reader:

```
'display the contents of the XmlReader object
objReader.MoveToContent()
outResults.InnerText = objReader.ReadOuterXml()
```

Writing the Transformed Result to Disk

The alternative "output device" for the Transform method of the XslTransform object is an XmlWriter object. This is ideal for piping the output back to a disk file. In our example page, we create an XmlTextWriter object (a public class that inherits from XmlWriter), using a path and filename that we created earlier in the page. The second parameter to the constructor is the encoding to use – if we specify Nothing it sets the encoding to the default "UTF-8":

```
'create an XMLTextWriter object to write result to disk
Dim objWriter As New XmlTextWriter(strOutPath, Nothing)
```

Now we can use our `XmlTextWriter` to create the disk file. We start with an XML declaration (by simply calling the `WriteStartDocument` method) and add a comment element:

```
'write the opening <?xml .. ?> declaration and a comment
objWriter.WriteStartDocument()
objWriter.WriteComment("List of authors created " & Now())
```

Then we can perform the transformation, sending the results directly to our `XmlTextWriter` – which writes them straight to the disk file. We finish by calling the `WriteEndDocument` method, to close any open elements and finalize the document, then close it and display a hyperlink so that you can examine the results:

```
'transform the XML into the XMLTextWriter
objTransform.Transform(objXPNav, Nothing, objWriter)

'ensure that all open elements are closed and end the document
objWriter.WriteEndDocument()

'flush the buffer to disk and close the file
objWriter.Close()
outFile.InnerHtml = "<a href=""" & strOutPath & """>" _
    & strOutPath & "</a>"
```

If you open the hyperlink at the bottom of the example page, you see the transformed result:

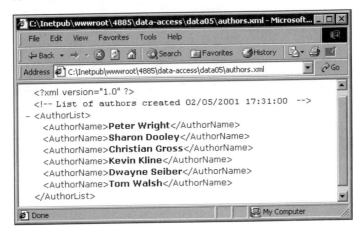

Summary

This chapter ends our voyage of exploration through the exciting new techniques available for accessing data under the .NET Framework. Over the previous four chapters, we've examined the main objects we use for both relational data and XML document access, seen how we can program with them, and showed you how these two traditionally opposing data-handling technologies are now integrated together.

This chapter completed the tour by concentrating on the ways we can work with objects drawn mainly from the System.XML namespaces – in particular we looked at how we can read, write, validate, and edit XML documents using a variety of methods. We also explored in more depth the way that integration between XML and relational data is achieved through the XmlDataDocument and DataSet objects.

Then, after looking at some of the options available for creating and editing XML documents, we finished up with a more detailed look at the capabilities of the XslTransform object. This object makes it easy to perform server-side XSL and XSLT transformations using style sheets.

Although we couldn't possibly cover all the topics of XML handling in .NET, you should now be familiar with the basics, the objects that are available, and how they can be used within your applications. To summarize, in this chapter we introduced:

- ❑ Accessing relational data as XML and vice versa
- ❑ Synchronization between an XML document and the DataSet object
- ❑ Validating XML documents using a schema
- ❑ Creating and editing XML documents in a range of different ways
- ❑ Some alternatives available when transforming XML using style sheets

We now leave data management behind and move on to pastures new. In the next two chapters you'll see how we go about configuring our ASP.NET applications.

"The Babel fish," says The Hitch Hiker's Guide to Galaxy "is small, yellow and leech-like, and probably the oddest thing in the Universe. It feeds on brainwave energy not from its carrier but from those around it. It absorbs all unconscious mental frequencies from this brainwave energy to nourish itself with. It then excretes into the mind of its carrier a telepathic matrix formed by combining the conscious thought frequencies with nerve signals picked up from the speech centres of the brain which has supplied them".

The practical upshot of all this is that if you stick a Babel fish in your ear you can instantly understand anything said to you in any form of language. The speech patterns you actually hear decode the brainwave matrix which has been fed into your mind by your Babel fish.

Web Applications and Global.asax

Classic ASP supported the concept of a Web Application. This was primarily a collection of .asp files plus the global.asa file. ASP.NET expands upon this concept, but includes additional resources such as ASP.NET Pages, Web Services, User Controls, configuration data, global.asax, and several other files (both user-defined and defined by ASP.NET).

This chapter has two key themes: first we'll look at how to create an ASP.NET Web Application, before going on to look at how we can use global.asax. Below is a breakdown of what we'll cover:

- ❑ **Creating IIS Web Roots and Applications** – In the first section we'll look at what a Web Application is, and how we can create new Web Applications using the Internet Information Services Manager (IIS). The steps covered in this section don't discuss ASP.NET features in their own right, but are relevant for using IIS as a host for ASP.NET.

- ❑ **ASP.NET Web Applications** – In this section we'll focus on two aspects of ASP.NET Web Applications: the \bin directory for compiled code deployment and the global.asax file format.

- ❑ **Application State** – Here we'll look at the three options in ASP.NET for maintaining application state: Application, Session, and Cache.

- ❑ **Application Events** – After discussing our choices for managing state in ASP.NET we'll look at the supported application level events, such as Application_OnStart and Application_OnError. Then we'll discuss the ordering of the events as well as some code examples showing use.

- ❑ **Advanced Topics** – In this last section of the chapter we'll cover some advanced topics. These topics include asynchronous application events, and using static variables.

Note that in the following chapter, we'll look at specific details of how we can configure our application – for example, how to set the Session state timeout using ASP.NET's new configuration system.

IIS Web Roots and Applications

An ASP.NET application consists of a collection of resources such as configuration information, global application files, compiled components, and other ASP.NET resources (pages, web services, etc.). These applications are defined using IIS application roots in the same manner as classic ASP. By default the **root directory** of a web site in IIS is an application root. This is the root level of a particular web site. For example, on a default Windows 2000 IIS 5.0 installation, the root directory of the default web site is http://localhost/ or http://<*servername*>, while the physical path of the root directory is c:\inetpub\wwwroot.

An application root is the starting point of an ASP.NET application and contains resources such as the global.asax file and the \bin directory. We'll discuss these in detail later in this chapter.

We can create applications in Internet Information Services (IIS) by using the IIS Microsoft Management Console (MMC) snap-in. Alternatively, both Visual Studio.NET and the command-line scripts included with IIS can be used to create web applications.

Let's look at two of the most common ways of creating an application:

❑ Create a new web site. By default the root directory of the web site will be an application root.

❑ Mark a **folder** (virtual or physical) as an application. The root of the folder will then be defined as an application root.

The IIS MMC displays both physical directories and virtual directories:

❑ A physical directory lives within the web site, for example, c: inetpub\wwwroot\ \Wrox, where c: \inetpub \wwwroot is the physical directory and \Wrox is a directory beneath it. This appears through the web server as: http://localhost/Wrox/.

❑ A virtual directory appears as a directory in the web site, but it exists in a separate physical path. For example c:\Wrox\ appears to be a directory available through the server as http://localhost/Wrox/). This is in fact a virtual directory since c:\Wrox's physical path is obviously not part of the root directory of our web site. For this reason, virtual directories are very useful, since multiple virtual directories can point to a common set of files, or live on the same file share.

Although we will go through the steps of creating both virtual directories and IIS applications this is only necessary if we want to create ASP.NET applications in directories other than the web's root directory, (usually c:\inetpub\wwwroot), as the web root is by default an application root. Most likely, we will be creating applications that are part of an existing site. For example, if we were hosting the HR site for our company, we'd have separate applications defined for Benefits, Claims, Hiring/Firing, etc.

Let's walk through creating a virtual directory and an IIS application.

Creating IIS Virtual Directories and Applications

Say we have a physical directory, c:\Wrox, and we want to expose that directory as a virtual directory in the web root of our web site, for example. http://localhost/Wrox.

Creating a Virtual Directory

To create a virtual directory we need to use the IIS MMC, which is available from Start | Programs | Administrative Tools | Internet Services Manager, or by selecting Start | Run and then typing inetmgr:

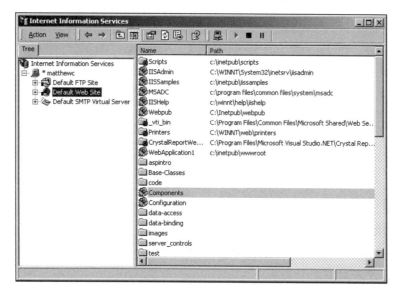

To create the Wrox virtual directory in the Default Web Site (highlighted) we simply right-click on Default Web Site and select New | Virtual Directory. This opens the Virtual Directory Creation Wizard, where we go through the following steps:

❑ Once the wizard is open, select Next to get past the opening screen. We will then be asked for the alias to use for the virtual directory. For this example, we'll enter Wrox, but this can be anything you like – you're not restricted to using the same name as the physical directory.

❑ We are then asked for the path to an existing directory we want to use as a virtual directory. We'll enter C:\Wrox (assuming we've already created it).

❑ Next, we're asked for the access permissions for the directory. The only required selections are Read and Run scripts (such as ASP). These are defaults and already selected.

❑ Finally, we're told that the virtual directory has been created and we press the Finish button to exit the wizard.

If we now view the available folders in our Default Web Site, we'll find a folder named Wrox. There are three types of icons next to folders in the root of this web site, as shown overleaf:

❑ **Normal explorer style folders** – For example if FrontPage server extensions are installed we'll see folders named: _vti_cnf, _vti_log, etc. – these folders exist as physical directories in the web server.

❑ **Normal explorer style folders with small globes in the bottom right corner** – These are virtual directories. Some common virtual directories include: Scripts and _vti_bin.

❑ **Web Application Folders** – These folders are represented by a package icon. Any virtual or physical directory on our server can be converted into a Web Application. By default the virtual directories we create are web application folders.

So the virtual directory Wrox that we just created is both a virtual directory and a Web Application. The fact that it is a Web Application takes precedence over its being a virtual directory, so it is represented by a package icon (as shown in the next figure):

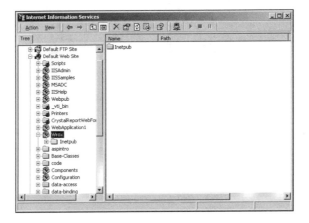

Marking a Folder as an Application

Instead of creating the Wrox directory as c:\Wrox and marking it as a virtual directory, we could have created a directory c:\inetpub\wwwroot\Wrox. Wrox is then a physical directory for the **Default Web Site**.

> *Note the default directory of the Default Web Site is c:\inetpub\wwwroot\.*

Because c:\inetpub\wwwroot\Wrox is a physical directory, we'll have to manually mark it as an application to use it as an ASP.NET application root.

We can do this by right-clicking on any virtual or physical folder in any IIS web and selecting Properties. This brings up a properties dialog for that folder, for example our \Wrox folder:

In the above dialog we can see the settings for the current folder, the Local Path value, and the permissions that folder allows. In this case the default permissions of Read, Log visits, and Index this resource are set.

In the lower half of the wrox Properties dialog box is a section defined as Application Settings. This is of interest to us, because here we can enable the physical directory as a web application. To do this we simply press the Create button. This changes some of the settings in the Application Settings section, as shown in the following figure:

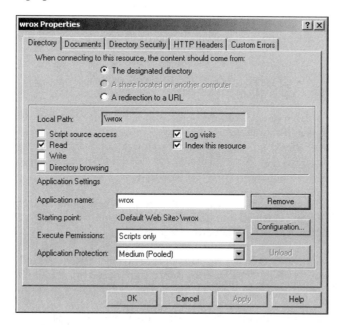

The Application name value has changed from Default Application (the name of the parent web application for this folder) to wrox. The Starting point value has changed from <Default Web Site> to <Default Web Site>\wrox, again noting that the application has changed. For simplicity, we'll skip over the smaller unimportant changes, except to note that the Create button has now become a Remove button.

> *For more detailed information on what the remaining options within the Properties dialog do, please see the Internet Information Server documentation, as they do not relate to further discussions of ASP.NET in this chapter. The only exception is mapping custom extensions to ASP.NET, which is covered later in the Advanced Topics section.*

> *Users familiar with the Application Protection settings should note that these do not affect ASP.NET since that runs in its own process, which is separate from IIS. Please see the IIS documentation for more information on this option.*

Finally, click Apply and then OK. The Wrox folder is now an application root, just as it was when we created it as a virtual directory.

Removing the Application

Removing a Web Application is just as simple as, if not easier than, creating it. Right-click on a folder marked as an application and select Properties. Within the Application Settings section of the dialog click the R*e*move button, then select Apply and OK. In the tree view of our Default Web Site we will now see the standard virtual or physical folder icon for Wrox.

> Keep in mind when we remove the application we are simply changing a configuration option in IIS. Removing the application does not delete any associated files.

Now that we've had a quick overview of creating a Web Application in IIS, let's relate this back to ASP.NET.

ASP.NET Web Applications

ASP.NET makes use of IIS web applications to identify distinct **application domains**, which are used by the Common Language Runtime (CLR). Each application domain is separate, secure, and does not share memory with other domains – for example, three web applications Wrox1, Wrox2, and Wrox3 will each be treated separately, so Wrox1 will not share data such as Session or Application state with either of the others, and likewise Wrox2 and Wrox3.

You can think of an application domain as a logical process. When it fails it doesn't take down the host process, so one failure won't crash all our ASP.NET applications. This is one of many new features provided by the CLR that ASP.NET takes advantage of.

An ASP.NET Web Application typically consists of three types of (user-created) resources, in addition to standard ASP pages or web services. These resource types are always found in the root of the application, and include:

❑   \bin – This directory lies immediately below the root of the application, and is used to hold .NET assemblies for use by the application. (An **assembly** is the technical term used to describe a component built with .NET. It is compiled reusable code, an example of which is ADO.NET.)

❑   global.asax – This file is ASP.NET's logical replacement for the ASP file global.asa. It allows us to execute code for ASP.NET application-level events, and to set application-level variables.

❑   web.config – Each web application can have its own ASP.NET configuration settings. These settings, depending upon the security configuration of the system, can override settings found in ASP.NET's machine.config.

> *The machine.config file applies global default settings for all ASP.NET applications. We'll cover ASP.NET configuration in more detail in the next chapter.*

Let's start by briefly looking at the ASP.NET \bin directory as it relates to ASP.NET web applications.

Registering Components

Rather than relying upon the system registry, ASP.NET uses a special directory, \bin, to register components as part of an application.

The next section will illustrate the differences between classic ASP/COM component registration and the new ASP.NET/Assembly registration.

Prior to .NET

If we wanted to use COM (reusable compiled code) in ASP, we always had to register the components on the server. For example, if we developed a simple data access component using Visual Basic 6 and wished to use that component in an ASP application, we would need to explicitly register it before we could make use of it.

Registering components was done either through a command-line tool, regsvr32.exe, or with COM+ Services (found in **Start | Programs | Administrative Tools | Component Services**). In either case an entry was made in the Windows registry describing the component, its threading model, and the location of the .dll file.

We could then write code in our ASP application using the Server.CreateObject() method:

```
<%
Dim myObject
Set myObject = Server.CreateObject("Example.DataAccess")
%>
```

Beneath the covers, the ProgID (in this case Example.DataAccess) would be used to find the entry for the required component in the registry. Once found, an instance of the component would be created and a reference set to the local variable myObject.

This is all well and good and many successful applications were (and still are!) built using this model. However, there are some caveats associated with using COM in ASP:

❑ **Deployment and update** – Deploying the component to multiple servers and replacing running components requires local server access.

❑ **Global registration and versioning** – In addition to requiring local server access to manage the components, registered components are available to *all* applications and versioning the component can be rather difficult.

> *Probably one of the most common problems that ASP developers ran into when using COM was the 'locking' of components by IIS when they attempted to replace an existing DLL with a new version.*

You'll be pleased to know that these kinds of ASP/COM issues – deployment, updates, global registration, and versioning – are no longer a problem in ASP.NET.

.NET Components

As we mentioned earlier, in .NET the term **assemblies** is used to describe components, that is packaged units of reusable, compiled code, built with .NET. Unlike ASP, ASP.NET does not require local server access to register a component. Instead we can simply copy our assemblies to an ASP.NET \bin directory using FTP, DAV, etc. Assemblies found in the \bin directory are then automatically loaded by ASP.NET, and the components made available to our application.

Note that there can only be one \bin directory per ASP.NET application.

Local Server Access Not Required

Deploying components in ASP.NET is simple. As described above, local server access is not required and all we need is the ability to copy the compiled assembly to the \bin directory. Once it's there, ASP.NET and the Common Language Runtime take care of everything else, and we can start using the component in our code right away.

So how does this type of registration work? Well, unlike a COM component, whose location and internal architecture need to be explicitly logged in the registry, a .NET assembly is self-describing. That's to say, the assembly's contents include metadata, that describes exactly what the compiled component can and cannot do. All information required to successfully use that component is held in one place, and no extra configuration is required.

Components Are Application Specific

Again, unlike ASP, the .NET components we register in a specific application's \bin directory are only available to that application – by contrast, classic ASP COM components were registered for the entire server.

Note that it is possible to register an assembly to be global for all applications using the Global Assembly Cache (GAC), which we'll cover in more detail in Chapter 23, but this is not the default behavior.

Component Updates

In ASP, when we wanted to replace a component we needed to stop and start IIS since the component was loaded in the IIS process. ASP.NET never locks the file, and thus we can simply delete, or copy over, the assembly when we remove or change the application – a procedure also done without local server access.

This dynamic loading and unloading of the components in the \bin directory works because ASP.NET specifically listens for file change notification events within the \bin directory. When a change is detected – such as the addition or deletion of a component – ASP.NET will create a new application domain to begin servicing the new requests. As soon as the original application domain has completed servicing any outstanding requests it is removed.

As far as the client is concerned, this process is completely transparent, and for the developer it means that updates can be implemented very simply without incurring any application downtime.

Example Use

Let's look at a simple example using our Wrox web application. We'll first need to create a \bin directory, for example, c:\Wrox\bin. Then we'll write a simple ASP.NET page, such as this:

VB.NET

```
<%@ Import Namespace="Component" %>
<%@ Import Namespace="System.Data" %>
<%@ Import Namespace="System.Data.SqlClient" %>

<Script runat="server">
  Public Sub Page_Load()
    Dim simpleComponent As New Simple ()

    Dim dataSet As New DataSet()
    dataSet = simpleComponent.LoadDataSet()

    datagrid1.DataSource = dataSet
    datagrid1.DataBind()
  End Function
</Script>
<font size=6>
<asp:DataGrid runat="server" id="datagrid1"/>
</font>
```

We'll look shortly at implementing the `Component.Simple` *assembly used above.*

This simple page creates a new instance, `simpleComponent`, of an assembly named `Simple`. It then uses the `LoadDataSet()` method of the `simpleComponent` to populate a `DataSet`, which is eventually used to data bind an ASP.NET `datagrid` server control.

At this point, if we requested the page in our browser, we'd receive an error message:

> The namespace or type 'Component' for the import 'Component' cannot be found.

This is because we've identified a namespace 'Component' that doesn't exist yet – we'll create it now.

Using either Visual Studio.NET or the command-line compiler, we can create and compile a simple VB.NET component named `Component.Simple`, which will be responsible for implementing the `LoadDataSet()` method – we're going to build it using VS.NET.

Open VS.NET, and select File | New | Project. Select the Visual Basic Projects type and Class Library for the template. Name the project `Component`, and, finally, implement the following code in the `Class1.vb` file created as part of the project:

```
Imports System.Data
Imports System.Data.SqlClient

Public Class Simple
    Public Function LoadDataSet() As DataSet
        Dim myConnection As SqlConnection
        Dim myCommand As SqlDataAdapter
        Dim products As New DataSet()
        Dim sql As String
        Dim dsn As String

        sql = "select address, city, state from Authors"
        dsn = "server=localhost;uid=sa;pwd=;database=pubs"
                myCommand = New SqlDataAdapter(sql, myConnection)
        myConnection = New SqlConnection(dsn)
```

```
        myCommand.Fill(products, "myAuthors")

        Return products
    End Function
End Class
```

This VB.NET class, named `Simple`, implements the `LoadDataSet()` method required by our ASP.NET page. We compile our VB.NET project by selecting Build | Build. Now, open the File Explorer and navigate to the location where the project was created. Within this location is a `\bin` directory, and we should find a `.dll` named `Component.dll`.

We'll simply copy (*Ctrl-C*) this file to the clipboard, navigate to the `c:\Wrox\bin` directory we created earlier, and paste (*Ctrl-V*) the copy of `Component.dll` there – and that's all there is to it. The act of copying the file into an application's `\bin` directory registers the component. Yes, it's that easy!

If we now request our simple ASP.NET page again, rather than throwing an error, it finds and uses the component, and returns an HTML table naming the address, city, and state (the columns selected in our `Simple` component).

So what if we now want to change the component? Perhaps we decide that we only want to return the address and state? Well, first we need to change our component's `sql` text (as below), and then we must re-compile it with VS.NET.

```
sql = "select address, state from Authors"
```

Once again, we copy the newly compiled component to the `c:\Wrox\bin` directory, and immediately request the ASP.NET page again. The response we see is an HTML table that only shows address and state. Behind the scenes, ASP.NET noticed that we'd replaced the old component, and restarted the application using the new one.

The `\bin` directory dramatically changes the way we build ASP.NET web applications. We no longer require local server access to register components and ASP.NET never locks those components. We can make updates and changes and ASP.NET will simply restart the application using the new version, without requiring us to do anything.

Now that we're somewhat familiar with the `\bin` directory we'll move on to another part of the ASP.NET Web Application, `global.asax`.

Application Code: global.asax

Like ASP, ASP.NET supports a global file for each web application. This file is used as an implementation point for global events, objects, and variables. If you're familiar with classic ASP, you'll recognize this file as `global.asa`. ASP.NET supports a similar file, called `global.asax`.

> The code contained in `global.asax` constitutes part of our application. It does not contain application configuration information – the `web.config` file deals with this, and is covered in the next chapter.

Running ASP.NET and ASP Together

ASP.NET's `global.asax` file uses a separate extension distinct from ASP's `global.asa` file. The extension `.asax` is used so as not to interfere with ASP's `global.asa`. This means that both a `global.asa` and `global.asax` can reside in the same web application root.

Microsoft worked very hard to ensure that installing ASP.NET wouldn't break any existing ASP applications. A caveat of this, however, is that although existing ASP applications will not break when ASP and ASP.NET are installed together, they also won't share any resources. This applies to **all ASP.NET and ASP resources**, not just the `global.asax`/`global.asa` files. ASP.NET maintains its `Application`, `Session`, global events, etc. in complete isolation from ASP. Additionally, in a manner similar to ASP, there can only be one `global.asax` file per web application, and it **must** be called `global.asax`.

Let's take a look at the `global.asax` file format.

File Format of global.asax

The `global.asax` file follows a similar format to ASP.NET pages. Below is a simple template of what a `global.asax` file looks like:

```
<%@ [Directive] [attribute]=[value] %>

<Script runat="server">
  [Application Event Prototypes]
</Script>
```

A `global.asax` file typically includes directives, events, and user code.

Directives

Similar to ASP.NET pages and web services, `global.asax` supports directives that provide ASP.NET with special instructions used in compilation of the `global.asax` file. Below is the prototype for directives – note that multiple attribute/value pairs are supported:

```
<%@ [directive name] [attribute]=[value] [attribute]=[value] %>
```

`global.asax` supports three directives, each with its own settings:

- ❑ **Application** – This allows us to define the base class `global.asax` will use, and additionally supports a simple documentation option. These features are implemented through two attributes: `Inherits` and `Description`.

  - ❑ The **Inherits** attribute allows us to name a .NET class that `global.asax` will use as the base class for all compiled instances of `global.asax`. This is useful if we want to add our own methods or properties to `global.asax`. This is quite a powerful feature and one that we'll discuss in more detail in the *Advanced Topics* section later in this chapter.

  - ❑ The **Description** attribute of the `Application` directive provides a simple way to add some descriptive text about our `global.asax`:

    ```
    <%@ Application Description="A sample global.asax description" %>
    ```

    The value of `Description` is discarded when `global.asax` is compiled.

❑ **Import** – This directive allows us to import .NET namespaces for use in `global.asax`, so giving us a shortcut to full qualification of classes within `global.asax`. This directive is similar in function to the `Imports` keyword in VB.NET or `using` in C#. It simply provides a reference to a namespace that contains classes we wish to make use of.

To use the Import directive, we must guarantee that the assembly in which the namespace exists is also available. If it is not, an ASP.NET exception will occur when the application is run. Support for adding the assembly is done either through the Assembly directive or the `<compilers>` section of our configuration file (configuration is covered in the next chapter). To reference assemblies that are not available, we can use the `Assembly` directive, outlined next.

The `Import` directive requires a single attribute: `Namespace`

❑ The **Namespace** attribute of `Import` is used to identify an assembly namespace for use in `global.asax`. For example, we could use the `Import` directive specifying the namespace attribute for the `System.Data` namespace.

```
<%@ Import namespace="System.Data" %>
```

If we include this directive in the `global.asax` file for our web application, we can use classes in `System.Data` without the need to fully qualify the class name.

For example, if we use the `DataSet` class we can refer to it as `System.Data.DataSet` (fully qualified class name), or use the `Import` directive naming the `System.Data` namespace and refer to the class simply as `DataSet`.

Using the `Import` directive and its `Namespace` attribute saves us from having to fully qualify the name of the class. However, in the event that two namespaces share a common class name (such as `Math`) we can't use the `Import` directive. Instead we would have to fully qualify the names, such as `Simple.Math` and `Complex.Math`, when we used them.

❑ **Assembly** – This directive is used to name assemblies containing classes we wish to use within our ASP.NET application. An assembly, which is a compiled unit of code in .NET with the extension `.dll`, exists either in the global assembly cache (covered in Chapter 23) or the `\bin` directory of the ASP.NET application.

The `Import` and `Assembly` directives are very different. `Import` assumes that the assembly (for example `System.Data.dll`) is already available to our application and allows us to use abbreviated class names for classes within that namespace. `Assembly`, on the other hand, is used to tell ASP.NET that there is an assembly that needs to be loaded. Remember, assemblies located in the `\bin` directory are automatically loaded.

Using the `Assembly` directive is simple. It has one attribute: `Name`.

❑ The `Name` attribute of `Assembly` identifies the assembly we wish to reference as part of our application. As mentioned above, some assemblies are available by default:

    ❑ `mscorlib.dll` – Base classes, such as the definition of Object, String, etc.

    ❑ `System.dll` – Additional base classes, such as the network class libraries

    ❑ `System.Web.dll` – Classes for ASP.NET

    ❑ `System.Data.dll` – Classes for ADO.NET

    ❑ `System.Web.Services.dll` – Classes for ASP.NET web services

- ❏ `System.Xml.dll` – Classes for XML

- ❏ `System.Drawing.dll` – Classes for graphics and drawing

- ❏ (Additionally, all assemblies within an application's `\bin` directory)

Included in this list are several `System` assemblies (for example, the assemblies provided as part of the .NET Framework), and those found in application `\bin` directories. We'd use the `Assembly` directive when an assembly is registered in the global assembly cache, or when we need System assemblies not already loaded.

For example, the assembly `System.DirectoryServices.dll` contains classes for working with Directory Services, such as Microsoft's Active Directory. This assembly is not one of the default assemblies loaded. If we wished to use the classes provided within it in `global.asax`, we'd need to use the `Assembly` directive:

```
<%@ Assembly Name="System.DirectoryServices" %>
```

Note that the extension of the assembly (`.dll`) is not included.

We can now write code in our `global.asax` file that uses classes found within this assembly, such as `DirectorySearcher`.

The directives for `global.asax` are straightforward to use, later, in the *Advanced Topics* section, we'll take a deeper look at one of these directives. For now, let's turn our focus to the code we can write within `global.asax`.

Code Declaration

Code is declared in `global.asax` using `<Script runat="server"/>` blocks. These are identical to the script blocks defined in ASP.NET pages, so we won't explain their syntax in detail again.

Later in the chapter, when we discuss global events, we'll implant the events created within these script blocks.

There are two additional ways of declaring code in `global.asax`:

- ❏ **Server-side Includes** – `global.asax` supports the use of server-side `#include` statements using both `File` and `Virtual` as the path type to the filename. Server-side includes are declared using the following syntax:

  ```
  <!--#Include [File | Virtual]="Path to file" -->
  ```

  `File` identifies the path as being on the file system, while `Virtual` identifies a virtual directory provided through the web server. The contents of the file included will be added to the `global.asax` file before it is compiled. Include files, especially those created using the `Virtual` option, can be quite useful as they allow us to define a common directory that can be shared among many applications, which may make our application more portable.

> If an include file is used within a `global.asax`, the application will automatically be restarted whenever the include file changes.

❑ **Declarative Object Tags** – `<Object>` tags enable us to declare and instantiate `Application` and `Session` objects in `global.asax` using a declarative tag-based syntax. These tags can be used to create .NET assemblies, or COM objects specified by either ProgID or CLSID.

The type of object to create is identified using one of three different tag attributes:

❑ `class`

❑ `progid`

❑ `classid`

Only one of these tag attributes can be used per `<Object>` tag declaration.

Using Object Tag Declarations

Here is a sample of how object tag declarations are used:

```
<object id="appData" runat="server"
        class="System.Data.DataSet" scope="Application"/>
```

We have declared an `Application`-scoped variable named `appData` that is of class type `System.Data.DataSet` – however, the object is not actually created until it is first used. The object then exists for the lifetime of the context in which it is created – in the above example this is the lifetime of the application. Likewise, if the scope were set to `"Session"`, the object would be valid for the life of the current user session, and once that session terminated, the object would be destroyed.

The attributes used in this declaration are:

Attributes	Description
ID	Unique name to use when referring to the object within the application.
runat	Must be set to `"server"` for the object to execute within ASP.NET.
scope	Determines where the object lives. The choices are `Application` for application state, `Session` for session state, or `Appinstance` allowing each application to receive its own object instance.
[Class, ProgID, ClassID]	Identifies either the assembly, or the COM ProgID or ClassID to create an instance of.

We have three options for adding code to a `global.asax` file. The first, and most common option, will be to use the `<script runat="server">` blocks to define application code. We can also define code from an include file and use the `<object/>` tag syntax to declaratively create an object. Now that we're familiar with how we code our `global.asax` file, let's take a quick diversion and discuss application state management before moving on to the supported application events.

Application State Management

State management is the persistence of objects or values throughout the lifetime of a web application or for the duration of a user's interaction with the application. ASP.NET provides four ways to manage state for our application (we'll cover each in more detail later in the chapter):

- **User State** (Session) – User state is controlled through the Session object. Session allows us to maintain data for a limited duration of time (the default is 20 minutes), for a particular user and isolate that data from other users. For example, if we wanted to track the ad banners we've shown a particular user we could do so using Session state. If the user doesn't interact with the site within the configurable Session time limit, their data expires and is deleted.

- **Application State** – Application state is controlled through the Application object. Application allows us to maintain data for a given ASP.NET application. Settings made in Application are accessible to all resources (ASP page, web services, etc.) within our web application. For example, if we wanted to retrieve some expensive records out of a database and needed to share this data throughout our application, storing the data in Application state would be very useful.

- **Transient Application State (Cache)** – Transient Application state is controlled through the Cache object. Cache is similar in functionality to Application, in that it is accessible (shared memory) for our entire web application. Cache, however, adds some functionality not available to Application, in the form of dependencies, callbacks, and expiration. For example, when our ASP.NET application started we might populate an object used by all ASP.NET pages from an XML file. We could store this object in the Cache and could also create a dependency for that item on the XML file the data originated from. If the XML file changed, ASP.NET will detect the file change and notify the Cache to invalidate the entry. Caching is a very powerful feature of ASP. NET. We'll summarize the key differences between Application and Cache later in the chapter.

- **Static Variables** – In addition to using Application or Cache to share data within our application, we can also use one of the object-oriented facilities of ASP.NET – static variables. We can declare static variables and only one copy of the variable is created no matter how many instances of the class are created. The static variable is accessible throughout our application and in some cases is more efficient than Application. This is a more advanced option and we'll discuss it at the end of the chapter.

The use of Application and Session (and now Cache) in ASP.NET is identical to the use of Application and Session in ASP. We simply use a string key and set a value:

```
' Set an Application value
Application("SomeValue") = "my value"

' Read an Application value
Dim someString As String
someString = Application("SomeValue")
```

These familiar semantics are carried forward and used for the Cache, too:

```
' Set a Cache value
Cache("SomeValue") = "my value"

' Read a Cache value
Dim someString As String
someString = Cache("SomeValue")
```

Let's take a deeper look at Session, Application, and Cache and how they relate to building web applications.

Session – Managing User State

Classic ASP's familiar Session object is new and improved for ASP.NET. The major caveats for Session use in classic ASP are:

❑ **Web farm challenges** – Session data is stored in memory on the server it is created upon. In a web farm scenario, where there are multiple web servers, a problem could arise if a user was redirected to a server other than the server upon which they stored their Session state. Normally this can be managed by an IP routing solution where the IP address of the client is used to route that client to a particular server. However, some ISPs use farms of reverse proxies, and therefore the client request may come through a different IP on each request. When a user is redirected to a server other than the server that contains their Session data, poorly designed applications can break.

❑ **Supporting clients that don't accept HTTP cookies** – Because the web is inherently a stateless environment, to use Session state the client and web server need to share a key that the client can present to identify its Session data on subsequent requests. Classic ASP shared this key with the client through the use of an HTTP cookie. While this scenario worked well for clients that accept HTTP cookies, it broke for the 1% of users that rejected HTTP cookies.

Both of these issues have been addressed in ASP.NET's Session state, which supports several new features to remedy these problems:

❑ **Web farm support** – ASP.NET Session now supports storing the Session data either in-process (in the same memory that ASP.NET uses), out-of-process using Windows NT Service (in separate memory from ASP.NET), and in SQL Server (persistent storage). Both the Windows Service and SQL Server solutions support a web farm scenario where all the web servers can be configured to share a common Session store. Thus, as users get routed to different servers each server is able to access that user's Session data. To the developer using Session, this is completely transparent and does not require any changes in the application code – rather we must configure ASP.NET to support one of these out-of-process options. We'll discuss configuring Session state in the next chapter.

❑ **Cookieless mode** – Although somewhat supported in ASP through the use of an ISAPI filter (available as part of the IIS 4.0 SDK), ASP.NET makes cookieless support for Session a first class feature, however, by default Session still uses HTTP cookies. When cookieless mode is enabled (details in the next chapter), ASP.NET will munge the URL that it sends back to the client with a Session ID (rather than storing the Session ID in an HTTP cookie). When the client makes a request using the munged URL containing the Session ID, ASP.NET is able to extract it and map the request to the appropriate Session data.

We'll cover how to configure both of these options in the next chapter when we discuss ASP.NET configuration. From our perspective, as a developer coding and using Session, the above features are completely transparent.

Programming with Session State

Session is dedicated data storage for each user within an ASP.NET application. It is implemented as a Hashtable and stores data based on key/value pair combinations.

Setting and Reading Session Value

Use of Session in ASP.NET follows the same usage pattern as classic ASP. To set a Session value we simply state:

VB.NET

```
Session("[String key]") = Object
```

C#

```
Session["[String key]"] = Object;
```

We provide Session with a key that identifies the item we are storing. This Session stores items of type Object. Since all types in .NET inherit from Object this allows us to store anything in Session. However, objects that contain live references, such as a DataReader containing an open connection to a database, should not be stored in Session.

For example, if we wished to store the String "Hello World" using a key of "SimpleSession" we would write the following code:

VB.NET

```
Session("SimpleSession") = "Hello World"
```

C#

```
Session["SimpleSession"] = "Hello World";
```

Underneath the covers the Common Language Runtime knows that the type String originated from type Object and is then able to store that value correctly in memory.

Because Session is available throughout our web application we can set values in global.asax code and access a Session value from ASP.NET pages.

For example to retrieve our "Hello World" value from Session we need only to provide Session with our key for it to return the value:

VB.NET

```
Dim sessionValue As String
sessionValue = Session("SimpleSession")
```

C#

```
string sessionValue;
sessionValue = Session["SimpleSession"];
```

For types other than `String` the semantics of accessing the value stored in `Session` are a bit more explicit. Because `Session` stores its data as an `Object` type, giving it the flexibility to store any .NET item, when we wish to retrieve data (other than type `String`) we have to cast the return value to the correct type.

For example, if we stored a custom class we defined called `PurchaseOrder` in `Session` here's how we would need to retrieve it:

VB.NET

```
Dim po As PurchaseOrder
po = CType(Session("po"), PurchaseOrder)
```

C#

```
PurchaseOrder po;
po = (PurchaseOrder) Session["po"];
```

In both examples we're casting the `Object` returned by the key "po" to type `PurchaseOrder`.

The `Session` API provides additional properties that we can use in code to determine what mode `Session` is in:

❑ **IsCookieless** – Returns `True` or `False` indicating whether or not `Session` is using cookieless mode to maintain the `Session` ID. By default this is `False`, meaning that `Session` is using cookies.

❑ **IsReadOnly** – Returns `True` or `False` indicating whether or not `Session` is in read-only mode. Read-only mode is an optimization that allows ASP.NET to not update `Session` data. This can be particularly useful for out-of-process modes on pages that only read `Session` state and don't need write access. When a `Session` is `ReadOnly` a lock does not have to be maintained and the round-trip back to an out-of-process `Session` store for an update can be skipped. By default this value is `False`, and `Session` is read/write. We'll discuss how to enable `ReadOnly` for `Session` in the next chapter.

❑ **Mode** – Returns the value of an enumeration, `SessionStateMode`, (found in `System.Web.SessionState`) which indicates the storage mode that `Session` is configured for. Values include: `InProc`, `Off`, `SQLServer`, and `StateServer`.

ASP.NET session state is quite different from ASP session state. The new capability of session state that is not bound to the ASP.NET process means that developers can begin to use session state in server farm environments without worrying about whether the client is coming through a proxy server. Additionally, with the cookieless state functionality, it is even easier to use session state and guarantee that all clients can take advantage of the session state feature. In the next chapter we'll learn how we can configure `Session` to support a read-only mode as well the other 'mode' options (in-process, Windows Service, and SQL Server).

Application – Managing Application State

Unlike `Session`, which is basically dedicated storage for each user, `Application` is shared application storage. This shared storage is quite useful, especially if there are resources that all users share, such as an XML representation of a site's shopping catalog. Similar to `Session`, `Application` state is simply a `Hashtable` that stores key/value pair combinations.

Unlike `Session`, however, `Application` does not support the concept of storing data separate from the ASP.NET process. Instead, `Application` stores its data in process with ASP.NET. If the ASP.NET process is recycled (covered in the next chapter) `Application` data is lost. The tradeoff is that storing the data in process is faster than going to another process, or possibly across the network, to retrieve data.

Setting and Accessing Values

The syntax used for setting and accessing values with `Application` is identical to that of `Session` – with one exception.

Since `Application` is accessible in a multi-user environment, updates to `Application` values should be **synchronized**. This simply means that whenever `Application` data is being updated, we should prevent other users or applications from updating the data simultaneously. Luckily for us `Application` provides us with the capability through a simple set of locking methods. Note these same locking methods `Lock()` and `UnLock()` are supported in ASP.

Reading and Writing Application Data

We read and write data in `Application` in a similar manner to `Session` using key/value pairs:

VB.NET

```
Application("HitCounter") = 10
```

C#

```
Application["HitCounter"] = 10;
```

Similarly, if we wish to read the value back we simply use our key:

VB.NET

```
Dim HitCount As Integer
HitCount = Application("HitCounter")
```

C#

```
int HitCount = Application["HitCounter"];
```

However, to update `HitCounter` we must synchronize access using the `Lock()` and `UnLock()` methods of `Application`. Otherwise the potential exists for two requests to attempt to update `HitCounter` simultaneously causing a potential deadlock or update failure.

579

> Although this is an illustrative example, when we **Lock** we are effectively blocking other applications that may be attempting to update the **HitCounter** value, causing them to serialize – that is, perform operations one after another.
>
> We definitely don't want to **Lock/UnLock** on each request, as this would negatively affect performance.
>
> If the data stored in **Application** must be updated frequently, it's probably not a good candidate for **Application** state, unless recreating the data is more costly than the time spent serializing the updates.

Let's look at an illustrative example using `Application.Lock` and `Application.UnLock`:

VB.NET

```
Public Sub Application_OnStart()
  Application("HitCount") = 0
End Sub

Public Sub Application_OnBeginRequest()
  Application.Lock()
  Application("HitCounter") = Application("HitCounter") + 1
  Application.UnLock()

End Sub
```

C#

```
public void Application_OnStart() {
  Application["HitCounter"] = 0;
}

public void Application_OnBeginRequest(){
  Application.Lock();
  int tmpInt = (int)Application["HitCounter"];
  Application["HitCounter"] = tmpInt + 1;
  Application.UnLock();
}
```

In the above code we call `Application.Lock()` to ensure that while we update `HitCounter`, some other thread can't also update the value simultaneously.

> *When the ASP.NET process is stopped or recycled* `Application` *state is lost. However, when the process is recycled the* `Application_OnEnd` *event (discussed later) is raised and values can be persisted to a database or file.*

Since ASP.NET is a multi-threaded system, this means that multiple threads can access `Application` memory simultaneously. When we use `Application` and we wish to set values we must either:

❏   Know that the object stored in `Application` is doing its own thread management (not shown).

or:

❑ Perform our own synchronization using `Application.Lock()` and `Application.UnLock()`.

Calling `Lock()` instructs ASP.NET to block any other threads from modifying this resource until `UnLock()` is called, giving your code exclusive access. However, if we don't explicitly call `UnLock()`, ASP.NET will call it when the application completes the request, the request times out, or an unhandled error occurs. Although this is done for us, we should always aim to write code that explicitly calls `UnLock()` for us.

Storing Objects in Application

Classic ASP VB objects could not be hosted in `Application` state due to the default threading model these components supported (Apartment Model threading). In effect, accessing an instance of a VB component stored in `Application` would cause ASP to serialize (read one request after another) access to that component. .NET components, by default, are free threaded and don't have this thread affinity problem. Thus there are no performance penalties for storing a VB.NET object in `Application` and accessing it across multiple requests.

Next, let's look at a new object, `Cache`, used to store transient application data.

Cache – Managing Transient State

Lots of developers use `Application` as a cache for frequently used resources – for example, reading an XML file that represents a product catalog and storing the object representing that XML file in `Application` memory.

However, what happens when this XML file representing the product catalog changes? In most cases developers who use `Application` to manage this data simply force the web application to restart, thus forcing `Application` to get refreshed.

The design goal of the `Cache` was to give developers the benefits of `Application`, but with additional features that went above and beyond those provided by `Application`, such as the ability to evict an item from the `Cache` when a file changes – it is then our responsibility through code to add the item back to the `Cache` if we desire.

Cache Overview

`Cache` is an instance of the `Cache` class found in the namespace `System.Web.Cache`. In addition to being a simple key/value pair `Hashtable` like `Application`, the `Cache` also supports:

❑ **Dependency-Based Expiration** – Dependencies can be other `Cache` keys, files, or a timestamp. When one of the dependencies changes or expires (timestamp) the `Cache` item is invalidated and removed from the `Cache`.

❑ **Lock Management** – Similar to `Application`, concurrent requests can attempt to modify the `Cache`. `Application` solves this by providing the `Lock()` and `UnLock()` methods.

Unlike `Application` though, the `Cache` class does its own internal lock management. Therefore, while `Application` required us to explicitly `Lock()` and `UnLock()` when updating `Application`, we don't need to do this with `Cache`.

Keep in mind that we do still need to manage concurrency for objects stored in the `Cache` just as we do with objects stored in `Application`.

❑ **Resource Management** – Items in the Cache that are under used are automatically removed, freeing up valuable memory. Therefore, before we request an item, we always need to check if the item exists.

❑ **Callbacks** – The Cache supports a capability allowing us to run code when items are removed from the Cache.

The Cache supports two methods of inserting items:

❑ **Implicit** – This is the syntax familiar to us from working with Session or Application using the key/value pairs:

VB.NET

```
Dim productDataSet As New DataSet()
' Populate DataSet
Cache("products") = productDataSet
```

C#

```
DataSet productDataSet = new DataSet();
// Populate DataSet
Cache["products"] = productDataSet;
```

❑ **Explicit** – Using the Insert() method. This allows us to set up special relationships such as dependencies:

VB.NET

```
Dim productDataSet As New DataSet()
' Populate DataSet
Cache.Insert("products", productDataSet, Nothing)
```

C#

```
DataSet productDataSet = new DataSet();
// Populate DataSet
Cache.Insert("products", productDataSet, null)
```

When using the Cache we'll most likely use the explicit Insert() most often; let's look at some examples.

Dependency-Based Expiration

Dependency-based expiration is very powerful. It allows us to create a relationship between an item in the Cache and either a file, another Cache key, or a defined point in time. For example, if our site used XML and XSL transforms to control aspects of content we could load the XML into an XmlDocument class and store the value within the Cache. We could also establish a relationship between the cached XmlDocument and the file that it is reading, using the file-based dependency feature of the Cache. Let's build this sample.

Below is the XML file:

```xml
<?xml version="1.0"?>
<books>
  <book>
    <name>Professional ASP.NET</name>
    <isbn>1861004885</isbn>
    <publisher>Wrox Press</publisher>
    <authors>
      <author name="David Sussman"/>
      <author name="Brian Francis"/>
      <author name="Alex Homer"/>
      <author name="Karli Watson"/>
      <author name="Rich Anderson"/>
      <author name="Rob Howard"/>
    </authors>
    <description>
    ASP.NET is a unified web development
    platform that provides the services necessary
    for developers to build enterprise-class web
    applications.
    </description>
  </book>
</books>
```

The file is saved as `1861004885.xml`, which is the ISBN number of this Wrox book. We also have an XSL transform for this file:

```xml
<xsl:stylesheet
      version="1.0"
      xmlns:xsl="http://www.w3.org/1999/XSL/Transform">
<xsl:output method="html"/>

  <xsl:template match="/">
    <html>
    <head>
      <title><xsl:value-of select="books/book/name"/></title>
    </head>
    <style>
        body { font-family: Arial; font-size: 18; color:white; }
        li { list-style: square outside; }
    </style>
    <body bgcolor="black">
        <xsl:apply-templates/>
    </body>
    </html>
  </xsl:template>

  <xsl:template match="name">
    <h1><font color="red"><xsl:value-of select="."/></font></h1>
  </xsl:template>

  <xsl:template match="description">
    <h6><xsl:value-of select="."/></h6>
  </xsl:template>
```

```
    <xsl:template match="isbn">
      <font size="1">ISBN: <xsl:value-of select="."/></font><br/>
    </xsl:template>

    <xsl:template match="publisher">
      <font size="1">Publisher: <xsl:value-of select="."/></font><br/>
    </xsl:template>
  </xsl:stylesheet>
```

Below is the ASP.NET page that uses the Cache and creates a file dependency on the XML file only –
in this particular example we're not caching the XSL file:

```
<%@ Import Namespace="System.Xml" %>
<%@ Import Namespace="System.Xml.Xsl" %>

<Script runat="server">
Public Sub Page_Load(sender As Object, e As EventArgs)
  Dim dom As XmlDocument
  Dim xsl As New XslTransform()

  ' Do we have the Wrox Pro ASP.NET book in the Cache?
  If (IsNothing(Cache("1861004885.xml"))) Then
    CacheStatus.Text = "Item not present, updating the Cache..."
    UpdateCache("1861004885.xml")
  Else
    CacheStatus.Text = "Retrieving from Cache"
  End If

  ' Load the transform
  xsl.Load(Server.MapPath("book.xsl"))

  dom = CType(Cache("1861004885.xml"), XmlDocument)

  BookDisplay.Document = dom
  BookDisplay.Transform = xsl

End Sub

Public Sub UpdateCache(strItem As String)

    Dim strPath As String
    Dim dom As New XmlDocument()

    ' Determine the file path the the file to monitor
    strPath = Server.MapPath(strItem)

    ' Load the file into an Xml Dom
    dom.Load(strPath)

    ' Create a CacheDependency on the file
    Dim dependency as new CacheDependency(strPath)

    ' Cache the XML document
    Cache.Insert(strItem, dom, dependency)
```

```
End Sub
</Script>
Status: <asp:label id="CacheStatus" runat=server/>
<br>
<asp:xml id="BookDisplay" runat=server/>
```

The interesting code happens in the UpdateCache subroutine, called if the Cache key 1861004885.xml is not present. We first map the path to the XML file, which is in the same directory, and load that XML file into an XmlDocument class. Then we create a new CacheDependency class passing in the path to the XML file. Finally, we use the Cache's Insert() method and create a new Cache entry using the name of the file (1861004885.xml), the XmlDocument instance, dom, and the CacheDependency class instance, dependency.

On the first request to this page, we would see:

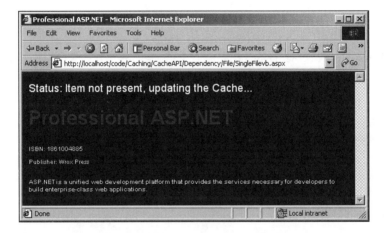

On subsequent requests we would see a Status of: Retrieving from Cache.

If we open the 1861004885.xml file and modify the name from Professional ASP.NET to Pro ASP.NET, our file change notification would be enforced and the XmlDocument storing the XML from our file would be removed from the Cache. Requesting our ASP.NET page would then yield:

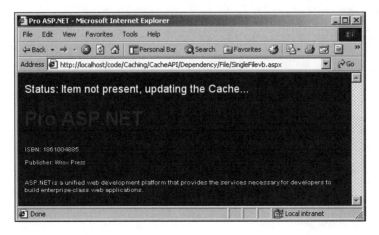

What if we didn't need to monitor a file, but instead wanted to remove an entry (or series of entries) from the `Cache` when another item in the `Cache` changed? This option is supported through a key-based dependency.

The syntax for supporting key-based dependencies is very similar to that for file-based dependencies. For example, we can easily change the above code to support a key-based dependency by modifying only a couple of lines.

If we cached multiple XML documents for each Wrox book on .NET, we could set up a dependency relationship where the `Cache` entries for the books could be invalidated (and reloaded) whenever a master key, for example `booksDependencyKey`, changed.

Below is a code example that creates such a relationship:

```
<%@ Import Namespace="System.Xml" %>

<Script runat="server">

  Public Sub Create(sender As Object, e As EventArgs)
    ' Create the Cache entry for the dependency realtionship
    ' the value of the key doesn't matter
    Cache("booksDependencyKey") = "Book Dependency"

    ' Create a string array with the key names for the
    ' dependencies to be created upon
    Dim dependencyKey(1) As String

    dependencyKey(0) = "booksDependencyKey"

    ' Create a CacheDependency on this key
    Dim dependency as new CacheDependency(nothing, dependencyKey)

    ' Cache the XML document
    Cache.Insert("1861004885.xml", Load("1861004885.xml"), dependency)

    Status()
  End Sub

  Private Function Load(xmlFile As String) As XmlDocument
    Dim dom As New XmlDocument()
    dom.Load(Server.MapPath(xmlFile))

    Return dom
  End Function

  Public Sub Invalidate(sender As Object, e As EventArgs)
    Cache.Remove("booksDependencyKey")
    Status()
  End Sub

  Public Sub Status()
    If (IsNothing(Cache("1861004885.xml"))) Then
      lblStatus1.Text = "No value..."
```

```
        Else
          lblStatus1.Text = "Cache entry exits..."
        End If
      End Sub

    </Script>
    <form runat=server>
      <input type="submit" OnServerClick="Create"
             value="Create Cache Entries" runat="server" />
      <input type="submit" OnServerClick="Invalidate"
             value="Invalidate Key" runat="server" />
    </form>
    Status for cache key: 1861004885.xml: <b><asp:label id="lblStatus1"
    runat=server/></b>
```

When we run this code we need to press the **Create Cache Entries** button to create the `Cache` entry for the XML file as well as the dependency relationship. We can then press **Invalidate Key**, which raises the `Invalidate` event. Within this event we explicitly remove the `Cache` key `booksDependencyKey`. This enforces the dependency and also removes the `Cache` entry for our XML document.

Finally, in addition to file- and key-based dependencies we can also create dependencies on time values. For example, if Wrox were to store all of its book titles in a single table in the database and we knew that this data was only updated once a week, we could `Cache` a `DataSet` that represents this data with an explicit expiration of 60 minutes. This will save us going to the database for every request, but in case an update occurs we can still guarantee that the data will be fresh within the following hour.

Here's the code that can do this:

```
<%@ Import Namespace="System.Data" %>
<%@ Import Namespace="System.Data.SqlClient" %>

<script runat=server>
  Private DSN As String

  Public Sub Page_Load(sender As Object, e As EventArgs)
    Dim strCacheKey As String
    Dim titlesDataSet As DataSet

    strCacheKey = "Titles"

    If (IsNothing(Cache(strCacheKey))) Then
      lblStatus.Text = "Getting data from database..."
      LoadTitles(strCacheKey)
    Else
      lblStatus.Text = "Getting data from Cache..."
    End If

    titlesDataSet = CType(Cache(strCacheKey), DataSet)
    TitleList.DataSource = titlesDataSet
    TitleList.DataBind()

  End Sub
```

```
Public Sub LoadTitles(strCacheKey As String)
   Dim connection As SqlConnection
   Dim command As SqlDataAdapter
   Dim sqlSelect As String
   Dim strDsn As String
   Dim dataset As New DataSet()

   sqlSelect = "Select title, pub_id, price, notes, pubdate FROM titles"
   strDsn = "server=localhost;uid=sa;pwd=00password;database=pubs"

   connection = New SqlConnection(strDsn)
   command = New SqlDataAdapter(sqlSelect, connection)

   command.Fill(dataset, "Author-Titles")

   Cache.Insert(strCacheKey, dataset, nothing, _
               DateTime.Now.AddMinutes(60), TimeSpan.Zero, _
               CacheItemPriority.High, _
               CacheItemPriorityDecay.Slow, nothing)
   End Sub
</script>
<font size=6>
<asp:label id="lblStatus" runat="server"/>
</font>
<P>
<ASP:DataGrid id="TitleList" HeaderStyle-BackColor="#aaaadd" BackColor="#ccccff"
runat="server" />
```

In the code example above, we have some logic at the beginning that checks for an entry in the Cache named Titles. If the Cache entry doesn't exist we then call the subroutine LoadTitles(), which connects to a database, performs a select on the titles table, fills a DataSet, and finally inserts the DataSet into the Cache. We're using the explicit Insert() method of the Cache:

```
Cache.Insert(strCacheKey, dataset, nothing, _
            DateTime.Now.AddMinutes(60), TimeSpan.Zero, _
            CacheItemPriority.High, _
            CacheItemPriorityDecay.Slow, nothing)
```

This adds a Cache entry with the key titles, the populated dataset, and also instructs the Cache to expire the item after 60 minutes. We've additionally instructed the Cache to set the priority of the item to High and that it should decay slowly. These two parameters simply control how the Cache will treat underused items. The last parameter, which is set to nothing, is what allows us to set up a callback – allowing us to execute code whenever the Cache removes our item.

The callback capability of the Cache is very useful. It allows us to run our code when an item is removed from the Cache giving us the opportunity to add it back.

We could make the following modification to the above code (highlighted), which would guarantee that our item is always served from the Cache:

```
      ...
      If (loadedFromCallback) Then
        lblStatus.Text = lblStatus.Text + "loaded from callback"
        loadedFromCallback = false
      End If

      sqlSelect = "Select title, pub_id, price, notes, pubdate FROM titles"

      connection = New
  SqlConnection("server=localhost;uid=sa;pwd=00password;database=pubs")
      command = New SqlDataAdapter(sqlSelect, connection)

      command.Fill(dataset, "Author-Titles")

      ' Create the a CacheItemRemovedCallback
      Dim onRemove As New CacheItemRemovedCallback(AddressOf _
                                              Me.RemovedCallback)

      Cache.Insert(strCacheKey, dataset, nothing,
               DateTime.Now.AddSeconds(5), TimeSpan.Zero, _
               CacheItemPriority.High, _
               CacheItemPriorityDecay.Slow, onRemove)
    End Sub

    ' This method represents the callback
    Public Sub RemovedCallback(key As String, value As Object,
                              reason As CacheItemRemovedReason)
      ' Let's always re-add the item if removed
      LoadTitles(key)
    End Sub
</script>
<font size=6>
<asp:label id="lblStatus" runat="server"/>
</font>
<P>
<ASP:DataGrid id="TitleList" HeaderStyle-BackColor="#aaaadd" BackColor="#ccccff"
runat="server" />
```

Caching adds a lot of powerful new features to managing data that we ordinarily would have stored in Application state. Dependencies allow us to set up relationships with items that can invalidate the Cache, and Callbacks allow us to execute our own code whenever an item is removed from the Cache.

State management in ASP.NET should be very familiar to developers who have worked with ASP. Both Session and Application state remain identical in use, and we also now have a new option: Cache. Understanding state management, and when to use each option is very important. Here are some basic guidelines:

❑ Session – Used to store data that you want available to the user on each request. Be efficient about what you store in Session since each Session will get its own individual copy of the data.

❑ Application – Used to store data that needs to be available to the entire application. A good candidate for Application is data that remains fairly static and must be available on each request.

❑ Cache – Use Cache to store data that may be used on each request, or data where a dependency relationship needs to be established.

Application Events

Although we don't have to take advantage of events to use ASP.NET, they do make our lives easier. Events provide great ways to organize and control execution of code. Examples here include creating instances of objects that we assign to `Application`, `Cache`, or `Session` when our application starts, validating custom user credentials before we allow the user to access the requested resource, or perhaps implementing a billing feature that will charge the user for each access to a page. The options are endless. The point is application events allow us to execute our own code during ASP.NET processing of the request.

We can use application events in one of two ways:

❑ **Implement event prototypes in `global.asax`** – We'll simply add event prototypes for the application events we wish to execute code for within our `global.asax` file; note this is similar to events we captured in ASP's `global.asa` file such as `Application_OnStart` or `Session_OnEnd`. We'll use `global.asax` to demonstrate application events in this chapter.

❑ **Author custom HTTP Modules** – An HTTP module is an advanced feature of ASP.NET. It is the equivalent of IIS's ISAPI filter concept. An HTTP module gives us an opportunity to work with the request before it is serviced by an ASP.NET page or web service (or custom HTTP handler), and again before the response is sent to the client. For example, we can use HTTP modules to author custom solutions for our ASP.NET applications, such as an authentication system that authenticates users against a Netscape LDAP.

> **ASP.NET application events are multi-cast events. This means that we can have both an HTTP module and `global.asax` respond to the same event.**

ASP.NET supports 18 application events, and also allows us to add our own custom events. ASP.NET also introduces support for asynchronous events. We'll discuss these at the end of the chapter in the *Advanced Topics* section.

Event Syntax and Prototypes

When implementing the event code in `global.asax` it is considered good practice to use `sender` as the `Object` parameter, and `e` as the `EventArgs` parameter. Below is the syntax in both VB.NET and C#:

VB.NET

```
Public Sub Application_OnStart(sender As Object, e As EventArgs)
End Sub
```

C#

```
public void Application_OnStart(Object sender, EventArgs e) {
}
```

The argument provided to our event prototype tells us who raised the event (`sender`), as well as providing a mechanism for the `sender` to provide additional event details through an `EventArgs` parameter (`e`).

In addition to using the prototypes above, we can also use a shorthand event prototype (shorthand since we're not naming the event parameters):

VB.NET

```
Public Sub Application_OnStart()
End Sub
```

C#

```
public void Application_OnStart() {
}
```

In the above event prototypes we don't have access to the `EventArgs` or the `sender`. It is considered best practice to include the parameters. However, you should be aware that the shorthand syntax is supported if you see it.

Supported Events

The 18 supported events can be divided into two categories: events that are raised on each request, and conditional events (such as when an error occurs). Below we've listed the two categories of events and provided a brief description of each event. For the per-request events we've also provide a figure that shows the ordering of the events. We'll implement some example uses for several of the events momentarily.

Per-Request Application Events

Per-request application events are those events raised during each and every request made to an ASP.NET application, such as the beginning or end of the request events:

❑   `Application_OnBeginRequest` – The `Application_OnBeginRequest` event is raised on **each** request that ASP.NET handles, for example, a page or web service. This is unlike the familiar ASP `Application_OnStart` event, which is only raised once when the application is started. We can use the `Application_OnBeginRequest` event to execute code before a page, web service, or any other HTTP Handler gets the opportunity to process the request.

❑   `Application_OnAuthenticateRequest` – This event is raised when ASP.NET is ready to perform authentication on the request (see Chapter 14 for more detail on authentication). Events such as this allow us to easily build in custom authentication systems to ASP.NET. Within this event we can examine the request and execute our own code to determine whether or not the request is authenticated. When enabled, ASP.NET authentication modes such as Windows Forms or Passport use this event.

❑   `Application_OnAuthorizeRequest` – Similar to `OnAuthenticateRequest`, this event is raised when ASP.NET is ready to authorize a request for a resource. We can use this event to examine the request and execute our own code that determines what privileges we grant or deny the request. Similar to the previous event, when enabled the ASP.NET authorization system relies on this event for its authorization support.

❑   `Application_OnResolveRequestCache` – Although not yet discussed, ASP.NET has a rich page and web service output caching feature that utilizes the `Cache` that we covered in this chapter. For example, rather than executing a page on each request, the page can be executed once and served statically for future requests. This event is raised when ASP.NET is ready to determine if the request should be served from the `Cache`. Internally, ASP.NET's output cache relies upon this event. We can use it to run application code independently of whether or not the actual response is served from the output cache.

❑ Application_OnAcquireRequestState – This event is raised when ASP.NET is ready to acquire Session state data from in-process, out-of-process Windows Service, or SQL Server. If we decided that we wanted to provide our own 'custom' Session, such as an XmlSession object, we could populate the values of that object using this event. Then when the request was handed to the page or web service, the XmlSession would already have its values populated.

❑ Application_OnPreRequestHandlerExecute – This event is the one raised before the handler servicing the request is called. In most cases the handler will be the Page Handler.

After the Application_OnPreRequestHandlerExecute event is raised the HTTP Handler receives the request. The next application event is raised when the handler is finished with the request.

❑ Application_OnPostRequestHandlerExecute – This event is the first raised after the handler has completed servicing the request. The Response object now has data to be sent back to the client.

❑ Application_OnReleaseRequestState – This releases the Session data and updates storage if necessary. After this event is raised we can no longer update Session data. In the corresponding Application_OnRequestState event we mentioned populating an XmlSession object. In this corresponding 'ReleaseState' event we could write the value of XmlSession back to the XML file that represented the session data for a particular user.

❑ Application_OnUpdateRequestCache – This event is raised when ASP.NET updates the output cache with the current request (if it is to be output cached).

❑ Application_OnEndRequest – The request is complete, this is the last event raised that allows us to affect the application response before we send the HTTP Headers and Body.

Below is a flow-chart showing the processing of a request by ASP.NET using the ten events detailed above:

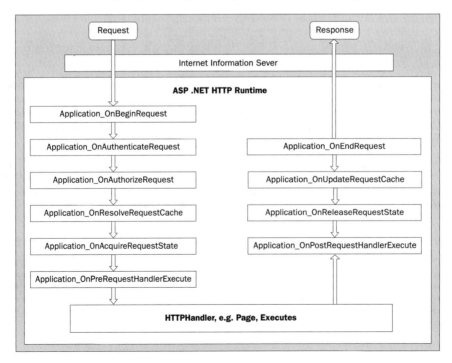

As shown above, IIS first receives the request and then hands it to ASP.NET. The ASP.NET Application Events are then raised starting with `Application_OnBeginRequest`. Immediately before an HTTP Handler (such as `default.aspx`) is called, the `Application_OnPreRequestHandlerExecute` event is raised. Immediately after the HTTP Handler has executed the `Application_OnPostRequestHandlerExecute` is raised. Finally, before the response is handed back to IIS to be sent back to the requestor the `Application_OnEndRequest` event is raised.

These ten per-request events are raised in a known order. However, there are two other per-request events that are raised during the processing of the request.

Per-Request Indeterminate Order

Unlike the other per-request events, the following two are raised as soon as data is ready to be sent back to the client. By default, ASP.NET enables response buffering – this simply means the server will not begin sending data to the requestor until all the data is ready. When buffering is enabled the following two events are raised after `Application_OnEndRequest`. However, if buffering is disabled, the response can be sent as data becomes available. In that case, the following two events will be raised when the data is sent to the client.

- ❑ `Application_OnPreSendRequestHeaders` – `OnPreSendRequestHeaders` is raised before the HTTP headers are sent to the client making the request. Once the headers are sent, we cannot modify the content of the response – we've already sent the content size of the response to the client.

- ❑ `Application_OnPreSendRequestContent` – `OnPreSendRequestHeaders` is raised before the HTTP body is sent to the client making the request.

Conditional Application Events

Conditional application events are events that may or may not be raised during the processing of a request. For example, when the application is first starting, we raise the `Application_OnStart` event or when an error occurs within our application we raise the `Application_OnError` event. These events are just as useful as our per-request events, sometimes even more so.

- ❑ `Application_OnStart` – This event is raised when an ASP.NET application first starts. This event is raised once when the application starts, unlike the `Application_OnBeginRequest` raised on each request. We can use this event to do any work to prepare our application to service requests; examples include: opening a connection to the database and retrieving some shared data, adding items to the cache, or simply setting `Application` or static variables to default values. If this event has not yet been raised when a request comes in, it will be raised before the per-request `Application_OnBeginRequest` event.

- ❑ `Application_OnEnd` – This event is another single occurrence event. It is the reciprocal event to `Application_OnStart` in that it is raised when the ASP.NET Web Application is shutting down. We can use this event for cleaning up code – for example: closing connections to the database, evicting items from the cache, or resetting `Application` and static variables.

  Most of these tasks won't be necessary, however, since once the application ends, the Common Language Runtime will eventually release the application's memory. However, it is still good practice to do the cleanup ourselves.

- ❑ `Session_OnStart` – This event is raised when a user's `Session` begins within an ASP.NET application. We can use this event to execute code that is user specific, such as assigning values to `Session`.

- ❑   Session_OnEnd – This is the reciprocal event to Session_OnStart, being raised when a user's Session ends. If we wish to save the Session data, we can use this to walk the object and save interesting information to a SQL database, or other permanent storage medium.

- ❑   Application_OnError – This event is raised whenever an unhandled application error occurs. This is a very powerful event, and we'll call it in one of our later examples. Just as an ASP.NET Page supports a Page_Error for unhandled page exceptions, the Application_OnError allows us to catch all unhandled exceptions for the entire application, such as logging an exception to the Windows event log, or sending the administrator an e-mail with details of the error.

- ❑   Application_OnDisposed – This event is raised when the ASP.NET application is eventually shut down and the Common Language Runtime removes the ASP.NET application from memory. This event gives us the opportunity to clean up or close any outstanding connections or write any last data back to a database or file system. In most scenarios this event will not be used.

Although ASP.NET supports 18 events, this doesn't necessarily mean that we need to use all of them. Now, we'll look at some examples of the more common events that we'll want to use most often in building ASP.NET applications.

Event Examples

Below are some code samples that demonstrate application events.

Adding a Footer to all Pages

The Application_OnEndRequest event is raised at the end of the request immediately before the response is sent to the requestor. Because this event is the last called, we can use it to run some code before the response is sent, or to modify the response. For example, an ISP running ASP.NET could use the Application_OnEndRequest event to add a footer to the bottom of all pages served by ASP.NET.

Here's the global.asax code:

VB.NET

```
<Script runat="server">

  Public Sub Application_OnEndRequest(sender As Object, e As EventArgs)
    Response.Write("<hr size=1>")
    Response.Write("<font face=arial size=2>This page was
                                    served by ASP.NET</font>")
  End Sub

</Script>
```

In the above global.asax code we implemented the Application_OnEndRequest event and within the event used Response.Write() to output a simple statement that says '...**served by ASP.NET**'.

We can then author an ASP.NET page:

VB.NET

```
<%@ Import Namespace="System.Data" %>
<%@ Import Namespace="System.Data.SqlClient" %>

<Script runat="server">

  Public Sub Page_Load(sender As Object, e As EventArgs)
    Dim connection As SqlConnection
    Dim command As SqlCommand
    Dim reader As SqlDataReader
    Dim sqlSelect As String
    Dim dsn As String

    ' Name dsn and sql select
    dsn="server=localhost;uid=sa;pwd=00password;database=pubs"
    sqlSelect="Select * From stores"

    ' Connect to the database
    connection = New SqlConnection(dsn)
    command = New SqlCommand(sqlSelect, connection)

    ' Open the connection
    connection.Open()

    ' Create the reader
    reader = command.ExecuteReader()

    ' Populate the datagrid
    datagrid1.DataSource = reader
    datagrid1.DataBind()

    ' Close the connection
    connection.Close()
  End Sub

</Script>
<asp:datagrid id="datagrid1" runat="server" />
```

The above code connects to a database and populates an ASP.NET `datagrid` with the results. If we save these two files into a web application, the result is that the code executed in `Application_OnEndRequest` will be added to the bottom of the requested page:

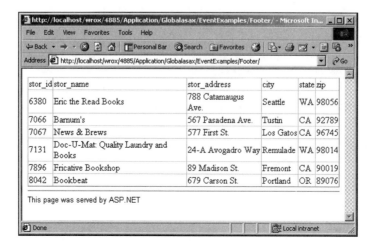

595

When we enable **page tracing** (which we'll learn more about in the following chapter on configuration), we output trace details at the end of the request. Internally, tracing is using the `Application_OnEndRequest` to ensure that the output details are the final addition to the request.

In the above example, we're using an event to output code, so as to better illustrate how the event is executed. This works well for ASP.NET pages, since the `Response.Write()` statements are appended to the end of the page results and simply add additional HTML. However, you would be well advised to remember that ASP.NET is no longer simply about displaying HTML pages. Good examples here include the rich set of server controls that can output WML, or ASP.NET web services, which return XML to the caller. The `global.asax` file is global for the ASP.NET application, and if we want to add logic into our `global.asax` file that outputs HTML, we should probably not serve ASP.NET web services out of that same application – unless we add additional code that checks the request type to see if HTML content can be returned.

Loading Custom User Data

ASP.NET provides some great facilities for storing per-request user state, `Session`, and per-application state, `Application` and `Cache`. However, what if we wanted to also support a scenario that fell somewhere in-between these, such as per-request group data?

Many sites personalize themselves based on the identity of the requestor. What if we didn't want to personalize for an individual user, but instead wanted to group a common set of users together and personalize our site based on group settings? For example, what if we divided our users into groups such as Gold, Silver, and Bronze. We want Gold customers to have access to common state for Gold customers, but not for Silver and Bronze customers. Similarly, we would want our Silver customers to only see their data.

We can build our own 'state manager' easily using ASP.NET, and use the `Application_OnAcquireRequestState` event to determine who the request is for and then to fetch the appropriate data. Let's look at a simple example that identifies the customer category from the URL – default.aspx?customerType=Gold, default.aspx?customerType=Silver, etc.

First, let's write the `global.asax` file:

VB.NET

```
<%@ Import Namespace="System.Xml" %>

<Script runat="server">

  Public Sub Application_OnAcquireRequestState(sender As Object,
                                               e As EventArgs)

    Dim dom As New XmlDocument()
    Dim customerType As String

    ' Grab the customerType from the QueryString
    customerType = Request.QueryString("customerType")

    ' Check for values
    If (IsNothing(customerType)) Then
      customerType = "Bronze"
    End If
```

```
        ' Load the appropriate XML file
        Select Case customerType
          Case "Gold"
            dom.Load(Server.MapPath("Gold.xml"))
          Case "Silver"
            dom.Load(Server.MapPath("Silver.xml"))
          Case Else
            dom.Load(Server.MapPath("Bronze.xml"))
        End Select

        Session("WelcomeMsg") = dom.SelectSingleNode("
                                        /customer/welcome").InnerText
      End Sub

</Script>
```

The above file's `Application_OnAcquireRequestState` event begins by executing some logic to determine the bucket that the current request fits in – we're simply passing a `customerType` value on the `QueryString` – and if no `customerType` is provided we default to Bronze.

The code then loads up an XML file for the appropriate customer type, for example `Gold.xml`, and loads the welcome message from that file. Here are the three XML files:

Gold.xml

```xml
<?xml version="1.0"?>
<customer>
 <welcome>
  You're a Gold customer -- you get a free product sample!
 </welcome>
</customer>
```

Silver.xml

```xml
<?xml version="1.0"?>
<customer>
 <welcome>
  You're a Silver customer -- thanks for your business!
 </welcome>
</customer>
```

Bronze.xml

```xml
<?xml version="1.0"?>
<customer>
 <welcome>
  You're a Bronze customer -- can we interest you in 30 days no interest?
 </welcome>
</customer>
```

Finally a session value is set for the current request, `Session("WelcomeMsg")`, with the appropriate welcome message for the customer type.

We can then write an ASP.NET page that extracts this session value and displays the welcome message for the correct group:

VB.NET

```
<Script runat="server">

  Public Sub Page_Load(sender As Object, e As EventArgs)
    WelcomeMsg.Text = Session("WelcomeMsg")
  End Sub

</Script>
<asp:label id="WelcomeMsg" runat="server" />
```

Although this is a simple example of using the `Application_AcquireRequestState` event (we could have written all of this code into our ASP.NET page), it shows how nicely we can encapsulate this work inside `global.asax` and not repeat it on each and every application file that wants to use the associated XML file for the customer type. Additionally when users access the ASP.NET page the values are already populated.

Finally, let's look at the `Application_OnError` event that we can use to catch unhandled exceptions from our ASP.NET application.

Handling Application Errors

Because ASP.NET uses the Common Language Runtime (CLR) we can use any CLR language to build our web application. One of the CLR's features is structured, try/catch, exception handling (no more of VB6's `On Error Resume Next`!). As great as this new structured error-handling model is, it doesn't prevent us from still writing buggy code. For example, we might write some code in our ASP.NET application that connects to and reads from a database. We also might then wrap that code in a try/catch block so that if we can't connect to the database we can handle the error appropriately.

However, what happens if an exception occurs outside of a try/catch block? If it's not handled ASP.NET will throw a run-time error (providing us with a detailed overview of where the error occurred and what the application was doing). For ASP.NET pages we can optionally implement a `Page_Error` event to catch all unhandled page errors. However, if we decide we would rather catch all unhandled ASP.NET errors at the application level, we have that option too, with the `Application_OnError` event.

We can use this event as a catch-all whenever an unhandled exception occurs, and log the exception to the Windows event log:

VB.NET

```
<%@ Import Namespace="System.Diagnostics" %>

<script language="VB" runat=server>
  Public Sub Application_Error(Sender as Object, E as EventArgs)

    Dim LogName As String = "Web_Errors"
    Dim Message As String
    Message = "Url: " & Request.Path
    Message = Message + " Error: " & Server.GetLastError.ToString

    ' Create Event Log if It Doesn't Exist
    If (Not EventLog.SourceExists(LogName)) Then
      EventLog.CreateEventSource(LogName, LogName)
    End if
```

```
      ' Fire off to Event Log
      Dim Log as New EventLog

      Log.Source = LogName
      Log.WriteEntry(Message, EventLogEntryType.Error)

    End Sub
  </script>
```

In the above example we first `Import` the namespace `System.Diagnostics` since we'll be using some of the classes found in this namespace to write to the event log. We then implement our `Application_Error` event handler and create some local variables, before using the `EventLog` class's static method `SourceExists()` to determine if the event log we're going to write to already exists – if it doesn't we create it. Finally we create a new `EventLog` instance named `Log` and use the `WriteEntry()` method to enter our `Message` into the Windows Event Log.

Whenever an error occurs within our application, that error is now logged into a custom event log named `Web_Errors`. It should be noted here that we wrote little more than 10 lines of code to accomplish a task that could potentially be 50-60 lines in VB/ASP.

Now that we've covered each of the application events, let's look at some Advanced Topics. These are areas that are left to the more advanced ASP.NET developer and the understanding of these topics is not required to build great ASP.NET applications, but they do help!

Advanced Topics

In this Advanced Topics section we'll cover five advanced topics related to building superior ASP.NET applications:

- ❑ **Using Static Variables** – It's not necessary in all cases to use `Application` to store persistent values in memory. Since ASP.NET is compiled, and the application is represented in an object-oriented manner, we can use global static variables in addition to `Application`.

- ❑ **Using Our Own Base Class for global.asax** – The earlier discussion of the `Application` directive for `global.asax` mentioned the `Inherits` attribute. We'll examine how we can use this to create our own class for `global.asax` to instantiate.

- ❑ **Mapping File Extensions** – If we want ASP.NET to support file extensions other than the defaults, such as the file extension `.wrox`, we must map the extension in IIS first. This is because IIS gets the first look at the request and acts as the router determining where to send requests.

- ❑ **Asynchronous Application Events** – Earlier in the chapter we discussed the application events that ASP.NET supported. What we didn't discuss in detail is the fact that ASP.NET also support some asynchronous representations of these events too.

Let's start with using static variables.

Static Variables

Although not covered in our earlier discussion of global.asax, another supported attribute of the Application directive is Classname. This attribute allows us to control the name of the class generated for our global.asax code when it's compiled. If we provide a Classname value, we can access the instance of global.asax. Since we now have access to the global.asax instance, this also means that public methods, properties, or variables declared within it are accessible anywhere in our application. An advanced design choice we can elect to make is to take advantage of one of the object-oriented features of ASP.NET, Static Members.

When a class is created, such as an instance of global.asax, each instance of the class also uses its own methods, properties, and variables to perform work. We can declare a method, property, or variable **static** and all instances of the class will share the one instance of that method, property, or variable. These static members can be used to store commonly accessed data, for instance, a string array containing the 50 states of the USA.

Using static members, in some cases, can be faster than accessing Application state. Application is an object, and loading Application requires memory allocations, etc. A simple example is the discount rate applied to all products for a one-time sale. Below is a sample global.asax file:

C#

```
<%@ Application Classname="CommerceApplication" %>

<Script Language="C#" runat=server>
// Set discount to 10%
public static float discountRate = .1F;
</Script>
```

VB.NET

```
<%@ Application Classname="CommerceApplication" %>

<Script runat=server>
' Set discount to 10%
Public Shared discountRate As Single = .1F
</Script>
```

In the above code sample we first identify the name of the global.asax's class using the Classname attribute of the Application directive. Then we declare a static member variable, discountRate.

We can now write code that accesses this class and its static member, discountRate. Below is a sample ASP.NET page, example.aspx:

```
<Script runat="server" >
  Public Sub Page_Load(sender As Object, e As EventArgs)
     ' Calculate the discount rate
     Dim discountRate As Single
     Dim productCost As Single

     ' Determine productCost value
     productCost = 19.99F
```

```
         ' Calculate discount rate and apply to product cost
         discountRate = CommerceApplication.discountRate
         productCost = productCost - (productCost * discountRate)

         ' Display calculation
         lblCost.Text = productCost.ToString()

      End Sub
   </Script>

   The cost of the product is: $<asp:label id="lblCost" runat="server" />
```

In the above example we have a simple VB ASP.NET page that calculates a product's cost with the applied discount rate. The value for discountRate is obtained from the static member defined in our global.asax file: CommerceApplication.discountRate.

Using Our Own Base Class for global.asax

The Inherits attribute of the global.asax Application directive allows us to name a .NET class that global.asax will use as the base class for all compiled instances of global.asax. This is useful if we want to add our own methods or properties as part of global.asax. It allows us to create a global.asax file that is customized to a particular application. For example, a commerce solution may provide a commerce-oriented global.asax that exposes properties or methods that are specific to its application, for example, a global.asax property such as AdTargetingEnabled. Developers who use this commerce framework don't see the implementation of this property, instead it's encapsulated within global.asax and they just need to know what happens when they set AdTargetingEnabled = true.

Inherits

To use Inherits, we first need to create our own custom class that inherits from the HttpApplication class. HttpApplication is the default base class used by global.asax, and it is what exposes the application and session events as well as any default properties. After creating a new class that inherits from HttpApplication, and adding the new functionality we desire, we can then use the global.asax Inherits directive to instruct ASP.NET to use our base class instead of HttpApplication. Let's illustrate this with an example.

Example

Below is a simple class, MyApplication, that inherits from HttpApplication. The MyApplication class implements a CurrentTime() method that simply returns the current date/time. Using the Inherits keyword we've told the compiler that the MyApplication class inherits all the methods, properties, events, etc. that HttpApplication implements. Essentially all this class does is add one more method.

```
   Imports System
   Imports System.Web

   ' To compile: vbc /t:library /r:system.web.dll /r:system.dll Inherits.vb

   Public Class MyApplication
     Inherits HttpApplication

     Public Function CurrentTime() As String
       ' Use ToString("r") to show seconds in Now output
       Return DateTime.Now.ToString("r")
     End Function
   End Class
```

Next, we need to compile and deploy the generated assembly to our Web Application's \bin directory. To compile, we can either create a new VB.NET Class project in Visual Studio.NET, or we can use the command-line compilers – either will work equally well. Here's the command-line compiler commands to compile this in case you don't have Visual Studio.NET:

```
vbc /t:library /r:system.web.dll /r:system.dll Inherits.vb
```

Next, we need to copy the resulting .dll to our Web Application's \bin directory. Remember, deploying it to the \bin directory makes it available to our application.

We can then write a global.asax file that uses the Application directive's Inherits attribute to inherit from our custom base class. Then within our global.asax code we have access to our new method:

```
<%@ Application Inherits="MyApplication" %>

<Script runat=server>
  Public Sub Application_OnBeginRequest()
    Dim TimeStamp As String
    TimeStamp = CurrentTime()

    Response.Write("Request Begining TimeStamp: " + TimeStamp)
    Response.Write("<HR size=1>")
  End Sub
</Script>
```

Since we inherited from the MyApplication base class (which itself inherits from HttpApplication), we have all of the standard behaviors of global.asax provided with the addition of a new CurrentTime() method.

In the above code example we created a simple local variable of type String named TimeStamp, then set TimeStamp using the inherited CurrentTime() method, before returning the result with Response.Write().

Mapping File Extensions to ASP. NET

A more advanced (but no more difficult) option that ASP.NET supports is mapping custom file extensions to ASP.NET resources. If for example, instead of using the extension .aspx for ASP.NET pages we decided to use the extension .wrox, we would need to make two changes to enable ASP.NET to serve default.wrox:

❑ First, we must create the following new entry in the <httpHandlers> section of either our web.config or machine.config files – more about these two files and the <httpHandlers> settings in the next chapter:

```
<configuration>
  <system.web>
    <httpHandlers>
      <add verb="*" path="*.wrox"
           type="System.Web.UI.PageHandlerFactory.System.Web" />
    </httpHandlers>
  </system.web>
</configuration>
```

❑ Second, we must tell IIS to send requests with the extension .wrox to ASP.NET. This is accomplished through the IIS Microsoft Management Console:

Open the IIS MMC, and right-click on either a web root or a web application folder (if we want to limit the mapping to a single application) and select the Properties option. Once the dialog is open, press the Configuration button, and select the App Mappings tab:

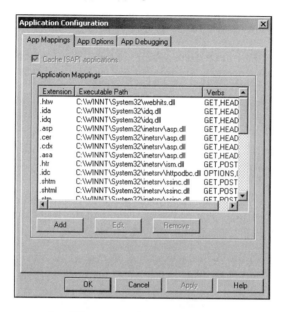

This tab lists all the extensions that IIS maps to ISAPI extensions. ISAPI is a low-level API that lets custom applications plug in to IIS. ASP used an ISAPI named asp.dll, and ASP.NET uses an ISAPI named aspnet_isapi.dll. The ASP.NET ISAPI simply takes the entire request from IIS and hands it to ASP.NET. If we want ASP.NET to handle the .wrox extension, we need to map it onto the aspnet_isapi.dll so that IIS sends the request to ASP.NET.

To add this application mapping press the Add button. This brings up the Add/Edit Application Extension Mapping dialog. We can then name the ASP.NET ISAPI (aspnet_isapi.dll), found in the directory: C:\[WinNt]\Microsoft.NET\Framework\[version]\. We can then also name our extension .wrox. Our completed entry should look similar to this:

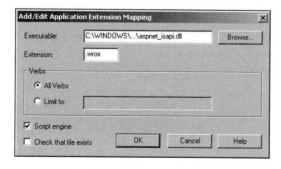

In the next chapter we'll look at how we can map the .wrox extension to ASP.NET resources through the ASP.NET configuration system.

Asynchronous Application Events

This is a more advanced discussion than the previous topics. Understanding asynchronous application events is not necessary to build good ASP.NET Applications. It is, however, an advanced feature that can prove very useful in some cases.

As we've mentioned earlier, ASP.NET code is executed in an ASP.NET worker process, not in the IIS process. Within this worker process, threads are used to execute code.

A thread is a resource, and there are a finite number of threads that ASP.NET will be able to use – otherwise the processor would spend all its time context switching (that is, switching threads of execution in the processor) rather than executing user code.

ASP.NET creates and manages a **threadpool** expanding and contracting the number of threads as required throughout the life of the application. This is in contrast to ASP, which used a fixed number of threads.

In some cases application code – such as network I/O – can potentially stall threads in the ASP.NET process. This is because the ASP.NET thread has to wait (it is blocked) until this slow operation is complete.

When a thread is blocked it can't be used to service requests, resulting in queuing of requests and degraded application performance. The ASP.NET team took this into consideration, and has added support for asynchronous events in addition to the existing synchronous ones we discussed earlier.

The only reason for using these asynchronous events in `global.asax` is in application code, within an event, that performs operations over the network where the network class supports I/O Completion ports, such as a web service proxy.

Supported Events

There are ten supported asynchronous events, which are raised in the following order:

- ❏ `AddOnBeginRequestAsync`
- ❏ `AddOnAuthenticateRequestAsync`
- ❏ `AddOnAuthorizeRequestAsync`
- ❏ `AddOnResolveRequestCacheAsync`
- ❏ `AddOnAcquireRequestStateAsync`
- ❏ `AddOnPreRequestHandlerExecuteAsync`
- ❏ `AddOnPostRequestHandlerExecuteAsync`
- ❏ `AddOnReleaseRequestStateAsync`
- ❏ `AddOnUpdateRequestCacheAsync`
- ❏ `AddOnEndRequestAsync`

No descriptions are given, as these events are synonymous with their synchronous counterparts described earlier.

When to Use Asynchronous Events

In Chapter 19, we'll start looking at ASP.NET Web Services. In a nutshell, ASP.NET allows us to easily build XML interfaces for application code. All we need to do is write the application logic and mark the methods with the `WebMethod` attribute.

Web services are very powerful, and easy to use. However, since they make calls over the network, and are subject to all the limitations of that network, we don't want to make a lot of web service calls within a web application (this is applicable to any web application, not just ASP.NET) because those network calls can potentially stall the threads used to process ASP.NET requests. For example, if our application gets twenty simultaneous requests and the application code that services that each request makes a call to a web service, we will potentially stall and queue subsequent requests as we wait for the threads making the web service calls to return.

However, by using asynchronous events, we could at least free up the threads that ASP.NET isn't using for the web service calls. Let's look at a sample of this.

The Web Service

First we need a sample web service. Below I've created a simple `StockQuote` web service:

VB.NET

```
<%@ WebService Class="QuoteService" %>

Imports System.Web.Services

Public Class QuoteService
  <WebMethod()> Public Function GetQuotes() As QuoteDetails()
    ' Create an array of 3 Quote objects for our return
    Dim quotes(3) As QuoteDetails

    quotes(0) = New QuoteDetails()
    quotes(0).Symbol = "MSFT"
    quotes(0).Price = 89.34F

    quotes(1) = New QuoteDetails()
    quotes(1).Symbol = "SUNW"
    quotes(1).Price = 11.13F

    quotes(2) = New QuoteDetails()
    quotes(2).Symbol = "ORCL"
    quotes(2).Price = 22.93F

    return quotes
  End Function
End Class

Public Class QuoteDetails
  Public Symbol As String
  Public Price As Single
End Class
```

This particular web service, written in VB.NET, simply returns an array of `QuoteDetails` with some pre-populated values. We can then write an ASP.NET application that uses this web service, and calls it asynchronously. When we build the proxy, ASP.NET automatically creates asynchronous implementations of our web service's methods.

Asynchronous Event Prototypes

Implementing asynchronous events is not trivial. Not only do you need to know whether or not the application code you're writing can benefit from asynchronous events, you also need to understand the asynchronous programming model supported by .NET.

To use these events within global.asax we need to wire up the provided event prototype ourselves. This is done by overriding the Init() method, which is marked as virtual in HttpApplication, and replacing it with our wire-up code. Unlike synchronous events, asynchronous event wire-up is not done for us.

Below is the code that calls the QuoteService web service asynchronously:

VB.NET

```
<%@ Import namespace="System.Threading" %>
<%@ Import namespace="System.Text" %>

<Script runat=server>
   Dim asyncResult As MyAsyncResult

   Public Overrides Sub Init()
      Dim beginEvent As New BeginEventHandler(AddressOf _Begin)
      Dim endEvent As New EndEventHandler(AddressOf _End)

      AddOnBeginRequestAsync(beginEvent, endEvent)
   End Sub
```

First we override the Init() method of HttpApplication so we can execute our code when global.asax is initialized. The code that we execute is an implementation of AddOnBeginRequestAsync(). We provide this event with both a begin and an end event handler. It is a code path within the begin event where we execute our code. Below is an implementation for both the BeginEventHandler and the EndEventHandler.

```
   ' Begin Event Handler
   Public Function _Begin(source As Object, e As EventArgs,_
                     callback As AsyncCallBack,
                     extraData As Object) As IAsyncResult
      asyncResult = new MyAsyncResult(Context, callback, extraData)

      Return asyncResult
   End Function

   ' End Event Handler
   Public Sub _End(ar As IAsyncResult)
   End Sub
```

The BeginEventHandler, _Begin, is raised when the OnBeginRequest is called. Within this event handler we create a new instance of a class called MyAsyncResult. It is within this class (defined further in the code) that we implement our code to call the web service.

The EndEventHandler, which can be used to clean up resources when the BeginEventHandler completes, is not used in this example.

Next, we find the implementation of `MyAsyncResult`; this class is an implementation of the `IAsyncResult` interface. The `IAsyncResult` interface is part of the asynchronous programming pattern defined by the Common Language Runtime. We provide an implementation (see the product documentation for a description of the implemented properties) that contains the code we want executed.

```
' Async implementation class
Private Class MyAsyncResult
  Implements IAsyncResult

  Dim _asyncState As Object
  Dim _callback As AsyncCallback
  Dim _thread As Thread
  Dim _context As HttpContext
  Dim _isCompleted As Boolean = false

  Public Sub New(context As HttpContext,
                 callback As AsyncCallback, asyncState As Object)
    _callback = callback
    _asyncState = asyncState
    _context = context

    _thread = New Thread(New ThreadStart(
                         AddressOf CallStockQuoteWebService))
    _thread.Start()
  End Sub

  Public ReadOnly Property AsyncState As Object
                                    Implements IAsyncResult.AsyncState
    Get
      Return _asyncState
    End Get
  End Property

  Public ReadOnly Property AsyncWaitHandle As WaitHandle
                              Implements IAsyncResult.AsyncWaitHandle
    Get
      Return Nothing
    End Get
  End Property

  Public ReadOnly Property CompletedSynchronously As Boolean
                          Implements IAsyncResult.CompletedSynchronously
    Get
      Return False
    End Get
  End Property

  Public ReadOnly Property IsCompleted As Boolean
                                  Implements IAsyncResult.IsCompleted
    Get
      Return _isCompleted
    End Get
  End Property
```

The constructor for `MyAsyncResult` creates a new thread and calls the `CallStockQuoteWebService` on that thread. This subroutine, below, creates a new instance of the proxy to our `QuoteService` ASP.NET web service, and uses the asynchronous implementation of the `GetQuotes()` method. It identifies a callback, `QuoteCallBack`, which is called when the I/O Completion port is reactivated. Within this callback we again create a new instance of the proxy class and then call its `EndGetQuotes` method. Finally, we save the proxy's `QuoteDetails` return to `Application` state memory so we can access it from anywhere within ASP.NET.

```
Public Sub CallStockQuoteWebService()
    Dim quote As New QuoteService()

    quote.BeginGetQuotes(New AsyncCallback(
                                AddressOf QuoteCallBack), Nothing)
End Sub

Public Sub QuoteCallBack(ar As IAsyncResult)
    Dim quote As New QuoteService()
    Dim d() As QuoteDetails

    d = quote.EndGetQuotes(ar)

    _context.Application("QuoteDetails") = d

    _isCompleted = true
    _callback(Me)
End Sub
End Class

</Script>
```

Finally, we can write a simple ASP.NET page that retrieves the values from `Application("QuoteDetails")`:

VB.NET

```
<Script runat="server">
  Dim quotes() As QuoteDetails

  Public Sub Page_Load(Sender As Object, e As EventArgs)
    quotes = CType(Application("QuoteDetails"), QuoteDetails())
  End Sub
</Script>

<%
Dim item As QuoteDetails

For Each item in quotes
  Response.Write("Symbol: " + item.Symbol + "<br>")
  Response.Write("Price: " + item.Price.ToString() + "<br>")
  Response.Write("<hr size=1>")
Next
%>
```

Executing this code provides the following result:

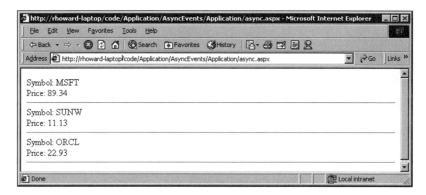

Because ASP.NET supports both synchronous and asynchronous application events we can have more options for how we build our application. Coding the event to be asynchronous will free the ASP.NET worker thread to service other requests until the code executed on the asynchronous thread completes. The result is better scalability, since we're not blocking the threads ASP.NET uses to service requests.

Summary

We've covered a lot of material in this chapter. Starting with a discussion of what a Web Application is, and how we create a new Web Application using Internet Information Services (IIS). We moved on to the important topic of developing an understanding of Web Applications, before we looked at the \bin directory and the global.asax file. We learned that the \bin directory is where we deploy compiled code in ASP.NET and that global.asax allows us to run application-level code. We additionally looked at the file format of global.asax.

Next, we discussed application state management and looked at three areas in detail: Application, Session, and Cache. We compared and contrasted Application versus Cache and gave some code examples showing the implicit and explicit methods used to add items to the Cache. We then looked at a Cache file dependency example.

Application events were covered next and in this section we looked at the eighteen events supported by ASP.NET. We gave brief overviews of each, covering their naming and syntax, before looking at specific examples of some of the more important events. One of the examples we gave showed how to use the Application_OnError event to write to the Windows Event Log.

Finally, we wrapped up the chapter with an Advanced Topics section covering some of the more advanced areas of ASP.NET including: asynchronous events, and mapping custom file extensions.

In the next chapter we're going to learn more about how we configure ASP.NET. We'll explore such topics as configuring Session to support the various modes discussed in this chapter.

"The Babel fish," says The Hitch Hiker's Guide to Galaxy "is small, yellow and leech-like, and probably the oddest thing in the Universe. It feeds on brainwave energy not from its carrier but from those around it. It absorbs all unconscious mental frequencies from this brainwave energy to nourish itself with. It then excretes into the mind of its carrier a telepathic matrix formed by combining the conscious thought frequencies with nerve signals picked up from the speech centres of the brain which has supplied them".

The practical upshot of all this is that if you stick a Babel fish in your ear you can instantly understand anything said to you in any form of language. The speech patterns you actually hear decode the brainwave matrix which has been fed into your mind by your Babel fish.

13

Configuration

Whenever we build an application, we also usually require the storage of details describing the behaviors and settings for the application, also known as configuration information. As it relates to web applications, configuration information includes details such as database connection strings, timeout values, and various other 'behaviors' such as how errors should be logged, or how state is to be maintained.

For those of us with a background in Active Server Pages, you'll no doubt recall that all of our application configuration information is stored in a binary repository called the Internet Information Services (IIS) metabase. When we want to configure an ASP application, such as changing the Session timeout – an example we'll use throughout the chapter – we need to modify the metabase, either through script or more commonly through the IIS Microsoft Management Console snap-in.

ASP.NET, unlike ASP, does not require extensive use of the IIS metabase. Instead, ASP.NET uses an XML-based configuration system. As we'll see in this chapter, ASP.NET's configuration system is much more flexible and accessible.

Below is a breakdown of what we'll cover:

- ❑ **Configuration Overview**. We'll start with a high-level overview of configuration, discussing both what's new in ASP.NET and how configuration has changed from ASP. We'll look at a common example, configuring Session state, to better frame the discussion. We'll also discuss the new configuration file format in detail.

- ❑ **Common Configuration Settings**. Here we'll look at several of the most common configuration settings that we'll use when working with ASP.NET. These settings include options for session state, security, and management of the ASP.NET worker process. The bulk of this chapter will be spent in this section.

- ❑ **Advanced Topics.** Finally, in this section of the chapter we'll discuss some more advanced topics such as the creation of our own configuration section handler and settings.

Let's get started with an overview of configuration.

Configuration Overview

ASP.NET configuration can be summarized in a single statement: **a simple, but powerful, XML-based configuration system**.

Rather than relying upon the Internet Information Services (IIS) metabase, as we have to for ASP applications, ASP.NET uses an XML-based configuration system. XML is used to describe the properties and behaviors for various aspects of ASP.NET applications.

The ASP.NET configuration system supports two types of configuration files:

❑ **Server Configuration** – Server configuration information is stored in a file named `machine.config`. This file represents the default settings used by all ASP.NET Web Applications. ASP.NET will install a single `machine.config` file on the server. We can find `machine.config` in `[WinNT]\Microsoft.NET\Framework\[version]\Config`.

> We will have a single **`machine.config`** file installed for each version of ASP.NET installed. The Common Language Runtime (CLR), and thus ASP.NET, supports the concept of side-by-side execution. Future versions of ASP.NET can run side-by-side with ASP.NET version 1.0 code. Each version provides its own **`machine.config`** file.

❑ **Application Configuration** – Application configuration information is stored in a file named `web.config`. This application configuration file represents the settings for an individual ASP.NET application. A server can have multiple `web.config` files, each existing in application roots or directories within our application. Settings made in a `web.config` file will override, or add new, settings to the default configuration information provided by `machine.config`. Later in the chapter we'll learn how the administrator can control which settings a `web.config` file is allowed to override.

We'll come back to these two configuration files and talk more about how to use them soon. Let's start our discussion of ASP.NET configuration with a brief discussion of ASP configuration (for those of us that used ASP).

ASP Configuration

Prior to ASP.NET, ASP web application configuration was either accomplished by script that modified the IIS metabase or through the IIS Manager.

The metabase is a binary data store that IIS uses for configuration settings.

Let's use a common task to illustrate ASP configuration. We'll use the example of setting `Session` state timeout from 20 minutes to 10 minutes.

Session State Example

To configure session timeout in ASP we go through the following steps (it should be noted that these steps need to be repeated for each server in your server farm):

- ❏   Open Internet Services Manager
- ❏   Right-click on a web application and select Properties
- ❏   Select the Home Directory tab
- ❏   Select Configuration
- ❏   Select the App Options tab

Finally, we're presented with the following dialog box in which we can configure session settings:

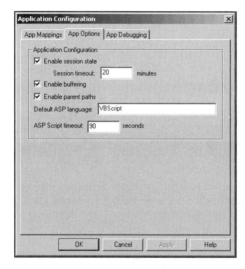

We can now change the session timeout value from 20 minutes to 10 minutes, press OK, and back out of all the menus. These settings are then applied to the metabase, but they don't apply to our application yet.

To apply these changes to our Web Application, we need to stop and start the web server by either using the IIS Manager (stop and start buttons), or shell to a command prompt and run `iisreset`.

Once these changes have been applied, and IIS is recycled, our application has the desired behavior of 10 minute `Session` timeout. If we maintained a web server farm, we would need to manually perform these steps for each server. Ideally we could replicate the IIS metabase to all the servers in our farm, but due to security reasons, the metabase uses a unique 'machine key' to encrypt some of the stored values. Even if we could manage to copy our updated metabase to another server, that server would most likely not be able to use it.

The above is obviously not ideal, especially when running a web server farm!

> *Application Center can replicate IIS settings to other IIS servers in our farm. It additionally includes other web farm manageability tools.*

Let's look at ASP.NET configuration.

ASP.NET Configuration

For completeness, we need to show the same configuration example of setting Session timeout from 20 minutes to 10 minutes for an ASP.NET application.

Session State Example

Fire up your favorite text editor and type the following XML into that file:

```
<configuration>
  <system.web>
    <sessionState timeout="10" />
  </system.web>
</configuration>
```

Next, save this file, naming it web.config, in a web application root (see the previous chapter for details on creating a Web Application).

> *While ASP.NET does not use the IIS metabase for application settings, the administrator is still required to mark folders as Web Applications.*

That's all there is to it – the ASP.NET application will now timeout the Session after 10 minutes of inactivity. Similar to ASP, ASP.NET Session timeout is set to 20 minutes. Although not shown, this default value is set in the server's machine.config file. However, our web.config has overridden that setting to 10 minutes.

> **Settings such as Session timeout made in the IIS metabase via the IIS MMC, as done for the ASP example, do not effect our ASP.NET applications.**

To update servers in our farm with these new settings we simply copy this web.config file to the appropriate application directory. ASP.NET takes care of the rest – no server restarts and no local server access is required – and our application continues to function normally, except now with the new settings.

As you can clearly see this new configuration system is very simple and straightforward to use. We simply write a configuration file and save that file to a web application and ASP.NET will automatically apply the changes. More on how all this works later.

Benefits of ASP.NET Configuration

As demonstrated above, instead of relying on the metabase for application configuration information, ASP.NET uses XML configuration files. The benefits of this include:

❑ **Human readable configuration settings** – It's very easy for us to open an XML file and read (or change) the settings. Tools that work with XML, such as Visual Studio.NET can be used to open the file and settings can easily be identified and updated.

❑ **Updates are immediate** – Unlike ASP, application configuration changes are immediate and do not require the web server to be stopped and restarted for the settings to take affect. Instead, the settings immediately affect a running system and are completely transparent to the end user.

❑ **Local server access is not required** – ASP.NET automatically detects when updates are made to the configuration system and then creates a new instance of the application. End users are then redirected to the new application and the configuration changes are applied without the need for the administrator to stop and start the web server. Although not covered in great detail, this is done through a feature of the Common Language Runtime known as Application Domains, mentioned in the previous chapter.

❑ **Easily replicated** – Unlike the metabase, which could not easily be replicated since the instance of the metabase is bound to the server it resides upon, ASP.NET configuration files can simply be copied to the appropriate location; they are simply XML files.

The ASP.NET configuration system eliminates 99% of the work of the metabase. However, there are two exceptions:

❑ **Creating web applications** – As discussed in the previous chapter, marking a folder, either virtual or physical, through the Internet Service Management Console as an application allows ASP.NET to treat components, files, and configuration information as a Web Application. This process must still be accomplished either by using script that modifies the IIS metabase, through the IIS Manager snap-in, or when we create a new project with Visual Studio.NET. This forces the administrator to decide what is or is not an ASP.NET application.

❑ **Custom file extension mappings** – Again, as discussed in the previous chapter, if we wish to use file extensions other than those already supported by ASP.NET, we need to add an entry in the application settings for IIS. For example, if we decide that we want to write applications that use the extension `.wrox`, we have to tell IIS that requests for resources ending with the extension `.wrox` should be handled by ASP.NET.

Both of the above exceptions are configuration decisions made when building the server. For all other application and server configuration options, such as configuring `Session` timeout, the execution timeout (how long an ASP.NET application executes before being timed out), or new settings such as timing out the worker process, we'll use the ASP.NET configuration exclusively.

How Configuration is Applied

When ASP.NET applies configuration settings for a given request, a union of the `machine.config` as well as any `web.config` files are applied for a given application. Configuration settings are inherited from parent web applications; `machine.config` being the root parent. This is best explained through the use of a diagram:

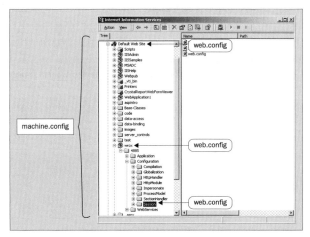

The previous screenshot is of the IIS MMC. On the left-hand side of the diagram `machine.config` is applied to all web applications on this server. We then see callouts, labeled 'web.config' that identify locations where a `web.config` file might exist within this server. The three configuration files apply to:

- ❑ The root of the web, for example http://localhost/.

- ❑ A sub-application, for example http://localhost/wrox/.

- ❑ A folder within the Wrox application, for example
  http://localhost/wrox/4885/Configuration/Session/.

The configuration for each of these applications is unique, but settings are inherited. For example, if the `web.config` file in the root of our web site defines session timeout as 10 minutes (overriding the server's default settings inherited from `machine.config`) and the `web.config` files in /wrox/ and /wrox/4885/Configuration/Session/ don't override these settings, both /wrox/ and /wrox/4885/Configuration/Session/ will inherit the settings of 10 minute session timeout, in addition to applying their own settings for their respective application.

Detecting Configuration File Changes

ASP.NET detects when files, such as `machine.config` or `web.config`, are changed by listening for file change notification events provided by the operating system. When a change is detected, such as an update to `machine.config`, ASP.NET creates a new Application Domain to service new requests. When the old Application Domain has completed servicing its outstanding requests it is destroyed.

> *An Application Domain is a feature provided by the Common Language Runtime (CLR) and was discussed in the previous chapter.*

There is no longer any need to stop and start IIS to apply configuration settings as we did with ASP. Instead, changes to ASP.NET configuration are immediate, handled behind the scenes through the use of Application Domains.

Configuration is Extensible

What happens if our application has configuration data we'd like to store? This wasn't a feasible option in ASP (using the metabase), but with ASP.NET configuration we've got a couple of choices:

- ❑ **Application Settings** – We can use the application settings section of ASP.NET configuration (which we'll look at a bit later in the chapter) to store key/value pairs representing our configuration settings.

- ❑ **Create a Custom Configuration Handler** – A more advanced option, and one we'll discuss at the end of the chapter, is extending the ASP.NET configuration system and creating our own configuration handler and settings.

We've discussed ASP.NET configuration at a highlevel, let's dig into the technical details. We'll start with the XML configuration file format.

Configuration File Format

As previously mentioned, there are two types of XML configuration files used by ASP.NET: `machine.config` and `web.config`. These two configuration files differ only in file name, where they live on the file system, and support of some settings. Both use the same XML format (pseudo schema below):

Items in brackets [ ] have unique values within the real configuration file.

```
<?xml version="1.0" encoding="UTF-8"?>
<configuration>
  <configSections>
    <section name="[sectionSettings]" type="[Class]"/>

    <sectionGroup name="[sectionGroup]">
      <section name="[sectionSettings]" type="[Class]"/>
    </sectionGroup>
  </configSections>

  <section name="[sectionSettings]" type="[Class]"/>

  <[sectionGroup]>
    <[sectionSettings] attribute="[value]"/>

    <[sectionSettings] attribute="[value]">
      <element attribute="[value]">
    </[sectionSettings]>
  </[sectionGroup]>
<configuration>
```

Note the camel-casing, the first letter of the first word is always lower-case and the first letter of subsequent words is upper-case, for example thisIsAnExample. Understanding the casing is very important since the ASP.NET configuration system is case sensitive.

The root element of the configuration file is always `<configuration>`. Within `<configuration>` there are two important sections:

❑   `<section name="[sectionSettings]">` – Referred to as a configuration section handler, this defines a class used to interpret the meaning of configuration data. It is important to note that configuration section handlers only need to be declared once for all applications if declared in `machine.config` (this is because applications inherit the settings in `machine.config`). Web Applications that wish to change the settings for a particular configuration option, such as the `Session` example shown earlier, do not need to re-declare the configuration section handler.

❑   `<[sectionSettings]>` – Referred to as configuration section settings, this defines the actual settings for a particular option. The sample `web.config` file shown earlier defines a configuration section setting for `sessionState` overriding the default of 20 minutes inherited from `machine.config`.

These two sections are intimately related. Whereas section settings, such as configuring the timeout value for `Session` state, define options for a particular feature, section handlers define the code that implements the desired behaviors. In a moment we'll look at some examples that clarify this better.

617

Each of the section handlers and settings are optionally wrapped in a <sectionGroup>. A <sectionGroup> provides an organizational function within the configuration file. It allows us to organize configuration into unique groups – for instance, the <system.web> section group is used to identify areas within the configuration file specific to ASP.NET.

Let's go a bit deeper here and look at some examples.

Configuration Handlers

Section handlers identify .NET classes, which are loaded when the configuration system is loaded. These classes are responsible for reading the settings for their respective features from the configuration section settings.

The name attribute of the <section name="[sectionSettings]"> tag defines the tag name, sessionState here, of the configuration section settings element, (<sessionState>). Let's use our Session state example to better illustrate how this works.

Session State Example

Within the machine.config file we can find the base definition for the sessionState section handler. Remember, since this section handler is defined in machine.config, we don't need to re-declare it on each use in web.config files.

Below is the XML that defines the sessionState section handler (highlighted):

```
<?xml version="1.0" encoding="UTF-8" ?>
<configuration>
  <configSections>
    <sectionGroup name="system.web">
          <section name="sessionState"
          type="System.Web.SessionState.SessionStateSectionHandler,
          System.Web"
      />
    </sectionGroup>
  </configSections>
...
```

The type="... SessionStateSectionHandler" identifies the class responsible for the configuration settings of ASP.NET session state. The name="sessionState" value defines the name of configuration section settings, <sessionState> here, an element found later in the configuration document, and System.Web identifies the assembly the class resides within.

Once a configuration section handler is declared, it does not need to be re-declared in configuration files that inherit from it. Since all web.config application configuration files inherit from machine.config, any configuration section handlers declared in machine.config are automatically available within web.config.

We can enforce settings found in the machine.config so that web.config files can't override settings. For example, if we are running ASP.NET in a hosted environment, the administrator can restrict the sessionState settings so they can't be changed in web.config files – we'll explore this option later in the chapter in the *Advanced Topics* section.

Let's take a look at the section settings that actually define our desired behaviors. We'll use the same sessionState example.

Configuration Settings

The second section of the configuration file is the configuration session settings. Whereas the handler (described above) names a class, the settings identify properties that affect the behavior of the application. In most cases we only need to understand the settings for the configuration option we wish to modify, such as the settings for `sessionState`.

Again, this is best explained through revisiting our session state example from above.

Session State Example

Below we have the `machine.config` section handler and settings for ASP.NET `sessionState` – the settings are highlighted – we'll come back to the values for `<sessionState>` later:

```xml
<?xml version="1.0" encoding="UTF-8" ?>
<configuration>
  <configSections>
    <sectionGroup name="system.web">
      <section name="sessionState"
            type="System.Web.SessionState.SessionStateSectionHandler,
            System.Web"
      />
    </sectionGroup>
    ...
  </configSections>
  ...
  <system.web>
    <sessionState
        mode="InProc"
        stateConnectionString="tcpip=127.0.0.1:42424"
        sqlConnectionString="data source=127.0.0.1;
                              user id=sa;password="
        cookieless="false"
        timeout="20"
    />
  </system.web>
</configuration>
```

In the session settings, properties are set. For example, the `sessionState` properties include: `mode`, `cookieless`, `timeout`, etc. ASP.NET `Session` uses these settings and when a request is made ASP.NET knows where to find the various resources it needs as well as how to use those resources. For example, if we were to set `cookieless="true"`, this would instruct ASP.NET to **not** use HTTP cookies to manage the `Session` ID and instead pass a key in the URL.

The above example shows both section handlers and session settings. As I mentioned earlier, we will use the settings most often as `web.config` files that we build for our applications inherit the handlers and settings found in `machine.config`. Below is a valid `web.config` file that enables cookieless session ID management – note we aren't re-declaring the handler:

```xml
<configuration>
  <system.web>
    <sessionState
        mode="InProc"
```

```
            stateConnectionString="tcpip=127.0.0.1:42424"
            sqlConnectionString="data source=127.0.0.1;
                              user id=sa;password="
            cookieless="true"
            timeout="20"
      />
    </system.web>
  </configuration>
```

It's good to understand section handlers, and we'll build our own at the end of the chapter, but it's definitely important that we understand the settings. When we build and deploy our applications we'll usually create our own web.config files and override the machine.config settings – without seeing machine.config. It is a recommendation to modify web.config files rather than changing machine.config, since changing machine.config affects all applications on the server.

Now that we've looked at the configuration file, let's discuss the most common configuration settings we'll use for our applications.

Common Configuration Settings

If you've examined machine.config, which I would suggest you do, you'll find around 30 configuration settings. Let's look at the 15 most commonly used configuration entries:

❑ **General Configuration Settings** – How long a given ASP.NET resource, such as a page, is allowed to execute before being considered 'timed-out'.

❑ **Page Configuration** – ASP.NET pages have configuration options such as whether buffering or view state is enabled.

❑ **Application Settings** – key/value combination that allows us to store data within the configuration system and access it within our application.

❑ **Session State** – Options for Session state, such as where data is stored, timeout, and support for cookieless state management.

❑ **Tracing** – Provides a trace of what our application is doing. This is configurable both at the page level and application level.

❑ **Custom Errors** – ASP.NET has several options for handling application errors, as well as common HTTP errors (404 file not found, etc.).

❑ **Security** – Although we'll cover security in more detail in Chapter 14, we will discuss some of the basic security configuration options.

❑ **Web Services** – The web services section allows us to configure some of the options for ASP.NET Web Services, such as the name and location of the DefaultWSDLHelpGenerator.aspx template used to generate an HTML view of our Web Service.

❑ **Globalization** – Application-level options for the request/response character encoding for ASP.NET to use.

❑ **Compilation** – The compilation options allow us to control some of the compilation behaviors of ASP.NET, such as changing the default language from VB.NET to C#.

❑ **Identity** – ASP.NET allows us to impersonate the user that ASP.NET acts on the behalf of.

❑ **HTTP Handlers** – HTTP Handlers are responsible for servicing requests for a particular extension in ASP.NET, such as `.aspx` or `.asmx`. Custom handlers can be added within this section or existing handlers can be removed.

❑ **HTTP Modules** – HTTP Modules are responsible for filtering each request/response in an ASP.NET application, such as determining whether a particular request should be served from the Cache or directed to an HTTP Handler.

❑ **Process Model** – By default, ASP.NET runs out-of-process from IIS and has the capability to recycle by itself. The settings found in this section allow us granular control over the behavior of the worker process. We'll also discuss the ASP.NET Worker process in this section.

❑ **Machine Key** – A key used for encryption or hashing of some values, such as the data in the Cookie used for Forms authentication. In a server farm environment all the servers must share a common machine key.

Let's get started by discussing General Configuration Settings.

General Configuration Settings

For general application configuration settings, such as how long a request is processed before being considered timed out, the maximum size of a request, or whether to use fully qualified URLs in redirects (a requirement for some mobile applications) we use the `<httpRuntime>` configuration settings:

```
<configuration>
  <system.web>
    <httpRuntime
          executionTimeout="90"
          maxRequestLength="4096"
          useFullyQualifiedRedirectUrl="false"
    />
  </system.web>
</configuration>
```

There are three configurable options:

❑ `executionTimeout`

❑ `maxRequestLength`

❑ `userFullyQualifiedRedirectUrl`

Let's discuss how each of these applies to an ASP.NET application.

Application Timeout

The `executionTimeout` setting is similar to the timeout option for ASP. The value of this attribute is the amount of time in seconds for which a resource can execute before ASP.NET times the request out. The default setting is 90 seconds.

If we have a particular ASP.NET page or web service that takes longer than 90 seconds to execute we can extend the time limit in the configuration. A good example here is an application that makes a particularly long database request, such as generating a sales report for an application in our company's intranet. If we know the report takes 120 seconds (on average) to execute we could set the timeout="300" and ASP.NET would not timeout our request prematurely. Similarly, we can set the value to less than 90 seconds and this will decrease the time ASP.NET is allowed to process the request before timing out.

Controlling the Maximum Request Length

The maximum request length attribute, maxRequestLength, identifies the maximum size in KB of the request. By default the maximum request length is 4MB.

For example, if our site allows customers to upload files, and we expect that content to be larger than 4MB, we can increase this setting. Good examples here include MP3s, unusually large images, such as an X-ray stored as a large, uncompressed TIFF for a medical site, and so on.

Controlling the maximum request length is important, since common denial of service attacks involve spamming a web site with unusually large requests.

Fully Qualified URLs for Redirects

Some devices that may use ASP.NET applications, such as mobile phones, require that a redirect URL be fully qualified. The default behavior is for ASP.NET to send an unqualified URL for client redirects, (/Wrox/Logon.aspx for example). Setting useFullyQualifiedRedirectUrl="true" will cause the server to send a redirect as http://[server name]/Wrox/Logon.aspx.

In addition to configuring the application, we also find settings that are particular to ASP.NET Pages.

Page Configuration

The Page configuration settings allow us to control some of the default behaviors for all ASP.NET Pages. These behaviors include options such as whether or not we should buffer the output before sending it, and whether or not Session state is enabled for Pages within the application.

Below is a web.config file that mirrors the default settings from machine.config:

```
<configuration>
  <system.web>
    <pages buffer="true"
           enableSessionState="true"
           enableViewState="true"
           enableViewStateMac="false"
           autoEventWireup="true"
    />
  </system.web>
</configuration>
```

The above settings automatically are all set to true, with the exception of enableViewStateMac – a one-way message authentication code (MAC) on the data that allows for the integrity of the data to be validated, but which can be costly to generate.

Here is what these settings allow us to control:

❑ `buffer` – Whether or not the response to a request is buffered on the server before being sent. If `buffer="false"` the response to a request is sent as the response is available. In some cases, buffering can be disabled and the end-user will perceive that the application is responding faster. In general, however, buffering should not be disabled and the default setting of `true` need not be changed.

❑ `enableSessionState` – By default Session is enabled for ASP.NET Pages. However, if `Session` is not going to be used for the application, you should disable Session state. Disabling Session will conserve resources used by the application.

In addition to `true`/`false` settings for this attribute, we can also set `enableSessionState` to `readonly`. We'll cover the `readonly` option later in the chapter when we discuss the `<sessionState>` settings.

❑ `enableViewState` – By default view state, a means of storing server control data on the client, is round-tripped within a hidden form element (`__VIEWSTATE`) in ASP.NET Pages. If our application will not use view state, we can set the value to `false` in the application's `web.config` file.

❑ `autoEventWireup` – ASP.NET can automatically wire up common Page events such as `Load` or `Error` – allowing us to simply author an event prototype such as `Page_Load`. Setting `autoEventWireup="false"`, the default behavior of Visual Studio.NET, forces us (done automatically with Visual Studio.NET) to override the appropriate Page events.

Note, all of the above settings can be overridden within a given ASP.NET Page. For example, we can disable view state at the control level on individual pages. Please see Chapter 5 for more details.

Application Settings

The application settings section, `<appSettings/>`, allows us to store application configuration details with the configuration file without needing to write our own configuration section handler. The use of these key/value pair settings simply populates a hashtable that we can access within our application. Below is a simple example that stores the DSN for a connection to a database:

```
<configuration>
  <appSettings>
    <add key="DSN"
         value="server=sql1;uid=cust;pwd=8d$net;database=pubs" />
    <add key="SQL_PRODUCTS"
         value="SELECT Name, Price FROM Products" />
  </appSettings>
</configuration>
```

We can then retrieve these settings within our ASP.NET application:

```
<%@ Import Namespace="System.Data" %>
<%@ Import Namespace="System.Data.SqlClient" %>
```

```
<Script runat=server>
   Private dsn As String
   Private sql As String

   Public Sub Page_Load()
     dsn = ConfigurationSettings.AppSettings("DSN")
     sql = ConfigurationSettings.AppSettings("SQL_PRODUCTS")

     Dim myConnection As New SqlConnection(dsn)
     Dim myCommand As New SqlCommand(sql, myConnection)
     Dim reader As DataReader

     myConnection.Open()

     If (reader.Read) Then
       datagrid1.DataSource = reader
       datagrid1.DataBind()
     End If

     myConnection.Close()
   End Sub
</Script>

<asp:DataGrid id=datagrid1 runat=server/>
```

Storing this type of commonly used information within the configuration system allows us to manage common application details in a single location, and if the configuration data changes – such as changing the password value of the DSN or the columns in the select statement – the application is automatically restarted and the new values used.

Session State

Session state is dedicated data storage for each user within an ASP.NET application. It is implemented as a Hashtable and stores data, based on key/value pair combinations (for details on how to use the Session programmatically see the previous chapter).

Classic ASP Session state has several short-comings:

❑   **Web farm Challenges** – Session data is stored in memory on the server it is created upon. In a web farm scenario, where there are multiple web servers, a problem could arise if a user was redirected to a server other than the server upon which they stored their Session state. Normally this can be managed by an IP routing solution where the IP address of the client is used to route that client to a particular server, in other words "sticky sessions". However, some ISPs use farms of reverse proxies, and therefore the client request may come through a different IP on each request. When a user is redirected to a server other than the server that contains their Session data, poorly designed applications can break.

❑   **Supporting clients that don't accept HTTP cookies** – Because the web is inherently a stateless environment, to use Session state the client and web server need to share a key that the client can present to identify its Session data on subsequent requests. Classic ASP shared this key with the client through the use of an HTTP cookie. While this scenario worked well for clients that accept HTTP cookies, it broke the 1% of users that rejected HTTP cookies.

Both of these issues are addressed in ASP.NET Session, which supports several new features to remedy these problems:

❑ **Web Farm Support** – ASP.NET Session supports storing the Session data either in-process (in the same memory that ASP.NET uses), out-of-process using Windows NT Service (in separate memory from ASP.NET), or in SQL Server (persistent storage). Both the Windows Service and SQL Server solutions support a web farm scenario where all the web servers can be configured to share a common Session store. Thus, as users get routed to different servers each server is able to access that user's Session data. To the developer programming with Session, this is completely transparent and does not require any changes in the application code – rather we simply configure ASP.NET to support one of these out-of-process options.

❑ **Cookieless mode** – Although somewhat supported in ASP through the use of an ISAPI filter (available as part of the IIS 4.0 SDK), ASP.NET makes cookieless support for Session a first class feature: however, by default Session still uses HTTP cookies. When cookieless mode is enabled, ASP.NET will embed the session ID, normally stored in the cookie, into the URL that is sent back to the client. When the client makes a request using the URL containing the Session ID, ASP.NET is able to extract the Session ID and map the request to the appropriate Session data.

Let's take a look at the configuration settings used to enable these options.

Configuration Settings

The sessionState configuration settings within web.config or machine.config allow us to configure how we take advantage of the Session features described above. Below is a sample web.config file that mirrors the defaults found in machine.config:

```
<configuration>
  <system.web>
    <sessionState
      mode="InProc"
      stateConnectionString="tcpip=127.0.0.1:42424"
      sqlConnectionString="data source=127.0.0.1; user id=sa;password="
      cookieless="false"
      timeout="20"
    />
  </system.web>
<configuration>
```

The <sessionState> configuration setting supports five attributes (we'll show their use shortly):

❑ mode – The mode setting supports four options: Off, InProc, SQLServer, and StateServer. The InProc option, the default, enables in-process state management. In-process state management is identical to the behavior of ASP Session. There are also two options for out-of-process state management: a Windows NT Service (StateServer) and SQL Server (SQLServer).

❑ stateConnectionString – Identifies the TCP/IP address and port used to communicate with the Windows NT Service providing state management facilities. We must configure the stateConnectionString when mode is set to StateServer.

❑ sqlConnectionString – Identifies the database connection string that names the database used for mode="SQLServer". This includes both the TCP/IP address identified by data source as well as a username and password to connect to the SQL Server database.

❑ cookieless – Enables support for Session key management without requiring HTTP Cookies.

❑ timeout – This option controls the life of a user's Session. timeout is a sliding value, and on each request the timeout period is reset to the current time plus the timeout value.

Next, let's implement some of the common scenarios we'll encounter when building applications using Session state.

Supporting Web Farms

By default ASP.NET ships with Session state configured to store Session data in the same process as ASP.NET. This is identical to how ASP Session data is stored. The session web farm feature allows several front-end web servers share a common storage point for Session data, rather than each web server maintaining its own copy. This creates a scenario in which the client making the request can be serviced from any server within the server farm. This additionally allows an individual server's process to recycle and access to Session data to be maintained.

We have two options for out-of-process Session state: a Windows NT Service, which stores the data (in memory) in a separate process from ASP.NET (either on the same server or on a different server), and a SQL Server option, which stores the data in SQL Server. Let's look at how we configure both of these options.

Out-of-Process: Windows Service

To support the out-of-process Windows Service option (mode="StateServer") we need first to decide which server is going to run the Windows Service used for Session state storage. ASP.NET ships with a Windows Service named aspnet_state that needs to be running in order for Session to function in mode="StateServer".

The service can be started by shelling to a command prompt and typing: net start aspnet_state .

Alternatively we can configure the service using the Services and Applications Microsoft Management Console MMC snap-in (available from Start | Programs | Administrative Tools | Computer Management). If we view the Services item in this tool we are presented with a list of the available services on the server:

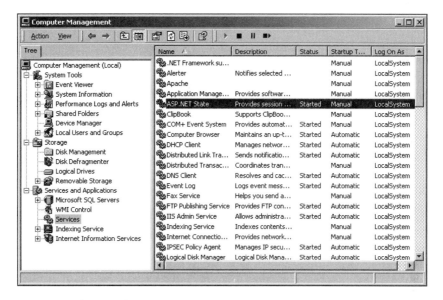

Right-clicking on the ASP.NET State item opens up a menu that allows us to configure how this service is to be run. We can select the start-up options (whether or not Windows should automatically start this service for us) as well as using the toolbar Start and Stop buttons to enable or disable this service ourselves.

Once the service has been started we then need to configure ASP.NET to use this particular service. This is done through our configuration file. We need to tell ASP.NET which server and port to use for communication with our ASP.NET State service as well as the fact that we want to use the Windows Service state option.

Here's our web.config, with the necessary settings highlighted:

```
<configuration>
  <system.web>
    <sessionState
        mode="StateServer"
        stateConnectionString="tcpip=127.0.0.1:42424"
        sqlConnectionString="data source=127.0.0.1; user id=sa;password="
        cookieless="false"
        timeout="20"
    />
  </system.web>
<configuration>
```

In the above example ASP.NET Session is directed to use the Windows Service for state management on the local server (address 127.0.0.1 is the TCP/IP loop-back address).

The default port that aspnet_state uses to communicate is port 42424; we can configure this to any other port we wish, but this configuration must be done through the system registry. To configure to the port 100, run RegEdit.exe, expand HKEY_LOCAL_MACHINE | System | CurrentControlSet | Services | aspnet_state | Parameters. Within Parameters we'll find a Port setting, which allows us to configure the TCP/IP port that the aspnet_state service uses to communicate on:

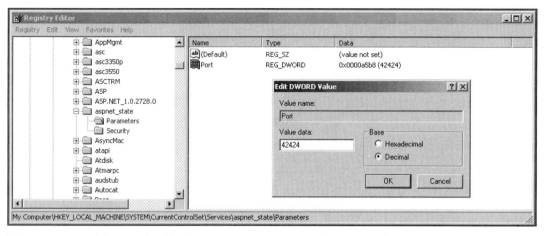

If we want to enable state for all of our servers in a server farm to point back to a single state server we need to change the IP address to reflect the IP address of the server running the Windows NT Service and we also need each of the server's machine keys to be identical.

This last point is very, very important. Each server, by default, is set to auto-generate its own machine key. This machine key is used to encrypt data or to create unique 'server-specific' values for data (known as hashing). The ID used for Session state is created using the machine key, and thus for the key to be understood by all the servers in the farm the servers need the same machine key.

The machine key has other applications besides sessionState and we'll cover it in more detail later in the chapter.

In addition to supporting an out-of-process Windows Service, ASP.NET additionally supports an out-of-process option that saves Session data to SQL Server.

Out-of-Process: SQL Server

Configuring ASP.NET to support SQL Server for Session state is just as simple as configuring the Windows Service; the only difference is we'll use SQL Server. To configure SQL Server we need to run a T-SQL script that ships with ASP.NET: InstallSqlState.sql.

Note that a T-SQL script to uninstall ASP.NET SQL Server support is also included: UninstallSqlState.sql.

> It should be noted that ASP.NET ships with a lightweight version of SQL Server 2000 that has several limitations (limited connections, throttled transactions, etc.) but is for all practical purposes a normal working version of SQL Server 2000. We can use this developer version of SQL Server 2000 for development purposes, but if we were to deploy and use SQL Server for state management in a production server farm we would want to use SQL Server 2000 Standard or Enterprise versions for optimal performance.

To run the InstallSqlState.sql script we'll use a tool that ships with SQL Server (and MSDE): OSQL.exe. OSQL allows us to apply a T-SQL script to a SQL Server. Our InstallSqlState.sql T-SQL script creates several stored procedures and creates several temporary databases for ASP.NET Session to use.

The script only needs to be run once on any given SQL Server, and we'll need sa (administrator) level access to run the script. To run the script shell to a command prompt and navigate to the \WINNT\Microsoft.NET\Framework\[version]\ directory and type:

OSQL -S localhost -U sa -P <InstallSqlState.sql

Note: for the purpose of example, I copied the T-SQL Script to c:\ before running OSQL.

Next, we need to configure our configuration settings to use SQL Server (highlighted):

```
<configuration>
  <system.web>
    <sessionState
      mode="SQLServer"
      stateConnectionString="tcpip=127.0.0.1:42424"
      sqlConnectionString="data source=127.0.0.1;
                           user id=session;password=&363test"
      cookieless="false"
      timeout="20"
    />
  </system.web>
<configuration>
```

First, we set mode="SQLServer" and then we configure the sqlConnectionString to point to the server that has the T-SQL script installed.

Session data stored in SQL is inaccessible to other applications. It is serialized as a protected type and should not be read or modified by applications other than ASP.NET.

> **ASP.NET accesses the data stored in SQL via stored procedures. By default Session data is stored in the TempDB database. The stored procedures may be modified, for example if we wished to store to tables other than TempDB. However, this is an option best saved for DBAs.**

From the developer's point of view, writing code that uses Session in any of the above modes is completely transparent. However, we should briefly discuss choosing a mode as the mode selection can impact on the performance of the application.

Choosing a Mode

There are three modes from which we can choose from when building an application.

- ❑ **In-process (default)** – In process will perform best because the Session data is kept within the ASP.NET process since local memory access will always be faster than having to go out of process. Additional reasons include: web applications hosted on a single server; applications in which the user is guaranteed to be re-directed to the correct server; or when Session data is not critical (in the sense that it can be easily re-created).

- ❑ **Windows Service** – This mode is best used when performance is important and there are multiple web servers servicing requests. With this out-of-process mode, you get the performance of reading from memory and the reliability of a separate process that manages the state for all servers.

- ❑ **SQL Server** – This mode is best used when the reliability of the data is fundamental to the stability of the application, as the data is stored in SQL Server. The performance isn't as fast as the Windows Service, but the tradeoff is the higher level of reliability.

Now that we've examined the supported options for web farms, let's turn our attention to another one of the great new features of ASP.NET Session: support for clients that don't accept HTTP cookies.

Cookieless Session

Because HTTP is a stateless environment, in order to maintain state across requests through Session both the client and the server need to maintain a key. This key is used to identify the client's Session across requests. The server can then use the key to access the data stored for that user. By default the server gives the client a key using an HTTP cookie. On subsequent requests to that server the client will present the HTTP cookie and the server then has access to the session key.

However, some clients choose not to accept HTTP cookies – for a variety of reasons, a common one being the perceived privacy issue. When this happens the site has to either 'adapt' and not support cookies (and Session), or build the application to not require use of Session. A third option, first provided with IIS 4, is an ISAPI filter that can extract the session ID out of the cookie and pass it as part of the URL. This concept is supported by ASP.NET as a first class feature. This feature is known as cookieless Session state, and it works with any of the supported mode options.

Individual applications can be configured to support either cookie or cookieless, not both.

We can enable cookieless Session support by simply setting a flag in our configuration system (highlighted):

```
<configuration>
  <system.web>
    <sessionState
      mode="inproc"
      stateConnectionString="tcpip=127.0.0.1:42424"
      sqlConnectionString="data source=127.0.0.1; user id=sa;password="
      cookieless="true"
      timeout="20"
    />
  </system.web>
</configuration>
```

Similar to all configuration changes in ASP.NET, the settings are applied immediately. After changing cookieless from `false` (default) to `true` the session ID is embedded in the URL of the page:

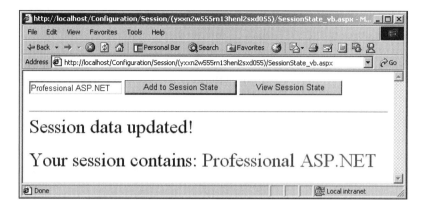

As you can see above, the session ID `yxxn2w555rn13henl2sxd055` is embedded within the URL. Below is the source for the above page; you'll notice that no special changes have been made to the source code to support embedding the `Session` ID in the URL:

VB.NET

```
<Script runat=server>
  Public Sub Session_Add(sender As Object, e As EventArgs)
    Session("cart") = text1.Value
    span1.InnerHtml = "Session data updated! <P>" + _
                     "Your session contains: <font color=red>" + _
                     Session("cart") + "</font>"
  End Sub

  Public Sub CheckSession(sender As Object, e As EventArgs)
    If (Session("cart") Is Nothing) Then
        span1.InnerHtml = "NOTHING, SESSION DATA LOST!"
    Else
        span1.InnerHtml = "Your session contains:" + _
                          "<font color=red>" + Session("cart") + "</font>"
    End If
  End Sub
</Script>

<form runat=server>
  <input id=text1 type=text runat=server>
  <input type=submit runat=server OnServerClick="Session_Add"
         Value="Add to Session State">
  <input type=submit runat=server OnServerClick="CheckSession"
         Value="View Session State">
</form>
<a href="SessionState_cs.aspx">C# Example</A>
<hr size=1>
<font size=6><span id=span1 runat=server/></font>
```

Additionally, for relative URLs (as viewed by the browser) within the page, such as:

```
<a href="SessionState_cs.aspx">C# Example</a>
```

ASP.NET will automatically add the session ID into the URL. Below is the link that the client receives:

```
<a href="/(yxxn2w555rn13hen12sxd055)/SessionState_cs.aspx">C# Example</a>
```

Note the ID is added directly after the name of the application root. In the above example /Session is marked as an application.

The new features for Session state in ASP.NET are very powerful. We can configure Session to be stored in a separate process from the ASP.NET worker process, which allows our Session data to be available in both a server farm and in the rare case that our web server crashes. In addition to the great support for out-of-process Sessions state, support for cookieless Sessions has also been added. Cookieless session allows us to use Session for clients that don't accept HTTP cookies. Next, let's look at a feature of ASP.NET that replaces Response.Write() debugging for ASP Pages.

Tracing

Tracing is a feature that did not exist in ASP and is a new feature introduced with ASP.NET. Tracing allows us trace the execution of an application and later view the trace results. Let's illustrate this with an example.

Trace Example

Below is a simple VB example of a page with a simple function:

```
<Script runat="server">
  Public Function Add(a As Integer, b As Integer) As Integer
    return a + b
  End Function
</Script>
Call the Add routine: 4 + 5 = <%=Add(4,5)%>
```

The output of which is:

Call the Add routine: 4 + 5 = 9

Classic ASP Tracing

Although a simple example, what if within the Add Function we wished to know the parameters of a and b as the code was executing? A common technique ASP developers use is to add Response.Write() statements in their code to trace the actions of their code as it's executed:

```
<Script runat="server">
Public Function Add(a As Integer, b As Integer) As Integer
  Response.Write("Inside Add() a: " + a.ToString() + "<BR>")
  Response.Write("Inside Add() b: " + b.ToString() + "<BR>")
  return a + b
End Function
</Script>
Call the Add routine: 4 + 5 = <%=Add(4,5)%>
```

The output of which is:

```
Inside Add() a: 4
Inside Add() b: 5
Call the Add routine: 4 + 5 = 9
```

Although this works well, it does introduce unnecessary code into the application. As we all know, unnecessary code usually results in bugs that break deployed applications. Examples of which include SQL statements, configuration flags, or output status details, which are all items that were never intended to be shown. We also couldn't trace a deployed application – since the users would see the Response.Write() trace results!

ASP.NET Tracing

Using ASP.NET's new tracing functionality, we replace the Response.Write() statements with Trace.Write() statements:

```
<Script runat="server">
  Public Function Add(a As Integer, b As Integer) As Integer
    Trace.Write("Inside Add() a: ", a.ToString())
    Trace.Write("Inside Add() b: ", b.ToString())
    return a + b
  End Function
</Script>
Call the Add routine: 4 + 5 = <%=Add(4,5)%>
```

If we request this page, using the default settings of ASP.NET (by default trace output is not enabled), we would see the following result in our browser:

Call the Add routine: 4 + 5 = 9

We can think of tracing as 'debug mode' for ASP.NET applications, since tracing code can be left in our code and when tracing is disabled the trace statements are simply ignored.

Viewing Trace Output

To view the results of the Trace.Write() statements, we have two options: enable page tracing or enable application tracing. By default, once tracing is enabled, the results are only presented to local clients – this is configurable, as we'll see momentarily.

Enable Page Tracing

We can enable page tracing by adding a directive to the top of our ASP.NET Page:

```
<%@ Page Trace="true" %>
  <Script runat="server">
    Public Function Add(a As Integer, b As Integer) As Integer
      Trace.Write("Inside Add() a: ", a.ToString())
      Trace.Write("Inside Add() b: ", b.ToString())
      return a + b
    End Function
  </Script>
Call the Add routine: 4 + 5 = <%=Add(4,5)%>
```

633

This will add a trace output to the bottom of the requested page. Included with this output are our `Trace.Write()` outputs:

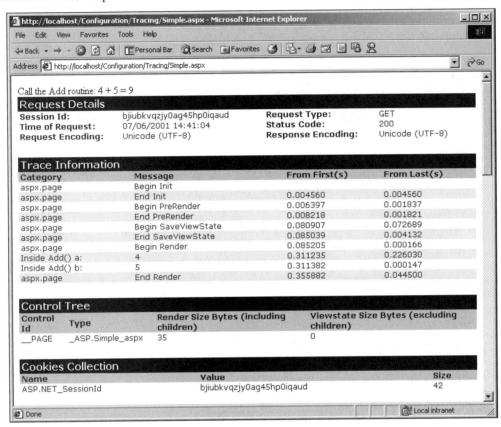

Enable Application Tracing

Adding `Trace="true"` statements to the top of our ASP.NET Pages isn't difficult, but what if we had a larger application consisting of several ASP.NET Pages? Or, what if we wanted to trace the output of our application and view the results, but at the same time not output the trace section at the end of each page? Application tracing allows us to accomplish all of this.

We can enable application tracing by creating a `web.config` file with trace settings in it for our web application:

```
<configuration>
  <system.web>
    <trace
        enabled="true"
        requestLimit="10"
        pageOutput="false"
        traceMode="SortByTime"
        localOnly="true"
    />
  </system.web>
</configuration>
```

We can set the enabled flag to true (the inherited machine.config default is false), request our page, and then use a special tool to view our application traces: trace.axd:

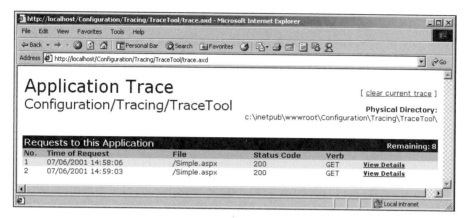

trace.axd is a special HTTP Handler used to view trace output for an application. We'll discuss this tool, tracing, and the Trace object in more detail in Chapter 22. Let's turn our attention to the configuration settings found in the web.config file we created.

Trace Configuration Settings

The <trace> section within the configuration file provides us with some additional options not available when enabling tracing on a page. These options include:

- ❑ enabled – We can set the enabled option to true or false. Tracing is either enabled at an application level, or it is disabled at the application level. If we set enabled=false, page tracing is still supported using the Trace directive discussed earlier. By default this value is set to false.

  enabled="[true | false]"

- ❑ requestLimit – The total number of trace requests to keep cached in memory on a per-application basis. Tracing exposes a special resource, trace.axd, used to view trace output when pageOutput is set to false. By default the value of requestLimit is 10.

  requestLimit = "[int]"

- ❑ pageOutput – When tracing is enabled through the configuration file, the administrator is given the option to either enable or disable tracing on each page. pageOutput tracing enables details to be traced for every page within an application. However, pageOutput tracing may be turned off while application-level tracing is still enabled (enabled = "true"). What this does is keep trace requests in memory, such that they are available via trace.axd but not within the output of a page. By default pageOutput is set to false.

  pageOutput = "[true | false]"

- ❑ traceMode – The tracemode setting gives us control over how trace detail information is output. Data may be sorted by time or category, where category is either the settings made by the system or the Trace.Write() settings enabled by the developer. By default traceMode is set to SortByTime.

  traceMode = "[SortByTime | SortByCategory]"

635

❑ localOnly – By default localOnly is set to true. When tracing is enabled, the localOnly flag determines whether or not the trace output is to be displayed to local requests (those made through http://localhost) or for any request. Since tracing is best used as a debug tool during development, it is suggested that the default setting be left as true.

```
localOnly = "[true | false]"
```

Tracing is a great tool for debugging applications during development. Tracing should not, however, be enabled for deployed applications. When tracing is enabled it does consume resources, and we want our applications as lean and mean as possible. This does not mean that we need to remove the Trace.Write() statements from our code. When tracing is not enabled these statements are ignored and do not affect the performance of our application.

For deployed applications, the recommendation is to use the Windows Event Log for application logging/tracing. A sample use of the Windows Event Log is shown for the Application_OnError event discussed in the previous chapter.

If you did any amount of coding in ASP, you'll no doubt remember those helpful error codes, such as 0x800A01A8. ASP.NET makes some dramatic improvements on the level of detail available when errors occur, however, we don't always want that type of 'rich' data displayed to end users. With ASP.NET's Custom Errors configuration option we can control how ASP.NET displays application error messages.

Custom Errors

When a run-time or design-time error occurs within our application, ASP.NET will display a very helpful error page. For example, a compilation error (such as forgetting to add a semi-colon to a line in C# code) generates an error page that describes the error, highlights the line of code, provides detailed compiler output, and the complete source for the page:

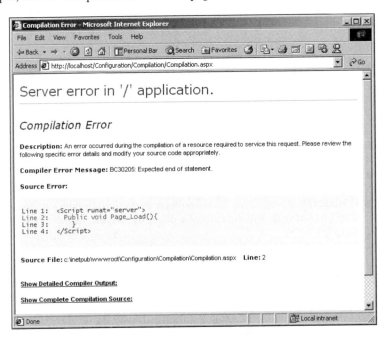

While this is unbelievably useful for aiding in debugging the application, we obviously don't want to display this type of error detail to end users. By default this type of error detail in only available to requests to http://localhost; requests from other domains will display a helpful error page, without the details, that describes how to enable the ASP.NET application to show richer error messages to remote clients:

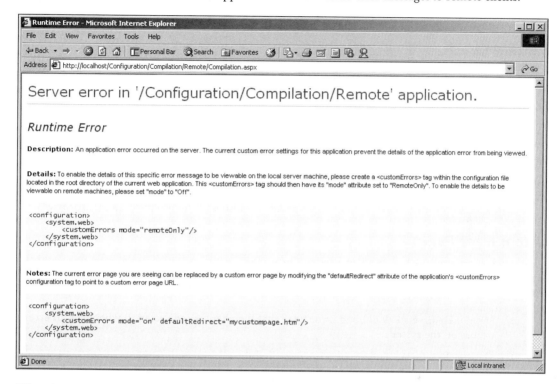

What this error page describes is the <customErrors> section of configuration:

```
<configuration>
  <system.web>
    <customErrors mode="RemoteOnly" />
  </system.web>
</configuration>
```

The <customErrors> section defines how ASP.NET behaves when an application error occurs, and provides us with a variety of options for how we want to handle these and other types of errors for our application.

Error Modes

When an error occurs, the mode attribute determines whether or not an ASP.NET error message is displayed. By default the mode value is set to RemoteOnly. Supported values include:

❏ RemoteOnly – ASP.NET error page is shown only to users accessing the server on the same machine (that is the localhost or 127.0.0.1). Non-localhost requests will first check the <error> settings, then use the defaultRedirect, or finally show an IIS error.

❑ On – ASP.NET will use user-defined error pages and will not use the rich, developer-oriented ASP.NET error page. If a custom error page is not provided, ASP.NET will show the error page describing how to enable remote viewing of errors.

❑ Off – ASP.NET will always use ASP.NET's rich error page, with stack traces and compilation issues, when an error occurs.

Always Showing ASP.NET Error Pages

If we want to always show the rich ASP.NET error page, such as when a team of developers are working against a single server, we could enable this mode by adding a web.config file with the following setting:

```
<configuration>
  <system.web>
    <customErrors mode="Off" />
  </system.web>
</configuration>
```

In a production environment we want to leave the default setting, mode="RemoteOnly", or mode="On", to ensure that remote users don't see rich error detail. We also want to provide custom error pages.

Custom Error Pages

For production applications we always want to provide ASP.NET with a custom error page so that an end user sees a friendly, helpful message rather than a developer-oriented message. There are two ways in which we can support custom error pages:

❑ Default Redirects – A defined error page that the client is redirected to whenever an error occurs on the system.

❑ Custom Redirects – A defined error page that the client is redirected to whenever a specific HTTP error occurs, for example the 404 Not Found error.

Let's look at both of these starting with default redirects.

Default Redirects

The defaultRedirect attribute of <customErrors> names the page to redirect to when an error occurs.

```
<configuration>
  <system.web>
    <customErrors defaultRedirect="/defaultError.aspx"/>
  </system.web>
</configuration>
```

In the example above, clients are redirected to the defaultError.aspx page whenever an error occurs. Note this only applies to ASP.NET-specific requests, so if we requested SomeRandomFile.aspx – an ASP.NET file that doesn't exist on our server – we would be redirected to /defaultError.aspx. However, if we requested SomeRandomFile.asp – an ASP file that doesn't exist – we would be redirected to the IIS-defined error page.

What happens if there is an error in the page we direct to when an error occurs, for example in defaultError.aspx? This could possibly lead to a circular reference: the page we're directed to causes an error and we're sent back to the same page again. ASP.NET detects this and will not cause the browser to continuously request the error page.

Custom Redirects

We can also send users to a custom error page depending upon the type of error that occurred. For instance, if we get a 404 Not Found error or an Access Denied error we can route the client to a specific error page tailored with an appropriate response, for example "Sorry, but you must be a valid user to access our site".

We can create that page, and then instruct ASP.NET to redirect HTTP requests that generate the matching statusCode value for the HTTP status code. This is done through a sub-element of <customErrors>: <error>.

<error> supports two attributes:

❑   statusCode – The HTTP status code to match. If a match is found the request is redirected to the value defined in redirect.

❑   redirect – The page that clients are re-directed to.

Let's look at a compound example that sets a defaultRedirect page, leaves mode to the default setting of RemoteOnly, and defines a <error> element for 404 Page Not Found errors.

> *Again, keep in mind that the <error> settings only apply to ASP.NET requests, so our earlier example of SomeRandomFile.aspx will now be redirected to /FileNotFound.htm.*

```
<configuration>
  <system.web>
    <customErrors defaultRedirect="/defaultError.aspx" mode="RemoteOnly">
      <error statusCode="404" redirect="/FileNotFound.htm"/>
    </customErrors>
  </system.web>
</configuration>
```

Configuring IIS and ASP.NET to Support the Same Error Pages

It is possible to configure ASP.NET and IIS to support the same set of error pages. For example, IIS uses the following error page for 404 errors:

C:\WINNT\Help\iisHelp\common\404b.htm.

We could create a virtual folder in our web site called /Errors and set the physical path of this virtual folder to c:\WinNt\Help\iisHelp\common\. We could then modify our ASP.NET <error> as follows:

```
<configuration>
  <system.web>
    <customErrors defaultRedirect="/defaultError.aspx" mode="RemoteOnly">
      <error statusCode="404" redirect="/Errors/404b.htm "/>
    </customErrors>
  </system.web>
</configuration>
```

We could also do the reverse and set up IIS to support an ASP.NET error page, 404.aspx for example. Please see the IIS documentation for how to configure IIS custom errors to specific URLs.

The ASP.NET error handling system is very rich. We can provide a default custom error page that we direct all errors to, or we can customize the error page depending upon the error case, 404 File Not Found for example. Additionally, we have control over what type of error page we show to what type of request. The default mode, RemoteOnly, shows custom (user friendly) errors to remote users, but shows rich ASP.NET errors to local clients.

As you can clearly see, ASP.NET is attempting to address many of the shortcomings of ASP. Another of the shortcomings it addresses is authentication and authorization. That is how we control access to resources served by our web server. Unless we used a custom solution, such as Site Server 3.0 or Commerce Server 2000 (and sometimes with these too), we had to have a good fundamental understanding of Windows security. ASP.NET still has great support for Windows security, but it extends the options to include Microsoft Passport and HTML Forms Based Authentication – as well as providing all the hooks allowing us to build custom authentication and authorization solutions, such as the Application_OnAuthenticate event discussed in the previous chapter.

Application authentication and authorization is, of course, also configured through the ASP.NET configuration system.

Authentication and Authorization

As it relates to ASP.NET, authentication is the process of establishing identity between the server and a request. We want to clearly establish that all the server really has is data sent to it over HTTP. In other words, the server knows nothing about the client other than what the client sends the server. This is important since the application making a request is not always a browser. In fact, we would be wise to get out of the mentality that only web browsers will be making requests against our server.

To establish the identity of a request, the request must follow a protocol that enables a pre-defined set of rules to be adhered to. For example, almost all HTTP servers support Clear Text/Basic authentication: the pop-up dialog box that asks for a username and password. Clear Text/Basic authentication follows a protocol such that the browser can properly formulate and encode the request in the format that the server expects.

ASP.NET provides four distinct options for assigning identity to a request:

- ❑ **Forms Authentication**. Allows us to authenticate requests using HTTP cookies and HTML forms. We can validate identity against any resource.

- ❑ **Passport Authentication**. Uses Microsoft's single sign-on Passport identity system.

- ❑ **Windows Authentication**. Allows us to authenticate requests using Windows Challenge/Response semantics. This consists of the server initially denying access to a request (a challenge) and the requestor responding with a hashed value of their Windows username / password, which the server can then choose to authenticate and/or authorize.

- ❑ **Custom Authentication**. Allows us to roll our own authentication system.

Authentication

ASP.NET's authentication system is very flexible. It supports four modes and various settings for each of these modes. The default mode is Windows, but we can configure support for the other modes using the mode attribute of the <authentication> element:

- ❑ mode – This attribute has four acceptable settings: Windows, Forms, Passport, and None. This value determines the authentication mode that ASP.NET will enforce. The default is Windows.

If the mode is set to Forms, we have a child element of <authentication> called <forms> that allows us to define behaviors for forms authentication.

Custom HTML Forms Login

Forms Authentication allows us to use HTML forms to request credentials, and then issue an HTTP cookie that the requestor may use for identity on subsequent requests. ASP.NET provides the infrastructure to support this, but also gives us the flexibility to choose how we wish to validate credentials. For example, once we obtain the username and password that has been sent to our ASP.NET application via HTTP POST (we'd rather not use HTTP GET as it passes the data on the query string), we can validate the credentials against an XML file, a database, an in-memory structure, an LDAP directory, or even through a Web Service!

The validation of credentials is completely up to us. Once the credentials are validated we can then call some of the APIs provided by Forms Authentication to issue an HTTP cookie to the requestor. On subsequent requests the cookie is provided along with the request body, and ASP.NET can use the information in the cookie to recreate a valid identity.

The <forms> element has the following attributes:

❑　name – Forms authentication uses a cookie that contains an ID of the authenticated user. The name of that cookie is defined by the name value of <forms>. The default setting is .ASPXAUTH.

❑　loginUrl – When a request comes into ASP.NET with forms authentication enabled, and the request doesn't present a cookie (new user) or has an invalid value within the cookie, ASP.NET will redirect the request to an ASP.NET page capable of logging in the user and issuing the cookie. loginUrl allows us to configure this value. By default it is set to login.aspx and we must provide our own implementation of this file.

❑　protection – The value within the cookie can optionally be encrypted or sent in plain text. For sites that simply use forms authentication as a means of identifying the user, we might choose to use no cookie encryption. Valid settings for protection are All, None, Encryption, and Validation.

❑　timeout – Specifies the time in minutes that the cookie is valid for. The timeout of the cookie is reset on each request to the current time plus the timeout value. The default value is 30 minutes.

❑　path – Specifies the path value of the cookie. By default this is set to "/", the root of the server. Cookies are only visible to the path and server that sets the cookie. ASP.NET forms authentication chooses to use the root of the server as the path, since the path value in a cookie is case sensitive.

Within <forms> there is also a <credentials> sub-element, which can **optionally** be used to define users.

As we'll learn in Chapter 14, when we use Forms Authentication we can validate users from any data store.

Defining Users for HTML Forms Authentication

Nested within the <forms> element we find a <credentials> element. <credentials> allows us to define users (identities) and passwords directly within our configuration file, although this is completely optional. We can choose to take advantage of this section, or we can choose to define identities in another location.

> **Use of the `<credentials>` section is not required. Instead, the validation of the username and password can be custom code, such as validation of username/password pairs stored in a database.**

The `<credentials>` section allows us to define `<user>` entries. We use this section to optionally store our usernames and passwords in the configuration file. `<credentials>` supports a single attribute:

❑ passwordFormat – The passwordFormat tells ASP.NET the password format used by the password value of `<user>`. Supported values include SHA1, MD5, and Clear. You should note, however, that simply setting this value does not automatically encrypt the value of password. It's the responsibility of the developer/administrator to add the value of the SHA1 or MD5 hashed password into the configuration file.

Nested within `<credentials>` are `<user>` entries. The `<user>` entries are used to define valid usernames and passwords used to authenticate against. A `<user>` entry contains two attributes: name and password, which together are compared against when we attempt to authenticate requests.

If we choose to store our usernames and passwords in the configuration file, we are provided with several options for password hiding. The `<credentials>` tag supports a single attribute: passwordFormat. This attribute can be set to one of three values:

❑ Clear – Value of the password for `<user>` entries is stored in clear text. For example, password="password".

❑ SHA1 – Value of the password for `<user>` entries is stored as a SHA1 hash. For example, password="5B9FEBC2D7429C8F2002721484A71A84C12730C7" (value is password). We'll discuss hash in the next chapter

❑ MD5 – Value of the password for `<user>` entries is stored as a MD5 hash. For example, password="2BF3023F1259B0C2F607E4302556BD72" (value is password). We'll discuss hash in the next chapter.

Rather than storing clear text values with the `<credentials>` section for `<user>` entries, we can store hashes of the password. If our configuration file is compromised, our user's passwords are safer than if they were stored in clear text.

An example of storing the username and password in the credentials section is below. The passwordFormat is set to SHA1 and the value for password represents a SHA1 hash of the user's password.

```
<configuration>
  <system.web>
    <authentication mode="Forms">
      <forms name=".ASPXAUTH" loginUrl="login.aspx"
             protection="all"  timeout="30" path="/" >
        <credentials passwordFormat="SHA1">
          <user name="SomeUser" password="83jksjfi3983ksl23dscdf"/>
        </credentials>
      </forms>
    </authentication>
  <configuration>
<system.web>
```

We'll explore authentication in more detail in Chapter 14.

Authorization (*<authorization>*)

The <authorization> configuration settings allow us to define access control permissions, defined as <allow> and <deny> settings, used to control access to resources. Both follow the same format for entries:

```
<[allow | deny] users="users | * | ?" roles="roles"/>
```

So for example:

```
<configuration>
  <system.web>
    <authentication mode="Forms">
      <forms name=".ASPXAUTH" loginUrl="login.aspx"
             protection="all"  timeout="30" path="/" >
      </forms>
    </authentication>
    <authorization>
      <allow users="Stephen, Brian, Rob" roles="Administrator, Customer" />
      <deny users="?" roles="BlackList" />
    </authorization>
  </system.web>
</configuration>
```

In the above configuration settings we define authorization settings that allow the users Stephen, Brian, and Rob as well as the roles Administrator and Customer. However all anonymous users (identified by "?") will be denied access, as well as those users that belong to the role/group BlackList.

Any users or roles that are denied access will be redirected to the loginUrl specified in the authentication settings – since the server will attempt to re-authenticate the user.

Web Services

ASP.NET Web Services allow us to easily expose programmable application logic over the Web using SOAP (Simple Object Access Protocol). Developers who want to use a web service do not need to know a thing about the implementation of our service; rather they simply need to know how to call our service using SOAP and know that they will get a SOAP reply in return: if the application is configured to send SOAP replies.

ASP.NET provides a flexible framework for building Web Services. As part of that framework we have the ability to configure aspects of ASP.NET Web Services.

Although there are other configuration options for Web Services, the only one we'll address is changing the ASP.NET Page used to create the Web Service Help Page:

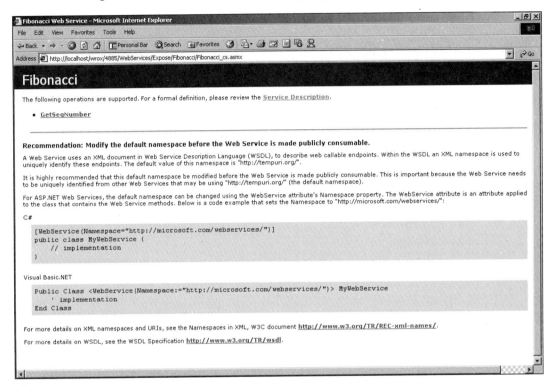

The ASP.NET Page used to create this view of our Web Service can be found at:

```
WinNt\Microsoft.NET\Framework\[version]\CONFIG\DefaultWSDLHelpGenerator.aspx
```

If we wish to customize `DefaultWSDLHelpGenerator.aspx`, we can instruct ASP.NET to use our custom file:

```
<configuration>
  <system.web>
    <webServices>
      <wsdlHelpGenerator href="MyWsdlHelpGenerator.aspx" />
    </webServices>
  </system.web>
</configuration>
```

We could use the above `web.config` file in our application and instruct ASP.NET to use a custom template page used to describe an ASP.NET Web Service.

Internationalization and Encoding

The settings defined within `<globalization>` allow us to configure the culture and encoding options, in other words the code page used by a request and the code page used by a response for our application. Below is a `web.config` file that mirrors the default settings found in `machine.config`:

```
<configuration>
  <system.web>
    <globalization
      requestEncoding="utf-8"
      responseEncoding="utf-8"
    />
  </system.web>
</configuration>
```

`<globalization>` supports five attributes that allow us to configure various globalization properties for our application:

❑ requestEncoding – The requestEncoding attribute allows us to set the assumed encoding of each incoming request; the default is utf-8. The values allowed for requestEncoding can be found within the Encoding class in the System.Text namespace. For example, if we wish to set the encoding to UTF-7, we could simply set:

> `<globalization requestEncoding="utf-7"/>`

❑ responseEncoding – The responseEncoding attribute allows us to set the encoding of outgoing responses. The default is utf-8. The values allowed can be found within the Encoding class in the System.Text namespace.

❑ fileEncoding – The fileEncoding attribute lets ASP.NET know the encoding type used for all ASP.NET file resources. The default is utf-8. The values allowed can be found within the Encoding class in the System.Text namespace.

❑ culture – The culture attribute is used to localize content using culture strings. For example, en-US represents United States English, while en-GB represents British English. This setting allows for strings to be formatted in both the appropriate language as well as using the appropriate format for dates, etc.

❑ uiCulture – The uiCulture attribute is used to define the culture string, described above, used to look up resources.

If, for example, we were building a web application that was used in France, we could configure the following globalization and culture settings:

```
<configuration>
  <system.web>
    <globalization
      requestEncoding="utf-8"
      responseEncoding="utf-8"
      culture="fr-FR"
      uiCulture="fr-FR"
    />
  </system.web>
</configuration>
```

We could then write a simple ASP.NET page to test our culture settings, such as ensuring that the current date value is formatted correctly:

VB.NET

```
<Script runat="server">
  Public Sub Page_Load(sender As Object, e As EventArgs)
    ' Use ToString("D") to format display: Week Day, Month Day, Year
    lblDateTime.Text = DateTime.Now.ToString("D")
  End Sub
</Script>
Server Date/Time: <b><asp:label id="lblDateTime" runat="server" /></b>
```

The default settings of culture, `en-US`, would display:

Server Date/Time: **Tuesday, May 01, 2001**

While our localized setting, using `fr-FR`, would display:

Server Date/Time: **mardi 1 mai 2001**

We obviously would still need to localize the string `'Server Date/Time:'`.

Compilation Options

The settings defined in the `<compilation>` section of `machine.config` allow us to control some of the settings that ASP.NET uses to compile ASP.NET resources, such as ASP.NET Pages. A common setting that we can change, if we don't want VB.NET to be our default language, is the `defaultLanguage` option. This is where we can also add additional Common Language Runtime compilers, such as COBOL or PERL. It is within the `<compilation>` settings that we also name the assemblies (compiled reusable code libraries) that ASP.NET will link to when compiling ASP.NET application files.

Below is the default configuration from `machine.config`:

```
<configuration>
  <system.web>
    <compilation debug="false" explicit="true" defaultLanguage="vb">
      <compilers>
        <compiler language="c#;cs;csharp" extension=".cs"
                  type="Microsoft.CSharp.CSharpCodeProvider,System" />
        <compiler language="vb;visualbasic;vbscript" extension=".vb"
                  type="Microsoft.VisualBasic.VBCodeProvider,System" />
        <compiler language="js;jscript;javascript" extension=".js"
             type="Microsoft.JScript.JScriptCodeProvider,Microsoft.JScript" />
      </compilers>

      <assemblies>
        <add assembly="mscorlib"/>
        <add assembly="System"/>
        <add assembly="System.Web"/>
        <add assembly="System.Data"/>
        <add assembly="System.Web.Services"/>
        <add assembly="System.Xml"/>
        <add assembly="System.Drawing"/>
        <add assembly="*"/>
      </assemblies>

    </compilation>
  </system.web>
</configuration>
```

The `<compilation>` tag supports three attributes: the list of which:

❑ `debugMode` attribute – Debug mode enables us to debug ASP.NET application files with the command-line debugger or Visual Studio.NET. When we build a project with Visual Studio.NET, VS.NET creates its own `web.config` file and sets the `debugMode` to `true` or `false` depending on whether or not the project is in debug mode (a compile option). The default setting is `false`.

One of the side benefits of setting `debugMode="true"` is that ASP.NET will save the source file it generates, which we can then view! Let's look at an example to show how this is done. ASP.NET takes a source file, such as the ASP.NET page below, compiles it, and saves the resulting .NET `.dll` file to disk in a directory under:

`\WinNt\Microsoft.NET\Framework\[version]\Temporary ASP.NET Files\`

Directories found within this directory are unique directories that ASP.NET creates automatically.

Let's look at what happens when we set `debugMode="true"`.

First, set `debugMode="true"` in `machine.config`. Next, we need a simple ASP.NET Page:

VB.NET

```
<Script runat="server">
  Public Sub Page_Load(sender As Object, e As EventArgs)
    lblHello.Text = "Hello!"
  End Sub
</Script>
<b><asp:label id="lblHello" runat="server" /></b>
```

We then need to request this page through a browser, here's the URL that I'm using to make the request: http://localhost/Configuration/Compilation/Hello.aspx.

We can then navigate to the ...`\Temporary ASP.NET Files\` directory. ASP.NET will create the directory based on the name of the Web Application. In this case the `Configuration` folder is marked as a Web Application. If we do a file search in the `Configuration` folder for `*`.vb, we'll find a single .vb file. Mine is named: `gh_2ci21.0.vb` – the name of the file is hashed to create a unique value.

If we open this file in Visual Studio.NET we see the following:

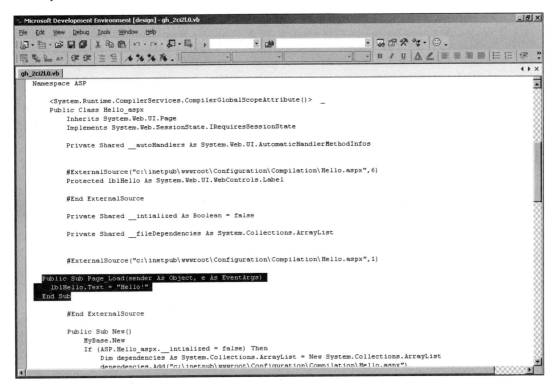

In the above screenshot we can see our code, `lblHello.Text = "Hello!"`, along with the rest of the code that ASP.NET automatically generated to build our ASP.NET page. If you ever want to know what an ASP.NET page is doing behind the scenes, this is a great resource.

Changing the Default Language

The `defaultLanguage` attribute of `<compilation>` allows us to configure the default language that ASP.NET resources use.

In code samples within this book we have been using both page directives and script blocks. When we've shown code examples in C#, or other languages, we've used one of three options to override the default language of VB.NET:

```
<%@ Page Language="C#" %>
```

```
<%@ WebService Language="C#" %>
```

```
<Script Language="C#" runat=server>
...
</Script>
```

If we decide that we would rather code all of our application logic in C#, we would set the defaultLanguage attribute in the <compilers> tag:

```
<compilation debug="false" explicit="true" defaultLanguage="C#">
```

The language value specified for defaultLanguage must be one of the supported languages named in a <compiler> sub-element of <compilers>. The <compilation> setting defines two sub-elements:

❑ <compilers> – Section pertaining to the supported .NET language compilers for ASP.NET.

❑ <assembly> – Section that allows us to define .NET assemblies that are added to the compilation of ASP.NET application files.

<compilers>

The <compilers> element is the parent element for <compiler> entries. The <compiler> element, which is a sub-element of the <compilers> tag, allows us to name and configure the languages supported by ASP.NET. By default ASP.NET supports the three languages that .NET ships with:

❑ Visual Basic.NET

❑ C#

❑ JScript.NET

The <compiler> element has three attributes:

❑ language – The value used when we name the language from Language = setting within our code files.

❑ extension – Names the extension for the code files when we're using a code-behind model.

❑ type – Both the language and extension setting are used so that ASP.NET knows the class named in the type attribute to use to compile the resource.

If we wished, for example, to include support for Perl we would need to make the following entry:

```
<configuration>
  <system.web>
    <compilation>
      <compilers>
        <compiler language="Perl" extension=".pl"
                  type="[Perl CodeDOM Class]"/>
      </compilers>
    </compilation>
  </system.web>
</configuration>
```

The final element found within <compilation> is the <assemblies> element.

<assemblies>

The <assemblies> element is used to add, remove, or clear assemblies that should be used in the compile path of our ASP.NET applications. Assemblies are units of compiled application logic, and contain classes and other information necessary for .NET applications to load and use the compiled application logic.

649

We need some assemblies to be available intrinsically for ASP.NET since we rely upon classes found in these assemblies in our ASP.NET applications. Below are the assemblies referenced in `machine.config` (and which are therefore available in all ASP.NET applications):

- ❑ `mscorlib.dll` – Contains the base classes, such as `String`, `Object`, `int`, etc., and the Root namespace of `System`. Additionally, defines other namespaces such as `System.IO`, etc.

- ❑ `System.dll` – Contains the code generators for C#, VB.NET, and JavaScript. Extends definition of the `System` namespace, and includes additional namespaces such as `Net` (the namespace for the network class libraries).

- ❑ `System.Web.dll` – The classes and namespaces used and required by ASP.NET, such as `HttpRequest`, `Page`, and namespaces such as `System.Web.UI` for ASP.NET server controls.

- ❑ `System.Data.dll` – Contains the classes and namespaces belonging to ADO.NET.

- ❑ `System.Web.Services.dll` – Contains the classes and namespaces, such as `System.Web.Services` used for building ASP.NET Web Services.

- ❑ `System.Xml.dll` – Contains the XML classes and namespaces, such as `XmlDocument` or `XmlNode` and namespaces, such as the `System.Xml.XPath`.

- ❑ `System.Drawing.dll` – Contains classes and namespaces for working with images, such as `Bitmap`.

- ❑ `*` – The special `*` entry tells ASP.NET also to include all assemblies found within ASP.NET application `\bin` directories. `\bin` directories, discussed in the previous chapter, are used to register assemblies that are specific to a Web Application.

The above assemblies are added using an `<add>` tag within `<assemblies>`, and the `.dll` extension of the assembly is not included in the reference.

<add>

The `<add>` tag is used to name .NET assemblies we wish to have available to our ASP.NET applications. For example, if we wished to use the classes found in `System.DirectoryServices.dll` in our web application we would need to add a reference for it in our `web.config` file (alternatively we could add it to `machine.config`, and make it available to all applications).

```
<configuration>
  <system.web>
    <compilation>
      <assemblies>
        ...
          <add assembly="System.DirectoryServices" />
        ...
      </assemblies>
    </compilation>
  </system.web>
</configuration>
```

<remove>

Just as we use the `<add>` tag to add the assemblies we want available within our application, we can use the `<remove>` tag to remove assemblies. This is very useful if `machine.config` names assemblies using the `<add>` tag, but we wish to restrict the use of assemblies within our ASP.NET application.

For example, `machine.config` lists `System.Drawing` as one of the assemblies to include in the compilation of ASP.NET application files. If we didn't need the classes found in `System.Drawing.dll`, we could ensure that ASP.NET didn't compile the assembly as part of our application. We could add an entry to a `web.config` file that used the `<remove>` tag to remove the `System.Drawing` assembly for that application only.

```
<configuration>
  <system.web>
    <compilation>
      <assemblies>
        <remove assembly="System.Drawing" />
      </assemblies>
    </compilation>
  </system.web>
</configuration>
```

<clear>

The `<clear>` entry goes one step further than the `<remove>` tag. Whereas the `<remove>` tag removes individual assemblies, `<clear>` removes any and all assembly references. When `<clear>` is used, no inherited assemblies are loaded.

The compilation settings in `machine.config` give us granular control over many settings that apply to our ASP.NET application files, such as the default language, support for other compilers, and the assemblies (libraries of code) we want available by default within our application.

Although the compilation settings allow us to control how the application is compiled, they don't allow us to control how the application is run. To control the identity of the process that ASP.NET uses for compiling, processing, and servicing requests of our ASP.NET application, we have the identity settings.

Controlling the Identity of Execution

We can use the `<identity>` setting of `machine.config` (note, `identity` can be set in `web.config` files too) to define which Windows user to impersonate when making requests from the operating system.

Note, this is separate from the trust level assigned to a particular application. The trust level, set in the configuration system for an application, determines what a particular application may or may not do. Trust levels are used to sand-box applications.

We have three attributes used with `<identity>`:

❑ `impersonation` – The `impersonation` attribute of `<identity>` is a Boolean value that determines the Windows NT user the ASP.NET worker process runs under. If `impersonation="true"`, ASP.NET will run under the identity provided by Internet Information Server. If set to `true` this would be `IISUSR_[server name]` – or whatever identity that IIS is configured to impersonate. However, if Windows NT authentication is enabled on the web server, ASP.NET will impersonate the authenticated user. Alternately, we can name a Windows NT user and password for the ASP.NET process to run as. The default setting of `impersonation` is `false`.

❑ name – Available when `impersonation="true"`, the name value names a valid Windows NT account to impersonate.

❑ password – Complementary to name, the password of the user to impersonate.

As mentioned above, the default setting is `impersonation="false"`, let's look at some examples where ASP.NET runs with `impersonation="true"` allowing the impersonation to flow from IIS, as well as configuring the user/password for ASP.NET to run as.

Impersonating the IIS User

To impersonate the user that IIS uses, we first need to set `impersonation="true"`:

```
<configuration>
  <system.web>
    <identity impersonation="true" />
  </system.web>
</configuration>
```

To test impersonation, we can use the following ASP.NET Page:

VB.NET

```
<%@ Import Namespace="System.Security.Principal" %>

<Script runat="server">
  Public Sub Page_Load(sender As Object, e As EventArgs)
    lblIdentity.Text = WindowsIdentity.GetCurrent().Name
  End Sub
</Script>
Current identity is: <asp:label id="lblIdentity" runat="server" />
```

This code simply uses the `WindowsIdentity` class's `GetCurrent()` method to return the name of the Windows user the request is processed as.

On my server, when `impersonation="false"` the result of a request to this page is:

Current identity is: NT AUTHORITY\SYSTEM

When `impersonation="true"` the result is:

Current identity is: RHOWARD-LAPTOP\IUSR_RHOWARD-LAPTOP

ASP.NET is impersonating the Windows user that Internet Information Services is using to process the request. In the above case this is the `IUSR_[machine name]` Windows account that IIS uses for anonymous requests. If we configured IIS to use a different anonymous account, or enabled IIS security to support NTLM authentication, we would see a different result.

For example, if we enable NTLM authentication for the server (see Chapter 14 for details on NTLM authentication), when I run the code I see:

Current identity is: REDMOND\RHOWARD

Since NTLM authentication is enabled, as is impersonation with ASP.NET, ASP.NET impersonates the Windows users that IIS NTLM authenticates. In this case the user Rhoward in the domain Redmond.

The last option we can configure with identity is to explicitly name a username and password. Note, the username and password values are stored in clear text in the configuration system:

```
<configuration>
  <system.web>
    <identity impersonation="true"
              name="ASPNET_Anonymous"
              password="93%dk12"
    />
  </system.web>
</configuration>
```

In the above example we've identified a user ASPNET_Anonymous as the user for ASP.NET to impersonate.

Keep in mind that the user impersonated needs to have the necessary file resources, in other words ASPNET_Anonymous needs to have access to the necessary ASP.NET files and common directory paths. Please see Chapter 14 for more details on ASP.NET security.

Controlling the identity of the impersonation account used by ASP.NET allows us to have granular system-level control over what any particular user may or may not do. However, we also have to provide the impersonation account with the appropriate levels of access to be able to accomplish meaningful work in our system.

Extending ASP.NET with HTTP Handlers

ASP.NET builds upon an extensible architecture known simply as the HTTP Runtime. The runtime is responsible for handling requests and sending responses. It is up to individual handlers, such as an ASP.NET Page or Web Service, to implement the work to be done on a request.

Much as Internet Information Server supports a low-level API known as ISAPI for letting developers implement custom solutions, such as building a JSP implementation that runs on IIS; ASP.NET implements a similar concept with HTTP Handlers. A request is assigned to ASP.NET from IIS, ASP.NET then examines entries in the <httpHandlers> section, based on the extension, .aspx for example, of the request to determine which handler the request should be routed to.

The most common entry used is the .aspx extension. Below is the entry in machine.config for the HTTP Handler used for the .aspx extension (as well as several other familiar extensions):

```
<configuration>
  <system.web>
    <httpHandlers>
      <add verb="*" path="*.aspx"
           type="System.Web.UI.PageHandlerFactory,System.Web" />
      <add verb="*" path="*.asmx"
           type="System.Web.Services.Protocols.WebServiceHandlerFactory,
                 System.Web.Services" validate="false"/>
      <add verb="*" path="*.ascx"
```

```
            type="System.Web.HttpForbiddenHandler,System.Web" />
        <add verb="*" path="*.config"
            type="System.Web.HttpForbiddenHandler,System.Web" />
      </httpHandlers>
    </system.web>
  </configuration>
```

In the above configuration code four common handlers are identified (note, the actual
machine.config file identifies about 18 entries). We have the HTTP handlers for Pages (.aspx), Web
Services (.asmx), User Controls (.ascx), and Configuration (.config).

Both Page and Web Services map to actual classes, while User Controls and Configuration map to a special
handler HttpForbiddenHandler. This handler explicitly denies access to these extensions when
requested directly, so a request for Address.ascx or web.config will send back an access denied reply.

As mentioned above, HTTP Handlers are the ASP.NET equivalent of IIS ISAPI extensions. However,
unlike ISAPI, which was only accessible to developers who could code C++, HTTP Handlers can be
coded in any .NET language – VB.NET developers can now author the equivalent of an ISAPI extension.

Let's look at a simple HTTP Handler written in VB.NET:

```
Imports System
Imports System.Web

Public Class HelloWorldHandler
  Implements IHttpHandler

  Sub ProcessRequest(ByVal context As HttpContext) _
                     Implements IHttpHandler.ProcessRequest
    Dim Request As HttpRequest = context.Request
    Dim Response As HttpResponse = context.Response

    Response.Write("<html>")
    Response.Write("<body>")
    Response.Write("<h1> Hello " + _
                     Request.QueryString("Name") + "</h1>")
    Response.Write("</body>")
    Response.Write("</html>")
  End Sub

  Public ReadOnly Property IsReusable As Boolean _
                     Implements IHttpHandler.IsReusable
    Get
      Return True
    End Get
  End Property
End Class
```

Above, we've written a VB.NET class, HelloWorldHandler, that implements the IHttpHandler
interface. This interface requires that we implement a single method, ProcessRequest(), as well as a
single property, IsReusable. Within the ProcessRequest() method, which is responsible for
processing the request, we Response.Write() some simple HTML. Within the body of the HTML we
use the Request to access the Name parameter passed on the query string.

To register this handler, we first must build it using either the command-line compilers or Visual Studio.NET. We then can deploy the compiled `.dll` file to an ASP.NET `\bin` directory and add the entry into our configuration file (in this particular case we're using a `web.config` file). We then use the `<add>` tag of `<httpHandlers>`.

Adding Handlers

The `<add>` tag is used to name a class that implements either the `IHttpHandler` or `IHttpHandlerFactory` interface. All HTTP Handlers must implement one of these two interfaces so that the HTTP runtime knows how to call them.

Below is the format that we use for this tag:

```
<configuration>
  <system.web>
    <httpHandlers>
      <add verb="[HTTP Verb]" path="[Request Path]" type="[.NET Class]"/>
    </httpHandlers>
  </system.web>
</configuration>
```

There are three attributes within the `<add>` tag that tell ASP.NET how the HTTP Handler is to be interpreted:

- ❏ verb – The `verb` attribute instructs the HTTP runtime about the HTTP verb type that the handler services request. Values for the `verb` attribute include: asterisks (`*`), which instructs the HTTP runtime to match on all HTTP verbs, a string value that names an HTTP verb. For example, the HTTP `Get` verb, `verb="Get"`, and finally, a string value of semi-colon separated HTTP verbs. For example `verb="Get; Post; Head"`.

- ❏ path – The `path` attribute instructs the HTTP runtime as to the request path, for example `/MyApp/test.aspx`, that this HTTP Handler is executed for. Valid values for the `path` include: asterisks (`*`) with an extension (`*.aspx`), which instruct the HTTP runtime to match on resources that match the extension, and a string value with an extension. We can name one resource that maps to an HTTP Handler. A good example here is the `Trace.axd` HTTP Handler, which uses the path value of: `path="trace.axd"`.

- ❏ type – The `type` attribute names the .NET class that implements the HTTP Handler code. The value for `type` follows the format: `[Namespace].[Class], [Assembly name]`.

If we compile the above sample, `HelloWorldHandler.vb`, to an assembly named, `Simple.dll`, we could make the following entry in a configuration file:

```
<configuration>
  <system.web>
    <httpHandlers>
      <add verb="*" path="HelloWorld.aspx"
           type="HelloWorldHandler, Simple"/>
    </httpHandlers>
  </system.web>
</configuration>
```

The above configuration entry names an assembly, Simple, that contains a class
HelloWorldHandler. ASP.NET will assume that HelloWorldHandler implements the
IHttpHandler interface. We then identify the path and verb that the ASP.NET HTTP Runtime uses to
route to this handler. In this case we've told the HTTP Runtime that we wish to route on all verbs (via
the *) and that we'll service requests for HelloWorld.aspx.

> *Note, we could use a custom extension, such as* `*.wrox`, *but this would further require us to map
> this* `.wrox` *extension to ASP.NET – as we discussed in the previous chapter.*

We're now ready to service requests for this handler. If we open a web browser, and point it to the Web
Application that contains \bin\Simple.dll as well as the above web.config file that we defined, we
can make a request for …/HelloWorld.aspx?Name=Rob:

ASP.NET maps the request HelloWorld.aspx to the HTTP Handler we built called Simple.dll.
The result is that the HTTP Handler is executed and our request is served – this is a somewhat simple
example, but it's easy to envision the types of applications that could be created.

What if this HTTP Handler was declared in machine.config, and we decided that we didn't want a
given application to have access to it? In that case we can use the <remove> tag of the
<httpHandlers> section.

Removing Handlers

The <remove> tag can be used to override <add> entries that are either inherited or declared within
the same configuration file. This is useful for removing HTTP Handlers from some Web Applications,
or commenting out HTTP Handlers so that the functionality is unavailable to end users.

```
<remove verb="[http verb | *]" path="[path]"/>
```

A good example is the trace.axd HTTP Handler used for tracing, which we may decide not to support
in all of our web applications. machine.config defines the following entry for the trace.axd:

```
<configuration>
  <system.web>
    <httpHandlers>
      <add verb="*"
        path="trace.axd"
        type="System.Web.Handlers.TraceHandler,System.Web"
      />
    </httpHandlers>
  </system.web>
</configuration>
```

We could remove support of this handler in web applications by creating a `web.config` file and making the following entry using the `<remove>` tag:

```
<configuration>
  <system.web>
    <httpHandlers>
      <remove verb="*" path="trace.axd"/>
    </httpHandlers>
  </system.web>
</configuration>
```

The web application using the above `web.config` file will generate a "file not found" error when a request is made for `trace.axd`.

HTTP Handlers allow us, at a low level, to handle the application request. We can build a simple example, such as the `HelloWorld` example above, or we could write more complex examples that take over well known extensions such as `.jpg` to add additional functionality, so for example a request for `chart.jpg?x=10&y=13` could draw a graph. The opportunities are endless! However, what happens in the case where we simply want to look at the request? Rather than replace the functionality that ASP.NET Pages provide us with we simply want to examine the request before or after the HTTP Handler processes it. For this we have HTTP Modules.

Extending ASP.NET with HTTP Modules

Whereas HTTP Handlers allow us to map a request to a specific class to handle the request, HTTP Modules act as filters (note, HTTP Modules are similar in function to ISAPI filters) that we can apply before the handler sees the request or after the handler is done with the request.

ASP.NET makes use of modules for cookieless session state, output caching, and several security-related features. In the advanced topics discussion in Chapter 20, we will look at an HTTP Module that authenticates Web Service requests. Before the request is 'handled' by the appropriate `.asmx` file, our HTTP Module looks at the request, determines if it is a SOAP message, and if it is a SOAP message it extracts out the username and password values from the SOAP header.

As it relates to configuration, we have the same three settings as we found for HTTP Handlers: `<add>`, `<remove>`, and `<clear>`. `<add>` is the only tag that differs from HTTP Handlers.

Adding Modules

The `<add>` entry for `<httpModules>` simply names the module and references the class that implements the `IHttpModule` interface and the assembly the class exists within. Just as HTTP Handlers implement a common interface, `IHttpHandler`, we have an interface that modules implement.

Below is an `<httpModules>` entry for the `OutputCache` module from `machine.config`:

```
<configuration>
  <system.web>
    <httpModules>
      <add name="OutputCache"
           type="System.Web.Caching.OutputCacheModule, System.Web" />
    </httpModules>
  </system.web>
</configuration>
```

Similar to HTTP Handlers, HTTP Modules require us to implement an interface. In this case that interface is IHttpModule. If we implement this interface, we can build a simple HTTP Module.

Handlers and modules are definitely an advanced feature of ASP.NET. They give us complete control over the request and allow us to look at the request as it comes in, execute the request, and then look at the request again as it goes out.

The machine.config file gives us access to a number of advanced configuration features, such as the two we just examined. Another of the configuration options found in machine.config is the process model settings. The process model settings allow us to configure the ASP.NET Worker Process.

Configuring the ASP.NET Worker Process

Unlike ASP, ASP.NET runs in a separate process from IIS. When code misbehaved in ASP – say we forgot to free memory in a COM object – the leak could degrade the server performance and even possibly crash the process ASP ran in. In some cases this could crash the IIS process, and if the IIS process is unavailable the application is not servicing requests!

ASP.NET, on the other hand, was designed to take into account the errors that can and will occur within the system. Rather than running in process with IIS, ASP.NET runs in a separate worker process: aspnet_wp.exe. ASP.NET uses IIS only to receive requests and to send responses (as a request/response broker). IIS is not executing any ASP.NET code. The ASP.NET process can come and go, and it doesn't affect the stability of IIS in any way.

We can view the ASP.NET process (aspnet_wp.exe) through the Windows Task Manager after a request for an ASP.NET resource has been made, as the process starts when ASP.NET applications are being used.

To view the process, first request an ASP.NET resource and then open up the Windows Task Manager (press *Control-Shift-Escape* simultaneously). Once the Task Manager is open, switch to the Processes tab and look for aspnet_wp.exe in the Image Name column:

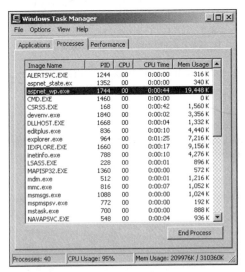

In the screenshot above we see the process, aspnet_wp.exe, the process ID (PID) of 1744, the CPU usage as a percentage 0%, CPU time, and memory usage in KB.

The <processModel> section of machine.config is used to configure ASP.NET process management. These settings can only be made in machine.config, as they apply to all ASP.NET applications on that machine. Within the <processModel> settings, we can configure options such as which processor each ASP.NET worker process should affinitize with, and we can additionally configure settings such as automatically recycling the process after *n* requests or *n* amount of time. Below is the default machine.config settings:

```
<configuration>
  <system.web>
      <processModel
          enable="true"
          timeout="Infinite"
          idleTimeout="Infinite"
          shutdownTimeout="0:00:05"
          requestLimit="Infinite"
          requestQueueLimit="5000"
          restartQueueLimit="10"
          memoryLimit="60"
          webGarden="false"
          cpuMask="0xffffffff"
          userName=""
          password=""
          logLevel="Errors"
          clientConnectedCheck="0:00:05"
      />
  </system.web>
</configuration>
```

As you can see, there are 14 options that we can configure. Let's examine each in detail, starting with the enable option.

Enabling the ASP.NET Worker Process

The enable attribute is a Boolean setting used to determine if ASP.NET should run in a separate worker process, the default, or in-process with Internet Information Server. If we set it to false the <processModel> settings are ignored.

```
enable="[true | false]"
```

If we do set the enable="false" we won't see the aspnet_wp.exe show up in the task manager, it's now loaded in-process with IIS.

Note, IIS has to be stopped and restarted if the enable option is changed.

It is recommended that this setting be left as true so our applications can reap the benefits that the ASP.NET worker process provides.

Timing Out the Process

The timeout attribute determines how long the worker process will live before a new worker process is created to take its place. The default value is Infinite. However, we can also set this value to a time using the following format: HH:MM:SS.

```
timeout = "[Infinite | HH:MM:SS]"
```

This value can be extremely useful if a scenario exists where the application's performance starts to degrade slightly after running for several weeks, such as in the case of a memory leak. Rather than having to manually start and stop the process, ASP.NET can restart automatically:

```
<configuration>
  <system.web>
        <processModel
            enable="true"
            timeout="336:00:00"
            idleTimeout="Infinite"
            shutdownTimeout="0:00:05"
            requestLimit="Infinite"
            requestQueueLimit="5000"
            restartQueueLimit="10"
            memoryLimit="60"
            webGarden="false"
            cpuMask="0xffffffff"
            userName=""
            password=""
            logLevel="Errors"
            clientConnectedCheck="0:00:05"
        />
  </system.web>
</configuration>
```

In the above setting the ASP.NET worker process will recycle itself automatically after approximately 336 hours (two weeks). The clock starts ticking on the life of the process when the process is started (on the first request after the changes have been made).

Shutting Down the Process Automatically

We can shut down the ASP.NET worker process automatically using the `idleTimeout` option. `idleTimeout` is used to shut down the worker process when it has not served any requests within a given period of time. By default, it is set to `Infinite` and once started will not shut down. We can also set this value to a time using the following format: `HH:MM:SS`.

```
idleTimeout = "[Infinite | HH:MM:SS]"
```

Starting a process for the first request can make a performance hit on the server. Two scenarios for use of `idleTimout` include:

❑   When we want to release resources that ASP.NET is using when we're not actively servicing requests.

❑   To recycle processes during down time. We could configure `idleTimout` to shutdown after 20 minutes of no requests. For example, if we don't receive requests between the hours of midnight to 3 A.M., ASP.NET can quietly exit the process. When a new request comes in, we start a new process.

Graceful Shutdown

The `shutDownTimeout` attribute is used to specify how long the worker process is given to shut itself down gracefully before ASP.NET calls the kill command on the process – kill is a low-level command that forcefully removes the process. By default, `shutDownTimeout` it is set to five seconds, but this is configurable:

```
shutDownTimeout = "[HH:MM:SS]"
```

This is a very useful configuration setting for processes that have crossed some threshold and appear to have crashed. ASP.NET can kill the process after it's given the opportunity to shutdown gracefully.

Recycling the Process after n Requests

`requestLimit` allows us to configure ASP.NET to recycle after a certain number of requests are served. The default value is `Infinite`, no request limit, but we can also set it to a number.

```
requestLimit = "[Infinite | int]"
```

If we notice that the performance of our application degrades after a certain number of requests – for example 5000 – we can configure the `requestLimit` property to a threshold of 5000. ASP.NET will then recycle the process after 5000 requests.

We can take this example a step further and show the `requestLimit` being enforced by ASP.NET. If we:

❑   Set the `requestLimit` to 5.

❑   Save our `machine.config` file.

❑   Open the Windows Task Manager, view the `aspnet_wp.exe` process, and take note of the process ID.

Next, if we make more than five requests for an ASP.NET application file, ASP.NET will recycle the process; to see this go back and check the process ID of `aspnet_wp.exe` – after five requests, we'll have a new process ID.

Recycling the Process if Requests are Queued

The `requestQueueLimit` option instructs ASP.NET to recycle the worker process if the number of queued requests limit is exceeded. ASP.NET uses threads within a process to service user requests. If a thread is blocked or is unable to service requests, requests can be queued. The `requestQueueLimit` option gives us the opportunity to detect if requests are queued and recycle the process if the queued requests exceed the allowed limit. The default setting is 5000.

```
requestQueueLimit = "[int]"
```

Recycling the Process if Too Much Memory is Consumed

The `memoryLimit` option determines how much physical memory the worker process is allowed to consume before it is considered to be misbehaving. The default value is 60 (representing 60%).

```
memoryLimit = "[int]"
```

We should never 'leak' memory in a .NET application, since the Common Language Runtime is performing garbage collection (memory management) for us. However, since .NET also supports the use of native code, and is able to interoperate with COM, it is possible to leak memory if either the native code or the COM object is mismanaging memory.

The simplest way to demonstrate the use of `memoryLimit` is with a simple ASP.NET page that fills application state memory with useless information – this simulates a memory leak.

VB.NET

```
<%@ Import Namespace="System.Diagnostics" %>
<%@ Import Namespace="System.Text" %>

<script runat=server>

  Sub Page_Load(Sender as Object, E as EventArgs)
    Dim i As Integer
    Dim garbage As New StringBuilder

    If Application("garbage") Is Nothing Then
      Dim c As Integer

      For c=1 to 1000
        garbage = garbage.Append("xxxxxxxxxx")
      Next c

      Application("garbage") = garbage
    Else
      garbage = Application("garbage")
    End If

    For i=1 to 500
      ' Make sure we create a unique entry
      Application(i.ToString + DateTime.Now.ToString("r")) =
                      (garbage.ToString() + DateTime.Now.ToString("r"))
    Next i

    Dim p as ProcessInfo
    p = ProcessModelInfo.GetCurrentProcessInfo()

    ProcessID.Text = p.ProcessID.ToString()

  End Sub

</script>

<html>
  <body>
      <h2>The Process ID serving this request is: <asp:label id="ProcessID"
forecolor=red runat=server/> </h2>
      <h2>There are <%=Application.Count.ToString()%> items in Application state
memory.</h2>
  </body>
</html>
```

We can then set `memoryLimit` to a very low threshold, such as 5%:

```
<configuration>
  <system.web>
        <processModel
            enable="true"
            timeout="336:00:00"
            idleTimeout="Infinite"
            shutdownTimeout="0:00:05"
            requestLimit="Infinite"
            requestQueueLimit="5000"
            restartQueueLimit="10"
            memoryLimit="5"
            webGarden="false"
            cpuMask="0xffffffff"
            userName=""
            password=""
            logLevel="Errors"
            clientConnectedCheck="0:00:05"
        />
  </system.web>
</configuration>
```

Next, we make requests for our ASP.NET page that simulates a leak.

Again, we'll open up the Windows Task Manager and watch the `aspnet_wp.exe` worker process. As we request the resource we'll see memory increase for the process. Finally, when 5% of memory has been utilized, we'll see a new process appear next to the old process, and then the old process will disappear. From the end user's perspective the application just keeps running.

The screenshot below shows the process (PID 748) that has exceeded the memory threshold, and the new process (PID 1828) that has just started:

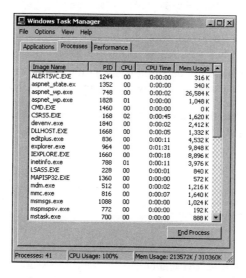

This is also evident in our sample ASP.NET page since we display the process ID.

Supporting Multiple Worker Processes

There are usually two ways to scale an application: write tighter and better code, or simply add more hardware. The term "web farm" is used to describe a collection of nearly identical web servers that can be used to service requests; as our user base grows we simply add more servers into our 'server farm' and we are able to increase the scalability of our application – this is very cost effective since adding a server is, in most cases, less expensive than re-writing the entire application.

When we build a server farm, all we're essentially doing is putting all the required hardware in place to host another process that can service requests. A new option that ASP.NET now supports is a **web garden**, in other words multiple processes on the same server.

A web garden lets us host multiple ASP.NET worker processes on a single server, thus providing the application with better hardware scalability.

Note: web garden mode is only supported on multi-processor servers.

To support a 'web garden' with ASP.NET we use two interrelated <processModel> configuration settings:

❑   webGarden – The webGarden attribute determines whether web garden mode is enabled. The default setting is false.

    webGarden = "[true | false]"

❑   cpuMask – The cpuMask, a hexadecimal value, is used to determine which processors should be affinitized to ASP.NET worker processes when webGarden="true". The default value is all processors, as 0xFFFFFFFF is a bit mask of 11111111111111111111111111111111, in other words if the server had 32 processors each would be affinitized to its own ASP.NET worker process.

    cpuMask="0xffffffff"

The settings of cpuMask do nothing if webGarden="false".

Setting the Identity of the Process

The username and password settings found in <processModel> are used to control the user that the ASP.NET Worker process runs as. By default it is the System account, however, by using these settings we can instruct the process to execute under another Windows identity.

For example, if we create a Windows user ASPNET_WP with a password of &dotnet$12 we could set these as our username and password values:

```
<configuration>
  <system.web>
      <processModel
          enable="true"
          timeout="336:00:00"
          idleTimeout="Infinite"
          shutdownTimeout="0:00:05"
          requestLimit="Infinite"
          requestQueueLimit="5000"
          restartQueueLimit="10"
          memoryLimit="5"
```

```
            webGarden="false"
            cpuMask="0xffffffff"
            userName="ASPNET_WP"
            password="&dotnet$12"
            logLevel="Errors"
            clientConnectedCheck="0:00:05"
      />
   </system.web>
</configuration>
```

When we view the process information in the Windows Task Manager we would see that the process is executing as user ASPNET_WP rather than System.

Logging Process Events

The logLevel attribute allows us to configure how the ASP.NET worker process logs events. The default setting is to log only errors.

```
logLevel="[All|None|Errors]"
```

In addition to logging errors that occur, we can also configure to log all events or log none of the events. The events are written to the Windows Application Event Log.

Checking if the Client is Connected

When an application is slow to respond, some users will simply issue a new request from the browser by hitting page refresh several times. This will force the web server to do unnecessary work, since the client may make 15 requests but only the last request completes – the web server will still do the associated work for the other 14 requests.

The clientConnectedCheck setting allows us to check if the client is still connected at timed intervals before performing work. Thus, rather than processing all the requests, ASP.NET will only process requests where the client is expecting a response. The other requests that sit in the queue waiting for work can then be discarded.

The default setting of this attribute is 5 seconds, meaning that for requests that are queued ASP.NET will check if the client is connected. If not the request can be discarded from the queue.

The following settings are supported:

```
clientConnectedCheck="[HH:MM:SS | Infinite]"
```

The process model settings of ASP.NET introduce a new level of flexibility and stability for our applications. All of the options for controlling the processing, including the identity that the process runs as, as well as which CPU the process should affinitize to, are provided.

The last machine.config setting we'll examine is the <machineKey>.

Machine Key

ASP.NET uses a key to encrypt or hash some data so that the data is only accessible from the server that created the data. In a single-server environment we'll never touch this setting. However, in a multi-server environment in which a request can be directed to a farm of web servers, each server in the farm needs to share the same machine key. This way server A and server B can both encrypt/decrypt or hash the same values, so that data created on A can be understood and used on B and vice-versa.

The default setting of <machineKey>, from machine.config, is below:

```
<machineKey validationKey="AutoGenerate"
            decryptionKey="AutoGenerate"
            validation="SHA1"
/>
```

There are three settings for <machineKey>:

❑   validationKey
❑   decryptionKey
❑   validation

Let's look at each of these in more detail.

validationKey

The validationKey is used for the validation of data, such as the hash that is done for Forms-based authentication cookies. The validationKey is used as part of the hash so that the hash can only be recomputed by ASP.NET applications that have the appropriate validationKey. The default setting is autogenerate (ASP.NET automatically creates a value for us), but in a server farm environment we would need to configure the value ourselves and ensure that each server, or application, has the same value. Below are the acceptable settings:

```
validationKey="[AutoGenerate | 40-128 hex Chars]"
```

If a user-defined validationKey is to be used, the recommendation is to use the full 128 chars. Below is a valid entry:

```
validationKey="0123456789abcdef0123456789abcdef0123456789abcdef
               0123456789abcdef0123456789abcdef0123456789abcdef
               0123456789abcdef0123456789abcdef"
```

Key lengths shorter than 40 or longer than 128 hex chars will generate an error.

validation

The validation attribute of machineKey is used to determine what type of hash is to be computed. Valid values include: MD5, SHA1, or 3DES.

The hash can be sent to the client along with, for example, the Forms Authentication cookie, and the data in the cookie can be validated by the server by re-hashing the values with the validationKey and the appropriate algorithm determined by validation. If the values match then the data is considered valid, if not, the data represented by the hash is considered invalid (it may have been tampered with). The validationKey guarantees the data is valid, another setting; decryptionKey, guarantees that the plain-text of the message cannot be read by non-trusted parties.

decryptionKey

The decryptionKey is used to encrypt data stored in the Forms Authentication cookie. The default is AutoGenerate (ASP.NET automatically generates the value). In a web farm environment, just as with the validationKey, each server needs to use an identical value for this key. The value of the string should be a 16 to 48 hex value.

The validationKey ensures that the information is valid; decryptionKey protects the information from prying eyes.

Advanced Topics

In this *Advanced Topics* section we'll cover three advanced topics related to ASP.NET configuration:

❑ Specifying Location
❑ Locking-down Configuration Settings
❑ Building a Custom Configuration Handler

Specifying Location

In all the examples we've discussed in this chapter we've either used machine.config to configure settings for the entire server or web.config to configure settings for an individual application.

Another option, not discussed previously, is using a <location> element within a configuration file. Using the <location> element we can specify application-specific settings in machine.config for different applications on our server, rather than creating a web.config file.

For example, if we have a virtual directory named Wrox accessible as http://localhost/Wrox, and that virtual directory is marked as an application, we could make the following entry in machine.config to configure Session settings for all applications as well as Session settings specific to the Wrox application:

```
<configuration>
  <system.web>
    <sessionState
      mode="InProc"
      stateConnectionString="tcpip=127.0.0.1:42424"
      sqlConnectionString="data source=127.0.0.1; user id=sa;password="
      cookieless="false"
      timeout="20"
    />
  </system.web>

  <location path="Default Web Site/Wrox">
    <system.web>
      <sessionState
        mode="StateServer"
        stateConnectionString="tcpip=127.0.0.1:42424"
        sqlConnectionString="data source=127.0.0.1; user id=sa;password="
        cookieless="true"
        timeout="10"
      />
    </system.web>
  </location>
<configuration>
```

In the above code-snip from `machine.config`, we've specified a default setting for all applications, but have also provide the settings specific to the Wrox application using the `<location>` element.

Setting the Path

The `<location>` element requires that we define a path. If a path is not provided, or the path value is set to an empty string the settings are applied as normal – in our example above, it would be an error to define `<location path="">`. This would cause `machine.config` to have two conflicting settings for `<sessionState>`.

> Note, that the value of path requires that we provide *[site name]/[application path]*. The value for *[site name]* is the description value of our web site. The description value of our web site can be obtained by opening the IIS MMC, right-clicking on a web site, selecting properties, selecting the tab **Web Sites**. The description value is then visible in the **Description** text box.

In addition to using `<location>` to define settings for our application, we can also lock down application configuration settings through the use of `<location>`.

Locking-down Configuration Settings

ASP.NET's configuration system is very flexible. For our applications, we can simply create a `web.config` file specifying the desired configuration options and our application will behave appropriately.

However, in some cases, as in a hosted environment, we may want to limit what configuration options a particular application is allowed to control. For example, we may decide that some applications cannot change the settings for Session state. We have two options for locking down configuration settings:

❑ Use the `<location>` `allowOverride` attribute

❑ Use the `allowDefinition` attribute on the configuration section handler

Let's look at both of these.

Lock-down via <location>

In addition to supporting a `path` attribute, we can additionally specify an `allowOverride` attribute in the `<location>` tag. The usage of `allowOverride` is:

```
<location path="[site description]/[application path]"
        allowOverride="[true|false]">
```

Let's look at an example to clarify the use. We could define the following in our `machine.config` file:

```
<configuration>
  ...
  <location path="Default Web Site/Wrox" allowOverride="true">
    <system.web>
      <sessionState
        mode="StateServer"
        stateConnectionString="tcpip=127.0.0.1:42424"
        sqlConnectionString="data source=127.0.0.1; user id=sa;password="
        cookieless="true"
        timeout="10"
      />
    </system.web>
  </location>
<configuration>
```

Within the Wrox application we could then define a `web.config` file that provides Session state settings, overriding the settings inherited from `machine.config`'s `<location>` settings:

```
<configuration>
  <system.web>
    <sessionState
      mode="InProc"
      stateConnectionString="tcpip=127.0.0.1:42424"
      sqlConnectionString="data source=127.0.0.1; user id=sa;password="
      cookieless="false"
      timeout="20"
    />
  </system.web>
<configuration>
```

However, if in `machine.config` we set `allowOverride="false"` in the `<location>` settings for Wrox, a `web.config` file for the Wrox application that attempted to set `<sessionState>` settings would result in an exception. The application is effectively prevented from 'redefining' the settings for `<sessionState>` configured by the administrator in `machine.config`.

Using the `allowOverride` attribute of `<location>` allows the administrator to control the default settings of a given application, as well as whether or not that application can change those settings in a `web.config` file.

If the default inherited settings from `machine.config` are acceptable, we can also lock down using the attributes on the configuration section handler.

Lock-down via Configuration Section Handler

If the settings specified in `machine.config` are acceptable defaults, and we don't want those settings changed by applications that inherit those settings, we can use the optional `allowDefinition` attribute on the configuration section handler.

Let's look at an example. Below are the values taken from `machine.config` for the `sessionState` section handler as well as the `<sessionState>` settings. The section handler is highlighted.

```xml
<?xml version="1.0" encoding="UTF-8" ?>
<configuration>
  <configSections>
    <sectionGroup name="system.web">
      <section name="sessionState"
             type="System.Web.SessionState.SessionStateSectionHandler",
                   System.Web
      />
    </sectionGroup>
    ...
  </configSections>
  ...
  <system.web>
    <sessionState
        mode="InProc"
        stateConnectionString="tcpip=127.0.0.1:42424"
        sqlConnectionString="data source=127.0.0.1;
                            user id=sa;password="
        cookieless="false"
        timeout="20"
    />
  </system.web>
</configuration>
```

In this configuration, applications can use a `web.config` file to redefine the configuration settings for `<sessionState>`. If we wished to restrict this we could use the `allowDefinition` attribute on the section handler:

```xml
<section name="sessionState"
       type="System.Web.SessionState.SessionStateSectionHandler,
             System.Web"
         allowDefinition="MachineOnly"
/>
```

Applications that use a `web.config` file attempting to change `<sessionState>` settings will now receive an error message, and will be prevented from defining `<sessionState>` settings – just as we did with `<location>`.

The `allowDefinition` attribute has three acceptable settings:

❑ Everywhere – Settings for the section handler can be declared in `machine.config` or within a `web.config` file; the `web.config` file may or may not reside within a directory marked as an application.

❑ MachineOnly – Settings for the section handler can be declared only by the `machine.config` file and cannot be overridden in a `web.config` file.

❑ MachineToApplication – Setting for the section handler can be declared in either `machine.config` or a `web.config` file residing within a directory marked as an application.

If `allowDefinition` is not present, the default setting is `allowDefinition="Everywhere"`.

Custom Configuration Handler

Earlier in the chapter we discussed the use of <appSettings> for storing our own configuration data. This allowed us to store simple key/value data in the configuration file and later access it through configuration APIs.

While <appSettings> is definitely useful, we also noted that in some cases we might want to add more complex configuration data. To do so, we can create our own configuration section handler that is capable of reading configuration settings. A custom configuration section handler is simply a class that implements the interface IConfigurationSectionHandler. This interface has one method that we are required to implement:

```
object Create(object parent, object configContext, XmlNode section)
```

Let's write a simple example of a configuration section handler.

Simple Configuration Handler

Let's say we want to provide all pages with a default background color. We also want to store the default value in the configuration system. Instead of using <appSettings> to accomplish this (for this example we could easily use it), we decide to write our own configuration handler.

Below is the C# code to our configuration section handler:

```csharp
using System;
using System.Collections;
using System.Xml;
using System.Configuration;
using System.Web.Configuration;

namespace Wrox {
  internal class PagePropertiesHandler : IConfigurationSectionHandler {
    public virtual object Create(Object parent,
                                 Object context,
                                 XmlNode node) {
      PagePropertiesConfig config;
      config = new PagePropertiesConfig((PagePropertiesConfig)parent);
      config.LoadValuesFromConfigurationXml(node);
      return config;
    }
  }

  public class PagePropertiesConfig {
    string _backColor;

    internal PagePropertiesConfig(PagePropertiesConfig parent) {
      if (parent != null)
        _backColor = parent._backColor;
    }
```

```
        internal void LoadValuesFromConfigurationXml(XmlNode node) {
          Exception error = null;
          XmlAttributeCollection attributeCollection = node.Attributes;
          _backColor = attributeCollection["backColor"].Value;
        }

        public string BackColor{
          get {return _backColor;}
        }
    }
  }
```

In the above code we've implemented a class, PagePropertiesHandler, that implements IConfigurationSectionHandler's Create method. We use a public class, PagePropertiesConfig, to both retrieve and store the values from the configuration settings.

When this handler is created it will pass in the XmlNode node value, and call LoadValuesFromConfigurationXml to load the setting: backColor.

After compiling the above source file and deploying it to our application's \bin directory, we can then write the following web.config file to use this configuration section handler:

```
<configuration>
  <configSections>
    <sectionGroup name="system.web">
      <section name="pageProperties"
               type="Wrox.PagePropertiesHandler, PageProperties" />
    </sectionGroup>
  </configSections>

  <system.web>
    <pageProperties backColor="blue" />
  </system.web>
</configuration>
```

Next, we can write the following ASP.NET Page:

```
<%@ Import Namespace="Wrox" %>

<Script runat="server">
  Public backColor As String

  Public Sub Page_Load(sender As Object, e As EventArgs)
    Dim _config As PagePropertiesConfig

    _config = CType(Context.GetConfig("system.web/pageProperties"),
                    PagePropertiesConfig)

    backColor = _config.BackColor

  End Sub
</Script>

<Body bgcolor="<%=backColor%>">

<Font face="arial" color="white" size=4>
This page has its backcolor set from the ASP.NET configuration system!
</Font>
```

Within our ASP.NET Page, we first import the `Wrox` namespace, as this includes the `PagePropertiesConfig`. Next, we use the `Context` object's `GetConfig` method and request the configuration information for `system.web/pageProperties`. We cast the return type to `PagePropertiesConfig`. Finally, we are able to access the `BackColor` property on the `PagePropertiesConfig` class, which returns the value we set in our `web.config` file: blue.

As you can clearly see, this is a simple example. However, it does show just how easy plugging into the ASP.NET configuration system is. We could easily write more complex configuration section handlers for personalization features or other extensions that we may want to add to ASP.NET.

Summary

As we learned in this chapter, the ASP.NET configuration system does not rely upon the IIS metabase as ASP did. Instead ASP.NET uses an XML configuration system. An XML configuration system is human readable/writable, replicates easily, and does not require local server access – since we can simply FTP the configuration files to our web servers.

ASP.NET's XML configuration system is divided into two distinct files: `machine.config` and `web.config`. A server will always have one `machine.config` file to represent the default settings for all web applications on that server. However, that same server may have multiple `web.config` files used to configure applications on an application-by-application basis.

We also learned that configuration files are inherited. The default settings in `machine.config` are inherited in `web.config` files, unless overridden – as we saw in the <sessionState> examples within this chapter.

After introducing configuration, we then spent the bulk of the chapter discussing various configuration settings used in ASP.NET. We covered topics from internationalization, to HTTP Handlers, to Process Model settings. The settings covered in this chapter should cover 90% of all the configuration settings we'll want to use for our applications.

Finally, we discussed how we could author our own configuration section handler by implementing a class that inherited from the `IConfigurationSectionHandler` interface.

"The Babel fish," says The Hitch Hiker's Guide to Galaxy "is small, yellow and leech-like, and probably the oddest thing in the Universe. It feeds on brainwave energy not from its carrier but from those around it. It absorbs all unconscious mental frequencies from this brainwave energy to nourish itself with. It then excretes into the mind of its carrier a telepathic matrix formed by combining the conscious thought frequencies with nerve signals picked up from the speech centres of the brain which has supplied them".

The practical upshot of all this is that if you stick a Babel fish in your ear you can instantly understand anything said to you in any form of language. The speech patterns you actually hear decode the brainwave matrix which has been fed into your mind by your Babel fish.

14

Securing ASP.NET Applications

Most of the pages that you create for a public web site are designed to be accessible to any visitor, so the default settings for ASP.NET pages are ideal – anyone can access the pages from anywhere on the network or the Internet. However, there will always be some pages that you don't want to be publicly available. For example, you might want to limit access to a complete site to users who have paid a subscription, or to limit access to administration pages to specific users only.

In previous versions of ASP, securing your pages was generally done in one of two ways. Either, you could create a custom security system that allowed users to login to your site or application (or a specific part of it). Alternatively, you could rely on the security features of IIS and Windows itself to control which users accessed certain pages, folders, or resources.

In ASP.NET our pages run under the .NET framework, and this introduces new concepts in managing security, while still retaining existing security features. In this chapter, we'll overview all the features that control user access, and then concentrate on the specific techniques designed for use with ASP.NET. The main topics of this chapter are:

- ❑ An overview of the security model in Windows 2000 and IIS
- ❑ An overview of the new security features in ASP.NET
- ❑ The different types of access control that we can implement with ASP.NET
- ❑ A detailed look at how we apply the ASP.NET security and access control features
- ❑ A brief overview of the "trust" model

Windows 2000 and IIS Security Overview

As this book is about ASP.NET, we'll only be providing an overview of the features in the Windows operating system and IIS for securing your web pages and web applications. Though we will be concentrating on Windows 2000 here, the concepts, configuration, and usage of these features is virtually unchanged from previous versions of ASP. However, they do provide the basis on which .NET security techniques are founded. If you are not familiar with the material in this section, you may wish to consult other documentation or books to gain a broader understanding.

> Securing your applications or web sites is one of the most important factors when connecting your server to the Internet. While the basics described here, and the techniques we use to control access will provide a secure environment, you must still implement all the other measures that are required for protecting your servers and applications against intruders. This includes physical security (that is locked doors and windows), internal user security (that is keeping passwords secret and monitoring usage), virus protection, prompt installation of operating system updates and patches, etc.

The Need for Security

When you come to secure your applications, you must first think about what it is you are actually trying to achieve. For example, does your application contain highly-sensitive information, or allow users to perform tasks that you absolutely must protect against misuse – such as a bank providing on-line account access to clients. Or, is the information less sensitive but still valuable, such as content that you want visitors to pay a subscription to access.

In the end, it all comes down to quantifying the risks involved and the effect of a security breech. Securing applications is more difficult than allowing everyone access, and can involve extra hardware to build complex multi-layer systems with firewalls, demilitarized zones, and all kinds of other highly-secure features. However this type of approach is normally used only when the highest levels of security are required, such as when you are protecting whole networks from access by external intruders.

Security as it concerns our ASP.NET applications will normally be limited to the configuration of the machine(s) on which it is run, and the connected resources such as database servers, etc. This involves limiting access to specific folders, files, components, and other resources, to only the appropriate users. These topics are the real focus of this chapter.

If you are building an application that requires the utmost in protection from intruders, you must base the ASP.NET servers in a secure environment, as well as configuring them correctly. This involves the kinds of extra equipment we mentioned earlier, and a thorough understanding of the risks involved. Books such as *Designing Secure Web-based Applications for Windows 2000* (MS Press, *ISBN 0-7356-0995-0*) and "*Hacking Exposed – Second Edition*" (Osborne *ISBN: 0-07-212748-1*) are useful. If in doubt, however, employ a professional to design and secure your network and servers as well.

Security Concepts

The basic concepts for securing your applications consist of four main topic areas:

- ❑ **Authentication** is the process of discovering the identity of the user, and making them prove that they are who they say they are.

- ❑ **Authorization** is the process of determining if a particular user is entitled to access the resource they've requested.

- ❑ **Impersonation** is the process whereby the resource is accessed under a different identity, usually the context of a remote user.

- ❑ **Data or functional security** is the process of securing the system through physical means, operating systems updates and the use of robust software. We don't cover this topic in this chapter.

Many elements of the operating system, IIS, and the .NET Framework combine to provide the features required to implement the first three of the topics we listed above. For example, Windows 2000 uses its own list of user accounts to help identify and authenticate users. IIS also identifies users based on the information provided by Windows as they access a web site, and it passes this information on to ASP.NET where it can be used as part of the overall authorization process.

To help you follow how the overall security process works, we'll look at each of the three topics separately. Just remember, however, that they are all part of the same chain of events involved in allowing or denying users access to resources.

Authentication

To be able to limit access to specific users, we have to be able to identify them. This doesn't mean we need to know everything about them – as in some "big-brother" scenario – but we do need to be able to tell each user apart, and identify those that should have access and those that should not.

Authentication involves challenging a user to prove that they are who they say they are – usually by means of a username and password, a digital certificate, perhaps a "smart card", or even a fingerprint reader. In theory, if they can provide a valid username and password combination, or some other user-specific "property" that can be identified, then they must be who they say they are. We depend on only one person having access to their "property".

In the most common case, a user provides their username and matching password when prompted – either when they log onto a machine or when they access the resource. If these details are valid, the user has been identified – they are "authenticated".

Authorization

Once we know who the user is, we can decide if they have permission to access the resource they've requested. This is done in a range of ways, depending on the resource. In Windows-based systems most resources have an Access Control List (ACL), which lists the users that can access a resource. The list will usually also specify what kind of access each user has – that is whether they can read it, write to it, modify it, delete it, etc.

For example, if they request an ASP page the operating system will check to see if they have **Read** access to the page, and if so, will allow IIS to fetch the page. However, IIS also has authorization settings that control what a user can do with a resource. If it's an ASP page, they will only be able to execute the script in that page if IIS has **Script Execute** permission set for the page.

So, in traditional ASP environments, you can see how several "layers" can be involved in the authorization process. If the identified user has permission to access the resource in the way that they've requested, the process succeeds. They have been "authorized". If not, they receive an error message of some type that is generated by the "layer" that refused them access to the resource.

Impersonation

There are times when a user will access a resource as though they were someone (or something) else. An example of this is when there is no access control in place for a web page – in other words it allows any users to access it.

> *In fact, this is an over-simplification, because Windows never allows anonymous access. All users must be authenticated and authorized using an existing account.*

For HTML pages, ASP pages, and components in version 3.0 and earlier, this is achieved through the two accounts named IUSR_*machinename* and IWAM_*machinename*. These accounts are set up when IIS is installed, and are automatically added to all the folders in every web site on the server.

If we allow anonymous access to a resource in IIS, every user will look the same – we won't be able to tell who is who. But we don't need to. When IIS receives a request for a web page or other resource for which anonymous access is permitted, it uses the IUSR_*machinename* account to access the resources on the user's behalf. If the resource they request is an ASP page that uses a COM or COM+ component, that component (by default) is executed under the context of the IWAM_*machinename* account.

In contrast, ASP.NET – when impersonation is turned off – makes all access to resources under the context of a "local system process" account. When we turn impersonation on, ASP.NET executes every resource under the account of a specified user that we authenticate when they make the request. As in a COM+ Application running under Windows 2000 or in MTS under Windows NT4, we can specify the account that will be used. If we specify the IUSR_*machinename* account, then ASP.NET will behave like previous versions of ASP, as far as the permissions required for accessing resources is concerned.

> One vital point to bear in mind is that the authentication process used by ASP.NET *only* applies to resources that are associated with ASP.NET. In other words, access control is only applied to files that are mapped to the ASP.NET ISAPI DLL in Internet Services Manager. This includes `.aspx` and `.asax` pages, `.ascx` components, `.vb` and `.cs` code files, web service files, and other resources that are mapped to `aspnet_isapi.dll`. It does *not* apply to resources like images, Word documents, zip files, PDF files, and other types of file. These types of files must be protected using standard Windows techniques such as ACLs. You'll see all these topics discussed in this chapter.

Security Within ASP.NET

From the preceding chapters, you'll have seen how many of the configuration settings you used to make within IIS under previous versions of ASP are now made through one or more instances of the new configuration file named `web.config`. This applies to most of the settings in the Internet Services Manager interface (in the MMC), as `web.config` replaces the metabase contents that this interface is used to manipulate.

However, security settings made in IIS are still effective in many areas. This is because, unlike the configuration of application settings, custom errors, etc., IIS is still actively managing the request and performing the base security process in conjunction with the operating system itself. In effect, a request for an ASP.NET page is received by IIS, which uses the **application mappings** defined for the site containing that page to direct the request to ASP.NET.

You can see the application mappings if you open the Application Configuration dialog from the Home Directory page of the Properties dialog for a site or directory in Internet Services Manager. The script mappings for all the ASP.NET resource types point to a file named `aspnet_isapi.dll` stored in the .NET frameworks folder:

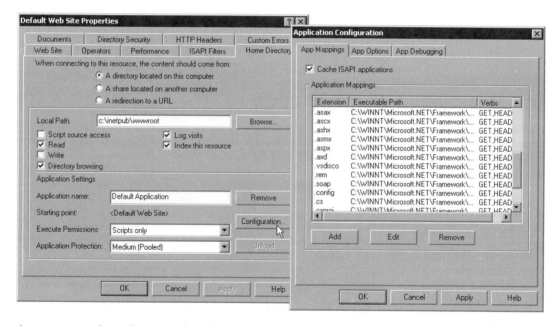

As you can see from the screenshot, the application mappings rely on file extensions. This is why you can still run existing ASP 3.0 pages on the same server as ASP.NET (they have a different file extension) – and of course publish other resources such as HTML pages, zip files, documents, etc. which aren't processed by ASP.NET.

> *If you hadn't realized it yet, this dialog proves that ASP.NET is an ISAPI DLL – as were ASP 3.0 and earlier. This DLL captures the request, processes it using managed code within the .NET Framework, and then passes the response back to IIS so it can be delivered to the client.*

So, IIS first authenticates a user, and then passes the request on to ASP.NET where it can perform its own security processes. The next schematic shows the overall flow of the request, and we'll briefly see how each part of the process is carried out in the following sections of this chapter.

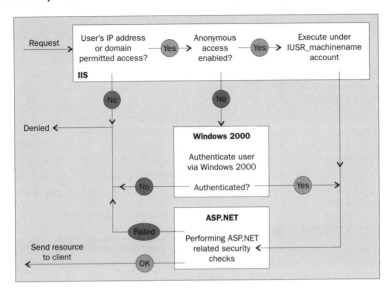

Authentication in Windows 2000

Windows 2000 maintains a list of users that are allowed to access resources on a machine. This is either stored on the machine itself, or on a domain controller elsewhere. The list is managed through the Computer Management tool, or through the Active Directory Users and Computers tool on a domain controller:

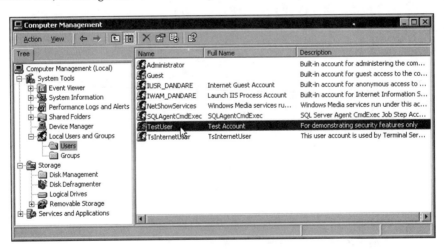

You can see the IUSR and IWAM accounts in the screenshot above that are used by IIS when anonymous access is enabled. Depending on the type of operating system and software you have installed, you'll probably see several other accounts listed as well. Within the list you can see an account with the username TestUser, which we created to experiment with the security features in ASP.NET and Windows 2000.

User Groups

The Properties dialog for this account shows that it is a member of two account groups – TestGroup and Users:

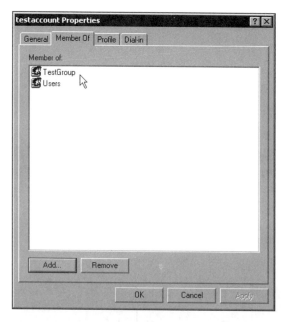

All accounts are automatically added to the Users group, but we created a new group named TestGroup and allocated this account to it. You can see a list of groups in the Computer Management dialog as well:

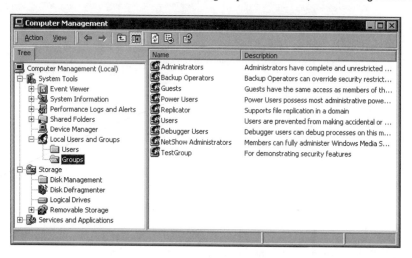

By allocating users to groups, we provide a way to minimize the amount of work required to change permissions. For example, if we have 500 users who can access a particular set of resources, we can allocate them all to one group and then give that group permission to access those resources. The alternative would be to add all 500 users to each resource individually. And any changes to the permissions afterwards would mean changing them for all 500 users rather than just once for the group as a whole.

Groups are also useful when we use "programmatic security". We can detect if a user is a member of a specific group, and make decisions based on the result. This means that we don't have to hard-code all of the usernames into our application (just the group name), and we don't have to change the code to add or remove individual users. We just configure the group in the ACL for the resource to add users to, or remove from, the group.

Authentication in IIS

When a user requests a resource over the web, IIS receives the request and performs the initial authentication of the user. IIS also performs other checks before deciding whether the user will be allowed access to the resource. We'll look at these next.

IP Address and Domain Name Restrictions

In Windows 2000 Server and Windows NT4 (but not Windows 2000 Professional), you can specify the IP addresses, or domain names, of clients that will be allowed access or denied access. This is achieved using the IP Address and Domain Name Restrictions dialog, available from the Directory Security page of the Properties dialog for a site or directory. This is useful if you always access the restricted site from a single machine, or if all your users come from a specific set of IP addresses or set of domains:

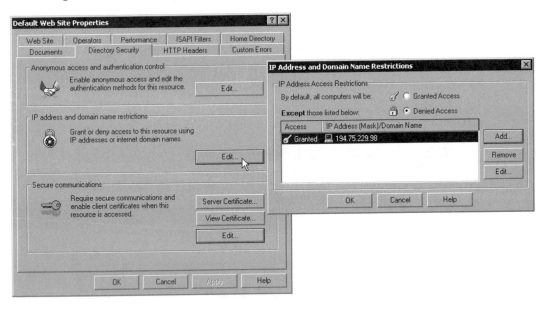

Using Certificates to Authenticate Users

You can also use the Properties dialog to set up server certificates that are to be used for a site or directory. As well as enabling secure communication through SSL, these certificates can be used in conjunction with client certificates to identify the machine that is accessing your server. For example, the following screenshot shows a configuration where the clients must provide a certificate to access the site. We've created a rule so that, if the organization that issued the certificate to the client is our own Certificate Server, the user will automatically be authenticated using the TestUser account we created earlier:

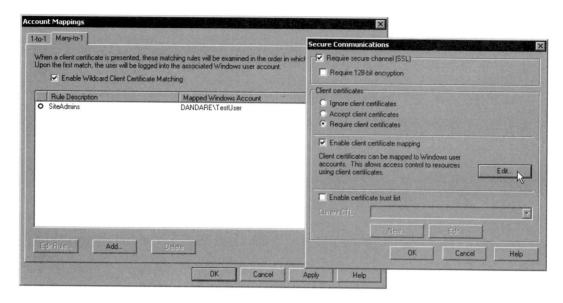

You can also access the content of a client certificate using code in an ASP.NET page, through the `Request.ClientCertificate` *collection.*

Specifying the Authentication Method

The third option in the Directory Security page of the Properties dialog for a site or directory allows us to specify the authentication method that should be used. The Authentication Methods dialog provides four options:

❑ **Anonymous Access** – Any user can access the web service providing that the settings for their IP address and domain name restrictions don't prevent them. IIS then accesses resources on their behalf using the IUSR account (or the IWAM account for components running out-of-process), and so they will be able to access all resources for which these accounts are valid.

❑ **Basic Authentication** – If anonymous access is disabled, users will be presented with a logon dialog generated by their browser or their client-side user agent application. The username and password they provide are Base64-encoded and passed to IIS. It then looks up this account in Windows (on the server), and will only allow the user to access the resource if the account is valid and has the appropriate permission for that resource. Base64 encoding is not very secure, and so this option is not suitable for high-security applications.

❑ **Digest Authentication** – If anonymous access is disabled, users will be prompted for their credentials (their logon information). The browser combines this with other information stored on the client, and sends an encoded hash (or digest) of it to the server. The server already has a copy of this information, and so can recreate the original details from its own hash and authenticate the user. This method only works with Internet Explorer and .NET Web Services, but will pass through firewalls, proxy servers, and over the Internet. It is also very secure. The user will be able to access the resource they requested only if the specified account exists in Windows, is valid, and has appropriate permission for that resource.

❏   **Integrated Windows Authentication** – This is the same method as is used when you log onto your local network. Sometimes called "NTLM" authentication or "Challenge Response" authentication, it can work with Windows NTLM or Kerberos. It also uses a hash algorithm to code and decode the client's credentials. However, it will not work through most proxy servers and firewalls, and some routers, so is not generally suitable for use on the Internet. However, it usually works fine on an Intranet or a corporate network. Like **Digest Authentication**, this is also a very secure technique. The user will be able to access the resource they requested only if the specified account exists in Windows, is valid, and has appropriate permission for that resource.

If anonymous access is disabled, and the other methods are all enabled, IIS will attempt to use Integrated Windows Authentication first, followed by Digest Authentication, with Basic Authentication used only as a last resort if the client does not support the other two methods.

We can also use the Authentication Methods dialog to specify which account is used for anonymous access. You can see that the default is our machine's IUSR account:

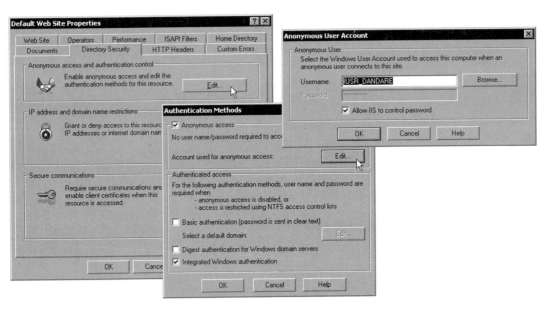

When set, the checkbox marked Allow IIS to control password specifies that IIS will automatically extract the correct password for the IUSR account from Windows and use it when requesting resources on behalf of the user. It is checked by default, which means that you won't break the web service if you change the password for this account in the Computer Management tool at some point in the future.

Authorization in Windows 2000

So, providing that our user has been successfully authenticated, what happens next? We mentioned in the previous section that a user will only be able to access the resource they requested if the account they authenticated with has appropriate permission for that resource. These permissions are held in an Access Controls List (ACL) for each resource. Windows manages these ACLs in a range of ways – for example Windows Explorer is used to manage the ACLs for files and folders on local and network drives.

Open the Properties dialog for any file or folder in Windows Explorer and select the Security page. This shows the accounts and groups that have access to the file or folder, and the permissions for each one. The Advanced button allows you to control the options in more detail, giving up to 13 different read/write/delete option combinations and the ability to propagate the permissions to child objects and inherit permissions from parent folders:

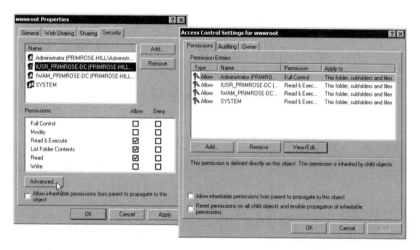

Other applications and services also rely on Windows accounts. For example, Microsoft SQL Server allows permissions to be set up for any Windows account. This means the account that the user is authenticated with can often be used to access all the resources they need:

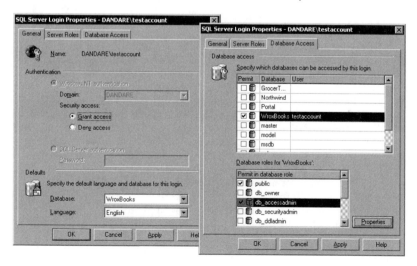

Authorization in IIS

There is one other area where security is applied to a web application or web site. IIS accesses resources on behalf of the user with either its own anonymous access account (the IUSR account) or with the account credentials that the user provides when anonymous access is disabled. However, on a different level, it also decides what they can do with the resource they have accessed.

The central section of the Home Directory page of the Properties dialog for a web site or directory specifies the type of operation that the user can perform within this site or directory. You can specify Script source access, Read, and/or Write:

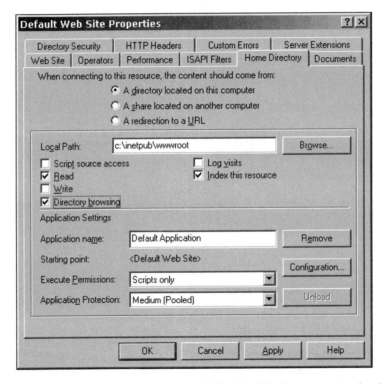

Remember, however, that this is separate from the ACLs that Windows contains for that resource. And this setting is applied on a web site or directory basis, and not on a per-user basis. The settings here affect all users.

What they do offer is an added layer of protection. For example, by default, users are prevented from writing to a web site directory through IIS, and they are also prevented from downloading any script files – these can only be executed so that the source code is not visible. Of course, you can change these settings (and others shown in this dialog) to suit your own application requirements.

However, if you decide to offer – for example – write access, you must also set the appropriate permissions on the Windows ACL for the disk folders. As in all security scenarios, when settings for a resource conflict like this, the most restrictive ones will be applied. In other words, if the ACL says you can't write to the folder, allowing Write access in IIS will have no effect.

ASP.NET Security Overview

Having briefly overviewed the security features provided by the operating system and IIS, the next step is to understand how these relate to the security features available within ASP.NET. As we said earlier, the process of authenticating users and authorizing their requests for resources is like a chain – the operating system and IIS have their own unique parts to play initially, as the request arrives at the server. Afterwards, providing that access is not denied by IIS, the request is passed to ASP.NET for processing and fulfilment.

The ASP.NET Security Process

The next schematic shows the process within ASP.NET in more detail. After IIS has checked the user's IP address and domain to ensure that they are allowed access, it authenticates the user. Remember that the "user" may be the IUSR account if anonymous access is enabled. At this point IIS spawns an instance of the ASP application that holds the resource the user requested, or passes the request into an already executing instance of the application:

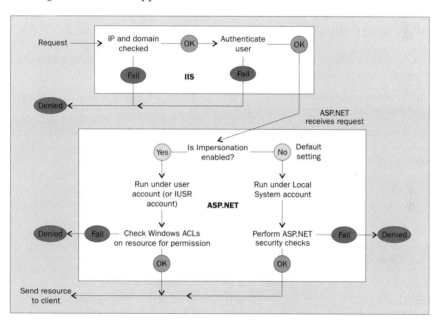

ASP.NET Impersonation

The first step within ASP.NET is to see if the application is configured to use **impersonation**. This is a similar concept to the way that IIS impersonates users with its own IUSR account. However, in this case, impersonation is used to decide whether the user's request should be executed under the context of their account, or that of a local system-process account that ASP.NET uses for anonymous requests.

This is a confusing concept to grasp at first. The added complexity comes from the fact that ASP.NET uses the dynamic compilation features of the .NET Framework. It needs to write to the drive in various places to create temporary files and compiled assemblies. The IUSR account has only limited permissions on the local machine, and so is not suitable without some reconfiguration. This is intentional because it is also the account used by IIS to access resources like HTML pages, documents, and zip files that are not executed as part of the .NET framework.

The account that is actually used for executing ASP.NET resources when impersonation is not enabled is controlled by the <processModel> *element in the* machine.config *configuration file. The username and password attributes specify which account is used. The defaults for normal use are* userName="SYSTEM" *and* password="AutoGenerate". *We'll look at this topic in more detail at the end of the chapter.*

If impersonation **is** enabled in an ASP.NET application then:

❑ If anonymous access **is** enabled in IIS (the default) the request is made under the context of the IIS anonymous access account (IUSR_*machinename* by default).

❑ If anonymous access is **not** enabled in IIS, the request is made under the context of the authenticated user (their own Windows account).

❑ In either case, permissions for the account are checked in the Windows ACL for the resource(s) the user requested, and a resource is only available if the account they are running under is valid for that resource.

If impersonation is **not** enabled in an ASP.NET application (the default) then:

❑ If anonymous access **is** enabled in IIS (the default) the request is made under the context of the system-level process account.

❑ If anonymous access is **not** enabled in IIS, the request is made under the context of the authenticated user (their own Windows account).

❑ In either case, permissions for the account are checked in the Windows ACL for the resource(s) the user requested, and a resource is only available if the account they are running under is valid for that resource.

Other security checks are also possible within ASP.NET. The availability of these checks depends on the type of security specified. We'll overview the various options next, and look at these in more detail as we go through the chapter.

The ASP.NET Security Options

ASP.NET provides a range of different options for implementing security and restricting user access in a web application. All these options are configured within the web.config file located in the root folder of the application. We looked at the main features of web.config and how it is used in chapter. In this chapter, we'll focus just on the security configuration sections.

Important Points When Using Security in ASP.NET

Before we get too involved, however, there are a couple of things that we need to keep in mind when working with ASP.NET security:

❑ You don't have to change any of the default settings in **Internet Services Manager**, or change the permissions assigned to files or resources when using the security features that are configured for ASP.NET in the web.config file. The examples we use in this chapter work fine with the default settings. However, you can tighten security by editing these settings as well, as we describe later in the chapter when we look at the various configuration options.

❑ Many of the options you configure within `web.config` are applied automatically to any directory in which you place the `web.config` file. This applies to the authorization settings you make in the `<authorization>` section. However, this is not the case with the authentication security configuration settings in the `<authentication>` section. To use the authentication techniques we describe here, you must place the `web.config` file in the root folder of a web site (the **Home Directory**) or configure the directory that contains `web.config` as a virtual root or virtual application in Internet Services Manager. Afterwards, remember to access the application through this alias.

The Types of Authentication and Authorization

ASP.NET provides three types of authentication and authorization, or you can just rely on IIS to do all the work for you. The options are:

Type	Name	Description
Windows built-in authentication	Windows	The initial authentication is performed by IIS through Basic, Digest, or Integrated Windows authentication. The requested resources are then accessed under the context of this account. The `web.config` file can specify the accounts that are valid for the whole or parts of the application.
Passport-based authentication	Passport	This option uses a centralized web-based authentication service provided by Microsoft that offers single login and core profile services for member sites.
Forms-based authentication	Forms	Unauthenticated requests are automatically redirected to an HTML form page using HTTP client-side redirection. This is similar to custom authentication methods used in previous versions of ASP, but it provides much of the functionality as part of the framework of ASP.NET. The user provides their login credentials and submits the form. If the application authenticates the request, the system issues a cookie that contains the credentials, or a key for re-acquiring the identity. The client browser then sends the cookie with all subsequent requests, and the user can access the application while they retain this cookie.
Default (IIS) authentication	None	*The default.* Impersonation can still be used, but access control is limited to that specified within IIS. Resources are accessed under the context of a local system process account, or the IUSR account if impersonation is enabled.

To specify the type of authentication we want to use in an ASP.NET application or directory we provide the **Name** shown above in the `<authentication>` section of `web.config`:

```
<configuration>
...
<system.web>

  <authentication mode="Windows|Passport|Forms|None">
    authentication options used for the application
  </authentication>
```

```
    <authorization>
       users and roles that have access to the application
    </authorization>

    <identity>
       if application should run under a different account
    </identity>

  </system.web>
  ...
  </configuration>
```

The other two elements within the `<system.web>` section of `web.config` that we're interested in are used to specify the details of how authentication should be carried out. The `<authorization>` section is used to specify which users or groups can and cannot access the application. The `<identity>` section is used to specify if impersonation is enabled – in other words whether to run under the user (or IUSR) account, the system process account, or a different account that you specify. You'll see how we use these sections of the file when we look at each type of authentication in more detail next.

Using Windows Authentication in ASP.NET

Windows authentication is best suited to situations like a corporate Intranet web site or web application where you know in advance which users will be accessing your site. This is because you have to set up an account within Windows for each user, and provide them with the username and password (the login credentials) they'll need to access the site.

Of course, in an Intranet scenario, or an application where you can classify users into groups, you can set up an account for each group and allow all users who know the relevant username and password to access the application under this single account.

> *Note that we aren't referring to Windows account groups here – we're using the term "group" simply to signify several users who will have the same access rights as each other.*

An example would be to set up a Windows account named siteadmins, and allow all administrators to log into the application using this account. Just bear in mind that this will not allow you to audit the actions of each user, as they will all be accessing resources under the same account credentials. However, this can be a suitable solution in many scenarios.

Setting Up Windows Authentication

To set up an application or a section of an application to use Windows authentication, you simply specify this authentication mode and then turn on impersonation within the `<identity>` element:

```
<configuration>
...
<system.web>
  <authentication mode="Windows" />
  <identity impersonate="true" />
</system.web>
...
</configuration>
```

Now, each user will access resources under the context of the account that they logged into IIS with. The `<identity>` element is only used with Windows authentication, and not with the other types of authentication that we'll meet later.

Specifying Users and Groups

As well as simply specifying Windows authentication, you can also provide a list of users and groups that will be able to access the application. This is done within the `<authorization>` section of the web.config file, with a series of `<allow>` and `<deny>` elements.

The general form of each of these elements is:

```
<allow roles="comma-separated list of Windows account group names"
       users="comma-separated list of Windows user account names"
       verb="GET|POST|HEAD"
/>
```

```
<deny roles="comma-separated list of Windows account group names"
      users="comma-separated list of Windows user account names"
      verb="GET|POST|HEAD"
/>
```

The `<allow>` and `<deny>` element must contain either a `roles` or a `users` attribute. It does not have to contain both, and the `verb` attribute is always optional. To specify a domain user account, you include the domain name followed by a backslash and the username, for example MyDomainName\MyUserName. There are also special values that refer to built-in account groups, such as Everyone, BUILTIN\Administrators, etc.

To specify a local (machine) account you just use the machine name in place of the domain name. There is no way to specify a domain account without the actual domain (that is no short-cut that means "use the local domain"), so you must edit the list if you change the domain name or move the application to another domain.

There are also two special symbols that you can use:

- ❏ An asterisk (`*`) means all `users`, `roles`, or `verbs`, depending on the attribute it is used in.

- ❏ A question mark (`?`) means 'anonymous access'. In the case of Windows authentication, this is the account set up in IIS for anonymous access. This character can only be used within the `users` attribute.

The default configuration for a server is in the file machine.config, stored in the directory C:\WINNT\Microsoft.NET\Framework\ [*version*]\CONFIG\. It contains a single `<allow>` element that permits all users to access ASP.NET resources:

```
<authorization>
  <allow users="*" />
</authorization>
```

The `<allow>` and `<deny>` elements are merged for all configuration files in the application path, starting with the root (default) configuration file machine.config, and including all web.config files in folders below this application directory. Rules that are higher up in the hierarchy (that is, nearer the application directory) take precedence over those in web.config files below them (nearer the root).

Once the merged list of `<allow>` and `<deny>` elements is created, they are processed from top to bottom, and the best match for a user or role is selected. Processing doesn't just stop when the first match is found, but continues throughout all the entries fine-tuning the selection. This means that a specific reference to a user will take precedence over a `role`, and over a wildcard rule that uses the asterisk character. The merge process also gives `<deny>` elements precedence over `<allow>` elements, so that you can allow a Windows account group using `<allow roles="..." />`, but deny specific users that are within that account group using `<deny users="..." />`.

So, to control access to a specific application or a directory within an application, we can add a `web.config` file to that directory, which contains something like this:

```
<configuration>
...
<system.web>
  <authorization>
    <allow roles="MyDomainName\SalesDept"
           users="MyDomainName\billjones,MyMachineName\marthasmith" />
    <deny users="*" />
  </authorization>
</system.web>
...
</configuration>
```

This will permit access to the application for the domain-level account named billjones from the domain named MyDomainName and the local (machine) account named marthasmith, plus all members of the domain-level account group named SalesDept. All other users will be denied access.

Specifying HTTP Access Types

We can also use the `<allow>` and `<deny>` elements to control the type of HTTP action that a user can take when accessing an application or directory by using the `verb` attribute:

```
<configuration>
...
<system.web>
  <authorization>
    <allow verb="GET" users="*" />
    <allow verb="POST" users="MyDomainName\marthasmith" />
    <deny verb="POST" users="*" />
  </authorization>
</system.web>
...
</configuration>
```

This will allow the domain-level account named marthasmith to send POST requests to the application (that is, to submit an HTML form), but all other users will only be able to send "GET" requests. And, of course, we can combine this access control setting with the list of groups and users, by adding the `verb` attribute to the previous example that used the `roles` and `users` attributes.

We can also use the `<location>` element to specify more than one `<system.web>` section, applying each of these sections to a specific path or file. This is useful for setting different permissions for subfolders or files using a single `web.config` file. For example we can specify that a file named `mypage.aspx` will have different authorization settings from the rest of the files in a folder using:

```
<configuration>
...
<system.web>  <!-- default for this application -->
  <authorization>
    <allow verb="GET" users="*" />
    <allow verb="POST" users="MyDomainName\marthasmith" />
    <deny verb="POST" users="*" />
  </authorization>
</system.web>
<location path="mypage.aspx">  <!-- only applies to this file -->
  <system.web>
    <authorization>
      <allow verb="GET" users="*" />
      <allow verb="POST" users="MyDomainName\billjones" />
      <deny verb="POST" users="*" />
    </authorization>
  </system.web>
</location>
...
</configuration>
```

Running Under Another Specific Account

Finally, we can instruct ASP.NET to execute resources under a specific account, rather than the user account that was authenticated by IIS or the local system process account (which is normally used when impersonation is not enabled). This is done within the `<identity>` element:

```
<configuration>
...
<system.web>
  <identity impersonate="true"
            name="MyDomainName\MyUserName
            password="MyPassword" />
</system.web>
...
</configuration>
```

Here we're specifying that impersonation is enabled but, instead of using the system process account, ASP.NET should access all resources under the context of the domain-level account named **MyUserName** from the domain named **MyDomainName**. We also have to provide the password for the account, so that ASP.NET can present it to the operating system and other applications and services when it requires access to them.

> Note that the password will be visible in the file, and this could introduce a security risk.

IIS and Windows Security Settings for Windows Authentication

Remember that authentication and access control using Windows authentication depends on a Windows account being available for ASP.NET to use to access the requested resources. You can tighten security by using the ACLs on resources to allocate permission to just specific users, or to the accounts that the user will be running under. This isn't required, but does provide a second level of protection.

To be able to do this, you must be aware of which account is actually being used to access the resource, and give that account the appropriate permissions while removing any permissions that are not required. The following schematic should help:

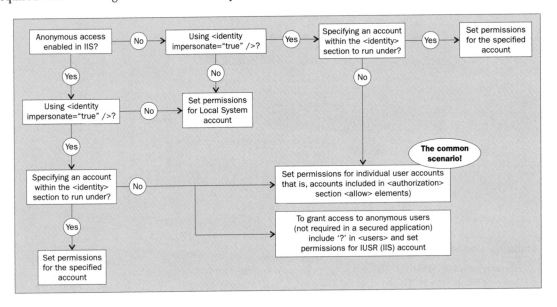

The Logon Process in Windows Authentication

When you access a resource in a secured application or virtual directory that does not allow anonymous access, you are always required to log on. However, if you are accessing the application or directory from the local machine or a machine on the same domain, you may not actually see the logon dialog. This is because – providing Integrated Windows authentication is enabled in Internet Services Manager (the default) – your browser will send your current Windows logon details in response to the logon challenge from the web server.

So, it's a good plan if you are building applications for the web (rather than for a corporate Intranet) to access the site from a machine that is not logged into the domain, as well as experimenting with one that is. On a machine that is not on the same domain (or a trusted domain), you will see the standard logon dialog:

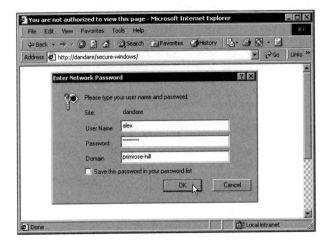

One useful way that you can tell what's going on as far as IIS authentication is concerned is to look at the page you get back if you make three attempts to access a secured resource with an invalid username or password. If anonymous access is **not enabled** in IIS, you get the standard IIS error page:

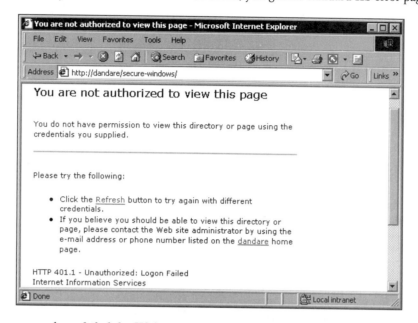

This is because you have failed the IIS logon process. However, if anonymous access **is enabled** within Internet Services Manager (the default), you are granted access and the request is passed to ASP.NET. It then detects that you don't have permission to access the resource (because your Windows account username and/or password are invalid) and it sends back its own error page:

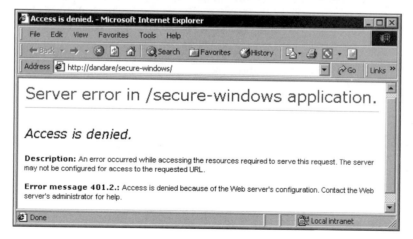

Later on in this chapter, we'll see an example of Windows authentication that you can use to help configure your applications and virtual directories.

Using Passport Authentication in ASP.NET

Windows authentication provides the most secure way of controlling access and securing your ASP.NET applications. However, it falls down if you want to establish a single-sign-on policy for several applications that are distributed across different servers and sites – especially if these are geographically separated. The only solution is to set up the same accounts on all the servers, perhaps by establishing a Windows 2000 "forest" using Active Directory so that all the servers are part of the same enterprise – even if they are on different domains.

But even this fails if you want to enable a system where users can be authenticated using the same credentials across multiple sites that you don't provide yourself. For example, you might want to build a solution where a user can log onto one of the well-known sites like Hotmail.com and then come to your site and be automatically authenticated based on the logon credentials they provided when they logged onto Hotmail.

This is possible using **Passport authentication**. Microsoft provides a "Passport Service" that can be used to authenticate users on any passport-enabled site, anywhere on the Internet. When they log onto a participating site, the browser or user agent sends their credentials to the passport service, which authenticates them and places a secure cookie on their machine. Then, when they access another participating site, the browser presents this cookie to the passport service to prove that the user has already been authenticated. The passport service then indicates who that user is to the new site so they can be properly authorized – that is, the new site can check if this user has permission to access the resource they've requested.

So, the power of the passport service is that a user can present the same credentials to any participating site, while only having to log in once during a session. When they close the browser, or indicate that they wish to log off, the cookie is destroyed and they must then log on again to re-access resources on any of the participating sites.

Setting Up Passport Authentication

Unfortunately, passport authentication doesn't come free – someone has to pay the running costs of the passport service. To set up passport authentication you must subscribe to the service and install special software on your web server to allow the process to work. Full details are available from http://www.passport.com/business/.

Once you've installed the software and subscribed to the service, you configure passport authentication in the web.config file:

```
<configuration>
...
<system.web>
  <authentication mode="Passport">
    <passport redirectUrl="internal|url" />
  </authentication>
</system.web>
...
</configuration>
```

The <passport> section supports a single attribute named redirectUrl. The default value (before you install and configure passport authentication) is internal, which means that unauthenticated requests will receive a generic error message created by your server. Any other string is assumed to be the URL of the passport service that unauthenticated requests will be redirected to for authentication.

696

Once passport authentication is enabled, the login process to your server goes something like this:

❑ The user requests a protected resource from your server. If they have already logged into the passport service, there will be an encrypted "ticket" in a cookie or the query string, and your server will access the passport service to get the user's identity.

❑ If there is no "ticket", or if it has expired, or is invalid, they are redirected to the passport service's login page on the main passport service servers. They present their credentials, are authenticated, and are redirected back to your server with an appropriate "ticket".

❑ Your server can now check the user's authorization and provide the protected resource if they have the relevant permission.

Using Forms-based Authentication in ASP.NET

The third type of authentication available in ASP.NET is an excellent solution for applications where the highest levels of security are not required. **Forms-based authentication** (sometimes referred to as cookie-based authentication) automates many of the tasks that you would normally perform in earlier versions of ASP to build custom authentication solutions. Forms-based authentication also removes the unintuitive Windows Logon dialog, allowing you to replace it with an attractive custom form or integrate the login controls (basically two text boxes and a button) into existing pages.

The following schematic describes the process. As usual, the request is received by IIS, which checks that the IP address and domain of the user are permitted. IIS also authenticates the user if anonymous access is disabled, although in this scenario you will almost always allow anonymous access, as the access control is being performed by ASP.NET.

Once IIS is happy with the user's request, it passes it to ASP.NET, where the first step is to see if there is an authentication cookie within the request headers:

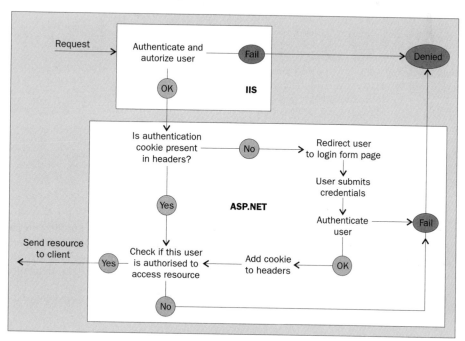

The forms authentication process generates this cookie when the user logs into the application. If it's present, we know that they have already been authenticated and the cookie contains their identity. ASP.NET then checks that this user is authorized to access the resource they requested, and if so sends it to them. If not, they are denied access.

If the cookie is not present in the request headers, the user is automatically redirected to a custom login page that we create ourselves. The user enters their credentials into this login page and submits it to our application, where these credentials are automatically checked to authenticate the user. Providing that they are recognized, an authentication cookie is added to the headers and the request is sent to the next stage of the process to be authorized. As before, ASP.NET checks to see if this user is authorized to access the resource they requested, and if so sends it to them. If not, they are denied access.

Setting Up Forms-based Authentication

Like all other ASP.NET security settings, forms-based authentication is configured within the web.config file for an application or a virtual directory. The <authentication> section carries the value forms for the mode attribute, and within the element itself we add more elements to specify how the authentication of users will behave:

```
<configuration>
...
<system.web>
  <authentication mode="Forms">
    <forms name="cookie-name"
           path="cookie-path"
           loginurl="url"
           protection="All|None|Encryption|Validation"
           timeout="number-of-minutes" >
      <credentials passwordformat="Clear|SHA1|MD5">
        <user name="user-name" password="user-password" />
        <user name="user-name" password="user-password" />
        ... more users listed here ...
      </credentials>
    </forms>
  </authentication>
  <machineKey validationKey="AutoGenerate|key"
              decryptionKey="AutoGenerate|key"
              validation="SHA1|MD5"/>
</system.web>
...
</configuration>
```

The attributes of the <forms> element define:

❑ The name that will be assigned to the cookie.

❑ The path that the cookie is valid for. This is usually set to "/" to indicate the complete site. If not, and the site contains links that are not in the correct letter case (that is an <a> element with href="mypage.aspx" where the actual page name is MyPage.aspx), then the cookie will not be returned by some browsers. This will cause the login form to be displayed again.

❑ The loginurl that specifies the virtual path to the login form page.

❑ The protection level required for the cookie. The settings are: All (the default), which uses both data validation (based on the <machineKey> element) and encryption (Triple DES if available if the key is at least 48 bytes long); None (should be used only for personalization purposes); Encryption (the cookie is encrypted but data validation is not performed); Validation (validation is performed but the cookie is not encrypted).

❑ The timeout in minutes before the cookie expires on the user's machine and the server.

Within the <forms> element is:

❑ An optional <credentials> element that specifies the encryption algorithm used to encrypt the users password in the web.config file. Within this element there can be a series of optional <user> elements, which between them specify the users who will be able to access the protected resources.

We can also specify an optional <machineKey> element within the <system.web> section, which specifies the keys and method to be used to encrypt the cookie contents. In general you will omit this element and allow a key to be created automatically. However, it can be useful in a situation like a web farm, where you want all machines to use the same key. The key length must match the number of characters required for the encryption level and method that is used. This entry in the default machine.config file specifies that the keys are auto-generated:

```
<machineKey validationKey="AutoGenerate"
            decryptionKey="AutoGenerate"
            validation="SHA1" />
```

So, an example web.config file might look like the following. Remember that the <credentials> and <machineKey> sections are optional. Our example also lists some users, and you can see that the passwords are encrypted in this case. We'll see where we get these values from later in the chapter.

```
<configuration>
...
<system.web>
  <authentication mode="Forms">
    <forms name="MyNewApp" path="/" loginUrl="/main/login.aspx"
           protection="All" timeout="30" >
      <credentials passwordFormat="SHA1">
        <user name="billjones"
              password="87F8ED9157125FFC4DA9E06A7B8011AD80A53FE1" />
        <user name="marthasmith"
              password="93FB8A49CC350BAEB2661FA5C5C97959BD328C50" />
        <user name="joesoap"
              password="5469541CA9236F939D889B2B465F9B15A09149E4" />
      </credentials>
    </forms>
  </authentication>
  <!-- keys usually only specified for a web farm -->
  <machineKey validationKey="3875f9...645a78ff"
              decryptionKey="3875f9...645a78ff"
              validation="SHA1" />
</system.web>
...
</configuration>
```

Note, that we do not use the <identity> element in forms-based authentication.

Creating a Login Form

After we've completed the configuration tasks with `web.config`, what about the things we have to do as developers to complete the setup of forms-based authentication? We need a form that will be used to collect the user's credentials, and code to process these credentials. The following listing shows a simple example of the HTML section of the page:

```
<%@Page Language="VB" %>
<html>
<body>
<form runat="server">
  UserName: <input id="txtUsr" type="text" runat="server" /><p />
  Password: <input id="txtPwd" type="password" runat="server" /><p />
  <ASP:CheckBox id="chkPersist" runat="server" />
  Remember my credentials<p />
  <input type="submit" value="Login" runat="server"
                        onserverclick="DoLogin" />
  <div id="outMessage" runat="server" />
</form>
</body>
</html>
... script section goes here ...
```

This creates a login form page containing textboxes for the username and password, and a checkbox where the user can specify that their credentials are to be "remembered" so that they won't have to login again next time they visit the site. This is followed by a Login button that fires an event handler named `DoLogin` on the server, and a `<div>` element where we display a message if the user's credentials are incorrect:

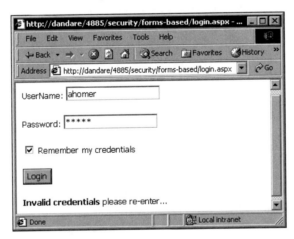

> To prevent the user's credentials being passed over the network in clear text, you should consider storing this form in a directory that has SSL (HTTPS) enabled. Once they are validated, the encrypted cookie can be used in the application over HTTP as usual. The content of the authentication cookie is just the encrypted session "ticket" – it does not contain the username or password.

Writing the Login Code

While forms-based authentication is a clever technology, it can't do everything automatically. We have to write code that authenticates the user and performs the other operations required, such as creating the cookie and redirecting the user to the page they originally requested. However, this is trivially simple.

All the classes used in ASP.NET security are in the `System.Web.Security` namespace of the class library. The class that handles forms-based security is called `FormsAuthentication`, and it exposes a whole range of properties and methods that we can use in our code. The most common methods are:

`Authenticate`	Checks to see if a username and password combination is valid by comparing it to the set of users specified within `web.config`.
`Redirect FromLoginPage`	Performs all the actions required once a user has been authenticated, including: creating the encrypted cookie, adding it to the request headers, and redirecting the user to the page they originally requested.
`SignOut`	Destroys the current encrypted cookie, effectively logging the user out of the application.
`SetAuthCookie`	Allows you to perform the tasks normally accomplished by the `RedirectFromLoginPage` method individually, and tailor them to a particular situation. This method creates the encrypted cookie, and adds it to the headers, but doesn't redirect the user.
`GetAuthCookie`	Returns the authentication cookie without adding it to the response headers. This is useful if you want to customize the cookie (for example change the path it applies to) before issuing it.
`GetRedirectUrl`	Returns the URL of the original page that the user requested before being redirected to the login page. Can be used in conjunction with `SetAuthCookie` to provide custom authentication when the `RedirectFromLoginPage` method is not being used.

So, to authenticate our user and return them to the page they originally requested, we just need to create an event handler that is executed when the Login button is clicked. In our login form, we specified the subroutine `DoLogin` as the value of the `onserverclick` attribute of the Login button. This is the event handler code we use to handle this event:

```
Sub DoLogin(objSender As Object, objArgs As EventArgs)
   If FormsAuthentication.Authenticate(txtUsr.Value, txtPwd.Value) Then
      FormsAuthentication.RedirectFromLoginPage(txtUsr.Value, _
                                          chkPersist.Checked)
   Else
      outMessage.InnerHtml = "<b>Invalid credentials</b> please re-enter."
   End If
End Sub
```

In this code, we start by checking to see if the username and password that were provided are valid within the list of users in `web.config`. If they are, the `Authenticate` method returns `True` and we can call the `RedirectFromLoginPage` method to create the cookie, add it to the request headers, and redirect the user to the page they originally requested. It's as simple as that.

How Long is a Login Valid for?

One interesting point is how long the authentication cookie will be valid for. If you don't specify a value for the `timeout` attribute in the `<forms>` element in `web.config`, the cookie only will remain on the user's machine for 30 minutes (the default setting in `machine.config`) or until they close their browser. However, we can set the `timeout` attribute in the `<forms>` element to over-ride this setting.

This means that they will be able to leave the site and come back to it again within 30 minutes providing that they haven't closed their browser (or deleted the cookie). Of course, as the user accesses pages within the site, the cookie will be updated with each response from the server, and so the timeout only comes into force the specified number of minutes after the last time they accessed a page. But, even if they leave their browser running, they will be effectively "logged out" after the timeout period. This provides a better level of security.

We also have the option to persist the cookie between sessions. When we call the `RedirectFromLoginPage` method, we specify a `Boolean` value for the second parameter. In our example code, this is the value of the `Checked` property of the checkbox control on the login page:

```
FormsAuthentication.RedirectFromLoginPage(username, persistcookie)
```

Passing the value `True` to the method causes it to create a cookie with a long expiry date and time (50 years from now!) so that the user will not have to log back into the site when they return again. Although most modern browsers store cookies on a per-user basis (providing that the client machine is set up to force users to log in), this can present a security risk. It's not difficult to hijack a cookie, and by doing so the hijacker will be automatically granted access to the site during the lifespan of that cookie. Nevertheless, it is a useful feature for low-security or personalization-only scenarios.

Finally, we can expire a cookie immediately on demand by calling the `SignOut` method. We can place a **Log Off** button or link on a page, and create an event handler that destroys the cookie and prevents the user accessing any other resources until they log in again. In the event handler all we need is:

```
FormsAuthentication.SignOut()
```

However, if a user has "stolen" a persistent cookie, this will not detect and remove it. Hence, persistent cookies should never be used for applications other than those performing basic personalization and requiring the minimum level of security.

Authorizing Users with Forms-Based Security

So far, we've only actually **authenticated** (or identified) the user – we haven't specified what resources they will be allowed to access. Unless we are happy for any authenticated user to access any of the resources within the site or directory (an unlikely scenario in a secured application), we **must** include an `<authorization>` section in `web.config` as well. If not, the default authorization level specified in the `machine.config` file will be used, and you'll recall that this file contains:

```
<authorization>
   <allow users="*" />
</authorization>
```

To allow only specified users to access the application, we add an appropriate `<authorization>` element to the `web.config` file for this site or directory. The format and content are the same as we described earlier when looking at Windows authentication and authorization – and the same rules apply:

```
<configuration>
...
<system.web>
  <authorization>
    <allow users="billjones,marthasmith,joesoap" verb="GET" />
    <allow users="marthasmith" verb="POST" />
    <deny users="?" />
  </authorization>
</system.web>
...
</configuration>
```

Note that we're using the '?' anonymous access wildcard in the `<deny>` element. In forms-based authentication, this indicates that only users we authenticate ourselves will be allowed access. Irrespective of which Windows account the user is running under (generally it will be the local system process in this case), they will only be permitted access if they are in the list of users in the `<allow>` element.

We can also get away with using just the single `<deny>` element that prevents unauthenticated access if we don't want to set any specific access permissions for the users we authenticate. In other words, providing that we are happy for all users that are listed in the `<authentication>` section to have access to all resources in the application using any type of HTTP method (POST, GET, HEAD), we can use:

```
<authorization>
  <deny users="?" />
</authorization>
```

> **Don't be tempted to try and set Windows ACL permissions on resources for the users you specify when using forms-based authentication. Even if Windows accounts do exist for these users, they are not used when the user logs on via forms-based authentication. All access will be performed under the context of the system process account (which must have access to the resource).**

Custom Lists of User Credentials

All our forms-based authentication configuration examples so far have used the `<credentials>` section of web.config to store the list of users that we authenticate requests against. In many cases this is not practical. Rather than manually editing a text file to add and remove users, you will often want to store user details elsewhere – maybe in a database table, an XML document, or even Active Directory. However, it's still useful to be able to take advantage of the other features that forms-based authentication provides, such as automatic redirection to a login page, encryption, and validation of the authentication cookie, and integration with the environment that allows you to retrieve the user's details elsewhere in your code (more details of this coming up later).

It's easy to accomplish lookups of user credentials in other data stores, as the examples at the end of the chapter demonstrate. For example, we can use the relational data access capabilities of .NET to retrieve values from a relational database using SQL statements or stored procedures, or we can use XML classes to read from XML documents.

Programmatic Security and Personalization

The techniques we've described so far can be used to control access to resources based on the principle of uniquely identifying a user through **authentication**, and then checking that user's access permission for a resource through **authorization**. This is sufficient to implement the common types of access control requirement for most applications.

However, there are times when we want to be able to control access on a more granular level, or just be able to tell within our code who the current user is. These two techniques are often referred to under the generic terms "**programmatic security**" and "**personalization**". We'll look at both of these next, as we see how we can get information about the currently logged-on user.

Roles and Identity Overview

Once a user has been authenticated, the system knows at least something about that user. At minimum, it knows the username (the **identity**) and the **type of authentication** that was carried out. In the case of a Windows authentication, it also knows which **roles** (that is, which Windows account groups) the user is a member of.

We can access this information in our code, and use it to tailor the way that our applications behave. For example, we can display different pages or change the content of pages depending on the specific user, or on the groups that they are members of. This is a very useful feature, as the only alternative would be to provide page content by creating multiple copies of the page, and setting up permission to access each page to the appropriate users. And even then, the only way that the user would know which page they should access would be to try them all. Not exactly a userfriendly approach!

There is also the situation where we allow each user to personalize their pages within an application – perhaps to show different content or perhaps just to change the font size, background color, etc. Again, we need to know who the user is so that we can build the appropriate pages. Perhaps one user wants to see the current news headlines on their "home" page in our application, while another just wants the daily "Dilbert" cartoon.

Getting the User Identity and Role

The technique we use to get the user's identity depends on the type of authentication we used originally. ASP.NET exposes a `User` object as a property of the current `HttpContext` object (the context within which the page is executing). The `User` object exposes a reference to an `Identity` object that describes the current user. This object provides a range of properties that we can use to identify our current user. The three we use most often are:

`Name`	Returns the username, or the name of the account that the user logged on with, including the domain name if it was a Windows domain account.
`IsAuthenticated`	Returns `True` if the current user has been authenticated.
`AuthenticationType`	Returns a string indicating the authentication method used – for example `"Forms"`, `"NTLM"`, `"Basic"`, `"Passport"`

Depending on the type of authentication used, the `Identity` property will actually be an instance of one of three different objects. For **Windows** authentication, the property returns a `WindowsIdentity` object, for **Passport** authentication it returns a `PassportIdentity` object, and for **Forms**-based authentication it returns a `FormsIdentity` object. The three properties listed above are common to all these objects:

```
strUserName = User.Identity.Name
blnAuthenticated = User.Identity.IsAuthenticated
strAuthType = User.Identity.AuthenticationType
```

However, the different `Identity` objects also expose properties that are specific to the type of authentication used. For example, the `WindowsIdentity` object exposes properties for the Windows security token, and `Boolean` values indicating if the account is a Guest account, an anonymous account, or a System account. The `FormsIdentity` object exposes the current users cookie "ticket" value, and the `PassportIdentity` object exposes a host of properties and methods that are specific to this type of authentication. A full list of all the properties and methods for each object is included in the .NET Framework Class Library section of the SDK.

The namespace containing the class that implements the `Identity` object (System.Web.Security) is imported by default, but to create a specific reference to a `WindowsIdentity` object we also need to import the `System.Security.Principal` namespace:

```
<%@Import Namespace="System.Security.Principal" %>
```

This allows us to cast the `User.Identity` to a `WindowsIdentity` object, and use the extra properties and methods it provides:

Checking the User's Role

If Windows authentication was used, it's possible to tell which Windows account group the current user is a member of. Or rather, to be more exact, it's possible to tell if the user is a member of the group that you specify. For security reasons, we can't enumerate the list of groups – instead we specify the group name in a call to the `IsInRole` method. This a method of the `User` object for the current context:

```
blnResult = User.IsInRole("MyDomainName\SalesDept")
```

This method is useful if we want to change the behavior of a page or application based on the Windows account group that the user is a member of. For example, we can display different menus or links pages for members of the Administrators group, or change the appearance of pages for members of a group named SalesDept compared to the appearance when a member of the AccountingDept group accesses them. To test for a local (machine-level) account group we include the machine name instead of the domain name:

```
blnResult = User.IsInRole("MyMachineName\SalesDept")
```

Using Built-in Account Groups

Windows 2000 includes several built-in groups, and it adds users to these groups automatically. For example, all user accounts are automatically members of the built-in Users group, and the administrator account is a member of the built-in Administrators group. To specify one of these built-in groups, we must include the word BUILTIN as though it is the domain name, for example:

```
blnResult = User.IsInRole("BUILTIN\Users")
blnResult = User.IsInRole("BUILTIN\Administrators")
```

However, instead of using the name of the group directly, we can substitute values from the enumeration named `WindowsBuiltInRole` to specify the groups that are built into Windows. This is useful because it will also detect the groups or individual accounts if we have renamed them, and will also work on platforms other than Windows 2000 and in other localized operating system languages. For example, using `WindowsBuiltInRole.Administrator` will include the built-in Administrator account even if we have renamed it. The full list of members of this enumeration is:

```
WindowsBuiltInRole.AccountOperator
WindowsBuiltInRole.Administrator
WindowsBuiltInRole.BackupOperator
WindowsBuiltInRole.Guest
WindowsBuiltInRole.PowerUser
WindowsBuiltInRole.PrintOperator
WindowsBuiltInRole.Replicator
WindowsBuiltInRole.SystemOperator
WindowsBuiltInRole.User
```

ASP.NET Security Examples

So far in this we've been involved mainly in the theory of security and access control in ASP.NET applications. In this section of the chapter, we'll look at some examples that use the different aspects of security and access control we've been exploring. The samples cover:

- ❑ Configuring a web application using Windows authentication
- ❑ Accessing the user's identity within this application
- ❑ Accessing the user's role within this application
- ❑ Configuring a web application using forms-based authentication
- ❑ Using different types of user credentials lists
- ❑ Accessing the user's identity within this application
- ❑ A simple personalization example

Obtaining the Example Files

The example files for this chapter can be downloaded from the Wrox Press web site at http://www.wrox.com/Books/Book_Details.asp?isbn=1861004885. Follow the links to the page containing the downloadable code. This includes a subfolder named `security`, in which you'll find the examples we use here. There is also a `default.htm` menu page in that folder:

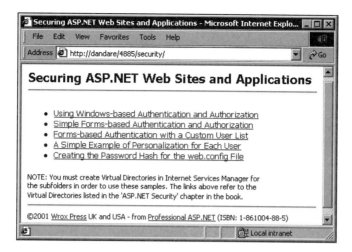

Setting Up the Examples on Your Server

Before you can use the examples we provide, there are a couple of things you need to do. First, you must create a virtual root to each of the subfolders containing the example pages with Internet Services Manager. In the Default Web Site on your server you create new virtual roots by right clicking and selecting New | Virtual Directory:

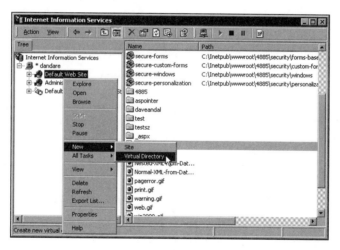

In the Wizard that appears, enter the appropriate alias from the list below, select the corresponding directory where you installed the example files, and then ensure that you leave the Read and Run Scripts permissions selected. The four aliases we used (and which are included in the links on the default.htm menu page) are:

❑ Alias `secure-forms` pointing to the folder in the examples named security\forms-based

❑ Alias `secure-custom-forms` for the folder named security\custom-forms-based

❑ Alias `secure-windows` for the folder in security\windows

❑ Alias `secure-personalization` for the folder named security\personalization

Creating the Windows Test Account and Groups

Our Windows authentication example uses a local user account named TestUser, and two local groups named TestGroup and NoMembers. You should create these using the Computer Management utility on your server – avoid using a domain controller machine as it will create domain-level accounts, rather than local accounts.

Right-click the Users entry in Local Users and Groups, and select New User. Enter the account name TestUser, a simple password that you can remember, uncheck User must change password at next logon, and check User cannot change password. Then click Create followed by Close:

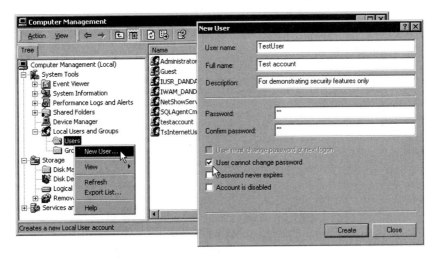

Now select the Groups entry, right-click, and select New Group. Name the new group TestGroup, click Add, and select the TestUser account and then your own domain or local user account as members of the group. Click Create to create this group, then enter the name NoMembers for another group and click Create again, followed by Close. As the name suggests, you shouldn't add any members to the NoMembers group:

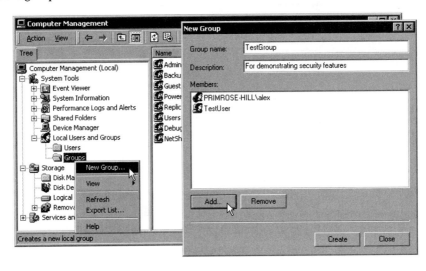

Creating the UserList Database

The only other task is to create the database of users for the "custom-forms-based" and "personalization" examples. We've provided a SQL script file named `make-security-db.sql` in the `security` folder of the samples that will do this for you. It adds a user named `anon` to SQL server for access to this database. Full instructions on creating the database are included in the file `database-readme.txt` in the same folder as the SQL script.

Windows Authentication Example

The first example, Using Windows-based Authentication and Authorization, demonstrates how we can use Windows authentication and authorization with a web site or web application directory. It uses a `web.config` file with the following structure:

```
<configuration>
<system.web>

  <authentication mode="Windows" />
  <identity impersonate="true" />

  <authorization>
    <allow roles="BUILTIN\Administrators"
           users="DANDARE\Administrator,DANDARE\TestUser" />
    <deny users="*" />
  </authorization>

</system.web>
</configuration>
```

> **Remember to edit the machine name when you run the example on your own server.**

This instructs the server to authenticate the user through IIS and Windows so they must login using a valid Windows account. We have also specified that we want to use impersonation, so the application will run under the context of this account. Then, in the `<authorization>` section, we specify that only members of the built-in Administrators group, the local Administrator account on the machine named DANDARE, and the local test user account named TestUser (on the same machine) can access the folder and its contents.

If we try and open the page under the context of a different account, we are denied access. In the following screenshot we've accessed the page from a machine that is not on the domain, and specified a username and password combination for an account that does exist on the target server, but which is not included in the list of users we specified within the `web.config` file:

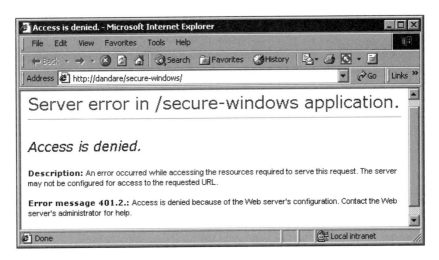

If we now log in using a suitable account that is included in the list in the web.config file, we see a page that shows our account login name (our username), and a selection of other information about our account. In the following screenshots, we've logged in using the TestUser account we created earlier and our own domain account that has the username alex. You can see the account name, complete with the machine or domain name, the authentication method used, the type of account, and the groups that the account is a member of:

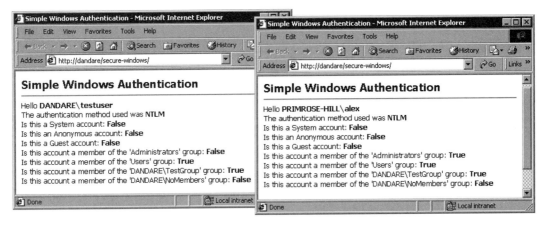

To experiment, you can edit the web.config file to specify different accounts and account groups that are to be permitted access to the folder and see the effects. Remember to close and reopen your browser each time you edit web.config so that you are not trying to access the pages using the previous logon credentials.

How This Example Works

Simply placing the web.config file into the folder containing our restricted pages is enough to look after authentication and authorization. The page you see when you do successfully log into the application (default.aspx) is just responsible for displaying the details of the account you use.

The page includes the `Import` directives required to use the Windows-based security features. We need this because we want to be able to access the account information using a `WindowsIdentity` object:

```
<%@Import Namespace="System.Security.Principal" %>
```

The HTML part of the page contains a single `<div>` element that we use to display the account details:

```
<div id="msgHello" runat="server" />
```

Checking If the User Has Been Authenticated

The code that gets information about the current user is in the `Page_Load` event, so it runs as the page is being created. The first thing we do is check that the user has in fact been authenticated. This will always be the case with the `web.config` file we're using, but it's a good idea to include this check. We access the `User` object via the current context of the page (it is a property of the integral `HttpContext` object), and get a reference to the user's `Identity` object from it. The `IsAuthenticated` property returns `True` if the user has been authenticated:

```
Sub Page_Load()

    'see if the user has been authenticated
    If User.Identity.IsAuthenticated Then
    ...
```

Accessing the User's Identity

Now we can get a reference to the actual `WindowsIdentity` object for this user. The `Identity` property returns an `Identity` object, and we cast this to a `WindowsIdentity` object (in VB this is done with the `CType` method). This is why we need to import the `System.Security.Principal` namespace, as it contains the definition of the `WindowsIdentity` class. From this `WindowsIdentity` object we can get more detailed information by calling the `GetCurrent` method, which also returns a `WindowsIdentity` object:

```
    ...
    'create a reference to a WindowsIdentity object that
    'represents this user's Indentity object
    Dim objIdentity = CType(User.Identity, WindowsIdentity)

    'get the current WindowsIdentity object for this user
    'this contains more specific information
    Dim objWinIdentity = objIdentity.GetCurrent()
    ...
```

We can use the original `WindowsIdentity` object returned by the `Users` property instead of creating the second one using the `GetCurrent` method. However, the `GetCurrent` method builds the identity using the operating system-level process token rather than just using the current HTTP Context object, and so contains information about the logon account that is not available when impersonation is turned off and we are running under the IIS anonymous (IUSR) account.

Displaying the Account Details

We can now access our `WindowsIdentity` object to display information about this user's account. We display the username and authentication type from the appropriate properties, and we can tell if the account is a System, Anonymous, or Guest account using three more of the properties of the `WindowsIdentity` object:

```
...
'display the properties
msgHello.InnerHtml = "Hello " & objWinIdentity.Name & "<br />" _
  & "The authentication method used was " _
  & objWinIdentity.AuthenticationType & "<br />" _
  & "Is this a System account: " _
  & objWinIdentity.IsSystem & "<br />" _
  & "Is this an Anonymous account: " _
  & objWinIdentity.IsAnonymous & "<br />" _
  & "Is this a Guest account: " _
  & objWinIdentity.IsGuest & "<br />" _
...
```

Accessing the User's Role

Now we can investigate which roles (that is, which Windows account groups) this user account belongs to. For this, we use the `IsInRole` method of the `User` object, and specify the account group we're checking for:

```
...
  & "Is this account a member of 'Administrators' group: " _
  & User.IsInRole("BUILTIN\Administrators") & "<br />" _
  & "Is this account a member of the 'Users' group: " _
  & User.IsInRole("BUILTIN\Users") & "<br />"
  & "Is this account a member of 'DANDARE\TestGroup' group: " _
  & User.IsInRole("DANDARE\TestGroup") & "<br />" _
  & "Is this account a member of 'DANDARE\NoMembers' group: " _
  & User.IsInRole("DANDARE\NoMembers")
...
```

Of course, you'll have to edit the code here to specify your own machine name – and you can add checks to see if the account is in other groups that exist on your own server and domain. However, it's easy to see from this how you can use "programmatic security" techniques to modify the behavior of an application based on the details of the user that are exposed by the `WindowsIdentity` object. We demonstrate a few of these techniques in conjunction with forms-based authentication in the final example of this chapter.

If Users Are Not Authenticated

The final few lines in the page complete the `If...Then` construct, and (just for completeness) display a message if the user accessed this page without being authenticated:

```
  Else
    msgHello.InnerHtml = "Hello, you were not authenticated"
  End If
End Sub
```

Forms-based Authentication Examples

The next two examples in this chapter demonstrate Forms-based authentication. The first one, Simple Forms-based Authentication and Authorization, uses the following `web.config` file:

```
<configuration>
<system.web>

  <authentication mode="Forms">
    <forms name="MyApp02" path="/" loginUrl="login.aspx"
           protection="All" timeout="30">
      <credentials passwordFormat="Clear">
        <user name="billjones" password="test" />
        <user name="marthasmith" password="test" />
        <user name="joesoap" password="test" />
      </credentials>
    </forms>
  </authentication>

  <authorization>
    <allow users="billjones,marthasmith,joesoap" />
    <deny users="?" />
  </authorization>

</system.web>
</configuration>
```

You can see that we've specified the page named `login.aspx` as the `loginUrl`, so this is the page that will be loaded when a user attempts to access the application when they have not been authenticated. We also include a `<credentials>` section that specifies the username and passwords for three users that will be permitted access to the application.

The `<authentication>` section that follows specifies that these three users are the only ones that will be permitted access – we include a `<deny users="?">` element to prevent any anonymous access to the application.

When you first access the `default.aspx` page in the protected folder, you are redirected to the login page. You must enter the credentials of one of the users specified in the `web.config` file (shown above):

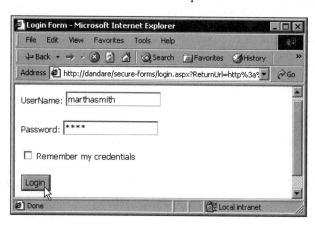

For the time being, leave the Remember my credentials checkbox unchecked, and click Login. If you got the username and password right, you'll be redirected to the default.aspx page. It displays the username that you entered and the type of authentication used:

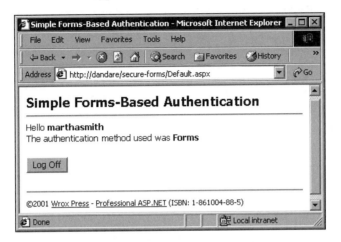

If you didn't get them right, you'll see a message appear below the Login button indicating that your credentials were invalid:

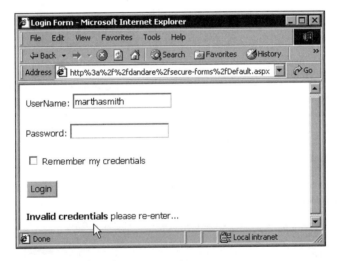

Using a Persistent Logon

Now close and reopen you browser and reload the default.aspx page. You will be redirected to the login page again. This time, check the Remember my credentials checkbox before you click Login to store a persistent cookie on your machine. Then close and reopen you browser, and reload the default.aspx page again. This time you are not redirected to the login page, and the server can extract and display your username and authentication method as before.

This is because you have the authentication cookie stored on your machine. To see the cookie that is used, open the Temporary Internet Files folder. The easiest way is to select Internet Options from the Tools menu in Internet Explorer, click Settings and View Files. Find the file named Cookie: [*Windows-user-name*] @ [*your-machine-name*] and double-click to open it and view the contents:

You can see that it doesn't make any sense at all due to the encryption – so it is quite safe to pass this cookie back and forth over the network or the Internet once the user has been authenticated.

Logging Off

Now go back to the page that displays your name and authentication type (the `default.aspx` page), and click the Log Off button. You are immediately redirected back to the logon page. The cookie holding your authentication details has been destroyed (not sent back to the browser), and so you must log in again to recreate it before you can access any restricted pages. You can also check your browser's Temporary Internet Files folder to confirm that the cookie is no longer there (press *F5* to refresh the list).

How This Example Works

When users first access an ASP.NET page in this folder, they are redirected to the page `login.aspx`. The HTML section of the `login.aspx` page contains a `<form>` with textboxes for the username and password, a checkbox where the user can specify a persistent logon, and a button to submit the form to the server. There is also a `<div>` element where we can display a message if the user cannot be authenticated:

```
<form runat="server">
   UserName: <input id="txtUsr" type="text" runat="server" /><p />
   Password: <input id="txtPwd" type="password" runat="server" /><p />
   <ASP:CheckBox id="chkPersist" runat="server" />
   Remember my credentials<p />
   <input type="submit" Value="Login" runat="server"
          onserverclick="DoLogin" /><p />
   <div id="outMessage" runat="server" />
</form>
```

The remainder of this page contains a single subroutine that is executed on the server when the user clicks the Login button. This is the same code as we discussed earlier in the chapter. First it authenticates the credentials provided against the list of users in `web.config` by calling the `Authenticate` method of the `FormsAuthentication` object, and passing it the username and password. If this returns `True` it redirects the user back to the page they originally requested – in our example this is `default.aspx`:

```
Sub DoLogin(objSender As Object, objArgs As EventArgs)

   If FormsAuthentication.Authenticate(txtUsr.Value, txtPwd.Value) Then
      FormsAuthentication.RedirectFromLoginPage(txtUsr.Value, _
                                               chkPersist.Checked)
   Else
      outMessage.InnerHtml = "<b>Invalid credentials</b> please re-enter."
   End If

End Sub
```

If the user cannot be authenticated, the `Else` section of the `If...Then` construct displays a message to this effect in the `<div>` element at the bottom of the page.

The default.aspx Page

If the user has been successfully authenticated, they will be redirected to the page default.apx (in our case, as this is the page that they attempted to load originally). The page contains a <div> element where we'll display some details about the user, and an HTML <form> on which there is a single submit button labelled Log Off:

```
<div id="msgHello" runat="server" /><p />
<form runat="server">
  <input type="submit" Value="Log Off" runat="server"
         onserverclick="DoSignOut" />
</form>
```

Accessing the User's Identity

Getting the user's name and authentication method is easy when using Forms-based authentication. We first check that they were authenticated (as in the previous Windows authentication example), and if so we access the properties of the User.Identity object. And, again as before, we display a message if the user was not authenticated:

```
Sub Page_Load()

  'see if the user has been authenticated
  If User.Identity.IsAuthenticated Then

    'display the properties
    msgHello.InnerHtml = "Hello " & User.Identity.Name & "<br />" _
                       & "The authentication method used was " _
                       & User.Identity.AuthenticationType

  Else

    msgHello.InnerHtml = "Hello, you were not authenticated"

  End If

End Sub
```

Logging a User Out of an Application

The Log Off button on this page has its onserverclick event set to DoSignOut. This is the name of the event handler that is executed when the user clicks this button. The code itself is trivial:

```
Sub DoSignOut(objSender As Object, objArgs As EventArgs)

  'destroy the users authentication cookie
  FormsAuthentication.SignOut()

  'and redirect them to the login page
  Response.Clear()
  Response.Redirect(Request.UrlReferrer.ToString())

End Sub
```

Once we've executed the SignOut method, we redirect the browser back to the referring page (in this case the "login" page), so that you can experiment and log on using a different account.

Encrypting the Passwords in web.config

One thing you may have noticed in the `web.config` file we used in this example is that the user's passwords are stored in plain text. We used this code:

```
   ...
   <credentials passwordFormat="Clear">
     <user name="billjones" password="test" />
     <user name="marthasmith" password="test" />
     <user name="joesoap" password="test" />
   </credentials>
   ...
```

This would be a security risk if anyone could get to see the `web.config` file. They cannot download the file from your site, as all requests for this file are blocked automatically by ASP.NET. However, local users might access it, and could then see the complete list of username/password combinations that are valid for the site. To prevent this, you can encrypt the passwords within the `web.config` file.

The delightfully named `HashPasswordForStoringInConfigFile` method (exposed by the `FormsAuthentication` object we used earlier) provides an easy way to do this. We've included an example page that takes a password and encrypts it using either the SHA1 or MD5 algorithm. These are the two encryption methods supported by ASP.NET.

Password Hashing Example

The page is named `hash-password.aspx` and is in the `security` folder of the samples we provide for this chapter. You can open it from the main menu page (`default.htm`) in the same folder. Simply select the encryption type, enter the password, and click the **Create Hash** button:

Now you can copy the password hash into the appropriate user's entry in web.config, and change the setting for the passwordFormat in the <credentials> element to suit the encryption method used:

```
...
<credentials passwordFormat="SHA1">
  <user name="billjones"
        password="87F8ED9157125FFC4DA9E06A7B8011AD80A53FE1" />
  <user name="marthasmith"
        password="2E1FA0D4D3B6CA2623EA6AF07624C3CD29D47344" />
<user name="joesoap"
        password="36854FAFECB73E79DC3DFF61E76CF24CF8B490CC" />
</credentials>
...
```

How the Password Hashing Example Works

The HTML section of this example page is just a simple <form> containing the two radio buttons, the textbox for the password, and a **Create Hash** button. There is also a <div> element that we use to display the result:

```
<form runat="server">
  Password Format:
  <input type="radio" value="SHA1" name="chkFormat"
         checked="true" runat="server" />
  SHA1  
  <input type="radio" value="MD5" name="chkFormat" runat="server" />
  MD5<p />
  Password: <input id="txtPwd" type="text" runat="server" /><p />
  <input type="submit" value="Create Hash" runat="server"
         onserverclick="DoHashPassword" /><p />
  <div id="outMessage" runat="server" />
</form>
```

Here's code to create the hash runs when the **Create Hash** button is clicked. It gets the encryption type from the selected radio button (using the Request.Form collection), and passes it, and the password, to the HashPasswordForStoringInConfigFile method. The result is then displayed in the <div> element:

```
Sub DoHashPassword(objSender As Object, objArgs As EventArgs)

  Dim strHash, strFormat As String

  'get the format name as a string from the radio button value
  strFormat = Request.Form("chkFormat")

  'create the hash using the password value provided
  strHash = FormsAuthentication.HashPasswordForStoringInConfigFile _
                                  (txtPwd.Value, strFormat)

  'and display the result
  outMessage.InnerHtml = strFormat & " Password Hash is: " & strHash

End Sub
```

Using Different Credential Lists

We mentioned earlier on, when looking at how forms-based authentication works, that you can substitute your own custom list of logon details for the list held in the `web.config` file. This is often a more robust solution – for example it allows you to store the list of users in a relational database or an XML document.

In particular, if you allow users to register themselves before being allowed access to resources, or if you're only using authentication to personalize the web site or application, a relational database is an obvious choice for the user list. You can update it with SQL statements or stored procedures on demand.

The example page, Forms-based Authentication with a Custom User List, demonstrates custom authentication against both an XML file and a relational database. It uses the following `web.config` file:

```
<configuration>
<system.web>

  <authentication mode="Forms">
    <forms name="MyApp01" path="/" loginUrl="login.aspx"
           protection="All" timeout="30">
    </forms>
  </authentication>

  <authorization>
    <deny users="?" />
  </authorization>

</system.web>
</configuration>
```

You can see that, in this case, we have no list of users (there is no `<credentials>` section). In the `<authorization>` section we have omitted the user list as well, simply leaving the `<deny users="?" />` element there. This means that we will allow anyone who **has** been authenticated to access the pages. Remember that the default `machine.config` file allows all users to access all resources unless you override this in an application.

An XML User List Document

We chose a simple format for our XML user list document to minimize the code required to access it. We've got a root element `<userlist>`, within which is a list of elements that are the usernames. The value of each element is that user's password:

```
<?xml version="1.0" ?>
<userlist>
  <billjones>test</billjones>
  <marthasmith>test</marthasmith>
  <joesoap>test</joesoap>
</userlist>
```

This file, named `userlist.xml`, is placed in the same folder as the login page. We'll see how we use it when we look at the code in that page shortly.

A User List in a Relational Database

We've also set up a simple table named Users in a relational database named UserList. It contains the same users, with varchar-type columns named UserName and Password. This table is used in the next example as well, so it contains an extra column named BGColor. There are also three more users, and you can see that the Password column values are encrypted for these users. Just ignore all this extra stuff for the time being:

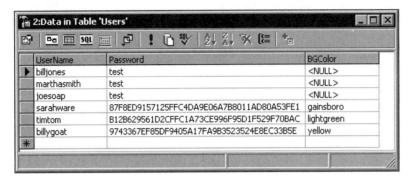

Running the Example

When you first access the example folder to load default.aspx, the forms-based security system detects that you haven't been authenticated and redirects you to the login page. This is similar to the previous example, but now contains a pair of radio buttons where you can select the user store you want to be authenticated against:

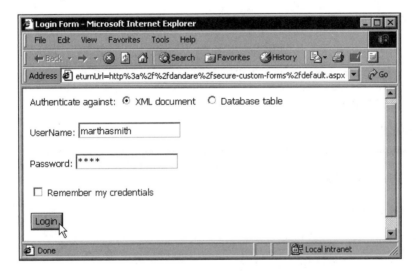

Note that you will have to install the database as described in the section "Creating the UserList Database" earlier in this chapter to be able to use the "Database table" option.

Enter the credentials of a suitable account (one with a plain-text password from the database table shown earlier – marthajones with the password test will do). If you get it wrong, a message is displayed as in the previous example. If you get it right, you can then access the default.aspx page:

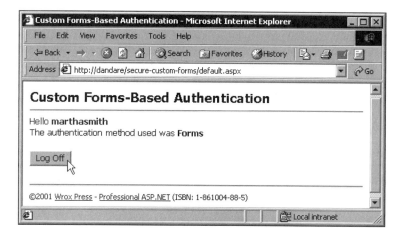

Again, as in the previous example, this page displays your username and the type of authentication used. It also contains the same Log Off button as the previous example.

How This Example Works

In the login.aspx page (where you are redirected if you haven't already been authenticated) we first import the namespaces we'll need. As code in this page contains references to classes for accessing relational data and XML documents, we need to add these namespaces to the page:

```
<%@Import Namespace="System.Data" %>
<%@Import Namespace="System.Data.OleDb" %>
<%@Import Namespace="System.Xml" %>
```

The HTML section of the page contains a `<form>` within which we place the same controls as the previous example for the username, password, persistent cookie checkbox, and Login button. However, at the top of the form, we also add the two radio buttons that allow you to choose the user list against which you want to be authenticated:

```
<form runat="server">

  Authenticate against:
  <input type="radio" id="chkXML" name="chkReadFrom" checked="true"
         runat="server" /> XML document  
  <input type="radio" id="chkSQL" name="chkReadFrom"
         runat="server" /> Database table<p />

  UserName: <input id="txtUsr" type="text" runat="server" /><p />
  Password: <input id="txtPwd" type="password" runat="server" /><p />

  <ASP:CheckBox id="chkPersist" runat="server" />
  Remember my credentials<p />

  <input type="submit" Value="Login" runat="server"
         onserverclick="DoLogin" /><p />

  <div id="outMessage" runat="server" />

</form>
```

The Login Code

When the Login button is clicked, our event handler named DoLogin is executed. In this, we first create a suitable connection string to access the database we're using. *You'll need to edit this to specify the server where you created the UserList database.* After that, we collect the values for the username and password from the form controls, and declare a flag variable to indicate if validation of the users credentials was successful. We set the default value of this variable to False:

```
Sub DoLogin(objSender As Object, objArgs As EventArgs)

  'specify the connection string - edit to suit your database
  Dim strConnect As String
  strConnect = "provider=SQLOLEDB.1;data source=[your-server];" _
    & "initial catalog=UserList;uid=anon;pwd="

  'get username and password from form
  Dim strUsr As String = txtUsr.Value
  Dim strPwd As String = txtPwd.Value

  'set a flag to indicate successful authentication
  Dim blnIsAuthenticated As Boolean = False    'default value
  ...
```

Validating the Credentials Against the XML User List Document

Now we can check to see which list of users was selected in the form by checking the value of the radio button with the id value of chkXML. If this is Checked we are authenticating against an XML document, so we can create the physical path to the document and load it into a new instance of an XmlDocument object:

```
  ...
  'see which method we're using to authenticate the user
  If chkXML.Checked Then

    'load the XML document containing the user credentials
    Dim strCurrentPath As String = Request.PhysicalPath
    Dim strXMLPath As String = Left(strCurrentPath, _
             InStrRev(strCurrentPath, "\")) & "userlist.xml"

    'create a new XmlDocument object
    Dim objXMLDoc As New XmlDocument()

    Try

      'load the XML file into the XmlDocument object
      objXMLDoc.Load(strXMLPath)

    Catch objError As Exception

      'display error details
      outMessage.innerHTML = "Error accessing XML document.<br />" _
          & objError.Message & "<br />" & objError.Source
      Exit Sub  ' and stop execution

    End Try
    ...
```

Providing that we loaded the file without an error, we can use the `GetElementsByTagname` method to return an `XmlNodeList` containing the node for this username. From that, we can access the value of the `#text` child node of the element to get the password. If this matches the value entered by the user, we know that they are a valid user so we set the `blnIsAuthenticated` flag variable to `True`:

```
...
'create a NodeList collection of all matching child nodes
'there should be only one for this user
Dim colUser As XmlNodeList
colUser = objXMLDoc.GetElementsByTagname(strUsr)

'see if we found an element with this username
If Not colUser Is Nothing Then

  'check if the value of the element (the child #text node)
  'is equal to the password that the user entered
  If strPwd = colUser(0).FirstChild().Value Then
    blnIsAuthenticated = True
  End If

End If
...
```

Validating the Credentials Against the Users Database Table

If the user specified authentication against our database table, the section of code in the `Else` part of the `If...Then` construct will be executed. Like the XML code we just used, this is quite simple, following the techniques we demonstrated in the data access chapters earlier in this book.

We create a suitable SQL statement that will extract the users' password from the row that contains their username and password (you'll see why we chose to return the password shortly). Then we create and open a connection to the database and execute the SQL statement, returning a `DataReader` object that contains the password if a matching row was found in the database:

```
...
Else

  'create a suitable SQL statement to retrieve the values
  Dim strSQL As String
  strSQL = "SELECT Password FROM UserTable WHERE UserName='" _
      & strUsr & "' AND Password='" & strPwd & "'"

  Try

    'create a new Connection object and open it
    Dim objConnect As New OleDbConnection(strConnect)
    objConnect.Open()

    'create a new Command using connection object and SQL statement
    Dim objCommand As New OleDbCommand(strSQL, objConnect)

    'declare a variable to hold a DataReader object
    Dim objDataReader As OleDbDataReader

    'execute SQL statement against Command to fill the DataReader
    objDataReader = objCommand.ExecuteReader()
    ...
```

Most relational databases are set up to do case-insensitive text matching in a WHERE clause unless you use a specific function or set options before executing the query. It's easier to return the password from the database and do a case-sensitive comparison in the event handler code (unless we aren't bothered about matching case). If the match succeeds, we can set our flag to indicate that this username and password combination is valid, then close the DataReader object and the database connection:

```
...
'if we get a row back, check password for same letter case
'(usually a SQL SELECT WHERE clause is not case sensitive)
If objDataReader.Read() Then
    If objDataReader("Password") = strPwd Then
      blnIsAuthenticated = True
    End If
End If

'close the DataReader and Connection
objDataReader.Close()
objConnect.Close()

Catch objError As Exception

'display error details
outMessage.InnerHtml = "Error accessing database.<br />" _
    & objError.Message & "<br />" & objError.Source
Exit Sub  ' and stop execution

End Try

End If
...
```

Authenticating the User

Now we can actually tell ASP.NET that we have validated the user's credentials and that they should be authenticated and receive the appropriate cookie so that they can access our application. If our flag variable is True, we simply call the RedirectFromLoginPage method, and specify the username and whether to persist the authentication cookie on their machine:

```
...
If blnIsAuthenticated Then
    FormsAuthentication.RedirectFromLoginPage(txtUsr.Value, _
                                              chkPersist.Checked)
Else
    outMessage.InnerHtml = Invalid credentials, please re-enter."
End If

End Sub
```

Encrypting the Passwords

Like our first example, we've used un-encrypted passwords in both the database table and the XML document. If there is a risk of these being viewed by unauthorized personnel, you may prefer to encrypt the passwords. One problem with this approach is if you need to provide passwords for users who forget them, as hashing can't be reversed to get the original value. Of course, if this feature isn't a requirement or if you'll just issue a new password, then that problem goes away.

With encrypted password hashes, the authentication process changes. The steps you would take are:

❑ Encrypt all the user passwords and replace the plain text ones in the database table and/or XML document with the encrypted version.

❑ In your login pages, get the password that the user provides from the login form controls and encrypt this using the same encryption algorithm.

❑ Compare the resulting hash with the encrypted password hash in your database or XML file.

We'll use this technique in the next example.

Simple Personalization Example

The final example in this chapter, A Simple Example of Personalization for Each User, demonstrates how we can implement personalization features much more easily in ASP.NET than in previous versions of ASP, and at the same time demonstrates more uses for "programmatic security".

When you open the example page, it immediately redirects you to the login page, as in the previous examples. You should login using the username timtom and password letmein. After being authenticated, you'll see a simple default.aspx page that contains a couple of (dummy) hyperlinks and the customary Log Off button:

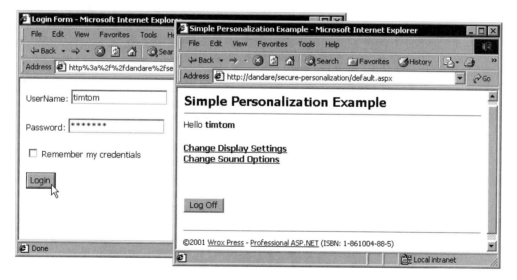

Now log off and login again using the username sarahware and password test. This time, you get a different colored background and more (dummy) hyperlinks:

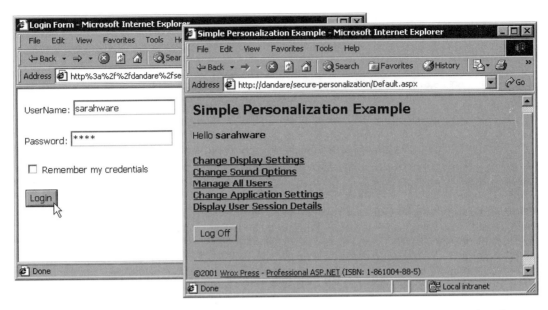

The login and `default.aspx` pages we use here are basically the same as those we used in the previous example, but with a few new twists. We still use a relational database to hold the user's credentials, but now (as you've seen) we also personalize the pages for each user. Try the username billygoat with the password help to see another example.

We also use encrypted passwords in the database in this example, as you can see in this screenshot of the database table contents. We include a column that contains the page background color for this user:

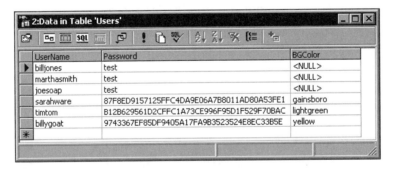

How This Example Works

The HTML section of the login page is identical to the earlier Forms-based examples, but it contains slightly different code in the `DoLogin` event handler. This time, after we create the connection string and collect the values entered by the user from the form controls, we create an SHA1 hash of the password:

```
Sub DoLogin(objSender As Object, objArgs As EventArgs)

  'specify the connection string - edit to suit your database
  Dim strConnect As String
  strConnect = "provider=SQLOLEDB.1;data source=[your-server-name];" _
          & "initial catalog=UserList;uid=sa;pwd=;"
```

```
'get username and password from form
Dim strUsr As String = txtUsr.Value
Dim strPwd As String = txtPwd.Value


'create the SHA1 hash of the password provided by the user
Dim strHash As String
strHash = FormsAuthentication.HashPasswordForStoringInConfigFile( _
                                            strPwd, "SHA1")


'set a flag to indicate successful authentication
Dim blnIsAuthenticated As Boolean = False    'default value
```

Next, we declare a variable to hold the value for the page background that we'll be extracting from the database table. Obviously, in your own applications, you'll add code, here and in the following SQL statement, to extract other values that you store in the table to personalize the application in other ways:

```
Dim strBGColor As String    'user's saved background color
```

Authenticating the User

To see if the username/password that the user entered is valid, we only have to look up the appropriate row in the database table. If it exists, we know that they can be authenticated. If not, we'll deny them access. In this case, because we've created an SHA1 hash for the password, we don't have to worry about matching letter case. The actual hash that the algorithm creates takes into account the case of the letters, and a different case for one or more characters will create a different password hash.

So, there's no need to extract the password from the database table – our SQL statement just needs to retrieve the personalization value (or values if we've added more personalization settings). If we get a row back, we know that the username/password combination is valid:

```
'create a SQL statement to retrieve personalization values
Dim strSQL As String
strSQL = "SELECT BGColor FROM Users WHERE UserName='" _
      & strUsr & "' AND Password='" & strHash & "'"
```

One point to watch out for here is that users can spoof your page by entering values into the UserName and Password textboxes that will always evaluate to True when the SQL statement is executed. For example, if they enter the text b'or'1'='1 for the user name and password, the result could produce matching rows. To protect from this, you should either parse the strings they enter and remove all single quotes, or use the technique of retrieving the password from the database and comparing it with the value that the user entered.

Now we execute the SQL statement and get the results back in a DataReader object. Providing that there is a row returned, we can set our authentication flag and collect the personalization value(s) into the string variable(s) we created earlier:

```
Try
   ...
   'code as used in previous examples to create and open
   'the connection and execute the SQL statement here
   ...
```

```
        'if we get a row back we know that the user is authenticated
     If objDataReader.Read() Then

          blnIsAuthenticated = True

          'get user's preferred background color
          strBGColor = objDataReader("BGColor")

          'get other preference values as required
          '... etc ...

     End If
     ...
  End Try
```

We can now save the personalization value(s) in the user's Session object so we can access them within the application pages without having to keep going back to the database. We also tell ASP.NET to create the authentication cookie and redirect the user back to the page they originally requested:

```
     If blnIsAuthenticated Then

          'save background color in Session object
          Session ("BGColor") = strBGColor

          '... save other personalization settings here


          'redirect user to original page
          FormsAuthentication.RedirectFromLoginPage(strUsr, chkPersist.Checked)
     Else
          outMessage.InnerHtml = "<b>Invalid credentials</b> please re-enter..."
     End If
  End Sub
```

The Personalized default.aspx Page

Following a successful login, the user is redirected to the page default.aspx. In it, we display their user name. We also include the same Log Off button – we won't be describing those features again here.

What is different is the way that we set the background color of the page, and display an appropriate set of hyperlinks depending on the current username. The opening <body> tag in the page includes a bgcolor attribute, with the value set to a variable named strColor:

```
  <body bgcolor="<% = strColor %>">
```

This variable is declared in the <script> section of the page, and so is globally available throughout the page:

```
  <script language="VB" runat="server">
  Dim strColor As String
  ...
  </script>
```

We placed five ASP:Hyperlink elements within the body of the page to create the HTML hyperlinks you can see in the screenshots above. The last three of these have their Visible property set to False so they won't normally be visible in the final page:

```
...
<ASP:Hyperlink id="lnkUser1" Text="Change Display Settings"
     NavigateUrl="http://dummy" runat="server" /><br />
<ASP:Hyperlink id="lnkUser2" Text="Change Sound Options"
     NavigateUrl="http://dummy" runat="server" /><br />
<ASP:Hyperlink id="lnkAdmin1" Text="Manage All Users"
     Visible="False" NavigateUrl="http://dummy" runat="server" /><br />
<ASP:Hyperlink id="lnkAdmin2" Text="Change Application Settings"
     Visible="False" NavigateUrl="http://dummy" runat="server" /><br />
<ASP:Hyperlink id="lnkAdmin3" Text="Display User Session Details"
     Visible="False" NavigateUrl="http://dummy" runat="server" /><br />
...
```

The <script> section of the page also contains an event handler that executes as the page is being created in response to the Page-Load event. This first checks that the user has been authenticated, and if so displays the authenticated user name:

```
Sub Page_Load()
   If User.Identity.IsAuthenticated Then

     'display welcome message
     msgHello.InnerHtml = "Hello <b>" & User.Identity.Name & "</b>"
     ...
```

Next, it extracts the BGColor value from the user's Session (stored there when they submitted their login details) and sets the strColor variable so that the background color of the page is set to the appropriate color for this user:

```
     ...
     'set preferred background color to the value that was
     'saved in this user's Session object by the "login" page
     strColor = Session("BGColor")
     ...
```

Now we can use the current login username to see if we should display the "administration" hyperlinks. In our example, we only display them if the user is **sarahware**:

```
     ...
     'if user is "sarahware" display admin hyperlinks in page
     If User.Identity.Name = "sarahware" Then
       lnkAdmin1.Visible = True
       lnkAdmin2.Visible = True
       lnkAdmin3.Visible = True
     End If
     ...
```

Other Personalization and Programmatic Security Options

This is a very simple example of personalization and programmatic security, but you can see how it can easily be extended. For example we could:

❑ Include more personalization options, such as the text color, font size and style, page layout, page content, etc.

❑ Include a page containing form controls where the user can select the personalization options and values, and then use a SQL statement or stored procedure to update these in the database.

❑ Store a custom "role" name for each user in the database table, giving us the ability to allocate users to separate "roles" (rather like Windows account groups). We could then extract the role name for each user as they log in and perform programmatic security checks using this role name rather than the username.

ASP.NET Process Model and Trust Levels

We've mentioned several times in this chapter how ASP.NET pages and associated resources such as Web Services, User Controls, Components, etc., run under a local system process account by default (if impersonation is not enabled). This is due to the fact that ASP.NET takes advantage of dynamic compilation and disk caching features. To be able to generate Intermediate Language (IL) code and binary executable files using the compilers included with the.NET Framework, the account under which the page executes requires more permissions than the equivalent in ASP 3.0.

By default ("out of the box"), ASP.NET runs in a mode called "Full Trust" level, which applies few security limits on the code that can be executed. This is fine for an Intranet scenario or a development machine, but once we place the server on the Internet, we should consider reducing the permissions that are available to the process running the ASP.NET pages.

There are several different ways that we can configure reduced permissions in ASP.NET. They all revolve around the ultimate decision that we have to make – which account should we run the pages under? Once we know which account is being used, or specify the one that we want to use, we can use the Windows ACLs on all the resources on our machine to limit and control access.

We can also control access permissions to access other applications and services by changing the trust level. We'll come back to this shortly.

The ASP.NET "Process Model"

The `<processModel>` element in machine.config (or in a web.config file placed in the application directory) specifies which account is used when impersonation is not enabled:

```
<processModel
  enable="[true|false]"
  userName="[user]"
  password="[AutoGenerate | password]"
/>
```

The default settings in `machine.config` are:

```
<processModel
  enable="true"
  userName="SYSTEM"
  password="AutoGenerate"
/>
```

So, by default, all our ASP.NET pages and resources will be executed under a local system process account – the account with the "moniker" of SYSTEM. This account generally has full permissions for all the resources on the machine, so ASP.NET will be able to run without any problems arising from permission settings. Of course, we can modify the permissions that this account has, thereby controlling how ASP.NET will be able to access that resource. However, many other processes use the SYSTEM account, and so changing its permissions could cause other applications to fail.

Instead, there is another "moniker" value you can use here instead, namely "MACHINE", and with the password also set to "AutoGenerate". This causes ASP.NET to run as an account called ASPNET (or ASPNET_E in the Enterprise version). This account is broadly equivalent to the normal ASP 3.0 IWAM_*machinename* account (that is, it is fairly unprivileged), but ASP.NET sets some ACLs for this account to help it work "out of the box". At minimum, ASP.NET needs permission to read its own binaries, configuration files (for example, the install `root` and the install `root/config` folders) and have full control over the ASP.NET Temporary Files folder, and the installation process automatically sets these. This option makes for a useful and simple method of tightening security on a public server.

An alternative is to specify that ASP.NET pages should be processed under the context of some other Windows account by changing the `userName` and `password` values in the `<processModel>` element – either for the entire machine (in `machine.config`), or for a specific application directory. As a trivial example, we can run our ASP.NET pages and resources under an account that we create named "MyProcess" with the password "secret" by specifying this account:

```
<processModel
  enable="true"
  userName="MyProcess"
  password="secret"
/>
```

Note that the settings specified in the `<processModel>` element are only applicable to ASP.NET, and do not affect other types of application or service running under the .NET Framework.

The Identity Element and Impersonation

The `<processModel>` element provides account details that are used only when impersonation is **not** enabled. Recall from our discussions near the start of this chapter that turning on impersonation means that ASP.NET will run under the context of the account that is authenticated by IIS when a request is received. If IIS is configured to allow anonymous access (the default for a web site), then the context is that of the IUSR account (or the account you specified that IIS use for anonymous access if you changed this).

Simply adding the `<identity impersonate="true">` element within the `<system.web>` section of the `machine.config` or `web.config` files means that anonymous access will take place under the IIS anonymous account (IUSR_*machinename*)

```
<system.web>
   ...
   <identity impersonate="true" />
   ...
</system.web>
```

Another possibility is to use the `userName` and `password` attributes of the `<identity>` element to specify the account that we want ASP.NET resources to be executed under. In this case we set the `impersonate` attribute to `"true"`:

```
<system.web>
   ...
   <identity impersonate="true"
            userName="account-name"
            password="account-password"
   />
   ...
</system.web>
```

Note that the settings specified in the `<identity>` element are applicable only to ASP.NET, and **not** to the rest of the .NET Framework. You also might like to consider the wisdom of using this last option where the password must be stored in the file as plain text.

> *In fact there is a little more to it than this. The `<processModel>` element specifies the account under which the worker process is run when it's enabled (it's not in IIS6 in native mode, for example). All threads start as the specified account. When impersonation is enabled, they temporarily take on the impersonated context. Calling the `RevertToSelf` method will always get back to the process account. There are a couple of events that fire without a `Request` context being available, such as `Application_OnEnd`, and these always run with the process account identity regardless of impersonation.*

Specifying the Trust Level

In the premium edition of .NET (the "Enterprise" version), there is another option for controlling the permissions for ASP.NET to process resources. This takes advantage of the `<trust>` element in `machine.config`, and it can be used to set a more stringent "trust level". The default setting is `"Full"`, specified by this line from the default `machine.config` file:

```
<trust level="Full" originUrl="" />
```

The other options are `"High"`, `"Low"`, and `"None"`, and these apply progressively more stringent limitations on the permissions that code running under the .NET Framework will have. The `<securityPolicy>` element specifies which security configuration file applies to each of the trust levels:

```
<securityPolicy>
   <trustLevel name="Full" policyFile="internal" />
   <trustLevel name="High" policyFile="web_hightrust.config" />
   <trustLevel name="Low"  policyFile="web_lowtrust.config" />
   <trustLevel name="None" policyFile="web_notrust.config" />
</securityPolicy>
```

Each of these files has sections that describe the permissions that are available to .NET framework applications and code. Some examples of the permissions that can be set are:

- ❑ Which environment variables the code can query

- ❑ Which directories the code can write to through the file I/O classes

- ❑ Whether DNS enquiries are allowed

- ❑ Whether blank passwords can be used with the ADO.NET data providers

- ❑ Whether messages can be sent to, and received from, the Message Queue Service

- ❑ Whether access to a printer is permitted

- ❑ Which performance counters can be accessed

You can change the trust level and edit the "trust" configuration files to finely control the permissions available to your code and resources. Remember that the settings specified in the `<trust>` element are applicable to the whole of the .NET framework, not just ASP.NET.

For a detailed explanation of the trust model, code-access security and other related topics check out the SDK that is provided with the .NET framework. The section "Programming in the .NET Framework" includes a whole subsection "Securing Your Application" that is devoted to all the topics we've mentioned in this chapter.

Summary

In this chapter, we've tackled a topic that is often considered to be the most difficult part of building ASP applications, and often doesn't get the attention it deserves (and, from a security point of view, requires). As you've hopefully gathered from the theory, explanations, and examples, ASP.NET makes it much easier to set up a secure web site or application to suit every kind of common scenario. But remember that security as a whole involves a lot more than just the topics we've covered here – you also need to consider physical network-and server-security implications, as well as application security settings and configuration. If in doubt, get an expert in!

The topic list for this chapter was:

- ❑ An overview of the security model in Windows 2000 and IIS.

- ❑ An overview of the new security features in ASP.NET.

- ❑ The different types of access control that we can implement with ASP.NET.

- ❑ A detailed look at how we apply the ASP.NET security and access control features.

- ❑ A brief overview of the "trust" model.

Web application security is based around the three fundamental concepts of **authentication** (forcing a user to prove that they are who they say they are), **authorization** (checking if the user has permission to access the resource they requested), and **impersonation** (allowing applications to be executed under the context of a different user).

We looked at each topic in turn, and saw how they are implemented and configured in IIS, in Windows 2000, and in ASP.NET. We also saw the whole chain of events that occurs as part of the overall process, and the various access control options that they provide.

We then concentrated on ASP.NET security configuration, and saw how our three fundamental concepts are implemented through the web.config files we place in our application folders. We completed this chapter with some examples of creating and configuring secured applications using the various techniques:

- ❏ Configuring a web application using Windows authentication
- ❏ Accessing the user's identity within this application
- ❏ Accessing the user's role within this application
- ❏ Configuring a web application using Forms-based authentication
- ❏ Using different types of user credentials lists
- ❏ Accessing the user's identity within this application
- ❏ A simple personalization example

In the next chapter, we change topics to start an in-depth look at some of the base classes that are provided by the Framework. In particular, we'll investigate data structures such as Collections and Lists.

"The Babel fish," says The Hitch Hiker's Guide to Galaxy "is small, yellow and leech-like, and probably the oddest thing in the Universe. It feeds on brainwave energy not from its carrier but from those around it. It absorbs all unconscious mental frequencies from this brainwave energy to nourish itself with. It then excretes into the mind of its carrier a telepathic matrix formed by combining the conscious thought frequencies with nerve signals picked up from the speech centres of the brain which has supplied them".

The practical upshot of all this is that if you stick a Babel fish in your ear you can instantly understand anything said to you in any form of language. The speech patterns you actually hear decode the brainwave matrix which has been fed into your mind by your Babel fish

15

Working with Collections and Lists

Over the years Microsoft Windows has grown into an enterprise-caliber operating system that millions of companies and users worldwide depend on daily. Windows NT and Windows 2000 have proved themselves as solid and stable operating systems, providing scalability, reliability, and return on investment (ROI).

The one area where Windows suffers badly today compared with its main rivals, is the complexity of its developer platform. Yes, Windows has fantastic tools like Visual Studio, but Windows supports ever-growing numbers of APIs and object models that have evolved to a point where they are becoming inconsistent, fragmented, and difficult to learn. Also, developers are penalized depending on individual programming languages or technologies (such as ASP) they choose.

Without doubt, the complexity of the Windows platform, from a development perspective, is a problem that Microsoft has clearly understood for some time. A major objective for .NET was to bring simplicity and consistency to the Windows development platform, making it more competitive with Java in that respect, without sand-boxing developers or sacrificing performance. From a consistency and accessibility viewpoint, the Common Language Runtime (CLR) provides the foundations that enable this. The .NET framework uses the CLR to provide a clean object-oriented approach to development, grouping classes within hierarchical namespaces, making locating and using the functionality of the platform simple, consistent, and universally available.

A key part of an object-oriented development platform like .NET is its Framework Base Class Library. These classes provide core functionality, with which developers can build their own application and class libraries. If you have ever programmed with the C/C++ Standard Template Library (STL), used the VB scripting runtime objects, or used the Java SDK, you'll have a good idea of the type of functionality that the .NET framework base classes provide.

In this chapter and the next one, we're going to examine some of the commonly-used classes in the .NET Framework Base Class Library, and look at how they have been carefully designed to allow applications to be built quickly and elegantly. There are quite simply too many classes in the framework to cover in detail in this book, so we're going to focus on collections in this chapter, then cover files and regular expressions in the next chapter.

Ever since I started programming, which feels like a very long time ago now, I've spent a reasonable percentage of time writing code to manage sets of data held in different types of data structures, such as queues, dictionaries, and stacks. I'm probably not the only one who's spent such a large amount of time doing this, since, after all, computers are essentially designed for storing and manipulating data.

Because working with different data structures is such a universal and common requirement, you shouldn't be surprised to learn that the .NET framework provides an impressive class library for dealing with common data structures.

By the end of this chapter you will:

❑ Understand the support provided by the .NET framework for working with common data structures such as lists, queues, stacks, and dictionaries

❑ Have a working knowledge of the collection interfaces and classes in the `System.Collections` and `System.Collection.Specialized` namespaces

❑ Know how to build your own strongly-typed collection classes

> **When writing this chapter, I used a virtual directory in IIS called `Collections` to map to the sample directory `Collections` located in the downloadable source code for this book. This is reflected in all screenshots.**

Working with Collections and Lists

The .NET framework contains thousands of types. A large proportion of these types of classes are data structures that are **enumerable**: they support the ability for a contained or associated collection of items to be accessed in a sequential or key-based (random access) way.

To help working with enumerable types, the .NET Framework `System.Collection` namespace provides:

❑ Collection Interfaces that define standard methods and properties implemented by different types of data structures. These interfaces allow enumerable types to provide consistency, and aid interoperability.

❑ Functionality-rich implementations of many common collection classes such as lists and dictionaries. These all implement one or more of the common collection interfaces.

Collection Interfaces

Since dealing with enumerable classes is a common task for developers, the .NET framework class library includes a set of interfaces in the `System.Collections` namespace, which define a contract of functionality that different enumerable classes implement. These interfaces provide consistency throughout the framework classes, making your life as a developer easier. Once you know how to work with one enumerable class that supports one or more common interfaces, you should, in theory, be able to work with any other enumerable class that supports the same interface in a uniform way. That includes the custom types that you or your fellow developers write.

As a developer, it is in your best interest to understand the collection interfaces in the `System.Collections` namespace. There aren't too many, and once you understand what is there, you can examine the interfaces that any enumerable type implements or returns as properties or methods, and determine what enumerable support a given type has. For example, any type that implements the `IEnumerable` interface supports forward-only iteration through its contained item. Support of this interface also means you can use the VB and C# for...each language keyword.

> During compilation, compilers convert **for...each** declarations into calls to **IEnumerable** and its associated interface **IEnumerator**.

It's worth mentioning early on that most of the collection classes have many members (methods, properties, etc.) that are not defined in standard collection interfaces. The reason for this is that the collection interfaces are there to define a usage pattern that is common across many different collection classes. Since the implementation of a given data structure, such as a queue, has many unique characteristics, these are not defined in a standard interface, and they are just defined as members of a particular type. While we'll focus mainly on the members defined by common interfaces in this chapter, be aware that there are many more methods available on most of the types we cover, all of which are documented in documentation provided with the .NET SDK.

Let's examine the core collection interfaces and look at some of the .NET framework classes that implement them.

The System.Collections Core Interfaces

The core collection interfaces defined in the `System.Collections` are:

- ❑ `IEnumerable`
- ❑ `IEnumerator` / `IDictionaryEnumerator`
- ❑ `ICollection`
- ❑ `IList`
- ❑ `IDictionary`

> If you're not familiar with interfaces please refer back to Chapter 3. In short, they are a specification that defines members that must be implemented if a type if going to conform to a polymorphic usage contract. Interfaces do not define how such exposed functionality will be implemented.

IEnumerable and IEnumerator

A type that implements the IEnumerable interface, indicates to consumers that it supports the notion of forward-only access to its items, using an **enumerator** object. An enumerator object provides a forward-only read-only cursor for a set of items.

The IEnumerable interface has one method, GetEnumerator:

```
public interface IEnumerable
{    IEnumerator GetEnumerator();
}
```

This method returns a new instance of an enumerator object each time it is called. The returned object implements the IEnumerator interface. This has methods that can be used to sequentially access the set of System.Object types exposed by an enumerable type. The enumerator object supports retrieving the item at the current cursor position, or resetting the cursor back to the beginning of the item set.

The built-in Array type supports the IEnumerable interface. The following code shows how to declare a simple string array (although any type of array could be used), call the GetEnumerator method to create an enumerator object, and use the methods of returned IEnumerator interface to sequentially access each item in the array:

C#

```
string[] authors = new string[6] {"Richard","Alex",
                                   "Dave","Rob","Brian","Karli"};

IEnumerator e;

e = authors.GetEnumerator();while( e.MoveNext() == true )
{
   Response.Write("<P>" + e.Current );
}
```

VB

```
dim authors as string()
authors = new string() { "Richard","Alex", _
                         "Dave","Rob","Brian","Karli"}

dim e as IEnumerator
e = authors.GetEnumerator()

Do While e.MoveNext() = true
   Response.Write("<P>" & e.Current )
Loop
```

In this code we declare a string array, called authors, which contains six authors. To get an enumerator object for the array, we call authors.GetEnumerator. All arrays implement the IEnumerator interface, so we know that calling GetEnumerator is possible. Once the enumerator object is created, the MoveNext method is called in a while loop. The MoveNext method moves the cursor forward by one logical record. The cursor is always positioned before the first record (think of this as position -1) when an enumerator object is created. This means you must always call MoveNext **before** retrieving the first item using the Current property. When the enumerator object is positioned past the last record in a collection, it returns false. We can therefore safely loop through all items in the collection by calling MoveNext while it returns true, exiting when it returns false.

The .NET framework guidelines say that once an enumerator object is created, it takes a snapshot of the items contained within an enumerable object at that point in time. If the original object is changed, the enumerator becomes invalid, and the enumerator object should throw an `InvalidOperationException` next time one of its methods is called. All of the .NET framework classes follow these guidelines, as should the enumerable types you write. However, for performance reasons, the actual implementation of enumerator objects in the framework doesn't actually copy all the items when an enumerable object is created. Instead, they just maintain a reference back to the enumerable object, and provide a logical snapshot. It's much cheaper to maintain a reference and an index into the original enumerable object, rather than copy each and every item, which could be a hugely expensive process for a large collection.

To implement the actual semantics of a logical snapshot, a simple versioning scheme is used. Each time an enumerable object is changed (an item is added or removed), it increments a version number (think of this as a change counter). When an enumerator object is created, it copies the current version number. Subsequently, each time an enumerator object method is called, it compares its stored version number to the enumerable object's version number. If these version numbers are different, it throws an `InvalidOperationException`.

It's worth mentioning that the `Current` property of the `IEnumerator` interface is defined as the `System.Object` type. In the code earlier, we didn't have to cast before using it, since `Response.Write` will call the `ToString` method for us, however, if you wanted to store the underlying string type in our example, you would typically cast it, for example:

C#

```csharp
string author
Author  = (string) e.Current;
```

VB

```vb
dim author as string
author = CType( e.Current, string )
```

All of the collection interfaces in the `System.Collections` namespace also use the `System.Object` type. This gives them great flexibility, because they can be used with any type. However, this generic approach does mean that the CLR must perform type-conversion checking for most calls, which imposes a small performance overhead.

For Each

As we discussed earlier, languages like VB and C# implement their `for...each` functionality using the `IEnumerable/IEnumerator` interfaces. This means that we could change the author example from earlier to use `for...each`:

VB

```vb
dim author as string

for each author in authors
  Response.Write("<P>" + author);
next
```

C#

```csharp
foreach( string author in authors )
{
  Response.Write("<P>" + author );
}
```

Depending on the type of developer you are, and the type of functionality you're writing, you'll typically enumerate collections using the for...each statement when you can, since it requires less code than using the IEnumerable/IEnumerator interfaces directly. Of course, there will be times when using for...each is not possible due to way your code is structured (for example a loop performed across several method invocations), or simply not advisable if you are trying to write generic functionality that doesn't deal with concrete types.

Providing that an enumerable type has a GetEnumerator method that returns a type derived from IEnumerable, a type does not have to implement the IEnumerable interface for the for...each statement to work in C# or VB. However, unless you have a very good reason, your enumerable types should always implement this interface in accordance with the guidelines that the rest of the framework follows.

All other enumerable types in the .NET framework class library derive from the IEnumerable interface. This means that, although other enumerable types provide additional members for accessing the items they contain, all of them support the forward-only cursor approach using enumerator objects too. The same is true for the IEnumerator interface. All other enumerator interfaces derive from it for the same reasons.

The following diagram shows the interface inheritance for the core interfaces:

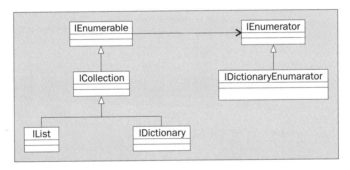

If you've not seen a UML class diagram before, don't worry, you would read this one as follows:

- The IList and IDictionary interfaces derive from ICollection, which in turn derives from IEnumerable
- The interface IEnumerable is associated with IEnumerator
- The interface IDictionaryEnumerator derives from IEnumerator

> Types that implement the IEnumerable interface can be enumerated in VB 6 and other COM-aware languages using COM interop, since the GetEnumerator method will be exposed with a DISPID of -4. See MSDN for more information.

ICollection and IList

Enumerating through a collection sequentially is a common task, but it's probably just as common to directly access items using a key or an index. For example, to check if a specific author exists in our author list from earlier, we could use the static `Array.IndexOf` method:

VB

```
dim index as integer
index = Array.IndexOf(authors,"Richard")
if index <> -1  then
   Response.Write("<P>" & authors(index) & " is in the author list")
end if
```

C#

```
int index;

index = Array.IndexOf( authors, "Richard");
if ( index != -1 )
{
   Response.Write("<P>" + authors[index] + " is in the author list");
}
```

In this code we use the `Array.IndexOf` method to retrieve the index of a specific author and store that in the `index` variable. If the `index` variable is not -1, we use the index to display the value held at that offset within the array. Under the hood, this method searches the array item by item, doing a comparison against each one. When an item match is found, the index is returned.

The `IList` interface defines methods and properties that allow you to work with arrays of `System.Object` items, such as our string array of authors.

The `IList` interface defines methods and properties that allow you to:

- ❑ Add an item to the end of the list using the `Add` method
- ❑ Insert an item at a specified offset in the list using the `Insert` method
- ❑ Determine if an item is contained within a list using the `Contains` methods
- ❑ Determine the index of an item within a list using the `IndexOf` method
- ❑ Retrieve or add an item by index using the `Item` property (in C# you have to use an indexer)
- ❑ Remove an item by reference, or by its index, using the `Remove` or `RemoveAt` methods
- ❑ Remove all items using the `Clear` method
- ❑ Determine if a list is read-only using the `IsReadOnly` property
- ❑ Determine if a list is of a fixed size using the `IsFixedSize` property

The `IList` interface derives from the `ICollection` interface, so inherits all of its members, as well as those of `IEnumerable` (since `ICollection` derives from `IEnumerable`)

The Array Type and IList

The built in Array type implements the `IList` interface, but it only implements a small number of the methods of the interface, namely: `IndexOf`, `Clear`, and `Contains`. It also has only one property: `Item`. If you try to call any of the other `IList` members, a `NotSupportedException` will be thrown. Because of this, the `IList` members are defined as **explicit interface member implementations**. You have to access the members using an `IList` interface reference. As we saw in Chapter 3, when implementing an interface, the author of a type can control whether or not the members of an interface can be used implicitly (as if they were just part of the type), or if an interface reference has to be used to access them. The former approach is typically used, but for types where the interfaces (or specific members of the interfaces) are not commonly used (or they are really only there for internal use), the latter approach is used. This keeps the list of the most commonly seen public interfaces (which, incidentally, are the methods, properties, and events listed in IntelliSense in VS.NET too) smaller and more intuitive.

To see `IList` in action we'll rewrite the last example where we determined if a specific author existed in an array. This time we'll use the `IList.Contains` method to determine if the item is present in the array, the `IList.IndexOf` method to determine the index of the item, and the `IList.Item` property to retrieve the value:

VB

```
dim list as IList

list = CType(authors, IList)
if list.Contains("Richard") then
   index = list.IndexOf( "Richard")
      Response.Write("<P>" & list(index) & " is in the author list")
end if
```

C#

```
IList list = (IList) authors;

if ( list.Contains("Richard") == true )
{
   index = list.IndexOf("Richard");
   Response.Write("<P>" + list[index] + " is in the author list");
}
```

Since the Item property is actually an indexer, in C# we can just use the array-style notation to access items in the list.

Using the `IList` interface is pretty simple. The code is certainly no more complex. To see more of the `IList` methods in use, let's take a look at the `System.Collections.ArrayList` type.

A Simple ArrayList

An `ArrayList` is capable of holding 0 to n items of the type `System.Object` in a dynamically sized array. The total number of objects that can be held in the array is defined by the `Capacity` property. The used space (the number of items in the array) is defined by the `Count` property. As you add or remove items from the list, the size of the `ArrayList` is automatically altered as needed. The only real difference between the built-in `Array` type and `ArrayList` is this automatic size management. Internally, the `ArrayList` uses the `Array` type to implement most of its functionality.

The following code shows how to create an `ArrayList` and populate it with a few items using the `Add` method. This time we're using movie names rather than authors:

C#

```
ArrayList movieList;

movieList = new ArrayList();
movieList.Add("Pulp Fiction");
movieList.Add("Aliens");
movieList.Add("The Good, the Bad and the Ugly");
```

Since the `ArrayList` supports any type derived from `System.Object` we could actually add lots of different item types to it:

VB

```
dim variedItems as ArrayList = new ArrayList()

variedItems.Add("Pulp Fiction")      ' add a string
variedItems.Add(1234)                ' add an integer
variedItems.Add(new ArrayList())     ' add another array list
```

The `ArrayList` type implements the `IList` interface, so all the other `IList` members that we've covered so far are implemented and available for use. The `IList` interface members are implemented **implicitly,** as public members by the `ArrayList` type, so you don't have to query for an `IList` interface, before the members can be called. Most of the types in the .NET framework do this to make using them simpler. You can, of course, use the interfaces if you want to, and doing so may have benefits if you're trying to write generic code that can work with any implementation of `IList`. In the code below we are using the `IList` interface of the `ArrayList`:

C#

```
IList movieList2;

movieList = new ArrayList();
movieList.Add("Pulp Fiction");
movieList.Add("Aliens");
movieList.Add("The Good, the Bad and the Ugly");
```

VB

```
dim movieList as IList

movieList = new ArrayList()
movieList.Add("Pulp Fiction")
movieList.Add("Aliens")
movieList.Add("The Good, the Bad and the Ugly")
```

In this code we have declared our `movieList` variable as `IList` and assigned an instance of a newly created `ArrayList` to it. We will only be able to use the members defined in the `IList` interface this way, and we will not be able to use any of the other `ArrayList` members without either casting back to `ArrayList` or another supported interface. Note that when assigning a newly instantiated type to a variable like this, there is no requirement to specify any casting. The compiler will interrogate the metadata of the type at compile time, and ensure that the interface is supported. If the interface isn't supported, a compile error will occur.

If you specify an explicit cast on any assignment such as new, this overrides the checks performed by the compiler. If a cast turns out to be invalid at run time, the CLR will throw an `InvalidCastException`.

To demonstrate using the various members of the `ArrayList` type, we'll write a simple web page that allows a user to enter a list of their favorite movies. The page will have options to add and delete movies, as well as sorting the list. We're not going to review the complete code for this application (the complete code is available in the download), we'll just review the important elements.

The application looks like this:

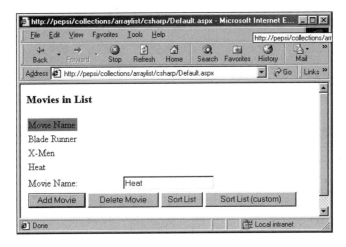

The ASP.NET page responsible for rendering the page (excluding the server-side code for events) is shown here:

C#

```
<h3>Movies in List</h3>

<%
  if ( movieList.Count != 0 )
  {
    Response.Write("<table>");
    Response.Write("<tr bgcolor=cornflowerblue>");
    Response.Write("<td>Movie Name");
    Response.Write("</tr>");

    foreach( string Movie in movieList )
    {
      Response.Write("<tr>");
      Response.Write("<td>" + Movie );
    }
    Response.Write("</table>");
  }
  else
  {
    Response.Write("<P>There are no movies in the list.");
  }
%>
```

If there are no movies in the list, the code renders the message "There are no movies in the list". If there are movies (the Count property of movieList is not equal to zero), the code renders a table containing the titles of the movies. We're using the for...each statement in this example to enumerate the ArrayList containing the movies, which, as you should recall from earlier, will use the IEnumerable interface under the hood.

The movieList variable is created in the Page_Load event. Let's look at two implementations of how to create and maintain state during postbacks, and examine some of the advantages and disadvantages of each approach.

The first implementation creates the list the first time the page is rendered, and places the instantiated object into the Session object using a key of 'movies'. On subsequent postbacks, the list is retrieved using the key from the Session object. Whether a page is being rendered for the first time or not, the ArrayList that is instantiated is held in a page-level member variable called movieList. I've used a variable in this way to make the subsequent page code more readable, since no casting is needed:

C#

```csharp
ArrayList movieList;

protected void Page_Load( object sender, EventArgs e )
{
    if ( IsPostBack == true )
    {
        movieList = (ArrayList) Session["movies"];
    }
    else
    {
        movieList = new ArrayList();
        Session["movies"] = movieList;
    }
}
```

> **Collection classes are reference types, not value types. When you assign a reference to collection type to one or more variables, all of those variables will reference the same object allocated on the managed heap.**

There are no COM-type threading issues with storing objects in the ASP intrinsic objects like Session. It's perfectly safe and you really don't have to worry about threading models ever again. However, storing the ArrayList in the Session object like this means that by default, your ArrayList objects reside in memory on a **specific** web server. This means you cannot load-balance requests to such a page across multiple web servers. There are two solutions to this problem. We could tell ASP.NET to use an external state store. This was discussed in Chapter 10 so we will not cover it here. Alternatively, we could store the list in **ViewState** instead of using the Session intrinsic object to hold the data.

The following code shows a new implementation of the Page_Load event using ViewState:

```
protected void Page_Load( object sender, EventArgs e )
{
  if ( IsPostBack == true )
  {
    movieList = (ArrayList) ViewState["movies"];
  }
  else
  {
    movieList = new ArrayList();
    ViewState["movies"] = movieList;
  }
}
```

From a code perspective, there is not a great deal of change here. All we have effectively done is replace occurrences of the text "Session", with "ViewState". Under the hood the ASP.NET page framework will persist the state held in the ArrayList as part of the HTML page returned back to the client. When the next postback occurs, ASP.NET will automatically recreate the ArrayList and any contained state, making it available to our page. This resolves the load-balancing problem discussed earlier, but it does mean pages sent back to the client are bigger, and of course, it does require a few more CPU cycles on the part of the web server to automatically create and destroy objects held in ViewState.

> When storing types in ViewState you should use the Page directive to enable tracing (<%@Page Trace=True%>) and keep an eye on the ViewState size. For more details, see Chapter 4.

Whether you use Session or ViewState to hold state comes down to a per-application choice with ASP.NET. For the most part you'll use both. All of the classic ASP problems associated with Session state are gone, thanks to the new external state stores such as SQL Server. One key benefit of using the Session object to hold the state is that the contents can survive across multiple pages, only getting destroyed when an ASP.NET session ends or when you delete the Session variable. For applications that require features like shopping carts, Session state combined with an external state store provides a good solution.

Unlike Session state, ViewState is limited to a single page, and can't be used beyond the scope of that page. It can't be used to pass data between pages, so any important data must be persisted elsewhere before navigating away from a page. The main advantage of using ViewState is that fewer server resources, such as memory, are consumed. The client HTML page is used as the state store, which potentially gives your application better scalability since fewer server resources will be consumed.

Now we've seen how the MovieList page is rendered, and the options for holding the list of movies in Session or ViewState, let's look at event handlers that manipulate the list when responding to user actions.

The MovieList Event Handlers

These allow the user to input a movie name and select one of the available buttons on the MovieList page using the following HTML form:

```
<form runat=server>
<table>
<tr>
 <td>Movie Name:</td>
 <td><asp:TextBox id=MovieName runat=server/>
<tr>
 <td colspan=2>
 <asp:Button OnClick="OnAddMovie" Text="Add Movie" runat=server />
 <asp:Button OnClick="OnDeleteMovie" Text="Delete Movie" runat=server />
 <asp:Button OnClick="OnSortList" Text="Sort List" runat=server />
 <asp:Button OnClick="OnCustomSortList" Text="Sort List (custom)" runat=server />
</table>

</form>
```

We're using server controls in this form, for the movie name text box, (id=MovieName) and each of the four buttons. Each button is associated with a server-side event handler by specifying the OnClick attribute.

When the user hits the **Add** button, the following event handler is invoked:

C#

```
protected void OnAddMovie( object sender, EventArgs e )
{
  movieList.Add( MovieName.Text );
}
```

This code retrieves the value of the MovieName server control using its Text property, adding it to movieList.

When the user hits the **Delete** button the following event handler is invoked:

C#

```
protected void OnDeleteMovie( object sender, EventArgs e )
{
  if ( movieList.IndexOf( MovieName.Text ) == -1 )
  {
    status.InnerHtml = "Movie not found in list";
    return;
  }
  movieList.Remove( MovieName.Text );
}
```

This code checks if the movie exists in the list by using the IndexOf method, and displays an error message if -1 is returned, which indicates the value was not in the list. To display the error message we're setting the InnerHtml property of a paragraph element (represented by the HtmlGenericControl control) below the main form:

```
<p style="color:red" id="status" EnableViewState="False" runat=server />
```

749

If the IndexOf method doesn't return -1, (indicating that the movie was in the list) the Remove method is called to delete the movie. The Remove method does not throw any exception if it's called with an argument that's not in the list, so you don't have to validate arguments as shown here, unless you want to give some type of feedback. It's worth noting that the Remove method of the ArrayList calls the IndexOf method internally, to determine the index of the passed item, and then calls the RemoveAt method, which removes the item at a specific position from the array. This means the above code isn't optimal, and should be written more efficiently as:

C#

```
protected void OnDeleteMovie( object sender, EventArgs e )

{
    int index;

    index = movieList.IndexOf( MovieName.Text );
    if ( index == -1 )
    {
        status.InnerHtml = "Movie not found in list";
        return;
    }
    movieList.RemoveAt(index);
}
```

In this code, we check for an item's index, and then store it in the index variable. We subsequently use this to delete the item. Small optimizations like this may seem minor, but it's well worth doing. The ArrayList type isn't particularly efficient, and will sequentially search an array, item by item, until a match is found. For a list with a few hundred items, the scan time can be significant, so removing redundant scans is certainly worthwhile.

When the user hits the Sort List button the following event handler is invoked:

C#

```
protected void OnSortList( object sender, EventArgs e )
{
    movieList.Sort();
}
```

The event handler calls the Sort method of the ArrayList. This method sorts the items in the list by using a **quicksort** algorithm (this cannot be changed), which results in the list being sorted efficiently, and alphabetically by default for string types:

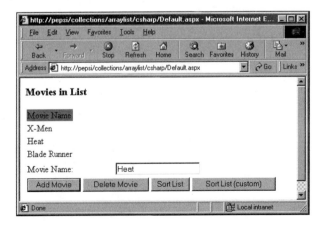

The `quicksort` algorithm works by dividing a list of items into two partitions based upon a **pivot** item. Items less than the pivot item end up in the **left partition**, items greater than the pivot item end up in the right partition, and the pivot item ends up in the middle. By recursively applying this algorithm to each of the left and right partitions that are created, until each partition only contains a single item, a list can be sorted with a minimal number of comparisons and exchanges.

> *If you want to understand how the `quicksort` algorithm works in more detail, then you won't have any problem, as most algorithm books cover elementary sorts like the quicksort, and also cover binary searching.*

Performance and Memory Optimizations

When adding items to an array list, the contained array is automatically expanded as needed when it's full. The default size for an array list allows it to hold sixteen items. If a seventeenth item is added, a new internal array is created which is twice the size, and the original items are copied to the array. When there are 32 items in the array, capacity will be expanded to 64. Since memory allocation and copying of items will be expensive, as a list grows in size, it's certainly worth optimizing the initial capacity of a list if you know how many items will be in it. For an array containing a large number of items, this can be a great performance boost.

To set the capability for the array list you can set the integer `Capacity` property:

```
ArrayList list = new ArrayList()
list.Capacity = 128;
```

Or you can use one of its overloaded constructors:

```
ArrayList list = new ArrayList( 128 );
```

Once a list is populated with items, you can release any unused slots by calling the `TrimToSize` method. However, be aware that this will require a new array to be allocated, and all of the existing items will be copied from the old array to the new one. You should only call this method if you know a list is likely to remain static in size for a period of time, or if you know that there are a large number of free slots that should be freed.

> **Most of the framework collection classes give you the ability to set the initial capacity or the grow size.**

Sorting the List – IComparer and IComparable

When sorting a collection, the framework classes like `ArrayList` and `Array` use the `System.Collections.IComparer` interface to determine equality: In other words, it establishes if one type instance is less than, equal to, or greater than another type instance.

This `IComparer` interface has a single method called `Compare`:

```
public int Compare( object x, object y )
```

Comparer objects that implement this interface have to check for equality between the two objects passed in, and return one of the following:

- Any negative value if Object x is less than Object y
- Any positive value is Object x is greater than Object y
- Zero if the objects are equal

The default implementation of IComparer, used by the ArrayList and other types, is implemented by the System.Collections.Comparer class. This implements its comparison of two objects by using the System.IComparable interface of the first object (x) passed in to the IComparer.Compare method.

The IComparable interface has a single method CompareTo:

```
Public int CompareTo(object x);
```

The return values from this method are the same as those of the IComparer Compare method.

Most value types such as string and integer implement the IComparable interface. This means you can compare most types like this:

```
String s1 = "richard";
String s2 = "anderson";

IComparable c1;

c1 = (IComparable) s1;

If ( c1.CompareTo(s2) != 0 )
  Console.WriteLine("The strings are different");

If ( c1.CompareTo(s2) < 0 )
  Console.WriteLine("string 1 is less than string 2");

If ( c1.CompareTo(s2) > 0 )
  Console.WriteLine("string 1 is greater than string 2");
```

When you create a custom type, you should always consider implementing the IComparable interface, so that the type can be easily sorted.

As the ArrayList type uses the System.Collections.Comparer implementation of IComparer to sort its list, which in turn uses the IComparable interface of the types within the list, there is a limitation to what can be sorted. Specifically, you can only sort an array containing items that can do equality checks on each other. Since most types can only do equality checks again the same type, you cannot sort array lists containing different types by default (which is acceptable for most applications). For example, the following code to compare a string and integer will throw an InvalidArgument exception:

```
string s1 = "richard";
int i1 = 1234;

IComparable c1;

c1 = (IComparable) s1;

if ( c1.CompareTo(i1) != 0 )
  Console.WriteLine("You'll never see this line");
```

When the `CompareTo` method is called, the string type checks the type of the argument passed. If the argument is not a string type, it throws an exception. You have to catch this at run time, since it cannot be caught at compile time.

To enable you to sort arrays containing different types, and to give you complete control over sorting an array of items, you can use an overload of the `Sort` method that allows you to pass in an `IComparer` interface to use when performing equality checks. The custom **Sort List** button in our movie list application uses this to sort the movie list in reverse order, as shown here:

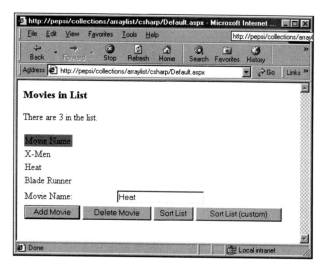

This is how we implement the reverse-ordered sort in our movie list:

```
// Custom Sort
protected void OnCustomSortList( object sender, EventArgs e )
{
  IComparer custom = new MyComparer();
  movieList.Sort( custom );
}
```

Our comparer class `MyComparer` was implemented as follows:

```
class MyComparer : IComparer
{
  public int Compare( object x, object y )
  {
    IComparable ic;
    int compareResult;

    ic = (IComparable) x;
    compareResult = ic.CompareTo( y );

    if ( compareResult != 0 )
      compareResult = compareResult * -1;

    return compareResult;
  }
}
```

When dealing with null values, an implementation of IComparer should always treat non-null values as being greater than a null value.

This class uses the IComparable interface of object x to compare it with object y. The result from the call to CompareTo is then checked, and the sign of the number inverted if the objects are not equal. By making negative values positive, and positive values negative, we effectively reverse-sort the list.

The ArrayList type does have a Reverse method, which you would typically use should you need to reverse-sort a list.

Efficient Searching – Binary Searching

When searching an ArrayList using methods like IndexOf, every item in the list is compared with the value being searched for, until a match is found. This 'brute force' approach to searching means the time taken to find an item can be significant, depending on the size of the list. As the number of items in a list increases, so does the number of comparisons that have to be performed to locate an item, especially when an item being searched for is located near the end of the list. The net result is pretty much a linear increase in search times as a list grows. For small lists this isn't a problem, but for large lists a more efficient solution is needed.

To search lists efficiently we use a binary search. Provided a list is sorted (this is a prerequisite of doing a binary search), a binary search can locate an item by doing significantly fewer comparisons, resulting in search times that are significantly less than for a regular linear search.

The following code shows how to binary search an ArrayList:

```
ArrayList someList;
Int ItemIndex;

SomeList = new ArrayList();

// Add code here to add lots of items to the list...

SomeList.Sort();
ItemIndex = someList.BinarySearch("Some item");
```

Binary searches do not work on an unsorted list. You will not receive an error if you call the BinarySearch method on an unsorted list, but you will get unpredictable results. Items that are in the list may not be found. You might wonder why the BinarySearch method doesn't just sort the list for you. There are two main reasons why it doesn't:

❑   Performance – the list may already be sorted so re-sorting would be wasteful.

❑   Custom sorts – the sorting of the list may require a custom IComparer implementation, so the BinarySearch method cannot make any assumptions on how to sort the list.

If you do sort a list using a custom IComparer interface, you must use the overloaded version of the BinarySearch method that accepts the comparer interface. If you don't use this overload, the search results will be unpredictable.

Indexers and Bounds Checking

When working with an `ArrayList` we can treat it just like an array, using an integer index to retrieve a specific item:

VB

```
BestMovieOfAllTime = CType(movieList[2], string)
```

C#

```
BestMovieOfAllTime = (string)movieList[2];
```

We can treat the `ArrayList` like an array because it implements an **indexer**. Indexers allow a type to be programmatically treated like an array, but under the hood, methods are called to set or retrieve values. Indexers can be declared to accept different types, meaning that an indexer value could be an integer, string, or another supported type. The ASP.NET `Session` object for example supports both integer and string indexers:

VB

```
dim SomeValue as string

SomeValue = CType(Session(0), string )
SomeValue = CType(Session("NamedValue"), string )
```

C#

```
string SomeValue;

SomeValue = (string) Session[0];
SomeValue = (string) Session["NamedValue"];
```

This code shows how to retrieve the first session variable using an integer index value of zero, and how to retrieve a named session variable.

Types that support indexers typically throw exceptions for invalid index values. If you don't know in advance if an index is valid, you should always write code that deals with exceptions:

C#

```
try
{
   BestMovieOfAllTime = (string)movieList[6];
}
catch( ArgumentOutOfRangeException rangeException )
{
   BestMovieOfAllTime = "index too big";
}
```

Since types like the `ArrayList` will throw an `ArgumentOutOfRangeException` if an index is invalid, I've declared an exception handler to catch an error and give the user some basic feedback.

You should also handle the general exception case too, since types could throw other unexpected exceptions:

```
try
{
   BestMovieOfAllTime = (string)movieList[6];
}
catch( ArgumentOutOfRangeException rangeException )
{
   BestMovieOfAllTime = "index too big";
}
catch( Exception e )
{
   // do something useful here
}
```

> **Always remember: Errors happen, deal with them! Refer back to Chapter 3 for an introduction to exception handling.**

ICollection

The `ArrayList` classes supports three collection interfaces: `IList`, `IEnumerable`, and `ICollection`. We've covered the first two, so let's look at `ICollection`.

The `ICollection` interface defines methods and properties that allow you to:

❑   Determine how many items are in a collection using a `Count` property

❑   Copy the contents of a collection into a specified array at a given offset using the `CopyTo` method

❑   Determine if the collection is synchronized and therefore thread-safe

❑   Determine the synchronization root object for the collection using the `SyncRoot` property: this is the object, which is locked and unlocked as collection operations on a synchronized collection are performed

The `ICollection` interface derives from the `IEnumerable` interface so it inherits the `GetEnumerator` method.

ICollection.Count Property

The following code shows how we use the `Count` property to display the number of items in our `MovieList`:

```
<P>There are <%=movieList.Count%> in the list.</P>
```

The implementation of the `Count` property, for the types in the class library, returns a cached field. It does not cause the size of a collection to be recalculated, so it isn't expensive to call. You don't need to worry about caching the `Count` property yourself for efficiency reasons.

ICollection.CopyTo Method

The CopyTo method allows the complete contents of a collection to be inserted into an array at a specified offset. The array to which the contents are copied must have sufficient capacity for the specific insertion or an ArgumentException will be thrown.

The following code shows how to copy the contents of the ArrayList into a string array (at the beginning) using the CopyTo method:

VB

```
dim Animals as ArrayList = new ArrayList()
dim ArrayOfAnimals() as string

Animals.Add( "Cat" )
Animals.Add( "Dog" )

dim a as Array
dim s as string

ArrayOfAnimals = Array.CreateInstance( GetType(String), 2 )

Animals.CopyTo( ArrayOfAnimals, 0 )
dim Animal as String

For Each Animal in ArrayOfAnimals
  Response.Write("<P>" + Animal )
Next
```

C#

```
ArrayList Animals = new ArrayList();
string[] ArrayOfAnimals;

Animals.Add( "Cat" );
Animals.Add( "Dog" );

ArrayOfAnimals = (string[]) Array.CreateInstance( typeof(string), 2 );
Animals.CopyTo( ArrayOfAnimals, 0 );

foreach( string Animal in ArrayOfAnimals )
{
  Response.Write("<P>" + Animal );
}
```

In this code, we create an ArrayList containing a couple of animals, dynamically create a string array, then use the CopyTo method to populate the created array with the contents of the ArrayList.

The ArrayList supports two additional overloads of CopyTo. The first overload doesn't require you to specify an index when copying the contents of the ArrayList and inserting it at the start of an array. The second overload allows you to copy a specified number of items from the ArrayList at a specified position, to a given index within another array.

As the ArrayList class does not expose its internal Array, you have to use either the AddRange or InsertRange methods when copying data from an array into an ArrayList. AddRange accepts an ICollection interface and adds all items within the collection to the end of the array. In this example we are copying the contents of two arrays into an ArrayList:

757

```
string[] Friends = { "Tom","Mark" };
string[] CoWorkers = { "Paul","Jon" };
ArrayList MergedList = new ArrayList();

MergedList.AddRange( Friends );
MergedList.AddRange( CoWorkers );

foreach( string Name in MergedList )
{
  Response.Write("<P>" + Name );
}
```

The code would result in the names being listed in this order: Tom, Mark, Paul, Jon.

InsertRange accepts an ICollection interface as the second parameter, but expects the first parameter to be the index at which the new items are copied. To make the names Paul and Jon appear at the front of the list, we could insert the second array using InsertRange with an index value of 0:

```
string[] Friends = { "Tom","Mark" };
string[] CoWorkers = { "Paul","Jon" };
ArrayList MergedList = new ArrayList();

MergedList.AddRange( Friends );
MergedList.InsertRange( 0, CoWorkers );

foreach( string Name in MergedList )
{
  Response.Write("<P>" + Name );
}
```

This code would result in the names being listed in this order: Paul, Jon, Tom, Mark.

ICollection.IsSynchronized Property

ASP.NET enables web applications to share objects using the application and cache intrinsic objects. If an object reference is shared this way, there is potential for multiple pages to be working simultaneously with the **same** object instance. If this happens, any changes to the object must be synchronized. If two pages try to modify an object at the same time without synchronization, there is a high probability that object's state will become corrupted. Objects that can safely be manipulated simultaneously are called **thread-safe**. The object takes on responsibility for guarding itself from concurrent access, providing any necessary synchronization.

The IsSynchronized property of the ICollection interface can be used to determine if an object is thread-safe. For performance reasons, most objects such as the ArrayList are not thread-safe by default. This means you should not share types like the ArrayList in a Web Application without performing some type of synchronization. In classic ASP you may have used the Application.Lock and Application.Unlock methods for synchronization. While they are available in ASP.NET too, they're not suitable for this task. They provide a coarse-grained lock (which is application-wide) that simply isn't suitable for scalable applications.

To safely share a collection object such as the ArrayList between multiple web pages, you need to use a synchronization helper object. Such a helper object provides the same public interface as a non-thread-safe type, but adds a synchronization wrapper around methods and properties that would otherwise not be thread-safe. Since this is such a common requirement, the collection types (and many other framework classes) follow a common pattern.

Types that need to work in a thread-safe way provide a public static `Synchronized` method that takes a non-thread-safe object reference, and creates and returns a thread-safe wrapper that can be used to synchronize calls. Both objects manipulate the same underlying state, so any changes by either the thread-safe or non-thread-safe object will be seen by any other code holding a reference to either object.

The following code shows how a non-thread-safe `ArrayList` adds an item then creates a thread-safe wrapper:

```
dim NotThreadSafeArrayList as ArrayList

NotThreadSafeArrayList = new ArrayList()
NotThreadSafeArrayList.Add("Hello")

dim ThreadSafeArrayList as ArrayList

ThreadSafeArrayList = ArrayList.Synchronized( NotThreadSafeArrayList )

if ThreadSafeArrayList.IsSynchronized = true then
   Response.Write("<P>It's synchronized")
end if
```

This diagram illustrates how the `ThreadSafeArrayList` shown in this example effectively works by protecting calls, then delegating the calls to the non-thread-safe object:

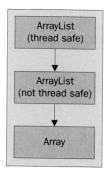

ICollection.SyncRoot Property

When writing thread-safe code, it's common to have a handle or object that's used by all the possible code paths in different threads (web pages) to synchronize access to shared state. The CLR automatically allows any .NET type instance to be a synchronization root (`SyncRoot`). A `SyncRoot` can be locked and unlocked to ensure one or more code statements are only ever executed by one thread at a time.

In VB you can use an object reference in conjunction with the `SyncLock` statement to make code thread-safe:

```
Sub DoSomethingWithAList( list as ArrayList )

   SyncLock list
     list.Add("abc")
   End SyncLock

End Sub
```

In C# you achieve the same result using the `lock` statement:

```
void DoSomethingWithAList( ArrayList list )
{
  lock(list)
  {
    list.Add("abc");
  }
}
```

Using SyncLocks, you can provide a very fine-grained level of locking inside ASP.NET pages. Rather than having one global lock, which is effectively what `Application.Lock` and `Application.Unlock` provide, you can have many smaller locks, reducing lock contention. The only disadvantage to this approach is that page developers need to really understand multi-threading. Since the writing of multi-threaded applications is not simple (and something ASP.NET does its best to protect you from), using the Synchronized method for automatically making a type thread-safe is often the preferred approach to take.

> Under the hood, both C# and VB use the **System.Threading.Monitor** object to perform their synchronization. Both cause the compiler to add exception handling around the statements being executed, ensuring that any unhandled exceptions in the code do not result in **SyncLocks** not being released.

When acquiring or releasing a SyncLock you need to know what SyncRoot object to use. This is the function of the `ICollection.SyncRoot` property. Since we cannot assume any implementation knowledge about the type providing an interface, we cannot make any assumptions about which SyncRoot object to use either. Consider this code:

```
dim NotThreadSafeArrayList as ArrayList

NotThreadSafeArrayList = new ArrayList()
NotThreadSafeArrayList.Add("Hello")

dim ThreadSafeArrayList1 as ArrayList
dim ThreadSafeArrayList2 as ArrayList
dim ThreadSafeArrayList3 as ArrayList

ThreadSafeArrayList1 = ArrayList.Synchronized( NotThreadSafeArrayList )
ThreadSafeArrayList2 = ArrayList.Synchronized( NotThreadSafeArrayList )
ThreadSafeArrayList3 = ArrayList.Synchronized( NotThreadSafeArrayList )
```

In this code we're creating an `ArrayList` and then creating three synchronization wrapper objects. Each of these wrapper objects exposes the `ICollection` interface. Since each of the wrapper objects actually manipulates the same underlying array, the `SyncRoot` object used by each of the wrappers is the non-thread-safe `ArrayList`:

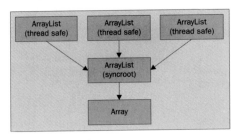

If we wanted to synchronize access to the array in a web page to perform an atomic operation, such as adding the contents of the array to a database and clearing it, we'd need to lock out all other threads from using the `ArrayList`. Assuming we only had a reference to an `ArrayList` object or an `ICollection` interface, and we didn't know whether or not that type was thread-safe, how would we achieve this? Assuming we had a thread-safe wrapper, and wrote our code like this, our code would fail miserably:

```
SyncLock ThreadSafeArrayList1

    ' Copy list to db and clear list (as an example)

End SyncLock
```

All this code does is acquire a lock on the thread-safe wrapper, and not the underlying list. Anybody using one of the other thread-safe wrappers would still be able to modify the list. The `ICollection.SyncRoot` property solves this problem. The implementation of this property should always return the appropriate `SyncRoot` object. We should therefore rewrite our code like this:

```
SyncLock ThreadSafeArrayList1.SyncRoot

    ' Copy list to db and clear list (as an example)

End SyncLock
```

Working with the Dictionary Objects

As ASP developers, we have all managed state using the `Session` or `Application` intrinsic objects. These classes enable you to store and retrieve a `variant` value using a string key. With ASP.NET the same functionality is provided by the intrinsic objects, but the value type stored is now `System.Object` rather than `variant`. Since all types in .NET derive from `System.Object`, any built-in type such as `string` or any custom type that you write can be held in Session or Application state.

The following code shows a simple example of storing and retrieving state using the Session intrinsic:

VB

```
Session("value1") = "Wrox"
Session("value2") = "Press"

Dim value as string

value = CType( Session("value1"), string )
value = CType( Session("value2"), string )
```

C#

```
Session["value1"] = "Wrox";
Session["value2"] = "Press";

string value;

value = (string) Session["value1"];
value = (string) Session["value2"];
```

In this code two values are being set using the keys `value1` and `value2`. The values associated with those keys are then retrieved.

Hashtable Class

The `Hashtable` class represents a **dictionary** of associated **keys** and **values**, implemented as a **hash table**. A hash table is a proven way of efficiently storing and retrieving values using the **hash** of a key value.

Internally, the ASP intrinsics like `Session` use the `System.Collections.Hashtable` class to implement key-based lookup functionality. This class is very similar to the scripting runtime `Dictionary` object you may have used in classic ASP pages, and provides all the methods of a dictionary type object you would expect.

Using the `Hashtable` class is straightforward. You can create an instance of the `Hashtable` class and use a text indexer to set and retrieve associated keys and values like this:

C#

```
Hashtable ourSession;

ourSession = new Hashtable();

ourSession["value1"] = "Wrox";
ourSession["value2"] = "Press";

string value;

value = (string) ourSession["value1"];
value = (string) ourSession["value2"];
```

You can determine if a key is contained within the hash table using the `ContainsKey` method:

VB

```
if ourSession.ContainsKey("value1") == true then
end if
```

You can also use the `Contains` method to determine if a key is present, but since all that does is call the `ContainsKey` method there is no point it using it.

You can determine if a specified value is held within the `hashtable` using the `ContainsValue` method:

VB

```
if ourSession.ContainsValue("Wrox") == true then
end if
```

Although the `Hashtable` allows any object type to be used as a key, only those types that override `System.Object.GetHashCode` and `System.Object.Equals` should be used. All of the primitive types in .NET, like integer and string, override these methods, and are safe to use as keys.

A hash table depends on hash codes to uniquely identify keys. Hash codes are numbers that, where possible, uniquely identify a single object instance of a specific type. A perfect hash code algorithm will always return a hash code that is unique to a single instance of a specific type. A good candidate for a hash code is something like the identity field for a row within a database. The `Hashtable` uses hash codes to provide efficient and fast lookups. When creating custom types you have to implement a good hash code algorithm.

As any type can be used with most of the collections in the .NET framework class library, the `System.Object` class has a method called `GetHashCode` that returns a hash code for any object instance. The system-provided implementation of this method returns a hash code that uniquely identifies an object instance, but it's not specific to a given type. The returned value is simply an index held internally by the CLR for identifying an object. This means that if the system-provided implementation of `GetHashCode` is not overridden by a type, then by default, if two hash code values are the same then it's the same object instance, as shown in this code:

```
Class SomeType {};

SomeType variable1 = new SomeType();
SomeType variable2;

variable2 = variable1;

if ( variable1.GetHashCode() == variable2.GetHashCode() )
{
   Console.WriteLine("The two variables reference the same object");
}
```

Hash codes enable classes like the `Hashtable` to efficiently store and retrieve values. When an item is added to a `Hashtable`, the hash code of its associated key is used to determine a slot where an item can be held. If a key with the same hash code doesn't already exist at the slot located using the hash code, the value can be saved. If the slot is already full, `System.Object.Equals` is called to determine if the key already in the slot is in fact equal to the one used to locate the slot. If both keys are equal, the existing value is overwritten. If the keys are in fact different, a new key and value is added to the hash table in a different slot.

For the reasons above, any type used as a key within a hash table must:

❑ Implement an efficient hash code algorithm that, where possible, uniquely identifies an object of a specific type. You must therefore override `System.Object.GetHashCode`.

❑ Override the `System.Object.Equals` and provide an efficient comparison of two object instances. Typically you'll implement this by comparing the hash codes (if you know the hash code is always unique), or key fields that are held within a type as fields.

You can enumerate all of the keys and values in a hash table using the `Keys` or `Values` properties. Both of these properties are defined as the type `ICollection`, so they can be accessed in numerous ways. For demonstration purposes, the following code uses the `foreach` statement of C# to enumerate the keys. Under the hood, this code will result in a call to `table.Keys.GetEnumerator` (remember `ICollection` inherits this from `IEnumerable`). This will return an enumerator object that implements `IEnumerator`, which is then used to walk through each key value:

C#

```
<%
Hashtable table = new Hashtable();

table["name"] = "Richard";
table["age"] = "Old enough";

foreach( string key in table.Keys )
{
   Response.Write("<br>" + key );
}
%>
```

And then we can use the `for...each` construct of VB to enumerate the values:

VB

```
<%

dim table as Hashtable = new Hashtable()
dim value as string

table("name") = "Richard"
table("age") = "Old enough"

for each value in table.Values
   Response.Write("<br>" & value )
next

%>
```

The `Hashtable` class implements the interface `IEnumerable`, so as expected, we can enumerate all contained keys and items. The enumerator object returned by the `Hashtable`'s implementation of `IEnumerable.GetEnumerator` call exposes contained items using the value type `System.Collections.DictionaryEntry`. This type has properties that enable us to access the associated `Key` and `Value` properties. To list all of the keys and current values held in a `hashtable` we could write the following code:

C#

```
foreach( DictionaryEntry entry in table)
{
   Response.Write("<BR>Key:" + entry.Key + " Value:" + entry.Value );
}
```

The public `GetEnumerator` method of the `Hashtable` returns the interface `IDictionaryEnumerator`. This enumerator interface has all the methods and properties of `IEnumerator`, but also has three additional properties that expose the `Key`, `Value`, and `DictionaryEntry` of the current item. The reason for returning a custom enumerator with these additional properties is to reduce casting when the `foreach` statement cannot be used. This in turn improves performance of an application, since a cast does incur some overhead, since CLR must check that a cast is type-safe.

This code shows how you'd use the `IDictionaryEnumerator` interface:

C#

```
IDictionaryEnumerator e;

e= table.GetEnumerator();

while(e.MoveNext())
{
   Response.Write("<BR>Key:" + e.Key +
                  " Value:" + e.Value );
}
```

When the type implements the `IEnumerable` interface, it still has to implement a version of the `GetEnumerator` interface, which returns an `IEnumerator` interface.

This code shows how you would implement an enumerable type that supports both the standard `IEnumerable.GetEnumerator` property using an explicit interface method definition, and a public `GetEnumerator` method that reduces the need for casting:

C#

```
class MyCollection : IEnumerable
{
  public MyCustomEnumerator GetEnumerator()
  {
    return new MyCustomEnumerator();
  }

  IEnumerator IEnumerable.GetEnumerator()
  {
    return new MyCustomEnumerator();
  }
}
```

Hashtable Behavioral Differences with the ASP.NET Intrinsics

This behavior of directly using the `Hashtable`, although similar to the ASP.NET intrinsic objects, has a few differences:

❑ The key values for a `Hashtable` are not restricted to strings. Any type can be used, providing the type used as a key overrides the `System.Object.Equals` and `System.Object.GetHashCode` methods.

❑ String keys are case-sensitive whereas the ASP.NET intrinsic objects are not.

❑ When enumerating over an ASP.NET intrinsic object, you are enumerating over the keys associated with each contained item value. The `hashtable` returns both the key and value using the `DictionaryEntry` class.

❑ When enumerating over an ASP.NET intrinsic object the `Current` property returns the type `System.String` (they key value) and not `System.Collections.DictionaryEntry`.

IDictionary – Working with Unordered Collections of Key-Value Pairs

The `IDictionary` defines methods and properties that allow you to work with an unordered collection of keys, and their associated values. Keys and values are both defined in this interface as the type `System.Object`. This means any type can be used as a key, and any type can be used as a value.

The `IDictionary` interface defines methods and properties that allow you to:

❑ Add items to the collection by calling the `Add` method, passing in the key and value

❑ Delete items from the collection by calling the `Remove` method, passing the key of the value to delete

❑ Determine if a specified key is associated with an item using the `Contains` method

❑ Empty the collection by calling the `Clear` method

❑ Enumerate all of the keys in the collection using the `Keys` property; this property is defined as `ICollection`

❑ Enumerate all of the values in the collection using the `Values` property; this property is defined as `ICollection`

❑ Enumerate key-value pairs by using the `GetEnumerator` method. This returns an `IDictionaryEnumerator` interface, which is discussed shortly

❑ Determine if the collection is read-only using the `IsReadOnly` property

❑ Determine if the collection is of a fixed size using the `IsFixedSize` property

The `IDictionary` interface derives from `ICollection` interface so it therefore inherits all of its methods and properties, as well as the basic interface `IEnumerable`.

Hashtable Keys are Case-Sensitive by Default

With the ASP.NET intrinsic objects, key values are case insensitive. This means the following code that uses the session intrinsic will happily set and retrieve the value correctly, even though the case in the key is different:

C#

```
Session["key"] = "value";
Response.Write("<P>value is " + Session["KEY"] );
```

The following code shows the hash codes for two objects that contain the same string value, but with differing case:

```
<%@Page Language="C#"%>
<%
string name1, name2;

name1 = "Richard";
name2 = "RICHARD";

Response.Write( "Hash code one is " + name1.GetHashCode() );
Response.Write( "<BR>");
Response.Write( "Hash code two is " + name2.GetHashCode() );
%>
```

Since the .NET framework is case-sensitive by default, the hash codes for these strings are unique:

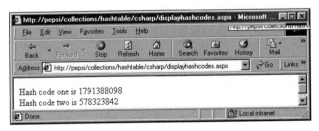

Although both strings contain the same name (Richard) the algorithm used to generate the hash code is case-sensitive. As key values, these string values are therefore considered unique. If we want two strings with different casing to be considered the same, we have to implement a **HashCodeProvider**. This class determines hash codes for other types, and can therefore use a different algorithm to create a hash code, which is not based on case-sensitive letters.

Since it's common to have case-insensitive keys, the .NET framework has a built-in hash code provider, which is case-insensitive:

```
<%@Page Language="C#"%>
<%
string name1, name2;
IHashCodeProvider hcp;

hcp = CaseInsensitiveHashCodeProvider.Default;
name1 = "Richard";
name2 = "RICHARD";

Response.Write( "Hash code one is " + hcp.GetHashCode( name1 ) );
Response.Write( "<BR>");
Response.Write( "Hash code two is " + hcp.GetHashCode( name2 ) );
%>
```

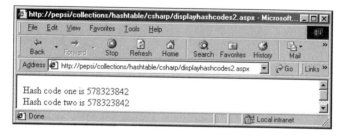

Classes like the Hashtable can use hash code providers to override their behavior. The following code shows how to create a hash table that is not case-sensitive when string keys are used, by using the standard framework classes CaseInsensitiveHashCodeProvider and CaseInsensitiveComparer:

C#

```
Hashtable ourSession;
ourSession = new Hashtable( CaseInsensitiveHashCodeProvider.Default,
        CaseInsensitiveComparer.Default );
Session["key"] = "value";
Response.Write("<P>value is " + Session["KEY"] );
```

In this code, the value will be correctly displayed in the browser since the value will be found, even though the casing of the key is different.

The CaseInsensitiveHashCodeProvider class provides an implementation of the IHashCodeProvider interface that creates a case-insensitive hash code of string types. For non-string types, the objects default hash code is returned, meaning that such types may still be case-sensitive depending on the algorithm used to create the hash. The CaseInsensitiveComparer provides an implementation of IComparer that for two string values will perform a case-insensitive comparison. If either of the objects being compared is not a string, it uses the default comparer object Comparer.Default, which we saw earlier in the chapter.

Both CaseInsensitiveHashCodeProvider and CaseInsensitiveComparer have a static property called Default that returns an instance of the class that is shared and always available.

Since creating a case-insensitive hash table is a common requirement, a helper class System.Collections.Specialized.CollectionsUtil can be used to create one:

```
Hashtable names;
names = CollectionsUtil.CreateCaseInsensitiveHashtable();
```

> With an ASP.NET page the `System.Collections.Specialized` is imported by default so you do not need to use fully qualified names or add your own import directive.

Stack

The `Stack` provides a Last-in First-Out (LIFO) collection of `System.Object` types. The last item pushed onto the stack is always the first item retrieved from the stack.

The `Stack` class can be extremely useful when performing recursive operations where you often need to save and restore values in order (such as the context within a XSLT processor), but the number of values saved and restored is not necessarily known in advance. A `Stack` class can also be useful if you simply need to save the values of some variables while performing a temporary calculation, after which you want to recall the original values.

The `Stack` class implements the `ICollection` and `IEnumerable` collection interfaces, and can therefore be enumerated using the `for...each` statement of VB and C#, have its size determined, have specific items accessed using an indexer, and so on.

The following code shows how to push several items on to a stack and then retrieve them:

```
<%@Page Language="VB" %>
<%
dim s as Stack = new Stack()

s.Push("Alex")
s.Push("Dave")
s.Push("Rich")
s.Push("Brian")
s.Push("Karli")
s.Push("Rob")

do while s.Count > 0
  Response.Write( "<BR>" & s.Pop() )
loop
%>
```

In this code we keep retrieving items from the stack and displaying them until the `Count` property tells us there are no more items. As expected, the items are listed in reverse order in the browser since the last item (Rob) is retrieved first, then Karli etc.:

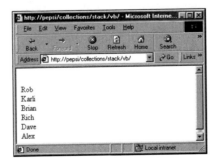

If we wanted to look at the item on the stack without actually removing it we could use the `Peek` method:

```
Response.Write( "<BR>" & s.Peek() )
```

The `Stack` class has a static `Synchronized` method that returns a thread-safe wrapper for a stack, enabling it to be called concurrently from different threads:

```
dim s as Stack = new Stack()
dim s2 as Stack
s2 = Stack.Synchronized( s )
```

> We should always use a thread-safe wrapper if multiple ASP.NET pages are going to access a shared object using application state, unless we provide our own synchronization.

Queue

The `Queue` class provides a First-In First-Out (FIFO) collection. This is useful when you need to process items in order, such as a list of in-memory work to do.

This code shows how to add items to the `Queue` and retrieve them, checking the `Count` property to ensure there are still items to be processed:

```
<%@Page Language="VB" %>
<%

dim q as Queue = new Queue()

q.Enqueue("Wake up")
q.Enqueue("Have a shower")
q.Enqueue("Get dressed")
q.Enqueue("Go to work")
q.Enqueue("Do a great job")
q.Enqueue("Come home and relax")

do while q.Count > 0

  Response.Write( "<BR>" & q.Dequeue() )
loop
%>
```

The output from this example shows the items are always retrieved in the order they are added (FIFO):

If we wanted to look at the item on the queue without actually removing it we could use the Peek method:

```
Response.Write( "<BR>" & q.Peek() )
```

The Queue class implements the ICollection and IEnumerable collection interfaces, and can therefore be enumerated using the for...each statement of VB and C#, have its size determined, have specific items accessed using an indexer, and so on.

The Queue class has a Synchronized method that can returns a thread-safe wrapper for a queue, enabling it to be called concurrently from different threads:

```
dim q as Queue = new Queue()
dim q2 as Queue
q2 = Queue.Synchronized( q )
```

A thread-safe wrapper should always be used if multiple ASP.NET pages are going to access a shared object using application state.

SortedList

The SortedList class is an interesting collection class, in that it's a cross between a hashtable and an ArrayList. The class implements the IDictionary interface and maintains key-value pairs like the Hashtable, but internally holds items in two arrays that are sorted.

The following code shows how to create and use a sorted list:

```
<%
SortedList alphabet = new SortedList();

alphabet.Add( "Z", "The Letter Z" );
alphabet.Add( "A", "The Letter A" );
alphabet.Add( "S", "The Letter S" );

Response.Write("<h3>A sorted list</h3>");

foreach( DictionaryEntry letter in alphabet )
{
  Response.Write( "<BR>" + letter.Key + " - " + letter.Value);
}
%>
```

This code creates an instance of the SortedList class, adds a couple of items that represent some letters of the alphabet, and then uses the foreach statement to display the items:

The `SortedList` always maintains a sorted collection of items. When an item is inserted, a binary search is performed to see if the key specified already exists. If the key is already in use, an `ArgumentException` is thrown since keys must be unique. If the key is not in use, the return code from the binary search (`Array.BinarySearch`) is used to determine the insert point of the new item.

The sort order for a `SortedList` is determined by the `IComparer` implementation used. The default comparer is `System.Collections.Comparer`. As we discussed earlier, this implementation uses the `IComparable` interface of the left object passed into the `IComparer.Compare` method. In our example the key is a string type, so the result is that our list is sorted alphabetically in ascending order (it will also be case-sensitive), since that's how the `string` type implementation of `IComparable` works.

An overloaded constructor of `SortedList` allows you to specify a custom `IComparer` interface if you need to override the sort order for a list of items:

```
IComparer ic = new SomeCustomTypeThatImplementsIComparer()
SortedList alphabet = new SortedList(ic);
```

If you need to create a case-insensitive sorted list, you could use the `System.Collections.Comparer` with this overload, or you can use the `CreateCaseInsensitiveSortedList` static method of the `CollectionsUtil` class, which basically just saves some typing:

```
SortedList alphabet;
alphabet = CollectionsUtil.CreateCaseInsensitiveSortedList();
```

> The **SortedList** class implements the **IDictionary** and **IEnumerable** interfaces. The **IEnumerable.GetEnumerator** method returns an **IDictionaryEnumerator** type.

From a performance perspective, accessing items using an indexer or searching for an item is very quick. Adding items to a sorted list can be slower than unsorted lists, since internally the `SortedList` class holds keys and values in two different arrays. Arrays are held contiguously in memory, when an item is inserted between two existing items, the items to the right of the insertion point have to be moved to make room. This copying of memory can be relatively slow for large lists, so you may want to consider an alternative approach.

Creating an Indexed/Sorted View of an Existing Collection

The `SortedList` class has a constructor that accepts an `IDictionary` parameter. When used, this constructor will copy the contents of a specified collection. This provides a great way of sorting/indexing existing collections of items, without changing the source collection. The two collections are detached, so the changing one does not affect the other once the copy is complete.

The following code creates an unordered list of names using a `Hashtable`, and then creates a sorted list using the `SortedList` class:

```
<%@Page Language="C#" %>
<%
// Create the unordered list of names and display them

Hashtable names = new Hashtable();
```

```
names.Add( "RA", "Richard Anderson" );
names.Add( "DS", "David Sussman" );
names.Add( "RH", "Rob Howard" );
names.Add( "AH", "Alex Homer" );
names.Add( "KW", "Karli Watson" );
names.Add( "BF", "Brian Francis" );

Response.Write("<h3>Unsorted list</h3>");

foreach( DictionaryEntry name in names )
{
  Response.Write( "<BR>" + name.Key + " - " + name.Value);
}

// Create a sorted copy of the list

SortedList sortedNameList = new SortedList( names );

Response.Write("<h3>Sorted list</h3>");

foreach( DictionaryEntry name in sortedNameList )
{
  Response.Write( "<BR>" + name.Key + " - " + name.Value);
}
%>
```

The output from this code is shown here:

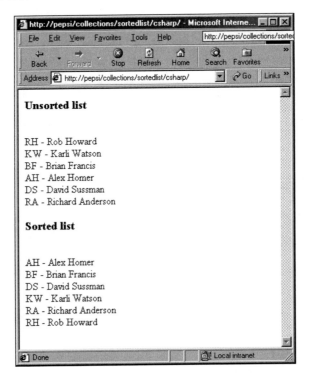

When a `SortedList` copies the contents of a source collection using the `IDictionary` interface, the list capacity is automatically resized to match the source. Once copied, no link between the collections is maintained. Any changes made to one of the collections do not affect the other.

The `SortedList` class has a `Synchronized` method that can return a thread-safe wrapper for a given `SortedList`.

BitArray

The `BitArray` class provides an efficient way of creating and manipulating a compact array of bit values. The bit array can be any size, and individual bits are represented as Booleans, where `True` equals **bit set**, and `false` equals **bit not set**.

This code shows how to create a bit array containing eight bits:

```
BitArray b = new BitArray(8);
```

By default all bits are set to `false`, although you can use an overloaded constructor to set the default value to `true`:

```
BitArray b = new BitArray(8,true);
```

The `BitArray` class implements the `IEnumerable` and `ICollection` interfaces. Using the `IEnumerable` interface we can display the values of the bit array:

```
<%@Page Language="C#" %>

<%
BitArray b = new BitArray(8,false);
int index;

Response.Write( "<br>Count property is :" + b.Count );
Response.Write( "<br>");

index = 0;

foreach( bool value in b )
{
  Response.Write( "<br>Bit " + index + " - value is : " + value );
  index++;

}

%>
```

The following shows the output you can expect to see from this code:

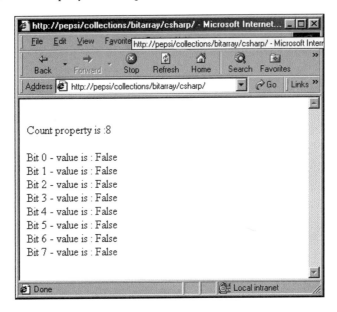

To set a bit, we can either use an indexer or the Set method. The following code sets bit 2 and bit 7 using both approaches:

```
<%@Page Language="C#" %>
<%
BitArray b = new BitArray(8,false);
int index;

Response.Write( "<br>Count property is :" + b.Count );
Response.Write( "<br>");

index = 0;

b[2] = true;  // using indexer - my preferred technique
b.Set(7,true);

foreach( bool value in b )
{
  Response.Write( "<br>Bit " + index + " - value is : " + value );
  index++;
}
%>
```

The output after this code runs shows that bit 2 and 7 are set as expected:

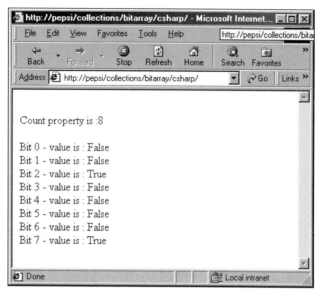

The `BitArray` class provides several methods that allow logical bit operations to be performed against a `BitArray`. These include:

❑ **And** – Perform a bitwise **AND** operation on the elements in the current `BitArray` against the corresponding elements in another `BitArray`.

❑ **Not** – Invert all bits in the array such that any 1's (`true`) become 0 (`false`) and vice versa.

❑ **Or** – Perform a bitwise **OR** operation on the elements in the current `BitArray` against the corresponding elements in another `BitArray`.

❑ **Xor** – Perform a bitwise **Exclusive OR (XOR)** operation on the elements in the current `BitArray` against the corresponding elements in another `BitArray`.

All of these logical operations work in the same way. The following code extends our previous example by creating a secondary bit array, setting bits 1 and 6, and then XOR-ing the second array with the first array:

```
<%@Page Language="C#" %>

<%

BitArray b = new BitArray(8,false);
BitArray b2 = new BitArray(8,false);
int index;

Response.Write( "<br>Count property is :" + b.Count );
Response.Write( "<br>");

index = 0;

b[2] = true;
b.Set(7,true);
```

```
   b2[0] = true;
   b2[1] = true;
   b2[6] = true;
   b.Xor( b2 );

   foreach( bool value in b )
   {
      Response.Write( "<br>Bit " + index + " - value is : " + value );
      index++;
   }
   %>
```

The expected result of an XOR is that a given bit is set to 1 if only one of the input bits is 1. If both bits are 0 or 1, the value should be zero.

The following screen shows the output of our XOR:

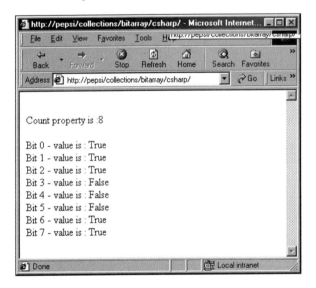

System.Collections.Specialized

The System.Collections.Specialized namespace contains collection classes that are suited to more specialized requirements, and collection classes that are strongly typed, which therefore limits the types that can be contained, and reduces the amount of casting needed.

StringCollection

The System.Collections.Specialized.StringCollection provides an implementation of an array list that can only contain string values. The class implements all of the functionality of the ArrayList type, but does all of the casting for you. The class implements the IList interface.

Here is a simple example of using the `StringCollection` class:

```
<%@Page Language="C#" %>
<%
StringCollection names = new StringCollection();

names.Add("Richard");
names.Add("Sam");
names.Add("Richard");
names.Add("Sam");

foreach( String name in names )
{
    Response.Write( "<BR>" + name );
}
%>
```

StringDictionary

The `System.Collections.Specialized.StringDictionary` provide an implementation of a hash table, where the key and value types are always `System.String`. The key is also case-insensitive. Internally, this class uses the `Hashtable` class for its implementation. You should use this class if you are only interested in dealing with string values.

The following code shows how to use the string dictionary to locate the surname of a given person:

```
StringDictionary names;
string surname;

names = new StringDictionary();
names["Richard"] = "Anderson";
names["Alex"] = "Homer";

surname = names["Alex"];
Response.Write("The surname for alex is " + surname );
```

Strongly Typed Collections

The fact that most collections classes in the .NET framework class library are designed to work with the `System.Object` type makes them very versatile. They can hold any type. However, this flexibility can also be a slight pain, since it means we have to do a lot of casting (assuming we know the type in the first place). For example, assuming a `Hashtable` contained a number of items of the type `Product`, you have to cast each item we retrieve:

C#

```
Hashtable products;
Product p;

p = (Product)product["ProductCode"];
```

VB

```
dim products as Hashtable
dim p as Product

p = CType( products("ProductCode"), Product )
```

Casting types like this isn't difficult, but it can make code less readable, and often leads to silly compiler errors when we forget to cast. Strongly-typed collections can resolve these problems. Rather than directly using the collection classes like `Hashtable` in our class, we instead provide a custom type that encapsulates the collection type being used, and also removes the need for casting. For example:

C#

```
ProductCollection products;
Product p;

p = products["ProductCode"];
```

VB

```
dim products as ProductCollection
dim p as Product

p = products("ProductCode")
```

Implementing a strongly-typed collection like this is relatively simple, and also enables us to build in additional build rules and error handling, saving us from duplicating throughout our code.

Let's look at the steps involved for writing a strongly-typed collection.

Step 1 – Define the Custom Type of the Item Held in the Collection

In our strongly-typed example, we used a `Product` type. When implementing a collection, you should always have a custom type, and a collection for that custom type, where the collection name is simply the custom type name appended with 'Collection', for example, `Product` and `ProductCollection`, `Address` and `AddressCollection`.

Here is a class definition for a `Product` type:

```
<%@Page Language="VB"%>
<script runat=server>

Public Class Product

' Private fields
```

```
Private _code as string
Private _description as string
Private _price as Double

' Constructor

    Sub New( initialCode as String, _
        initialDescription as String, _
        initialPrice as Double   )

    Code = initialCode
    Description = initialDescription
    Price = initialPrice
End Sub

    Public Property Description as String
        Get
            Description = _description
    End Get

    Set
        _description = Value
        End Set
    End Property

    Public Property Code as String
        Get
            Code = _code
    End Get

    Set
        _code = Value
        End Set
    End Property

    Public Property Price as Double
        Get
        Price = _price
    End Get

    Set
        _price = Value
    End Set
    End Property

    End Class
</script>
```

The Product type has three public properties:

- ❑   Code – a unique code assigned to the product

- ❑   Description – a description of the product

- ❑   Price – the cost of the product

All of the properties have a get and set accessor, and their implementation simply stores or retrieves the property value in a private field. The field name is the same as the property name, but prefixed with an underscore. The `Product` type has a constructor that accepts three parameters, thus allowing for quick initialization, for example:

```
dim p as Product
p = new Product( "PROASP3", _
        "Professional ASP 3.0", _
        39.99 )
```

> For demonstration purposes I'm defining classes inside of an ASP.NET page. Typically you would define these in a separate compiled assembly. That topic was introduced in Chapters 3 and 4, and is covered in more detail in Chapter 17.

Step 2 – Create the Collection Class

The `ProductCollection` class we're going to create will support two key features:

- ❑ Unordered enumeration of all the contained products
- ❑ Direct access of a product using a product code

Since the `Hashtable` provides the collection functionality we need to implement these features, we'll use that internally within our collection class for holding our items. We'll then aggregate the functionality of `Hashtable` and expose it, providing access to our items in a type safe way that doesn't require users of it to do any casting.

Since we're using a `Hashtable` internally to hold our `Product` items, we define a private field called `_products` of the type `Hashable` within our collection class, creating a new object instance assigned to it in the constructor:

```
...
dim _products as Hashtable

Public Sub New()
  _products = new Hashtable()
End Sub
...
```

The Add Method

The `Add` method allows a new `Product` to be added to the collection:

```
Public Sub Add( Item as Product )
  if Item is Nothing then
    throw new ArgumentException("Product cannot be null")
  end if
  _products.Add(Item.Code,Item)
End Sub
```

The `Add` method throws an `ArgumentException` if a null item parameter is passed. If the parameter is not null, the `Code` property of the passed `Product` is used as the key for the `Product` in the contained `Hashtable`. We could perform additional business logic validation here and throw additional exceptions depending on our requirements.

The Remove Method

The `Remove` method removes a `Product` from the collection. The implementation of the method simply calls the `Remove` method of the `Hashtable`:

```
Public Sub Remove( Item as Product )
  _products.Remove( Item.Code )
End Sub
```

The Item Property

The `Item` Property allows a `Product` to be retrieved from, or added to the collection using the Product Code:

```
Public Default Property Item(Code as String) as Product
  Get
     Item = CType( _products(Code), Product )
  End Get

  Set
     Add( Value )
  End Set
End Property
```

The implementation of the `Set` accessor calls the `Add` method to add the new product to the internal `Hashtable`. It is implemented like this so that any business logic in the `Add` method (such as the null check) is not duplicated or missed.

The GetEnumerator method

To enable our collection class to be used with the `for...each` statements in VB and C#, our collection class must have a method called `GetEnumerator`. Although not strictly necessary, we also implement the `IEnumerable` interface using the VB `Implements` keyword. This requires very little work and is good practice:

```
Public Class ProductCollection
  Implements IEnumerable
...
' Implement an enumerator for the products

Public Function GetEnumerator() As IEnumerator _
  Implements IEnumerable.GetEnumerator

  GetEnumerator = _products.Values.GetEnumerator()
End Function


...

End Class
```

The `GetEnumerator` method has to return an enumerator object that implements the `IEnumerator` interface. We could implement this interface by creating another class, but since our collection class is using a `Hashtable` internally, it makes much more sense for us to reuse the enumerator object provided by that class when its values are enumerated. As you should recall from earlier, the `Hashtable.Values` property returns an `ICollection` interface. Since the `ICollection` interface derives from `IEnumerable`, we can call `GetEnumerator` to create an enumerator object for the collection of values.

Using the Collection Class

With the `Product` and `ProductCollection` classes created, we can use them just like the other
collections we have seen in this chapter, but with no casting:

```
<%

' List products where the price is greater than 40 dollars

dim products as ProductCollection
dim p as product

products = new ProductCollection()

p = new Product("CAR", "A New Car", 19999.99 )
products.Add( p )

p = new Product("HOUSE", "A New House", 299999.99 )
products.Add( p )

p = new Product("BOOK", "A New Book", 49.99 )
products( p.Code ) = p

Response.Write("<h4>Product List</h4>")

for each p in products
   Response.Write (p.Code & "-" & p.Description & "-" & p.Price )
   Response.Write("<BR>")
next

products.Remove( products("HOUSE") )

Response.Write("<h4>Product List (HOUSE removed)</h4>")

for each p in products
   Response.Write (p.Code & "-" & p.Description & "-" & p.Price )
   Response.Write("<BR>")
next

Response.Write("<p>")

Response.Write("<BR>Description for code CAR is:" & _
               products("CAR").Description )

%>
```

The output of this code is shown here:

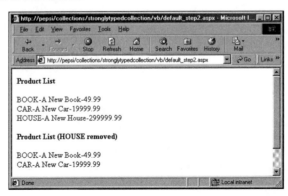

Here is the complete ASP.NET code written in VB for the `Product` and `ProductCollection` classes, as well as the ASP.NET page:

```vb
<%@Page Language="VB"%>

<script runat=server>

    ' Defines a product

    Public Class Product

    ' Private members

        dim _code as string
        dim _description as string
        dim _price as Double

    ' Constructor

    Sub New( initialCode as String, _
             initialDescription as String, _
             initialPrice as Double   )

        Code = initialCode
        Description = initialDescription
        Price = initialPrice

    End Sub

    Public Property Description as String

    Get
        Description = _description
    End Get

    Set
        _description = Value
        End Set

    End Property

    Public Property Code as String
        Get
            Code = _code
        End Get

    Set
        _code = Value
        End Set
    End Property

    Public Property Price as Double

        Get
            Price = _price
        End Get
```

```
        Set
            _price = Value
        End Set

    End Property

End Class

' Define a Products Collection

Public Class ProductCollection

Implements IEnumerable

dim _products as Hashtable

Public Sub New()
    _products = new Hashtable()
End Sub

' Implement an enumerator for the products

Public Function GetEnumerator() As IEnumerator _
    Implements IEnumerable.GetEnumerator

    GetEnumerator = _products.Values.GetEnumerator()
End Function

Public Default Property Item(Code as String) as Product
    Get
        Item = CType( _products(Code), Product )
    End Get

Set
    Add(Value)
    End Set
End Property

Public Sub Add( Item as Product )
    if Item is Nothing then
        throw new ArgumentException("Product cannot be null")
    end if

    _products.Add(Item.Code,Item)
End Sub

Public Sub Remove( Item as Product )
    _products.Remove( Item.Code )
End Sub

End Class

</script>

<%
```

```
' List products where the price is greater than 40 dollars

dim products as ProductCollection
dim p as product

products = new ProductCollection()

p = new Product("CAR", "A New Car", 19999.99 )
products.Add( p )

p = new Product("HOUSE", "A New House", 299999.99 )
products.Add( p )

p = new Product("BOOK", "A New Book", 49.99 )
products( p.Code ) = p

Response.Write("<h4>Product List</h4>")

for each p in products
    Response.Write (p.Code & "-" & p.Description & "-" & p.Price )
    Response.Write("<BR>")
next

products.Remove( products("HOUSE") )

Response.Write("<h4>Product List (HOUSE removed)</h4>")

for each p in products
    Response.Write (p.Code & "-" & p.Description & "-" & p.Price )
    Response.Write("<BR>")
next

Response.Write("<p>")

Response.Write("<BR>Description for code CAR is:" & _
               products("CAR").Description )

%>
```

Here is the same code written in C#:

```
<%@Page Language="C#"%>

<script runat=server>

    // Defines a product

    public class Product
    {

    // Private members

        string _code;
        string _description;
        double _price;
```

```
   // Constructor

      public Product( string initialCode,
         string initialDescription,
         double initialPrice)
   {

      Code = initialCode;
      Description = initialDescription;
      Price = initialPrice;
   }

   public string Description
   {

      get { return _description; }

      set { _description = value; }

   }

   public string Code
   {

      get { return _code; }
      set { _code = value; }
   }

   public double Price
   {
      get { return _price; }

      set { _price = value; }
   }
 }

// Define a Products Collection
   public class ProductCollection : IEnumerable
   {

      Hashtable _products;

      public ProductCollection()
   {
      _products = new Hashtable();
   }

// Implement an enumerator for the products

   public IEnumerator GetEnumerator()
   {

      return _products.Values.GetEnumerator();
   }
```

```
      public Product this[ string Code ]
      {

         get { return (Product) _products[Code]; }

         set { Add(value); }
      }

      public void Add( Product Item )
      {

         if ( Item == null )
         throw new ArgumentException("Product can not be null");

      _products.Add(Item.Code,Item);
      }

      public void Remove( Product Item )
      {
         _products.Remove( Item.Code );
      }

      }

</script>

<%

// List products where the price is greater than 40 dollars
ProductCollection products;
Product p;

products = new ProductCollection();

p = new Product("CAR", "A New Car", 19999.99 );
products.Add( p );

p = new Product("HOUSE", "A New House", 299999.99 );
products.Add( p );

p = new Product("BOOK", "A New Book", 49.99 );
products[p.Code] = p;

Response.Write("<h4>Product List</h4>");

foreach( Product p2 in products )
{
  Response.Write (p2.Code + "-" + p2.Description + "-" + p2.Price );
  Response.Write("<BR>");
}

products.Remove( products["HOUSE"] );

Response.Write("<h4>Product List (HOUSE removed)</h4>");
```

```
foreach( Product p2 in products )
{
  Response.Write (p2.Code + "-" + p2.Description + "-" + p2.Price );
  Response.Write("<BR>");
}

Response.Write("<p>");
Response.Write("<BR>Description for code CAR is:" +
               products["CAR"].Description );
%>
```

DictionaryBase and CollectionBase

The DictionaryBase and CollectionBase classes allow you to respectively create a Hashtable or ArrayList collection that can validate, and therefore restrict the types it contains. It's a simple process to create your own collection class by deriving from these classes.

This simple ASP.NET page defines a collection class called MyStringCollection, adds three strings and one integer, then displays the contents:

```
<%@Page Language="VB" %>

<script runat="server">

' Our custom collection

Class MyStringCollection
  Inherits CollectionBase
End Class

</script>

<%
    dim names as IList
    dim name as string

    names = new MyStringCollection

    names.Add("Richard")
    names.Add("Alex")
    names.Add("Dave")
    names.Add( 2002 )

    for each name in names
    Response.Write( name & "<BR />" )
    next
%>
```

The Collection base class implements the interfaces IList and ICollection. All the members of these interfaces are defined explicitly, which is why in the sample code we have defined the names variables as the type IList.

Each of the collection base classes provides a number of virtual functions that are called when the collection is modified. For example, `OnClear` is called when a collection is cleared; `OnInsert` is called when an item is added; `OnRemove` when an item is deleted, and so forth. By overriding one of these methods, you can perform additional checks and potentially throw an exception if you're not happy that a given precondition has been met. For example, we could implement an `OnInsert` method in our collection class that throws an `ArgumentException` if anything other than a string is added to it as follows:

```
Class MyStringCollection
  Inherits CollectionBase

  Overrides Protected Sub OnInsert( index as Integer, _
          item as Object )

     if not (typeof item is string) then
        throw new ArgumentException("Collection only supports strings")
     end if

  End Sub

End Class
```

The `DictionaryBase` class is used in the same way as the `CollectionBase` class. It implements the `IDictionary` and `ICollection` interfaces.

ReadOnlyCollectionBase

The `ReadOnlyCollectionBase` class provides functionality for exposing a read-only collection. The class implements the `ICollection` and `IEnumerable` interface. The items exposed are internally held in a protected `ArrayList` variable called `InnerList`. To use this class you have to derive your own class from it, and populate the contents of the `InnerList` array.

Disposable Enumerators – IEnumerator and IDisposable

When enumerating a collection, the enumerator objects that implement the `IEnumerator` interface may require expensive resources. For example, depending on how underlying items are stored, a custom enumerator could potentially be using a database connection, or be holding temporary files on disk. In these scenarios, it is important that the enumerable object releases its held resources as soon as possible. Due to the non-deterministic way the CLR releases object references, any code you write that directly uses an `IEnumerator` interface must always check if the enumerator objects that provided the interface supports the `IDisposable` interface, and call the `Dispose` method when you have finished with the enumerator. If you do not do this, the resources held by the enumerator may not be released for some time due to the way the CLR garbage collector works. When using the `foreach` language statement in C# and VB this is automatically done for you.

When using the `IEnumerator` interface directly (or any other enumerable type), if you do not know if an enumerator object supports the `IDisposable` interface you should always check once you have finished with it:

```
IEnumerator e = c.GetEnumerator();
try
{
  while (e.MoveNext())
  {
    Foo x = e.Current;
      ...;
  }
}
finally
{
    IDisposable d = e as IDisposable;
    if (d != null) d.Dispose();
}
```

If you know an enumerator object supports IDisposable you can call it directly:

```
IEnumerator e = c.GetEnumerator();
try
{
  while (e.MoveNext())
  {
  Foo x = e.Current;
        ...;
  }
}
finally
{
    ((IDisposable)e).Dispose();
}
```

Summary

In this chapter we've covered most of the interfaces and classes that comprise the `System.Collections` and `System.Collecton.Specialized` namespaces. We've examined the standard interfaces such as `IEnumerable`, `IEnumerator`, and `ICollection`, and we've discussed how these interfaces work together to provide a consistent way of using and creating collections. We've not covered every single collection class or method in this chapter (that's the job of the .NET SDK help), but hopefully you now have a pretty good feel for the type of functionality available.

In this chapter we looked at:

- ❑ How to use the standard collection classes such as `ArrayList`, `Hashtable`, `Queue`, and `Stack`.
- ❑ How to derive from collection base classes to quickly implement your own collection classes that restrict contained types.
- ❑ How to create strongly-typed collections that make using collections more intuitive for specific applications, leading to more readable code due to less casting.

In the next chapter, we'll look at the classes provided for working with text files, sockets, and regular expressions.

"The Babel fish," says The Hitch Hiker's Guide to Galaxy "is small, yellow and leech-like, and probably the oddest thing in the Universe. It feeds on brainwave energy not from its carrier but from those around it. It absorbs all unconscious mental frequencies from this brainwave energy to nourish itself with. It then excretes into the mind of its carrier a telepathic matrix formed by combining the conscious thought frequencies with nerve signals picked up from the speech centres of the brain which has supplied them".

The practical upshot of all this is that if you stick a Babel fish in your ear you can instantly understand anything said to you in any form of language. The speech patterns you actually hear decode the brainwave matrix which has been fed into your mind by your Babel fish.

16

Working with Other Base Classes

In the last chapter we introduced the .NET Framework class library, and spent a fair amount of time looking at the collection classes it provides for dealing with common data structures such as lists, queues, and stacks.

In this chapter we're going to continue our examination of the .NET Framework class library, this time looking at the classes provided for working with directories, files, regular expressions, and web requests.

In this chapter we'll cover:

- ❑ Examining the contents of the file system, working with files and directories
- ❑ Reading and writing data from backing stores such as the file system or memory
- ❑ Retrieving data in a generic way using stream objects
- ❑ Using regular expressions to parse text and extract values using captures

We'll start the chapter by looking at the classes used for working with the file system.

Working with Directories and Files

The .NET Framework base class library makes working with directories and files a joy. It provides an easy-to-understand set of classes located in the `System.IO` namespace that can be used to:

❏   Retrieve and change information about directories and files

❏   Manipulate paths, combining them or extracting individual elements of a path

❏   Read and write bytes of data from generic streams such as files and memory buffers

It's important to understand early on that the classes in `System.IO` are not just designed for working with the file system. They are designed to work with any number of **backing stores** that are accessed using **stream** objects.

A backing store is the .NET Framework term used to define a source from which data can be read or to which it can be written using a **stream** object. Each backing store provides a stream object that is used to communicate with it. For example, as we'll see later in this chapter, the `FileStream` class can be used to read and write data the file system, and the `MemoryStream` class can be used to read and write data memory. All stream classes derive from a common base class `Stream`. Just like the collection interfaces described in the last chapter, once you know what the common `System.IO` classes are, you'll find working with new data sources is a breeze.

Class Overview

The following classes are primarily used when working with directories, files and streams:

Class	Description
Directory	Provides static (shared) methods for enumerating directories and logical drives.
DirectoryInfo	Used to work with a specific directory and its sub-directories.
File	Provides static methods for working with files.
FileInfo	Used to work with a specific file.
Stream	Base class used to read from and write a backing store, such as the file system or network.
StreamReader	Used in conjunction with a stream to read characters from a backing store.
StreamWriter	Used in conjunction with a stream to write characters to a backing store.
TextReader	Abstract class used to defines methods for reading characters from any source (backing store, string etc.).
TextWriter	Abstract class used to defines methods for writing characters to any source (backing store, string etc.).
BinaryReader	Used to read primitive types such as string, integer, and Boolean from a stream.
BinaryWriter	Used to write primitive types such as string, integer, and Boolean to a stream.
FileStream	Used to read and write data in the file system.
MemoryStream	Used to read and write data in a memory buffer.

DirectoryInfo and Directory

The base class library provides two classes for working with directories, the `Directory` and `DirectoryInfo` classes. The `Directory` class contains a number of **static** methods (if you're a VB.NET programmer you'll know these as **shared** methods) that can be used to manipulate or query information about any directory. The `DirectoryInfo` class contains a series of **instance** methods (non-static or if you prefer non-shared) and properties that can be used to manipulate and work with a single named directory.

For the most part these classes have equivalent functionality, and can be used to:

❑ Create and delete directories

❑ Determine if a directory exists

❑ Get a list of sub-directories and/or files for a given directory

❑ Retrieve information about directories such as creation times and attributes, and allow changes to that information

❑ Get and set the current working directory (`Directory` class only)

❑ Get a list of available drives (`Directory` class only)

❑ Move directories

Although confusing at first, the reason for having two classes is actually to increase the degree of simplification and performance. For example, if we wanted to determine whether or not a given directory existed, we could use the static `Exists` method of the `Directory` class as follows:

```
<%@ Import Namespace="System.IO" %>
<%
if Directory.Exists("C:\Wrox") then
    Response.Write("C:\Wrox directory exists")
else
    Response.Write("C:\Wrox directory does not exist")
end if
%>
```

Since the `Exists` method is static, we've not had to declare a variable and instantiate an instance of the `Directory` class. This has made the code more readable, and also saved us a few CPU cycles by not instantiating the object.

> The constructor of the Directory class is declared as private so you cannot instantiate an instance of the class.

To check if a directory exists using the `DirectoryInfo` class, we first have to instantiate an instance of the `DirectoryInfo` class, passing the directory name we want to work with into the constructor. Then we call the `Exists` method of the object to determine if the directory exists:

```
<%@ Import Namespace="System.IO" %>
<%
dim dir as DirectoryInfo

dir = new DirectoryInfo("C:\Wrox")

if dir.Exists = true then
    Response.Write("C:\Wrox directory exists")
else
    Response.Write("C:\Wrox directory does not exist")
end if
%>
```

As the `DirectoryInfo` has instance members (they are not static) we have to use an object reference to access them. If all we want to do is check for the existence of a directory, using `DirectoryInfo` is overkill – we'd be better off using the `Directory` class. However, if we want to perform several operations against a single directory, then using the `DirectoryInfo` class is the right approach. Its code readability and general style is much improved, as shown by this additional line of code displaying the creation time of a directory, if it exists:

```
<%@ Import Namespace="System.IO" %>
<%
dim dir as DirectoryInfo

dir = new DirectoryInfo("C:\Wrox")

if dir.Exists = true then
    Response.Write( "<br>C:\Wrox directory exists")
    Response.Write( "<br>Created: " & dir.CreationTime )
else
    Response.Write( "C:\Wrox\Hello.Txt file exists does not exist")
end if
%>
```

Instantiating an object in this way and then using its members, or passing it as a parameter to method calls, is a fundamental concept in object-oriented programming. This is something we're all familiar with doing in classic ASP, using objects like ADO `Connection` or `Recordset`. If I were tasked with writing a method to display the contents of a directory in ASP.NET, I'd probably have the method accept a `DirectoryInfo` object rather than a `string` containing the directory name. It just looks neater, feels right, and can have performance benefits if the method was going to use the `DirectoryInfo` class to do a lot of work. Also, why create a new instance of the `DirectoryInfo` class when the caller might already have one?

Another more subtle benefit of using the `DirectoryInfo` class is that it will typically execute multiple operations against a single directory more efficiently. Once instantiated, it can maintain state such as the creation time and last modification date of a directory. When subsequent members are used, such as the `CreationTime` property, this state can be used to provide the results. In contrast, the `Directory` class cannot do this. It must go out and retrieve information about a directory each time a method is called. Although traditionally this wasn't a terribly expensive operation, in the land of the CLR this type of operation requires code access permissions to be granted by the runtime. This means the runtime has to ensure the code calling the method is allowed to know about the directory. These checks can be relatively expensive and should be avoided where possible, so using the `DirectoryInfo` class wherever possible makes good coding sense.

> The **DirectoryInfo** class performs different code access permission checks depending on the methods called. While some methods will not cause permission checks, others, such as **Delete**, always will.

File and FileInfo

When working with files we can use the File and FileInfo classes to discover information about them, and get access to a **stream** object enabling us to read and write the contents of a file.

The File and FileInfo classes provide equivalent functionality and can be used to:

❑   Create, delete, open, copy, and move files (these classes are not used for reading, writing, appending to, or closing files)

❑   Retrieve information about files, such as creation times and attributes, and also change that information

Like the Directory class, the File class has a series of static methods to manipulate or query information about a file. The FileInfo class on the other hand has a series of instance methods and properties that can be used to manipulate and work with a single named file.

Here is a simple code example showing how to use the File class to determine if a file exists:

```
<%@ Import Namespace="System.IO" %>
<%
if File.Exists("C:\Wrox\Hello.txt") then
        Response.Write( "C:\Wrox\Hello.Txt file exists")
else
        Response.Write( "C:\Wrox\Hello.Txt file does not exist")
end if
%>
```

The Exists method returns true if the file exists, and false if it does not.

Here is the same code using FileInfo, although this time we're also showing the file's creation time, like we did in our previous DirectoryInfo sample for the same reason:

```
<%@ Import Namespace="System.IO" %>
<%
dim myfile as FileInfo

myfile = new FileInfo("C:\Wrox\Hello.Txt")

if myfile.Exists = true then
        Response.Write("<br>C:\Wrox\Hello.Txt file exists")
        Response.Write("<br>Created: " & myfile.CreationTime)
else
        Response.Write("C:\Wrox\Hello.Txt file does not exist")
end if
%>
```

As with the DirectoryInfo class, FileInfo is the preferred class to use when performing multiple operations for reasons of readability, style, and performance.

Common Directory and File Tasks

Having introduced the various directory and file classes, now we'll look at some examples of how they can be used to perform common tasks, and some of the common exceptions that are thrown in error conditions.

Setting and Getting the Current Directory

When an ASP.NET page is executed, the thread used to execute the code that generates the page will by default have a current working directory of C:\Windows\System32. If you pass a relative filename into any System.IO class, the file is assumed to be located within the current working directory.

Retrieving the current working directory and/or changing it is a function of the Directory class. The following example shows how to change the working directory using SetCurrentDirectory and retrieve it again using GetCurrentDirectory:

```
<%@ Import Namespace="System.IO" %>
<%
Directory.SetCurrentDirectory("C:\Wrox")
Response.Write("The current directory is " & Directory.GetCurrentDirectory() )
%>
```

When writing an ASP.NET page you should make no assumptions about the current working directory. Typically you should never need to change it, since you should not use relative filenames within ASP.NET pages. You should use the Server.MapPath method to create a fully qualified filename from a relative filename.

Common Exceptions

In most of the code samples for this chapter we're not including exception handling. We've done this to keep our examination of the methods as clear as possible. However, you should be aware that like most other classes in .NET, the System.IO classes throw exceptions when an error condition occurs. The most common exceptions include:

❑   IOException – a general problem has occurred during the method

❑   ArgumentException – one or more of the method input parameters are invalid

❑   UnauthorizedAccessException – a specified directory, file or other resource is read-only and cannot be accessed or modified

❑   SecurityException – the code calling the method doesn't have enough runtime privileges to perform the operation

When writing code you should always use exception handling, as discussed in Chapter 22.

Listing Available Logical Drives

The GetLogicalDrives method of the Directory class returns a string array containing available drives:

```
<%@ Import Namespace="System.IO" %>
<%

dim Drives() as string
dim Drive as string
```

```
    Drives = Directory.GetLogicalDrives()

    For Each Drive in Drives
        Response.Write(drive)
        Response.Write("<BR>")
    Next
%>
```

Here is the output from this code, showing the server-side logical drives returned by the method call:

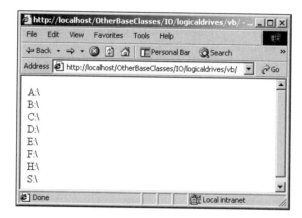

Creating a Directory

The following code shows how to create a hierarchy of directories in one method call using `Directory.CreateDirectory`:

```
<%@ Import Namespace="System.IO" %>
<%
Directory.CreateDirectory("C:\Create\Several\Directories")
%>
```

When the `CreateDirectory` method is called it will first check if the `C:\Create` directory exists. If it doesn't exist it will be created. Next, it will check if the `Several` directory exists within the `Create` directory. Again, if it doesn't exist it will create it. Finally, it will check if the `Directories` directory exists within the `Several` directory, creating it if it does not exist.

If you try to create a directory that already exists, an exception will **not** be thrown. An `ArgumentException` will only be thrown if part of the directory path is invalid. If you need to determine if a directory exists before creating it, you can use the `Directory.Exists` method.

The `DirectoryInfo` class has a `Create` method that provides the same functionality.

Listing the Contents of a Directory

The `Directory` class has the following methods for retrieving a list of its contents:

Method Name	Parameters	Description
GetDirectories	Pathname	Returns a string array filled with the fully qualified names of each contained directory.
GetDirectories	Pathname, SearchPath	Returns a string array filled with the fully qualified names of each contained directory that matches the search pattern.
GetFiles	Pathname	Returns a string array filled with the fully qualified names of each contained file.
GetFiles	Pathname, SearchPath	Returns a string array filled with the fully qualified names of each contained file that matches the search pattern.
GetFile SystemEntries	Pathname	Returns a string array filled with the fully qualified names of each contained directory and file.
GetFile SystemEntries	Pathname, SearchPath	Returns a string array filled with the fully qualified names of each contained directory and file that matches the search pattern.

The following code demonstrates using the `GetDirectories` method:

```
<%@ Import Namespace="System.IO" %>
<%
      dim dir as string
      dim subdirs() as string

      subdirs = Directory.GetDirectories("c:\")

      For Each dir in subdirs
         Response.Write(dir & "<BR>")
      next

         subdirs = Directory.GetDirectories("c:\","t*")

      For Each dir in subdirs
         Response.Write(dir & "<BR>")
   next
%>
```

This code demonstrates using the `GetFiles` method:

```
<%@ Import Namespace="System.IO" %>
<%
      dim f   as string
      dim files() as string
```

```
            files = Directory.GetFiles("C:\Wrox\")
            For Each f in files
                Response.Write( f & "<BR>" )
            next

            files = Directory.GetFiles("C:\Wrox\","h*")

        For Each f in files
            Response.Write( f & "<BR>" )
        next
    %>
```

Demonstration using the `GetFileSystemEntries` method:

```
<%@ Import Namespace="System.IO" %>
<%
        dim item as string
        dim items() as string

        items = Directory.GetFileSystemEntries("C:\Wrox\")

        For Each item in items
            Response.Write( item & "<BR>" )
        next

        items = Directory.GetFileSystemEntries("C:\Wrox\","h*")

        For Each item in items
            Response.Write( item & "<BR>" )
        next
    %>
```

The `DirectoryInfo` class also has the methods `GetDirectories`, `GetFiles`, and `GetFileSystemEntries`. These provide equivalent functionality, but with two important differences:

- ❏ No pathname is passed as an argument to the methods, since the class already knows the path as it was passed in as a parameter to the constructor when the `DirectoryInfo` object was created.

- ❏ The methods do not return string arrays. The `GetDirectories` method returns an array of `DirectoryInfo`. The `GetFiles` method returns an array of `FileInfo`. The `GetFileSystemEntries` method returns an array of `FileSystemInfo`, which is discussed shortly.

Deleting a Directory

You can delete a directory using `Directory.Delete` or `DirectoryInfo.Delete`:

```
<%@ Import Namespace="System.IO" %>
<%
        Directory.Delete("C:\Create",true)

        dim dir as DirectoryInfo
        dir = new DirectoryInfo("C:\Create")
        dir.Delete()
    %>
```

801

If you attempt to delete a non-existent directory a `DirectoryNotFound` exception will be thrown.

If you attempt to delete a directory that contains other files or directories, an `IOException` will be thrown unless you use an overloaded version of the `Delete` method that allows you to specify whether or not any contained files or directories should also be deleted:

```
<%@ Import Namespace="System.IO" %>
<%
        Directory.Delete("C:\Create",true)

        dim dir as DirectoryInfo
        dir = new DirectoryInfo("c:\Create")
        dir.Delete(true)
%>
```

Deleting a File

You can delete a file using the `File.Delete` or `FileInfo.Delete` methods:

```
<%@ Import Namespace="System.IO" %>
<%
        File.Delete("C:\myfile.txt")

        dim f as FileInfo
        f = new FileInfo("myfile.txt")
        f.Delete()
%>
```

If you attempt to delete a file that does not exist, no exceptions are thrown unless part of the path does not exist, in which case a `DirectoryNotFoundException` is thrown.

Working with Attributes, Creation Time, Last Modified Time, and so On

When working with directories and files, there are common operations that can be performed against both of them, such as deleting them. They also share common properties, such as their creation time, fully qualified name, and attributes.

The `FileSystemInfo` class defines members that are common to both files and directories. Both the `DirectoryInfo` and `FileInfo` classes are derived from this class.

The `FileSystemInfo` class has the following properties:

Name	Type	Read/Write	Description
Attributes	FileAttributes	Read/Write	Delete the file or directory.
CreationTime	System.DateTime	Read/Write	When the file or directory was created.
LastAccessTime	System.DateTime	Read/Write	When the file or directory was last accessed.
LastWriteTime	System.DateTime	Read/Write	When the file or directory was last updated.

Name	Type	Read/Write	Description
Exists	Boolean	Read	Indicates if the file or directory exists.
Extension	String	Read	Returns the file or directory extension, including the period. For a directory, the extension is the text located after the last period in the name.
Name	String	Read	Returns the name of the file/directory relative to its containing directory. This includes the extension.
FullName	String	Read	Returns the fully qualified name for the file/directory.

The `FileSystemInfo` class has the following methods:

Name	Description
Delete	Delete the file or directory.
Refresh	Update any cached state such as creation time and attributes with those present on disk.
Exists	Determines whether the file or directory exists.

> **FileSystemInfo is marshaled by reference, and therefore derives from MarshalByRefObject.**

To demonstrate using attributes, and other interesting methods and properties of the `DirectoryInfo` and `FileInfo` classes, let's take a look at the code required to write a simple web-based file browser:

This application accepts a path, and then lists any directories and files it contains. It also displays the last modified time for each directory and file, and their various attributes, such as if they have been archived.

The application uses a form to capture the path to be examined. This has an input control, which is marked as a server control using the `runat="server"` attribute, with the ID `DirName`:

```
<form runat="server" action="default.aspx">
  Directory Name: <input type="text" id="DirName" size="60"
              value="c:\program files\internet explorer"
                    runat="server" >
  <input type="submit" value="List">
</form>
```

When the page renders, it uses the `DirName.Value` server control property to initialize an instance of the `DirectoryInfo` class:

```
dim dir as DirectoryInfo
dim anchor as string
dir = new DirectoryInfo(DirName.Value)
```

The `DirectoryInfo` class is used rather than the `Directory` class, since we want to display details about the contained directories and files, such as their last modification date. The `Directory` class's `GetDirectories` method does not give us this information – it only provides the name.

The first block of rendering logic for the application outputs a table, listing the directory name being listed, and its subdirectories. The sub-directories are retrieved using the `GetDirectories` method of the `dir` object:

```
Response.Write("<h3>Sub Directories in " + DirName.Value + "</h3>")
Response.Write("<table>")
Response.Write("<tr bgcolor=cornflowerblue>")
Response.Write("<td>")
Response.Write( "Name" )
Response.Write("<td>")
Response.Write( "Last Modified" )
Response.Write("</tr>")

dim SubDir as DirectoryInfo

    for each SubDir in dir.GetDirectories()

......anchor = "<a href='" & "default.aspx?dir=" & _
        SubDir.FullName & "'>" + SubDir.Name & "</a>"
        Response.Write("<tr>")
        Response.Write("<td>")
        Response.Write( anchor )
        Response.Write("<td>")
        Response.Write( SubDir.LastWriteTime )
        Response.Write("</tr>")
    next

    Response.Write("</table>")
```

When listing each contained directory, we output an anchor tag that points back to our page with a URL that contains a `dir` parameter holding the fully qualified name of the sub-directory. This fully qualified name is returned by the `FullName` property. The actual text of the anchor is just the directory's relative name within its parent, which is accessed using the `Name` parameter:

```
for each SubDir in dir.GetDirectories()
   anchor = "<a href='" & "default.aspx?dir=" & _
      SubDir.FullName & "'>" + SubDir.Name & "</a>"

next
```

When a postback occurs, if the `dir` parameter is present in the query string, the `Page_Load` event sets the value of the `DirName.Text` property to its value. This allows our application to navigate down to sub-directories and list their contents:

```
<script runat="server">
   Sub Page_Load( sender as object, e as EventArgs)
      if not Request.Form("dir") is nothing   then
         DirName.Value = Request("dir")
      end if
   End Sub
</script>
```

The next section of the page has an anchor tag that shows the parent directory of the one being listed. This is determined using the `Parent` property. This value can be `null` if there isn't a parent directory, so our code checks for this, before rendering:

```
if ( not dir.Parent is nothing ) then
   anchor = "<a href='" & "default.aspx?dir=" & dir.Parent.FullName & _
      "'>" & dir.Parent.FullName & "</a>"
   Response.Write("<p>Parent directory is " + anchor )
end if
```

The parent directory is rendered as an anchor tag, which also uses the `dir` parameter, but this time to allow the user to navigate up from the current directory to the parent directory.

The final section of the page uses the `GetFiles` method to list files within the directory. As well as displaying the file name and its last modified date, this code shows what attributes are set on the file, such as if it's a system or a hidden file. These attributes are held in the `Attributes` property of the `FileInfo` class, which is declared as the enumeration type `FileAttributes`. The code uses the bit-wise and operator to determine if these attributes are set for a given file. If they are, we do some simple custom formatting to shows its presence:

```
Response.Write("<tr>")
Response.Write("<td>")
Response.Write(f.Name)

if ( (f.Attributes and FileAttributes.ReadOnly) <> 0 ) then
   Response.Write(" (read only)")
end if
if ( (f.Attributes and FileAttributes.Hidden) <> 0 ) then
   Response.Write(" (hidden)")
```

```
    end if
    if ( (f.Attributes and FileAttributes.System) <> 0 ) then
       Response.Write(" (system)")
    end if
    if ( (f.Attributes and FileAttributes.Archive) <> 0 ) then
       Response.Write(" (archive)")
    end if
       Response.Write("<td>")
    Response.Write( f.LastWriteTime )
    Response.Write("<td>")
    Response.Write( f.Length.ToString() )

    Response.Write("</tr>")
```

All enumeration types support the ability to convert a numeric enumeration value into a text value. This is very cool for debugging, and if we didn't want any custom formatting in our application, we could replace our explicit checks for given attributes, with the `ToString` method and let the enumeration type do the conversion for us, like this:

```
... Response.Write( f.Attributes.ToString() )
```

This would list out each of the attributes specified separated by a comma.

Working with Paths

When working with files and directories you often need to manipulate paths. The `Path` class provides members for:

❑ Extracting the elements of a path, such as the root path, directory, filename, and extension

❑ Changing the extension of a file or directory

❑ Combining paths

❑ Determining special characters, such as the path and volume separator characters

❑ Determine if a path is rooted or has an extension

The `Path` class has the following methods:

Method Name	Parameters	Description
ChangeExtension	Path, Extension	Takes a path (with or without an extension) and a new extension (with or without the period) as input and returns a new path with the extension.
Combine	Path1, Path2	Concatenates two paths. The second path should not be rooted. For example: `Path.Combine("c:\rich", "anderson" )` returns `c:\rich\anderson`.
GetDirectoryName	Path	Returns the directory or directories within the path.
GetExtension	Path	Returns the extension of the path if present.

Method Name	Parameters	Description
GetFileName	Path	Returns the filename if present.
GetFileNameWithoutExtension	Path	Returns the filename without its extension.
GetFullPath	Path	Given a non-rooted path, returns a rooted path name based on the current working directory. For example, if the path was `"test"` and the working directory was `"c:\wrox"`, the return path would be `"c:\wrox\test"`.
GetPathRoot	Path	Returns the root path.
GetTempFileName	None	Returns a temporary filename, located in the temporary directory returned by `GetTempPath`.
GetTempPath	None	Returns the temporary directory name.
HasExtension	Path	Returns a Boolean value indicating whether a path has an extension or not.
IsPathRooted	Path	Returns a Boolean value indicating if a path is rooted or not.

The `Path` class uses a number of static constants for defining special characters used with paths:

Constant Name	Type	Description
DirectorySeparatorChar	Char	The default character used to separate directories within a path. This returns the backslash character '\'.
AltDirectorySeparatorChar	Char	The alternative character that can be used to separate directories within a path. This returns the forward slash character '/'.
PathSeparator	Char	The character used when a string contains multiple paths. This returns the semi-colon character ';'.
VolumeSeparatorChar	Char	The character used to separate the volume name from the directory and/or filename. This returns the colon character ':'.
InvalidPathChars	Char Array	Returns all of the characters that cannot be used in a path because they have special significance.

The following application lets you enter a path, and then displays the component parts of a path such as the root path (logical drive), the directory, filename, and extension:

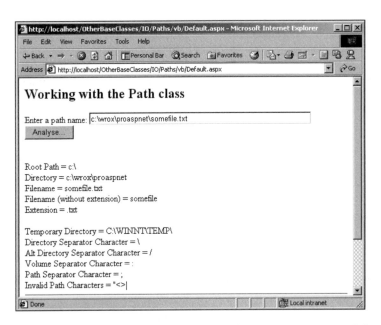

The code for this page shows how the various methods and constant properties of the Path class have been used to create this application:

```
if ( Page.IsPostBack ) then
    Response.Write("<BR>Root Path = ")
    Response.Write( Path.GetPathRoot(PathName.Text) )
    Response.Write("<BR>Directory = ")
    Response.Write( Path.GetDirectoryName(PathName.Text) )

    Response.Write("<BR>Filename = ")
    Response.Write( Path.GetFileName(PathName.Text) )
    Response.Write("<BR>Filename (without extension) = ")
    Response.Write(Path.GetFileNameWithoutExtension(PathName.Text) )

    if ( Path.HasExtension(PathName.Text) ) then
        Response.Write("<BR>Extension = ")
        Response.Write( Path.GetExtension(PathName.Text) )
    end if

    Response.Write("<BR>Temporary Directory = ")
    Response.Write( Path.GetTempPath() )
    Response.Write("<BR>Directory Separator Character = ")
    Response.Write( Path.DirectorySeparatorChar )
    Response.Write("<BR>Alt Directory Separator Character = ")
    Response.Write( Path.AltDirectorySeparatorChar )
    Response.Write("<BR>Volume Separator Character = ")
    Response.Write( Path.VolumeSeparatorChar )
    Response.Write("<BR>Path Separator Character = ")
    Response.Write( Path.PathSeparator )

    Response.Write("<BR>Invalid Path Characters = ")
    Response.Write( HttpUtility.HtmlEncode( new String(Path.InvalidPathChars)) )
end if
```

One point worth noting about this code is that we have used the `HttpUtility.HtmlEncode` method to HTML encode the `Path.InvalidPathChars` character array. We have to do this because the characters returned would otherwise be interpreted as HTML elements. The returned character array contains the greater than (>) and less than (<) characters.

Reading and Writing Files

The `File` and `FileInfo` classes provide a number of helper methods that can open an existing file, or create a new file. These methods do not perform the reading and writing of files, they actually instantiate and return other classes, such as `FileStream`, which are responsible for reading and writing **bytes** of data to and from a file; the `StreamReader` class, which can be used to read **characters** from a stream, or the `StreamWriter` class for writing **characters** to a stream.

The following code example shows the opening of a text file using `File.OpenText` and the reading of several lines of text from it:

```
<%@ Import Namespace="System.IO" %>
<HTML>
<BODY>
<%
    dim myfile as StreamReader
    dim name as string

    myfile = File.OpenText( Server.MapPath("names.txt") )
    name = myfile.ReadLine()

    do while not name is nothing
       Response.Write( name & "<BR>" )
       name = myfile.ReadLine()
    loop

    myfile.Close()
%>
</BODY>
</HTML>
```

In this code we use the `File.OpenText` method to open up the `names.txt` file. If successful, this method returns a `StreamReader` object that can be used to read characters (not bytes) from the file. The code uses the `ReadLine` method that reads all characters up to the next carriage return line feed. This method reads the carriage return line feed from the stream, but those characters are not returned as part of the string. When the end of the file is reached, a null string is returned. We check for this and use it to terminate our `while` loop. Calling the `Close` method closes the file.

> For scalability reasons and due to the non-deterministic finalization of the garbage collection you should always close files as soon as you can.

Creating a new text file and writing a few lines to it is shown in this example code:

```
<%@ Import Namespace="System.IO" %>
<%
dim books as StreamWriter

books = File.CreateText( Server.MapPath("books.txt") )

books.WriteLine("Professional ASP.NET")
books.WriteLine("Professional C#")
books.Close()
%>
```

We use the `File.CreateText` method to create a new file. This method returns an instance of a `StreamWriter` object that can be used to write data to the file. The code calls the `WriteLine` method of the object (which is inherited from the base class `TextWriter`) and outputs the names of the two books, after which the `Close` method is called to close the file.

Once you've written code to read or write data from a **backing store,** such as the file system, using the `StreamReader` or `StreamWriter` classes, you can easily read and write character data from other backing stores, such as memory buffers or network connections, using the **same** classes. This makes working with streams of data very consistent and very easy.

The main role of the `StreamReader` and `StreamWriter` classes is essentially to convert bytes of data into characters. As you are probably aware, different character encoding types, such as Unicode, ASCII, or UTF-8, use different byte sequences to represent their characters. No matter where bytes are read from, or written to, these same translations are performed, so it makes sense to always use the same classes for this purpose. To support this, the classes read and write bytes of data using a `Stream` class as shown in this diagram:

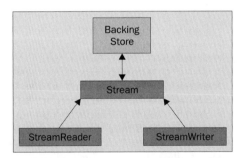

This generic model is very powerful. To support reading character data from different backing stores, all that is required is a stream object for each backing store. Each of these stream objects inherits from the `Stream` class and overrides several abstract methods that can be used for reading and writing bytes of data, providing the current position in the stream as well as changing it, determining the length of the stream, and exposing the capabilities of the backing store (for example, read-only, or write-only.)

This following diagram shows how reading and writing from the file system, network sockets, and a memory buffer is supported by this model:

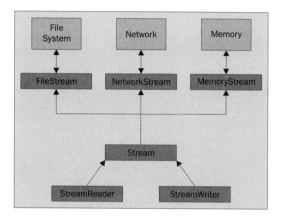

The `FileStream`, `NetworkStream`, and `MemoryStream` classes all derive from the `Stream` class.

The `StreamReader` and `StreamWriter` classes contain a reference to the stream object they use to access the associated backing store. This is held in the `BaseStream` property that is defined as the type `Stream`. Assuming we just had a reference a `StreamReader`, and we knew the backing store was actually a `FileStream`, we could use this property to get a reference to the original `FileStream` object:

```
dim myfile as StreamReader
dim backingStore as FileStream

' assuming backingStore and myfile are already initialized
...

backingStore = CType(myfile.BaseStream,FileStream)
backingStore.Seek(0,SeekOrigin.Begin)
```

The capabilities of a stream object will depend on the backing data store. For example, if we're using a `StreamReader` to read data from a socket (like a web page over HTTP), we cannot change the position of the stream since we cannot push data back into a socket once it has been read. To determine the capability of a backing store the `Stream` class has a number of read-only properties:

❑ `CanRead` – determines if data can be read from a stream. If this returns `true`, the `Read` method can be used to read a specified number of bytes from the `Stream` into a byte array at a given offset, or `ReadByte` can be used to read a single byte.

❑ `CanWrite` – determines if data can be written to a stream. If it returns `true`, the `Write` method can be used to write a specified number of bytes from a byte array to the `Stream`, or `WriteByte` can be used to write a single byte.

❑ `CanSeek` – indicates if a stream supports random access. If it does, the `Position` property of the stream class can be used to set the stream position, or the `Seek` method can be used to set a relative position from the start of the stream, end of the stream, or current position of the stream. The `SetLength` method can also be called to change the size of the underlying backing data store object.

> If you have used the `IStream` interface in COM before, you can consider the `Stream` its replacement in .NET. In future versions of .NET the `Stream` object will automatically expose the `IStream` interface through COM interop.

FileStream

The FileStream class provides all of the functionality you would expect to have available when reading and writing data to files. It derives from the Stream class, so inherits all of the properties and methods mentioned previously.

The FileStream class has the following constructors that you can use for opening and/or creating new files in various modes:

Parameters	Description
path as string, mode as FileMode	Specifies a path/file and how you want to work with it. FileMode is an enumeration that defines how you want to work with a file, and what actions you want to take if it already exists. We'll cover the values of FileMode shortly.
path as string, mode as System.IO.FileMode, access as FileAccess	As for the previous constructor, but allows you to specify if you want permissions to read, write, or read and write from the stream. Values for FileAccess are Read, ReadWrite and Write. The default is to request read and write access.
path as string, mode as System.IO.FileMode, access as FileAccess, share as FileShare	As with the previous constructor, but allows you to specify what access if any other people will have to the file while you're working with it. Values for FileShare are None, Read, ReadWrite, Write, and Inheritable. The default is None: nobody else can access the file.
path as string, mode as System.IO.FileMode, access as FileAccess, share as FileShare, bufferSize as Integer	As with the previous constructor, but allows you to specify the size of the internal buffer used to reduce calls to the underlying operation system. The default value is 4KB. You should not change the size of this buffer unless you have good reasons to do so.
path as string, mode as System.IO.FileMode, access as FileAccess, share as FileShare, bufferSize as Integer, useAsync as Boolean	As with the previous constructor, but tells the class the application calling it is using asynchronous IO. This can result in better performance for large reads and writes. The default value of this parameter is False.

The following code shows how you can create a new text file using the FileStream:

```
<%@ Import Namespace="System.IO" %>
<%
dim fs as FileStream
fs = new FileStream("MyFile.Txt", FileMode.Create )
fs.Close()
%>
```

Since we've specified the `FileMode.Create` parameter, any existing file called `MyFile.Txt` will be truncated (all existing content overwritten) when the file is opened. Other `FileMode` values include:

❑   `Append` – opens the specified file and seeks to the end of the stream. If a file does not exist, creates it.

❑   `CreateNew` – creates the specified file. If the file already exists, an exception is thrown.

❑   `Create` – creates the specified file, truncating the file content if it already exists.

❑   `Open` – opens the specified file. If the file does not exist, a `FileNotFound` exception is thrown.

❑   `OpenToCreate` – opens the specified file, creating it if it does not already exist.

❑   `Truncate` – opens the specified file and clears the existing contents. If the file does not exist, a `FileNotFound` exception is thrown.

Once a file is opened and you have a `FileStream` object, you can create a reader or writer object to work with the file's contents. This code shows how to write a few lines of text to a file by using the `StreamWriter`:

```
<%@ Import Namespace="System.IO" %>
<%
    dim fs as FileStream
    dim sw as StreamWriter
    fs = new FileStream("MyFile.Txt", FileMode.Create )
    sw = new StreamWriter(fs)
    sw.WriteLine("Professional ASP.NET")
    sw.WriteLine("Professional C#")

    sw.Close()
%>
```

When using a writer object to write data to a stream, you should only use one writer. You should never have multiple writers per stream. Writer objects buffer data in an internal cache to reduce calls to the underlying backing store. Having multiple writers active on one stream will result in unpredictable results.

The lifetime of the writer is tied to that of the stream. When the writer is closed, the stream is also closed by the writer, which is why we call `sw.Close` in this code rather than `fs.Close`.

When a stream is closed (assuming the writer didn't close it) the writer can no longer write to the stream. The same is true for reader objects. Any attempt to perform an operation on a closed stream will result in an exception.

The following code shows how you can open an existing file using the `FileStream` and read lines of text from it using the `StreamReader`:

```
<%@ Import Namespace="System.IO" %>
<%
    dim fs as FileStream
    dim sr as StreamReader
    dim line as String

    fs = new FileStream("MyFile.Txt", FileMode.Open )
    sr = new StreamReader(fs)
```

```
    line = sr.ReadLine()
    Response.Write(line & "<BR>" )

    line = sr.ReadLine()
    Response.Write(line & "<BR>" )

    sr.Close()
%>
```

In this code we're using the `FileMode.Open` parameter to tell the `FileStream` that we're opening an existing file. We use the `ReadLine` method to read two lines from the file and write that to our ASP.NET page using `Response.Write`.

MemoryStream

The memory stream allows you to read and write bytes of data from memory. It has several constructors that allow you to initialize the buffer to a given size (the default is 256 bytes), indicate whether the buffer is read-only – and can therefore not be written to, and also copy a specified amount of data from an existing array.

The following code demonstrates how we can use the `MemoryStream` class to create a byte array containing the text "Professional ASP.NET". Although something of an esoteric example, it demonstrates how to use a stream writer to fill the memory stream with some text, and then create a byte array containing that text:

```
<%@ Import Namespace="System.IO" %>
<%
dim memstream as MemoryStream
dim writer as StreamWriter
dim array() as Byte

memstream = new MemoryStream()
writer = new StreamWriter( memstream )

writer.Write("Professional ASP.NET")
writer.Flush()

array = memstream.ToArray()

writer.Close()
%>
```

The `StreamWriter` class uses an internal 1KB buffer to write blocks of data to the underlying stream and its associated backing store more efficiently. Calling its `Flush` method causes any buffered data to be written to the underlying stream prematurely before the 1KB limit is reached, and resets the buffer to an empty state. The `Flush` method is automatically called by the `Close` method of the `StreamWriter`.

In our code we use the `ToArray` method of the `MemoryStream` to convert the memory buffer into a byte array. We have to explicitly call the `Flush` method before calling this method, since the amount of data written to the stream using the `Write` method is less than 1KB. If we didn't call `Flush` first, we'd simply end up with an empty array, as no data would have actually been written to the memory stream. In this case we have to call `Flush`, since calling the `ToArray` method after calling `Close` would also result in an empty array, since the memory stream releases its resources (memory) when `Close` is called.

The `Capacity` property can be used to determine the amount of data a memory stream can hold before it will need to reallocate its buffer. You can set this property to increase or shrink the size of the memory buffer. However, you cannot set the capacity of the memory stream to be less than the current length of the memory stream, the length being how much data has been written to the memory stream. To determine how much data is currently in a memory stream you can use the read-only `Length` property.

The `MemoryStream` automatically manages its own capacity expansion. When a memory stream is full it doubles in size, allocating a new buffer and copying the old data across.

> Remember, when using classes like the **StreamWriter** to populate a memory stream, the memory stream's **Length** property will not be accurate until the stream writer's **Flush** method is called, due to the buffering it performs.

TextReader and TextWriter

The `StreamReader` class derives from the abstract class `TextReader`. This class defines the base methods that are useful to applications reading character data. It does not define any methods for opening or connecting to an underlying data source (backing store), those are provided by derived classes like the `StringReader` and `StreamReader`.

The `TextReader` has the following methods:

Method Name	Parameters	Description
Close	None	Closes the underlying backing store connection and/or dispose of any held resources.
Read	None	Reads the next character from the input stream.
Read	Char Array, index, count	Reads a specified number of characters from the input stream into an array at the specified offset. The number of characters read is returned.
ReadBlock	Char Array, index, count	Reads a specified number of characters from the input stream into an array at the specified offset. The number of characters read is returned. This method will **block** (the method will not return) until data is available.
ReadLine	None	Returns a string containing the next line of characters.
ReadToEnd	None	Reads all of the remaining content from the input stream into a string. You should not use this method for large streams, since it can potentially consume a lot of memory.
Synchronized	TextReader	Accepts a `TextReader` object as input and returns a thread-safe wrapper. This is a static method.

One of the reasons the `TextReader` class exists is so that non-stream-oriented backing stores, such as a `string`, can have an interface consistent with streams. It provides a mechanism by which classes can expose or consume a text stream without being aware of any implementation details about where the underlying data stream is. For example, the following code shows how a function can output the data read from a text-oriented input stream using an ASP.NET page (written using C#):

```
<script runat=server>

   protected void WriteContentsToResponse( TextReader r )
   {
      string line;
      line = r.ReadLine();

      while ( line != null )
      {
         Response.Write(line);
         Response.Write( "<BR>" );
         line = r.ReadLine();
      }
   }
</script>
```

Given a `TextReader`, this function reads lines of text using the `ReadLine` method, and then writes that back to the client browser using the `Response` object's `Write` method. As the HTML standard defines line breaks using the `<BR>` element, the function writes that element out after each line.

The `StringReader` class derives from `TextReader` to provide a way of accessing the contents of a string in a text-stream-oriented way. The `StreamReader` class extends `TextReader` to provide an implementation that makes it easy to read text data from a file. You could derive your own classes from `TextReader` and provide an implementation that makes it easy to read from your internal data source. This same model is used for the `TextWriter`.

The `StreamWriter` class derives from the abstract class `TextWriter`. This defines methods for writing character data. It provides many overloaded methods for converting primitive types like `Boolean` and `Integer` into character data:

Method Name	Parameters	Description
Close	None	Closes the underlying backing store connection and/or disposes of any held resources.
Flush	None	Flushes any buffered data to the underlying backing store.
Synchronized	TextWriter	Accepts a `TextWriter` object as input and returns a thread safe wrapper. This is a static method.
Write	Numerous overloads	Writes the passed parameter to the underlying data stream. The primitive types `string`, `char`, `char array`, `bool`, `integer`, `unsigned integer`, `long`, `unsigned long`, `float`, and `decimal` are valid parameter types. If a string and an object parameter are passed, the string is assumed to contain formatting specifications, so the `String.Format` method is called. There are method overloads for formatting that either take 1-3 object parameters or an array of objects as input.
WriteLine	Numerous overloads	Implemented as per the `Write` method, but also outputs the carriage return line feed characters.

The following code shows how the `Write` method can be used to write formatted strings using the various available overloads:

```
<%@ Import Namespace="System.IO" %>
<%

Dim myfile as TextWriter

myfile = File.CreateText("c:\authors.txt")
myfile.WriteLine("My name is {0}", "Richard")
myfile.WriteLine("My name is {0} {1}", "Richard", "James")
myfile.WriteLine("My name is {0} {1} {2}", "Richard", "James", _
                "Anderson" )

dim authors(5) as object
authors(0) = "Alex"
authors(1) = "Dave"
authors(2) = "Rich"
authors(3) = "Brian"
authors(4) = "Karli"
authors(5) = "Rob"
myfile.WriteLine( "Authors:{0},{1},{2},{3},{4},{5}", authors)

myfile.Close()
%>
```

The `authors.txt` file created by this code is shown here:

```
My name is Richard
My name is Richard James
My name is Richard James Anderson
Authors:Alex,Dave,Rich,Brian,Karli,Rob
```

StringReader and StringWriter

The `StringReader` derives from the `TextReader` class and uses a string as the underlying input stream. The string to read from is passed in as a parameter to the constructor.

The `StringWriter` class derives from the `TextWriter` class and uses a string as the underlying output stream. For efficiency reasons, this underlying string is actually built using a string builder. You can optionally pass in your own `StringBuilder` object as a constructor parameter if you want to add data to existing strings.

The following code shows how to build a multi-line string using the `StringWriter`:

```
<%@ Import Namespace="System.IO" %>
<HTML>
<BODY>
<%
    dim sw as StringWriter = new StringWriter()

    sw.WriteLine("The Cow")
    sw.WriteLine("Jumped Over")
    sw.WriteLine("The Moon")
    Response.Write("<pre>")
    Response.Write( sw.ToString() )
    Response.Write("</pre>")
```

```
    sw.Close()
%>
</BODY>
</HTML>
```

In this code we allocate a `StringWriter` and use the `WriteLine` method to build up the contents of the string. We retrieve the string using the `ToString` method, and render it within an HTML `<pre>` element to ensure that the carriage return line feeds within the string are not ignored by the browser:

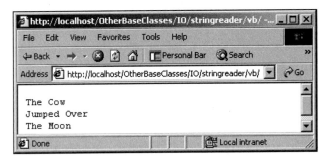

Reading and Writing Binary Data

When working with streams of binary data you often need to read and write primitive types. To achieve this you can use the `BinaryReader` and `BinaryWriter` classes.

The following code demonstrates how to use the `BinaryWriter` with a `FileStream` to write a few primitive types to a file:

```
<%@ Page Language="C#" %>
<%@ Import Namespace="System.IO" %>
<%
    BinaryWriter bw;
    FileStream fs;
    string filename;

    filename = Server.MapPath("myfile.bin");
    fs = new FileStream( filename, FileMode.Create );

    bw = new BinaryWriter(fs);

    string s = "a string";
    long l = 0x123456789abcdef;
    int i = 0x12345678;
    char c = 'c';
    float f = 1.5f;
    Decimal d = 100.2m;

    bw.Write( s );
    bw.Write( l );
    bw.Write( i );
    bw.Write( c );
    bw.Write( f );
    bw.Write( d );

    fs.Close();
%>
```

The following code shows how you could re-read the binary file created with the `BinaryWriter` using the `BinaryReader` class:

```
<%@ Page Language="C#" %>
<%@ Import Namespace="System.IO" %>
<%
    BinaryReader br;
    FileStream fs;
    string filename;

    filename = Server.MapPath("myfile.bin");
    fs = new FileStream( filename, FileMode.Open );
    br = new BinaryReader( stream );

    string s;
    long l;
    int i;
    char c;
    float f;
    Decimal d;

    s = br.ReadString();
    l = br.ReadInt64();
    i = br.ReadInt32();
    c = br.ReadChar();
    f = br.ReadSingle();
    d = br.ReadDecimal();

    fs.Close();
%>
```

Encodings

The `StreamReader` class, by default, will attempt to determine the encoding format of a file. If one of the supported encodings, such as UTF-8 or UNICODE, is detected it will be used. If the encoding is not recognized the default encoding of UTF-8 will be used. Depending on the constructor you call you can change the default encoding used, and optionally turn off encoding detection.

The following code shows how to specify a default encoding of `Unicode` when reading from a file:

```
Dim Reader as StreamReader
Reader = new StreamReader("somefile.txt", System.Encoding.Text.Unicode );
```

The default encoding for `StreamWriter` is also UTF-8, and you can override it in the same manner as the `StreamReader` class.

The following example code creates a file using each supported encoding:

```
<%@Page Language="C#"%>
<%@Import Namespace="System.IO" %>
<%@Import Namespace="System.Text" %>
<%
    StreamWriter stream;
    char HiChar;
    HiChar = (char) 0xaaaa;
```

```
        stream = new StreamWriter( Server.MapPath("myfile.utf8"), false,
                                          System.Text.Encoding.UTF8 );
    stream.Write( "Hello World");
    stream.Write( HiChar );
    stream.Close();

        stream = new StreamWriter( Server.MapPath("myfile.utf7"), false,
                                          System.Text.Encoding.UTF7 );
    stream.Write( "Hello World");
    stream.Write( HiChar );
    stream.Close();

        stream = new StreamWriter( Server.MapPath("myfile.ascii"), false,
                                          System.Text.Encoding.ASCII );
    stream.Write( "Hello World");
    stream.Write( HiChar );
    stream.Close();

        stream = new StreamWriter( Server.MapPath("myfile.unicode"), false,
                                          System.Text.Encoding.Unicode );
    stream.Write( "Hello World");
    stream.Write( HiChar );
    stream.Close();
%>
```

The size of each created file varies due to the way the different encodings work. As you might expect, the largest file is the Unicode-encoded one at 26 bytes. The smallest file is the ASCII file at 12 bytes. But, since the ASCII encoding can only encode 8-bit characters, and we've got a 16-bit character (0xaaaa) we're actually losing data. As a general rule, you should avoid ASCII encoding whenever possible and either stick with the default UTF-8 encoding, or use Unicode. UTF-8 is the preferred encoding since it typically requires less space than Unicode (17 bytes for our example) and is the standard encoding for web technologies (XML, HTML, and so on).

BufferedStream

The BufferedStream class reads and writes data to another stream through an internal buffer, the size of which can be specified in the constructor. This class is designed to be composed with other stream classes that do not have internal buffers, thus enabling you to reduce potentially expensive calls, by reading large chunks of data and buffering it.

The BufferedStream should not be used with FileStream or MemoryStream because they buffer their own data.

Copying Between Streams

One of the functions of the stream object not included in version 1.0 of .NET is writing the contents of one stream into another. This is something you may want to do, so here is some C# code that shows you how it can be implemented:

```csharp
public static long Pump(Stream input, Stream output)
{
    if (input == null)
        throw new ArgumentNullException("input");
    if (output == null)
        throw new ArgumentNullException("output");
```

```
        const int count = 4096;
        byte[] bytes = new byte[count];
        int numBytes;
        long totalBytes = 0;
        while((numBytes = input.Read(bytes, 0, count)) > 0)
        {
            output.Write(bytes, 0, numBytes);
            totalBytes += numBytes;
        }
        return totalBytes;
    }
```

This code uses a 4KB buffer to read data from the input stream and write it to the output stream. If the copy is successful the total number of bytes copied is returned. The function throws an `ArgumentNullException` if the input parameters are invalid.

Always call Close(), and Watch for Exceptions!

In the non-deterministic world of .NET you should **always** make sure you call `Close` on your streams. If you do not call `Close`, the time at which the buffered contents of a stream will be written to the underlying backing store is not predictable, due to the way the CLR garbage collector works. Furthermore, since garbage collection does not guarantee the order in which objects are finalized, you may also find your data is not written correctly and may even get corrupted. For example, it is possible for a stream to be closed before a writer object has flushed its data.

Because of this non-deterministic behavior, you should also always add exception handling to your code when using streams. There is no performance overhead at run-time for doing this in non-exceptional cases (that is when exceptions are not thrown), and by putting your stream cleanup code in the `finally` section of the exception handler, you can ensure resources aren't held for an unpredictable amount of time in the unlikely case that error conditions do arise.

If you're developing code in C# you should consider the `using` statement. This can be used to automatically close a stream for you when it goes out of scope, even if an exception is thrown. Here is a simple example of the `using` statement:

```
<%@ Page Language="C#" %>
<%@ Import Namespace="System.IO" %>
<%
FileStream fs = new FileStream("MyFile.Txt", FileMode.Create );

using(fs)
{
 ...
}
%>
```

In this code we create a file stream, then begin a new scope by using the `using` statement. When this `using` statement is exited (either normally or if an exception occurs), the resources held by the stream are released. Under the hood the `using` statement causes code to be generated that calls the `IDiposable.Dispose` method implemented by the `FileStream`.

> **For more information on the `using` statement check out the book *Professional C#, ISBN 1-861004-99-0*, also published by Wrox Press.**

ASP.NET and Streams

The ASP.NET page framework allows you to read and write content to a page using a stream:

❑ `Page.Response.Output` property returns a `TextWriter` than can be used to write text content into the output stream for a page.

❑ `Page.Response.OutputStream` property returns a `Stream` object that can be used to write bytes to the output stream for a page.

❑ `Page.Request.InputStream` property returns a `Stream` object that can be used to read bytes of data from a posted request.

Assuming content was posted to an ASP.NET page (such as an XML file), the following shows how we could read and display the data using the `Page.Request.InputStream`:

```
<%@ Import Namespace="System.IO" %>
<%
dim reader as StreamReader
dim line as String

reader = new StreamReader( Page.Request.InputStream )
line = reader.ReadLine()

do while not line is nothing
    Response.Write( line & "<BR>" )
    line = reader.ReadLine()
loop
%>
```

Writing Custom Streams

Depending on the type of applications or components you write, you may want to create your own stream class. Custom streams are fairly easy to write, and once written can be used just like the other stream classes such as `FileStream`, and used in conjunction with classes like `StreamReader` and `StreamWriter`.

There are essentially two types of stream you are likely to want to write:

❑ Streams that provide access to some type of custom backing store
❑ Streams that are composed of other streams to provide services such as filtering, compression, or encryption

To implement either of these you create a new class that derives from the `Stream` class and override the following properties:

Name	Get/Set	Type
CanRead	Get	Bool
CanWrite	Get	Bool
CanSeek	Get	Bool
Length	Get	Long
Position	Get/Set	Long

and these methods:

Name
Close
Flush
Seek
SetLength
Read
Write

The other methods of the Stream object, like ReadByte and WriteByte, use these members in their implementation. You can also override these methods and provide custom implementation. You should considering doing this for performance reasons.

Here is a simple custom stream implementation written in C# that you can compose from other stream objects. It accepts a Stream object as a constructor parameter, and implements all of the stream members by directly delegating to that object, except for the Read and Write methods:

```csharp
using System;
using System.IO;

namespace CustomStreams
{
    public class UpperCaseStream : Stream
    {

        Stream _stream;

        public UpperCaseStream(Stream stream)
        {
            _stream = stream;
        }

        public override bool CanRead
        {
            get { return _stream.CanRead; }
        }

        public override bool CanSeek
        {
            get { return _stream.CanSeek; }
        }

        public override bool CanWrite
        {
            get { return _stream.CanWrite; }
        }

        public override long Length
        {
```

```
      get { return _stream.Length; }
   }

   public override long Position
   {
      get { return _stream.Position; }
      set { _stream.Position = value; }
   }

   public override void Close()
   {
      _stream.Close();
   }

   public override void Flush()
   {
      _stream.Flush();
   }

   public override long Seek( long offset, System.IO.SeekOrigin origin)
   {
      return _stream.Seek( offset, origin );
   }

   public override void SetLength( long length )
   {
      _stream.SetLength( length );
   }

   public override int Read( byte[] buffer, int offset, int count )
   {
      int bytesRead;
      int index;

      // let base class do the read
      bytesRead = _stream.Read( buffer, offset, count );

      // if something was read

      if ( bytesRead > 0)
      {
         for( index = offset; index < (offset+bytesRead);
                              index++)
         {
            if ( buffer[index] >= 'a' && buffer[index] <= 'z')
            {
               buffer[index] = (byte) (buffer[index] - 32 );
            }
         }
      }

      return bytesRead;
   }
```

```
            public override void Write( byte[] buffer, int offset, int count )
            {
                int index;

                // if something was to be written
                if ( count > 0)
                {
                    for( index = offset; index < (offset+count); index++)
                    {
                        if ( buffer[index] >= 'a' && buffer[index] <= 'z')
                        {
                            buffer[index] = (byte) (buffer[index] - 32 );
                        }
                    }
                }

                // write the content
                _stream.Write( buffer, offset, count );
            }
        }
    }
```

The Read and Write methods scan the data passed in to them and convert any lower case characters to upper-case. In the case of the Read method, this is done after the Read method of the contained stream class is called. For the Write method it is done before the Write method of the contained stream is called.

The following code shows how we could create this custom stream and then code it to interact with a FileStream to automatically read and convert characters contained within a file to uppercase:

```
static void Main()
{
    UpperCaseStream customStream;

    // Create our custom stream, passing it a file stream

    customStream = new UpperCaseStream( new FileStream( "file.txt",
                                                        FileMode.Open ) );

    StreamReader sr = new StreamReader( customStream );
    Console.WriteLine("{0}",sr.ReadToEnd() );
    customStream.Close();
}
```

The following code shows how we could use this custom stream, in conjunction with a FileStream, to automatically convert written data to uppercase:

```
static void Main()
{
    UpperCaseStream customStream;

    customStream = new UpperCaseStream( new FileStream( "fileout.txt",
                                                        FileMode.Create ) );
```

```
        StreamWriter sw = new StreamWriter( customStream,
                                              System.Text.Encoding.ASCII );

        sw.WriteLine("Hello World!");
        sw.Close();
    }
```

If we examine the `fileout.txt` file we can see it contains the text "HELLO WORLD!"

This is a fairly simple custom stream implementation, but using the same technique you could write a more sophisticated composable stream class, maybe dynamically compressing, or securing data. Although not covered in this book, the `System.Security` namespace does contains a `CryptoStream` class for encrypting data, and third-party vendors are already working on compression streams.

Web Request Classes and Streams

Once you understand that streams provide a generic mechanism by which data can be read and written to a backing store, and that reader and writer objects provide higher-level functions to a stream such as the ability to read and write text, it's really easy to work with numerous backing stores in .NET.

To demonstrate how other namespaces in the .NET framework build upon the stream paradigm, we'll take a brief look at the `HttpWebRequest` and `HttpWebResponse` classes in `System.Net`. These classes make it a breeze to download a file over the HTTP protocol. We're not going to examine the `System.Net` namespace in depth, since it's outside the scope of this book.

HttpWebRequest and HttpWebResponse

To make an HTTP request you create an instance of the `HttpWebRequest` class using the static method `WebRequest.CreateRequest` method. This is a factory method that accepts the URI of an internet resource, and based upon that protocol, creates an instance of a protocol-specific request object. All protocol-specific request objects derive from the abstract class `WebRequest`.

When a URI is determined to use the HTTP protocol the actual concrete class created by the `WebRequest.CreateRequest` method is `HttpWebRequest`. When we write code to create a URI starting with http:// we can safely cast the object returned from `WebRequest.CreateRequest` back to an `HttpWebRequest` type.

Once you have a request object you use the `GetResponse` method to go out and start retrieving the resource. As with request objects, each protocol implements its own response object that derives from a common abstract class, `WebResponse`. This is the type returned by the `GetResponse` method of the request object. For the HTTP protocol the response object can be cast back to the concrete class `HttpWebResponse`.

The `HttpWebResponse` class has a method called `GetResponseStream` that returns a `Stream` object. This can be used to read the response data in exactly the same way you would read data from a file, or any other stream.

The following code shows how to download the **amazon.com** home page using the `System.Net` classes:

```
<%@ Import Namespace="System.IO" %>
<%@ Import Namespace="System.Net" %>
```

```
<H3>HTML for http://www.amazon.com</H3>

<%
dim myRequest as HttpWebRequest
dim myResponse as HttpWebResponse
dim sr as StreamReader
dim line as String

myRequest = CType(WebRequest.Create("http://www.amazon.com"), HttpWebRequest)

myResponse = CType(myRequest.GetResponse(), HttpWebResponse )

sr = new StreamReader( myResponse.GetResponseStream() )

line = sr.ReadLine()
do while not line is nothing

   line = HttpUtility.HtmlEncode(line)
   if line.Length <> 0 then
   Response.Write( line & "<BR>" )
   end if
   line = sr.ReadLine()
loop

sr.Close
%>
```

The output this page generates is shown here:

Let's take a look a closer look at what the code does.

The code initially constructs a web request using `WebRequest.Create` and casts the returned object back to an `HttpWebRequest`:

```
myRequest = CType(WebRequest.Create("http://www.amazon.com"), HttpWebRequest)
```

Next, the request is executed and the response object is retrieved. Once again, we can safely cast the `Response` object back to the `HttpWebResponse` type since we know the protocol being used:

```
myResponse = CType( myRequest.GetResponse(), HttpWebResponse )
```

Once we have the web response object we can call the `GetResponseStream` method to get back a `Stream` object that will let us read the web page data:

```
sr = new StreamReader( myResponse.GetResponseStream() )
```

To display the underlying HTML in a useful form, we create a `StreamReader` so we can read the web page line by line, and display it as you'd see the page if you viewed the source in Internet Explorer.

Since we want to see the underlying HTML and not have it interpreted by the browser, we use the `HttpUtility.EncodeHtml` method to escape any characters that would otherwise be interpreted:

```
    line = sr.ReadLine()
do while not line is nothing

    line = HttpUtility.HtmlEncode(line)
    if line.Length <> 0 then
        Response.Write( line & "<BR>" )
    end if
    line = sr.ReadLine()
loop
```

Finally, we close the stream using the `Close` method of the `StreamReader`.

The `HttpWebRequest/HttpWebResponse` classes make it really simple to work with resources located anywhere over the Internet or indeed a local network. They do not use the `WinInet` APIs under the hood, so they can be safely used in ASP.NET without any scalability worries.

To finish our coverage of the `HttpWebRequest/HttpWebResponse` classes, and to introduce our next topic, **Regular Expressions**, we'll introduce a simple application that allows you to determine the ranking of a book on amazon.com. OK, it's not that useful to anybody who isn't an author or a publisher, but hopefully it will inspire you, and give you an idea of how you can apply these classes in real-world applications. The technique shown is often called screen scraping.

Our application accepts the URL of a book on Amazon.com and displays the book ranking along with details about the response such as the content length, encoding, and HTTP response code:

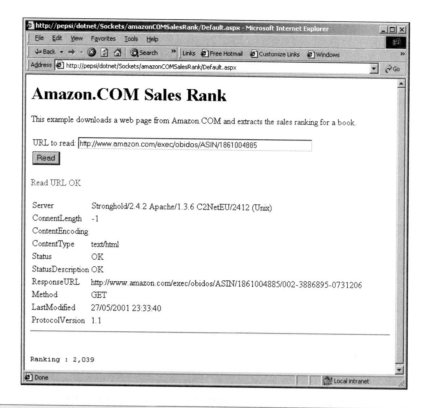

We're only showing edited highlights of this application. The full source is located in the book download at www.wrox.com.

The application works by downloading the page specified and placing the retrieved HTML into a string. To get the page content into a string we create a `StreamReader` object, as in the previous example, after which we call its `ReadToEnd` method, which returns a string containing all of the stream content:

```
HttpWebRequest myRequest;
HttpWebResponse myResponse;
Stream s;

myRequest = (HttpWebRequest) WebRequest.Create(URLToRead.Value);
myResponse = (HttpWebResponse) myRequest.GetResponse();

s = myResponse.GetResponseStream();
_HtmlContent = new StreamReader(s).ReadToEnd();
s.Close();
```

Once the page content is retrieved, the string containing the HTML content is processed and the ranking extracted using regular expressions:

```
void RenderStreamIntoPage()
{
    // Stream the return string for the expected ranking

    Regex re;
    Match m;

    re = new Regex("(?<x>Amazon.com Sales Rank: </b>.*\n)(?<rank>.*)");
    m = re.Match( _HtmlContent );

    // Check for multiple matches

    while( m.Success == true )
    {
        foreach( Capture c in m.Captures )
        {
            Response.Write("<BR>Ranking : " + m.Result("${rank}" ) );
        }
        m = m.NextMatch();
    }

}
```

Regular Expressions

Let's now look at the regular expression objects the .NET Framework provides, so we can understand how we're extracting the book ranking. Regular expressions are an area that generates lots of confusion, but they can be great if you have to deal with any form of text input or perform some text processing. In Chapter 5 we looked at the validation controls, including the regular expression validator that used a regular expression to check the value of an e-mail entry field. For validating entry fields this works very well, but there are times when you need to process text outside of the validators, perhaps when writing custom text or when writing screen scraping Web Services.

For example, without regular expressions, how easy would it be to, say, extract all the links from the HTML of a web page? You could search for the string href, but then you have to be flexible about the contents of the attribute string. It's this flexibility that regular expressions allow, by way of pattern matching.

Pattern Matching

The use of regular expressions allows you to search, extract, or replace sub-strings based on an expression, or a pattern, and these expressions are where the power lies. If you've ever searched for files using Windows Explorer then you're probably used to the * wildcard character as an expression meaning 'any group of characters'. The patterns available in regular expressions use this same notion of special characters and sequences to identify what is being searched for. We won't cover them fully here, as they are extensively covered in the SDK help files, but it's worth a brief outline. Thefollowing table lists some of the main pattern elements:

Element	Description
*	Zero or more matches.
+	One or more matches.
( )	Captures the matched substring into the next available capture group. A capture group is zero, one, or more strings.
(?<name>)	Captures the matched substring into the capture group identified by name.
\n	Return the nth captured group.
|	Either of the expressions separated by the | character.
.	Any character (except newline).
[]	Any single character within the brackets.
[^]	Any single character not within the brackets.
\s	Any whitespace character.
\S	Any non whitespace character.
\d	Any digit character.
\D	Any non-digit character.

For example:

Example	Matches
abc*	abc followed by none or more characters.
abc+	abc followed by one or more characters.
abc(def)ghi	abcdefghi, and places def in the first capture group.
ab(cd)ef(gh)i	abcdefghi, placing cd into capture group 1, and gh into capture group 2.
hello|goodbye	Either hello or goodbye.
[abcdef]	Any of the characters abcdef.
[a-f]	Any of the characters abcdef.
[^a-f]	Any character other than abcdef.

There are many other elements you can use, and you should consult the documentation for a comprehensive list.

Pattern Ordering and Length

When searching for patterns it's important to note two points. The first is that the searched pattern will be the largest available, which may not be what you expect. For example, consider the following string:

```
Alex Homer is an author. Despite his years, he's not the Homer that wrote Greek
epics.
```

Let's say we use the following expression:

```
Homer(.*)
```

This looks for the word `Homer`, and places any characters found after it in a capture group. The thing to watch for is that the first expression found in the search string is used. So, what's captured is the following:

```
 is an author. Despite his years, he's not the Homer that wrote Greek epics.
```

There are two instances of `Homer`, and it's the first one that is matched.

This rule changes when the search expression is widened to include any characters at the start of the search string. If we now use:

```
.*Homer(.*)
```

This looks for any characters, followed by `Homer`, and places any characters found after it in a capture group. However, since the entire expression is widened, it now matches a larger number of characters, so the largest match is returned, but the group now contains less characters. In this case:

```
 that wrote the Greek epics.
```

The rules for these matches are consistent, but it does mean that you have to be careful in selecting your match string.

Text Replacement

If you are using patterns to search and replace within a string, remember that the replacement text may invalidate the expression used to search. You should therefore be careful of search patterns that pick the widest match. It's nearly always best to be as explicit as possible, and use the narrowest pattern.

Pattern Example

Earlier in this chapter, we showed how to use the network classes to retrieve a web page from Amazon.com and extract the sales ranking for a book (we authors are rather shallow). Let's take a look at the HTML that the web page uses first:

```
<b>Amazon.com Sales Rank: </b>
8,712
</font><br>
```

Now let's look at this expression in detail:

```
(?<x>Amazon.com Sales Rank: </b>.*\n)(?<rank>.*)
```

There are several parts to this, some of which aren't directly relevant to the ranking. However, we'll take the whole expression so you can see exactly what it's built from. Firstly you'll notice that we have two groups (these are the parts contained within parentheses), each of which is given a name. The name is defined by use of the ? character followed by a name contained within angle-brackets. So we have x and rank. The groupings don't affect how the expression is parsed – they are just used to allow easy access to parts of the expression once parsing has taken place.

For the sales rank alone, we need to extract the middle line from the three lines of HTML. The first line is guaranteed to be the same (assuming Amazon doesn't change its HTML pages too often) – we search for the specific words followed by any number of characters. We also need to include the new line character, as the .* expression doesn't match new line. The actual sales rank comes after the new line so we can use .* again to extract everything on that line.

Now let's compare this to the one for Barnes and Noble (covered more in Chapter 20). Here's the HTML produced:

```
<b><font size="-1">sales rank: 2,640</font></b><br>
```

Notice that this is all on one line, so we need to extract the rank from the middle of text, rather than from a line on its own. Here's the search expression, this time only using one group, since we really only require the sales rank:

```
<b><font size=\"-1\">sales rank: (?<rank>.*)</font></b>
```

You can clearly see which characters we need to match – those after the : and before the closing font tag. These are extracted by the group labeled rank.

The Regular Expression Classes

The System.Text.RegularExpressions namespace contains eight classes for the manipulation of regular expressions. These are:

Class	Represents
Regex	A regular expression.
Match	The results from a single expression match.
MatchCollection	A collection of results from iteratively applied matches.
Group	The results from a single captured group.
GroupCollection	A collection of captured groups.
Capture	The results from a single sub-expression capture.
CaptureCollection	A collection of captured sub-expressions.
RegexCompilationInfo	Information about the compilation of expressions.

Like the pattern matching, we're not going to cover an exhaustive list of all the classes, properties, and methods. Instead we'll concentrate on the most useful scenarios.

The Regex Class

This is the root class for regular expressions, and represents an individual regular expression. It contains a number of methods to allow the creation and matching of expressions, for example:

```
Dim expr As String = "hello"
Dim re As New Regex(expr)

re.Match("Hello everyone, hello one and all.")
```

This creates an expression and then uses the Match method to match the expression with the supplied string. In this case there would only be one match – the second hello – since the matching by default is case-sensitive.

The Regex class constructor can be overloaded, also allowing options to be specified. For example:

```
Dim expr As String = "hello"
Dim re   As New Regex(expr, RegexOptions.IgnoreCase)

re.Match("Hello everyone, hello one and all.")
```

Now there are two matches, since case is being ignored.

The options can be one of the RegexOptions shown below (and set the Options property of the class):

RegexOption	Description
Compiled	Specifies that the expression should be compiled to MSIL.
ECMAScript	Enables ECMAScript-compliant behavior for the expression.
ExplicitCapture	Only captures explicitly named or numbered groups, allowing parentheses to be matched without escaping.
IgnoreCase	Case-insensitive match.
IgnorePattern Whitespace	Ignores un-escaped whitespace in the pattern.
Multiline	Make ^ and $ match the beginning and end of any line, rather than the entire string.
None	No set options.
RightToLeft	Searches from right to left. This sets the RightToLeft property of the class.
SingleLine	Treat the search string as a single line (where all characters are matched, including new line).

The Match Class

The Match class contains the details of a single expression match, as returned from the Match method of the Regex class. For example:

```
Dim mt   As Match
Dim expr As String = "hello"
Dim re   As New Regex(expr, RegexOptions.IgnoreCase)

mt = re.Match("Hello everyone, hello one and all.")
```

You can then use the Success property to determine if any matches were made, and the Groups and Captures collections to identify what was matched.

The Group Class

The Group class identifies a single captured group. Since an expression can contain multiple groups, the Match class has a Groups collection, containing a Group object for each group matched. For example, consider the match expression:

```
(he(ll)o)
```

This contains two explicit groups. One for the entire word "hello", and one for the two "l" characters. There is also a third group, which is the entire expression. So, as far as matching is concerned the above expression is equivalent to:

```
he(ll)o
```

The only difference is the number of groups created.

Unlike the book-ranking examples, these groups aren't explicitly named, so they are given names equivalent to their position in the collection (1, 2, etc.). You can access the groups directly, or through enumeration. For simple expressions, it's marginally quicker to let the class name the groups for you, but for more complex expressions, explicit names make it clear exactly which groups correspond to which match expression.

For example, consider the following expression:

```
(1)+
```

This matches one or more occurrences of the character 1.

The following example shows simple grouping in use:

```
Dim mt   As Match
Dim gp   As Group
Dim expr As String = "h(e(ll)o) "
Dim re   As New Regex(expr, RegexOptions.IgnoreCase)

mt = re.Match("Hello everyone, hello one and all.")

For Each gp In mt.Groups
  Response.Write(gp.Value)
Next
```

This returns the following:

```
hello
ello
ll
```

There are three matches. The first is the entire match expression, the second corresponds to the group within the first set of parentheses, and the third the group within the second set of parentheses.

The `Group` class also includes `Index` and `Length` properties, indicating the position of the match within the search string, and the length of string matched.

The Capture Class

The `Capture` class represents a single sub-expression capture. Each `Group` can have multiple `Captures`. The `Capture` class really comes into its own when quantifiers are used within expressions. Quantifiers are where much of the power of regular expressions lies, as they add the optional quantity to finding patterns. Examples of quantifiers are `*` for `zero` or more occurrences and `+` for `one` or more occurrences.

For example, consider the following expression:

```
(1)+
```

This searches for the first occurrence of one or more 1 characters. So, putting this into a full sample:

```
Dim mt   As Match
Dim gp   As Group
Dim cp   As Capture
Dim expr As String = "(1)+"
Dim re   As New Regex(expr, RegexOptions.IgnoreCase)

mt = re.Match("Hello everyone, hello one and all.")

For Each gp In mt.Groups
  Response.Write("Group: " & gp.Value)
  For Each cp In gp.Captures
    Response.Write(" Capture: " & cp.Value)
  Next
Next
```

This gives the following result:

```
Group: ll
  Capture: ll
Group: l
  Capture: l
  Capture: l
```

Both a single 1 and multiple 1 characters are matched, because the + quantifier means one or more. So, the first group matches the 11 in the first `Hello`. For the second group there are two occurrences of single 1 characters. This becomes clearer with another example – consider the following match expression:

```
(abc)+
```

This matches one or more occurrences of the string abc. When matched against:

```
QQQabcabcabcWWWEEEabcab
```

we get the following output:

```
Group: abcabcabc
    Capture: abcabcabc
Group: abc
    Capture: abc
    Capture: abc
    Capture: abc
```

The first group matches the widest expression, and there is only one occurrence of this. The second group matches the explicit group, and there are three occurrences of this.

Substitutions

When using groups in expressions, you can reuse the group without having to retype it. This is known as substitution. For example, consider the expression:

```
(abc)def
```

This matches abcdef but places abc into the first group. If you then wanted to match abcdefabc you could use:

```
(abc)def\1
```

Summary

The File and Directory classes provide static methods for enumerating files and directories.

The FileInfo and DirectoryInfo classes enable you to work with a single file or directory. For the most part, they provide equivalent functionality to File and Directory classes, but deal with a single object.

Backing stores are responsible for the physical storage and management of bytes of data.

The Stream class is the programmatic interface used to communicate to a backing store. Each backing store such as the file system or memory buffer provides its own class derived from Stream. This implements the basic functionality required from a backing store, and can also provide additional methods and properties specific to a given backing store.

Reader and writer classes layer functionality over a stream to abstract you from the underlying byte representation of primitive types, such as characters, strings, and floats.

Reader and writer classes use internal buffers for performance reasons.

The System.Net classes provide a powerful way of writing network applications. The classes are safe to use in an ASP.NET page and are scalable.

Finally, we covered how to use regular expressions as a means of searching data using simple or very complex patterns.

In the next chapter we'll take a look at building business objects.

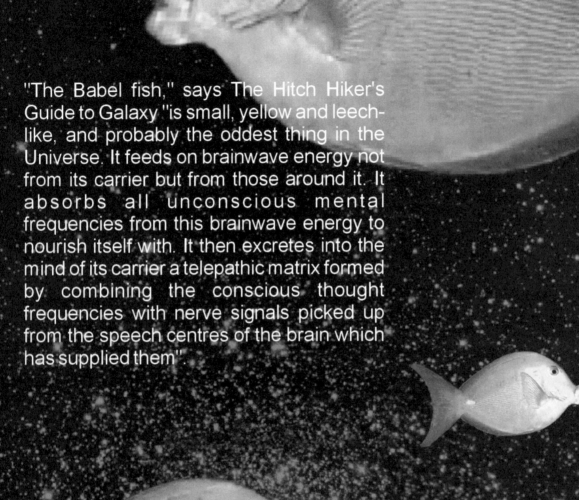

"The Babel fish," says The Hitch Hiker's Guide to Galaxy "is small, yellow and leech-like, and probably the oddest thing in the Universe. It feeds on brainwave energy not from its carrier but from those around it. It absorbs all unconscious mental frequencies from this brainwave energy to nourish itself with. It then excretes into the mind of its carrier a telepathic matrix formed by combining the conscious thought frequencies with nerve signals picked up from the speech centres of the brain which has supplied them".

The practical upshot of all this is that if you stick a Babel fish in your ear you can instantly understand anything said to you in any form of language. The speech patterns you actually hear decode the brainwave matrix which has been fed into your mind by your Babel fish.

17

.NET Components

Even with the great changes that Microsoft has cooked into the Common Language Runtime and the .NET Frameworks, there are still some basics of application design that remain constant. One of those constants is the benefit of components. Even with the advent of compiled ASP.NET pages written in multiple languages, good application design still requires the use of components.

While we may no longer gain the absolute benefits of speed that we saw when moving to COM components from scripted ASP pages, we can still gain the benefits of encapsulation and reusability that components provide. I don't know who came up with the adage that says "just because you can doesn't mean that you should", but that definitely holds true with the .NET platform when it comes to application design.

In the past, one of the main reasons for moving script code to components was to gain execution speed. Now with pages being compiled and executed, that benefit is gone. So, does this mean that we should forego good application design and throw all our code into our ASP.NET pages? Just because you can doesn't mean that you should!

Components are still critical in the .NET Framework. While we won't go into detail about why you should use components, we will talk about how to use components. It is important to know how to build components, how to use the features of the Common Language Runtime to extend components, and then as important – how to deploy components.

In this chapter, we will be looking at building and deploying .NET components for use within ASP.NET applications. Specifically, we will be looking at:

- ❑ Writing Business Objects using the .NET Framework
- ❑ Creating a class in one language, and then inheriting from that class in a different language
- ❑ Using COM+ Services, such as transactions, from within .NET components
- ❑ How to deploy components in .NET

Writing Business Objects

First, we will look at creating business objects that can be used by .NET applications. These business objects will perform the same types of functions that business objects in COM or other objects models do, plus they will be able to take advantage of all of the advantages offered by the .NET architecture and the Common Language Runtime.

In this section, we will look at how to create an object and then extend that object through inheritance. We will then look at how we can extend the functionality of an existing class and also how to utilize some of the COM+ component services within our .NET object. After creating the object, we will then compile it and place it in an assembly. Once we have the assembly created, we can create an ASP.NET page to test our new object.

We will be looking at two concurrent examples as we move through the chapter. They will share exactly the same functionality, except that one will be written in VB.NET and the other will be written in C#. We will test these objects from an ASP.NET page, but you could just as easily test them from a Windows Forms application or from a command-line application. We will be using a simple text editor to create the files, and using the command-line compilers and tools to create the assemblies.

Building the Object

When we begin to create our object, there are a number of things that we need to look at. First off, we need to take a look at various guidelines for creating a component. And then finally before getting started, we need to look at the various attributes that can be set to describe a component. With all of that out of the way, we can move on to actually creating the example objects.

Class Design Guidelines

As we begin to write components for .NET, some of our existing design guidelines can still be used. However, just as the .NET Framework is different from COM and COM+, some of the design guidelines we have used in the past are now implemented in a different way. In the past, we may have even had different guidelines depending on the language we were using. Now with .NET, those guidelines are unified. One of the other keys to using these design guidelines is that they have been adhered to by Microsoft in the creation of the System Frameworks themselves, along with all of the sample code that comes with the SDK.

Error Handling

Now that robust error handling, including structured exception handling, is part of the CLR, and therefore available to all languages supported by the CLR, you should use it wherever possible. The former practice of using error codes and checking return values or even `On Error Goto` has been replaced with catching exceptions and handling the errors at that point.

This doesn't mean you should use exceptions everywhere – exceptions are designed to handle *errors* – not something you should expect to happen. That being said, there are instances where error codes can come in handy. For example, if you are trying to open a file and the file doesn't exist, then return a null value – since that error could be expected in normal use – but if the file system returns an I/O error, then throw an exception – since that condition isn't one normally expected.

Properties versus Methods

One of the most difficult choices in designing a component is choosing what type of interface to use. This holds true for all component-based architectures – not just .NET. Knowing when to use a property as opposed to using a method, and vice versa, is as much a matter of personal taste as it is the following of design guidelines. The basic guidelines to follow are:

❑ If there is an internal data member being exposed outside the component, you should use a property.

❑ If the execution of the code causes some measurable side effect to the component or the environment, then use a method.

❑ If the order of code execution is important, then use a method. Since the Common Language Runtime has the ability to short-circuit expression testing, a property may not be accessed when you expect it will. Take a look at this example of a short-circuited expression:

You have an object X that has two properties A and B. These properties do more than just expose an internal data member – they actually do some work as they return a value. For this example, let's say that they each return an integer between 1 and 10. They are being used in code that looks like this:

```
if (X.A > 5) and (X.B < 7) then
    ... ' do something
end if
```

If the evaluation of X.A returns a 4, then we know that the first part of the Boolean expression is false. We know that for an AND statement to be true, both parts have to be true. The CLR knows this too, and seeing that the first part is false, it will skip, or short-circuit, the evaluation of X.B, since its value doesn't matter. However, because we violated good design principles and did work during the evaluation of B – that work will not be performed in this case. This is not something we want happening if we are assuming that work is being done.

Memory Management

Memory management has to be one of the most difficult things that most programmers have faced. Now that we have gone to a flat memory model, we don't have the issues from the days of Windows 3.1 about allocating memory. However, we still have had to deal with how and when to discard the memory. With the Common Language Runtime handling most of the memory management for our .NET components, there are only a few things that we need to do differently when dealing with memory than we did in the past.

The Common Language Runtime has the ability to create small, short-lived objects very quickly and cheaply. This means that you shouldn't be worried about creating objects that make your development easier to follow. According to performance testing done by Microsoft, the runtime can allocate nearly 10 million objects per second on a moderately fast machine. Also, objects running in the Common Language Runtime will be garbage-collected by the runtime after they are no longer being referenced. This will happen automatically, and keeps the developer from having to deal with memory leaks from improperly-freed objects. While automatic garbage collection does deal with a lot of headaches, there still has to be processor cycles dedicated to the garbage collector running. When it actually runs is also unpredictable, and could cause a temporary hiccup in performance.

Using Attributes

Attributes in the Common Language Runtime allow developers to add additional information to the classes they have created. These are then available to the application using the component by using the `System.Reflection` classes. You can use attributes to provide hints or flags to a number of different systems that may be using your component. Attributes can be used as compiler flags to tell the compiler how to handle the compilation of the class. They can be used by tools to provide more information about the usage of the component at design time. This means that we can get away from having to embed comments in code simply as clues for the tool to know where certain parts of the code are. Attributes can also be used to identify the transaction characteristics of a class when interacting with the components services of the operating system.

These are a set of standard attributes for properties and events that are defined in the `System.ComponentModel` class in the Common Language Runtime. As these attributes are already defined, they can be used by the developer without having to create a corresponding class for a custom attribute.

Attributes for Events and Properties

Attribute	Used for	Usage – default in bold
Browsable Attribute	Declares if this property should appear in the property window of a design tool.	[Browsable (false | **true**)]
Category Attribute	Used to group properties when being displayed by a design tool.	[Category (categoryName)]
Description Attribute	Help text displayed by the design tool when this property or event is selected.	[Description (descriptionString)]

Attributes for Properties

Attribute	Used for	Usage – default in bold
Bindable Attribute	Declares if data should be bound to this property.	[Bindable (**false** | true)]
Default Property Attribute	Indicates that this is the default property for the class.	[DefaultProperty]
DefaultValue Attribute	Sets a default value for the property.	[DefaultValue (value)]
Localizable Attribute	Indicates that a property can be localized. The compiler will cause all properties with this attribute to store the property in a resource file. You can then localize the resource file without having to modify any code.	[Localizable (**false** | true)]

Attributes for Events

Attribute	Used for	Usage
`DefaultEvent` `Attribute`	Specifies the default event for the class.	`[DefaultEvent]`

Our Sample Object

In this chapter, we will be creating a sample object. The sample object will be used to encapsulate business and data access functionality – this is the typical usage for objects in the applications that most developers are creating. Our business object will encapsulate the interaction with the `IBuyAdventure` database that we will use with our case study later in the book. Since this is more an example of how to build components, rather than a full case study on a business and data component, our component will have limited functionality.

The component will have one property:

Property Name	Type	Usage
`DatabaseConnection`	String	The database connection string.

The component will have three methods:

Method Name	Returns	Parameters	Usage
`GetProductTypes`	`String` `Collection`	*none*	Returns a string collection of all of the Product Types in the database.
`GetProducts`	`DataSet`	`productType`	Returns a `DataSet` containing the records for a specific product type.
`AveragePrice`	`Single`	`productType`	Returns a Single value that represents the average price of the items of a specific product type.

Now that we know what the interface to our component is going to be, we can set about writing it. As we stated earlier, we will show how to develop the component in both Visual Basic.NET and in C#. We will start with the VB version.

VB Class Example

Here is how the final class looks when written in VB. We will then break down each part and describe what it does and how.

```
Option Explicit
Option Strict

Imports System
Imports System.Data
Imports System.Data.SqlClient

Namespace BusObjectVB

  Public Class IBAProducts

    private m_DSN as String

    public Sub New ()
      MyBase.New
      m_DSN = ""
    end sub

    public Sub New(DSN as string)
      MyBase.New
      m_DSN = DSN
    end sub

    public Property DatabaseConnection as string
      set
        m_DSN = value
      end set
      get
        return m_DSN
      end get
    end Property

    public function  GetProducts ( productType as String)  as DataSet
      if m_DSN = "" then
        throw(new ArgumentNullException("DatabaseConnection", "No value for the_
                                        database connection string"))
      end if
      dim myConnection as new SqlConnection(m_DSN)
      dim sqlAdapter1 as new SqlDataAdapter("SELECT * FROM Products WHERE_
                             ProductType='"+productType+"'", myConnection)

      dim  products as new DataSet()
      sqlAdapter1.Fill(products, "products")

      return products
    end function

    public function GetProductTypes () as DataSet
      if m_DSN = "" then
        throw(new ArgumentNullException("DatabaseConnection", "No value for the_
                                        database connection string"))
      end if
      dim myConnection as new SqlConnection(m_DSN)
```

```
          dim sqlAdapter1 as new SqlDataAdapter("SELECT DISTINCT ProductType FROM_
                                                Products", myConnection)

          dim types as new DataSet()
          sqlAdapter1.Fill(types, "ProdTypes")

          return types
       end function

       public function AveragePrice ( productType as string) as Double
          if m_DSN = "" then
             throw(new ArgumentNullException("DatabaseConnection", "No value for the_
                                             database connection string"))
          end if
          dim myConnection as new SqlConnection(m_DSN)

          dim sqlAdapter1 as new SqlDataAdapter("SELECT AVG(UnitPrice) AS
AveragePrice_
                   FROM Products WHERE ProductType='"+productType+"'", myConnection)

          dim AvgPrice as new DataSet()
          sqlAdapter1.Fill(AvgPrice, "AveragePrice")

          dim priceTable as DataTable
          priceTable = AvgPrice.Tables("AveragePrice")
          if (not priceTable.Rows(0).IsNull("AveragePrice"))
             return CDbl(priceTable.Rows(0)("AveragePrice"))
          else
             return 0
          end if
       end function
    end class
end namespace
```

Now, let's take a look at the object in detail. The first two statements are unique to Visual Basic. With its roots as a loosely-typed language, Visual Basic.NET has had some directives added to it to tell the compiler that it should do some level of type checking when compiling the application. The Option Explicit statement is familiar to Visual Basic programmers. It forces the declaration of all variables before they are used, and will generate a compiler error if a variable is used before it is declared. The Option Strict statement is new to Visual Basic.NET. It greatly limits the implicit data type conversions that VB has been able to do in the past. Option Strict also disallows any late binding. This will increase the performance in your components since types are checked at compile time, and not at run time.

```
Option Explicit
Option Strict
```

The next thing we do in the file is state which parts of the System Frameworks we will be using in this object.

```
Imports System
Imports System.Data
Imports System.Data.SqlClient
```

We can actually use any part of the System Frameworks at any time in our code by simply referencing the full path to it – System.Data.SqlClient.DataTable – but that would begin to make our code cumbersome and unnecessarily long. By explicitly stating which parts of the System Frameworks we will be using, we can refer to the particular class without having to state the full path – DataTable – as we do in the example.

In this object, we will be using the System namespace, which contains the necessary base classes to build our object. The System.Data namespace contains the classes that make up the ADO.NET data access architecture. Since we will be accessing our data in a SQL Server 2000 database, we will also include the System.Data.SqlClient namespace. This namespace contains the classes to access the SQL Server managed provider.

```
namespace BusObjectVB

  public class IBAProducts
```

We will be encapsulating our object within its own unique namespace – BusObjectVB – so we need to declare all of the classes that make up our object within that namespace. Our business component is defined as a class – when we actually create an instance of it in our program we will then have an object.

```
      private m_DSN as String

      public  Sub New ()
        MyBase.New
      end sub

      public  Sub New(DSN as string)
        MyBase.New
        m_DSN = DSN
      end sub
```

Within our object there will be one private variable, which will be used to hold the database connection string. The next two methods are the constructors for the class. The constructor is automatically called by the runtime when an object is instantiated. We have actually created two constructors. The first one takes no parameters and is therefore called the default constructor. The second constructor takes a parameter, DSN, and will set the database connection string at the same time that the object is created.

Since a constructor cannot return any values, it is declared as a Sub rather than a Function. In Visual Basic, we must also *explicitly* call the constructor for our base class – using the MyBase.New statement.

```
    public Property DatabaseConnection as string
      set
        m_DSN = value
      end set
      get
        return m_DSN
      end get
    end Property
```

While the second constructor allows us to set the database connection string when the object is created, we also need to provide a way to set and read it at other times. Since the member variable holding this data is marked as private, we need to provide a property function to set and retrieve the value. The external name of the property is `DatabaseConnection`. Next, we will look at the methods that allow us to work with the information in the database.

```
public function GetProductTypes () as DataSet

  if m_DSN = "" then
    throw(new ArgumentNullException("DatabaseConnection", "No value for the_
                                     database connection string"))
  end if
  dim myConnection as new SqlConnection(m_DSN)
```

The first method, `GetProductTypes`, will let us retrieve a listing of the product types of the products stored in the database. We will return the listing to the calling program in a `DataSet`. A `DataSet` represents an in-memory cache of data. This means that it is a *copy* of the data in the database, so there is no underlying connection to the stored data. To access the database, we first will need to connect to it. The `SqlConnection` object provides this functionality and when the `Open` method is called, it will connect to the database using the connection string that was stored in the private member variable m_DSN.

It is therefore important that this value be set properly. If the user of the component does not set the value of the `DatabaseConnection` property, then we won't be able to open the database. The best way to indicate this is to throw an exception. We are using the `throw` statement and passing it an instance of the `ArgumentNullException` class. This version of the constructor for this class takes two strings – the parameter that was null and a text description of the error.

```
dim sqlAdapter1 as new SqlDataAdapter("SELECT DISTINCT ProductType FROM_
                                       Products", myConnection)
```

To retrieve the desired information from the database, we will be using a SQL Query. To process the query, we will be using the `SqlDataAdapter`. When we create the object, we will pass in the text of the SQL Query that will be executed by this object. We also tell the object which database connection object to use to access the data. That is the object that was created in the previous steps. The creation of this object will automatically open the database connection.

```
dim types as new DataSet()
sqlAdapter1.Fill(types, "ProdTypes")

return types
end function
```

Now that we have the mechanism for retrieving the data from the database, we need a place to store it to pass it back to the caller. This will be in a `DataSet` object. We will create a new instance of this class and call it types. The data will be placed in this object by using the `Fill` method of the `SqlDataAdapter` class. This method takes the destination `DataSet` object as well as a name to represent the data within the data set. To send the data back to the caller, we will return the `DataSet` object types.

```
public function  GetProducts ( productType as String) as DataSet
   if m_DSN = "" then
      throw(new ArgumentNullException("DatabaseConnection", "No value for the_
                                       database connection string"))
   end if
   dim myConnection as new SqlConnection(m_DSN)
   dim sqlAdapter1 as new SqlDataAdapter("SELECT * FROM Products WHERE_
                            ProductType='"+productType+"'", myConnection)

   dim products as new DataSet()
   sqlAdapter1.Fill(products, "products")

   return products
end function
```

The next method will allow us to retrieve the list of products for a specified product type. We will specify the product type by passing in the product type string. The list of products will be returned as a DataSet. The main part of the method is the same as the previous method, in that we connect to the database and fill up a DataSet object with the information we want.

The resulting filled DataSet object can then be returned to the calling application. Next, we will look at the method to calculate the average selling price of the items of a particular type.

```
public function AveragePrice ( productType as string) as Double
   if m_DSN = "" then
      throw(new ArgumentNullException("DatabaseConnection", "No value for the_
                                       database connection string"))
   end if
   dim myConnection as new SqlConnection(m_DSN)

   dim sqlAdapter1 as new SqlDataAdapter("SELECT AVG(UnitPrice) AS
AveragePrice_
            FROM Products WHERE ProductType='"+productType+"'", myConnection)
```

The method to calculate the average selling price for a product type will pass that value back as a return value of type double. Just as with the previous method, the one parameter for this method will be the product type of the desired product group. The database access code is again very similar – the primary difference being that the SQL statement will be calculating an average rather than returning a set of rows from the database.

```
dim AvgPrice as new DataSet()
sqlAdapter1.Fill(AvgPrice, "AveragePrice")

dim priceTable as DataTable
priceTable = AvgPrice.Tables("AveragePrice")
```

With the results of the database query in the DataSet object, we will want to take a look at the contents of the data to see what the average price was. To examine the data directly, we first need to grab the table that contains the result of the query from the DataSet. In the Fill method, we told ADO.NET to put the results of our query into a table named AveragePrice. Then to get a reference to that specific table from the DataSet, we retrieve that table by name from the Tables collection.

```
        if (not priceTable.Rows(0).IsNull("AveragePrice"))
          return CDbl(priceTable.Rows(0)("AveragePrice"))
        else
          return 0
        end if
      end function
    end class
  end namespace
```

If there was no data returned, we will have a table with no rows in it. If this is the case, then we can return the average price as 0. If there is one row in the table – a SQL statement to calculate an average will return at most one row – then we will look at the value contained in the field named AveragePrice and return that value as the average price for the product type. The field named AveragePrice does not exist in the physical database, but is rather an alias that we created with the SQL SELECT statement to hold the results of the AVG() function.

This brings us to the end of our VB class. Before we look at how to compile and test it, we will look at exacyly the same component coded in C#.

C# Class Example

Here is a look at the same class when written in C#. We will then look at the differences between this version and the VB version we just finished looking at.

```
using System;
using System.Data;
using System.Data.SqlClient;


namespace BusObjectCS {

public class IBAProducts {

  private string m_DSN;

    public  IBAProducts () {
      m_DSN="";
    }

  public  IBAProducts (string DSN) {
    m_DSN = DSN;
  }

  public string DatabaseConnection {
    set { m_DSN = value; }
    get { return m_DSN; }
  }

  public DataSet GetProducts (string productType) {
    if (m_DSN == "")
    {
      throw new ArgumentNullException("DatabaseConnection", "No value for the
                                      database connection string");
    }
    SqlConnection myConnection = new SqlConnection(m_DSN);
    SqlDataAdapter sqlAdapter1 = new SqlDataAdapter("SELECT * FROM Products WHERE
                            ProductType='"+productType+"'", myConnection);
```

```
    DataSet products = new DataSet();
    sqlAdapter1.Fill(products, "products");

    return products;
  }

  public DataSet GetProductTypes () {

    if (m_DSN == "")
    {
      throw new ArgumentNullException("DatabaseConnection", "No value for the
                                          database connection string");
    }
  SqlConnection dbConnection = new SqlConnection(m_DSN);
    dbConnection.Open();

    SqlDataAdapter sqlAdapter1 = new SqlDataAdapter("SELECT DISTINCT ProductType
                                          FROM Products", dbConnection);

    DataSet types = new DataSet();
    sqlAdapter1.Fill(types, "ProdTypes");

    return types;
  }

  public Double AveragePrice (string productType) {
    if (m_DSN == "")
    {
      throw new ArgumentNullException("DatabaseConnection", "No value for the
                                          database connection string");
    }
    SqlConnection dbConnection = new SqlConnection(m_DSN);
    dbConnection.Open();

    SqlDataAdapter sqlAdapter1 = new SqlDataAdapter(
    "SELECT AVG(UnitPrice) AS AveragePrice FROM Products WHERE
                            ProductType='"+productType+"'", dbConnection);

    DataSet AvgPrice = new DataSet();
    sqlAdapter1.Fill(AvgPrice, "AveragePrice");

    DataTable priceTable;
    priceTable = AvgPrice.Tables["AveragePrice"];
    if (priceTable.Rows.Count > 0)
    {
      return (Double)priceTable.Rows[0]["AveragePrice"];
    }
    else
      return 0;
    }
  }
}
```

Let's now look at this object in detail. We will be focusing on the differences between the C# version and the VB.NET version. The functionality is exactly the same.

```
using System;
using System.Data;
using System.Data.SqlClient;
```

The first set of statements is used to specify the System Framework namespaces that will be used by this class. Rather than using the VB keyword Imports, C# uses the keyword using. As before, we will be using the same three namespaces as we did in the VB.NET version. In the VB.NET version, we had an Option Explicit and an Option Strict statement. Since by default C# is a strongly-typed language, these statements (or rather a C# equivalent) are not necessary.

```
namespace BusObjectCS {

  public class IBAProducts {
```

The next step is to declare the namespace and the class that we will be creating. Note that the name of the class is exactly the same as the VB version. This is OK – and we can even run both at the same time – because of the namespace. Class names only need to be unique within a namespace.

```
    public  IBAProducts () {
      m_DSN="";
    }


    public  IBAProducts (string DSN) {
      m_DSN = DSN;
    }
```

The next major difference in the two implementations comes with the way that constructors are defined. In C#, a constructor is defined with a method that has the same name as the class. In Visual Basic, the constructor for a class is always named New(). In C#, the base class constructor is called automatically by the compiler.

```
    public string DatabaseConnection {
      set { m_DSN = value; }
      get { return m_DSN; }
    }
```

A property is defined in a similar way to VB, but we just use a different syntax to declare the accessor methods. Whereas in C# you use a set or get statement followed by a block delimited by braces, in Visual Basic.NET you use a specific set...end set or get...end get block to denote the accessor methods.

The remainder of the component is identical to the C# version, except for the language syntax differences. With both of our components created, we can move on to the next step – compilation.

Compiling the Classes

As we saw earlier in the book, the .NET architecture executes code stored in the MSIL format. This intermediate language is created from the source code of the various languages supported by the Common Language Runtime. We have already created the source code for our components. The next step is to compile this source code into the MSIL version. This is done by executing the appropriate compiler with the proper arguments, based on the language and our destination.

Compiling the VB.NET Class

To compile our Visual Basic.NET component, we will use a batch file, which should be run from the command line. This file is named `makevb.bat` and is shown below:

```
vbc /out:bin\BusObjectvb.dll /t:library sampleObject.vb /r:System.Data.dll
/r:System.dll /r:System.XML.dll
```

Let's take a look at the parameters that we pass to the compiler. The first parameter, `/out`, defines the output file that the MSIL code will be placed in. In this example, the compiled output will be placed in the file named `BusObjectvb.dll`, and will be stored in the subdirectory named `bin` below the directory where the source file resides. If we did not include an `/out` parameter, then the compiler would have automatically created the filename based on the name of the source file and the target type and placed it in the current directory.

The next parameter, `/t`, is used to specify the type of output file format the compiler should create. This is a shortened version of the `/target` parameter, and either version can be legally used. There are four possible values for this parameter:

❑   `/target:exe` – this tells the compiler to create a command-line executable program. This is the default value, so if the `/target` parameter is not included, an `.exe` file will be created.

❑   `/target:library` – this tells the compiler to create a DLL file that will contain an assembly that consists of all of the source files passed to the compiler. The compiler will also automatically create the manifest for this assembly.

❑   `/target:module` – this tells the compiler to create a DLL, but not to create a manifest for it. This means that in order for the module to be used by the .NET Framework, it will need to be manually added to an assembly using the Assembly Generation tool (`AL.EXE`). This tool allows you to create the assembly manifest information manually, and then add modules to it.

❑   `/target:winexe` – this tells the compiler to create a Windows Forms application.

The next parameter is the name of the file to be compiled. In our example, the source file is named `sampleObject.vb`. The file extension is not critical, but it does make it easier to recognize the type of source file it is without having to open it up. If there are multiple source files, you can specify multiple source files on the same command line. They will be combined into the file type specified by the `/target` parameter. The final set of parameters indicates the other assemblies that are referenced from within our component.

Compiling the C# Class

To make it easier to run the compiler during development, we have also created a batch file that will execute the C# compiler with all of the proper parameters. This file is called `makecs.bat` and looks like this:

```
csc /out:bin\BusObjectcs.dll /t:library sampleObject.cs /r:System.Data.dll
/r:System.dll /r:System.XML.dll
```

As you can see, it is identical to the `makevb.bat` file except for three small changes. First, since we are calling the C# compiler rather than the VB compiler, the file to execute is `csc` instead of `vbc`. The next difference is the name of the output file; since we are creating a separate assembly for the C# component, we gave it a different name of `BusObjectcs.dll`. Finally, the source file that contains the C# source code is called `sampleObject.cs`

Testing the Class

Now that we have created our two identical objects, we need a way to test them. For this test, we will access these components from within an ASP.NET page.

The first page that we will have, `ProductTypes.aspx`, will test the `GetProductTypes()` method. This page will simply be used to display the results of a call to this method. The source code for the page looks like this:

```
<%@ Page Language="C#" Description="Component Test Program" %>
<%@ Import Namespace="System.Data" %>
<%@ Import Namespace="BusObjectCS" %>
<%@ Import Namespace="BusObjectVB" %>
<html>
<script language="C#" runat=server>


void Page_Load(Object sender, EventArgs evArgs){
// BusObjectCS.IBAProducts objProducts = new BusObjectCS.IBAProducts();
   BusObjectVB.IBAProducts objProducts = new BusObjectVB.IBAProducts();

   String dsn = "server=localhost;uid=sa;pwd=;database=IBuyAdventure";

   objProducts.DatabaseConnection = dsn;

   DataSet prodTypes = objProducts.GetProductTypes();

   productList.DataSource = prodTypes;
   productList.DataBind();

}

</script>

<body>
   <h3><font face="Verdana">List of Product Types</font></h3>

<asp:DataList id="productList" runat="server">
```

```
<headertemplate>
 <table border=1>
   <tr><th>Click to Display list of products</th></tr>
</headertemplate>

<itemtemplate>
     <tr>
     <td align=center>
     <%# DataBinder.Eval(Container.DataItem, "ProductType",
                       "<a href=\"displayProducts.aspx?PID={0}\">{0}</a>") %>

     </tr>
  </itemtemplate>

<footertemplate>
 </table>
 </footertemplate>

</asp:DataList>

</body>
</html>
```

The first part of the page sets up the language we will be using, as well as the namespaces of the assemblies that will be used on the page.

```
<%@ Page Language="C#" Description="Component Test Program" %>
<%@ Import Namespace="System.Data" %>
<%@ Import Namespace="BusObjectCS" %>
<%@ Import Namespace="BusObjectVB" %>
```

The code in this page will be written using C#. The language we use in our ASP.NET page does not have to correlate to the language that we use in our business components. Since both the page and the components will be compiled down to MSIL before they are executed, the language they are written in does not need to correspond.

We will also need to include the namespaces of the assemblies we are using. Even though we are not calling any of the methods from the System.Data namespace, we are using one of the classes (DataSet) as a return value from the method in our component. In order for the page to understand how to deal with this class, we have to add the namespace that contains it as an @Import to the page. Since this page will be used to test both the C# and VB versions of our component, we need to import the namespaces for both. There are no drawbacks in doing this, as the different namespaces guarantee that there will be no name conflicts, and the compiler is smart enough not to load a namespace if there is nothing in the code that references it.

```
void Page_Load(Object sender, EventArgs evArgs){
// BusObjectCS.IBAProducts objProducts = new BusObjectCS.IBAProducts();
   BusObjectVB.IBAProducts objProducts = new BusObjectVB.IBAProducts();
```

Within our Page_Load method, we will be working with the data provided by our business component. This test page will be used to test both components. Since each component has *exactly* the same interface (properties and methods), we can use the same local variable to represent the one we want. We simply will have two lines in the page – one of which will be commented out – that create the object in the language that we want to test. In our test page, the first line will create the C# version of the component, and the second the VB version.

```
String dsn = "server=localhost;uid=sa;pwd=; database=IBuyAdventure";

objProducts.DatabaseConnection = dsn;
```

This example uses the database from the IBuyAdventure case study in Chapter 24. Please follow the instructions in the readme.txt *file in the* /database *folder to set up the database in SQL Server 2000.*

The component needs to know where to retrieve its data. We will pass in a database connection string as the DatabaseConnection property of the object. This value is simply stored in the page as a string. In a production environment, values like database connection strings are usually stored in the web.config file for the ASP.NET application.

```
DataSet prodTypes = objProducts.GetProductTypes();

productList.DataSource = prodTypes;
productList.DataBind();
```

Once the instance of our class has been created and initialized with the proper database connection string, we can call the GetProductTypes() method to return the list of product types. This data will be passed back as a DataSet. This DataSet will serve as the data source for the asp:DataList element named productList that will actually display the data for us. By calling the DataBind() method, the values in the DataSet will be rendered out into the DataList element.

```
<itemtemplate>
    <tr>
    <td align=center>
    <%# DataBinder.Eval(Container.DataItem, "ProductType",
            "<a href=\"displayProducts.aspx?PID={0}\">{0}</a>") %>
    </td>

    </tr>
</itemtemplate>
```

Our asp:DataList will use a template to add some formatting to the data. The header and footer will simply begin and end the TABLE element being used to display the data. The itemtemplate template sets up the format for each row in the table. In each row, there will be one column. This will be the product type string as a hyperlink to the page named displayProducts.aspx. The value of the product type will be passed to this page as part of the Query String.

When we display this page in our browser we see the following:

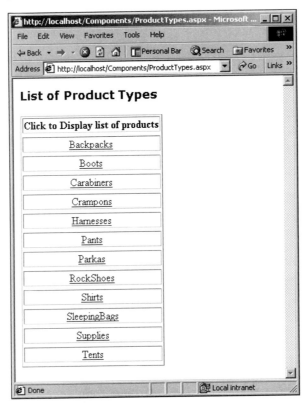

When the user clicks on any of the hyperlinks, they will be taken to the detail test page that we have created called displayProducts.aspx. This page's source code looks like this:

```
<%@ Page Language="VB" Description="Component Test Program" %>
<%@ Import Namespace="BusObjectCS" %>
<%@ Import Namespace="BusObjectVB" %>
<%@ Import Namespace="System.Data" %>

<html>
<script runat=server>
sub Page_Load(sender as Object, evtArgs as EventArgs)
  dim dsn as String = "server=localhost;uid=sa;pwd=;database=IBuyAdventure"

' dim objProducts = new BusObjectCS.IBAProducts()
  dim objProducts = new BusObjectVB.IBAProducts()

  objProducts.DatabaseConnection = dsn

  dim products as DataSet = objProducts.GetProducts(Request.Params("PID"))

  prodGrid.DataSource = products
  prodGrid.DataBind()
```

```
    avgPrice.Text = objProducts.AveragePrice(Request.Params("PID")).ToString()
end sub

</script>

<body>

<h2>Average price for products in this category = <asp:Label runat="server"
id=avgPrice /></h2>

  <h3>List of Products</h3>

<asp:DataGrid id="prodGrid" runat="server" ShowHeader="False">
</asp:DataGrid>

</body>
</html>
```

In this page, we will be using the final two methods of our business component. The first thing we need to do in the page, however, is to make sure that the proper namespaces are included with the page.

```
<%@ Page Language="VB" Description="Component Test Program" %>
<%@ Import Namespace="BusObjectCS" %>
<%@ Import Namespace="BusObjectVB" %>
<%@ Import Namespace="System.Data" %>
```

From the methods that we will be using in this page, we will be returning a double value from one and a DataSet object from the other. In order for the code on this page to understand how to work with the DataSet class, we need to import the System.Data namespace into the page. As we did in the previous page, we will be importing both the C# and VB versions of the components.

```
sub Page_Load(sender as Object, evtArgs as EventArgs)
   dim dsn as String = "server=localhost;uid=sa;pwd=;database=IBuyAdventure"

' dim objProducts = new BusObjectCS.IBAProducts()
   dim objProducts = new BusObjectVB.IBAProducts()


   objProducts.DatabaseConnection = dsn
```

The first part of the Page_Load method is the same as the previous page. We have statements to create the object in both VB and in C#, but only one of these will be active when the page is run – the other will be commented out. In fact, if for some reason both lines were left in the page when it was executed, the C# object will be created first. Then the VB object will be created and assigned to the same variable name. When that happens the C# object will be marked for disposal, and will be destroyed the next time the Common Language Runtime garbage collector is run. So we will end up with a VB component.

```
   dim products as DataSet = objProducts.GetProducts(Request.Params("PID"))

   prodGrid.DataSource = products
   prodGrid.DataBind()
```

We will retrieve the list of products for the requested product type by using the GetProducts method of our class. The product type has been passed in on the URL, and can be retrieved from the Request.Params collection. The information is returned as a DataSet object. We want to use the values in this collection as the source to populate our DataGrid.

```
avgPrice.Text = objProducts.AveragePrice(Request.Params("PID")).ToString()
end sub
```

The other piece of information that we want to display on the page will be the average price for all of the products of this product type This is retrieved by calling the AveragePrice() function of our business component. When we call this method, it will return a double value. Since the Text property of our Label control requires a string, we need to convert the double value to a string using the ToString function.

```
<h2>Average price for products in this category = <asp:Label runat="server"
id=avgPrice /></h2>

  <h3><font face="Verdana">List of Products</font></h3>

<asp:DataGrid id="prodGrid" runat="server" ShowHeader="False">
</asp:DataGrid>
```

All of the difficult work in our page is done in the Page_Load() method. All that we need to do in the display portion is provide the proper server-side controls to display the information. The asp:Label element is a server-side control that we use to display the average selling price for the product type. The asp:DataGrid element will display a simple table that contains the list of products for that product type.

When we select one of the hyperlinks from the previous page, the browser will show something like the following:

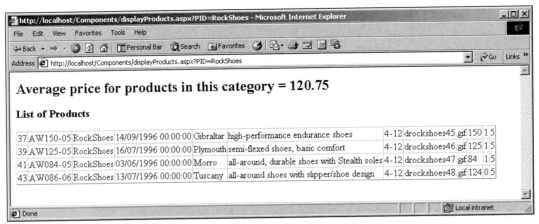

Cross-Language Inheritance

In the past, it has been quite difficult – nearly impossible actually – to have components written in one language subclass and extend a component written in another. You couldn't take a class written in C++ and inherit from it in Visual Basic to create a new object – things like that just weren't possible. You also had no way of taking a compiled binary component – even one written in the same language – and deriving a new object from it without having the source code for the parent object, or at least a header file. It came down to the fact that there just wasn't enough information about the compiled components embedded in them to allow you to derive a new object from it.

However, now, with the Common Language Runtime, we have the ability to do just that. The metadata that is associated with a .NET class provides enough information – even in compiled form – to allow you to derive a new class from an existing class. The other cool thing that the Common Language Runtime allows is for you to derive a new class in a different language. In the past, you actually had to have the source code for your base class in order for you to derive a new class – and that new class had to be written in the same language as the base class. But since all CLR languages compile down to an intermediate language – MSIL – your new class can be in whatever CLR-compliant language you choose.

Cross-Language inheritance, as this is known, also makes debugging much easier. It doesn't matter what language the code was written in when we are debugging. We simply run the debugger on our code, and then the Common Language Runtime will allow us to trace from one language to the next *automatically* and *transparently* to the developer. We can even handle exceptions across languages and not have to worry about translating or modifying the information as it switches languages – the Common Language Runtime makes that all transparent to us.

The other key advantage to cross-language inheritance is that it makes a great way to create class libraries. If you remember back a few years to the Microsoft Foundation Classes (MFC) that were introduced by Microsoft to build Windows applications, you have an example of a class library. MFC was written in C++, so it could be used to create C++ Windows applications or components. But since MFC is innately tied to C++, a Visual Basic developer could not directly use any of the capabilities of MFC. With the .NET Frameworks, Microsoft has written those in C#, but the cross-language inheritance capabilities of the Common Language Runtime allow any supported language to both use the Frameworks as well as create new classes that inherit from classes within the Framework.

Cross-Language Inheritance Example

To show how cross-language inheritance works, we will look at a quick example component. In this example, we will be taking the C# class that was created earlier in the chapter and deriving another class from it. This class will be written in Visual Basic.NET and will override the function that calculates the average selling price. The first step is to modify the C# class so that we can override the function that we need to.

```
public virtual Double AveragePrice (string productType) {
```

We will be overriding the `AveragePrice()` method in our new class. In order to do this, we must add the `virtual` modifier to the function declaration in the C# class. By default in C#, properties and methods are non-virtual, meaning they can't be overridden in any derived classes. If we didn't add the `virtual` keyword, then we would get an error message when we tried to compile our derived class that was trying to override this method.

This points out an interesting design dilemma when creating your classes. If there are methods that you think might be overridden in a derived class, then it probably makes sense to mark these as `virtual` when you first create the class. In our example, we didn't do that, so now we have to go back and re-deploy the original component. Likewise, if there is a function that you don't want overridden in a derived class, make sure that it is not defined as `virtual`, and anyone that derives from your class will not be able to override it.

Next, we can look at the new class, written in VB.NET, that is derived from this C# class.

```
Option Explicit
Option Strict

Imports BusObjectCS
Imports System.Data

namespace SubBusinessClass
  public class SubIBAProducts
  Inherits IBAProducts
    public Overrides function AveragePrice ( productType as string) as Double

      dim iAverage as Double

      iAverage = MyBase.AveragePrice(productType)

      return CDbl(iAverage * 0.65)
    end Function

    public function GetNewestProduct (productType as string) as String

      dim myProducts as DataSet
      myProducts = GetProducts(productType)

      Dim myDataView As DataView = New DataView(myProducts.Tables("products"))
      myDataView.Sort = "ProductIntroductionDate DESC"

      return myDataView(0)("ProductCode").ToString()

    end Function

  end Class
end Namespace
```

As with all Visual Basic.NET components, we should set both `Option Explicit` and `Option Strict` so that the compiler takes care of a lot of the error checking and code validation. These will greatly help to reduce any run-time errors that may occur.

```
Imports BusObjectCS
Imports System.Data
```

Since this class will be derived from the C# version of our business component, we need to import the namespace for that class so that the compiler will understand the references to that class that are made in our new component.

We will also be using a `DataSet` object in our derived class, so we need to import the namespace that contains that class as well. This is an important concept. Even though our base class imported this namespace, we still need to import it here. This is because the namespaces are not inherited by the derived class – they are internally used by the base class, but not available externally.

```
namespace SubBusinessClass
  public class SubIBAProducts
  Inherits IBAProducts
```

The next two lines are nearly identical to the VB component that we created earlier. We are defining a namespace called `SubBusinessClass` and then within that namespace we are creating a public class called `SubIBAProducts`. Remember that class names only have to have unique names within the same namespace. This means that we could have named our class `IBAProducts`, as we did in both original classes, and still no naming conflicts will occur. The key line in this class is the next line. The `Inherits` statement defines the class that the class we are defining is inheriting from. It must be the *first* line in the class definition after the class declaration.

```
public Overrides function AveragePrice ( productType as string) as Double

    dim iAverage as Double

    iAverage = MyBase.AveragePrice(productType)

    return CDbl(iAverage * 0.65)
end Function
```

The first method in the derived class will be the one that we want to override. When we are defining a derived class, any public properties and methods from the parent class automatically become public properties or methods of the derived class. This means that we automatically get the two constructors of the parent class, along with the one property and three methods.

However, we want to change the implementation of the third method. This is why in the base class we added the `virtual` keyword to the method declaration – so that we can change its implementation. The new implementation will not have the `virtual` keyword (unless we want to further derive from this class and override the method again) but rather an `overrides` keyword. This keyword means that the function we are declaring here will replace the base class version of this function. In order to override a function in a base class, the overriding function must have the same declaration – function name, parameter list, and return type.

In the body of the function, we want to utilize some of the functionality of the base class implementation. To do this, we can actually call the base class version of the function directly. To do that, we use the `MyBase` keyword as a preface to the function call, so that the compiler knows which version to call. The value that is returned from the function is then modified and returned as the new return value for this function. There is no requirement that we use any of the base class implementation – we just want to leverage the code that is in there rather than having to rewrite it ourselves.

```
public function GetNewestProduct (productType as string) as String

    dim myProducts as DataSet
    myProducts = GetProducts(productType)
```

```
    Dim myDataView As DataView = New DataView(myProducts.Tables("products"))
    myDataView.Sort = "ProductIntroductionDate DESC"

    return myDataView(0)("ProductCode").ToString()

end Function
```

The other method in our derived class is not found in the base class. This new method will only be accessible to instances of the derived class. In this method, we want to calculate the newest product in a specific product category. There are two ways we could do this. We could write a whole new method from scratch that had all of the database code necessary to execute the proper SQL query to obtain this information. This would in essence duplicate a great deal of code from the base class – not normally the most efficient way to write code.

The other way to do this is to leverage a method from the base class – GetProducts – and then perform some other work to determine the newest product. Notice that the call to GetProducts does not have to be prefaced with MyBase. This is because we don't have a function declared in our class that overrides the function in the base class. The compiler automatically figures out that it needs to call the implementation of this method from the base class.

Once we have the DataSet that contains all of the products for a particular product type, we can then obtain a DataView that represents the table containing the information. By sorting the DataView in reverse order by ProductIntroductionDate, this ensures that the first product in the table is the newest. We can then just grab that row's ProductCode and return it from our new function.

To test this component, we will first compile it, and then modify the test ASP.NET page so that this component is used instead of the original component. When we execute the page, displayProducts_ovr.aspx, we can see that the new value for average price is now displayed. We will also add some code to display the newest product.

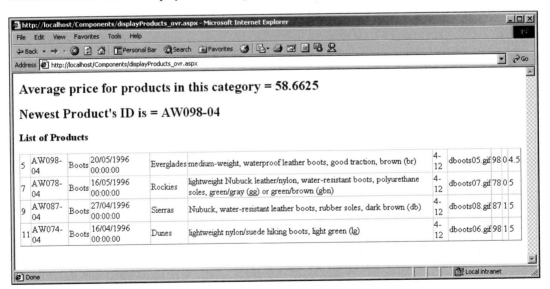

Transactions in .NET

To provide integration with COM+, the CLR provides the same declarative transaction model. This allows managed objects to participate in existing transactions. We can use these transactions from within ASP.NET pages, and also from within .NET Components.

At the ASP.NET page level you can add a page-level directive for this:

```
<%@ Page Transaction="Required" %>
```

The allowable values are:

Value	Description
Disabled	Transactional context will be ignored. This is the default.
NotSupported	The page does not run within a transaction. The object context is created without a transaction.
Supported	The page runs within the scope of an existing transaction, if one is active. If no transaction scope is active, the page runs without a transaction.
Required	The page runs within the scope of a transaction, either an existing one, or creating one if no existing transaction exists.
RequiresNew	The page requires a new transaction, and one will be created for each page request.

To participate in the transaction success or failure, you can either rely on transaction AutoComplete or explicitly commit or abort the transaction. With AutoComplete enabled, your page will vote to commit the transaction if the page runs without throwing an exception. AutoComplete is enabled by default on a page, so if the page completes successfully, then the page will vote to commit.

You can also explicitly control the transaction result by calling the methods of the ContextUtil class. To vote to abort a transaction, you call:

```
ContextUtil.SetAbort()
```

And, if you want to vote to commit a transaction, you call:

```
ContextUtil.SetComplete()
```

For components, we need to create a Serviced Component.

Serviced Components

A **Serviced Component** is one that is automatically serviced by the Windows Component Services, allowing managed classes to live within the existing ObjectContext. The key thing here is that the code is still managed, so you get all of the managed benefits, with the addition of transactional integration. A Serviced Component is a .NET component, but it is hosted inside of a COM+ Application, and therefore can access the services offered by COM+.

A serviced component has its configuration information held by the COM+ catalog. When you use a serviced component within your application, COM+ will create a context service layer based on the attributes you have assigned to your serviced component. Basically, the context service layer runs within COM+ Services, and communicates with your serviced components, which are still running within .NET.

There are several steps to go through to create serviced components:

❑ Derive your class from the `System.EnterpriseServices.ServicedComponent` class.

❑ Add the `TransactionAttribute` to your class.

❑ Create a strong name for the assembly.

❑ Add assembly attributes to identify the strong name, and the COM+ application name.

❑ Register the assembly with the COM+ catalog. This can be manually done, or under certain circumstances, done automatically (this is called Lazy Registration).

Creating a Serviced Component Class

Creating the class and adding the attributes is simple:

VB.NET

```
Option Explicit
Option Strict

Imports System.EnterpriseServices
Imports System.Reflection

<assembly:AssemblyKeyFile("BankVB.snk")>
<assembly:ApplicationName("DotNetBank")>

Namespace Wrox

<Transaction(TransactionOption.RequiresNew)> Public Class BankVB
   Inherits ServicedComponent

    Public Sub Transfer(FromAC As String, ToAC As String, Amt As Decimal)
       Dim f As String = "Transferring " & Amt.ToString() & " from " & FromAC
                                                       & " to " & ToAC

       ContextUtil.SetComplete()
    End Sub

  End Class

End Namespace
```

Let's take a look at the attributes that have been added to this class. The first two are:

```
<assembly:AssemblyKeyFile("BankVB.snk")>
<assembly:ApplicationName("DotNetBank")>
```

The `AssemblyKeyFile` attribute is used to indicate the file that contains the public and private keys for the **strong name** for this assembly. Later in this chapter, we will look at strong-named assemblies. These types of assemblies are required if we want to have multiple versions of an assembly executable at the same time on the same system. The `ApplicationName` attribute defines the COM+ application that this .NET component will execute within. If the application is not found, then COM+ will create an application with the name supplied – in this case `DotNetBank`.

```
<Transaction(TransactionOption.RequiresNew)>
```

The other attribute that has been included with this component is the `Transaction` attribute. This attribute specifies the transaction parameter for this component. In this case, we want to make sure that the component executes inside a new transaction. The parameter that we pass is an enum defined as `TransactionOption.RequiresNew`.

C#

```csharp
using System.EnterpriseServices;
using System.Reflection;

[assembly:AssemblyKeyFile("BankCS.snk")]
[assembly:ApplicationName("DotNetBank")]

namespace Wrox

  [Transaction(TransactionOption.Required)]
  public class BankVB : ServicedComponent
  {
    public void Transfer(string FromAC, string ToAC, decimal Amt)
    {
      string f = "Transferring " + Amt.ToString() + " from " + FromAC + " to "
                                                                   + ToAC;

      ContextUtil.SetComplete();
    }
  }
}
```

The C# version of the serviced component is nearly identical to the VB.NET version. The only difference is the syntax that is used to denote the attributes within the code. Where in the VB.NET version, we used <...> to delineate the attributes, the C# version uses [...] to indicate the attributes.

Additional Assembly Attributes

As well as the `ApplicationName` attribute, you can also add COM+ Component details, such as:

❑ `ApplicationActivation`, to determine how the assembly is activated (`Library` or `Server`).

❑ `ApplicationID`, to specify a GUID.

❑ `Description`, to give the assembly a description.

For example, in VB.NET these would be:

```
<assembly:ApplicationActivation(ActivationOption.Library)>
<assembly:ApplicationID("guid")>
<assembly:Description(".NET bank assembly")>
```

Accessing COM+ Context

To access the COM+ Context from the .NET Serviced Component you use the `System.EnterpriseServices.ContextUtil` class. There are no major performance penalties since the cost to transition into COM+ context is very small. The context (including transactions) flows with the call, so transactions automatically flow.

Registering the Serviced Component

Classes using COM+ services must be registered, which can be done using the Register Services Tool. The syntax is:

```
regsvcs [Options] AssemblyName
```

where *Options* can be one of:

Option	Description
/fc	Find or create a target application. This is a default.
/c	Create the target application, generating an error if it already exists.
/exapp	Expect an existing application.
/tlb:tlbfile	Filename for the exported type library.
/appname:name	Use the specified *name* for the application.
/parname:name	Use the specified *name* or ID for the target partition.
/extlb	Use an existing type library.
/reconfig	Reconfigure the existing target application. This is a default.
/noreconfig	Do not reconfigure the existing target application.
/u	Uninstall the target application.
/componly	Configure only the components, not methods or interfaces.
/nologo	Suppress logo output.
/quiet	Suppress logo and success output.

Using this utility performs the following actions:

- ❏ Loads the assembly
- ❏ Registers the assembly
- ❏ Generates a type library
- ❏ Registers the type library
- ❏ Installs the type library into the COM+ application
- ❏ Configures the COM+ application

For example, to register the bank assemblies:

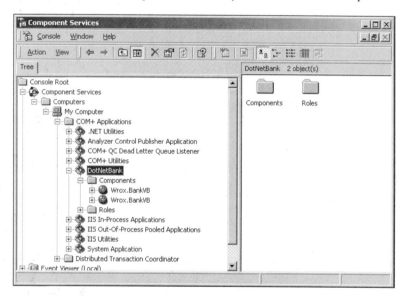

If you then examine the COM+ Component Services, you'll see the .NET components.

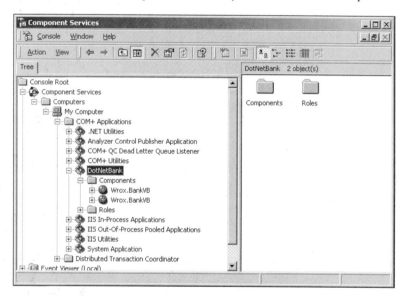

These can be treated like any other transactional COM+ component.

Lazy Registration

If a serviced component is used from managed code, and it is not already registered as part of a COM+ application, then the registration and configuration is performed automatically for you. This may seem like an ideal solution, but it does require administrative privileges, so is not suitable for all scenarios. By and large it's best to manually register components, perhaps as part of the installation.

Serviced Component Security

Integration with COM+ security is also provided as part of serviced components, allowing access to the `SecurityContext` object of the COM+ application. For this to succeed the managed code needs to obtain an NT Security token and perform impersonation before calling the COM object.

Component Deployment

The assembly is used by the .NET architecture to support the sharing and re-use of code. All classes must exist within an assembly in order to be creatable by the Common Language Runtime. The assembly contains the metadata that the Common Language Runtime uses to allow the object to function. Without an assembly, the component cannot function. In the past, you could store code in a DLL, and you could use DLLs as loadable modules within an application. But the difference is in the metadata – a DLL was just a block of code – there was no knowledge of what it did outside of the developer that was familiar with it. The metadata associated with an assembly provides that kind of information.

What are Assemblies?

There is no concept of an assembly as a file – there is no such thing as a `.assembly` file that we have to worry about now. The assembly is a collection of files that together make up the assembly. The only requirement is that these files need to all reside in the same directory on the disk. When they are placed into an assembly, the Common Language Runtime treats all these as a single unit.

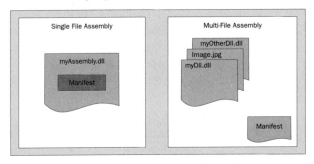

As you can see from the picture above, the manifest is what is used to describe the contents of the application. The manifest can either be embedded within a single DLL, as seen in the single file assembly, or can be in a separate file, as is the case with the multi-file assembly. When we talk about DLLs in .NET, they are just a bit different from what they were in COM or Win32. While the extension is the same, they are executed by the Common Language Runtime, instead of being executed as native code.

The assembly can be thought of as a logical DLL. In the past, we would distribute components or resources through the deployment of a DLL. Now, we can distribute the pieces of an assembly in the same way. The main difference is that the DLL needed some other information somewhere – usually in the registry – to tell the system that it was there ready to run. With an assembly, it carries that information along with it – in its metadata.

An assembly is **not** an application. An application is built from one or more assemblies. The assemblies that make up an application can be deployed in a number of different ways. Since an assembly contains its own metadata, it is capable of telling the operating system all about itself. It does not rely on entries into the registry to describe itself.

This association of metadata with executable code simplifies the distribution of an application. All you need to do to deploy an application is simply to copy all of the assemblies that make up the application to a directory on the disk. This is known as XCOPY deployment, since the only tool required to deploy the files to disk is the XCOPY console command. When the application is first executed, the metadata within the assemblies tells the system all that it needs to know in order to execute the application. As we saw earlier, this may not always be the case, as if you are using serviced components, these need to be registered with COM+.

You can also use more traditional installation mechanisms to distribute applications built out of assemblies. You can build an `.msi` file and use the Windows Installer to deploy the files into the correct location. Likewise, you can build a `.CAB` file and have a browser download the file to the system and then execute the application. In either case, all that the installation mechanism is responsible for is getting the proper files into the proper location on the destination system – no information about the assemblies needs to be added to the registry of the target system.

Assemblies and Versioning

There are currently two problems with the Win32 architecture that have combined to give us what is known as DLL Hell. In DLL Hell, there is no control entity that is responsible for all of the DLL files installed onto a system. Information about a COM DLL is held in the registry. It can be easily overwritten by another application. For DLLs that aren't COM DLLs, there is no entry whatsoever in the registry. An application install program can also overwrite an existing DLL. This can play havoc with any existing application that was relying on that particular DLL performing a specific function when a method is called.

One of the specific problems with Win32 is that there is no system-level enforcement of versioning rules between components. It is left up to "best practices" coding, which says that once an interface is published it can never be changed – but there is nothing in the operating system that explicitly prevents this. The other problem is that there is no common way for an application to say that it needs version 1.2.1.1234 of a particular component. It is left up to the developer to check the version of a DLL before calling into it. If that check is not done, and the application finds a different version, then the code that it is relying on may no longer be there, or it may not perform the function that it expects – even if the interface is still intact. To attempt to combat this, Windows 2000 added System File Protection. This is an OS feature that can stop any installation program from overwriting any system DLLs.

The Common Language Runtime extends this support by allowing developers to specify the specific version of a component that they want their application to use. It provides all of the support to make sure that the proper version is located and used for the requesting application. In doing this, it also allows for the execution of code from two similar components – only differing in version. This is known as side-by-side execution and we will look at that a bit later in the chapter.

Assembly Manifest

In order for an assembly to describe itself to the Common Language Runtime it must contain a set of metadata. This metadata is contained in the assembly's manifest. The manifest contains the metadata required to specify:

- The assembly version
- The security information for the assembly
- The scope of the assembly
- Information to resolve references to the resources and classes of the assembly

The manifest for an assembly can either be stored in an EXE or DLL file, or in a standalone file. Remember that the assembly can be made up of one or more files – there isn't a specific file that contains the entire assembly. In a single-file assembly, the manifest is part of the DLL or EXE file that is the assembly.

The manifest of an assembly lists all of the files and resources that make up the assembly. It also lists all of the classes and types defined in the assembly, and specifies which resources or files within the assembly map to which classes or types. The manifest also identifies any other assemblies on which it is dependent.

In creating a multi-file assembly, the Assembly Generation tool (AL.EXE) is used to create the manifest for the assembly. To create a multi-file assembly, you compile the individual source files without an assembly. Then the AL tool is used to read through the compiled modules and create an assembly for the full set of modules.

Metadata

The manifest will specifically contain these pieces of metadata:

❑ **Assembly Name** – this is a textual string name that identifies the assembly. When an assembly is used by one application, the developer can generally enforce a unique name for each assembly – thus preventing name collisions. However, when an assembly is designed to be shared, a more unique naming method must be used. This is called a **strong name**, and creating one allows the assembly to be stored in the **global assembly cache**. The global assembly cache is used to store assemblies that can be used by several applications on a machine.

To store an assembly into the global assembly cache, there are three steps that have to be followed:

First, you must create a strong name for the assembly using the SN.EXE tool. This tool will generate a file that contains the necessary public and private keys to define a strong name.

Second, the contents of that file are passed to the Assembly Generation Tool (AL.EXE) to create an assembly with a strong name associated with it.

Finally, to install the assembly into the global assembly cache, you will use the Global Assembly Cache Tool (GACUTIL.EXE). This is a tool is used to manipulate the contents of the global assembly cache, including adding components to the GAC.

❑ **Version Information** – the components of the version number are the major and minor version numbers, a build number, and a revision number. This is represented as a set of four numbers with the format:

```
<major version>.<minor version>.<build number>.<revision>
```

When the Common Language Runtime is checking to see an assembly is the proper version, it first checks the major and minor version numbers. These **must** match in order for the assembly to be compatible. If these two numbers match but the build number is different, then as long as the build number of the assembly is greater than the build required by the application, it can be assumed to be backwards-compatible with the version expected by the application.

❑ **Assembly File List** – lists each file contained in the assembly, along with the relative path to the file. For version 1 of the .NET Framework, all files in an assembly must be in the same directory as the manifest file. This only holds true for a multi-file assembly.

❑ **Type reference information** – maps all of the types included in the assembly to the specific file in the assembly that contains the type. This is necessary so that any types referenced within the classes contained in the assembly can be resolved by the Runtime.

❑ **Referenced Assemblies** – lists all of the other assemblies that are statically referenced within the types contained in this assembly. Each entry contains the name of the assembly along with the required version information.

There is also custom metadata that can be included by the developer. Only the developer can use this information – the Common Language Runtime does not use this information in any way. In the first release of the .NET architecture, there are two sets of custom assembly metadata. The first set is made up of nine classes from the `System.Reflection` namespace. You can use this namespace to query the values for this metadata at run time. `System.Reflection` metadata includes:

❑ Company information

❑ Build information, such as "Retail" or "Debug"

❑ Copyright information

❑ Additional naming and version information

❑ Assembly Title and Description

❑ Product and Trademark Information

The second set is made up of classes from the `System.Runtime.CompilerServices` namespace. This metadata includes:

❑ Cultures or spoken languages supported by the assembly – not programming languages

❑ OS and Processors the assembly has been built to support. Version 1 of the Common Language Runtime does not use this information

Self-Describing Components

With other application architectures, the only way for components to communicate is through a binary interface. If these components were written in different languages, then there is a good chance that the way that data was stored is different as well. This leads to problems in the communication between these two components. In the .NET architecture, the metadata that is presented by each assembly helps to alleviate this confusion. The confusion is further alleviated through the common types of the Common Language Runtime.

Since the components within an assembly are so thoroughly defined by the metadata, you can even define a new class that inherits from an existing class directly from the compiled code – you don't need to access the source code to do this. In fact, the components don't even need to be in the same language – as long as both are managed components. We saw an example of this earlier.

The assemblies and the components within them are said to be "self-describing". This means that they carry all the information that other components need to know in order to interact with them. This information is all carried within the metadata of the assembly. There are no more IDL files in the .NET architecture or public header files that get out of sync with the executables, and you can always be sure that the metadata information being used by the runtime is the proper metadata for the code being executed – since they are held together in the assembly.

Side-by-Side Execution

The ability to run multiple versions of the same component at the same time is a very valuable feature of the Common Language Runtime. It can even execute two versions of the same component within the same process. The ability to do this is called side-by-side execution. By allowing this, the .NET architecture offers the developer an advantage over architectures such as COM. While there have been ways in the past to do side-by-side execution, the implementation of it in .NET frees the developer from most of the worries associated with doing it. By handling it in the plumbing of the Common Language Runtime, the developer only has to worry about the business-specific code in their application.

When creating new versions of a component, a developer doesn't have to worry as much about maintaining compatibility with previous versions. Since the older component can run right alongside the new component, and the application using the component knows which version of the component to use, both can coexist peacefully on the same machine. There are some precautions that the developer must take into account when having components that will run side-by-side with previous versions. For example, if the component is relying on a physical file as a data cache, then two components executing side-by-side will try to access the same file. The components would need to be written such that they keep the file in a location that is dependent on the version of the component being executed.

Summary

The flexibility and power of the .NET architecture extends beyond just creating applications, web services, and ASP.NET pages. We can create powerful business components using the .NET Frameworks and the Common Language Runtime that have just as much power and flexibility as COM objects. In some cases, the capabilities offered by the Common Language Runtime provide distinct advantages over COM. Now we can actually derive new objects from classes written in different languages. And we can do this even if all we have is the compiled version of the base class. However, that doesn't mean that we can't have COM and .NET work together in the same application.

In this chapter, we have specifically looked at:

- ❑ How to write a business object in two different languages, and then use the same test program to work with both objects

- ❑ How to take a class written in one language and extend its functionality by deriving a new class in a totally different language

- ❑ How to make use of transactions in your ASP.NET pages and within your .NET components.

- ❑ How assemblies and metadata provide a way to package the executable code along with detailed descriptions of the code that is executing

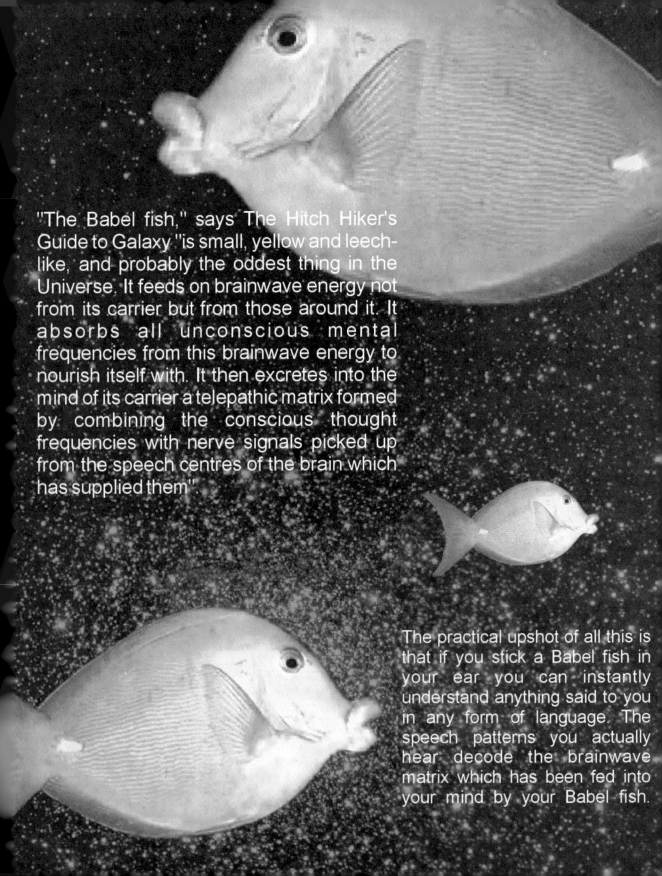

"The Babel fish," says The Hitch Hiker's Guide to Galaxy "is small, yellow and leech-like, and probably the oddest thing in the Universe. It feeds on brainwave energy not from its carrier but from those around it. It absorbs all unconscious mental frequencies from this brainwave energy to nourish itself with. It then excretes into the mind of its carrier a telepathic matrix formed by combining the conscious thought frequencies with nerve signals picked up from the speech centres of the brain which has supplied them".

The practical upshot of all this is that if you stick a Babel fish in your ear you can instantly understand anything said to you in any form of language. The speech patterns you actually hear decode the brainwave matrix which has been fed into your mind by your Babel fish.

18

Building ASP.NET Server Controls

Since the early days, COM developers around the world have been building reusable visual controls. In the early 90's, building such controls required significant time and investment in understanding the myriad of COM interfaces that a control had to implement and use.

Later in the decade, C/C++ frameworks like the Microsoft Foundation Classes (MFC) and the Active Template Library (ATL) made control development a little easier. They provided reusable classes and templates that implemented a lot of plumbing code required for controls. But the true breakthrough in popular control development didn't really happen until 1996 when the release of the Visual Basic Control Creation edition made control creation far simpler, and consequently very popular globally.

The upside of control development, and the reason why people still write so many controls today, is reusability. Once you have conquered visual control development, the reward of being able to write a control once (the grid control being the canonical example) and then reuse it in numerous **control containers** (such as Word, Excel, etc.) makes it worth all the pain. You can, of course, reuse the control in your own suite of products, not to mention the fact that you could make a good living selling them to other developers. These same advantages apply in the world of ASP.NET controls, but there is one big difference: **ASP.NET controls are easy to get started with**.

ASP.NET allows you to build reusable visual controls that can render themselves as HTML or any other mark-up language such as WML. Many high level similarities can be drawn between COM controls and ASP.NET controls, as they both enable reuse within UIs. But in reality, they are very different in the way they are implemented. ASP.NET provides a clean and easy-to-use class hierarchy for implementing controls, and there are no esoteric interfaces or threading models that are difficult to understand. ASP.NET still uses interfaces, but there really aren't more than a couple you'll use on a regular basis.

In this chapter we're going to look at ASP.NET control development covering:

❑ When, why, and how you can build ASP.NET controls in both VB.NET and C#.

❑ How controls form the basis of **all** page rendering in ASP.NET.

❑ How controls persist state across page invocation.

❑ How controls interact with postback and can raise events.

❑ Building controls that, themselves, use other controls to render their UI.

Writing a Simple Control

To demonstrate the basic principles of control development and to show how easy ASP.NET control development is, we'll kick off this chapter by writing a simple Label control, which can render a text message. We'll initially develop the control in C#, review the code, and then rewrite it using VB. This example will hopefully prove to you that control development really isn't that difficult, and it is, at the very least, worth understanding how controls are written so you can better understand how ASP.NET renders pages.

Creating a C# Control

Fire up your text editor or IDE of choice and enter the following C# code:

```
using System;
using System.Web;
using System.Web.UI;

namespace WroxControls
{
    public class MyFirstControl : Control
    {
        protected override void Render(HtmlTextWriter writer)
        {
            writer.Write("<h1>ASP.NET Control Development in C#</h1>");
        }
    }
};
```

Save the file and call it MyFirstControl.cs. Let's briefly examine the code. The first few lines import three **namespaces** that controls typically use:

❑ System – contains core system classes like String. The code will compile without this, but as most controls make use of the core classes it is always good practice to include it.

❑ System.Web – the parent namespace for all ASP.NET classes. This contains classes like HttpRequest (the ASP.NET Request object) and HttpResponse (the ASP.NET Response object). Again, the code will compile without this, but as with the System namespace, most control classes will use the ASP.NET intrinsic objects so it is good practice to include it.

❑ System.Web.UI – contains the ASP.NET control classes, many of which are divided up into namespaces based upon their family (System.Web.UI.WebControls, System.Web.UI.HtmlControls, etc.). This reference is needed as we are using the Control and HtmlTextWriter classes.

The next line of the code marks the beginning scope of a new namespace we have chosen for our control called WroxControls:

```
namespace WroxControls
{
```

Anything declared within the next section of the code, until the closing namespace statement seven lines later, is a member of the WroxControls namespace. This means that the full namespace-qualified reference to our control is WroxControls.MyFirstControl. Any code using our class must use this full name unless the Using directive is included to import all definitions within our namespace into its default scope.

The next five lines of code declare the class for our server control:

```
public class MyFirstControl : Control
{
    protected override void Render(HtmlTextWriter writer)
    {
        writer.Write("<h1>ASP.NET Control Development in C#</h1>");
    }
}
```

The class is called MyFirstControl. It's derived from the class Control, (which is part of the System.Web.UI namespace) declared as public, and has one protected method called Render. The Control class implements the basic plumbing code required by a server control to be used within an ASP.NET page.

The name of the class is arbitrary and you can call your controls whatever you like, as they are defined in your own namespace. You should avoid using names that are already used by ASP.NET (or any other part of the runtime), as name conflicts will occur if two namespaces are imported using the @Import directive by a page, or the using directive inside of a source file. If you decided to create your own label control do not call it Label; call it YourLabel or some other meaningful name such as WroxLabel.

> By marking our class as **public,** we are stating that *anybody* can create an instance of our class and use it. If we specify that it is private (by omitting the **public** attribute), the class will only be usable by other classes within the same namespace. If an ASP.NET page attempts to access a private class, the runtime will raise an error saying the class/type is not defined. This is somewhat confusing when trying to track down an error, so it is always worth checking the access control of a class as it is easy to forget to add the **public** keyword when developing.

The Render method is declared using the override attribute. This attribute tells the compiler that the base class Control implements the Render member, but our class wants to override the method so that it can control the output created at run-time itself. The implementation of this method calls the Write method of the HtmlTextWriter object, which results in the HTML "<h1>ASP.NET Control Development in C#</h1>" being written to the page output stream.

Once you have created a server control and compiled it, you can use it in an ASP.NET page. To do this, you use the @Register page directive to associate a tag prefix with a namespace containing a server control, and then use the tag prefix plus the class name of a server control as show here:

```
<%@ Register TagPrefix="Wrox" Namespace="WroxControls"
             Assembly="MyFirstControl" %>
<html>
<body>

<Wrox:MyFirstControl runat="server" />

</body>
</html>
```

Create a new file called myfirstcontrol.aspx *to contain this ASP.NET page.*

This page tells the ASP.NET page compiler that when it sees any element starting with 'Wrox:' it should search the namespace WroxControls for a class whose name matches the element name (that is, MyFirstControl). Furthermore, the assembly attribute defines the physical assembly in which the class is contained. At run-time, assuming ASP.NET located the class, it creates an instance of it, and calls its Render method to allow it to write data to the output stream being created (for example, the page).

The position of the HTML that a control creates in the final page depends upon where that control is declared inside the ASP.NET page code. In this page we'd expect the server controls output to be rendered after the body tag.

In this example, once our control has inserted its HTML into the output stream, the final page sent down to the client browser will look like this:

```
<html>
<body>

<h1>ASP.NET Control Development in C#</h1>

</body>
</html>
```

The actual rendering of which is shown here:

To test the ASP.NET page yourself and view the output, you need to compile the C# source code to create an assembly. This is placed in the bin directory of the application on your web server, causing the ASP.NET runtime to scan the assembly and make an internal note of the namespaces and classes/controls within it.

Compiling the C# Control and Creating an Assembly

To compile our server control class, bring up your text editor, enter the following batch commands, and save the file as make.bat:

```
set outdir=..\bin\MyFirstControl.dll
set assemblies=System.dll,System.Web.dll

csc /t:library /out:%outdir% /r:%assemblies% MyFirstControl.cs
```

> For the class to compile correctly, you'll need to change the outdir parameter '..', in line one, to match a directory on your machine that is configured as a virtual directory.

The first two lines of the make.bat file declare a couple of variables. These make the line that actually does the compilation more readable. The compiler options are discussed in Chapter 3. The important points to note about this file are:

❑ A reference to the System.dll and System.Web.dll assemblies is added using the /r parameter. We have to do this so that the compiler knows where to search for the namespaces/classes we're importing into our control with the using directive. If you do not add a reference to the assembly containing referenced classes you'll get a compile error.

❑ The output of the compiler (MyFirstControl.DLL) is placed directly into our web application's bin directory. When ASP.NET has to create a class at runtime, this directory is searched. Using the metadata contained in our assembly, ASP.NET will know where to locate the WroxControls namespace specified in the page's @Register directive. By compiling our control directory to the bin directory, we are less likely to forget to copy the assembly.

Run the make.bat file, and you'll see some output like this:

If all goes well, check that the bin directory contains the compiled assembly. If it exists, you should be able to open the ASP.NET page we created earlier and see the output of the control.

First Control Complete

Although the C# control we've just developed is about as simple as it gets, and doesn't really have any practical use as yet, you've just seen the full development cycle required for a simple ASP.NET control. Hopefully you now think that: (a) control development is nothing like it was in the COM days, and (b) maybe control development is worth checking out in more detail. Things will get more advanced from here on in, but all of the code is clean and fairly easy to understand once you've grasped the basic concepts that we've been discussing.

To show that control development in Visual Basic is just as painless, we'll create an almost identical control called `MyFirstControlInVB`.

Control Development in Visual Basic

One of the great things about VB.NET is that the language has arrived in the 21st Century with a bang. It now has all the object-oriented (OO) features that make it a first-class programming language. However, as you'd expect, the VB team and C# teams at Microsoft are competing with each other for adopters, and as a result they have used different names for certain attributes and directives within their respective languages, that they feel are more suitable for their audience of programmers. This is fair enough, but it does means that switching between the languages can be a little confusing at first.

Here are a few notes on the language differences that should help you convert any of the samples in this chapter between C# and VB:

C# Example	VB Example

`Using System;`
 	
`Namespace WroxControls {`
`    ...`
`};`
	`Imports System`
	
	`Namespace WroxControls`
	`    ...`
	`End Namespace`

`Public class A : B {`
`    ...`
`}`
	`Public Class A`
	`        Inherits B`
	`    ...`
	`End Class`

`Public class A : B {`
`    ...`
`}`
	`Public Class A`
	`        Implements B`
	`    ...`
	`End Class`

> In this chapter we'll mainly write the samples in C#, but whenever a new technique is introduced we will show the equivalent VB code.

Creating Your First VB ASP.NET Server Control

Create a new file for the VB control called `MyFirstControlInVB.vb` and enter this code:

```
Imports System
Imports System.Web.UI

Namespace WroxControls
```

```
    Public Class MyFirstControlInVB

    Inherits Control

      Overrides Protected Sub Render(writer as HtmlTextWriter)
        writer.Write("<h1>ASP.NET Control Development in VB</h1>")
      End Sub

    End Class

  End Namespace
```

Using the table above, you should be able to see how the code has been translated from C#. The main changes are:

❑   All references to Using have been replaced with Imports.

❑   All the trailing C-style syntax semicolons have been removed.

❑   All opening curly brackets have been removed, and the closing curly brackets replaced with the more verbose VB syntax of End Class, End Namespace, etc.

❑   The Class declaration has had the trailing ': Control' text removed, and a separate line, Inherits Control, has been added to replace it.

❑   The method declaration order has been switched around, as VB declares the name of a variable first and then the type, whereas C# does the opposite.

The other change to note is that we have changed the HTML output to say VB rather than C#, so the browser output is now rendered like this:

To build the assembly containing this new class, create a file called makevb.bat and enter the following commands:

```
  set outdir=..\..\bin\MyFirstControlInVB.dll
  set assemblies=System.dll,System.Web.dll

  vbc /t:library /out:%outdir% /r:%assemblies% MyFirstControlInVB.vb
```

Again, substitute the '..' in the first line to point to your virtual directory.

This is similar to the C# make file except that the compiler name is now vbc rather than csc, and the output file is MyFirstControlInVB.DLL.

Run the make file to compile the control, then bring up your text editor and enter the following ASP.NET page code, and save it:

```
<%@ Register TagPrefix="Wrox" Namespace="WroxControls"
             Assembly="MyFirstControlInVB" %>
<html>
<body>

<Wrox:MyFirstControlInVB runat="server" />

</body>
</html>
```

The page is pretty much identical to the ASP.NET page that used the C# version of the control, but we have changed the line in the <body> element to specify the class MyFirstControlInVB instead of MyFirstControl.

Two Controls on One Page

After you have viewed the page to prove your VB control is working, update the page with the additional lines shown here:

```
<%@ Register TagPrefix="Wrox" Namespace="WroxControls"
             Assembly="MyFirstControlInVB" %>
<%@ Register TagPrefix="WroxCSharp" Namespace="WroxControls"
             Assembly="MyFirstControl" %>
<html>
<body>
<Wrox:MyFirstControlInVB runat="server" />
<WroxCSharp:MyFirstControl runat="server" />
</body>
</html>
```

The additional register directive associates the assembly containing the C# control with the tag prefix WroxCSharp. Since the controls we're using on this page are in different assemblies, we have to do this. If two controls were in the same assembly, we'd only need one directive.

View this updated page in the browser and you should see the output from the two controls:

As expected, both controls have rendered themselves in the output stream depending upon their location in the ASP.NET page. The ASP.NET page framework doesn't care what language the controls are written in, as long as they are directly, or indirectly, derived from the Control class.

Multi-Step Page Rendering

The rendering of a control is just one of many events that occur during its lifetime. As we progress through this chapter, we'll discuss the other events that occur, and how these events are fired during the lifetime of an ASP.NET page. Unlike ASP, where a page essentially had one execution step, 'render', an ASP.NET page has many executions steps or phases. As such, control events are fired during different execution stages within a page.

Control Properties

For a server control to be useful it needs to allow a page developer to have influence over how the control renders its UI. In ASP.NET pages, the basic way of achieving this is using attributes.

For example, assuming we had a server control called `MyLabel`, which had a `Text` attribute specifying a label to be printed, we could declare the control a couple of times and make different labels appear:

```
<%@ Register TagPrefix="Wrox" Namespace="WroxControls"
             Assembly="MyLabel" %>
<html>
<body>

<Wrox:MyLabel runat="server" Text="Hello" />
<Wrox:MyLabel runat="server" Text="World" />

</body>
</html>
```

When the ASP.NET page framework processes attributes of an HTML element that are part of a server control declaration, it maps them to the **public properties** of the associated class. These values of the properties are set in the **initialization stage** of a page. During this stage, for each control, the `OnInit` method is called once all properties for a control have been set. In this method a control can perform validation of the properties, and/or perform other operations such as default values.

> During the initialization stage a control should not try and access other server controls declared on a page, except child controls. Until the initialization stage is reached, other controls on the page will be in an inconsistent state.

The following code implements the `MyLabel` control discussed:

```
using System;
using System.Web;
using System.Web.UI;

namespace WroxControls
{
    public class MyLabel : Control
    {
        string _text;

        public string Text
        {
            get{ return _text; }
            set{ _text = value; }
        }
    }
```

```
    protected override void OnInit(EventArgs e)
    {
        base.OnInit(e);
        if ( _text == null )
            _text = "Here is some default text";
    }

    protected override void Render(HtmlTextWriter writer)
    {
        writer.Write("<h1>" + _text + "</h1>" );
    }
  }
};
```

The main areas of interest in this code are:

❑   The Text property now allows the value of the label to be set and retrieved.

❑   The OnInit method sets the Text property to a default value if it's not specified. For our example, this shows that properties of the class are set just before OnInit is called.

❑   The Render method has been updated to write the control's Text property out between the <h1> elements.

❑   With these code changes in place, we can create a new ASP.NET page that has three MyLabel controls:

```
<%@ Register TagPrefix="Wrox" Namespace="WroxControls"
             Assembly="MyLabel" %>
<html>
<body>

<Wrox:MyLabel runat="server" Text="Hello" />
<Wrox:MyLabel runat="server" Text="World" />
<Wrox:MyLabel runat="server"/>

</body>
</html>
```

This page should render two <h1> elements with the text "Hello" and "World", and one <h1> element with the text "Here is some default text", since not specifying the Text attribute should result in the default text appearing.

Here is the output from this page:

Attribute Value Conversion

When ASP.NET matches an attribute to a property, it will perform intelligent conversion of the attribute value. If a class property is a `string`, ASP.NET will just do a simple mapping and initialize the attribute. If the property is an `integer` or `long`, the attribute value will be converted to a number, then set. If a value is an enumeration, ASP.NET will match the `string` value against an **enumeration name**, and then set the correct enumeration value. The same type of logical conversion occurs for other types such as `Boolean`. If a value cannot be converted, for example, if you try and use a `string` value for a numeric property, ASP.NET will generate a parse error.

To demonstrate some of these conversions, we'll add a `RepeatCount` property to our control, which is defined as an `integer`, and a `ForeColor` property defined as `System.Drawing.Color`. These new properties will enable page developers to specify how many times a label should appear, and the color used for the text.

In this updated page we use the `RepeatCount` attribute to tell the first label to draw itself three times. We use the `ForeColor` attribute to set the second label to `Green` and the third label to `Orange`. Since we do not specify a `ForeColor` attribute for the first label it will appear as the default color we've selected, `Blue`:

```
<%@ Register TagPrefix="Wrox" Namespace="WroxControls"
             Assembly="MyLabel" %>
<html>
<body>

<Wrox:MyLabel runat="server" RepeatCount=3 Text="Hello" />
<Wrox:MyLabel runat="server" Text="World" ForeColor=Green />
<Wrox:MyLabel runat="server" ForeColor=Orange />

</body>
</html>
```

The output for this new page is shown here, where "**Hello**" now appears three times, and the text is in different colors (or different shades of gray in the case of the printed book text):

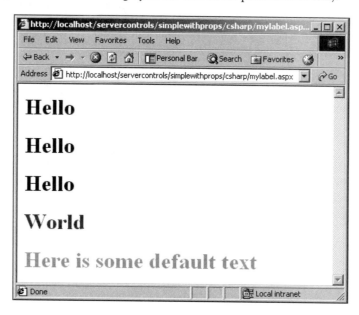

Implementing these new properties in our server control is straightforward because ASP.NET provides all of the conversion processing for us, keeping our code clean and simple. There is nothing specific to ASP.NET in the code we write:

```
public class MyLabel : Control
{
    int _repeatCount = 1;
    public int RepeatCount
    {
        get { return _repeatCount; }
        set { _repeatCount = value; }
    }

    Color _foreColor = Color.Blue;
    public Color ForeColor
    {
        get { return _foreColor; }
        set { _foreColor = value; }
    }
};
```

The Color enumeration is defined in the System.Drawing namespace.

In this code we have made the default RepeatCount equal to 1, and the default color Blue. Both of these defaults are set using member initializers rather than adding code to the OnInit method. Typically this is the best way to specify default values for a variable. You only really need to add initialization code in OnInit for more complex initialization. For example, in OnInit you could ensure the RepeatCount is within a valid range, throwing an ArgumentException if the count exceeds a reasonable number.

With these new properties in place, the Render method is updated to output the <h1> element and its associated text RepeatCount times. The color of the text will be set using a style attribute and a color selector. To convert the Color enumeration we use the System.Drawing.ColorTranslator class. The ToHtml method of this class is used in our code to convert the _foreColor enumeration value into the HTML color value. Here is the updated Render method:

```
protected override void Render(HtmlTextWriter writer)
{
    int loop;

    for( loop=0; loop < _repeatCount; loop++ )
    {
        writer.Write("<h1 style='color:" +
                ColorTranslator.ToHtml(_foreColor) +
                "'>" + _text + "</h1>" );
    }
}
```

Using HtmlTextWriter Rendering Services

Our label server control is starting to become more useful now we've enabled basic customizations such as the repeat count, and foreground color. The only problem with these customizations is that they have increased the complexity of the HTML we are creating. As the number of attributes a control supports increases, so does the complexity of the HTML it has to emit, and the code needs to create. To keep code readable, and to reduce the likelihood of HTML formatting errors, we can use the rendering services of the `HtmlTextWriter` class to manage HTML tag and attribute creation.

The `HtmlTextWriter` class provides services for:

❑   Writing HTML or other markup languages to the output stream.

❑   Managing the creation of well-formed elements.

❑   Creating attributes.

❑   Creating a style attribute.

Using the services of the `HtmlTextWriter`, we can rewrite the `Render` method as follows:

```
protected override void Render(HtmlTextWriter writer)
{
    int loop;
    for( loop=0; loop < _repeatCount; loop++ )
    {
        writer.AddStyleAttribute( "color",
            ColorTranslator.ToHtml(_foreColor) );
        writer.RenderBeginTag("h1");
        writer.Write( _text );
        writer.RenderEndTag();
    }
}
```

This code is much more readable, maintainable, and less error prone, since the `HtmlTextWriter` class takes on responsibility for formatting the HTML.

The call to `AddStyleAttribute` tells the `HtmlTextWriter` that the next element it starts should have a style element called `color` with a specified value. You can call this multiple times, and the `HtmlTextWriter` will automatically emit a style element.

The call to `RenderBeginTag` tells the `HtmlTextWriter` to output a start tag for the element `<h1>`, outputting any attributes that have previously been added using `AddStyleAttribute`, or `AddAttribute`. `AddAttribute` can be used to output a normal HTML attribute.

The call to `Write` tells the `HtmlTextWriter` to output the specified content to the HTML stream. There are various overloads for `Write` that allow you to pass in any type. All types will be converted to a string and written to the output stream. If there is not a specific overload for a type, the `Object.ToString` method will be used.

The `RenderEndTag` call tells the `HtmlTextWriter` to output the close tag for the last tag opened using `RenderStartTag`. These two methods automatically stack, and recursively manage, element tags, and can be used to emit complex nested HTML elements.

The HTML output from our page using the rendering services of `HtmlTextWriter` looks like this:

```
<html>
<body>

<h1 style="color:Blue;">
  Hello
</h1><h1 style="color:Blue;">
  Hello
</h1><h1 style="color:Blue;">
  Hello
</h1>
<h1 style="color:Green;">
  World
</h1>
<h1 style="color:Orange;">
  Here is some default text
</h1>

</body>
</html>
```

As you can see, the `HtmlTextWriter` also performs automatic indentation of the markup it creates.

Object Properties

Server controls can expose other objects, as well as primitive types, as properties. A server control declaration within an ASP.NET can directly set the properties of an object property in two ways. The first method of setting object properties is using the **Object Walker** syntax for attribute names, when a hyphen (–) character is used to specify a property of an object:

```
<Wrox:MyFirstControl MyObject-A="hello" MyObject-B="World"
                     runat="server" />
```

The object walker syntax can walk any number of sub-objects of an object property too:

```
<Wrox:MyFirstControl MyObject-AnotherObject-A="hello"
                     runat="server" />
```

Supporting an object property is straightforward. For example, this simple class definition allows two string values to be set using the properties A and B:

```
public class SampleClassProperty {

    string _valueA;
    string _valueB;

    public string A {
        get {
            return _valueA;
        }
        set {
            _valueA = value;
```

```
            }
        }
        public string B {
            get {
                return _valueB;
            }
            set {
                _valueB = value;
            }
        }
    };
```

A server control could use it for one of its object properties, MyObject, as follows:

```
SampleClassProperty _exampleObjectProperty
    = new SampleClassProperty();

public SampleClassProperty MyObject
{
    get { return _exampleObjectProperty; }
}
```

By enabling object properties to be initialized, server controls can group logically related attributes together and easily expose them on one or more controls, with very little code. The style object, used by most ASP.NET controls, is a good example of this.

Another way of initializing object properties within a server control is by using nested elements:

```
<Wrox:MyFirstControl runat=server>
    <MyObject A="Hello" B="Hello" />
</Wrox:MyFirstControl>
```

Most of the ASP.NET web controls support this. However, for it to work you need to annotate your server control class definition with the ParseChildren attribute, specifying a value of True:

```
namespace WroxControls
{
    [
        ParseChildren(true)
    ]
    public class MyLabel : Control
    ...
```

When the ASP.NET page compiler sees this attribute, the default **control builder** that ASP.NET uses to parse sub-content for a server control declaration, then knows that each element is an object property. If you do not specify this attribute, or you specify false, ASP.NET assumes that nested elements should be added as child controls, a topic covered later in this chapter.

> **A control builder is the parser used by ASP.NET to process the inner content of a server control declaration. Control builders are an advanced topic covered at the end of this chapter.**

891

If sub-elements of control declarations also contain elements, such elements are assumed to be object properties of the outer object property. For example, assuming the mythical `MyObject` element mapped to an object called my `MyObject`, which had two object properties called `SomeObjectPropertyA` and `SomeObjectPropertyB`, we could declare and initialize the control like this:

```
<Wrox:MyFirstControl runat=server>
    <MyObject A="Hello" B="Hello">
    <SomeObjectPropertyA  SomeAttribute="Another value" />
    <SomeObjectPropertyB  SomeAttribute="Another value" />
  </MyObject>
</Wrox:MyFirstControl>
```

We could also use the object-walker syntax, although that is less readable for complex server-control declarations:

```
<Wrox:MyFirstControl MyObject-A="hello" MyObject-B="World"
            MyObject-SomeObjectPropertyA-SomeAttribute="Another value"
            MyObject-SomeObjectPropertyB-SomeAttribute="Another value"
            runat="server" />
```

To demonstrate using object properties in a server control let's take a look at the `Style` object.

Using the System.Web.UI.WebControls.Style Object

The `Style` class has methods and properties that make working with style attributes more intuitive, and very consistent through all server controls. This class handles style attributes for colors, borders, fonts etc. If your server control is going to expose style elements, it should use the `Style` class.

To use the style object we can add a new member variable called _style to our control, along with a read-only property accessor to enable our ASP.NET pages to access it:

```
Style _style = new Style();
public Style LabelStyle
{
    get { return _style; }
}
```

Only properties of the `LabelStyle` property can be set, so it is read-only.

As we are going to use the `Style` for building the `style` attribute eventually rendered down to the browser, we need to change our `ForeColor` property accessor to use the `Style` object to set and retrieve the `ForeColor` value. This removes the need for the `_foreColor` member variable, so it can be deleted. Our updated `ForeColor` property accessor code looks like this:

```
public Color ForeColor
{
    get { return _style.ForeColor; }
    set { _style.ForeColor = value; }
}
```

Finally, we update our `Render` method to use the `AddAttributesToRender` method of the `Style` class. This takes an `HtmlTextWriter` object as an input parameter, and calls `AddStyleAttribute` depending on the various style attributes that have been set using the `Style` object:

```
protected override void Render(HtmlTextWriter writer)
{
    int loop;
    for( loop=0; loop < _repeatCount; loop++ )
    {
        _style.AddAttributesToRender( writer );
        writer.RenderBeginTag("h1");
        writer.Write( _text );
        writer.RenderEndTag();
    }
}
```

With these changes in place, we can create a label with the text "Server Controls Are Cool", displayed in a yellow font, on a black background, using a 36-point font size as follows:

```
<%@ Register TagPrefix="Wrox" Namespace="WroxControls"
            Assembly="MyLabel" %>
<html>
<body>

<Wrox:MyLabel runat="server"
            ForeColor="Yellow"
            LabelStyle-BackColor="Black"
            LabelStyle-Font-Size="36"
            Text="Server Controls Are Cool" />
</body>
</html>
```

The rendered output for this new page is shown here:

Using the WebControl Class for Server Controls that use Style

For controls like our label that need style management you should derive from the `System.Web.UI.WebControl` class. This class adds the following functionality to a server control:

❑ Exposes properties that allow style colors to be set using properties like `ForeColor`, `BackColor`, and `Font`.

❏ Allows expando attributes to be specified in a server-control declaration. Expando attributes are not interpreted and are written directly to the output HTML stream. By default, the `Control` class throws an exception if an attribute is not a property of the server control.

❏ Provides consistency with the standard ASP.NET web controls, since they derive from the class.

❏ Persists the style object and any settings/state during postbacks using view state. In the control example earlier when we used the style object, any style changes made in event handlers or in other code would not have been remembered after a postback, since the state of the style object was not being round tripped using viewstate. For our control to remember any style changes, we'd need to implement custom statement management, by overriding the `LoadViewState` and `SaveViewState` methods. Viewstate is discussed later in the chapter.

The `WebControl` class is designed to either assist with the rendering of a control, or take complete control of the rendering. For a simple control like our label, the `WebControl` class can be used to replace most of the code we have written.

To make use of the `WebControl` class we have to make the following changes to our code:

❏ Derive from the `WebControl` class rather than `Control` class.

❏ Declare a public constructor that calls the base constructor, specifying which HTML element to render.

❏ Override the `RenderContents` method to emit the content we want within our `<h1>` element. The `WebControl` class takes responsibility for rendering the attributes and the begin/end tags, so we remove the `Render` method.

❏ Remove all of the style properties we implemented earlier, since the `WebControl` will automatically have implemented them for us.

After making these changes, our C# control code looks like this:

```
using System;
using System.Web;
using System.Web.UI;
using System.Web.UI.WebControls;

namespace WroxControls
{
    public class MyLabel : WebControl
    {
        string _text;

        public MyLabel() : base ("H1")
        {
        }

        public string Text
        {
            get{ return _text; }
            set{ _text = value; }
        }
    }
}
```

```
        protected override void OnInit(EventArgs e)
        {
            base.OnInit(e);
            if ( _text == null)
                _text = "Here is some default text";
        }

        protected override void RenderContents(HtmlTextWriter writer)
        {
            writer.Write( _text);
        }
    }
};
```

The same control in VB.NET is shown here:

```
Imports System
Imports System.Web
Imports System.Web.UI
Imports System.Web.UI.WebControls

Namespace WroxControls

    Public Class MyLabel
        Inherits WebControl

        Private _text As String

        Public Sub New()
            MyBase.New("H1")
        End Sub 'New

        Public Property Text As String
            Get
                Return _text
            End Get
            Set
                _text = value
            End Set
        End Property

        Protected Overrides Sub OnInit(e As EventArgs)
            MyBase.OnInit(e)
            If _text Is Nothing Then
                _text = "Here is some default text"
            End If
        End Sub

        Protected Overrides Sub RenderContents(writer As HtmlTextWriter)
            writer.Write(_text)
        End Sub

    End Class

End Namespace
```

With these changes, we need to change our ASP.NET page since the available properties names for our control have changed. You can use the WebControl class documentation to get a list of all the available properties.

Here is our updated page, which now uses properties consistent with all the server controls provided as part of ASP.NET, which were discussed in Chapter 5:

```
<%@ Register TagPrefix="Wrox" Namespace="WroxControls"
             Assembly="MyLabel" %>
<html>
<body>

<Wrox:MyLabel  runat="server"
               ForeColor="Yellow"
               BackColor="Black"
               Font-Size="36"
               Text="Web Controls" />

</body>
</html>
```

For controls that only require one HTML root element to be rendered, our updated control code provides a good model to follow when building server controls. Your server controls should always derive from the WebControl class unless they do not render any UI, in which case the services provided by WebControl do not provide any benefit.

You can use all the other techniques we've used to render HTML so far with server controls derived from WebControl, the only difference is that your code is moved to the RenderContents method.

In this revised code demonstrating the use of WebControl I removed support for the RepeatCount property, since that would require one or more HTML elements to be rendered at the root level (you can have any number of controls within the root element). This is something a basic web control can do. If you need to do this, you have to override the Render method.

To implement the RepeatCount property in our implementation, the overridden Render method calls the base implementation of Render RepeatCount a number of times. The following code just calls the base Render method 3 times to demonstrate the technique:

C#

```
protected override void Render(HtmlTextWriter writer)
{
    for(int i=0; i < 3; i++ )
    {
        base.Render( writer );
    }
}
```

VB.NET

```
Protected Overrides Sub Render(writer As HtmlTextWriter)
    Dim i As Integer
    For i = 0 To 2
        MyBase.Render(writer)
    Next i
End Sub 'Render
```

As expected, the control will render the label three times:

To show our server control can also be programmatically manipulated, just like any other ASP.NET server control provided out of the box, the following ASP.NET page sets all the properties of our server-control properties within the Page_Init event:

```csharp
<%@ Register TagPrefix="Wrox" Namespace="WroxControls"
             Assembly="MyLabel" %>
<%@ Import Namespace="System.Drawing" %>

<script runat="server" language="C#">

  void Page_Init( object sender, EventArgs e )
    {
      ourLabel.Text = "Web Controls";
      ourLabel.ForeColor = Color.Yellow;
      ourLabel.BackColor = Color.Black;
      ourLabel.Font.Size = 36;
    }
</script>

<html>
<body>
   <Wrox:MyLabel runat="server" id="ourLabel" />
</body>
</html>
```

Now that we've created a couple of server controls that generate their UI by emitting HTML, let's take a look at composite controls. These controls render their UI by reusing other server controls. An ASP.NET page is a good example of a composite control – so let's take a look at how they work in detail.

Composite Controls

All ASP.NET dynamic pages are created by the ASP.NET run-time using ASP.NET controls. Although you may not have realized it, we have already built several ASP.NET controls in the earlier chapters of this book just by creating ASP.NET pages and user controls. The ASP.NET page framework automatically converts and compiles pages into server controls contained within a dynamically created assembly the first time a page is requested:

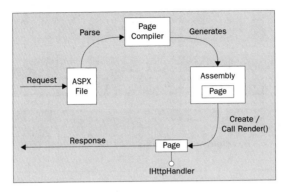

This server control is then used to render the page. Subsequent times, when a page is requested, the precompiled server control can just be instantiated and called, resulting in great performance:

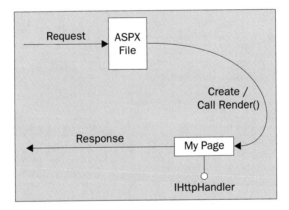

The assemblies created for ASP.NET pages are automatically managed for you. If you search around your Windows system directory, you'll find a directory called Temporary ASP.NET Files. Within this you'll find sub-directories for the various web sites on your machine, which in turn will contain the assemblies for ASP.NET pages.

If we open up one of these generated assemblies using the ILDASM tool, we'll see that they typically contain a single class with the same name as the ASP.NET page. This class extends (derives from) the class System.Web.UI.Page: (see the sixth item from the root in the tree control.)

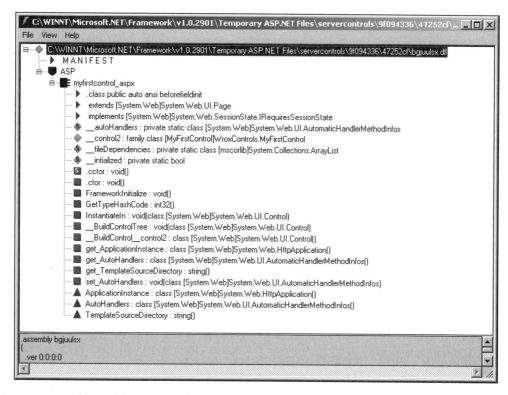

The page object (located in the assembly `System.Web.dll`) derives from the `TemplateControl` class, which in turn derives from the `Control` class. This diagram shows the main ASP.NET control classes and their inheritance hierarchy:

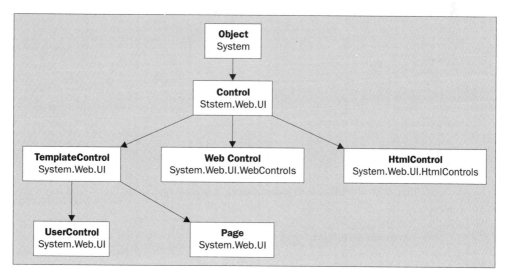

Here is a brief description of the role of each of these classes:

❑ `Control` – provides a common base class for all other control types.

❑ `WebControl` – provides methods and properties for dealing with the style. This class is the base class for all ASP web controls. These are always declared in an ASP.NET page using an `ASP:` prefix.

❑ `HtmlControl` – base class for standard HTML elements, such as `input`. Typically you will never derive from this control.

❑ `TemplateControl` – contains functionality that is shared between user controls and pages, such as support for loading user controls (`.ascx`) or templates.

❑ `UserControl` – base class from which all user controls derive.

❑ `Page` – base class from which all dynamically compiled ASP.NET pages derive.

The actual code generated by ASP.NET for these dynamically generated classes is not that different to the code we have just written for our label control. One key difference is that it uses **control composition** to actually generate the page. That is, a page is a server control that uses other server controls to render its UI.

Building a Composite Control

A server control can be a **container** for other controls. The `Control` class has a `Controls` property of the type `ControlsCollection`. This collection class can hold zero or more child controls. When a control is rendered, each of its child controls are called upon to render themselves. If these child controls also contain child controls, this process repeats, until all controls have been rendered.

By default, if you derive a server control from the `Control` class, nested elements declared within an ASP.NET page will be added to the `Controls` collection, assuming you haven't used the `ParseChildren` attribute discussed earlier to change the default behavior.

Assuming we had a server control with a class definition that basically did nothing:

```
using System;
using System.Web;
using System.Web.UI;

namespace WroxControls
{
    public class CompositeControl : Control
    {
    }
};
```

And then declared that control with nested sub-controls (a button and some literal text) on a page:

```
<%@ Register TagPrefix="Wrox" Namespace="WroxControls"
             Assembly="MyFirstControl" %>
<html>
<body>

<Wrox:CompositeControl runat="server">
```

```
       <asp:button Text="A Button" runat=server />
       Some Text

   </Wrox:CompositeControl>

   </body>
   </html>
```

> **The ASP.NET page parser automatically creates a `LiteralControl` for each block of text or significant whitespace.**

The control would actually render the button and the literal text, since the default `Render` implementation invokes the `Render` method of each Control in the `Controls` collection:

When writing a composite control, the control itself typically decides on what child controls to create, rather than the user. If the user is going to create all the UI, you should use the user controls rather than a custom server control.

Server controls override the `CreateChildControls` method and populate the `Controls` collection. The ASP.NET framework calls this method to signal to a control that it should create its child controls. What controls you populate the controls collection with depends on the UI your control rendered. Any class can be used as long as it derives from the `Control` class.

The code required to implement our first server control using control composition is shown here:

```
using System;
using System.Web.UI;

namespace WroxControls
{
   public class CompositeControl : Control, INamingContainer
   {
      protected override void CreateChildControls()
      {
         LiteralControl text;

         text = new LiteralControl(
                  "<h1>ASP.NET Control Development in C#</h1>" );
          Controls.Add(text);
      }
   }
};
```

In this code we have removed the Render method and replaced it with the CreateChildControls method. When called, this code creates a single LiteralControl and adds it to the child control collection. We have also modified the class to derive from the INamingContainer interface to indicate that it is a **naming container**. We'll discuss naming containers in more detail later in this chapter, but as a general rule all composite controls should implement this.

By removing the Render method from our class, the default implementation of the Render method defined in the Control class is called during the render phase of a page. The default Render method enumerates the Controls collection and invokes the RenderControl method of each child control in turn. This effectively causes a control's UI to be drawn, by allowing each child control to output their own HTML, by either using the HtmlTextWriter object, or, again, by also using child controls.

When deriving from the WebControl class and overriding the RenderContents methods, you should always call the base implementation of RenderContents if your WebControl uses control composition. This is because it's the method that calls its base classes' (the Control class) Render method. The same is true if you derive from Control and override Control.Render (assuming you want child controls declared in a page to be rendered.)

CreateChildControls

The CreateChildControls method can be called at different stages in the life cycle of a composite control, but it will only ever be called once, unless you explicitly reset the state of a control using the ChildControlsCreated property. It this respect it is a non-deterministic event that occurs during the lifetime of a control, unlike the Init and Render events already discussed, which occur at fixed times in the life cycle of a page, so are deterministic.

If not called before, the CreateChildControls method will always be called in the pre-render stage of a page. The method will be called prior to this if either the public FindControl method of the control is called, or if the Control itself calls the protected EnsureChildControls method. The FindControl method is used when pushing postback data into a control, so CreateChildControls will also be called during the postback stage of a page, if there is postback data associated with a given control.

As a control author you should always use the EnsureChildControls method if you need your populate your own controls collection prematurely. This method calls CreateChildControls only if the public property ChildControlsCreated is false. If the property is false, it is set to true once CreateChildControls is called. This method ensures child controls are only ever created once.

If the ChildControlsCreated property is set to false in your code, all child controls are released automatically. Subsequently, CreateChildControls may be called again.

ASP.NET Pages and Composite Controls

An ASP.NET page is essentially compiled into a composite control. Consider this simple page:

```
<html>
    <body>
        <form method="post" runat=server>
            Name: <asp:textbox runat=server/>
        </form>
    </body>
</html>
```

When it's compiled, the page will be rendered using the following server controls, which effectively form a hierarchical tree of server controls:

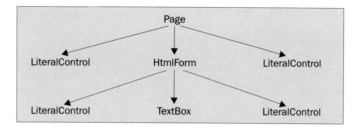

The Page object's Controls collection will contain the child controls LiteralControl, HtmlForm, and LiteralControl. The HtmlForm control will contain the child controls LiteralControl, TextBox, and LiteralControl. When the page is rendered, each of these controls will be rendered in turn, starting at the top, recursively rendering each child control before moving onto the next sibling. So, for this page the rendering sequence would be Page, LiteralControl, HtmlForm, LiteralControl, TextBox, LiteralControl, LiteralControl.

Control Tree Navigation

A server control tree can be navigated using different methods of the Control class. To navigate down one level you use the Control.Controls collection. To navigate up the tree one level, from a control to its parent, you use the Parent property. To navigate from a Control to the container Page you use the Control.Page property. To recursively search down the tree for a control you use the Control.FindControl method.

The Advantages of Control Composition

Using control composition for simple controls really doesn't have much advantage over rendering the HTML directly using HtmlTextWriter. To see when there is a much greater benefit, let's create a more complex control. This control will create an HTML table below an <h1> element. The table will contain 10 rows, each with 5 cells. We could render this using the HtmlTextWriter or by creating lots of LiteralContent objects, but it makes a lot more sense to use the high-level ASP.NET web controls we have seen in earlier chapters of this book. Although we have typically only made references to these controls in ASP.NET pages before, creating these controls dynamically within a control is straightforward:

```
using System;
using System.Web;
using System.Web.UI;
using System.Web.UI.WebControls;

namespace WroxControls
{
    public class CompositeTableControl : Control, INamingContainer
    {
        Table _table;  // Make table a member so we can access it at any point

        protected override void CreateChildControls()
        {
            LiteralControl text;
```

```
        text = new LiteralControl(
                    "<h1>ASP.NET Control Development in C#</h1>");
        Controls.Add(text);

        TableRow row;
        TableCell cell;

        // Create a table and set a 2-pixel border

        _table = new Table();
        _table.BorderWidth = 2;

        Controls.Add(_table);

        // Add 10 rows each with 5 cells

        for(int x = 0; x < 10; x++) {
            // Create a row and add it to the table

            row = new TableRow();
            _table.Rows.Add(row);

            // Create a cell that contains the text

            for(int y = 0; y < 5; y++) {

                text = new LiteralControl("Row: " + x + " Cell: " + y);

                cell = new TableCell();
                cell.Controls.Add(text);

                row.Cells.Add(cell);
                }
            }
        }
    }
};
```

This code may look at bit complex at first, but what it's doing is very simple. Firstly, it adds the LiteralControl containing the <h1> element as a child control. Next, it creates a Table object (System.Web.UI.WebControls.Table), sets the border width to two pixels and adds that as a child control:

```
_table = new Table();
_table.BorderWidth = 2;

Controls.Add( _table );
```

The table is then populated with rows by running a for loop for ten iterations, creating, and adding a TableRow object using the Rows collection property:

```
row = new TableRow();
_table.Rows.Add( row );
```

Finally, for each row that is added, an inner loop is executed for five iterations adding a `TableCell` object that has a `LiteralControl` as its child. The `Text` of the `LiteralControl` is set to indicate the current row and cell. Compiling and executing this code produces the following:

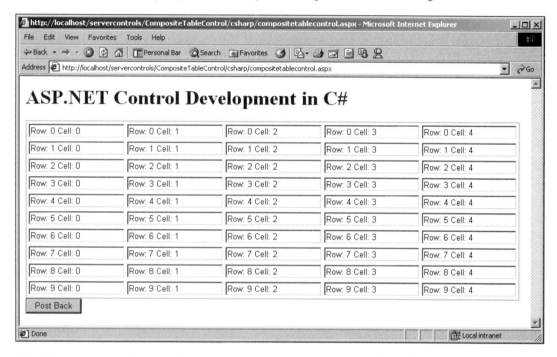

All of the controls we have used (`Table`, `TableRow`, `TableCell` etc.) derive from the `Control` class somewhere in their inheritance hierarchy. Each of these controls also uses control composition to render their UI. The control tree for our page actually looks something like this:

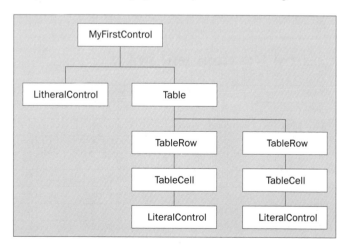

If you view the source for this generated page you'll see around **130** lines of HTML. We didn't directly create any of that, and we have gained a number of key advantages by using control composition over direct rendering:

- ❏ We have saved ourselves a great deal of error-prone HTML creation via code, and therefore saved time and increased our productivity.

- ❏ We have programmatically created objects, called methods, and set properties. The code we've written is therefore simple to read, and easily extendable at a later date.

- ❏ We have not been exposed to the underlying HTML generated by the various controls we have used.

- ❏ The fact that they actually render `table`, `tr`, and `td` HTML elements to the page is an implementation detail that we do not have to concern ourselves with. In theory, the output could just as easily be WML or any other markup language – our control will still work just fine.

The argument for using composite controls becomes more apparent as the child controls we use, such as the `Table` control, provide more and more functionality – and hence save us more time and effort. For example, let's modify our table so the user can edit each of the cells within it by using a `TextBox` control within our `TableCell` control, rather than a `LiteralControl`:

```
for( int y=0; y < 5; y++ ) {

    TextBox textbox;

    textbox = new TextBox();
    textbox.Text = "Row: " + x + " Cell: " + y;

    cell = new TableCell();
    cell.Controls.Add(textbox);
...
```

By changing four lines of code we now have an editable table:

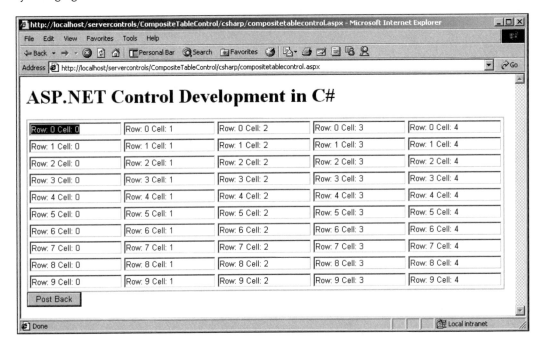

The underlying HTML generated by our control is now even more complex; with the child controls creating all the input elements needed within the td elements:

```
<html>
<body>

<form name="ctrl0" method="post" action="compositetablecontrol.aspx" id="ctrl0">
<input type="hidden" name="__VIEWSTATE" value="dDwtNTMxODUzMzMxODs+" />

   <h1>ASP.NET Control Development in C#</h1>

   <table border="0" style="border-width:2px;border-style:solid;">
     <tr>
       <td>
         <input name="grid:ctrl2" type="text" value="Row: 0 Cell: 0" />
       </td><td>
         <input name="grid:ctrl3" type="text" value="Row: 0 Cell: 1" />
       </td><td>
         <input name="grid:ctrl4" type="text" value="Row: 0 Cell: 2" />
       </td><td>
         <input name="grid:ctrl5" type="text" value="Row: 0 Cell: 3" />
       </td><td>
         <input name="grid:ctrl6" type="text" value="Row: 0 Cell: 4" />
       </td>
     </tr><tr>...
```

You'll notice within this HTML that each of the input elements has a name attribute. By default, these ids are assigned sequentially by ASP.NET as the child controls are created and added to our control. When a postback occurs, ASP.NET uses these ids to automagically push **postback** data into server controls that are created with the same id. This automatic management of postback data is part of the magic that gives the impression to page developers that controls are intelligent – since they don't have to write lots of code to manually make controls, like a textbox, remember their state. Of course, under the hood, a control author has to implement some code that maps the postback data to properties, but once that is done, page developers and custom control writers can simply reuse an intelligent self-maintaining control.

Writing a TextBox Control

To understand some of the more advanced development aspects of server control, the clearest way of explaining them is to actually write a simple control like a textbox. Although this isn't the most exciting control in the world to write, especially since it already exists, it clearly demonstrates some important aspects that control authors need to understand including:

❑ Interacting with postback.

❑ Using viewstate.

❑ Raising events from a control.

To render a textbox our server control needs to output an HTML input element with a type attribute containing the value "text". Using the WebControl as our control's base class makes this first task simple. We have to perform three main tasks:

❑   Create a new class that derives from the WebControl class.

❑   Implement a public constructor that calls the base class constructor specifying that our server control should output an input element.

❑   Override the AddAttributesToRender method. This is called to allow derived classes to add attributes to the root element (input). We override it and add the type attribute with a value of "text". We also need to add a name attribute whose value is derived from the UniqueID property. This property is used by ASP.NET to hold the unique id of each control. We have to output the name property containing this value since an HTML form will not postback the value entered into an input field without a name.

Here is the source code that implements these steps:

```
using System;
using System.Web;
using System.Web.UI;
using System.Web.UI.WebControls;

namespace WroxControls
{
    public class MyTextBox : WebControl
    {
      public MyTextBox() : base("input")
      {
      }

      protected override void AddAttributesToRender(HtmlTextWriter writer)
      {
          base.AddAttributesToRender(writer);
          writer.AddAttribute(HtmlTextWriterAttribute.Name, UniqueID);
          writer.AddAttribute(HtmlTextWriterAttribute.Type, "input" );
      }
    }
};
```

The implementation of the AddAttributesToRender method calls the base-class implementation. This is called since the base-class implementation will add various other attributes to our element depending on other properties that have been set in the base class, such as style attributes.

Once compiled, we can use the following ASP.NET page to reference our control (assuming the control is called MyTextBox and is compiled to the assembly MyTextBox.dll):

```
<%@ Register TagPrefix="Wrox" Namespace="WroxControls"
            Assembly="MyTextBox" %>
<html>
<body>

<form runat="server">
```

```
    <H3>TextBox Control</H3>
    <P>Enter a value: <Wrox:MyTextBox runat="server" />
    <BR>
    <ASP:Button Text="Postback" runat="server" />

</form>

</body>
</html>
```

In this ASP.NET page we've declared an instance of our `MyTextBox` control, and a button within a form element so that we can cause a postback to occur.

When viewed in the browser this page initially renders like this:

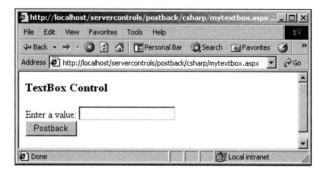

If we enter some text into our textbox and click the postback button we will find that after the postback occurs, the textbox is blank again. This demonstrates that as a control developer, you have to do some work for a control to become intelligent.

For our textbox to become intelligent, we need to access the postback data submitted as part of a form. If data is present for our control, we need to add a `value` attribute to our `input` element. Assuming we can populate a member variable `_text` with the postback for our textbox, we could add the following code to output a `value` attribute:

```
public MyTextBox() : base ("input")
{
}

string _value;

protected override void AddAttributesToRender(HtmlTextWriter writer)
{
   base.AddAttributesToRender(writer);
   writer.AddAttribute(HtmlTextWriterAttribute.Name, UniqueID);
   writer.AddAttribute(HtmlTextWriterAttribute.Type, "input" );

   if ( _value != null )
      writer.AddAttribute( "value", _value );
}
```

To access postback data a server control has to implement the `IPostBackDataHandler` interface. This interface has two methods:

```
bool IPostBackDataHandler.LoadPostData(string postDataKey,
                                 NameValueCollection postCollection);

void IPostBackDataHandler.RaisePostDataChangedEvent()
```

IPostBackDataHandler

The `LoadPostData` method is called when postback occurs and a control has postback data. The method is called in sequence for all controls on a page that need to access postback data. If a control does not have any postback data (for example if the control was disabled), the method is not called. A control can explicitly ask for this method to be called even if does not have postback, by calling the `Page.RegisterRequiresPostBack` method.

The `LoadPostData` call passes all of the postback data submitted in a form using a `NameValueCollection`. A control can access any of the data. To access the specific postback data item associated with a control, the `postDataKey` variable is used as the key into the collection. The value of this key field is the **unique name** assigned to the control either automatically by ASP.NET, or the value assigned by a user if an `id` attribute was specified in the control declaration.

The `LoadPostData` method returns a `Boolean` value. If `true` is returned the `RaisePostDataChangedMethod` will be called after the `LoadPostData` method has been called for all other server controls on a page with postback data. If `false` is returned the `RaisePostDataChangedMethod` will not be called.

A control should return `true` in the `LoadPostData` method if it wants to raise an event as the result of certain data being present, or changes to data caused as a result of postback data. Events must be raised in the `RaisePostDataChangedEvent` method since raising events in `LoadPostData` will cause unpredictable results. Any event handler that caught and processed an event raised in `LoadPostData` would not be able to depend on consistent state being present in other controls, since such controls may not have initialized or updated their state based upon postback.

To make our textbox control intelligent we'll implement the `IPostBackDataHandler` interface as follows:

```
bool IPostBackDataHandler.LoadPostData(string postDataKey,
                                 NameValueCollection postCollection)
{
    _value = postCollection[postDataKey];
    return false;
}

void IPostBackDataHandler.RaisePostDataChangedEvent()
{
}
```

> The **NameValueCollection** class is defined in the namespace
> **System.Collections.Specialized** so it has to be imported into any class files
> before this code will compile.

The `LoadPostData` method uses the `postDataKey` variable to copy the postback data for our control into the `_value` variable. Since we are already using this variable to render a value, if present, our textbox should now appear intelligent. We return `false` from `LoadPostData` since we're not yet interested in raising any events. For the same reason our implementation of the `RaisePostDataChangedEvent` is also empty.

With these changes in place, we can enter a value into our textbox, hit the postback button to cause a roundtrip to the server, and any value we entered will be remembered since the value attribute will be emitted by our control:

If we look at the HTML output for this page we'll see the value attribute, which is why the value redisplays correctly:

```html
<html>
<body>

<form name="ctrl0" method="post" action="mytextbox.aspx" id="ctrl0">
 <input type="hidden" name="__VIEWSTATE" value="dDwtMTAxMTg4NzIyODs7Pg==" />

 <H3>TextBox Control</H3>
 <P>Enter a value: <input name="ctrl1" type="input"
                          value="An Intelligent Control!!" />
 <BR>

 <input type="submit" name="ctrl2" value="Postback" />
</form>

</body>
</html>
```

If we declared a couple more `MyTextBox` controls in our ASP.NET page, entered values and used the button to cause postback, we would see that they all remember their state, just as you have seen with other standard server controls in earlier chapters of the book. Each declared server control has a unique name assigned to it, so each manages its own postback and renders itself correctly, without interfering with other controls. All control behavior we have added to our textbox is encapsulated and reusable. This makes server controls very powerful, and makes complex page development much simpler. Once individual controls are written they take care of all the plumbing code to remember their state.

A Control that Raises Events

ASP.NET provides a powerful server-side event model. As a page is being created, server-controls can fire events that are caused either by aspects of a client-side postback, or by controls responding to page code that is calling their methods or changing properties. These events can be captured in an ASP.NET page, or can be caught by other server controls.

ASP.NET server controls support events using delegates just like any other .NET class does. With ASP.NET the `EventHandler` delegate is used when defining most events. This delegate defines a method signature with two parameters that you will have seen time, and time again, in event handlers like `Page_Load`. The first parameter of the delegate is of type `object`. When a server control raises an event, this parameter will contain a reference to the server control. The second delegate parameter is declared as the type `EventArgs`. Depending on the parameters you need your controls to raise, you can replace the `EventHandler` delegate with your own custom one.

To demonstrate events, we'll add an event to our textbox control that is raised when its value changes.

Events in Action

To support an event in our textbox control we first define a public `event` of the type `EventHandler` called `TextChanged`:

```
public event EventHandler TextChanged;
```

or in VB:

```
Event TextChanged As EventHandler
```

Next, we change the `LoadPostData` implementation to always return `true`:

```
bool IPostBackDataHandler.LoadPostData(string postDataKey,
                               NameValueCollection postCollection)
{
    _value = postCollection[postDataKey];
    return true;
}
```

This will cause the `RaisePostDataChangedEvent` to be called, from which we know it is safe to raise events caused by postback. In this method we use the delegate to raise a TextChanged event, assuming there are listeners (for example the delegate is not `null`):

```
void IPostBackDataHandler.RaisePostDataChangedEvent()
{
  if ( TextChanged != null )
     TextChanged( this, EventArgs.Empty );
}
```

You're probably wondering if these changes will always raise a `TextChanged` event when postback occurs, even if the text has not changed. As it stands, you would be correct. We'll shortly refine the event handler later to only call the event when the value actually changes. But for now, we'll just demonstrate how events are raised.

To use our new event we declare an event handler in our ASP.NET page called `OnNamedChanged`:

```
<script runat="server" language="C#">

    private void OnNameChanged( object sender, EventArgs e )
    {
        status.Text = "Value changed to " + name.Text;
    }
</script>
```

To wire the event handler up to our text changed event, we add an attribute called 'OnTextChange' and specify the name of the method to be called when the event is fired. In this case, 'OnNameChanged':

```
<P>Enter a value: <Wrox:MyTextBox id="name" runat="server"
                              OnTextChanged="OnNameChanged" />
```

Prefixing an event name with 'On' is the way in which event handlers are associated with server-control events in server control declarations. If our control had an additional event called `TextInvalid`, the attribute used to wire up the event handler would be `OnTextInvalid`.

The `OnNameChanged` event handler displays the value of text in a label field when the event is fired:

```
<ASP:Label runat="server" id=status />
```

For our event handler code to work, we have to declare a `Text` property on our server control that exposes the held value so it can be displayed:

```
public string Text
{
    get { return _value; }
}
```

With all these changes in place, entering a value of 'Events in ASP.NET' in our textbox and calling the postback button will cause a message to appear below the postback button:

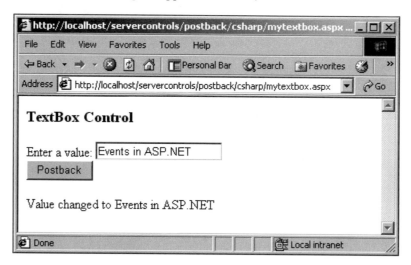

The following code shows how to implement a server-side control that supports events in VB:

```vb
Imports System
Imports System.Web
Imports System.Web.UI
Imports System.Web.UI.WebControls
Imports System.Collections.Specialized

Namespace WroxControls

  Public Class MyTextBoxVB
    Inherits WebControl

    Implements IPostBackDataHandler

    Public Sub New()
       MyBase.New("input")
    End Sub 'New

    Public Event TextChanged As EventHandler

    Private _value As String

    Public ReadOnly Property Text As String
      Get
          Return _value
      End Get
    End Property

    Protected Overrides Sub AddAttributesToRender(writer As HtmlTextWriter)

      MyBase.AddAttributesToRender(writer)
      writer.AddAttribute(HtmlTextWriterAttribute.Name, UniqueID)

      writer.AddAttribute(HtmlTextWriterAttribute.Type, "input")
      If Not (_value Is Nothing) Then
        writer.AddAttribute("value", _value)
      End If

    End Sub

    Function LoadPostData(postDataKey As String, _
                   postCollection As NameValueCollection) As Boolean_
                   Implements IPostBackDataHandler.LoadPostData

       _value = postCollection(postDataKey)

       Return True
    End Function

    Sub RaisePostDataChangedEvent() _
       Implements IPostBackDataHandler.RaisePostDataChangedEvent

       RaiseEvent TextChanged(Me, EventArgs.Empty)
    End Sub
  End Class

End Namespace
```

The Framework Event Pattern

When supporting events, classes in the .NET framework define a protected method called OnEventName that actually raises the event. The reason for this is that it enables derived classes to perform event handling by overriding a method instead of attaching a delegate. This is simpler and more efficient. To follow this pattern for our TextChange event, we could implement our IPostBackDataHandler.RaisePostDataChangedEvent method from earlier as follows:

```
void IPostBackDataHandler.RaisePostDataChangedEvent()
{
   OnTextChanged(EventArgs.Empty );
}
protected void OnTextChanged (EventArgs e)
{
   if ( TextChanged != null )
     TextChanged ( this, e);
}
```

In this code the RaisePostDataChangedEvent method calls the OnTextChanged method to raise the event. Derived classes that want to raise events can simply override the OnTextChanged method to catch the event, and optionally call the base-class implementation if they want other listeners to receive the event.

Causing Postback from Any Element – IPostBackEventHandler

In HTML only the button and imagebutton elements can actually cause a postback to occur. When designing controls you may want other elements of a control's user interface such as an anchor element to cause postback. You may also want a control's user interface to be able to raise different types of postback events it can process, to manipulate its user interface. For example, a calendar control may want to have previous-month and next-month events.

To show how to support postback events we're going to write a simple counter control. The control's user interface displays a counter (starting at 50) and provides two hyperlinks that allow you to increase or decrease the value:

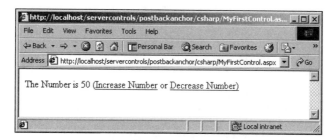

If we click Increase Number twice the count would increase to 52:

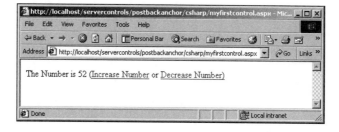

If we click **Decrease Number** four times the number goes down to 48:

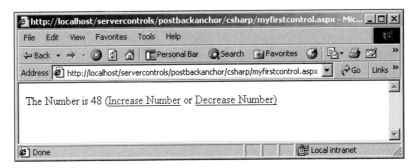

This control is raising postback events back to itself. To achieve this a control must do two things:

❑ Derive from the `IPostBackEventHandler` interface and implement the `RaisePostBackEvent` method.

❑ Call the `Page.GetPostBackEventReference` method to create some script code that can be rendered into a page to force a postback to occur. This of course means the browser must support JavaScript for this feature.

The `IPostBackEventHandler.RaisePostBackEvent` method is called when a postback is caused by script code calling `Page.GetPostBackEventReference`. The `RaisePostBackEvent` method accepts a single `string` parameter that can be used to determine what event has been raised. In the case of our counter control we use the value "inc" to signal our counter should be increased, and "dec" to signal it should be decreased:

```csharp
public void RaisePostBackEvent(string eventArgument)
{
    if ( eventArgument == "inc" )
      Number = Number + 1;

    if ( eventArgument == "dec" )
      Number = Number - 1;

}
```

When a control renders its user interface it calls the `Page.GetPostBackEventReference` method passing itself as a parameter. The return value is a string containing JavaScript code that will cause a postback event to be raised when it is called. In our control, we place this JavaScript into an anchor element, so when the user clicks the anchor, a postback occurs.

The following code shows how this method was used to generate the "inc" postback event:

```csharp
writer.Write("<a href=\"javascript:" +
    Page.GetPostBackEventReference(this,"inc") +
    "\">Increase Number</a>");
```

Here is the complete source code for the counter control which demonstrates how to:

❑ Derive and implement the `IPostBackEventHandler`
❑ Use the `Page.GetPostBackEventReference` to raise two events

The next section in the chapter covers viewstate, so for now ignore the implementation of the number property:

```
using System;
using System.Web;
using System.Web.UI;

namespace WroxControls
{
  public class MyFirstControl : Control,
      IPostBackEventHandler
  {
    public int Number
    {
      get
      {
        if ( ViewState["Number"] != null )
        return (int) ViewState["Number"];
        return 50;
      }
      set
      {
        ViewState["Number"] = value;
      }
    }

    public void RaisePostBackEvent(string eventArgument)
    {
      if ( eventArgument == "inc" )
      Number = Number + 1;

      if ( eventArgument == "dec" )
      Number = Number - 1;
    }

    protected override void Render(HtmlTextWriter writer)
    {
      writer.Write("The Number is " + Number.ToString() + " (" );

      writer.Write("<a href=\"javascript:" +
              Page.GetPostBackEventReference(this,"inc") +
              "\"'>Increase Number</a>");

      writer.Write(" or " );

      writer.Write("<a href=\"javascript:" +
              Page.GetPostBackEventReference(this,"dec") +
              "\">Decrease Number)</a>");
    }
  }
}
```

The following HTML is rendered by this control:

```
<html>
<body>

<form name="ctrl0" method="post" action="myfirstcontrol.aspx" id="ctrl0">
<input type="hidden" name="__VIEWSTATE"
value="dDwtMTM0MTQ1NDExNjt0PDtsPGk8MT47PjtsPHQ8O2w8aTwxPjs+O2w8dDxwPGw8TnVtYmVyOz4
7bDxpPDQ4Pjs+Pjs7Pjs+Pjs+" />

The Number is 48 (<a href="javascript:__doPostBack('ctrl1','inc')"'>Increase
Number</a> or <a href="javascript:__doPostBack('ctrl1','dec')">Decrease
Number)</a>

<input type="hidden" name="__EVENTTARGET" value="" />
<input type="hidden" name="__EVENTARGUMENT" value="" />
<script language="javascript">
<!--
  function __doPostBack(eventTarget, eventArgument) {
    var theform = document.ctrl0;
    theform.__EVENTTARGET.value = eventTarget;
    theform.__EVENTARGUMENT.value = eventArgument;
    theform.submit();
  }
// -->
</script>
</form>
</body>
</html>
```

Notice how a script block containing the __doPostBack function is automatically rendered into the output stream when an ASP.NET server control calls the Page.GetPostBackEventReference reference:

```
<script language="javascript">
<!--
  function __doPostBack(eventTarget, eventArgument) {
    var theform = document.ctrl0;
    theform.__EVENTTARGET.value = eventTarget;
    theform.__EVENTARGUMENT.value = eventArgument;
    theform.submit();
  }
// -->
</script>
```

This function is called by the script code returned from Page.GetPostBackEventReference:

```
<a href="javascript:__doPostBack('ctrl1','inc')"'>
```

Now we have covered handling postback and events, let's look at how a control can persist state during postback using viewstate.

Using ViewState

After an ASP.NET page is rendered the page object, which created the page and all of its server controls, is destroyed. When a postback occurs, a new page object and new server-control objects are created.

When writing a server control you often need to store and manage state. Since a control is created and destroyed with each page request, any state held in object member variables will be lost. If a control needs to maintain state, it has to do so using another technique. As we have seen with our textbox control, one way of managing statement is to use postback. When a postback occurs, any postback data associated with a control is made available to it via the `IPostBackData` interface. A control can therefore re-populate its class variables, making the control appear to be stateful.

Using postback data to manage the state of a control is a good technique when it can be used, but there are some drawbacks. The most obvious one is that only certain HTML elements like `input` can use postback. If you had a label control that needed to remember its value, you couldn't use postback. Also, postback is only really designed to contain a single item of data. For example, our textbox control needs to remember its last value so it can raise a changed text event when the value changes. To maintain this additional state, one option would be hidden fields. When a control renders its output, it could also output hidden fields with other values that need to be remembered. When a postback occurs, these values would be retrieved into the `LoadPostData` method. This approach would work for a single control, but could be problematic when there are potentially many instances of the same control on a page. For example, what would you call the hidden fields? How could you ensure the names do not clash with names a page developer may have used?

To resolve the problems of managing state ASP.NET has a feature called viewstate. In a nutshell, viewstate is a hidden input field that can contain state for any number of server controls. This hidden field is automatically managed for you, and as a control author you never need to access it directly.

Introducing the StateBag

All server controls have a property called `ViewState`. This is defined in the `Control` class as the type `StateBag`, and allows server controls to store and retrieve values that are automatically round-tripped and recreated during a postback.

During the **save state stage** of a page, the ASP.NET framework enumerates all server controls within a page and persists their **combined state** into a hidden field called __VIEWSTATE. If you view any rendered ASP.NET containing a form element you will see this field:

```
<input type="hidden" name="__VIEWSTATE" value="dDwtMTcxOTc0MTI5NDs7Pg==" />
```

When a postback occurs, ASP.NET decodes the __VIEWSTATE hidden field and automatically repopulates the viewstate for each server control as they are created. This reloading of state occurs during the **load state stage** of a page for controls that are declared on an ASP.NET page. If a control is dynamically created, either on a page or within another composite control, the state will be loaded at the point of creation. ASP.NET keeps track of what viewstate hasn't been processed, and when a new control is added to the `Controls` property of a `Control` (remember a page is a control), it checks to see if it has any viewstate for the control. If it has, it is loaded into the control at that point.

To see viewstate in action, we will change our textbox control to store its current value in viewstate, rather than the _value field. By doing this, when `LoadPostData` is called to enable our textbox control to retrieve its new value, we can compare it to the old value held in viewstate. If the values are different we will return `true`, causing a `TextChanged` event to be raised in `RaisePostDataChangedEvent`. If the values are the same, we will return `false` so `RaisePostDataChangedEvent` is not called, and no event is raised.

The StateBag class implements the IDictionary interface, and for the most part is used just like the Hashtable class used with a string key. All items stored are of the type System.Object, so any type can be held in the viewstate, and casting is required to retrieving an item.

In our earlier textbox control we used a string member variable _value to hold the current value of our textbox. We'll delete that variable and rewrite the property to use viewstate:

```csharp
public string Text
{
  get
  {
    if ( ViewState["value"] == null )
    return String.Empty;

    return (string) ViewState["value"];
  }
  set
  {
    ViewState["value"] = value;
  }
}
```

Since we have deleted the _value member variable and replaced it with this property, we need to change all references to it, with the Text property. We could directly reference the ViewState where we previously used _value, but it's good practice to use properties to encapsulate our usage of viewstate, making our code cleaner and more maintainable. (For example, if we changed the viewstate key name used for the text value, we'd only have to do it in one place.)

With this new property in place, we can revise the LoadPostData to perform the check against the existing value as discussed:

```csharp
bool IPostBackDataHandler.LoadPostData(string postDataKey,
                            NameValueCollection postCollection)
{
  bool raiseEvent = false;

  if ( Text != postCollection[postDataKey] )
    raiseEvent = true;

  Text = postCollection[postDataKey];

  return raiseEvent;
}
```

Before testing this code to prove that our TextChanged event is now only raised when the text changes, we need to make a small change to our ASP.NET page. As you'll recall from earlier we have an event handler that sets the contents of a label to reflect our textbox value when our event is raised:

```csharp
<script runat="server" language="C#">

private void OnNameChanged( object sender, EventArgs e )
{
  status.Text = "Value changed to " + name.Text;
}

</script>
```

The label control uses viewstate to remember its value. When a postback occurs, even if this event is not raised, the label will still display the text from the previous postback, making it look like an event was raised. So to know if an event really was raised, we need to reset the value of the label during each postback. We could do this within the page `init` or `load` events, but since the label uses viewstate to retain its value, we can simply disable viewstate for the control using the `EnableViewState` attribute as follows:

```
<ASP:Label runat="server" EnableViewState="False" id=status />
```

During the save state stage of a page, the ASP.NET page framework will not persist viewstate for the controls with an `EnableViewState` property of `true`. This change to the page will therefore make our label forget its value during each postback.

> Setting **EnableViewState** to **false** does not prevent a control from remembering state using postback. As such, should you need to reset the value of a textbox, you'd have to clear the **Text** property in a page's **init/load** event.

With all these changes made, if we enter a value of "Wrox Press" and press the postback button, we will see that during the first postback our event is fired, and our label control displays the value:

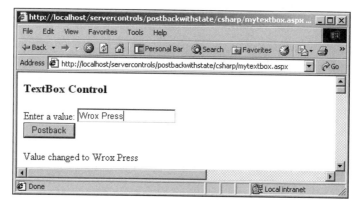

If we click the postback button again, the textbox control will use its viewstate to determine that the postback value has not changed, and it will not fire its `TextChanged` event. Since the label control does not remember its state, as we disabled viewstate for it, the value-changed message will not appear during the second postback since the label will default back to its original blank value:

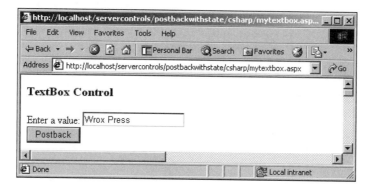

Our textbox control is now pretty functional for a simple control: It can remember its value during postback, can raise events when its text changes, and can have style properties applied in the same way as other web controls using the various style attributes:

```
<Wrox:MyTextBox id="name" runat="server"
                BackColor="Green"
                ForeColor="Yellow"
                BorderColor="Red"
                OnTextChanged="OnNameChanged" />
```

More on Events

Any server control that derives from the `Control` base classes automatically inherits several built-in events that page developers can also handle:

❑   **Init** – called when a control has to be constructed and its properties have been set.

❑   **Load** – called when a control's viewstate is available.

❑   **DataBinding** – called when a control with a data source should enumerate that source and build its control tree.

❑   **PreRender** – called just before the UI of a control is rendered.

❑   **Unload** – called when a control has been rendered.

❑   **Disposed**– called when a control is destroyed by its container.

These events behave just like any other event. For example, we could catch the `PreRender` event of our `TextBox` and restrict its length to seven characters by adding an `OnPreRender` attribute to our control declaration:

```
<P>Enter a value: <Wrox:MyTextBox id="name" runat="server"
                   BackColor="Green"
                   ForeColor="Yellow"
                   BorderColor="Red"
                   OnTextChanged="OnNameChanged"
                   OnPreRender="OnPreRender" />
```

And an event handler that restricts the size of the `TextBox` value if it exceeds 7 characters:

```
private void OnPreRender( object sender, EventArgs e )
{
  if ( name.Text.Length > 7 )
    name.Text = name.Text.Substring(0,7);
}
```

As a control author you can also catch these standard events within your controls. You can do this by either wiring up the necessary event wire-up code, or as we've seen already, you can override one of these methods:

❑   OnInit(EventArgs e)

❑   OnLoad (EventArgs e)

❑   OnDataBinding(EventArgs e)

❑   OnPreRender(EventArgs e)

❑   OnUnload(EventArgs e)

❑   Disposed()

The default implementation of each of these methods raises the associated events listed earlier. For example, OnInit fires the Init event, and OnPreRender fires the PreRender event. When overriding one of these methods, you should call the base-class implementation of the method so that events are still raised, assuming that is the behavior you want:

```
protected override void OnInit(EventArgs e)
{
    base.OnInit(e);
    if ( _text == null )
        _text = "Here is some default text";
}
```

Event Optimization in C# Using the EventHandlerList

When an event is declared within a class definition, additional memory must be allocated for an object instance at run-time for the field containing the event. As the number of events a class supports increases, the amount of memory consumed by each and every object instance increases. Assuming that a control supports 10 events (the 6 built-in ones and 4 custom events), and assuming an event declaration requires roughly 16 bytes of memory, each object instance will require 160 bytes of memory. If nobody is interested in any of these events, this is a lot of overhead for a single control.

To only consume memory for events that are in use, ASP.NET controls can use the EventHandlerList class.

The EventHandlerList is an optimized list class designed to hold delegates. The list can hold any number of delegates, and each delegate is associated with a key. The Control class has an Events property that returns a reference to an instance of the EventHandlerList. This instantiates the class on demand, so if no event handlers are in use, there is almost no overhead:

```
protected EventHandlerList Events
{
    get
    {
        if (_events == null)
            _events = new EventHandlerList();
    }
        return _events;
}
```

The EventHandlerList class has two main methods:

```
void AddHandler( object key, Delegate handler );
void RemoveHandler( object key, Delegate handler );
```

AddHandler is used to associate a delegate (event handler) with a given key. If the method is called with a key for which a delegate already exists, the two delegates will be combined and both will be called when an event is raised. RemoveHandler simply performs the reverse of AddHandler.

Using the `Events` property, a server control should implement support for an event using a property declared as the type event:

```
private static readonly object _textChanged = new object();

public event EventHandler TextChanged
{
    add { Events.AddHandler(EventPreRender, value); }
    remove { Events.RemoveHandler(EventPreRender, value); }
}
```

Since this property is declared as an event, we have to use the add and remove property accessor declarations, rather than get and set. When add or remove are called, the value is equal to the delegate being added or removed, so we use this when calling `AddHandler` or `RemoveHandler`.

> As VB does not support the **add/remove** accessor, we can't use optimized event handlers in VB.

To create a unique key for our events, which we know will not clash with any events defined in our base classes, we define a static, read-only member variable called _textChanged, and instantiate it with an object reference. We could use other techniques for creating the key, but this approach adds no overhead for each instance of our server control, and is also the technique used by the built-in ASP.NET server controls. By making the key value static, there is no per-object overhead.

Checking and raising an event using the `Events` property is done by determining if a delegate exists for the key associated with an event. If it does, we raise it to notify one or more subscribed listeners:

```
void IPostBackDataHandler.RaisePostDataChangedEvent()
{
    EventHandler handler = (EventHandler) Events[_textChanged];
    if (handler != null)
        handler(this, EventArgs.Empty);
}
```

Using the `EventHandler` technique, a control can implement many events without causing excessive overhead for controls that do not have any event listeners associated with them. Since the `Control` class already implements most of the work you do, you should always implement your events in this way.

Tracking ViewState

When adding, and removing, items from viewstate, they are only persisted by a control if its viewstate is being tracked. This tracking only occurs after the initialization phase of a page is completed. This means any changes a server control makes to itself, or to another control before this phase, and the `OnInit` event has been raised will not be saved.

Types and ViewState

We mentioned earlier that the `StateBag` class that is used to maintain viewstate allows any type to be placed into it. Whilst this is true, this **does not** mean that you can use any type with it. Only types that can be safely persisted can be used. As such, types that maintain resources such as database connections or file handles should not be used.

`ViewState` is optimized and designed to work with the following types:

❑ `Int32`, `Boolean`, `Strings`, and other primitive types.

❑ Arrays of `Int32`, `Boolean`, `Strings`, and other primitive types.

❑ `ArrayList`, `Hashtable`.

❑ Types that have a **type converter**. A type converter is a class derived from `System.ComponentModel.TypeConverter` that can convert one type into another. For example, the type converter for the `Color` class can convert the string "red" into the enumeration value for red. ASP.NET requires a type converter that can convert a type to and from a string.

❑ Types that are **serializable** (marked with the serializable attribute, or support the serialization interfaces).

❑ `Pair`, `Triplet` (defined in `System.Web.UI`, and respectively hold 2 or 3 of the other types listed).

`ViewState` is converted from these types into a string by the Limited Object Serialization (LOS) formatter class (`System.Web.UI.LosFormatter`).

The LOS formatter used by ASP.NET encodes a hash code into viewstate when a page is generated. This hash code is used during postback to determine if the static control declarations in an ASP.NET page have changed (for example, the number and ordering of server controls declared within an ASP.NET page). If a change is detected, all viewstate is discarded, since viewstate cannot reliably be processed if the structure of a page has changed. This limitation stems from the fact that ASP.NET automatically assigns unique identifiers to controls, and uses these identifiers to associate viewstate with individual given controls. If a page structure changes, so do the unique identifiers assigned to controls, so the viewstate/control relationship is meaningless. In case you're wondering, yes, this is one technical reason why ASP.NET only allows a page to postback to itself.

More on Object Properties and Template UI

Earlier, we discussed how the default control builder of a server control would automatically map sub-elements defined within server-control public properties of that control. For example, given the following server-control declaration:

```
<Wrox:ICollectionLister id="SessionList" runat=server>

    <HeadingStyle ForeColor="Blue">
       <Font Size=18/>
    </HeadingStyle>

    <ItemStyle ForeColor="Green" Font-Size="12"/>

</Wrox:ICollectionLister>
```

The control builder of the `ICollectionLister` control shown here would try and initialize the object properties `HeadingStyle` and `ItemStyle`, determining the type of the object properties by examining the metadata of the `ICollectionLister` class using reflection. As the `HeadingStyle` element in this example has a `Font` sub-element, the control builder would determine that the `HeadingStyle` object property has an object property of `Font`.

The `ICollectionLister` server control is a simple composite control we've created that can enumerate the contents of any collection class implementing the `ICollection`. For each item in the collection it creates a `Label` control, and sets the text of the label using the `ToString` method of the current item in the collection. This causes a line-break because for each item in the collection, the label starts with "`<BR>`". The control also has a fixed heading of "`ICollection Lister Control`" which is also created using a label control.

The `ICollectionLister` control has three properties:

- ❏ **DataSource** – A public property of the type `ICollection`. When `CreateChildControls` is called this property is enumerated to generate the main output of the control.

- ❏ **HeadingStyle** – a public property of the type `Style`. This allows users of the control to specify the style attributes used for the hard-coded heading text. The `Style.ApplyStyle` method is used to copy this style object into the `Label` control created for the header.

- ❏ **ItemStyle** – a public property of the type `Style`. This allows users of the control to specify the style attributes used for each of the collections that is rendered. The `Style.ApplyStyle` method is used to copy this style object into the `Label` control created for the header.

The code for this server control is shown here:

```
using System;
using System.Web;
using System.Web.UI;
using System.Collections;
using System.Web.UI.WebControls;

namespace WroxControls
{

    public class ICollectionLister : WebControl, INamingContainer
    {
      ICollection _datasource;

      public ICollection DataSource
      {
        get { return _datasource; }
        set { _datasource = value; }
      }

      Style _headingStyle = new Style();

      public Style HeadingStyle
      {
        get{ return _headingStyle; }
      }

      Style _itemStyle = new Style();

      public Style ItemStyle
      {
        get{ return _itemStyle; }
      }
```

```
protected override void CreateChildControls()
{
IEnumerator e;
Label l;

// Create the heading, using the specified user style

l = new Label();
l.ApplyStyle( _headingStyle );
l.Text = "ICollection Lister Control";
Controls.Add( l );

// Create a label for each key/value pair in the collection

if ( _datasource == null )
  throw new Exception("Control requires a datasource");

e = _datasource.GetEnumerator();

while( e.MoveNext() )
{
  l = new Label();
  l.ApplyStyle( _itemStyle );
  l.Text = "<BR>" + e.Current.ToString();
  Controls.Add( l );
}
  }
 }
};
```

There is nothing new in this code that we haven't already discussed. If you've skipped the chapter on collection classes, refer back to Chapter 15 for an explanation of using `IEnumerator` and `ICollection`.

The following ASP.NET page uses the `ICollectionLister` control to list the contents of a string array. This array is created in the `Page_Load` event and associated with a server control which has been given a name/id of `SessionList` in this page:

```
<%@ Register TagPrefix="Wrox" Namespace="WroxControls"
        Assembly="DictionaryLister" %>

<script runat=server language="C#">

  void Page_Load( object sender, EventArgs e )
  {

    string[] names = new string[3];

    names[0] = "Richard";
    names[1] = "Alex";
    names[2] = "Rob";

    SessionList.DataSource = names;
  }
</script>
```

```
<Wrox:ICollectionLister id="SessionList" runat=server>

  <HeadingStyle ForeColor="Blue">
    <Font Size=18/>
  </HeadingStyle>

  <ItemStyle ForeColor="Green" Font-Size="12"/>

</Wrox:ICollectionLister>
```

The output from this page (if viewed in color) is a blue header with green text for each item in the collection:

For controls that have fixed style and layout requirements, initializing them using object properties like we have in the ICollectionLister control is a good approach. You will have seen the same approach used throughout the standard ASP.NET server controls, such as the data grid and data list. However, for a control to provide ultimate flexibility, it's better to enable the user of the control to define what the UI of a control looks like by using template UI. Again, you'll have seen this in earlier chapters, with controls like the data grid.

Using Templates

As we saw in Chapter 7, templates allow the users of a control to define how chunks of its UI – such as the header or footer – should be rendered.

Templates are classes that implement in the ITemplate interface. As a control developer, to support one or more templates you declare public properties of the type ITemplate. When the default control builder sees a property of this type, it knows to dynamically build a class that supports the ITemplate interface, which can be used to render the section of UI the template defines.

Supporting template properties in a server control is relatively straightforward, although when using them within a data-bound control things can initially seem a little complex, since the way child controls are created has to be handled slightly differently.

Let's introduce templates by rewriting our ICollectionLister control to support a heading and item template. We need to make the following changes to our code:

❑ Change the HeadingTemplate and ItemType properties to the Itemplate type.

❑ Make the HeadingTemplate and ItemType properties writeable. This has to be done since the objects implementing the ITemplate interface are dynamically created by the ASP.NET page and then associated with our server control.

❏ Use the `TemplateContainer` attribute to give the control builder a hint about the type of object within which our templates will be instantiated. This reduces the need for casting in databinding syntax.

Our changed code is shown here:

```
ITemplate _headingStyle;

[TemplateContainer(typeof(ICollectionLister))]
public ITemplate HeadingStyle
{
  get{ return _headingStyle; }
  set{ _headingStyle = value; }
}


ITemplate _itemStyle;

[TemplateContainer(typeof(ICollectionLister))]
public ITemplate ItemStyle
{
  get{ return _itemStyle; }
  set{ _itemStyle = value; }
}
```

At run-time, if a user specifies a template the properties will contain a non-null value. If they are null, no template has been specified.

The `ITemplate` interface has one method called `InstantiateIn`. This method accepts one parameter of the type `Control`. When called, this method populates the `Controls` collections of the control passed in with one or more server controls that represent the UI defined within a template by a user. Any existing controls in the collection are not removed, so you can instantiate a template against another server control one or more times.

> A server control could use the **Page.LoadTemplate**(string filename) to dynamically load templates, but this is not recommended. It is very slow and is known to be unreliable. If you need dynamic templates you should write your own class that implements the **ITemplate** interface.

Using the `InstantiateIn` method we can change our `CreateChildControls` to use our new template properties to build the server controls for the header and each item.

Since we're not supporting the data-binding syntax yet, the UI created for each item in the collection will not contain any useful values.

In the following code, we only call the `InstantiateIn` method if a template is not null. If a template is null, we simply assume the user didn't want that part of the controls UI to appear.

```
protected override void CreateChildControls()
{
    IEnumerator e;
```

```
    if ( _headingStyle != null )
      _headingStyle.InstantiateIn( this );

    if ( _datasource == null )
      throw new Exception("Control requires a data source");

    e = _datasource.GetEnumerator();

    while( e.MoveNext() )
    {
      if( _itemStyle !=null)
        _itemStyle.InstantiateIn( this);
    }
  }
}
```

With our new template properties and revised `CreateChildControls`, we can now declare a page that uses templates to style our controls UI. Here is a basic example that uses an `<H3>` element for the heading, and some bold text for each item (remember we're not showing the item value yet):

```
<Wrox:ICollectionLister id="SessionList" runat=server>

  <HeadingStyle>
    <h3>ICollection Lister</H3>
  </HeadingStyle>

  <ItemStyle>
    <BR><Strong>An item in the collection</Strong></BR>
  </ItemStyle>

</Wrox:ICollectionLister>
```

With these changes, our UI will now render like this:

Although not visually stunning, these changes allow the UI of our control to be completely controlled and changed by the user in their declaration of our server control. As you'll have seen in previous chapters, this is a very powerful technique.

Without any additional changes, our controls template support can use databinding syntax, but it is limited to the data it can access. Without any additional changes we can access public properties, or methods, on the page within which the control is declared, or any public property or method of any other server control we can access.

For example, if we had a public property declared in our ASP.NET page called Name, we could bind our item template to this using the databinding syntax, which was introduced in Chapter 7:

```
<ItemStyle>
  <BR><Strong>An item in the collection: <%#Name%></Strong></BR>
</ItemStyle>
```

When this expression is evaluated, ASP.NET will try and locate the Name property on the naming container first (the control in which the template was instantiated, in our case); if its not found there, it will check the ASP page. Assuming we defined this property to return the string 'Templates Rock', we'd see this output from our control:

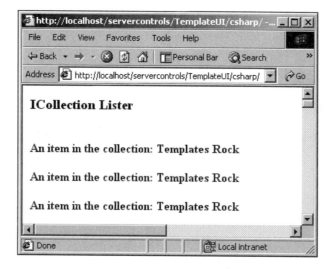

To bind to the text field of a label field, on the same page called mylabel, we would use this syntax:

```
<ItemStyle>
  <BR><Strong>An item in the collection: <%#mylabel.Text%></Strong></BR>
</ItemStyle>
```

If we only want to bind to the naming container in which the template is instantiated, we can use the Container. syntax:

```
<ItemStyle>
  <BR><Strong>An item in the collection: <%#Container.DataItem%></Strong></BR>
</ItemStyle>
```

Using this last syntax we could be forgiven for thinking we could enable our item template to access the current collection item being enumerated. To achieve this, it looks as if we'd simply add a public object property to our server control called DataItem:

```
    object _dataitem;

public object DataItem
    {
       get{   return _dataitem; }
    }
```

Then we set that property to the current item being enumerated in the loop that instantiates the item template, like this:

```
...
e = _datasource.GetEnumerator();

while( e.MoveNext() )
{
if ( _itemStyle != null )
  {
     // Set the current item
     _dataitem = e.Current;
     _itemStyle.InstantiateIn( this );
  }
}
...
```

But if we were to make these changes, and compiled them, we'd encounter an interesting problem:

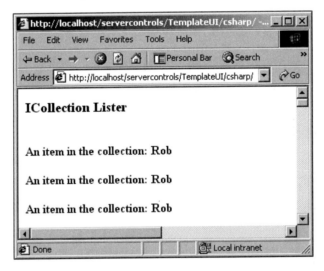

Each template item instantiated has the same value! This occurs because the data binding for controls instantiated using a template, or just added using `Controls.Add` by hand, are not data bound **until** the parent control is data bound. This means our collection has already been enumerated, and the `DataItem` will always point to the last item in the collection as the controls instantiated by the item templates are data bound. To resolve this problem, we need to instantiate our template on a control that has a `DataItem` property that holds the correct value. This control will not render any UI, and basically, will do very little except expose the `DataItem` property:

```
public class CollectionItem : WebControl, INamingContainer
{
  object _dataitem;

  public object DataItem
  {
    get{ return _value; }
  }

  public CollectionItem(object value)
  {
    _dataitem = value;
  }
}
```

The class derives from the `Control` since it will be the container for the controls instantiated by the item template. It also derives from the `INamingContainer` to signal that it is a naming container for any child controls. This is important. Without this, our data-binding syntax would still refer to the parent control.

Using this new class, we can change our enumeration code to create an instance of it for each item enumerated in the collection, passing in the current item being enumerated as a parameter to the constructor. The item template is then instantiated against the `CollectionItem` object created, before being added as a child control of the `ICollectionLister`.

Here is the revised section of our enumeration code:

```
...
e = _datasource.GetEnumerator();

CollectionItem item;

while( e.MoveNext() )
{
  if ( _itemStyle != null )
  {
    item = new CollectionItem( e.Current );
    _itemStyle.InstantiateIn( item );
    Controls.Add( item );
  }
}
...
```

The end result of these changes is that the following server control hierarchy will be created:

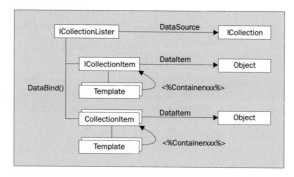

At the top of this diagram we have the instance of our `ICollectionLister` control declared on the page. Assuming for a moment the `DataSource` associated with the control only contained two items, the `CollectionItem` object would have two `CollectionItem` child server controls. Each of these has a `DataItem` property that exposes the associated collection item, passed in via the constructor. The item template is instantiated within each of the `CollectionItem` objects, so its child controls will vary depending on the "what's defined in the item" template. However, any data binding using the `Container.` syntax will always refer back to its parent `CollectionItem`, and therefore the correct `DataItem`.

As our **item template** is now being instantiated within the `CollectionItem` class, we have to update the `TemplateContainer` attribute declared on the `ItemTemplate` property to reflect this. Without this ASP.NET would throw a cast exception when evaluating a data-binding expression:

```
ITemplate _itemStyle;

[TemplateContainer(typeof(CollectionItem))]
public ITemplate ItemStyle
{
  get{ return _itemStyle; }
  set{ _itemStyle = value; }
}
```

With these changes in place, our UI renders each item in the collection and displays its value:

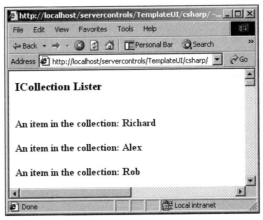

When implementing a control that supports templates, here are a few simple rules you should follow:

❑ If you are going to instantiate a template more than once, **do not** instantiate it against the same instance of a control, unless you have very good reason to do so. For example, if a template does not contain any data-binding syntax and you can ensure none of the controls will be assigned an `id` (`ids` must always be unique within a naming container).

Remember, `ids` must be unique within a naming container.

❑ If a control is going to support a header template, it should always support a footer template, as well. This is important for scenarios where a user may want to create an HTML table, or any other item that has a start element, several items, then an end item.

❑ Try and be consistent with the intrinsic controls, and follow the same naming conventions that they use.

DataBind/OnDataBinding

When a server control can be data bound, it should support a couple of additional features:

❑ The ability for the page developer to determine when (and if) a control should databind itself. This high degree of control over when a control accesses its data source, allows a page developer to optimize data source usage, keeping it to a minimum.

❑ The ability to recreate itself and all child controls during postback, without being connected to its data source. The goal here is to reduce load on the data source provider.

To signal a control to connect to its data source, and create its child controls, a page developer calls the Control.DataBind method. When called, this method will result in the Control.OnDataBinding method being called, and the DataBinding event being raised. This behavior is inline with all other stages of pages.

When a server control's OnDataBinding method is called, it should create its child control tree as we did previously in the CreateChildControls method, but with a few changes:

❑ The number of controls instantiated (the numbers of items in the collection) is remembered using ViewState. We have to do this since we need to recreate the same number of controls when a postback occurs. All other state will automatically be remembered by the other server controls instantiated as part of the template.

❑ Because OnDataBinding may be called one or more times, the ClearChildViewState and Controls.Clear methods are called to clear any existing viewstate for the control, and delete all child controls.

❑ The ChildControlsCreated property is set to true. Setting this flag ensures that CreateChildControls is not subsequently called.

The follow code implements these changes:

```
protected override void OnDataBinding( EventArgs args )
{
  base.OnDataBinding(args);

  if ( _datasource == null )
    throw new Exception("Control requires a data source");

  // Clear all controls and state

  ClearChildViewState();
  Controls.Clear();

  IEnumerator e;
  int iCount;

  if ( _headingStyle != null )
    _headingStyle.InstantiateIn( this );

  e = _datasource.GetEnumerator();
```

```
      CollectionItem item;
      while( e.MoveNext() )
      {
        if ( _itemStyle != null )
        {
          item = new CollectionItem( e.Current );
          _itemStyle.InstantiateIn( item );
          Controls.Add( item );
          iCount++;
        }
      }

      // Remember the number of controls, so we can recreate the
      // same controls, without the data source.

      ViewState["count"] = iCount;

      // stop CreateChildControls() being called again

      ChildControlsCreated = true;

      // Ensure viewstate is being tracked
          TrackViewState();
      }
```

When a postback occurs, a server control's `CreateChildControls` method will typically be called, unless a page developer explicitly calls `DataBind`. This method should recreate the control tree, using only information stored in viewstate.

Here is the implementation of `CreateChildControls`. The basic creation logic is similar to `OnDataBinding`, but we do not use the data source at all:

```
    protected override void CreateChildControls()
    {
      int iCount;
      int i;
      CollectionItem item;

      if ( _headingStyle != null )
        _headingStyle.InstantiateIn( this );

        iCount = (int) ViewState["count"];
        for( i=0; i< iCount; i++ )
        {
          if ( _itemStyle != null )
          {
            item = new CollectionItem( null );
            _itemStyle.InstantiateIn( item );
            Controls.Add( item );
          }
        }
      }
```

The changes in this code are:

- ❑ We have not used the data source.
- ❑ The number of controls to create was determined by the count property held in viewstate.
- ❑ A null value was passed to the constructor of CollectionItem, since the DataItem will not be used.

With these changes in place, we have a data-bound templated control. The control should behave just like any of the built-in controls you have used.

Miscellaneous Topics

In this section of the chapter we'll show some techniques you may find useful, depending on the types of server controls you write.

Accessing the ASP.NET Intrinsics

The Control class has a Context property that enables a server control to access ASP.NET intrinsic objects such as Application, Session, Request, Response, Error, and Cache.

The Context property is defined as the type System.Web.UI.HttpContext, which is the same type as the Page.Context property, which means it is used in the same way (for example,. for tracing, etc.)

The following code shows a simple server control that will output HTML to display the keys and values held in the application and session intrinsics:

```
using System;
using System.Web;
using System.Web.UI;
using System.Web.UI.WebControls;

namespace WroxControls
{
  public class IntrinsicDisplay : WebControl
  {
    protected override void Render(HtmlTextWriter writer)
    {
      writer.Write("<H3>Application Variables</H3>");

      foreach( string key in Context.Application )
      {
        writer.Write( "<BR>Key = '" + key +
                "' , Value = '" +
                Context.Application[key] + "'" );
      }

      writer.Write("<H3>Session Variables</H3>");
```

```
        foreach( string key in Context.Session )
        {
          writer.Write( "<BR>Key = '" + key +
              "' , Value = '" +
              Context.Session[key] + "'" );
        }
      }
    }
};
```

Assuming that we have an ASP.NET page that sets some application and session variables in the Page_Load event and declares an instance of this control:

```
<%@ Register TagPrefix="Wrox" Namespace="WroxControls"
        Assembly="Intrinsic" %>
<script runat=server language="VB">

  Sub Page_Load( sender as object, args as EventArgs )

    Application("Name") = "Richard"
    Application("Age") = 27

    Session("Year") = "1972"
    Session("Car") = "Audi"

  End Sub
</script>
<html>
<body>

<Wrox:IntrinsicDisplay runat="server" />

</body>
</html>
```

Our control would render the following output:

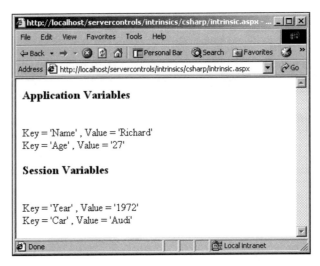

Writing Adaptive Controls

When writing a server control the HTML (or other markup) a control generates can be varied depending on the capabilities of the client browser. Using the Browser property of the Page object property, a control can determine the capabilities of the browser where its output will be sent. Most of the built-in ASP.NET server controls use this capability to reduce postback when a browser supports client-side Java Script.

Here is a simple server control that determines the capabilities of a browser and reports some of them back to the client browser:

```
using System;
using System.Web;
using System.Web.UI;
using System.Web.UI.WebControls;
using System.ComponentModel;

namespace WroxControls
{
  public class AdaptiveControl: WebControl
  {
    override protected void Render( HtmlTextWriter objWriter )
    {
      objWriter.Write("<BR>");
      objWriter.Write("Browser is: ");
      objWriter.Write(Page.Request.Browser.Browser );

      objWriter.Write("<BR>");
      objWriter.Write("Browser version is: ");
      objWriter.Write(Page.Request.Browser.Version );
      objWriter.Write("<BR>");

      if  ( Page.Request.Browser.JavaScript == true )
      {
        objWriter.Write("Browser supports JavaScript");
      }

      if  ( Page.Request.Browser.VBScript == true )
      {
        objWriter.Write("Browser supports VBScript");
      }

      if  ( Page.Request.Browser.Browser == "IE" )

      {
        objWriter.Write("<BR>IE rocks!");
      }

      if  ( Page.Request.Browser.Browser == "Netscape" )

      {
        objWriter.Write("<BR>Netscape rolls!");
      }
    }
  }
}
```

The output from this server control, when viewed in IE 5.5 is shown here:

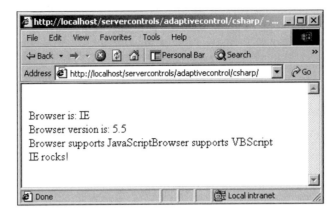

The output from the same server control when viewed in a Netscape browser is shown below:

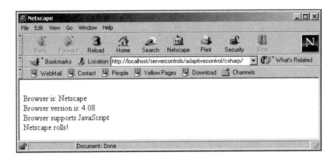

Using the `HttpBrowserCapabilities` class exposed through the `Page.Browser` property a server control can become adaptive. For example, if the `Page.Request.Browser.JavaScript` property returns `true`, a textbox control could generate some client-side JavaScript to perform an advanced client-side behavior – such as limiting the number, or type, of characters that can be entered into it.

Control Attributes

When developing server controls you can annotate your classes with attributes that give the ASP.NET page compiler instructions of how it should be compiled and used. Attributes can also affect the way your control is displayed by a visual designer such as Visual Studio.NET.

This table lists a few of the common attributes used by ASP.NET server controls:

Bindable	Whether a property should be displayed in the DataBindings dialog in VS.NET.
Category	If the property grid is sorted by category, this determines which category the property should appear in.
DefaultValue	The default value of the property.

Description	Text describing the property. This appears at the bottom of the property grid in the "Description" box.
PersistenceMode	How (or whether) changes made to the value of this property should be persisted.
Browsable	Whether a property is displayed in the designer.
TypeConverter, Editor	Hooks up extended UI for setting the property.

The following example shows how we'd use the Browsable property to hide the SomeProperty from the properties window:

```
[
Browsable(false),
]
protected virtual string SomeProperty
{
    get { ... }
}
```

Custom Control Builders

A custom control builder is a class that derives from the class ControlBuilder, and overrides one or more methods that influence how a server deals with declaration within an ASP.NET page.

The following control builder class overrides the AllowWhitespaceLiterals method and returns false to indicate that spaces are not significant. If this method returned true, a LiteralControl containing spaces would be created and added the to Controls collection:

```
public class NoWhiteSpaceBuilder: ControlBuilder
{

    public override bool AllowWhitespaceLiterals()
    {
        return false;
    }
}
```

A control builder is associated with a given server control using the ControlBuilder attribute:

```
[
ControlBuilderAttribute(typeof(NoWhiteSpaceBuilder)),
Designer("System.Web.UI.Design.WebControls.XmlDesigner, " +
AssemblyRef.SystemDesign)
]
public class SomeControl : Control {…}
```

User Controls

Although we have not explicitly discussed creating user controls in this chapter (see Chapter 4), all of the features we have shown can be pretty much applied to them as is.

One of the key benefits of using user controls is complex sections of the UI can be declared using nothing but control declarations. In a server control, you'd have to write code to achieve this. Although not difficult, this can be time consuming, changing or maintaining it can take longer, and also it's more error prone.

Why Create Your Own Server Controls?

"Why Create Your Own Controls?" isn't really the right question to ask. Instead, the decision you have to make as an ASP.NET developer is whether you let ASP.NET build server controls automatically for you (by just building your sites using ASP.NET pages and/or user controls), or whether you take over some of the control creation yourself. In the latter case, you can build your site using a mixture of ASP.NET pages, user controls, and custom server controls.

So there's no right answer to the original question. However, here are a few pointers that should help you decide for yourself:

❑ ASP.NET controls enable a fine-grained level of black box reuse. ASP.NET user controls and pages can also provide this reuse, but since they are far more coarse-grained and typically have fixed UI traits (pages don't support templates, although user controls can), they are likely to provide far less re-use.

❑ ASP.NET controls ultimately provide the most flexibility, but take longer to write and require more coding skill.

❑ If you think you want a custom control, but are not 100% sure, start with a user control as you can always change it to become a custom control later. All the code you write will work as a control, but you will need to convert any HTML sections of your user control into code using control composition.

❑ Only custom controls and user controls can be 'lookless', and therefore support templates. If you want people to be able to extend and manage the UI of your control, you must use these control types.

❑ User controls and custom controls can be written in different languages, and then used within the same hosting page. At present only one language can be used directly within any single ASP.NET page.

❑ Only custom controls are compiled. You may therefore want to use them if you need to protect your source code.

Summary

In this chapter we've examined how to develop ASP.NET server controls using C# and VB. There are many topics we have not covered in this chapter, such as advanced state management, but we've hopefully given you enough information to start developing server controls.

We started the chapter by looking at how to develop a really elementary server control with a hard-coded user interface. We then evolved this into a more useful label control supporting attributes to allow the text content of a label to be specified, along with server style attributes to define font size and text control.

Then we saw how the WebControl class is designed for server controls that require styles, and also want to provide an object model consistent with the built-in ASP.NET server controls. Next we looked at how server controls can interact with postback and use viewstate to become intelligent – automatically round tripping their values in the browser, and raising events to allow server-side event handlers to react to changes in state.

We also looked at several miscellaneous topics, including how to use attributes to influence the design-time experience of a server control, and how to determine the capabilities of a browser to enable a control's user interface to be adaptive.

Finally, we looked at some of the reasons why you might want to write server controls in preference to user controls or plain ASP.NET pages.

In the next chapter we'll look at how to expose Web Services, allowing you to share information across networks and the Internet.

"The Babel fish," says The Hitch Hiker's Guide to Galaxy "is small, yellow and leech-like, and probably the oddest thing in the Universe. It feeds on brainwave energy not from its carrier but from those around it. It absorbs all unconscious mental frequencies from this brainwave energy to nourish itself with. It then excretes into the mind of its carrier a telepathic matrix formed by combining the conscious thought frequencies with nerve signals picked up from the speech centres of the brain which has supplied them".

The practical upshot of all this is that if you stick a Babel fish in your ear you can instantly understand anything said to you in any form of language. The speech patterns you actually hear decode the brainwave matrix which has been fed into your mind by your Babel fish.

19

Exposing Web Services

Web Services, in theory, aren't a new concept. They allow distributed applications to share business logic over a network. For example, the classic Web Service scenario is a stock quote service: one company provides a service that can accept requests for stock symbols and respond with stock quote details. A company building an investing site can then use the application logic provided by the stock quote company to retrieve stock quote detail.

This problem sounds relatively simple, but it has been quite difficult to solve in the past. That's due largely to proprietary protocol formats, such as RMI, and the lock-down of open ports to only port 80 and port 443 (for HTTP and HTTPS traffic only).

However, what is new is the use of XML and HTTP, rather than proprietary serialization formats (DCOM, RMI, or CORBA – OK, CORBA isn't "proprietary", but we've included it here since each vendor's CORBA implementation is "unique" to that vendor).

Microsoft's Web Services use standard web protocols such as HTTP, and data description languages such as XML, to exchange data over common ports, utilizing the ubiquitous HTTP infrastructure support already in place.

The technical definition of a Web Service is programmable application logic accessible via standard web protocols. Behind this definition are two important points:

❑ **Programmable application logic**. A Web Service is implementation-non-specific. The application logic can be implemented by components, by PERL scripts, or by any other mechanism that supports XML.

❑ **Standard web protocols**. Web Services use Internet transport protocols such as HTTP or SMTP.

The union of XML and HTTP forms one of the new industry buzz words: **Simple Object Access Protocol (SOAP)**. SOAP is a W3C submitted note (as of May 2000) that uses HTTP and XML to encode and transmit application data.

Consumers of a Web Service don't need to know anything about the platform, object model, or programming language used to implement the service; they only need to understand how to send and receive SOAP messages.

ASP.NET makes building Web Services easy, and since it continues the ASP "just hit save" development model, ASP developers already have the necessary skills to build Web Services with ASP.NET. Although a Web Service makes use of XML and HTTP as part of the plumbing, ASP.NET abstracts this for us and makes building SOAP based end-points as simple as coding application logic. Of course, the plumbing is also accessible if we wish to work with the transport or serialization mechanisms.

Here's what we'll cover in this chapter:

❑ **Web Services Overview**. We'll start with an overview of what a Web Service is, look at some of the common problems associated with building distributed applications, and briefly discuss the public specifications used for building Web Services.

❑ **ASP.NET Web Services Programming Model**. We'll look at how we build Web Services with ASP.NET, starting with some simple application logic that we'll enable.

❑ **Protocols and Data types**. ASP.NET Web Services support three protocols for exchanging data through a Web Service: HTTP GET and POST and SOAP. In this section we'll take a look at these protocols and the supported data types.

❑ **Attributes**. In the ASP.NET Web Services Programming Model section we'll look at how we can build a simple Web Service using only the required set of classes and attributes. In this section we'll look at the additional attributes and classes we can use when creating ASP.NET Web Services.

❑ **Designing ASP.NET Web Services**. In this section we'll look at some strategies for building Web Services and tracing Web Service requests, as well as how we can build services that operate asynchronously on the server. Additionally, we'll look at some of the general ASP.NET features we can leverage.

> **For the purpose of this chapter, any discussion of Web Services implies the use of SOAP unless otherwise stated.**

Let's get started with an overview of what a Web Service is.

Web Services Overview

Today the most common way to access information on the Internet is through a browser sending and receiving messages that contain HTML markup via HTTP. This HTML markup is then parsed in a web browser to render the user interface.

The web browser only begins to scratch the surface of what can be done with Internet when it comes to building applications. Already we're seeing a migration to other Internet applications, which use a similar set of underlying protocols, but don't always rely on HTML to control the user interface or exchange data. Examples here include PDAs, cellular phones, blackberry devices, and other rich-client peer-to-peer applications such as Napster or gaming applications.

Web Services are designed to facilitate the move to this next generation of the Internet. Using Web Services it's simpler to enable scenarios such as peer-to-peer and distributed application development, by providing the common protocol that connected web applications can share. It's very easy to envision applications using a broad set of Web Services for authentication, e-mail, buddy lists, etc.

The protocol format is standardized, so any application that understands SOAP can take advantage of Web Services. For example, if E-Bay built an auction Web Service, or Hotmail built an e-mail Web Service, SOAP-aware applications would be able to utilize each together or independently. It should be noted, however, that various implementations can "interpret" the meaning of the SOAP 1.1 specification differently. Microsoft is working extremely hard to ensure that ASP.NET Web Services are compatible with other common SOAP implementations.

As great as all this sounds, there are obviously some common issues and questions surrounding Web Services.

Common Issues

Solving the problem of exposing application logic or details through XML and HTTP isn't difficult. In the past we could have used languages such as ASP, Java, or Perl to write a simple application that exposed data via XML. For example, we could use ASP to write a simple application that accepts values passed on the query string, and generates an XML return document representing a specific database table. Applications could simply make calls against an end-point – say a URL exposing our database tables – and fetch, parse, and derive values from the document.

However designs like this are tightly coupled. The client is expecting a highly structured XML document, and if the application providing this document changes, the client implementations will most likely break. In the majority of cases this can be addressed by using public XML schemas, but maintaining and managing a disparate set of schemas for each application can be cumbersome. Also, the XML document will be dependent upon the server implementation.

Typically, even minor changes to the application logic can become large changes in the code used to expose that application logic as an XML document. The classic example of this problem is encountered with screen-scraping, where the HTML of a site is parsed for specific values. As long as the HTML remains static the known values can easily be extracted. If the HTML changes, it usually completely breaks the application consuming the HTML.

Other common issues include:

- ❏ **Publishing the service**. Once the service is available, how do clients find or discover the Web Service? Just as we have web sites such as www.msn.com or www.yahoo.com for publishing the location of web sites, shouldn't we have something similar for Web Services?

- ❏ **Describing the service**. How do consumers of the service call the service? For example, what protocol does the service support? How does the protocol serialize data? What data types does the service support? That is, should binary data be treated as big endian or little endian (the byte ordering of data – the big/little endian terms come from an analogy to Gulliver's Travels' Big-Endians and Little-Endians, who bickered over which end to crack open a hardboiled egg)? Does the Web Service require a schema?

- ❏ **Network**. One of the problems with other protocols such as DCOM, RMI, or CORBA is that technologies such as these use TCP/IP ports that are closed or restricted, or in some cases require additional software or a specific OS. Administrators use firewalls to lock down their Internet exposure, with only ports 80 and 443 left open for HTTP/HTTPS traffic respectively. If the required ports are not accessible, or are blocked, building successful distributed applications is more difficult. Additionally, most web applications are an amalgamation of technologies and operating systems.

- ❏ **Development Framework/Tools**. Given some application logic, is there a common development framework – as opposed to a choice of language, or even platform – that we can use to easily enable the creation of Web Services (as opposed to writing the framework ourselves)?

- ❏ **Plumbing**. Most developers don't have time to deal with building all of the underlying HTTP, XML, and serialization mechanisms and so forth; not to mention security! That's not necessarily due to a lack of interest, but rather time. We don't reinvent the engine every time we decide to buy a new car – we understand how the engine works, but we trust someone else to put it together.

These challenges are not particularly difficult to overcome. In fact, with the work being done by Microsoft, IBM, Intel, and HP (to name just a few), many of these issues have already been addressed. This is either through development frameworks (such as Microsoft's .NET) or through specifications that have been submitted to standards organizations.

The specifications address how to solve many of the problems listed above. Rather than each company driving its own view of the world, each can agree upon the specification and provide an implementation of that specification. Standards-based specifications work especially well at the network level since each application can then leverage all the features provided by the platform.

Let's review some of the specifications.

Specifications

To solve these types of integration, protocol, discovery, and description problems, Microsoft is working with companies like those listed above, who believe that Web Services are the key to building the next generation of web applications.

The specifications fall into three categories:

❑ **Discovery**. There are two specifications that address the discovery of Web Services. **Universal Description, Discovery and Integration** (**UDDI** – see http://www.UDDI.org for more details) is the (soon to be) well-known directory in the sky that we'll use to either publish or discover public Web Services. Another specification, **DISCO** (abbreviated from **Discovery**) can also be used to group common services together on a server, and provide links to the schema documents the services it describes may require. We will discuss DISCO and UDDI in the next chapter.

❑ **Description**. **Web Service Description Language** (**WSDL**), another Microsoft co-submitted W3C specification, defines an XML grammar for describing Web Services. This description includes details such as where we find the Web Service (URI), what methods and properties that service supports, the data types, and the protocols used to communicate with the service. Tools can consume this WSDL, and build proxy objects that clients use to communicate with the Web Services. We'll talk more about what proxies are and how to build them in Chapter 15. You can also see the WSDL specification at http://www.w3.org/TR/wsdl for more details.

❑ **Protocol**. As we've already mentioned, a specification called **Simple Object Access Protocol** (**SOAP**) submitted to W3C in May 2000 describes an extensible XML serialization format that uses HTTP to transport data. We will discuss SOAP in this chapter, but not in any great detail. Please see the public specification – http://www.w3.org/TR/SOAP – for more information.

Using Discovery, Description, and Protocols

When we want to build a Web Service, UDDI, DISCO, and WSDL are, for the most part, solutions that are used at design time. Here is a common scenario of usage for a theoretical Credit Card Web Service:

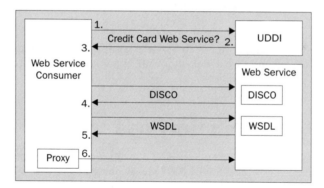

The steps here are as follows:

❑ **Step 1**. Either through UDDI's public Web Services, or through the browser, we communicate our interest in a Credit Card Web Service to a UDDI node (nodes maintain the available services).

❑ **Step 2**. UDDI responds with a listing of credit card services – if they're available, which we'll assume they are.

❑ **Step 3**. The list of services returned by UDDI provides us with URIs that map either to DISCO documents or to WSDL documents. We'll use the DISCO documents. In addition to the programmatic details provided by UDDI, we can also discover documentation for the service at one of the UDDI.org nodes. Hopefully the provider of the service would give us additional details about what the service offered.

❑ **Step 4**. We follow the URI for the DISCO document. Within the DISCO document we find a listing of the location of WSDL documents.

❑ **Step 5**. After parsing the DISCO document, we follow the URI for the WSDL document related to the credit card validation and posting Web Services.

❑ **Step 6**. We parse the WSDL document, and build a proxy object based on the details provided within the WSDL.

Note: although the DISCO and the WSDL documents can reside on the same server as the Web Service, it is not a requirement. Rather, the DISCO can live anywhere since it is only responsible for linking to WSDL documents. Similarly the WSDL document can exist anywhere as long as it accurately describes the Web Service (the description includes the end point of the Web Service).

We now have a proxy object that we can use locally within our code, which looks and feels like the application logic it represents – it exposes the same methods and properties, but rather than the application logic executing locally, the proxy encapsulates the calls to the Web Service.

We're now ready to use our Web Service at runtime.

We can build an application, such as an e-commerce application, that uses the proxy – we'll call it the `CreditCardWebService` proxy. The proxy encapsulates all the details for using the remote Web Service. From our perspective, we are working with a local class/object. If the company providing the Credit Card Web Service decides to add some more functionality to the Web Service, they can simple update the WSDL. If they only add new methods, and don't change the method/property signatures of existing methods, our proxy continues to work fine.

A lot of companies, including Microsoft and IBM, believe strongly that Web Services will be the next great enabler of the Internet. Support for Web Services is one of the most important features in ASP.NET, and in the next chapter we'll look at how we can use the services we build. First though, let's discuss using ASP.NET to build Web Services.

Building ASP.NET Web Services

As we already mentioned, ASP.NET Web Services follow the "just hit save" programming model of ASP.NET pages. Tools such as Visual Studio.NET make coding easier, with language highlighting, inline help, and code completion, but the tool is not necessary to create ASP.NET Web Services.

> **ASP.NET Web Service files are simply source files with the extension `.asmx` that are part of an ASP.NET application.**

Also like ASP.NET Pages, ASP.NET Web Services are compiled on the first request, and support a 'code behind' model, where the code for the Web Service can reside in a pre-compiled .NET Assembly.

`asmx` is not an acronym and has no overloaded meaning.

In this section we'll discuss the programming model with emphasis on the requirements to expose application logic as a Web Service, rather than upon the application logic itself.

The Simple Web Service

We're going to take as our example a simple Math class that calculates the value of an index in a Fibonacci series. A Fibonacci series is a series of numbers beginning with 0 and 1, in which the next number in the sequence is calculated by adding the previous two numbers. So, the third number in the sequence is $0 + 1 = 1$, the fourth number is $1 + 1 = 2$, the seventh is $3 + 5 = 8$, and so on. The first seven numbers of the Fibonacci series are 0, 1, 1, 2, 3, 5, and 8.

Now, let's implement this in code.

Fibonacci Application Logic

Below is the logic that allows us to interact with a Fibonacci series.

VB.NET

```vb.net
Public Class Fibonacci

   Public Function GetSeqNumber (fibIndex As Integer) As Integer

     If (fibIndex < 2) Then
        Return fibIndex
     End If

     Dim FibArray(2) As Integer
     Dim i As Integer

     FibArray(0) = 0
     FibArray(1) = 1

     For i = 2 To fibIndex
        FibArray(1) = FibArray(1) + FibArray(0)
        FibArray(0) = FibArray(1) - FibArray(0)
     Next

     Return FibArray(1)
   End Function
End Class
```

C#

```csharp
public class Fibonacci {

  public int GetSeqNumber(int fibIndex){

    if (fibIndex < 2)
      return fibIndex;

    int[] FibArray = {0,1};

    for (int i = 1; i< fibIndex; i++){
      FibArray[1] = FibArray[0] + FibArray[1];
      FibArray[0] = FibArray[1] - FibArray[0];
    }

    return FibArray[1];
  }
}
```

Both of these examples create a class named `Fibonacci` with a single method: `GetSeqNumber`. `GetSeqNumber` accepts a single parameter, `fibIndex`, of type `Integer/int`, and returns the value of the index in the Fibonacci series (note the index into the series begins with 0). For example, `GetSeqNumber(6)` returns the value 8.

A two-element array is created and initialized with the first series values of 0 and 1. For these numbers in the series, the value is the same as the index number, so we can just use that as a return value. Next, if the `fibIndex` parameter is greater than 0 or 1, we iterate in a `For Next` (VB) or `for` loop (C#), performing the necessary math to calculate the current values. Finally we return the requested element in the array – the last value we calculated in the loop.

Essentially, we've written some very simple business logic that we could compile and deploy as a component. We could if we wished save either of the two source files into a `.vb` or `.cs` file for the corresponding VB.NET and C# code, and compile and use the `Fibonacci` class in any .NET language. For example, we could use the VB.NET implementation from a C# application or vice versa, or we could use that component in an ASP.NET page.

The point is it's simply application logic, and is no different from the type of application logic we author when building ASP.NET pages or components. However, there are some special considerations that we need to be aware of when designing the application logic to be a Web Service, such as supported data types and behaviors specific to Web Services. We'll cover those later in the chapter.

Next, let's see what we need to do to enable this simple application logic as a Web Service using ASP.NET. The end goal is that we want another application to easily call and use our `Fibonacci` class. The difference is that our `Fibonacci` class needs to be able to communicate using SOAP. ASP.NET lets us do that very easily.

Fibonacci ASP.NET Web Service

We can use ASP.NET to expose application logic as a Web Service by simply adding attributes to our code. An attribute is declarative code that adds additional behavior to our code – such as the ability to support SOAP – without us having to add new programmatic code that changes the behavior of our application logic. It sounds complicated, but it's really not.

There are several attributes that a Web Service makes use of. The most notable attribute is the `WebMethod` attribute. The methods or properties that have this attribute are treated as Web Services. They can receive and process XML messages, as well as respond with XML messages. All of the internal serialization and de-serialization (that is, how the data being sent back-and-forth as XML is represented) is handled internally.

Let's look at our reworked Fibonacci code as an ASP.NET Web Service that shows the use of the `WebMethod` attribute. We'll look at a more complex Web Service later, but for now we want to examine what needs to be done to our simple `Fibonacci` class to enable its `GetSeqNumber` method as an ASP.NET Web Service; changes are highlighted.

VB.NET

```
<%@ WebService class="Fibonacci"%>

Imports System.Web.Services

Public Class Fibonacci

  <WebMethod> Public Function GetSeqNumber (fibIndex as Integer) as Integer

    If (fibIndex < 2) Then
      Return fibIndex
    End If

    Dim FibArray(2) as Integer
    Dim i as Integer

    FibArray(0) = 0
    FibArray(1) = 1

    For i = 2 To fibIndex
      FibArray(1) = FibArray(1) + FibArray(0)
      FibArray(0) = FibArray(1) - FibArray(0)
    Next

    Return FibArray(1)
  End Function
End Class
```

C#

```
<%@ WebService Language="C#" class="Fibonacci" %>

using System.Web.Services;

public class Fibonacci : WebService{

  [WebMethod]
  public int GetSeqNumber(int fibIndex){

    if (fibIndex < 2)
      return fibIndex;

    int[] FibArray = {0,1};

    for (int i = 1; i< fibIndex; i++){
      FibArray[1] = FibArray[0] + FibArray[1];
      FibArray[0] = FibArray[1] - FibArray[0];
    }

    return FibArray[1];
  }
}
```

What's important to notice here is that the application logic for both files remains identical. The difference is that the code now exists within an ASP.NET Web Service source file (Fibonacci_vb.asmx or Fibonacci_cs.asmx), and has some additional declarative changes, such as the use of the WebMethod attribute.

We'll discuss the details of these changes in a moment, but first let's test our Web Service.

Testing Our Web Service

At this point our Fibonacci ASP.NET Web Service code is a functional Web Service. To test the functionality we can use a browser and request the URL that is represented by the ASP.NET Web Service file.

> *Keep in mind that a Web Service is not intended to service requests for web browsers. The web browser functionality shown is only for testing, or design-time informational purposes. In the next chapter we'll look at an IE 5.5 behavior that lets us consume Web Services for rich browser clients.*

To run our `fibonacci_cs.asmx` or `fibonacci_vb.asmx` file, we must make it accessible through a web server, just as we would do for an ASP.NET page. When you save the code above to a file on your web server, and navigate to it with your browser, you should see something like this:

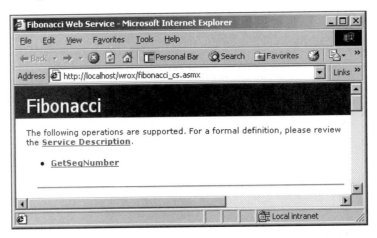

ASP.NET provides an ASP.NET Web Service Help file template. On receiving an HTTP `Get` request, the Web Service Help file template programmatically examines (the programmatic term is **reflection**) the code in the .asmx file, and generates the UI seen above. You'll notice this includes details such as the class and method name, and later we'll see how we can get even more details out of this file. This UI also provides some handy ways of testing the functionality of the Web Service.

The template page that performs this magic is called `DefaultWsdlHelpGenerator.aspx`, and can be found in the `\WinNt\Microsoft.NET\Framework\[version]` directory. Since `DefaultWsdlHelpGenerator.aspx` is just an ASP.NET page, we can easily customize it for our application. We can, in fact, have custom Help file templates files for each ASP.NET application.

In the screenshot above, you can see a Service Description link. This link provides us with the **Web Service Description Language** (**WSDL**), our XML contract for this Web Service. The WSDL for any ASP.NET Web Service is available as `[webservice name].asmx?WSDL`: so in this case that would be `fibonacci_cs.asmx?WSDL`. We'll come back to WSDL in the next chapter when we talk about using Web Services and how we use the WSDL to build our proxy.

The other link on the page names the `GetSeqNumber` method. This represents the method that we marked as a `WebMethod` in our Fibonacci class. If we select this link we are presented with information about the `GetSeqNumber` method exposed as a Web Service:

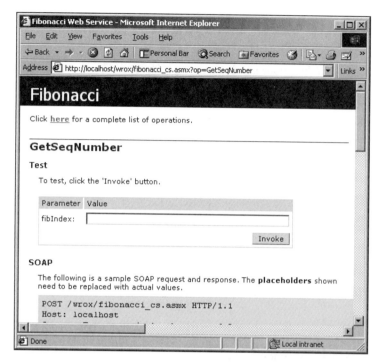

We can use the HTML forms that this provides to pass values to the GetSeqNumber method – just enter a number into the parameter textbox and press the **Invoke** button to view the results:

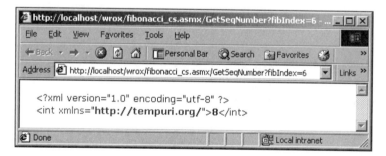

What's shown above is the XML returned from the GetSeqNumber method call. The element is named `<int/>`, and the return value is 8. Also note that the value of fibIndex=6 is passed as an argument in the query string. We could change this argument's value, and the Web Service would return the appropriate result.

This isn't a SOAP return, but another protocol type that ASP.NET Web Services support: HTTP-GET. The Web Service help page is generating a simple HTML form that makes a GET request to the Fibonacci_cs.asmx file. SOAP is not the return type, since by default this is using another ASP.NET Web Service protocol HTTP-GET. In the next chapter when we build proxies to use our Web Service, the default protocol will be SOAP.

Let's take a closer look at the changes we just made to our code.

Coding ASP.NET Web Services

The .asmx file format is very straightforward. We have two options for exposing application logic as an ASP.NET Web Service. Both options involve creating a file with the extension .asmx:

❑ **Inline** – Application logic exists within the .asmx file

❑ **Code-behind** – Application logic exists outside the .asmx file

Let's examine each of these options in more detail.

Inline

The first option, and the one we'll use for our examples, is to code the application logic within the .asmx file. This is similar to inline ASP.NET pages – we take the Fibonacci VB.NET or C# code and create the corresponding Fibonacci_vb.asmx and Fibonacci_cs.asmx – exactly as we did above.

For example, here's the C# Fibonacci example from earlier to demonstrate this:

```
<%@ WebService Language="C#" class="Fibonacci" %>

using System.Web.Services;

public class Fibonacci : WebService{

  [WebMethod]
  public int GetSeqNumber(int fibIndex){

    if (fibIndex < 2)
      return fibIndex;

    int[] FibArray = {0,1};

    for (int i = 1; i< fibIndex; i++){
      FibArray[1] = FibArray[0] + FibArray[1];
      FibArray[0] = FibArray[1] - FibArray[0];
    }

    return FibArray[1];
  }
}
```

Next, let's look at the code-behind option, which lets us store our source code in a separate assembly.

Code-behind

Just as we have a code-behind option for ASP.NET pages, we have a code-behind option for ASP.NET Web Services as well. Code-behind is the default behavior for ASP.NET Web Services created with Visual Studio.NET. Rather than the application logic existing within the .asmx file, the application logic lives in an external CLR assembly.

To reference an external assembly, the assembly must reside in the ASP.NET application's `bin` directory. The `bin` directory is a special directory used by the ASP.NET application, which assemblies can be deployed to and 'automatically' registered.

To use the code-behind option we simply craft a small ASP.NET Web Service `.asmx` file (here `Fibonacci_Codebehind.asmx`) with one simple line of implementation:

```
<%@ WebService Codebehind="Fibonacci.vb" Class="Fibonacci" %>
```

We then need an implementation of the `Fibonacci` class in a separate assembly, compiled and deployed in our ASP.NET application's `bin` directory, or an assembly named directly in our configuration file. Here's what the source would look like for our Fibonacci example (`Fibonacci.vb`):

```
Imports System
Imports System.Web
Imports System.Web.Services

Public Class Fibonacci
  <WebMethod()> Public Function GetSeqNumber (fibIndex As Integer) _
                                             As Integer

    If (fibIndex < 2) Then
      Return fibIndex
    End If

    Dim FibArray(2) As Integer
    Dim i As Integer

    FibArray(0) = 0
    FibArray(1) = 1

    For i = 2 To fibIndex
      FibArray(1) = FibArray(1) + FibArray(0)
      FibArray(0) = FibArray(1) - FibArray(0)
    Next

    Return FibArray(1)
  End Function
End Class
```

To compile this code we can simply use the command line compiler to compile the source into a .NET assembly:

```
vbc /t:library /r:System.Web.dll /r:System.Web.Services.dll Fibonacci.vb
```

The output of this is a single file: `Fibonacci.dll`, which we need to place in a directory named `bin` located below the root directory of the application.

We can easily deploy the assembly (`fibonacci.dll`) such that both ASP.NET pages and Web Services may use it, as it's simply a component with a `WebMethod` attribute. For example, say we develop a data access class that we compile into an assembly for an ASP.NET web application, and use this data access class in our ASP.NET pages. Later we decide that the functionality encapsulated within the data access class would be a great Web Service. By making some minor changes to the assembly's application logic, and by creating a one line ASP.NET Web Service `.asmx` file (as above), we could easily enable that application logic as a SOAP based end-point.

> As code-behind is the default behavior, the use of the `Codebehind` statement in `Fibonacci.asmx` is optional. Visual Studio.NET will use the `Codebehind` attribute, but we can just as easily remove it and still achieve the same functionality, as long as the assembly contains the class our ASP.NET Web Service references. It should also be noted, that there is no performance difference for using inline or code-behind.

All further discussion of Web Services will use the inline style, unless otherwise noted. The only tangible benefit for using code-behind over the inline style is:

- ❏ Code is compiled and the source cannot be viewed once deployed
- ❏ Since the code-behind option is an assembly, the assembly can also be used in ASP.NET pages

Both the inline and code-behind options share a common set of directives used to give ASP.NET special instructions when handling ASP.NET Web Service requests.

The WebService Directive

Like ASP.NET pages, ASP.NET Web Services support directives that instruct ASP.NET how to process the request. For example, when we converted our Fibonacci examples to ASP.NET Web Services, the first thing we added was a directive at the top of the `.asmx` file.

VB.NET

```
<%@ WebService Class="Fibonacci" %>
```

C#

```
<%@ WebService Language="C#" Class="Fibonacci" %>
```

The `WebService` directive is a required addition for all ASP.NET Web Services. Let's first look at the directive syntax, then we'll look at the attributes we'll use most often.

Syntax

The directive syntax is identical to ASP.NET pages. It is declared within `<%@ %>` tags, contains a single directive, and may contain multiple attributes that apply to that directive:

```
<%@ DirectiveName Attribute="Value" %>
```

or:

```
<%@ WebService Attribute="Value" Attribute="Value"%>
```

An ASP.NET Web Service may contain multiple classes. However only one of the classes can contain methods marked with `WebMethod` attributes. This relationship is enforced with a `WebService` directive attribute named `Class`.

Class

The `Class` attribute is special, since it is required and forces us to always declare the `WebService` directive within a `.asmx` file.

Fortunately, it's by no means complicated. The `Class` simply names the .NET class, whether inline or in a separate assembly (code-behind), that contains methods or properties exposed as web callable:

```
<%@ WebService Class="[Namespace.Class | Class]" %>
```

Class Example

The `Fibonacci` class must be named in the `Class` attribute since the `Fibonacci` class contains the logic to be exposed as web callable:

```
<%@ WebService Class="Fibonacci" %>
```

If the `Fibonacci` class existed within a namespace, we would need to further qualify it:

```
<%@ WebService Language="C#" Class="MyMath.Fibonacci" %>
namespace MyMath{
   public class Fibonacci{
      // implementation
   }
}
```

In addition to the class attribute, we may also use the language attribute if we wish to use a language other than the ASP.NET default language: VB.

Language

The `Language` attribute is used to override the default language specified in the configuration file. By default the language setting is set to VB (Visual Basic.NET), but we can easily override this setting with the `Language` attribute.

Of course Microsoft's .NET platform supports any language that provides a .NET compiler – for example, .NET compilers exists for COBOL and Perl. This feature of .NET allows us to build Web Services, or for that matter, any .NET solution, in a multitude of languages. To use these other languages the appropriate compiler must be named in the ASP.NET configuration system.

If we wish to use C# as the language for our Fibonacci implementation, we add the `Language` directive:

```
<%@ WebService Language="C#" Class="Fibonacci"%>
```

That's all the basic knowledge you need for coding ASP>NET Web Services. Next, let's look at the changes required to our application logic.

Application Code

Application code for an ASP.NET Web Service may exist inline or in an assembly named through the code-behind support in Web Services. However, the requirements for both resources remain the same:

❑ Include a reference to the `System.Web.Services` namespace

❑ Use attributes found within the `System.Web.Services` namespace to identify methods and properties as web callable

❑ Optionally inherit from the `WebService` base class

Let's look at these three important areas in more detail, starting with the `System.Web.Services` namespace.

The System.Web.Services Namespace

The `System.Web.Services` namespace contains classes that ASP.NET relies upon to enable ASP.NET Web Services. The implementation of these classes can be found in the assembly `System.Web.Services.dll` in the `\WinNt\Microsoft.NET\Framework\[version]\` directory.

We declare the use of this namespace in our ASP.NET Web Service file differently depending upon the language we are coding our logic with.

VB.NET

```
Imports System.Web.Services
```

C#

```
using System.Web.Services;
```

Importing the `System.Web.Services` namespace is a requirement, and it is this namespace that gives us access to the `WebMethod` attribute.

The WebMethod Attribute

The `WebMethod` attribute is the declarative code that we use to enable our application logic to be 'web callable'. By that we mean we're able to support serialization and de-serialization of XML, mapping of XML values to correct types, and transporting of requests and responses – the 'infrastructure' that enables Web Services.

Again, the syntax of the attribute declaration varies from language to language.

VB.NET

```
<WebMethod> Public Function GetSeqNumber (fibIndex as Integer) as Integer
```

C#

```
[WebMethod]
public int GetSeqNumber(int fibIndex)
```

As you can clearly see, the syntax for VB.NET and C# is quite different. For VB.NET we declare the attribute inline with the function or property declaration, and for C# we declare the attribute on the line above the method or property declaration.

A WebMethod Example

The following is an example of using `WebMethod` in VB.NET (`WebMethod1.asmx`). This just returns the sum of two integers provided by the user:

```
<%@ WebService class="WebMethod1" %>

Imports System.Web.Services

Public Class WebMethod1
  <WebMethod> Public Function Add(a As Integer, b As Integer) As Integer
    Return a + b
  End Function
End Class
```

Once the `WebMethod` attribute is added, the `Add` method is web callable, and when requested through the browser it is available as one of the selectable options:

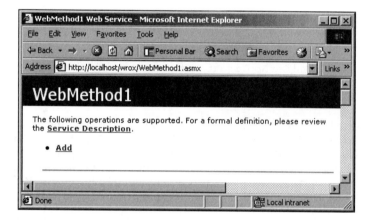

The last change we can make to our application code is to optionally inherit from the `WebService` base class, another resource available after importing the `System.Web.Services` namespace.

WebService Base Class

An ASP.NET Web Service is part of the ASP.NET application it resides in. Just as we have application-specific configuration, session, and data for ASP.NET pages, we have the same capabilities for ASP.NET Web Services.

We have a couple of choices for how we gain access to the ASP.NET intrinsic objects, such as `Application` or `Session`. The easiest way to enable access to ASP.NET intrinsics within a Web Service is to inherit from the `WebService` base class.

WebService Base Class Example

Below we use the VB.NET `Inherits` keyword to inherit from the `WebService` base class. This base class gives us access to an `Application` property, just as we would expect to find on an ASP.NET page:

```
<%@ Webservice class="WebServiceBaseClass" %>

Imports System.Web.Services

Public class WebServiceBaseClass
   Inherits WebService

  <WebMethod> Public Sub SetApplicationState(state As String)
    Application("state") = state
  End Sub

  <WebMethod> Public Function GetApplicationState() As String
     Return Application("state").ToString()
  End Function
End Class
```

The above code sample (`WebServiceBaseClass1.asmx`) exposes two web-callable methods, `SetApplicationState` and `GetApplicationState`. `SetApplicationState` accepts a string value and sets an application key/value pair to the value passed in. `GetApplicationState` simply retrieves the value of the data set in `SetApplicationState`.

It's important to note here that an ASP.NET page has access to the same application state memory that ASP.NET Web Services do, and the same is true with `Cache` and `Session` too. Therefore items added to application state memory, or the cache, can be shared between both page and Web Services. This allows for powerful reuse – for example, an e-commerce site can load the store catalog into `Application` state memory from the database one time, and then both the ASP.NET Pages and Web Services can share that data.

The `WebService` base class adds five public (not web-callable) properties, whose use we are already familiar with from ASP.NET pages:

❑   `Application` – Application state memory

❑   `Context` – Instance class passed throughout the life of the request

❑   `Session` –Session state memory

❑   `Server` – Server intrinsic, provides us with access to methods such as `CreateObject`

❑   `User` – Identity of the user making the request (security feature)

To re-iterate, inheriting from the `WebService` base class is optional. Classes **do not need to** inherit from the `WebService` base class to be a functional Web Service – it is only for convenience. In fact, since an ASP.NET Web Service is simply another ASP.NET resource, the `HttpContext`, which contains the raw information for the request and response, is available by default.

Thus classes that do not inherit from the `WebService` base class can still implement similar functionality – for example, accessing the `Application` intrinsic.

Example Without Inheriting the WebService Base Class

Let's take, for example, the same code as we had above, but without the inheritance of the `WebService` base class:

```
<%@ Webservice class="WebServiceBaseClass" %>

Imports System.Web
Imports System.Web.Services

Public class WebServiceBaseClass

  <WebMethod()> Public Sub SetApplicationState(state As String)
    Dim Application As HttpApplicationState

    Application = HttpContext.Current.Application

    Application("state") = state
  End Sub

  <WebMethod()> Public Function GetApplicationState() As String
    Dim Application As HttpApplicationState

    Application = HttpContext.Current.Application

    Return Application("state").ToString()
  End Function
End Class
```

In the above example (`WebServiceBaseClass2.asmx`), we're using the Web Service's instance of the `HttpContext` to retrieve the `Application` intrinsic. This forces us to import the `System.Web` namespace, since `HttpContext` is defined in the `System.Web` namespace. We can then use the `HttpContext` instance to access the `Application` intrinsic, which we set to a local variable of type `HttpApplicationState` named `Application`. Our code then uses the `Application` intrinsic in an identical manner to the code that inherited from the `WebService` base class.

Since a class can only inherit from a single base class, the only advantage of not using the `WebService` base class is the case when we wish to inherit from a different class.

As stated earlier, having access to the ASP.NET intrinsic objects means that ASP.NET pages and Web Services can share common data and settings. For example, a `DataSet` that is loaded when the application begins, and is then placed into `Application` state memory, can be shared between both pages and Web Services – or, for that matter, any ASP.NET related resource.

We now have all the basic knowledge necessary for building ASP.NET Web Services. At this point we could skip directly to the next chapter and discuss consuming ASP.NET Web Services. However, there are of course more options for building ASP.NET Web Services. For example the `WebMethod` attribute has configurable properties, and it's not the only available attribute.

Later in this chapter, we're going to focus on some of the more advanced options. However, first we need to talk a little about the protocols and data types supported by Web Services.

Protocols and Data Types

Protocols define how communication takes place. For example, in diplomatic exchange certain protocols must be followed to ensure that the communication that takes place is accurate. Just as diplomatic exchanges between nation states must use a protocol to exchange information correctly, technologies also use protocols so various systems can agree upon how to exchange information.

Protocol Support

ASP.NET supports three default protocols – HTTP-GET, HTTP-POST, and SOAP – but it can be extended to support others.

The first two protocols, HTTP-GET and HTTP-POST, are implemented primarily as helper protocols, and for backwards compatibility. We will use these protocols through ASP.NET Web Services to test these Web Services, and to provide a mechanism for existing ASP applications to build and immediately use ASP.NET technologies.

The backwards compatibility is for ASP applications that accepted parameters either through FORM GET or POST mechanisms, and returned an XML document. ASP.NET supports this exact same behavior, but in a more robust manner. If you're used to authoring ASP applications that emit XML this should be a simple transition. However, for application-to-application communication, SOAP is the default.

The Simple Object Access Protocol (SOAP) is the default protocol that we need to be most familiar with. SOAP combines XML and HTTP to provide a simple but powerful mechanism, which allows developers to build applications that can communicate through strongly typed XML documents.

Let's examine each of these protocols in more detail.

HTTP-GET

The HTTP-GET protocol implementation is the one that we see the most of when we're building an ASP.NET Web Service. That's because HTTP-GET is the protocol used in the page generated by DefaultWsdlHelpGenerator.aspx.

For example, when we built the Fibonacci Web Service, viewed it through the browser, and called the method, the result we received was a simple XML document:

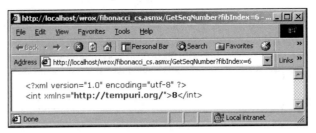

However, this document is nothing to do with SOAP. Instead, parameters are passed on the query string in the form GetSeqNumber?fibIndex=6. We can also modify the query string directly, and get different results.

Our Web Service help page only supports HTTP-GET (by default) and HTTP-POST. The reason for this is that a simple HTML form POST/GET mechanism cannot support the POST format used by SOAP. SOAP requires the body of the POST to be an XML SOAP document. However, HTML form POSTs will attempt to send a name/value pair, which cannot be used to generate a valid XML document in the POST body.

HTTP-POST

The output from HTTP-POST is similar to HTTP-GET, the only difference being how HTTP-POST is input – that is, how the data is sent to the endpoint. Rather than passing data in the query string, the data is posted as name/value pairs within the body of the HTTP request.

For example, we could telnet into the web server and issue the following command:

```
POST /code/4885/WebServices/Expose/Fibonacci/Fibonacci_cs.asmx HTTP/1.1
Connection: Keep-Alive
Content-Length: 14

IndexIntoFib=6
```

We'd expect the result to be an XML document identical to the one we got through the HTTP-GET request in the previous section.

If we want to use HTTP-POST in our Web Service description Help page, and have it provide us with an HTML form similar to that created for HTTP-GET, we can modify `DefaultWsdlHelpPage.aspx`, setting the flag `showPost` to `true`.

SOAP

The Simple Object Access Protocol is a simple, lightweight XML protocol for exchanging structured and typed information on the Web. SOAP 1.1 was submitted to the World Wide Web Consortium and became a W3C note on 8 May 2000.

> *This chapter is not going to cover SOAP in great detail. Firstly because there are other great resources for learning about SOAP, such as the specification, and secondly because it's a protocol and this chapter is about building solutions. If you want more details on SOAP, you'll find some useful resources listed at the end of the chapter.*
>
> *At the time of writing, SOAP is not yet a standard. It is currently a document that has been submitted to the W3C for the express purpose of going through the standardization process.*

The W3C has officially created the XML Protocol Activity using SOAP 1.1. The XML Protocol Group has four deliverables:

- ❑ Protocol envelope
- ❑ Mechanism for serializing abstract data models
- ❑ Convention for use with RPC
- ❑ Binding to HTTP

Although SOAP is not yet an official standard, several companies have developed solutions using the SOAP 1.1 specification, including Microsoft .NET, Microsoft Soap Toolkit v2, and the Apache Soap Toolkit from IBM.

The Microsoft Soap Toolkit v1 was intended to be an SDK. Version 2 is a supported solution, but with the availability of .NET you would be wise to use ASP.NET.

Implementation Details

A SOAP protocol message contains four parts:

❑ An envelope

❑ Encoding rules

❑ RPC representation

❑ Protocol bindings

The implementation of SOAP in ASP.NET uses HTTP as a transport, and thus is two-way – we send a message and we get a response. This is a design of HTTP and not of SOAP.

The SOAP envelope is the basic unit of exchange between the listener and sender of the SOAP message. Envelopes can be nested, in which case the outer envelope is considered active to the receiving SOAP end-point.

Headers are one of the extensibility mechanisms of SOAP, and are used to pass additional information about the envelope, or data that pertains to the particular protocol exchange. A good example of SOAP headers is for the use of authentication – for example, rather than passing in an identification token as part of the envelope, which would assume the token was part of a method in ASP.NET, the token can be passed as part of the header.

We'll see more about SOAP later in this chapter, and in Chapter 20 we'll look at using the header to pass authentication information, which we can then use verify credentials and authorize actions.

Now that we've looked at the supported protocols for Web Services, let's look at the supported data types.

Data Types

ASP.NET Web Services support all the primitive types supported in the Common Language Runtime – including String, Integer, Long, and so on. (For a full listing of these types refer to the product documentation.) In addition to the simple primitive types, arrays of primitives are also supported.

More interesting, however, is the support for user-defined classes and structs. Essentially anything that can be represented by an XSD schema can be a parameter or return type of an ASP.NET Web Service.

Custom Types

Let's say, for example, that we want to build an ASP.NET Web Service that returns a user-defined class named CustomerRecord. This returns some string and integer values, as well as an array of another user-defined class named Order:

```
Public Class CustomerRecord
    Public Customer As String
    Public Address1 As String
    Public Address2 As String
    Public Phone As String
    Public Email As String
    Public CustomerOrder(2) As Order
End Class
```

```
Public Class Order
  Public OrderNumber As Integer
  Public Name As String
  Public Cost As String
  Public ShipDate As String
End Class
```

We could write the following WebMethod that returned an instance of CustomerRecord:

```
Public Class OrderDetails
  <WebMethod()> Public Function RequestOrderDetails() As CustomerRecord
    Dim customerRecord As New CustomerRecord

    ' Set data...
    customerRecord.Customer = "JohnDoe"
    customerRecord.Address1 = "22913 Crestpark Dr"
    customerRecord.Address2 = "Houston, Tx 79043"
    customerRecord.Phone = "281-475-0938"
    customerRecord.Email = "john@customer.com"

    customerRecord.CustomerOrder(0) = New Order()
    customerRecord.CustomerOrder(0).OrderNumber = 12
    customerRecord.CustomerOrder(0).Name = "Product A"
    customerRecord.CustomerOrder(0).Cost = "$23.45"
    customerRecord.CustomerOrder(0).ShipDate = "8/6/01"

    customerRecord.CustomerOrder(1) = New Order()
    customerRecord.CustomerOrder(1).OrderNumber = 15
    customerRecord.CustomerOrder(1).Name = "Product C"
    customerRecord.CustomerOrder(1).Cost = "$13.41"
    customerRecord.CustomerOrder(1).ShipDate = "7/1/01"

    Return customerRecord
  End Function
End Class
```

As long as the user-defined class represents its data using primitive types, and those types are public, the data will be sent correctly to the caller. If, however, the class used Get/Set properties and modified private variables within the class, the data would not be sent correctly – as XML is not used to describe the binary representation of the object in memory.

We'll talk more about user-defined classes later in the chapter when we discuss shaping the XML document.

Now that we're more familiar with the data types and the general ASP.NET Web Service .asmx file, let's take a deep look at two of the attributes we'll use most often when building ASP.NET Web Services.

WebMethod and WebService Attributes

Although the WebMethod attribute will be the attribute we use most often when authoring ASP.NET Web Services, there are other attributes at our disposal for additional functionality. As well as simply marking a method or property with an attribute, we can set some attribute properties that affect the behavior of attributes, and which in turn affect the target of the attribute. We'll use the following syntax to set attribute properties.

VB.NET

```
    ... <AttributeName(PropertyName:="Value")> ...
```

Note the colon in `PropertyName:="Value"`; *this syntax is only required for VB.NET.*

C#

```
    [AttributeName(PropertyName="Value")]
```

We won't be discussing all the available attributes here – in this section we'll be concentrating on the `WebMethod` and `WebService` attributes.

If you want to know more about available attributes, try the .NET Framework SDK Documentation.

Let's take a detailed look at the `WebMethod` attribute.

WebMethod

As previously mentioned, the `WebMethod` attribute is used to mark either a method or property as web callable – that's web callable in the sense that the method is able to communicate using one of the supported ASP.NET Web Service protocols for sending and receiving data. These protocols include HTTP-GET, HTTP-POST, and SOAP. We'll examine the protocols in detail later in the chapter.

The `WebMethod` attribute is represented by the `WebMethodAttribute` class, which is found in the `System.Web.Services` namespace in the `System.Web.Services.dll` assembly.

There are six properties on the `WebMethod` attribute that we can manipulate:

- ❏ `Description`
- ❏ `EnableSession`
- ❏ `MessageName`
- ❏ `TransactionOption`
- ❏ `CacheDuration`
- ❏ `BufferResponse`

We'll examine each of these in turn.

Commenting the Web Method

The `Description` property is used to provide a brief description of the functionality of the web-callable method or property.

VB.NET

```
...<WebMethod(Description:="[string]")>...
```

C#

```
[WebMethod(Description="[string]")]
```

The value of Description is added to the Web Service Description Language (WSDL) – more on WSDL in the next chapter. It is also added to the Web Service Help page, which is displayed when the .asmx page is requested through the browser.

Example Use of Description

If we add a Description property to our Fibonacci example, and then request this through the browser, we'll see the description show up under the link for the web-callable method:

```
<%@ WebService Language="C#" class="Fibonacci" %>

using System.Web.Services;

public class Fibonacci : WebService{

  [WebMethod(Description="Returns value of index into Fibonacci series")]

   public int GetSeqNumber(int fibIndex){

     if (fibIndex < 2)
       return fibIndex;

     int[] FibArray = {0,1};

     for (int i = 1; i< fibIndex; i++){
       FibArray[1] = FibArray[0] + FibArray[1];
       FibArray[0] = FibArray[1] - FibArray[0];
     }

     return FibArray[1];
   }
}
```

When displayed in a browser, the result is:

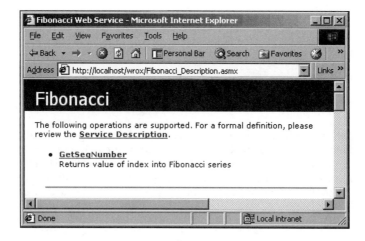

Above we see the output through the browser in the Web Service Help page, and if we view the Service Description (WSDL) we'll see it there as well:

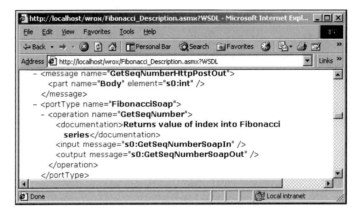

The entries in the Description property may contain HTML formatting. This formatting is then used to display a description in the Help page. However, keep in mind that the description text is entered into the WSDL. Other applications may consume the WSDL – such as a Windows Forms application – and they might not understand the HTML tags found in the description.

Enabling Session State

Classes that inherit from the WebService base class, or that use the HttpContext, can take advantage of session state to maintain state between calls.

Session state, however, is additional overhead, and is bound to the HTTP protocol since it uses HTTP cookies. SOAP is theoretically transport independent, but when we use HTTP cookies we are relying on the transport protocol for application functionality. If we moved the SOAP message to SMTP we wouldn't have the HTTP cookies functionality available.

By default, session state is disabled. To enable session state support we can use one of the WebMethod properties, EnableSession.

VB.NET

```
...<WebMethod(EnableSession:="[true/false]")>...
```

C#

```
[WebMethod(EnableSession="[true/false]")]
```

To enable session state, we simply set the value to true, since it is set to false by default.

One caveat of session state is that the session state is only valid as long as the caller presents the same session ID. In Chapter 20, when we build proxies to use against our Web Services, session state is available only for the duration of the existence of the proxy instance. The HTTP cookie is never stored on disk, and a new session is created for each new proxy instance, since the proxy, by default, isn't persisting the session cookie containing the ID. In Chapter 20 we'll look at an example of how to persist and reuse the session cookie.

Aliasing Web Method Names

The `MessageName` property is used to alias method or property names. The most common use of the `MessageName` property is to uniquely identify polymorphic methods within a class that we wish to mark as web callable.

VB.NET

```
...<WebMethod(MessageName:="[string]")>...
```

C#

```
[WebMethod(MessageName="[string]")]
```

Example Use of MessageName

Here's a snippet of C# code that has two `Add` methods that differ only by method signature:

```
...
[WebMethod]
public int Add(int a, int b){
  return a+b;
}

[WebMethod]
public int Add(int a, int b, int c){
  return a+b+c;
}
...
```

This generates an exception when requested through the browser.

Both `Int32 Add(Int32, Int32, Int32)` and `Int32 Add(Int32, Int32)` use the message name `Add`. We can use the `MessageName` property of the `WebMethod` custom attribute to specify unique message names for the methods.

The problem is that ASP.NET cannot discern the difference between the two methods, and requires that we use the `MessageName` property to differentiate between the method names:

```
...
[WebMethod]
public int Add(int a, int b){
  return a+b;
}

[WebMethod(MessageName="Add2")]
public int Add(int a, int b, int c){
  return a+b+c;
}
...
```

Additionally, the WSDL that is generated must also be able to uniquely identify the element name when it is used to construct a message. When we use the `MessageName` property, this is also reflected in our WSDL:

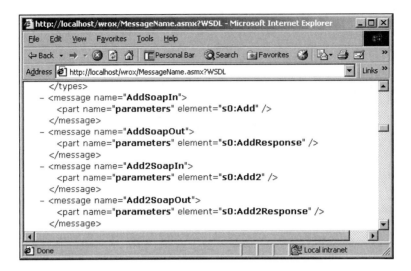

The MessageName property simply aliases our method name.

Building Transacted Web Services

ASP.NET Web Services support transactions, but only transactions that the Web Service originates. In other words, a transaction cannot be started by another application and then flow into a Web Service.

VB.NET

```
...<WebMethod(TransactionOption:="[TransactionOption]")>...
```

C#

```
[WebMethod(TransactionOption="[TransactionOption]")]
```

Example Use of TransactionOption Property

For example, say we have a banking transaction, where the client makes a Web Service remote call to a method named DebitAccount. The transaction started by the client cannot be stretched through the Web Service remote call:

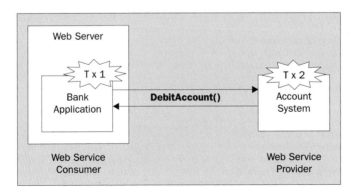

In the above diagram a Bank Application begins a transaction (Tx1). It then calls a Web Service, which begins another transaction (Tx2). The transaction (Tx1) begun by the Bank Application does not flow through the Web Service.

If the Web Service transaction (Tx2) succeeds, it will allow the application's transaction (Tx1) to continue. However, the failure of the DebitAccount call will fail the application's transaction.

The DebitAccout call that is actually executed on the server providing the Web Service can also choose to participate in a transaction, but it is a new transaction context, not the transaction context started by the calling application.

The options for using transacted web methods are:

❑   Disabled – We cannot control automatic transactions on the object.

❑   NotSupported – The object does not run within the scope of a transaction, irrespective of whether a transaction already exists or not.

❑   Supported – If a transaction exists, the object runs in the context of that transaction. If there is no existing transaction, the object runs without one.

❑   Required – The object requires a transaction in order to execute. It will either use an existing transaction, or create a new one if none exists.

❑   RequiresNew – The object requires a new transaction, so a new transaction is created for each request.

The default is Required.

Calling SetComplete or SetAbort in code is no longer necessary. Simply raising an exception is considered as a SetAbort, and successful completion of the call is considered a SetComplete().

If you're unfamiliar with the calls SetAbort and SetComplete these methods are used to indicate to MTS or COM+ whether the transaction completed or failed.

Caching Web Services

Like ASP.NET pages, ASP.NET Web Services support output caching. Output caching allows for the result of a particular resource to be saved to a cache rather than executed on each request. Caching is a performance win, since high traffic resources whose data change infrequently can take advantage of caching for better scalability.

The use of caching for Web Services is configured on a method-by-method basis through the use of the WebMethod attribute's CacheDuration property.

VB.NET

```
...<WebMethod(CacheDuration:=[int])>...
```

C#

```
[WebMethod(CacheDuration=[int])]
```

Example Use of Caching

The following is a VB.NET example use of CacheDuration (WebMethodCacheDuration_vb.asmx):

```
<%@ WebService class="CacheDurationExample" %>

Imports System
Imports System.Web.Services

Public Class CacheDurationExample

  <WebMethod(CacheDuration:=30)> Public Function TimeLastCached As String
    Return DateTime.Now.ToString("r")
  End Function

End Class
```

This simple sample returns the value of the current time on its first execution. This result is then cached for 30 seconds, and the same result is returned until the cached entry has expired (30 seconds after the initial call), at which time the code will execute again.

Although this simple example highlights that caching is working, what about a more complex example where the WebMethod has parameters? We obviously don't want to serve the same response for all requests: rather we want to vary the response based on the request.

For example, if the result our Web Service returned from a SQL Server database depended on one of the parameters of the WebMethod, we still might want to cache the result (for the performance win) but we would want different variations of that cached result based on the parameters. This is supported by default.

Let's take a look at a code sample to better illustrate this (WebMethodCacheData_vb.asmx).

```
<%@ WebService class="DataExample" %>

Imports System.Web.Services
Imports System.Data
Imports System.Data.SqlClient

Public Class DataExample : Inherits WebService
  <WebMethod(CacheDuration:=30)> Public Function _
                  GetDataSet(City As String) As DataSet
    If (Application("ProductData" + City) Is Nothing) Then
      Application("ProductData" + City) = LoadDataSet(City)
    End If

    Return CType(Application("ProductData" + City), DataSet)
  End Function

  Private Function LoadDataSet(City As String) As DataSet
    Dim dsn As String
    Dim sql As String

    dsn = "server=localhost;uid=sa;pwd=;database=pubs"
    sql = "SELECT * FROM Authors WHERE City = '" + City + "'"
```

```
      Dim myConnection As New SqlConnection(dsn)
      Dim myCommand As New SqlDataAdapter(sql, myConnection)

      Dim products As New DataSet

      myCommand.Fill(products, "products")

      Return products
   End Function
End Class
```

You might have to alter the `server` *name in the code above to reflect your own database.*

In the example code above, a `WebMethod` named `GetDataSet` accepts a single parameter: `City`. The result from the request will be output cached – the ASP.NET Web Service is executed once and served statically on subsequent requests for 30 seconds – and the cache will vary based on the different value for `City`. If we have a request where the value of `City` is `Dallas`, the Web Service will execute once and the result will be cached. If there is another request for `City=Dallas` within the allotted time period of 30 seconds, it will be served from the cache – the ASP.NET Web Service does not need to execute and query the database.

This can be a serious performance enhancement, but should be used wisely – only items that vary by a few parameters are good candidates for Web Services output caching. For example, an `Add()` `WebMethod` would not be a good candidate.

Buffering the Server Response

Buffering allows the server to buffer the output from the response, and transmit it only once the response is completely buffered. For long running methods this might not be optimal – we'll probably want to send the response as we receive it rather than waiting for the complete response.

By default ASP.NET Web Services buffer the response before sending it as this is usually most optimal for the server, but the `BufferResponse` property allows us to configure ASP.NET Web Services to not buffer the response. By default this property is set to `true`.

VB.NET

```
...<WebMethod(BufferResponse:="[true|false]")>...
```

C#

```
[WebMethod(BufferResponse="[true|false]")]
```

In summary, the `WebMethod` attribute is used for exposing methods or properties as web callable, as well as to enable special functionality on methods and properties through the use of the properties of the `WebMethod` attribute.

The other attribute we're going to look at, the `WebService` attribute, gives us additional control over the class containing the web-callable methods rather than the individual methods.

WebService

The WebService attribute is used to configure properties for the class – rather than the method or property – named in the WebService directive. These properties apply both to the Web Service Help page, as well as the WSDL. It **does not**, however, mark the methods within the class as web callable.

There are three properties of the WebService attribute that we can manipulate:

❑ Description

❑ Namespace

❑ Name

Commenting the Web Service

The Description property is used to provide a brief description of the functionality of the class containing web-callable methods and/or properties. It is similar to the WebMethod's Description property, but it's a description for the entire class, not individual methods and properties.

VB.NET

```
<WebService (Description:="[string]")> Public Class [Class Name]
```

C#

```
[WebService(Description="[string]")]
public class [Class Name]
```

Example Use of Description

The value from the Description is added to the WSDL, and is also added to the output generated when the ASP.NET Web Service is requested through the browser.

For example, we can add a Description property to our Fibonacci example (WebServiceDescription_cs.asmx):

```
<%@ WebService Language="C#" class="Fibonacci" %>

using System.Web.Services;

[WebService (Description=
            "This class contains methods for working with Fib series")]
public class Fibonacci : WebService{

  [WebMethod]
  public int GetSeqNumber(int fibIndex){

    if (fibIndex < 2)
      return fibIndex;

    int[] FibArray = {0,1};
    for (int i = 1; i< fibIndex; i++){
      FibArray[1] = FibArray[0] + FibArray[1];
      FibArray[0] = FibArray[1] - FibArray[0];
    }

    return FibArray[1];
  }
}
```

We would see the output both in the browser:

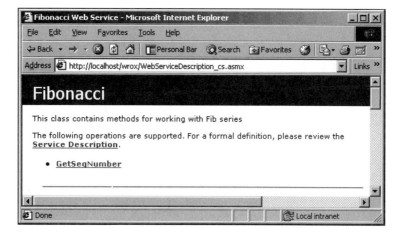

as well as in the WSDL:

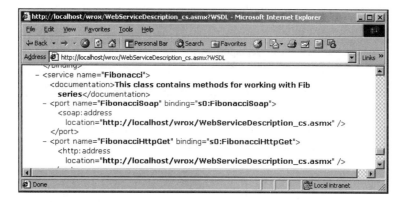

Controlling the Namespace

XML uses namespaces to uniquely identify sections of an XML document. Multiple documents can share markup vocabularies for describing particular regions of information. For example, if you have two XML documents that both contain an <Add> element, how does software differentiate between the two elements in the composite document?

Organizations may qualify their markup vocabulary with a universal name that is unique to their markup vocabulary through the use of XML namespaces.

The default namespace that ASP.NET assigns to ASP.NET Web Services is http://tempuri.org. We'll talk more about tempuri.org in the WSDL section in the next chapter. For now, all we need to know is that we can use the Namespace property of the WebService attribute to change the namespace value to a value we choose.

VB.NET

```
<WebService(Namespace:="[string]")> Public Class [Class Name]
```

C#

```
[WebServiceNamespace="[string]")]
public class [Class Name]
```

Example Use of Namespace

If we viewed the WSDL from either our VB or C# Fibonacci Web Service, we would see
http://tempuri.org/ used for the value of the namespace:

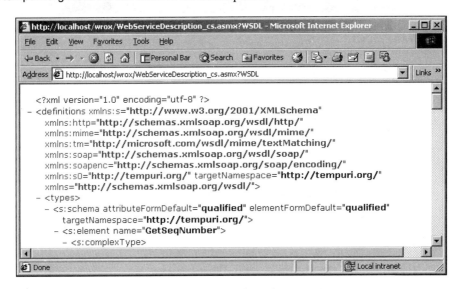

If we wanted to change the namespace to http://rhoward/Fibonacci/, we would make the
following change to our code (WebServiceNamespace_cs.asmx):

```
<%@ WebService Language="C#" class="Fibonacci" %>

using System.Web.Services;

[WebService(Namespace="http://rhoward/Fibonacci/")]
public class Fibonacci : WebService{

  [WebMethod]
  public int GetSeqNumber(int fibIndex){

    if (fibIndex < 2)
      return fibIndex;
    int[] FibArray = {0,1};

    for (int i = 1; i< fibIndex; i++){
      FibArray[1] = FibArray[0] + FibArray[1];
      FibArray[0] = FibArray[1] - FibArray[0];
    }

    return FibArray[1];
  }
}
```

Now our WSDL appears as follows:

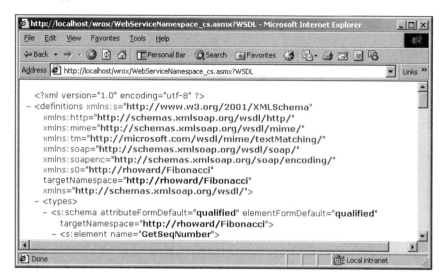

This affects what our SOAP looks like:

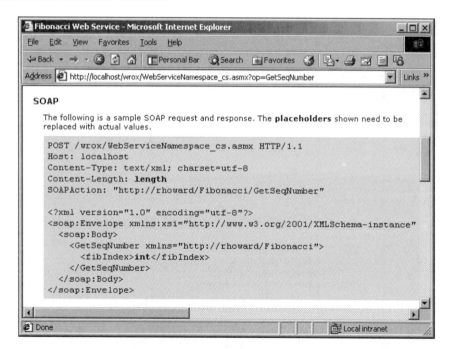

Changing the Name of the Web Service

When the WSDL is generated for an ASP.NET Web Service, the name of the class is used for the service name value within the WSDL. When a proxy uses the WSDL and builds a proxy class, the name of the class generated corresponds to the name value of service. The Name property of the WebService attribute allows us to override the default value.

VB.NET

```
<WebService(Name:="[string]")> Public Class [Class Name]
```

C#

```
[WebService(Name="[string]")]
```

Example Use of Name

For example, if we view the WSDL of our Fibonacci class we would see the following:

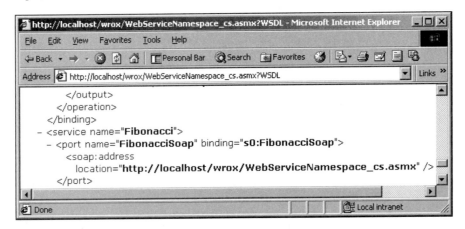

If we were to set the Name value to WebServiceExample in the WebService attribute (as in WebServiceName.asmx):

```
[WebService(Name="WebServiceExample")]
```

we would see the following change in our WSDL:

All instances of Fibonacci in the WSDL will then be replaced with WebServiceExample.

This property becomes more useful once we wish to control the name of the class that proxies generate, as tools that consume the WSDL to build the proxy will now build a `WebServiceExample` class as the proxy instead of building a class with the name `Fibonacci`.

Now that we've looked at the two attributes we will use most often to build ASP.NET Web Services, we're ready to discuss designing Web Services, and look at some more advanced areas.

Designing ASP.NET Web Services

Web Services provide access to application logic, and application logic can take many forms, from stored procedures to components. Although ASP.NET Web Services take the form of classes with implementations, this should not imply that normalized object-oriented design principles should always be adhered to. Nor should we ever consider a Web Service a class, method, or property. Rather a Web Service is an endpoint that we send data to and receive data from.

Let's start the discussion of building ASP.NET Web Services by discussing API design, namely "chunky versus chatty" patterns.

Chunky Versus Chatty

Web Services rely on XML and HTTP to encode and transmit serialized application data. The combination of these two technologies provides a powerful means for cross-platform distributed applications, and the ability to push application requests through proxies. However, there are some downsides to this technology as well. It's an extremely verbose way of describing what should be a simple exchange of data between two applications, and it's stateless.

The design recommendation is that you should try to reduce the number of network calls to the Web Service wherever possible.

Stateless Versus Stateful

HTTP is a stateless protocol, and this doesn't change for ASP.NET Web Services that use HTTP to transport SOAP messages. ASP.NET provides workarounds for this stateless barrier, but the workarounds rely upon the use of a session token which can either be stored in an HTTP cookie, or embedded within the URL (for more details on either of these options, see Chapter 13).

You should definitely take into account the stateless nature of HTTP when building your web applications. If you need to solve that stateless problem with a solution such as `Session` state, you should consider the implications to the Web Service – using HTTP cookies builds reliance upon the protocol rather than the SOAP message.

The discussion of stateless versus stateful applies most to discussions of design – how we expose our application logic and how end-users interact with that logic. A great example here is the differences between using methods or properties in our classes.

Methods or Properties

ASP.NET Web Services use a class with methods marked with the `WebMethod` attribute to enable us to send and receive SOAP messages. Although we've shown how to use the `WebMethod` attribute applied to methods within the class, this attribute can also be applied to properties within the class:

```
<%@ WebService Class="MethodsAndProperties" %>

Imports System.Web.Services

Public Class MethodsAndProperties
  Private Dim _name As String

  Public Property YourName() As String
    <WebMethod()> Get
      Return _name
    End Get

    <WebMethod()> Set
      _name = value
    End Set
  End Property
End Class
```

In the above code example (`StatelessMethodsAndProperties_vb.asmx`) we've applied the `WebMethod` attribute to the `Get` and `Set` of the `YourName` property.

It's probably best not to mark properties with the `WebMethod` attribute. Although functionally the behavior can be made to work, it requires that the class instance hold state. For example, running the code example above (using our handy Web Service Description Help page) we can call `set_YourName` and pass it Rob. If we then call `get_YourName` we get no result. Since ASP.NET Web Services are stateless, the instance of our `MethodsAndProperties` class is created and destroyed for each request.

We can fix this by enabling session state (`StatefulMethodsAndProperties_vb.asmx`):

```
<%@ WebService Class="MethodsAndProperties" %>

Imports System.Web.Services

Public Class MethodsAndProperties
  Private Dim _name As String

  Public Property YourName() As String
    <WebMethod(EnableSession:=true)> Get
      Return _name
    End Get

    <WebMethod(EnableSession:=true)> Set
      _name = value
    End Set
  End Property
End Class
```

However, this solution will only work when we use a proxy to access this Web Service (which we'll do in the next chapter). Even with these changes, we will not get the desired behavior when we test this code in our Web Service help page.

The design recommendation is that you design your web services to be stateless, and that using properties in Web Services is bad design.

Caching Versus Static

Caching is another feature that can really help us build great ASP.NET Web Services. It's ideal for data that is requested often and doesn't change frequently. As we've already seen, we can control caching using the `CacheDuration` property of the `WebMethod` attribute.

Response Caching

The `CacheDuration` property allows us to specify a time duration that the response to the request should be served from the ASP.NET cache. Serving requests from the cache can dramatically improve the performance of our application, since we don't need to execute code on each request.

Requests to a web-callable method using the `CacheDuration` property will vary the entries for the response in the cache based upon the request – so for a SOAP request, the contents of the cache will depend on the POST data.

Data Caching

However, there are some cases where caching the entire response simply doesn't make sense. In these cases we can use the cache API to cache interesting data within our Web Service. Take for example the code below (`DataCaching_vb.asmx`):

```
<%@ WebService class="DataCachingExample" %>

Imports System.Web.Services
Imports System.Data
Imports System.Data.SqlClient
Imports System.Web.Caching
Imports System.Web

Public Class DataCachingExample
  <WebMethod()> Public Function GetDataSet(column As String) As DataSet
    Dim AppCache As Cache

    AppCache = HttpContext.Current.Cache

    If (AppCache(column) Is Nothing) Then
      AppCache(column) = LoadDataSet(column)
    End If

    Return CType(AppCache(column), DataSet)
  End Function

  Private Function LoadDataSet(column As String) As DataSet
    Dim myConnection As SqlConnection
    Dim myCommand As SqlDataAdapter
    Dim products As DataSet
```

```
        myConnection = _
          New SqlConnection("server=localhost;uid=sa;pwd=;database=pubs")
        myCommand = _
          New SqlDataAdapter("select " + column + " from Authors", myConnection)
        products = New DataSet()

        myCommand.Fill(products, "products")

        Return products
      End Function
    End Class
```

Although this code would work equally well with the `WebMethod CacheDuration` property set, it does illustrate how we can use the lower-level cache API to save work. In this example we accept a single parameter: the name of a column in a database. We then use this parameter to create a `DataSet`, which we then add to the cache. On subsequent requests we can service the request dynamically, but we get a serious performance win since we don't have to fetch the data from the database.

Although you're recommended to use caching when (and where) possible for performance enhancements, you should understand how the resources within the Web Service are being cached. For example, in the database example above we had a fairly simple matrix of items to be served from the cache (limited by the number of columns in a particular database table). However, caching is useless for application logic that might have an unlimited amount of variations, for example `Add(a As Integer, b As Integer)`.

Asynchronous Versus Synchronous

Web Services can be designed to be synchronous or asynchronous.

A synchronous design allows the ASP.NET thread of execution to run until it's complete. If action within the code has the potential to block, such as network I/O or an extensive database lookup, this can stall the ASP.NET worker thread. Since a thread is a resource, and there are only a limited number of resources available on the system, this can force other applications' requests to queue. This all translates to an impact on the performance and scalability of the system.

An asynchronous design, on the other hand, allows the ASP.NET thread of execution to start up another thread, which can call back onto an ASP.NET thread when the work is complete. That way, the ASP.NET application is not stalled due to resource constraints on available threads.

Advanced ASP.NET Web Services

In this section of the chapter we're going to focus more on some of the esoteric areas of Web Services. We'll cover topics such as integrating with Windows DNA, shaping the SOAP/XML document exposed by our Web Services.

Controlling and Shaping the XML

ASP.NET provides us with several additional attributes that we didn't discuss earlier, which allow us to shape the XML generated by the XML serializer used by ASP.NET. There are two separate types of attributes: those that apply to the XML documents generated by the HTTP-GET and HTTP-POST protocols, and those that apply to SOAP. It is not an error to use the attributes together.

The following is a listing of these attributes, along with a brief description of their purpose:

Attribute	Description
XML Documents: `XmlAttribute` SOAP Documents: `SoapAttribute`	Allows us to control the XML attribute representation, or convert an XML element into an attribute.
XML Documents: `XmlElement` SOAP Documents: `SoapElement`	Allows us to control the XML element representation, or convert an XML attribute into an element.
XML Documents: `XmlArray` SOAP Documents: `SoapArray`	Allows us to treat elements as an XML array.

These attributes allow us to have fine granular control over the shape of the XML document used as part of the HTTP-GET, HTTP-POST, or SOAP responses.

These attributes are very straightforward, and are most often used when we return an instance of a class. We haven't discussed returning classes yet, so a brief example is necessary. Below is a simple ASP.NET Web Service (`Books_vb.asmx`) that returns a `Books` class:

```
<%@ WebService Class="ReturnBooks" %>

Imports System.Web.Services

Public Class ReturnBooks
  <WebMethod()> Public Function GetBooks() As Books
    Dim b As New Books
    b.Title = "Professional ASP.NET"
    b.Price = 59.99
    b.Description = "This book covers Microsoft's ASP.NET technology " & _
                    "for building Web Applications"
    ReDim b.Authors(6)
    b.Authors(0) = "Alex Homer"
    b.Authors(1) = "David Sussman"
    b.Authors(2) = "Rob Howard"
    b.Authors(3) = "Brian Francis"
    b.Authors(4) = "Rich Anderson"
    b.Authors(5) = "Karli Watson"

    Return b
  End Function
End Class

Public Class Books
  Public Title As String
  Public Description As String
  Public Price As Double
  Public Authors() As String
End Class
```

Calls made to the `GetBooks` WebMethod will return an XML document with a root node of `<Book>`, and elements within `<Book>` such as `<Authors>`, `<Title>`, `<Price>`, etc. for each of our classes members. Here's the XML document returned from an HTTP-GET request:

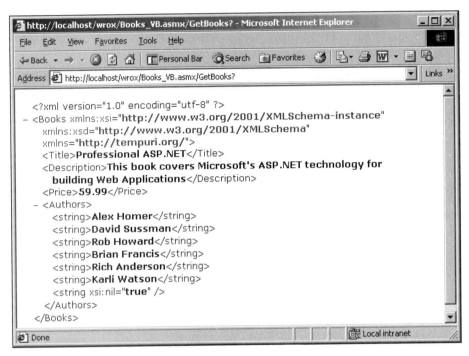

If we wanted to change the shape of the XML document – say by returning the title as an attribute of `Books`, and renaming the `<Price>` element to `<DiscountPrice>` – we would use the `XmlAttribute` and `XmlElement` attributes.

Note that to affect the SOAP message we would also need to add the SOAP equivalent attributes.

We need to make two changes to our `Books` class. First, we need to add the `System.Xml Serialization` namespace, as both the `XmlAttribute` and `XmlElement` live within this namespace. Second, we need to add the attributes to the book class member variables we want them applied to (`Books2_vb.asmx`):

```
<%@ WebService Class="ReturnBooks" %>

Imports System.Web.Services
Imports System.Xml.Serialization

Public Class ReturnBooks
   <WebMethod()> Public Function GetBooks() As Books
      Dim b As New Books
      b.Title = "Professional ASP.NET"
      b.Price = 59.99
      b.Description = "This book covers Microsoft's ASP.NET technology " & _
                      "for building Web Applications"
      ReDim b.Authors(6)
```

```
      b.Authors(0) = "Alex Homer"
      b.Authors(1) = "David Sussman"
      b.Authors(2) = "Rob Howard"
      b.Authors(3) = "Brian Francis"
      b.Authors(4) = "Rich Anderson"
      b.Authors(5) = "Karli Watson"

      Return b
   End Function
End Class

Public Class Books
   <XmlAttribute> Public Title As String
   Public Description As String
   <XmlElement("DiscountedPrice")> Public Price As Double
   <XmlArray("Contributors")> Public Authors() As String
End Class
```

All of these attributes allow us to rename either the attribute or the element, as shown in the modification of Price to DiscountedPrice and the renaming of the Authors array from Authors to Contributors.

Here's our new XML document:

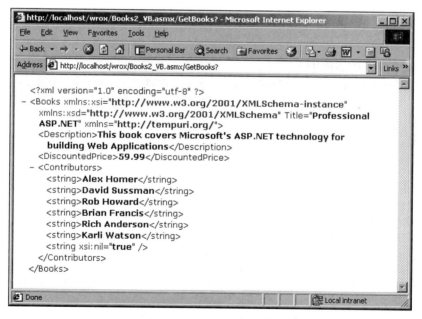

These attributes are very powerful in that they allow us fine granular control over the shape of the XML document, without requiring us to make any complex changes to our application code.

Next, let's look at the Web Service Help page. This is what we use when we view our Web Service through the browser.

Modifying the Web Service Help Page

The default Web Service Help page, implemented in the file `DefaultWsdlHelpGenerator.aspx`, can be found in the `\WinNt\Microsoft.NET\Framework\[version]` directory. This file is the default template used for all ASP.NET Web Services when a request is made through the browser to a particular Web Service.

In Chapter 16, when we discussed ASP.NET configuration, we've also covered how each application can support its own Web Service Help page; it's simply a configuration option to tell the application which ASP.NET page to use.

Since the Web Service Help page is implemented as an ASP.NET page, we can obviously make modifications to it. For example, we can customize this page with graphics that are specific to our application, or provide additional details about the Web Services that our server provides.

> *A good example of how this customization can be done is accomplished in the IBuySpy Store example: http://www.ibuyspy.com/store/InstantOrder.asmx. This is an example of a customized Web Service Help page.*

Keep in mind that any modification to the server's `DefaultWsdlHelpGenerator.aspx` will apply to all ASP.NET Web Services on that server, unless you alter the ASP.NET configuration. However, there are some modifications that we can make to this file which will be useful for helping to debug our ASP.NET Web Service.

HTML Form (Post Support)

If an ASP.NET Web Service is capable of supporting the HTTP-POST protocol and we wish to test that functionality, we can open `DefaultWsdlHelpGenerator.aspx` and modify a `showPost` flag:

```
// set this to true if you want to see a
// POST test form instead of a GET test form
bool showPost = false;
```

By default this flag is set to `false`, but when set to `true` it will generate another HTML form available on the detail page for a particular WebMethod supporting HTTP-POST.

Protocol Request/Response Sample

When we drill into a particular WebMethod detail page we are provided with a view of what the protocol request/response messages should look like. Within `DefaultWsdlHelpGenerator.aspx` we have three flags that allow us to change the behavior of the view of these protocol messages.

Flag	Default Value	Description
dontFilterXml	false	By default the XML shown in the protocol messages is not URL encoded. If we set this flag to true, we can view the URL encoded XML in the message.

Flag	Default Value	Description
maxObjectGraphDepth	int = 4	When objects, such as the Books object we used earlier, are described in the sample protocol sections, this setting allows us to control the depth of the number of objects to show. This would be applicable for our Books class if it contained a public member Authors that was another class, and Authors contained a public member which was another class, etc.
maxArraySize	int = 2	Similar to the control for object depth, this option allows us to control the maximum number of array element examples shown within the protocols. For example, our Books class contained an array of six authors. The array representing these items in the protocol samples only show two items.

Next, let's look at one of the features of SOAP headers, which we can use to send out-of-band information.

SOAP Headers

We've mentioned several times that SOAP is a simple lightweight XML protocol for exchanging structured and typed information on the Web. A SOAP message contains four parts:

❑ An extensible envelope

❑ A set of encoding rules

❑ A convention for representing RPC

❑ Protocol bindings for HTTP

Note the use of headers is only supported within the SOAP protocol, not HTTP-GET or HTTP-POST.

ASP.NET Web Services that we create use SOAP as the default protocol for application-to-application communication. For example, here is the SOAP response to a call to our Fibonacci Web Service:

```
<?xml version="1.0"?>
<soap:Envelope xmlns:xsi="http://www.w3.org/2000/10/XMLSchema-instance"
               xmlns:xsd="http://www.w3.org/2000/10/XMLSchema"
               xmlns:soap="http://schemas.xmlsoap.org/soap/envelope">
  <soap:Body>
    <GetSeqNumber xmlns="http://tempuri.org/">
      <FibIndex>6</FibIndex>
    </GetSeqNumber>
  </soap:Body>
</soap:Envelope>
```

The HTTP headers have been stripped out, and what we're left with is the body of an HTTP request containing the SOAP message. The SOAP message contains an envelope, `<soap:Envelope ...>`, which encapsulates a body, `<soap:Body>`, and optionally headers, `<soap:Headers>`, (not shown). To use SOAP headers we need to specify a `SoapHeader` attribute on our web-callable method or property.

The `SoapHeader` attribute allows us to optionally set a SOAP header, either on the consumer or provider of the service. SOAP does not define headers for us: headers are simply an extensibility mechanism that we can use in our ASP.NET Web Services.

For example, here's the SOAP for our Fibonacci example with a simple header, which we'll create below:

```xml
<?xml version="1.0"?>
<soap:Envelope xmlns:xsi="http://www.w3.org/2000/10/XMLSchema-instance"
               xmlns:xsd="http://www.w3.org/2000/10/XMLSchema"
               xmlns:soap="http://schemas.xmlsoap.org/soap/envelope">
  <soap:Header>
    <SimpleSoapHeader xmlns="http://tempuri.org/">
      <value>string</value>
    </SimpleSoapHeader>
  </soap:Header>
  <soap:Body>
    <GetSeqNumber xmlns="http://tempuri.org/">
      <FibIndex>int</FibIndex>
    </GetSeqNumber>
  </soap:Body>
</soap:Envelope>
```

To use SOAP headers, we first need to create our own class that inherits from the `SoapHeader` base class.

In the code below we'll use both a `SoapHeader` attribute and the `SoapHeader` class. They are two separate classes – it just so happens that with attributes we don't need to explicitly add `Attribute` onto the end of the attribute when we declare it, such as in `SoapHeaderAttribute`.

SoapHeader Class

To make use of a SOAP header we need to first create a class that derives from the `SoapHeader` base class. This class can be found in the namespace `System.Web.Services.Protocols` in the assembly `System.Web.Services.dll`:

```
public abstract class SoapHeader{
  public bool MustUnderstand{get; set;}
  public string Actor{get; set;}
  public bool DidUnderstand{get; set;}
}
```

Here's a simple example of a `SimpleSoapHeader` class that inherits from `SoapHeader`:

```
Imports System.Web.Services.Protocols

Public Class SimpleSoapHeader
  Inherits SoapHeader

  Public value As string
End Class
```

In the above code sample we first create a small class, `SimpleSoapHeader` that inherits from the `SoapHeader` base class. Within this class we define a single public member, `value`. Applications that wish to use this SOAP header can pass data within `value`.

Let's add this class to our Fibonacci example (`FibonnaciSOAP_vb.asmx`):

```
<%@ WebService class="Fibonacci"%>

Imports System.Web.Services
Imports System.Web.Services.Protocols

Public Class SimpleSoapHeader
  Inherits SoapHeader

  Public value As string
End Class

Public Class Fibonacci

  Public simpleHeader As SimpleSoapHeader

  <WebMethod, SoapHeader("simpleHeader")> Public Function _
                          GetSeqNumber (fibIndex as Integer) as Integer

    If (fibIndex < 2) Then
      Return fibIndex
    End If

    Dim FibArray(2) As Integer
    Dim i As Integer

    FibArray(0) = 0
    FibArray(1) = 1

    For i = 2 To fibIndex
      FibArray(1) = FibArray(1) + FibArray(0)
      FibArray(0) = FibArray(1) - FibArray(0)
    Next

    Return FibArray(1)
  End Function
End Class
```

You won't be able to test this in the same way as we did our earlier examples – we'll see why in a moment.

In our modified `Fibonacci` class we first declare a local member variable `simpleHeader` of type `SimpleSoapHeader`:

```
Public simpleHeader As SimpleSoapHeader
```

This will represent an instance of our custom SOAP header that a client will set. Next, we use the `SoapHeader` attribute, which has been added to `GetSeqNumber`, and pass in the name of our member variable `simpleHeader`:

```
<WebMethod, SoapHeader("simpleHeader")> Public Function _
                          GetSeqNumber (fibIndex as Integer) as Integer
```

Without going into too much detail, setting the SoapHeader attribute to the value of simpleHeader creates a SOAP header containing a single item – named value – which we can set, as defined in our SimpleSoapHeader class.

When we created the SimpleSoapHeader class above, we inherited from the SoapHeader class. Let's take a look at the inherited properties our class receives.

SoapHeader Class Inherited Properties

The SoapHeader class provides us with three additional properties. We won't be discussing these in detail, but you can review the SOAP 1.1. specification (http://www.w3.org/TR/SOAP) to learn more about why they exist. These properties are:

- ❑ Actor – Section 4.2.2 of the SOAP 1.1 specification states that an actor header message may be used by a SOAP document to name the intended recipient, as a SOAP message can pass through many applications capable of routing the message. The Actor property allows us to set the URI value – that is the endpoint that the SOAP message is ultimately going to be routed to. Alternatively, we can set a special URI – http://schemas.xmlsoap.org/soap/actor/next as defined by the SOAP 1.1 specification – which indicates that the next recipient of the SOAP message should process the message.

- ❑ MustUnderstand – Section 4.2.3 of the SOAP 1.1 specification states that a SOAP header can use an attribute, mustUnderstand, to indicate whether it is mandatory or optional for a recipient to process the header entry. This value is set to false by default.

- ❑ DidUnderstand – A Boolean flag that the receiver of the SOAP message may set if the SOAP header was understood.

When we applied the SoapHeader attribute above, we set a value. This value represents a property of a SoapHeader attribute called MemberName. Let's take a look at MemberName, as well as the other properties supported by the SoapHeader attribute.

SoapHeader Attribute

The SoapHeader attribute is the attribute we add to web callable methods or properties to instruct those methods and properties to support SOAP headers. We've already learned that to use a SOAP header we need to create a class that inherits from the SoapHeader base class. We then expose a member variable of the type of our class that inherits from SoapHeader.

Consumers of our Web Service use the member variable, as we'll learn in the next chapter, to create an instance of our class and set values. The SoapHeader attribute is provided with the name of this class – for example <SoapHeader("simpleHeader")> – and is thus able to access the class instance. This constructor sets the MemberName property of the SoapHeader attribute.

The SoapHeader attribute supports three properties:

- ❑ MemberName
- ❑ Direction
- ❑ Required

Let's start by discussing the MemberName property.

MemberName

The MemberName property identifies the name of the member within the class that the header is to be created for. This is best demonstrated by visiting the code:

```
public simpleHeader As SimpleSoapHeader

<WebMethod, SoapHeader("simpleHeader")> public Function
                          GetSeqNumber (FibIndex as Integer) as Integer
```

simpleHeader is variable of type SimpleSoapHeader, where SimpleSoapHeader is our class that inherits from the SoapHeader base class.

Next we see our SoapHeader attribute and the value passed in its constructor – the name of our SimpleSoapHeader variable, simpleHeader. simpleHeader is the name of the member that represents the SimpleSoapHeader class. In the next chapter when we discuss consuming Web Services, we'll see how the consumer can create an instance of SimpleSoapHeader, set its value property, and assign that instance to simpleHeader.

In a nutshell the MemberName allows the SoapHeader attribute to name the class variable that it will be a type of.

The Direction Property

SOAP headers by default are inbound only – that is the server servicing SOAP requests expects to receive SOAP headers, not set and send SOAP headers. This becomes immediately obvious if you try to test the example we have above, the Fibonacci Web Service with a simple SOAP header, using the Web Services Help page – the HTML form for testing the results is no longer available:

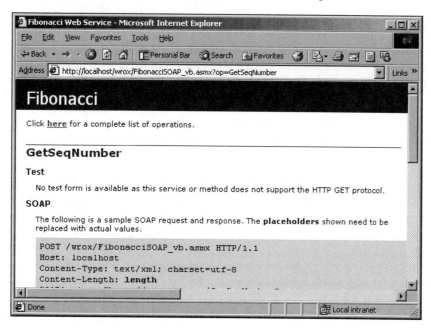

The Direction property allows this to be configured. The Direction property uses the SoapHeaderDirection enumeration to determine the direction of the header.

VB.NET

```
<SoapHeader("simpleHeader", Direction:=SoapHeaderDirection.InOut)>
```

C#

```
[SoapHeader("simpleHeader", Direction=SoapHeaderDirection.InOut)]
```

The `SoapHeaderDirection` enumeration supports three values, whose meaning is fairly obvious:

- ❑   `SoapHeaderDirection.In`
- ❑   `SoapHeaderDirection.Out`
- ❑   `SoapHeaderDirection.InOut`

The Required Property

Headers defined by a method are required by default, meaning they must be present in the request or an exception will be generated. Setting the `Required` property to `false` allows headers to be optional.

VB.NET

```
<SoapHeader("simpleHeader", Required:="false")>
```

C#

```
[SoapHeader("simpleHeader", Required="false")]
```

Summary

As we've learned, ASP.NET, and for that matter all Microsoft .NET branded products, have deep support for XML. This support for XML includes technologies such as SOAP, a technology that Microsoft has clearly identified as important. In the very near future we can expect to see a plethora of third-party web services such as credit card validation/verification, address verification, billing services, the list goes on.

In this chapter we attempted to provide an introduction, with some extra advanced material, that clearly illustrates how we can build Web Services easily with ASP.NET. We've discussed:

- ❑   Some of the common issues associated with building applications that can share data, and how Web Services address these by using a common protocol, SOAP, that all parties can adhere to.
- ❑   Some of the public specifications in addition to SOAP, namely WSDL and UDDI, and how all these pieces can fit together in a real-world application.
- ❑   Building a simple ASP.NET Web Service using some straightforward application logic. We walked through examples both in VB and C#, and showed how – with a few small modifications – our application logic can be "Web Service enabled". We tested that logic by calling it through a browser, and examining the richly detailed description that ASP.NET was able to generate for us.

- ❑ The details of the ASP.NET `.asmx` file – the file format used to expose our application logic. We discussed the directives, the `System.Web.Services` namespace, and the `WebMethod` attribute. We also saw how using the `WebService` base class within our code is not a requirement.

- ❑ The `WebMethod` and `WebService` attributes, including some of their more esoteric aspects such as the properties that each supports.

- ❑ Design suggestions, and some of the more advanced aspects of ASP.NET Web Services, specifically shaping the XML document and SOAP Headers.

Finally, here are a couple of links to some locations where you can learn more about ASP.NET Web Services, SOAP, and other aspects of general Web Services:

- ❑ http://msdn.microsoft.com
- ❑ http://www.asp.net
- ❑ http://www.gotdotnet.com
- ❑ http://www.uddi.org
- ❑ http://www.w3c.org
- ❑ http://www.webservicesarchitect.com
- ❑ http://www.webservices.org
- ❑ http://www.xmethods.com

In the next chapter we'll take a look at consuming the Web Services that we learned to build in this chapter, as well as discussing security with ASP.NET Web Services.

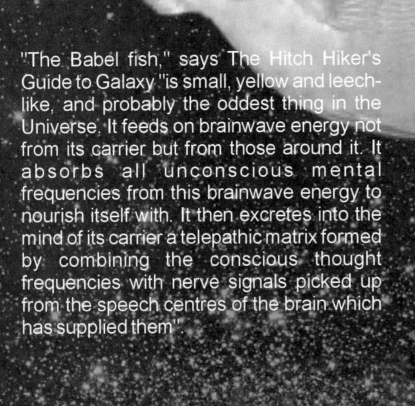

"The Babel fish," says The Hitch Hiker's Guide to Galaxy "is small, yellow and leech-like, and probably the oddest thing in the Universe. It feeds on brainwave energy not from its carrier but from those around it. It absorbs all unconscious mental frequencies from this brainwave energy to nourish itself with. It then excretes into the mind of its carrier a telepathic matrix formed by combining the conscious thought frequencies with nerve signals picked up from the speech centres of the brain which has supplied them".

The practical upshot of all this is that if you stick a Babel fish in your ear you can instantly understand anything said to you in any form of language. The speech patterns you actually hear decode the brainwave matrix which has been fed into your mind by your Babel fish.

20
Using Web Services

In the previous chapter we discussed using ASP.NET to create Web Services. We learned that we could simply author application logic, as we did with the Fibonacci examples, and use the `WebMethod` attribute to enable methods as SOAP end points.

In this chapter we're going to look at how we to use Web Services in our applications. Whether those Web Services are built with Microsoft solutions, such as ASP.NET, or some other technology, such as IBM's Apache SOAP module. Although, in theory, we can use other Web Services we'll use the same ones we created in the previous chapter, that is Fibonacci written in ASP.NET.

In addition to examining how we use Web Services in our applications, we'll also discuss some other concepts related to ASP.NET Web Services. Namely: HTML screen scraping and Security.

Here's what we'll be looking at:

- **Finding and Describing Web Services.** When we build a Web Service we still face the problem of both describing what the capabilities of the service are, and also where the server hosting it can be found. In this section we'll discuss two technologies that address finding and describing Web Services: UDDI and WSDL.

- **Building Web Service Proxies.** Rather than us doing the work to serialize and de-serialize SOAP messages or understand the various transport protocols for SOAP messages, we'll build proxy or 'stub' objects that applications can use. We'll look at building proxies both with Visual Studio.NET and the command line tool: `wsdl.exe`.

- **Using the .NET Proxy Class.** The proxy class that's generated for us by either Visual Studio.NET or `wsdl.exe` has additional properties and methods that let us control various aspects of how the proxy calls the Web Service, such as request timeout and access to the HTTP cookies collections.

❑ **HTML Screen Scraping.** After we describe how to use the proxy class, we'll look at another feature that ASP.NET Web Services support: the ability to use regular expression 'pattern matching' syntax to extract information from a web page. We'll look at how we can create a custom WSDL document, then use that document with either of our .NET proxy generation tools to create a proxy that is capable of extracting information from any web page – turning any web page into a Web Service that we can program.

❑ **Design Decisions.** Here we'll discuss some common design decisions that you might encounter when building applications that use Web Services..

❑ **Web Services Security.** Security, as it relates to Web Services, is an important application feature that must be addressed in any application. In this section we'll look at how we can use the various security options provided by .NET to secure our Web Service

❑ **Advanced Topics.** Finally at the end of the chapter we'll look at some advanced topics. We'll discuss custom authentication and authorization strategies for Web Services, as well as something known as Soap Extensions – a feature of ASP.NET for interacting with .NET Web Services at a low level.

Let's get started by discussing how we find and describe Web Services.

Finding and Describing Web Services

If we're building an e-commerce application and decide that we'd like to use a Web Service to support credit card purchasing on our site, how do we find one that meets our needs? It's, of course, obvious to us where to find a given SOAP end point if we author it ourselves, such as the Fibonacci examples in the previous chapter, but how do we find Web Services that are offered by third parties?

Just as we would use a tool such as Lycos to find web documents we can use a similar directory-oriented tool to find Web Services: it's called UDDI.

Although not well publicized at the time of writing, **Universal Description Discovery and Integration** (UDDI) will become the standard location to find and register Web Services. Let's briefly take a look at UDDI and how it works.

Universal Description, Discovery, and Integration

Universal Description Discovery and Integration (UDDI) is a project that strives to define how businesses describe and publish Web Services. Microsoft, IBM, and Ariba jointly announced UDDI in September 2000. There are now upwards of 160 companies that have joined the project.

UDDI consists of two main elements:

❑ **UDDI XML Schema for Business Description** – This schema is used to define XML documents that describe various elements of a business, for example, contact information, business categorization, and Web Services offered. When we search UDDI for a service, we are searching against XML documents conforming to this schema.

❑ **Web-Based Registry** – The business description data is available either through a standard browser interface, or through published, SOAP-based, Web Services. We can use the Web Services for programmatic interaction with the UDDI schema repository.

Since UDDI is still a work in progress, we won't discuss it in great detail in this book, but please visit **http://www.uddi.org** to learn more, as well as to find the public specifications.

Just as we use a phone book to find companies that provide services, we use the UDDI Web Services directory as the yellow, white, and green pages for services offered by organizations.

Drawing on our earlier example, a company that provides a credit card Web Service can register that service at UDDI.org. Then, customers needing a credit card Web Service can visit UDDI.org and, either through UDDI's public SOAP Web Services or through their browser, query UDDI for the existence of credit card services. If services matching the criteria of the request are found, we then have the necessary information to access those services, such as the location and description of the Web Service.

Implementations of UDDI

UDDI allows organizations to register Web Services, as well as discover Web Services that other organizations have registered. The specification, at the time of writing, is implemented by three of the companies supporting UDDI:

- ❑ **Microsoft** – UDDI implementation available at: http://uddi.microsoft.com/
- ❑ **Ariba** – UDDI implementation available at: http://www.ariba.com/corporate/news/uddi.cfm
- ❑ **IBM** – UDDI implementation available at: http://www-3.ibm.com/services/uddi/

These three UDDI nodes mirror each other. If any one node is unavailable, another node can be used, thus eliminating single points of failure. In the future, additional UDDI nodes will most likely become available.

It is also perfectly possible that private UDDI servers will be made available. This would allow organizations to host their own intranet UDDI nodes for intra-organizational Web Service registration and discovery.

We're not going to look at how we use UDDI programmatically in this chapter, since it's still in beta, but we'll discuss the necessary steps to find Web Services using a browser at one of the existing UDDI nodes.

Let's look at Microsoft's UDDI node, available at http://uddi.microsoft.com.

Microsoft UDDI Node

When we point our browser at http://uddi.microsoft.com, we're served a simple HTML page that contains news and information about the UDDI project. We can search this node for services (after logging in through Passport).

Let's take a look at how we find Web Services offered by Microsoft.

Search

The Search UDDI link brings us to another HTML page that details how we can search for services. An HTML form is provided for entering our search parameters. Since we know we're looking for Web Services offered by Microsoft, we can select to search for the value "Microsoft" in Business names. Other search options include:

Option	Searches by	Example
Business Location	Location of the business.	Redmond
Service type by name	Services that support a certain type of service.	SOAP
Business identifier	A D-U-N-S reference number for business lookup.	08-146-6849 for Microsoft
Discovery URL	The location at which a service exists. For a known service this allows us to determine if the service is registered with UDDI.	A URL for a service that we already know exists: reverse lookup
GeoWeb Taxonomy	By geographic classification.	North America
NAICS Codes	North American Industry Classification.	Software Publisher
SIC Codes	Standard Industrial Classification.	Classification code used to classify business types.
UNSPSC Codes	Universal Standard Products and Services Codes.	Software

After we query UDDI we are presented with the results. In this case a link to a 'detail page' that describes the registered services for the Microsoft Corporation.

Detail Page

The detail page is broken down into several sections. The section of interest to us is the Services section, which lists the Web Services offered by Microsoft. One of the selectable options, at the time of writing, is Web Services for Smart Searching. Selecting this link gives us details, such as the bindings, for this Web Service provided by Microsoft.

Bindings

Once the Service Detail page for Web Services for Smart Searching is open, we are presented with a list of bindings. The bindings represent the available end points for the Web Service(s). In this case we have a reference in the Binding section to two ASP.NET Web Services (identified by the *.asmx extension). We now have the location of a service that we wish to use – later in the chapter we'll talk about how we can use the technologies found in .NET to easily build proxy classes that can use these SOAP-based Web Services.

In summary, UDDI allows us to search a common repository for published Web Services. If we find a Web Service that meets our needs we can then access that Web Service using the binding details provided by UDDI.

UDDI solves the problem of Web Service discovery. However, once we've found the Web Service, we still have some problems that need to be addressed. These include:

- ❏ How do we describe what the Web Service can, and can't, do?
- ❏ What does the SOAP request look like?
- ❏ What does the SOAP response look like?
- ❏ What data types does the Web Service support?
- ❏ Does the Web Service require an XML schema?

While UDDI makes finding Web Services easy, another technology, **Web Service Description Language** (WSDL), is used to describe the capabilities of a Web Service, answering the above questions.

Web Service Description Language

WSDL is a W3C submitted specification (at the time of writing it is not yet a W3C standard) supported by a number of industry leaders, including Microsoft and IBM.

The public specification, available at http://msdn.microsoft.com/xml/general/wsdl.asp, states:

> *"Web Service Description Language is an XML format for describing network services as a set of end-points operating on messages containing either document-oriented or procedure-oriented information."*

Simply put, WSDL is an XML document that describes:

- ❏ **How the Web Service is used.** For example, how both the client and the server send and receive messages.
- ❏ **The location of a Web Service.** For example, the URI that messages are sent to, for interacting with the Web Service.
- ❏ **The nature of the message exchange.** For example, SOAP allows for either an XML document or XML RPC view of messages.

> *If you come from an object development background and have used Interface Definition Language (IDL) in the past to describe an object, its methods, and the interfaces it supports, WSDL is similar in concept but uses XML and describes a Web Service rather than a component.*

Interoperability

The beauty of Web Services is interoperability at the network level. The implementation of a Web Service is completely independent of the Operating System or the technology used to implement the service, and the description of the Web Service is encapsulated in an XML document (WSDL). For example, if a JSP developer wanted use ASP.NET Web Services in his or her application. He or she would simply need to examine the WSDL for the Web Service and format the correct message to a named end point. The return message could then also be interpreted, again using the WSDL, and the appropriate value extracted. However, it doesn't need to be this complicated. With .NET, using Web Services requires only a trivial amount of work.

WSDL is an incredibly important technology for enabling Web Service interoperability because it fully describes the capabilities and use of the service. In fact, the description is so complete that tools can use WSDL to automate the creation of code. Let's look at a sample WSDL document that describes the Fibonacci Web Service we implemented in the previous chapter.

WSDL Example: Fibonacci

If you remember from the previous chapter, an ASP.NET Web Service provides a Web Service Description Help Page:

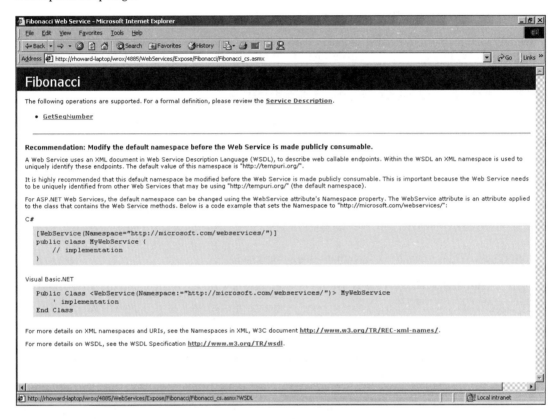

This help page allows us to interact and 'test' the Web Service through a browser.

The help page additionally provides a link called Service Description. This requests the current document, Fibonacci.asmx, and appends ?WSDL: Fibonacci.asmx?WSDL. Selecting the Service Description link provides us with WSDL:

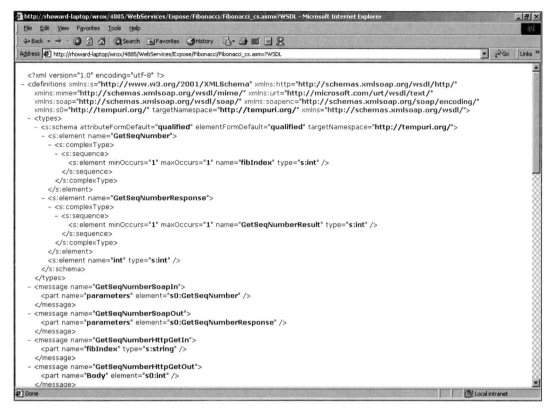

Below is the WSDL document that describes the Fibonacci ASP.NET Web Service. We implemented the Web Service in both C# and VB.NET, but as you can see below this is completely abstracted by the WSDL:

> *Sections of the WSDL that describe the use of the HTTP-GET and HTTP-POST protocols have been removed in this example (to decrease the size). This WSDL document only describes Web Services using SOAP.*

```xml
<?xml version="1.0" encoding="utf-8"?>
<definitions xmlns:s="http://www.w3.org/2001/XMLSchema"
             xmlns:http="http://schemas.xmlsoap.org/wsdl/http/"
             xmlns:mime="http://schemas.xmlsoap.org/wsdl/mime/"
             xmlns:urt="http://microsoft.com/urt/wsdl/text/"
             xmlns:soap="http://schemas.xmlsoap.org/wsdl/soap/"
             xmlns:soapenc="http://schemas.xmlsoap.org/soap/encoding/"
             xmlns:s0="http://tempuri.org/" targetNamespace="http://tempuri.org/"
             xmlns="http://schemas.xmlsoap.org/wsdl/">
  <types>
    <s:schema attributeFormDefault="qualified"
              elementFormDefault="qualified"
              targetNamespace="http://tempuri.org/">
      <s:element name="GetSeqNumber">
        <s:complexType>
          <s:sequence>
```

```
              <s:element minOccurs="1"
                         maxOccurs="1"
                         name="fibIndex"
                         type="s:int" />
          </s:sequence>
        </s:complexType>
      </s:element>
      <s:element name="GetSeqNumberResponse">
        <s:complexType>
          <s:sequence>
            <s:element minOccurs="1"
                       maxOccurs="1"
                       name="GetSeqNumberResult"
                       type="s:int" />
          </s:sequence>
        </s:complexType>
      </s:element>
      <s:element name="int" type="s:int" />
    </s:schema>
  </types>
  <message name="GetSeqNumberSoapIn">
    <part name="parameters" element="s0:GetSeqNumber" />
  </message>
  <message name="GetSeqNumberSoapOut">
    <part name="parameters" element="s0:GetSeqNumberResponse" />
  </message>
  <portType name="FibonacciSoap">
    <operation name="GetSeqNumber">
      <input message="s0:GetSeqNumberSoapIn" />
      <output message="s0:GetSeqNumberSoapOut" />
    </operation>
  </portType>
  <binding name="FibonacciSoap" type="s0:FibonacciSoap">
    <soap:binding
        transport="http://schemas.xmlsoap.org/soap/http" style="document" />
    <operation name="GetSeqNumber">
      <soap:operation
          soapAction="http://tempuri.org/GetSeqNumber" style="document" />
      <input>
        <soap:body use="literal" />
      </input>
      <output>
        <soap:body use="literal" />
      </output>
    </operation>
  </binding>
  <service name="Fibonacci">
    <port name="FibonacciSoap" binding="s0:FibonacciSoap">
      <soap:address location="http:// ... /Fibonacci_cs.asmx" />
    </port>
  </service>
</definitions>
```

The above WSDL document is divided into five major sections:

❑ **types** – The `<types>` section of our WSDL is simply an XML schema used by the Web Service to define the schema for the message sections. The XML schema is used as a set of rules for how XML data should be formatted, and the resulting XML can be validated against the schema.

❑ **message** – For each Web Service described in our WSDL there will be at least one `<message>`. There may be only one as a Web Service can be one-way (read-only) as opposed to two-way (request/response). In our example above, the `GetSeqNumber` Web Service is two-way and we therefore have both a request message `GetSeqNumberSoapIn` and a response message `GetSeqNuberSoapOut`. The message describes the format that the Web Service expects to receive the request in, as well as the format the Web Service will use when it responds. Both of the message examples in the above WSDL support parameters and use an XSD (XML Schema) to describe the message format defined in the `<types>` section.

❑ **portType** – The WSDL may describe multiple Web Services. The `<portType>` is used to describe the request and/or response messages (defined by `<message>` sections) that these Web Services support. In this particular example, the only Web Service described is the `GetSeqNumber`. This is the name value of the `<operation>` tag in `<portType>`. If we exposed additional Web Methods, such as `Add`, we would expect to find a definition for them as well. Within the `<operation>` tag we then find the `<input>` and `<output>` tags. These reference `<message>` sections within the WSDL.

❑ **binding** – The `<binding>` tag describes the message format, either SOAP section 5 RPC-style encoding, or XML document-style encoding. Each method supported by the Web Service can vary in its support of message encoding and thus each Web Service described by the WSDL receives its own section within `<binding>`. The only Web Service described by this WSDL is `GetSeqNumber`; remember this is the method that we authored in our ASP.NET Web Service to calculate the value of an index into a Fibonacci series.

❑ **service** – The name of the Web Service the WSDL document describes. In the above WSDL the `<service>` name value is `Fibonacci`. Also defined in the `<service>` is the `<port>`, which identifies the location of the Web Service – in other words the end point that services calls, as well as any bindings that the Web Service uses. The values in the `<port>` tag are further described by the `<binding>` and `<portType>` tags. By default, the service name corresponds to the class name of the ASP.NET Web Service we authored – this service name is configurable using the `WebService` attribute on the Web Service.

As you many have noticed in the above WSDL, XML namespaces are used extensively.

Namespaces applied to WSDL

XML uses namespaces to uniquely identify sections of an XML document. Namespaces are Universal Resource Indicators (URIs), such as http://microsoft.com. XML namespaces allow the markup language used to be unique within a given namespace. Software can use namespaces to differentiate between the `<GetSeqNumber>` tag from Microsoft and the `<GetSeqNumber>` tag from a third party – if the two XML documents are combined or described in the same WSDL.

The default namespace ASP.NET assigns to Web Services is http://tempuri.org, as is evident in the above WSDL.

As we learned in the previous chapter, we can use the `Namespace` property of the `WebService` attribute to change the default namespace from http://tempuri.org to a namespace we choose:

VB.NET

```
<%@ WebService class="Fibonacci" %>

Imports System.Web.Services

<WebService(Namespace:="http://rhoward/Fibonacci")> _
Public Class Fibonacci
  <WebMethod> _
  Public Function GetSeqNumber (fibIndex as Integer) as Integer
    If (fibIndex < 2) Then
      Return fibIndex
    End If

    Dim FibArray(2) as Integer
    Dim i as Integer

    FibArray(0) = 0
    FibArray(1) = 1

    For i = 2 To fibIndex
      FibArray(1) = FibArray(1) + FibArray(0)
      FibArray(0) = FibArray(1) - FibArray(0)
    Next

    Return FibArray(1)
  End Function
End class
```

> It's important to note that even though a URI might take the shape of an **http://**
> address, this does not imply that some value or meaning exists at this end point, it is
> simply a unique string.

*Although the above statement is correct, that there is no implied value or meaning for the URI used
by a namespace, Microsoft does own the http://tempuri.org URI and has provided some detail
explaining what http://tempuri.org is as well as details related to changing the namespace for
ASP.NET Web Services.*

The WSDL that ASP.NET generates describes three protocols: SOAP, HTTP-POST, and HTTP-GET –
all covered in the previous chapter. You'll also recall, from the previous chapter, that through some of
the attributes provided by ASP.NET, we can modify the WSDL, such as the namespace settings,
through the WebService attribute.

We do not need a thorough understanding of WSDL to build Web Services. It is useful, but definitely
not required. For those of us building Web Services with ASP.NET, the WSDL is created automatically
as part of the Web Service Help Page by simply requesting the ASP.NET Web Service and appending
?WSDL, for example Fibonacci.asmx?wsdl.

Now that we've had a foundation in UDDI and WSDL, let's shift the discussion to using WSDL to build
a proxy class that is capable of calling a Web Service.

For further references on UDDI or WSDL, I would suggest the following:

❏ http://www.uddi.org

❏ http://msdn.microsoft.com/webservices/

Building Web Service Proxies

In software, a proxy is code that does work on behalf of other code.

A good example is proxy web server software. Users first configure their web browser to use a proxy server and then make requests for Internet resources, such as http://msdn.microsoft.com/. Since a proxy has been specified, rather than this request being forwarded to a gateway and directly to the Internet, the request is forwarded to the proxy. The proxy then makes a request on the behalf of the browser/user to the requested URL.

In the case of Web Services, we can use proxy classes to represent the Web Service we wish to call. For example, the Fibonacci Web Service is implemented as follows:

VB.NET

```
<%@ WebService class="Fibonacci"%>

Imports System.Web.Services

Public Class Fibonacci
  <WebMethod> _
  Public Function GetSeqNumber (fibIndex as Integer) as Integer
    If (fibIndex < 2) Then
      Return fibIndex
    End If

    Dim FibArray(2) as Integer
    Dim i as Integer

    FibArray(0) = 0
    FibArray(1) = 1

    For i = 2 To fibIndex
      FibArray(1) = FibArray(1) + FibArray(0)
      FibArray(0) = FibArray(1) - FibArray(0)
    Next

    Return FibArray(1)
  End Function
End Class
```

We have a class named `Fibonacci`, and that class supports a single method `GetSeqNumber`. With some minor modifications, we could compile the above code into a .NET assembly and deploy it to an ASP.NET application's \bin directory (on the server). We could then use the assembly as both a Web Service – because of the `<WebMethod>` attribute – and a local class inside an ASP.NET page.

For example, if we compiled and deployed the assembly to an ASP.NET application's \bin directory we could write the following valid ASP.NET Page:

```
<script runat="server">
  Public Sub Page_Load(sender As Object, e As EventArgs)
    Dim fibonacci As New Fibonacci()
    lblResult = Fibonacci.GetSeqNumber(5)
  End Sub
</script>
Index of 5 in the Fibonacci Series is: <asp:label id="lblResult" runat="server"/>
```

The point is that our Fibonacci Web Service is application logic stored in a reusable class. We can compile the class, create an instance of Fibonacci, and then make calls to methods. However, we've also implemented it as a Web Service, meaning we additionally support the ability to call our Fibonacci's GetSeqNumber via SOAP over the network.

However, can we expect applications that wish to use our Fibonacci Web Service to work with the raw SOAP messages (the HTTP and XML) directly? I think not.

Consumers of this Web Service should not have to formulate their own XML messages, and encapsulate those messages in HTTP to send them to the appropriate destination. The same is true for receiving messages. Instead, what consumers should use is a proxy representation of the Fibonacci Web Service.

Fibonacci Proxy

As we learned earlier, the WSDL describes the Web Service. Because the WSDL is so complete, we can use it to create a proxy class using tools capable of reading the WSDL. For example, using the WSDL discussed earlier we can build a proxy class for the Fibonacci Web Service. This proxy will have a class named Fibonacci and a method named GetSeqNumber.

Although these details are described in the WSDL, and can therefore be used to create a local class named Fibonacci with a GetSeqNumber method the proxy class obviously does not contain the actual implementation (the code that calculates the sequence number), since this is not described in the WSDL. The implementation still resides within the Web Service we're calling.

However, the proxy does look and feel the same. It has the same class name and same method name/parameters, like a local Fibonacci class, but the methods wrap calls to the remote Fibonacci Web Service. For example, here's the pseudo-code for a **proxy** implementation of Fibonacci:

VB.NET

```
Public Class Fibonacci
  Inherits SoapHttpClientProtocol

  Public Sub New()
    MyBase.New
    Me.Url = "http://[Server]/Fibonacci_cs.asmx"
  End Sub

  Public Function GetSeqNumber(ByVal fibIndex As Integer) As Integer
    Dim results() As Object = Me.Invoke("GetSeqNumber", New Object() {fibIndex})
    Return CType(results(0),Integer)
  End Function

End Class
```

In the above code sample (pseudo-code – this is the actual proxy code we'll create later minus some details) we have a class named `Fibonacci`, and a single function named `GetSeqNumber`.

The major difference between the above proxy and the Fibonacci ASP.NET Web Service is the code in the `GetSeqNumber` function:

```
Public Function GetSeqNumber(ByVal fibIndex As Integer) As Integer
   Dim results() As Object = Me.Invoke("GetSeqNumber", New Object() {fibIndex})
   Return CType(results(0),Integer)
End Function
```

The proxy function name and parameters look identical to the Web Service implementation, but the actual implementation (highlighted above) is obviously different.

In the above sample we have two lines of code. The first line uses the proxy method's `Invoke()` function to call the Web Service and return a result. The second line uses the VB.NET `CType()` function to cast the return data, `results(0)`, to an `Integer`.

Let's expand this explanation a little further. Imagine if our Fibonacci Web Service was implemented on a server residing in New York, while the application that wished to call it was in Seattle. Our Seattle application could examine the WSDL of the New York Fibonacci Web Service, and construct a proxy class similar to the example above. The application could then write the following valid ASP.NET page (below) which when requested would use the local proxy to call the Fibonacci Web Service in New York. The New York Web Service would then perform the work and return the result back to the application in Seattle that called it:

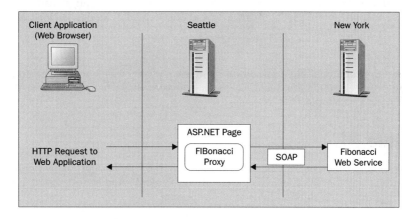

Below is what the ASP.NET Page that uses the Fibonacci proxy might look like.

VB.NET

```
' Seattle ASP.NET application
<script runat="server">
   Public Sub Page_Load(sender As Object, e As EventArgs)
      Dim fibonacci As New Fibonacci()
      lblResult = Fibonacci.GetSeqNumber(5)
   End Sub
</script>
Index of 5 in the Fibonacci Series is: <asp:label id="lblResult" runat="server"/>
```

To the Seattle developer coding the application, it appears as if Fibonacci is a local class, when in fact the class is a proxy of the New York Fibonacci Web Service.

Now that we have an idea of what a proxy is used for, let's talk about how we automate the creation of a proxy.

Creating Proxy Classes

There are four ways to create proxies for Web Services:

- ❏ Use Visual Studio.NET and add a **Web Reference** to a new project.

- ❏ Use the command-line `wsdl.exe` utility available with the .NET framework.

- ❏ Use another solution, such as the Microsoft SOAP toolkit.

- ❏ Roll your own. Using PERL, Java, VB, C++, and so on. As long as the platform is capable of sending and receiving HTTP and is capable of parsing strings (or supports XML) you've got everything you need to communicate with a Web Service.

> **It should be noted that although all the examples in this chapter will use ASP.NET Web Services, the .NET technology used to create the proxies could be applied to any Web Service as long as it used SOAP.**

Because this book is about .NET, we're only going to focus on the first two options for building proxies: Visual Stuido.NET and the `wsdl.exe` command-line tool. The second option, using the command-line tool `wsdl.exe`, is applicable if you don't have Visual Studio.NET. The first option, using Visual Studio.NET, is by far the easiest.

Let's start by looking at how we build a proxy using Visual Studio.NET. After we use both Visual Studio.NET and the command-line tool to build and use a proxy, we'll come back and examine the auto-generated proxy class in more detail. For both examples we'll use the Fibonacci Web Service we created in the previous chapter.

Visual Studio.NET

If you've built an application using Visual Basic 6 (before .NET), you're probably familiar with the **Add Reference** option, available from any VB project under **Project | Add Reference**, that allowed us to reference a component we wanted to include in our project.

Including the reference allowed us to early-bind to the object, instead of late binding. Early binding simply allows us to know the data types at run time/compile time, while late binding would force the code to determine the data types at run time. For example, late-bound code would be as follows:

```
Dim objAdo As Object
objAdo = CreateObject("ADODB.Connection")
```

Note, that the above code is written in Visual Basic 6 and hence makes use of the Object *data type.*

With late-bound code we would treat an instance of ADODB.Connection as an Object type and VB would be responsible for calling the appropriate methods at run time. We would additionally have no statement completion (intellisense), since at design time VB would not know that objAdo was of type ADODB.Connection. Late binding is expensive, and we want to avoid it where possible, mainly because the application needs to infer the appropriate data types to use at run time.

Instead of writing late-bound code, as shown above, we could use the **Add Reference** option in VB to add a reference to the ADO object at design time. Our code would then look as follows:

```
Dim objAdo As New ADODB.Connection
```

We would have statement completion and VB would treat objAdo as an instance of type ADODB.Connection at run-time.

Visual Studio.NET continues to support the concepts of early and late binding, as well as the **Project | Add Reference** option. However, we have a new option specifically designed for Web Services: **Project | Add Web Reference**.

Add Web Reference

Just as we can early-bind to local classes, Visual Studio.NET supports the capability to early-bind to Web Services.

When we add a **Web Reference** to a Visual Studio.NET project – note the **Add Web Reference** option is available to all Visual Studio.NET projects and languages – Visual Studio.NET will do all the work required to connect to the Web Service, parse the WSDL, and generate a proxy class that we use to program with the Web Service.

Using the Fibonacci Web Service

Let's look at an example using our Fibonacci Web Service created in the previous chapter.

Before we can create the Web Reference we need to know the address to the WSDL of the Web Service we want to create the reference to. For example, here is the address of the WSDL for the VB.NET Fibonacci implementation of the ASP.NET Web Service on my server:

```
http://localhost/wrox/4885/WebServices/Expose/Fibonacci/Fibonacci_vb.asmx?WSDL
```

Next, let's create a new Visual Studio.NET project. Since this book is about ASP.NET, we'll create a new ASP.NET Web Application using Visual Basic.NET as our language.

Once Visual Studio.NET creates the new Web Application we're presented with a design page. We can drag-and-drop elements onto this page. For the purpose of this example, we'll need a textbox, a label, and a button (it doesn't need to be pretty for this example):

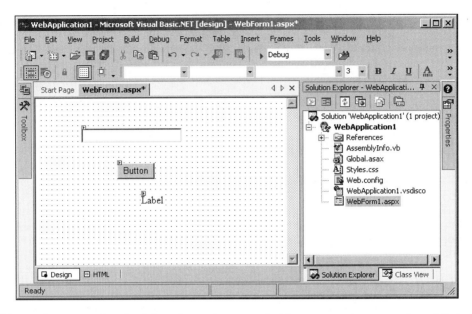

We'll leave the names of each of these items the same, that is, `TextBox1`, `Button1`, and `Label1`. We are now ready to add our **Web Reference**.

We have two options, we can either select **Project | Add Web Reference** or we can right-click on the on **References** in the **Solution Explorer** and select **Add Web Reference**. Either selection opens the **Add Web Reference** dialog box:

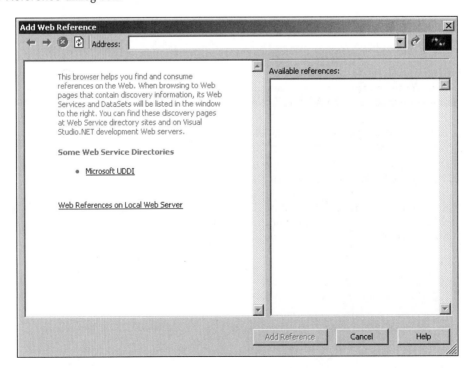

Within this dialog box we can browse services provided by UDDI (the link to Microsoft UDDI takes us to the Microsoft UDDI implementation), browse Web References on the local server (for Web Services we created with Visual Studio.NET), or enter the address ourselves.

Let's enter in the address of our Fibonacci Web Service:

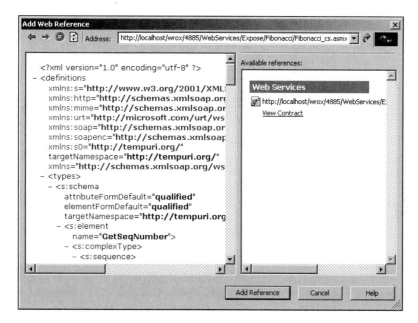

In the above screenshot we've entered in the address of the location of the WSDL document that describes the Fibonacci Web Service. On the left-hand side of the **Add Web Reference** dialog we can view the WSDL. Additionally, the **Add Reference** button of this dialog is now enabled.

Essentially what has happened is this:

❑ Visual Studio.NET fetched the WSDL from the location we specified and validated it.

❑ The **Add Reference** button is enabled and we are able to add a reference to the Web Service(s) described by this WSDL to our current project (whereby Visual Studio.NET will create a proxy).

Let's go ahead and press **Add Reference**.

Once we've done this the dialog closes, and Visual Studio.NET quietly creates a new section in our **Solution Explorer** entitled: **Web References**. Behind the scenes VS.NET has parsed the WSDL, created a proxy object that represents the Web Service (the namespace of the proxy is the name of the server the WSDL was served from, in our case localhost), and cached a local copy of the WSDL. This is all visible to us if we expand the **Web References** section with the **Solution Explorer**:

We can now write code in our Web Application to use the Fibonacci Web Service. Let's double-click on **Button1** and write some code for the Button1_Click event. Once the code view is open, we can write the following to call the GetSeqNumber of the Fibonacci Web Service:

```
Private Sub Button1_Click(ByVal sender As System.Object,
                          ByVal e As System.EventArgs) Handles Button1.Click
    Dim fibonacci As New localhost.Fibonacci()
    Dim indexIntoSeries As Integer

    indexIntoSeries = TextBox1.Text

    Label1.Text = fibonacci.GetSeqNumber(indexIntoSeries)
End Sub
```

In the above code we first create an instance of the proxy, fibonacci, by calling New localhost.Fibonacci(). The Web Reference we created uses the namespace localhost and within that namespace we find the proxy class Fibonacci.

> Although we didn't change the namespace in this example, changing it from **localhost** to some more meaningful value, such as **MathServices**, is as simple as right-clicking on **localhost** in the **Solution Explorer** and selecting **rename**.

Next, we declare a local variable, indexIntoSeries. This is used as the parameter value for the call to GetSeqNumber(). Next, we extract the value from TextBox1 and assign it to indexIntoSeries – so the user must enter an Integer value. We then use our instance, fibonacci, calling its GetSeqNumber() method, passing in the value of indexIntoSeries. Finally, when the call completes an Integer is returned, the value of which we assign to Label1.Text.

Here's a high-level rundown of what occurs when we run this application and click on Button1: ASP.NET creates an instance of the proxy, and calls it, passing in the value of TextBox1. The proxy then calls, via SOAP, to the Fibonacci Web Service, which, in turn, computes the result, and sends it back to the proxy via SOAP. The proxy then deserializes the SOAP message (converts the values within the SOAP message to .NET types) and returns an Integer value, which is finally displayed to the end user.

Now that we've seen the proxy in action, let's take a look at the source code that Visual Studio.NET created.

Viewing the Source for the Proxy

Behind the scenes Visual Studio.NET has obviously done a lot of work for us – namely, creating the proxy and sending and receiving the SOAP requests and responses.

We can access, and modify, the source code that Visual Studio.NET compiles for our proxy. It's not available to us by default, but if we right-click on our project in Solution Explorer and select Add Existing Item a file selection dialog box is opened. The location that the file dialog box is currently accessing is the root directory of our project. We should see a folder named `localhost` (or another name if we renamed the Web Reference). If we open this folder we find the source to our proxy. On my server the source file is: `Fibonacci_cs.vb`.

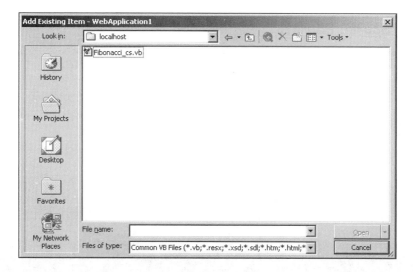

> The proxy is created in whatever language the project is using. For this particular example, the proxy source is using VB.NET since it is a VB.NET ASP.NET Web Application.

This file contains the source for our Proxy. If we open it, it'll be added to our current project and we can view and/or modify its source.

Creating a proxy using Visual Studio.NET is simple. As long as we have the URL to the WSDL Visual Studio.NET takes care of the rest. We can write code, and call methods, just as we expect to call on a local class, when in fact the proxy is exchanging SOAP messages with a Web Service.

While Visual Studio.NET definitely makes using Web Services easy, Visual Studio.NET isn't a requirement for creating proxy classes. If we're using .NET, but don't have a copy of Visual Studio.NET, we can still automate the process of building proxies to Web Services using the command-line tool `wsdl.exe`.

Command-Line Tool (wsdl.exe)

The command-line tool, installed by the .NET framework, used to generate proxy classes from Web Service Description Language (WSDL) contracts is: `wsdl.exe`. This tool is found in the `\Program Files\Microsoft.NET\FrameworkSDK\Bin` directory. This directory is added to the `PATH` when .NET is installed.

Using `wsdl.exe` to generate a proxy for a .NET application isn't as easy as it is with Visual Studio.NET. For example, the output of `wsdl.exe` is always a source file, which we then have to compile. However, the command-line tool does give us more options, such as the language (any .NET language) used for the proxy source file.

Creating the Source File

Let's start by using `wsdl.exe` to generate a proxy for a WSDL document available, for argument's sake, at the following URL (the same WSDL used for Visual Studio.NET example):

```
http://localhost/wrox/4885/WebServices/Expose/Fibonacci/Fibonacci_cs.asmx?WSDL
```

We first need to shell to a command, where we then type:

```
wsdl http://localhost/.../Fibonacci_cs.asmx?WSDL
```

The result is a source file, by default in C#: `Fibonacci.cs`.

Here's the screenshot of `wsdl.exe` in action:

By default, if we name an HTTP-based WSDL location, `wsdl.exe` will use the proxy settings configured for Internet Explorer. Alternatively, we can copy the WSDL locally and run it through `wsdl.exe`:

```
wsdl Fibonacci_vb.wsdl
```

We get the same result – a C# source file that represents the proxy.

As previously mentioned, `wsdl.exe` creates a C# source file for our proxy. But the language is configurable, and if we wish to generate our proxy in VB.NET we simply need to set the `language` flag:

```
wsdl /language:VB http://localhost/.../Fibonacci_cs.asmx?WSDL
```

If we execute the above statement `wsdl.exe` will generate another proxy source file, this time in VB:

```
Command Prompt                                                    _ □ X
Microsoft Windows 2000 [Version 5.00.2195]
(C) Copyright 1985-2000 Microsoft Corp.

C:\>wsdl /language:vb http://localhost/wrox/4885/WebServices/Expose/Fibonacci/Fi
bonacci_cs.asmx?WSDL
Microsoft (R) Web Services Description Language Utility
[Microsoft .NET Framework Version 1.0.2728.2]
Copyright (C) Microsoft Corp 2000. All rights reserved.

C:\Fibonacci.vb
Writing file 'C:\Fibonacci.vb'.

C:\>
```

When we open up the source files we are presented with similar implementations differing only in the syntax of the language.

Below are the auto-generated proxy sources for our Fibonacci Web Service in both VB.NET and C#:

VB.NET

```vbnet
Option Strict On
Option Explicit On

Imports System
Imports System.Web.Services
Imports System.Web.Services.Protocols
Imports System.Xml.Serialization

<WebServiceBindingAttribute(Name:="FibonacciSoap", _
[Namespace]:="http://tempuri.org/")>
Public Class Fibonacci
  Inherits System.Web.Services.Protocols.SoapHttpClientProtocol

  Public Sub New()
    MyBase.New
    Me.Url = "http://localhost/wrox/4885/WebServices" _
                               /Expose/Fibonacci/Fibonacci_cs.asmx"
  End Sub

  <SoapDocumentMethodAttribute("http://tempuri.org/GetSeqNumber", _
          Use:=Description.SoapBindingUse.Literal, _
          ParameterStyle:=SoapParameterStyle.Wrapped)>
  Public Function GetSeqNumber(ByVal fibIndex As Integer) As Integer
    Dim results() As Object = Me.Invoke("GetSeqNumber", New Object() {fibIndex})
    Return CType(results(0),Integer)
  End Function

  Public Function BeginGetSeqNumber(ByVal fibIndex As Integer, _
                        ByVal callback As System.AsyncCallback, _
                        ByVal asyncState As Object) _
                        As System.IAsyncResult
    Return Me.BeginInvoke("GetSeqNumber", New Object() {fibIndex}, _
                        callback, asyncState)
```

```
    End Function

  Public Function EndGetSeqNumber(ByVal asyncResult As System.IAsyncResult) _
                                 As Integer
    Dim results() As Object = Me.EndInvoke(asyncResult)
    Return CType(results(0),Integer)
  End Function
End Class
```

C#

```
using System.Xml.Serialization;
using System;
using System.Web.Services.Protocols;
using System.Web.Services;

[WebServiceBindingAttribute(Name="FibonacciSoap",Namespace="http://tempuri.org/")]
public class Fibonacci : SoapHttpClientProtocol {

  public Fibonacci() {
    this.Url = "http://localhost/wrox/4885/" +
                        "WebServices/Expose/Fibonacci/Fibonacci_cs.asmx";
  }


  [SoapDocumentMethodAttribute("http://tempuri.org/GetSeqNumber",
                        Use= Description.SoapBindingUse.Literal,
                        ParameterStyle=SoapParameterStyle.Wrapped)]
  public int GetSeqNumber(int fibIndex) {
    object[] results = this.Invoke("GetSeqNumber", new object[] {fibIndex});
    return ((int)(results[0]));
  }

  public System.IAsyncResult BeginGetSeqNumber(int fibIndex,
                                    System.AsyncCallback callback,
                                    object asyncState) {
    return this.BeginInvoke("GetSeqNumber",
                        new object[] {fibIndex},
                        callback, asyncState);
  }

  public int EndGetSeqNumber(System.IAsyncResult asyncResult) {
    object[] results = this.EndInvoke(asyncResult);
    return ((int)(results[0]));
  }
}
```

Compiling the Source File

Now that we have the proxy source files we need to compile them. Included with .NET are several command-line compilers, two of which are for C# (csc.exe) and VB.NET (vbc.exe). We'll use these to build our proxy classes into assemblies.

> For more language-specific details and information on the respective command-line compilers, please see Wrox's *Professional C#* and *Professional VB.NET* books.

Compiling the VB.NET Source

To compile the VB.NET source file we'll execute the following statement at a command prompt:

vbc /t:library /out:fibonacci_vb.dll fibonacci.vb

This instructs the VB.NET command-line compiler to create an output target of library (.dll), rather than an executable or other output type, and to create a file named `fibonacci_vb.dll` – an optional statement we need to use since we're creating both a VB and a C# version – and finally the above statement instructs the VB.NET compiler to use `fibonacci.vb` as the input source file.

The result is a .dll file named `fibonacci_vb.dll`.

Compiling the C# Source

To compile the C# source file we'll execute the following statement:

csc /t:library /out:fibonacci_cs.dll fibonacci.cs

The syntax for the VB.NET and C# compilers is nearly identical – after executing the above statement the result is a .dll file named `fibonacci_cs.dll`.

We can now copy either of these .dll files – we only need one of them – to an ASP.NET application's \bin directory. We can then build an ASP.NET application that uses this proxy, just as we did with Visual Studio.NET:

```
<Script runat="server">
Private Sub Page_Load(sender As Object, e As EventArgs)
  Dim fibonacci As New Fibonacci ()

  lblResult.Text = fibonacci.GetSeqNumber(6)
End Sub
The value of the 6th element in the Fibonacci series is: <asp:label id="lblResult"
runat="server"/>
```

In the Visual Studio.NET version of this example, we used a Fibonacci proxy that was part of the namespace, `localhost`. Our example of the proxy using the command-line tool didn't use a namespace – this is simply a choice we made, we could make the above class part of a namespace with another simple command-line switch: `namespace`:

wsdl /language:VB /namespace:localhost http://localhost/.../Fibonacci_cs.asmx?WSDL

The `namespace` and `language` parameters are just two of the parameters that `wsdl.exe` supports. Let's look at the others.

wsdl.exe Usage and Parameters

WSDL supports several parameters used to configure the behavior of the tool. A description of these parameters can be found by typing the following at a command prompt:

wsdl.exe /?

This returns a full listing of the switches the tool supports:

Parameters	Description
`<url or path>`	The URL or file path to one of these supported documents types that `WSDL.exe` recognizes: WSDL Contract XSD Schema DISCO Document

`/nologo`	Hides the banner output when the tool is run. The banner is as follows:
	
	`Microsoft (R) Web Services Description Language Utility`
	
	`[Microsoft .NET Framework Version ##]`
	
	`Copyright (C) Microsoft Corp 2000. All rights reserved.`

`/language:<language>`	WSDL generates a proxy class source file. The language option (short form `/l:`) allows us to create the proxy in any .NET language. Three languages are available as part of the SDK that the tool supports: C# – `/language:CS` VB.NET – `/language:VB` JScript. – `/language:JS` To use a language other than the above three we must name the class implementing the interface `ICodeGenerator`. For example, if we wish to use PERL we would use a CodeDOM class provided by the .NET PERL compiler. *If not specified the language defaults to C#.*
`/server`	By default `wsdl.exe` will create client proxies for a given wsdl. However, if we use the `/server` option `wsdl.exe` will generate a source file with abstract members that represents the server implementation of the Web Service. This option is useful if several organizations agree upon the structure of the Web Service (as defined by the WSDL), but would like to provide their own implementations. .NET can automate the creation of the classes, methods, and properties based on the WSDL.

Parameters	Description
/namespace: <namespace>	The /namespace (short form /n:) allows us to set the namespace that the proxy class is generated within. By default no namespace is used. For example, if we wish to generate a proxy class for our Fibonacci Web Service, we can generate a proxy class within a namespace of MathSamples by simply setting /n:MathSamples. We would then refer to our Fibonacci class as MathSamples.Fibonacci.
/out:<filename>	The /out parameter allows us to name the source file created by wsdl.exe. By default the name of this source file is the [service name].[language extension] and does not need to be specified unless we wish the source file to have a different name.
/protocol:<protocol>	ASP.NET Web Services support three protocols: HTTPGet, HTTPPost, and SOAP. By default SOAP is the protocol used for client proxies and is what WSDL will instruct the proxy class to use (through attributes in the source). We can override this setting by specifying a different protocol with the /protocol parameter. Valid values include: HttpGet, HttpPost, and SOAP
/username:<username>	The /username parameter (short form /u:) is set when we use a URL to access the WSDL, DISCO, or XSD Schema and the server requires authentication.
/password:<password>	The /password parameter (short form /p:) is set when we use a URL to access the WSDL, DISCO, or XSD Schema and the server requires authentication.
/domain:<domain>	The /domain parameter (short form /d:) is set when we use a URL to access the WSDL, DISCO, or XSD Schema and the server requires authentication.
/proxy:<url>	The proxy server used for HTTP requests. By default the proxy settings defined by IE will be used.
/proxyusername: <username>	Name of the user to authenticate to the proxy server with.
/proxypassword: <password>	Value of the proxy user's password to authenticate to the proxy server with.
/proxydomain: <domain>	Name of the proxy user's domain to authenticate to the proxy server with.
/appsettingsurlkey: <key>	Rather than using the URL specified in the WSDL document, for example, hard coding the URL into the proxy, a URL may be stored in ASP.NET configuration system's <appSettings> section. We can use the appsettingsurlkey parameter with wsdl.exe to name the key that corresponds to the value stored in the configuration file.
/appsettingsbaseurl: <baseurl>	Used in conjunction with the appsettingsurlkey this parameter allows us to name the base URL for the Web Service.

As we learned in the previous chapter, ASP.NET makes creating Web Services almost trivial. Similarly, using Web Services, whether built with ASP.NET or with other technologies, is equally trivial through the use of Visual Studio.NET or `wsdl.exe`. Either option creates a source file that is either compiled for us, as in the case of Visual Studio.NET, or that we need to compile, as in the case of `wsdl.exe`. However, both options take care of wrapping the calls to the SOAP end points in a rich, object-oriented manner.

> *Although we've focused on the high-level features that we'll use 95% of the time, later in the chapter we'll look at how we get to the more advanced features through the use of SOAP Extensions.*

Now that we know how to use both Visual Studio.NET and `wsdl.exe` to create a proxy class, let's discuss the proxy that's generated. It inherits some properties and methods from a base class, and as we'll see, these properties and methods give us even more options and control over the interaction with the Web Service the proxy represents.

Using the Proxy Class

If you build and use the proxy class in Visual Studio.NET you'll notice (through statement completion) that the class contains additional methods and properties beyond the methods used in our Web Service.

For example, the `Fibonacci` class supported a `GetSeqNumber()` method, however, if we examine the proxy for Fibonacci in Visual Studio.NET we'll see several other methods and properties that `Fibonacci` supports – in addition to `GetSeqNumber`.

This is because the Fibonacci proxy class inherits these methods and properties from a base class.

> The base class that a proxy inherits from is **SoapHttpClientProtocol**, which inherits from **HttpWebClientProtocol**, which in turn inherits from **WebClientProtocol**. All of which add properties and methods to the proxy class.

Let's examine some of the common methods and properties we might use.

Controlling Timeout

Providers of Web Services will base their business model on the availability of their service. However, we still need to write our applications to behave correctly when the service is not performing optimally. For example, the network connection between the provider and the consumer of the service could become saturated and responses start to take too long or requests can be issued and the consumer of the service simply waits until the request times out – if not specified, the default timeout for a request from our proxy is ninety seconds.

The code below illustrates a simple `Add` Web Service that performs slowly – due to a call to `Thread.Sleep(20000)` – which forces the thread to wait 20 seconds before continuing:

VB.NET

```
<%@ WebService Class="Timeout" %>

Imports System.Threading
Imports System.Web.Services

Public Class Timeout
  <WebMethod()> Public Function Add(a As Integer, b As Integer) As Integer
    Thread.Sleep(20000)

    Return a + b
  End Function
End Class
```

The above code introduces false latency into our application. However, if this latency were real, such as from network congestion, the client using the Web Service would most likely not want to wait 20 seconds for a response.

One of the inherited properties in the proxy class is Timeout. If we built a proxy for the Add Web Service, named Timeout, we could write the following code to time out the request automatically if the Web Service did not respond within five seconds:

VB.NET

```
<Script runat="server">
Public Sub Page_Load(sender As Object, e As EventArgs)
  Dim example As New Timeout()
  example.Timeout = 5000

  Try
    lblResult.Text = example.Add(4,5)
  Catch err As Exception
    lblResult.Text = err.Message
  End Try
End Sub
</Script>
The result of 4 + 5 is: <asp:label id="lblResult" runat="server" />
```

> **The above code demonstrates the use of a Try...Catch block surrounding a Web Service call. We'll talk more about handling Web Service exceptions later in the chapter. A timeout is an exception, and if not handled will generate an error.**

Using the Timeout property of the proxy ensures that our application won't wait for a slow Web Service. Another inherited property of the proxy, Url, allows us to set the end-point URL that the proxy sends requests to.

Setting the URL

When we build a proxy from a WSDL document generated by ASP.NET, the default end point of the service is already provided. Here's a snippet of the WSDL for our Fibonacci Web Service:

```
<service name="Fibonacci">
  <port name="FibonacciSoap" binding="s0:FibonacciSoap">
    <soap:address location="http:// ... /Fibonacci_cs.asmx" />
  </port>
</service>
```

The `location` attribute defined in `<soap:address/>` names the end point to which SOAP calls are sent. The proxy that is generated uses this setting. For example, if we look at the constructors of both the VB.NET and C# code:

VB.NET

```
Public Sub New()
  MyBase.New
  Me.Url = "http://localhost/wrox/4885/WebServices" _
                          /Expose/Fibonacci/Fibonacci_cs.asmx"
End Sub
```

C#

```
public Fibonacci() {
  this.Url = "http://localhost/wrox/4885/" +
                    "WebServices/Expose/Fibonacci/Fibonacci_cs.asmx";
}
```

Both set the `Url` property to the value of `location` in our WSDL. Although the value is 'pre-configured' for us in the proxy, we can either remove this setting or reset the value of the property ourselves at run time using the `Url` property of the proxy.

Because we can reset the `Url` that the proxy uses, this means we can dynamically choose the Web Service we want to use, or use a common proxy for multiple Web Services. For example, if we built an e-commerce site and wanted to use credit card Web Services for credit card validation we could use the `Timeout` and the `Url` properties together. If a given call to a service timed out, for example a call to a Credit Card Web Service, we can write code that changes the `Url` to a Web Service provided by another vendor and call that 'backup' service. This of course assumes that either proxy supports all these services, or all the services implement a common Web Service API.

Proxy Web Server Access

By default the Web Service proxy will use the settings configured for Internet Explorer to access the Internet. If our local network relies on a proxy server for external Internet access, which most companies do, and if IE isn't already configured to use this proxy – or if we desire to use a different proxy server – we have that option in the Web Service proxy through the `Proxy` property.

To use the `Proxy` property, we need to set its value to a class that implements `IWebProxy`, such as the `WebProxy` class found in the `System.Net` namespace. For example, if our local network requires us to use a proxy server named `'AcmeCoProxy'` through port 80, we could write the following code:

VB.NET

```
<%@ Import Namespace="System.Net" %>
<Script runat="server">
Private Sub Page_Load(sender As Object, e As EventArgs)
  Dim fibonacci As New Fibonacci()
  Dim webProxy As New WebProxy("AcmeCoProxy", 80)

  Fibonacci.Proxy = webProxy
  lblResult.Text = fibonacci.GetSeqNumber(6)
End Sub
The value of the 6th element in the Fibonacci series is: <asp:label id="lblResult"
runat="server"/>
```

Calls made through the `Fibonacci` proxy object are now routed to the `AcmeCoProxy` server on port 80. The web proxy server then issues the request and returns the result to the caller.

> If the web proxy server requires credentials, these can be set as part of the `System.Net.WebProxy` class.

Maintaining State

ASP.NET Web Services utilize HTTP as the transport protocol for messages. Additional transport protocols can be used to route SOAP, such as SMTP or UDP, but HTTP will be the most commonly used protocol. Our proxy provides us with access to common HTTP protocol features, such as cookies.

As we do with a browser-based web application, we can also use HTTP cookies to pass 'additional' data along with SOAP messages. The most common use of cookies in an ASP.NET Web Service will most likely be for maintaining a `Session` on the server providing the Web Service. For example, the following Web Service uses `Session` state to retain values on the server:

VB.NET

```
<%@ WebService Class="SessionStateExample" %>

Imports System.Web.Services

Public Class SessionStateExample
  Inherits WebService

  <WebMethod(EnableSession:=true)> _
  Public Function SetSession(key As String, item As String)
    Session(key) = item
  End Function

  <WebMethod(EnableSession:=true)> _
  Public Function GetSession(key As String) As String
    Return Session(key)
  End Function
End Class
```

The above ASP.NET Web Service has two functions defined as Web Services:

❑ `SetSession()` – Allowing us to pass a key and item (both strings) and use the key value to create an entry in `Session` for the value.

❑ `GetSession()` – Allows us to pass the key and retrieve the result of the item stored for that key.

The `WebMethod` attribute explicitly enables Session, which by default is not-enabled, by setting `EnableSession:="true"` for each of the above methods. The server will issue a Session cookie to the caller containing a unique Session ID. On each subsequent request the caller, in our case the Web Service proxy, presents the cookie and the server is able to load the appropriate Session data.

There are two caveats for using HTTP cookies with the proxy:

❑ If we create a proxy for a Web Service, and the Web Service requires the use of HTTP cookies we need to explicitly support HTTP cookies within our proxy. This is done by creating an instance of a `CookieContainer` class and assigning that instance to the proxy's `CookieContainer` property.

❑ If we intend to maintain state through the use of ASP.NET session state within the Web Service we need to re-present the HTTP cookie on subsequent uses of the proxy with our application. The `Cookie` that the proxy receives is only valid for the life of the proxy. When the proxy instance goes out of scope or is destroyed, the cookie is lost and on subsequent requests we no longer have access to our Session (since we no longer have the Session cookie to send to the server).

The following code illustrates both of the above caveats:

VB.NET

```
<Script runat="Server">
Public Sub Page_Load(sender As Object, e As EventArgs)
   Dim sessionExample As New SessionStateExample()

   sessionExample.SetSession("name", "rob")
   lblSession1.Text = sessionExample.GetSession("name")
End Sub
</Script>
<Font face=arial>
Value: <asp:label id="lblSession1" runat="server"/>
</Font>
```

In the `Page_Load` event we create an instance of `SessionStateExample` and create a new Session on our Web Service by calling `SetSession()`. We then retrieve the value by calling `GetSession("name")`. In this case no value is returned, since the proxy is not using HTTP cookies, therefore `lblSession1` would not contain a value.

Supporting Cookies within a Web Service Proxy

To enable cookie support within our Web Service proxy we need to create a `CookieContainer`. Here is the fixed code:

VB.NET

```
<%@ Import Namespace="System.Net" %>

<Script runat="Server">
Public Sub Page_Load(sender As Object, e As EventArgs)
  Dim sessionExample As New SessionStateExample()

  Dim cookieContainer As New CookieContainer()
  sessionExample.CookieContainer = cookieContainer

  sessionExample.SetSession("name", "rob")
  lblSession1.Text = sessionExample.GetSession("name")
End Sub
</Script>
<Font face=arial>
Value: <asp:label id="lblSession1" runat="server"/>
</Font>
```

In the above 'fixed' example, we first import the namespace `System.Net`. The `System.Net` namespace contains the `CookieContainer` class that we need. Then, within our `Page_Load` event we add two lines of code to create an instance of the `CookieContainer` class and set that instance to the `CookieContainer` property of the Web Service proxy.

When we execute the above code, we now get the desired result. The `GetSession()` call returns the value set by `SetSession()`.

Although this is a simplistic example, it effectively illustrates how to maintain state through the use of an HTTP cookie using a Web Service proxy. We can go one step further.

Persisting the Web Service Cookie for Multiple Requests

Since the proxy does not persist the Session cookie, and we want to use Session state in our Web Service across multiple requests, we need to do our own cookie persistence.

Take the following example:

```
<%@ Import Namespace="System.Net" %>

<Script runat="Server">

Public Sub Page_Load(sender As Object, e As EventArgs)
  Dim sessionExample As New SessionStateExample()
  Dim cookieContainer As New CookieContainer()
  Dim sessionCookie As Cookie
  Dim cookieCollection As New CookieCollection()

  sessionExample.CookieContainer = cookieContainer

  sessionCookie = CType(session("sessionCookie"), Cookie)
```

```
   If (IsNothing(sessionCookie)) Then
      sessionExample.SetSession("name", "rob")
      cookieCollection = sessionExample.CookieContainer.GetCookies( _
            New Uri("http://localhost"))
      Session("sessionCookie") = cookieCollection("ASP.NET_SessionId")
   Else
      sessionExample.CookieContainer.Add(sessionCookie)
   End If

   lblSession1.Text = sessionExample.GetSession("name")
End Sub

</Script>
<Font face=arial>
Value: <asp:label id="lblSession1" runat="server"/>
</Font>
```

The above is a more advanced example that demonstrates how we can store the Web Service's Session cookie in Session state with the Web Application that is using the Web Service.

The above example uses two new local variables: `sessionCookie` and `cookieCollection` used to store the Web Service's Session cookie.

The code first attempts to retrieve a value for `sessionCookie` by attempting to access a local Session variable. The code then determines if `sessionCookie` references an instance of a `Cookie`. If it does not it walks through the procedure of calling the proxy's `SetSession()` method and then stores the Web Service's Session cookie.

Alternativley, we could simply add the `sessionCookie` to the existing proxy's `CookieContainer` and request the method, `GetSession()`. We've encapsulated all of this work in one ASP.NET page, but this could just as easily be applied to an entire web application – allowing us to use ASP.NET Session state for Web Services across our application.

There are several other properties and methods of the proxy object that we're not covering. However, there are additional properties that we will cover later in this chapter, as they relate to security, `ClientCertificates`, and `Credentials`.

Next, let's look at another feature that ASP.NET Web Services enable: converting any web site into a Web Service.

From Web Site to Web Service: Screen Scraping

HTML Screen Scraping is the practice of connecting to a web site, retrieving a result, usually HTML, and then sifting through the unstructured HTML to extract a useful value. For example, if we wanted to find the current sales rank for the Wrox precursor to this book, *A Preview of ASP+*, we could look it up by ISBN (1-861004-75-3) on BarnesAndNoble.com using the following URL:

http://shop.barnesandnoble.com/booksearch/isbnInquiry.asp?isbn=1861004753

We could then view the HTML source and search for 'sales rank'. We would find:

```
<font size="-1">sales rank: 2,823</font>
```

In the past, if we wanted to automate this through code, we could write a small application that would connect to BarnesAndNoble.com through `WinInet`, or the `XMLHttp` component, and request the document, and then we would write some code to search the HTML for a string that matched '`<font size="-1">sales rank: `' and also search for a string immediately following the previous string of '`</font>`'. Anything found between these two strings would be our result.

Not exactly efficient, and our code to perform this match would be very fragile – in the sense that if the HTML changed, our code would no longer function correctly.

.NET makes much of this a lot easier. For example, there is support for Regular Expression (RegEx) pattern matching. Finding the sales rank value in the above string is now simply a matter of creating the appropriate RegEx syntax, and then searching the document:

```
"size=.-1.>sales rank:.(.*?)</"
```

The above RegEx search string returns the sales rank value of 2,823.

While RegEx does simplify searching for strings, we still need to write all the other code to access the site and return the HTML, as well as wrapping all of this in a friendly API.

ASP.NET Web Services automates much of this for us by allowing us to build custom WSDL documents that specify the location, parameters, regular expression to match, and return types all using XML. We can then use one of our proxy generation tools, such as Visual Studio.NET or `wsdl.exe` to generate a proxy object to encapsulate this – turning any web site into a Web Service.

Authoring the WSDL

Let's write an example that returns the sales rank for any book, for a provided ISBN. First we'll need to write the WSDL.

```xml
<?xml version="1.0"?>
<definitions xmlns:s="http://www.w3.org/2000/10/XMLSchema"
             xmlns:http="http://schemas.xmlsoap.org/wsdl/http/"
             xmlns:mime="http://schemas.xmlsoap.org/wsdl/mime/"
             xmlns:soapenc="http://schemas.xmlsoap.org/soap/encoding/"
             xmlns:soap="http://schemas.xmlsoap.org/wsdl/soap/"
             xmlns:s0="http://tempuri.org/"
             targetNamespace="http://tempuri.org/"
             xmlns="http://schemas.xmlsoap.org/wsdl/"
             xmlns:msType="http://microsoft.com/wsdl/mime/textMatching/">
  <types/>
  <message name="GetBookDetailsHttpGetIn">
    <part name="isbn" type="s:string"/>
  </message>
  <message name="GetBookDetailsHttpGetOut"/>
  <portType name="BarnesAndNobleHttpGet">
    <operation name="GetBookDetails">
```

```
          <input message="s0:GetBookDetailsHttpGetIn"/>
          <output message="s0:GetBookDetailsHttpGetOut"/>
      </operation>
  </portType>
  <binding name="BarnesAndNobleHttpGet" type="s0:BarnesAndNobleHttpGet">
    <http:binding verb="GET"/>
    <operation name="GetBookDetails">
      <http:operation location="/booksearch/isbnInquiry.asp"/>
      <input>
        <http:urlEncoded/>
      </input>
      <output>
        <msType:text>
          <msType:match name="Rank"
                        pattern="size=.-1.&gt;sales rank:.(.*?)&lt;/"
                        ignoreCase="true"/>
        </msType:text>
      </output>
    </operation>
  </binding>
  <service name="BarnesAndNoble">
    <port name="BarnesAndNobleHttpGet" binding="s0:BarnesAndNobleHttpGet">
      <http:address location="http://shop.barnesandnoble.com"/>
    </port>
  </service>
</definitions>
```

The above WSDL defines a `<service>` named `BarnesAndNoble`, which also names the end point http://shop.barnesandnoble.com we'll make queries against. This service does not use SOAP, but instead uses HTTP GET to make requests. There are two other areas of interest in the above WSDL: `<binding>` and `<message name="GetBookDetailsHttpGetIn">`.

The `<binding>` section defines an operation, `GetBookDetails`, which further qualifies the end point we'll send our HTTP-GET request to (`/booksearch/isbnInquiry.asp`). It also defines, in the `<output>` section, a `<msType:match ...>`. It is within a `<match>` tag that we declare the RegEx syntax used for our string match. The `name` value allows us to control the name of the property the proxy will create, which we'll use to access the 'sales rank' of a given ISBN. The `pattern` value is the RegEx pattern we'll use to search the document and return results with. Finally, the `ignoreCase` option is self-explanatory.

The other section of interest to us is `<message name="GetBookDetailsHttpGetIn">`. We use this section to define parameters that we want to send as part of the HTTP GET request. The defined value, `isbn`, of type `string`, will be used to formulate a request, such as:

http://shop.barnesandnoble.com/booksearch/isbnInquiry.asp?isbn=1861004753

or:

http://shop.barnesandnoble.com/booksearch/isbnInquiry.asp?isbn=1861004885

We're now ready to build a proxy for this WSDL using either Visual Studio.NET or `wsdl.exe`.

Building the Proxy

Since Visual Studio.NET makes building the proxy so easy (to the point of trivializing it), let's use the command-line tool.

First we need to open a command prompt and move to the directory where the above WSDL was created. We can then issue the following command:

```
wsdl.exe /language:VB bn.wsdl
```

If there were no errors in our WSDL, we should now have a VB source file named BarnesAndNoble.vb. Let's look at the source of this file (we've removed some elements not relevant to this discussion, namely comments and the asynchronous methods):

```
Option Strict On
Option Explicit On

Imports System
Imports System.Web.Services
Imports System.Web.Services.Protocols
Imports System.Xml.Serialization

Public Class BarnesAndNoble
    Inherits System.Web.Services.Protocols.HttpGetClientProtocol

    Public Sub New()
        MyBase.New
        Me.Url = "http://shop.barnesandnoble.com"
    End Sub

    <HttpMethodAttribute(GetType(TextReturnReader), _
                    GetType(UrlParameterWriter))> _
    Public Function GetBookDetails(ByVal isbn As String) As GetBookDetailsMatches
        Return CType(Me.Invoke("GetBookDetails", _
            (Me.Url + "/booksearch/isbnInquiry.asp"), _
            New Object() {isbn}), _
            GetBookDetailsMatches)
    End Function
End Class


Public Class GetBookDetailsMatches
    <MatchAttribute("size=.-1.>sales rank:.(.*?)</", IgnoreCase:=true)> _
    Public Rank As String
End Class
```

The above auto-generated source file contains two classes. The first class, BarnesAndNoble, has a single function GetBookDetails and accepts isbn as a parameter and returns an instance of GetBookDetailsMatches. The returned type, GetBookDetailsMatches, is the second class defined in our source file, and it contains a single member variable Rank. The Rank member variable has an attribute applied to it; this <MatchAttribute> represents the RegEx syntax we declared in our WSDL.

Let's compile this source file. Again, we'll use the command-line tools since Visual Stuido.NET automates this for us. We'll execute the following statement:

```
vbc.exe /t:library /r:System.dll /r:System.Web.dll /r:System.Web.Services.dll
/r:System.Xml.dll BarnesAndNoble.vb
```

This will generate an assembly named `BarnesAndNoble.dll`.

Using the Screen Scrape Proxy

Now that we've built an assembly, we can deploy it to the `\bin` directory of a web application. We can then write the following VB.NET or C# ASP.NET Pages that load and use our `BarnesAndNoble` proxy:

VB.NET

```
<%@ Import Namespace="System.Net" %>

<Script runat=server>
Public Sub GetSalesRank(sender As Object, e As EventArgs)
  Dim bn As New BarnesAndNoble()
  Dim match As GetBookDetailsMatches
  match = bn.GetBookDetails(isbn.Value)

  rank.Text = match.Rank
End Sub
</Script>
<font face=arial>
  <form runat=server>
  ISBN number: <input type=text id="isbn" runat=server/>
  <input type=submit id=submit onserverclick="GetSalesRank" runat=server/>
  </form>
  Sales Rank: <font color=red><b><asp:label id=rank runat=server/></b></font>
</font>

<!-- Sample ISBNs
A Preview of ASP+: 1861004753
Professional ASP.NET: 1861004885
-->
```

C#

```
<%@ Page Language="C#" %>
<%@ Import Namespace="System.Net" %>

<Script runat="server">
public void GetSalesRank(Object sender, EventArgs e) {
  BarnesAndNoble bn = new BarnesAndNoble();
  GetBookDetailsMatches match;
  match = bn.GetBookDetails(isbn.Value);
  rank.Text = match.Rank;
}
</Script>
<font face=arial>
  <form runat=server ID="Form1">
```

```
    ISBN number: <input type=text id="isbn" runat=server />
    <input type=submit id=submit onserverclick="GetSalesRank" runat=server/>
    </form>
    Sales Rank: <font color=red><b><asp:label id=rank runat=server/></b></font>
</font>

<!-- Sample ISBNs
A Preview of ASP+: 1861004753
Professional ASP.NET: 1861004885
-->
```

Both of the above code samples create a new instance of the BarnesAndNoble proxy object in their GetSalesRank() event raised when the input button is clicked. The BarnesAndNoble instance, bn, is used to call the GetBookDetails() method, passing in the ISBN number:

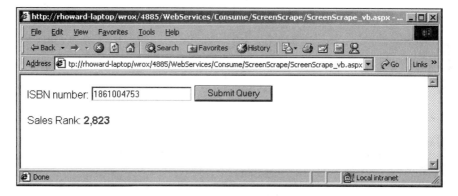

In the above screenshot we can see that our ASP.NET, ScreenScrape_vb.aspx, successfully queried BarnesAndNoble.com for the sales rank of a *Preview of ASP+*.

This screen scraping feature of ASP.NET Web Services allows us to turn any web site into a Web Service. We simply author the WSDL and either VS.NET or wsdl.exe takes care of the rest.

Design Decisions

Just as there are design decisions made when we build a Web Service, we also have design decisions related to how we use a Web Service. One of the most obvious is handling exceptions.

Handling Exceptions

In an ideal scenario whenever we call a Web Service, some type of application logic is executed performing the desired task according to our request. However, in the real world all code has bugs. SOAP takes this fact into account and defines the response a Web Service should use when an error has occurred. This error takes the form of a SOAP message, but it is known as a **SOAP Exception**.

SOAP Exceptions

Requests to ASP.NET Web Services that generate an exception will return a SOAP Exception. Within the `System.Web.Services.Protocols` namespace is a class named `SoapException`. Clients using .NET can wrap `try...catch` blocks around calls to Web Services and catch SOAP Exceptions as instances of a `SoapException` class. Let's look at an example: below is the code to a simple ASP.NET Web Service that can generate a run-time "divide by zero" error:

VB.NET

```
<%@ WebService Class="ExceptionExample" %>

Imports System.Web.Services

Public Class ExceptionExample
  <WebMethod()> Public Function Divide(a As Integer, b As Integer) As Integer
    Return a / b
  End Function
End Class
```

Using Visual Studio.NET or `wsdl.exe` we can build a proxy class. We'll name it `ExceptionExample`, deploy it to a web application's `\bin` directory and call the `ExceptionExample` Web Service:

VB.NET

```
<Script runat="server">
Public Sub Page_Load(sender As Object, e As EventArgs)
  Dim example As New ExceptionExample()

  lblDiv1.Text = example.Divide(6,2)
  lblDiv2.Text = example.Divide(5,0)
End Sub
</Script>
The result of 6 divided by 2 is: <asp:label id="lblDiv1" runat="server" />
<br>
The result of 5 divided by 0 is: <asp:label id="lblDiv2" runat="server" />
```

If we execute the above code the statement `example.Divide(6,2)` is valid and should complete, however, the statement `example.Divide(5,0)` is a divide-by-zero error. Here's the result:

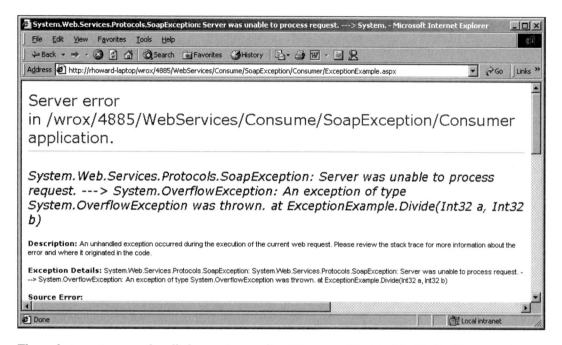

The code is raising an unhandled exception on line 6 in our call to `Divide(5,0)`. The exception type that is bubbled up and displayed in the ASP.NET error page is of `SoapException`. Let's make a few modifications to our code to handle this exception:

VB.NET

```
<%@ Import Namespace="System.Web.Services.Protocols" %>

<Script runat="server">
Public Sub Page_Load(sender As Object, e As EventArgs)
  Dim example As New ExceptionExample()

  Try
    lblDiv1.Text = example.Divide(6,2)
  Catch err As SoapException
    lblDiv1.Text = "Unable to compute..."
  End Try

  Try
    lblDiv2.Text = example.Divide(5,0)
  Catch err As SoapException
    lblDiv2.Text = "Unable to compute..."
  End Try

End Sub
</Script>
The result of 6 divided by 2 is: <asp:label id="lblDiv1" runat="server" />
<br>
The result of 5 divided by 0 is: <asp:label id="lblDiv2" runat="server" />
```

Unlike ASP/VBScript, ASP.NET supports structured error handling (no more `On Error Resume Next`) thanks to the Common Language Runtime. In the above code we've made a few modifications to catch errors. We've first added a namespace, `System.Web.Services.Protocols`; within this namespace is the `SoapException` class. We then added `Try...Catch` blocks around our code. With each attempt to call to the Web Service, if an exception of type `SoapException` occurs we can catch the exception and display a meaningful result.

Now when we run this code, we get the following result:

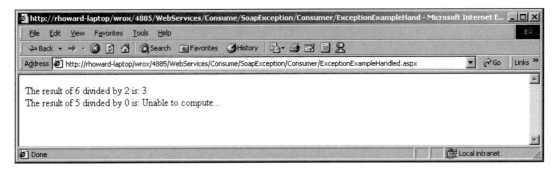

Another design decision is using SOAP headers to send additional data with our Web Service. In the previous chapter we examined how to support SOAP headers on the server, let's look at how we use SOAP headers with our proxy.

Using SOAP Headers

Below is a simple ASP.NET Web Service that implements a SOAP header:

```
<%@ WebService Class="UsingSoapHeaders" %>

Imports System.Web.Services
Imports System.Web.Services.Protocols

Public Class MySoapHeader : Inherits SoapHeader
  Public Value As String
End Class

Public Class UsingSoapHeaders
  Public sHeader As MySoapHeader

  <WebMethod(), SoapHeader("sHeader")> _
  Public Function GetValueOfSoapHeader() As String
      Return sHeader.Value
  End Function
End Class
```

In this example `GetValueOfSoapHeader()` returns the value of the SOAP header that the caller presents.

Described in WSDL

The information for `SimpleSoapHeader` is described in the WSDL for the service, since the application using the Web Service will require knowledge of the `SoapHeader` to call the service:

```
<s:element name="MySoapHeader" nillable="true" type="s0:MySoapHeader" />
<s:complexType name="MySoapHeader">
  <s:sequence>
    <s:element minOccurs="1"
               maxOccurs="1"
               name="Value"
               nillable="true"
               type="s:string" />
  </s:sequence>
</s:complexType>
```

The above section of WSDL uses an XML Schema to define a SOAP Header: `MySoapHeader`. Our proxy generator, VS.NET or `wsdl.exe`, will then create a class `MySoapHeader` with a single member variable `Value`.

SOAP Header Proxy

Below is the VB.NET source for a proxy generated by Visual Studio.NET for the WSDL of the above Web Service:

```
Namespace Simple

  <WebServiceBindingAttribute(Name:="UsingSoapHeadersSoap")
                            [Namespace]:="http://tempuri.org/")>
  Public Class UsingSoapHeaders
    Inherits SoapHttpClientProtocol

    Public MySoapHeaderValue As MySoapHeader

    Public Sub New()
      MyBase.New
      Me.Url = "http://localhost/.../SoapHeaders_vb.asmx"
    End Sub

    <SoapHeaderAttribute("MySoapHeaderValue")> _
    <SoapDocumentMethodAttribute("http://tempuri.org/GetValueOfSoapHeader",
                            Use:=SoapBindingUse.Literal,
                            ParameterStyle:= SoapParameterStyle.Wrapped)>
    Public Function GetValueOfSoapHeader() As String
      Dim results() As Object = Me.Invoke("GetValueOfSoapHeader", _
                                        New Object(0) {})
      Return CType(results(0),String)
    End Function

  End Class

  <XmlRootAttribute([Namespace]:="http://tempuri.org/", IsNullable:=true)>
  Public Class MySoapHeader
    Inherits SoapHeader

    Public Value As String
  End Class
End Namespace
```

As you can see, the proxy class contains a sub-class `MySoapHeader` with a member variable of `Value`. The proxy class additionally contains a member variable `MySoapHeaderValue` that we use to set the SOAP header.

Using the SOAP Header

Let's look at how we use this proxy, along with its SOAP header to send additional data with the Web Service request. Below is a simple ASP.NET Page that uses the proxy:

```
<%@ Import Namespace="Simple" %>

<script runat=server>
Public Sub Page_Load(sender As Object, e As EventArgs)
  ' Create a new instance of the UsingSoapHeaders
  ' proxy class used to call the remote .asmx file
  Dim soapHeaderExample As New UsingSoapHeaders()

  ' Create a new instance of the mySoapHeader class
  Dim myHeader As New MySoapHeader()

  ' Set the value of myHeader
  myHeader.Value = "Sample Header Text"

  ' Set the MySoapHeader public member of the
  ' UsingSoapHeaders class to myHeader
  soapHeaderExample.MySoapHeaderValue = myHeader

  ' Get the result of the call
  Dim result As String
  result = soapHeaderExample.GetValueOfSoapHeader()
  span1.InnerHtml = result
End Sub
</script>
<font size=6>The value of the SOAP header is: <font color=red>
<span id=span1 runat=server/></font></font>
```

In the above `Page_Load` event we first create a new instance of the Web Service proxy: `soapHeaderExample`. We then also create an instance of the class, `MySoapHeader` that represents the SOAP Header: `myHeader`. We then set the `Value` field of `myHeader` to `"Sample Header Text"`. Next, we set `myHeader` to the `soapHeaderExample` member variable `MySoapHeaderValue`. Finally we call the `GetValueOfSoapHeader()` Web Service. The `MySoapHeader` class instance `myHeader` is serialized as a SOAP header for the message and is sent along with the request. When the call completes we display the value that was sent as a SOAP header.

Using SOAP Headers is easy. The WSDL of the service describes what the SOAP Header is, and the proxy generation tool turns the XML description found in the WSDL into a .NET class that we program with. As we'll see later in the chapter, SOAP Headers are very powerful since they allow us to pass out-of-band data, that is data that is part of the request, but doesn't belong as part of the method marked as a Web Service. For example, if we wish to send a user ID with each request we obviously don't want to design each of the methods in our Web Service to accept that user ID as a parameter – it would be much easier to simply make use of a SOAP header.

The above example is relatively simple, but is definitely enough to allow us to build some meaningful applications that use SOAP headers. Later in the chapter, in our advanced topics section, we'll look at a real-world example of how we could use SOAP headers. Specifically we'll look at using SOAP headers to send authentication details with each request. Using SOAP headers for authentication is obviously a 'custom' implementation of authentication and authorization, so before we extend the ASP.NET security system for Web Services let's first review the features that are already available.

Web Services Security

Security, as it relates to Web Services, almost seems to be a taboo topic. Individuals and companies are still trying to understand just what exactly they can build with Web Services, but still aren't quite sure how they protect those investments.

Because ASP.NET Web Services are simply part of an ASP.NET application, we can take advantage of all the security features provided by ASP.NET.

This includes solutions for granting or denying access to resources based on the identity of the user (their username, password, and the groups/roles that the user may belong to) as well as protecting the data through the use of encryption, such as using Secure Sockets Layer (SSL) with HTTP (HTTPS). We can additionally step outside the bounds of what ASP.NET provides and implement some custom solutions, which we'll discuss at the end of the chapter.

Let's start with the authentication and authorization security features provided by ASP.NET

ASP.NET Authentication and Authorization

As we learned in Chapter 14 ASP.NET has several offerings for authenticating and authorizing access to ASP.NET resources:

❑ **Windows Authentication** – Uses existing Windows users, groups and security concepts, such as Access Control Lists (ACLs), to protect resources. To enable Windows authentication/authorization, IIS must also enforce Windows authentication, either through NTLM or Clear-Text/Basic Authentication.

❑ **Forms Authentication** – Uses user-defined users and roles and ASP.NET's URL authorization features. The developer instructs ASP.NET as to what a given user or role is allowed to access using the ASP.NET configuration system. ASP.NET then enforces these permissions and redirects the user to a login page if they do not present a valid Forms Authentication cookie.

❑ **Passport Authentication** – Uses a distributed authentication store to validate usernames and passwords.

Let's start by examining how we enable Windows Authentication for a Web Service:

Windows Authentication

To enable Windows Authentication for our Web Service we first need to instruct IIS to use Windows authentication. This is done through the IIS Administration tool (Start | Programs | Administrative Tools | Internet Services Manager). We then find the resource we want to enforce Windows security upon, such as /Wrox/WebServices/BasicAuthentication/Server, right-click, select Properties from the menus and then select the Directory Security tab:

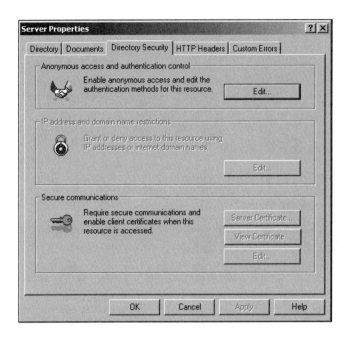

From here we'll select the **Anonymous access and authentication control Edit** button. This brings up the **Authentication methods** dialog:

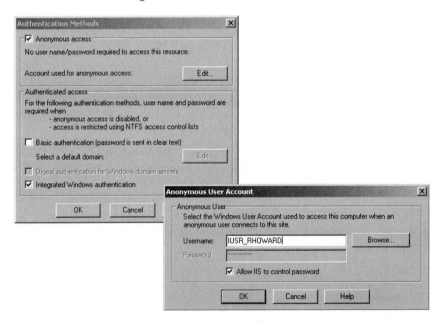

Above we see the default settings. **Anonymous access** is checked and **Authenticated Access** is set to use **Integrated Windows authentication**. By default with **Anonymous access** checked, IIS will not require the client to present identity to the server. Instead the server will treat all requests, including Web Services, as anonymous – unless the resource, such as a file, requested does not allow anonymous access in which case the client will be challenged for credentials.

If we uncheck **Anonymous access,** and leave **Integrated Windows authentication** checked, we'll instruct IIS to enforce NTLM authentication challenges for resources requested in the directory `/Wrox/WebServices/BasicAuthentication/Server`. We can then write a simple ASP.NET Web Service to validate the credentials used:

VB.NET

```
<%@ WebService Class="SecureSample" %>

Imports System.Web.Services

Public Class SecureSample
  Inherits WebService

  <WebMethod> _
  Public Function WhoAreYou() As String
    Return User.Identity.Name
  End Function
End Class
```

The above Web Service simply uses the ASP.NET `User` object's `Identity.Name` property to return the name of the authenticated user back to the caller. We can now build a proxy for this Web Service and test to see if the credentials are enforced. Below is a simple ASP.NET page that uses the proxy to call the `SecureSample` Web Service:

VB.NET

```
<%@ Import Namespace="System.Net" %>

<Script runat="server">
Public Sub Page_Load(sender As Object, e As EventArgs)
  ' Create an instance of the SecureSample proxy
  Dim secureSample As New SecureSample()

  ' Create a new NetworkCredential class
  Dim credentials As New NetworkCredential()

  ' Set username and password values
  credentials.UserName = "demo"
  credentials.Password = "00password"
  credentials.Domain = "rhoward"

  ' Set the credentials
  secureSample.Credentials = credentials

  ' Call its WhoAreYou() function
  lblSecureSample.Text = secureSample.WhoAreYou()
End Sub

</Script>
<asp:label id="lblSecureSample" runat="server"/>
```

The above code first creates an instance of the `SecureSample` proxy, `secureSample`, and then creates an instance of a class found in `System.Net`: `NetworkCredentials`. The `NetworkCredentials` class is used to specify a `UserName`, `Password`, and `Domain`. These 'credentials' are then used along with the network request. For our proxy class we assign the `NetworkCredentials` instance, `credentials`, to an inherited property of the proxy: `Credentials`. We can then make our request to the Windows authenticated Web Service. If the credentials are valid the user is authenticated, otherwise they are denied access.

The above sample uses NTLM authentication. When we make a request to the web server, the web server determines that Windows authentication is required and issues a challenge response back to the caller. The caller then has the opportunity to send a hashed value of the username, password, and domain to the server. The server will then attempt to create the same hash and if the values match the user is considered 'authenticated'. Sometimes, however, we can't use NTLM authentication. For example if our client was a non-Windows application. In that case we might decide to use Clear-Text/Basic Authentication.

Clear-Text/Basic Authentication

Whereas Windows NTLM authentication sends a hash of the credentials, this hash can only be computed by an application that is able to create the hash. Some Web Service clients may not wish to use NTLM authentication, but will most likely still be able to use Clear-Text/Basic Authentication.

Clear-Text/Basic Authentication works in a similar manner to NTLM, in that the server issues a challenge, but rather than sending a hashed value of the credentials, the client Base64-encodes the values. The format is BASIC: Domain\Username: Password. Basic authentication hides the data, but any reasonably intelligent developer can easily extract the credentials. The value is sent using the AUTHORIZATION HTTP header and the value of this header is the Base64 encoded value. Clear-Text/Basic Authentication, by itself, is not considered a secure form of authentication. However, when used with HTTPS, which encrypts all communication between the client and server, it is quite useful.

We can enable this authentication option in IIS, by revisiting our Authentication methods dialog and selecting Basic authentication only.

When we enable Basic authentication, IIS will display a warning telling us that this authentication method will pass credentials in clear text.

We can now use our same proxy class to make calls to the Web Service. However, instead of using a secure authentication mechanism, our credentials are passed in Base64-encoded clear text.

Another option is to use ASP.NET Forms Authentication to validate the user. However, we have to make some special arrangements to use this type of authentication with Web Services. This is because Forms Authentication uses cookies, and we have already learned how a cookie is kept in memory and is lost when the proxy is destroyed. Additionally, Forms Authentication makes use of HTTP redirects to an HTML form for unauthenticated users.

Forms Authentication

ASP.NET Forms Authentication allows us to use an HTML form to request the credentials for a user. The provided credentials can then be validated against any data store, and if the credentials are considered valid, an HTTP cookie is sent to the client. This cookie is used on subsequent requests to authenticate the user.

While Forms Authentication is a very flexible system, it is somewhat cumbersome to use with Web Services. The main issue is: **when configured for Forms Authentication, ASP.NET will redirect requests to an HTML forms login page**. This obviously will cause problems for a Web Service proxy, which is expecting a SOAP response. To use Forms Authentication with ASP.NET Web Services, we have to bend the rules a little. Let's look at how this is done – we'll use the same SecureSample Web Service we used earlier with one minor modification:

```
<%@ WebService Class="SecureSample" %>

Imports System.Web.Services
Imports System.Web.Security

Public Class SecureSample
  Inherits WebService

  <WebMethod> _
  Public Function WhoAreYou() As String
    Return User.Identity.Name
  End Function

  <WebMethod> _
  Public Function Authenticate(username As String, password As String)
    If (username = "John") AND (password = "password") Then
      FormsAuthentication.SetAuthCookie(username, true)

      Return true
    End If

    Return false
  End Function
End Class
```

We've added a new function, Authenticate(), which accepts both a username and a password. We then write code to determine the validity of the username and password values, but we must use the FormsAuthentication static method SetAuthCookie to write the Forms Authentication cookie to the client. We also need a web.config file that configures this Web Service to use Forms Authentication:

```
<configuration>
  <system.web>
    <authentication mode="Forms">
      <forms name=".ASPXAUTH" loginUrl="login.aspx"
             protection="All"  timeout="30" path="/" />
    </authentication>
  </system.web>
</configuration>
```

Note, that we don't specify an `<authorization>` section. This allows us to get around the problem of redirecting the user to `login.aspx`, but still allows us to use the Forms Authentication cookie for validation purposes.

After we properly authenticate by calling the Web Service `Authenticate()` method, we can then call `WhoAreYou()` and see that the ASP.NET `User` object recognizes us as a valid user. We can then authorize actions for this user in our code, for example for users in the 'customer' role we could allow access to direct database requests, but for users in the role 'anonymous' we could send them cached data – data that is old, or data that we don't take the hit of generating for non-customers.

Another solution to the authentication problem is to use client certificates. Client certificates usually go hand-in-hand with SSL, let's discuss these together.

HTTPS Encryption and Client Certificates

The recommended strategy for hiding data in transmission is to use the HTTPS protocol. HTTPS uses public/private asymmetric cryptography to provide a secure communication between the caller and the server.

Please see the IIS documentation for directions on how to install and use a server certificate for secure communication.

Once a server certificate is installed, we can enforce the use of the certificate on our Web Application by simply opening the properties dialog for our Web Application, selecting the **Directory Security** tab, and pressing the **Edit** button under **Secure Communications**, then checking the **Require secure channel (SSL)** checkbox:

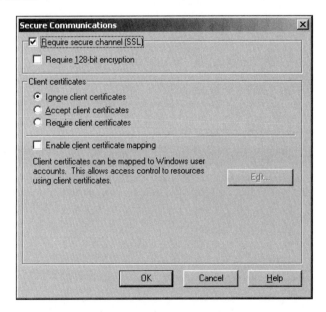

Requests to this web application will now require HTTPS to request data from the server, thus encrypting content. We can simply add an ASP.NET Web Service to this application and use of HTTPS will be transparent.

An ASP.NET Web Service served from a web application with HTTPS enabled will generate WSDL that correctly identifies the Web Service as using HTTPS; described via the `location` attribute of the port setting in our WSDL. When we build a proxy using the WSDL, the proxy will automatically be configured to use HTTPS for secure communication with the server.

Another option, only available when the server has an installed certificate, is to enable the server to recognize client certificates.

Client Certificates

Server certificates are issued by a third party to ensure that the identity of the server is valid or can be trusted. A client certificate is also issued by a trusted third party, but is used to ensure that the identity of the client is valid or can be trusted. A client can send a request to the server along with the client certificate. The server can then determine if the certificate is trusted and then use the certificate to authenticate and authorize the client.

The most common use of client certificates is a certificate installed with the browser. For example, if we obtain a client certificate we can view the certificate in Internet Explorer. For IE 5.5, this is done by selecting Tools | Internet Options. This opens the Internet Options dialog, and from this dialog we select the Content tab:

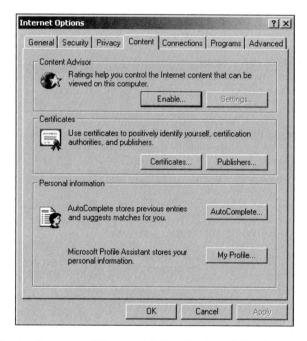

If we press the Certificates button we'll be provided with a list of the client certificates installed. For example, I have the following certificate installed:

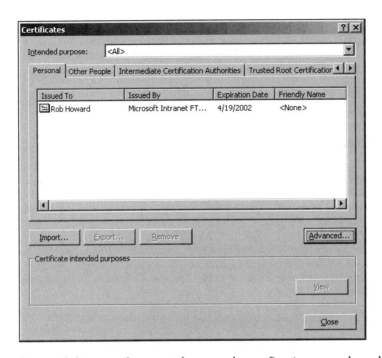

We can require the use of client certificates on the server by configuring our web application through the same Secure Communication dialog box we used to enable HTTPS – note, this requires that we have a server certificate as well. To enable support for client certificates, we simply check the Require or Accept client certificates option.

Clients that make requests to this web application are then required to present a client certificate. If the client does not present a certificate, access is denied. If certificates are accepted, it is then our responsibility to determine whether or not to authenticate the request. We validate the certificate through code, as we'll see in a moment.

Before we use the certificate from our proxy, we'll test the certificate using a browser that has a client certificate installed and access an ASP.NET Web Service on a server that requires the use of client certificates – this all happens transparently within our code.

If client certificates are installed, we can also write some code on the server that examines the certificate and extracts meaningful information from it. Below is a simple ASP.NET Web Service that accesses certificates presented by the client and extracts meaningful details:

VB.NET

```
<%@ WebService Class="CertExample" %>

Imports System.Security.Principal
Imports System.Web.Services
Imports System.Web
Imports System

Public Class CertExample
```

```
<WebMethod> _
  Public Function GetCertDetails() As CertDetails
    Dim request As HttpRequest = HttpContext.Current.Request
    Dim cert As New CertDetails()

    cert.Issuer = Request.ClientCertificate.Issuer
    cert.Subject = Request.ClientCertificate.Subject
    cert.Valid = Request.ClientCertificate.IsValid
    cert.KeySize = Request.ClientCertificate.KeySize
    cert.PublicKey = Convert.ToBase64String(Request.ClientCertificate.PublicKey)
    cert.Cookie = Request.ClientCertificate.Cookie

    Return cert
  End Function
End Class

Public Class CertDetails
  Public Issuer As String
  Public Subject As String
  Public Valid As Boolean
  Public KeySize As Integer
  Public PublicKey As String
  Public Cookie As String
End Class
```

If we test this Web Service through a browser and the client presents a certificate, we should see a result similar to this:

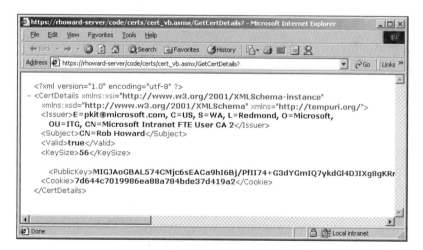

The above example demonstrates how a certificate sent by the client is used on the server to recognize the client's identity. Now we'll look at the same example, but instead of using a browser to present the certificate we'll use our ASP.NET proxy to present it along with the request.

Using Client Certificates with Web Services

To use client certificates with our proxy, we first need to export the client certificate. If we select Tools | Internet Options from Internet Explorer, and select the Content tab and view the installed certificates (as we did earlier), we can select a certificate and export it.

If we select the certificate and press the Export button, the Certificate Export Wizard will open. We can simply press the Next button, accepting the defaults, until we arrive at the File to Export dialog. Here we need to provide a filename for the exported certificate as well as a location, for example c:\cert. We can then click the Finish button and our certificate is exported (c:\cert.cer).

We now need to modify our application that's using the Web Service proxy to supply the certificate with the call:

VB.NET

```
<%@ Import Namespace="System.Security.Cryptography.X509Certificates" %>

<script runat="server">
  Public Sub Page_Load(sender As Object, e As EventArgs)
    Dim cert As new CertExample()
    Dim details As CertDetails
    Dim x509 As X509Certificate.CreateFromCertFile("c:\\cert.cer")

    cert.ClientCertificates.Add(x509)

    details = cert.GetCertDetails()

    lblIssuer.Text = details.Issuer
    lblSubject.Text = details.Subject
    lblValid.Text = details.Valid
    lblKeySize.Text = details.KeySize
    lblPublicKey.Text = details.PublicKey
    lblCookie.Text = details.Cookie
  End Sub
</script>
Issuer: <asp:label id="lblIssuer" runat=server/>
<br>
Subject: <asp:label id="lblSubject" runat=server/>
<br>
Valid: <asp:label id="lblValid" runat=server/>
<br>
KeySize: <asp:label id="lblKeySize" runat=server/>
<br>
PublicKey: <asp:label id="lblPublicKey" runat=server/>
<br>
Cookie: <asp:label id="lblCookie" runat=server/>
```

In the above code sample we use a .NET class X509Certificate to load the client certificate from the c:\cert.cer file. We then add the certificate to our proxy and issue the request.

As you can see we have several options for both authentication and authorization using Windows, Basic, Forms, or Certificate authentication and authorization, as well as a way to encrypt the data exchanged using Secure Sockets to create an HTTPS session.

Next, in the *Advanced Topics* section, we're going to delve a bit deeper into security as it relates to Web Services.

Advanced Topics

In this advanced topics section we're going to look at an advanced example of SOAP authentication using SOAP headers, as well as a feature of ASP.NET Web Services known as SOAP Extensions.

All of the options we've discussed so far, as they relate to security, rely upon the HTTP transport protocol for the security details; Windows NTLM, Basic, and Forms authentication all rely on either an HTTP header or an HTTP cookie.

Now, let's look at an advanced example that demonstrates a custom Authentication and Authorization example using SOAP Headers.

Custom Authentication and Authorization

As mentioned earlier, SOAP headers provide a great way to send 'out-of-band' data. Just as we use HTTP headers to send details that aren't directly part of the body with the HTTP message, we can do the exact same thing with SOAP headers. This allows us to decouple application details such as session cookies, authentication, and so on from the HTTP transport and instead pass them as part of the SOAP message. This way, no matter what transport the SOAP message is sent over (HTTP, SMTP, etc.) these details remain with the message – instead of being lost when we change transport protocols.

Let's look at an example that uses SOAP headers to send an 'authentication' header, rather than relying upon a cookie or an HTTP header. This example shows off several great features of ASP.NET:

❑ **Custom Authentication** – We bypass the provided authentication features that ASP.NET offers, such as Forms or Windows, and plug our own authentication system into ASP.NET.

❑ **SOAP Headers** – Use SOAP headers to transmit credentials and decouple the information from the HTTP headers, theoretically making the message transport-independent.

❑ **HTTP Module** – Our example makes use of an HTTP module that looks at each request and determines if it is a SOAP message.

❑ **Custom Application Events** – The HTTP module raises a custom global.asax event, within which we implement our application logic to verify credentials.

Let's start by examining the Web Service.

ASP.NET Web Service

Below is the code for a Web Service that implements an authentication SOAP header:

VB.NET

```
<%@ WebService Class="SecureWebService" %>

Imports System
Imports System.Web.Services
Imports System.Web.Services.Protocols

Public Class Authentication : Inherits SoapHeader
  Public User As String
  Public Password As String
End Class
```

```
Public Class SecureWebService : Inherits WebService
  Public authentication As Authentication

  <WebMethod> _
  <SoapHeader("authentication")> _
  Public Function ValidUser() As String
    If User.IsInRole("Customer") Then
      Return "User is in the Customer role..."
    Else If User.Identity.IsAuthenticated Then
      Return "User is valid..."
    Else
      Return "Not authenticated"
    End If
  End Function
End Class
```

The above code implements a single WebMethod: ValidUser(). The ValidUser() function simply uses the ASP.NET User intrinsic object to determine if the request is from a validated user. If the user is in the role "Customer", then the function returns "User is in the Customer role...", if the user is simply authenticated and not in the Customer role the function returns "User is valid...", and finally if the user is not authenticated the function returns "Not authenticated". As you can see, the code is quite simple. The Web Service uses the ASP.NET User intrinsic object to validate the authentication of a request.

The Web Service also defines a SOAP header, Authentication. Applications using the Web Service will set this header with appropriate values, and our application will validate the credentials and create a valid User object – we'll see how that's done next, when we look at an example of that service.

Sample Application

Below is the source code for a simple ASP.NET page that makes use of a proxy, SecureWebService. The proxy is used to make calls to the ASP.NET Web Service described above.

VB.NET

```
<%@ Import Namespace="Security"%>
<%@ Import Namespace="System.Web.Services.Protocols" %>

<script runat=server>
  Public Sub Page_Load(sender As Object, e As EventArgs)
    span1.InnerHtml = ""
    span2.InnerHtml = ""
  End Sub

  Public Sub Authenticate_Click(sender As Object, e As EventArgs)
    Dim secureWebService As New SecureWebService()

    ' Create the Authentication header and set values
    Dim authenticationHeader As New Authentication()
    authenticationHeader.User = user.Value
    authenticationHeader.Password = password.Value

    ' Assign the Header
    secureWebService.AuthenticationValue = authenticationHeader
```

```
        ' Call method
        Try
            span1.InnerHtml = s.ValidUser()
        Catch soap As SoapException
            span2.InnerHtml = soap.Message
        End Try
    End Sub
</script>
```

This ASP.NET Page simply renders an HTML form that allows the user to enter credentials. These credentials are then made part of the request sent to the server. In fact, here is the SOAP message that a caller makes to the server (minus HTTP headers):

```
<?xml version="1.0" encoding="utf-8"?>
<soap:Envelope xmlns:soap="http://schemas.xmlsoap.org/soap/envelope/"
               xmlns:xsi="http://www.w3.org/2001/XMLSchema-instance"
               xmlns:xsd="http://www.w3.org/2001/XMLSchema">
  <soap:Header>
    <Authentication xmlns="http://tempuri.org/">
      <User>John</User>
      <Password>password</Password>
    </Authentication>
  </soap:Header>
  <soap:Body>
    <ValidUser xmlns="http://tempuri.org/" />
  </soap:Body>
</soap:Envelope>
```

And here is the response (minus HTTP headers):

```
<?xml version="1.0" encoding="utf-8"?>
<soap:Envelope xmlns:soap="http://schemas.xmlsoap.org/soap/envelope/"
               xmlns:xsi="http://www.w3.org/2001/XMLSchema-instance"
               xmlns:xsd="http://www.w3.org/2001/XMLSchema">
  <soap:Body>
    <ValidUserResponse xmlns="http://tempuri.org/">
      <ValidUserResult>Not authenticated</ValidUserResult>
    </ValidUserResponse>
  </soap:Body>
</soap:Envelope>
```

As you can clearly see, the SOAP header is passed in clear-text – we'll address encryption shortly.

Calls to the Web Service are obviously getting processed, but, as I'm sure you can tell, we've left a few details out, such as how the credentials are authenticated. Let's look at how the Web Service validates credentials.

Validating SOAP Header Credentials

The ASP.NET Web Service, the source of which we examined earlier, also requires a `global.asax` file in its application root. Here's what the `global.asax` file contains:

```
<%@ Import Namespace="Microsoft.WebServices.Security" %>
<%@ Import Namespace="System.Security.Principal" %>

<script runat=server>
  Public Sub WebServiceAuthentication_OnAuthenticate(sender As Object,_
                                        e As WebServiceAuthenticationEvent)
    If (e.User = "bwhite@bar.com") AND (e.Password = "password") Then
      e.Authenticate()
    Else If (e.User = "sswienton@foo.com") AND (e.Password = "password") Then
      Dim s(1) As String
      s(0) = "Customer"
      e.Authenticate(s)
    End If
  End Sub
</script>
```

Our `global.asax` file implements an event named `WebServiceAuthentication_OnAuthenticate()` – we'll talk about where this event comes from shortly. It is raised whenever a request is made to a Web Service within the current application. Inside the event, application logic is used to determine the validity of a given set of credentials. In this case we have two hard-wired cases: one simply authenticates the user and the other authenticates the user and also adds the user to the `Customer` role. Although the usernames and passwords are hard-coded into the logic, it is easy to envision replacing this with calls to a database, an XML file, or any other resources that we want to verify credentials against. The option is there, just as it was with Forms Authentication.

The `WebServiceAuthentication_OnAuthenticate()` event is raised by a custom HTTP module. The HTTP module looks at each request, and for requests that are Web Services, the HTTP module opens the message; parses the SOAP value for an authentication header (and values), raises a custom event, and finally implements the necessary calls to both authenticate a user and add a given user to the role. By the time the request actually reaches the Web Service, all of this has already taken place.

Let's look at a couple snips from the HTTP module, the entire contents of which are too large to include in this chapter but are available for download with the source code from this book from www.wrox.com.

WebServiceAuthentication HTTP Module

The HTTP module encapsulates all the work of authenticating the request. Although all of the work done by the module could be achieved using `global.asax`, this method provides a clean level of abstraction and allows the developer to focus on authenticating the request.

The HTTP module listens for an ASP.NET authenticate event (discussed in Chapter 12). When this ASP.NET application event is raised the HTTP module has the opportunity to execute code; in this case the module raises its own `OnEnter()` event:

C#

The `OnEnter` event starts by examining the request for the `HTTP_SOAPACTION` header. The existence of this header is required by the SOAP 1.1 specification, but the value it contains is optional. If the header exists, we know the HTTP request contains a SOAP message.

```csharp
void OnEnter(Object source, EventArgs eventArgs) {
    HttpApplication app = (HttpApplication)source;
    HttpContext context = app.Context;
    Stream HttpStream = context.Request.InputStream;

    // Current position of stream
    long posStream = HttpStream.Position;

    // If the request contains an HTTP_SOAPACTION
    // header we'll look at this message
    if (context.Request.ServerVariables["HTTP_SOAPACTION"] == null)
        return;

    // Load the body of the HTTP message
    // into an XML document
    XmlDocument dom = new XmlDocument();
    string soapUser;
    string soapPassword;
    try {
        dom.Load(HttpStream);
```

If the request is a valid SOAP message, we will then attempt to load the SOAP (XML) into an XML document. If this succeeds, we'll reset the location in the stream (so that the ASP.NET Web Service still has the chance to read the request). We'll then attempt to read the `User` and `Password` values of the `Authentication` header. Because these operations are wrapped in a `try...catch` block, if it fails, we'll throw an exception.

```csharp
        // Reset the stream position
        HttpStream.Position = posStream;

        // Bind to the Authentication header
        soapUser = dom.GetElementsByTagName("User").Item(0).InnerText;
        soapPassword = dom.GetElementsByTagName("Password").Item(0).InnerText;
    } catch (Exception e) {
        // Reset Position of stream
        HttpStream.Position = posStream;

        // Throw exception
        throw soapException
    }
```

If no exceptions are raised we'll then call the code to raise the event that we can listen for in `global.asax` (as mentioned above).

```
    // Raise the custom global.asax event-C#
    OnAuthenticate(new WebServiceAuthenticationEvent(context,
                                           soapUser,-C#
                                           soapPassword));

    return;
}
```

Finally, the function returns, and the processing of the request is handed to the ASP.NET `.asmx` handler.

The above example, which we didn't cover in depth, demonstrates how we can use SOAP headers to pass additional information, such as authentication details, as part of the SOAP message, decoupling those details from the transport. In this particular example we passed the data in clear text, obviously a less than ideal solution – however, this example is only meant to be a conceptual sample that you can extend, not a solution in itself.

Next, we'll look at another advanced feature of ASP.NET Web Services: SOAP Extensions.

SOAP Extensions

ASP.NET provides a great programming model for working with and building Web Services, and in some senses it has trivialized the work required to build SOAP-based applications. We simply author our application logic, sprinkle some `WebMethod` attributes on the functions and *voilà!* It's done.

However, life isn't always so easy. The use of the `WebMethod` is simple, but it also abstracts a lot of what is happening behind the scenes. A special base class, `SoapExtension`, allows us to implement our own custom extensions that are able to manipulate ASP.NET Web Services at a very low level.

The `SoapExtension` base class, which our own class must inherit from, requires that we implement some virtual functions. As it relates to this discussion the most important function that we must implement is `ProcessMessage()`.

The `ProcessMessage()` function allows us to look at the raw message before and after it is serialized from a .NET class into SOAP or de-serialized from SOAP back into a .NET class. This functionality is available for both the Web Service as and the proxy.

Let's look at a simple SOAP Extension that enables us to trace the SOAP request/response data to disk – this is a very helpful attribute written by some of the developers on the ASP.NET Web Services team.

Tracing

If you've done any development with Web Services, you know that one of the most frustrating aspects can be the lack of tools available to view the SOAP message exchange. The trace extension, the source of which is opposite, outputs the incoming and outgoing SOAP message to a file.

The usage is as follows:

```
<WebMethod()> _
<TraceExtension(Filename:="c:\\trace.log")> _
Public Function Add(a As Integer, b As Integer) As Integer
  Return a + b
End Function
```

We simply compile the trace extension attribute and deploy it to our application's \bin directory. We then use the attribute, as shown above, providing it with the name of a file to log results to. The result of which is:

```
==================================== Request at 6/6/2001 2:10:20 AM
<?xml version="1.0" encoding="utf-8"?>
<soap:Envelope xmlns:soap="http://schemas.xmlsoap.org/soap/envelope/"
               xmlns:xsi="http://www.w3.org/2001/XMLSchema-instance"
               xmlns:xsd="http://www.w3.org/2001/XMLSchema">
  <soap:Body>
    <Add xmlns="http://tempuri.org/">
      <a>10</a>
      <b>5</b>
    </Add>
  </soap:Body>
</soap:Envelope>


--------------------------------- Response at 6/6/2001 2:10:20 AM
<?xml version="1.0" encoding="utf-8"?>
<soap:Envelope xmlns:soap="http://schemas.xmlsoap.org/soap/envelope/"
               xmlns:xsi="http://www.w3.org/2001/XMLSchema-instance"
               xmlns:xsd="http://www.w3.org/2001/XMLSchema">
  <soap:Body>
    <AddResponse xmlns="http://tempuri.org/">
      <AddResult>15</AddResult>
    </AddResponse>
  </soap:Body>
</soap:Envelope>
```

Above we see the trace results of a request to our Add Web Service and the response from that came back

Here's the source to the trace extension attribute:

```
using System;
using System.IO;
using System.Web.Services.Protocols;

[AttributeUsage(AttributeTargets.Method)]
public class TraceExtensionAttribute : SoapExtensionAttribute {

  private string filename = "c:\\log.txt";
  private int priority;

  public override Type ExtensionType {
    get { return typeof(TraceExtension); }
  }
```

```
      public override int Priority {
        get { return priority; }
        set { priority = value; }
      }

      public string Filename {
          get {
          return filename;
        }
        set {
          filename = value;
        }
      }
    }
```

In this first class, `TraceExtensionAttribute`, we inherit from `SoapExtensionAttribute`, implementing both our public property for configuring the filename used for logging: `Filename`, and the `Extension` type attribute, which returns a class of type `TraceExtension`:

```
public class TraceExtension : SoapExtension {

  Stream oldStream;
  Stream newStream;
  string filename;

  public override object GetInitializer(LogicalMethodInfo methodInfo,
                                        SoapExtensionAttribute attribute) {
    return ((TraceExtensionAttribute) attribute).Filename;
  }

  public override object GetInitializer(Type serviceType){
    return typeof(TraceExtension);
  }

  public override void Initialize(object initializer) {
    filename = (string) initializer;
  }
```

In the `TraceExtension` class, we first override some methods that are marked as `virtual` in `SoapExtension`. The most important of which is `ProcessMessage`, which allows us to interact with the message at four different stages of processing:

❑ **BeforeSerialize** allows us to interact with the message before we serialize the data as a SOAP message.

❑ **AfterSerialize** allows us to interact with the message after we serialize the data as a SOAP message. In our case we use this stage to call the `WriteOutput()` function to write the current SOAP message to our log.

❑ **BeforeDeserialize** allows us to interact with the message before we de-serialize the SOAP message back into .NET data types. Here we call `WriteInput()` to write the current SOAP message to our log.

❑ **AfterDeserialize** allows us to interact with the message after we de-serialize the SOAP message back into .NET data types.

Below is the code:

```
public override void ProcessMessage(SoapMessage message) {
  switch (message.Stage) {

  case SoapMessageStage.BeforeSerialize:
    break;

  case SoapMessageStage.AfterSerialize:
    WriteOutput( message );
    break;

  case SoapMessageStage.BeforeDeserialize:
    WriteInput( message );
    break;

  case SoapMessageStage.AfterDeserialize:
    break;

  default:
    throw new Exception("invalid stage");
  }
}

public override Stream ChainStream( Stream stream ){
  oldStream = stream;
  newStream = new MemoryStream();
  return newStream;
}

public void WriteOutput( SoapMessage message ){
  newStream.Position = 0;
  FileStream fs = new FileStream(filename, FileMode.Append, FileAccess.Write);
  StreamWriter w = new StreamWriter(fs);
  w.WriteLine("-------------------------- Response at " + DateTime.Now);
  w.Flush();
  Copy(newStream, fs);
  fs.Close();
  newStream.Position = 0;
  Copy(newStream, oldStream);
}

public void WriteInput( SoapMessage message ){
  Copy(oldStream, newStream);
  FileStream fs = new FileStream(filename, FileMode.Append, FileAccess.Write);
  StreamWriter w = new StreamWriter(fs);
  w.WriteLine("============================= Request at " + DateTime.Now);
  w.Flush();
  newStream.Position = 0;
  Copy(newStream, fs);
  fs.Close();
  newStream.Position = 0;
}

void Copy(Stream from, Stream to) {
  TextReader reader = new StreamReader(from);
  TextWriter writer = new StreamWriter(to);
  writer.WriteLine(reader.ReadToEnd());
  writer.Flush();
}
}
```

Although we're not covering it in detail as it's an advanced topic, it should be obvious how powerful SOAP extensions are. We could have, for example, written the custom authentication example demonstrated earlier using SOAP extensions. Another possibility would have been to use SOAP extensions for custom encryption of data.

Custom Encryption

This sample was originally written to demonstrate an alternative to using HTTP/SSL to send data. The scenario is as follows: as long as the SOAP message is sent via the HTTP protocol, we can use a complementary protocol such as HTTPS to encrypt the data. However, if the SOAP message is routed between various servers, each of those servers must have a trust relationship with the others – since each will have to establish a new SSL connection to transmit the data to the next server.

In the public Internet environment the scenario exists where we want to route over public networks, but exchange private data. The custom encryption attribute discussed below allows a valid SOAP message to be routed over the public network, but the contents of that SOAP message can be encrypted.

For example, we could write the following Web Service and using the tracing extensions mentioned earlier to see exactly what is exchanged via SOAP on the wire:

```
...
<WebMethod()>
<TraceExtension(Filename:="c:\\trace.log")>
Public Function SayHello() As String
  Return "Secret message"
End Function
...
```

Below is the log result of the exchange:

```
--------------------------------- Response at 6/7/2001 3:11:47 AM
<?xml version="1.0" encoding="utf-8"?>
<soap:Envelope xmlns:soap="http://schemas.xmlsoap.org/soap/envelope/"
               xmlns:xsi="http://www.w3.org/2001/XMLSchema-instance"
               xmlns:xsd="http://www.w3.org/2001/XMLSchema">
  <soap:Body>
    <SayHello xmlns="http://tempuri.org/" />
  </soap:Body>
</soap:Envelope>

=================================== Request at 6/7/2001 3:11:49 AM
<?xml version="1.0" encoding="utf-8"?>
<soap:Envelope xmlns:soap="http://schemas.xmlsoap.org/soap/envelope/"
               xmlns:xsi="http://www.w3.org/2001/XMLSchema-instance"
               xmlns:xsd="http://www.w3.org/2001/XMLSchema">
  <soap:Body>
    <SayHelloResponse xmlns="http://tempuri.org/">
      <SayHelloResult>Secret message</SayHelloResult>
    </SayHelloResponse>
  </soap:Body>
</soap:Envelope>
```

To prevent prying eyes from examining the details of our message exchange we could:

❑   Use HTTPS and encrypt the entire data exchange

❑   Use a custom SOAP Extension and encrypt only part of the data

Let's look at a custom SOAP Extension that is capable of encrypting only part of the data:

```
...
<WebMethod()>
<EncryptionExtension(Encrypt=EncryptMode.Response)>
<TraceExtension(Filename:="c:\\trace.log")>
Public Function SayHello() As String
   Return "Secret message"
End Function
...
```

We've now added an attribute to our SayHello() function, EncryptionExtension, and also set a property in this new attribute that sets EncryptMode.Response. Now, when we make a SOAP request to this service and trace the result our data is encrypted:

```
------------------------------- Response at 6/7/2001 3:18:25 AM
<?xml version="1.0" encoding="utf-8"?>
<soap:Envelope xmlns:soap="http://schemas.xmlsoap.org/soap/envelope/"
               xmlns:xsi="http://www.w3.org/2001/XMLSchema-instance"
               xmlns:xsd="http://www.w3.org/2001/XMLSchema">
  <soap:Body>
    <SayHello xmlns="http://tempuri.org/" />
  </soap:Body>
</soap:Envelope>

=================================== Request at 6/7/2001 3:18:27 AM
<?xml version="1.0" encoding="utf-8"?>
<soap:Envelope xmlns:soap="http://schemas.xmlsoap.org/soap/envelope/"
               xmlns:xsi="http://www.w3.org/2001/XMLSchema-instance"
               xmlns:xsd="http://www.w3.org/2001/XMLSchema">
  <soap:Body>
    <SayHelloResponse xmlns="http://tempuri.org/">
      <SayHelloResult>
        158 68 233 236 56 189 240 27 73 27 17 214 65 142 207 77
      </SayHelloResult>
    </SayHelloResponse>
  </soap:Body>
</soap:Envelope>
```

As you can clearly see in the highlighted section of the above trace result, the <SayHelloResult> is now an array of bytes. These bytes are a single-pass, symmetric (DES) encryption of the string "Secret Message".

The EncryptionExtension attribute that we added to the function encrypts the value after the message is serialized into SOAP – thus allowing us to send a valid SOAP message that can be routed between various intermediaries as well as sent over alternative protocols – our data remains secure as it is sent over the network.

To decrypt the message, we use the same attribute, but add it to the proxy that the application using our service uses:

```
<EncryptionExtension(Decrypt=DecryptMode.Request)> _
<SoapDocumentMethodAttribute("http://tempuri.org/SayHello",
                        Use:=SoapBindingUse.Literal,
                        ParameterStyle:= SoapParameterStyle.Wrapped)> _
Public Function SayHello() As String
   Dim results() As Object = Me.Invoke("SayHello", New Object(0) {})
   Return CType(results(0),String)
End Function
```

Instead of setting an Encrypt property in the EncryptionExtension attribute, we now set a Decrypt property. This instructs the EncryptionExtension to decrypt any incoming messages. The result is that data is encrypted on the wire as it's exchanged, and decrypted again by the intended recipient.

Below is the ProccessMessage function of EncryptionExtension:

```
public override void ProcessMessage(SoapMessage message) {
  switch (message.Stage) {

    case SoapMessageStage.BeforeSerialize:
      break;

    case SoapMessageStage.AfterSerialize:
      Encrypt();
      break;

    case SoapMessageStage.BeforeDeserialize:
      Decrypt();
      break;

    case SoapMessageStage.AfterDeserialize:
      break;

    default:
      throw new Exception("invalid stage");
  }
}
```

As you can see it's very similar to the tracing extension we looked at earlier. However, instead of writing the SOAP message to a file, this extension is capable of using DES encryption to both encrypt and decrypt the SOAP message. Here's the Encrypt() routine that is called:

```
private void Encrypt() {
  newStream.Position = 0;

  if (encryptMode == EncryptMode.Response)
    newStream = EncryptSoap(newStream);
    Copy(newStream, oldStream);
  }
```

If the `Encrypt` property of the attribute is set to `EncryptMode.Response`, then the `Encrypt()` function will call another routine, `EncryptSoap`:

```
public MemoryStream EncryptSoap(Stream streamToEncrypt) {
   streamToEncrypt.Position = 0;
   XmlTextReader reader = new XmlTextReader(streamToEncrypt);
   XmlDocument dom = new XmlDocument();
   dom.Load(reader);

   XmlNamespaceManager nsmgr = new XmlNamespaceManager(dom.NameTable);
   nsmgr.AddNamespace("soap", "http://schemas.xmlsoap.org/soap/envelope/");
   XmlNode node = dom.SelectSingleNode("//soap:Body", nsmgr);
   node = node.FirstChild.FirstChild;

   byte[] outData = Encrypt(node.InnerText);

   StringBuilder s = new StringBuilder();

   for(int i=0; i<outData.Length; i++) {
     if(i==(outData.Length-1))
        s.Append(outData[i]);
     else
        s.Append(outData[i] + " ");
   }

   node.InnerText = s.ToString();

   MemoryStream ms = new MemoryStream();
   dom.Save(ms);
   ms.Position = 0;

   return ms;
}
```

`EncryptSoap()` reads in the memory stream that represents the SOAP message and navigates down to the appropriate node. Once the this is found, another `Encrypt()` method that accepts a string and returns the DES encrypted byte array is called. Afterwards `EncryptSoap()` simply converts the encrypted byte array to a string and adds that string back into the SOAP message stream, which is then returned.

Although this is quite a complex sample, it should provide an excellent start to building more secure Web Services. Here are some recommendations:

❑ Ideally this encryption extension should be using asymmetric encryption, rather than both the web service and the proxy sharing the same key.

❑ A SOAP header should be used to send additional details about the message relating to the encryption, for example the public key (if you re-implement this to support asymmetric encoding), as well as an encrypted timestamp to prevent replay attacks.

❑ Currently the message exchange only supports clear-text requests (from the proxy) and encrypted results. Ideally, the extension should support encrypted requests.

These suggestions are beyond the scope of what can be reasonably covered in this chapter. Hopefully someone will implement them in the near future and release the code into the public domain.

Summary

We started this chapter discussing the general problem of finding Web Services that we may want to use. To address the problem we first introduced Universal Description, Discovery, and Integration (UDDI), and how organizations can use UDDI, a yellow-pages style directory, to both find and register Web Services. We then stepped through the use of UDDI, using Microsoft's UDDI node, to demonstrate its typical use in discovering SOAP Web Services.

After discussing the uses of UDDI, we then mentioned that we still needed a way of describing the capabilities of Web Services, such as the protocols they support and the data types, or XML schemas that may be used. To address this problem, we introduced Web Service Description Language (WSDL). We used WSDL to describe the capabilities of our Web Service through XML – we additionally mentioned that WSDL has been submitted to W3C by Microsoft and IBM (among others) for standardization.

Thanks to WSDL, we can build software based on the XML blueprint of a web service. We discussed the use of both Visual Studio.NET, and the command-line tool `wsdl.exe` to create this 'proxy' software. After creating proxies with both of these tools we demonstrated how to use them and stepped through some common scenarios, such as setting the timeout value, or using HTTP cookies.

Following our discussion of building .NET proxies for Web Services, we diverted the discussion to HTML Screen Scraping and how we could use a simple WSDL document and .NET's regular expression support to easily turn any web site into a Web Service – very handy indeed!

Next we mentioned several design decisions for Web Services. Specifically we looked at handling exceptions and using SOAP headers to send out-of-band data (data that doesn't belong as part of the body of the SOAP message).

Finally, we spent the remainder of the chapter discussing Security – both the options provided by ASP.NET, such as Forms or Windows authentication, and some custom security and encryption options in the *Advanced Topics* section.

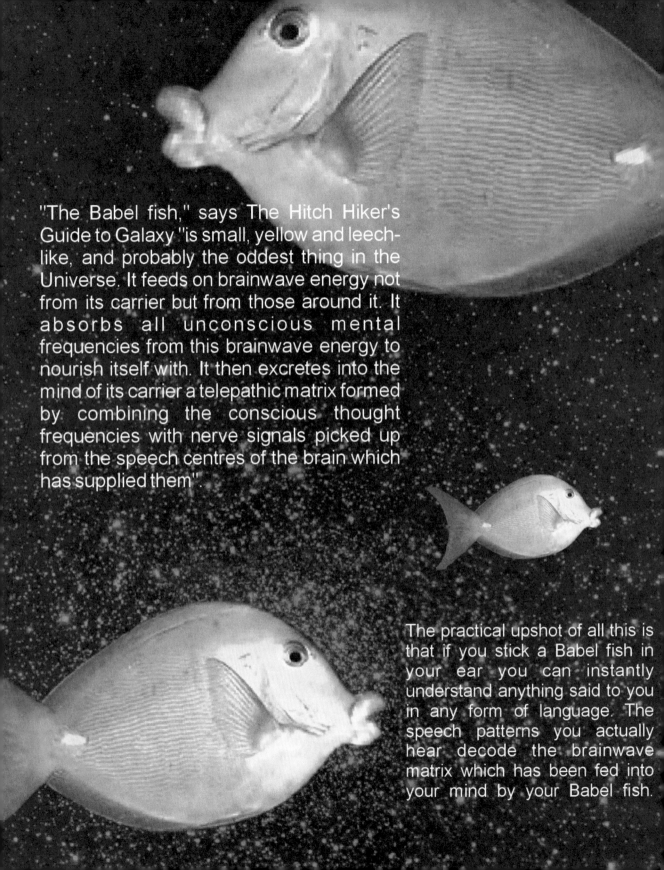

"The Babel fish," says The Hitch Hiker's Guide to Galaxy "is small, yellow and leech-like, and probably the oddest thing in the Universe. It feeds on brainwave energy not from its carrier but from those around it. It absorbs all unconscious mental frequencies from this brainwave energy to nourish itself with. It then excretes into the mind of its carrier a telepathic matrix formed by combining the conscious thought frequencies with nerve signals picked up from the speech centres of the brain which has supplied them".

The practical upshot of all this is that if you stick a Babel fish in your ear you can instantly understand anything said to you in any form of language. The speech patterns you actually hear decode the brainwave matrix which has been fed into your mind by your Babel fish.

21
Mobile Controls

The Mobile Internet Toolkit is an extension to the controls available in the .NET framework that adds support for mobile devices. It is a collection of controls that, when placed in ASP.NET pages, will vary their output depending on the browsing device, and allow for content types other that HTML, such as WML.

In this chapter we will detail the use of these controls and give examples of their use. We'll start with a tour of the wireless Web, with a look at what is available today and a discussion of WAP. Next we'll look at the mobile controls, including a reference section on the controls available. Moving on, we'll see some of the more advanced techniques we can use to streamline mobile web applications, before finishing off with a few guesses as to what the future holds for mobile controls, and wireless internet access.

A Summary of the Wireless Web

Recently, there has been a huge surge of interest in wireless internet access, and indeed in mobile computing in general. As we have become increasingly dependant on the World Wide Web we have developed a desire to access it from anywhere. The technology now exists to enable us to do this, although the exact nature of this access is quite different from 'traditional' internet access.

This difference has caused many problems, for both device manufacturers and consumers, as it has frequently been overlooked. Often, consumers have expected to get an all-singing all-dancing, web-surfing gadget, and have been disappointed with what they have ended up with. However, the underlying potential of such devices is unquestionable. In order to make sense of this we need to look at features inherent in the types of devices that can be used for mobile Internet access. The most obvious of these features is that the device will be small. It follows on from this that:

❏ Display area is limited, being far smaller than a PC monitor and likely to lack the associated color capabilities in order to maximize battery life and minimize cost.

❏ Processing power and memory is unlikely to compete with PCs.

❏ Multimedia capabilities will be severely challenged.

Already it's obvious that we cannot expect the sort of web experience that we are becoming accustomed to using web browsers on our PC. To further illustrate this, consider the Wrox web site displayed on the screen of an internet-capable mobile phone:

I think you'd have a hard time navigating through this site – if you could even read it!

Of course, larger screened devices are available, such as the (significantly more expensive) Personal Digital Assistant (PDA) type devices out there. Some of the cutting edge ones even claim to support resolutions up to 640x480 pixels, so perhaps there is hope for viewing complex HTML pages. Most standard PDAs with smaller screens are also capable of viewing HTML, although the experience can be quite different from using a traditional web browser.

There are also concerns when we consider the 'wireless' aspect of mobile internet access. Put plainly, we can never expect the sort of bandwidth that is possible in hardwired systems. Not only that, but the signal quality is likely to be variable – we might temporarily lose communications by driving through a tunnel, for example.

Current systems allow a data transfer rate of around 9600 baud, which is comparable to the modems of yesteryear, and about six times slower than you might expect on a standard modem line (and orders of magnitude slower than more professional systems). Although many mobile networks will implement systems allowing for faster access in the future, speeds will always be slower than we might achieve on a PC. When this is taken into account we can hardly expect streaming multimedia web sites on mobile devices, unless there is some interesting paint drying near you that you can watch while things download.

Up till now we've been considering the bad points. After reading the above you may well be asking yourself how mobile internet access ever got off the ground. But, there are many things that are possible with mobile devices that aren't with PCs. It is only when we consider these possibilities that the true power becomes clear. The key point to remember is that mobile Internet access is **mobile**. It is available anywhere and anytime, without having to lug much hardware around with you. In addition, the fact that you carry it with you means that you are likely to be interested in information that pertains to your current situation and position (such as "Where's the closest Indian restaurant?"). In theory this kind of 'location-dependant' information should be accessible without actually entering information about where you are. After all, the network operator knows more or less where you are from the network cell you are in. Unfortunately, this kind of application has yet to appear at the time of writing. It seems that network operators aren't too keen on handing out this information yet, although developments are occurring regularly, and I wouldn't be surprised if this was possible by the time you read this.

So, we **know** that mobile internet access is a good idea, but, in the face of all the problems mentioned earlier, how do we make it work? Luckily, this isn't something we have to work out for ourselves. A lot of serious thought has been expended to come up with standards to get things moving. The standard that has the greatest prominence, in most of the world, is the **Wireless Application Protocol** (**WAP**).

WAP

If you've had any experience using mobile devices to connect to internet services, you've more than likely used a WAP-enabled device. Not only that, but I'd say it was very likely that you've heard the term 'WAP' on TV, seen it in magazines, and heard how much people seem to hate it. However, if you analyze the problems that people have with WAP, such as "It's too slow", "There's no color", "All the WAP sites look rubbish", and so on, you may notice that these can in all cases be explained by the limitations we looked at in the last section – and we weren't even considering WAP there.

Even so, it seems perfectly reasonable to wonder why we should bother with WAP at all.

In actual fact, WAP does quite a good job of dealing with these limitations, but the end result is still not enough to satisfy the e-generation. However, WAP is ready for the next generation of mobile communication networks – without major changes – and is likely to start to become more accepted as bandwidth increases. Of course, many people ask whether WAP will be here at all, or whether it will be replaced with something else. In order to address this point we need to take a step back and look at exactly what WAP is, and how it works.

The objective of WAP is, logically enough, getting information from the Internet to a mobile client. This isn't exactly simple, not least due to the fact that there is no physical connection between the Internet and the wireless network. In addition, building up any communication protocol is a lengthy process (I, for one, wouldn't fancy sitting down and reading through the specifications drawn up for internet communications, even if I did have a spare month or two). Deciding what form data should take, what security measures should be taken, how data should be compressed and transmitted etc. is by no means simple.

This is one thing that we can relax about though, the architects of WAP (the **WAP forum**) have analyzed the issues involved, and the results work fine. To summarize, the gap between the Internet and the wireless network is filled by what is known as a **WAP gateway**, which acts primarily as a protocol converter. Resources on the Internet are accessed by this gateway in much the same way as internet clients do – using HTTP. The gateway does this when it receives a request from a WAP-enabled device, which is transmitted using WAP protocols. Once it has fetched the resource required, the gateway may perform additional processing (such as compressing files to optimize transmission) if necessary, and then will transmit the result back to the mobile client, again using WAP protocols. This is illustrated in the figure below:

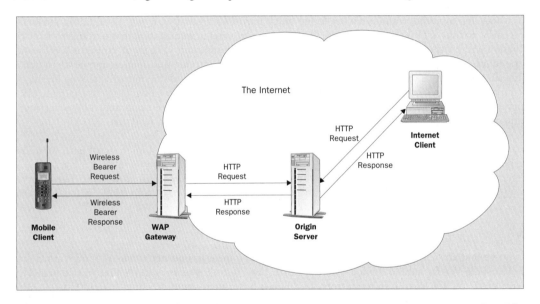

This leads to a few questions, such as "What form do WAP resources take on the Internet?" and "How is security propagated between the mobile client and the origin server?" Again, these questions have been thought of already, which is part of the reason why the WAP specification (freely available from www.wapforum.org, now in version 1.2, and last updated June 2000) is so large and consists of so many sections. Instead of listing all the documents, I'll just point out the categories to which they belong:

- ❏ **General WAP technologies** – a selection of documents setting out the objectives of the WAP specification, and the various enabling technologies.

- ❏ **The WAP protocol stack and WAP gateways** – the means by which information is exchanged with the Internet, optimized to be as efficient as possible in a low-bandwidth environment.

- ❏ **WAP language specifications** – specifics on the way in which applications may be created for WAP-enabled devices.

- ❏ **The WAP push specification** – information on server-initiated WAP exchanges (that is, how information may be transmitted to WAP-enabled devices without a direct request for it).

Much of this specification is advanced, certainly more advanced than we want to get into here, but it's reassuring to know that it is there.

Consider the WAP language specification section. This is the part of the specification that details how resources should be formatted on servers (as well as how they may be compressed for wireless transmission). From the discussion in the last section, it shouldn't be too much of a surprise to find out that HTML isn't the language used by WAP devices. HTML is a relatively heavyweight language, containing much functionality that just doesn't fit in with the idea of quick mobile internet access. It makes far more sense to create something new for the bulk of cheap mobile devices, something relatively simple, optimized for the considerations we looked at earlier, and lightweight. Something, in fact, like **WML** – the **Wireless Markup Language**. We'll take a look at this in the next section.

Note that more complex devices, such as PDAs, don't suffer from quite such strict limitations when it comes to internet content. Since they typically have larger screens than WAP-enabled mobile phones they are more suited to HTML – or at least very simple HTML to avoid the low-bandwidth problem.

After looking at all this, I hope I can convince you that WAP is here to stay. So many technical challenges have been overcome, and so much groundwork is in place, that launching a new and completely different means of wireless internet access would be like reinventing the wheel. Of course, there are places where improvements may be made (as we will see later), but WAP is much more likely to evolve than to die.

WML

The Wireless Markup Language (WML) is the WAP forum's solution to the problem of formatting content for display on WAP browsers. It is an XML application and shares some features with HTML, although comparisons between these languages aren't that simple to draw. As we saw earlier, a web 'page' (taken here as the atomic unit of a web site) isn't an obvious choice for a fragment of a WAP site. For a start many web pages contain far more information than would be usable on a mobile device, and the concept of separate frames containing extra information is also not easily translatable.

A single WML file is often called a **deck**, and contains one or more **cards**. Each card can be thought of as a screen-full of information, complete with text, graphics, hyperlinks, etc. Depending on the characteristics of the browser, and the device used to display a given card, this 'screen' may fit completely into the device display area, be accessible via scrolling keys, or require other modes of user intervention to navigate through. Navigation between cards may be within a single deck, or between decks:

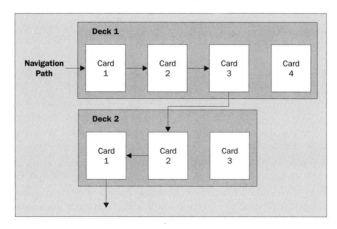

Owing to the limitations detailed earlier a size restriction has been placed on WML decks. A *compiled* WML deck may be no larger than 1,440 bytes. This is quite a small limit, and means that complete WML applications will rarely fit into a single deck, unless they are very simple.

Also, as is apparent from the diagram in the last section, WML files may be stored on any existing web server, such as IIS, PWS, Apache, etc. All that is required in order to do this is to configure the MIME types for WML and compiled WML files. When doing this it is worth adding the other MIME types that are used by WAP, as shown in the table below:

Description	MIME Type	Associated Extension
Plain WML file	`text/vnd.wap.wml`	`.wml`
Compiled WML file	`application/vnd.wap.wmlc`	`.wmlc`
WMLScript file	`text/vnd.wap.wmlscript`	`.wmls`
Compiled WMLScript file	`application/vnd.wap.wmlscriptc`	`.wmlsc`
Wireless Bitmap Image	`image/vnd.wap.wbmp`	`.wbmp`

WAP browsers may then access WML files using standard URL format.

Let's look at an example of a WML deck. This file can be found in the downloadable code for this chapter with the filename `example1.wml`:

```
<?xml version="1.0"?>
<!DOCTYPE wml PUBLIC "-//WAPFORUM//DTD WML 1.1//EN"
                     "http://www.wapforum.org/DTD/wml_1.1.xml">

<wml>
    <card id="first" title="First Card">
        <p>
            Welcome!<br/>
            <a href="#second">Continue</a>
        </p>
        <do type="accept" label="Next">
            <go href="#second"/>
        </do>
    </card>
    <card id="second" title="Second Card">
        <p>
            Now into content...
        </p>
        <do type="prev">
            <prev/>
        </do>
    </card>
</wml>
```

Before we analyze this code let's have a quick look at the results on a WAP device simulator. For this example we'll use the Nokia WAP toolkit version 2.1 (the most recent version at the time of writing) simulating a Nokia 7110 phone. This toolkit is freely available at http://forum.nokia.com/ if you register for it, and comes with all the documentation necessary to set up and use the device simulators included (for brevity I won't cover this aspect here). Upon loading the example deck into the simulator we see the content of the first card:

Note that if you are using Windows NT, 2000, or XP you must launch the toolkit from the command line (details in the `UsersGuide.pdf` *file included in the installation).*

Here we have two choices – we can follow the highlighted Continue link by pressing the default selection button on the device (on the simulator this involves clicking the mouse on it) or select Options by pressing the button beneath this text. A labeled button such as Options is called a **softkey**. If we follow the Continue link we'll reach the next card in the deck:

This card has no hyperlink but contains text content and an additional softkey – Back. This softkey will take us one place back in the history stack, and return us to the first card.

Now let's look at the code that achieved this. The code starts with the standard XML declaration necessary for any XML file:

```
<?xml version="1.0"?>
```

Next we have the DOCTYPE for the XML file, that is, the resource that specifies the WML 1.1 syntax and enables validation:

```
<!DOCTYPE wml PUBLIC "-//WAPFORUM//DTD WML 1.1//EN"
                     "http://www.wapforum.org/DTD/wml_1.1.xml">
```

Note that we're not using WML 1.2 here. This is because many current devices (and emulators) don't support it. Using this version isn't a problem for us, as I won't be looking at anything WML 1.2-specific in this chapter.

Next we have the root element, `<wml>`, which contains the WML deck:

```
<wml>
   ...
</wml>
```

Within this root element we have the two cards that make up the deck:

```
<card id="first" title="First Card">
   ...
</card>
<card id="second" title="Second Card">
   ...
</card>
```

Each of these card elements has two attributes (there are many more possible, but these two are fine for a simple example): `id` and `title`. `id` is used to identify each card within the deck, and is essential for navigation between cards, as we will see in a moment. `title` provides a string for the browser to use in the presentation of the card. The Nokia 7110 places this text at the top of its display area as shown in the earlier screenshots, but it should be noted that this is not always the case – some browsers will display this in alternative ways, and some will ignore it completely. We'll look at this kind of behavior in more detail later, in the section on device interoperability.

Next we'll look at each card in turn, starting with the one with the `id` attribute of `"first"`. This card contains two elements: `<p>`, a paragraph element that contains (among other things) text to display, and `<do>`, which defines a softkey:

```
<p>
   Welcome!<br/>
   <a href="#second">Continue</a>
</p>
<do type="accept" label="Next">
   <go href="#second"/>
</do>
```

The paragraph element contains the simple text "Welcome!", a line break using the `<br/>` empty element (note that we need the trailing slash here to signify that the element is empty, unlike the similar `<br>` tag in HTML), and a hyperlink. WML hyperlinks use either the `<anchor>` element or the slightly less versatile `<a>` element. Here we use the `<a>` element, as this is all that is required for simple navigation. Enclosed in the element is the text that we want to display for the link, Continue, and the navigation itself is detailed by the element attributes. The only attribute used here, `href`, contains the destination for the link. This link is meant to provide navigation to the other card in the deck, which has an `id` of second, so this is what we use for the attribute value. Note that we use a '#' symbol here, which is essentially XML fragment syntax, and points the browser at a specified card within a deck. We could use a fully qualified URL here, such as `http://www.somewhere.com/somedeck.wml#card1`. If we point at a separate deck in this way then the card specifying section (`"#card1"`) is optional; if omitted then the first card contained in the target deck will be navigated to.

The <do> element is a versatile one, and allows several different types of softkey to be created, the type being chosen by the type attribute. Here the type "accept" is used, which means this is a simple "press to activate" type key. The label attribute is used when displaying the softkey. The Nokia 7110 browser requires the user to access the Options menu to accept type softkeys, where they are placed along with built-in device options:

The Next softkey is shown highlighted in the above list.

The functionality of this softkey is determined by the content of the <do> element. In this case the element contains a <go> element, which specifies navigation. This code uses the same destination for the softkey as for the #second hyperlink and so we have two ways of navigating to the other card in the deck. If there were more text contained in the <p> element, so that the Continue hyperlink didn't appear without scrolling down, this softkey provides an alternative and possibly quicker method of getting to the second card.

The second card contains another <p> element, this time containing just some simple text, and another <do> element:

```
<p>
   Now into content...
</p>
<do type="prev">
   <prev/>
</do>
```

This time the <do> element is of type prev and contains a simple empty element, <prev/>. This is a quick way of adding a Back link to a card, and is worth using a lot!

That completes our brief WML example, which although only scratching the surface of what is possible does show us the basics, and gives a general idea of the structures used. If you want to learn more about the WML language you can find a more in-depth treatment in *Beginning WAP, WML and WMLScript*, ISBN 1-861004-58-3, also from Wrox Press. This book also details the client-side scripting language detailed in the WAP specification. We won't cover this in our chapter to save space, but for completeness I'll say that it is a language similar to JavaScript (it is in fact a subset of ECMAScript) and enables simple client-side calculations. This can save round trips to the server (important in the low-bandwidth WAP world), and can be useful for simple user input validation, for example.

However, this knowledge isn't essential to use the techniques found in the rest of this chapter, although it may be useful to get a wider understanding of wireless internet access.

Device Interoperability

Before we move on to look at the ASP.NET mobile controls, it is worth considering what is probably the main problem with WML. WML was designed to specify content, not layout, meaning that different devices will often display the same WML in different ways. In itself this isn't a real problem, as in most cases the information contained in a file will be preserved. However, in certain situations this becomes much more serious, and usability may be severely hampered. In some cases, WML code that works fine on one device may be difficult or even impossible to make sense of when rendered on others.

In addition, many devices have certain quirks that may be exploited to enhance usability, but the syntax for these varies greatly. In particular, devices equipped with the Openwave (the new name for Phone.com) Browser may use a proprietary set of WML extensions, requiring a different DTD file (DOCTYPE). If files using these are loaded into other browsers they will likely fail to work at all.

As a simple demonstration, let's look at an example from the last section on the Openwave Simulator (also available free of charge, from http://developer.phone.com/download/index.html, and comes with full instructions for use). The most recent version at the time of writing is version 4.1. If we load our deck into this browser we will see that the first card looks like this:

Image Courtesy of Openwave Systems Inc.

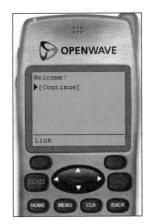

Copyright © 2001 Openwave Systems Inc.

The first thing to realize here is that the title attribute for the <card> element isn't displayed. In fact, the WAP specification says that this attribute is optional, and only intended as a suggestion to the browser to be used for display purposes if it chooses. This can cause problems, however, if you've only tested a WAP application on a browser that displays these titles, and use them as an important source of information for the user. This is an example of a common pitfall to avoid when developing in WML – you must test code on multiple browsers!

Going back to the screenshot, we also see a Link softkey. This appears because the Continue link is selected, and the Link softkey enables us to follow this link. With this browser we can specify the text that should be displayed for this softkey using the title attribute of the <a> element that specifies that link – another example of an attribute whose value may or may not be used by a browser. We should also note that the softkey defined by the <do> element is not displayed. However, if we look at how the screen looks when the hyperlink isn't selected:

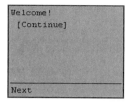

We see that a **Next** softkey appears – which is the one specified by our <do> element. accept type <do> elements on this browser are overridden by, among other things, softkeys created to follow hyperlinks.

Let's look at the other card in the deck:

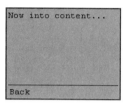

The **Back** softkey here acts as a back link. However, this is shown regardless of whether a prev type <do> element appears in the code – it is the default display for the left softkey on this browser. Also, devices equipped with this browser are expected to have a button for going back (an example of which can be seen in the first screenshot in this section), meaning that this functionality is always available.

The above browser comparison is a very basic one, but does illustrate some of the differences that often occur between browsers (although not fatal ones in this case). There are many more of these, but a discussion of the situation in greater depth is beyond the scope of this chapter.

There are several solutions to this problem. The simplest, but also the highest maintenance, is to provide different WML files for different devices. It is possible to detect the browser type by examining the HTTP_USER_AGENT header then redirect the browser accordingly.

Slightly more advanced is the technique of generating WML dynamically, using ASP.NET or any other code generation technology. However, this can be tricky to implement, as many minor things can need changing, which can make the code very confusing. This may also result in you creating more work for yourself as different decks may end up with quite different processing.

Another strategy is to make use of the fact that WML is an XML application and transform raw data with XSLT, using different stylesheets for different browsers. I have used this to good effect, although it is tricky to get started and requires a great deal of foresight to structure your stylesheets in an appropriate fashion.

Finally, you can use ASP.NET mobile controls. These may not allow as much versatility as other methods, but certainly seem to work OK and require much less effort on your part. As well as being able to generate WML they also cater for HTML, making them suitable for sites that should work on both WAP-enabled devices and HTML browsers on PDAs. In theory this means that knowledge of WML is unnecessary, although I feel that a basic knowledge of the structure of WML pages can help you to design mobile web forms in a better way. We'll spend the rest of this chapter examining these controls.

Introduction to Mobile Controls

Mobile controls are the ASP.NET solution to creating Web Applications that are usable by multiple platforms. The current release supports HTML 3.2, WML 1.1, and cHTML browsers, and allows third-party customization for other types of output (such that the controls could be extended to cover whatever odd internet access technologies might appear in the future). The motivation behind this is to create a set of controls that will perform equally well on multiple devices and yet be programmable using device-independent syntax.

At the time of writing the beta version of the mobile controls SDK is freely available from http://msdn.microsoft.com/downloads/. If you select the Software Development Kits entry from the table of contents on the left you should see the .NET Mobile Web SDK Beta 1 entry, which contains the controls. Simply download and install this SDK (it's only about half a megabyte) and you're ready to use the examples in this chapter.

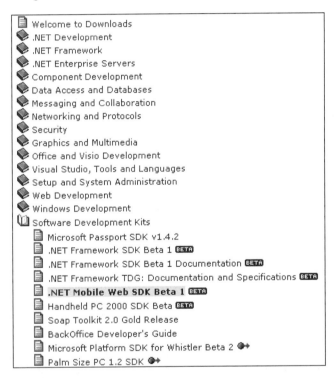

The techniques for using mobile controls are similar to those required for other ASP.NET controls, so much of the code may look familiar to you, particularly that required for event handling, etc. However, there are differences in the way we need to structure our pages to contain mobile web controls, many of which are due to the limitations of mobile devices as discussed earlier. In particular, multiple forms can be contained within a single mobile control web page, necessary to create a system analogous to multiple WML cards in a single deck.

As is often the case when trying to explain a new programming paradigm, it is easiest to start with an example to show the basic operation of mobile controls in action.

Simple Example

For this example we'll create a mobile controls page similar to the simple example we used earlier in the chapter. The code, `example1.aspx`, is as follows:

```
<%@ Page Inherits="System.Web.UI.MobileControls.MobilePage" Language="VB" %>
<%@ Register TagPrefix="mobile" Namespace="System.Web.UI.MobileControls"
   Assembly="System.Web.Mobile" %>

<mobile:Form Runat="server" id="first" Title="First Page">
   Welcome!<br/>
   <mobile:Link Runat="server" NavigateURL="#second">
      Continue
   </mobile:Link>
   <mobile:Link Runat="server" NavigateURL="http://www.somewhere.com/">
      Home
   </mobile:Link>
</mobile:Form>

<mobile:Form runat="server" id="second" Title="Second Page">
   Now into content...
</mobile:Form>
```

The first two lines of code are required for any mobile web form application, setting up the base class for the page:

```
<%@ Page Inherits="System.Web.UI.MobileControls.MobilePage" Language="VB" %>
```

And the mobile controls namespace:

```
<%@ Register TagPrefix="mobile" Namespace="System.Web.UI.MobileControls"
   Assembly="System.Web.Mobile" %>
```

These two lines of code are often called the **prolog** of a mobile web form.

Note that the `TagPrefix` *attribute here specifies* `mobile` *as the prefix for mobile controls. Although you can use a different prefix this is not advised, as this may cause compatibility problems with pages made using Visual Studio.NET.*

The body of the page consists of two `<mobile:Form>` controls. Each of these can be thought of as a card for display on a WAP device, or a page for display in an HTML browser. The first of these forms contains some plain text and two `<mobile:Link>` controls, to display hyperlinks – complete with `NavigateURL` attributes pointing to the second form and an external link. The second form just contains some text.

Don't worry too much about the exact functionality of these controls for now; all of this will be covered later in the chapter.

Again, let's take a brief look at the results, first on the Nokia 7110 simulator:

 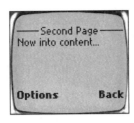

Points to notice for this device (in comparison with the earlier example and in a general sense):

❑ A back link is placed in both cards. The mobile controls automatically place these in every card generated.

❑ Both links are generated as hyperlinks.

Next let's look at the Openwave Simulator:

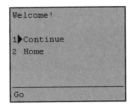 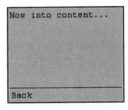

Although it looks slightly different, the functionality is the same. However, the code is quite different, as we will see in the next section.

Finally, as mobile control pages can also generate HTML, we should look at the results in an HTML browser on a PDA. One way of doing this, and the method I'll use, is to use the Pocket PC Emulator available as an MSDN download. This will give us a fair idea of how HTML will be rendered on a real-life PDA. We could also use Microsoft Explorer and simply reduce the window size, but this way is more accurate:

The first page shows the specified text along with a hyperlink to the second page, while the second simply produces the expected string. No softkeys are generated, as PDAs don't generally have them, and the concept of a softkey doesn't fit in with HTML code.

The HTML results here do look quite bare, although, as we will see later on, it is possible to customize HTML output such that it could be considered for a professional web site – using templates and style properties.

Viewing Generated Code

In each browser used in the last section different code was generated. Most browsers allow us to view the source code for the page being displayed (that is, the code generated by the ASP.NET processor, not the ASP.NET code itself). However, this is not always the case.

It can be useful to see the code generated by an ASP.NET page containing mobile controls, to see exactly what is happening and allow you to further customize your code as required. The easiest way to do this is to impersonate the device from a separate ASP.NET page, which will call pages containing mobile controls sending the required headers (HTTP_USER_AGENT, HTTP_ACCEPT, and a few others related to device capabilities) to get the tailored response.

Well, to save you the trouble I've created just such a page: impersonate.aspx, which is available in the code download for this chapter. The interface looks like this:

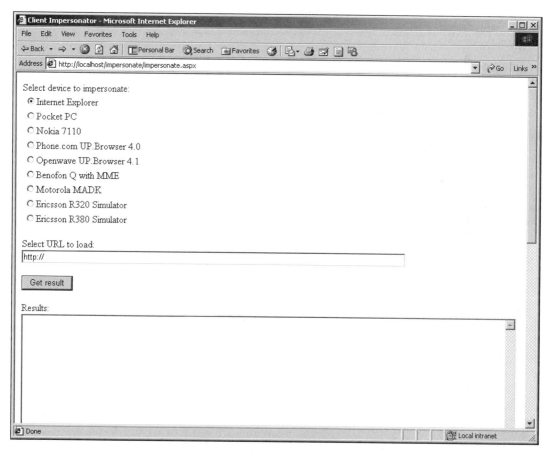

If we select a device (I've included a few more browsers here – it's simple enough to add more to the code if you know the HTTP headers for a device), enter a URL (try the example from the last section) and press Get Result we will see the resultant code in the text box:

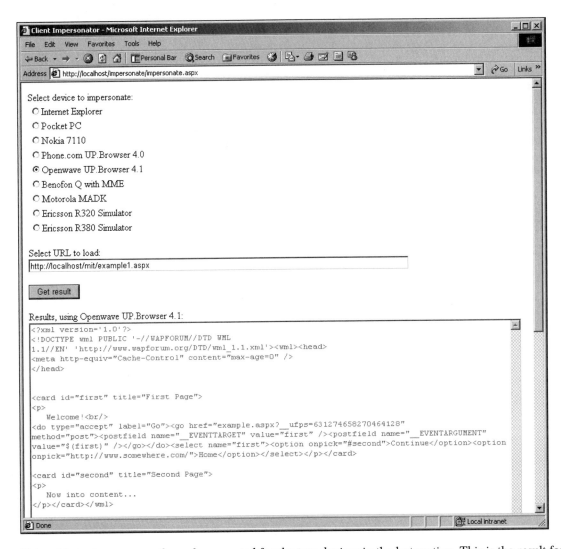

Using this tool we can see the code generated for the two devices in the last section. This is the result for the Nokia 7110:

```
<?xml version='1.0'?>
<!DOCTYPE wml PUBLIC '-//WAPFORUM//DTD WML 1.1//EN'
'http://www.wapforum.org/DTD/wml_1.1.xml'>

<wml>
    <head>
        <meta http-equiv="Cache-Control" content="max-age=0" />
    </head>
```

```
      <card id="first" title="First Page">
         <do type="prev" label="Back">
            <prev />
         </do>
         <p>
            Welcome!
            <br/>
            <a href="#second">Continue</a>
            <a href="http://www.somewhere.com/">Home</a>
         </p>
      </card>

      <card id="second" title="Second Page">
         <do type="prev" label="Back">
            <prev />
         </do>
         <p>
            Now into content...
            <br/>
         </p>
      </card>
   </wml>
```

And this is the result for the Openwave Simulator:

```
<?xml version='1.0'?>
<!DOCTYPE wml PUBLIC '-//WAPFORUM//DTD WML 1.1//EN'
'http://www.wapforum.org/DTD/wml_1.1.xml'>

<wml>
   <head>
      <meta http-equiv="Cache-Control" content="max-age=0" />
   </head>

   <card id="first" title="First Page">
      <p>
         Welcome!
         <br/>
         <do type="accept" label="Go">
            <go href="example.aspx?__ufps=631274387883062944" method="post">
               <postfield name="__EVENTTARGET" value="first" />
               <postfield name="__EVENTARGUMENT" value="$(first)" />
            </go>
         </do>
         <select name="first">
            <option onpick="#second">Continue</option>
            <option onpick="http://www.somewhere.com/">Home</option>
         </select>
      </p>
   </card>

   <card id="second" title="Second Page">
      <p>
         Now into content...
         <br/>
      </p>
   </card>
</wml>
```

As you can see, the two versions are quite different. Don't worry about any WML elements you don't recognize – in most cases you don't need to know exactly what they mean. However, it is worth looking at those that make up the main differences between these pieces of code.

The `<select>` and `<option>` elements are used by WML to build list selection fields. On the Openwave Simulator these are rendered as numbered lists, allowing selection either by hitting a softkey or by pressing the appropriately numbered button on the device – a quick and intuitive solution to lists of up to 10 choices. Unfortunately, list selection fields aren't rendered like this on other devices. It can be tricky to select an item from these on, for example, the Nokia 7110, and no numeric keypad shortcuts are available. This is why hyperlinks are used instead on the Nokia simulator, and the `<a>` element is used as shown above.

Also the code for the Openwave Simulator contains code that is common to ASP.NET pages – the postback information. This isn't required for simple links such as the one used for the Nokia 7110 simulator. But, when we use many controls to generate more complex pages it is worth keeping an eye on this added info. Remember that there is quite a small size limit for WML pages – if the compiled version gets to be larger than around one and a half KB we'll start to run into problems.

> *As a final note on this link rendering, be aware that the code generated can vary in certain circumstances – see the notes on the `<mobile:Link>` control in the control reference section of this chapter.*

This is the first example we've seen of different WML being generated for different devices – without any intervention on our part. This is good – we can relax in the knowledge that (assuming the mobile controls development team do their job properly and keep up with current devices) the code we write will be effectively tailored for multiple client devices.

Wherever WML code is detailed in this chapter it has been extracted using this simple tool, which will save you the effort of downloading and installing multiple WAP browsers. Note, however, that some of the devices, such as the Motorola MADK, are not supported by the version of the mobile controls available at the time of writing. If you generate code using these you will see the HTML code as generated for IE.

Mobile Control Forms

All mobile controls in ASP.NET pages are held in `<mobile:Form>` forms. As we saw in the last example, each of these corresponds to a single display. The form currently being displayed is held in the `ActiveForm` property of the page, which we can set programmatically to change the display – something we will often do in event handlers for controls.

We can see a quick example of this by making use of one of the events that `<mobile:Form>` forms generate. They create two events, which (unsurprisingly) occur when a given form is activated or deactivated, and are called `OnActivate` and `OnDeactivate` accordingly. We can assign event handlers for these controls using identically named attributes on any given form, and create event handlers in the standard way. So, to view the ID for the currently active form we could use the following (not particularly useful, but illustrative) code:

```
<%@ Page Inherits="System.Web.UI.MobileControls.MobilePage" Language="VB" %>
<%@ Register TagPrefix="mobile" Namespace="System.Web.UI.MobileControls"
      Assembly="System.Web.Mobile" %>
```

```
<mobile:Form runat="server" id="first" OnActivate="first_OnActivate">
   Now in form:
   <mobile:Label runat="server" id="content"/>
</mobile:Form>

<script runat="server" language="VB">
   Sub first_OnActivate(sender As Object, e As System.EventArgs)
      content.Text = ActiveForm.id
   End Sub
</script>
```

Here we are setting the `Text` property for the `<mobile:Label>` control with the `id` attribute of `content` to the `id` property of the currently active form – in this case `first`. The result for this is simply:

As this is simple text there is no need to show the result in other browsers (throughout this chapter I'll only show multiple browsers where the results are pertinent).

In addition to the `runat`, `id`, `title`, `OnActivate`, and `OnDeactivate` properties for forms there are a few more we should take a brief look at. Several of these allow you to set styles for form content. These are common to all mobile controls, and any that are set for a form will propagate down into contained controls. We can also set up common style references elsewhere using simple stylesheets, and use the `StyleReference` attribute of a form or contained control to set up multiple style properties simultaneously, using reusable styles. We'll look at how we go about doing this in the Styling section later in the chapter.

For now, here is a list of the common style attributes:

❑   StyleReference
❑   Font (broken down into sub-properties as per standard server controls)
❑   ForeColor
❑   BackColor
❑   Alignment
❑   Wrapping

There are also some properties that concern pagination. As we can't fit huge amounts of text on a mobile screen it is often useful to split text over several cards, and perhaps even decks. The pagination properties are as follows:

❑   Pagination
❑   PagerStyle

We'll look at the use of these later in the chapter, in the section on *Pagination*.

Finally, there are two properties controlling the postback operation of the form. `Action` is used to specify an alternative URL to use for posting information if required, and `Method` selects the HTTP method (`GET` or `POST`) used for postback information.

Control Reference

In this section we will look at each of the controls available in the mobile controls collection (with the exception of `<mobile:StyleSheet>`, which we will examine in the *Styling* section) along with examples of their usage and details of their properties and available events. We'll start with the simpler visual controls and finish up with the validation controls, which are similar to their standard ASP.NET control counterparts.

Note that all controls contain the standard `id` and `runat` attributes (where `runat` must be `server` for all controls) as well as the styling attributes listed in the last section, so these won't be listed with the attributes for each control. Also, attributes pertaining to events will be listed in a separate *Events* section where appropriate.

<mobile:Label>

The first control we'll look at is the simplest of all, allowing us to output simple text to a browser. We can do this using plain text as we've already seen, but this control lets us make programmatic changes to its text via the `Text` property, in the same way as the `<asp:Label>` control does for non-mobile ASP.NET pages.

On WAP devices this control will result in text being placed inside a `<p>` element in the card created by the `<mobile:Form>` form that contains the `<mobile:Label>` control. For HTML, output text is placed within `<div>` tags.

Attributes

Attribute	Description
Text	The text to output to the browser.

Code Generated

On the WAP simulators this generates the following code in a card:

```
<p>
    Text<br/>
</p>
```

For HTML browsers the following is generated:

```
<div>Text</div>
```

This is contained inside the `<form>` for the page.

Example Usage

As we saw in the earlier example:

```
<mobile:Form runat="server" id="frmFirst">
   <mobile:Label runat="server">Welcome!</mobile:Label>
</mobile:Form>
```

The label text may be set either by the Text attribute or by enclosing text inside the element (although the attribute value always takes precedence). The above code could be rewritten, with no change to the results, as:

```
<mobile:Form runat="server" id="frmFirst">
   <mobile:Label runat="server" Text="Welcome!"/>
</mobile:Form>
```

As this example generates simple text, the like of which we have already seen, I won't show screenshots of the resultant displays here.

<mobile:Link>

This control is another one that we have already seen in action, and generates the UI code required to create a simple hyperlink.

Attributes

Attribute	Description
NavigateUrl	The destination URI for the link. If preceded with a # character this refers to the id of a mobile form within the current page.
SoftkeyLabel	The label to display on a softkey when the link is selected, if supported on the target browser.
Text	The text to output to the browser.

Code Generated

This control can generate three types of code, depending on: whether the target of the link is another form in the same page, whether further processing is required for a second page, and whether several links are placed next to each other in a single form. In simple cases, the WML generated for a single link control will be as follows:

```
<a href="NavigateURL" title="SoftKeyLabel">Text</a>
```

On some WAP devices, a softkey alternative will also be generated, meaning the link can be followed even if it isn't visible on screen owing to scrolling. In this case the code generated will be:

```
<do type="accept" label="SoftKeyLabel">
   <go href="NavigateURL" />
</do>
```

The HTML generated is generally along the lines of:

```
<a href="NavigateURL">Text</a>
```

Or:

```
<a href="javascript:__doPostBack('ctrl5','frmSecond')">Text</a>
```

Depending on the task required and the various forms that postback operations can take (simply adding a `SoftkeyLabel` attribute will result in the latter code). There will also be a `__doPostBack()` function defined on the page, together with the usual hidden data for the viewstate, etc.

As demonstrated in the earlier example, the WML created for multiple links can vary a great deal depending on the device, and may be rendered as several `<a>` elements or a `<select>` / `<option>` list.

Example Usage

The following code generates simple, postback, and `<select>` / `<option>` links depending on the browser:

```
<mobile:Form runat="server" id="first" Title="First">
    <mobile:Link runat="server"
                  NavigateUrl="http://www.somewhere.com/somefile.aspx">
        External Link
    </mobile:Link>
    <mobile:Link runat="server"
                  NavigateUrl="http://www.somewhere.com/somefile.aspx"
                  SoftkeyLabel="Ext">
        External Link with label
    </mobile:Link>
    <mobile:Link runat="server" NavigateUrl="#second">
        Internal Link
    </mobile:Link>
    <mobile:Link runat="server" NavigateUrl="#second" SoftkeyLabel="Int">
        Internal Link with label
    </mobile:Link>
</mobile:Form>

<mobile:Form runat="server" id="second" Title="Second">
    2nd Card
</mobile:Form>
```

Try using this along with additional forms etc. to see the various code generated, using `Impersonate.aspx`.

\<mobile:Command\>

This control allows you to place a UI element that the user can interact with in some way, resulting in a call to an event handler (either a simple click event or a custom item event, which will be bubbled up to parent controls). For HTML output this control results in a button; the WML result varies (see below).

Attributes

Attribute	Description
SoftkeyLabel	The label to display on a softkey when the link is selected, if supported on the target browser.
CommandName	The name that identifies the command in OnItemCommand.
CommandArgument	The argument associated with the command in OnItemCommand.
Text	The text to output to the browser.

Events

Event	Description
OnItemCommand	Occurs when the user interacts with the UI element generated and bubbled up to parent controls, if any.
OnClick	Occurs when the user interacts with the UI element generated.

Code Generated

For HTML pages this results in an `<input>` element, for example:

```
<input name="id" type="submit" value="Text"/>
```

The WML again varies. A softkey may be generated:

```
<do type="accept" label="Text">
  <go href="command.aspx?631151558034057424" method="post">
    <postfield name="__VIEWSTATE"
    value="YjU2NTJiNTktODVlNS00YTVhLThjZWMtYWJjYmRkZmIzOTQ3LDA=f0da65f6" />
    <postfield name="__EVENTTARGET" value="id" />
    <postfield name="id" value="$(id)" />
  </go>
</do>
```

Alternatively, and particularly on the Openwave Simulator, a `<select>` list may be generated with an `<option>` element allowing the command to be called, in much the same way as we saw for `<mobile:Link>`.

Example Usage

The following code contains some text that changes when the **Press** button is pressed:

```
<mobile:Form runat="server" id="first" Title="First">
  <mobile:Label runat="server" id="result">
    Button not pressed.
  </mobile:Label>
  <mobile:Command runat="server" id="button1" Text="Press"
                  SoftkeyLabel="Press" OnClick="button1_OnClick"/>
</mobile:Form>
```

```
<script runat="server" Language="VB">

Sub button1_OnClick(sender As Object, e As System.EventArgs)
   result.Text = "Button pressed!"
End Sub

</script>
```

The button appears on various devices as follows:

Pocket PC:

Nokia 7110 (also accessible through the Options softkey):

Openwave Simulator (softkey also generated):

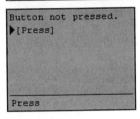

<mobile:Image>

This control allows you to embed images in your forms. WAP supports a single image format, known as Wireless Bitmap Images, or WBMPs. This format is (once again) optimized for low-bandwidth systems, as it can display only two color (one bit) images. Various editors are available on the Web for creating such images, and various plug-ins are available for existing image editors (see http://www.wapjournal.net/developer/utils.cfm, for example).

This control requires you to make a choice of image based on the browser being used. Later on in the chapter we'll cover such things in more detail, but for now we'll look at the simple case of distinguishing between HTML and WML browsers.

The Mobile Internet Toolkit requires us to add filters to the `web.config` file for our application in order to check against device capabilities stored in `machine.config`. A simple filter for WML 1.1 and HTML 3.2 devices requires the following code to be added to `web.config`:

```xml
<?xml version="1.0" encoding="utf-8" ?>
<configuration>
    <system.web>


        ...


        <deviceFilters>
            <filter name="isHTML32" compare="preferredRenderingType"
                    argument="html32" />
            <filter name="isWML11" compare="preferredRenderingType"
                    argument="wml11" />
        </deviceFilters>
    </system.web>
</configuration>
```

We can then refer to these filters by placing a `<DeviceSpecific>` element inside the `<mobile:Image>` element, which in turn contains one or more `<Choice>` elements. These `<Choice>` elements allow us to make modifications to the `<mobile:Image>` control based on specified filters. These modifications take the form of overriding properties of the `<mobile:Image>` control. The following usage selects one of two images depending on whether the browser is WML 1.1:

```xml
<mobile:Image runat="server" ImageURL="NonWML1.1URL">
    <DeviceSpecific>
        <Choice ImageURL="WML1.1URL" Filter="isWML11"/>
    </DeviceSpecific>
</mobile:Image>
```

Attributes

Attribute	Description
AlternateText	Text to display if no image can be displayed in the browser being used (rendered as a label control).
ImageReference	The id of another `<mobile:Image>` control containing the image to display.
NavigateURL	A URL to navigate to if the image is interacted with, if desired.

Code Generated

The code generated is identical for all browsers, as the WML syntax is identical to the HTML syntax:

```html
<img src="Filename" alt="AlternateText"/>
```

The only difference in the generated code will be the filename specified.

Example Usage

The following code displays a picture I took of a cat I met in Turkey, in one of two formats, depending on the browser used:

```
<mobile:Form runat="server" id="first">
    <mobile:Image runat="server" AlternateText="Cat" ImageURL="cat.bmp">
        <DeviceSpecific>
            <Choice ImageURL="cat.wbmp" Filter="isWML11"/>
        </DeviceSpecific>
    </mobile:Image>
</mobile:Form>
```

The results are as follows:

Pocket PC:

Nokia 7110 (scrolling necessary for large images such as this):

Openwave SDK:

<mobile:TextBox>

This control enables user input. The output in all cases will be a text box, although the functionality of the WML rendition of this varies significantly between browsers (see below).

It is possible to change the type of text box displayed using the Numeric and Password attribute. If both of these are false we get a plain text box, setting Numeric to true gives a number-only text box, and setting Password to true renders a password mode text box, where asterisks are written to the screen to prevent unwanted reading of passwords. However, I personally think that the Password type only causes confusion on mobile devices, as it makes the already awkward text input even harder (it's easy to lose your place) and – to be honest – who's likely to read your password over your shoulder on a tiny LCD screen?

Attributes

Attribute	Description
MaxLength	The maximun number of characters allowed in the text box.
Numeric	true or false. Whether the text box is numeric.
Password	true or false. Whether the text box acts in password mode.
Size	The size of the control in characters.
Text	The text to output to the browser.

Events

Event	Description
OnTextChanged	Occurs when the user modifies the text in the text box (and a postback is triggered).

Code Generated

For HTML and WML browsers (again, the syntax is identical):

```
<input name="id" [type="password"]/>
```

Example Usage

The following code uses text input for a simple login page:

```
<mobile:Form runat="server" id="first">
   Enter name
   <mobile:TextBox runat="server" id="name"/>
   Enter password:
   <mobile:TextBox runat="server" id="password" Password="true"/>
   <mobile:Link runat="server" NavigateUrl="#second" Text="Login"
               SoftkeyLabel="Login"/>
</mobile:Form>

<mobile:Form runat="server" id="second" OnActivate="second_OnActivate">
   <mobile:Label runat="server" id="result"/>
</mobile:Form>

<script runat="server" Language="VB">

Sub second_OnActivate(sender As Object, e As System.EventArgs)
   if ((name.Text = "Karli") AND (password.Text = "Cheese")) then
      result.Text = "Welcome Karli!"
   Else
      result.Text = "Sorry, " & name.Text & ", your password is not " _
               & "recognized."
   End If
End Sub

</script>
```

The first form takes a name and password; the second displays the login result. This result is calculated by `frmSecond_OnActivate()`, which is called when the name and password are submitted (or, more accurately, when `frmSecond` is activated). The simple algorithm used simply checks if the name is "Karli" and the password is "Cheese"; if not it displays a failure message.

It is worth noting another fairly major difference between browsers here. Although the code generated for different WAP devices is very similar the user experience can vary a great deal. The Nokia 7110 browser looks similar to the Pocket PC interface:

Here, selecting a field in the Nokia simulator takes you to a separate data entry screen, and when you return the fields are updated.

However, the Openwave Simulator interface only allows a single input field to be displayed at a time:

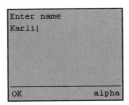

When text is entered and the **OK** softkey is selected the display moves on to the password entry field, and finally to the **Login** link. The end effect is the same, but the routes there can vary.

<mobile:List>

This control allows for simple non-interactive lists of items in plain text, lists of commands, or lists of links. Whatever you want to do with this control you can specify the items it contains using `<Item>` elements within the control, or programmatically (using the exposed `Items` collection). A very simple list, used for display only, might therefore look like this:

```
<mobile:List runat="server">
   <Item Text="Richard Anderson"/>
   <Item Text="Brian Francis"/>
   <Item Text="Alex Homer"/>
   <Item Text="Dave Sussman"/>
   <Item Text="Karli Watson"/>
</mobile:List>
```

Each of the <Item> elements may also have a `Value` property, which specifies a destination when link lists are used. To obtain a link list we simply set the `ItemsAsLinks` property to `true`:

```
<mobile:List runat="server" ItemsAsLinks="true">
   <Item Text="Richard Anderson" Value="http://www.richardanderson.com/"/>
   <Item Text="Brian Francis" Value="http://www.brianfrancis.com/"/>
   <Item Text="Alex Homer" Value="http://www.alexhomer.com/"/>
   <Item Text="Dave Sussman" Value="http://www.davesussman.com/"/>
   <Item Text="Karli Watson" Value="http://www.karliwatson.com/"/>
</mobile:List>
```

Alternatively, we can specify an event handler to execute when an item is selected using `OnItemCommand`, although this won't work properly if `ItemsAsLinks` is `true`.

The control also supports standard ASP.NET data binding.

Attributes

Attribute	Description
DataMember	When databinding, this attribute specifies the table of a `DataSet` to use.
DataSource	When databinding, this attribute specifies the data source to use.
DataTextField	When databinding, this attribute specifies the field to use for item text values.
DataValueField	When databinding, this attribute specifies the field to use for item value values.
Decoration	`None`, `Bulleted`, or `Numbered` – allows for extra formatting of item text by adding bullet marks or numbering items.
ItemsAsLinks	`true` or `false`. Whether to render items as links.
ItemCount	The amount of items to display when using pagination, where a value of 0 means to choose this value automatically.

Events

Event	Description
OnItemCommand	Occurs when an individual list item generates a command event. Note that this won't work if `ItemsAsLinks` is `true`.
OnItemDataBind	Occurs when an item is databound.
OnLoadItems	Occurs when pagination is being used and the items to display are requested.

Code Generated

Obviously, this control can generate varied code. For simple lists the output will be plain text, with appropriate line breaks, or formatted as a table. Link lists will generate code appropriate to the device, such as `<select>` fields or anchors. For example, the code above generates the following HTML on a Pocket PC:

```
<table>
   <tr>
      <td>
         <a href="http://www.richardanderson.com/">Richard Anderson</a>
      </td>
   </tr>
   <tr>
      <td>
         <a href="http://www.brianfrancis.com/">Brian Francis</a>
      </td>
   </tr>
   <tr>
      <td>
         <a href="http://www.alexhomer.com/">Alex Homer</a>
      </td>
   </tr>
   <tr>
      <td>
         <a href="http://www.davesussman.com/">Dave Sussman</a>
      </td>
   </tr>
   <tr>
      <td>
         <a href="http://www.karliwatson.com/">Karli Watson</a>
      </td>
   </tr>
</table>
```

The WML generated on a Nokia 7110 is as follows:

```
<a href="http://www.richardanderson.com/">Richard Anderson</a>
<a href="http://www.brianfrancis.com/">Brian Francis</a>
<a href="http://www.alexhomer.com/">Alex Homer</a>
<a href="http://www.davesussman.com/">Dave Sussman</a>
<a href="http://www.karliwatson.com/">Karli Watson</a>
```

And the WML generated on Openwave browsers is along the lines of:

```
<do type="accept" label="Go">
   <go href="example.aspx?__ufps=631274647595414160" method="post">
      <postfield name="__VIEWSTATE"
                 value="aDxfX1A7QDw7MmI1YjhiMTgtYWROGExOTg1LDA7Pjs+" />
      <postfield name="__EVENTTARGET" value="ctrl0" />
      <postfield name="__EVENTARGUMENT" value="$(ctrl0)" />
   </go>
</do>
```

```
<select name="ctrl0">
  <option onpick="http://www.richardanderson.com/">Richard Anderson</option>
  <option onpick="http://www.brianfrancis.com/">Brian Francis</option>
  <option onpick="http://www.alexhomer.com/">Alex Homer</option>
  <option onpick="http://www.davesussman.com/">Dave Sussman</option>
  <option onpick="http://www.karliwatson.com/">Karli Watson</option>
</select>
```

Each of these pieces of code is entirely appropriate for the target device.

If we are generating a list of commands then appropriate post-back code will also be generated.

Example Usage

As a quick example of a command list, consider the following modified code:

```
<mobile:Form runat="server" id="first">
  <mobile:List runat="server" id="List1"
            OnItemCommand="List1_OnItemCommand">
    <Item Text="Richard Anderson"
          Value="http://www.richardanderson.com/"/>
    <Item Text="Brian Francis"
          Value="http://www.brianfrancis.com/"/>
    <Item Text="Alex Homer"
          Value="http://www.alexhomer.com/"/>
    <Item Text="Dave Sussman"
          Value="http://www.davesussman.com/"/>
    <Item Text="Karli Watson"
          Value="http://www.karliwatson.com/"/>
  </mobile:List>
</mobile:Form>

<mobile:Form runat="server" id="second">
  Follow this link for <mobile:Label runat="server" id="name"/> homepage:
  <mobile:Link runat="server" id="homepage" Text="Link"
            SoftkeyLabel="Link"/>
</mobile:Form>

<script runat="server" Language="VB">

Sub List1_OnItemCommand(sender As Object,_
                   e As System.Web.UI.MobileControls.ListCommandEventArgs)
  name.Text = e.ListItem.Text & "'s"
  homepage.NavigateURL = e.ListItem.Value
  ActiveForm = second
End Sub

</script>
```

When the user selects an item from the list they are redirected to the second card by the command event handler, which also provides a link to the homepage specified in the item value attributes.

<mobile:SelectionList>

This control is similar to <mobile:List>, but has a few important differences. First, it doesn't support pagination. Second, multiple item selection is permitted, aided by the fact that selecting individual items doesn't necessarily trigger a postback. Third, it maintains a list of what items are selected. Finally, the UI is different.

There are two methods of accessing selected items. For single selection lists we can look at the Selection and SelectedIndex properties of the control. However, for multiple selection lists we must examine the Selected property of each item in the Items collection of the control.

Attributes

Attribute	Description
DataMember	When databinding this attribute specifies the table of a DataSet to use.
DataSource	When databinding this attribute specifies the data source to use.
DataTextField	When databinding this attribute specifies the field to use for item text values.
DataValueField	When databinding this attribute specifies the field to use for item value values.
SelectType	DropDown (the default), ListBox, Radio, MultiSelectListBox, or CheckBox. Determines the rendering style.

Events

Event	Description
OnItemDataBind	Occurs when an item is data bound.
OnSelectedIndexChanged	Occurs when a postback is performed and the selected items have changed.

Code Generated

The code generated for this control varies a great deal from HTML output, to cater for the various input methods, although for WML it is always a <select> / <option> list. As a postback isn't generated by default we also need to add a method of doing this manually, such as a button or link.

Example Usage

The following code generates a multiple selection check box list and displays the items selected when a <mobile:Command> control is manipulated:

```
<mobile:Form runat="server" id="first">
    <mobile:SelectionList runat="Server" id="List1" runat="server"
                          SelectType="CheckBox">
        <Item Text="Richard Anderson" />
        <Item Text="Brian Francis" />
```

1096

```
                <Item Text="Alex Homer" />
                <Item Text="Dave Sussman" />
                <Item Text="Karli Watson" />
        </mobile:SelectionList>
        <mobile:Command id="nextForm" runat="server" SoftkeyLabel="Next"
                        Text="Next" onClick="nextForm_click"/>
    </mobile:Form>

    <mobile:Form runat="server" id="second">
        Selected:
        <mobile:Label id="names" runat="server"/>
    </mobile:Form>

    <script runat="server" Language="VB">

    Sub nextForm_click(sender As Object, e As System.EventArgs)
        Dim selectionCount As New Integer()
        Dim item As MobileListItem
        selectionCount = 0
        names.Text = ""
        For Each item In List1.Items
            If item.Selected Then
                If selectionCount <> 0 Then
                    names.Text += ", "
                End If
                names.Text += item.Text
                selectionCount += 1
            End If
        Next
        If selectionCount = 0 Then
            names.Text = "None"
        End If
        ActiveForm = second
    End Sub

    </script>
```

Remember that we can only use the `Selection` and `SelectedIndex` properties of `List1` to get info on single selection lists, hence the `For...Each` loop in the above code to interrogate all items in the list.

On the Pocket PC this is rendered as follows:

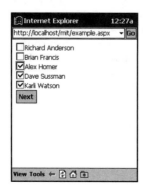 

On the Openwave simulator it looks like:

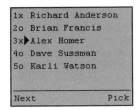 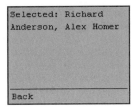

The Nokia 7110 interface is slightly trickier to use and involves more steps, but it still works. The most awkward thing here is that the command doesn't render as a link, just as a softkey option in the Options menu:

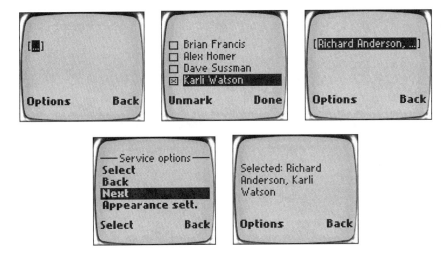

There is plenty more you can do with this control, so have a play!

<mobile:ObjectList>

This control enables more complex lists to be defined, where each item is the visual representation of an object. This representation may vary significantly between browsers.

This object allows for a lot more flexibility – even in its default usage it allows the user to view additional object information. We can also define multiple fields to view and commands to execute for items, leading to interesting possibilities, as we will see when we look at an example in a moment. Due to this additional functionality, and the difference in rendering when compared to simple lists, no selection attributes exist and items can only be defined by databinding. However, we still have access to the Selection and SelectedIndex properties of a list, which becomes important once a command is executed for an item, as it allows us to tell which item generated the command.

Attributes

Attribute	Description
AutoGenerateFields	true or false – If true (the default value) then object properties are automatically converted into extra fields for each ObjectListItem object that the list contains.
DataMember	When databinding to a DataSet this attribute specifies the table to use.
DataSource	This attribute specifies the data source to use.
DefaultCommand	The default command to execute for an item.
LabelField	The field to use for primary display purposes.
TableFields	The fields to display in table view, as a series of identifiers separated by semicolons.

Events

Event	Description
OnItemCommand	Occurs when an individual list item generates a command event.
OnItemDataBind	Occurs when an item is databound.
OnShowItemCommands	Occurs when the defined commands for an item are rendered.

Code Generated

The generated code can be quite involved, so it is better to look at examples.

Example Usage

To illustrate this object, let's expand the author list from the last section such that information about each author is stored in an object. First of all, we need to define an author class:

```
<script runat="server" Language="VB">

Public Class author
    Private authorName, authorInitials, authorFavoritefood As String

    Public Sub New(ByVal name As String, ByVal initials As String, _
                ByVal favoritefood As String)
        authorName = name
        authorInitials = initials
        authorFavoritefood = favoritefood
    End Sub

    Public ReadOnly Property name() As String
        Get
            Return authorName
        End Get
    End Property
End Class
```

```
        Public ReadOnly Property initials() As String
            Get
                Return authorInitials
            End Get
        End Property

        Public ReadOnly Property favoritefood() As String
            Get
                Return authorFavoritefood
            End Get
        End Property
End Class
```

We can then populate the list control, `itemList`, with an array of `author` objects. The easiest place to do this is in the `Page_Load()` event handler (although we only need to do this once, so we can check to see if there is a postback going on):

```
public Sub Page_Load(o As Object, e As EventArgs)
    if (IsPostBack = false) then
        Dim authors As new ArrayList
        authors.Add(new author("Richard Anderson", "RJA", "Pizza"))
        authors.Add(new author("Brian Francis", "BF", "Pasta"))
        authors.Add(new author("Alex Homer", "AH", "Steak "))
        authors.Add(new author("Dave Sussman", "DS", "Whisky"))
        authors.Add(new author("Karli Watson", "KCW", "Fondue"))
        lstItems.DataSource = authors
        lstItems.DataBind()
    end if
end sub

</script>
```

The code for the form itself is then very simple. The only thing we need to add is a `LabelField` attribute, which specifies which field to use for the primary list display:

```
<mobile:Form runat="server" id="frmFirst">
    <mobile:ObjectList runat="server" id="lstItems" LabelField="name"/>
</mobile:Form>
```

The result of all this is more complex then you might expect. On the Pocket PC the following is generated:

Clicking on an author name has no effect (we haven't implemented a handler), but the hyperlink automatically shows us additional information based on the field created. Notice that the field names are exactly the same as the class property names. This is because we have `AutoGenerateFields` set to `true` – the default. If we change this to `false` we can specify how fields are rendered, or even if they are rendered at all. We do this by adding `<Field>` elements inside the control. Each of these elements specifies a field to add to the `ObjectListItems` in the control. We specify these by what property they should represent (using the `DataField` attribute), the display name for the field (using the `Title` attribute), and an `id` for accessing the field. We can also use the `Visible` attribute to control whether a given field appears when we follow the automatically generated `more` link:

```
<mobile:Form runat="server" id="first">
    <mobile:ObjectList runat="server" id="itemList"
                    AutoGenerateFields="False" LabelField="fName">
        <Field Name="fName" Title="Author Name"
            DataField="name" Visible="True"/>
        <Field Name="fInitials" Title="Author Initials"
            DataField="initials" Visible="True"/>
        <Field Name="fFood" Title="Author's Favorite Food"
            DataField="favoritefood" Visible="False"/>
    </mobile:ObjectList>
</mobile:Form>
```

The above changes result in the following:

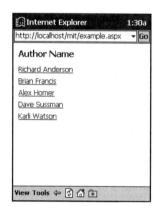

As well as adding fields we can also define commands for the items, using `<Command>` elements. Let's add two commands, to query for a biography or a favorite food:

```
<mobile:Form runat="server" id="frmFirst">
    <mobile:ObjectList runat="server" id="lstItems" AutoGenerateFields="False"
                    LabelField="name">
        <Field id="fName" Title="Author Name" DataField="name"
            Visible="True"/>
        <Field id="fInitials" Title="Author Initials" DataField="initials"
            Visible="True"/>
        <Field id="fFood" Title="Author's Favorite Food" DataField="favoritefood"
            Visible="False"/>
        <Command Name="Bio" Text="Author biography"/>
        <Command Name="Food" Text="Find out the author's favorite food!"/>
    </mobile:ObjectList>
</mobile:Form>
```

This command appears as follows:

In order to hook up the commands (we have two now) we use the `OnItemCommand` event. First we specify a handler by modifying the opening tag for the control:

```
<mobile:ObjectList runat="server" id="itemList"
                   AutoGenerateFields="False" LabelField="fName"
                   OnItemCommand="itemList_itemCommand">
```

Next we implement the handler. Here we'll simply use the item data to specify information for two new forms, shown beneath the code that goes in the `<script>` section of the page:

```
public sub itemList_itemCommand(sender As Object, _
                                e As ObjectListCommandEventArgs)
   Dim currentAuthor as author
   if (e.CommandName = "Food") then
     foodLabel.Text = itemList.Selection.Item("fName") & "
('s favorite food is " &) _
                   itemList.Selection.Item("fFood") & "!"
     ActiveForm = second
   else
       bioLabel.Text = itemList.Selection.Item("fName") & " biography..."
       ActiveForm = third
   end if
end sub
```

```
<mobile:Form runat="server" id="second">
   <mobile:Label runat="server" id="foodLabel"/>
</mobile:Form>

<mobile:Form runat="server" id="third">
   <mobile:Label runat="server" id="bioLabel"/>
</mobile:Form>
```

Clicking on an author name then yields the first screenshot below, and on a 'favorite food' link the second:

This is all very well, but how does it appear on a WAP device? Well, on the Openwave Simulator we see the following card first:

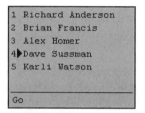

When we select an author we get to see the available commands:

And these links take us to the relevant command-generated forms:

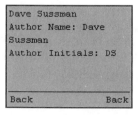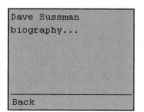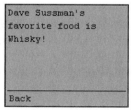

This is a very powerful control, as we can do far more with the commands than just display information. We could trigger whole chains of business logic in this manner. Again, I'll leave it to you to play with that!

<mobile:Call>

This control allows the user to call a phone number. Obviously, this isn't appropriate for all devices, so provision is made for those without this capability.

Attributes

Attribute	Description
AlternateFormat	Text to output to devices incapable of making a phone call. This text should include the two placeholders {0} and {1}, which will be replaced with Text and PhoneNumber respectively. The default it "{0} {1}".
AlternateURL	Target URL for non-calling devices. If specified, the text in AlternateFormat will be rendered as a hyperlink pointing at this URL.
PhoneNumber	Phone number to dial.
Text	Descriptive text to output to the browser.

Code Generated

If the device cannot dial a number then the AlternateFormat text will be output. If the AlternateURL attribute is specified, then the text will be rendered as a hyperlink pointing at the specified URL.

Devices that can dial numbers fall into two categories: some devices, including those using the Openwave Browser version 4.1, such as the Openwave Simulator, make use of **Wireless Telephony Application Interface** (**WTAI**) type commands, in which case the following WML code will do the job:

```
<a href="wtai://wp/mc;PhoneNumber" title="Text">Text</a>
```

Other devices, allow the user to use a number that appears in text, in which case the number will simply be rendered to the screen:

```
<p>Text PhoneNumber</p>
```

Example Usage

We could use this control in code such as:

```
<mobile:Form runat="server" id="first">
   <mobile:Call runat="server" Text="Call Karli's mum"
                PhoneNumber="555-1234" AlternateFormat="{0} on: {1}"/>
</mobile:Form>
```

The Pocket PC simply renders text, as it cannot dial phone numbers (it renders links if we specify `AlternateURL`):

The Openwave Simulator renders a link that will dial the number:

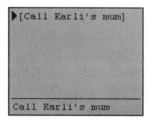

And the Nokia 7110 renders the phone number such that it can be selected with the Use Number menu option:

<mobile:Calendar>

This control is basically the same as the web control with the same name, but is capable of allowing date selection from WAP devices. The UI required to do this is quite different from the HTML version, due to the impossibility of fitting a similar calendar onto a WAP device screen and keeping functionality intact.

The WML version of this control allows you to select dates in two different ways. You can either type one in manually, following the suggested format of MM/DD/YYYY, or choose one by selecting a month, a week, and a day (although not a year for some reason.)

All of the attributes associated with the standard ASP.NET `Calendar` control are also available, although not declaratively. We can gain access to these using the `WebCalendar` property of this control, which returns a web forms calendar control that we can manipulate.

Attributes

Attribute	Description
FirstDayOfWeek	The first day of the week (such as Sunday). The default value (default) uses the locale settings to determine this attribute.
SelectedDate	The currently selected date, which defaults to TodaysDate.
SelectionMode	day, dayweek, dayweekmonth, none – what selections are possible from the calendar. The default is day.
ShowDayHeader	true or false. Whether to show day names or just date numbers.
VisibleDate	The month to display – set by choosing any date in a given month.

Events

Event	Description
OnSelectionChanged	Occurs when a selection is made.

Code Generated

Once again, the code generated by this control is complex, and voluminous. Knowing exactly what this code is doesn't really tell us anything useful, and it would waste a lot of space!

Example Usage

As an example, let's create a page that asks the user what their birthday is. To start off with I'll initialize the calendar to my birthday (once you know what it is you can all send me presents), and then prompt for a selection. When the OnSelectionChanged even is raised the user will be asked to confirm the date, which will either complete the procedure or take the user back to the calendar selection. The code is as follows:

```
<script runat="server">

public Sub Page_Load(o As Object, e As EventArgs)
    if (IsPostBack = false) then
        birthdayCal.SelectedDate = new DateTime(2001, 9, 17)
        birthdayCal.VisibleDate = birthdayCal.SelectedDate
    end if
end sub

public Sub birthdayCal_selectionChanged(sender As Object, _
                                    e As System.EventArgs)
    confirmLabel.Text = "Your birthday is " & _
                    birthdayCal.SelectedDate.Month.ToString() & "/" & _
                    birthdayCal.SelectedDate.Day.ToString() & "?"
    ActiveForm = confirm
end sub

</script>
```

```
<mobile:Form runat="server" id="calendar">
    When is your birthday?
    <mobile:Calendar runat="server" id="birthdayCal"
                    OnSelectionChanged="birthdayCal_selectionChanged"/>
</mobile:Form>

<mobile:Form runat="server" id="confirm">
    <mobile:Label runat="server" id="confirmLabel"/>
    <mobile:Link runat="server" NavigateURL="#done" Text="Yes"/>
    <mobile:Link runat="server" NavigateURL="#calendar" Text="No"/>
</mobile:Form>

<mobile:Form runat="server" id="done">
    Done.
</mobile:Form>
```

Using the Pocket PC we see the following calendar display:

From here we can select a date easily by following any of the day links.

The Openwave Simulator gives us the following screen to start off with:

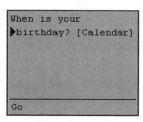

When we follow this link we get three more options:

The first link, which shows the currently selected date, allows us to confirm a date choice, the other two allow the user either to enter a date, either by manually typing it in (with an error message appearing if we enter an invalid date):

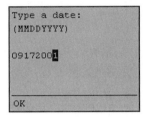

or, via a series of selection screens:

```
1  25 Feb  -  03 Mar
2  04 Mar  -  10 Mar
3  11 Mar  -  17 Mar
4  18 Mar  -  24 Mar
5▶25 Mar  -  31 Mar
6  01 Apr  -  07 Apr

Go
```

Whichever method is used the same confirmation message appears, where we can choose to keep or discard the selected date.

The Nokia 7110 version is similar, although only really works properly if you enter a date manually. Going through the other selections is awkward, requiring you to select Go from the Options menu to proceed past each step, and seems to result in the wrong date being chosen – more evidence that this product is still a beta version.

> *This control also supports advanced styling using style objects if we extract the web form control from* WebCalendar.

<mobile:TextView>

This control is designed for displaying large volumes of text set at run-time. The only time this control is useful is when you have dynamic text, as it is easier to use literal text in static cases.

This control has a single method, SetText(), which can be used to set the text in the control.

<mobile:AdRotator>

This control is practically identical to the ASP control of the same name, including the way it gets data from an XML file. The only difference is that it can render WML – it just outputs the AlternateText text for the advert chosen. Since this is the case I will not reiterate its functionality here.

<mobile:Panel>

This control can be used as a container for other controls, including other panels. The main reason for using it is that it can be templated, which lends itself to interesting formatting possibilities, as we will see shortly.

Validation Controls

The Mobile Web SDK contains the following validation controls:

- ❏ `<mobile:RequiredFieldValidator>`
- ❏ `<mobile:RangeValidator>`
- ❏ `<mobile:CompareValidator>`
- ❏ `<mobile:RegularExpressionValidator>`
- ❏ `<mobile:CustomValidator>`
- ❏ `<mobile:ValidationSummary>`

If these look familiar, it's probably because they are – once again – very similar to their non-mobile counterparts. As such, I'm not going to go into a huge amount of detail about these controls, save to provide an example of their use and the results they provide.

Example Usage

Let's use a couple of controls in a login form:

```
<mobile:Form runat="server" id="first">
   Enter name:
   <mobile:TextBox runat="server" id="name"/>
   Enter password:
   <mobile:TextBox runat="server" id="password" Password="true"/>
   Confirm password:
   <mobile:TextBox runat="server" id="confirm" Password="true"/>
   <mobile:Command runat="server" id="enter" Onclick="enter_click"
                   Text="Enter"/>
   <mobile:RequiredFieldValidator runat="server" ControlToValidate="name"
                                  ErrorMessage="Please enter a name" />
   <mobile:RequiredFieldValidator runat="server"
                                  ControlToValidate="password"
                                  ErrorMessage="Please enter a password" />
   <mobile:RequiredFieldValidator runat="server" ControlToValidate="confirm"
                          ErrorMessage="Please confirm your password" />
   <mobile:CompareValidator runat="server" ControlToValidate="confirm"
                        ControlToCompare="password"
                        ErrorMessage="Confirmation must match password" />
</mobile:Form>

<mobile:Form runat="server" id="second">
   <mobile:ValidationSummary runat="server" formToValidate="first"
                          HeaderText="Invalid input"/>
</mobile:Form>

<mobile:Form runat="server" id="third">
   <mobile:Label runat="server">Input accepted.</mobile:Label>
</mobile:Form>

<script runat="server">

public sub enter_click(sender As Object, e As System.EventArgs)
   if (Page.IsValid) then
      ActiveForm = third
   else
      ActiveForm = second
   end if
end sub

</script>
```

We prompt for a name, a password, and a password confirmation, then check to see if the input is valid. If it is, then we display a confirmation message, otherwise we use the `<mobile:ValidationSummary>` control to output the reasons why the input is invalid. This code also uses the `Page.IsValid` property to see whether a validation summary is required.

Advanced Mobile Control Topics

We've now covered all of the controls and their basic usage. However, there will often be times when you want to display them in better ways, particularly in HTML pages to avoid them looking too bland, or change their default behavior in some way. There are four ways we can achieve this:

- **Styling** – all the controls give us a degree of influence over the way they look, from basic color schemes to more involved styling.

- **Using Device Capabilities** – the controls give us access to many of the capabilities specific to a device, so we can tailor content accordingly.

- **Templating** – adding templates to controls allows us to add extra code to output, both HTML and WML.

- **Pagination** – splitting lengthy text over several pages

In this section we will examine these four areas.

Styling

As mentioned earlier, all the mobile controls have a set of styling attributes we can use. The basic ones are:

Attribute	Description
Alignment	NotSet, Center, Left, or Right – for text alignment.
BackColor	The background color for the control.
ForeColor	The foreground color for the control.
Font	The font to use for text display. This is split into Font-Name, Font-Size (Normal, Small, or Large), Font-Bold (true or false), and Font-Italic (true or false).
Wrapping	Wrap, or NoWrap. Whether to 'wrap' text, where wrapping text means to place it on multiple lines if possible.

Most of these are self explanatory, but you must bear in mind that many WAP browsers will ignore many of these attributes. As an example, let's look at a very simple `<mobile:Label>` control with added formatting:

```
<mobile:Form runat="server" BackColor="Azure">
    <mobile:Label runat="server" ForeColor="BlueViolet" Alignment="Center"
            Font-Bold="true" Font-Size="large"
            Font-Name="Arial">This is some formatted text.</mobile:Label>
</mobile:Form>
```

On the various browsers we've been using, the results are as follows:

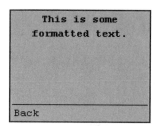

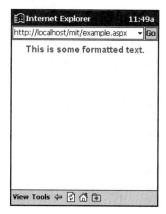

The `BackColor` attribute from the form propagates through to the label. Notice also, that the Nokia 7110 only applies centering formatting. The Openwave Simulator does as much as is feasible, and successfully writes the text in bold. This is about as much as we can expect from mobile devices – or at least ones without color displays.

In addition to the attributes shown above, there is one more: `StyleReference`. This attribute allows us to refer to a separate style, defined in a `<mobile:StyleSheet>` control by a `<Style>` element. `<mobile:StyleSheet>` controls result in no rendering at all, and are not contained in `<mobile:Form>` controls, but they allow us to specify named collections of style attributes that we can apply to multiple controls in our page. For example, we could rewrite the above code as:

```
<mobile:StyleSheet runat="server">
   <Style Name="textStyle" ForeColor="BlueViolet" Alignment="Center"
          Font-Bold="true" Font-Size="large" Font-Name="Arial"
          BackColor="Azure"/>
</mobile:StyleSheet>

<mobile:Form runat="server" StyleReference="textStyle">
   This is some formatted text.
</mobile:Form>
```

We can define as many styles as we want in this way and use them in as many controls as we like.

Using Device Capabilities

In the last section, and in the earlier discussion of `<mobile:Image>`, we capitalized on the fact that we can detect whether a browser supports HTML or WML using a filter. The use of `<DeviceSpecific>` and `<Choice>` elements along with information added to `web.config` allowed us to customize the output of mobile controls. In actual fact we've only scratched the surface of what is possible here so far.

If you look in your `machine.config` file after installing the Mobile Internet Toolkit you'll see that a large volume of text has been added. Much of this is concerned with determining the capabilities of connecting devices by interrogating the HTTP headers received.

There is no worldwide standard implemented for this. Some browsers, such as the Openwave, send additional device capability headers to servers. Others, like the Nokia 7110, don't. Because of this, many capabilities have been found out manually, and are hard coded in `machine.config`. The reasoning goes that if you have enough information to identify a device then you can specify its capabilities.

The list of capabilities that is set in `machine.config` is quite a long one, and I won't reproduce it here. It includes entries as simple as whether a device has a color screen (`isColor`), entries on specific WML rendering characteristics (such as `rendersBreaksAfterWmlAnchor`), screen dimensions (including `defaultScreenPixelsWidth`), and so on. There are sections for many current devices, for example Nokia, which starts by assigning some general Nokia browser characteristics:

```
<!-- Nokia -->
            <case
                match="Nokia.*">
                browser = "Nokia"
                mobileDeviceManufacturer = "Nokia"
                preferredRenderingType = "wml11"
                preferredRenderingMIME = "text/vnd.wap.wml"
                preferredImageMIME = "image/vnd.wap.wbmp"
                screenCharactersWidth = "20"
                screenCharactersHeight = "4"
                screenPixelsWidth="90"
                screenPixelsHeight="40"
                screenBitDepth = "1"
                isColor = "false"
                inputType = "telephoneKeypad"
                numberOfSoftkeys = "2"
                hasBackButton = "false"
                rendersWmlDoAcceptsInline = "false"
                isMobileDevice = "true"
```

And has additional sections for individual devices, such as the 7110:

```
                <case
                    match="Nokia7110/1.0 \((?'versionString'.*)\)">
                    type = "Nokia 7110"
                    version = ${versionString}
                    <filter
                        with="${versionString}"
                        match=
```

```
                  "(?'browserMajorVersion'\w*)(?'browserMinorVersion'\.\w*).*">
                        majorVersion = ${browserMajorVersion}
                        minorVersion = ${browserMinorVersion}
                  </filter>
                  mobileDeviceModel = "7110"
                  screenCharactersWidth="22"
                  screenCharactersHeight="4"
                  screenPixelsWidth="96"
                  screenPixelsHeight="44"
                  canInitiateVoiceCall = "true"
                  canSendMail = "true"
                  rendersBreaksAfterWmlAnchor = "true"
                  requiresPhoneNumbersAsPlainText = "true"
            </case>
```

Here the `match` attributes are compared with the `HTTP_USER_AGENT` header to identify the device, and set the capabilities accordingly.

The important thing to realize here, is that this is an **extensible** system. There are plenty of devices already in this file, but we can add our own, perhaps including the capabilities of the browser built into your fridge or whatever. We could even add devices that support some odd proprietary format should we wish to.

Once these device capabilities have been set we have access to them from our code in two ways: The simplest is through the `System.Mobile.MobileCapabilities` class.

This class has a number of properties that relate to device characteristics, such as the number of characters that can fit in a screen row, whether color is supported, and what markup language is preferred. `<Choice>` elements can access these properties via their `capability` attribute, which is how we chose the preferred markup type earlier. We were actually testing for the value of the `preferredRenderingType` property of the `MobileCapabilities` object containing information about the current browser.

We can also access these capabilities programmatically. The following code outputs the value of `preferredRenderingType` to the screen (note the additional namespace import required):

```
<mobile:Form runat="server" id="first" OnActivate="first_activate">
   <mobile:Label runat="server" id="devCaps"/>
</mobile:Form>

<script runat="Server">

public Sub first_activate(o As Object, e As EventArgs)
   devCaps.Text = "preferredRenderingType = " & _
               Device.PreferredRenderingType
end sub

</script>
```

Resulting in:

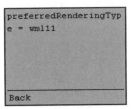

and:

Using this method we can make dynamic choices in our code based on device capabilities.

The other method is the one we briefly saw earlier, involving setting up filters and using them declaratively in our code. Setting filters involves adding `<filter>` elements to the `<deviceFilters>` section of the `<system.web>` section, of the `web.config` file for your application.

The format of these `<filter>` elements is simple:

```
<filter name="filterName" compare="devCap" argument="comapareString" />
```

We specify a name for the filter with `filterName`, a device capability (as specified in `machine.config`) with `devCap`, and a string to compare with the string content of the capability. The filters we set up earlier are now pretty self-explanatory:

```
<deviceFilters>
    <filter name="isHTML32" compare="preferredRenderingType"
            argument="html32" />
    <filter name="isWML11" compare="preferredRenderingType"
            argument="wml11" />
</deviceFilters>
```

Once we have configured our filters we can use them in any mobile control with `<DeviceSpecific>` and `<Choice>` elements. The simplest use of these is simply to override or provide extra properties, as with the earlier example:

```
<mobile:Image runat="server" AlternateText="Cat" ImageURL="cat.bmp">
    <DeviceSpecific>
        <Choice ImageURL="cat.wbmp" Filter="isWML11"/>
    </DeviceSpecific>
</mobile:Image>
```

Here, the only attribute of <Choice> that is specific to the <Choice> element is Filter; all others are applied to the parent control.

<Choice> elements can also be used to contain templates, which is the subject of the next section.

Templates

Much like the standard ASP.NET controls, it is possible to extend the way mobile controls are displayed using templates. Unlike ASP.NET controls we can do this on a device-by-device basis using the <DeviceSpecific> and <Choice> elements discussed in the last section. A given template will specify markup to use for display purposes, which, for example, might be as simple as specifying a section of HTML that is always output prior to the standard HTML output of a mobile control in a web browser, or might be more subtle.

There are five mobile controls that allow templating: <mobile:Form>, <mobile:Panel>, <mobile:Image>, <mobile:List>, and <mobile:ObjectList>. There are eight available templates:

- ❑ ContentTemplate – markup for replacing entire control output

- ❑ HeaderTemplate – markup to place before the control

- ❑ FooterTemplate – markup to place after the control

- ❑ LabelTemplate – markup to use for rendering the label of an item in an ObjectList

- ❑ ItemTemplate – markup to use for each item contained in the control

- ❑ AlternatingItemTemplate – markup to use for every other item contained in the control

- ❑ ItemDetailsTemplate – markup to use for rendering the details for an item in an ObjectList

- ❑ SeparatorTemplate – markup to place between each item contained in the control

These apply to the templatable controls as shown in the table below.

		Template							
		ContentTemplate	HeaderTemplate	FooterTemplate	LabelTemplate	ItemTemplate	AlternatingItemTemplate	ItemDetailsTemplate	SeparatorTemplate
Control	`<mobile:Form>`	Y	Y	Y	N	N	N	N	N
	`<mobile:Panel>`	Y	N	N	N	N	N	N	N
	`<mobile:Image>`	Y	N	N	N	N	N	N	N
	`<mobile:List>`	N	Y	Y	N	Y	Y	N	Y
	`<mobile:ObjectList>`	N	Y	Y	Y	Y	Y	Y	Y

Templates are specified within elements having the same name as the template in question, and contain markup to use.

The clever part here is that these elements are contained within <Choice> elements, allowing us to provide different templates for different devices (in much the same way as we saw different images being used in the <mobile:Image> control), for example:

```
<mobile:Form runat="server" id="first" title="Back to Front">
    <DeviceSpecific>
        <Choice Filter="isHTML32">
            <HeaderTemplate>
                <table width="100%" cellpadding="4" cellspacing="2"
                    bgcolor="black">
                <tr>
                    <td align="center" colspan="2" bgcolor="blanchedalmond">
                        <font face="Arial Black" size="5" color="black">
                        Back to Front
                        </font>
                    </td>
                <tr>
                    <td width="25%" bgcolor="Gold" valign="top">
                        <font face="Verdana, sans-serif" size="2"><b>
                            <a href="/index.aspx">Home</a><br>
                            <a href="/links.aspx">Links</a><br>
                            <a href="/about.aspx">About</a><br>
                            <a href="/discuss.aspx">Discuss</a><br>
                            <a href="/contact.aspx">Contact</a>
                        </b></font>
                    </td>
```

```
                    <td bgcolor="coral" valign="top">
            </HeaderTemplate>
            <FooterTemplate>
                    </td>
                <tr>
              </table>
            </FooterTemplate>
          </Choice>
          <Choice Filter="isUP4x">
              <HeaderTemplate>
                  <b>Back to Front</b><br/>
              </HeaderTemplate>
          </Choice>
      </DeviceSpecific>
      The site that talks about what you don't want to hear about in a way that
      makes it too confusing to follow anyway!
   </mobile:Form>
```

This code uses the header and footer templates to customize form layout. It requires the following filters in `web.config`:

```
<filter name="isHTML32" compare="preferredRenderingType"
        argument="html32" />
<filter name="isUP4x" compare="type"
        argument="Phone.com 4.x Browser" />
```

On a WML browser the HTML template is ignored, and an additional plain text title is added to the display on an Openwave browser:

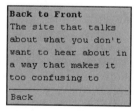

On the Nokia 7110 this extra title isn't necessary, as the `Title` attribute of `<mobile:Form>` works:

However, on an HTML browser such as the Pocket PC we make much more use of the available capabilities:

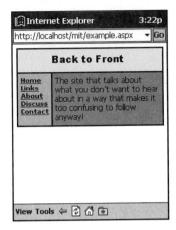

The other templates, when used with lists, can also be used to create excellent results, but I won't give an example of this here as their use is identical to formatting lists using the standard ASP.NET controls (although using a structure like the previous example's).

Templates can also be placed in stylesheets such that they can be reused in multiple forms. The template used in the last example is a good candidate for this, as it provides a structure for containing body text that might apply well to several forms.

Pagination

Pagination is specified and controlled from `<mobile:Form>` controls. In most cases the pagination functionality supplied by default is enough for us, so `Paginate` is set to `'off'`. It can be turned on as follows:

```
<mobile:Form runat="server" id="first" Paginate="true">
    ...
</mobile:Form>
```

Any text we specify in the form will then be split across screens where appropriate. For example:

```
<mobile:Form runat="server" id="first" Paginate="true">
Tyger! Tyger! burning bright<br/>
In the forest of the night<br/>
What immortal hand or eye<br/>
Could frame thy fearful symmetry?<br/>
<br/>
In what distant deeps or skies<br/>
Burnt the fire of thine eyes?<br/>
On what wings dare he aspire?<br/>
What the hand dare seize the fire?<br/>
<br/>
And what shoulder, and what art,<br/>
Could twist the sinews of thy heart?<br/>
And when thy heart began to beat,<br/>
What dread hand? and what dread feet?<br/>
```

```
<br/>
What the hammer? what the chain?<br/>
In what furnace was thy brain?<br/>
What the anvil? what dread grasp<br/>
Dare its deadly terrors clasp?<br/>
<br/>
When the stars threw down their spears,<br/>
And watered heaven with their tears,<br/>
Did he smile his work to see?<br/>
Did he who made the lamb make thee?<br/>
<br/>
Tyger! Tyger! burning bright<br/>
In the forests of the night,<br/>
What immortal hand or eye<br/>
Dare frame thy fearful symmetry?<br/>
</mobile:Form>
```

This text is rendered over several pages on the Nokia and Openwave browsers, with Next and Previous links added automatically:

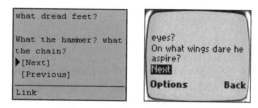

The Pocket PC fits all this on one page:

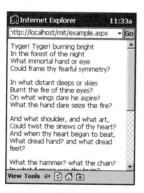

This device does support pagination, but can fit more text in one page. In fact, it will fit another two paragraphs on the end of the Blake poem I've used here.

Summary and Future Possibilities

To conclude this chapter I'd like to take a quick peek into the future and attempt to predict the fortunes of the mobile web and mobile controls.

The Future of the Mobile Internet

There is one thing we can say with absolute certainty – the mobile web is here to stay. In fact, it may become so pervasive that we cease to use wires at all in the future. However, this situation is a long way off, so let's just consider the next few years for now.

For a start, more and more people will gain mobile internet access. More devices will be available at a lower cost and will be more useful. We can expect the available bandwidth to increase rapidly, and enhanced usability will come with this speed and with packet networks. It will soon become essential for most organizations with a web presence to develop for mobile devices.

However, many of the limitations of mobile devices are impossible to surmount. We will always be stuck with a tiny display area when compared to desktop PCs – at least until we can display information directly onto the human retina I suppose! We will also be hampered when it comes to other capabilities important for multimedia applications.

The upshot of this is that we will still need to design classic and mobile web applications in different ways – even if we don't end up using WML. In fact, it has been announced that the next version of WAP will use XHTML in some form (although the dialect used is likely to be related to WML). This may mean that it will be easier for web designers to make the leap to mobile applications, but still doesn't change the fact that a single web application is unlikely to be suitable for all browsers unless specific customizations are made; and, of course, one candidate for this could rely on mobile controls.

The Future of the Mobile Controls

The mobile controls, as we have seen in this chapter, provide a viable alternative to low-level mobile application design. Although their use can be tricky to get to grips with for traditional web designers, their power is obvious. However, there are problems.

For a start there are currently many devices with many browsers and subtle differences. The best developer team in the world would surely have a tough time keeping up with developments. This means that interoperability issues will continue to abound. This is particularly true when proprietary device enhancements are taken into account. To maximize usability it is often desirable to make use of these, resulting in significant code differences between even quite similar devices. Can mobile controls account for this? In theory, they can. However, this may mean a fair bit of effort is required on the part of developers to write device-specific code. Mind you, the extensibility framework is in place, so all is not lost!

I would not advise production-quality code to be released using the mobile controls covered in this chapter. However, when they emerge from their beta stage, any familiarity with them is likely to pay off, as general principles are likely to be unchanged.

Perhaps, in a few years time, the mobile controls covered here will form the basis of a significant amount of multi-browser Web Applications. If the development team at Microsoft continues to develop them then I for one will be very interested in the results.

"The Babel fish," says The Hitch Hiker's Guide to Galaxy "is small, yellow and leech-like, and probably the oddest thing in the Universe. It feeds on brainwave energy not from its carrier but from those around it. It absorbs all unconscious mental frequencies from this brainwave energy to nourish itself with. It then excretes into the mind of its carrier a telepathic matrix formed by combining the conscious thought frequencies with nerve signals picked up from the speech centres of the brain which has supplied them".

The practical upshot of all this is that if you stick a Babel fish in your ear you can instantly understand anything said to you in any form of language. The speech patterns you actually hear decode the brainwave matrix which has been fed into your mind by your Babel fish.

22

Debugging, Tracing, and Error Handling

I often wonder whether the panacea of error-free software will ever happen. Humans aren't error free, so while we're writing software it's likely we'll make at least one mistake. That's why software companies have teams of people testing their products: because developers are fallible. Not only do mistakes happen, but also compatibility between components can cause other errors. One of the error-handling specifications for ASP.NET says, "Errors happen. Deal with it", and one developer I know says "Errors suck". Both are true – however bad errors are, they do happen, and we have to find ways of tracking them down and preventing further errors.

In this chapter we're going to look at the features ASP.NET provides to help during the development cycle. In particular we'll look at:

❑   Tracing, and how to track progress through ASP.NET pages and components.

❑   Profiling, and how to identify areas of slow performance.

❑   Debugging, showing how to find errors, and use the debugger.

❑   Error handling, showing how to handle errors gracefully, and prevent further ones.

These topics were all available in ASP, but they were always hampered by the environment or language. The .NET platform has freed us from some of the constraints and restrictions that ASP imposed, and the languages have improved other areas. Overall .NET not only gives us a far better way of developing applications, but also better facilities for making those applications as robust and error free as possible.

Tracing

Tracing is the art of tracking the progress of an application – finding out what's happening and when. It's a fairly safe bet that you use the tried and tested method of tracing that everyone else does – scattering `Response.Write` statements through your code. It may not be elegant, but it works. There are, however, problems with this approach:

❑ Where to output the tracing information. Putting it inline just makes the output hard to read, and the trace statements hard to interpret. Ways of getting around this are to build a string of tracing information, and then output that as the last thing on the page, or write the tracing information externally (such as to a text file, database, or event log).

❑ How to enable or disable tracing. There are two ways to achieve this in ASP. The first is the laborious method of just commenting out the tracing information. This is time consuming, not very flexible, and error prone (ever commented out too many lines?). The second approach is to encapsulate the tracing within a procedure in an include file. You can then just comment out the code in one place, or replace the procedure with one that does nothing, but this is also inefficient. Alternatively you can use a switch (perhaps a registry setting or configuration file) to identify whether tracing is enabled. But, again, this can lead to performance problems.

❑ How to have tracing, but not have it visible to users. When testing applications you often want to trace the path of execution without your users being aware of the information. Writing output to a text file or database would probably be the best solution here.

You can actually create some quite elegant solutions for tracing, but with ASP.NET we have everything neatly encapsulated for us. What's particularly cool is that you can decide if you want tracing managed on a page-by-page basis, or for the entire application.

Page-Level Tracing

Page level tracing is achieved with the simple addition of a page level directive. For example, let's consider the following page (`SimpleTrace.aspx`):

```
<html>
<body>

This is a simple page showing tracing in action.
<br/>
At the moment the page does nothing.

</body>
</html>
```

It doesn't do anything, and you can see there are just a couple of lines of text. To enable tracing for this page, you add the following page directive:

```
<%@ Page Trace="True" %>
```

Adding this to the top of your ASP.NET page will give you the following output:

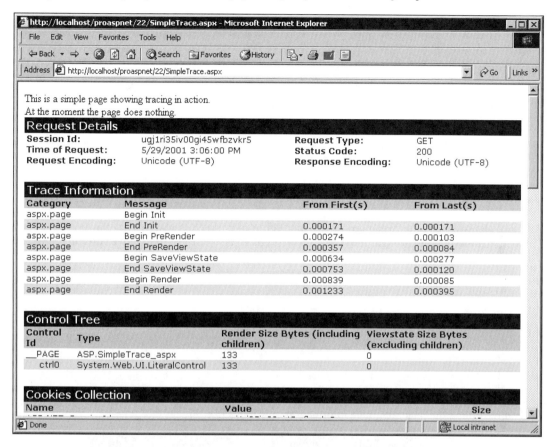

Apart from that one line of code, nothing has changed in the page, and yet we've got a whole heap of information. This is all automatically generated and added to the bottom of the page, and consists of the following sections (not all of which are shown above, purely due to the screen size):

Section	Contains...
Request Details	Information about the request, such as the type, HTTP code, and so on.
Trace Information	Details of execution order, showing time taken to execute for each section. When adding your own custom message (you'll see how to do that in a while), they will appear in this section.
Control Tree	Hierarchical list of all controls on the page, including their size.
Session State	Details of each item (if any) held in Session state.
Application State	Details of each item (if any) held in Application state.

Table continued on following page

Section	Contains...
Cookies Collection	Details of each cookie.
Headers Collection	The HTTP headers.
Forms Collection	Name and value of each of the Form contents.
QueryString Collection	Name and value (if applicable) of each of the QueryString contents.
Server Variables	A complete list of all server variables and their contents.

Not all sections appear for all pages. For example, if your page doesn't contain Form or QueryString information then these sections are not rendered.

Writing Trace Information

To add your own trace information to the Trace Information section you can use the `TraceContext` object, made available through the `Trace` property of a page. For example, if we add the following to our simple page:

```
<script language="VB" runat="sever">

Sub Page_Load(Sender As Object, E As EventArgs)

  Trace.Write("Page_Load", "Here we are")

End Sub

</script>
```

Upon refreshing the page, the trace information now looks like this:

Category	Message	From First(s)	From Last(s)
aspx.page	Begin Init		
aspx.page	End Init	0.000097	0.000097
Page_Load	Here we are	0.000793	0.000696
aspx.page	Begin PreRender	0.000935	0.000143
aspx.page	End PreRender	0.001055	0.000119
aspx.page	Begin SaveViewState	0.001511	0.000457
aspx.page	End SaveViewState	0.002008	0.000497
aspx.page	Begin Render	0.002130	0.000122
aspx.page	End Render	0.038919	0.036789

You can see that our line of text has been added. If we now add a button to the page, and have the following as the event:

```
Sub btn_Click(Sender As Object, E As EventArgs)

  Trace.Warn("btn_Click", "Button was pressed")

End Sub
```

Upon postback, we now see:

Category	Message	From First(s)	From Last(s)
aspx.page	Begin Init		
aspx.page	End Init	0.000160	0.000160
aspx.page	Begin LoadViewState	0.000329	0.000169
aspx.page	End LoadViewState	0.000747	0.000418
aspx.page	Begin ProcessPostData	0.000867	0.000119
aspx.page	End ProcessPostData	0.000997	0.000130
Page_Load	Here we are	0.001116	0.000119
aspx.page	Begin ProcessPostData Second Try	0.001253	0.000137
aspx.page	End ProcessPostData Second Try	0.001366	0.000113
aspx.page	Begin Raise ChangedEvents	0.001471	0.000105
aspx.page	End Raise ChangedEvents	0.001575	0.000105
aspx.page	Begin Raise PostBackEvent	0.001679	0.000104
btn_Click	Button was pressed	0.002678	0.000999
aspx.page	End Raise PostBackEvent	0.002822	0.000143
aspx.page	Begin PreRender	0.002972	0.000150
aspx.page	End PreRender	0.003093	0.000121
aspx.page	Begin SaveViewState	0.007514	0.004421
aspx.page	End SaveViewState	0.007829	0.000315
aspx.page	Begin Render	0.007947	0.000118
aspx.page	End Render	0.009401	0.001454

The new line has been added in red because we used the `Warn` method (trust me – it really is red), and you can see the extra events that are called as part of the postback. Using `Warn` allows you to easily spot lines in the trace information.

The TraceContext Object

Tracing is actually handled by the `TraceContext` object, which has two properties and two methods:

Method / Property	Description
IsEnabled	Indicates whether or not tracing is enabled, and equates to the page level directive. This is a read/write property, so it can be used to enable or disable tracing from within code.
TraceMode	Indicates the sort order of messages in the Trace Information section, and can be either `SortByCategory` or `SortByTime`. Like `IsEnabled`, this is also available through a page directive.
Write	Writes information to the Trace Information section.
Warn	The same as `Write`, except for the text being shown in red.

Both of the methods for writing to the log can be overloaded:

```
Trace.Write (message)
Trace.Write (category, message)
Trace.Write (category, message, errorInfo)
```

```
Trace.Warn (message)
Trace.Warn (category, message)
Trace.Warn (category, message, errorInfo)
```

The three parameters are:

Parameter	Type	Description
category	String	The category for the message
message	String	The message to display
errorInfo	System.Exception	Any exception information, to be displayed after the message

For example:

```
Trace.Write("A simple message")
Trace.Write("Button", "Message here")

Try
   ' some code goes here
Catch E As Exception
   Trace.Warn("Error", "Message here", E)
End Try
```

Turning Off Tracing

One of the problems with the old ASP method of tracing was that we had to remove the trace statements, when we were done. With ASP.NET all you do is turn off tracing, either by setting the page directive or using the IsEnabled property. You don't have to remove the Trace statements themselves, or comment them out, because if tracing isn't enabled, the compiler automatically removes them. So, this is where the great improvement comes – you're free to put as many trace statements into your code as you feel is warranted, without the worry of having to clean them up after testing, and without worrying about performance.

One great thing about this is that you can make the tracing dynamic, perhaps by use of the query string. For example, consider the following code:

```
Sub Page_Load(Sender As Object, E As EventArgs)

   If Request.QueryString("Trace") = "True" Then
      Trace.IsEnabled = True
   End If

End Sub
```

You could then call a page with:

```
http://localhost/TestPage.aspx?Trace=True
```

This would turn on tracing, but if called normally no tracing would appear. Alternative solutions, such as using the registry or a configuration file to identify whether tracing is enabled or not, are also possible.

Tracing from Components

The same method of tracing is available to components called from an ASP.NET page, allowing them to integrate seamlessly with your pages. To access the `Trace` functionality you have to import the `System.Web` namespace, and then reference the current HTTP context. For example:

```
Imports System
Imports System.Web

Namespace People

  Public Class PersonTrace

    Private ctx As HttpContext

    Public Sub New()
      ctx = HttpContext.Current
      ctx.Trace.Write("PersonTrace", "New")
    End Sub
```

These messages just become part of the existing trace messages, appearing in the order in which they are called:

aspx.page	Begin Raise PostBackEvent
btn_Click	Button was pressed
PersonTrace	New
PersonTrace	FirstName:Set
PersonTrace	FirstName:Get
aspx.page	End Raise PostBackEvent
aspx.page	Begin PreRender

The tracing output is only displayed if tracing is turned on for the page in which the component is called.

Application-Level Tracing

Application-level tracing expands on the page idea, but allows tracing to be controlled for an entire application. To configure this option you need to create, or edit, the `Web.config` file in the root directory of your application. Application-level tracing works by collecting the trace information for each request, which can be optionally displayed in each page, or just collected for later examination.

You can add a `Trace` element as part of the `<system.web>` section, which takes the following attributes:

Attribute	Default	Description
enabled	False	Indicates whether or not application-level tracing is enabled.
requestLimit	10	The number of HTTP requests for which to store tracing information in the trace log. This works on a rolling system, where the last n requests are kept.
pageOutput	False	Indicates whether or not the tracing information is displayed at the end of each page. The information is still collected whether or not it is displayed.

Table continued on following page

Attribute	Default	Description
traceMode	SortByTime	Indicates the sort order of messages in the **Trace Information** section, and can be either SortByCategory or SortByTime.
localOnly	True	Indicates whether the trace information is only shown to local clients, or is available to remote clients as well.

For example:

```
<trace enabled="true" localOnly="false" />
```

The interesting thing about application-level tracing is that the trace details are collected for each request (up to the number set in the requestLimit attribute), irrespective of whether they are shown on the page. This means that tracing can be enabled for a live application without the users seeing anything.

Viewing Trace Information

To view the trace information you navigate to trace.axd held in the root directory of the application. This file doesn't actually exist, but is instead a special URL that is intercepted by ASP.NET. It will give you a list of requests:

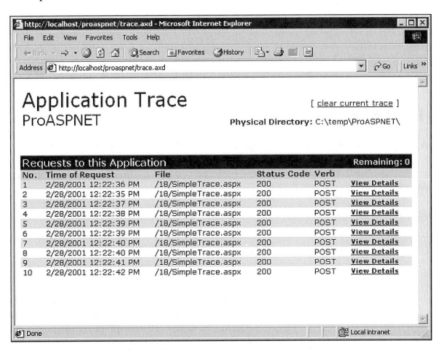

Clicking on the **View Details** link for a request will then show the same trace details that would normally be shown at the end of each page.

Error Handling

Error handling has always been a bit of a juggling act – that fine line between what you need to protect your code against and what you don't. While it would be nice to assume that all data handled by your code is correct (it **was** validated wasn't it?) and that all resources will be available, that's not something you can take for granted. As applications become more complex they rely on other programs, components, external resources, and so on, and you have to assume that at some point something might go wrong. Taking this defensive attitude will lead to more robust applications, as well as making development easier in the future.

In previous versions of ASP you've probably relied upon the VBScript `On Error` statement (or `try/catch` if you're one of the few who used JScript server side). While acceptable, it was never a good solution, as it was difficult to build centralized error routines and provide a neat way to manage the errors. The CLR has solved this by providing support for structured error handling.

Structured Exception Handling

Structured exception handling is a fundamental part of the CLR, and provides .NET programmers with a great way of managing errors, and has a good set of features:

❑ It is cross-language; therefore exceptions can be raised in one language and caught in another.

❑ It is cross-process and cross-machine, so even when remote .NET components raise exceptions, they can be caught locally.

❑ It is a hierarchical system, allowing exceptions to be layered, with each exception able to encompass another. This means that components can trap exceptions from underlying objects (such as data access layers), and raise their own exception, including the original as part of it. This allows programs to trap exceptions at a high level, but drill-down through the exception list to find more fine-grained exception information.

❑ It obviates the need to check for return values from every function or method call – errors that are raised as exceptions will never be missed.

❑ There's no performance downside unless an exception is raised.

All exceptions in the CLR are derived from a single base class, and many of the classes in the framework extend from this to provide finer-grained errors.

The Exception Class

The exception class provides the following properties to detail the problem:

Property	Description
HelpLink	A URN or URL indicating the Help file associated with this error.
HResult	For COM interoperability, the Windows 32bit HRESULT.
InnerException	For nested exceptions, an exception object representing the inner exception.
Message	The textual error message.

Table continued on following page

Property	Description
Source	The name of the application, or object, that raised the error. This will be the assembly name if left blank.
StackTrace	A string containing the stack trace.
TargetSite	A MethodBase object detailing the method that raised the exception.

There is also one method, GetBaseException, for use with nested exceptions that returns the original exception that was raised.

Try/Catch

The way in which you manage exceptions is by use of the Try/Catch statements. In Visual Basic the general syntax is:

```
Try

    ' code block to run

[Catch [exception [As type]] [When expression]

    ' code to run if the exception generated matches
    ' the exception and expression defined above

    [Exit Try]
]

Catch [exception [As type]] [When expression]

    ' code to run if the exception generated matches
    ' the exception and expression defined above

    [Exit Try]

[Finally
    ' code that always runs, whether or not an exception
    ' was caught, unless End Try is called
]
End Try
```

There can be multiple Catch blocks to allow for fine-grained control over exceptions. For example, imagine a function that returns the contents of a file:

```
Public Function GetFileContents(file As String) As String

    Dim contents As String = ""

    Try
        Dim sr As New StreamReader(file)
        contents = sr.ReadToEnd()
        sr.Close()
```

```
        Catch exArg As ArgumentException
          ' argument not supplied

        Catch exFNF As FileNotFoundException
          ' file wasn't found - handle error

        Finally
          Return contents

        End Try

    End Function
```

When using multiple Catch blocks you should put the finest-grain exception first, and the widest (the base class Exception, for example) last. This is because these blocks are tried in the order of declaration. So, putting the widest exception first could shadow a narrower one.

The Finally block will always be run, whether or not an exception is thrown. Even if used within a procedure, and the procedure is exited from within a Catch block, the Finally block still runs.

Raising Exceptions

To raise exceptions you use the Throw statement. For example, if you forget the file name to the constructor of the StreamReader you normally get this message:

But if you wanted to provide your own error message, you could throw a new error containing the new details:

```
Public Function GetFileContents(file As String) As String

   Dim contents As String = ""

   Try
      Dim sr As New StreamReader(file)
      contents = sr.ReadToEnd()
      sr.Close()
```

```
      Catch exArg As ArgumentException
         Throw New ArgumentException("Doh - you forgot the filename.")

      End Try

   End Function
```

This gives you:

This gives you the new error message, but the source error is shown on the line where you raised the error, rather than where the error was actually generated. If this isn't acceptable you can pass in the original exception as an argument when you throw the new exception. For example:

```
   Catch exArg As ArgumentException
      Throw New ArgumentException("Doh - you forgot the filename.", exArg)
```

This now gives you:

Hmm, but wait a minute – where has the new error message gone. Well, if you look at the stack trace you see it:

```
Stack Trace:


[ArgumentException: Empty path name is not legal.]
    System.IO.StreamReader..ctor(String path, Encoding encoding,
    System.IO.StreamReader..ctor(String path) +29
    ASP.TryCatch_aspx.GetFileContents(String file) in C:\temp\Pr

[ArgumentException: Doh - you forgot the filename.]
    ASP.TryCatch_aspx.GetFileContents(String file) in C:\temp\Pr
    ASP.TryCatch_aspx.Page_Load(Object Sender, EventArgs e) in C
    System.Web.UI.Control.OnLoad(EventArgs e) +55
    System.Web.UI.Control.LoadRecursive() +65
    System.Web.UI.Page.ProcessRequestMain() +394
```

The original exception is shown first, and then your error second. This may not seem what you'd want, and it's probably not a scenario you'd use that often. But the reason for generating exceptions is so that you can catch them and take some appropriate action, such as displaying a message to the user (who doesn't need to see the stack trace or the errors).

Custom Exceptions

Taking the custom error message one step further allows you to create your own exception class, derived not from the `Exception` class, but from `ApplicationException`. For example I was recently writing a parser for a text file of a specific format, and wanted to have parsing errors integrated with the exception-handling system. So, I created a new exception like so:

```
Imports System

Namespace Wrox

  Public Class InvalidContentException
    Inherits ApplicationException

    Public Sub New()
        MyBase.New()
    End Sub

    Public Sub New(message As String)
      MyBase.New(message)
    End Sub

    Public Sub New(message As String, inner As Exception)
      MyBase.New(message, inner)
    End Sub

  End Class

End Namespace
```

This simply defines a new class derived from `ApplicationException`. The class can be any name, but by convention it should end in `Exception`. Within the class I implement the three standard constructors to call the base class constructors. Now when you throw this error you get:

> **Content is invalid**
>
> **Description:** An unhandled exception occurred during the execution of the current web request, where it originated in the code.
>
> **Exception Details:** Wrox.InvalidContentException: Content is invalid
>
> **Source Error:**
>
> ```
> Line 9:     Sub RaiseException(Sender As Object, E As EventArgs)
> Line 10:
> Line 11:        Throw New InvalidContentException("Content is invalid")
> Line 12:
> Line 13:    End Sub
> ```

Notice that this is the same layout as standard exceptions – the only difference is that your exception name is used. The great advantage of this system is that you can just trap your custom exception. For example:

```
Try
    ' run custom parser

Catch ex As InvalidContentException
    ' notify user of error

End Try
```

Within the new exception class you can do more than just call the base class methods. For example you could add extra tracing information, or even overload the properties to provide further information.

Exception Types

Many of the internal classes define their own exceptions that you can catch. For example, when connecting to SQL Server a data access problem might raise a SQLException. Although the documentation details what exceptions will be raised, the simplest way to find a list of the exceptions available is to use a tool like WinCV, and search for exception. This gives you a list as shown below:

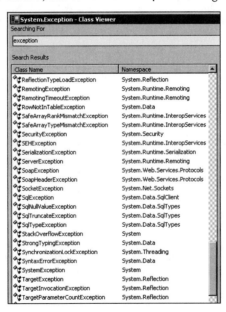

Here you can see exactly what exceptions are available, and to which namespace they belong. WinCV is in the bin directory of the SDK install.

Exceptions and COM

The exception handling system in .NET integrates well with the error handling of COM components, whatever type of interoperability you are performing. If you are using .NET components from COM then exceptions raised in the .NET component will lead to a Windows HRESULT being passed to the COM component. If using COM components from .NET, and the COM component returns an HRESULT, this will be mapped to a .NET exception. What type of exception depends on the HRESULT – for example the HRESULT E_ACCESSDENIED error will be mapped to UnauthorizedAccessException, while unknown HRESULTS will be mapped to COMException. Additionally, COM components that support IErrorInfo will have these details mapped to the properties of the exception.

This topic is covered in more detail in Chapter 23 where we look at migration and interoperability.

ASP.NET Error Handling

In addition to the CLR exception system, ASP.NET also provides ways of handling errors. There are three ways in which this can be done:

❑   At the page-level error event, for errors on an individual page.

❑   At the application-level error event, for errors in an application.

❑   In the application configuration file, to perform declarative error handling for an application.

Which method you use depends on what you want to do when handling errors, and what sort of structure you wish your application to have.

Page_Error Event

At the page level you can use the Page_Error event to trap errors on a page. For example:

```
<%@ Import Namespace="System.Data.SqlClient" %>

<script runat="server">

  Sub Page_Load(Sender As Object, E As EventArgs)

    Dim conn As SqlConnection
    Response.Write(conn.ToString())

  End Sub

  Sub Page_Error(Sender As Object, E As EventArgs)

    Dim err As String = "Error in: " & Request.Url.ToString() &  "<p/>" & _
                        "Stack Trace Below:<br/>" & _
                        Server.GetLastError().ToString()

    Response.Write(err)
    Server.ClearError()

  End Sub

</script>
```

This uses the Page_Load event to generate a run-time error (by trying to display the connection string details when the connection hasn't been opened), which can be caught by the Page_Error event. The error details are available by calling the GetLastError method to return the exception object generated by the error. In this case we just output the details, but you could log the error or notify the web site administrator (see the notifying section a little later in this chapter for details).

Application_Error Event

Like the Page_Error event, there's also an Application_Error event, which is declared in the global.asax file. For example, using similar code to above:

```
Sub Application_Error(Sender As Object, E As EventArgs)

    Dim err As String = "<h1>Application Error</h1>" & _
                        "Error in: " & Request.Url.ToString() &  "<p/>" & _
                        "Stack Trace Below:<br/>" & _
                        Server.GetLastError().ToString()

    Response.Write(err)
    Server.ClearError()

End Sub
```

This event will be run if no Page_Error event traps the error. This event is one place where you could put application-wide error logging information.

Application Error Configuration

As well as programmatic handling of errors, there's also the declarative method, utilizing the web.config file. This method is for handling HTTP errors, and providing a simple way to return custom error pages, and is configured with the customErrors element of the system.web section.

```
<system.web>
  <customErrors defaultRedirect="url" mode="On|Off|RemoteOnly">
    <error statusCode="code" redirect="url"/>
  </customErrors>
</system.web>
```

The defaultRedirect indicates the page that should be shown if no other errors are trapped – it should be the last-resort page for completely unexpected errors. The mode can be:

❏   On – to specify that custom errors are enabled.

❏   Off – to specify that custom errors are disabled.

❏   RemoteOnly – to specify that custom errors are only enabled for remote clients.

The latter of these allows you to define custom errors for all users except those accessing the page locally. This allows users to see a nice error page while you can log onto the server and see the exception details and stack trace.

The `error` subelement allows individual pages to be shown for individual errors. For example:

```
<system.web>
  <customErrors defaultRedirect="DefaultErrorPage.aspx" mode="RemoteOnly">
    <error statusCode="404" redirect="FileNotFound.aspx"/>
  </customErrors>
</system.web>
```

Here the 404 (not found) error will redirect to `FileNotFound.aspx`, while all other HTTP errors will go to `DefaultErrorPage.aspx`. You can have multiple `error` elements to cater for multiple HTTP errors.

Notifying Administrators of Errors

The rich set of error handling that ASP.NET provides is a great way to trap errors, but the users aren't the only people who need to know that something has gone wrong. A user will see the error page, but administrators and developers also need to know when things go wrong. There are many ways in which you can do this, but by far the simplest is to automatically write an event to the **Event Log** or to mail the administrator. Both of these are techniques you could add to the error pages so that whenever an error occurs the details are logged somehow.

Writing to the Event Log

Writing to the Event Log is extremely simple, as there is an `EventLog` class in the `System.Diagnostics` namespace. Consider the following function:

```
<%@ Import Namespace="System.Diagnostics" %>

... ' rest of page here

Sub WriteToEventLog(LogName As String, Message As String)

  ' Create Event Log if It Doesn't Exist
  If (Not EventLog.SourceExists(LogName)) Then
    EventLog.CreateEventSource(LogName, LogName)
  End if

  ' Fire off to Event Log
  Dim Log as New EventLog
  Log.Source = LogName
  Log.WriteEntry(Message, EventLogEntryType.Error)

End Sub
```

This first creates a custom event log if it doesn't already exist, and then writes a new entry into the log. You could call this function like this:

```
Try
  ' do something here
Catch ex As Exception
  WriteToEventLog("Wrox", ex.ToString())
End Try
```

The result appears in the Event Log like any other event. Notice that this is in a custom Log:

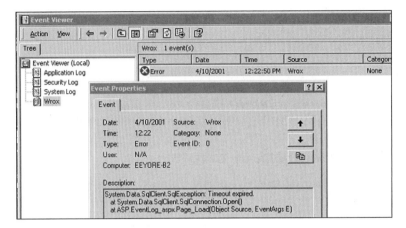

Sending E-Mail Error Notifications

An alternative approach would be to send an automatic mail message, using the `MailMessage` class of the `System.Web.Mail` namespace. For example:

```
<%@ Import Namespace="System.Web.Mail" %>

    ... ' rest of page here

  Public Sub SendMail(message As String)

    Dim MyMessage as New MailMessage

    MyMessage.To = "davids@ipona.co.uk"
    MyMessage.From = "davids@ipona.co.uk"
    MyMessage.Subject = "Unhandled ASP.NET Error"
    MyMessage.BodyFormat = MailFormat.Text

    MyMessage.Body = message

    SmtpMail.Send(MyMessage)

  End Sub
```

Notice that the `Send` method is a static method, and therefore you don't need to create an instance of the `SmptMail` component.

You could call this like so:

```
  Try
    ' do something here
  Catch ex As Exception
    SendMail(ex.ToString())
  End Try
```

Debugging

With previous versions of ASP debugging has always been a bit of a chore. `Response.Write` was the primary method of finding out what's going on in a program, and even the **Script Debugger** was weak in comparison to the debuggers that Windows developers had for Visual Basic and C++ code. All that has now changed with .NET, as the CLR provides integrated debugging for all applications. The primary goals of this were:

- ❑   Both in-process and out-of-process debugging.
- ❑   Remote process debugging.
- ❑   Managed and unmanaged code debugging.
- ❑   Mixed language support.
- ❑   Edit and Continue.

Some of these aren't actually implemented as part of the CLR, but the rest of the framework provides the required support. There are two ways to do debugging in the .NET framework. The first is to use the SDK debugger, and the second is to use Visual Studio.NET. This section isn't going to give a comprehensive list of all debugger features, as most are fairly obvious. What we'll concentrate on are the most used features.

The SDK Debugger

The SDK debugger (`DbgCLR.exe`) ships with the .NET SDK, and can be found in the `GuiDebug` directory. It provides the same features as the Visual Studio debugger, except that it doesn't support remote debugging or Edit and Continue. Despite the lack of these two features, it is far above anything we've been used to in the ASP world.

Enabling Debugging

Earlier in this chapter we showed that to allow tracing you added a page directive to your web pages. The same is true for debug, where you use the following directive:

```
<%@ Page debug="True" %>
```

This tells the compiler to emit debugging symbols into the compiled page, and allows the debugger to attach to the running program.

The debug symbols are also required for components, and to enable them you use the `/debug` flag on the compiler (the flag is the same whichever compiler you are using). When you compile with this an extra file is created, ending in `.pdb` – this contains the debugging symbols. You don't have to do anything with this file, as it's only used by the debugger.

Before using the debugger, you'll also need to view the web page in the browser so that the debugging symbols are loaded for the page. You can still start the debugger and load the page, but you won't be able to do any debugging until the page has been compiled once with the debugging enabled.

> *Remember to disable debugging and compile components without the debug symbols when you deploy applications, to reduce any overhead.*

Starting Debugging

To start debugging your ASP.NET applications you launch the debugger, and from the Tools menu select Debug Process…, to show the following dialog:

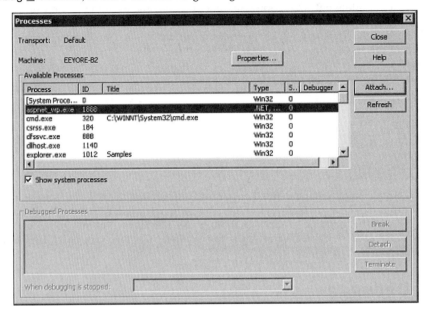

This shows the processes you can pick to debug. Make sure you have the Show system process checkbox box selected, and pick the aspnet_wp.exe process – this is the ASP.NET worker process. Click the Attach… button to attach the debugger to the process, and then close the dialog.

You can now load a page into the debugger (by using File | Open) and set break points (by clicking in the gray margin):

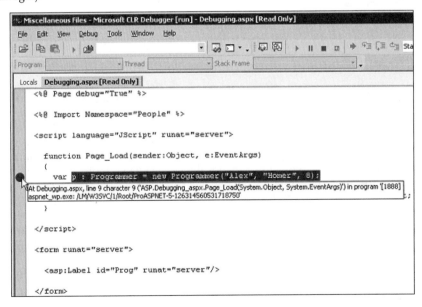

This shows a breakpoint in a simple ASP.NET page coded using JScript (unlikely for most people, but there's a point to it – bear with me). This page simply instantiates a class called `Programmer`. If you now hit the page you are flipped into the debugger at the set line:

```
Locals  Debugging.aspx [Read Only]
    <%@ Page debug="True" %>

    <%@ Import Namespace="People" %>

    <script language="JScript" runat="server">

      function Page_Load(sender:Object, e:EventArgs)
      {
          var p : Programmer = new Programmer("Alex", "Homer", 8);
```
This is the next statement that will be executed. To change which statement is executed next, drag the arrow. This may have unintended consequences.

You can now step into the code for the component (assuming it was compiled with the `/debug` option):

```
Locals  Debugging.aspx [Read Only]  Programmer.vb [Read Only]

    Public Sub New()
      MyBase.New()
    End Sub

    Public Sub New(firstName As String, lastName As String)
      MyBase.New(firstName, lastName)
    End Sub

 ⇨  Public Sub New(firstName As String, lastName As String, hoursSleep As Integ
      MyBase.New(firstName, lastName)
      _avgHoursSleepPerNight = hoursSleep
    End Sub
```

Now we've stepped into the constructor of the `Programmer` class, and notice that it's a Visual Basic class. We're almost at that point I was trying to make – let's go one step further and step into the base class:

```
Locals  Debugging.aspx [Read Only]  Programmer.vb [Read Only]  person.cs [Read Only]
    public class person
    {
      private string _firstName;
      private string _lastName;

      public person() {}

 ⇨    public person(string firstName, string lastName)
      {
        _firstName = firstName;
        _lastName = lastName;
      }
    }
```

Now the point is made. We have a base class written in C#, which is subclassed by a Visual Basic class, and used in a JScript ASP page. This becomes obvious when examining the call stack:

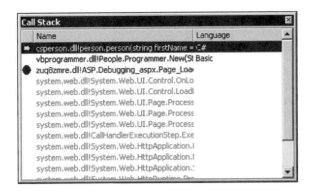

This really reinforces the concept of language equality in the run-time, since you can debug through components written in different languages. Even if it were restricted to a single language, the fact that we have such a good debugger would be a great benefit in itself.

SDK Debugger Features

The SDK Debugger has all of the great features that you'd expect from a high-end development environment, including:

❑   Stepping into, out of, and over code.

❑   Setting breakpoints on specific lines.

❑   Setting breakpoints on specific exceptions.

❑   Setting breakpoints on expressions.

❑   Viewing contents of variables.

❑   Viewing the call stack, threads and modules.

The two major features that aren't supported are debugging remote processes and Edit-and-Continue. The latter of these means that the SDK Debugger is a read-only debugger, so you can't edit code inline and continue the debugging process. You can only edit code externally, and the debugger recognizes that the file has changed (and will reload it if you desire), but the new changes will not take effect until the request is rerun. For these features you need the Visual Studio Debugger.

Debugging in Visual Studio.NET

In Visual Studio debugging is just a part of working with an integrated development tool. When building an application all you have to do is set a breakpoint from within the code editor window and run your application:

This looks similar to the SDK debugger, and supports the same set of features such as stepping and viewing of code and variables.

Edit and Continue

Edit and Continue gives you the ability to alter code while programs are running. This is due to the ability of the run time to inject code into a running process. There are, however, some limitations:

❑ For running functions (anywhere in the call stack) you are limited to 64 bytes of additional variables. Outside of the call stack there is no limit.

❑ You cannot change resource files.

❑ You cannot change exception-handling blocks.

❑ You cannot change data types.

❑ You cannot remove functions.

In most cases you couldn't really call these limitations, as they are the sorts of alterations that would require more than a simple change.

There's nothing special you have to do to enable this functionality. There are options to disable Edit and Continue, and to specify its various functions, but the defaults are all acceptable. All you have to do is retype code in the debugger when in break mode and the new code takes effect.

Remote Debugging

Remote debugging works in the same way as local debugging, except you have the option to debug a remote process. This is useful in situations where you have a separate server hosting the application.

Profiling and Performance

Profiling is often one of those areas that never seems to have great value in some people's minds, but in certain respects it's the most important area of development. A slow web site is a great way to put off users and lose customers, and remains the bane of many administrators' lives. The simple fact is that performance testing often gets cut due to time constraints, as when deadlines get tight people cut things that don't have an immediate impact. The attitude is often to get the product shipped, and then release a performance-enhanced version at a later date. The reality is, of course, that users expect great things from a first release, and there should be no excuses for not delivering the best-performing application.

So, if we want the best possible performance from an application, how do we go about it? How do we find the areas of an application that need improvement, and go about testing those areas? Profiling is the act of gathering that data about an application, allowing us to see which areas take longest to execute.

Performance testing isn't only about seeing how well an application performs in its current incarnation, but also includes:

- ❑ **Baselining**. This is the act of collecting performance data to be used as a comparison for future tests. Collecting metrics is important as applications and loads change – you need to have some base figures against which you can compare future analysis.

- ❑ **Loading**. Application performance decreases as the load increases, so you need to see how your application will perform under increasing load. That's the thing about web sites – the load is never guaranteed to stay the same – it can increase and decrease sharply as usage trends change.

- ❑ **Stability**. Web sites have to have constant availability as they have global reach. It's not possible to assume that no one will use your site at night, because your night may be your user's day. Therefore you have to ensure your application stays stable, especially under load.

As applications become more complex, so does testing. This is especially true now, where ASP.NET applications may be written with interoperability in mind, to provide integration with, or reuse of, existing technology. An example of this is the reuse of an existing COM data layer. This layer may be performing optimally in a current application, but when used from a .NET application does it become a bottleneck? At this stage you have to ask if performance could be improved by rewriting the layer? This sort of question is discussed further in Chapter 23, where we look at migration and interoperability issues.

There are three steps in the process of profiling:

- ❑ **Instrumentation**, where you add profiling to your code. This could be adding Windows performance counters, or custom profiling statements to identify the execution of the code, as well as logging and tracing information.

- ❑ **Sampling**, where you run your application to collect the profiling data.

- ❑ **Analysis**, where you examine the collected data, and validate it against your baseline data.

We'll be concentrating on the first of these, although we will discuss the latter two options to show how the instrumentation process is used.

Instrumentation

Instrumentation is a bit like Schrödinger's Cat, where the act of viewing changes the outcome. In performance testing you are examining how your application performs under certain conditions, and you add profiling to detect this. However, the profiling you add affects those very things you are testing – the performance metrics. The more profiling code you add to applications, the more you affect performance. So, the act of instrumentation is one that should be carefully handled. There is no harm in adding large amounts of profiling code as long as you understand the implications.

The Trace class shown earlier provides some performance data for events, but this has to be manually viewed, and is not really designed for profiling. To profile you want a simple way of adding profiling code as well as collecting information. This is provided by Performance Monitor Counters. Both the .NET framework and ASP.NET have counters (which we'll look at under the analysis section), but to provide custom profiling you'll need to create custom counters.

When to Create and Remove Counters

The creation and removal of counters is something you should think carefully about, as they are really installer and uninstaller features. If your application requires custom counters, then the counters should be created when the application is installed, and removed when the application is uninstalled. One problem with this approach is fitting it into ASP.NET applications where the xcopy deployment method is used. Ways to solve this could be:

- ❑ Create an application installer so that the counters are created and removed in the correct place.

- ❑ Create a separate script or page to create and remove the counters.

- ❑ Check for the existence of counters in your application (perhaps the `Application_OnStart` event), and if missing create them. This leaves the problem of removing counters if the application is uninstalled, as well as a performance problem since you are checking for them every time the application starts.

Of these solutions, the first option is certainly the best.

Along with the question of when to create counters, is the one of why? The answer is simple – create custom counters when you need to profile areas within your application. The supplied counters are perfect for looking at the application or ASP.NET as a whole, but aren't fine-grained enough to show you how the individual parts of your application are performing. So, it's only if you need this amount of information that you need to create custom counters.

Custom Performance Counters

The base class library supplies a set of classes for interacting with the Windows performance monitor, allowing both read-and-write access, as well as the creation of custom objects and counters. These objects are:

Object	Description
`PerformanceCounterCategory`	A counter category, to contain individual counters.
`PerformanceCounter`	The details of an individual performance counter.
`CounterCreationData`	The details required for the creation of a counter.
`CounterCreationDataCollection`	A collection of performance counter creation details, for creating multiple counters in a category.
`CounterSample`	A sample of data from a counter.

The first two of these objects are easy to relate to, by looking at the Add Counters screen of the Windows Performance Monitor:

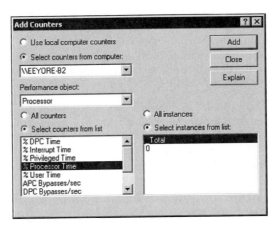

The `Performance` object corresponds to the `PerformanceCounterCategory`, and the counters correspond to the `PerformanceCounter`. Just like the above dialog, the use of the counter objects isn't limited to the local machine – many of the methods allow the addition of a machine name, allowing manipulation of counters on remote machines (assuming the correct permissions).

The PerformanceCounterCategory object

Lets first look at the category object, as this contains details for the category itself, allowing creation of new categories and counters as well as the retrieval of category and counter information. It has three properties:

Property	Description
CategoryName	The name of the category.
CategoryHelp	Text describing the category.
MachineName	The machine upon which the category is installed.

The methods are more extensive:

Method	Description
CounterExists	Indicates whether or not the selected counter exists.
Create	Creates a category and a counter or counters.
Delete	Deletes a category and counters.
Exists	Indicates whether or not the category exists.
GetCategories	Returns an array of categories.
GetCounters	Returns an array of counters for the category.
GetInstanceNames	Returns an array of names of counter instances.
InstanceExists	Indicates whether or not the counter instance exists.
ReadCategory	Returns a collection of all category and instance data.

Many of these methods are overloaded, allowing several forms of use. For example, the `CounterExists` method has three forms:

```
CounterExists(CounterName)
CounterExists(CounterName, CategoryName)
CounterExists(CounterName, CategoryName, MachineName)
```

The first case of these requires the `PerformanceCounterCategory` object to have been initialized to an existing category. For example:

```
Dim PC As New PerformanceCounterCategory("Wrox")
If PC.CounterExists("MyCounter") Then ...
Then
    ...
End If
```

The latter two cases are static methods, and don't require an object instance. For example:

```
If PerformanceCounterCategory.CounterExists("MyCounter", "Wrox") Then ...
Then
    ...
End If
```

or

```
If PerformanceCounterCategory.CounterExists("MyCounter", "Wrox", "Eeyore") Then
...
"MC1") Then
    ...
End If
```

Creating Custom Performance Counters

The first point to note about creating counters is that they can only be created in new categories. This means that you cannot modify any of the existing categories, and that if you want to add counters to a custom category you need to remove the category first. To create counters you use the `Create` method of the `PerformanceCounterCategory` object, which has several forms:

```
Create(CategoryName, CategoryHelp, CounterName, CounterHelp)
Create(CategoryName, CategoryHelp, CounterName, CounterHelp, MachineName)
Create(CategoryName, CategoryHelp, CounterCreationDataCollection)
Create(CategoryName, CategoryHelp, CounterCreationDataCollection, MachineName)
```

The first two of these allow a category and a single counter to be created. For example:

```
PerformanceCounterCategory.Create("Wrox", "Wrox Press Counters", _
                    "Counter1", "This counter is counter 1")
```

The second two use a collection of `CounterCreationData` objects, allowing the creation of multiple counters, as well as being able to specify the type of counter (which defaults to `RateOfCountsPerSecond32` – more on types later). This object can be constructed like so:

```
Dim CCD As CounterCreationData
CCD = New CounterCreationData("Counter1", "This counter is counter 1", _
                        PerformanceCounterType.NumberOfItems32)
```

Or, alternatively using the properties:

```
Dim CCD As New CounterCreationData

CCD.CounterName = "Counter1"
CCD.CounterHelp = "This counter is counter 1"
CCD.CounterType = PerformanceCounterType.NumberOfItems32
```

Once created, the object can be added to the collection:

```
Dim CCDC As New CounterCreationDataCollection

CCDC.Add(CCD)

PerformanceCounterCategory.Create("Wrox", "Wrox Press Counters", CCDC)
```

This process can be abbreviated by combining creation and addition into one line, making adding multiple counters easier to read:

```
Dim CCDC As New CounterCreationDataCollection

CCDC.Add(New CounterCreationData("Counter1", "This counter is counter 1", _
                        PerformanceCounterType.NumberOfItems32)
CCDC.Add(New CounterCreationData("Counter2", "This counter is counter 2", _
                        PerformanceCounterType.NumberOfItems32)
CCDC.Add(New CounterCreationData("Counters/sec", _
                        "Counters per second", _
                PerformanceCounterType.RateOfCountersPerSecond32)

PerformanceCounterCategory.Create("Wrox", "Wrox Press Counters", CCDC)
```

The allowable values for `PerformanceCounterType` are:

Type	Description
AverageBase	Used as the base data in the computation of time or count averages (AverageCounter64 and AverageTimer32).
AverageCount64	A count that usually gives the bytes per operation when divided by the number of operations.
AverageTimer32	A timer that usually gives time per operation when divided by the number of operations.
CountPerTimeInterval32	Count per time interval. Typically used to track number of items queued or waiting.
CountPerTimeInterval64	Large count per time interval. Typically used to track number of items queued or waiting.

Type	Description
CounterDelta32	Difference between two counters.
CounterDelta64	Large difference between two counters.
CounterMultiBase	Used as the base data for the Multi counters. It defines the number of similar items sampled.
CounterMultiTimer	Timer sampling of multiple but similar items. Result is an average sampling among the items.
CounterMultiTimer100Ns	Timer sampling of multiple, but similar items, every 100 nanoseconds. Result is an average sampling among the items.
CounterMultiTimer 100NsInverse	The inverse of CounterMultiTimer100Ns. Used when the object is not in use.
CounterMultiTimer Inverse	The inverse of CounterMultiTimer. Used when the object is not in use.
CounterTimer	A common timer for percentage values.
CounterTimerInverse	The inverse of CounterTimer. Used when the object is not in use.
ElapsedTime	The data is the start time of the item being measured.
NumberOfItems32	A raw counter value.
NumberOfItems64	A large raw counter value.
NumberOfItemsHEX32	A raw counter value for display in hexadecimal.
NumberOfItemsHEX64	A large raw counter value for display in hexadecimal.
RateOfCounts PerSecond32	Rate of counters per second.
RateOfCounts PerSecond64	Large rate of counts per second.
RawBase	Used as the base data for RawFraction. The counter value holds the denominator of the fraction value.
RawFraction	Instantaneous value, to be divided by the base data (RawBase).
SampleBase	Used as the base data for SampleCounter and SampleFraction.
SampleCounter	A count that is either 1 or 0 on each sampling. The counter value is the counter of 1s sampled.
SampleFraction	A count that is either 1 or 0 on each sampling. The counter value is the counter of 1s sampled. For display in terms of a percentage.
Timer100Ns	Timer sampling every 100 nanoseconds.
Timer100NsInverse	The inverse of Timer100Ns. Used when the object is not in use.

The type of counter you create depends upon what you are trying to measure. For simple count values (for example the total number of orders in an e-commerce system) you can use `NumberOfItems32` or `NumberOfItems64` (the difference being the size of number allowed). For a performance metric (such as the number of orders per second) you can use `RateOfCountsPerSecond32` or `RateOfCountsPerSecond64`. The difference between the large and normal counters (those ending in 32 and 64) is the size of data they can hold. Those ending in 32 are 32 bits wide (holding 4 bytes) and those ending in 64 are 64 bits wide (holding 8 bytes).

The counter type also comes into effect when we look at sampling, as shown later in the chapter.

Creating Counter Instances

The term **instance** can be confusing when dealing with performance counters, as it's easy to think in terms of class instantiation giving you an instance of a class. This is, in fact, the right way to think of it – the difference is that an instance of a performance counter is reflected as part of the instrumentation. For example, consider the Performance Monitor application, where you have the choice to add counters:

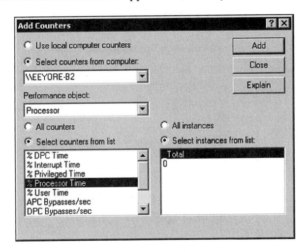

At the bottom right of this dialog you see instances of a counter dealing with the `Process` object. The instances here reflect the number of processors in the monitored machine (sadly I only have 1 CPU). There is also a `_Total` instance, which aggregates the values for other instances. Some counters, such as `Memory`, don't have specific instances, as they are concerned with a single object. What's especially noteworthy about this is that instances apply to a `Performance` object (or category), and not to individual counters. You cannot have two counters in the same category with different instances.

Creating instances is different from creating the counters themselves, because instances are created for existing custom counters. You use the `PerformanceCounter` object for this:

```
Dim pc As New PerformanceCounter("Wrox", "Counter1")
Dim pc As New PerformanceCounter("Wrox", "Counter1", "Instance1")
Dim pc As New PerformanceCounter("Wrox", "Counter1", "Instance2")
Dim pc As New PerformanceCounter("Wrox", "Counter1", "_Total")
```

The first line creates a counter with the default instance. The latter three lines show the creation of explicit instances. These examples create read-only counters – the constructor is overloaded to allow a `boolean` flag to indicate a read/write counter:

```
Dim pc As New PerformanceCounter("Wrox", "Counter1", "Instance2", True)
```

There is also another form allowing the addition of a machine name:

```
Dim pc As New PerformanceCounter("Wrox", "Counter1", "Instance2",
                                 "EEYORE", True)
```

We'll look at the use of counters in more detail a little later when we discuss updating counter values and sampling.

Counter Lifetime

It is important to understand that performance counter values are values rather than entries – when you write a value to a performance counter, you are not making a permanent entry in the counter as you do when you write an entry to an event log. Rather, performance counter values are transitory, and reflect a point in time. When the last `PerformanceCounter` component to reference a particular system counter is disposed of, the counter resets itself to zero.

There are several ways you can manage the lifetime of a performance counter if you want to retain values for a longer period of time than the default counter behavior allows:

❑   You can run the Performance Monitor application on the server where the counter lives. As long as Performance Monitor is open, the reference to the counters is maintained and counter values continue to accumulate.

❑   You can make sure that there is always an instance of the `PerformanceCounter` component connected to the particular counter for which you want to maintain values.

❑   You can write a Windows service that keeps a reference to the counter.

While these solutions are perfectly acceptable, you should realize that performance counters aren't meant to hold stateful data. Their very nature is for measuring metrics at a particular point in time. So, if no one is running your application it makes sense for the counter values to be 0.

Removing Counters

Custom counters can be removed by use of the `Delete` method of the `PerformanceCounterCategory` object, which removes the category and all counters associated with it. For example:

```
PerformanceCounterCategory.Delete("Wrox")
```

What's important to remember is the lifetime of counters, because the counter will not be removed if another application is using it. The counters use shared memory underneath, so this memory won't be released until all monitoring and instrumentation applications have been closed. This means that you could remove counters, and then recreate them immediately, and the old values would be retained. To guarantee their instant removal you can use the `CloseSharedResources` method of the performance counter object. For example:

```
Dim cat As New PerformanceCounterCategory("Wrox")
Dim pc As New PerformanceCounter

For Each pc In cat.GetCounters()
  pc.CloseSharedResources()
Next
PerformanceCounterCategory.Delete("Wrox")
```

The trouble with this code is that you'd need to add more to check for instances. As a general rule it's best to just use the `Delete` method to delete the category and counters – the counter values will be reset once all references are removed.

Updating Performance Counter Values

Once your counters have been created, there are several ways to update counter values. The first is to simply set the `RawValue` property:

```
Dim pc As New PerformanceCounter("Wrox", "Counter1", True)

pc.RawValue = 10
```

The other ways all rely on a similar set of methods:

```
pc.Increment()
pc.IncrementBy(5)
pc.Decrement()
pc.DecrementBy(5)
```

These just increment or decrement the counter, either by 1 or by a supplied value.

Sampling

The .NET framework doesn't provide any new tools for performance testing, but instead integrates with the Windows Performance Log, so you can use existing tools to track how your application performs. If you don't have an existing performance-testing tool, then the **Web Application Stress Tool** (WAST) is freely available from Microsoft at http://webtool.rte.microsoft.com/. This allows you to run automated tests against a web site, simulating large numbers of users. A description of WAST is outside the scope of this book, but there are two good chapters on performance testing, including the use of WAST, in *ISBN 1861004478 Professional Application Center 2000*, also by Wrox Press.

Monitoring custom counters with Performance Monitor is just the same as for Windows counters – you just pick your custom category and counters:

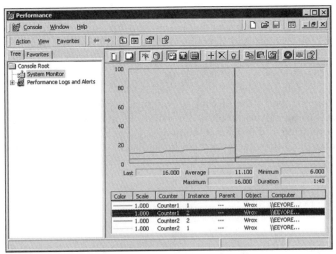

In itself this is an acceptable form of monitoring, but if you want to build some form of custom graphs, you'll need to take sample data and perform calculations on it.

Custom Sampling

There are several ways in which you can extract the values from performance counters. The simplest, and quickest, is to examine the value of the RawValue property, which gives the uncalculated value of the counter. When using this value you should remember that it represents the counter value at its last sampling, and may only represent a transient state. For example, a counter measuring CPU utilization may have high fluctuations, and the RawValue will not reflect that. You can also use the NextSample method to fetch the next raw value for the counter. For example:

```
Dim pc As New PerformanceCounter("Wrox", "Counter1", True)
Dim ValueNow As Integer
Dim ValueNew As Integer

ValueNow = pc.RawValue
ValueNew = pc.NextSample().RawValue
```

This example introduces the concept of the CounterSample object, which contains the following properties:

Property	Description
BaseValue	Returns the base value. Only for samples that are based upon multiple counters.
CounterFrequency	Returns the frequency at which the counter is read. This is the number of milliseconds between samples.
CounterTimeStamp	The time at which the sample was taken.
CounterType	The type of counter. This will be one of the PerformanceCounterType constants.
RawValue	Returns the raw value of the counter.
SystemFrequency	The frequency at which the system reads from the counter.
TimeStamp	The system time stamp.
TimeStamp100nSec	The system time stamp, to within 0.1 milliseconds.

There is also a single method, Calculate, to calculate sample values:

```
Dim pc      As New PerformanceCounter("Wrox", "Counter1", True)
Dim samp1   As CounterSample
Dim result  As Single

samp1 = pc.NextSample()

result = CounterSample.Calculate(samp1)
```

You can also use this method to calculate between two samples:

```
Dim pc        As New PerformanceCounter("Wrox", "Counter1", True)
Dim samp1     As CounterSample
Dim samp2     As CounterSample
Dim result    As Single

samp1 = pc.NextSample()
samp2 = pc.NextSample()

result = CounterSample.Calculate(samp1, samp2)
```

This takes two samples, and then uses the `Calculate` method to perform the calculation between them. When dealing with counters that could have fluctuations sampling gives a more accurate picture of the trends within your application.

The calculation performed depends upon the type of counter (from the `PerformanceCounterType` enumeration), and the details are shown below:

AverageCount64

A standard average counter, giving the result of the average count per operation.

$$\frac{NewSample - OldSample}{NewCount - OldCount}$$

AverageTimer32

The average of a time value, giving the result of the average time per operation.

$$\frac{\left(\dfrac{NewSample - OldSample}{SampleFrequency}\right)}{NewTime - OldTime}$$

CountPerTimeInterval32, CountPerTimeInterval64

Represents the number of counts per time interval.

$$\frac{NewSample - OldSample}{NewTime - OldTime}$$

CounterDelta32, CounterDelta64

Difference between two counter values.

$$NewSample - OldSample$$

CounterMultiTimer

Result is an average sampling among multiple items.

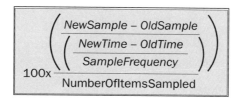

$$100x \frac{\left(\dfrac{NewSample - OldSample}{\dfrac{NewTime - OldTime}{SampleFrequency}} \right)}{NumberOfItemsSampled}$$

CounterMultiTimerInverse

The inverse of CounterMultiTimer.

$$100x \frac{NumberOfItemsSampled - \left(\dfrac{NewSample - OldSample}{\dfrac{NewTime - OldTime}{SampleFrequency}} \right)}{NumberOfItemsSampled}$$

CounterMultiTimer100Ns

Result is an average sampling among multiple items per 100 nanoseconds.

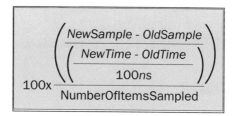

$$100x \frac{\left(\dfrac{NewSample - OldSample}{\dfrac{NewTime - OldTime}{100ns}} \right)}{NumberOfItemsSampled}$$

CounterMultiTimer100NsInverse

The inverse of CounterMultiTimer100NsInverse.

$$100x \frac{NumberOfItemsSampled - \left(\dfrac{NewSample - OldSample}{\dfrac{NewTime - OldTime}{100ns}} \right)}{NumberOfItemsSampled}$$

CounterTimer

The percentage of items over the sample period

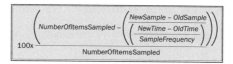

$$100x \left(\frac{NewSample - OldSample}{NewTime - OldTime} \right)$$

1157

CounterTimerInverse

The inverse of CounterTimer.

$$100x \left(1 - \left(\frac{NewSample - OldSample}{NewTime - OldTime}\right)\right)$$

ElapsedTime

The elapsed time for the measurement.

$$\frac{SampleTime - SampleStartTime}{SampleFrequency}$$

NumberOfItems32, NumberOfItems64, NumberOfItemsHEX32, NumberOfItemsHEX64

These counters have no calculation since they indicate fixed values.

RateOfCountsPerSecond32, RateOfCountsPerSecond64

Number of counts per time base.

$$\frac{\left(\dfrac{NewSample - OldSample}{NewTime - OldTime}\right)}{SampleFrequency}$$

RawFraction

The raw fraction between two values.

$$100x \frac{Sample}{Base\ Value}$$

SampleCounter

The difference between samples.

$$\frac{NewSample - OldSample}{NewBaseValue - OldBaseValue}$$

SampleFraction

The fractional difference between samples.

$$100x \frac{NewSample - OldSample}{NewBaseValue - OldBaseValue}$$

Timer100Ns

The percentage of time (in 100Ns units) for the counter.

$$100x \frac{NewSample - OldSample}{NewTime100ns - OldTime100ns}$$

Timer100NsInverse

The inverse of Timer100Ns.

$$100x\left(1- \frac{NewSample - OldSample}{NewTime100ns - OldTime100ns}\right)$$

Analysis

There are two sets of information you can use to evaluate the performance of your web applications – the .NET performance counters, and custom counters. ASP.NET has an extensive list of counters, which are well documented in the framework SDK.

Analysis of custom counters is application specific, and there are no hard rules as to what you should analyze. It really depends upon what counters you have created and when you update them. Remember that custom counters can easily be tracked in the Performance Monitor. Using tools such as WAST you can test your application and collect performance counters for analysis, perhaps in a spreadsheet. You can also use the `PerformanceCounter` object to query counters, although this is a task best left to applications other than ASP.NET. This is because accurate monitoring depends on regular sampling of data, and this isn't a task that ASP.NET is suited to. In this case you'd be better off building a Windows Forms application that could sample the data at regular intervals.

Summary

In this chapter we've examined the less exciting parts of development – those things that many programmers find a drudge, but in some respects are the most important. Maybe these topics have always been shied away from because we just haven't had the facilities to make their implementation and use easy. After all, that was pretty much the case with ASP. It's a great product, but the surrounding toolset wasn't industrial strength. With ASP.NET we have that strength – great support for error handling and tracing, and a fully featured debugger.

In particular we've looked at:

- ❏ **Tracing**, and how you can trace the flow of your applications.

- ❏ **Error handling**, to show how robust applications can be created.

- ❏ **Debugging**, with the rich debuggers allowing cross-language and cross-machine application debugging.

- ❏ **Profiling**, seeing how to add performance counters so performance and scalability can be assessed.

Together these features provide a great environment for developing applications.

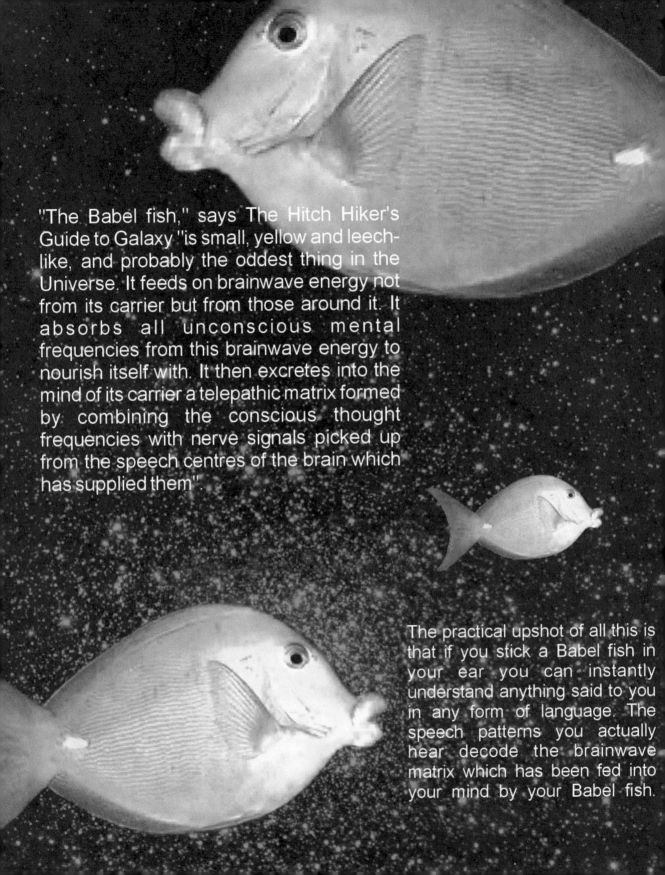

"The Babel fish," says The Hitch Hiker's Guide to Galaxy "is small, yellow and leech-like, and probably the oddest thing in the Universe. It feeds on brainwave energy not from its carrier but from those around it. It absorbs all unconscious mental frequencies from this brainwave energy to nourish itself with. It then excretes into the mind of its carrier a telepathic matrix formed by combining the conscious thought frequencies with nerve signals picked up from the speech centres of the brain which has supplied them".

The practical upshot of all this is that if you stick a Babel fish in your ear you can instantly understand anything said to you in any form of language. The speech patterns you actually hear decode the brainwave matrix which has been fed into your mind by your Babel fish.

23

Migration and Interoperability

Wouldn't it be great if, when a new version of a development product was released, we could forget about all our existing projects using old versions of the software? Unfortunately, for the majority of people, existing applications take up a good deal of their time – and rightly so. If we restarted development with every new version of a product, then we'd never get anything finished. Organizations have a duty to their staff and shareholders, so throwing away existing investment (in both products and expertise) is not something that can be done lightly. Therefore new developments may have to work alongside, and in cooperation with, existing products.

This chapter is about that situation – how to manage the story of getting .NET to work with the pre-.NET world. In particular we will look at:

- ❑ Migrating ASP applications to ASP.NET.
- ❑ Changing from JScript and Visual Basic to their .NET equivalents.
- ❑ Using existing COM components from .NET.
- ❑ Using .NET components from COM.

Despite the fact that ASP.NET is such a radical change from ASP, there's an excellent migration path, as well as great support for working alongside existing applications.

Migrate, Integrate, or Rewrite?

The first question that needs to be asked is, should you migrate at all? Is the effort going to be worth it? No-one can deny that ASP.NET is better than ASP in many (if not all) areas for developers. The whole environment promotes cleaner code, better reuse, and faster applications – many developers would love to work in this better world. However you move forward with your development, there's going to be costs involved, and you must weigh up those costs carefully to decide which option you should choose.

For example, ask yourself the following questions:

- ❏ Is the application purely ASP pages?
- ❏ Does it use COM components?
- ❏ Do you have a data tier in MTS or COM+ Services?
- ❏ Which browsers is it targeted at?
- ❏ Does it use client-side script?
- ❏ Do you need to convert at all?

The answers to these questions will help you decide the action you need to take. Unfortunately, there's no simple answer – every application is different and must be taken on its own merits. The one thing that's critical about the process of migration is to set your expectations at the right level. Don't think you can just rename your pages to `.aspx` and expect miracles to happen.

Migrate

We can describe migration as the movement of all parts of an application to a new environment, with the minimal amount of code change. This is often the goal many people aim for, but it can have hidden costs.

For example, will the new application be easily maintainable? Will you add code to bring the application into line with ASP.NET, but in doing so leave code that is even more confusing than it was before? The short-term cost of performing the least work might actually turn out to be more expensive, if, further down the line, more work is required. You should analyze the cost of this approach, comparing it to the cost of rewriting, and see which has the greatest long-term benefit.

Integrate

Integration gives us the ability to add new ASP.NET features to existing ASP applications, or perhaps to migrate only selected parts of an application. In many ways this is a good approach, but it also comes with dangers, the two most obvious of which are:

- ❏ Built-in **Session and Application state cannot be shared** between ASP and ASP.NET applications.
- ❏ **Performance**, as crossing the managed/un-managed code boundary incurs a minor performance cost.

You may decide that the latter of these is acceptable for your particular application – after all, the application will still work, and the new ASP.NET code should run faster, so the benefit of using new code might equal out any performance drop. Also, when all things are considered, the boundary crossing is light compared to some other actions (such as database access). The former option, though, is a big problem – you can easily integrate ASP.NET pages into an ASP application, but there's no way of sharing built-in state. So, unless your application uses its own form of session storage (such as a database), your options are limited.

Integrating ASP.NET applications with existing COM components only suffers from the minor performance hit of the unmanaged/managed code border, unless they use the ASP context. In this case you may need to alter your ASP.NET pages. We'll look at this topic later.

Rewrite

Rewriting is the option many of us would like. Starting again from scratch is not only a great opportunity to get the best from the new platform, but it's also a chance to cure some of those things about the original application that you never liked. This option will, of course, get the best from .NET, and in the long run may be the cheapest solution. One of the reasons why the ASP.NET team decided to break compatibility with ASP was because we have more Internet time ahead of us than behind us. Microsoft wants a platform that will last for a long time.

Of course, one of the big problems with the rewrite method isn't with the code itself, it's with education. With a new technology such as .NET, it's often the training and experience that prove too much of a hindrance to this option.

Do Nothing

No matter how much we might want to take one of the above steps, doing nothing might actually be the best bet for your applications. After all, do you really need to move to .NET? What sort of business case can you put forward to justify it? How much will it cost? Conversion (whatever form it takes) means time (and therefore money) for developers, testers, bug fixing, and so on. The whole development cycle has to be gone through again.

Remember the old adage – "if it ain't broke, don't fix it". It's nice to play with new toys, but sometimes a good old-fashioned wooden train set works fine.

ASP.NET

There are many changes to take into account when looking purely at ASP pages. The most obvious are the server controls and the postback architecture. These have been covered extensively in earlier chapters of the book, so now we'll move on to other features that still exist in ASP.NET, but that are different from ASP. We'll also abbreviate explanations of changes that are explained in detail elsewhere in this book, and instead provide a summary and reference to them. Since ASP.NET is fully class based, we'll also provide references to the underlying classes, so you can easily find full information in the documentation, or look up the classes in tools such as WinCV and ILDasm.

The first things to look at are changes to the ASP API.

Preparing the Way

Before we delve into the changes in detail, here's a quick list of things you can do now, in your current ASP pages, to pave the way for migrating to ASP.NET.

Note that these are only relevant to server-side code – client-side code is still browser related.

❑ Use only a single language within each ASP page.

❑ Use `Option Explicit` to enforce declaration of variables.

❑ Use `<script>` blocks for function declaration instead of `<% %>` blocks.

❑ Avoid render functions.

❑ Use the `Call` keyword for calling functions, to force the use of parenthesis around arguments.

❑ Avoid default properties, such as `Recordset("column")` instead of `Recordset.Fields("column").Value`.

❑ Explicitly close open resources (such as the file system or recordsets).

Many of these are best practices anyway, but we all tend to take shortcuts. Adhering to the above list will ease your migration path. We'll be looking at these in detail as we go through the chapter.

Intrinsic Objects

Most ASP intrinsic objects remain available and unchanged, providing excellent support for existing applications. However, there are changes to some properties and methods, as well as the addition of new ones. One significant change is the removal of the `ASPError` object, as error handling is now managed by exceptions.

The Application Object

ASP.NET application state handling is implemented by the `HttpApplicationState` class in the `System.Web` namespace. Although ASP.NET supports ASP functionality by way of the `Contents` and `StaticObjects` collections, there are some minor differences, which may confuse you if you check the documentation. The reason is that `HttpApplicationState` is a first class object that implements a collection (used to hold the items in application state). Therefore methods such as `Remove` and `RemoveAll` are members of the `HttpApplicationState` object itself. However, to preserve compatibility, there is also a `Contents` property, which simply points back to the parent object. Thus, the following lines of code are equivalent:

VB.NET

```
Application.Remove("Item1")
Application.Contents.Remove("Item1")
```

C#

```
Application.Remove("Item1");
Application.Contents.Remove ("Item1");
```

The first line in these examples is how you'd see examples in .NET code samples, whereas the second line is how you'd do it in ASP. However, because compatibility has been preserved, they both work.

New features of the application object are:

Property/Method	Description
AllKeys	Returns an array of strings containing the names of stored application state members.
Count	Returns a count of items in application state.
Add	Adds a new item to the state.
Clear	Removes all items from the state. This is equivalent to RemoveAll, and is provided as part of the standard collection handling features.
Get	Returns an individual item (either by name or by ordinal).
GetKey	Returns the key for the supplied ordinal.
Set	Updates the value of a stored item.

It's important to note that although there are explicit Add and Get methods, the existing way of accessing the collection still works fine.

Objects in Application State

In ASP it was always taboo to store single-threaded objects in application state, which was a real problem for Visual Basic programmers developing components. Given that the .NET languages (including Visual Basic) allow the production of free-threaded components, has this problem now gone away? Well, to a degree yes, as long as you understand the following:

❑ You can store free-threaded components as long as they provide thread synchronization.

❑ You can store single-threaded components if you use Lock and Unlock to protect against thread blocks.

❑ Application state has no guaranteed durability. The application domain can be torn down at any time (synchronized restart for example), so for durability you need an external store.

By and large, the storage of objects in application state should be discouraged because of the resources used, and the potential for scalability and performance problems. However, the storage of scalar type data (such as string) is a great way to get some performance improvement, as long as it is used carefully. You might think that the classic case of wanting to store Recordsets in application state is now easy, since you can store the XML from a DataSet, but remember that memory (although cheap) is finite. Frequent use of a 10Mb set of data stored in application state may give great benefits, but 100Mb may not. This sort of scenario needs full testing before the implications are really known.

1165

The Session Object

Session state is implemented by the `HttpSessionState` class in the `System.Web.SessionState` namespace. The `Contents` and `StaticObjects` follow the same rules as `Application` state – the structure of the class is different from ASP, but access works in the same way. Thus, the following examples are equivalent:

VB.NET

```
Session.Remove("Item1")
Session.Contents.Remove("Item"1)
```

C#

```
Session.Remove("Item1");
Session.Contents.Remove("Item1");
```

The *changed* and **new** features of the session object are shown below, in corresponding fonts:

Property/Method	Description
Count	Returns a count of items in session state.
IsCookieless	Indicates whether or not session state is being handled in a cookieless manner.
IsNewSession	Indicates whether or not the session has been created with the current request.
IsReadOnly	Indicates whether or not the session is read-only.
IsSynchronized	Indicates whether or not access to the session state values is thread safe.
Mode	Indicates how session state is being stored. Will contain one of the `SessionStateMode` constants: ❑ `InProc`, for in process ❑ `Off`, for no session state ❑ `StateServer`, for the out-of-process state service ❑ `SQLServer`, for SQL Server
SessionID	In ASP.NET the `SessionID` property returns a `String` (as opposed to a `Long` in ASP)
SyncRoot	An object that provides synchronous access to the session contents.
Add	Adds a new item to the session state.
Clear	Removes all items from the session state. This is equivalent to `RemoveAll`, and is provided as part of the standard collection handling features.
CopyTo	Copies the contents of the session state to an array of strings.

Property/Method	Description
Equals	Compares an object in session state with the supplied one to see if they are the same.
Remove	In ASP the Remove method could take either the key name of the item or its index. In ASP.NET you can only supply the name. To remove by index use the RemoveAt method.
RemoveAt	Removes an item at the selected ordinal.

The Request Object

The request is implemented by the HttpRequest class in the System.Web namespace. All of the existing properties and methods are supported, although there are some notable exceptions regarding the use of collections (see below). Where appropriate the ASP 3.0 ServerVariables equivalent has been mentioned.

New and *changed* properties or methods are detailed below, in corresponding fonts:

Property/Method	Description
AcceptTypes	Returns a string array of the MIME types supported by the client. For ASP this could be extracted from the comma separated ServerVariables HTTP_ACCEPT entry.
ApplicationPath	The virtual application path.
BinaryRead	Returns a Byte array containing the binary information sent to the server. In ASP the return type is variant.
Browser	Returns an HttpBrowserCapabilities object describing the features of the browser.
ClientCertificate	Returns an HttpClientCertificate object (as opposed to an array of values in ASP).
ContentEncoding	The character set of the entity body.
ContentLength	The length (in bytes) of the request. Equivalent to CONTENT_LENGTH.
ContentType	The MIME type of the request. Equivalent to CONTENT_TYPE.
Cookies	Returns an HttpCookieCollection object (as opposed to an array of values in ASP).
FilePath	The virtual path of the request. Equivalent to SCRIPT_NAME.
Files	Returns an HttpFileCollection of uploaded files (for multi-part form posts).
Filter	Identifies the stream filter to use for the request. All content will be passed through the filter before being accessible by the page.

Table continued on following page

1167

Property/Method	Description
Form	Returns a collection (NameValueCollection) of Form contents. Accessing this collection is different from accessing the Form collection under ASP (see the **Request Collections** sections below).
Headers	A collection (NameValueCollection) of HTTP headers. In ASP these values are space-separated *name:value* pairs; in .NET they can be accessed via HTTP_*name*.
HttpMethod	The HTTP method used for the request. Equivalent to REQUEST_METHOD.
InputStream	A Stream containing the input for the request.
IsAuthenticated	Indicates whether or not the user has been authenticated.
IsSecureConnection	Indicates whether or not the connection is using HTTPS. Equivalent to HTTPS in ASP.
Params	A combined collection of QueryString, Form, ServerVariables, and Cookies.
Path	The virtual path of the request. Equivalent to PATH_INFO.
PathInfo	Additional path information.
Physical ApplicationPath	The physical path of the application root. Equivalent to APPL_PHYSICAL_PATH.
PhysicalPath	The physical path of the request. Equivalent to PATH_TRANSLATED.
QueryString	Returns a collection (NameValueCollection) of QueryString contents. Accessing this collection is different from accessing the QueryString collection under ASP (see the **Request Collections** sections below).
RawUrl	The raw URL of the request. Equivalent to RAW_URL.
RequestType	The HTTP method used for the request. Equivalent to REQUEST_METHOD.
TotalBytes	The number of bytes in the input stream.
Url	A Uri object containing details of the request. A Uri object (from the System namespace) encapsulates information about a specific resource, such as port and DNS information.
UrlReferrer	A Uri object detailing referrer information.
UserAgent	The browser user agent string. Equivalent to HTTP_USER_AGENT.
UserHostAddress	The IP address of the user. Equivalent to REMOTE_ADDR.
UserHostName	The DNS name of the user. Equivalent to REMOTE_NAME.

Property/Method	Description
UserLangauges	An array of langauges preferences. Equivalent to HTTP_ACCEPT_LANGUAGE.
MapImage Coordinates	Maps the image-field parameter to *x* and *y* coordinates.
MapPath	Maps the virtual path to a physical path. The method is now overloaded taking two forms. The first is the same as ASP where the parameter is the URL of the virtual path. The second takes three parameters: the virtual path, the virtual base directory for relative resolution, and a Boolean indicating whether or not the virtual path may belong to another application.
SaveAs	Saves the HTTP request to disk.

Some of this information is still available through the ServerVariables collection, but has now been abstracted out into more accessible properties.

Request Collections

The Request object supports collections for accessing the contents of a form or query string, and there are some major implications where those contents contain elements of the same name. This is typically the case where check boxes, radio buttons, or multi-select list boxes are used. For example, consider the following ASP form:

```
<form action="foo.asp" method="post">

Select your favorite editor:

<select name="editor" multiple="multiple">
   <option>Notepad
   <option>Textpad
   <option>Visual Studio.NET
</select>

<p/>
<input type="submit" value="Send">

</form>
```

To extract the selected values from the multi-select list we could use:

```
For item = 1 To Request.Form("editor").Count
   Response.Write Request.Form("editor")(item) & "<br/>"
Next
```

However, this code will not work in ASP.NET, as a NameValueCollection represents the form contents. There are two points about this:

❑   The collection is zero based.

❑   You have to explicitly get the values.

For example:

```
Dim item As Integer
For item = 0 To Request.Form.GetValues("editor").Length - 1
   Response.Write (Request.Form.GetValues("editor")(item) & "<br/>")
Next
```

Here we have to use the GetValues of the collection, and index into that (using a base of 0) to get the required value.

The Response Object

The response to a request is implemented by the HttpResponse class. Like the request, all existing functionality is kept, with the following *changes* or **additions**:

Property/Method	Description
BufferOutput	Indicates whether or not to buffer output. This is the same as the Buffer property, and is the preferred method of changing buffering in ASP.NET.
Cache	Returns an HttpCachePolicy object, containing details about the caching policy of the current response.
CacheControl	Although still supported, this property is deprecated in favor of the HttpCachePolicy methods.
ContentEncoding	Identifies the character set of the output. The value can be one of the Encoding enumerations (ASCIIEncoding, UnicodeEncoding, UTF7Encoding, UTF8Encoding).
Cookies	Returns a collection (HttpCookieCollection) of HttpCookie objects (as opposed to an array of attributed values in ASP). The ASP cookie attributes appear as properties of the HttpCookie object.
Expires	Although still supported, this property is deprecated in favor of the HttpCachePolicy methods.
ExpiresAbsolute	Although still supported, this property is deprecated in favor of the HttpCachePolicy methods.
Filter	The Stream object that acts as the output filter. All output will go through this filter before being returned to the client.
Output	Returns a TextWriter object through which custom output can be returned to the client.
OutputStream	Returns a Stream object representing the raw data of the content body.
Status	Sets the HTTP status code to return to the client. This property has been deprecated in favor of the StatusDescription property.

Property/Method	Description
StatusCode	The HTTP status code of the response.
StatusDescription	Sets the HTTP status description to return to the client. This is preferred over the Status property.
SuppressContent	Indicates whether or not content is to be returned to the client.
AddFileDependencies	Adds a group of file names to the dependency list upon which the response is based. Changes to these files will invalidate the output cache.
AddFileDependency	Adds a single file name to the dependency list upon which the response is based. Changes to this file will invalidate the output cache.
AddHeader	This method has been deprecated in favor of the AppendHeader method.
AppendHeader	Appends an HTTP header to the content stream. This method is preferred over AddHeader.
ApplyAppPathModifier	Applies the Cookieless Session ID to a given relative or virtual path. This allows HREFS with fully qualified names to be modified to include the current Session ID.
BinaryWrite	Writes binary data (a Byte array) to the output stream. In ASP the array is a variant array of unsigned integers.
ClearContent	Clears the content from the buffer stream.
ClearHeaders	Clears the headers from the buffer stream.
Close	Closes the socket connection to the client.
Redirect	This method is now overloaded. The first form is the same as ASP, taking a URL, and the second form takes a URL and a Boolean indicating whether or not Response.End is called after the redirection.
Write	This method is overloaded, and can take one of four sets of parameters: ❑ A Char ❑ An Object ❑ A String ❑ A Char array, along with the start index and number of characters to write
WriteFile	Writes the specified file directly to the output stream.

The Server Object

The Server object is implemented by the `HttpServerUtility` class in the `System.Web` namespace. The **additions** and *changes* are detailed below:

Property/Method	Description
MachineName	Returns the name of the server.
ClearError	Clears the previous exception.
CreateObject	This method is now overloaded. The original form taking a string of the `ProgID` is still allowed, as well as the new form taking a `Type` object.
CreateObjectFromClsid	Creates an instance of a COM object from the Class identifier (`CLSID`).
Execute	This method is now overloaded. The original form taking a string of the path of the new request is still allowed, as well as the new form taking the path and a `TextWriter` used to capture the output. This allows requests to be executed and then manipulated.
GetLastError	This now returns an `Exception` object (as opposed to an `ASPError` object in ASP).
HtmlDecode	Decodes an HTML encoded string.
HtmlEncode	This method is now overloaded, with an additional form taking a `string` to encode and a `TextWriter` into which the encoded text should be placed.
Transfer	This method is now overloaded, with an additional form taking a `string` for the path, and a `Boolean` to indicate whether or not the `Form` and `QueryString` collections should be preserved across the transfer.
UrlDecode	Decodes an HTML encoded URL.
UrlPathEncode	Encodes only the URL portion of a string (as opposed to `UrlEncode` which encode the URL and any `QueryString`).
UrlEncode	This method is now overloaded, with an additional form taking a `string` of the URL to encode, and a `TextWriter` into which the encoded URL is placed.

The ASPError Object

The `ASPError` object has been removed, as errors are now represented by exceptions. For example, the following code extracts the last error:

```
Dim lastError As Exception

lastError = Server.GetLastError()

Response.Write("Error was: " & lastError.Message)
```

The ObjectContext Object

The `ObjectContext` object in ASP is designed for the integration of ASP pages with external transacted components, such as those in **Microsoft Transaction Server** (MTS) or COM+ Services. Within ASP.NET you have the ability to run pages with **ASP Page Compatibility**, by setting a page directive:

```
<%@ Page AspCompat="true" %>
```

This allows the page to be run on a single threaded apartment (STA) thread, allowing it to call STA components, such as those written in VB6. This is particularly useful for those components that reference the ASP intrinsic objects and generate HTML.

The Page Object

The `Page` object (in the `System.Web.UI` namespace) was not a part of ASP, but plays an important role in ASP.NET. The `Page` is the parent object for the objects mentioned above, apart from the `ObjectContext`. Many of the features of the page you'll already have seen (such as the `IsPostBack` and `IsValid` properties), and the rest are extensively documented in the help files. We mention this object here in case you see code such as `Page.Session`, `Page.Response`, or `Page.Request`, and wonder how the objects relate.

Page Changes

Along with changes to the common objects, the structure and usage of ASP pages have changed. You've already seen how the event model and postback architecture changes the layout of pages, so what we'll concentrate on here are the things that need changing from existing ASP pages.

Single Language per Page

I've never actually seen any code that used more than one server-side language, but with ASP.NET you must use a single language per page. If you need to use multiple languages then you'll have to use `User Controls` or custom controls, which can be in any language.

This only affects individual pages – multiple pages in an application can be in different languages.

Script Blocks

Procedures in ASP.NET pages have to reside within proper script tags. So, the following is no longer allowed:

```
<%
   Sub Foo()
      ...
   End Sub
%>
```

Instead you must use:

```
<script language="VB" runat="server">

  Sub Foo()
    ...
  End Sub

</script>
```

You can still use the `<% %>` tags for inline placement of variables or function results.

Code Render Functions

The changes to script block usage mean that render functions are no longer allowed. Render functions were where the body of a function actually contained HTML. For example:

```
<% Sub ShowSeparator() %>
  <img src="sep.gif" width="100%"></img>
<% End Sub %>
```

This now has to be:

```
<script language="VB" runat="server">

  Sub ShowSeparator()
    Response.Write("<img src='sep.gif' width='100%'></img>")
  End Sub

</script>
```

Language Changes

One of the most major changes in .NET has been in the use of languages. We looked at the specifics of these language changes in Chapter 2, but it's worth reiterating some of them here, to remind ourselves of the implications.

Visual Basic probably has the changes that affect people most, purely because most ASP pages are written in VBScript. Microsoft made a brave (but correct) move in updating the language – breaking functionality in certain areas and adding functionality in others. The main reasons for this are to bring Visual Basic into the fold of the .NET CLR, and to take the opportunity to update the language with some much-needed features.

For JScript, the changes will have less impact, for the simple reason that most JScript is client-side coding (which is not CLR related). I know of only a few people who use JScript as their preferred ASP language.

Visual Basic.NET

The details we listed in Chapter 2 regarding Visual Basic related to the language as a whole. In this section we'll look at the differences between VBScript and Visual Basic.NET and the sort of things you'll need to change when migrating applications.

Variables and Strong Typing

The first point is that VBScript is no longer used – being replaced by Visual Basic. This means we now have the ability to have data types. For example:

```
Dim Name As String
Dim Age  As Integer
```

The second point about variables is that by default they have to be declared, as the `explicit` option is set to `true`. We can set this option on a page-by-page basis by:

```
<%@ Page Explicit="False" %>
```

Alternatively it can be set in the `web.config` file:

```
<compilation explicit="false"/>
```

As a general rule, explicit variable declaration is better, as it reduces the potential for errors.

Variant and Data Type Conversion

The `Variant` data type has been removed, and replaced by a generic `Object`. For example, in VBScript we could do this:

```
Dim o
o = 1
Response.Write "o=" & o & "<br/>"

o = "hello"
Response.Write "o=" & o & "<br/>"
```

and the output we would get would be:

o=1
o=hello

In Visual Basic.NET, we can declare a variable as type `Object`, although the effect this has depends on whether you have strict typing enabled or not. This can be set either at the page level with:

```
<%@ Page Strict="True" %>
```

or in the `web.config` file:

```
<compilation strict="true"/>
```

Without strict typing the following code works fine:

```
Dim o As Object
o = 1
Response.Write("o=" & o & "<br/>")

o = "hello"
Response.Write("o=" & o & "<br/>")
```

That's because the object type automatically converts its value to a `string`. With strict typing however, the code needs to be changed to:

```
Dim o As Object
o = 1
Response.Write("o=" & o.ToString() & "<br/>")

o = "hello"
Response.Write("o=" & o.ToString() & "<br/>")
```

Automatic conversion cannot be done on the `Object` type with strict conversion, so we have to convert explicitly. Implicit conversion is limited to widening, for example from an `Integer` to a `Long`.

Explicit Type Conversion

To perform data type conversion you use the `CType` function or the `cast` keywords:

```
CType (expression, DataType)
```

The *expression* is the variable to be converted, and *DataType* is the new type. For example:

```
Dim d As Double = 123.456

Dim i As Integer = CType(d, Integer)
```

The alternative method of conversion is to use the cast types:

```
Dim i As Integer = CInt(d)
```

Since every primitive data type ultimately inherits from `Object`, you can also utilize the `ToString` method provided by `Object`. For example:

```
Dim d As Double = 123.456

Response.Write(d.ToString())
```

Methods

The main change to methods has been the way in which they are called. In Visual Basic.NET all methods must be surrounded by parentheses, as opposed to VBScript where parentheses were only required for functions. For example, the following is no longer allowed:

```
Response.Write "Hello there"
```

and has to be replaced by:

```
Response.Write("Hello there")
```

This has its biggest impact when switching between the ASP and ASP.NET environments.

Method Arguments

By default, arguments to methods in Visual Basic.NET are now passed by value, rather than by reference. This means the following code will not work as expected:

```
Sub Foo(X As Integer)

  X = X + 1

End Sub

Dim Y As Integer = 3

Foo(Y)

Response.Write("Y=" & Y.ToString())
```

The output here will be 3, rather than 4. To correct this you need to change the procedure declaration to:

```
Sub Foo(ByRef X As Integer)
```

Default Properties

The use of default properties is not allowed in Visual Basic.NET. This doesn't affect .NET components, since there's no way to define a default property, but it has an impact when accessing COM objects. For example, the following would not be allowed:

```
Dim rs    As New ADODB.Recordset
Dim Name As String

rs.Open("...", "...")

Name = rs("Name")
```

The last line in .NET would be:

```
Name = rs("Name").Value
```

While this does mean more typing, it makes the code much more explicit, and therefore less prone to potential errors.

Set and Let

The Set and Let keywords are no longer required for object references. For example, the following is now the accepted syntax:

```
Dim conn As SQLConnection

conn = SQLConnection
```

There's no need for the Set keyword before the object assignment.

Single and Multiple Lines

In Visual Basic.NET, all If statements must be constructed across multiple lines. For example, in VBScript you could do this:

```
If x > y Then foo()
```

In Visual Basic.NET this becomes:

```
If x > y Then
   foo()
End If
```

JScript.NET

JScript.NET remains much closer to its pre .NET version. As far as ASP.NET programmers are concerned, the most obvious difference is in data types. Variables can now be declared using the following syntax:

```
var variableName : DataType [= value]
```

For example:

```
var Name : String
var Age: Integer = 24
```

Functions also have the addition of data types:

```
function foo() : Boolean
{
  return True;
}
```

Implicit Type Conversion

Data types can be implicitly converted using the following syntax:

```
TypeName(expression)
```

For example:

```
var d : double = 123.456

var i : Integer = int(d)
```

Interoperability

No matter how much we'd like to do all our coding in .NET, we have to face reality. There is an enormous amount of traditional ASP and COM code being used in web applications, and businesses cannot afford to just throw that away. The success of MTS/COM+ Services as a middle-tier business object layer has led to a large number of COM objects being used as, amongst other things, data layers, abstracting the data management code from the ASP code. With .NET, Microsoft has provided good interoperability for several reasons:

❑ **To preserve existing investment**. Compatibility with existing applications means we can continue to use existing code, as well as preserve our existing investment.

❑ **Incremental Migration**. There is no need to migrate everything at once if your new code can exist alongside other applications.

❑ **Some code will never change**. There is probably plenty of code where the investment, time, or skill to migrate is not available.

Although .NET is independent from COM, Microsoft has realized the need for interoperability, and provided ways to use not only COM objects from within .NET, but also .NET components from within COM. They've realized that there had to be a way to call down to the Windows API, for those that need to.

This chapter uses the term COM as a generic term for COM and COM+ purely to improve legibility. From the interoperability point of view there is no difference.

Crossing the Boundary

We know that .NET code is managed by the CLR, and that COM code is not, so there has to be some way to cross the managed/unmanaged code boundary. One of the major problems is the conversion of data types, but the CLR handles this for us:

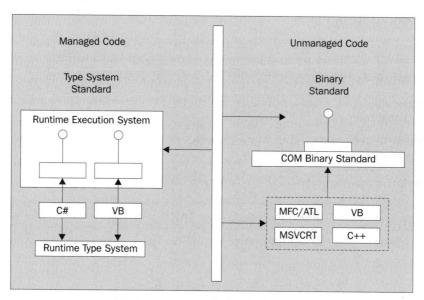

When crossing this boundary we have to think about the differences between the two systems. Architecturally these are:

Unmanaged Code has ...	Managed Code has ...
Binary standard	Type standard
Type libraries	Metadata
Immutable types	Version binding
DLL hell	Versioned assemblies
Interface based	Object based
HResults	Exceptions
GUIDS	String names

Additionally, there are the programming differences:

Unmanaged Code has ...	Managed Code has ...
CoCreateInstance	new operator
QueryInterface	Cast operator
Reference counting	Memory management and Garbage collection
GetProcAddress	Static methods

The unmanaged way of doing things doesn't affect ASP or ASP.NET, but does affect those of us who also write COM and use components.

Data Type Marshalling

When we cross the managed/unmanaged boundary, the wrappers automatically perform data type mapping for you. So, although we don't need to know how this works, it's useful to see what language types map to in .NET. There are two kinds of data types as far as marshalling goes:

❑ **Isomorphic types**. These are the same on both sides of the boundary, and therefore don't need any conversion.

❑ **Non-Isomorphic types**. These are different on either side of the boundary, and therefore require conversion.

The table below details the pre-.NET data types, and what they map into in .NET:

C++	Visual Basic 6	.NET	Isomorphic
signed char	Not supported	SByte	Yes
unsigned char	Byte	Byte	Yes
short	Integer	Short	Yes

C++	Visual Basic 6	.NET	Isomorphic
unsigned short	Not supported	UInt16	Yes
int	Long	Integer	Yes
unsigned int	Not supported	UInt32	Yes
__int64	Not supported	Long	Yes
unsigned __int64	Not supported	UInt64	Yes
float	Single	Single	Yes
double	Double	Double	Yes
BSTR	String	String	No
BOOL	Boolean	Boolean	No
VARIANT	Variant	Object	No
IUnknown	object	UnmanagedType.IUknown	No
DATE	Date	Date	No
CURRENCY	Currency	Decimal	No
__wchar_t	Char	Char	Yes
void	Not supported	Void	Yes

Simple arrays (single dimensional arrays of isomorphic types) are themselves defined as isomorphic types.

Custom Type Marshalling

For isomorphic types, the marshaller always knows both the managed and unmanaged type, but this isn't so for non-isomorphic types (such as strings or multi-dimensional arrays). By default the following conversion takes place:

Managed Type	Unmanaged Type
Boolean	A 2 or 4 byte value (VARIANT_BOOL or Win32 BOOL), with True being 1 or −1.
Char	A Unicode or ANSI char (Win32 CHAR or CHAR).
String	A Unicode or ANSI char array (Win32 LPWSTR/LPSTR), or a BSTR.
Object	A Variant or an interface.
Class	A class interface
Value Type	Structure with fixed memory layout
Array	Interface or a SafeArray

For non-isomorphic types, we can specify how they are marshalled across the boundary. This is really beyond the scope of this book, but is well detailed in the .NET SDK help file, under "Programming with the .NET Framework", "Interoperating with Unmanaged Code", and "Data Marshalling".

HRESULTS

In Windows, the standard method of handling errors is via the use of HRESULTS. When crossing the boundary to .NET these are automatically converted to exceptions, with the HRESULT details being stored as part of the exception object. This means that we can use COM objects without sacrificing the structured exception handling that .NET brings us. For this to work the COM object must support the ISupportErrorInfo and IErrorInfo interfaces.

Using COM Objects from .NET

Using COM components from .NET is extremely simple, as there is a tool that takes a COM component or type library and creates a managed assembly (a callable wrapper) to manage the boundary transition for us. The diagram below shows how this wrapper is used:

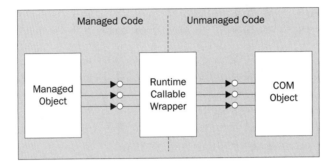

From the programming perspective all we have to do is call methods and access properties as we would with the COM component. The difference is that we'll be calling the wrapper class, which will take the .NET types, convert them to COM types, and call the COM interface methods. The CLR maintains the reference to the COM object, so COM reference counting works as expected, while also providing the simplicity of garbage collected references for the .NET usage of the object.

There are several ways in which we can generate the wrapper class:

❏ Adding a reference in Visual Studio.NET.

❏ Using the type library import tool.

❏ Using the type library convert class.

❏ Creating a custom wrapper.

Of these, the first two are by far the easiest.

Using Visual Studio.NET

In Visual Studio.NET all we have to do is create a reference to the COM object, and the wrapper class is created for us. First select References from the Solution Explorer, and then pick Add Reference....

Then, from the dialog that appears, select the COM tab, and pick your COM object:

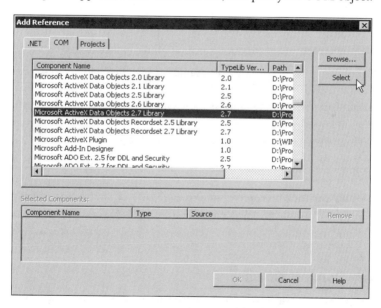

Once you've clicked Select and then OK, the reference is added. The wrapper class (in this case it would be ADODB.dll) is placed in the bin directory of the application.

The Type Library Import Tool

If you don't have Visual Studio.NET (or are a die-hard Notepad user) then you can use the type library import tool to create the wrapper class for you. The syntax is:

```
tlbimp TypeLibrary [Options]
```

where *Options* can be:

Option	Description
/out:*FileName*	The filename of the wrapper assembly to create.
/namespace:*Namespace*	Namespace of the assembly to be produced.
/asmversion:*version*	Version number of the assembly to be produced.
/reference:*FileName*	Assembly filename used to resolve references. This can be specified multiple times for multiple references.
/publickey:*FileName*	Filename containing the strong name public key.
/keyfile:*FileName*	Filename containing the strong name key pair.
/keycontainer:*FileName*	Key container holding the strong name key pair.
/delaysign	Force strong name delay signing.
/unsafe	Produce an interface without runtime security checks.
/nologo	Don't display the logo.
/silent	Don't display output, except for errors.
/verbose	Display full information.
/primary	Produce a primary interop assembly.
/strictref	Only use assemblies specified with /reference

By default the output name will be the same as the COM type library, not the filename. For example:

```
tlbimp msado15.dll
```

will produce a wrapper assembly called ADODB.dll, **not** msado15.dll.

The resulting assembly can then be copied into the application bin directory (or placed in the Global Assembly Cache), and referenced as with other .NET assemblies:

```
<%@ Import Namespace=" ADODB" %>
```

The Type Library Convert Class

The System.Runtime.InteropServices namespace contains a class called TypeLibConverter, which provides methods to convert COM classes and interfaces into assembly metadata. This is really only useful if you are building tools that examine COM type libraries at runtime, and is outside the scope of this book.

Custom Wrappers

If your COM component doesn't have a type library then it's possible to create a custom wrapper that directly calls the COM component. This is outside the scope of the book, but for more information, see the topic "Programming with the .NET Framework", "Interoperating with Unmanaged Code", and "Customizing Standard Wrappers" in the SDK help file.

Using the Wrapper Assembly

Using the wrapper assembly is simply a case of treating it like any other managed assembly. For example, if you import the ADO namespace, you can use it in your ASP.NET pages like so:

```
<%@ Import Namespace="ADODB" %>

<html>

<script language="VB" runat="server">

  Sub Page_Load(Sender As Object, e as EventArgs)

    Dim rs As New ADODB.Recordset

    rs.Open("publishers", "Provider=SQLOLEDB; Data Source=.; " & _
                        "Initial Catalog=pubs; User Id=sa")

    While Not rs.EOF
      Response.Write(rs.Fields("pub_name").Value & "<br/>")
      rs.MoveNext()
    End While

    rs.Close

  End Sub

</script>

</html>
```

Deploying Applications that Use COM

However great the COM interoperability story is, it doesn't get around the fact that COM components need to be registered. This as not a fault of .NET, more an issue of the way COM works, and you don't need to do anything other than the standard COM registration. However, the big problem this causes is with the xcopy deployment model, for which it isn't suitable. You can still xcopy the deployment, but you'd need to provide some form of script to register the COM components before the application is activated.

Using .NET Components from COM

The interoperability story doesn't end with using COM code in .NET, as the reverse is also possible. This allows the new language and class features to be used, but without getting rid of old applications. The workings of the wrapper class are shown below – it marshals the COM calls through to the managed object.

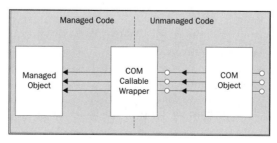

The story is very similar to its opposite that we've just examined, as COM type libraries are created for the .NET assemblies. The difference is that there's slightly more work, as you have to explicitly decide which interfaces and methods you want exposed to COM. This is a crucial point, because for .NET components to be available in COM they have to have an **Interface** (see Chapter 3 for more details on Interfaces), and there are two ways to have this exposed – manually or automatically.

Manually Created Interfaces

Manually creating interfaces means you use the language features to explicitly declare the interface. For example, consider a `Person` class with two properties (`FirstName` and `LastName`) and one method (`FullName`). The interface and class could be defined like this:

Visual Basic.NET

```
Public Interface IPersonVB
   Property FirstName() As String
   Property LastName()  As String
   Function FullName()  As String
End Interface

Public Class PersonVB
   Implements IPersonVB

   Private _firstName As String
   Private _lastName  As String

   Public Sub New()
      ' default constructor - required for interop
   End Sub

   Public Property FirstName() As String Implements IPersonVB.FirstName
      Get
         FirstName = _firstName
      End Get
      Set
         _firstName = value
      End Set
   End Property

   Public Property LastName() As String Implements IPersonVB.LastName
      Get
         LastName = _lastName
      End Get
      Set
         _lastName = value
      End Set
   End Property

   Public Function FullName() As String Implements IPersonVB.FullName
      Return _firstName & " " & _lastName
   End Function

End Class
```

One thing to notice is that the class must have a public default constructor.

C#

```
public interface IPersonCS
{
  string FirstName{get; set;}
  string LastName{get; set;}
  string FullName();
}

public class PersonCS : IPersonCS
{
  private string _firstName;
  private string _lastName;

  // default constructor - required for interop
  public PersonCS() {}

  public string FirstName
  {
    get { return _firstName; }
    set { _firstName = value; }
  }

  public string LastName
  {
    get { return _lastName; }
    set { _lastName = value; }
  }

  public string FullName()
  {
    return _firstName + " " + _lastName;
  }
}
```

Automatic Interfaces

The alternative approach is to use the **Interop Services** attributes to have an interface automatically created from the class. To do this you must use the `InteropServices` namespace, and then add an attribute in front of the class. This attribute will be one of the `ClassInterfaceType` attributes, which can be one of:

Attribute	Description
None	No class interface is generated for the class. Using COM `QueryInterface` for `IDispatch` will fail. An interface needs to be manually created.
AutoDispatch	An interface that supports `IDispatch` is created for the class. However, no type information is produced, so `DispIds` cannot be cached.
AutoDual	A dual interface is created for the class. `Typeinfo` is produced and made available in the type library.

The use of this attribute form is shown below:

Visual Basic.NET

```
Imports System.Runtime.InteropServices

<ClassInterfaceAttribute(ClassInterfaceType.AutoDual)>
Public Class PersonVB
```

C#

```
using System.Runtime.InteropServices;

[ClassInterfaceAttribute(ClassInterfaceType.AutoDual)]
public class PersonCS
```

The attribute can also be applied to the assembly, whereby it affects all classes within it.

Interop Attributes

As well as the ClassInterfaceAttribute, there are others that control how various parts of the assembly are exposed to COM. For example, the attribute GuidAttribute allows you to specify the GUID of the exposed item (class, interface, or assembly), and ComVisibleAttribute can be used to hide .NET types from COM.

Attributes that relate to the marshalling of data are covered in the API Calls section, a little later in the chapter, while the others are fully covered in the SDK help, under "Programming with the .NET Framework", "Interoperating with Unmanaged Code", "Exposing .NET Framework Components to COM", and "Applying Interop Attributes".

Which Interface Method to Use

We've seen that there are three ways of interface creation, and each has its own advantages and disadvantages. The real problem that arises is that of versioning – as COM interfaces are immutable, and .NET has the ability to bind to version interfaces. So, the type of interface you expose to COM depends on how your .NET components are going to change over time. For example, consider the following:

Visual Basic.NET

```
Public Class A
  Public Sub Foo()
  End Sub
End Class

Public Class B
    Inherits A
  Public Sub Foo()
  End Sub
End Class
```

C#

```
public class A
{
  public void Foo(){}
}
public class B : A
{
  public void Foo(){}
}
```

Since class interfaces do not support versioning, consider what happens if class A is updated to version 2 by adding a new method. Managed users of the class are unaffected, but for unmanaged users of either class A or class B the code will break. This affects both early-bound clients (who rely on the layout of the class interface being immutable) as well as late-bound clients (who use DispIds, which change between versions). So, there are great dangers in exposing class interfaces.

By and large the safest option is for the manual creation of interfaces – although it involves more work, you get complete control over the interface. The pros and cons of each method are explained below:

ClassInterfaceType. None & Manual Interface

Advantages

- ❑ There are no versioning problems because users can only call through explicitly created interfaces.
- ❑ The class author has full control over versioning of the class.

Disadvantages

- ❑ More work, as the interface has to be created manually for each class.
- ❑ No scripting support.
- ❑ Less design time support from some RAD tools.

ClassInterfaceType. AutoDispatch

Advantages

- ❑ No versioning problems because classes only support late binding, but without caching DispIds.
- ❑ Does not require user to create separate interface for each class.
- ❑ Supports scripting.

Disadvantages

- ❑ More work for class user.
- ❑ Less support in Visual Basic, as everything must be of type Object.
- ❑ Slower.

1189

ClassInterfaceType. AutoDual

Advantages

- ❏ No extra work for class author or user.
- ❏ Easy to use from all COM clients.

Disadvantages

- ❏ Does not support versioning at all. Any class changes will break COM clients.

Exporting the Type Library

Once the .NET assembly has been created, you need to create a COM type library so that COM clients can set references to the classes. This is done using the Type Library Export tool, the syntax of which is:

```
tlbexp AssemblyName [Options]
```

where *Options* can be:

Option	Description
/out:FileName	The filename of the type library to create.
/nologo	Don't display the logo.
/silent	Don't display output, except for errors.
/verbose	Display full information.

For example, if the Person class were compiled into a Person.dll assembly, we would use:

```
tlbexp Person.dll
```

By default this creates Person.tlb.

Registering the DLL for Local Use

Once the type library is created, the class needs to be registered in the Registry. Even though it's a .NET class, which ordinarily doesn't require registration, its use with COM means the wrapper must be registered. The registration is done using the regasm tool:

```
regasm AssemblyName [Options]
```

where *Options* can be:

Option	Description
/unregister	Unregister the type.
/tlb[:FileName]	Export the assembly to the specified type library, and then register it.

Option	Description
/regfile[:FileName]	Generate a registry merge file with which the type library can be registered.
/codebase	Set the code base in the registry.
/registered	Only refer to type libraries that are already registered.
/nologo	Don't display the logo.
/silent	Don't display output, except for errors.
/verbose	Display full information.

For example, we could register the Person class with:

```
ragasm Person.dll
```

We could also save on the explicit tlbexp step by doing:

```
regasm /tlb:Person.tlb Person.dll
```

This creates the type library and then registers it.

Once registered, the classes can be used as if they were COM-created classes. The DLL created must be in the same directory as the application executable.

Registering the DLL for Global Use

If you wish the .NET assembly to be used in multiple applications, then it must be registered in the Global Assembly Cache (GAC). This applies not only to .NET components used from .NET, but also to .NET components used from COM.

Generating a Strong Name

Before adding assemblies to the GAC they need to be strongly-named. A **Strong Name** consists of the assembly identity (name, version and culture), plus a public key and digital signature. A strong name is useful for several reasons:

❑ **Guarantees uniqueness**. Key pairs are globally unique, and no two will ever be the same.

❑ **Guarantees version protection**. Because the key pair includes a digital signature, they ensure protection against spoofed versions of code.

❑ **Guarantees code integrity**. The digital signature is part of the procedure that ensures code hasn't been changed since it was built.

You can create strong names with the sn utility, which has the following syntax:

```
sn [-q(quiet)] Options [parameters]
```

There are plenty of options (detailed in the help), but the one we are interested in is the generation of key pairs:

```
sn -k Person.snk
```

This generates a key pair and stores it in the file named `Person.snk`. The suffix can be anything, although by convention it is .snk.

At this stage the assembly doesn't know anything about the strong name. To guarantee the link between the assembly and the strong name file you need to add an attribute to the assembly:

Visual Basic.NET

```
<assembly:AssemblyKeyFile("Person.snk")>

Namespace People
```

C#

```
[assembly:AssemblyKeyFile("PersonCS.snk")]

namespace People
```

Installing in the Global Assembly Cache

Once the key pair has been constructed the assembly can be installed into the GAC, in one of two ways.

❑   By using the Windows Installer.

❑   By using the Global Assembly Cache tool (`gacutil`).

We'll use the latter of these, with either the `/i` switch to install the assembly, or `/u` to uninstall the assembly. For example:

```
gacutil /i Person.dll
```

or:

```
gacutil /u Person
```

You can also use the `/l` option to list all assemblies in the cache. Alternatively, you can use the Assembly Cache Viewer (search the SDK for more information on this).

Using the .NET Component from COM

Once the .NET component has been created and made available to COM (either in the application directory or the GAC), then it's available for use. All we have to do is reference it in the usual way:

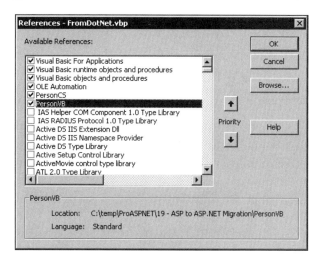

Then we can use it:

```
Dim p As New PersonVB.PersonVB

p.FirstName = "Dave"
p.LastName = "Sussman"

MsgBox p.FullName
```

And, unsurprisingly, the result is:

API Calls

The compatibility story doesn't stop with COM, as .NET provides a way to access DLLs that aren't COM based, using the Platform Invoke Services (**P/Invoke**). This gives you the ability to call APIs in a manner similar to the way Visual Basic 6 does it – by specifying the DLL and API call before it's used.

Visual Basic.NET

The Visual Basic.NET syntax is the same as Visual Basic 6:

```
Declare StringConversionType (Function | Sub) MethodName Lib "DllName" ([Args]) As
Type
```

where:

❑ *StringConversionType* identifies the type of conversion that takes place for strings. This can be Ansi (the default) to convert all strings to Ansi values, Unicode to covert all strings to Unicode values, or Auto to convert strings according to the .NET runtime rules.

❑ *MethodName* is the name of the API to call.

❑ *DllName* is the name of the DLL.

❑ *Args* are any arguments to the API call.

❑ *Type* is the return type of the API call.

For example:

```
Declare Auto Function GetSystemMetrics _
            Lib "User32.dll" (nIndex As Integer) As Integer
```

You can place this within a class if you wish to encapsulate several API calls:

```
Namespace Wrox

   Public Class Metrics

      Declare Auto Function GetSystemMetrics _
               Lib "User32.dll" (nIndex As Integer) As Integer

   End Class

End Namespace
```

You can then call this API like so:

```
Dim mt  As New Metrics
Dim val As Integer

val = mt.GetSystemMetrics(…)
```

Alternatively you can wrap the API call in a class method, giving you the option of pre- or post-processing the data.

```
Namespace Wrox

   Public Class Metrics

      Declare Auto Function GetSystemMetrics _
               Lib "User32.dll" (nIndex As Integer) As Integer

      Public Function GetMetrics(Index As Integer) As Integer)

         Return GetSystemMetrics(Index)

      End Function

   End Class

End Namespace
```

This approach allows you to wrap many API calls into a single class.

C#

For C# you use the DllImport attribute, using the following syntax:

```
[DllImport("LibraryName", CallingConvention := "CallingConvention", _
                          CharSet := "CharSet", _
                          EntryPoint := "EntryPoint", _
                          ExactSpelling := "ExactSpelling", _
                          PreserveSig := "PreserveSig", _
                          SetLastError := "SetLastError")> _
          static extern FunctionName(Arguments)
```

The fields of DllImport are detailed below:

Field	Description
CallingConvention	Indicates the value to use when passing method arguments. This can be one of the CallingConvention enumerations:
	❑ Cdecl, to use the __cdecl format.
	❑ FastCall, to use the __fastcall format.
	❑ StdCall, to use the __stdcall format.
	❑ ThisCall, to use the thiscall format.
	❑ Winapi, to use the __far or __pascal format.
	For Win32 API calls you should use StdCall, which is the default.
CharSet	Indicates the character set to use for names and string passing. This can be one of the CharSet enumerations:
	❑ Ansi, to marshal strings as ANSI 1-byte characters.
	❑ Auto, to automatically marshal strings appropriate to the target system.
	❑ None, to indicate no specific marshalling.
	❑ Unicode, to marshal string as Unicode 2-byte characters. This also appends the letter 'A' to the EntryPoint, in convention with many Windows API calls.
	The default is Ansi.
EntryPoint	The name, or ordinal, of the entry point in the DLL to be called.
ExactSpelling	Indicates whether or not the name of the EntryPoint should be modified to correspond with the CharSet. The default value is False.
PreserveSig	Indicates whether or not the HRESULT from the API call should be converted to a managed failure. The default is True.
SetLastError	Indicates whether or not the GetLastError API call can be called to determine if an error occurred. The default is False.

For many Win32 API calls you can accept the default values, for example:

```
[DllImport("User32.dll")]
static extern int GetSystemMetrics(int nIndex);
```

This can be wrapped in a class to allow external use:

```
namespace Wrox
{
  public class Metrics
  {
    [DllImport("User32.dll")]
    static extern int GetSystemMetrics(int nIndex);
  }
}
```

Alternatively you can wrap the API call in a class method, giving you the option of pre- or post-processing the data.

```
namespace Wrox
{
  public class Metrics
  {
    [DllImport("User32.dll")]
    static extern int GetSystemMetrics(int nIndex);

    public int GetMetrics(int Index)
    {
      return GetSystemMetrics(Index);
    }
  }
}
```

Using the API Class

Using this API class wrapper is just like using any other class. For example, consider the following ASP.NET page:

```
<%@ Import Namespace="Wrox" %>

<html>

<script Language="VB" runat="server">

  Sub Page_Load(Sender As Object, E As EventArgs)

    Dim mt     As New Metrics()
    Dim Width  As Integer = mt.GetMetrics(MetricsValues.SM_CXSCREEN)
    Dim Height As Integer = mt.GetMetrics(MetricsValues.SM_CYSCREEN)

    VBScreen.Text = "VB Screen = " & Width.ToString() & " * " & _
                                     Height.ToString()

  End Sub
```

```
    </script>

    <asp:Label id="Screen" runat="server"/>

    </html>
```

This displays the current screen resolution of the server. The values passed into the `GetMetrics` method are defined in the class as an `enum` (see the Platform SDK under **GetSystemMetrics** for more details on these).

Type Marshalling

When dealing with API calls we often have to pass structures into the call, and the structure gets filled with the appropriate information. When doing this we need to tell the CLR how the structure is going to be arranged in memory, so that it matches the equivalent Win32 structure. This is done by using the `StructLayout` attribute. For example, consider the `GetSystemTime` API call:

Visual Basic.NET

```
<StructLayout(LayoutKind.Sequential)> Public Structure SystemTime
    Public wYear         As Short
    Public wMonth        As Short
    Public wDayOfWeek    As Short
    Public wDay          As Short
    Public wHour         As Short
    Public wMinute       As Short
    Public wSecond       As Short
    Public wMilliseconds As Short
End Structure

Public Class API
    Declare Auto Sub GetSystemTime _
                Lib "Kernel32.dll" (ByRef sysTime As SystemTime)
End Class
```

The API call could then be used like this:

```
Dim st As New SystemTime()
Dim t  As New API()

t.GetSystemTime(st)

Response.Write("Month = " & st.Month)
```

C#

In C# we also specify attributes on the API arguments.

```
[StructLayout(LayoutKind.Sequential)]
public class SystemTime
{
    public short wYear;
    public short wMonth;
    public short wDayOfWeek;
```

```
    public short wDay;
    public short wHour;
    public short wMinute;
    public short wSecond;
    public short wMilliseconds;
  }

public class API
{
  [DllImport("Kernel32.dll")]
  static extern void GetSystemTime(
               [Out, MarshalAs(UnmanagedType.LPStruct)]SystemTime sysTime)
}
```

The API call could then be used like this:

```
SystemTime st = New SystemTime();
API t = New API();

t.GetSystemTime(st);

Response.Write("Month = " + st.Month);
```

Marshalling Attributes

The `StructLayout` attribute determines how the CLR aligns the members of a class, allowing them to line up with their unmanaged equivalent. The possible values are:

Type	Description
Automatic	Allows the runtime to choose the most appropriate layout.
Explicit	Used in conjunction with the `FieldOffsetAttribute` to allow exact positioning of each member.
Sequential	To layout each member sequentially, in the order they are declared.

The `MarshalAs` attribute gives the CLR explicit instructions on how the type is to be marshalled. The possible values for the `UnmanagedType` enum are:

Type	Description
AnsiBStr	Length prefixed ANSI (single byte) character string.
AsAny	The type is determined at runtime.
Bool	4-byte Boolean, where `False` is 0, and `True` is not 0.
BStr	Length prefixed Unicode (double byte) character string.
ByValArray	An array of items whose type (an `UnmanagedType` value) is defined by the `ArraySubType` field.
ByValTStr	Fixed length character array within a structure.

Type	Description
Currency	Used to marshal a `System.Decimal` type to an unmanaged `Currency` type.
CustomMarshaller	A custom marshaller type.
Error	A signed or unsigned integer, equivalent to an HRESULT.
FunctionPtr	A function pointer.
I1	A 1-byte signed integer.
I2	A 2-byte signed integer.
I4	A 4-byte signed integer.
I8	An 8-bye signed integer.
IDispatch	A COM `IDispatch` pointer.
Interface	A COM interface pointer.
IUnknown	A COM `IUnknown` pointer.
LPArray	An array whose size is determined at runtime.
LPStr	An ANSI (single byte) character string.
LPStruct	A pointer to a C-style structure.
LPTStr	A platform-dependent character string (ANSI on Win9x, Unicode on NT/Windows 2000/XP).
LPWStr	A Unicode (double byte) character string.
R4	A 4-byte floating point number.
R8	An 8-byte floating point number.
RPrecise	Size agnostic floating point number.
SafeArray	A self-describing array.
Struct	A C-style structure.
SysInt	Platform-dependent signed integer (4-bytes on 32-bit Windows, 8-bytes on 64-bit Windows).
SysUInt	Hardware natural sized unsigned integer.
TBStr	Length prefixed platform-dependent character string (ANSI on Windows 9x, Unicode on Windows NT/2000/XP).
U1	A 1-byte unsigned integer.
U2	A 2-byte unsigned integer.
U4	A 4-byte unsigned integer.

Table continued on following page

Type	Description
U8	An 8-bye unsigned integer.
VariantBool	An 8-bye unsigned integer.
VBByRefStr	Visual Basic specific array passed by reference.

Dangers of P/Invoke

When calling DLLs through the P/Invoke method, you should be aware that the CLR cannot apply any security checks to unmanaged code. With managed code we have great security control (safe types, no unmanaged memory, code security, versioning, and so on), but none of these is available in unmanaged code.

This issue shouldn't be confused with the integration of Windows Component Services security, which is covered in the **Serviced Components** section in Chapter 17.

Summary

As mentioned earlier in the chapter, there's no denying that .NET is an exceptional platform for application development. Throughout this book you've seen the great features ASP.NET provides for writing first-class applications, and how those applications will have less code, be more reusable, and provide easier maintenance. It would have been easy for Microsoft to leave it there, and just provide a great new platform, but the reality of life means that this platform has to interoperate with existing applications. There's a huge investment, not only in ASP, but also in Visual Basic and COM, and this cannot be thrown away.

So, Microsoft has provided a way to integrate that existing investment with new development on the .NET platform. In this chapter we've examined the differences between ASP and ASP.NET, and how moving from VBScript to Visual Basic.NET can be achieved with the least pain. We've also examined how to allow .NET to leverage existing COM infrastructures, as well as showing how COM can use .NET. So, if the features of .NET weren't enough to persuade you that this is a great platform, maybe the ability to run alongside existing applications will tip the balance.

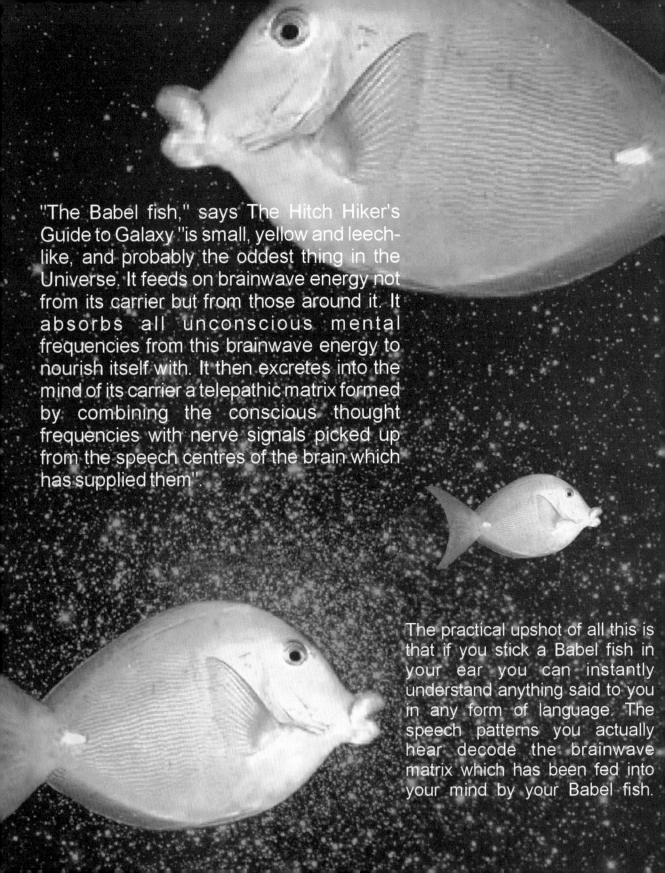

"The Babel fish," says The Hitch Hiker's Guide to Galaxy "is small, yellow and leech-like, and probably the oddest thing in the Universe. It feeds on brainwave energy not from its carrier but from those around it. It absorbs all unconscious mental frequencies from this brainwave energy to nourish itself with. It then excretes into the mind of its carrier a telepathic matrix formed by combining the conscious thought frequencies with nerve signals picked up from the speech centres of the brain which has supplied them".

The practical upshot of all this is that if you stick a Babel fish in your ear you can instantly understand anything said to you in any form of language. The speech patterns you actually hear decode the brainwave matrix which has been fed into your mind by your Babel fish.

24

Case Study – IBuyAdventure.NET

In the previous chapters of this book we've looked at the individual features of ASP.NET, such as web controls, data binding, configuration, and security. Powerful though they are, these features are like pieces of a jigsaw puzzle: the final objective is to figure out how to put them together to create the big picture.

In this chapter we're going to show you how to use ASP.NET to create a simple *n*-tier e-commerce application that is scalable, yet still relatively simple to code and understand. Along the way we'll discuss and review:

- ❑ How to design and write an *n*-tier e-commerce application on the .NET platform
- ❑ Using HTML form-based authentication to secure an e-commerce application
- ❑ Scalability considerations when creating an e-commerce site that must scale in a web farm
- ❑ Using business objects to encapsulate business logic and data access
- ❑ Using 'code behind' to share common page logic

Overview of the Application

For those who can remember back to ASP 2.0, you may recall that it shipped with a sample application called **AdventureWorks**. This application allowed you to shop for climbing equipment suitable for extreme conditions. AdventureWorks featured all the basic features of a typical e-commerce application, including product viewing and selection, user registration, and a shopping basket. In this chapter we are going to use ASP.NET to extend the AdventureWorks application into a new one called **IBuyAdventure.NET**, or IBA for short. Throughout the rest of this chapter we're going to review the code and functionality of this application, and discuss some of the design decisions we made while creating it.

> All the files for the IBuyAdventure.NET application are available for download from the Wrox website, **www.wrox.com**, and include setup and installation instructions.

IBuyAdventure.NET (IBA.NET)

If you haven't seen or used the old ASP AdventureWorks application before, don't worry. We'll be covering the IBA.NET application from the ground up, and we will only be porting a small subset of features from the original application. This approach allows us to demonstrate how to use ASP.NET to create real-word e-commerce applications, without getting distracted by too many application-specific features that would simply dilute the goals of the chapter.

> *If you do have access to the original AdventureWorks application we recommend that you spend some time comparing the original ASP code and ASP.NET code in this chapter. Sections such as the shopping basket and page layout code really show the power and simplicity of ASP.NET.*

The Target Audience

The IBA.NET application is aimed at allowing climbing enthusiasts to check out and buy the latest climbing equipment over the Internet from the comfort of their home, or tent! The application will let customers view different products grouped by category (boots, pants, tents, etc.), and enable them to add items to their shopping cart at any time. The application uses just-in-time registration, so customers can fill their shopping carts with products and not have to register or login until they actually proceed to the checkout. This approach is pretty common on most major sites like Amazon.com, and really is a must-have feature in any e-commerce application today.

Scalability – Web Solution Platform

The IBA.NET application needs to be scalable and capable of supporting hundreds, if not thousands, of concurrent users. To achieve this goal the application has been designed according to the guidelines set out by the **Microsoft Web Solution Platform** (http://microsoft.com/business/products/webplatform). The application therefore adopts an *n*-tier architecture as described by Windows DNA, where the application is split into a number of tiers for presentation, business logic, and data:

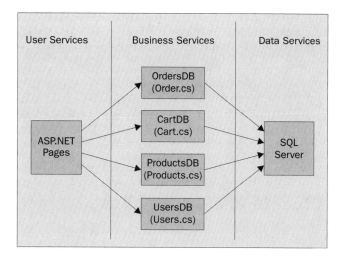

By adopting an *n*-tier approach the IBuyAdventure.NET application can easily be deployed on a single machine or multiple machines (one or more physical tiers). It should be possible, using this architecture, to deploy ASP.NET pages, .NET components, and SQL Server on their own dedicated servers. All the ASP.NET pages in IBuyAdventure.NET access the backend database using a set of .NET components that enforce business logic and encapsulate the underlying database. These components are fairly thin, and for the most part simply wrap a series of ADO.NET routines, similar to those that were covered in Chapter 8, returning a `DataSet` from the methods that are called to retrieve data.

Designing for Enterprise Scalability

To cater for enterprise-level scalability (the use of web farms) the application uses **no ASP.NET session-level state**. All state is either stored client-side within hidden fields, or in the backend SQL server database. When a user first visits the site, the ASP.NET session ID is used to track the user and any shopping items they add to their shopping cart. This information is stored in the database, and the session ID is used as the primary key to identify the user. While this is not normally recommended, the transient nature of the shopping cart data makes it pretty safe. Alternatively, we could generate a GUID and use that to track the anonymous users. After registering or logging in, any references to the ASP.NET session ID stored in the database are updated with the customer name.

By taking this approach, the application can easily be deployed in a web farm without the need to use session state that is specific to an individual server. Each web server receiving a request can simply use the session ID or user name (provided by the forms-based authentication) to look up user details and cart items from a central database.

> **"Sticky Sessions" is a term used to describe ASP/ASP.NET user sessions that must always be redirected to the same front-end web server in a web farm. Generally, sticky sessions are required in applications that depend upon state stored in the `Session` object. This is typically a bad design decision because if the machine hosting the sticky session crashes or has to be restarted, all session state is lost and the user effectively has to start again.**

Using a database to store session state (such as the shopping cart) does add a degree of overhead to our application, but it makes it more resilient in the case of failures. If a web server, or two, fails during a user's request, another server can handle it and no information will be lost. If we'd used a session-based shopping cart, our customers would lose everything created during their session if the machine hosting that session failed.

> **ASP.NET was designed around the principle that servers do fail and applications/ components do leak memory and crash from time to time. By designing the IBuyAdventure application to use no session state we work well with the ASP.NET philosophy.**

The Business Objects and Assemblies

Four business objects written in C# provide the various ASP.NET pages with all the business logic and data access code they require. As all of the .NET classes are fairly similar in terms of structure, and the ADO.NET code they use to access the SQL server database, we won't review every single method of every single object. Instead we'll look at one of the components in detail (ProductsDB) to see the basic structure of our components, and then use the ILDASM utility to show the methods and properties of each of the remaining business objects for reference purposes. As we encounter pages that use these functions we'll expand on their purposes.

ProductsDB Business Object

The ProductsDB class provides functions for retrieving product information. The complete C# code for the class is shown here:

```csharp
using System;
using System.Data;
using System.Data.SqlClient;

namespace IBuyAdventure
{
    public class ProductsDB
    {
        string m_ConnectionString;
        public ProductsDB( string dsn ) {
            m_ConnectionString = dsn;
        }

        public DataSet GetProduct(string productCode) {

            SqlConnection myConnection = new SqlConnection(m_ConnectionString);
                    SqlDataAdapter sqlAdapter1 = new SqlDataAdapter("SELECT * FROM
                        Products WHERE ProductCode='"+productCode+"'",
myConnection);

            DataSet products = new DataSet();
            sqlAdapter1.Fill(products, "products");

            return products;
        }
```

```
        public DataSet GetProducts(string category) {

            SqlConnection myConnection = new SqlConnection(m_ConnectionString);
            SqlDataAdapter sqlAdapter1 = new SqlDataAdapter("SELECT * FROM Products
                            WHERE ProductType='"+category+"'", myConnection);

            DataSet products = new DataSet();
            sqlAdapter1.Fill(products, "products");

            return products;
        }

        public DataSet GetProductCategories() {

            SqlConnection myConnection = new SqlConnection(m_ConnectionString);
            SqlDataAdapter sqlAdapter1 = new SqlDataAdapter("SELECT Distinct
    ProductType FROM Products", myConnection);

            DataSet products = new DataSet();
            sqlAdapter1.Fill(products, "products");

            return products;
        }
    }
}
```

This class has four methods, including the constructor:

- ProductsDB – Initializes the class with a data source string.

- GetProduct – Returns a dataset containing details for a single product.

- GetProducts – Returns a dataset containing the details for all products in a specified category.

- GetProductCategories – Returns a dataset containing the list of product categories.

The first three lines of the component declare the namespaces we are using:

```
using System;
using System.Data;
using System.Data.SqlClient;
```

All of our class files have these lines and they indicate that we are using the standard system namespace, the namespaces for ADO.NET, and the SQL Server-specific parts of ADO.NET (System.Data.SqlClient). We use the SQL-specific elements of ADO.NET because they provide high performance SQL Server access using TDS (Tabular Data Stream) via the classes SqlConnection and SqlDataAdapter. If we needed to support a different backend database we could recode our classes to use the OleDbConnection and OleDbDataAdapter classes, which perform database access through OLEDB. These classes were discussed in Chapter 8.

One important point to note about all of the ADO.NET code in the business object is that it does not contain any exception handlers. It is therefore up to the code that uses these classes to catch exceptions like SqlException, which can be thrown if any error occurs when performing the data access (such as the existence of duplicate rows, etc.) We haven't included any exception handling in our ASP.NET pages to keep them terse, but the basic format is shown here:

```
try
{
  someObject.SomeMethodUsingAdoDotNet()
}
catch (SqlException e)
{
  if (e.Number == 2627)
     Message.InnerHtml = "Record exists with the same primary key";
  else
     Message.InnerHtml = e.Message;
}
```

In this code we are checking for a known SQL server error code using the `SqlException Number` property. If the error code we are checking for is matched, we display a custom error message. If the known error code is not encountered we display the exception's `Message` property. The `Message` property of an exception object typically contains very descriptive and helpful text that can help resolve a problem quickly. In your applications you're unlikely to check for specific error codes unless you want to perform some type of action. For example, you may check for the error code above if you want to delete a row that may already exist.

> You should always proactively add exception-handling code to your production applications. The ADO.NET classes (including `SqlException`) are located in the assembly `System.Data.dll`. Use the IL Disassembler (**ILDASM.exe**) tool for the class browser example from the quick start to explore the classes in more detail.

The Connection String Constructor

The `ProductsDB` class has a constructor that accepts the connection string used to establish a connection to the backend database. By passing the string in like this we prevent people from forgetting to specify it, and hopefully we prevent the business objects from containing hard-coded strings, which is always bad practice.

The string passed in is stored in the member `m_ConnectionString` in the constructor code:

```
...
string m_ConnectionString;

public ProductsDB( string dsn ) {
   m_ConnectionString = dsn;
}
...
```

The `m_ConnectionString` member is then used when constructing the `SqlConnection` object:

```
public DataSet GetProduct(string productCode) {

SqlConnection myConnection = new SqlConnection(m_ConnectionString);
SqlDataAdapter sqlAdapter1 = new SqlDataAdapter("SELECT * FROM Products
            WHERE ProductCode='"+productCode+"'", myConnection);

DataSet products = new DataSet();
sqlAdapter1.Fill(products, "products");

return products;
}
```

Anybody using the `ProductsDB` business object (and any of the other business objects) must therefore pass the connection string when creating an instance of the class:

```
IBuyAdventure.ProductsDB inventory = new IBuyAdventure.ProductsDB(getConnStr());
```

The `getConnStr` function in this example retrieves the connection string from the `web.config` file:

```
<configuration>
  <appSettings>
    <add key="connectionString"
       value="server=localhost;uid=sa;pwd=;database=IBuyAdventure" />
    <add key="specialOffer" value="AW048-01" />
  </appSettings>
...
```

By using the `web.config` file to store the connection string for our components we do not have connection strings duplicated throughout business objects and ASP.NET pages, making it much easier to manage the connection string should we decide to rename the database or change any of the connection string properties.

> The `getConnStr` function is implemented using a 'code behind' class that we'll review later in this chapter. You could alternatively use an include file to define such functions in your application, but the 'code behind' approach is my preferred option.

Now we have reviewed the `ProductsDB` class lets take a brief look at a couple of ILDASM screenshots showing the methods for our other business objects.

The ILDASM Output for IBuyAdventure.dll

The follow screen shows the ILDASM output for the `IBuyAdventure.dll` assembly:

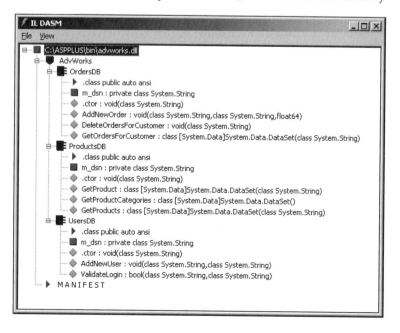

The ILDASM Output for IBuyAdventureCart.dll

The follow screen shows the ILDASM output for the IBuyAdventureCart.dll assembly:

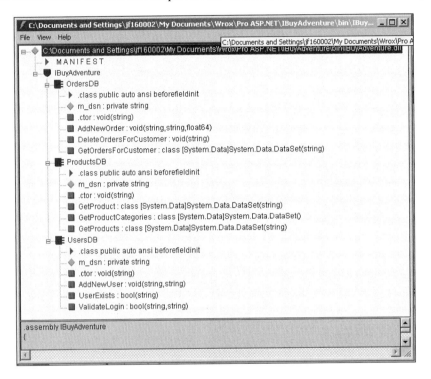

Assemblies

As we discussed in Chapter 17, assemblies are the key deployment mechanism in ASP.NET applications. The business objects for IBuyAdventure.NET are divided into two assemblies that are both dependant upon the System.Data.dll assembly, because they use ADO.NET:

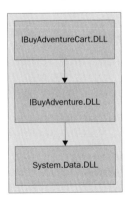

The IBuyAdventureCart.DLL contains the CartDB business object, which is used for manipulating the shopping cart. This is dependant upon the ProductsDB class contained within the IBuyAdventure.DLL assembly.

> Although assemblies have a **dll** extension, they are, for the most part, not DLLs! The extension was kept only to aid interoperability between COM+ managed code and classic COM unmanaged code.

The IBuyAdventureCart.dll assembly isn't strictly necessary, but it does show that partitioning classes into different assemblies in an ASP.NET application isn't a difficult task. The decision as to when to create assemblies will typically be influenced by a number of real-life factors:

- ❑ The functionality of the classes within the assembly – assemblies should ideally contain functionally related classes.

- ❑ The number of developers working on an application – assemblies are key units of deployment in ASP.NET applications so it makes sense for different development teams to create their own assemblies to ease co-development.

Compiling the Assemblies

All of the business object source code for the IBuyAdventure application is located in the components directory. This directory contains the file make.bat that uses the C# command-line compiler (csc.exe) to create the two assemblies:

```
csc /out:..\bin\IBuyAdventure.dll /t:library productsdb.cs ordersdb.cs usersdb.cs
/r:System.Data.dll,System.dll,System.Xml.dll
```

```
csc /out:..\bin\IBuyAdventureCart.dll /t:library cartdb.cs
/r:System.Data.dll,System.dll,System.Xml.dll /r:..\bin\IBuyAdventure.dll
```

The first statement compiles the business objects ProductsDB, OrdersDB, and UsersDB, which are respectively located within the files productdb.cs, ordersdb.cs, and usersdb.cs. The output from this statement is the IBuyAdventure.dll assembly. The second statement compiles the business CartDB, which is located in the file cartdb.cs. The output from this is the IBuyAdventureCart.dll assembly. Both assemblies are compiled into our ASP.NET application bin directory so that they are available to our ASP.NET pages.

Naming Conventions

The IBuyAdventure business objects ProductsDB, OrdersDB, and UsersDB are declared within the namespace **IBuyAdventure**. This reflects the name of the assembly they are contained in, making it easy to locate and determine what files to ship when it comes to deploying an application that contains pages that are dependant upon those classes. The same naming convention applies to the CartDB business object, which is declared within the namespace IBuyAdventureCart, and contained in the assembly IBuyAdventureCart.dll. Microsoft also uses this naming convention for most of its assemblies. The exceptions to the rule are core classes, such as strings, which tend to live in assemblies called mscor[*].dll.

The IBuyAdventure.NET Database

IBuyAdventure is driven by a SQL Server 7 or 2000 database, with four tables (Accounts, Products, ShoppingCarts, and Orders) as shown in the next diagram:

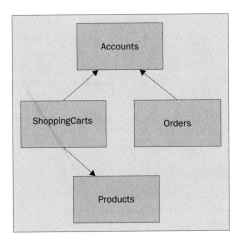

The business objects encapsulate each of these tables, so the ASP.NET pages never perform direct database access.

The Accounts Table

The Accounts table is used to store the login information for registered customers and has the following structure:

Column Name	Type	Length	Description
CustomerName	nvarchar	50	The name, or e-mail address, of the registered user. This field is used as the key against all of the tables, and should therefore be unique.
Password	nvarchar	30	The password specified by the user during their registration.

The Orders Table

The Orders table is used to store a summary of all the orders made by customers and has the following structure:

Column Name	Type	Length	Description
CustomerName	nvarchar	50	The name, or e-mail address, of the registered user. This field is used as the key against all of the tables, and should therefore be unique.
Ordered	DateTime	8	The date the order was placed.
TotalValue	float	8	The total value of the order.

When a user hits the **Confirm Order** button, and moves to the checkout page to confirm an order, an entry is added to this table. The individual items within the shopping cart are not saved to the database when an order is confirmed, although this would be a requirement for a commercial application.

The Products Table

The `Products` table contains a list of all products that a customer can purchase from IBuyAdventure. The table has the following structure:

Column Name	Type	Length	Description
ProductID	int	4	A unique ID for the product.
ProductCode	nvarchar	10	The unique code for the product.
ProductType	nvarchar	20	The category for the product.
Product Introduction Date	small datetime	4	The date when the product was first added to the catalogue.
ProductName	nvarchar	50	The name of the product shown in the catalogue.
Product Description	nvarchar	255	A description of the product.
ProductSize	nvarchar	5	The size of the product.
ProductImageURL	varchar	255	The URL of the image to display for the product.
UnitPrice	float	8	The price for this product.
OnSale	Int	4	A flag to indicate whether or not the unit price is a sale price: 1 = on sale, 0 = not on sale.
Rating	float	8	A rating out of five for this product in terms of overall quality.

IBuyAdventure has slightly less than 50 products, grouped in 12 categories.

The ShoppingCarts Table

The `ShoppingCarts` table holds all of the current product details for each user's shopping cart. The table has the following structure:

Column Name	Type	Length	Description
ShoppingCartID	Int	4	Auto-generated ID field.
ProductCode	nvarchar	10	The unique code for the product.
ProductName	Char	50	The name of the product.
Description	nvarchar	255	A description of the product.

Table continued on following page

Column Name	Type	Length	Description
UnitPrice	money	8	The price for this product.
Quantity	Int	4	The number of units wanted.
CustomerName	nvarchar	50	The name or e-mail address of the registered user that currently has the specified product in their basket. If the user is not currently registered or logged in, this is a GUID to represent the anonymous user.

Every time an item is added to a user's shopping cart, an entry is added to this table.

> The IBuyAdventure sample application does not clean up the database, or remove rows that are associated with sessions that have expired. This would need to be done in a production application. You could handle the `Session_OnEnd` event and do your database cleanup there.

The Application User Interface

When a user first visits the IBuyAdventure site they are presented with an ASP.NET page that gives them a brief introduction to the site contents, and provides all the standard promotion material, special offers, and navigation buttons you'd expect from an e-commerce application:

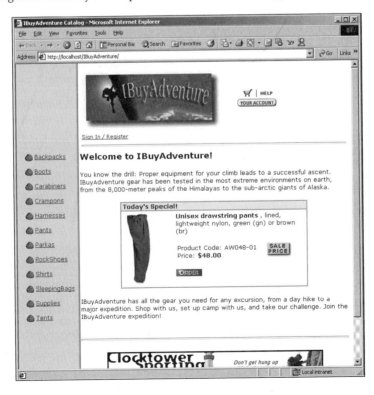

The welcome page provides a fairly intuitive user interface that should enable customers to browse, register, and buy goods. The top of the page contains the IBuyAdventure logo and navigation buttons that let the user register, login, and view their current/previous orders. The left-hand side of the screen details all of the product categories that are defined in the IBuyAdventure database. The bottom of the screen contains the product-advertising banner and the rest of the screen's middle section contains the special offers.

All pages on the site have the same basic structure as the front page, so each page uses at least three User Controls:

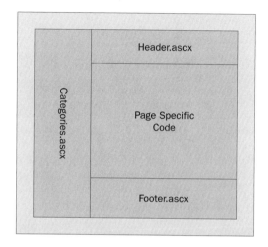

User Controls in IBuyAdventure.NET

The User Controls are defined at the top of each page using the `@Register` directive. As discussed in Chapter 4, this allows you to associate a User Control with an ASP.NET tag prefix (that is, an element **namespace**). When the ASP.NET runtime finds these special tags it knows to create the appropriate User Control and render the necessary output.

The `@Register` directives common to each page are shown here:

```
<%@ Register TagPrefix="IBA" TagName="Header" Src="UserControl\Header.ascx" %>
<%@ Register TagPrefix="IBA" TagName="Categories"
Src="UserControl\Categories.ascx" %>
<%@ Register TagPrefix="IBA" TagName="Special" Src="UserControl\Special.ascx" %>
<%@ Register TagPrefix="IBA" TagName="Footer" Src="UserControl\Footer.ascx" %>
```

The User Controls we've registered are then inserted into a page in the same way as we've seen in previous chapters:

```
<IBA:Header id="Header" runat="server" />
```

Most of the pages in the IBuyAdventure application have the same basic format, containing an HTML table. We will therefore review the complete page code for `Default.aspx` that shows all of the User Controls being declared, the language, 'code behind' page directive, the default output cache directive, and the basic HTML page structure:

```
<%@ Page Language="C#" Inherits="IBuyAdventure.PageBase"
src="components/stdpage.cs" %>
<%@ Register TagPrefix="IBA" TagName="Header" Src="UserControl\Header.ascx" %>
<%@ Register TagPrefix="IBA" TagName="Categories"
Src="UserControl\Categories.ascx" %>
<%@ Register TagPrefix="IBA" TagName="Special" Src="UserControl\Special.ascx" %>
<%@ Register TagPrefix="IBA" TagName="Footer" Src="UserControl\Footer.ascx" %>
<%@ OutputCache Duration="60" VaryByParam="*" %>

  <script language="C#" runat="server" >

    private String GetCustomerID() {

      if (Context.User.Identity.Name != "")
      {
        return Context.User.Identity.Name;
      }
      else {
      if (Session["AnonUID"] == null)
        Session["AnonUID"] = Guid.NewGuid();
        return Session["AnonUID"].ToString();
      }
    }

    void Page_Load(Object sender, EventArgs e) {

      if (Request.Params["Abandon"] == "1")
      {
        IBuyAdventure.CartDB cart = new
IBuyAdventure.CartDB(ConfigurationSettings.AppSettings["connectionString"]);
        cart.ResetShoppingCart(GetCustomerID());
        Session.Abandon();
        FormsAuthentication.SignOut();
      }

    }
  </script>

<HTML>
  <HEAD>
    <TITLE>IBuyAdventure Catalog</TITLE>
  </HEAD>

  <BODY BACKGROUND="images/back_sub.gif">
    <form runat="server">
    <FONT FACE="Verdana, Arial, Helvetica" SIZE=2>
    <TABLE BORDER=0 cellpadding=0 cellspacing=0>
        <tr>
          <td colspan=5>
            <IBA:Header id="Header" runat="server"/>
          </td>
        </tr>
```

```
<TR>
  <TD colspan=3 ALIGN=LEFT VALIGN=TOP>
    <IBA:Categories id="Categories" runat="server"/>
  </TD>
  <td>
      
  </td>
  <TD align=left valign=top>
    <h3>Welcome to IBuyAdventure!</h3>
    <p>
    <FONT FACE="Verdana, Arial, Helvetica" SIZE=2>
    You know the drill: Proper equipment for your climb leads to
    a successful ascent. IBuyAdventure gear has been tested in the
    most extreme environments on earth, from the 8,000-meter
    peaks of the Himalayas to the sub-arctic giants of Alaska.
    <p>
    <IBA:Special runat="server"/>
    <p>
    IBuyAdventure has all the gear you need for any excursion,
    from a day hike to a major expedition. Shop with us, set up
    camp with us, and take our challenge. Join the IBuyAdventure
    expedition!
    <BR>
    <BR>
    <BR>
    <IBA:footer runat="server"/>
    </FONT>
  </TD>
</TR>
</TABLE>
</FONT>
</form>
</BODY>
</HTML>
```

Although the appearance of the front page is fairly rich, the amount of code within the page is actually quite small because much of the HTML and code is encapsulated within the three User Controls. `Default.aspx`, like most pages, uses the `@OutputCache` directive to specify that pages be cached for 60 seconds. This reduces database overhead, but you should consider a couple of issues:

❏   Cached information is stored in memory so the amount of memory used by your application will be larger.

❏   The same page will be cached multiple times if it has different query parameters, so you will have to allow for that increase in the working set.

❏   If a page is cached, then all the output for that page is also cached. This might sound obvious, but it does mean that, for example, the **AdRotator** control for the Adventure Work application doesn't rotate as often as a normal site (the advert changes once every 60 seconds on the pages that use caching). If we wanted portions of the page to be cached, while the rest is rendered afresh every time, we could use fragment caching. Fragment caching works by caching the information in a User Control – so that the .aspx page is rendered each time – but when the time comes to add the contents of the User Control to a page, those contents are drawn from the cache.

1217

Only One Server-Side <form> Element

One important point to note about the default.aspx page is that it contains a single <form> element with the runat="server" attribute. This form contains the majority of the page's HTML, including all of the C. None of the User Controls have a server-side <form> element. This is important because <form> elements **cannot** be nested, so the single form must include **all** User Control code. If you attempt to define a <form> element with the runat="server" attribute anywhere within the outer <form> element, you will generate an error.

Using C# for the User Controls and Code

The first line of all our pages in IBuyAdventure contains the @Page directive:

```
<%@ Page Language="C#" Inherits="IBuyAdventure.PageBase"
        src="components/stdpage.cs" %>
```

We first saw this kind of directive in Chapter 4. The one we're using here informs the ASP.NET compiler of two key points about our pages:

❏ All of the page code is written using C#. (Although we could just as easily have used many other languages.)

❏ Each page uses 'code behind', and derives from the .NET class PageBase that provides common functionality.

The main motivation for using C# to write the IBuyAdventure application was to show that it really isn't so different from JScript and VB, and it's easy to read and understand. ASP.NET, itself, is written in C#, which indicates that it has a solid future ahead of it. Since all .NET languages compile down to MSIL before they're executed, it really doesn't matter which language the code is written in – as we said earlier in the book, you should use the one that your most comfortable with.

The 'code behind' class specified using the Inherits and Src attributes, causes the ASP.NET compiler to create a page that derives from the class PageBase rather than Page. The implementation of PageBase is very simple:

```
using System;
using System.Collections;
using System.Web.UI;
using System.Web.Security;
using System.Configuration;

namespace IBuyAdventure
{
    public class PageBase : Page
    {
        public string getConnStr() {
        string dsn;
        dsn = ConfigurationSettings.AppSettings["connectionString"];
        return dsn;
        }
    }
}
```

By deriving each page from this class we make the `getConnStr` function available within each of our ASP.NET pages. This function retrieves the database connection string from the `web.config` file, and is called in our pages when constructing business objects that connect to the backend data source. The `web.config` file is cached, so accessing it frequently in our pages should not have any detrimental effect on performance. Should you want to cache just the connection string you could use the data cache to hold it, only accessing the `web.config` file initially to retrieve the value when creating the cache entry:

```
// An alternative way of accessing the DSN via the data cache

public String getConnStrCached() {

  string connectionString;

  // Check the Cache for the ConnectionString
  connectionString = (string) Context.Cache["connectionString"];

  // If the ConnectionString is not in the cache, fetch from Config.web

  if (connectionString == null) {
    connectionString =
              ConfigurationSettings.AppSettings["connectionString"];

  //store to cache
  Cache["connectionString"] = connectionString;
  }

  // Return the Connection String

  return connectionString;
  }
```

One point to consider when using the data cache is that the values held within it **will** be updated if somebody changes the `web.config` file. ASP.NET automatically creates a new application domain and essentially restarts the web application to handle all new web requests when the `web.config` file is changed. As this results in a new data cache being created, the new connection string will be cached after the first call to `getConnStrCached`.

> As discussed in Chapter 13 applications settings should always be stored in the `appsettings` section of `web.config`. Values within that section are cached automatically.

However, should you decide to store application configuration in another location (maybe your own XML file on a central server) you can still invalidate the cache when your files change by creating a file dependency. This allows a cache item to be automatically flushed from the cache when a specific file changes:

```
//store to cache
Cache.Insert("connectionString", connectionString,
        new CacheDependency(Server.MapPath("\\someserver\myconfig.xml")));
```

File dependencies are just one of the cache dependency types ASP.NET supports. The other types supported include:

❑ **Scavenging** – flushing cache items based upon their usage, memory consumption, and rating

❑ **Expiration** – flushing cache items at a specific time or after a period of inactivity/access

❑ **File and key dependencies** – flushing cache items when either a file changes or another cache entry changes

The Specials User Control – Specials.ascx

As you might have noticed, the default.aspx page we saw earlier, which implements the welcome page, actually uses an additional User Control (UserControl\Special.ascx) to display today's special product, so the page structure is slightly more complex than it would otherwise be:

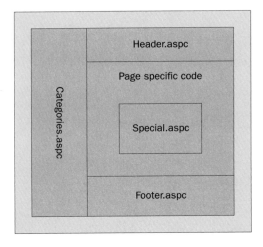

The product on offer is stored in the web.config file, making it easy for the site administrator to change the product displayed:

```
<configuration>
  <appSettings>
    <add key="connectionString"
value="server=localhost;uid=sa;pwd=;database=IBuyAdventure" />
    <add key="specialOffer" value="AW048-01" />
  </appSettings>
    ...
</configuration>
```

The special User Control reads this value in its Page_Load event handler, retrieving the product information using the ProductDB component and then updates the page using server-side controls:

```
...
<script language="C#" runat="server">

    void Page_Load(Object sender, EventArgs e) {
```

```
            // Obtain today's special product.

            IBuyAdventure.ProductsDB inventory = new
                                    IBuyAdventure.ProductsDB(getConnStr());
            string specialOffer;

            specialOffer = ConfigurationSettings.AppSettings["specialOffer"];

            DataSet specialDetails = inventory.GetProduct(specialOffer);

            // Update UI with product details

            ProductImageURL.Src = Context.Request.ApplicationPath + "/images/" +
                    (String) specialDetails.Tables[0].Rows[0]["ProductImageURL"];

            ProductName.Text = (String)
                              specialDetails.Tables[0].Rows[0]["ProductName"];

            ProductDescription.Text = (String)
                        specialDetails.Tables[0].Rows[0]["ProductDescription"];

            ProductCode.Text = (String)
                              specialDetails.Tables[0].Rows[0]["ProductCode"];

            UnitPrice.Text = String.Format("{0:C}",
                              specialDetails.Tables[0].Rows[0]["UnitPrice"]);

            OrderAnchor.HRef = Request.ApplicationPath +
                        "/ShoppingCart.aspx?ProductCode=" + (String)
                        specialDetails.Tables[0].Rows[0]["ProductCode"];

        if ( (int) specialDetails.Tables[0].Rows[0]["OnSale"] == 0 ) {
            sale.Visible = false;
            }
    }


    ...
    }
</script>

<table width=400 align=center border=1 cellpadding=0 cellspacing=0>

  <tr bgcolor="#F7EFDE">
    <td>
      <font face="verdana" size=2 ><b>  Today's Special! </b></font>
    </td>
  </tr>

  <tr>
    <td>
      <table>
        <tr>
          <td align=left valign=top width=110>
             <IMG id="ProductImageURL" runat="server">
          </td>
```

```
        <td align=left valign=top>

          <FONT SIZE=2>
            <B>
              <asp:label id="ProductName" runat="server"/>
            </B>,
            <asp:label id="ProductDescription" runat="server"/><BR>
            <BR>

            <table>
              <tr>
                <td>
                  <FONT SIZE=2>
                  Product Code: <asp:label id="ProductCode" runat="server"/>
                  <BR>
                  Price: <B><asp:label id="UnitPrice" runat="server"/></B>
                  </FONT>
                </td>

                <td>
                  
                <img src="../images/saleTag1.gif" id="sale" runat="server" >
                </td>
              </tr>
            </table>

            <br>
            <A id="OrderAnchor"
          HREF='../ShoppingCart.aspx?ProductCode=AW109-15' runat="server">
            <IMG SRC="images/order.gif" WIDTH="55" HEIGHT="15"
                                            ALT="Order" BORDER=0>

            </A>

            <br><br>
          </FONT>
        </td>
      </tr>
    </table>
  </td>
 </tr>
</table>
```

The User Control code is very simple and just updates the server controls with values from the
DataSet returned by the function call to GetProduct. The String.Format function is called using a
format string of {0:C} to show the UnitPrice as a numerical value that represents a locale-specific
currency amount.

The Categories User Controls – Categories.ascx

The product category list (`categories.ascx`), shown on the left-hand side of most of the pages (it's not on the checkout or account pages), is dynamically built using the `asp:DataList` control and the `ProductsDB` business object. The `DataSource` property for the control is set in the `Page_Load` event:

```
<%@ Control Inherits="IBuyAdventure.ControlBase" src="../components/stdctrl.cs" %>

<script language="C#" runat="server">

    void Page_Load( Object sender, EventArgs e ) {
        String dsn = getConnStr();
        IBuyAdventure.ProductsDB inventory = new
                                IBuyAdventure.ProductsDB(getConnStr());
        CategoryList.DataSource = inventory.GetProductCategories();
        CategoryList.DataBind();
    }


</script>
```

The `ItemTemplate` for this data list control is detailed in the User Control, and specifies the layout of the data:

```
<asp:datalist id="CategoryList" border="0" runat="server">

  <ItemTemplate>
    <tr>
      <td valign=top>
        <asp:image ImageURL="/IBuyAdventure/images/bullet.gif"
                              AlternateText="bullet" runat="server" />
      </td>
      <td valign=top>
        <font FACE="Verdana, Arial, Helvetica" SIZE=2>
          <asp:hyperlink NavigateURL='<%#
          "/IBuyAdventure/catalogue.aspx?ProductType=" +
          DataBinder.Eval( Container.DataItem, "ProductType" )%>'
          Text='<%# DataBinder.Eval( Container.DataItem, "ProductType" )%>'
          runat="server"/>
        </font>
      </td>
    </tr>

  </ItemTemplate>

</asp:datalist>
```

The `asp:DataList` control was first seen in Chapter 7. It is bound to a data source of items in a collection, and renders the `ItemTemplate` for each of them.

The `asp:DataList` control outputs an HTML table; so the `ItemTemplate` we've written outputs a `<tr>` element containing two columns (`<td>` elements), which ensure the table and page are correctly rendered. The first column contains an `asp:image` control that renders the small 'rock' bullet bitmap, the second column contains an `asp:hyperlink` control that has two fields (`NavigateURL` and `Text`). These fields are bound to the current row of the `DataSet` returned by the `ProductDB` business object.

The hyperlink rendered in `ItemTemplate` allows the user to view the product details for a specific category. The `NavigateURL` attribute is a calculated field consisting of a fixed URL (`/IBuyAdventure/catalogue.aspx`) and a dynamic query parameter, `ProductType`, whose value is set to equal the `ProductType` field in the current dataset row. Finally, the `Text` attribute is a simple attribute with its value also assigned to equal the `ProductType` field in the current dataset row.

The `DataBinder` class is used to retrieve the values stored in these properties. In case you're wondering, the `DataBinder` class is just a 'helper' class provided by ASP.NET to keep our code simpler (fewer casts) and more readable, especially if we also need to format a property.

Alternatively, we could also have directly accessed the current `DataSet` row ourselves and retrieved the `ProductType` value using the following code:

```
((DataRowView)Container.DataItem)["ProductType"].ToString()
```

This format is slightly more complex, but may be preferable if you're happy using casts and prefer the style. One advantage of this code is that it is early bound, so it will execute faster than the late-bound `DataBinder` syntax.

When one of the product category hyperlinks is clicked, the ASP.NET page `Catalogue.aspx` is displayed:

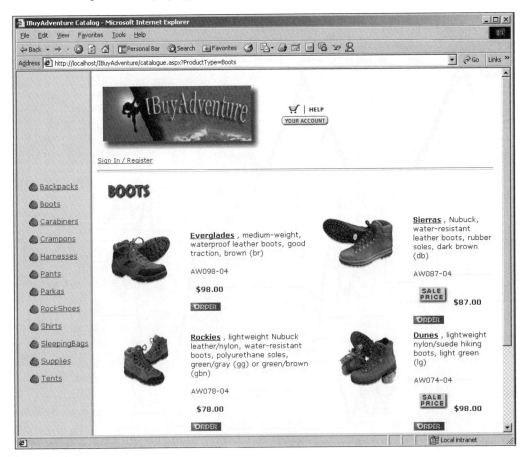

This page shows the products for the selected category by using the `ProductType` query string parameter in the `Page_Load` event to filter the results returned from the `ProductDB` component:

```
void Page_Load(Object sender, EventArgs e) {

    String productType = Request.Params["ProductType"];
    CatalogueSectionImage.Src = "images/hd_" + productType + ".gif";

    IBuyAdventure.ProductsDB inventory = new
                        IBuyAdventure.ProductsDB(getConnStr());
    MyList.DataSource = inventory.GetProducts(productType);
    MyList.DataBind();
}
```

A design issue here is that we have used a hyperlink, and not a postback, to change the products shown.

Each of the products displayed for the selected category has a number of details:

- ❑ **Product Name** – the name of the product (Everglades, Rockies, etc.)

- ❑ **Product Info** – facts about the product that will interest customers and help them make purchasing decisions (whether the item is waterproof, its color, etc.)

- ❑ **Product Code** – the unique ID for the product across the site

- ❑ **Price** – the price of the product

- ❑ **On Sale** – if the price is reduced, the 'SALE PRICE' image is displayed

- ❑ **Order Button** – to add the product to the shopping basket the user clicks the 'Order' image

The main body of this page is also generated using an `asp:DataList` control, by setting the data source in the `Page_Load` event and using an `ItemTemplate` to control the rendering of each product. Unlike the category's User Control, the `asp:datalist` on this page takes advantage of the `RepeatDirection` and `RepeatColumns` attributes:

```
<asp:datalist id="MyList" BorderWidth=0 RepeatDirection=vertical RepeatColumns=2
runat="server" OnItemCreated="ItemCreated">
```

These attributes automatically perform the page layout for us, and make the application look professional. All we do in our `ItemTemplate` is define a two-column table that contains the image in the first column, and the details in the second. The `asp:DataList` control then works out how to flow the rows – so changing the page to use horizontal flowing is simply a matter of changing one attribute value:

```
<asp:datalist id="MyList" BorderWidth=0 RepeatDirection=horizontal
RepeatColumns=2 runat="server" OnItemCreated="DataList_ItemCreated">
```

Now, we get a different layout of the items:

Without the `asp:DataList` control providing this functionality, we'd have to have written a not inconsiderable amount of code ourselves to achieve this.

> *If you review the original ASP Adventure Works application, you'll see it required around 100 lines of code in total.*

When an item is in a sale this bitmap is shown:

To determine whether or not this image is displayed, we will handle the `ItemCreated` event of the `asp:datalist` object. This event is raised whenever an item in the datalist is created. We do this by setting the `Visible` property of the `saleItem` server control (our img element) to `false` if the `OnSale` property is equal to zero. In order to get a reference to the `saleItem` control, we need to use the `FindControl` method of the `datalist` item object. This method will search all the child controls of the `datalist` item being added to the page so we can get a reference to the `saleItem` control of that item.

```
    ...
        void DataList_ItemCreated(Object sender , DataListItemEventArgs e ) {

      DataRowView myRowView;
      DataRow myRow;

      myRowView = (DataRowView) e.Item.DataItem;
      myRow = myRowView.Row;

      if  ( (int) myRow["OnSale"] == 0 )
        e.Item.FindControl("saleItem").Visible = false;
    ...

  <img src="images/saleTag1.gif" id="saleItem" runat="server" />

    ...
```

By setting the `Visible` property to `false`, the ASP.NET runtime does not render the control or any child controls – as it would if we'd used something like a `<span>` element to contain the image and text. This is a very powerful approach for preventing partial page generation, and is much cleaner than the inline `if...then` statements that classic ASP required us to write.

An advantage of this approach is that the code is somewhat cleaner and easier to maintain, but, more importantly, any changes made by the code to controls that persist their state survive postbacks. As `inline` is executed during the render phase of ASP.NET page, viewstate (state saved by the page and/or any child controls) has **already** been saved, so any changes made in inline code will not be round-tripped during a postback. The reason for using inline code in this chapter is to show that while ASP.NET applications can still make use of inline code, better (and sometimes mandatory) alternative approaches exist that allow you to maintain a much stronger separation of code from content.

Product Details

For each product shown in the `catalogue.aspx` page, the product name is rendered as a hyperlink. If a customer finds the product overview interesting, they can click the link to see more details about it (admittedly there is not a great deal of extra detail in our sample application):

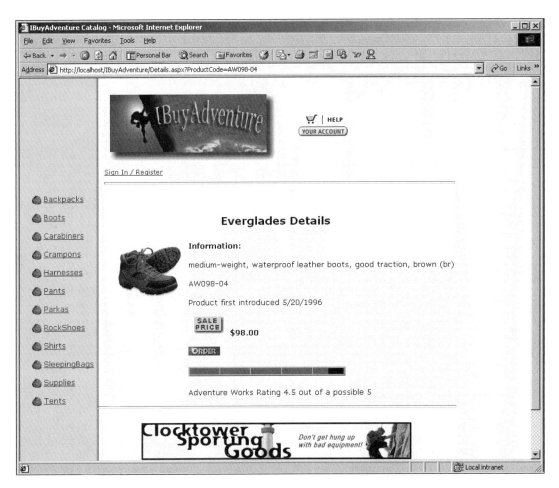

The additional information on this screen includes the date when the product was first introduced and a product rating assigned by the reviewer team at IBuyAdventure. The team always tests out the gear it sells first hand and assigns a rating. The Rating field in the Products table determines the rating bar shown for each product. The bar itself is generated using a custom server control written for IBuyAdventure. The source code for this rating meter control is located in the Controls directory, and should be easily understood if you have read Chapter 6. Like the Components directory, the Controls directory contains a make.bat file for building the control.

The control is registered and assigned an element name (tag prefix) at the top of the details page:

```
<%@ Register TagPrefix="Wrox" Namespace="WroxControls" %>
```

Although it only shows a single product, the details.aspx page still uses an asp:DataList control. The motivation for this was that future versions of IBuyAdventure could potentially allow multiple products to have their details viewed at the same time for product comparison purposes. The rating control is therefore declared within the ItemTemplate for the asp:DataList control as the Score property, using the field named Rating in the database table:

```
<Wrox:RatingMeter runat="server"
Score=<%#(double)DataBinder.Eval(Container.DataItem, "Rating")%> Votes=1
MaxRating=5
CellWidth=51
CellHeight=10 />
```

While the properties of the rating control may seem a little confusing at first, you should understand that it is a generic control that suitable for many tasks. If you have seen the ASPToday.com article rating system it will probably makes sense, but if not, consider the case where 200 people have rated a product, so you have 200 votes. For each vote a score between 0 and `MaxRating` is assigned, and the `Score` attribute reflects the total sum for all votes.

The rating control actually supports more functionality than is needed by the IBuyAdventure application, so we set the **Votes** property to 1, since only a single staff member rates the products. The idea is that future versions of the application will support customer ratings and reviews.

We won't be covering the functionality of the rating control any further in this chapter, so to help you out, here is a run down of the properties that will hopefully set you in the right direction:

Property	Description
CellWidth	The size of each cell within the bar.
MaxRating	The maximum rating that can be assigned by a single vote. This value determines the number of cells that the bar has.
CellHeight	The height of each cell.
Votes	The number of votes that have been cast.
Score	The current score or rating.

The Shopping Cart

When surfing through the site, a customer can add items to their shopping basket at any time by hitting the **Order** image hyperlink:

This image is inserted into the `catalogue.aspx` page as it is created, and clicking it results in the browser navigating to the `ShoppingCart.aspx` page:

```
<a href='<%# DataBinder.Eval(Container.DataItem, "ProductCode",
"ShoppingCart.aspx?ProductCode={0}") %>'>
   <img src="images/order.gif" WIDTH="55" HEIGHT="15" ALT="Order" BORDER=0>
</a>
```

The page looks like this:

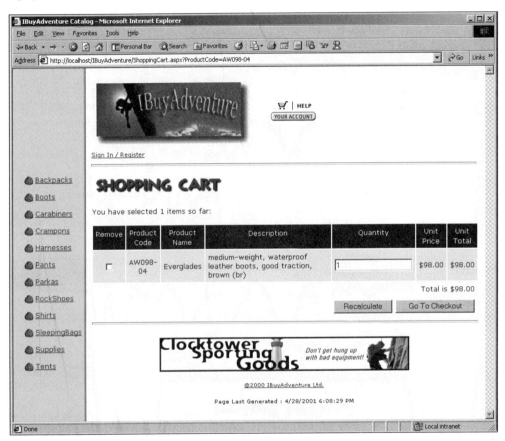

When the `ShoppingCart.aspx` page is being generated, the `Page_Load` event checks to see if a new product is being added to the cart by looking for a `Request` parameter called `ProductCode`. This is added to the URL as a query string by the code in the `Catalogue.aspx` page (as shown earlier). The `AddShoppingCartItem` function of the `CartDB` object is then invoked to add it to the shopping cart for the current user.

The Page_Load event handler for the `ShoppingCart.aspx` page is shown here:

```
void Page_Load(Object sender, EventArgs e) {

    IBuyAdventure.CartDB cart = new IBuyAdventure.CartDB(getConnStr());

        if (Request.Params["ProductCode"] != null) {
    cart.AddShoppingCartItem(GetCustomerID(),Request.Params["ProductCode"]);
        }

        if (Page.IsPostBack == false) {
            PopulateShoppingCartList();
            UpdateSelectedItemStatus();
        }
    }
```

The `ProductCode` parameter is optional because the shopping cart can also be displayed by clicking on the shopping cart symbol shown in the navigation bar. If this is the method by which the page is accessed, then we don't want to add any items to the shopping cart. The `CustomerID` function used here returns the unique ID for the current customer, which is then passed as a parameter to the `AddShoppingCartItem` function. If the customer has not registered and logged in, the ID returned by the `CustomerID` function is the current ASP.NET session ID; otherwise it is the current user name:

```
String GetCustomerID() {
  if (User.Identity.Name != "") {
    return Context.User.Identity.Name;
  }
  else {
    return Session.SessionID;
  }
}
```

The implementation of the `AddShoppingCartItem` method of the `CartDB` business object is worth reviewing at this point, because it contains two interesting sections of code:

```
public void AddShoppingCartItem(string customerName, string productCode) {

    DataSet previousItem = GetShoppingCartItem(customerName, productCode);

    if (previousItem.Tables[0].Rows.Count > 0) {
                UpdateShoppingCartItem((int)
                previousItem.Tables[0].Rows[0]["ShoppingCartID"],
                ((int)previousItem.Tables[0].Rows[0]["Quantity"]) + 1);
    }
    else {

    IBuyAdventure.ProductsDB products;
    products = new IBuyAdventure.ProductsDB(m_ConnectionString);
    DataSet productDetails = products.GetProduct(productCode);

    String description = (String)
                productDetails.Tables[0].Rows[0]["ProductDescription"];
    String productName = (String)
                productDetails.Tables[0].Rows[0]["ProductName"];
    double unitPrice = (double)
                productDetails.Tables[0].Rows[0]["UnitPrice"];
    String insertStatement = "INSERT INTO ShoppingCarts (ProductCode,
        ProductName, Description, UnitPrice, CustomerName,
        Quantity) values ('" + productCode + "', @productName,
        @description, " + unitPrice + ", '" + customerName + "' , 1)";

    SqlConnection myConnection = new SqlConnection(m_ConnectionString);
    SqlCommand myCommand = new SqlCommand(insertStatement, myConnection);

    myCommand.Parameters.Add(new SqlParameter("@ProductName",
                                SqlDbType.VarChar, 50));
    myCommand.Parameters["@ProductName"].Value = productName ;

    myCommand.Parameters.Add(new SqlParameter("@description",
                                SqlDbType.VarChar, 255));
    myCommand.Parameters["@description"].Value = description;
```

```
        myCommand.Connection.Open();
        myCommand.ExecuteNonQuery();
        myCommand.Connection.Close();
    }
}
```

The first interesting point about the code is that it checks if the item is already in the shopping cart by calling GetShoppingCartItem, and if it does already exist it simply increases the quantity for that item and updates it in the database using the UpdateShoppingCartItem function.

The second interesting point comes about because the ADO.NET code that adds a new cart item uses the SqlCommand class. Since the IBuyAdventure product descriptions can contain single quotes, we need to ensure that any quotes within the description do not conflict with the quotes used to delimit the field. To do this we use the SqlCommand object to execute our query, making use of parameters in our SQL, like @description, to avoid any conflict. The values for the parameters are then specified using the Parameters collections of the SqlCommand object:

```
myCommand.Parameters.Add(new SqlParameter("@description",
                                        SqlDbType.VarChar, 255));
```

Once the SQL statement is built, the command object can be connected, the statement executed, and then disconnected:

```
        myCommand.Connection.Open();
        myCommand.ExecuteNonQuery();
        myCommand.Connection.Close();
```

Displaying the Shopping Cart and Changing an Order

The shopping cart allows customers to specify a quantity for each product in the cart, and displays the price per item, and total price for the quantity ordered. At any time, a customer can change the order quantity or remove one or more items from the cart by checking the **Remove** box and clicking **Recalculate**. An item will also be removed if the customer enters a quantity of zero.

To implement this functionality we have used the asp:Repeater control. Implementing this functionality in straight ASP isn't an easy task, and requires significant code. In ASP.NET it's fairly simple.

The asp:Repeater control was used as the base for building the shopping cart as it doesn't need to use any of the built-in selection and editing functionality provided by the other list controls such as the asp:DataList and asp:DataGrid. All of the items are always checked and processed during a postback, and the cart contents (the dataset bound to the asp:Repeater control) is always generated during each postback.

The asp:Repeater control is also 'lookless' (it only generates the HTML element that we specify using templates), which fits in well with the design our shopping cart page – we don't need a complete table to be generated by the control (the table's start and header rows are part of the static HTML).

Data Source/HTML/ASPX for the Shopping Cart

The shopping cart data source is provided by the `CartDB` component, which is bound to the `myList` `asp:repeater` control:

```
void PopulateShoppingCartList() {

    IBuyAdventure.CartDB cart = new IBuyAdventure.CartDB(getConnStr());

    DataSet ds = cart.GetShoppingCartItems(GetCustomerID());

    MyList.DataSource = ds;
    MyList.DataBind();
    ...
```

The HTML used to render the shopping cart, including the `ItemTemplate` rendered for each item in the `MyList.DataSource` is shown next, although some parts of the HTML page formatting (for example the font settings) have been removed to keep it short and easily readable:

```
<table colspan="8" cellpadding="5" border="0" valign="top">
<tr valign="top">
  <td align="center" bgcolor="#800000">Remove</td>
  <td align="center" bgcolor="#800000">Product Code</td>
  <td align="center" bgcolor="#800000">Product Name</td>
  <td align="center" bgcolor="#800000" width="250">Description</td>
  <td align="center" bgcolor="#800000">Quantity</td>
  <td align="center" bgcolor="#800000">Unit Price</td>
  <td align="center" bgcolor="#800000">Unit Total</td>
</tr>

<asp:Repeater id="MyList" runat="server">

  <itemtemplate>
    <tr>
    <td align="center" bgcolor="#f7efde">
      <asp:checkbox id="Remove" runat="server" />
    </td>
    <td align="center" bgcolor="#f7efde">
      <input id="ShoppingCartID" type="hidden" value=
               '<%#DataBinder.Eval(Container.DataItem,"ShoppingCartID",
               "{0:g}")%>'
        runat="server" />
      <%#DataBinder.Eval(Container.DataItem, "ProductCode")%>
    </td>
    <td align="center" bgcolor="#f7efde">
      <%#DataBinder.Eval(Container.DataItem, "ProductName")%>
    </td>
    <td align="center" bgcolor="#f7efde">
      <%#DataBinder.Eval(Container.DataItem, "Description")%>
    </td>
    <td align="center" bgcolor="#f7efde">
      <asp:textbox id="Quantity"
               text='<%#DataBinder.Eval(Container.DataItem,
               "Quantity", "{0:g}")%>' width="30" runat="server" />
```

```
            </td>
            <td align="center" bgcolor="#f7efde">
              <asp:label id="UnitPrice"
                runat="server">
                <%#DataBinder.Eval(Container.DataItem, "UnitPrice", "{0:C}")%>
              </asp:label>
            </td>
            <td align="center" bgcolor="#f7efde">
              <%# String.Format("{0:C}",
                (((int)DataBinder.Eval(Container.DataItem, "Quantity"))
                * ((double) DataBinder.Eval(Container.DataItem, "UnitPrice")) )) %>
            </td>
          </tr>
        </itemtemplate>

    </asp:Repeater>

    <tr>
      <td colspan="6"></td>
      <td colspan="2" align="right">
      Total is <%=String.Format(fTotal.ToString(), "{0:C}") %>
      </td>
    </tr>
    <tr>
      <td colspan="8" align="right">
    <asp:button text="Recalculate" OnClick="Recalculate_Click" runat="server" />
    <asp:button text="Go To Checkout" OnClick="Checkout_Click" runat="server" />
      </td>
    </tr>
    </table>
```

The code shown above is similar to that which we've seen earlier, so it should be easy to follow. The important point to note, is that all the fields that need to be available when a postback occurs are marked with the ID and `runat="server"` attributes. When the customer causes a postback by pressing the **Recalculate** button, the ASP.NET page can access the **Remove** checkbox control, the database cart ID hidden field control, and the **Quantity** field control for each list item – and update the database accordingly.

For each row in the `ShoppingCarts` table for this customer, the `asp:Repeater` control will contain a list item containing these three controls – which can be programmatically accessed:

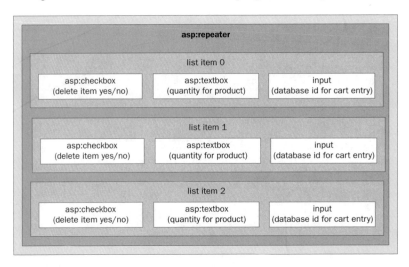

To associate each list item within the `asp:Repeater` control with a specific database cart item, a hidden field is used to store the unique ID for the entry:

```
<input id="ShoppingCartID" type=hidden
    value='<%#DataBinder.Eval(Container.DataItem, "ShoppingCartID", "
    {0:g}") %>' runat="server">
```

As discussed earlier, the contents of the shopping cart are always stored in the SQL server table named `ShoppingCarts`, and manipulated using the business object named `CartDB`. To populate the shopping cart with items, the ASP.NET page invokes the `PopulateShoppingCartList` function. This occurs when the page is loaded for the first time (that is, when `Page.PostBack` is `false`), and after each postback that leads to the database being modified – items added, deleted, or changed. To retrieve the cart items and data bind the `asp:Repeater` control, this function uses the `GetShoppingCartItems` method of the `CartDB` object:

```
void PopulateShoppingCartList() {

    IBuyAdventure.CartDB cart = new IBuyAdventure.CartDB(getConnStr());

    DataSet ds = cart.GetShoppingCartItems(GetCustomerID());

    MyList.DataSource = ds;
    MyList.DataBind();
    ...
```

Once the list is bound, the dataset is then enumerated to calculate the total value of the items within the cart:

```
DataTable dt;
dt = ds.Tables[0];

int lIndex;
double UnitPrice;
int Quantity;

for ( lIndex =0; lIndex < dt.Rows.Count; lIndex++ ) {

    UnitPrice = (double) dt.Rows[lIndex]["UnitPrice"];

    Quantity = (int) dt.Rows[lIndex]["Quantity"];

    if ( Quantity > 0 ) {
        fTotal += UnitPrice * Quantity;
    }
  }
}
```

The total stored in the `fTotal` parameter is defined as a `Double` earlier in the page definition:

```
// Total for shopping basket
double fTotal = 0;
```

and then referenced by inline code that executes just after the `asp:Repeater` control:

```
    . . .
  </asp:repeater>
  <tr>
    <td colspan="6"></td><td colspan="2" align="right">
        Total is <%=String.Format("{0:C}", fTotal ) %>
    </td>
  </tr>
    . . .
```

When a customer changes the order quantity for products in their cart, or marks items to be removed, they click the **Recalculate** button. This button was created using the `asp:button` control with its `OnClick` event wired up to the `Recalculate_Click` function:

```
<asp:button text="Recalculate" OnClick="Recalculate_Click" runat="server" />
```

The `Recalculate_Click` function updates the database based on the changes the user has made to the quantities, and the items they've added or deleted. It then retrieves the updated cart items from the database, rebinds the repeater control to the updated data set, and finally creates a status method informing the user how many items (if any) are currently in the cart. These functions are, in turn, delegated within the event handler to three different functions:

```
void Recalculate_Click(Object sender, EventArgs e) {

  // Update Shopping Cart
  UpdateShoppingCartDatabase();

  // Repopulate ShoppingCart List
  PopulateShoppingCartList();

  // Change status message
  UpdateSelectedItemStatus();
}
```

The `UpdateShoppingCartDatabase` method is called first in the event handler, when the postback data for the `asp:Repeater` control describing the cart, and any changes made, will be available. The function can therefore access this postback data before any database updates and deletions that may be required. Next, calling `PopulateShoppingCartList` causes the shopping cart to be re-read from the database and bound to the `asp:Repeater` control. This will cause the page to render an updated view of the cart to the user.

To perform the required database updates, the `UpdateShoppingCartDatabase` function iterates through each of the list items (the rows) within the `asp:Repeater` control and checks each item to see if it should be deleted or modified:

```
void UpdateShoppingCartDatabase() {

  IBuyAdventure.ProductsDB inventory = new
                          IBuyAdventure.ProductsDB(getConnStr());
  IBuyAdventure.CartDB cart = new IBuyAdventure.CartDB(getConnStr());

  for (int i=0; i<MyList.Items.Count; i++) {
    TextBox quantityTxt = (TextBox)
                          MyList.Items[i].FindControl("Quantity");
    CheckBox remove = (CheckBox)
```

```
                               MyList.Items[i].FindControl("Remove");
        HtmlInputHidden shoppingCartIDTxt = (HtmlInputHidden)
                               MyList.Items[i].FindControl("ShoppingCartID");

        int Quantity = Int32.Parse(quantityTxt.Text);

      if (remove.Checked == true || Quantity == 0) {
        cart.DeleteShoppingCartItem(Int32.Parse(shoppingCartIDTxt.Value));
      }
      else {
        cart.UpdateShoppingCartItem(Int32.Parse(shoppingCartIDTxt.Value),
        Quantity );
      }
    }
}
```

This code takes a brute-force approach by updating every item in the shopping cart that isn't marked for deletion. In a commercial application, you should consider having a hidden field that stores the original quantity and only updates items when the two quantity fields differ. This could potentially reduce database I/O considerably if you have users who keep changing their order quantities and deleting items. Another alternative would be to handle the `OnChange` events for the controls in the list, and only update the database when events are invoked.

Checkout Processing and Security

When a customer is ready to commit to purchasing the goods that are currently in their shopping cart, they can click the Go to Checkout button in the shopping cart page, or click the shopping basket image located on the navigation bar. The security system used in IBuyAdventure takes advantage of forms-based authentication (also called cookie-based security), as introduced in Chapter 14. When a customer hits any of the pages that require authentication, if they haven't already signed in, the page `login.aspx` is displayed:

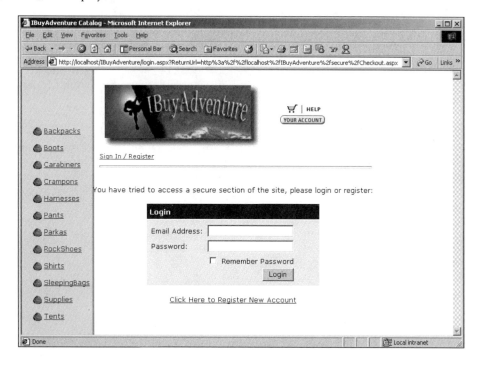

The ASP.NET runtime knows to display this page if a user is not logged in because all pages that require authentication are located in a directory called SECURE. It contains a web.config file, which specifies anonymous access is **not** allowed:

```
<configuration>
  <system.web>
    <authorization>
      <deny users="?" />
    </authorization>
  </system.web>
</configuration>
```

Remember that '?' means 'anonymous users'.

Using a specific directory to contain secure items is a simple yet flexible way of implementing security in ASP.NET applications. When the ASP.NET runtime determines that an anonymous user is trying to access a page in a secure directory of our application, it knows which page to display because the web.config file located in the root directory has a cookie element with a loginurl attribute that specifies it:

```
<configuration>
  <system.web>
    <authentication mode="Forms">
      <forms name=".ibuyadventurecookie" loginUrl="login.aspx"
                                   protection="All" timeout="60">
      </forms>
    </authentication>
    <authorization>
      <allow users="*" />
    </authorization>
  </system.web>
</configuration>
```

This configuration basically says if the .ibuyadventurecookie cookie is present and it has not been tampered with, the user has been authenticated and so can access secure directions, if authorized; if not present, redirect to the URL specified by loginurl.

Forms-Based Authentication in Web Farms

For forms-based authentication to work within a web farm environment, the decryptionkey attribute of the cookie element must be set, and not left blank or specified as the default value of autogenerate. The decryptionkey attribute should be set the same on all machines within the farm. The length of the string is 16 characters (as in the example above) for DES encryption (56/64 bit), or 48 characters for Triple-DES encryption (128 bit). If you do use the default value it will cause a different encryption string to be generated by each machine in the farm, and cause the session authentication to fail between different machines as a user moves between servers. If this happens a CryptographicException will be thrown and the user will be presented with a screen saying the data is bad, or could not be decoded.

The Login.aspx Page Event Handlers

The Login button on the login form is created using an `asp:button` control, which has the `OnClick` event wired up to the `LoginBtn_Click` event handler:

```
...
<td colspan="2" align="right">
  <asp:button Text=" Login "OnClick="LoginBtn_Click" runat="server" />
</td>
```

When the button is clicked the `LoginBtn_Click` event handler is invoked. It validates the user, and then redirects them to the original page. The validation and redirection code is shown here:

```
void LoginBtn_Click(Object sender, EventArgs e)
{
   IBuyAdventure.UsersDB users = new IBuyAdventure.UsersDB(getConnStr());
      IBuyAdventure.CartDB cart = new IBuyAdventure.CartDB(getConnStr());

      if (users.ValidateLogin(UserName.Text, Password.Text)) {

         cart.MigrateShoppingCartItems(Session.SessionID, UserName.Text);
         FormsAuthentication.RedirectFromLoginPage(UserName.Text,
                                                Persist.Checked);
      }
      else {
         Message.Text = "Login failed, please check your details and
                                              try again.";
      }
   }
```

The code initially creates the two business objects that are required, using the 'code behind' function `getConnStr` to collect details of the data source to connect to. Once the `UsersDB` object is created, its `ValidateLogin` method is invoked to determine if the user credentials are OK (the user details are stored in the `Account` table rather than the `web.config` file). If the details are invalid, the `Text` property of the `Message` control is updated to show the error. If the login is successful, the following steps occur:

1. The client is marked as authenticated by calling the `RedirectFromLoginPage` method of the `FormsAuthentication` object, which we discussed in Chapter 14.

2. This causes the cookie named `.ibuyadventurecookie` to be sent back to the client, so we know from here on in that the client has been authenticated.

3. The user is redirected back to the page that initially caused the login form to be displayed.

If a customer has previously registered, they can login via the Login page. This will then redirect them back to the original page that caused the Login page to be displayed. This redirection code is actually implemented by the Login page we've created, and does require some extra work on our part. We'll see this next.

Handling Page Return Navigation During Authentication

When the ASP.NET runtime determines that a secure item has been accessed, it will redirect the user to our Login page, and include a query string parameter named ReturnURL. As the name suggests, this is the page that we will redirect the user to once we are happy that they should be allowed access to it. When displaying our page, we need to save this value, as it will be lost during the postbacks where we validate the user. The approach used in our page is to store the value in a hidden field during the Page_Load event:

```
void Page_Load(Object sender, EventArgs e)
{
  // Store Return Url in Page State
  if (Request.QueryString["ReturnUrl"] != null)
  {
      ReturnUrl.Value = Request.QueryString["ReturnUrl"];
  ((HyperLink)RegisterUser).NavigateUrl = "Register.aspx?ReturnUrl=" +
                                                  ReturnUrl.Value;

  }
}
```

The hidden field is defined as part of the Login form, and includes the runat="server" attribute so that we can programmatically access it in our event handlers:

```
<input type="hidden" value="/advworks/default.aspx"
       id="ReturnUrl" runat="server" />
```

We've given the hidden field a default value, as it is possible for the user to go directly to the login page via the navigation bar. Without a default value, the redirection code that is executed after login would not work.

So, when the customer clicks the Login button, we can validate their details and then redirect them to the page whose value is stored in the ReturnUrl hidden control.

First Time Customer – Registration

If a customer has not registered with our application before, they can click the Registration hyperlink, and will be presented with a user registration form to fill in:

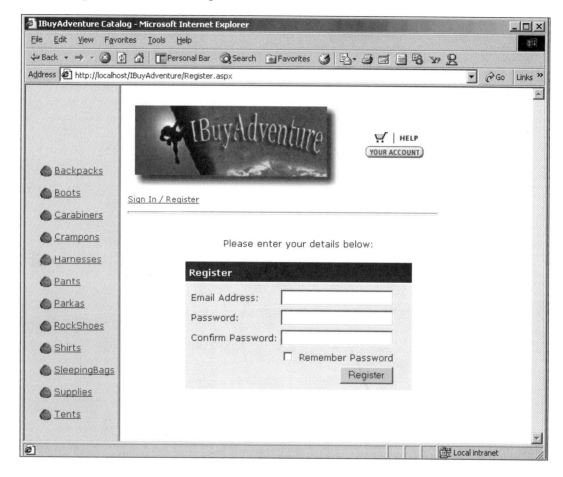

We've kept the form simple for this case study, and only ask for an e-mail address and password. In a commercial application, this form would probably include additional information such as the name and address of the customer.

As the registration page (`Register.aspx`) is opened from a hyperlink in the login page (`login.aspx`), we have to ensure that we pass on the `ReturnUrl` parameter – so that the registration page knows where to redirect the user once they have completed the form. To do this we dynamically create the hyperlink in the registration form during the `Page_Load` event of the login page:

```
((HyperLink)RegisterUser).NavigateUrl =
                    "Register.aspx?ReturnUrl=" + ReturnUrl.Value;
```

We also need to make sure that the hyperlink is marked as a server control in the `login.aspx` page:

```
...
<font size="2">
<asp:HyperLink NavigateUrl="Register.aspx" id="RegisterUser"
    runat="server" />
  Click Here to Register New Account
</asp:hyperlink>
</font>
...
```

Those of you with a keen eye will have spotted that customers can actually login at any time by clicking the 'Sign In or Register' hyperlink located in the page header. Once a user is successfully authenticated, this hyperlink changes to say 'Sign Out':

The sign in or out code is implemented in the header User Control (`UserControl/header.ascx`) where the `Page_Load` event handler dynamically changes the text of the `signInOutMsg` control, depending on the authentication state of the current user:

```
<%@ Import Namespace="System.Web.Security" %>
<script language="C#" runat="server">

    private void Page_Load( Object Sender, EventArgs e ) {
        updateSignInOutMessage();
    }

    private void SignInOut( Object Sender, EventArgs e ) {

        if ( Context.User.Identity.Name != "" ) {
           IBuyAdventure.CartDB cart = new
IBuyAdventure.CartDB(ConfigurationSettings.AppSettings["connectionString"]);
           cart.ResetShoppingCart(GetCustomerID());
           FormsAuthentication.SignOut();
           Response.Redirect("/IBuyAdventure/default.aspx");
        }
        else {
           Response.Redirect("/IBuyAdventure/login.aspx");
        }
    }

    private void updateSignInOutMessage() {

        if ( Context.User.Identity.Name != "" ) {
           signInOutMsg.Text = "Sign Out (" + Context.User.Identity.Name+ ")";
        }
        else {
           signInOutMsg.Text = "Sign In / Register";
        }
    }

}
</script>
...
```

The `updateSignInOutMessage` function actually updates the text, and the `SignInOut` method is called when the user clicks the sign in/out text. If a user is signing out, the `CookieAuthentication.SignOut` function is called to invalidate the authentication cookie. If signing in, the user is redirected to the login page.

The `SignInOut` code is wired up as part of the control declaration:

```
...
<td>
   <asp:linkbutton style="font:8pt verdana" id="signInOutMsg"
                                       runat="server" OnClick="SignInOut" />
</td>
...
```

Checkout Processing

Once a customer is authenticated, they are taken to the checkout page (`secure/checkout.aspx`), presented with their shopping list, and asked to confirm that the list is correct:

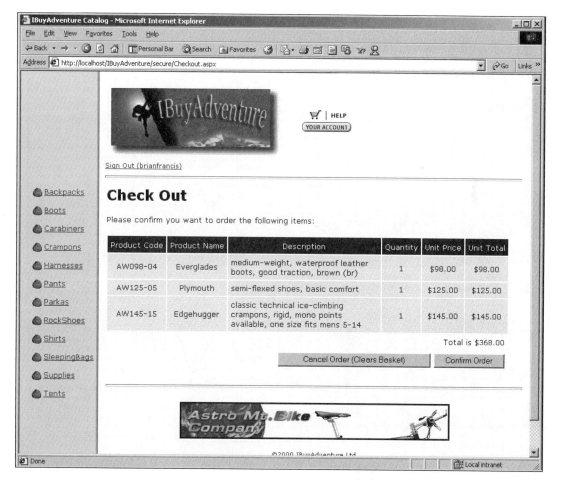

The checkout page uses very similar code to the `ShoppingCart.aspx` page, except we have omitted the controls that allow the customer to remove items or edit the order quantities. If the customer confirms an order by pressing the Confirm Order button, a new database record is created for the order containing the date, and the total order value. Then the current shopping basket is cleared, and the customer is presented with a confirmation screen:

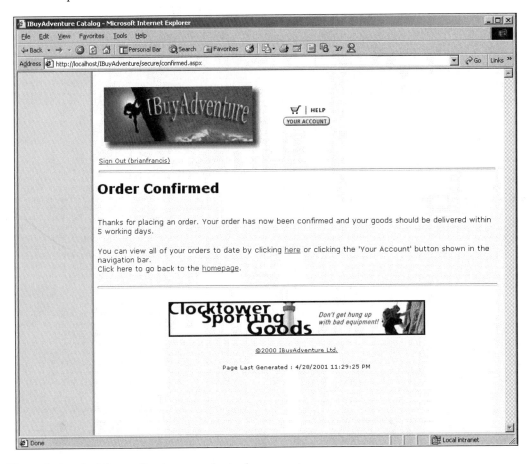

The code invoked for confirming an order is shown next:

```
void Confirm_Order(Object sender, EventArgs e) {

  IBuyAdventure.CartDB cart = new IBuyAdventure.CartDB(getConnStr());
  double totalOrderValue;

  totalOrderValue = cart.GetOrderValueForCart(GetCustomerID());

  IBuyAdventure.OrdersDB orders = new IBuyAdventure.OrdersDB(getConnStr());
  orders.AddNewOrder(GetCustomerID(), DateTime.Now.ToString("G",
                     DateTimeFormatInfo.InvariantInfo), totalOrderValue );

  cart.ResetShoppingCart( GetCustomerID() );
  Response.Redirect("confirmed.aspx");
}
```

The total value of the order is calculated using the `GetOrderValueForCart` function of the `CartDB` object. The customer name that is passed into this function, as returned by a call to `GetCustomerID`, will always be the name that the user entered when registering, as it is not possible to access this page without being authenticated.

Once the total value of the order has been calculated, the `AddNewOrder` function of the `OrdersDB` object is called to create an entry in the `orders` table. Since we will be adding the date and time of the order to the database, we need to make sure that the date is in a known format – as the standard formatting routines take into account the locale of the server, we may end up with a date format that SQL Server doesn't recognize.

To get around this, we're using an overloaded version of the `ToString()` method. Usually, this method takes no parameters – but in this case we are using two. The first specifies that we want the general date and time format. The `DateTimeFormatInfo.InvariantInfo` is a static object that ensures that the date string will be formatted the same regardless of the locale of the server. Finally, the shopping cart contents are cleared from the database and the browser is redirected to the order confirmation screen.

> In a commercial application you would want to keep the contents of the shopping cart so you could actually process the order. As this is only a simple demonstration application, we have not implemented this here.

Canceling the Order

If an order is canceled before it is completed, the current shopping cart is cleared and the customer is taken back to the IBuyAdventure home page (`default.aspx`). The code for canceling an order is shown here:

```
void Cancel_Order(Object sender, EventArgs e) {

  IBuyAdventure.ProductsDB inventory = new
                             IBuyAdventure.ProductsDB(getConnStr());
  IBuyAdventure.CartDB cart = new IBuyAdventure.CartDB(getConnStr());
  cart.ResetShoppingCart( GetCustomerID() );

  Response.Redirect("/IBuyAdventure/default.aspx");
}
```

Order History and Your Account

Customers can review their order history at any time by clicking the 'Your Account' image located at the top of each page. When clicked, this page displays all the orders they have previously placed to date, showing the date when the order was created and the total value of the order:

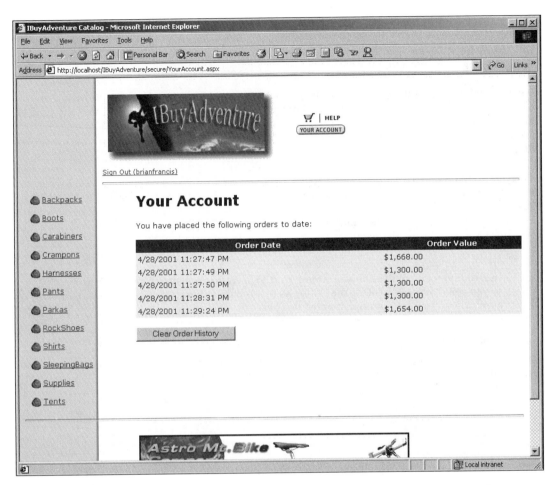

This page is generated using the asp:Repeater control, and simply shows the entries in the Orders table for the current customer. The PopulateOrderList function databinds the controls just as in previous pages:

```
void PopulateOrderList() {

   IBuyAdventure.OrdersDB orders = new IBuyAdventure.OrdersDB(getConnStr());

   DataSet ds = orders.GetOrdersForCustomer(GetCustomerID());

   MyList.DataSource = ds;
   MyList.DataBind();

   if ( MyList.Items.Count == 0 ) {
     ClearButton.Visible = false;
     MyList.Visible = false;
     Status.Text = "No orders have been placed to date.";
   }


}
```

The last few lines of our code hide the 'Clear Order History' button if there are no orders for the customer. If there are orders, then clicking this button invokes the `ClearOrderHistory` function:

```
void ClearOrderHistory(Object sender, EventArgs e) {

   IBuyAdventure.OrdersDB orders = new IBuyAdventure.OrdersDB(getConnStr());
   orders.DeleteOrdersForCustomer( GetCustomerID() );
   PopulateOrderList();
}
```

This code clears all orders for the customer by calling the `DeletesOrdersForCustomer` function provided by the `OrdersDB` object.

Summary

That's it, your first ASP.NET e-commerce application!

In this chapter we've seen how clean and easy it is to write an e-commerce application using ASP.NET. The rich server-side control and event model makes ASP.NET development much more like traditional VB event-based programming, which dramatically reduces the amount of code we have to write in our pages.

We have not had the space to cover every single feature that you could potentially use in an application in this chapter. However, hopefully the code presented here covers the most common aspects of an application, and when combined with the information provided in the other chapters, will give you the confidence to build your own applications.

"The Babel fish," says The Hitch Hiker's Guide to Galaxy "is small, yellow and leech-like, and probably the oddest thing in the Universe. It feeds on brainwave energy not from its carrier but from those around it. It absorbs all unconscious mental frequencies from this brainwave energy to nourish itself with. It then excretes into the mind of its carrier a telepathic matrix formed by combining the conscious thought frequencies with nerve signals picked up from the speech centres of the brain which has supplied them".

The practical upshot of all this is that if you stick a Babel fish in your ear you can instantly understand anything said to you in any form of language. The speech patterns you actually hear decode the brainwave matrix which has been fed into your mind by your Babel fish.

The Common System Namespaces

Due to the huge number of classes that make up the .NET class library, we don't have room to list them all, let alone their properties, methods and events. The SDK provided with the Framework contains a full reference section, which you can access through .NET Framework Reference | .NET Class Library Reference.

To help you find the classes you need, we've provided below a list of the most commonly used namespaces, together with a description of the classes they contain.

Fundamental System Namespaces

System	Fundamental classes and base classes that define commonly-used value and reference data types, events and event handlers, interfaces, attributes, and processing exceptions. Plus services that support data type conversion, method parameter manipulation, mathematics, remote and local program invocation, application environment management, and supervision of managed and unmanaged applications.
System.Collections	Interfaces and classes that define various collections of objects, such as the List, Queue, ArrayList, HashTable, and Dictionary objects.

Table continued on following page

System.ComponentModel	Classes that are used to implement the run-time and design-time behavior of components and controls. Includes the base classes and interfaces for implementing attributes, type converters, binding to data sources, and licensing components.
System.Configuration	Classes that are used to configure an assembly and allow custom installers to be created.
System.IO	Classes and types that provide synchronous and asynchronous reading from and writing to data streams and files.
System.Reflection	Classes and interfaces providing a managed view of loaded types, methods, and fields, with the ability to dynamically create and invoke types.
System.Security	Classes that provide the underlying structure for the common language runtime security system, including base classes for permissions.
System.Text	Classes representing ASCII, Unicode, UTF-7, and UTF-8 character encodings, abstract base classes for converting blocks of characters to and from blocks of bytes, and a helper class that manipulates and formats String objects without creating intermediate instances.
System.Text.RegularExpressions	Classes that provide access to the .NET Framework regular expression engine.
System.Threading	Classes and interfaces to enable multi-threaded programming, including the ThreadPool class, a delegate timer class and the Mutex class. Also contains classes for thread scheduling, wait notification, and deadlock resolution.
System.Timers	Contains the programmable Timer component, which allows events to be raised at specified intervals.

.NET Languages Namespaces

Microsoft.CSharp	Classes that support compilation and code generation for the C# language.
Microsoft.JScript	Classes that support compilation and code generation for the JScript language.
Microsoft.VisualBasic	Classes that support compilation and code generation for the Visual Basic language.

Data Management Namespaces

System.Data	Classes that constitute the ADO.NET relational data access and management architecture for multiple data sources.
System.Data.OleDb	Classes that support the OLE DB .NET data provider.
System.Data.SqlClient	Classes that support the SQL Server .NET data provider.

`System.Data.SqlTypes`	Classes for native data types within MS SQL Server.
`System.Xml`	Classes that provide standards-based support for processing XML.
`System.Xml.Schema`	Classes that provide standards-based support for processing XML schemas.
`System.Xml.XPath`	Contains the `XPath` parser and evaluation engine.
`System.Xml.Xsl`	Classes that provide support for XSL/T transformations.

Debugging and Monitoring Namespaces

`System.Diagnostics`	Classes for debugging applications and for tracing code execution, starting system processes, reading and writing to event logs, and monitoring system performance using performance counters.
`System.Management`	Classes for working with Windows Management Instrumentation (WMI).

Application Services Namespaces

`System.DirectoryServices`	Classes that provide access to Active Directory.
`System.EnterpriseServices`	Classes that are used to manage component activation and associated activities in an enterprise scenario.
`System.Messaging`	Classes for working with message queues, sending messages to queues, and receiving or peeking messages from queues. Note, this is not used for SMTP messaging.

Graphics and Printing Namespaces

`System.Drawing`	Provides access to GDI+ basic graphics functionality.
`System.Drawing.Design`	Classes that extend design-time user interface logic and drawing.
`System.Drawing.Drawing2D`	Advanced 2-dimensional and vector graphics classes.
`System.Drawing.Imaging`	Advanced GDI+ imaging classes.
`System.Drawing.Printing`	Classes that allow customized printing.
`System.Drawing.Text`	Advanced GDI+ typography classes for creating and using fonts.

Fundamental Networking Namespaces

`System.Net`	Provides simple programming interfaces to many common network protocols. Includes the `WebRequest` and `WebResponse` classes that enable applications to use Internet resources.
`System.Net.Sockets`	Provides a managed implementation of the Windows Sockets interface in the same way as the Winsock API.

Windows Forms Application Namespaces

`System.Windows. Forms`	Classes for creating Windows-based executable applications to run under the .NET Framework.
`System.Windows. Forms.Design`	Classes for extending design-time support for Windows Forms.

Fundamental Web Application Namespaces

`System.Web`	Classes and interfaces to enable browser/server communication. Includes `HTTPRequest` and `HTTPResponse`, and the `HTTPServerUtility` object that provides access to server-side utilities and processes. Also includes classes for cookie manipulation, file transfer, exception information, and output cache control.
`System.Web.Caching`	Classes for caching frequently used resources on the server.
`System.Web. Configuration`	Classes that are used to configure ASP.NET applications.
`System.Web.Hosting`	Classes for working with application domains, worker requests and interfacing with IIS.
`System.Web.Mail`	Classes for creating and managing SMTP e-mail messages and attachments.
`System.Web.Security`	Classes that implement security in ASP.NET applications.

Web Forms Application Namespaces

`System.Web.UI`	Classes and interfaces for creating user interface pages and controls in web applications. Includes the `Control` base class, the `Page` class and classes to implement data binding, `viewstate` management, and control parsing.
`System.Web.UI. Design`	Classes for extending design-time support for Web Forms.

`System.Web.UI.` `Design.WebControls`	Classes for extending design-time support for Web Controls.
`System.Web.UI.` `HtmlControls`	Classes for creating HTML server controls that map directly to standard HTML elements.
`System.Web.UI.` `WebControls`	Classes for creating ASP.NET Web Controls, which provide a consistent and abstract control.

Web Service Application Namespaces

`System.Web.Services`	Classes for building and using Web Services.
`System.Web.` `Services.Description`	Classes for publicly describing Web Services via Service Description Language (SDL).
`System.Web.` `Services.Discovery`	Classes for implementing Web Service Discovery.
`System.Web.` `Services.Protocols`	Classes that define the data transmission protocols between ASP.NET Web Services and clients.

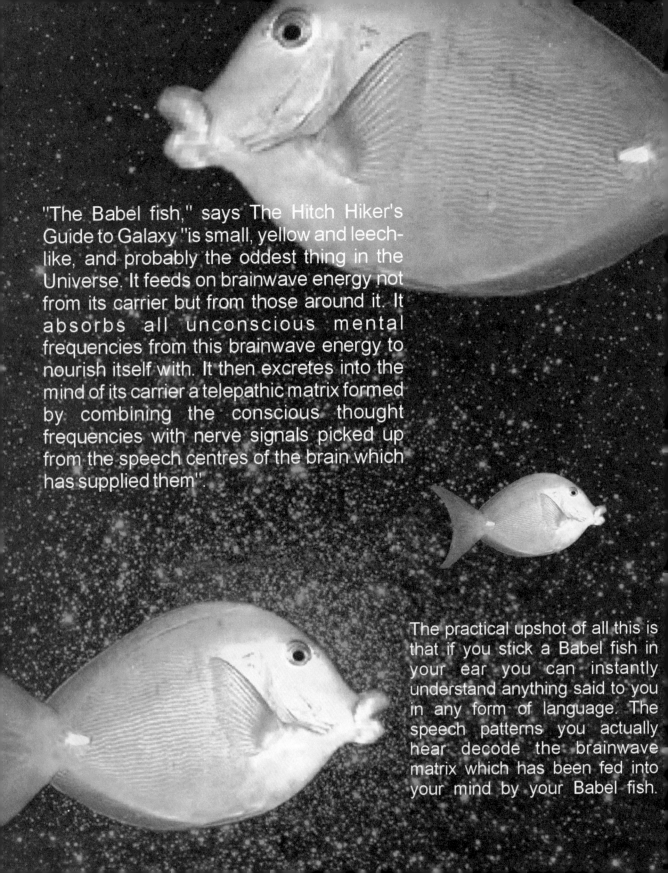

"The Babel fish," says The Hitch Hiker's Guide to Galaxy "is small, yellow and leech-like, and probably the oddest thing in the Universe. It feeds on brainwave energy not from its carrier but from those around it. It absorbs all unconscious mental frequencies from this brainwave energy to nourish itself with. It then excretes into the mind of its carrier a telepathic matrix formed by combining the conscious thought frequencies with nerve signals picked up from the speech centres of the brain which has supplied them".

The practical upshot of all this is that if you stick a Babel fish in your ear you can instantly understand anything said to you in any form of language. The speech patterns you actually hear decode the brainwave matrix which has been fed into your mind by your Babel fish.

Scott Guthrie's Top Performance Tips

With thanks to Scott Guthrie, the inventor of ASP. Here are Scott's top tips for maximizing performance of your ASP.NET applications – plus a few things to watch out for.

In general, ASP.NET pages take longer to respond on the first "hit" due to the extra instantiation and compilation sequence. However, after they are first compiled they are faster for all subsequent accesses. Although pages with very little code may provide around the same performance as ASP 3.0 pages, more complex pages are actually a lot faster due to the compilation of the code they contain.

The best cost/benefit for an ASP.NET server is a two-processor machine. With ADO.NET data access, a four-processor machine can be beneficial, but is far more costly – two to three thousand dollars will buy a good twin-processor server, whereas a four-processor machine is into the twenty thousand dollar price range.

Manage Your Viewstate

Depending on the size of the viewstate, transmitting your viewstate across a network can entail a performance hit. You can check the viewstate for any control on the complete page by turning on tracing in a page using the page directive:

```
<%@ Page Trace="true" ... %>
```

To disable viewstate maintenance for a page, use the page directive:

```
<%@ Page MaintainState="false" ... %>
```

To disable viewstate maintenance for a single control, use the `MaintainState` property:

```
<ASP:Datagrid MaintainState="false" ... runat="server"/>
```

To disable viewstate maintenance for an entire application, change the setting on `web.config`:

```
<pages enableViewState="false" ... />
```

Manage Your SessionState

You should only use sessions where they are actually required for the application. Turn them off in any pages that don't require access to them. Alternatively, use read-only session state where you don't need to update the values.

To disable session state maintenance for a page, use the page directive:

```
<%@ Page EnableSessionState="false" %>
```

To disable session state maintenance for an entire application, change the setting on `web.config`:

```
<sessionState mode="off" />
<pages enableSessionState="false" ... />
```

To specify read-only session state maintenance for a page, use the page directive:

```
<%@ Page EnableSessionState="ReadOnly" %>
```

To specify read-only session state maintenance for an entire application, change the setting on `web.config`:

```
<pages enableSessionState="ReadOnly" ... />
```

Where possible, use the default in-process session management. The out-of-process state service can produce a performance hit of 20% over the in-process session manager, and the remote SQL Server state management session adds around another 50% performance hit over out-of-process session state management – use it only for a Web Farm.

Use Output Caching

The judicious use of output caching can provide a ten-fold performance increase, depending on whether or how much of a page can be cached and how many variations there are for different users. To enable output caching for a page, use the page directive:

```
<%@ OutputCache Duration="#ofseconds"
    Location="Any | Client | Downstream | Server | None"
    VaryByControl="control-name" VaryByCustom="browser | custom-string"
    VaryByHeader="headers" VaryByParam="parameter-name" %>
```

Only Use Server Controls Where Appropriate

However, if you need to access an HTML element's properties, methods, or events in server-side code, you have to create it as a server control. But it's always worth considering which elements actually do need to be server controls when we build a page. For example, the following situations **do not** require a server-side control:

- ❑ When the element is only used to run some client-side script, for example, a button that opens a new browser window, or that interacts with a client-side ActiveX control or Java applet, or that calculates some value for display in the page using DHTML, or in an `alert` dialog.

- ❑ When the element is a hyperlink that opens a different page or URL and there is no need to process the values for the hyperlink on the server.

- ❑ Any other times when access to the element's properties, methods, or events in server-side code is not required.

A page containing server control will take a performance hit compared to one that does not use server controls, perhaps as much as 30%. However, using code to set or access the element content directly will also cause a performance hit, so if you do need to access the element programmatically (even just to set the text or value), use a server control for that element.

Use a DataReader Instead of a DataSet

In general, the only times that a `DataSet` must be used in preference to a `DataReader` are:

- ❑ When the data will be remoted (that is, sent as a disconnected package) to the client or a remote instance of the application or a component – for example, when using a Web Service that returns a `DataSet`.

- ❑ When you need to retrieve and store more than one set of rows, and, optionally, the relationships between them.

The `DataReader` can be used as the source for data binding controls if required.

Use the SQL TDS Classes for Data Access

There are two sets of objects for accessing a data source:

- ❑ Objects prefixed `OleDb` (from the **System.Data.OleDb** namespace) use an OLE-DB provider to access that data store.

- ❑ Objects prefixed `Sql` (from the **System.Data.SqlClient** namespace) use the Microsoft SQL Server Tabular Data Stream (TDS) interface to access that data store.

In general, the `Sql` prefixed objects are much faster and more efficient, and should always be used where you know that the data store will be Microsoft SQL Server.

Both the `OleDb` and `Sql` objects automatically provide connection pooling.

Use Data Binding Where Possible

Traditionally, ASP has been used to iterate through a rowset extracting values and placing them in the page. In ASP.NET the List controls can do this automatically through data binding, and provide a huge performance increase.

Compared to using ASP 3.0 with ADO to create an HTML table explicitly from a `Recordset`, ASP.NET with a data-bound `DataList` control fed by a `DataReader` object using the `OleDb` data provider can be three times quicker. Switch to the `Sql` TDS data provider and it can be up to five times faster.

If you do need to bind to a `DataSet`, use the `DataMember` property of the control to specify the table rather than creating a `DataView` object first.

Use Option Explicit or Strict On Visual Basic

Early binding provides much better performance than late binding. To ensure that only early binding is used, always include the `Option Explicit` statement in code to force variables to be pre-declared.

```
<%@ Page Language="VB" Strict="true" %>
```

Also, always specify a data type for variables when they are declared. This provides strong typing of variables for best performance. For example, use:

```
Dim intThis As Integer
```

Rather than:

```
Dim intThis
```

As a comparison, failing to declare variable types and therefore forcing late binding can lead to performance that is about the same as using VBScript in ASP 3.0.

It's also worth using `Option Strict` where possible to enforce strict variable typing. This means that variables must be explicitly cast to the correct data type for each operation that requires a type conversion. Again, it can provide better performance, though it does involve more code and so may not always be appropriate.

```
<%@ Page Language="VB" Strict="true" %>
```

Use Early-binding to Components

Early binding provides a noticeable performance increase for components that are used in ASP.NET pages. The actual performance hit from late-bound components depends on the amount of data that is transferred, however for a component that has to marshal strings an approximate measure of performance can be gaged from the following comparisons:

- ❏ COM or COM+ components using late binding provide around the same performance as in ASP 3.0 with VBScript.

- ❏ COM or COM+ components using early binding (for example, components wrapped with the `tlbimp` utility) provide around 50% better performance than in ASP 3.0 with VBScript.

- ❏ Early bound .NET components provide around three times better performance than the equivalent COM or COM+ components using late binding in ASP 3.0 with VBScript.

All the .NET objects provided by the frameworks, including all ASP.NET server controls, are automatically early-bound. The instantiate/destroy cycle is also very efficient under the .NET framework, and "stateful" components (components that cannot be pooled in Component Services or MTS) are acceptable.

Avoid ASP Compatibility

To use an apartment-threaded component in an ASP.NET page, you must set the compatibility mode to "ASP" using the page directive `AspCompat="true"`. This allows the page to be executed on a single-threaded apartment (STA) thread, so that it can call into STA components (for example a component developed with VB6.0). However, in this mode, performance of the ASP.NET page can be quite severely degraded.

Remember the New Request and Response Objects

In ASP.NET, the `Request` and `Response` objects have been extended to provide many new features that can improve performance. For example, to write the contents of a disk file into a page use the new `Response.WriteFile` method rather than opening the file, reading it from disk and writing it to the `Response`.

Finally, avoid the `ServerVariables` collection where possible by using the new `Request` properties like `Request.Url`, `Request.Referrer`, `Request.PhysicalPath`, `Request.UserAgent`, etc.

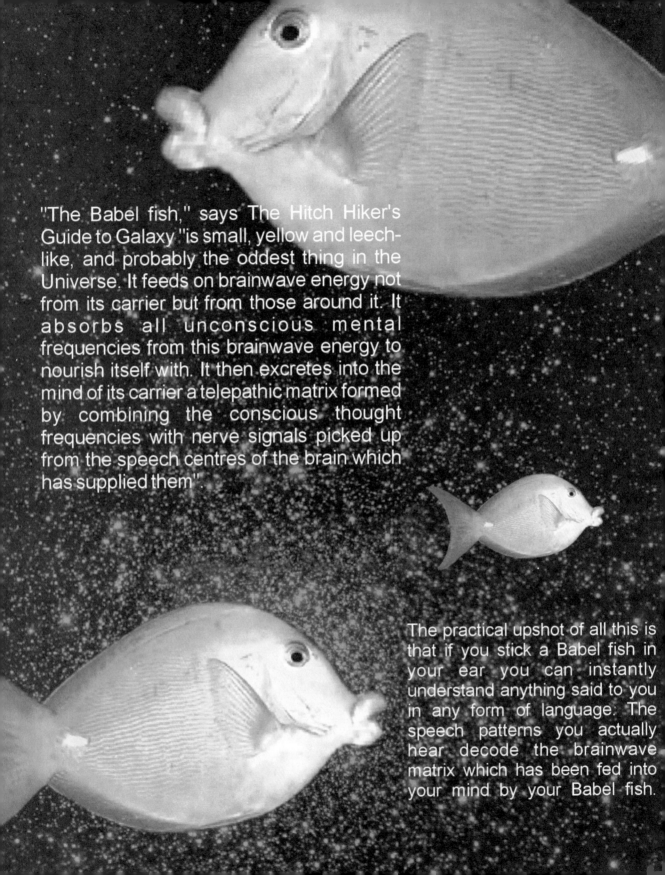

"The Babel fish," says The Hitch Hiker's Guide to Galaxy "is small, yellow and leech-like, and probably the oddest thing in the Universe. It feeds on brainwave energy not from its carrier but from those around it. It absorbs all unconscious mental frequencies from this brainwave energy to nourish itself with. It then excretes into the mind of its carrier a telepathic matrix formed by combining the conscious thought frequencies with nerve signals picked up from the speech centres of the brain which has supplied them".

The practical upshot of all this is that if you stick a Babel fish in your ear you can instantly understand anything said to you in any form of language. The speech patterns you actually hear decode the brainwave matrix which has been fed into your mind by your Babel fish.

References and Further Information

Although .NET is a new product, there are already many web sites that provide discussion lists, reference information, community support, components, and other useful resources. Some of those that were available when we went to press are listed below.

ASP.NET Web Sites and Discussion Lists

MSDN .Net Start Page	http://msdn.microsoft.com/net/
Visual Studio	http://msdn.microsoft.com/net/
ASP.NET	http://msdn.microsoft.com/net/aspnet/default.asp
Wrox Press ASP discussion list	http://p2p.wrox.com/
Microsoft Framework team web site	http://www.asp.net/
ASPNG ASP.NET community site	http://www.aspng.com/
A Tale of Two Authors	http://daveandal.com/
.NET Advocacy Discussion Lists	http://discuss.develop.com/dotnet-advocacy.html
.NET101	http://www.dotnet101.com/
.NETWire	http://www.dotnetwire.com/
123aspx.com	http://www.123aspx.com/

411 ASP.NET Directory	http://www.411asp.net/
4GuysFromRolla.com	http://www.4guysfromrolla.com/
ActiveZ.com (in Turkish)	http://activez.cu.edu.tr/
Angry Coder	http://www.angrycoder.com/
ASP Index	http://www.aspin.com/
ASP Wire	http://www.aspwire.com/
ASP101.com	http://www.asp101.com/
aspalliance	http://www.aspalliance.com/
ASPFree.com	http://www.aspfree.com/aspnet/Default.aspx
ASPLists Windows Forms	http://www.asplists.com/asplists/winforms.asp
ASPNextGen.com	http://www.aspnextgen.com/
ASPToday.com	http://www.asptoday.com/
BipinJoshi.com	http://www.bipinjoshi.com/
C# Corner	http://www.c-sharpcorner.com/
C# Corner Discussion Forums	http://www.c-sharpcorner.com/forum/
Code Guru	http://www.codeguru.com/
DevX.com	http://www.devx.com/dotnet/
DOTNET Distribution List	http://discuss.develop.com/dotnet.html
DotNET French .NET news portal	http://www.dotnet-fr.org/
IBuySpy.com	http://www.ibuyspy.com/
KOSOB.com	http://www.kosob.com/
Learn C# The Easy Way	http://learncsharp.cjb.net/
Mailing list DOTNET (in French)	http://www.neoxia.com/fr/mailing-lists.php3
MCPCentral.com	http://www.mcpcentral.com/
St. Louis .NET User Group	http://www.stlnet.org/
The Code Project	http://www.codeproject.com/
ThinkDOTNET	http://www.thinkdotnet.com/
VB-Joker	http://www.vb-joker.com/
VBXML.com	http://www.vbxml.com/
Visual.NET Advisor	http://www.advisor.com/www/VisualNetAdvisor/
VSJ	http://www.net.vsj.co.uk/

Third Party ASP.NET Component Vendors

Software Artisans	http://softwareartisans.com/
Aylo's Charting Engine	http://chart.aylo.com/
Combit	http://www.combit.net/us/default.asp?content=/us/support/msdotnet.asp
Component Source	http://www.componentsource.com/build/msnet.asp
Dart Communications	http://www.dart.com/dotnet.asp
Dataphor	http://www.dataphor.com/
Desaware Inc.	http://www.desaware.com/net.htm
Developer Express	http://devexpress.com/index.shtm
DevPower Components	http://www.devpower.com/net/
FarPoint Technologies	http://www.fpoint.com/newtech/
Infragistics	http://www.infragistics.com/
LEADTOOLS Imaging Development	http://www.leadtools.com/
Mabry Software	http://www.mabry.com/dotnet.htm
Sax Software Corporation	http://www.saxsoft.net/
Seagate Software	http://www.seagatesoftware.com/x-jump/scr_net/default.asp
Software FX - Chart FX	http://www.softwarefx.com/
VisualSoft Technologies	http://www.visualmart.com/dotnetreq.asp
WebGecko Software	http://www.webgecko.com/products/dotnet.asp
Xceed Software Inc.	http://www.xceedsoft.com/dotnet/

ASP.NET Hosting

2COOLWEB	http://www.2coolweb.com/
Brinkster.com	http://www.brinkster.com/aspxinfo.asp
Eraserver.net	http://www.eraserver.net/
Extreme Web Works	http://extremewebworks.com/
Franklins.net	http://www.franklins.net/
IIS Host List	http://www.actionjackson.com/hosts/
MaximumASP.com	http://www.maximumasp.com/
ORCSWEB.com	http://www.orcsweb.com/
SecureWebs.com	http://www.securewebs.com/hosting/net.htm

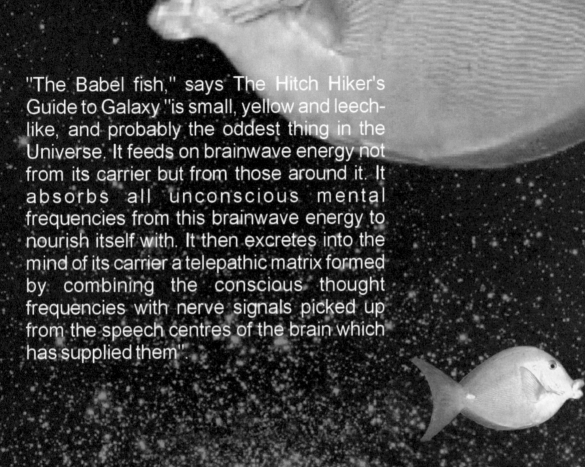

"The Babel fish," says The Hitch Hiker's Guide to Galaxy "is small, yellow and leech-like, and probably the oddest thing in the Universe. It feeds on brainwave energy not from its carrier but from those around it. It absorbs all unconscious mental frequencies from this brainwave energy to nourish itself with. It then excretes into the mind of its carrier a telepathic matrix formed by combining the conscious thought frequencies with nerve signals picked up from the speech centres of the brain which has supplied them".

The practical upshot of all this is that if you stick a Babel fish in your ear you can instantly understand anything said to you in any form of language. The speech patterns you actually hear decode the brainwave matrix which has been fed into your mind by your Babel fish.

D

Support, Errata, and p2p.wrox.com

One of the most irritating things about any programming book is when you find that the bit of code that you've just spent an hour typing simply doesn't work. You check it a hundred times to see if you've set it up correctly, and then you notice the spelling mistake in the variable name on the book page. Of course, you can blame the authors for not taking enough care and testing the code, the editors for not doing their job properly, or the proofreaders for not being eagle-eyed enough, but this doesn't get around the fact that mistakes do happen.

We try hard to ensure that no mistakes sneak out into the real world, but we can't promise that this book is 100% error free. What we can do is offer the next best thing by providing you with immediate support and feedback from experts who have worked on the book, and who try to ensure that future editions eliminate these gremlins. We are also committed to supporting you not just while you read the book, but once you start developing applications as well – through our online forums you can put your questions to the authors, reviewers, and fellow industry professionals.

In this appendix we'll look at how to:

- ❑ Enroll in the peer to peer forums at http://p2p.wrox.com
- ❑ Post and check for errata on our main site, http://www.wrox.com
- ❑ E-mail a query, or feedback on our books in general, to our technical support team

Between all three support procedures, you should get an answer to your problem in no time.

The Online Forums At p2p.wrox.com

We provide **programmer to programmer™ support** on mailing lists, forums, and newsgroups, all in addition to our one-to-one e-mail system, which we'll look at in a minute. You can be confident that your query is not just being examined by a support professional, but by the many Wrox authors and other industry experts present on our mailing lists.

How to Enroll for Support

Just follow this four-step system:

> **1.** Go to p2p.wrox.com in your favorite browser:

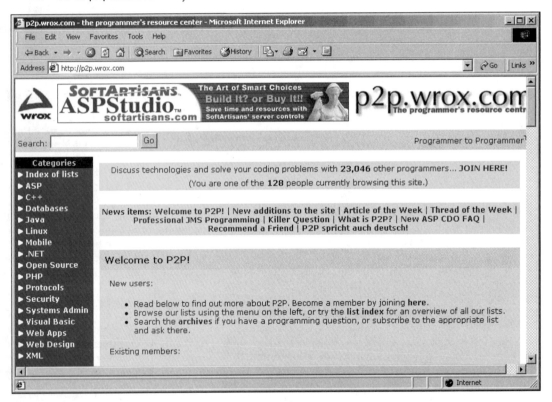

2. Click on the .NET entry in the left hand column. You'll be presented with the lists that are currently available:

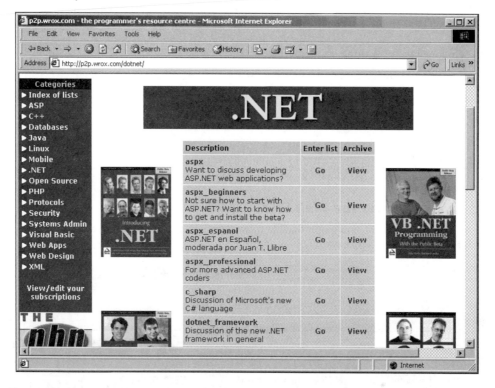

3. Choose to access the list you're interested in by clicking on its entry in the Description column.

4. If you are not a member of the list, you can choose to either view the list without joining it, or create an account in the list, by hitting the respective buttons.

5. If you choose to join, you'll be presented with a form in which you'll need to fill in your e-mail address, name, and a password (of at least 4 digits). Choose how you would like to receive the messages from the list and then hit Subscribe.

6. Congratulations. You're now a member of the mailing list.

Why This System Offers the Best Support

You can choose to join the mailing lists, or you can receive them as a daily digest. If you don't have the time or facility to receive the mailing list, then you can search our online archives.

As these lists are moderated, you can be confident of finding good, accurate information quickly. Mails can be edited or moved by the moderator into the correct place, making this a most efficient resource. Junk and spam mail are deleted, and your own e-mail address is protected by the unique Lyris system from web-bots that can automatically hoover up newsgroup mailing list addresses. Any queries about joining or leaving lists, or any query about the list should be sent to listsupport@wrox.com.

Checking the Errata Online At www.wrox.com

The following section will take you step by step through the process of posting errata to our web site to get that help. The sections that follow, therefore, are:

- ❏ Finding a list of existing errata on the web site
- ❏ Adding your own errata to the existing list
- ❏ What happens to your errata once you've posted it (why doesn't it appear immediately)?

There is also a section covering how to e-mail a question for technical support. This comprises:

- ❏ What your e-mail should include
- ❏ What happens to your e-mail once we've received it

Finding an Erratum on the Web Site

Before you send in a query, you might be able to save time by finding the answer to your problem on our web site – http://www.wrox.com:

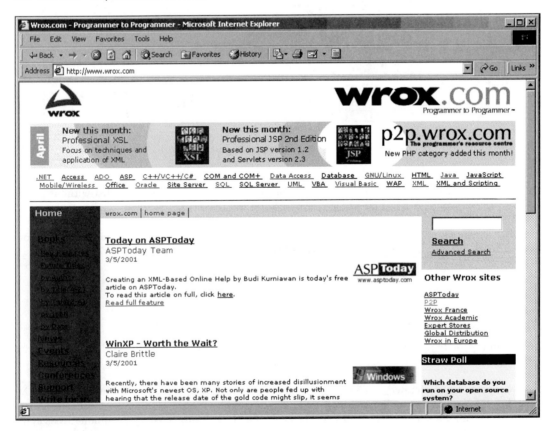

1. Each book we publish has its own page and its own errata sheet. You can get to any book's page by clicking on the subject list below the banner at the top of the page – so for this book click on .NET or ASP.

2. This will list the books available in that subject area. Click on Professional ASP.NET, and then the Book Errata link.

3. This will take you to the errata page for the book. We update these pages daily to ensure that you have the latest information on bugs and errors. You can get more details on a specific listing by clicking on the link for that error, or you can list all the errata in more detail by clicking on the view all errata link.

Add an Erratum: E-mail Support

If the errata page doesn't solve your problem, then you should contact our customer support team. You can point out an error to put up on the web site, or directly query a problem in the book page with an expert who knows the book in detail. Either click on the submit errata link on the book support page, or send an e-mail to support@wrox.com.

A typical e-mail should include the following things:

- ❏ The **name, last four digits of the ISBN**, and **page number** of the problem in the Subject field.
- ❏ Your **name, contact info** and the **problem** in the body of the message.

We won't send you junk mail. We need the details to save your time and ours. When you send an e-mail, it will go through the following chain of support.

Customer Support

Your message is delivered to one of our customer support staff, who are the first people to read it. They have files on most frequently asked questions, and will answer anything general immediately. They answer general questions about the book and the web site.

Editorial

Deeper queries are forwarded to the technical editor responsible for that book. They have experience with the programming language or particular product, and are able to answer detailed technical questions on the subject. Once an issue has been resolved, the editor can post any errata to the web site.

The Authors

Finally, in the unlikely event that the editor can't answer your problem, s/he will forward the request to the author. We try to protect the author from any distractions from writing. However, we are quite happy to forward specific requests to them. Most Wrox authors help with the support on their books. They'll mail the customer and the editor with their response, and again all readers should benefit.

What We Can't Answer

Obviously with an ever-growing range of books and an ever-changing technology base, there is an increasing volume of data requiring support. While we endeavor to answer all questions about the book, we can't answer bugs in your own programs that you've adapted from our code. But do tell us if you're especially pleased with the routine you developed with our help.

How to Tell Us Exactly What You Think

We understand that errors can destroy the enjoyment of a book and can cause many wasted and frustrated hours, so we seek to minimize the distress that they can cause.

You might just wish to tell us how much you liked or loathed the book in question. Or you might have ideas about how this whole process could be improved. In that case you should e-mail feedback@wrox.com. You'll always find a sympathetic ear, no matter what the problem is. Above all you should remember that we do care about what you have to say and we will do our utmost to act upon it.

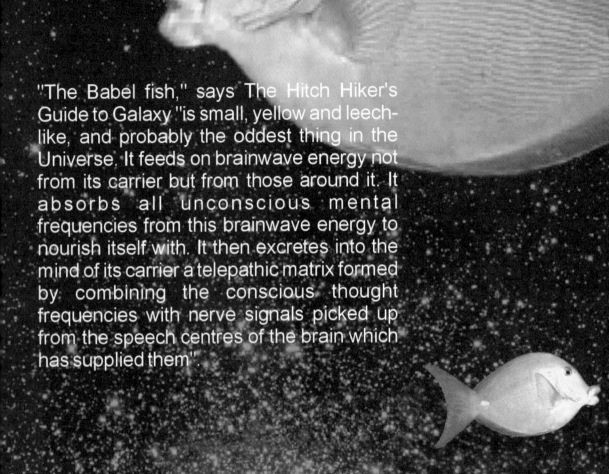

"The Babel fish," says The Hitch Hiker's Guide to Galaxy "is small, yellow and leech-like, and probably the oddest thing in the Universe. It feeds on brainwave energy not from its carrier but from those around it. It absorbs all unconscious mental frequencies from this brainwave energy to nourish itself with. It then excretes into the mind of its carrier a telepathic matrix formed by combining the conscious thought frequencies with nerve signals picked up from the speech centres of the brain which has supplied them".

The practical upshot of all this is that if you stick a Babel fish in your ear you can instantly understand anything said to you in any form of language. The speech patterns you actually hear decode the brainwave matrix which has been fed into your mind by your Babel fish.

Index

A Guide to the Index

The index is arranged hierarchically, in alphabetical order, with symbols preceding the letter A. Most second-level entries and many third-level entries also occur as first-level entries. This is to ensure that users will find the information they require however they choose to search for it.

I

M

"The Babel fish," says The Hitch Hiker's Guide to Galaxy "is small, yellow and leech-like, and probably the oddest thing in the Universe. It feeds on brainwave energy not from its carrier but from those around it. It absorbs all unconscious mental frequencies from this brainwave energy to nourish itself with. It then excretes into the mind of its carrier a telepathic matrix formed by combining the conscious thought frequencies with nerve signals picked up from the speech centres of the brain which has supplied them".

The practical upshot of all this is that if you stick a Babel fish in your ear you can instantly understand anything said to you in any form of language. The speech patterns you actually hear decode the brainwave matrix which has been fed into your mind by your Babel fish.

p2p.wrox.com
The programmer's resource centre

A unique free service from Wrox Press
with the aim of helping programmers to help each other

Wrox Press aims to provide timely and practical information to today's programmer. P2P is a list server offering a host of targeted mailing lists where you can share knowledge with your fellow programmers and find solutions to your problems. Whatever the level of your programming knowledge, and whatever technology you use, P2P can provide you with the information you need.

ASP Support for beginners and professionals, including a resource page with hundreds of links, and a popular ASP+ mailing list.

DATABASES For database programmers, offering support on SQL Server, mySQL, and Oracle.

MOBILE Software development for the mobile market is growing rapidly. We provide lists for the several current standards, including WAP, WindowsCE, and Symbian.

JAVA A complete set of Java lists, covering beginners, professionals,and server-side programmers (including JSP, servlets and EJBs)

.NET Microsoft's new OS platform, covering topics such as ASP+, C#, and general .Net discussion.

VISUAL BASIC Covers all aspects of VB programming, from programming Office macros to creating components for the .Net platform.

WEB DESIGN As web page requirements become more complex, programmer sare taking a more important role in creating web sites. For these programmers, we offer lists covering technologies such as Flash, Coldfusion, and JavaScript.

XML Covering all aspects of XML, including XSLT and schemas.

OPEN SOURCE Many Open Source topics covered including PHP, Apache, Perl, Linux, Python and more.

FOREIGN LANGUAGE Several lists dedicated to Spanish and German speaking programmers, categories include .Net, Java, XML, PHP and XML.

How To Subscribe

Simply visit the P2P site, at **http://p2p.wrox.com/**

Select the 'FAQ' option on the side menu bar for more information about the subscription process and our service.

ASP Today

ASPToday - Your free daily ASP Resource . . .

A discount off your ASPToday subscription with this voucher!!! see below for more details.

Expand your knowledge of ASP.NET with ASPToday.com - Wrox's code source for ASP and .NET applications, with free daily articles!

Every working day, we publish free Wrox content on the web:

- Free daily article
- Free daily tips
- Case studies and reference materials
- Index and full text search
- Downloadable code samples
- 11 Categories
- Written by programmers for programmers

And for just-in-time, practical solutions to real world problems, subscribe to our Living Book - our 600+ strong archive of code-heavy, useable articles.

Find it all and more at http://www.asptoday.com

This voucher entitles you to a discount off your annual ASPToday subscription, to claim your reduced rate please visit:

http://www.asptoday.com/special-offers/

If you have any questions please contact customersupport@wrox.com